W9-CTE-464

FREQUENTLY USED SYMBOLS

β	beta coefficient, a measure of an asset's riskiness.
b	the fraction of a firm's earnings retained rather than paid out. It is equal to $(1 - D/E)$, where D/E is the ratio of dividends (D) to earnings (E).
CAPM	capital asset pricing model.
CAR	cumulative average residuals.
CF	cash flow; CF_t is cash flow in period t.
CML	capital market line.
COV_{ij}	the covariance of the returns between assets i and j.
D	dividend per share of stock; D_t is dividend per share during period t.
EBIT	earnings before interest and taxes.
EPS	earnings per share.
E(R)	the expected return; $E(R_t)$ is the expected return during period t.
FV	future value.
FVIF	future value interest factor for a lump sum.
FVIFA	future value interest factor for an annuity.
g	growth rate in earnings, dividends, or stock prices.
I	rate of inflation.
i	required rate of return.
IRR	internal rate of return.
NPV	net present value.
P	price of a share of stock; P_o is price of a share of stock today.
p/e	the price/earnings ratio.
PV	the present value
PVIF	the present value interest factor for a lump sum.
PVIFA	the present value interest factor for an annuity.
r_{ij}	the correlation coefficient between assets i and j.
RFR	the rate of return on a risk-free asset.
ROA	return on assets.
ROE	return on equity.
SML	security market line.
Σ	summation sign (capital sigma).
σ	standard deviation (lower case sigma).
t	tax rate time when used as a subscript (e.g., D_t — the dividend in year t).
V	the value of an asset; V_j is the value of asset j.
YTM	yield to maturity.

*Investment
Analysis and
Portfolio
Management*

Second Edition

Frank K. Reilly
*BERNARD J. HANK PROFESSOR
UNIVERSITY OF NOTRE DAME*

The Dryden Press
CHICAGO   NEW YORK   PHILADELPHIA
SAN FRANCISCO   MONTREAL   TORONTO
LONDON   SYDNEY   TOKYO   MEXICO CITY
RIO DE JANEIRO   MADRID

Acquisitions Editor: Elizabeth Widdicombe
Developmental Editor: Paul Psilos
Project Editor: Nancy Shanahan/Rebecca Ryan
Managing Editor: Jane Perkins
Design Director: Alan Wendt
Production Manager: Mary Jarvis
Permissions Editor: Doris Milligan

Text and Cover Designer: Paul Uhl
Copy Editor: Kathy Richmond
Indexer: Sheila Ary
Compositor: Progressive Typographers, Inc.

Library of Congress Cataloging in Publication Data

Reilly, Frank K.
    Investment analysis and portfolio management.

    Includes bibliographies.
    1. Investments.   2. Investment analysis.
3. Portfolio management.   I. Title.
HG4521.R396   1985   332.6   84-13800
ISBN 0-03-063204-8

Printed in the United States of America
678-016-9876

Copyright 1985 CBS College Publishing
Copyright 1979 The Dryden Press
All rights reserved

Address orders:
383 Madison Avenue
New York, NY 10017

Address editorial correspondence:
One Salt Creek Lane
Hinsdale, IL 60521

CBS COLLEGE PUBLISHING
The Dryden Press
Holt, Rinehart and Winston
Saunders College Publishing

to
my best friend and wife
Therese
and our four greatest gifts
Frank K. III
Clarence R. II
Therese B.
Edgar B.

THE DRYDEN PRESS
SERIES IN FINANCE

PREFACE

Preparing this new edition has been a joy and a frustration. The frustration came in attempting to find the time such a task requires. Since the publication of the first edition, many changes have occurred in the investments field and I have truly enjoyed revising the material to reflect these changes. As an instructor, I am also a perennial student whose life work is to remain current in my field, to increase my store of knowledge, and to share it with others. The textbook is the epitome of the teacher profession: In this instance I have the opportunity to impart knowledge to students by helping others in their teaching function.

Making this book current, accurate, and readable has been an exciting challenge. My goal is to help you understand the concepts and to integrate this knowledge into a total framework as it relates to making investment and portfolio decisions. I welcome your suggestions and comments.

Intended Market

Investment Analysis and Portfolio Management is addressed to both graduate and advanced undergraduate students who are looking for an in-depth discussion of investments and portfolio management. The presentation of the material is intended to be rigorous and empirical, without being overly quantitative. A proper discussion of the modern developments in investments and portfolio theory must be rigorous. The detailed discussion of numerous empirical studies reflects my personal belief that it is essential for our theories to be exposed to the real world and to be judged on the basis of how well they help us understand and explain reality. As much as possible, I attempt to discuss studies that are relevant to each topic and consider the implications of the results for the various theories.

Changes in the Second Edition

Since the publication of the first edition, the investments literature has undergone several major changes. These are incorporated in this second edition. Beyond the new studies in the efficient market areas related to the small firm effect and the January anomaly, there are new chapters on the following subjects:
Financial statement analysis (Chapter 11); Empirical studies related to the Capital asset pricing model (CAPM) (Chapter 20); Arbitrage pricing theory (APT) (Chapter 20); New techniques in bond analysis and portfolio management (Chapters 18 and 19); Evaluation of Bond Portfolio Management (Chapter 22); Commodity and financial futures (Chapters 24 and 25). The reader will also find a new section on "How to become a CFA" immediately following this preface. Finally, sample CFA questions have been added to the end of the analysis chapters.

Acknowledgments

So many people have helped me in a myriad of ways that I almost hesitate to list them since I may miss someone. I must begin with the University of Notre Dame because of the direct support the University has provided and the understanding of my superiors and associates. Also, I want to thank the Bernard J. Hank Family who have endowed the Chair that helped bring me back to this beautiful place called Notre Dame. Shanta Hegde, my colleague at Notre Dame, was a terrific help, under great time pressure, on the futures chapters. Also, I cannot forget those who helped with prior editions, including my deceased friend, Ken Carey, who helped me with the portfolio chapters, and Michael Joehnk from Arizona State for assistance on the bond chapters. Reviewers for this revision were very patient with my production of material and provided valuable input: Dr. Gerald A. Blum of Babson College, Dosoung Choi of the University of Tennessee, Eurico J. Ferreira of Clemson University, A. James Ifflander of Arizona State University, George A. Racette of the University of Oregon, James Rosenfeld of Emory University, Stanley D. Ryals from Chartered Financial Analysts, and David E. Upton of the Texas Tech University.

I was also fortunate to have the following excellent reviewers for past manuscripts: Robert Angell, East Carolina University; Brian Belt, University of Missouri at Kansas City; Eugene F. Drzycimski, University of Wisconsin at Oshkosh; Joseph E. Finnerty, University of Massachusetts; Stephen Goldstein, University of South Carolina; Ronald Hoffmeister, Arizona State University; Ron Hutchins, Eastern Michigan University; John Mathys, DePaul University; Dennis McConnell, University of Maine; George Pinches, University of Kansas; Douglas Southard, Virginia Polytechnic Institute; Harold Stevenson, Arizona State University.

Great comments and suggestions have come from my former graduate students at the University of Illinois: Paul Fellows, University of Iowa; R. H. "Unk" Gilmer, Jr., University of Oklahoma; Daniel Lehmann, DeKalb Pfizer Genetics; Wenchi Wong, Washington State University; and David Wright, University of Notre Dame.

I continue to be blessed with terrific research assistants who are bright and dedicated. Rian Gorey spent a summer with me, and I am especially grateful to Jim Stork who worked on numerous tasks related to the book for two years prior to getting a "real" job with Duff and Phelps.

Current and former colleagues have been very helpful: Yu Chi Chang and Bernie Kilbride, University of Notre Dame; C. F. Lee, University of Illinois; Don Panton, University of New Mexico; Donald Tuttle, Indiana University; and John M. Wachowicz, University of Tennessee. While we don't get to jog together as much as in the past, I continue to receive very insightful thoughts from my very good friend, Jim Gentry, of the University of Illinois.

One of the great risks of writing an investments book amidst the corn fields of Indiana or Illinois is the tendency to drift from the real world. I have tried to avoid this and have received gracious help from friends whom I refer to as my "connections with reality." These include:

Richard Cacchione
Fitch Investors Service, Inc.

Thomas Coleman
Adler, Coleman and Co. (NYSE)

William Cornish
Duff and Phelps

Peter Dietz (and his associate
Leslie Bailey)
Frank Russell, Inc.

Ray Dixon
Goldman, Sachs and Co.

William Dwyer
Moody's Investors
Service, Inc.

John Flanagan
Stokes, Hoyt and Co. (NYSE)

Russ Fraser
AMBAC Indemnity Corporation

William J. Hank
Conlon–Moore Corporation

Jim Johnson
Options Clearing Corporation

John W. Jordan, II
The Jordan Company

Martin Leibowitz
Salomon Bros.

Doug Lempereur
Standish, Ayer and Wood, Inc.

John Maginn
Mutual of Omaha

Robert Milne
Duff and Phelps

Robert G. Murray
First Interstate Bank of Oregon

John Phelan
New York Stock Exchange

Philip J. Purcell, III
Dean Witter Financial Services Group

Robert Quinn
Salomon Brothers

Stanley Ryals
Investment Counselor

Barry Schnepel
Merrill Lynch, Pierce,
Fenner and Smith

Richard H. Tierney
The Bond Buyer

Thomas V. Williams
Kemper Financial Services

Robert Wilmouth
National Futures Association

I have also gained a great deal from my association with the Institute of Chartered Financial Analysts and the dedicated people at the Institute: Darwin Bayston, Whit Broome, Hap Butler, and David McLaughlin.

Liz Widdicombe was a terrific editor to work with, and Paul Psilos applied his gentle pressure once more. Kathy Richmond did a great job copyediting and Nancy Shanahan was wonderful as project editor until her daughter Erin's birth. Also, thanks to Becky Ryan who filled in after the blessed event. It is difficult to describe the patience and effort of my secretary, Phyllis Sandfort, who did so much with enormous grace, efficiency, and good humor.

As it has been and always will be, my greatest gratitude is to my family. This includes my parents who gave of themselves and my in-laws who give perennially through their daughter. Most important is my wonderful wife and our fabulous children who have given me more love and understanding than I deserve.

Frank K. Reilly   Notre Dame, Indiana   October 1984

About the Author

Frank K. Reilly is Dean of the College of Business Administration and Bernard J. Hank Professor of Business Administration at the University of Notre Dame. He holds degrees from the University of Notre Dame (B.B.A.), Northwestern University (M.B.A.), and the University of Chicago (Ph.D). Professor Reilly has taught at the University of Illinois, the University of Kansas, and the University of Wyoming, in addition to the University of Notre Dame. He has several years of experience as a senior securities analyst as well as in stock and bond trading. A Chartered Financial Analyst and a member of the Council of Examiners and the Grading Committee of the Institute of Chartered Financial Analysts, Professor Reilly has been President of both the Midwest Business Administration Association and Eastern Finance Association. He is currently President of the Financial Management Association. The author of more than one hundred articles, monographs and papers, Professor Reilly's work has appeared in numerous publications including *Journal of Finance, Journal of Financial and Quantitative Analysis, Financial Management, Financial Analysts Journal, Financial Review,* and *Journal of Portfolio Management.* In addition to *Investment Analysis and Portfolio Management,* Professor Reilly is the author of another textbook, *Investments* (Dryden Press, 1982). In 1974 Professor Reilly was named on the list of *Outstanding Educators in America.* He has received both the University of Illinois Alumni Association Graduate Teaching Award (1980), and the Outstanding Educator Award from the MBA class of 1981 at the University of Illinois. Professor Reilly is Editor of *Readings and Issues in Investments,* as well as a member of the editorial boards of *Financial Management, The Financial Review, Journal of Financial Education,* and *Quarterly Review of Economics and Business.* He is included in *Who's Who in Finance and Industry, Who's Who in America,* and *Who's Who in the World.*

How to Become a
Chartered Financial Analyst

The professional designation of Chartered Financial Analyst (CFA) is becoming a significant requirement for a career in investment analysis and/or portfolio management. For that reason, we include here the general guidelines for acquiring the CFA designation, and the history and objectives of the Institute of Chartered Financial Analysts.

The CFA Program

The CFA Program is directed toward the professional development of financial and investment analysts and portfolio managers. The study program covers:
1. Ethics and professional standards
2. Financial accounting
3. Fixed-income securities analysis
4. Equity securities analysis
5. Portfolio management.

The program requires the successful completion of three examinations of increasing difficulty. Examinations are taken in their numbered sequence, and only one examination may be taken in a given year. Regardless of educational background and professional experience, every candidate must successfully complete all three examinations. The examinations are given annually in early June at some 90 sites in the U.S., Canada, and abroad.

Members and candidates are typically employed in the investment field. From 1963 to 1984, more than 10,000 charters have been awarded. Currently, about 5000 individuals are registered in the CFA Candidate Program.

A college degree or equivalent is necessary to enter the program. No work experience per se is required to take any of the three examinations. To take the Level II and Level III examinations, the candidate should be a member of a Society of The Financial Analysts Federation. Although experience is no longer a specific requirement for the examinations, professional experience could help the individual answer questions on the Level II and Level III examinations. Before being awarded the Charter, however, the candidate must have at least four years' experience in financial analysis as related to investments. The professional conduct of a candidate must conform to the Institute's code of ethics and standards of professional conduct.

x CFA Objectives and History

The Institute is an autonomous professional organization composed of members who have been awarded the registered professional designation Chartered Financial Analyst (CFA). The Institute's objectives are:

— To encourage and promote high standards of education and professional development in financial analysis.

— To conduct and foster programs of research, study, discussion, and publishing that improve the practice of financial analysis.

— To administer for CFA candidates a study and examination program with the threefold purpose of guiding analysts in mastering a professional body of knowledge, developing analytical skills, and testing the competency of financial investment analysts.

— To award the professional designation, Chartered Financial Analyst (CFA), to persons who meet recognized standards of competency and stipulated standards of conduct for the professional practice of financial analysis, and

— To sponsor and enforce a code of ethics and standards of professional conduct.

The Institute of Chartered Financial Analysts was formed in 1959 and was incorporated under the laws of Virginia in 1962. Its headquarters is in Charlottesville, Virginia. The CFA candidate examinations were first offered in 1963. The ICFA has close ties with the University of Virginia, The Financial Analysts Federation, and The Financial Analysts Research Foundation.

For More Information

If you are interested in learning more about the CFA program, the Institute has a booklet that describes the program and includes an application form. The address is: Institute of Chartered Financial Analysts, University of Virginia, P.O. Box 3668, Charlottesville, Virginia 22903.

Contents

xi

Part 1

The Investment Background

The chapters in this section are meant to give you a background in the total area of investments by answering the following questions:
— Why do people invest?
— What are some of the investments available?
— How do securities markets function?
— How and why are these securities markets changing?
— How can you determine what common stocks are doing?
— Where do you get relevant information on various potential investments?
In the first chapter we consider why individuals invest and discuss in detail the factors that determine an investor's required rate of return on an investment. The latter point will be very important in subsequent analyses. Because one of the most important tenets of investment theory is the need to diversify, in the second chapter we discuss a number of alternative investment instru-

ments and consider several studies that contain the rates of return and risk experienced by some of these alternative investments.

In Chapter 3, we examine the function of markets in general, and of the securities markets specifically, concentrating on the markets for bonds and common stocks. There have been significant changes in the operation of the securities market since 1965, that are dealt with in Chapter 4. We also consider what the future may hold for these markets and the implication of these changes for investors.

The behavior of the stock market is often measured in terms of changes in various stock market series. Because these series are used in a number of ways, in Chapter 5 we examine them in depth, and compare several of them. The final chapter in this section contains a description of sources of information on various aspects of investments.

Chapter 1   *The Investment Setting*

THE CONCEPT OF INVESTMENT[1]

F or most of our lives, we will be earning money and we will want to purchase certain things. Usually, though, there will be an imbalance between our current money income and our consumption desires at any given point in time and in the future. We will either have more money than we want to spend, or we will want more things than we can afford. In most cases, these imbalances will cause us to save either negative or positive amounts in order to maximize the benefits (utility) from our income.

When your current money income exceeds your current consumption desires, you will save the excess. You can put the savings under your mattress or bury it in the back yard until some future time when your consumption desires exceed current income. Or you may believe it is worthwhile to give up the immediate possession of these savings for a future larger amount of money that will be used for consumption. This trade-off of *present* consumption for a higher level of *future* consumption is the essence of saving and investment. In contrast, when your current money income is less than your current consumption desires, you will attempt to trade part of your *future* money income stream for a higher level of *current* consumption. When current consumption desires exceed current money income, you engage in *negative saving,* commonly referred to as *borrowing.* The funds borrowed can be used for consumption *or* be invested at rates of return above the cost of borrowing.

Obviously the individual who forgoes part of his current money income

---

[1] The discussion in this section draws heavily on Irving Fisher, *The Theory of Interest* (New York: Macmillan, 1930: reprinted Augustus M. Kelley, 1961); J. Hirshleifer, "Investment Decision Under Uncertainty: Choice — Theoretic Approaches," *Quarterly Journal of Economics* 79 no. 4 (November 1965): 509–536; and Eugene F. Fama and Merton H. Miller, *The Theory of Finance* (New York: Holt, Rinehart and Winston, 1972) Chapter 1.

4

stream and thereby defers current consumption will want more than the same amount in the future. At the same time, the individual attempting to consume or invest more than his current income is willing to pay back more than a dollar in the future for a dollar today. The rate of exchange between *certain* future consumption (future dollars) and *certain* current consumption (current dollars) is the *pure rate of interest* or the *pure time value of money.* The rate of exchange between current and future consumption is established in the capital market and is influenced by the supply of excess income available to be invested at a point in time and the demand for excess consumption (borrowing). If the cost of exchanging $100 of certain income today is $104 of certain income one year from today, the pure rate of exchange on a risk-free investment is said to be 4 percent $(104/100 - 1)$.

The pure time value of money is a "real" rate in that it indicates the increase in "real" goods and services desired. The investor is giving up $100 of consumption today in order to consume $104 of goods and services *at today's prices.* If investors expect a change in prices, they will adjust their required rate of return to compensate for this change. If they expect prices to increase (i.e., inflation) at the rate of 2 percent during the period of investment, one would expect them to increase their rate of exchange by this 2 percent (from 4 percent to 6 percent).

Finally, if an individual believes that the future payment is not certain, he will require a return which exceeds the pure time value of money plus the inflation rate. The amount required in excess of the pure time value of money plus the inflation rate is called a *risk premium.* Extending the example, when the investor is not certain about future repayment, he would require something in excess of $106 one year from today, possibly $110. In this example, the investor is requiring a $4 or 4 percent risk premium.

Investment Defined

Following the previous discussion, an investment is defined as *the current commitment of funds for a period of time in order to derive a future flow of funds that will compensate the investing unit for the time the funds are committed, for the expected rate of inflation, and also for the uncertainty involved in the future flow of funds.* This encompasses all types of investments, whether they be corporate investments in machinery, plant and equipment, government investments in flood control, or investments by individuals in stocks, bonds, commodities, or real estate. In all cases the investor is trading a *known* dollar amount today for some *expected* future stream of payments or benefits that will exceed the current outlay by an amount which will compensate the investor for the time the funds are committed, for the expected changes in prices during the period, and the uncertainty involved in expected future cash flows.[2] The alternative investments that are considered by various investing units (corporations, governments, and individuals) noted above only differ with regard to the institu-

---

[2] It is recognized that the uncertainty involved is a function of the asset's unique uncertainty and also its relationship with all other assets in the investing unit's portfolio. The exact nature of this uncertainty is considered in detail in a later chapter. At this point it is only necessary to recognize that the investor requires that the expected cash flows compensate for this uncertainty, however defined.

tional characteristics of the investment and some unique factors which must be considered in the analysis (e.g., differential taxes).

MEASURES OF RETURN AND RISK

In our discussion we referred to the return derived from an investment and contended that this return is influenced by the uncertainty or risk involved. Prior to discussing specific factors that determine the required rate of return, it is necessary to discuss briefly how the return is measured. In addition, it is important to generate an operational definition of risk and determine how it is measured.

Measure of Return

The purpose of investing is to defer current consumption and thereby add to our wealth so that it will be possible to consume more in the future. Therefore, when we talk about a return on an investment, we are concerned with the increase in wealth resulting from this investment. As an example, if you commit $100 to an investment at the beginning of a year and you get back $110 at the end of the year, your return on the investment (i.e., increase in wealth) was $10. Because the actual dollar amount committed to alternative investments differs, it is typical to express a *rate* of return in terms of a relationship between the amount invested and the amount returned:

$$\text{Rate of Return} = \frac{\text{Ending Wealth} - \text{Beginning Wealth}}{\text{Beginning Wealth}}$$

$$= \frac{\$110 - \$100}{\$100} = \frac{\$10}{\$100} = 10\%.$$

This 10 percent represents the rate of increase in wealth. Many investments provide you with a flow of cash in addition to changing value while the funds are invested. These cash flows must also be considered an addition to wealth. Because a particular investment may only be a portion of your wealth, it is appropriate to consider the rate of return on each investment. Therefore, a more general specification of rate of return is:

$$\text{Rate of Return} = \frac{\text{Ending Value} - \text{Beginning Value} + \text{Cash Flows}}{\text{Beginning Value}}$$

If we consider the prior example and add a $3 cash flow to it, the rate of return would be:

$$\text{Rate of Return} = \frac{\$110 - \$100 + \$3}{\$100}$$

$$= \frac{\$10 + \$3}{\$100} = \frac{\$13}{\$100} = 13\%.$$

The rate of increase in wealth for this portion of your portfolio would therefore be 13 percent. This *total* rate of return of 13 percent can be broken down into capital appreciation (the change in price) which was 10 percent, and cash flow (i.e., dividend income), which was 3 percent.

Risk and Uncertainty

Although in a formal sense, there is a difference between risk and uncertainty, our discussion will not make such a distinction since, in fact, there is a tendency to use the terms interchangeably or to use one term to explain the other. Risk is thought of as *uncertainty regarding the expected rate of return from an investment.* When an investor is considering an investment it is possible to ask what rate of return he "expects." The answer might be 10 percent, which is really a point estimate of his total expectation. If you were to press him further, he might acknowledge that he is not certain of this return and he recognizes that, under certain conditions, the return might go as low as negative 10 percent or as high as 25 percent. The point is, the larger the range of possible returns, the more uncertain the investor is regarding the actual return, and, therefore, the greater the risk.

It is possible to determine how certain an investor is regarding the expected rate of return on an investment by analyzing the probability distribution of expected returns. A probability distribution indicates the *possible* returns and assigns probabilities to each of them. The probabilities of a specified return might range from zero (no chance of this return) to one (complete certainty). The probabilities that can be assigned to a particular return are either subjective estimates by the investor or are based upon past frequencies (e.g., about 30 percent of the time the return on this particular investment was 10 percent). Let us begin with an example of perfect certainty; i.e., the investor is supposedly certain of a return of 5 percent. This can be envisioned as:

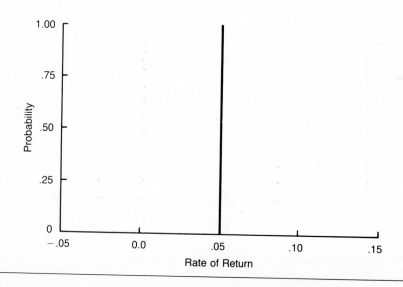

In the case of certainty there is only one possible return and the probability of receiving that return is 1.0. The *expected* return from an investment is defined as:

$$\text{Expected Return} = \Sigma \text{ (Probability of Return) (Possible Return)}$$
$$= \Sigma \, (Pi) \, (Ri).$$

In this case it would be:

$$\text{Expected Return} = (1.0) \, (.05) = .05.$$

An alternative example would be a case in which an investor believed several rates of return were possible under different conditions. If there is a strong economic environment with high corporate profits and little or no inflation, the investor may believe that his return on common stock could be as high as 20 percent. In contrast, if there is an economic decline and a higher than average rate of inflation, similar to what happened during 1974, he might feel that the return on common stock could be a negative 20 percent. Finally, the investor may believe that, if there is no major change in the economic environment, the return on common stock will approach the long-run average of 10 percent. The investor's estimated probabilities for each of these potential states based upon past experience are as follows:

State of Nature	Probability	Rate of Return
Strong Economy—No Inflation	.15	.20
Weak Economy—Above Average Inflation	.15	−.20
No Major Change in the Economy	.70	.10

This set of potential outcomes can be visualized as follows:

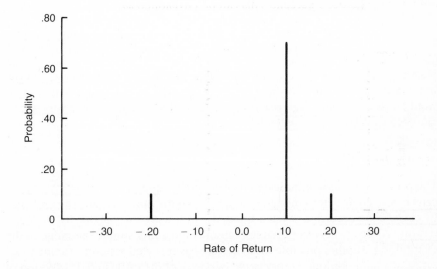

The computation of the expected rate of return is as follows:

Expected Rate of Return = (.15) (.20) + (.15) (− .20) + (.70) (.10)
$$= (.03) + (− .03) + (.07)$$
$$= .07.$$

Obviously, the investor is more uncertain regarding this investment than he was with the prior investment with a single possible return. One can visualize an investment with ten possible outcomes ranging from negative 40 percent to 50 percent with equal probabilities for each rate of return. A graph of such a set of expectations would look like this:

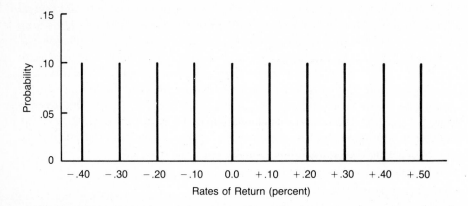

In this case there are numerous outcomes from a wide range of possibilities. The expected return would be:

Expected Rate of Return = (.10) (− .40) + (.10) (−.30) + (.10) (− .20)
$$+ (.10) (−.10) + (.10) (0.0) + (.10) (.10)$$
$$+ (.10) (.20) + (.10) (.30) + (.10) (.40)$$
$$+ (.10)(.50)$$
$$= (−.04) + (−.03) + (−.02) + (−.01)$$
$$+ (.00) + (.01) + (.02) + (.03) + (.04) + (.05)$$
$$= .05.$$

Note that the *expected* rate is the same as it was in the certainty case, but the investor is obviously not very certain about what the *actual* return will be. This would be considered a high risk investment because the investor is very uncertain regarding the actual realized return.

Measure of Risk

The previous discussion indicated that the uncertainty or risk of an investment can be derived by determining the range of possible outcomes and the probability of each one occurring. What is needed now is a *measure* of the dispersion of returns. There are several possible measures including simply the range of the distribution. Another possible measure that has received support in some theoretical work on portfolio theory is *the variance* of the estimated distribution of expected returns or the square root of the variance, i.e., *the standard deviation* of the distribution. These statistics are meant as indicators of deviations of possible returns from the expected return and are computed as follows:

$$\text{Variance } (\sigma^2) = \Sigma \text{ (Probability) (Possible Return} - \text{Expected Return)}^2$$
$$= \Sigma \ (Pi) \ (Ri - \overline{R})^2.$$

The larger the variance, everything else remaining constant, the greater the dispersion of expectations and the greater the uncertainty or risk of the investment.

The variance for the perfect certainty example would be as follows:

$$(\sigma^2) = \Sigma \ Pi(Ri - \overline{R})^2.$$
$$= 1.0(.05 - .05)^2 = 1.0(0.0) = 0.$$

Note that in the case of the perfect certainty there is *no variance of return* because there is *no deviation from expectations* and, therefore, *no risk or uncertainty.*

The variance for the second example would be:

$$\sigma^2 = \Sigma \ Pi(Ri - \overline{R})^2.$$
$$= [(.15) \ (-.20 - .07)^2 + (.15) \ (.20 - .07)^2 + (.70) \ (.10 - .07)^2]$$
$$= (.15) \ (-.27)^2 + (.15) \ (.13)^2 + (.70) \ (.03)^2$$
$$= (.15) \ (.0729) + (.15) \ (.0169) + (.70) \ (.0009)$$
$$= .010935 + .002535 + .00063$$
$$= .0201.$$

As noted, the standard deviation is the square root of the variance and so is equal to:

$$\text{Standard Deviation} = \sqrt{\Sigma \ Pi(Ri - \overline{R})^2}.$$

For the second example, the standard deviation (σ) would be:

$$\sigma = \sqrt{.0201}$$
$$= .14177.$$

In some cases, an unadjusted variance or standard deviation can be misleading if all else is not held constant; i.e., there are major differences in the mean rate of return. In such cases, a popular measure of *relative variability* is the coefficient of variation:

$$\text{Coefficient of Variation} = \text{Standard Deviation of Returns/Expected Returns}$$

$$CV = \frac{\sigma i}{\overline{Ri}}.$$

The *CV* for the second example would be:

$$CV = \frac{.14177}{.07000}$$

$$= 2.025.$$

It is generally assumed that investors are *risk averse*. If investors are given a choice between two investments which both have an expected return of 5 percent, and the standard deviation of the probability distribution for one investment is .001, while the standard deviation for the second distribution is .1, the investor would choose the investment with the smaller standard deviation (smaller risk).

DETERMINANTS OF REQUIRED RATES OF RETURN

Once an individual has excess income (savings) and decides to invest it, the rate of return for the investment instrument selected (savings account, bond, stock, real estate, etc.) becomes a crucial question. There are two important points to consider regarding required rates of return. First, *the overall level of required rates of return for all investments changes dramatically over time*. An example of such changes can be seen in what happened to the promised yield on Moody's Aaa corporate bonds (the highest grade corporate bonds), which was over 5 percent during the 1930s, declined to about 3 percent in the 1940s, and rose to over 14 percent in the early 1980s.[3] Obviously, it is important to understand why the required rate on a security changes over time. The second point regarding required returns in that *there is a wide range of required returns for alternative investments*. As an example, Table 1.1 contains a list of promised yields on alternative bonds. The point is, all of these are bonds and yet the yields differ significantly. One could detect even greater differences in expected returns if one could observe promised yields on common stock, real estate, etc.

Because the required returns on all investments change over time, and because of the large differences in required rates of return for alternative investments, investors should be aware of what determines the required return.

The Risk-Free Rate[4]

The risk-free rate (RFR) is the basic exchange rate assuming no uncertainty of future flows; i.e., the investor knows with certainty what cash flows he will receive and when he will receive them. There is no probability of default on the investment. Earlier this was referred to as the pure time value of money because the only sacrifice the lender made was to give up use of the money (consumption) for a period of time. This rate of interest is the price charged for the exchange between current goods (consumption) and future goods. There are

---

[3] For a graph of the long-term rates extending back to the 1920s see *Historical Chart Book* (Board of Governors of the Federal Reserve System, 1984).

[4] This subsection draws heavily from Irving Fisher, *The Theory of Interest* (New York: Macmillan, 1930; reprinted Augustus M. Kelley, 1961) Chapters 4, 7, and 16.

TABLE 1.1
Promised Yields on Alternative Bonds

Type of Bond	1978	1979	1980	1981	1982	1983
U.S. Govt.—3-Month Treasury Bills	7.19	10.07	11.43	14.03	10.61	8.61
U.S. Govt.—Long Term	7.89	8.74	10.81	12.87	12.23	10.84
Aaa Utility	8.96	10.03	12.74	15.56	14.41	12.10
Aaa Corporate	8.73	9.63	11.94	14.17	13.79	12.04
Baa Corporate	9.45	10.69	13.67	16.04	16.11	13.55

SOURCE: *Federal Reserve Bulletin*, various issues.

two factors, one psychological and one objective, that influence this price. The subjective factor is the *time preference of individuals for the consumption of income*. When individuals give up $100 of consumption this year, how much consumption do they want a year from now to compensate for this sacrifice? The level of this human desire for consumption influences the rate of compensation required. The time preference will vary among individuals with a composite rate determined by the market. While this composite time preference rate will change over time, one would expect any aggregate changes to be gradual and slow.

The objective factor that influences the risk-free rate is *the investment opportunities available in the economy*. The investment opportunities are a function of *the long-run real growth rate of the economy*. Therefore, a change in the economy's long-run growth rate causes a change in *all* investment opportunities and a change in the required returns on all investments. There are three factors that influence the real growth rate of the economy: (1) the long-run growth rate of the labor force; (2) growth in the average number of hours worked by the labor force; and (3) the growth rate of the productivity of the labor force. When examining these variables, you should emphasize *long-run* trends and not be mislead by short-run changes caused by cyclical fluctuations. The overall performance of these factors has generally suggested a real growth rate of about 3 percent as follows:

Long-Run Growth Rate of the Labor Force	1.5 to 2.0 percent
Average Number of Hours Worked	− 0.5 to 0.0 percent
Rate of Growth of Labor Productivity	2.0 to 3.0 percent

Unfortunately, the growth of productivity declined to about 1.5 percent during the 1970s. As a result, the real growth rate of the U.S. economy was between 3.0 and 3.5 percent during the 1950s and 1960s, but only about 2.5 percent during the 1970s and early 1980s.[5]

As the investment opportunities in an economy increase or decrease due to changes in the long-run real growth rate, the risk-free rate of return should likewise increase or decease; i.e., there is a *positive* relationship between the

[5] For a discussion of the components and changes over time, see *Economic Report of the President* (Washington, D.C.: U.S. Government Printing Office, 1981) and Arthur E. Rockwell, *"Long-Term U.S. Economic Outlook,"* (Los Angeles Security Pacific National Bank).

investment opportunities in an economy and the RFR. Again, while investment opportunities and, therefore, the RFR can change over time, one would expect these changes to be slow and gradual.

Factors Influencing the Nominal (Money) Rate on Risk-Free Investments

Because the factors that determine the level of the risk-free rate are long-term variables that change only gradually, one might expect the required rate on a risk-free investment to be quite stable over time. As noted previously, this has *not* been true for long-term government bonds over the period from 1930 through 1983. A more specific example can be derived from an analysis of the average yield on U.S. government treasury bills for the period 1967–1984 (see Table 1.2). This analysis is appropriate because government T-bills are a prime example of a default-free investment because of the government's unlimited ability to derive income from taxes or the creation of money. Especially notable is the steady increase in 1968 and 1969 followed by a sharp decline in 1971 and a mammoth increase (75 percent) in 1973. Again, following a decline to below 5 percent in 1976, rates increased from 7 percent in 1978 to over 14 percent in 1981 before declining to less than 9 percent in 1983. This indicates that rates almost tripled in a period of five years and then declined by almost one-third in two years.

The nominal (money) rate of interest on a default-free investment is definitely *not* stable in the long run or the short run, even though the underlying determinants of the RFR *are* quite stable. Therefore, it is important to consider the other factors that influence the *nominal* risk-free rate. Recall that these nominal rates are also referred to as money rates or market rates. The two factors that influence the *market* rates are relative ease or tightness in the capital market and the expected rate of inflation.

Relative Ease or Tightness.   This is a short-run phenomenon caused by a temporary disequilibrium in the supply and demand of future income streams or capital. As an example, starting from a point of equilibrium in the capital market, one can visualize a disruption caused by a change in monetary policy as evidenced by a sharp decrease in the growth rate of the money supply. In the short run, assuming no immediate adjustment in demand, there would be relative tightness and interest rates would increase. If one assumes a relatively stable supply of funds and a sudden increase in the government's demand for capital because of an increase in the deficit, there would also be an increase in money rates reflecting the relative tightness. Therefore, the market rate on risk-free investments can change in the short run because of temporary ease or tightness in the capital market. One would expect this to be a short-term effect because in the long run the higher or lower rates would affect supply and demand.

Expected Inflation.[6]   Up to this point the discussion has been in "real" terms

---

[6] This section draws heavily on Irving Fisher, *The Theory of Interest* (New York: Macmillan, 1930; reprinted Augustus M. Kelley, 1961) Chapter 2.

TABLE 1.2
Average Yields on U.S. Government Three-Month Treasury Bills

1967	4.29	1973	7.03	1979	10.07
1968	5.34	1974	7.84	1980	11.43
1969	6.67	1975	5.80	1981	14.03
1970	6.39	1976	4.98	1982	10.61
1971	4.33	1977	5.27	1983	8.61
1972	4.07	1978	7.19		

SOURCE: *Federal Reserve Bulletin*, various issues.

unaffected by changes in the price level. In discussing the rate of exchange between current consumption and future consumption, it was assumed that the 4 percent required return meant that you as an investor were willing to give up $1 of consumption today in order to consume $1.04 worth of goods and services one year from now. The exchange rate assumed *no change in prices* so a 4 percent increase in money wealth would mean a 4 percent increase in potential consumption of goods and services. If the price level is going to increase during the period of investment, you should increase your required rate of return by the rate of inflation to compensate. Assume that you want a 4 percent rate of return on a risk-free investment. The 4 percent required return is a "real" required rate of return. Assuming you expect prices to increase by 3 percent during the investment period, you should increase your required rate of return by approximately the same amount to about 7 percent $\{(1.04 \times 1.03) - 1\}$. If you do not increase your required return, you will receive $104 at the end of the year. Yet because prices have increased by 3 percent during the year, what previously cost $100 now costs $103 and you can only consume about 1 percent more at the end of the year ($104/103) - 1. Your ability to consume "real" goods and services has only increased by about 1 percent, and your "real" return is only 1 percent, not 4 percent. If you had required a 7 percent nominal return (in current dollars), your real consumption would have increased by 4 percent ($107/103) - 1. Therefore, an investor's *nominal* required rate of return (in current dollars) on a risk-free investment should be:

$$\text{Nominal RFR} = (1 + \text{RFR})(1 + \text{Expected Rate of Inflation}) - 1.$$

The nominal (market) rate of interest on a risk-free investment is *not* a good estimate of the "real" RFR because it can be changed dramatically in the short run by temporary ease or tightness in the capital market and in the long run by changes in the expected rate of inflation. Albert Burger of the St. Louis Federal Reserve developed a model to explain short-term interest rates that included growth of the monetary base (a proxy for the supply of funds), state of economic activity (demand for funds), and actual and expected rate of inflation.[7] The model did an excellent job of explaining past movements in short-term rates. A study by Fama not only found a strong relationship between short-term rates and inflation, but it contended that short-term rates were good *predictors* of infla-

---

[7] Albert E. Burger, "An Explanation of Movements in Short-Term Interest Rates," St. Louis Federal Reserve *Review* 58 no. 7 (July 1976): 10–22.

tion.[8] Prior to these studies, Yohe and Karnosky examined the relation between interest rates and past inflation and derived preliminary estimates of a "real" rate of interest of between 3 and 3.5 percent for the period 1952–1969.[9]

The Common Effect.   Note that all the factors discussed thus far regarding the required rate of return *affect all investments equally.* Irrespective of whether the concern is with stocks, bonds, real estate, or machine tools, if the expected rate of inflation increases from 2 percent to 6 percent, the required return on *all* investments should increase by 4 percent. On the other hand, if there is a general easing in the capital market because of an increase in the growth rate of the money supply that causes a decline in the market RFR of 1 percent, then the required return on *all* investments will decline by 1 percent.

A Risk Premium

A risk-free investment was defined as one for which the investor is certain of the amount and timing of his income stream. In contrast, an investor in the real world is not certain of the income he will receive, when he will receive it, or if he will receive it. Not only is there uncertainty involved in most investments, but there is a wide spectrum of uncertainty running from basically risk-free items, such as government T-bills, to highly uncertain items like the common stock of small companies engaged in a speculative operations such as oil exploration. Because most investors do not like uncertainty, they will require an additional return on an investment to compensate for the uncertainty. This additional required return is referred to as a *risk premium* that is added to the nominal RFR.

While the risk premium is a composite of all uncertainty, it is possible to consider several major sources of uncertainty. The three major ones discussed most frequently are: business risk, financial risk, and liquidity risk.

Business risk is the uncertainty of income flows caused by the nature of the firm's business. When a firm or an individual borrows money, his ability to repay the loan and pay interest on it is a function of the certainty of his income flows. As the income flows of the borrower become more uncertain, the uncertainty of the flows to the lender increases. Therefore, the lender will consider the basic pattern of income flows he receives and assign a risk premium on the basis of this distribution of flows. An example of a borrower with no uncertainty of income flows is the U.S. government because of its power to tax and print money. In contrast, there is the small oil drilling firm which has a potential range of returns from a large probability of no income to a small probability of a very large income. This uncertainty of income caused by the basic business of the firm is typically measured by the distribution of the firm's operating income over time;

---

[8] Eugene F. Fama, "Short-Term Interest Rates as Predictors of Inflation," *American Economic Review* 65 no. 3 (June 1975): 513–518.

[9] William P. Yohe and Denis S. Karnosky, "Interest Rates and Price Level Changes, 1952–69," St. Louis Federal Reserve *Review* 51 no. 12 (December 1969): 18–38.

i.e., the more volatile the firm's operating income over time relative to its mean income, the greater the business risk.[10]

In turn, the firm's operating income volatility is a function of its sales volatility and its operating leverage. Assuming a constant profit margin, if sales fluctuate over time, operating income will fluctuate. Hence, one can consider sales volatility the prime determinant of operating earnings volatility (business risk). One must also consider the production function of the firm. If all production costs are variable costs, then operating income will vary according to sales variability. In contrast, if some costs are fixed, (e.g., depreciation, administration, research), then operating income will be more volatile than sales. Depending upon where the firm is operating relative to its breakeven point, its earnings can increase by more than sales during good times and decline by more than sales during bad times. This effect of fixed costs on the volatility of operating earnings is referred to as *operating leverage*.[11] Therefore, a firm's business risk is measured in terms of the coefficient of variation of operating earnings. In turn, operating earnings volatility is a function of sales volatility and operating leverage.

$$\text{Business Risk} = f(\text{Volatility of Operating Earnings})$$

$$\text{Operating Earnings Volatility} = f(\text{Sales Volatility; Operating Leverage}).$$

Financial risk is the uncertainty introduced by the method of financing an investment. If a firm uses equity to finance a project, there is only business risk involved; the variability of income to the ultimate owner is the same as the variability of operating income (assuming a constant tax rate). If, in addition to using equity, a firm borrows money to help finance an investment, it introduces fixed financing charges (interest) that must be paid prior to paying the owners (the equity holders). As a result, the uncertainty (variability) of returns to the investor increases because of the method of financing the investment. This increase in uncertainty due to fixed cost financing is referred to as *financial risk* and causes investors to increase their risk premium.[12]

Liquidity risk is the uncertainty introduced by the secondary market for an investment. When an investor gives up current consumption (commits funds) by investing, there is an expectation that at some future time the investment will mature (as with a bond) or that the investor will be able to sell it to someone else (convert it into cash) and use the proceeds for current consumption or other investments. Given a desire to liquidate an investment (convert it into the most

---

[10] For a more detailed discussion of the measure see J. Fred Weston and Eugene F. Brigham, *Managerial Finance,* 7th ed. (Hinsdale, Ill.: The Dryden Press, 1981), 607–609 and James C. Van Horne, *Financial Management and Policy,* 6th ed. (Englewood Cliffs, N.J.: Prentice-Hall, 1983), 142–147.

[11] For a general discussion of operating leverage, see Eugene Brigham, *Financial Management,* 3d ed. (Hinsdale, Ill.: The Dryden Press, 1982), 598–602, and Steven E. Bolten and Robert L. Conn, *Essentials of Managerial Finance* (Boston: Houghton Mifflin Co., 1981), 40–47; J.R. Percival, "Operating Leverage and Risk," *Journal of Business Research* 2 no. 2 (April 1974).

[12] For a detailed discussion of financial leverage, see O. Maurice Joy, *Introduction to Financial Management,* 3d ed. (Homewood, Ill., Richard W. Irwin, Inc. 1983), 478–493.

liquid of all assets—cash), the investor is faced with two uncertainties: (1) how long will it take to make the conversion? (2) what price will be received? There is similar uncertainty for a buyer: how long will it take to acquire the asset and what will be the price? *The ability to buy or sell an investment quickly without a substantial price concession is known as liquidity.*[13] The greater the uncertainty regarding when the investment can be bought or sold, or the greater the price concession required to buy or sell it, the greater the liquidity risk. An example of an asset with almost no liquidity risk would be a U.S. Government treasury bill. A treasury bill can be bought or sold in minutes at a price almost identical to the quoted price. Purchase or conversion into cash is almost instantaneous and the price is known with almost perfect certainty. In contrast, an example of an illiquid asset would be a specialized machine or a parcel of real estate in a remote area. In both cases it might take a considerable period of time to find a potential seller or buyer and the expected selling price could vary substantially from expectations; i.e., the selling price is uncertain because it is a "unique" investment.

The risk premium on an investment is, therefore, determined by the basic uncertainty of expected returns to the investor. The specific factors influencing this uncertainty are sales volatility and operating leverage (business risk), any added uncertainty of returns caused by how the investment is financed (financial risk), and the uncertainty involved in buying or selling the investment (liquidity risk).[14]

Risk Premium = f(Business Risk; Financial Risk; Liquidity Risk).

Risk Premium and Portfolio Theory

An alternative view of risk has been derived based upon extensive work in portfolio theory and capital market theory by Markowitz, Sharpe, and others. These theories are dealt with in greater detail in Chapters 7 and 8, but the impact on the risk premium should be mentioned briefly. Their work indicated that investors should use an *external market* measure of risk. It has been shown that all rational, profit maximizing investors want to hold a completely diversified portfolio of risky assets, called the *market portfolio,* and they borrow or lend to arrive at the desired risk level. Under such conditions, the relevant risk measure for an individual asset is its *comovement with the market portfolio.* This covariance with the market portfolio of risky assets is referred to as an asset's *systematic risk.* It is that portion of an individual asset's total variance that is attributable

---

[13] For a discussion of a measure of liquidity applied to common stocks, see Michael D. Hirsch, "Liquidity Filters: Tools for Better Performance," *Journal of Portfolio Management* 2 no. 1 (Fall 1975): 46–50. For an analysis of the impact, see William L. Fouse, "Risk and Liquidity: The Keys to Stock Price Behavior," *Financial Analysts Journal* 32 no. 3 (May–June 1976): 35–45; and William L. Fouse, "Risk and Liquidity Revisited," *Financial Analysts Journal* 33 no. 1 (January–February, 1977): 40–45.

[14] For an empirical analysis of factors influencing the risk premium on bonds see Lawrence Fisher, "Determinants of Risk Premiums on Corporate Bonds," *Journal of Political Economy* 67 no. 3 (June 1959): 217–237. For an application to common stock see Fred D. Arditti, "Risk and the Required Return on Equity," *Journal of Finance* 22 no. 1 (March 1967): 19–36; and Richard S. Bower and Dorothy Bower, "Risk and the Valuation of Common Stock," *Journal of Political Economy* 83 no. 2 (May–June 1969): 437–453.

to the variability of the total market portfolio. In addition, individual assets have variance that is due to unique features called *unsystematic* variance. This unsystematic risk is not generally considered to be important because it is eliminated in any large portfolio composed of different earning assets—i.e., a diversified portfolio. At the same time, if an investor's portfolio is not large and well diversified this unsystematic variability will be important. Still, it is typically assumed that investors can become diversified by acquiring shares of an investment company that owns a diversified portfolio of assets.

Therefore, under these assumptions *the risk premium for an individual earning asset is a function of the asset's systematic risk with the aggregate market portfolio of risky assets.*

Risk Premium = f(Systematic Market Risk).

Some may believe that there might be a conflict between these two alternative measures of risk—i.e., the market measures of risk (systematic risk) and the fundamental determinants of risk (business risk, etc.). The fact is a number of studies have examined the relationship between the market measure of risk (systematic risk) and numerous corporate accounting variables used to measure business risk, financial risk, and liquidity. Notably, these studies have generally concluded that *there is a significant relationship between the two measures.*[15] Therefore, the two definitions of risk are *not* contradictory but are parallel and complementary. This consistency seems logical because, in a properly functioning capital market, one would expect that the market measure of the risk would reflect all the fundamental risk characteristics of the asset—not only internal risk but also external liquidity characteristics.[16] Therefore one can specify:

Risk Premium = f(Business Risk; Financial Risk; Liquidity Risk)

or

Risk Premium = f(Systematic Market Risk).

Summary of Required Return

The overall required rate of return on alternative investments is determined by three major sets of variables. The first is the economy's RFR which is influenced by the investment opportunities in the economy (i.e., the long-run real growth rate) and investors' time preferences for consumption. These factors are generally quite stable and change only gradually. The second set of variables influences the market rate on risk-free investments and includes short-run ease or tightness in the capital market and expected changes in the price level (infla-

---

[15] This will be discussed more fully in later chapters. A brief review of several of these studies is contained in Donald J. Thompson II, "Sources of Systematic Risk in Common Stocks," *Journal of Business* 49 no. 2 (April 1976): 173–188. A listing of these studies is contained in the reference section at the end of the chapter.

[16] In fact, some authors have advocated the use of "fundamental betas." In this regard, see Barr Rosenberg and Walt McKibben, "The Prediction of Systematic and Specific Risk in Common Stocks," *Journal of Financial and Quantitative Analysis* 8 no. 1 (March 1973): 317–333.

18   tion). *The first two sets of variables are the same for all investments.* The final set are those variables that influence the risk premium on investments, which is the factor that causes differences among investments. One can visualize the risk premium as being affected by fundamental factors such as business risk, financial risk, and liquidity risk. One can also envision the risk premium as a function of a composite market risk variable derived from portfolio theory and referred to as systematic risk. Therefore:

— Required Rate of Return
    Risk-Free Rate
        Time Preference for Consumption
        Investment Opportunities (long-run real growth rate)
— Factors Influencing the Market RFR
    Ease or Tightness of Capital Market
    Expected Rate of Inflation
— Risk Premium
    Business Risk
    Financial Risk
    Liquidity Risk
    or
    Systematic Risk.

RELATIONSHIP BETWEEN RISK AND RETURN

To better illustrate the forgoing material, this section contains a graph of the relationship between risk and return with an emphasis on what causes changes

FIGURE 1.1
Relationship between Risk and Return

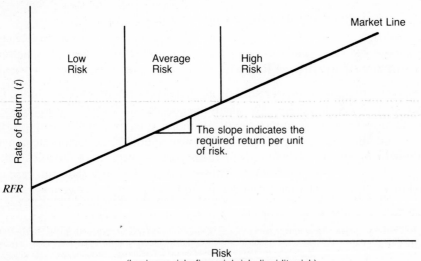

FIGURE 1.2
Effect of Capital Market on Investment Risk

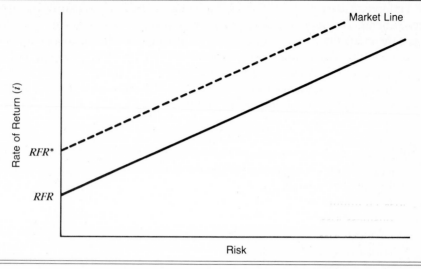

RFR* = nominal risk-free rate

in required returns over time. The basic relationship is shown in Figure 1.1. This graph indicates that investors want the risk-free return on riskless investments and that they increase their required return as perceived uncertainty increases. As noted, the slope of the market line indicates the composite return per unit of risk required by all investors. Investors who are more risk averse would have a steeper line, while others would be willing to accept a lower slope.

Given the market line indicating the average relationship, investors select investments that are consistent with their risk preferences. Some will only consider low risk, while others will welcome high risk investments.

Figure 1.2 indicates what happens to the market line when the notion of ease or tightness in the capital market or expected inflation is considered. The dotted line indicates a parallel *shift* in the market line caused by either temporary tightness in the capital market or an increase in the expected rate of inflation. The parallel shift in the line reflects the fact that these changes affect *all* investments irrespective of their level of risk.

SUMMARY

Individuals have expected income streams and patterns of desired consumption. Except in rare cases, these streams of income and desired consumption do not match. Therefore, there are certain economic units that have more income than they want to consume (savings), and they are willing to trade current consumption for a larger amount of future consumption. In contrast, others have more current consumption desires than income and want to dis-save (borrow future income). The rate of exchange between current and future consumption, assuming no risk, is the time value of money.

Because the required rate of return differs substantially between alternative investments and the required return on specific investments changes over time, it is important to examine the factors that influence the required rate of return on investments. The three major variables affecting it are the RFR, factors that influence the market rate on risk-free investments (most notably inflation), and the risk premium. The required rate of return on all investments is affected by changes in the RFR, by market ease or tightness, or by changes in the expected rate of inflation. Therefore the factor causing all differences *between* investments at a point in time is the risk premium.

QUESTIONS

1. Why do people invest? Be specific regarding when they are willing to invest and what they are looking for in the future.
2. Define an investment.
3. Why do people engage in negative saving or dis-saving? Be specific.
4. As a student are you saving or dis-saving? What do you expect to derive from this activity?
5. Divide a person's life from ages 20 to 70 into ten-year segments and discuss what the saving or dis-saving patterns during each of these periods are likely to be and why.
6. Would you expect the saving–dis-saving pattern to differ by occupation, e.g., for a doctor versus a plumber? Why or why not?
7. The *Wall Street Journal* reported that the yield on common stocks is about 4 percent, while a study at the University of Chicago contends that the rate of return on common stocks has averaged about 9 percent. Reconcile these statements.
8. The variance of the distribution of expected rates of return has been suggested as a good measure of uncertainty. What is the reasoning behind this measure? What is its purpose? Discuss.
9. What are the three *major* determinants of an investor's required rate of return on an investment? Discuss each of these briefly.
10. Discuss the two major factors that determine the market's risk-free rate (RFR). Which of these factors would you expect to be more volatile over the business cycle? Why?
11. Discuss the three factors that contribute to the risk premium of an investment.
12. You own stock in the Edgar Company and you notice that after a recent bond offering their debt/equity ratio has gone from 30 percent to 45 percent. What effect will this change have on the variability of the net income stream, other factors being constant? Discuss. Would you change your required rate of return on the common stock of the Edgar Company? Discuss.
13. Draw a properly labeled graph of the market line and indicate where you would expect to plot the following investments along that line. Discuss your reasoning for this placement.
    a. Common stock of large firms
    b. U.S. government bonds
    c. Low-grade corporate bonds
    d. Common stock of a new, small firm.
14. Discuss in nontechnical terms why you would change your nominal required

rate of return if you expected the rate of inflation to go from zero (no inflation) to 7 percent. Give an example of what would happen if you did not change your required rate of return under these conditions.

15. Assume the long-run growth rate of the economy increased by 1 percent, and the expected rate of inflation increased by 4 percent. What would happen to the required rate of return on government bonds, common stocks, and real estate? How would the effect differ? Show this graphically.

16. Discuss an example of a liquid investment asset and an illiquid asset. Indicate specifically why they are liquid or illiquid.

17. On February 1, you bought a stock for $24 a share and a year later you sold it for $29 a share. During the year you received a cash dividend of $1 a share. Compute the rate of return that you received on this stock.

18. On August 15, you purchased a stock at $40 a share and a year later you sold it for $36 a share. During the year, you received dividends of $2 a share. Compute your rate of return on this investment.

19. During the past five years, you owned two stocks that had the following annual rates of return:

Year	Stock T	Stock B
1	.17	.08
2	.08	.03
3	− .12	− .07
4	− .03	.02
5	.15	.04

a. Compute the average annual rate of return for each stock. Which is most desirable?

b. Compute the standard deviation of the annual rate of return for each stock (use the appendix if necessary). Which is the preferable stock in the terms of this measure of absolute risk?

c. Compute the coefficient of variations for each stock (use the appendix if necessary). Which stock is preferable on the basis of this *relative* measure of risk?

20. *CFA Examination III (June 1981)* As part of your portfolio planning process, it is suggested that you estimate the "real" long-run growth potential of the economy.

a. **Identify** and **explain** three major determinants of the economy's real long-run growth potential.

(15 minutes)

b. **Briefly discuss** the outlook for each of these three determinants of long-term growth. **Present** approximate estimates for each of these components and **calculate** the composite *real* growth potential for the next five years. (While you should provide a calculation, the emphasis should be on the process rather than on specific numbers.)

(10 minutes)

22   REFERENCES

Arditti, Fred D. "Risk and the Required Return on Equity." *Journal of Finance* 22 no. 1 (March 1967).

Beaver, William, Kettler, Paul and Scholes, Myron. "The Association between Market-Determined and Accounting-Determined Risk Measures," *Accounting Review* 45 no. 4 (October 1970).

Beaver, William, and Manegold, James. "The Association between Market-Determined and Accounting-Determined Measures of Systematic Risk: Some Further Evidence," *Journal of Financial and Quantitative Analysis* 10 no. 2 (June 1975).

Ben-Zion, Uri, and Shalit, Sol S. "Size, Leverage and Dividend Record as Determinants of Equity Risk," *Journal of Finance* 30 no. 4 (September 1975).

Bildersee, John S. "The Association between a Market-Determined Measure of Risk and Alternative Measures of Risk," *Accounting Review* 50 no. 1 (January 1975).

Bowman, Robert G. "The Theoretical Relationship Between Systematic Risk and Financial (Accounting) Variables," *Journal of Finance* 34 no. 3 (June 1979).

Breen, William, J., and Lerner, Eugene. "Corporate Financial Strategies and Market Measures of Risk and Return," *Journal of Finance* 28 no. 2 (May 1973).

Burger, Albert E. "An Explanation of Movements in Short-Term Interest Rates," St. Louis Federal Reserve *Review* 58 no. 7 (July 1976).

Fama, Eugene F., and Miller, Merton H. *The Theory of Finance.* New York: Holt, Rinehart and Winston, 1972.

Fisher, Irving. *The Theory of Interest.* New York: Macmillan, 1930; reprinted Augustus M. Kelley, 1961.

Fisher, Lawrence. "Determinants of Risk Premiums on Corporate Bonds," *Journal of Political Economy* 67 no. 3 (June 1959).

Fouse, William L. "Risk and Liquidity: The Keys to Stock Price Behavior," *Financial Analysts Journal* 32 no. 3 (May–June 1976).

Fouse, William L. "Risk and Liquidity Revisited," *Financial Analysts Journal* 33 no. 1 (January–February 1977).

Gonedes, Nicholas. "Evidence on the Information Content of Accounting Numbers: Accounting-Based and Market-Based Estimates of Systematic Risk," *Journal of Financial and Quantitative Analysis* 8 no. 2 (June 1973).

Hamada, Robert. "The Effect of the Firm's Capital Structure on the Systematic Risk of Common Stocks," *Journal of Finance* 27 no. 2 (May 1972).

Haugen, Robert, and Wichern, Dean. "The Intricate Relationship between Financial Leverage and the Stability of Stock Prices," *Journal of Finance* 30 no. 5 (December 1975).

Hirsch, Michael D. "Liquidity Filters: Tools for Better Performance," *Journal of Portfolio Management* 2 no. 1 (Fall 1975).

Lev, Baruch. "On the Association between Operating Leverage and Risk," *Journal of Financial and Quantitative Analysis* 9 no. 2 (June 1974).

Logue, Dennis, and Merville, Larry. "Financial Policy and Market Expectations," *Financial Management* 1 no. 2 (Summer 1972).

Melicher, Ronald W. "Financial Factors which Influence Beta Variations within a Homogeneous Industry Environment," *Journal of Financial and Quantitative Analysis* 9 no. 1 (March 1974).

Reints, William, and Vanderberg, Pieter A. "The Impact of Changes in Trading Location on a Security's Systematic Risk," *Journal of Financial and Quantitative Analysis* 10 no. 5 (December 1975).

Robichek, Alexander, and Cohn, Richard. "The Economic Determinants of Systematic Risk," *Journal of Finance* 29 no. 2 (May 1974).

Rosenberg, Barr, and McKibbon, Walt. "The Prediction of Systematic and Specific Risk in Common Stocks," *Journal of Financial and Quantitative Analysis* 8 no. 1 (March 1973).

Rosenberg, Barr, and Guy, James. "Prediction of Beta from Investment Fundamentals," *Financial Analysts Journal* 32 no. 3 (May–June 1976).

Thompson, Donald J., II. "Sources of Systematic Risk in Common Stocks," *Journal of Business* 49 no. 2 (April 1976).

Yohe, William P., and Karnosky, Denis S. "Interest Rates and Price Level Changes, 1952–1969," St. Louis Federal Reserve *Review* 51 no. 12 (December 1969).

Appendix 1A

Computation of Variance and Standard Deviation

The variance or standard deviation is a measure of how the actual values (rates of return) differ from the expected value (mean) of a given series of values. As noted, it is possible to conceive of other measures of this difference (dispersion), but the variance and standard deviation are the best known because of their uses in statistics and probability theory. Variance is defined as follows:

$$\text{Variance } (\sigma^2) = \Sigma(\text{Probability})(\text{Possible Return} - \text{Expected Return})^2$$
$$= \Sigma(Pi)(Ri - \bar{R})^2.$$

Consider the following example discussed in the chapter:

Probability of Possible Return (Pi)	Possible Return (Ri)	Pi Ri
.15	.20	.03
.15	−.20	−.03
.70	.10	.07
		$\Sigma = .07$

Therefore, the expected return ($\bar{R}$) is 7 percent. The dispersion of this distribution in terms of the variance is as follows:

Probability (Pi)	Return (Ri)	$Ri - \bar{R}$	$(Ri - \bar{R})^2$	$Pi(Ri - \bar{R})^2$
.15	.20	.13	.0169	.002535
.15	−.20	−.27	.0729	.010935
.70	.10	.03	.0009	.000630
				$\Sigma = .014100$

Thus, the variance (σ^2) is equal to .014100, i.e., 1.41 percent. The standard deviation is equal to the square root of the variance as follows:

$$\text{Standard Deviation } (\sigma) = \sqrt{\Sigma Pi(Ri - \bar{R})^2}.$$

Therefore, the standard deviation for the example above would be:

$$\sigma_t = \sqrt{.014} = .11874.$$

This would indicate a standard deviation of approximately 11.87 percent. Therefore, one could describe this distribution as having a mean (expected value) of 7 percent and a standard deviation of 11.87 percent.

In many instances an investor might want to compute the variance or standard deviation for a historical series. As an example, assume that you are given the following information on annual rates of return for common stocks listed on the New York Stock Exchange (NYSE):

Year	Annual Rate of Return
19_1	.07
19_2	.11
19_3	−.04
19_4	.12
19_5	−.06

In this case, we are not dealing with expected rates of return, but actual returns. Therefore, we can assume equal probabilities, and the expected value of the series is simply the sum of the series divided by the number of observations. In this example it is .04 (.20/5). The variance and standard deviation would be as follows:

Year	Ri	$Ri - \bar{R}$	$(Ri - \bar{R})^2$	
19_1	.07	.03	.0009	$\sigma^2 = .0286/5$
19_2	.11	.07	.0049	$= .00572$
19_3	−.04	−.08	.0064	
19_4	.12	.08	.0064	$\sigma = \sqrt{.00572}$
19_5	−.06	−.10	0100	$= .0756$
			$\Sigma = .0286$	

Therefore, regarding the performance of stocks during this period of time, one would say that the average rate of return was 4 percent and the standard deviation of annual rates of return was 7.56 percent.

COEFFICIENT OF VARIATION

In some instances one might want to compare the dispersion of two different series. A problem with the variance or the standard deviation is that they are *absolute* measures of dispersion; therefore, they can be influenced by the magnitude of the original numbers. When it is necessary to compare series with very different values, it is desirable to have a *relative* measure of dispersion. A potential measure that indicates this relative dispersion is the coefficient of variation which is defined as follows:

$$\text{Coefficient of Variation } (CV) = \frac{\text{Standard Deviation}}{\text{Expected Return}}.$$

The larger this value, the greater the dispersion *relative* to the expected return. For the previous example, the *CV* would be:

$$CV = \frac{.0756}{.0400} = 1.89.$$

It would be possible to compare this value to a comparable figure for a very different distribution. Assume you wanted to compare this to another investment alternative that had a mean return of 10 percent and a standard deviation of 9 percent. On the basis of the standard deviations alone, the second series has greater dispersion and might be considered higher risk (i.e., 9 percent versus 7.56 percent). In fact, the relative dispersion is much less.

$$CV_1 = \frac{.0756}{.0400} = 1.89$$

$$CV_2 = \frac{.0900}{.1000} = 0.90.$$

Considering the relative dispersion and the total distribution, most investors would probably prefer the second series.

Chapter 2

Alternative Investments— A Brief Overiew

I n any book on investments, the emphasis is usually on common stocks. Although this is also true, to a great extent, of the book in your hands, at the outset you should be aware that *there are numerous investment instruments available and the astute investor should consider a broad range of alternatives.* The principles of valuation and portfolio management discussed here are applicable to a variety of investments, with which we will deal. In some cases there may be problems in deriving inputs for the valuation models, but the concept will be the same.

One of the main reasons that you should consider numerous different investments is that you can derive substantial benefits from *diversification.* In the context of investments, diversification means *owning alternative investments with different return patterns over time* such that when one investment is yielding a low or negative rate of return, another investment will hopefully be enjoying above normal returns. The overall result is relatively stable earnings for the collection of investments (also referred to as *the portfolio*). Several subsequent chapters contain a discussion of the principle of diversification in greater detail. At this point it is important only to recognize that *proper diversification results in less variability in the rates of return for a portfolio over time* and, therefore, *helps reduce the uncertainty or risk of the portfolio.* Investors should consider a variety of investment instruments in order to diversify their portfolio so that the rates of return for the total portfolio will yield a relatively stable earnings pattern over time.

TYPES OF INVESTMENTS

The purpose of this chapter is to briefly discuss some of the major investment alternatives that all investors should consider for their portfolios. It will become apparent that some are not appropriate for particular investors given their individual risk or liquidity preferences. Hopefully, though, exposure to the numer-

28   ous alternatives will ensure that an investor considers the full range and does not miss some very worthwhile and interesting investment opportunities. We will begin our discussion with the most obvious alternatives, bonds and stocks, but will eventually consider some rather unusual possibilities as well as the rates of return on a number of the investments. We conclude the chapter with an analysis of the risk and return experience for several investment instruments and consider the relationship among the returns for these various investments.

Fixed-Income Investments

Within this category are investments that have a *fixed payment schedule*. With securities of this type, the owner is promised specific payments at predetermined times, although the legal force behind the promise varies. At one extreme, if the contractual payment is not made at the appointed time, the issuing firm can be declared bankrupt. In other cases, the payments must be made only if they are earned (an income bond); while in some instances, the payment does not have to be made unless the board of directors votes for it (preferred stock).

Savings Accounts.   It is probably not necessary to describe savings accounts except to indicate that they are an example of a fixed-income investment. When an individual deposits funds in a savings account at a bank or savings and loan association, he is really lending money to the institution to derive a fixed payment. Such investments are considered very low risk (almost all are insured), convenient, and liquid. Therefore, the rate of return is generally low compared to that for other alternatives.

Banks and savings and loan associations have created several new savings account instruments that should also be considered. The *passbook savings account* is the basic account; no minimum amount is required to open such an account and no minimum balance must be maintained at any point in time. In addition, it is generally possible to withdraw funds at any time with very little loss of interest. (Generally the loss is of interest for the current quarter only on the amount withdrawn.) Due to the flexibility involved, the promised interest on passbook accounts is lower than on the other types of accounts to be discussed.

For investors with larger amounts of funds who are willing to give up the use of the money for a specified period (i.e., give up liquidity), banks and S & Ls developed *certificates of deposits* (CDs) which involve minimum amounts (typically $500) and specified time periods (e.g., three months, six months, one year, 2.5 years). The promised rates on these CDs are higher than those for passbook savings, and the rate increases with the length of deposit of the CD. As an example, assume the rate on passbook savings is 5.25 percent; the rates on alternative CDs might be as follows: three month, 5.75 percent; six month, 6.00 percent; one year, 6.35 percent; 2.5 year, 9.25 percent. As stated, an investor can receive a higher rate because he makes a higher initial deposit, but also, and mainly, because he is willing to forgo the use of the money for a definite period of time. The longer the time period, the higher the rate. If the investor wants to cash in a CD prior to its stated expiration date, there is a heavy penalty in terms of the interest received on the money.

For investors with large sums of money (a minimum of $10,000), it has always been possible to invest in treasury bills (T-bills), which are short-term obligations (three or six months) of the U.S. government. The T-bills are sold at auction each week by the government, and the rate is determined by the current supply and demand for short-term money. To compete for the funds that might be invested in T-bills, banks and S & Ls developed *money market certificates* which are similar to CDs but involve a minimum investment of $10,000 and a minimum maturity of six months. A unique feature is that the promised rate on these certificates fluctuates at some premium over the weekly rate on six-month T-bills. As an example, if the rate on six-month T-bills were 8.50 percent, the rate on six-month money market certificates would be about 8.75 percent. These certificates are like regular CDs as they can only be redeemed at the bank of issue and there is a penalty for early withdrawal of funds.

Government Securities.[1]   All government securities are fixed-income instruments that generally differ in terms of the time to maturity when they are initially issued. Specifically, bills are for less than a year, notes are from one to ten years, and bonds are for over ten years. Because these are obligations of the U.S. government, they are riskless in terms of default and they are very liquid in terms of the ability to buy or sell them quickly at a known price.

Municipal Bonds.   These are similar to the bonds mentioned above, but they are issued by municipalities (states, cities, towns, etc.). Municipal bonds can be *general obligation* bonds wherein the full taxing power of the municipality is used to pay for them. Also there are municipal *revenue* bonds for which the revenue comes from a particular project (e.g., sewer bonds for which the revenue comes from water taxes).

A major feature distinguishing municipal bonds is that they are *tax-exempt,* which means the interest earned is exempt from taxation by the federal government and by the state that issued the bond, if the investor is a resident of that state. This feature is important to investors in high-tax brackets. Assume that an individual has an income such that his marginal tax rate is 49 percent. If he buys a regular bond with an interest rate of 8 percent, because he must pay 49 percent tax on this income, his net return after taxes is only 4.08 percent ($.08 \times [1 - .49]$). Such an investor would be better off with a tax-free bond that had a yield of 5 percent. As a result, yields on municipal bonds are below yields on comparable taxable bonds. (The yield is generally about 60 to 70 percent of the yield on taxable bonds).[2]

Corporate Bonds.   Corporate bonds can be broken down in terms of issuer (industrial corporations, public utility corporations, or railroads), in terms of quality (i.e., the rating assigned by an agency on the basis of probability of

[1] Chapter 14 contains a detailed discussion of marketable bonds including government securities, municipal bonds, and corporate bonds. For a readable discussion of bonds see the latest edition of *The Bond Book* (New York: Merrill Lynch, Pierce, Fenner & Smith).

[2] A readable article on the subject is "Investing in Tax-Exempts," *Business Week,* July 25, 1977, pp. 127–129.

30 default), or in terms of maturity (short term, intermediate term, or long term). In addition, they can be considered on the basis of their internal characteristics or the contractual promise to the investor implied, e.g., whether a bond is a debenture, a mortgage bond, an income bond, or a convertible bond, as described below.

Debentures.   These are promises to pay interest and principal, but typically there is no collateral put up and the lender is dependent upon the success of the borrower to receive the promised payment. Debenture owners usually have first call on the earnings and uncollateralized assets of a firm. If an interest payment is not made, the debenture owners can declare the firm bankrupt and claim the assets of the firm to pay off the bonds. A bond can take an almost unlimited variety of potential forms.

Mortgage bonds.   These bonds are similar to debentures, but in case of bankruptcy, there are specific assets pledged as backing for them. Examples would include land, buildings, or equipment.

Income bonds.   These have a stipulated coupon and interest payment schedule, but the interest is only due and payable *if the company earns the interest payment* by a stipulated date. If the required amount is not earned, the interest payment does not have to be made and the firm cannot be declared bankrupt. Instead, the interest payment is considered in arrears and, if subsequently earned, must be paid off. Given the lack of legal guarantees, an income bond is not considered as safe as a debenture or a mortgage bond.

Convertible bonds.   These bonds have all the characteristics of other bonds with the added feature that *they can be converted into the common stock of the company that issued the bond.* A firm could issue a $1,000 face value bond and stipulate that owners of the bond could, at their discretion, convert the bond into 40 shares of common stock. Such bonds are considered very attractive, especially when issued by growth firms. In this case, investors acquire an investment with a fixed income feature but also have the potential opportunity to convert the bond into the common stock of the firm and become an owner if the company does well. The interest rates on convertible bonds are generally lower than those on comparable straight debentures of the firm. The greater the potential of the company, the greater the yield differential because the conversion potential is of greater value.[3]

Zero coupon bonds.   As indicated, the typical bond promises the holder a series of interest payments and the payment of the principal at maturity. An alternative instrument that has become quite popular during the last several years is a zero coupon bond that does *not* promise any interest payments during

[3] For further discussion of bonds see Chapters 16–18. Also David M. Darst, *The Complete Bond Book* (New York: McGraw-Hill, 1975); David M. Darst, *The Handbook of the Bond and Money Markets* (New York: McGraw-Hill, 1981); and Marcia Stigum, *The Money Market: Myth, Reality and Practice* (Homewood, Ill.: Dow Jones-Irwin, 1978).

the life of the bond, but *only* promises the payment of the principal at maturity. In this case, the value of the bond is the discounted value of the principal payment at the required rate of return. As an example, the value of a bond that promises to pay $10,000 in five years is $6,806 if you require 8 percent on this bond—i.e., the present value factor for five years at 8 percent assuming annual compounding is .6806. The idea is that you would pay $6,806 now, you would not receive any interest payments, but you would receive $10,000 at the end of five years.

These instruments have some unique advantages for corporations issuing them and for tax-free investors (including IRA investments by individuals). They will be discussed further in Chapter 19.

Preferred Stock.   Preferred stock is a fixed-income security because a yearly payment is stipulated that is either a coupon (e.g., 5 percent of the face value) or a stated dollar amount (e.g., $5 preferred). The major difference between preferred stock and bonds is that the preferred stock payment (which is a dividend) is not legally binding and, for each period, must be voted on by the firm's board of directors as is a common stock dividend. Even if the firm earned enough money to pay the preferred stock dividend, the board of directors could vote to withhold it and, because most preferred stock is cumulative preferred, the dividend would accumulate.

Although preferred dividends are not legally binding, they are considered binding in a practical sense because of the credit implications of a missed dividend. Because preferred stock payments cannot be deducted from the taxes of the issuing firm, as the interest on bonds can, preferred stock has not been a very popular source of financing for most corporations except utilities. Ignoring the latter category, preferred stocks constitute less than 3 percent of all new corporate financing. At the same time, because corporations can legally exclude 85 percent of dividends from taxable income, preferred stocks have become popular investments for some financial corporations. The demand by these corporations has been such that, during many periods, the yield on high-grade preferred stock has been *below* the yield on high-grade bonds.[4]

Equity Instruments

Common Stock.   When considering investing, many investors think of common stock. Such stock represents *ownership* of a firm and, therefore, an investor who buys shares in a company is basically buying part of the company. Like any business owner, he will share in the company's successes and problems. If, like IBM or Xerox, the company does very well, the value of common stock will increase tremendously and the investor can become very wealthy. In contrast to such success stories, one can think of several instances in which the firms went

[4] For a detailed analysis of trends regarding preferred stock, see Donald E. Fischer and Glenn A. Wilt, Jr., "Non-Convertible Preferred Stock as a Financing Instrument, 1950–1965," *Journal of Finance* 23 no. 4 (September 1968): 611–624; and John S. Bildersee, "Some Aspects of the Performance of Non-Convertible Preferred Stocks," *Journal of Finance* 28 no. 5 (December 1973).

bankrupt (e.g., Penn Central) or eventually were forced to liquidate their assets. The point is, common stock entails all the advantages *and* disadvantages of ownership and is a relatively risky investment compared to fixed-income securities.

Other Common Stock Classifications

In addition to classifying equity investments according to the risk involved, the nature of the firm invested in should also be considered, both in terms of the type of business it represents and in terms of its earnings potential.

Classification by Business Line.   Common stocks can be categorized in a number of ways. An obvious broad classification is by function or general business line: industrial firms, utilities, transportation, or financial institutions.

The best-known firms are the *industrial* companies such as General Motors, General Electric, and IBM, a category which includes a wide variety of specific industries. In fact, Standard & Poor's has constructed a stock price index for 400 industrial firms and has broken these 400 firms down into about 80 separate industries including autos, electrical equipment, retail stores, and computers. Clearly, the industrial category includes a wide variety of different economic groups.

The *utility* category includes companies providing telephone service, electricity, gas, etc. Major factors differentiating these firms from industrial companies are their competitive position, the regulation involved, and their geographical limitations.

The *transportation* group includes the railroads that, at one point, were the only companies in this category. In recent years airlines have been added along with trucking companies and shipping firms.

Finally, the *financial* category includes banks, savings and loan companies, loan companies, and insurance firms.

Classification by Operating Performance.   Another technique for classifying companies is in terms of their internal operating peformance, e.g., growth companies, cyclical companies, and defensive companies. Such a classification helps the investor analyze the companies and subsequently make a valuation of the stock.

Growth companies.   These companies have opportunities to invest capital at rates of return that exceed the firm's required cost of capital. As a result of these opportunities, such firms retain a large amount of earnings (have low dividend payments) and their earnings grow rapidly—almost certainly faster than the average firm's. Growth firms can provide outstanding opportunities, but they can also be very risky if their growth rates decrease.

Cyclical companies.   These are closely tied to cyclical fluctuations in the economy and typically experience changes in earnings over the business cycle that are *greater* than the earnings changes for the aggregate economy. The industries that fall into this category are automotive, steel, and industrial machinery.

Defensive companies.   These are firms whose sales and earnings are expected to move countercyclically to the economy, especially during recessions. These firms are not expected to feel the effects of a recession. Typically these companies produce or sell products that are considered necessities. A prime example is retail food stores. These firms are also generally defensive during expansions, which means they do not feel the full benefits of an expansion because consumers generally reduce the proportion of income spent on necessities during expansions.

Investment Companies

Up to this point we have been discussing individual securities that can be acquired from the government, a state or municipality, or a corporation. However, rather than buy an individual stock or bond issued by one of these sources, an investor may choose to acquire shares in an investment company that owns a number of individual stocks and/or bonds. Specifically, an investment company sells shares in itself and uses the proceeds (the money invested in the investment company) to acquire bonds, stocks, or other investment instruments. As a result, an investor who acquires shares in an investment company is a partial owner of the investment company that, in turn, owns the stock or bonds. Therefore, the investor owns part of the *portfolio* of stocks or other investment instruments.

Investment companies are usually identified by the types of investment instruments they acquire. Some of the major types are as follows:[5]

Money market funds.   These are companies that generally invest in high-quality money market instruments like T-bills, high-grade commercial paper (public short-term loans) from various corporations and large CDs from the major money center banks. The yields on the money market portfolios are always above those on normal bank CDs because the investment is larger and there is a longer maturity than the typical individual CD involves. In addition, the returns on the commercial paper the fund acquires are above the prime rate. The typical minimum initial investment is $1,000 and there is no sales commission. Minimum additions are $250–$500. Notably, it is possible to withdraw the money invested in a money market fund at any time without any penalty; you receive the current interest to the day of withdrawal. Because of the high yields available and the extreme flexibility and liquidity, these funds that were introduced in 1975 have experienced phenomenal growth to over $200 billion in 1984 according to the Investment Company Institute.

Bond Funds.   These generally invest in various long-term government, cor-

---

[5] There is a detailed discussion of investment companies in Chapter 26.

porate, or municipal bonds. The funds differ in terms of the quality ratings assigned by various rating services to the bonds the funds invest in.

Common Stock Funds.   These invest in a variety of common stocks depending upon the stated investment objective of the fund. As a result of these objectives, a fund may invest in a range of stocks from income stocks to growth stocks to gold-mining stocks.

Balanced Funds.   These invest in a combination of bonds and stocks of various sorts depending on the stated objective of the fund.

Because the basic concept of an investment company is to pool the money of a number of individuals and have a group of professionals invest the money in a portfolio of investment instruments for a variety of objectives, it is possible to conceive of an investment company for almost every investment instrument discussed. We will see that this is true not only for the instruments discussed, but also for foreign securities, real estate, and commodities.

Special Equity Instruments

In addition to straight common stock investments, it is also possible to invest in *options* to acquire common stock at a specified price. The two major option instruments available are *warrants* and *puts and calls*.

Warrants.   A warrant is an option issued by a corporation that gives the holder the right to acquire the common stock of the company from the company at a specified price within a designated time period. The warrant does not constitute ownership of the stock, only the option to buy the stock.

Warrants are generally issued by corporations in conjunction with fixed-income instruments (bonds) to increase the appeal of the bonds. A firm with common stock selling at $45 a share can issue a $1,000 bond with ten warrants attached that will allow the bondholder to buy shares of the company's common stock from the company at $50 a share for the next five years. Assuming that investors have confidence in the growth prospects of the firm, these common stock warrants could become very valuable.

Quantities of warrants are currently available from large, well-known firms. We will deal in depth with the valuation of warrants in a subsequent chapter. For now, the reader merely should be aware of their availability and their usefulness in creating a well-balanced portfolio.[6]

Puts and Calls.   A call option is somewhat similar to a warrant in that it is an option to buy the common stock of a company at a specified price (referred to as the *striking price*) within a certain period. The difference is that the call option is *not* issued by the company but by another investor willing to "write" such an option and stand behind it. It also differs because it is typically for a much shorter period (less than a year compared to an initial term of over five years for warrants).

[6] For further discussion and references, see Chapter 23.

A put is an option that allows the holder to sell a given stock at a specified price during a designated time period. It is used by investors who expect the stock price to decline during the period or by investors who own the stock and want to have downside protection (i.e., protection from a price decline).

Prior to 1973, the put and call market was very small and was not used by the typical individual investor or by institutions because it did not have enough volume and liquidity. In April 1973, this changed dramatically with the establishment of the Chicago Board Options Exchange (CBOE). The CBOE introduced many features that helped to standardize this market. The numerous articles and books on the subject indicate that the options market is certainly a viable investment alternative and allows a wide range of risk for those who want to buy or sell options.[7]

Initial Stock Issues. An investor can occasionally acquire shares of a stock that was not public prior to the sale; an example was Coors Brewing in 1975. Because there is no public market for the stock when it is sold, the initial pricing is uncertain so the risk of these stocks is quite high. The new-issue market was very active during 1968 and 1969 and almost disappeared during 1974. A recovery after 1976 reached a peak in early 1981 followed by a decline in late 1981 and a substantial boom in late 1982 and 1983. The 1983 new-issue market was the most active and this carried into 1984.[8] The point is, unseasoned new issues provide substantial opportunities for high returns and risk. At various times, they have become "the hottest game in town," so investors should become aware of the potential risks and returns available in this area.[9]

Foreign Securities. American citizens think nothing of buying TV sets and automobiles produced by companies in Japan, Germany, and France, but they seldom consider the common stock of these firms. This is a mistake because the earnings of many foreign firms have grown substantially as a result of increasing sales to the U.S. market.

In addition to the potential rates of return, foreign securities are attractive because of the diversification possibilities. Specifically, foreign companies have sales and earnings patterns that are substantially different from those of U.S. firms. Hence, the correlation between the returns on foreign stock and those on U.S. stocks is much lower than is among alternative U.S. stocks. Therefore, even leaving aside the possibility of superior returns from the stocks of fast-growing

[7] Further discussion and extensive references are contained in Chapter 23. Also, in Chapter 23 there is a discussion of options on stock market indicator series such as the NYSE Index and even special industries (e.g., hotels, transportation).

[8] For a discussion of the revivals, see Peter C. DuBois, "Hot-and-Cold Issues," *Barron's,* July 19, 1976, p. 3; John C. Boland, "Avantek to Xidex," *Barron's,* October 30, 1978, p. 7; "Going Wild Over Going Public," *Business Week,* December 6, 1982, pp. 100–101; John C. Boland, "High-Flying Fledglings," *Barron's,* December 13, 1982, pp. 8–9; Diane Harris, "New Issues Stampede," *Financial World,* April 30, 1983, pp. 16–24.

[9] For a more detailed analysis of the historical short-run returns on initial stock issues, see Frank K. Reilly, "New Issues Revisited," *Financial Management* 6 no. 4 (Winter 1977): 28–42. Several earlier studies are reviewed in this article and listed in the references to this chapter.

36 foreign companies, there are substantial diversification advantages to be derived from foreign stocks.[10]

Commodities Trading

Almost all individuals who have excess funds to invest will consider buying either stocks or bonds. In contrast, very few potential investors ever consider trading commodities. While some characteristics of commodities trading probably justify this attitude, there are many aspects of this trading that are very similar to buying and selling stock.[11] Investors should be aware of the similarities between stocks and commodities and not be intimidated by some of the unique characteristics of commodity trading.

Spot Contracts.   In one sense, the commodity exchanges function like any other market, simply dealing in the purchase and sale of commodities (corn, wheat, etc.) for current delivery and consumption. This is obviously a very necessary function, bringing together those who produce commodities (farmers) and those who consume them (food processors). When someone wants to buy a commodity for current delivery, he goes to a "spot" market and acquires the available supply. There is a spot market for each commodity and prices fluctuate depending upon current supply and demand.

Future Contracts.   The bulk of trading on the commodity exchanges is in future contracts, which are contracts for the delivery of a commodity at some future date, usually within nine months. The price reflects what the participants believe the future will be for the commodity. In July of a given year one could speculate on the future prices for wheat on the Chicago Board of Trade in September, December, and March, and May of the next year. If investors expected the eventual price to rise, they could buy contracts now and sell them later; if they expected the prices to fall, they could sell contracts now and buy similar contracts later to cover the sale when the price declines. The number of commodities available for trading is quite large and increasing over time, as shown by the quotations in the *Wall Street Journal.*

There are several factors that distinguish investing in commodities from investing in stocks.[12] One of these is the greater use of leverage which increases the volatility of returns. Specifically, because an investor only puts up a small

---

[10] Chapter 22 contains a detailed analysis of international diversification including a discussion of several previous empirical studies of this topic. For a discussion of how to engage in foreign investing through American depository receipts (ADRs), see Anna Merjos, "How to Invest Abroad," *Barron's,* July 24, 1978, p. 9. Also, see Jill Bertner, "Foreign Stocks Catch on with Small Investors; Gains Are Bigger Lure than Diversification," *Wall Street Journal,* April 20, 1981, p. 36; Laurie Cohen, "International Stock Funds Attracting American Investors," *Chicago Tribune,* May 19, 1981, p. 3; Daniel Hertzberg, "Pension Managers Invest More Overseas, Aware of Risks but Hopeful about Profits," *Wall Street Journal,* July 2, 1981, p. 36.

[11] For a discussion of some of these similarities, see Charles V. Harlow and Richard J. Teweles, "Commodities and Securities Compared," *Financial Analysts Journal* 28 no. 5 (September–October 1972): 64–70.

[12] For a detailed discussion of these differences, see Richard J. Teweles, Charles V. Harlow, and Herbert L. Stone, *The Commodity Futures Trading Guide* (New York: McGraw-Hill, 1969), and Chapter 24 of this book where commodities are discussed in detail.

proportion of the contract (10–15 percent), when the price of the commodity changes, the change in the *total* value of the contract is large compared to the amount invested. Another unique aspect is the term of the investment. While stocks can have an infinite maturity, commodity contracts are almost never for more than a year.

Financial Futures. In addition to futures contracts on commodities, a recent innovation has been the introduction of futures contracts on financial instruments such as T-bills, Treasury bonds, etc. These futures contracts allow bond portfolio managers and financial managers to hedge against volatile interest rates. These are discussed in detail in Chapter 25, along with futures on stock market series such as the S&P 500, and the *Value Line* Index.

Real Estate

Real estate investments are somewhat like commodities in that most investors consider this area interesting and probably profitable but believe that it is limited to a select group of experts with large capital bases. The fact is there are real estate investments that are feasible for all investors because they do not require large capital commitments. We will begin our discussion by considering low-capital alternatives.

Real Estate Investment Trusts (REIT). An REIT is basically a closed-end mutual fund (these terms are defined in Chapter 26) designed to invest in various real estate properties. The idea is similar to a common stock mutual fund except that the purpose is to invest in property and buildings rather than in stocks and bonds. There are several types.

Construction and development trusts and mortgage trusts. Construction and development trusts lend the money required during the initial construction of a building, shopping center, etc. Mortgage trusts are involved in long-term financing of various properties, acquiring the long-term mortgage once the construction is completed.

Equity trusts. Equity trusts own various income-producing properties such as office buildings or apartment houses. As a result, an investor who buys an equity trust is buying a portfolio of income-producing properties.

REITs were very popular during the period 1969–1970 and grew substantially. They experienced problems during 1973–1974 due to general economic and money market conditions. While they are subject to unique risks, it appears that the concept is viable for investors interested in real estate investments.[13]

---

[13] For a general description of REITs, see Peter A. Schulkin, "Real Estate Investment Trusts," *Financial Analysts Journal* 27 (1971): 33–40. More recent appraisals are contained in Mary Greenbaum, "Searching for Bargains Among the REITs," *Fortune,* March 12, 1979, pp. 153–156; Michael Brody, "Sounder Ground," *Barron's,* May 21, 1979, pp. 4–5; James Carberry, "Many REITs Stage Comeback, Aided by an Attraction of Foreign Investors," *Wall Street Journal,* August 6, 1979, p. 6; Mary Greenbaum, "The Return of the REITs," *Fortune,* May 18, 1981, pp. 111–112.

Direct Real Estate Investments.   The most common type of direct real estate investment is the purchase of a home. It is often said that this will be the largest investment you will make in your career. This is certainly possible when you consider that the purchase of a single-family house will probably cost a minimum of over $80,000.[14] The purchase of a home is considered an investment because the buyer is committing a sum of money for a number of years and hopes to get that money back along with some excess return when the house is sold. The financial commitment includes a down payment and specific payments made over a 20- to 30-year period.

Raw land.   Another form of direct real estate investment is the purchase of raw land with the intent of selling it in the future at a profit. From purchase to sale it is necessary to make payments on the mortgage and pay all taxes until the time at which someone will want to buy the lot. Obviously, a major risk is the general lack of liquidity of such an asset compared to that of most stocks and bonds.[15]

Apartment buildings.   It is possible to acquire a building with rental apartments with a low down payment. Once the initial down payment is made, the intent is to derive enough from the rents to pay the expenses of the building including the mortgage payments. For the first few years following the purchase, there is generally no reported income from the building because of deductible expenses. Subsequently, there is a cash flow and an opportunity to profit from the sale of the building after the equity has increased.[16]

Land development.   The idea of buying raw land, splitting it into individual lots, and building houses on it is a feasible form of investment, but such an undertaking requires a substantial commitment of capital and time and extensive expertise. Clearly, the returns from a successful development can be significant.[17]

Low-Liquidity Investments

All of the investment alternatives mentioned thus far are generally traded on national markets and have good liquidity. The investments briefly discussed in

[14] The average price of a new home in early 1984 was in excess of $100,000 according to the Federal Home Loan Bank.

[15] Some indication of the returns on this form of investment can be derived from Frank K. Reilly, Raymond Marquardt, and Donald Price, "Real Estate as an Inflation Hedge," *Review of Business and Economic Research* 12 no. 3 (Spring 1977): 1–19.

[16] A well-known article on this topic is Paul F. Wendt and Sui N. Wong, "Investment Performance: Common Stocks Versus Apartment Houses," *Journal of Finance* 20 no. 3 (June 1965): 633–646.

[17] For a general review of studies of returns on real estate see Stephen E. Roulac, "Can Real Estate Returns Outperform Common Stocks?" *Journal of Portfolio Management* 2 no. 2 (Winter 1976): 26–43; C. F. Sirmans and James R. Webb, "Investment Yields in the Money, Capital and Real Estate Markets: A Comparative Analysis for 1951–1976," *The Real Estate Appraiser* 44 no. 4 (July–August 1978): 40–46; Michael S. Young, "Comparative Investment Performance: Common Stocks Versus Real Estate," *Real Estate Issues* 2 no. 1 (Summer 1977): 30–47; Harold A. Davison and Jeffrey E. Palmer, "A Comparison of the Investment Performance of Common Stocks, Homebuilding Firms, and Equity REITs," *The Real Estate Appraiser* 44 no. 4 (July–August 1978): 35–39. For a somewhat concerned view of the outlook for real estate syndications, see Howard Rudnitsky and John Heins, "The Fellow Who Sold the Brooklyn Bridge to Tourists Might Have Done Better Packaging Real Estate Syndications," *Forbes,* December 19, 1983, pp. 143–150.

this section are certainly viable alternatives for individual investors, but they have never been considered by financial institutions because they have low liquidity and high transaction costs. Many of these assets are sold at auctions and there is substantial uncertainty regarding the expected price under such conditions. It may take a long time to get the "right" price for some of them. The transaction cost on these investments is usually very high compared to that on bonds and stocks. This is because there is no national market for these investments, so local dealers must be compensated for the added carrying costs and the cost of searching for buyers or sellers. Given these two attributes, many observers consider these investment alternatives to be more in the nature of hobbies, although the returns have often been substantial.

Antiques.   The most obvious antique investors are antique dealers who specifically acquire antiques in order to refurbish them and sell them at a profit. From the few specific instances in which the value of antiques can be established based upon sale prices at large public auctions, it can be estimated that returns to serious collectors may be substantial.[18]

Art.   There are many examples of paintings that have subsequently increased in value and the implied rates of return could be significant. These returns are generally realized on the works of well-known artists which enjoy some liquidity. Therefore, art can be used as an investment vehicle, but it typically requires a large capital base to acquire the work of known artists.[19]

Coins and Stamps.   The market for coins and stamps is fragmented compared to the stock market, but it is more liquid than most of the markets for art and antiques. The reason is that the volume of coins and stamps traded has prompted the publication of several price lists on a weekly and monthly basis.[20] These areas are therefore much more amenable to investment because the investor can use a grading specification to determine the correct market price on most coins or stamps. Once graded, a coin or stamp can usually be disposed of quite quickly through a dealer.[21]

---

[18] Richard H. Rush, *Antiques as an Investment* (New York: Bonanza Books, 1968); Peter Keresztes, "Collecting for Profit: Art, Antique Market Is Booming, but Gains Still Can Be Illusory," *Wall Street Journal,* March 13, 1978, p. 34; Roger Ricklefs, "Some Tips on Collecting Art and Antiques: Prices on Most Pieces Aren't Exorbitant," *Wall Street Journal,* October 1, 1979, p. 40.

[19] Richard H. Rush, *Art as an Investment* (Englewood Cliffs, N.J.: Prentice-Hall, 1961). Also, James Winjum and Joanne Winjum, "The Art Investment Market," *Michigan Business Review,* November 1974: 1–5; and Gigi Mahon, "Investing in Art," *Barron's,* July 16, 1979, p. 4 et seg.; Jean Ross-Skinner, "Art: How Good an Investment?" *Dun's Review* (May 1980): 60–68; "The Incredible Art Market," *Institutional Investor* 14 no. 9 (September 1980): 99 et seg; Cynthia Saltzman, "Once Touted as Good Investments, Art, Stamps and Other 'Collectibles' Have Plunged in Price," *Wall Street Journal,* July 12, 1982, p. 34.

[20] There are several monthly coin magazines including *Coinage* (Encino, CA.: Behn-Miller Publications, Inc.). Besides providing current prices for a wide range of coins, the magazine contains articles on investing in specific types of coins. Also see Nicholas Ronalds, "While Money in Your Pocket Loses Value, Rare Old Coins are Appreciating Smartly," *Wall Street Journal,* August 27, 1979, p. 28; Bob Wolenik, "Coins: The Inflation Killers," *Coinage* (April 1979): 80, 81, 84, 86.

[21] For a discussion of grading stamps, see Richard Cabeem, *Standard Handbook of Stamp Collecting* (New York: Thomas Y. Corwell, 1957). For a discussion of a stamp auction, see Myron Keller, "Above Catalog," *Barron's,* April 12, 1976, p. 11.

Diamonds.   Everyone knows that diamonds are forever and a girl's best friend. A more relevant question is, are they a good investment? They can be and have been during most recent periods, but it is important to recognize that they can be *very illiquid,* the grading process is still generally *quite subjective,* most investment grade gems require *substantial investments,* and there is no return during the holding period until the stone is sold. In fact, during the holding period there are storage costs and appraisal costs when you go to sell it.[22]

HISTORICAL RETURNS ON ALTERNATIVE INVESTMENTS

Given the previous discussion of some of the investments available, it seems appropriate to examine the historical performance of some of them. Therefore, this section contains a discussion of several studies that have dealt with the rates of return for some of these investment instruments. This should provide the reader with a better background on the returns that are possible and the relationship among returns. As noted, information about the relationship among returns is important for optimal diversification.

During the past two decades a number of studies have been done on the rates of return available on common stocks. These studies were prompted by the interest in common stocks as an investment and because the data on stocks, as compared to other investments, were readily available. Recently there has been a growing interest in bonds and their performance has been dealt with in several studies. The impact of inflation has also been a subject of growing interest, and studies have examined the computed nominal and "real" rates of return on investments. Finally, a few studies have examined the performance of other assets, e.g., real estate, foreign stocks, commodities. In this section we will review results of some of the major studies.

The 50-Year Fisher – Lorie Study

The most famous work in this area involved the Fisher – Lorie studies done at the University of Chicago.[23] These studies were substantially more complete than all prior studies. They included *all* common stocks listed on the NYSE since 1926 and considered all capital changes such as splits and mergers. In addition, they included taxes and commissions as well as showing the effect of reinvesting dividends. The results were widely publicized and became a new benchmark for all portfolio managers. Subsequently, the authors updated the returns through

---

[22] For a discussion of problems and opportunities, see Jonathan Kwitny, "Average Diamond Buyer May Find that Gains Are Elusive Even as Prices on Stones Increase," *Wall Street Journal,* April 10, 1978, p. 38; Jonathan Kwitny, "Our Man Takes a Flier in Emeralds, Only to Discover All that Glitters Isn't Gold," *Wall Street Journal,* March 5, 1979, p. 30; "When to Put Your Money into Gems," *Business Week,* March 16, 1981, pp. 158 – 161.

[23] James H. Lorie and Lawrence Fisher, "Rates of Return on Investment in Common Stock," *Journal of Business* 37 no. 1 (January 1964): 1 – 17; Lawrence Fisher and James H. Lorie, "Rates of Return on Investment in Common Stock: The Year-by-Year Record, 1926 – 1965," *Journal of Business* 40 no. 3 (July 1968): 219 – 316; Lawrence Fisher, "Outcomes for Random Investments in Common Stocks Listed on the New York Stock Exchange," *Journal of Business* 38 no. 2 (April 1965): 149 – 161.

TABLE 2.1
Long-Run Rates of Return for Common Stocks Listed on the New York Stock Exchange under Various Assumptions

	12/25 to 12/76		12/56 to 12/76		12/66 to 12/76	
	Equal Weighted	Value Weighted	Equal Weighted	Value Weighted	Equal Weighted	Value Weighted
Dividend Reinvested; Cash to Portfolio:						
Tax Exempt; Current Dollars	9.0	9.1	9.6	8.5	8.4	7.4
Tax Exempt; Deflated Dollars	6.5	6.6	5.6	4.5	2.4	1.4
Lower Tax Rate; Current Dollars	8.3	8.3	8.7	7.5	7.4	6.2
Lower Tax Rate; Deflated Dollars	5.8	5.9	4.7	3.6	1.5	0.3
Higher Tax Rate; Current Dollars	7.2	7.1	7.4	6.1	6.2	4.9
Higher Tax Rate; Deflated Dollars	4.7	4.7	3.5	2.2	0.4	-0.9
Without Dividend Reinvested; Cash to Portfolio:						
Tax Exempt; Current Dollars	7.3	7.9	9.9	8.6	8.4	7.1
Tax Exempt; Deflated Dollars	5.8	6.7	6.4	5.1	2.5	1.3
Lower Tax Rate; Current Dollars	7.0	NA[a]	9.0	NA	7.5	NA
Lower Tax Rate; Deflated Dollars	5.4	NA	5.4	NA	1.6	NA
Higher Tax Rate; Current Dollars	6.4	6.8	7.6	6.2	6.3	4.8
Higher Tax Rate; Deflated Dollars	4.6	5.3	3.9	2.6	0.4	-0.9
Rates of Change in Prices; Cash to Portfolio:						
Tax Exempt; Current Dollars	4.6	4.3	5.9	4.5	4.9	3.4
Tax Exampt; Deflated Dollars	2.2	1.9	2.0	0.7	-0.9	-2.3

[a] Not available.

SOURCE: Lawrence Fisher and James H. Lorie, *A Half Century of Returns on Stocks and Bonds* (Chicago: The University of Chicago Graduate School of Business, 1977). Reprinted by permission.

42

1976.[24] The recent study expanded the earlier work in three ways: (1) in addition to computing rates of return for an equal weighted portfolio (there is an equal dollar amount invested in each stock), the authors computed rates of return for a value weighted portfolio (the amount of stock in the portfolio is proportional to its market value); (2) besides computing rates of return on a current dollar basis, the rates of return are adjusted for changes in the price level (inflation); (3) this study includes rates of return for long-, intermediate-, and short-term government securities.

The rates of return reported in Table 2.1 were taken from over 20 tables and were limited to three time intervals considered to be of interest: the longest period available (12/25 to 12/76); the latest 20-year period (12/56 to 12/76); and the latest 10-year period (12/66 to 12/76).

The first block of returns are based on the assumption that all dividends are reinvested and that the portfolio is held at the end of the period. An analysis of these returns allows for several interesting observations. The first figure in the upper left hand corner (9.0) is of prime interest since it is widely quoted as the long-run rate of return on common stocks. This figure does not take into account any taxes, the effects of inflation, or commissions or taxes entailed in selling the portfolio. The long-run effect of inflation over the 50-year period was about 2.5 percent, but this increased to about 4 percent for the last 20 years, and to almost 6 percent during the last 10 years of the study. Because of this increase, Fisher and Lorie felt compelled to report both sets of returns. The effect of taxes indicates that the difference between tax exempt and lower tax rates was about 1 percent with another 1 percent due to higher tax rates. Finally, the effect of weighting the stocks in the portfolio also had a changing impact. For the longest period (51 years) there was *very little difference* in returns due to the weighting. In contrast, during the last 20 years and 10 years the rates of return differed by at least 1 percent. This indicates that recently stocks with a higher market value did not do as well as other stocks.

A comparison of the rates of return in the first and second blocks indicates the effect of reinvesting dividends compared to consuming dividends. Finally, the last set of returns indicates the effect of dividends on the total rates of return. In general the impact was significant. Between 4 and 5 percent a year and over 50 percent of the total return is due to the dividend return.

The total listing of common stock results clearly shows that investors in common stock listed on the NYSE have received positive rates of return during the great majority of periods since 1926. Also investors have received fairly substantial positive returns during most periods even when considering commissions and taxes.

Table 2.2 contains selected annual rates of return on U.S. treasury securities of different maturities for different time intervals (51 years, 20 years, 10 years). All of these securities are considered to be risk-free in the sense that there is no probability of default.

An analysis of the rates of return *across* a line indicates the influence of

[24] Lawrence Fisher and James H. Lorie, *A Half Century of Returns on Stocks and Bonds* (Chicago: The University of Chicago Graduate School of Business, 1977).

TABLE 2.2
**Long-Run Rates of Return on U.S. Treasury Securities
for Different Maturities under Various Assumptions**

Interest Reinvested	12/25 to 12/76			12/56 to 12/76			12/66 to 12/76		
	Long	Inter-mediate	Short	Long	Inter-mediate	Short	Long	Inter-mediate	Short
Tax Exempt; Current Dollars	3.4	3.6	3.0	4.2	4.7	5.3	5.4	5.7	7.0
Tax Exempt; Deflated Dollars	1.1	1.2	0.7	0.4	0.8	1.4	−0.4	−0.1	1.0
Lower Tax; Current Dollars	2.7	2.9	2.4	2.8	3.3	3.9	3.5	3.8	5.0
Lower Tax; Deflated Dollars	0.4	0.6	0.1	−1.0	−0.5	0.1	−2.2	−1.9	−0.8
Higher Tax; Current Dollars	1.7	2.0	1.6	1.0	1.5	2.1	1.3	1.6	2.7
Higher Tax; Deflated Dollars	−0.6	−0.3	−0.7	−2.7	−2.2	−1.6	−4.3	−4.0	−3.0

SOURCE: Lawrence Fisher and James H. Lorie, *A Half Century of Returns on Stocks and Bonds* (Chicago: The University of Chicago Graduate School of Business, 1977). Reprinted by permission.

maturity on rates of return. (The long-term bonds have a maturity of at least ten years, the intermediate bonds have maturities of between five and ten years, and it was assumed that the short-term bonds were acquired when they had about a year left to maturity and were sold after six months.) For the 51-year period, the intermediate securities consistently provided the highest rates of return. The effect of taxes on bond returns was similar to the effect on stock returns, about 1 percent for lower taxes and an additional 1 percent for the higher tax rates. The most important effect was that of inflation. For the total period the returns adjusted for inflation were about 2 percent lower but were typically positive. For the last 20 years, the "real" returns (returns adjusted for inflation, i.e., deflated dollars) were only about 1 percent without taxes and were negative after taxes. During the last ten years, *almost all* deflated returns were negative. Therefore, individuals who invested in government securities during the last ten years were not able to increase their consumption of goods and services as a result of this investment.

The rates of return on U.S. treasury securities have generally been consistent with expectations over the long run (51 years). In contrast, recent experience has been unique because of the effect of inflation on relative returns. This indicates the importance of considering the effect of inflation when analyzing individual investments and constructing portfolios, i.e., the returns from an investment must be adjusted for inflation.

Ibbotson – Sinquefield Studies

A second set of major studies dealing with the nominal and real rates of return on common stocks, bonds, and bills was done by Ibbotson and Sinquefield at the

University of Chicago.[25] The authors present year-by-year historical rates of re-turn for six major classes of assets in the United States: (1) common stocks, (2) small capitalization stocks, (3) long-term U.S. government bonds, (4) long-term corporate bonds, (5) U.S. treasury bills, and (6) consumer goods (a measure of inflation). For each asset, the authors present total rates of return that reflect dividend or interest income as well as capital gains or losses. None of the returns is adjusted for taxes or transaction costs.

Given the monthly and annual rates of return, the authors computed geo-metric mean returns over longer periods and the arithmetic mean returns to derive the average returns on the assets analyzed. In addition to the six basic series, the authors computed seven monthly returns series derived from the basic series. The first four of these were net returns reflecting different pre-miums. The first was a net return from investing in common stocks rather than in U.S. treasury bills. This net return is referred to as the *risk premium* involved in investing in a risky alternative, rather than in something basically risk-free like treasury bills. There was also a *small stock premium* which is the return on small capitalization stocks minus the return on total stocks (the S&P 500). The third net return was the difference in investing in long-term government bonds and U.S. treasury bills. This is referred to as a *maturity premium* because in both cases the securities are considered default-free; the only difference between them is their maturity dates. Finally, the difference in net returns from long-term corporate bonds and long-term government bonds was determined. This is re-ferred to as a *default premium* because the difference between the two long-term bond series is that the corporate bonds involve a possibility of default. The final five series derived are basically inflation-adjusted returns for the initial five. The authors ascertained the *real* rates of return on common stocks, small capital-ization stocks, treasury bills, long-term government bonds, and long-term corpo-rate bonds.

A summary of the results for the basic and derived series is contained in Table 2.3. The geometric mean returns are always lower than the arithmetic returns, and the difference increases with the standard deviation of returns.[26]

Over the period 1926–1981, common stocks returned 9.1 percent a year compounded annually. Excluding dividends, stocks increased at a rate of 4.0 percent a year. For the total period, the risk premium on common stocks was 5.9 percent and the inflation-adjusted "real" returns were 6.1 percent per year. Beyond the performance by a broad cross section of common stocks as repre-sented by the S&P 500, the authors also examined the performance by small capitalization stocks which included the smallest 20 percent of stocks listed on the NYSE where size was measured in terms of the market value of common

[25] The original study was Roger G. Ibbotson and Rex A. Sinquefield, "Stocks, Bonds, Bills and Inflation: Year-by-Year Historical Returns (1926–1974)," *Journal of Business* 49 no. 1 (January 1976): 11–47. The results were updated in 1977, 1979 and 1982 as follows: Idem, *Stock, Bonds, Bills, and Inflation: The Past (1926–1976) and the Future (1977–2000)* (Charlottesville, Va.: Financial Analysts Research Founda-tion, 1977); *Stocks, Bonds, Bills, and Inflation: Historical Returns (1926–1978)* (Charlottesville, Va.: Financial Analysts Research Foundation, 1979); *Stocks, Bonds, Bills, and Inflation: The Past and the Future,* 1982 ed. (Charlottesville, Va.: Financial Analysts Research Foundation).

[26] There is a discussion of the difference between the arithmetic and geometric mean in the appendix to this chapter. Readers not familiar with the difference are encouraged to read this before proceeding further.

TABLE 2.3
Basic and Derived Series: Historical Highlights (1926–1981)

Series	Annual Geometric Mean Rate of Return	Arithmetic Mean of Annual Returns	Standard Deviation of Annual Returns	Number of Years Returns are Positive	Number of Years Returns are Negative
Common Stocks	9.1%	11.4%	21.9%	37	19
Small Capitalization Stocks	12.1	18.1	37.3	38	18
Long-Term Corporate Bonds	3.6	3.7	5.6	42	14
Long-Term Government Bonds	3.0	3.1	5.7	40	16
U.S. Treasury Bills	3.0	3.1	3.1	55	1
Consumer Price Index	3.0	3.1	5.1	47	9
Equity Risk Premium	5.9	8.3	22.0	34	22
Small Stock Premium	4.1	6.0	20.5	33	23
Default Premium	0.5	0.5	3.2	35	21
Maturity Premium	0.0	0.2	6.5	27	29
Common Stock—Inflation Adjusted	5.9	8.3	21.9	35	21
Small Capitalization Stocks—Inflation Adjusted	8.8	14.7	36.4	38	18
Long-Term Corporate Bonds—Inflation Adjusted	0.5	0.9	8.2	33	23
Long-Term Government Bonds—Inflation Adjusted	−0.1	0.3	8.3	31	25
U.S. Treasury Bills—Inflation Adjusted	0.0	0.1	4.5	31	25

SOURCE: Roger G. Ibbotson and Rex A. Sinquefield, *Stocks, Bonds, Bills, and Inflation: Historical Returns (1926–1981)* Charlottesville, Va.: Financial Analysts Research Foundation, 1982.

stock outstanding. The results indicated that these stocks experienced a geometric mean return of 12.1 percent and an arithmetic return of 18.1 percent. The geometric mean premium return for these small firms compared to the broad cross section of stocks was 4.1 percent.

Although the small capitalization stocks and the cross section of stocks outperformed the other asset groups in terms of rates of return, the returns for these assets were also more volatile as measured by the standard deviation of annual returns. These results for the small capitalization stocks should be kept in mind when reading Chapter 7 on efficient markets since a number of studies have examined this relative performance in detail.

Long-term U.S. government bonds experienced a 3.0 percent annual return over the period 1926–1981. During the same period, the real return on these bonds was 1 percent and the maturity premium for these bonds, compared to treasury bills, was 0.7 percent. The returns on these bonds were far less volatile than the annual returns on common stocks.

The annual compound rate of return on long-term corporate bonds was 3.6 percent over the total period. The default premium on these bonds, compared to that on long-term government bonds, was only 0.5 percent. The inflation adjusted return was 0.5 percent. The volatility of these bonds was similar to the volatility on government bonds.

During the entire period, U.S. treasury bills returned 3.0 percent a year, which was equal to the rate of inflation for the total period. As a result, the inflation-adjusted return on T-bills for the entire period was 0.0 percent. The return on T-bills was not very volatile; the standard deviation was the lowest for all of the series examined. In contrast, the inflation-adjusted T-bill series was more volatile.

This study generally confirmed the results of the Fisher-Lorie studies and extended the analysis to other alternatives. The returns were as expected and were generally consistent with the uncertainty measured using the standard deviation of annual returns.

Robichek – Cohn – Pringle Study

The R–C–P study deals with the rates of return on a number of investments including stocks, bonds, commodities, real estate, and foreign securities.[27] In the study *ex post* rates of return and correlation coefficients are computed for 12 investment media for the period 1949–1969 inclusive, and the implications of the results for portfolio construction are analyzed. The purpose of the study was to show the difference in returns for alternative investments. The specific media considered were: (1) Standard & Poor's Industrial Common Stock Index, (2) S&P Utility Index, (3) U.S. government 2 percent bonds of 1970–1965, (4) Bethlehem Steel 2 3/4 percent bonds due in 1970, (5) Canadian Pacific Perpetual 4 percent bonds, (6) farm real estate, (7) cotton future contracts, (8) wheat future contracts, (9) copper future contracts, (10) Japanese common stocks,

[27] Alexander A. Robichek, Richard A. Cohn, and John J. Pringle, "Returns on Alternative Media and Implications for Portfolio Construction," *Journal of Business* 45 no. 3 (July 1972): 427–443.

TABLE 2.4
Mean Rates of Return and Variability of Annual Returns
for Alternative Investment Media: 1949–1969

	Arithmetic Mean	Geometric Mean	Standard Deviation[a]	Coefficient of Variation[b]
S&P Industrials	12.97	11.63	17.55	1.51
S&P Utilities	9.31	8.60	12.43	1.45
Japanese Stocks	24.07	18.94	41.30	2.18
Australian Stocks	7.80	6.82	14.22	2.09
Treasury Bill Yields	3.01	3.00	1.60	0.53
U.S. Government 2 percent bonds, 1970–1065	2.48	2.37	4.68	1.97
Bethlehem Steel, 2 3/4 Percent Bonds (Maturity 1970)	2.06	2.00	3.40	1.70
Canadian Pacific Perpetual 4 Percent Bonds	1.56	1.40	5.71	4.08
Farm Real Estate	9.56	9.47	4.50	0.48
Cotton Futures	17.10	3.80	66.77	17.57
Wheat Futures	−0.49	−22.88	64.07	2.80
Copper Futures	121.02	26.60	244.02	9.17

[a] Standard deviation about geometric mean.
[b] Coefficient of Variation = Standard Deviation ÷ Geometric Mean.
SOURCE: Alexander A. Robichek, Richard A. Cohn, and John J. Pringle, "Returns on Alternative Investment Media and Implications for Portfolio Construction," *Journal of Business* 45 no. 3 (July 1972). Copyright © 1972 by The University of Chicago Press. Reprinted by permission of The University of Chicago Press.

(11) Australian common stocks, and (12) treasury bill yields. A summary of the mean returns and the standard deviation of returns for the total period 1949–1969 are contained in Table 2.4. The authors felt that the returns on U.S. equities were as expected. Industrials had a higher mean return and a higher standard deviation than did utilities. The returns on Japanese stocks indicated that the mean annual return for the 20 one-year periods was a surprising 24.07 percent. The holding period return over the entire time was 18.94 percent. The coefficient of variation of returns for Japanese stocks was higher than it was for U.S. stocks. Returns from Australian common stocks, at 6.8 percent, were considerably lower than returns from other groups. On the other hand, the relationship between the instability of returns and the mean return was about the same for Australian stocks as for Japanese issues and somewhat higher than it was for American stocks.

The *ex post* compound rates of return over the 20-year period for the three bonds studied were 2.4 percent for the U.S. government 2 percent bonds, 2.0 percent for the Bethlehem Steel bonds, and 1.4 percent for the Canadian Pacific Perpetual 4 percent bonds. All of these *ex post* returns exhibited a high degree of variance in relation to the mean return, and all three bonds produced negative returns during many years. The *ex post* returns on these bonds were lower than the average rate of return on treasury bills, which was 3 percent.

The most notable characteristic of the results on farm real estate was the apparent stability of returns over time. The geometric mean rate of return was 9.47 percent and the standard deviation was only 4.5 percent, resulting in a

TABLE 2.5
Matrix of Correlation Coefficients

	S&P Indus-trial	S&P Utilities	U.S. Govern-ment	Bethle-hem Steel	Canadian Pacific	Farm Real Estate	Cotton Futures	Wheat Futures	Copper Futures	Japanese Stocks	Australian Stocks
S&P Utilities	.59[a]	—									
U.S. Govt. 2 percent of Bonds 1970–65	−.54[b]	−.17	—								
Bethlehem Steel 2 3/4 Percent Bonds 1970	−.30	−.08	.81[a]	—							
Canadian Pacific Perpetual 4 Percent Bonds	.23	.34	.02	.10	—						
Farm Real Estate	−.13	−.15	−.19	−.26	−.13	—					
Cotton Futures	.29	−.04	−.21	−.12	−.01	−.09	—				
Wheat Futures	.29	.06	−.31	−.41	.14	−.24	.67[a]	—			
Copper Futures	.32	−.24	−.20	−.10	.12	−.21	.23	.38	—		
Japanese Stocks	−.07	.11	−.21	−.19	.05	.48[b]	−.31	−.09	−.13	—	
Australian Stocks	.22	−.17	−.28	−.05	−.44[b]	−.29	.33	.04	.13	−.15	—
Treasury Bill Yields	−.55[a]	−.66[a]	.26	.20	−.40	.06	−.41	−.35	.05	−.02	.14

[a] Significant at the .01 level. Critical values and corresponding significance levels as follows: .55 (1 percent), .43 (5 percent), .37 (10 percent), and .29 (20 percent).
[b] Significant at the .05 level.

coefficient of variation of only .48. This relative measure of volatility was considerably lower than that of any other long-term investment medium.

Returns on commodity futures showed very large year-to-year variations. Comparison of the returns on futures contracts in the three different commodities shows that wheat provided a high negative mean return (minus 22.88 percent), copper a high positive rate of return (26.60 percent), and cotton a very low mean return (3.8 percent).

The authors examined the correlation among the rates of return over time for the alternative investment media (for a discussion of covariance and correlation, see Appendix 2B at the end of this chapter). The matrix of correlation coefficients is contained in Table 2.5.

The correlation coefficients among the various media were generally low and the signs of the coefficients were almost equally divided between positive and negative values. The common stock returns for the different countries had very low correlation coefficients. This is especially true for the Japanese stocks, which are negatively correlated with U.S. industrial stocks and Australian stocks. Given the high rates of return on these Japanese stocks, the negative correlations indicate that they would be very desirable additions to the portfolio of a U.S. investor.

The returns from real estate were very stable and not significantly correlated with any other media. Commodity futures, on the other hand, were extremely volatile year-to-year and variability among the commodities were quite different than that among other media. These general findings indicate that enlarging the universe of investment alternatives would be of benefit in portfolio construction in terms of the risk-return opportunities. Given the correlation coefficients, the authors specifically constructed a number of portfolios and found that there was a significant improvement in their risk-return characteristics based upon the multimedia diversification. The authors contended that *the results support the arguments that investors should look beyond common stocks and treasury bills in constructing investment portfolios.*

SUMMARY

The purpose of this chapter was to briefly describe some of the major investment alternatives available to individuals. In addition, a major intent was to help the reader become aware of *the vast variety of these alternatives.*[28] The reader should be aware of *all* of the alternatives for two reasons. The first is that they provide a wide variety of risk and return choices that may be of interest to different investors. One man's garbage may be another man's feast. As an example, one reader, after becoming familiar with commodities trading, may decide that it is much too speculative and would not consider it at all, while another reader may believe that it is very exciting and may decide to commit a large share of resources to this area.

In addition, it is widely acknowledged that considering several areas in

---

[28] There are obviously a number of investment alternatives we are not able to cover. For a collection of articles on alternative investments by a number of authors, see Leo Barnes and Stephen Feldman (eds.) *Handbook of Wealth Management* (New York: McGraw-Hill, 1977).

terms of risk can benefit the investor's portfolio. Assuming that the alternatives are not highly correlated, it can be shown that the variance of returns for an investor's total portfolio can be substantially reduced through diversification.

The chapter finished with a discussion of three studies concerned with the historical rates of return on common stocks and a number of other investment alternatives including bonds, commodities, and real estate. The results of these studies pointed toward two generalizations:

1. There was typically a positive relationship between the rates of return on an investment medium and the variability of the rate of return over time. This is consistent with expectations in a world of risk-averse investors who require a higher return to assume more uncertainty.

2. The correlation of the rates of return for alternative investments were typically quite low, which indicates that there are definite benefits to diversification among investments in order to reduce the variability of the investor's total portfolio.

QUESTIONS

1. What are the major advantages to investing in the common stock rather than the corporate bonds of the same company? What are the major disadvantages?

2. Discuss briefly why an investor might prefer utility common stocks to industrial common stocks.

3. Would you expect the returns on industrial common stocks to have the same pattern over time as the common stock of financial firms? Why or why not?

4. Assume that the returns from transportation stocks are not correlated with the returns from financial stocks. Will this benefit an investor who has both types of stock in his portfolio? Why or why not?

5. How does a bond differ from a common stock in terms of the certainty of returns over time? Draw a simple time-series graph to demonstrate the pattern of returns you might imagine.

6. Assume that you had the opportunity to acquire convertible bonds from a growth company or a utility. Both firms have straight debentures that yield 9 percent. Given the conversion feature, which convertible bond would have the lower yield? Why?

7. Define a spot commodity contract and a future commodities contract.

8. A contract involves 5,000 bushels of wheat. Assuming wheat is selling for $3.50 a bushel, the total value of the contract is $17,500. Given a margin of 15 percent, an investor would have to put up $2,625 to purchase such a contract. Ignoring commissions, if the price of wheat increases to $3.75 a bushel, what is the percentage of change in the value of the contract, and what is the investor's return on his investment? Assuming a decline in price to $3.35, what is his return? Show all calculations.

9. Define an REIT and briefly discuss the alternative types.

10. Discuss the difference in liquidity between an investment in raw land and an investment in common stock. Be specific as to why there is a difference and how they differ. (Hint: begin by defining liquidity.)

11. Define a stock warrant. Define a call option. Discuss how a warrant differs from a call option.

12. What has the CBOE contributed to the call option market that has caused significant growth in the market since 1973? Be specific.

13. Would you expect the price of an initial public offering to fluctuate more when it is first offered than the price of a listed stock involved in a new offering? Why or why not?

14. It is contended that the returns on foreign stocks should have low correlation with the returns on U.S. stocks. What is the rationale behind such an assumption?

15. Why is it contended that antiques and art are generally illiquid investments? Be specific in your discussion. Why are coins and stamps considered to be more liquid than antiques and art? Again be specific and consider what it would require to sell the various assets.

16. Look up in the *Wall Street Journal* the current *maturity premium* on U.S. government securities. The long-term security should have a maturity of at least 20 years.

17. Each week in *Barron's* on the last two or three pages there is a set of stock indexes for foreign countries. For a recent week, determine the percent of change in the index for Japanese and Australian stock and compare this to the percent of change in the Dow-Jones Industrial Average for the same period. Do the results of the comparison indicate any benefits to diversification among securities from these countries? Why or why not?

18. *CFA Examination I (June 1980)* The following information is available concerning the historical risk and return relationships in the U.S. capital markets:

U.S. Capital Markets
Total Annual Returns, 1947–1978[a]

Investment Category	Arithmetic Mean	Geometric Mean	Standard Deviation of Return[b]
Common Stocks	11.80%	10.30%	18.0%
Preferred Stocks	3.30	2.90	9.2
Treasury Bills	3.53	3.51	2.1
Long Government Bonds	2.60	2.40	6.2
Long Corporate Bonds	2.40	2.20	6.7
Real Estate	8.19	8.14	3.5

[a] Adapted from R. G. Ibbotson and C. L. Fall, "The U.S. Market Wealth Portfolio," *The Journal of Portfolio Management.*

[b] Based upon arithmetic mean.

a. **Explain** why the geometric and arithmetic mean returns are not equal and whether one or the other may be more useful for investment decision-making.

(5 minutes)

b. For the time period indicated, **rank** these investments on a risk adjusted basis from most to least desirable. **Explain** your rationale.

(6 minutes)

c. Assume the returns in these series are normally distributed.
   1. **Calculate** the range of returns that an investor would have expected to achieve 95 percent of the time from holding common stocks.

(4 minutes)

2. Suppose an investor holds real estate for this time period. **Determine** the probability of at least breaking even on this investment.

(5 minutes)

d. Assume you are holding a portfolio composed entirely of real estate. **Give** the justification, if any, for adopting a mixed asset portfolio by adding long government bonds.

(5 minutes)

REFERENCES

Agmon, Tamir. "The Relations among Equity Markets: A Study of Share Price Co-Movements in the United States, United Kingdom, Germany and Japan." *Journal of Finance* 27 no. 3 (September 1972).

Barnes, Leo, and Feldman, Stephen eds. *Handbook of Wealth Management*. New York: McGraw-Hill, 1977.

Bildersee, John S. "Some Aspects of the Performance of Non-Convertible Preferred Stocks." *Journal of Finance* 28 no. 5 (December 1973).

The Bond Book. New York: Merrill Lynch, Pierce, Fenner & Smith, 1982.

Cabeem, Richard. *Standard Handbook of Stamp Collecting*. New York: Thomas Y. Crowell Company, 1957.

Darst, David M. *The Complete Bond Book*. New York: McGraw-Hill, 1975.

Darst, David M. *The Handbook of the Bond and Money Markets*. New York: McGraw-Hill, 1981.

Davidson, Harold A., and Palmer, Jeffrey E. "A Comparison of the Investment Performance of Common Stocks, Homebuilding Firms, and Equity REITs." *The Real Estate Appraiser* 44 no. 4 (July–August 1978).

Fischer, Donald E., and Wilt, Glenn A. Jr. "Non-Convertible Preferred Stock as a Financing Instrument, 1950–1965." *Journal of Finance* 23 no. 4 (September 1968).

Fisher, Lawrence, and Lorie, James H. "Rates of Return on Investments in Common Stock: The Year-by-Year Record, 1926–1965." *Journal of Business* 40 no. 3 (July 1968).

Fisher, Lawrence, and Lorie, James H. *A Half Century of Returns on Stocks and Bonds*. Chicago: University of Chicago Graduate School of Business, 1977.

Grubel, Herbert G. "Internationally Diversified Portfolios: Welfare Gains and Capital Flows." *American Economic Review* 58 no. 5 (December 1968).

Harlow, Charles V., and Teweles, Richard J. "Commodities and Securities Compared." *Financial Analysts Journal* 28 no. 5 (September–October 1972).

Ibbotson, Roger G., and Sinquefield, Rex A. "Stocks, Bonds, Bills, and Inflation:

Year-by-Year Historical Returns (1926–1974)." *Journal of Business* 49 no. 1 (January 1976).

Ibbotson, Roger G., and Sinquefield, Rex A. *Stocks, Bonds, Bills, and Inflation: Historical Returns (1926–1981).* Charlottesville, Va.: Financial Analysts Research Foundation, 1982.

Lessard, Donald R. "International Portfolio Diversification: A Multivariate Analysis of a Group of Latin American Countries." *Journal of Finance* 28 no. 3 (June 1973).

Logue, Dennis E. "On The Pricing of Unseasoned Equity Issues, 1965–1969." *Journal of Financial and Quantitative Analysis* 8 no. 1 (January 1973).

McDonald, J. G., and Fisher, A. K. "New Issue Stock Prices Behavior." *Journal of Finance* 27 no. 1 (March 1972).

Reilly, Frank K. "Further Evidence on Short-Run Results for New Issue Investors." *Journal of Financial and Quantitative Analysis* 8 no. 1 (January 1973).

Reilly, Frank K. "New Issues Revisited." *Financial Management* 6 no. 4 (Winter 1977).

Reilly, Frank K., and Hatfield, Kenneth. "Investor Experience with New Stock Issues." *Financial Analysts Journal* 25 no. 5 (September–October 1969).

Reilly, Frank K., Marquardt, Raymond, and Price, Donald. "Real Estate as an Inflation Hedge." *Review of Business and Economic Research* 12 no. 3 (Spring 1977).

Robichek, Alexander A., Cohn, Richard A., and Pringle, John H. "Returns on Alternative Investment Media and Implications for Portfolio Construction." *Journal of Business* 45 no. 3 (July 1972).

Roulac, Stephen E. "Can Real Estate Returns Outperform Common Stocks?" *Journal of Portfolio Management* 2 no. 2 (Winter 1976).

Rush, Richard H. *Antiques as an Investment.* New York: Bonanza Books, 1968.

Rush, Richard H. *Art as an Investment.* Englewood Cliffs, N.J.: Prentice-Hall, 1961.

Schulkin, Peter A. "Real Estate Investment Trusts." *Financial Analysts Journal* 27 no. 3 (May–June 1971).

Sirmans, C. F. and Webb, James R. "Investment Yields in the Money, Capital and Real Estate Markets: A Comparative Analysis for 1951–1976." *The Real Estate Appraiser* 44, no. 4 (July–August 1978).

Stigum, Marcia. *The Money Market: Myth, Reality and Practice.* Homewood, Ill.: Dow Jones-Irwin, 1978.

Teweles, Richard J., Harlow, Charles V., and Stone, Herbert L. *The Commodity Futures Trading Guide.* New York: McGraw-Hill, 1969.

Wendt, Paul F., and Wong, Sui N. "Investment Performance: Common Stocks Versus Apartment Houses." *Journal of Finance* 20 no. 3 (June 1965).

Young, Michael S. "Comparative Investment Performance: Common Stocks Versus Real Estate." *Real Estate Issues* 2 no. 1 (Summer 1977).

53

Appendix 2A

Geometric Mean Returns

When examining the average returns on an investment over an extended period of time, the typical measure used is the arithmetic average of annual rates of return. As will be shown, the arithmetic average return can be biased upward if there is substantial variability in the returns over time. An alternative measure of the central tendency is the geometric mean of the annual returns. This measure is considered superior by some investigators because it is the same formulation that is used to derive compound interest and provides a proper measure of the true ending wealth position for the investment involved.

ARITHMETIC MEAN BIAS

As is known, the arithmetic mean (designated $\overline{X}$) is the sum of each value in a distribution divided by the total number of values.

$$\overline{X} = \Sigma X/n.$$

A problem occurs if there are large changes in the annual returns over time. Consider the example in which a nondividend paying stock goes from \$50 to \$100 during Year 1 and back to \$50 during Year 2. The annual returns would be:
— Year 1: 100%
— Year 2: −50%
Obviously, during the two years there was *no* return on the investment. Yet the arithmetic mean return would be:

$$[(+100) + (-50)]/2 = 50/2 = 25\%.$$

In this case, although there was *no* change in wealth and, therefore, no return, the arithmetic mean return is computed at 25 percent.

GEOMETRIC MEAN

The geometric mean (designated G) is the nth root of the product arrived at by multiplying the values in the distribution by each other. Specifically, it is:

$$G = \Pi X^{1/n}$$

where Π stands for *product*. When calculating the geometric mean returns, it is customary to use holding-period returns, which are the yield plus 1.0 (e.g., a positive 10 percent return is designated 1.10; a negative 15 percent return is designated 0.85). This is done because a negative yield causes the geometric mean calculation to be meaningless. As an example, consider the extreme example used in the previous discussion of the arithmetic mean:

	Yield (percent)	Holding-Period Return
Year 1:	100	2.00
Year 2:	−50	0.50

$$G = (2.00 \times 0.50)^{1/2} = (1.00)^{1/2} = 1.00 - 1.00 = 0\%.$$

To get the yield, 1.00 is subtracted from the geometric holding-period return. As can be seen, this answer is consistent with the ending wealth position of the investor. He ended where he began and had a 0 percent return during the period.

Extended Example

Consider the following, more complete example using rounded percentage of price changes for a stock market series during a recent ten year period.

Year	Percentage of Price Change	Holding Period Change
1	15.00	1.15
2	−17.00	0.83
3	−28.00	0.72
4	38.00	1.38
5	18.00	1.18
6	−17.00	0.83
7	−3.00	0.97
8	4.00	1.04
9	12.00	1.12
10	8.00	1.08

$$\bar{X} = \Sigma X/n = 30/10 = 3.0\%$$
$$G = \Pi X^{1/n}$$
$$= 1.1334^{1/10} = 1.012604 - 1.00 = 1.3\%.$$

As shown, the arithmetic mean price change is more than two times as large as the geometric mean price change. Because of the upward bias in the arithmetic mean, it will *always* be larger (except where all returns are equal), and the discrepancy will be wider with a more volatile series. If there is a large difference between the arithmetic mean and the geometric mean, it can be inferred that the returns were very volatile.

Appendix 2B

Covariance and Correlation

COVARIANCE

It is assumed that almost all students have been exposed to the concept of covariance, so the following discussion is set forth in intuitive terms with an example that will, hopefully, help the reader recall the concept.[1]

Covariance is an absolute measure of the extent to which two sets of numbers move together over time, i.e., move up or down together. In this regard *move together* means they are generally above their means or below their means at the same time. Covariance between i and j is defined as:

$$Cov_{ij} = \frac{\Sigma(i - \bar{i})(j - \bar{j})}{N}.$$

If we define $(i - \bar{i})$ as i' and $(j - \bar{j})$ as j', then

$$Cov_{ij} = \frac{\Sigma i'j'}{N}.$$

Obviously, if both numbers are consistently above or below their individual means at the same time, their products will be positive and the average will be a large positive value. In contrast, if the i value is below its mean when the j value is above its mean or vice versa, their products will be large negative values and you would find negative covariance. Table 2B.1 should make this clear. In this example the two series generally moved together, so there was positive covariance. As noted, this is an *absolute* measure of their relationship and, therefore, can range from $+\infty$ to $-\infty$. Note that the covariance of a variable with itself is its *variance*.

---

[1] For a more detailed, rigorous treatment of the subject the reader is referred to any standard statistics text including Ya-lun Chou, *Statistical Analysis* (New York: Holt, Rinehart and Winston, 1975), 152–156.

TABLE 2B.1
Calculation of Covariance

Observation	i	j	$i - \bar{i}$	$j - \bar{j}$	$i'j'$
1	3	8	-4	-4	16
2	6	10	-1	-2	2
3	8	14	$+1$	$+2$	2
4	5	12	-2	0	0
5	9	13	$+2$	$+1$	2
6	11	15	$+4$	$+3$	12
Σ	$= 42$	72			34
Mean	$= 7$	12			
Cov_{ij}	$= \dfrac{34}{6} = +5.67$				

CORRELATION

To obtain a relative measure of a given relationship we use the correlation coefficient (r_{ij}) which is a normalized measure of the relationship:

$$r_{ij} = \frac{Cov_{ij}}{\sigma_i \sigma_j}.$$

You will recall from your introductory statistics course that $\sigma_i = \sqrt{\dfrac{\Sigma(i - \bar{i})^2}{N}}$ so, if the two series move *completely* together, then the covariance would equal $\sigma_i \sigma_j$ and

$$\frac{Cov_{ij}}{\sigma_i \sigma_j} = +1.0.$$

The correlation coefficient would equal unity and we would say the two series are perfectly correlated. Because we know that

$$r_{ij} = \frac{Cov_{ij}}{\sigma_i \sigma_j},$$

we also know that $Cov_{ij} = r_{ij}\sigma_i\sigma_j$, which is a relationship that may be useful when computing the standard deviation of a portfolio because, in many instances, the relationship between two securities is stated in terms of the correlation coefficient rather than the covariance.

Continuing the example given in Table 2B.1, the standard deviations are computed in Table 2B.2 as is the correlation between i and j. As shown, the two standard deviations are rather large and similar but not the same. Finally, when the positive covariance is normalized by the product of the two standard deviations, the results indicate a correlation coefficient of .898, which is obviously quite large and close to 1.00. Apparently these two series are highly related.

TABLE 2B.2
Calculation of Correlation Coefficient

Observation	$i - \bar{i}$[a]	$(i - \bar{i})^2$	$j - \bar{j}$[a]	$(j - \bar{j})^2$
1	-4	16	-4	16
2	-1	1	-2	4
3	$+1$	1	$+2$	4
4	-2	4	0	0
5	$+2$	4	$+1$	1
6	$+4$	16	$+3$	9
		42		34

$\sigma^2 = 42/6 = 7.00 \qquad\qquad \sigma^2 = 34/6 = 5.67$

$\sigma_i = \sqrt{7.00} = 2.65 \qquad\qquad \sigma_j = \sqrt{5.67} = 2.38$

$$r_{ij} = Cov_{ij}/\sigma_i\sigma_j = \frac{5.67}{(2.65)(2.38)} = \frac{5.67}{6.31} = .898.$$

[a] from Table 2B.1

Chapter 3

Organization and Functioning of Securities Markets

T he stock market, Wall Street, and the Dow Jones Industrials are part and parcel of our everyday experience. Each evening we find out how they fared on the television news broadcasts; each morning we read about their prospects for a rally or decline in the pages of our daily newspaper. Yet the operation of the securities market remains a given to most investors. What this market is, how it functions, and who is involved in it are imperfectly understood at best. It is the purpose of this chapter to define the securities market, both primary and secondary, and to indicate those persons who are key to its operation, especially the specialists.

FINANCIAL MARKETS

What is a Market?

Prior to discussing the organization and functioning of the stock and bond markets, it seems appropriate to consider the general question of what a market is, or, more specifically, what is its purpose. Most people have been exposed to numerous markets in their lives without really being aware of what they do and why they exist. Basically, we take markets for granted. *A market is the means through which buyers and sellers are brought together to aid in the transfer of goods and/or services.* Several aspects of this general definition seem worthy of emphasis. First, it is not necessary for a market to have a physical location. It is only necessary that the buyers and sellers can communicate regarding the relevant aspects of the purchase or sale.

Second, the market does not necessarily own the goods or services involved. When we discuss what is required for a "good" market, the reader will note that ownership is not involved; the basic criterion is the smooth, cheap transfer of goods and services. In the case of most financial markets, those who establish and administer the market do not own the assets, but they simply provide a location for potential buyers and sellers to meet and they help the market to function by providing information and transfer facilities.

Finally, a market can deal in any variety of goods and services. For any commodity with a diverse clientele a market should develop to aid in its transfer and both buyers and sellers will benefit from its existence.

Factors that Determine a "Good" Market

A buyer or seller of goods or services enters a market in order to buy or sell the commodity quickly at a price justified by the prevailing supply and demand in the market. So he would like to have timely and accurate information on past transactions in terms of volume and price and on all currently outstanding bids and offers. Therefore, one attribute of a good market is *availability of information regarding price and volume for past transactions and current market conditions.*

Another prime requirement is a *liquid* market, where we define liquidity as *the ability to buy or sell an asset quickly at a known price,* i.e., a price not substantially different from the prior price, assuming no new information is available. Therefore, there are two aspects of liquidity: *the time involved to complete the transaction* and *the certainty of the price.* An instance in which a broker can assure the owner of a specified price, but indicates that it might take six months to sell the asset at that price, would not be considered a very liquid market because the time involved is excessive. In contrast, if a broker tells an owner that he can sell an asset very quickly but at a substantial discount from the prior market price for a comparable asset, this, likewise, is not a very liquid market because of the significant price change that accompanies a quick transaction. The latter case, in which it is possible to sell *quickly,* is sometimes referred to as *marketability,* i.e., *the asset can be turned into cash quickly,* but there is nothing certain about price. Therefore, marketability is a necessary, but *not* a sufficient, condition for liquidity.

One of the factors that contributes to liquidity is a *price continuity.* Continuity refers to prices which do not change much from one transaction to the next, unless substantial new information becomes available. Given a case in which new information is not forthcoming and the last transaction was at a price of $20, if the next trade was at 20 1/8[1] it would probably be considered a reasonably continuous market. Obviously, *it is necessary to have a continuous market without large price changes between trades in order to have a liquid market.*

A continuous market also requires *depth.* There must be numerous potential buyers and sellers who are willing to trade at figures above and below the current market price. These buyers and sellers enter the market when there are price changes and thereby ensure that there are no major price moves.

Another factor contributing to a good market is the *cost of a transaction.* The

---

[1] The reader should be aware that common stocks are sold in increments of eighths which are equal to $0.125. Therefore, 20 1/8 means the stock sold at $20.125 per share.

lower the cost of the transaction (in terms of the percentage of the value of the trade), the more efficient the market. Assuming that an individual is comparing two markets, if the cost of a transaction on one was 2 percent of the value of the trade, while the other market charged 5 percent, the individual would trade in the 2 percent market. Most microeconomic textbooks define an *efficient* market as *one in which the cost of the transaction is minimized.* Papers by West and Tinic define this attribute of a market as "internal" efficiency.[2]

Finally, a buyer or seller would want the prevailing market price to adequately reflect all the available supply and demand factors in the market. If supply and demand conditions change as a result of new information, participants would want this information to be reflected in the price of the commodity. Therefore, another requirement for a good market is that *prices adjust quickly to new information regarding supply or demand.* This attribute is referred to as "external" efficiency.

In summary, a good market for goods and services would have the following characteristics:

1.   Timely and accurate information on the price and volume of past transactions and similar information on prevailing supply and demand.
2.   Liquidity. A buyer or seller of a good or service can buy or sell the asset quickly at a price which is close to the price of previous transactions, assuming no new information has been received. In turn, a liquid market requires price continuity, i.e., prices do not change very much from transaction to transaction. Price continuity itself requires depth. There must be a number of buyers and sellers willing and able to enter the market at prices above and below those prevailing.
3.   Low transaction cost. This "internal" efficiency means that all aspects of the transaction entail low costs, including the cost of reaching the market, the actual brokerage cost involved in the transaction, as well as the cost of transferring the asset.
4.   Rapid adjustment of prices to new information. This "external" efficiency ensures that the prevailing price reflects all available information regarding the asset.

Organization of the Securities Market.   Before discussing the specific operation of the securities market, it is important that we understand the overall organization of the market. This understanding will provide insight into the purpose of the different segments of the securities market and their interrelationships. In this context, the principal distinction is between *primary* markets, where new securities are sold, and *secondary* markets, where outstanding securities are bought and sold. Within each of these markets there is a further division based upon the economic unit that issued the security, e.g., the U.S. government, local municipalities, or corporations. In the following discussion, we will consider each of these major segments of the securities market with an emphasis on the individuals involved and the functions they perform.

---

[2] Richard R. West and Seha M. Tinic, "Corporate Finance and the Changing Stock Market," *Financial Management* 3 no. 3 (Autumn 1974): 14–23; Richard R. West, "On the Difference between Internal and External Market Efficiency," *Financial Analysts Journal* 31 no. 6 (November–December 1975): 30–34.

64 PRIMARY MARKETS

Seasoned and Initial Primary Offerings

The primary market for corporate offerings is the one in which new issues, bonds, preferred stock, or common stock are sold by companies to acquire new capital. The proceeds of the sale of securities goes to the firm as new capital. These new issues are typically broken down into two groups. The first and largest group are *seasoned* new issues offered by companies with existing public markets for their securities. An example would be General Motors selling a new issue of common stock. There is an existing public market for General Motors common stock and the company is increasing the number of outstanding shares to acquire new equity capital.[3]

The second major category in the new issues market is generally referred to as *initial* public offerings. An example would be a small company selling common stock to the public for the first time. In this case, there is no existing public market for the stock, i.e., the company has been closely held.[4]

New issues (seasoned or initial) are typically underwritten by investment bankers who acquire the total issue from the company and, in turn, sell the issue to interested investors. The underwriter gives advice to the corporation on the general characteristics of the issues, its pricing, and the timing of the offering. He also accepts the risk of selling the new issue after acquiring it from the corporation.[5]

Alternative Relationship with Investment Banker. Arrangements made by the company and the underwriter typically take one of three forms. The first is the most common: an existing corporation negotiates with a specific underwriter or investment banker, usually one with whom it has worked on a continuous basis. When the firm decides to sell a new issue of securities (stocks or bonds), the investment banker advises the firm on what type of issue to sell, the price of the issue, and when the firm should come to the market with the issue. He also forms an underwriting syndicate and selling group for the sale of the issue.[6]

A corporation may also specify the type of securities to be offered (common stock, preferred stock, or bonds) and then may solicit competitive bids from

[3] An extensive analysis of this segment of the new issues market is contained in I. Friend, J. R. Longstreet, M. Mendelson, E. Miller and A. P. Hess, Jr., *Investment Banking and the New Issues Market* (Cleveland: The World Publishing Co., 1967).

[4] A popular example of an initial public offering was that made by Coors Brewing Company in June 1975. The company had a history of very successful operation but had been privately held prior to this time. The price performance of these new issues was discussed in Chapter 2 and specific studies that have examined this price performance are contained in the references for Chapter 2.

[5] For a more detailed discussion and analysis of the investment banking industry, see Samuel L. Hayes, III "The Transformation of Investment Banking," *Harvard Business Review* 57 no. 1 (January–February 1979): 153–170; Dennis E. Logue and John R. Lindvall, "The Behavior of Investment Bankers: An Econometric Investigation," *Journal of Finance* 29 no. 1 (March 1974): 203–215; Gershon Mandelker and Arthur Ravic, "Investment Banking: An Economic Analysis of Optimal Underwriting Contracts," *Journal of Finance* 32 no. 3 (June 1977): 683–694.

[6] For a detailed discussion of the underwriting process, see J. Fred Weston and Eugene F. Brigham, *Managerial Finance,* 7th ed. (Hinsdale, Ill.: The Dryden Press, 1981), Chapter 18.

investment banking firms. This is typically done by utilities, which, in many cases, are *required* to submit their issues for competitive bids. It is contended that the cost of the issue is reduced in this manner, although it is also acknowledged that there is a reduction in the services provided by the investment banker. He will give the issuing firm less advice but will still underwrite the issue.[7]

Alternatively, an investment banker can agree to become involved with an issue and sell it on a "best efforts" basis. This is usually done with speculative new issues. The point is, the investment banker does *not* really underwrite the issue since he does *not* buy it. The stock is owned by the company, and the investment banker is acting as a broker trying to sell what he can at a stipulated price. The investment banker's commission on such an issue is less than on an issue he underwrites.

With either a negotiated relationship or a "best efforts" arrangement, the lead investment banker typically will form an *underwriting syndicate* of other investment bankers to spread the risk and also help in the sales. In addition, if the issue is very large, the lead underwriter and underwriting syndicate will form a *selling group* of smaller firms to help in the distribution.

This typical practice of negotiated arrangements and numerous investment banking firms in the syndicate and selling group has changed recently with the introduction of *Rule 415*. This rule was introduced by the SEC during 1982 on an experimental basis and subsequently approved on a permanent basis during 1983. The Rule basically stipulates that large firms are allowed to register security issues and sell the issues piecemeal during the two years following the initial registration (these are referred to as "shelf registrations"). Notably, the subsequent sales can be carried out on very short notice. As an example, IBM could register an issue of five million shares of common stock during 1985 and sell a million shares in early 1985, another million late in 1985, two million shares in early 1986 and the rest in late 1986. Each of these offerings could have been done with little notice or paperwork by one underwriter or several. In fact, in many instances the lead underwriter will handle the whole deal without a syndicate, or may only use one or two other firms. This arrangement has been supported by large corporations because it provides great flexibility for them, is less costly in

---

[7] Several studies have examined the cost differences between negotiated versus competitive bid underwritings. In this regard, see Michael Joehnk and David S. Kidwell, "Comparative Costs of Competitive and Negotiated Underwritings in the State and Local Bond Market," *Journal of Finance* 34 no. 3 (June 1979): 725–731; Dennis E. Logue and Robert A. Jarrow, "Negotiation vs. Competitive Bidding in the Sales of Securities by Public Utilities," *Financial Management* 7 no. 3 (Autumn 1978): 31–39; Louis H. Ederington, "Negotiated Versus Competitive Underwritings of Corporate Bonds," *Journal of Finance* 31 no. 1 (March 1976): 17–28; Reuben Kessel, "A Study of the Effects of Competition in the Tax-Exempt Bond Market," *Journal of Political Economy* 79 no. 3 (July–August 1971): 706–738; George G. C. Parker and Daniel Cooperman, "Competitive Bidding in the Underwriting of Public Utility Securities," *Journal of Financial and Quantitative Analysis* 13 no. 5 (December 1978): 885–902; Eric H. Sorensen, "The Impact of Underwriting Method and Bidder Competition upon Corporate Bond Interest Cost," *Journal of Finance* 34 no. 4 (September 1979): 863–869; Gary D. Tallman, David F. Rush and Ronald W. Melicher, "Competitive Versus Negotiated Underwriting Costs for Regulated Industries," *Financial Management* 3 no. 2 (Summer 1974): 49–55; Edward Dyl and Michael Joehnk, "Competitive Versus Negotiated Underwriting of Public Utility Debt," *Bell Journal of Economics* 7 no. 2 (Autumn 1976): 680–689; M. Chapman Findlay III, Keith B. Johnson, and T. Gregory Morton, "An Analysis of the Flotation Cost of Utility Bonds, 1971–76," *Journal of Financial Research* 2 no. 2 (Fall 1979): 133–142; Frank J. Fabozzi and Richard R. West, "Negotiated versus Competitive Underwritings of Public Utility Bonds: Just One More Time," *Journal of Financial and Quantitative Analysis*, 16 no. 3 (September 1981): 323–339.

66

terms of registration fees and expenses, and in some instances has allowed the firms issuing the securities to request competitive bids from several investment banking firms on the underwriting arrangement. Alternatively, there has been some concern expressed that the use of these shelf registrations does not allow enough time to examine the firm issuing the securities. Also it reduces the ability of small underwriters to participate (i.e., the syndicates are smaller and selling groups are almost nonexistent).[8]

Finally, primary offerings can be placed *privately* rather than being sold publicly. In such an arrangement, referred to as a *private placement,* the firm, with the assistance of an investment banker, designs an issue and finds a small group of institutions willing to acquire a significant position in the firm involved. The firm benefits because the costs of the offering are less since it is not necessary to prepare the extensive registration statement for a public offering. On the other side, the institution typically benefits because the firm issuing the securities is willing to provide a higher return due to the cost savings. Further, the buyer (e.g., institution) should *require* a higher return because of the lower liquidity of the security—i.e., there is generally no secondary market for these issues after the original sale.[9]

SECONDARY MARKETS

Importance of Secondary Markets

In secondary markets there is trading in outstanding issues. In this case, an issue has already been sold to the public, and it is traded between current and potential owners. Again, there are secondary markets for bonds, preferred stock, and common stock. The proceeds from a sale in the secondary market do *not* go to the company but to the current owner of the security.

Prior to discussing the various segments of the secondary market, we must consider its overall importance. As noted, the secondary market involves trading securities initially sold in the primary market. Therefore, the secondary market provides *liquidity* to individuals who acquired securities in the primary markets. After an individual has acquired securities in the primary market, he wants to be able to sell the securities at some point in the future in order to acquire other securities, buy a house, or go on a vacation. Such a sale takes place in the secondary market. The investor's ability to convert the asset into cash (liquidity) is heavily dependent upon the secondary market. *The primary market would be seriously hampered in its function of helping firms acquire new capital without*

---

[8] For further discussion of this rule, see Tim Carrington, "Investment Bankers Enter a Different Era, and Many are Uneasy," *Wall Street Journal,* June 12, 1982, p. 1, 12; A. F. Ehbar, "Upheaval in Investment Banking," *Fortune,* August 23, 1982, 90ff.; Beth McGoldrick, "Life With Rule 415," *Institutional Investor* 17 no. 2 (February 1983): 129–133; "The Traders Take Charge," *Business Week* (February 20, 1984): 58–62.

[9] For further discussion of these issues, see Patrick J. Davey, "Private Placements: Practices and Prospects," *Conference Board Information Bulletin* (January 1979): 1–14; Patrick A. Hays, Michael Joehnk, and Ronald W. Melicher, "Differential Determinants of Risk Premiums in the Public and Private Corporate Bond Markets," *Journal of Financial Research* 2 no. 2 (Fall 1979): 143–152; Adi S. Karna, "The Cost of Private Versus Public Debt Issues," *Financial Management* 1 no. 2 (Summer 1972): 65–67.

the liquidity provided by the secondary market. Investors would be hesitant to acquire securities in the primary market if they felt they would not subsequently have the ability to sell the securities quickly at a known price in the secondary market.

Secondary markets are also important to a corporation because the prevailing market price of the security is determined by action in the secondary market. Therefore, any new issue of that security sold in the primary market will necessarily be priced in line with the current price in the secondary market. As a result, the firm's capital costs are determined in the secondary market.

Secondary Bond Markets

Types of Bonds.   When considering the secondary markets for bonds, the distinction that should be made is the division between the vast number of bonds issued by the government, bonds issued by state and local government units, and bonds issued by individual business firms.

Government bond issues can be divided into several groups. The first group are those issued by the federal government and include long-term bonds and notes that have maturities of from one year to 25 years. In addition, there are short-term treasury bills that have maturities, at the time of issue, of from 90 to 180 days. There are a number of governmental agencies that likewise are authorized to issue their own bonds. Examples would include the Federal Home Loan Banks, the Federal Land Bank, the Federal National Mortgage Association (FNMA), and the World Bank. There is a more detailed discussion of these bonds in later chapters.

There is also a large market for bonds issued by state and local government units known as municipal bonds. These issues are typically broken down into general obligation securities (GOs), which are backed by the full taxing power of the municipality, and revenue issues, which are backed by the expected revenues generated from a particular governmental service.

Corporate bonds are issued by industrial companies, railroads, and utilities. There can be a large difference in the quality of these bonds depending upon the firm that issued them. Quality in this case refers to the ability of the firm to meet all required interest payments and the face value at maturity.[10]

Secondary Government and Municipal Bond Markets.   All government bonds are traded by bond dealers specifically concerned with government bonds. These dealers are typically distinguished by the type of government bonds they handle. Some deal almost wholly in federal bonds, others are involved in agency bonds, and there is a virtually completely separate group of municipal bond dealers. Some of the most active government bond dealers are large banks in major cities like New York and Chicago and some of the large investment banking firms.

Banks are likewise active in municipal bond trading because a large part of

---

[10] For a discussion of bond ratings, see Hugh C. Sherwood, *How Corporate and Municipal Debt Is Rated* (New York: John Wiley & Sons, 1976), and the discussion in Chapter 14.

their investment portfolios are committed to them. Many large investment banking firms also have municipal bond departments because such firms are active in underwriting these issues.

Secondary Corporate Bond Market. The secondary market for corporate bonds has two major segments, the exchanges and the over-the-counter market. The major exchange for bonds is the New York Stock Exchange (NYSE). As of the end of 1983 there were over 3,200 bond issues listed on the NYSE with a par value of over $790 billion and a market value of approximately $766 billion.[11] On a typical day about 1,000 of the issues are traded, and the volumes of trading is about $28 million. In addition, there are about 200 issues listed on the American Stock Exchange (ASE) which has a typical daily volume of about $2 million. All corporate bonds not listed on one of the exchanges are traded over the counter by dealers who buy and sell for their own account.

Financial Futures Market. In addition to the market for the bonds, recently there has been a market for futures contracts for these bonds — i.e., a contract that allows the holder to buy or sell a specified amount of a given bond issue at a stipulated price. These futures contracts and the futures market is discussed in detail in Chapter 25.

Secondary Equity Markets

Secondary equity markets are usually broken down into three major groups: the major national exchanges, including the New York Stock Exchange and the American Stock Exchange; what are usually called "regional exchanges" in cities like Chicago, San Francisco, Boston, Philadelphia, and Washington; and the over-the-counter market trading in securities not listed on an organized exchange. The first two groups are similar in that they are referred to as listed securities exchanges; they differ in terms of size and geographic emphasis.

The listed securities exchanges are formal organizations that have a specified group of members that may use the facilities of the exchange and a specified group of securities (stocks or bonds) that have qualified for "listing." In addition to limitations on membership and the securities eligible for trading, these exchanges are similar in that the prices of securities listed on them are determined via an auction process, whereby interested buyers and sellers submit bids and asks for a given stock to a central location for that stock. The bids and asks are recorded by a "specialist" assigned to that stock. Shares of stock are then sold to the highest bidder and bought from the investing unit (individual, institution, etc.) with the lowest asking price (the lowest offering price).

National Securities Exchange. Two securities exchanges are generally referred to as national in scope: the New York Stock Exchange (NYSE) and the American Stock Exchange (ASE). They are considered national because of the

---

[11] *Fact Book* (New York: New York Stock Exchange, 1983), p. 77.

TABLE 3.1
Listing Requirements for NYSE

Pre-Tax Income Last Year	$ 2,500,000
Pre-Tax Income Last 2 Years	$ 2,000,000
Net Tangible Assets	$16,000,000
Shares Publicly Held	1,000,000
Market Value Publicly Held Shares[a]: Maximum	$16,000,000
Minimum	$ 8,000,000
Number of Round Lot Holders (100 shares or more)	2,000

[a] This required market value depends upon the value of the NYSE Common Stock Index. For specifics see the 1983 *Fact Book*, p. 31.
SOURCE: *Fact Book* (New York: New York Stock Exchange, 1984). Reprinted by permission.

TABLE 3.2
Average Daily Reported Share Volume Traded on the NYSE (thousands)

1940	751	1971	15,381
1945	1,422	1972	16,487
1950	1,980	1973	16,084
1955	2,578	1974	13,904
1960	3,042	1975	18,551
1961	4,085	1976	21,186
1962	3,818	1977	20,928
1963	4,567	1978	28,591
1964	4,888	1979	32,237
1965	6,176	1980	44,871
1966	7,538	1981	46,853
1967	10,080	1982	65,052
1968	12,971	1983	85,344
1969	11,403		
1970	11,564		

SOURCE: *Fact Book* (New York: New York Stock Exchange, various years). Reprinted by permission.

large number of securities they list, the geographic dispersion of the firms listed, and their clientele of buyers and sellers.

The New York Stock Exchange (NYSE).   This is the largest organized securities market in the United States. The initial constitution that formally established the exchange was adopted in 1817. The NYSE was originally named the "New York Stock and Exchange Board." This was changed to the New York Stock Exchange in 1863.

At the end of 1983, there were 1,550 companies with stock listed on the NYSE, and 2,307 stock issues (common and preferred) with a total market value of $1,584 billion. The specific listing requirements for the NYSE as of 1983 are contained in Table 3.1.

The average number of shares traded on the exchange has increased steadily, as has the number of issues listed and the turnover of shares. The average daily volume in recent years is contained in Table 3.2. These figures indicate that prior to the 1960s, the average daily volume was less than 3 million shares. Daily volume increased to about 5 million shares in the early 1960s, increased again to

TABLE 3.3
Shares Sold on Registered Exchanges

	Number of Shares Traded (percent of total)			Market Value of Shares Traded (percent of total)		
	NYSE	ASE	Other	NYSE	ASE	Other
1935	77.6	12.8	9.6	87.3	7.9	4.8
1940	76.0	12.9	11.1	85.3	7.7	7.0
1945	66.6	20.5	12.9	83.0	10.6	6.4
1950	76.5	13.4	10.1	86.0	6.8	7.2
1955	67.7	20.1	12.2	86.5	6.8	6.7
1960	69.0	21.6	9.3	83.9	9.2	6.8
1965	69.9	22.5	7.5	82.0	9.7	8.3
1970	70.8	19.4	9.8	78.7	10.9	10.4
1971	72.1	17.7	10.2	79.5	9.6	10.0
1972	71.4	17.5	11.1	78.3	10.0	11.7
1973	75.7	12.9	11.4	82.3	5.9	11.9
1974	79.0	9.8	11.2	83.9	4.3	11.9
1975	81.1	8.7	10.2	85.2	3.6	11.2
1976	80.3	9.1	10.7	84.4	3.8	11.8
1977	79.9	9.3	10.8	84.0	4.6	11.4
1978	80.3	10.5	9.2	84.4	6.1	9.5
1979	79.9	10.7	9.4	83.7	6.9	9.4
1980	80.0	10.7	9.3	83.6	7.3	9.1
1981	80.7	9.3	10.0	84.8	5.4	9.9
1982	81.1	7.0	11.9	85.1	3.4	11.4
1983	80.5	7.3	12.2	85.2	3.3	11.5

SOURCE: Securities and Exchange Commission, *Annual Report* (Washington, D.C.: U.S. Government Printing Office); *Fact Book* (New York: New York Stock Exchange, various years). Reprinted by permission.

about 10 million shares in the second half of the 1960s. Daily trading volume averaged about 15 million during the first half of the seventies and went to over 30 million by the end of the decade. Volume literally exploded in the eighties to over 85 million by 1983 and this volume continued in 1984.

The domination of other listed exchanges by the NYSE is indicated by Table 3.3, which contains the percentage breakdown of share volume and the value of trading on that exchange. The NYSE has consistently accounted for about 75–80 percent of all shares traded on listed exchanges, as compared to about 10 percent for the ASE, and about 10 percent for all regional exchanges combined (the "other" category). Because the price of shares on the NYSE tends to be higher than that of shares on the ASE, the percentage of value of trading on the NYSE has averaged from 80 to 85 percent with much lower figures for the ASE. The regional exchanges are typically comparable in shares traded and the value of trading.

Based upon this clearly dominant position and the history of the NYSE, the exchange has been called a monopolist.[12] The volume of trading and dominant position are also reflected in the price of membership on the exchange (referred

[12] Robert W. Doede, "The Monopoly Power of the New York Stock Exchange," (Ph.D. dissertation, University of Chicago, June 1967).

TABLE 3.4
Membership Prices on the NYSE and the ASE (in thousands of dollars)

	NYSE		ASE			NYSE		ASE	
	High	Low	High	Low		High	Low	High	Low
1925	150	99	38	9	1971	300	145	150	65
1935	140	65	33	12	1972	250	150	145	70
1945	95	49	32	12	1973	190	72	100	27
1955	90	80	22	18	1974	105	65	60	27
1960	162	135	60	51	1975	138	55	72	34
1961	225	147	80	52	1976	104	40	68	40
1962	210	115	65	40	1977	95	35	52	21
1963	217	160	66	53	1978	105	46	65	25
1964	230	190	63	52	1979	210	82	90	40
1965	250	190	80	55	1980	275	175	252	95
1966	270	197	120	70	1981	285	220	275	200
1967	450	220	230	100	1982	340	190	285	180
1968	515	385	315	220	1983	425	310	325	261
1969	515	260	350	150					
1970	320	130	185	70					

SOURCE: *Fact Book* (New York: New York Stock Exchange, various issues); *Amex Statistical Review* (New York: American Stock Exchange, various issues). Reprinted by permission of the New York Stock Exchange and the American Stock Exchange.

to as a "seat"). As shown in Table 3.4, the price of membership has fluctuated in line with trading volume and other factors that influence the profitability of membership.

The American Stock Exchange (ASE).   The ASE was begun by a group of persons who traded unlisted shares at the corner of Wall and Hanover Streets in New York and was referred to as the Outdoor Curb Market. It made several moves along the streets of the financial district and, in 1910, formal trading rules were established and the name was changed to the New York Curb Market Association. The members moved inside a building in 1921 and continued to trade mainly in unlisted stocks (i.e., stocks not listed on one of the registered exchanges). The predominance of unlisted stocks continued until 1946 when listed stocks finally outnumbered unlisted stocks. The current name was adopted in 1953.[13]

The ASE is distinct because of its desire to be different from the NYSE. A major factor in this uniqueness was that, prior to August 1976, no stocks were listed on the NYSE and ASE at the same time. This was changed in August 1976 when a request by the ASE to abolish "The New York Rule" was approved by the SEC.[14] This rule was an agreement between the two exchanges that no stock would be listed on both. Then several firms listed on the ASE applied for listing

[13] For a further discussion of the development of the ASE, see Robert Sobel, *The Curbstone Brokers: The Origins of the American Stock Exchange* (New York: Macmillan, 1970).

[14] "SEC Clears Trading on Amex of Stocks Listed on Big Board," *Wall Street Journal,* August 23, 1976, p. 3.

TABLE 3.5
Average Daily Reported Share Volume Traded on the American Stock Exchange
(thousands)

1940	171	1966	2,741	1976	2,562
1945	583	1967	4,544	1977	2,582
1950	435	1968	6,353	1978	3,923
1955	912	1969	4,963	1979	4,349
1960	1,113	1970	3,319	1980	6,427
1961	1,948	1971	4,233	1981	5,310
1962	1,225	1972	4,454	1982	5,287
1963	1,262	1973	3,015	1983	8,225
1964	1,479	1974	1,906		
1965	2,120	1975	2,138		

SOURCE: *Amex Databook* (New York: American Stock Exchange, various issues). Reprinted by permission.

on the NYSE but retained their ASE listing. Subsequently, most of them gave up their ASE listing because the great majority of trading was on the NYSE.[15]

The ASE has been quite innovative in listing foreign securities over the years. There were over 60 foreign issues listed in 1984, and trading in these issues constituted over 20 percent of total volume.[16] Further, there were warrants listed on the ASE for a number of years before the NYSE would list them. The most recent innovation by the ASE has been the trading of call options on listed securities, introduced after option trading became widespread with the establishment of the Chicago Board Options Exchange (CBOE). Again, because options are not traded on the NYSE (as of mid-1984), almost all options traded on the ASE are for stocks listed on the NYSE.

At the end of 1983, there were approximately 1,400 stock issues listed on the ASE.[17] As can be seen from the figures in Table 3.5, average daily trading volume has fluctuated substantially over time as the demand for smaller and younger firms, which are mainly traded on the ASE, has changed. Prior to 1955, average daily volume was below 500,000 shares. Average daily volume reached 1 million shares in 1959, almost 2 million in 1961, and exceeded 2 million in 1965 and 1966. In 1967, the average daily volume increased to 4.5 million and reached a high of 6.3 million shares in 1968. Trading volume declined to between 3 and 4 million shares a day during 1970–1973 and declined further to about 2 million shares a day during the period 1974–1977. Since 1977 there has been an overall increase, with a small decline in 1981 and 1982, to a new record in 1983 in excess of 8 million shares a day. Volume has continued in this area during 1984.

The American Stock Exchange is national in scope and, although also located in New York, is distinct from the NYSE. The companies listed on the ASE are almost completely different from those listed on the NYSE. In addition, ASE firms are generally smaller and younger than the firms listed on the NYSE, which is consistent with the difference in listing requirements contained in Table 3.6.

[15] The topic of dual listing on the NYSE and ASE is discussed further in the next chapter.

[16] American Stock Exchange Research Department.

[17] The requirements for listing on the ASE are contained in Table 3.6.

TABLE 3.6
Listing Requirements for ASE

Pre-Tax Income Last Year	$ 750,000
Net Income Last Year	$ 400,000
Net Tangible Assets	$4,000,000
Shares Publicly Held	400,000
Market Value Publicly Held Shares	$3,000,000
Number of Round Lot Holders	1,200

SOURCE: American Stock Exchange Research Department.

To prosper and compete against the NYSE, the ASE has had a history of innovation. Because of the differences, most of the large brokerage firms are members of both the NYSE and the ASE.

Regional Securities Exchanges

Regional exchanges have basically the same operating procedures as the NYSE and ASE but differ in terms of their listing requirements and the geographic distribution of the firms listed. There are two main reasons for the existence of regional stock exchanges: they provide trading facilities for local companies that are not large enough to qualify for listing on one of the national exchanges. To accommodate these companies, the listing requirements are typically less stringent than are those of the national exchanges as set forth in Tables 3.1 and 3.6. Their second purpose is that they list firms that are listed on one of the national exchanges for local brokers who are not members of a national exchange. As an example, American Telephone and Telegraph and General Motors are both listed on the NYSE, but they are *also* listed on several regional exchanges. This *dual* listing allows a local brokerage firm that is not large enough to purchase a membership on the NYSE (for $200,000 or more) to buy and sell shares of dual listed stock (e.g., General Motors) using its membership on a regional exchange. As a result, the broker will not have to go through the NYSE and give up part of his commission. Currently, between 65 and 90 percent of the volume on regional exchanges is attributable to trading in dual listed issues.[18]

The major regional exchanges are:
— Midwest Stock Exchange (Chicago)
— Pacific Stock Exchange (San Francisco – Los Angeles)
— PBW Exchange (Philadelphia – Baltimore – Washington)
— Boston Stock Exchange (Boston)
— Spokane Stock Exchange (Spokane, Washington)
— Honolulu Stock Exchange (Honolulu, Hawaii)
— Intermountain Stock Exchange (Salt Lake City)

The first three exchanges (Midwest, Pacific, PBW) account for about 90 percent of all regional exchange volume. In turn, total regional volume is about 9 to 10

---

[18] For an extended discussion of the regional exchanges see James E. Walter, *The Role of Regional Security Exchanges* (Berkeley: University of California Press, 1957). In the next chapter we will discuss the current and future status of the regional stock exchanges more extensively.

percent of total exchange volume as shown in Table 3.3. Table 3.3 shows that the fortunes of the regional exchanges have fluctuated substantially over time. The regional exchanges prospered during the late 1960s when there was widespread interest in small, young firms. Their recent relative growth has been influenced by institutional interest in stocks dual listed on national and regional exchanges and changes in the institutional arrangements discussed in the next chapter.

The Over-the-Counter Market (OTC).   The over-the-counter market includes trading in all stocks not listed on one of the exchanges. It can also include trading in stocks that are listed. This latter arrangement, referred to as the *third market,* is discussed in the following section. The OTC market is not a formal market organization with membership requirements or a specific list of stocks deemed eligible for trading. In theory, it is possible to trade *any* security on the OTC market as long as someone is willing to "take a position" in the stock. This means an individual or firm is willing to buy or sell the stock (i.e., make a market in the stock).

Size.   The OTC market is the largest segment of the secondary market in terms of the number of issues traded and is also the most diverse in terms of quality. As noted earlier, there are about 2,300 issues traded on the NYSE and about 1,400 issues on the ASE. In terms of active issues, there are over 3,000 traded on the OTC quotation system (NASDAQ),[19] inclusion in which requires certain size and at least two active market-makers. In addition, there are at least another 3,000 to 4,000 stocks that are traded fairly actively but are not on NASDAQ. Therefore, there are between 6,000 and 7,000 issues traded on the OTC market — more than on the NYSE and ASE combined. While the OTC is dominant in terms of the numbers of issues, the NYSE is still dominant in terms of the total *value* of the stocks.

There is tremendous diversity in the OTC because there are no minimum requirements for a stock to be traded. Therefore, it is possible for OTC listings to range from the smallest, most unprofitable company, to the largest, most profitable firm. On the upper end, all U.S. government bonds are traded on the OTC market, as are the vast majority of bank stocks and insurance stocks. Finally, the 100 listed stocks that are *also* traded on the OTC (the third market), includes AT&T, General Motors, IBM, Xerox, and a host of other stocks with active third markets.

Operation of the OTC.   As noted, any stock can be traded on the OTC as long as someone indicates he is willing to "make a market" in the stock, i.e., buy or sell for his own account. Therefore, *participants in the OTC market act as dealers because they buy and sell for their own account.*[20] This is in contrast to the situation on the listed exchanges where the specialist is generally acting as an agent for other investors. The specialist keeps the book and attempts to match

[19] NASDAQ is an acronym for National Association of Securities Dealers Automatic Quotations. The system is discussed in detail in a subsequent subsection.

[20] Dealer and market-maker are synonymous.

the buy and sell orders left with him. Because of this, the OTC market is referred to as a *negotiated* market in which investors directly negotiate with dealers. Exchanges are *auction* markets with the specialist acting as the intermediary (auctioneer).

The NASDAQ system.   NASDAQ is an acronym that stands for National Association of Securities Dealers Automatic Quotations. It is an electronic quotation system that serves the vast OTC market. Because any number of dealers can elect to make a market in an OTC stock, it is possible to have 10, 15, or more market-makers for a given stock, and it is common to have three to five. A major problem has always been determining the current quotations by specific market-makers. Prior to the introduction of NASDAQ, it was necessary for a broker to make phone calls to three or four dealers to determine the prevailing market and then, after such a "survey," go back to the one with the best market for his client (i.e., the one with the highest bid or lowest asking price). This process was very time consuming and frustrating, and when there were 10 or 15 dealers making a market for a stock, even after three or four phone calls a broker was not certain he had found the best market. With NASDAQ, all quotes by market-makers are available immediately and the broker can make one phone call to the dealer with the best market, verify that the quote has not changed, and make the sale or purchase. The National Association of Securities Dealers (NASD) has specified three levels for the NASDAQ system to serve firms with different needs and interests.[21]

Level 1 is for firms that want current information on OTC stocks but do not consistently buy or sell OTC stocks for their customers and are not market-makers. For these brokerage firms, a current quote on alternative OTC stocks is most important. Level 1 provides a single *median quote* ("representative") for all stocks in the system that considers all the market-makers (half the quotes are higher and half the quotes are lower). This composite quote is changed constantly to adjust for any changes by individual market-makers.

Level 2 is for firms that seriously trade in OTC stocks for themselves or their customers. For this clientele, Level 2 provides *instantaneous current quotations by all market-makers in a stock.* Given a desire to buy or sell, the broker simply calls the market-maker with the best market for his purpose (highest bid if he is selling or lowest offer if he wants to buy) and consummates the deal.

Level 3 is for investment firms that make markets in OTC stocks. Such firms want to know what everyone else is quoting (Level 2), but they also need the capability to enter their own quotations and the ability to *change* their quotations. This is what Level 3 provides—everything in Level 2 plus the ability to enter the system and change quotes.

Listing requirements for NASDAQ.   The reporting of quotes and volume of

---

[21] A detailed description of the NASDAQ system is contained in *NASDAQ and the OTC* (Washington, D.C.: National Association of Securities Dealers), or *The NASDAQ Revolution: How Over-the-Counter Securities are Traded* (New York: Merrill Lynch, Pierce, Fenner & Smith, 1978). An analysis of the impact is contained in A. M. Santomero, "Economic Effects of NASDAQ," *Journal of Financial and Quantitative Analysis* 9 no. 1 (January 1971), and Hans R. Stoll, "Dealer Inventory Behavior: An Empirical Investigation of NASDAQ," *Journal of Financial and Quantitative Analysis* 11 no. 3 (September 1976): 359–380.

trading for OTC is contained in two lists: a national list and a smaller additional list. Prior to November 1981 the criteria for being included on the national list was based on the dollar volume of trading during a specified period. This criteria caused problems because it resulted in numerous shifts over time as volume changed; it was also inconsistent with the listing requirements used by the other exchanges. Therefore, as of November 1981, the NASDAQ determined what stocks would be on the national list using two alternative sets of financial criteria as follows:

1. a.   Annual net income of at least $300,000 in the previous fiscal year or in two of the past three years
    b.   A market value of publicly held shares of at least $2 million
    c.   A minimum bid price of $3
    d.   350,000 publicly held shares.
2. a.   Net worth of at least $8 million
    b.   A market value of publicly held shares of at least $8 million
    c.   800,000 publicly held shares
    d.   Minimum incorporation of four years.

The second set of criteria was designed for companies that have substantial net worth but that are too new to generate income.[22] Given the new criteria about 1,800 companies initially qualified for the national list and NASDAQ included 1,000 stocks on the additional list.

A sample trade.   Assume you are considering the purchase of 100 shares of Pabst Brewing. Although Pabst is large enough and profitable enough to be eligible for listing on a national exchange, the company has never applied for listing because it enjoys a fairly active market on the OTC. (Daily volume is typically above 20,000 shares and often exceeds 40,000 shares.) Therefore, when you contact your broker, the broker will consult the NASDAQ electronic quotation machine to determine the current markets for PABT, the trading symbol for Pabst Brewing.[23] The display screen on his Level 2 machine would indicate that about 10 dealers are making a market in PABT. An example of differing markets might be as follows:

Dealer	Bid	Ask
1	14 1/4	14 5/8
2	14 3/8	14 5/8
3	14 1/4	14 1/2
4	14 3/8	14 3/4
5	14 1/4	14 3/4

If we assume for the moment that these are the best markets available from the total group, the investor's broker would then call Dealer 3 because he had the

---

[22] "NASDAQ Is Changing Criteria for Stocks on Its National Lists," *Wall Street Journal,* November 16, 1981, p. 48.

[23] Trading symbols are one-to four-letter codes used to designate stocks. Whenever a trade is reported on a stock ticker the trading symbol is used. Many are obvious, like GM (General Motors), F (Ford Motors), GE (General Electric), T (American Telephone and Telegraph).

lowest offering price, i.e., Dealer 3 was willing to sell at the lowest price. He would verify the quote and tell Dealer 3 that he wants to buy 100 shares of PABT at 14 1/2 ($14.50 a share). Because the investor's firm was not a market-maker in the stock, the firm would act as a broker for the customer and charge $1,450 plus a commission for the trade. If the customer had been interested in *selling* 100 shares of Pabst Brewing, the broker would have contacted Dealer 2 or 4 because they had the highest bids, i.e., they were willing to pay the most to buy the stock. If the broker was also a market-maker in PABT and had the quote of 14 1/4 to 14 1/2, then he would have sold the stock to the customer at 14 1/2 "net" (without commission).[24]

Changing dealer inventory.   It seems useful at this point to consider the quotation an OTC dealer would give if he wanted to change his inventory on a given stock. For example, assume Dealer 1 with a current quote of 14 1/4 bid – 14 5/8 ask decides that he wants to *increase* his holdings of PABT. An examination of the quotes on his NASDAQ quote machine indicates that the highest bid is currently 14 3/8. He can increase his bid to 14 3/8 and get some of the business currently going to Dealers 2 and 4, or, if he wants to be very aggressive, he can raise his bid to 14 1/2 and buy all the stock that is offered, including some from Dealer 3 who is offering it at 14 1/2. In this example, the dealer raises his bid but does not change his asking price, which was above another dealer's. Thus he is going to buy stock but probably will not sell any. If the dealer had more stock than he wanted, he would keep his bid below the market (lower than 14 3/8) and reduce his asking price to 14 1/2 or less. Dealers are constantly changing their bid and/or their asking price, depending upon their current inventory or the outlook for the stock.[25]

The Third Market.   The term *third market* is used to describe *over-the-counter trading of shares listed on an exchange.* When a stock is listed on an exchange, members of that exchange are generally required to execute all buy and sell orders through the exchange.[26] Further, since most investors are aware that the stock is listed on an exchange, they will likely consider it the best place

---

[24] An analysis of marketmaking on NASDAQ is contained in, Hans R. Stoll, "Dealer Inventory Behavior: An Empirical Investigation of NASDAQ," *Journal of Financial and Quantitative Analysis* 11 no. 3 (September 1976): 359–380.

[25] A number of studies have examined the determinants of the dealers bid-ask spread. In this regard, see: Amir Barnea and Dennis E. Logue, "The Effect of Risk on the Market Maker's Spread," *Financial Analysts Journal* 31 no. 6 (November–December 1975): 45–49; George J. Benston and Robert L. Hagerman, "Determinants of Bid-Asked Spreads in the Over-the-Counter Market," *Journal of Financial Economics* 1 no. 4 (December 1974): 353–364; Ben Branch and Walter Freed, "Bid-Ask Spreads on the AMEX and the Big Board," *The Journal of Finance* 32 no. 1 (March 1977): 159–163; Kalman J. Cohen, Stephen F. Maier, Robert A. Schwartz, and David K. Whitcomb, "Market Makers and the Market Spread: A Review of Recent Literature," *Journal of Financial and Quantitative Analysis* 14 no. 4 (November 1979): 813–836; Harold Demsetz, "The Cost of Transacting," *Quarterly Journal of Economics* 82 no. 1 (February 1968): 33–53; James L. Hamilton, "Competition, Scale Economics, and Transaction Cost in the Stock Market," *Journal of Financial and Quantitative Analysis* 11 no. 5 (December 1976): 779–802; Seha M. Tinic, "The Economics of Liquidity Services," *Quarterly Journal of Economics* 86 no. 1 (February 1972): 79–93; Seha M. Tinic and Richard R. West, "Competition and the Pricing of Dealer Service in the Over-the-Counter Stock Market," *Journal of Financial and Quantitative Analysis* 7 no. 3 (June 1972): 1707–1726.

[26] This requirement is being changed over time and is discussed in detail in Chapter 4 when we consider the national market system.

to go to trade this stock. Therefore, one would expect most of the transactions in listed stocks to take place on an exchange. Still, an investment firm that is not a member of an exchange can make a market in a listed stock in the same way that it would make a market in an unlisted stock. Most of the activity on this market is conducted by large financial institutions trading in large well-known stocks like AT&T, IBM, and Xerox. The success or failure of this segment of the market will obviously depend upon whether the OTC market in these stocks is as good as the exchange market and/or how does the relative cost of the transaction compare to the cost on the exchange.

This segment of the market grew dramatically from 1965 through 1972 because it provided a means for large institutions to avoid the high commissions charged for large NYSE transactions. As is discussed in Chapter 4, since negotiated commissions were introduced, there has been a decline in third market activity because this market no longer provides a large cost savings relative to commissions on the NYSE.

The Fourth Market.   The term *fourth market* is used to describe *the direct trading of securities between two parties* with no broker intermediary. In almost all cases, both parties involved are institutions. When you think about it, a direct transaction is really not that unusual. If you own 100 shares of AT&T and decide to sell it, there is nothing wrong with simply asking your friends or associates if any of them would be interested in buying the stock at a mutually agreeable price and making the transaction directly. Investors typically buy or sell stock through a broker because it is faster and easier. Also, you may get better execution because there is a good chance of finding the "best" buyer through a broker. You are willing to pay a fee for these services, which is the brokerage commission.

The fourth market evolved because the brokerage fee that is charged to institutions with large orders is substantial. At some point it becomes worthwhile for institutions to attempt to deal directly with each other and save the brokerage fee. Consider an institution that decides to sell 100,000 shares of AT&T. Assuming that AT&T is selling for about $50 a share, the value of the 100,000 shares is $2 million. The average commission on such a transaction, prior to fully negotiated rates, was about 1 percent of the value of the trade which, for this trade, would be *$20,000*. Given this cost, it becomes attractive for the selling institution to spend some time and effort finding another institution interested in increasing its holding of AT&T and attempt to negotiate a direct sale. Because of the diverse nature of the fourth market and the lack of reporting requirements, there are no data available regarding its specific size or growth.

DETAILED ANALYSIS OF THE EXCHANGE MARKET

Because of the importance of the listed exchange market, it must be dealt with at some length. In this section we discuss the several types of membership on the exchanges, the major types of orders used, and finally the function of the specialist who is considered the main determinant of a "good" exchange market.

Exchange Membership

Listed securities exchanges typically have five major categories of membership: (1) specialist, (2) odd-lot dealer, (3) commission broker, (4) floor-broker, and (5) registered trader.

Specialists constitute about 25 percent of the total membership on exchanges. They are considered by some observers to be the most important group because, as will be discussed, they are responsible for maintaining a fair and orderly market in the securities listed on an exchange.

Odd-lot dealers stand ready to buy or sell less than a round lot of stock. (A round lot is typically a multiple of 100 shares.) When an individual wants to buy fewer than 100 shares, his order is turned over to an odd-lot dealer who will buy or sell from his own inventory. Note that the dealer is *not* a broker—i.e., he is buying and selling from his own inventory. Prior to 1976, all odd-lot transactions were handled by an odd-lot house. Since then, the NYSE has taken over the function. On most other exchanges, the specialist in a stock is also the odd-lot dealer for the stock. Some large brokerage firms (most notably Merill Lynch, Pierce, Fenner & Smith), have been acting as odd-lot dealers for their own customers.

Commission brokers are employees of a member firm who buy or sell for the customers of the firm. When an investor places an order to buy or sell stock through a registered representative of a brokerage firm and the firm has a membership on an exchange, it will contact its commission broker on the floor of the exchange; he will go to the appropriate post on the floor and buy or sell the stock as instructed.

Floor brokers are members of an exchange who act as brokers on the floor for other members. They are typically not connected with a member firm but own their own seat. When the commission broker for Merrill Lynch becomes too busy to handle all of his orders, he will ask one of the floor brokers to help him. At one time they were referred to as "$2 brokers" because that is what they received for each order. Currently they receive about $4 per 100 share order.

Registered traders are allowed to use their membership to buy and sell for their own account. They therefore save the commission on their own trading and observers believe they have an advantage because they are on the floor. The exchanges and others believe they should be allowed these advantages because registered traders provide the market with added liquidity. Because of possible abuses, there are regulations regarding how they trade and how many registered traders can be in a trading crowd around a specialists' booth at a point in time.

Types of Orders

The reader should have a full understanding of the different types of orders used by individual investors and by the specialist in his dealer function.

Market Orders.   The most frequent type is a market order. A *market order* is an order to buy or sell a stock at the best price currently prevailing. An investor who wants to sell some stock using a market order indicates that he would be willing to sell *immediately* at the highest bid available at the time the order reaches the specialist on the exchange. A market buy order indicates the investor is willing to pay the lowest offering price available at the time the order reaches the floor of the exchange. Market orders are used when an individual wants to effect a transaction *quickly* (wants immediate liquidity) and is willing to accept the prevailing market price. Assume an investor is interested in American Telephone and Telegraph (AT&T) and called his broker to find out the current "market" on the stock. Using a quotation machine, the broker determines that the prevailing market is 20 bid – 20 1/4 ask. This means that currently the highest bid on the books of the specialist, i.e., the most that anyone has offered to pay for AT&T, is 20. The lowest offer is 20 1/4, which is the lowest price someone is willing to accept for selling the stock. If an investor placed a market buy order for 100 shares, he would buy 100 shares at $20.25 a share (the lowest ask price) for a total cost of $2,025 plus commission. If an investor submitted a market sell order for 100 shares, he would sell the shares at $20 each and receive $2,000, less commission.

Limit Orders.   The second major category is a *limit order,* which means that the individual placing the order has specified the price at which he will buy or sell the stock. An investor might submit a bid to purchase 100 shares of AT&T stock at $18 a share when the current market is 20 bid – 20 1/4 ask with the expectation that the stock will decline to $18 in the near future. Such an order must also indicate *how long* the limit order will be outstanding. The alternatives, in terms of time, are basically without bounds — they can be instantaneous ("fill or kill"— fill instantly or cancel it), for part of a day, for a full day, for several days, a week, a month, or open-ended, which means the order is good until canceled (GTC). Rather than wait for a given price on a stock, a broker will give the limit order to the specialist, who will put it in his book and act as the broker's representative. When and if the market reaches the limit order price, the specialist will execute the order and inform the broker. The specialist receives a small part of the commission for rendering this service.

Short Sales.   While most investors purchase stock with the expectation that they will derive their return from an increase in value, there are instances in which an investor believes that a stock is overpriced and wants to take advantage of an expected decline in the price. The way to do this is to *sell the stock short.* A *short sale* is the sale of stock that is not owned with the intent of purchasing it later at a lower price. The investor *borrows* the stock from another investor through his broker and sells it in the market. He will subsequently repurchase the stock (hopefully, at a price lower than the one at which he sold it) and thereby replace it. The investor who lent the stock has the use of the money paid for it, because it is left with him as collateral on the stock loan. While there is no time limit on a short sale, the lender can indicate that he wants to sell his shares, in which case the broker must find another investor to make the loan.

Two technical points in connection with short sales are important. First, *a short sale can only be made on an uptick trade* (the price of the sale must be higher than the last trade price). The reason for this restriction is that the exchanges do not want traders to be able to *force* a profit on a short sale by pushing the price down through continually selling short. Therefore, the transaction price for a short sale must be an uptick or, if there is no change in price, the previous price must have been higher than its previous price (a zero uptick). An example of a zero uptick is a transaction at 42, 42 1/4; you could sell short at 42 1/4 even though it is no change from the previous trade at 42 1/4. Second, *the short seller is responsible for the dividends to the investor who lent the stock.* The purchaser of the short sale stock receives the dividend from the corporation, so the short seller must pay a similar dividend to the lender.

Special Orders.   In addition to these general orders, there are several special types of orders. One is a *stop loss order,* which is a conditional market order, whereby the investor indicates that he wants to sell a stock *if* the stock drops to a given price. Assume you buy a stock at 50 and expect it to go up. If you are wrong, you want to minimize or limit your losses. To do this, you would put in a stop loss order at 45, in which case, *if* the stock dropped to 45, your stop loss order would become a *market sell order,* and the stock would be sold at the prevailing market price. The order does not guarantee that you will get the $45; you can get a little bit more or a little bit less. Because of the possibility of market disruption caused by a large number of stop loss orders, exchanges, on occasion, have canceled all stop loss orders on certain stocks and have not allowed brokers to accept further stop loss orders on the issues involved.

Another type of stop loss, but on the other side, is a *stop buy order.* This is used by an investor who has sold stock short and wants to minimize any loss if the stock begins to increase in value. This order makes it possible to place a conditional buy order at a price above the price at which he sold the stock short. Assume you sold a stock short at 50, expecting it to decline to 40. To protect yourself from an increase, you could put in a stop buy order to purchase the stock if it reached a price of 55. This would hopefully limit any loss on the short sale to approximately $5 a share.

Margin Transactions.   Given any type of order, the investor can pay for the stock with cash or can borrow part of the cost, i.e., can *leverage* the transaction. Leverage is accomplished by *buying or selling on margin,* which means that the investor pays some cash and borrows the rest through his broker, putting up the stock for collateral. The determination of the maximum proportion that can be borrowed is set by the Federal Reserve Board under Regulations T and U. These regulations were enacted during the 1930s because it was contended that the excessive credit extended for stock acquisition was a reason for the stock market collapse of 1929. Since the enactment of the regulations, the margin requirement (the proportion of total value that must be paid for in cash) has varied from 40 percent (you could borrow 60 percent of the value) to 100 percent (no borrowing allowed). As of June 1984, the *initial margin requirement* is 50 percent. After the initial purchase, the market price of the stock will vary such that the proportion of *equity* will change (equity equals the market value of the collateral stock minus the amount borrowed). Obviously, if the stock price increases, the investor's equity as a proportion of the total value of the stock will increase (i.e., the investor's margin will exceed the initial margin requirement). In contrast, if the stock price declines, the investor's equity will decline. At this point, the relevant criterion is the *maintenance margin,* the proportion of equity to the total value of the stock. At present, the maintenance margin is 25 percent. If the stock price declines to the point where the investor's equity drops below 25 percent of the total value of the stock position, the account is considered undermargined, and the investor must provide more equity (the investor will receive a margin call), or the stock will be sold to pay off the loan.

It is important to recognize that buying on margin provides all the advantages *and* disadvantages of leverage; i.e., the *lower* the margin, the more you can borrow and the *greater* the percentage gain or loss on your investment when the stock price increases or decreases. The leverage factor is equal to 1-percent margin. Thus, if the margin is 50 percent, the leverage factor is two. This means that if the rate of return on the stock is plus or minus 10 percent, the return on the equity for an investor who borrowed 50 percent of the purchase price would be plus or minus 20 percent. If the margin declines to 33 percent, you can borrow more (67 percent) and the leverage factor is three (1/.33). Therefore, when you acquire stock or other investments using margin, you are increasing the financial risk of the investment beyond that which is inherent in the security itself, and you should increase your required return accordingly.

The Specialist[27]

With justification, the stock exchange specialist has been referred to as the center of the auction market for stocks. As noted, three requirements for a "good" market are depth, price continuity, and liquidity. The existence of these characteristics is heavily dependent upon how the specialist does his job.

The specialist is a member of the exchange who applies for his position by asking the exchange to assign stocks to him. The typical specialist will handle about 15 stocks. He must possess substantial capital to carry out this function, either $500,000 or enough to purchase 5,000 shares of the stock, whichever is greater. He must also have the knowledge to fulfill the functions of a specialist.

Functions of the Specialist.   The specialist has two major functions. The first is that of a *broker* who handles the limit orders or special orders placed with member brokers. An individual broker who receives a limit order to purchase a stock at $5 below the current market does not have the time or inclination to constantly watch the stock to see when and if the decline takes place. Therefore, he leaves the limit order (or a stop loss or stop buy order) with the specialist who enters it in his book and executes it when appropriate. For this service the specialist receives a portion of the broker's commission on the trade.

---

[27] An excellent booklet describing the specialist is *The New York Stock Exchange Market* (New York: New York Stock Exchange, June 1984). It also describes other facets of the Exchange and is free.

The second major function is to act as a *dealer* in the stocks assigned to him in order to maintain a "fair and orderly market." He is expected to buy and sell *for his own account* when there is insufficient public supply or demand to provide a continuous, liquid market. In this function he is acting like a dealer on the OTC market. If a stock is currently selling for about $40 per share, one could envision a situation in an auction market in which the current bid and ask (without the intervention of the specialist) might be a 40 bid–41 ask. Assuming the specialist does not intercede, and market orders to buy and sell the stock come to the market in a random fashion, the price of the stock would fluctuate between 40 and 41 constantly—a movement of 2.5 percent between trades. Most investors would probably consider such a price pattern to be too volatile; it would not be considered a very continuous market. The specialist is expected to provide an alternative bid and/or ask that will narrow the spread and thereby provide greater price continuity over time. In the above example this would entail *either* entering a bid of 40 1/2 or 40 3/4 or an ask of 40 1/2 or 40 1/4 to narrow the spread to one-half or one-quarter point. The specialist can enter *either* side of the market. Which side he enters will depend upon several factors. The first is *the trend of the market.* Since he is committed to being a stabilizing force in the market, he is expected to buy or sell *against* the market when prices are clearly moving in one direction; i.e., he is expected to buy stock for his own inventory when there is an excess of sell orders and the market is definitely declining, or to sell stock from his inventory or sell it short when there is an excess of buy orders and the market is rising. He is not expected to prevent the price from rising or declining, but only to ensure that the price changes in an orderly fashion.

Another factor is *his current inventory position in the stock.* If a specialist already has a large inventory position in a given stock, all other factors being equal, he would probably enter on the ask (sell) side in order to reduce his heavy inventory. In contrast, if previous market action had prompted a number of sales from his inventory or short sales, the specialist would tend toward the bid (buy) side in order to accumulate stock to rebuild his inventory or close out his short positions.

Finally, *the position of his book* (i.e., the specialist's information on all limit orders for a stock) will influence his actions, assuming no current trends to which he must react. If the specialist notes a large number of limit buy orders (bids) close to the current market and very few limit sell orders (asks), he might surmise that the most likely future move for the stock, in the absence of any new information, is toward a higher price because there is apparently heavy demand and limited supply. Under such conditions, one would expect the specialist to attempt to accumulate some stock in anticipation of an increase—i.e., he would tend to be on the bid side of the quote.[28]

Income.   The specialist derives income from both of his major functions. The actual breakdown between income from acting as a broker for limit orders and

---

[28] An analysis of the impact of specialists' market-making on stock price movements is contained in Victor Neiderhoffer and M. F. Osborne, "Market Making and Reversal on the Stock Exchange," *Journal of the American Statistical Association* 22 no. 4 (December 1966): 865–877.

84   income from acting as a dealer to maintain an orderly market will depend upon the specific stock. In the case of a very actively traded stock (e.g., American Telephone and Telegraph), there is not much need for the specialist to act as a dealer because substantial public interest in the issue creates a tight market. In this case the major concern of the specialist (and his main source of income for this stock) is maintaining the limit orders for the stock. In contrast, in the case of a stock with low trading volume and substantial price volatility, the specialist would be an active dealer and his income would depend upon his ability to trade in the stock profitably. A major advantage for the specialist in his trading of the stock is his access to the "book" that contains all limit orders for the stock in question. The specialist is the only one who is supposed to see the book, which means that he has a monopoly source of very important information. One can visualize the specialist's book containing the full set of limit orders as representing the current supply and demand curve for the stock. Therefore, it should provide the specialist with significant information regarding the probable direction of movement for the stock, at least in the short run.

Although specialists may be forced to buy or sell against the market for short periods of time, over longer periods they should make substantial profits on their dealer transactions because of the monopoly source of information contained in the specialist's book.[29] In addition, the income derived from acting as a broker can be substantial and is basically without risk. Most specialists attempt to balance the stocks assigned to them between the two types: they will have some strong broker stocks that provide a steady riskless source of income and some stocks that require an active dealer role.

Given the capital committed to the specialist function and the risk involved in acting as a dealer, one might wonder about the rate of return that specialists receive on their capital. Because most individual investors typically have received about 10 percent on common stock investments, one might expect a return to specialists of 20 percent. The fact is, a study by the Securities and Exchange Commission (SEC) indicated that there is substantial variation in the monthly income of specialist units, with the greatest variability experienced by units that have high inventory activity, i.e., among those specialists that are most active in market-making. An analysis of gross income per month relative to the aveage dollar of investment indicated that the annual rate of return for high activity units was *over 80 percent,* the return for the medium activity group was about *110 percent,* while the low activity group had an average rate of return of almost *190 percent.*[30] Besides indicating returns that seem clearly excessive for the risk involved, it is notable that the *least* active specialist units receive the *greatest* return.

---

[29] There is evidence that the specialists do not fare too badly even in instances in which they are forced to trade against the market. In this regard see Frank K. Reilly and Eugene F. Drzycimski, "The Stock Exchange Specialist and the Market Impact of Major World Events," *Financial Analysts Journal* 31 no. 4 (July–August 1975): 27–32. Also, if there is a major imbalance in trading due to new information, the specialist can request a temporary suspension of trading. For an analysis of what occurs during the period surrounding these suspensions, see Michael H. Hopewell and Arthur L. Schwartz, Jr. "Temporary Trading Suspensions in Individual NYSE Securities," *Journal of Finance* 33 no. 5 (December 1978): 1355–1373.

[30] United States House Committee on Interstate and Foreign Commerce, subcommittee on Commerce and Finance. *Securities Industry Study: Report and Hearings.* 92nd Congress, 1st and 2nd sessions, 1972, Chapter 12.

The value of being able to trade using the monopoly information contained in the specialist's book should not be underrated. The specialist performs a very useful function on the exchange, but it also appears that the rate of return he receives is excessive for the risk involved. These excess returns seem to be the result of the very strong position of the NYSE in the secondary exchange market and the monopoly position of the specialists in terms of information regarding their respective stocks. The service is useful, but the returns are excessive.[31] Because of these excess returns, one of the stated goals of the SEC is to introduce more competition into the market-making function. The idea is to maintain the basic structure but introduce more competition in order to reduce the costs to the investor. In Chapter 4, we will consider some of the changes that have taken place in the securities markets during the past decade and their effect on the specialist and other members of the securities market.

SUMMARY

The chapter has been concerned with what a market is, why markets exist, and what constitutes a "good" market. It also included a discussion of the division of the securities market into primary and secondary markets and why secondary markets are important for primary markets. We then considered the major segments of the secondary markets, including listed exchanges (the NYSE, the ASE, and regional exchanges); the over-the-counter market; the third market; and the fourth market. The final section included a detailed analysis of the exchange market and a discussion of the membership on an exchange, a consideration of the types of orders used on the exchange, and an in-depth look at the specialist function.

QUESTIONS

1. Define a market.
2. You own 100 shares of General Motors stock and you want to sell it because you need the money to make a down payment on a car. Assume there is *absolutely no secondary market system* in common stocks. How would you go about selling the stock? Discuss what you would have to do to find a buyer, how long it might take, and the price you might receive.
3. Briefly discuss the major characteristics of a "good" market.
4. Define liquidity and discuss what factors contribute to liquidity. Give an example of a liquid asset, an illiquid asset, and discuss why they are considered liquid and illiquid.
5. Define a primary market for securities.
6. Give an example of an initial public offering in the primary market. Give an example of a seasoned issue in the primary market. Which would involve greater risk to the buyer? Why?
7. Find an advertisement for a recent primary offering by a corporation in the *Wall Street Journal*. Based upon the information in the ad, indicate the characteristics

---

[31] For a proposed means of evaluating specialists, see Amir Barnea, "Performance Evaluation of NYSE Specialists," *Journal of Financial and Quantitative Analysis* 9 no. 4 (September 1974): 511–535.

of the security sold and the major underwriters. How much new capital did the firm derive from the offering before commissions were paid?

8. Briefly explain the difference between a competitive bid and a negotiated underwriting.

9. What is a secondary market for securities? How does it differ from the primary market?

10. Some observers would contend that without a good secondary market for securities, the primary market would be less effective. Discuss the reasoning behind this contention.

11. In the section of the *Wall Street Journal* on government bonds entitled "Treasury Bonds and Notes," what is the current bid and yield on the 8 1/4 of 1990?

12. How do the two national stock exchanges differ from each other?

13. Based upon the figures in Table 3.4, there is typically a major difference in the price paid for a seat on the NYSE compared to the ASE. How would you explain this difference?

14. What are the major reasons for the existence of the regional exchanges? How do they differ from the national exchanges?

15. How does the OTC market differ from the listed exchanges?

16. Which market segment of the secondary market (listed or OTC) is larger in terms of the number of issues? In terms of the value of the issues traded?

17. Which segment of the secondary market has more diversity in terms of the size of the companies and the quality of the issues? Why is this so?

18. What is the NASDAQ system? Discuss the three levels of NASDAQ in terms of what they provide and who would subscribe to each.

19. What are the benefits derived from NASDAQ? What has it done for the OTC market?

20. Define the third market. Give an example of a third market stock.

21. Why is there a limited number of stocks that are actively traded on the third market?

22. Define the fourth market. Why would a financial institution use the fourth market?

23. What is the major advantage of the fourth market? What is its major disadvantage?

24. Define a market order and give an example for a person selling 100 shares of a stock.

25. Briefly define each of the following terms and give an example:
    a.   Limit order
    b.   Short sale
    c.   Stop loss order.

26. The initial margin requirement is 60 percent. You have $30,000 to invest in a stock selling for $75 a share. Ignoring taxes and commissions, show in detail the impact in terms of rate of return if the stock rises to $100 a share and if it declines to $40 a share assuming: (a) you pay cash for the stock; (b) you buy it using the maximum amount of leverage available.

27. What are the two major functions of the specialist?

28. Over a long-run period (e.g., six months), would you expect the specialist to make money in his dealer function? Why or why not?

29. What are the two main sources of income for the specialist?

30. Other than the example in the chapter, give an example of a stock that would be a broker stock for the specialist. Why is it a broker stock?

31. What is the high risk segment of the specialists' dealer function? Why is it high risk? What aspect of the specialist position reduces the risk involved and also increases potential return? Be specific.

REFERENCES

Amex Statistical Review. New York: American Stock Exchange, published annually.

Barnea, Amir. "Performance Evaluation of NYSE Specialists." *Journal of Financial and Quantitative Analysis* 9 no. 4 (September 1974).

Barnea, Amir, and Logue, Dennis E. "The Effect of Risk on the Market Maker's Spread." *Financial Analysts Journal* 31 no. 6 (November–December 1975).

Basi, Bart A. "The Responsibility of the Broker-Dealer to the Investing Public." *American Business Law Journal* 14 no. 3 (Winter 1976).

Baumol, William J. *The Stock Market and Economic Efficiency.* New York: Fordham University Press, 1965.

Benston, George J., and Hagerman, Robert L. "Determinants of Bid-Asked Spreads in the Over-the-Counter Market." *Journal of Financial Economics* 1 no. 4 (December 1974).

Branch, Ben, and Freed, Walter. "Bid-Ask Spreads on the AMEX and the Big Board." *The Journal of Finance* 32 no. 1 (March, 1977).

Cohen, Kalman J., Maier, Stephen F., Schwartz, Robert A., and Whitcomb, David K. "Market Makers and the Market Spread: A Review of Recent Literature." *Journal of Financial and Quantitative Analysis* 14 no. 4 (November 1979).

Demsetz, Harold, "The Cost of Transacting." *Quarterly Journal of Economics* 82 no. 1 (February 1968).

Doede, Robert W. "The Monopoly Power of the New York Stock Exchange." Ph. D. dissertation, University of Chicago, June 1967.

Eiteman, W.J., Dice, C.A., and Eiteman, D.K. *The Stock Market.* 4th ed. New York: McGraw-Hill, 1966.

Fact Book. New York: New York Stock Exchange, published annually.

Friend, Irwin. "The Economic Consequences of the Stock Market." *American Economic Review* 62 no. 2 (May 1972).

Friend, I., Longstreet, J., Mendelson, M., Miller, E., and Hess, A. *Investment Banking and the New Issues Market.* New York: World, 1967.

Friend, Irwin, and Winn, W.J. *The Over-the-Counter Securities Markets.* New York: McGraw-Hill, 1958.

Hamilton, James L. "Competition, Scale Economies, and Transaction Cost in the Stock Market." *Journal of Financial and Quantitative Analysis* 11 no. 5 (December 1976).

88

Hamilton, James L. "Marketplace Organization and Marketability: NASDAQ, the Stock Exchange, and the National Market System." *Journal of Finance* 33 no. 2 (May 1978).

Hopewell, Michael H., and Schwartz, Arthur L. Jr. "Temporary Trading Suspensions in Individual NYSE Securities." *Journal of Finance* 33 no. 5 (December 1978).

Leffler, George L., and Farwell, Loring. *The Stock Market* 3d ed. New York: The Ronald Press, 1963.

Logue, Dennis. "Market-Making and the Assessment of Market Efficiency." *Journal of Finance* 30 no. 1 (March 1975).

Loll, Leo M., and Buckley, Julian G. *The Over-the-Counter Securities Markets* 4th ed. Englewood Cliffs, N.J.: Prentice-Hall, 1981.

Moore, Thomas G. "Stock Market Margin Requirements." *Journal of Political Economy* 74 no. 1 (April 1966).

NASDAQ and the OTC. New York: National Association of Securities Dealers, 1974.

Niederhoffer, V., and Osborne, M.F. "Market-Making and Reversal on the Stock Exchange." *Journal of the American Statistical Association* 22 no. 4 (December 1966).

Regan, Donald T. *A View From the Street.* New York: New American Library, 1972.

Reilly, Frank K., and Drzycimski, Eugene F. "The Stock Exchange Specialist and the Market Impact of Major World Events." *Financial Analysts Journal* 31 no. 4 (July–August 1975).

Reilly, Frank K., and Slaughter, William. "The Effect of Dual Markets on Common Stock Market Making." *Journal of Financial and Quantitative Analysis* 8 no. 1 (March 1971).

Robbins, Sidney. *The Securities Markets: Operations and Issues.* New York: The Free Press, 1966.

Santomero, A.M. "Economic Effects of NASDAQ." *Journal of Financial and Quantitative Analysis* 9 no. 1 (January 1974).

Sobel, Robert. *The Big Board.* New York: The Free Press, 1965.

Sobel, Robert. *The Curbstone Brokers: The Origins of the American Stock Exchange.* New York: Macmillan, 1970.

Sobel, Robert. *N.Y.S.E.: A History of the New York Stock Exchange, 1935–1975.* New York: Weybright and Talley, 1975.

Stoll, Hans R. "Dealer Inventory Behavior: An Empirical Investigation of NASDAQ." *Journal of Financial and Quantitative Analysis* 11 no. 3 (September 1976).

Tinic, Seha M. "The Economics of Liquidity Services." *Quarterly Journal of Economics* 86 no. 1 (February, 1972).

Tinic, Seha M., and West, Richard R. "Competition and the Pricing of Dealer Service in the Over-the-Counter Stock Market." *Journal of Financial and Quantitative Analysis* 7 no. 3 (June 1972).

Walter, James E. *The Role of Regional Security Exchanges.* Berkeley: University of California Press, 1957.

West, Richard R., and Tinic, Seha M. *The Economics of the Stock Market.* New York: Praeger Publishers, 1971.

West, Richard R. "On the Difference between Internal and External Market Efficiency." *Financial Analysts Journal* 31 no. 6 (November–December 1975).

Chapter 4   *The Securities Market: Past and Future Changes*

T he previous chapter contained a general description of securities markets including what they are intended to do and how they function. In textbooks written prior to 1970, such a discussion would have completed the analysis of securities markets. In 1965, however, a series of changes began which, by 1970, had profoundly affected the securities markets. It is necessary, therefore, to consider *what* these changes were and *why* the markets have changed. This analysis will also provide you with an insight into possible future developments.

CHANGES IN THE SECURITIES MARKETS

Why the Market is Changing

Prior to discussing the specific changes in the securities markets that have transpired over the past 20 years, you should fully appreciate *why* these changes have occurred. The answer is that *almost all the changes have been prompted by the significant and rapid growth of trading by large financial institutions* like banks, insurance companies, pension funds, and investment companies. As the figures show, the amount of trading by these institutions (in both absolute and relative terms) has grown dramatically since 1965. The trading patterns and requirements of institutions are different from those of individual investors. The market mechanism was basically developed and shaped to serve individuals who were the main customers of the securities exchanges. When a mechanism developed to serve individual investors was faced with completely different customers whose trading patterns were significantly different, there were problems.

    Therefore, regarding the question of why the market changed, the answer is simply that *the changes were prompted by a new dominant clientele with substantially different requirements from the original clientele.*

TABLE 4.1
Average Shares Per Sale Printed on the NYSE Tape

1961 — 197	1967 — 257	1973 — 449	1979 — 787
1962 — 204	1968 — 302	1974 — 438	1980 — 872
1963 — 213	1969 — 356	1975 — 495	1981 — 1,013
1964 — 218	1970 — 388	1976 — 559	1982 — 1,305
1965 — 224	1971 — 428	1977 — 641	1983 — 1,434
1966 — 240	1972 — 443	1978 — 717	

SOURCE: *Fact Book* (New York: New York Stock Exchange, various issues). Reprinted by permission.

Evidence of Institutionalization.   An indication of the growing impact of large financial institutions can be derived from data on size of trades, block trades, and overall institutional trading. It is assumed, because of the size of institutional portfolios, that institutional portfolio managers buy and sell large quantities (blocks) rather than 100–200 share lots. (A *block* is defined as a transaction involving at least 10,000 shares.)

Average size of trades.   One indication of increased institutional trading, therefore, is an increase in the average size of trades as reflected in the average number of shares per sale printed on the NYSE ticker tape. As shown in Table 4.1, the size of an average trade has grown steadily and has more than quadrupled during the last 23 years. Note especially the rapid growth since 1967.

Growth of block trades.   Because financial institutions are the main source of large block trades, further evidence of institutional involvement can be derived from the data on block trades contained in Table 4.2. The number of large block trades grew steadily at a very high rate from 1965 through 1972. There was a slight leveling off in 1973 and a definite decline in 1974 coincident with a decline in stock prices. The growth resumed in 1975 and has continued into 1984. One can derive an appreciation for the tremendous growth in block trades by considering the average number of block trades per day. As recently as 1965 there were only nine block trades *a day;* obviously they were a relatively rare occurence. Since 1982, the average has generally exceeded 1,000 such trades a day. This means that in a six-hour trading day there is currently at least one block trade *every 30 seconds.* A block trade is no longer rare. In fact, such trades constitute a major part of the volume on the exchange, about 40 percent.

Value of trading by institutions.   Institutional interest in common stock is also indicated by the value of purchases and sales of common stock by major financial institutions, as shown in Table 4.3. The financial institutions included are noninsured private pension funds, open-end investment companies, life insurance companies, and fire and casualty companies.

   A rough measure of the *relative* amount of trading by institutions can be derived by comparing the dollar value of purchases and sales by institutions with the total value of shares sold on registered exchanges during the year. While the total value figure is lower than the true total of all transactions in the United States because it does not include the OTC market or the third market, the series

TABLE 4.2
Block Transactions on the NYSE (10,000 shares or more)

Year	Total Number of Transactions	Total Number of Shares (000)	Percent of Reported Volume	Average Number of Block Transactions per Day
1965	2,171	48,262	3.1	9
1966	3,642	85,298	4.5	14
1967	6,685	169,365	6.7	27
1968	11,254	292,680	10.0	50
1969	15,132	402,063	14.1	61
1970	17,217	450,908	15.4	68
1971	26,941	692,536	17.8	106
1972	31,207	766,406	18.5	124
1973	29,233	721,356	17.8	116
1974	23,200	549,387	15.6	92
1975	34,420	778,540	16.6	136
1976	47,632	1,001,254	18.7	188
1977	54,275	1,183,924	22.4	215
1978	75,036	1,646,905	22.9	298
1979	97,509	2,164,726	26.5	305
1980	133,597	3,311,132	29.2	528
1981	145,564	3,771,442	31.8	575
1982	254,707	6,742,481	41.0	1,007
1983	363,415	9,842,080	45.6	1,436

SOURCE: *Fact Book* (New York Stock Exchange, various issues). Reprinted by permission.

TABLE 4.3
Purchases and Sales of Common Stock by Major Financial Institutions: Total Dollar Value and Relationship to the Value of Stock Transactions on Registered Exchanges

Year	Value of Purchases and Sales by Institutions (000)	Market Value of Total Shares Sold on Registered Exchanges (000)	Institutional Purchases and Sales as Percent of Total Value of Shares Sold
1965	23,160	89,214	.260
1966	33,120	123,034	.269
1967	48,645	161,758	.300
1968	67,245	196,358	.342
1969	79,960	175,298	.456
1970	68,435	130,908	.523
1971	92,340	184,931	.499
1972	101,575	204,026	.498
1973	85,910	178,037	.483
1974	51,546	118,249	.436
1975	66,430	157,092	.423
1976	73,694	194,969	.378
1977	71,422	187,203	.382
1978	90,346	249,217	.363
1979	104,956	299,750	.350
1980	196,115	475,850	.412

SOURCE: *Annual Report* (Washington, D. C.: Securities and Exchange Commission, various issues).

is internally consistent and so should indicate relative growth. As shown, the percentage of institutional trading doubled from 1965 to 1970. Following declines in the percentage during 1978 and 1979, there was an increase during 1980. Unfortunately, the SEC stopped reporting those data in 1980. Even so, these figures indicate substantial overall growth and recent stability at a relatively high ratio. Clearly, the impact of financial institutions on U.S. equity markets has substantially increased since the middle 1960s. Studies by Freund and Minor[1] and Soldofsky[2] projected continued growth.

EFFECTS OF INSTITUTIONAL INVESTMENTS ON THE SECURITIES MARKETS

The prior discussion indicated that institutions currently dominate the total equity capital market and they differ in how they trade (e.g., 2,000–20,000 shares versus 200–1,000 shares for individuals). This difference in trading patterns has had a profound effect on the functioning of the market in several areas.[3]

The major effects of an institutional market can be divided into five factors as follows:

1. The imposition of negotiated (competitive) commission rates
2. The influence of block trades
3. The creation of a tiered trading market
4. The impact of institutions on stock price volatility
5. The development of a national market system (NMS)

The first and last factor were basically changes *imposed* on the securities industry by the Securities and Exchange Commission (SEC). In contrast, the other three are *economic* changes caused by the response of the free market to this change in clientele. As an example, block trades are a natural result of an institutional market. The question then becomes, how did the market respond to this change in the trading environment?

Negotiated Commissions

Background.   When the NYSE was formally established in 1792 by the signing of the Buttonwood Agreement, the major points of the agreement were that the members would carry out all trades in designated stocks on the exchange, and that they would charge nonmembers on the basis of a *minimum commission schedule.* Obviously, this stipulation means that while it was possible to charge more than everyone else, nobody could engage in price cutting.

Because the securities markets were designed for the individual investor,

---

[1] William C. Freund and David F. Minor, "Institutional Activity on the NYSE: 1975 and 1980," *Perspectives on Planning* (New York: New York Stock Exchange, June 1972).

[2] Robert M. Soldofsky, *Institutional Holdings of Common Stock, 1900–2000* (Ann Arbor: University of Michigan Bureau of Business Research, 1971).

[3] Notably, while institutions account for about 40 percent of the trading, they only own about 30 percent of the stock. The difference is because they trade more actively — i.e., have higher trading turnover which is defined as the ratio of the dollar value of trading to the dollar value of stock owned. Individuals have an average annual turnover of about 20–25 percent, while institutions range from 30–45 percent.

the system was established to handle transactions involving less than 1,000 shares, and the pricing of trading services was developed to compensate for the handling of small orders. A major effect of heavy institutional trading came in the area of the fixed commission structure. The initial commission structure compensated members for handling many relatively small orders; it made no allowance for the substantial economies of scale involved in trading large orders. The increased cost of trading 10,000 shares as opposed to 300 or 400 shares is relatively small. If it costs $20 to sell 300 shares, it probably costs no more than $30 or $40 to sell 10,000 shares, and possibly less. These economies of scale were not adequately allowed for in the commission structure. The commission charged for a 10,000 share block was approximately five times as much as the charge for a 1,000 share trade.[4]

When institutions began trading heavily, they recognized that, because of the fixed minimum commission schedule, they were required to pay substantially more in commissions than the cost of transactions when trading large blocks.

Response to Fixed Minimum Commissions.   When institutions began trading heavily, the first reaction to the high prices the commission schedule involved was the introduction of "give-ups." The practice of give-ups evolved because brokers acknowledged that they received more for large transactions than was justified by the costs involved. Brokers consequently agreed to pay part of their commissions to other brokerage houses or research firms designated by the institution making the trade. If a brokerage house received $2,000 for a trade by a mutual fund, they were instructed to give up some portion of this commission (sometimes as much as 80 percent) to another brokerage house that had been selling the mutual fund or to a research firm that had provided research to the mutual fund. As a consequence, institutions used part of their excess commission dollars to pay for services other than brokerage. (These commission dollars were referred to as "soft" dollars.) When the two national exchanges (NYSE and ASE) attempted to reduce the use of give-ups, the regional exchanges became a major conduit for such transactions.

Another response to the high commission was the increased use of the third market. One of the advantages of trading in the third market was that commissions were not fixed and regulated as they were on the NYSE. Therefore, institutions could negotiate commissions for trades in the third market. Trading costs for large block trades were generally substantially lower than they were for comparable trades on the NYSE or ASE. The stock was typically acquired for one quarter point above the last trade on the NYSE *net,* meaning no additional commission was charged. Because of the lower commissions, from 1965 to 1972, the volume of trading on the third market grew steadily in absolute terms and in terms of the percentage of volume on the NYSE. There was a decline after 1972 because of the change in commission structure, as will be discussed in the following section.

---

[4] Using the commission schedule in effect in 1970, the commission charge for selling 1,000 shares of a $30 stock would be $262; the commission charge for selling 10,000 shares of this stock would be $1,342.

The fixed commission structure also fostered the development and use of the fourth market where two institutions deal directly with one another and, therefore, save the full commission. While there was probably substantial growth in this area, the extent of growth cannot be documented because no published figures are available on these trades.

A final response to the high commission costs was an attempt by some institutions to become members of one of the exchanges. The NYSE and ASE would not allow institutional members, but some of the regional exchanges admitted the institutions to increase trading volume.

Imposition of Negotiated Commissions.   All of the aforementioned ploys to offset or avoid commissions were attempted because the institutions felt there was little chance of changing the fixed minimum commission structure. Beginning in 1970, however, the SEC considered implementing negotiated commissions; i.e., for certain specified trades, the fixed commission structure would not hold and the broker and customer would negotiate the commission involved. The NYSE and almost all member firms vehemently opposed the concept, arguing that negotiated commissions would bring about the demise of the NYSE auction market because members would have no incentive to remain on the exchange if the commissions they received were limited.[5]

This argument was eventually rejected by the SEC, which began a program of allowing negotiated commissions on large transactions and finally allowed negotiated commissions on all transactions. In April 1971, it was ruled that the commission on that part of an order exceeding $500,000 could be negotiated between the broker and the customer. On April 24, 1972, the commission on that part of an order exceeding $300,000 became subject to negotiation. Finally, all commissions became fully negotiated on May 1, 1975 ("May Day").[6]

Impact of Negotiated Commissions

Effect on commissions.   The effect on commissions charged has been dramatic, especially for large trades by institutions. Initially, the negotiated commissions were stated in terms of discounts from the fixed rates that prevailed just prior to "May Day." The discounts started at 30 percent and slowly increased to over 40 percent on "no brainers" (i.e., relatively small trades on very liquid stocks, such as 2,000 shares of AT&T). Subsequently there was a tendency to quote some commissions in cents per share irrespective of price, which could involve a very large discount on high-priced shares.

Initially there was little discounting in trades by individuals, and in some instances, the commissions charged on small trades *increased*. Eventually a number of discount brokers appeared who did charge less for individuals wanting only straight transactions (no research advice, no safekeeping, etc.) carried

[5] A very insightful discussion of some potential effects of negotiated rates written prior to their imposition is contained in Chris Welles, "Who Will Prosper? Who Will Fail?" *Institutional Investor* 5 no. 1 (January 1971): 36–40.

[6] Thomas T. Murphy, ed., *Fact Book* (New York: New York Stock Exchange, 1977).

out.[7] As was true for institutional trades, the discounts varied according to the size of the trade. The discount firms advertise extensively in the *Wall Street Journal* and *Barron's*.

Effect on industry makeup. Because of the lower commissions, there have been numerous mergers and liquidations by smaller investment firms and many observers believe that this consolidation trend will continue, although at a slower pace, for several more years.[8] Therefore, it appears that there will be fewer, but larger and stronger, firms in the industry that have a full range of investment services. Even with fewer firms, there is limited concern over the industry's ability to meet the needs of investors and corporations.[9]

Effect on research firms. During the period of fixed minimum commissions, institutions used soft dollars to pay for research, and it was cheaper for most institutions to buy research from external sources than to establish extensive in-house research staffs. Therefore, numerous independent research firms were established to serve the institutions, and they were paid with soft commission dollars. With the introduction of competitive rates, there were almost no excess commissions available to give up, and the institutions concentrated their business with the large brokerage firms that had good trading capability *and* research departments. As a result, almost all of the independent research firms either disbanded or merged with full-service brokerage firms that were anxious to acquire experienced analysts with a reputation.

Effect on regional exchanges. Regional stock exchanges flourished during the early 1970s because they helped institutions distribute soft dollars and because some of them allowed institutions to become members. As a result, many institutions traded some of their blocks on these exchanges. With fully negotiated rates, there were few excess commission dollars to distribute and little incentive to maintain memberships. Therefore, some observers expected regional exchanges to be adversely affected by negotiated commissions. Apparently, the unique trading capability developed by these exchanges and their ability to implement block trades were relatively effective. A study by Reilly and Perry indicated that overall relative trading on the major regional exchanges during the period 1976–1978 was very similar to what had prevailed prior to 1975.[10] While there were differences between exchanges (e.g., the Detroit ex-

[7] See, Harvey D. Shapiro, "Shakeout in the Discount Game," *Institutional Investor* 15 no. 12 (December 1981): 146–156; Sherry Siegel, "The Compensation Revolution," *Institutional Investor* 16 no. 11 (November 1982): 217–221. Tim Carrington, "Discounters Are Taking Even-Wider Slice of Broker Commissions, SIA Study Finds," *Wall Street Journal* March 7, 1983, p. 7.

[8] Carol J. Loomis, "The Shakeout on Wall Street Isn't Over Yet," *Fortune* May 22, 1978, pp. 58–64; Richard Rustin, "Wall Street Mergers May Basically Change U.S. Financial System," *Wall Street Journal* April 22, 1981, p. 1; Carol J. Loomis, "The Fight for Financial Turf," *Fortune* December 28, 1981, pp. 54–65.

[9] Carol J. Loomis, "Where Does Wall Street's Shakeout Leave Its Customers?" *Fortune* June 19, 1978, pp. 140–144.

[10] Frank K. Reilly and Gladys Perry, "Negotiated Commissions and Regional Stock Exchanges," (presented at Southwest AIDS Meeting, Nashville, Tenn., February 1979). Faculty working paper no. 543 (University of Illinois at Urbana).

change went out of existence while the Cincinnati Exchange grew substantially), *the overall range of relative trading was similar.*

Effect on third market.   The third market expanded rapidly in the late 1960s and early 1970s because of trading by institutions anxious to save on commissions. A major question was whether it would continue to get the business when the commission advantage was lost after May Day. An analysis of the data strongly supported the prophets of doom; relative trading volume peaked in 1972 at over 8.5 percent of NYSE volume (shortly after the second change in commission rates) and declined steadily thereafter to less than 4 percent by 1977. It still exists in 1984 but is apparently only about 1 percent of NYSE volume.

Legal problems.   In a fixed-commission situation in which everyone charged the same price (commission), the only factor to consider was the execution of sale or purchase; i.e., making the best "deal" for the securities. In a world of negotiated commissions, both commission and execution must be considered, and institutional investors contended that low commissions are not worthwhile if execution is poor. As an example, on a 30,000 share block, you might save $2,000 in commissions, but if the sale is made at one-quarter point below another dealer's price, the loss in value ($7,500) will more than offset the savings in commissions. This is a complex legal issue, because a suit could be brought for poor execution of a trade.

Another legal issue involves payment for research. Many large investment houses still provide research support for their institutional customers, and this is obviously worth some difference in commission. However, the initial feeling was that the SEC would not allow houses to introduce any price difference for such help. Subsequent statements indicated that the SEC would allow a slightly higher price for "service," including research.

Summary of Effects.   Clearly the effects of negotiated commissions have been substantial, but they have varied for different segments of the industry. There has been a significant decline in total commissions paid and a consequent change in the size and structure of the industry. Definite casualties have been numerous independent research firms and the third market. On the other hand, there has apparently been little or no impact on the regional stock exchanges. Finally, price competition has introduced added legal considerations, but the impact has not been as great as expected.[11]

The Impact of Block Trades.   You will recall that a block trade is a transaction that involves a minimum of 10,000 shares. The increase in institutional trading resulted in a major increase in block trading which is a major test of the market's liquidity because it is obviously difficult to sell a block of 10,000 shares quickly

---

[11] Articles that discuss some of these factors are, Chris Welles, "Discounting: Wall Street's Game of Nerves," *Institutional Investor* 11 no. 11 (November 1976): 27–33; Seha M. Tinic and Richard R. West, "The Securities Industry under Negotiated Brokerage Commissions: Changes in the Structure and Performance of New York Stock Exchange Member Firms," *Bell Journal of Economics* 11 no. 1 (Spring 1980): 29–41; Sherry Siegal, "The Compensation Revolution," *Institutional Investor,* 16, no. 11 (November 1982): 217–221.

without effecting a major price change.[12] Also, even small price changes due to liquidity are obviously very significant to an institution that wants to buy or sell a "major position" (i.e., a large block of a given security). A half-point price change on a 10,000 share order entails a gain or loss of $5,000; on a 50,000 share order it would constitute a gain or loss of $25,000.

Block trades and specialists.   The increase in block trading has had a large impact on specialists because the specialist system had three problems with regard to block trading: *capital, commitment, and contacts* (the three Cs.). The first and most obvious problem was that specialists were *undercapitalized* when it came to dealing in large blocks. As the size of blocks has become larger, it has become more difficult for the specialist to come up with the capital needed to acquire the shares involved. Needless to say, large sums would be involved in the acquisition of 10,000 shares, much less the numerous blocks that exceed 20,000 shares. Further, even when the specialist has the capital to finance a position, he may not be willing to *commit* himself because of the risk involved in such an acquisition. Finally, the specialist is not allowed to deal directly with a customer who is not a broker (Rule 113 of the NYSE). Therefore, when an institution brings a block to the exchange, the specialist *cannot contact* another institution to determine whether it would have an interest in some part of the block. He is, therefore, cut off from the major source of demand for blocks and may be reluctant to take a large position if the stock involved is "thinly" traded; to whom is he going to sell it?

Block houses.   This lack of capital, commitment, and contacts on the part of specialists created a vacuum in the trading of blocks and resulted in the development of a new institution on Wall Street — *block houses.* Block houses evolved because some institutions needed help from institutional brokerage firms in locating other institutions with an interest in buying or selling given stocks. This practice of helping in the movement of blocks eventually became rather widespread.

Block houses are brokerage firms that stand ready to help buy or sell blocks for institutions. They may or may not be members of an exchange. A good block house has the requisites mentioned before in connection with the specialist: it must have the *capital* required to position a large block; it must be willing to *commit* this capital to an individual block; and, finally, it must have *contacts* among other institutions.

Example of a block trade.   The following example may help clarify what transpires in a block trade. Assume a mutual fund owns 250,000 shares of Ford Motors and decides that it wants to sell 50,000 shares of this position so that it can establish a position in another stock. Assume further that the fund decides to attempt the sale through Goldman Sachs & Company (GS&Co.), one of the larger, more active block houses which is a lead underwriter for Ford and knows institutions with an interest in the stock. The trader for the mutual fund would

---

[12] Recall that we defined liquidity as the ability to convert an asset into cash *quickly* at a known price, i.e., at a price similar to the previous market price.

contact a block trader at Goldman Sachs, tell him that he wants to sell the 50,000 share block, and ask what GS&Co. can do about it. At this point, several traders at Goldman Sachs would contact some of the institutions that currently own Ford to see if any of them would like to add to their position and to determine the price the institution would be willing to bid. After several phone calls, let us assume that GS&Co. receives commitments from four different institutions for a total of 40,000 shares at an average price of 49 5/8 (the last sale of Ford on the NYSE was 49 3/4). At this point, Goldman Sachs might go back to the mutual fund and bid 49 1/2 minus a negotiated commission for the total 50,000 shares. The fund can reject the bid and try another block house. Assuming they accept the bid, Goldman Sachs now owns the block and will immediately sell 40,000 shares to the four institutions that made prior commitments while "positioning" 10,000 shares themselves. (This means that they own the 10,000 shares and must eventually sell them at the best price possible.) Because GS&Co. is a member of the NYSE, the block will be processed ("crossed") on the Exchange as one transaction of 50,000 shares at 49 1/2. In the process, a specialist may take some of the stock to fill limit orders on his book at prices between 49 1/2 and 49 3/4. For working on this trade, Goldman Sachs has received a negotiated commission, but it has committed almost $500,000 to position the 10,000 shares. The major risk to GS&Co. is the possibility of a subsequent price change on the 10,000 shares. If Goldman can sell the 10,000 shares for 49 1/2 or more, it will just about break even on the position and have the commission as income. If the price weakens, they may have to sell the position at 49 1/4 and take a loss on it. This loss of about $2,500 will offset the income from the commission.

Such an example indicates the importance of having the contacts to quickly find institutions with an interest, the capital to position a certain portion of the block, and the willingness to commit that capital to the block trade. Without all three, the transaction would not have taken place.

DEVELOPMENT OF TIERED TRADING MARKETS

In addition to the creation of specific trading mechanisms to accommodate the institutions, the dominance of trading by institutions has resulted in a distinction among individual stocks based upon their appeal to institutions. Such a distinction results in a situation known as a *tiered market*. There have been many instances of tiered markets occurring over time. The two-tiered market that developed in the 1970s will probably be more long term than past tiered markets have been. For our purposes, it is important to define a tiered market in a general way. A tiered market occurs when *investors are willing to pay different price-earnings ratios for alternative stocks with basically the same characteristic in terms of risk and growth*. Typically, such differences in valuation have been short run.

Prior Tiered Markets

Using this definition, one can see that there have been tiered markets over the years because of the existence of numerous "hot" groups. Examples would include electronic stocks, mobile homes, fast-food franchisers, computer companies, and genetic engineering firms. In all these cases investors paid substantial premiums beyond what one would expect based upon growth and risk for stocks within these industry groups. Typically, the period of popularity did not exceed nine months to a year. A major difference between previous tiered markets and the recent tiered market is the broad specification of favored stocks and the length of time they were popular.

In the early 1970s the institutions showed a strong interest in a total *group* of stocks — large growth companies. They wanted growth firms to provide performance and large capitalization stocks (large market value of outstanding shares) for liquidity.[13]

Current Tiered Market

The tiered market that has prevailed and apparently has carried into the 1980s is concentrated on simply *large capitalization firms.* It appears that institutions will shift between industries and types of companies (growth, cyclical, etc.), but the overriding criterion is size; i.e., regardless of other characteristics, they will generally *not* acquire a small firm. The fact is, this preference for large capitalization firms is a logical consequence of institutional portfolio management. Institutions want to maximize return for a given level of risk or minimize risk for a given level of return. A major tool for minimizing risk is *diversification* which is intended to eliminate all unique or unsystematic risk from the portfolio. A common belief is that a portfolio with more securities is more diversified. Unfortunately, *there is a cost to diversification* because of the costs of administration and research. The more stocks in a portfolio, the higher the administrative costs, the higher the research costs, and, other factors being equal, the lower the net returns. Therefore, a portfolio manager should not overdiversify if he can avoid it.

In terms of overdiversification, several studies have shown that it is possible to derive most of the benefits of diversification with a portfolio consisting of from 12 to 18 stocks.[14] To be adequately diversified does *not* require 200 stocks in a portfolio. Moreover, at some point the costs of further diversification exceed the additional benefits. Therefore, managers should attempt to minimize the number of different issues in a portfolio while still being properly diversified. Although most large institutions would probably need more than the minimum 20 stocks, a number much over 100 is probably excessive. Given a portfolio with a large dollar value and a self-imposed limit on the number of stocks included, *the value of each holding must be substantial.* Assume an institutional portfolio has a value of $1 billion. (This size is not at all unusual.) In such a portfolio containing 50 stocks, each holding must have *an average value of $20 million;* if

[13] C. J. Loomis, "How the Terrible Two Tier Market Came to Wall Street," *Fortune* July 1973, pp. 82–89.

[14] John L. Evans and Stephen H. Archer, "Diversification and the Reduction of Dispersion: An Empirical Analysis," *Journal of Finance* 23 no. 5 (December 1968): 761–767; Lawrence Fisher and James H. Lorie, "Some Studies of Variability of Returns on Investments of Common Stock," *Journal of Business* 43 no. 2 (April 1970): 99–134; Jack E. Gaumnitz, "Maximal Gains from Diversification and Implications for Portfolio Management," *Mississippi Valley Journal of Business and Economics* 6 no. 3 (Spring 1971): 1–14.

the portfolio contains 100 stocks, each holding must have *an average value of $10 million.*

In order to insure the liquidity of the holdings, institutions will limit their ownership of an issue. The usual limit set by portfolio managers is 5 percent of the outstanding issue. (This is a legal limit for mutual funds, but most managers impose their own limit which is lower than this.) Assuming the self-imposed limit is 5 percent and the average value of each holding is $10 million, the market value of each firm's total outstanding stock must be $200 million ($10 million ÷ .05). If each holding by the institution averages $20 million and the limit is set at 5 percent, the average total market value of each company in the portfolio must be $400 million.

Therefore, when institutions become interested in companies for performance reasons, they *also* require that these companies be *large.* Because of this constraint, *the large institutions concentrate their attention on a universe of less than 700 stocks.*[15] Many observers contend that they concentrate on a substantially smaller number i.e., 300–400. The point is, this preference for large capitalization firms means the large institutions who currently do the majority of the trading in the secondary market are concentrating on a relatively small proportion of available public firms. Specifically, based on the size preference, it appears that most institutions will only consider about *700* firms *at most,* while there are about 6,500 public stocks with reasonable markets (1,700 on the NYSE; 1,300 on the ASE; and about 3,500 on the OTC market including 2,700 on NASDAQ). The result is that the majority of trading is concentrated in about 11 percent of the available stocks.[16]

Effect of a Tiered Secondary Market

The previous discussion indicated that the primary market for securities, in which companies sell stock or bonds to get new outside capital, is heavily dependent upon the liquidity provided by the secondary market. In the future, we will probably face a substantial problem in the secondary market because of the liquidity requirements of institutions; i.e., they will concentrate their investments in a limited number of large companies. A generous estimate of the total number of companies that qualify for most institutional portfolios is about 700, while the number of public companies likely exceeds 6,500.[17] Because institutions are looking at a relatively small number of companies, the secondary market for the remaining stocks traded by individuals will deteriorate. Institutions are concentrating their attention on a smaller group of companies while a shrinking segment of the trading market, the individual investor, is left with a growing number of stocks. Therefore, the secondary markets for the large institutional

---

[15] Frank K. Reilly, "A Three Tier Stock Market and Corporate Financing," *Financial Management* 4 no. 3 (Autumn 1975): 7–15.

[16] Subsequent discussions of the two tier market are contained in Daniel Seligman, "The Terrible Two-Tier Market (cont.)," *Fortune* (October 1973): 105–111; and "The Two-Tier Market Lingers On, Sort Of," *Fortune* (February 1974): 41–45.

[17] For a detailed estimate of the number of companies in the alternative tiers, see Frank K. Reilly, "A Three Tier Market and Corporate Financing," *Financial Management* 4 no. 3 (Autumn 1975): 7–15.

stocks will improve substantially and will be very viable.[18] The secondary market for the great bulk of medium to small firms will deteriorate and this will seriously affect the primary market for these companies.[19]

A study by Reilly and Drzycimski examined a sample of common stocks in three market tiers based on market value.[20] They examined specific changes in trading activity, stock price volatility, and financing characteristics during the 15-year period 1964–1978. The authors hypothesized that because of the tiered market, the firms in the bottom tier would experience a decline in trading activity, an increase in price volatility, and undesirable changes in financial structure. The results indicated that while almost all the changes were as hypothesized, not all of them were statistically significant. Clearly the lower tier firms experienced a decline in relative market liquidity and dividend payout while experiencing an increase in stock price volatility and financial leverage. The authors concluded:

> Almost all the changes are detrimental to the lower tier stocks because these stocks have become riskier relative to top tier stocks. The impact could cause further deterioration in the secondary markets for these stocks which, in turn, will make it more difficult for them to acquire new equity capital from the primary market.[21]

INSTITUTIONS AND STOCK PRICE VOLATILITY

Many observers believe that there should be a strong *positive* relationship between institutional trading and stock price volatility. It is reasoned that institutions trade in large blocks and such a trading pattern causes a decline in liquidity for the securities markets and, hence, an increase in stock price volatility.[22] Others contend that institutions tend to trade together (i.e., trade in parallel), which likewise would cause major price changes.[23] Notably articles that make these contentions base them on intuitive arguments or very *ad hoc* evidence. In contrast to this folklore, several empirical studies have examined the relationship between the amount or proportion of trading by large financial institutions and stock price volatility. The fact is, the empirical evidence has *never* supported the folklore. Because the folklore is so persuasive and appears to have intuitive appeal, it seems worthwhile to discuss some of these studies briefly.

---

[18] For a discussion of how market changes will benefit some corporations, see Richard R. West and Seha M. Tinic, "Corporate Finance and the Changing Stock Market," *Financial Management* 3 no. 3 (Autumn 1974): 14–23.

[19] This problem is discussed in, "Are the Institutions Wrecking Wall Street?" *Business Week,* June 2, 1973, pp. 58–64.

[20] Frank K. Reilly and Eugene F. Drzycimski, "An Analysis of the Effects of a Multi-Tiered Stock Market," *Journal of Financial and Quantitative Analysis* 16 no. 4 (November 1981), pp. 559–575.

[21] *Ibid.,* p. 571.

[22] Jonathan Laing, "Fiduciary Grants: Huge Sums Managed by Bank Trusts Units Stirs up Controversy, " *Wall Street Journal,* January 7, 1975, p. 114; John F. Lyons, "What Happens When Liquidity Disappears?" *Institutional Investor* 3 no. 11 (November 1969): 29–36; David McClintok, "Illiquid Stock, Lack of Ready Buyers and Sellers Imperils the Stock Market," *Wall Street Journal,* December 10, 1971, p. 1.

[23] Steven C. Leuthold, "The Causes (and Cures?) of Market Volatility," *Journal of Portfolio Management* 2 no. 2 (Winter 1976): 21–25.

104   Empirical Studies on Relationship

A study by Reilly examined the relationship between several series published by the SEC that indicate common stock transactions by financial institutions (pension funds, investment companies, and insurance companies) and several measures of stock price volatility.[24] The correlations among the measures of institutional trading activity and measures of stock price volatility were either positive and insignificant or negative and insignificant. Clearly the results did *not* support the folklore that institutional trading causes an increase in stock price volatility.

A subsequent study by Reilly and Wachowicz considered a larger and more detailed set of institutional trading variables and more measures of stock price volatility.[25] An analysis of percentage changes in the two sets of series indicated that almost all the correlations were significantly *negative*. Overall, the results indicated that during periods when the institutions experience a large *increase* in trading activity, there is generally a *decline* in the various measures of stock price volatility.

A study by Berkman came to similar conclusions following a set of studies.[26] After an analysis of overall market volatility and institutional trading volume and practices, Berkman specifically examined the trading behavior of mutual funds to see if trading patterns and practices tended to cause an increase in stock price volatility. A detailed analysis of transactions indicated that "in and out" trading has not been a frequent practice during the postwar period nor has such trading increased during this period. In fact, sample funds commonly spread purchases and sales over two or more quarters. He also tested for concentration among mutual fund purchases and sales (i.e., the herd effect). The results provided little evidence of a consistent tendency toward herdlike trading among mutual funds. These results are consistent with earlier findings by Kraus and Stoll.[27]

Rather than examining all transactions by institutions, Reilly and Wright examined only block trades, which are generally considered the ultimate test of liquidity.[28] The analysis considered whether the level of block trades in absolute terms or as a proportion of total volume was related to various measures of stock price volatility. The relationship between percentage changes in the measures was significantly *negative*. This indicated that when there was a large *increase* in total block trading or the proportion of block trading, there was a *decline* in stock price volatility. Again, these results are consistent with studies by Scholes; Kraus and Stoll; Nielsen and Joehnk; and Carey, who found that the price impact

---

[24] Frank K. Reilly, "Institutions on Trial: Not Guilty," *Journal of Portfolio Management* 3 no. 2 (Winter 1977): 5–10.

[25] Frank K. Reilly and John M. Wachowicz, "How Institutional Trading Reduces Market Volatility," *Journal of Portfolio Management* 5 no. 2 (Winter 1979): 11–17.

[26] Neil Berkman, "Institutional Investors and the Stock Market," *New England Economic Review* (November–December 1977): 60–77.

[27] Alan Kraus and Hans R. Stoll, "Parallel Trading by Institutional Investors," *Journal of Financial and Quantitative Analysis* 7 no. 5 (December 1972): 2107–2130.

[28] Frank K. Reilly and David J. Wright, "Block Trades and Stock Price Volatility," *Financial Analysts Journal* 40, no. 2 (March–April, 1984).

related to block trades was generally quite small and rapid and the price change reflected a permanent change in value rather than a liquidity cost.[29]

Following an analysis which indicated there had been significant changes in the level of stock price volatility over time, Wachowicz and Reilly examined a number of variables that might cause such changes in volatility using a multiple regression model.[30] Besides a number of macroeconomic variables like interest rate volatility, the authors included measures of institutional trading activity. The regression results indicated that the coefficient for the institutional trading variable was always statistically significant and *negative*.

Effects of Institutions on Price Volatility.   In summary, the empirical evidence regarding the impact of institutional trading on stock price volatility is both extensive and consistent. The results indicate either there is *no relationship* between institutional trading and stock price volatility, or the relationship is *negative*. This indicates that an increase in trading by institutions is related to a decline in stock price volatility. In a capital market where trading has become dominated by institutions, the best environment is one where all institutions are active since *they provide liquidity for one another and for noninstitutional investors* because they are active simultaneously but not necessarily on the same side of the market. (That is, there is *no* evidence of a herd instinct.) Therefore, there is *no* support for the folklore and *no* justification for restricting or inhibiting trading by financial institutions.

The final change caused by the increase in institutional trading is the development of a National Market System (NMS) which is intended to provide greater efficiency and competition. The requirements of a NMS and progress in this area is discussed in the following section.

A NATIONAL MARKET SYSTEM (NMS)

In addition to suggesting that negotiated commissions be introduced, the Institutional Investor Report, prepared by the SEC at the request of Congress, strongly recommended the creation of a national, competitive market. Although there is no one generally accepted definition of what a national market would constitute, there are four major characteristics that are generally included in a description of such a market:
1.   Centralized reporting of all transactions
2.   A centralized quotation system

---

[29] Myron S. Scholes, "The Market for Securities: Substitution versus Price Pressure and the Effects of Information on Share Prices," *Journal of Business* 45 no. 2 (April 1972): 179–211; Alan Kraus and Hans R. Stoll, "Price Impact of Block Trading on the New York Stock Exchange," *Journal of Finance* 27 no. 3 (June 1972): 710–717, James F. Nielsen and Michael D. Joehnk, "Further Evidence on the Effects of Block Transactions on Stock Price Fluctuations," *Mississippi Valley Journal of Business and Economics* 9 no. 2 (Winter 1973–1974): 27–34; Kenneth J. Carey, "Nonrandom Price Changes in Association with Trading in Large Blocks: Evidence of Market Efficiency in Behavior of Investor Returns," *Journal of Business* 50 no. 4 (October 1977): 407–414.

[30] John M. Wachowicz and Frank K. Reilly, "An Analysis of Factors that Influence Aggregate Stock Market Volatility," Southern Finance Association Meeting, Atlanta, (November 1979).

3.   A centralized limit-order book (CLOB)
4.   Free and open competition among all qualified market-makers.

A Composite Tape

A central market must involve *centralized reporting of transactions, i.e.,* a composite tape on which all transactions in a stock would be reported regardless of where the transactions took place. As one watched the tape, he might see a trade in GM on the NYSE, another on the Midwest, and a third on the OTC. The intent is to report all completed trades on the tape and thereby provide full information on all securities traded. As of June 16, 1975, the NYSE began operating a central tape that includes all NYSE stocks traded on other exchanges and on the OTC.[31] Therefore, this aspect of a National Market System (NMS) has already been introduced for stocks listed on the NYSE.

Centralized Quotations

The second requirement for an NMS is a centralized quotation system that contains the quotes for a given stock from all market-makers, including those on the national exchanges, the regional exchanges, and the OTC. With a centralized quotation system, a broker who requested the market for GM would be given the prevailing quotes on the NYSE and the Midwest Stock Exchange, those from other regional exchanges on which GM is listed, and the several markets made by OTC dealers. The broker should complete the trade on the market with the best quote for his client.

ITS.   Currently there are two centralized quotation systems available. One is the *Intermarket Trading System (ITS)* developed by the American, Boston, Midwest, New York, Pacific, and Philadelphia Stock Exchanges.[32] ITS consists of a central computer facility with interconnected terminals in the participating market centers. Brokers and market-makers in each market center can indicate to those in other centers specific buying and selling commitments by way of a composite quotation display. These displays show the current quote for each eligible stock in that market center, and the current quotes in all other participating market centers or system-wide. A broker or market-maker in any market center can thus exercise *his own best judgment* in determining, on the basis of current quotations, where to execute a customer's orders. If a better price is available in another market, he simply sends a message to that market center, committing himself to buy or sell at the price shown on the quotation display. When his commitment is accepted, he receives a message telling him that the transaction has taken place. The following example illustrates how ITS works:

A broker on the NYSE has a market order to sell 100 shares of XYZ stock. The

---

[31] Murphy, Thomas T. ed., *Fact Book* (New York: New York Stock Exchange, 1977), 7.

[32] This discussion draws heavily on *ITS: A Cornerstone of the National Market System,* (New York: New York Stock Exchange, 1981). The publication is available from any of the participating exchanges.

quotation display on the floor of the NYSE shows that the best current bid for XYZ has been entered on the Pacific Stock Exchange (PSE), and he decides to take advantage of that bid. He enters a firm commitment on the NYSE terminal to sell 100 shares at the bid on the PSE. Within seconds, the commitment is flashed on the CRT screen and is also printed out at the PSE specialists' post, where it is executed against the PSE bid.

After the commitment is accepted, a short message is entered into the system which immediately reports an execution back to New York, and the trade is reported on the consolidated tape. Brokers on both sides of the transaction receive an immediate confirmation, and a journal of all transactions is transmitted to the appropriate market centers at the end of the day. Thereafter, each broker completes his own clearance and settlement procedure.

As it currently operates, the ITS system provides centralized quotations for the stocks listed, and on the NYSE screen it specifies whether a bid or ask away from the NYSE market is superior to that on the New York market. Note that there are several characteristics that the system does *not* have. One is that it does not have the capability for automatic execution at the best market; it is necessary to contact the market-maker and indicate that you want to buy or sell at his bid or ask. It is possible that, when a NYSE broker goes to "hit" another market, the bid or ask will be withdrawn. Also, it is *not* mandatory that a broker go to the best market. Although the best price is elsewhere, a broker might consider it inconvenient to transact on that exchange if the price difference is not substantial. It is almost impossible to audit such actions.[33]

NSTS.   Another centralized quotation system that has the capability to become the core of an NMS is the *National Securities Trading System* (NSTS), which is currently operating on the Cincinnati Stock Exchange.[34] With this system it is possible for any qualified broker to enter a bid, ask, or limit order for any of the 16 stocks on NSTS. (All are listed on the NYSE.) As a consequence, the system encompasses multiple competing market-makers, and all orders are exposed to a national market. Further, once an order is entered and accepted, the trade is executed automatically and subsequent confirmations are automatic.

In contrast to ITS, the NSTS has a public, central limit-order file. All limit orders list a price and time priority, and the system automatically executes the order with the best price and earliest time. The SEC has allowed operation of this system which has been used by Merrill Lynch, Pierce, Fenner, & Smith on an experimental basis. The experiment apparently ended in 1983.[35]

In summary, there has been substantial progress in development of a central

---

[33] For a discussion of the actual operation of ITS, see Burt Schorr, "Fledgling Market Line Works, but Can't Cope during Hectic Trading," *Wall Street Journal,* May 5, 1980, p. 1.

[34] This discussion draws heavily from the booklet *The National Securities Trading System* (Jersey City, N.J.: The Service Bureau Company, 1979).

[35] "Extensions of Electronic Trading System at Cincinnati Exchange is Issued by SEC," *Wall Street Journal,* December 14, 1979, p. 9; Richard E. Rustin, "Inclusion of Cincinnati Exchange, NASD in Intermarket Trading System Proposed," *Wall Street Journal,* May 9, 1980, p. 3; "Cincinnati Exchange, First Electronic One, Is Linked to Others," *Wall Street Journal,* February 12, 1981, p. 3; Tim Carrington, "Merrill Lynch Ends Computer Trading Role," *Wall Street Journal,* July 13, 1983, p. 5.

quotation system, which clearly indicates that the required technology is available and operational. The question remaining is, who can use these quotes and who can enter them.

Central Limit-Order Book (CLOB)

A major area of controversy has been the establishment of a central limit-order book that would contain all limit orders from *all* exchanges. Ideally, the CLOB would be visible to everyone, and all market-makers and traders could fill orders on the CLOB. Currently most limit orders are placed with the specialist on the NYSE and, when a transaction *on the NYSE* reaches the stipulated price, the order is filled by the NYSE specialist who receives some part of the commission for rendering this service. The NYSE has opposed a CLOB because the NYSE specialists do not want to share this very lucrative business.

Two versions of CLOB have been proposed. One is a "soft" CLOB that would only be accessible to specialists and specified market-makers, although not limited to those on the NYSE. This version would probably not entail automatic execution of transactions. In contrast, a "hard" CLOB would be available to all market-makers and would involve automatic execution of orders. Generally, advocates of an NMS support the "hard" CLOB with rigid time and price guarantees built into the system. The SEC has proposed a rule that would basically entail creation of a CLOB. The technology for a CLOB is already available with the NSTS. Given the SEC requirement, it apparently will become a reality eventually.

Competition between Market-Makers (Rule 390)

Competing market-makers have always prevailed on the OTC market, but competition has been opposed by the NYSE. The argument in favor of competition among market-makers is that it forces dealers to make better markets or they will not do any business. Assume Dealer A quotes 49–50 for a stock, and Dealer B makes a quote of 49 1/4–49 3/4. Dealer B should do all the business in the stock because he has a higher bid and a lower ask. If Dealer A wants to do any business, he must at least match the quote by the other market-maker or improve on it by bidding 49 3/8 and/or offering stock at 49 5/8. If competition improves the market for the stock (i.e., reduces the bid-ask spread), this improvement should be reflected in market data. Several studies that examined the relationship between the spread on a sample of stocks and the number of dealers trading those stocks, holding other relevant variables constant, indicated that the more competition (dealers), the smaller the spread.[36]

In contrast, the NYSE argues that a *central* auction market provides the best

[36] Seha M. Tinic and Richard R. West, "Competition and the Pricing of Dealer Service in the Over-the-Counter Stock Market," *Journal of Financial and Quantitative Analysis* 7 no. 3 (June 1972): 1707–1727; George J. Benston and Robert L. Hagerman, "Determinants of Bid-Asked Spreads in the Over-the-Counter Market," *Journal of Financial Economics* 1 no. 4 (December 1974): 353–364.

market because, under such an arrangement, all orders are forced to the one central location; this concentration of orders will ensure the best auction market. The principal device used by the NYSE to create a concentrated market was Rule 394, which was subsequently modified and called Rule 390. This rule states that, unless specifically exempted by the Exchange, members must obtain the permission of the exchange before carrying out a transaction in a listed stock off the Exchange. The stated purpose of the rule is to ensure that all volume comes to the NYSE so that the Exchange can provide the most complete auction market. The Exchange contends that Rule 390 is necessary to protect the auction market, arguing that if the rule is eliminated, members will be tempted to trade on or off the Exchange and many orders will be *internalized* (i.e., brokers will match orders from the holdings of their own customers and, the orders will not come to the exchange at all). In general, a "fragmented" dealer market is envisioned, which the exchange contends is not as good as the central auction market.[37] An alternative view by Hamilton contends that the adverse effects of fragmentation are more than offset by the benefits of competition.[38]

The contrasting view is that market-making should be on a *free competitive basis* similar to what occurs on the OTC market where anybody who wants to make a market in a stock and can meet specified basic capital requirements is allowed to do so. In addition, members of the exchange could and *should* trade with the market-maker offering the best market. Advocates of this competitive market contend that such a structure has served well for decades in the OTC market, and several competing dealers would have more capital with which to make markets than does a single specialist.[39]

Competing arguments aside, the SEC contends that its mandate from Congress under the Investment Act of 1975 is to help establish an open, competitive market without restrictions like Rule 390. The question is *when* and how Rule 390 will be eliminated. The NYSE and a number of brokerage firms have suggested implementing a modified form of Rule 390 *until* the central market is established because they believe that, until the NMS is working, participants will need a strong auction market such as exists on the Exchange. The contrasting view is that the abolition is necessary *before* a central market can be established because, as long as Rule 390 exists, about 80 percent of the volume of the NYSE stocks is restricted to the Exchange, and it is not reasonable to expect a potential market-maker to establish a competitive market under such conditions. Therefore, it is argued that there will not be a truly competitive market *until* this rule is eliminated.

Progress in achieving this final phase of the NMS has been slow due to strong

---

[37] This is the implication derived from a panel discussion reported in Shelby White, "The New Central Marketplace: The Debate Goes On," *Institutional Investor* 10 no. 8 (August 1976): 30–31.

[38] James L. Hamilton, "Competition, Scale Economics, and Transaction Cost in the Stock Market," *Journal of Financial and Quantitative Analysis* 11 no. 5 (December 1976): 779–802; James L. Hamilton, "Marketplace Fragmentation Competition and the Efficiency of the Stock Exchange," *Journal of Finance* 34 no. 1 (March 1979): 171–187; James L. Hamilton, "Marketplace Organization and Marketability: NASDAQ, the Stock Exchange and the National Market System." *Journal of Finance* 33 no. 2 (May 1978): 487–503.

[39] For a further discussion of this view, see Seymour Smidt, "Which Road to an Efficient Stock Market?" *Financial Analysts Journal* 27 no. 5/(September–October 1971):18–20.

opposition and caution on the part of the SEC.[40] However, changes are being made which indicate that Rule 390 will be eliminated or greatly modified at some point. A step in this direction is a proposal that stocks newly listed on the exchange would *not* be bound by Rule 390; exchange members could trade these newly listed securities away from the exchange.[41] As of 1984 there were over 300 stock freed of off-board trading restrictions.

Impact of NMS without Rule 390

It is reasonable to assume that the SEC will eventually have its way and establish a true NMS with the characteristics mentioned earlier (consolidated tape and quotes, a CLOB, and no Rule 390). Therefore, let us consider the effect of this on various segments of the industry.[42]

Dealer markets.   One major effect of eliminating Rule 390 would be that any interested market-maker could become a dealer in any stock. Until Rule 390 is eliminated, a member firm of the NYSE obviously can not make a market in AT&T or GM because all such trades must be made through the exchange, even the large block trades that are matched ''upstairs'' (away from the floor of the exchange) by block houses like Goldman Sachs and Salomon Bros. Without Rule 390, member firms like Goldman Sachs and Salomon Bros. will probably not bring the blocks to the exchange, but they will simply trade them as dealers off the exchange.

A more significant effect would be the creation of dealer markets for smaller trades by firms such as Merrill Lynch which could begin making dealer markets in stocks like AT&T and GM and make trades for smaller orders in these stocks for their many individual investors. This cannot be done with Rule 390 because all trades must go to the NYSE. As mentioned previously, this practice is referred to as *internalization*. If a number of large brokerage firms did this for a large number of stocks, volume on the NYSE could be substantially reduced. However, this line of reasoning appears to be rather drastic and implies that there is little value in the NYSE auction market. The fact is, major firms that have discussed establishing dealer markets when Rule 390 is eliminated have made it quite clear that they will only become dealers in stocks with reasonable spreads

---

[40] Stan Crock and Richard E. Rustin, ''Work on a National Stock-Trading System Lags Badly: Some Blame Brokers and SEC,'' *Wall Street Journal,* February 2, 1979, p. 32; ''Chiefs of National Stock Market Hearings Assert Industry, SEC Proceed Too Slowly,'' *Wall Street Journal,* September 25, 1979, p. 12; ''SEC Hit by House Unit for Slow Progress in Creation of National Securities Market,'' *Wall Street Journal,* September 12, 1980, p. 3; Stan Crock, ''SEC's Aim to Start National Stock Market Triggers Partisan Crossfire in Congress,'' *Wall Street Journal,* February 26, 1981, p. 9; ''SEC Delays Test of Electronic Trade Link for OTC, 7 Exchanges to March 1, 1982,'' *Wall Street Journal,* April 22, 1981, p. 3.

[41] ''Two Rules that Move the Securities Industry Nearer National System Proposed by SEC,'' *Wall Street Journal,* April 27, 1979, p. 4; ''SEC Eases Curb on Off-Board Trading by Brokers in Exchange-Listed Issues,'' *Wall Street Journal,* June 6, 1980, p. 7; Tim Carrington, ''Share Trading Away from Exchanges Can Start Tomorrow at Brokerage Firms,'' *Wall Street Journal,* July 20, 1980, p. 3; Richard Hudson, ''SEC Drops Its Plan for Off-Board Trading That Split the Brokerage Industry,'' *Wall Street Journal,* July 29, 1983, p. 4.

[42] For other discussions on this topic, see William C. Melton, ''Corporate Equities and the National Market System,'' Federal Reserve Bank of New York, *Quarterly Review* (Winter 1978–1979): 13–25; Robert C. Klemkosky and David J. Wright, ''The Changing Structure of the Stock Market: The National Market System,'' *Business Horizons* (July–August 1981): 10–20.

from which there is a potential for reasonable returns.[43] These firms have no desire to compete with the NYSE specialists in stocks like AT&T and GM where the typical spread is one-eighth or one-fourth point at best, because trading such stocks is not worth their time and effort. They will become dealers in stocks with spreads of three-eighths or one-half point, because the returns will justify the effort and capital required. The added competition could cause a reduction in the spread, which means the investor will gain. Also, because all trades will be reported on the composite tape, the broker *must* go to the best market or be liable for poor execution.

Effect on the specialist.   Clearly the position of the specialist will change dramatically after Rule 390 is abolished. First, he will lose his protected position as the lone market-maker in many stocks and will have to compete with numerous potential dealers. In some cases, the specialist may choose to stop being the market-maker in less active issues. Assuming that the major order flow for stocks like AT&T and GM will continue to come to the NYSE, the specialist could continue to make this market, but he would lose income that previously came from running the limit book, if we assume that a hard CLOB will be introduced. Therefore, the specialists' returns will clearly be less than those reported in the late 1960s. One contemplated change that will be beneficial to the specialists is the elimination of Rule 113 prohibiting the specialist from dealing with institutions. This may enable the specialists to be more active in block transactions, although they will no longer be involved in the block trades that are matched "upstairs."

Effect on NYSE.   There will be less overall volume because there will no longer be block crosses (i.e., block transactions will no longer be required to be processed on the exchange); the off-exchange dealer markets in stocks with large spreads will increase; and the limit-order book will be replaced by the hard CLOB. The final effect will probably not be as great as some observers envision because the exchange will probably continue to serve as the major auction market in high-volume stocks like AT&T and IBM; i.e., the stocks the exchange will lose are the low-volume stocks with large spreads. Much of this will depend upon how well the specialist is able to compete for the block business in these large-volume stocks.

Effect on block houses.   The block houses will not be forced to take their trades to an exchange to be crossed. This should save money and make the trades easier, although the block houses will not have the benefit of the specialist in some issues. Still, most block trades are in the large, active stocks in which the specialist will stay active. In fact, the specialist may begin to offer some competition to the block houses after Rule 113 is eliminated.

---

[43] For a discussion of this point and the future without Rule 390, see Chris Welles, "The Showdown over Rule 390," *Institutional Investor* 11 no. 12 (December 1977): 33–38. An article that likewise discusses some of the effects and makes a strong case for the NMS is Junius W. Peake, "The National Market System," *Financial Analysts Journal* 34 no. 4 (July–August 1978): pp. 25–28.

Effect on regional exchanges.   The regional exchanges should benefit from wider exposure of their markets on the consolidated quotation machine and their ability to participate in the limit orders that were formerly restricted to the NYSE. At the same time, they could be seriously affected by the loss of numerous blocks that are crossed on the regionals because block houses will not be required to cross blocks on an exchange.

Summary of Effects of an NMS without Rule 390.   Without Rule 390, one should expect the creation of more dealer markets and some internalization of orders. Most new dealer markets will be in stocks with relatively low trading volumes and large spreads, while the specialist will probably retain the large active stocks with competitive markets. The specialist will lose control of the limit-order book and some of the income from this and from blocks crossed on the exchange, but overall he should benefit from the cancellation of Rule 113. The NYSE may lose some volume but will probably still be the major auction market for the large, active stocks. Block houses will not have to cross blocks on an exchange, but they may lose some liquidity if the specialists stop dealing in small issues, and they may feel competition from the specialist on large issues after Rule 113 is eliminated. Finally, regional stock exchanges will lose most of their block cross business but gain from greater exposure and from the hard CLOB.

FUTURE DEVELOPMENTS

Besides the expected effects of the specific factors discussed (the NMS, etc.), there are some overall changes expected in capital markets. Being aware of potential changes, you can concentrate on understanding why the changes are happening and contemplate the effect of them on your investment program.

Institutional Growth and Diversification

From the late 1960s through 1970s there was a tendency for individuals to reduce their equity holdings, apparently due to poor stock performance. It was also during this period that the institutional impact grew. Notably, the latest survey report by the NYSE indicated a major reversal of this trend; there was a substantial increase in individuals owning common stock. Some have suggested that this might cause a reversal in the institutional impact. It is possible to envision that more individuals will own common stock, but still to expect a strong and possibly growing institutional impact. The question is, how do individuals own common stock? Obviously, if they own it *directly,* they will do the trading. Alternatively, individual investors may choose to own stock *indirectly* through financial institutions like investment companies. In the latter case, individuals would have decided that they want to invest in equities, but they do *not* want to do their own analysis and make the investment decisions. The author anticipates the latter scenario because many individuals do not believe they have the time or the expertise to engage in security analysis and specific stock selection decisions.

Therefore, the expectation is for more individual owners *and* a stable or growing institutional market.

Although individuals may want to invest through institutions, this does not mean that they do not want variety in investment instruments. In this regard, we will see *an expansion in the types of investments available* through institutions. Just as the investment industry responded to the need of small investors for money market funds, we will see the development of numerous mutual funds that concentrate on such alternatives as small firms, foreign firms, and possibly investment alternatives such as stamps, coins, and precious metals. While there are a few examples of these, the numbers and variety will increase substantially during the coming decade. The point is, in the past the investment industry has displayed terrific ability to respond to the needs of investors, and it is anticipated that the industry will respond to this need for variety.

Financial Supermarkets

If one examines the structure that prevailed in the investment industry prior to the 1960s, it is best described as a collection of specialty shops — i.e., stocks, bonds, commodities, real estate. A firm usually concentrated in only one phase of the business; for example, it could specialize in stocks *or* commodities but never both. This age of numerous specialty shops has clearly passed and we are on our way to an era of financial supermarkets where it is one-stop shopping for all your financial assets. This trend is already well under way within the securities industry.[44] The apparent leaders at this point are the largest factors in the various segments. Specifically, securities firms are acquiring insurance companies and vice versa; both groups are acquiring real estate operations. In anticipation of the elimination of the Glass-Steagill Act, some banks have acquired discount brokerage firms although there is substantial opposition.[45] Ultimately, individuals will be able to deal with one firm regardless of whether it is securities, insurance, real estate or any banking needs. Besides consolidating services, this will lead to more automation and competition among the giants and generally lower costs and prices.[46]

Financial Boutiques

While the vast majority of financial transactions will take place through financial supermarkets, there will also be a *limited number* of financial specialty firms known as "boutiques." These firms will provide a unique financial product (similar to women's boutique stores that carry designer clothes). The product must be unique because the cost typically will be higher than that offered by the

[44] Richard E. Rustin, "Wall Street Mergers May Basically Change U.S. Financial System," *Wall Street Journal,* April 22, 1981, p. 1.

[45] Richard L. Hudson, "SEC Seeks Tighter Rules for Most Banks that Offer Full-Line Brokerage Services," *Wall Street Journal,* October 28, 1983, p. 5; Daniel Hertzberg and Tim Carrington, "Controversy Engulfs Banking Industry In Wake of Fed's Latest Nonbank Ruling," *Wall Street Journal,* December 16, 1983, p. 6.

[46] Tim Carrington, "Securities Industry Group Is Urging Plan to Increase Automation for Small Trades," *Wall Street Journal,* December 4, 1980, p. 4.

efficient, automated supermarket. For example, firms might do special research in a limited segment of the market like small firms (e.g., capitalization under $50 to $75 million), or concentrate in smaller regional firms (e.g., those in the south), or do research on low grade bonds (below BA rating). It is even possible to become a specialist in one industry if it is large and popular among investors — like oil or computers. Alternatively, one might attempt to become even more efficient than the giants in one segment of the business, e.g., become the cheapest discount broker.[47]

Consolidated Financial Markets

The discussion has emphasized the consolidation of all segments of the equity market. The obvious next step is *the consolidation of markets for different financial assets*—e.g., stocks, bonds, options, commodities. This is already occurring somewhat since the ASE is involved in stocks, bonds and options although the trading floors are separate. The point is, why should there be separate exchanges for these assets? Possibly when institutions become involved in the stamp and coin markets because of mutual funds in these areas, the volume of trading will justify a national market for these assets.

SUMMARY

In this chapter we considered the many changes in our securities markets since 1965, why the changes transpired, and several significant potential future changes. The market changes mainly resulted from the substantial growth of institutional trading, which we documented with empirical evidence. We discussed the specific changes in five sections:

1. Negotiated commissions
2. Impact of block trades
3. Development of a tiered trading market
4. Institutions and stock price volatility
5. A national market system (NMS).

In each instance we considered why it happened, current effects, and potential future effects.

We concluded the chapter with a discussion of possible future developments to capital markets beyond those directly related to these factors.

This chapter is important because numerous extensive changes have already occurred. More importantly, many more changes are yet to come, and the effects will continue to affect the industry and capital markets.[48] This discussion pro-

---

[47] The opposite approach might also be a possibility. In this regard, see Marilyn Chase, "Major Discount Brokerage House Finds a Luxurious Image Doesn't Hurt, Either," *Wall Street Journal,* April 7, 1980, p. 3.

[48] A major change that does not directly affect the securities markets, but one that has impacted investment banking firms and corporations is the introduction of Rule 415 which allows corporations to register large issues of securities and sell segments of the issue "off the shelf" during the following two years. For a discussion of this rule and its impact, see Tim Carrington, "Investment Bankers Enter a Different Era, and Many are Uneasy," *Wall Street Journal,* June 21, 1982, pp. 1, 12; A.F. Ehbar, "Upheaval in Investment Banking," *Fortune,* August 23, 1982, pp. 90–94; Beth McGoldriek, "Life with Rule 415," *Institutional Investor* 17, no. 2 (February 1983): 129–133.

vides the reader with the background to understand these changes and their effects.

QUESTIONS

1. The secondary equity market has experienced major changes since 1965. What is the overall reason for these changes?
2. Discuss three pieces of empirical evidence that attest to the growth in institutional trading in an absolute sense and in a relative sense.
3. Briefly discuss *why* trading by financial institutions has grown dramatically since 1965. Why do the institutions own more stock and trade more stock?
4. Would you expect the large financial institutions to continue to dominate trading in the secondary equity market in the future? Why or why not?
5. Describe the fixed commission schedule. Why did it exist and whom did it protect? Why was it a problem for large financial institutions?
6. What were give-ups? Why did they exist in the fixed commission world?
7. Why did the third market grow so rapidly from 1965 to 1972?
8. Why do you believe the fourth market grew during the period 1965–1974?
9. Why did institutions want to become members of an exchange? Why did some of the exchanges not allow it? Why did some of the exchanges welcome institutions?
10. What is meant by the term *negotiated commissions?* When was May Day?
11. Discuss the impact of fully negotiated rates on each of the following segments of the securities industry. Indicate what you think will happen *and why* you believe it will happen.
    a. Research firms
    b. Regional exchanges
    c. The third market.
12. Discuss why block trades are considered the ultimate test of the liquidity of a market.
13. In the discussion of block trades and the specialist, it was noted that the specialist is hampered by the three Cs. Discuss each of the three Cs as it relates to block trading.
14. Describe block houses and why they evolved.
15. Describe what is meant by *positioning* part of a block. What is the risk involved?
16. Define a tiered trading market.
17. What were the main characteristics of the tiered trading market that developed in the early 1970s? Why did it develop and what sort of companies were in the top tier?
18. It is contended that the tiered market of the mid-1970s is heavily concerned with the *size* of the companies involved. Why is size important to an institutional portfolio manager? Discuss the logic of this contention.
19. The value of an institutional portfolio is $2 billion. The portfolio managers decide they do not want more than 100 issues in the portfolio, and they do not believe they should own more than 4 percent of any firm. What will be the average value of each holding? What must be the average market value of each firm? Show all computations.

116

20. What will be the effect of a tiered market on firms in the top tier? Why? What will be the effect of a tiered market on firms in the bottom tier? Why?
21. Set forth the intuitive argument for the expectation that there will be a positive relationship between institutional trading and stock price volatility.
22. Describe the empirical tests suggested to test whether there is a positive relationship between institutional trading and stock price volatility.
23. In general, in the tests described in Question 22, what was the relationship between the various measures of institutional trading and the measures of stock price volatility? Do these results support the intuitive expectations set forth in Question 21?
24. Would the results discussed in Question 23 support those who want to restrict institutional trading? Why or why not?
25. Describe the major attributes of the national market system (NMS).
26. Briefly describe the ITS and what it contributes to an NMS. What are its deficiencies regarding the NMS?
27. Briefly describe the NSTS and how it fits into the requirements for the NMS. What charateristics does it have that are not present with ITS?
28. Briefly discuss Rule 390. What is its purpose?
29. Discuss why the NYSE believes Rule 390 should not be eliminated; i.e., what are the supposed benefits of this rule to the participants (buyers and sellers of stock)?
30. Discuss the free competition argument against Rule 390. What are the supposed advantages of eliminating Rule 390 in terms of market-making and capital?
31. Briefly give the arguments for and against eliminating Rule 390 before a central market is established.
32. Given the several future developments described at the end of the chapter, select one and discuss what has transpired—e.g., what has happened regarding the development of financial supermarkets?

REFERENCES

"Are the Institutions Wrecking Wall Street?" *Business Week,* June 2, 1973.

Black, Fischer. "Toward a Fully Automated Stock Exchange." *Financial Analysts Journal* 27 no. 4 (July–August 1971) and 27 no. 6 (November–December 1971).

Bostian, David B., Jr. "The De-Institutionalization of the Stock Market in American Society." *Financial Analysts Journal* 29 no. 6 (November–December 1973).

Carey, Kenneth J. "Nonrandom Price Changes in Association with Trading in Large Blocks: Evidence of Market Efficiency in Behavior of Investor Returns." *Journal of Business* 50 no. 4 (October 1977).

Farrar, Donald E. "The Coming Reform on Wall Street." *Harvard Business Review* 50 no. 5 (September–October 1972).

Farrar, Donald E. "Toward a Central Market System: Wall Street's Slow Retreat into the Future." *Journal of Financial and Quantitative Analysis* 9 no. 5 (November 1974).

Farrar, Donald E. "Wall Street's Proposed 'Great Leap Backward'." *Financial Analysts Journal* 27 no. 5 (September–October 1971).

Freund, William C. "The Historical Role of the Individual Investor in the Corporate Equity Market." *Journal of Contemporary Business* 3 no. 1 (Winter 1974).

Freund, William C., and Minor, David F. "Institutional Activity on the NYSE: 1975 and 1980." *Perspectives on Planning No. 10.* New York Stock Exchange, June 1972.

Gaumnitz, Jack E. "Maximal Gains from Diversification and Implications for Portfolio Management." *Mississippi Valley Journal of Business and Economics* 6 no. 3 (Spring 1971).

Hamilton, James L. "Competition, Scale Economies, and Transaction Cost in the Stock Market." *Journal of Financial and Quantitative Analysis* 11 no. 5 (December 1976).

Hamilton, James L. "Marketplace Organization and Marketability: NASDAQ, the Stock Exchange, and the National Market System." *Journal of Finance* 33 no. 2 (May 1978).

Hamilton, James L. "Marketplace Fragmentation, Competition, and the Efficiency of the Stock Exchange." *Journal of Finance* 34 no. 1 (March 1979).

Klemkosky, Robert C. "Institutional Dominance of the NYSE." *Financial Executive* 41 no. 11 (November 1973).

Klemkosky, Robert C., and Scott, David F., Jr. "Withdrawal of the Individual Investor from the Equity Markets." *MSU Business Topics* 21 no. 2 (Spring 1973)

Klemkosky, Robert C., and Wright, David J. "The Changing Structure of the Stock Market: The National Market System." *Business Horizons* (July–August 1981).

Kraus, Alan, and Stoll, Hans R. "Parallel Trading by Institutional Investor." *Journal of Financial and Quantitative Analysis* 7 no. 5 (December 1972).

Kraus, Alan, and Stoll, Hans R. "Price Impact of Block Trading on the New York Stock Exchange." *Journal of Finance* 27 no. 3 (June 1972).

Leuthold, Steven C. "The Causes (and Cures?) of Market Volatility." *Journal of Portfolio Management* 2 no. 2 (Winter 1976).

Loomis, Carol J. "How the Terrible Two-Tier Market Came to Wall Street." *Fortune* (July 1973).

Lorie, James H. *Public Policy for American Capital Markets.* Washington, D.C.: Department of the Treasury, February 7, 1974.

Lyons, John F. "What Happens When Liquidity Disappears?" *Institutional Investor* 3 no. 11 (November 1969).

Martin, William McChesney, Jr. *The Securities Markets: A Report with Recommendations.* Submitted to the Board of Governors of the New York Stock Exchange, August 5, 1971.

Melton, William C. "Corporate Equities and the National Market System." Federal Reserve Bank of New York *Quarterly Review* (Winter 1978–1979).

Mendelson, Morris, "From Automated Quotes to Automated Trading: Restructing the

118   Stock Market in the U.S." *Bulletin of the Institute of Finance.* Graduate School of Business Administration, New York University (March 1972).

National Bureau of Economic Research. "Regional Stock Exchanges in a Central Market System." *Explorations in Economic Research* 2 no. 3 (Summer 1975).

Nielsen, James F., and Joehnk, Michael D. "Further Evidence of the Effects of Block Transactions on Stock Price Fluctuations." *Mississippi Valley Journal of Business and Economics* 9 no. 2 (Winter 1973–1974).

Ofer, Aharon R., and Melnick, Arie. "Price Deregulation in the Brokerage Industry: An Empirical Analysis." *Bell Journal of Economics* 9 no. 2 (Autumn 1978).

Officer, Robert R. "The Variability of the Market Factor of the New York Stock Exchange." *The Journal of Business* 46 no. 3 (July 1973).

Peake, Junius W. "The National Market System." *Financial Analysts Journal* 34 no. 4 (July–August 1978).

Reilly, Frank K., and Wright, David J. "Block Trades and Stock Price Volatility." *Financial Analysts Journal* 11, no. 2 (March–April, 1984).

Reilly, Frank K. "Institutions on Trial: Not Guilty." *Journal of Portfolio Management* 3 no. 2 (Winter 1977).

Reilly, Frank K. "A Three Tier Stock Market and Corporate Financing." *Financial Management* 4 no. 3 (Autumn 1975).

Reilly, Frank K., and Drzycimski, Eugene F. "An Analysis of the Effects of a Multi-Tiered Stock Market." *Journal of Financial and Quantitative Analysis* 16 no. 4 (November 1981).

Reilly, Frank K., and Perry, Gladys. "Negotiated Commissions and Regional Exchanges." Working paper no. 543, University of Illinois (August 1978).

Reilly, Frank K., and Slaughter, William. "The Effect of Dual Markets on Common Stock Market-making." *Journal of Financial and Quantitative Analysis* 8 no. 2 (March 1973).

Reilly, Frank K., and Wachowicz, John. "How Institutional Trading Reduces Market Volatility." *Journal of Portfolio Management* 5 no. 2 (Winter 1979).

Robertson, Wyndham. "A Big Board Strategy for Staying Alive." *Fortune* (March 1977).

Rosenberg, Marvin. "Institutional Investors: Holdings, Prices and Liquidity." *Financial Analysts Journal* 30 no. 2 (March–April 1974).

Scholes, Myron S. "The Market for Securities: Substitution Versus Price-Pressure and the Effects of Information on Share Prices." *Journal of Business* 45 no. 2 (April 1972).

Smidt, Seymour. "Which Road to an Efficient Stock Market?" *Financial Analysts Journal* 27 no. 5 (September–October 1971).

Snyder, Linda. "Wall Street's Discount Houses are Selling Hard." *Fortune* (March 1977).

Soldofsky, Robert M. *Institutional Holdings of Common Stock, 1900–2000.* Ann Arbor: Bureau of Business Research, University of Michigan, 1971.

Stoll, Hans R. "The Supply of Dealer Services in Securities Markets." *Journal of Finance* 33 no. 4 (September 1978).

Stoll, Hans R. "The Pricing of Security Dealer Services: An Empirical Study of NAS-DAQ Stocks." *Journal of Finance* 33 no. 4 (September 1978).

Tinic, Seha M., and West, Richard R. "Competition and the Pricing of Dealer Service in the Over-the-Counter Market." *Journal of Financial and Quantitative Analysis* 7 no. 2 (June 1972).

Tinic, Seha, M., and West, Richard R. "The Securities Industry under Negotiated Brokerage Commissions: Changes in the Structure and Performance of New York Stock Exchange Member Firms." *The Bell Journal of Economics* 11 no. 1 (Spring 1980).

"The Two-Tier Market Lingers On, Sort Of." *Fortune* (February 1974).

United States House of Representatives. *Securities and Exchange Commission, Institutional Investor Study Report.* H. Doc. 92–64, 92nd Congress, 1st session. Washington, D.C., U.S. Government Printing Office, 1971.

Welles, Chris. "Discounting: Wall Street's Game of Nerves." *Institutional Investor* 10 no. 11 (November 1976).

Welles, Chris. "The Showdown Over Rule 390." *Institutional Investor* 11 no. 12 (December 1977).

West, Richard R. "Institutional Trading and the Changing Stock Market." *Financial Analysts Journal* 27 no. 3 (May–June 1971).

West, Richard R., and Tinic, Seha M. "Corporate Finance and the Changing Stock Market." *Financial Management* 3 no. 3 (Autumn 1974).

West, Richard R., and Tinic, Seha M. *The Economics of the Stock Market.* New York: Praeger Publishers, 1972.

Chapter 5

Stock Market Indicator Series

A fair statement regarding stock market indicator series is that everybody talks about them, but few people know how they are constructed and what they represent. Although portfolios are obviously composed of individual stocks, there is a tendency on the part of investors to ask, "What happened to the market today?" The reason for this question is that, if an investor owns more than a few stocks, it is cumbersome to follow each stock individually in order to determine the composite performance of the portfolio. Also there is an intuitive notion that most individual stocks move with the aggregate market. Therefore, if the overall market rose, an individual's portfolio probably also increased in value. To supply investors with a composite report on market performance, some financial publications have developed market indicator series. The general purpose of a market indicator series is to provide an overall indication of aggregate market changes or market movements.

In this chapter we will consider some specific uses of market indicator series, discuss the factors determining what a market indicator series can tell us, and examine some of the major types of indicator series. Finally, we will analyze long- and short-run price movements for some well-known series.

USES OF MARKET INDICATOR SERIES

There are at least four specific uses for stock market indicator series. A primary application is in examining total market returns over a specified time period and using derived returns as a benchmark *to judge the performance of individual portfolios.* A basic assumption is that any investor should be able to derive a rate of return comparable to the "market" return by randomly selecting a large number of stocks from the total market. Hence, it is reasoned that a superior portfolio manager should consistently do better than the market. Therefore, the indicator series are used to judge the performance of professional money managers. In addition to examining the rates of return on the portfolios, one should analyze the differential risk for the institutional portfolios as compared to the market indicator series; i.e., the evaluation of performance should be on a risk-adjusted basis.

Securities analysts, portfolio managers, and others use the series to examine the *factors that influence aggregate stock price movements*. Studies of the relationship between economic variables and aggregate stock market movements require some measurement of overall stock market movements, i.e., a composite stock market indicator series.

Another group interested in an aggregate market series are "technicians," who believe past price changes can be used to predict future price movements. Technicians interested in aggregate market forecasting would obviously want to examine past movements of different market indicator series.

Finally, work in portfolio theory has shown that the relevant risk for an individual security is its "systematic" risk with the market. The systematic risk for a stock is determined by the relationship between the rates of return for the security and the rates of return for a market portfolio of risky assets.[1] Therefore, it is necessary for an analyst or portfolio manager attempting to determine the systematic risk for an individual security to relate its returns to the returns for an aggregate market indicator series.

DIFFERENTIATING FACTORS IN CONSTRUCTING MARKET INDICATOR SERIES

Because indicator series are intended to indicate the overall movements of a group of stocks, it is necessary to consider which factors are important in computing any average intended to represent a total population.

Sample. Our initial concern is with the sample used to construct the series. When talking about samples, three factors must be considered: *the size of the sample, the breadth of the sample,* and *the source of the sample.*

A small percent of the total population will provide valid indications of the behavior of the total population if the sample is properly selected. In fact, at some point the costs of taking a larger sample will almost certainly outweigh any benefits in terms of generating information that is closer to total market performance. The sample should be *representative* of the total population or the size of the sample will be meaningless; a large biased sample is no better than a small biased sample. The sample can be generated by completely random selection or by a nonrandom but well-designed selection process in which the characteristics desired are taken into consideration. The *source* of the sample becomes important if there are any differences between alternative segments of the population, in which case samples from each segment are required.

Weighting. Our second concern is with *the weight given to each member in the sample*. In computing stock market indicator series, three principal weight-

---

[1] William F. Sharpe, "Capital Asset Prices: Theory of Market Equilibrium under Conditions of Risk," *Journal of Finance* 19 no. 3 (September 1964): 425–442.

ing schemes are used: (1) a price-weighted series, (2) a value-weighted series, and (3) an unweighted series, or what would be described as an equally weighted series.

Computational Procedure.   Our final consideration is with *the computational procedure used*. One alternative is to take a simple arithmetic average of the various members in the series. Another is to compute an index and have all changes, whether in price or value, reported in terms of the basic index. Finally, some prefer using a geometric average.

ALTERNATIVE INDICATOR SERIES

Price-Weighted Series

A price-weighted series is an arithmetic average of current prices which means that, in fact, movements are influenced by differential prices.

Dow-Jones Industrial Average.   The best-known price series is also the oldest and certainly the most popular market indicator series, the Dow-Jones Industrial Average (DJIA). The DJIA is a price-weighted average of 30 large, well-known industrial stocks that are generally the leaders in their industry (blue chips) and are listed on the New York Stock Exchange. The index is derived by totaling *the current prices* of the 30 stocks and dividing the sum by a divisor that has been adjusted to take account of stock splits and changes in the sample over time.[2] The adjustment of the divisor is demonstrated in Table 5.1 on page 124.

$$DJIA_t = \sum_{i=1}^{30} P_{it}/D_{adj},$$

where:

$$DJIA_t = \text{the value of the DJIA on day } t$$
$$P_{it} = \text{the closing price of stock } i \text{ on day } t$$
$$D_{adj} = \text{the adjusted divisor on day } t.$$

In Table 5.1 three stocks are employed to demonstrate the procedure used to derive a new divisor for the DJIA when a stock splits. When stocks split, the divisor becomes smaller. An idea of the cumulative effect of splits can be derived from the fact that the divisor as of April 1984 was 1.194.

The idea is to derive a new divisor that will ensure that the new value for the series is the same as it would have been without the split. In this case, the presplit index value was 20. Therefore, after the split, given the new sum of prices, the divisor is adjusted downward to maintain this value of 20. The divisor is also changed if there is a change in the makeup of the series. This does not happen

---

[2] A complete list of all events that have caused a change in the divisor since the DJIA went to 30 stocks on October 1, 1928, is contained in Phyllis S. Pierce, ed., *The Dow-Jones Investor's Handbook* (Princeton, N.J.: Dow-Jones Books, 1984).

TABLE 5.1
Example of Change in DJIA Divisor When a Sample Stock Splits

	Before Split	After 3 for 1 Split by Stock A	
	Prices	Prices	
A	30	10	
B	20	20	
C	10	10	
	60 ÷ 3 = 20	40 ÷ X = 20	X = 2 (new divisor)

very often with the series; there were only three changes during the 21 years from 1959 to 1980. In August 1976, Minnesota Mining and Manufacturing (3M) replaced Anaconda. A major change occurred in June 1979, when IBM and Merck & Co. replaced Chrysler and Esmark.[3] Interestingly, IBM was in the sample in 1932, but it was deleted in 1939 to make room for American Telephone and Telegraph.

Because the series is price weighted, a high-priced stock carries more weight in the series than does a low-priced stock; i.e., as shown in Table 5.2, a 10 percent change in a $100 stock ($10) will cause a larger change in the series than a 10 percent change in a $30 stock ($3). In Case A, the $100 stock increases by 10 percent, which causes a 5 percent increase in the average; in Case B, the $30 stock increases by 10 percent and the average only rises by 1.8 percent.

The DJIA was created in the late 1800s by Charles Dow, publisher of *The Wall Street Journal.* Initially, there were only 15 stocks included in the average, but it was later expanded to 30. The initial computation was the sum of the prices of the stocks divided by 15 to generate an average price. When stocks split, the after-split price was multiplied by the split factor and divided by the initial 15. It was later determined that using current prices but changing the divisor was an easier method of supposedly achieving the same effect. As will be discussed, the effect is *not* the same because the weighting changes.

The DJIA has been criticized over time on several counts, the first of which is that the sample used for the series is limited. It is difficult to conceive of how 30 nonrandomly selected blue-chip stocks can be representative of the 1,800 stocks listed on the NYSE. Beside the fact that their number is limited, the stocks included are, by definition, offerings of the largest and most prestigious companies in various industries. Therefore, the DJIA probably reflects price movements for large, mature blue-chip firms rather than for the typical company listed on the NYSE. Several studies have pointed out that price movements of the DJIA have not been as volatile as they have been on other market indicator series and that the long-run returns on the DJIA are not comparable to those implied by more representative price indicator series.

In addition, the stocks in the DJIA are weighted on the basis of their relative prices. Therefore, when a high-priced stock such as duPont moves even a small percent, it has an inordinate effect on the overall index. In contrast, when compa-

---

[3] For a discussion of the change, see "Revised Dow-Jones Industrials to Add IBM and Merck, Delete Chrysler and Esmark," *Wall Street Journal* June 28, 1979, p. 31; and H. L. Butler, Jr. and J. D. Allen, "The Dow-Jones Industrial Average Re-Reexamined," *Financial Analysts Journal* 35 no. 6 (November–December 1979): 23–30; Andrew T. Rudd, "The Revised Dow-Jones Industrial Average: New Wine in Old Bottles?" *Financial Analysts Journal* 35 no. 6 (November–December 1979): 57–63.

TABLE 5.2
Demonstration of Price Effect

	Period T	Period T + 1	
		Case A	Case B
A	100	110	100
B	50	50	50
C	30	30	33
Sum	180	190	183
Divisor	3	3	3
Average	60	63.3	61
Percentage Change		5.0	1.8

nies have a stock split their prices decline and, therefore, their weight in the DJIA is reduced, even though they may be large and important. Therefore, the weighting scheme causes a downward bias in the DJIA because the stocks that have higher growth rates will have higher prices and such stocks tend to split consistently, and thereby consistently lose weight within the index.[4] Regardless of the several criticisms made of the DJIA, a comparison of short-run price movements of the DJIA and of other NYSE indicators shows a fairly close relationship between the daily percentages of price changes for the DJIA and comparable price changes for other NYSE indicators.

In addition to a price series for industrial stocks, Dow-Jones also publishes an average of 20 stocks in the transportation industry and an average for utilities that includes 15 stocks. Detailed reports of the averages are contained in *The Wall Street Journal* and *Barron's,* including hourly figures.

National Quotation Bureau Average. There is another price-weighted series which is, in contrast to the DJIA, probably one of the least known of all stock market indicator series, the National Quotation Bureau (NQB) Average of 35 over-the-counter industrial stocks. The NQB index, like the DJIA, is composed of only industrial stocks and also includes the large, well-established, blue-chip companies traded on the OTC market.[5]

Value-Weighted Series

A value-weighted index is generated by deriving the initial total market value of all stocks used in the series (Market Value = Number of Shares Outstanding ×

---

[4] For an extensive discussion of these problems see the following studies: H. L. Butler, Jr. and M. B. Decker, "A Security Check on the Dow-Jones Industrial Average," *Financial Analysts Journal* 9 no. 1 (February 1953): 37–45; R. B. Shaw, "The Dow-Jones Industrials vs. the Dow-Jones Industrial Average," *Financial Analysts Journal* 11 no. 5 (November 1955): 37–40; Lawrence Fisher, "Some New Stock Market Indexes," *Journal of Business* 39 no. 1, Part II (January 1966 Supplement): 191–225; R. D. Milne, "The Dow-Jones Industrial Average Re-Examined," *Financial Analysts Journal* 22 no. 6 (December 1966): 83–88; E. E. Carter and K. J. Cohen, "Bias in the DJIA Caused by Stock Splits," *Financial Analysts Journal* 22 no. 6 (December 1966): 90–94; Paul Cootner, "Stock Market Indexes — Fallacies and Illusions," *Commercial and Financial Chronicle,* September 29, 1966, pp. 18–19; Lewis L. Schellbach, "When Did the DJIA Top 1200?" *Financial Analysts Journal* 23 no. 3 (May–June 1967): 71–73; E. E. Carter and K. J. Cohen, "Stock Averages, Stock Splits, and Bias," *Financial Analysts Journal* 23 no. 3 (May–June 1967): 77–81.

[5] Since the creation of the NASDAQ price indicator series in 1971 (to be discussed in a few pages), it is very difficult to get figures for the NQB series. Apparently they are available daily only in the NQB "pink" sheets, weekly in the *OTC Market Chronicle,* and monthly in the *OTC Securities Review.*

Current Market Price). This figure is typically established as the base and as-signed an index value of 100. Subsequently, a new market value is computed for all securities in the index; this is compared to the initial "base" value to deter-mine the percentage of change which, in turn, is applied to the beginning index value of 100.

$$\text{Index}_t = \frac{\Sigma P_t Q_t}{\Sigma P_b Q_b} \times \text{Beginning Index Value,}$$

where:

Index_t = index value on day t
P_t = ending prices for stocks on day t
Q_t = number of outstanding shares on day t
P_b = ending prices for stocks on base day
Q_b = number of outstanding shares on base day.

A simple example for a three stock index is shown in Table 5.3.

As can be seen, there is an *automatic adjustment* for stock splits and other capital changes in a value-weighted index because the decrease in the stock price is offset by an increase in the number of shares outstanding. In a value-weighted index, the importance of individual stocks in the sample is dependent on the market value of the stocks. Therefore, a change in the value of a large company has a greater impact than a comparable percentage change for a small company. As an example, consider the figures in Table 5.3. If we begin with a base value of $200 million and there is a 20 percent increase in the value of Stock A, which has a beginning value of $10 million, the ending index value will be $202 million or an index of 101. In contrast, if Stock C increases by 20 percent from $100 million, the ending value will be $220 million or an index value of 110.

Standard & Poor's Indexes.   The first company to widely employ a market value index was Standard & Poor's Corporation. The firm developed an index using 1935–1937 as a base period and computed a market value index for 425 industrial stocks. They also computed an index of 50 utilities and 25 transporta-tion firms. Finally, they developed a 500-stock composite index. The base period was subsequently changed to 1941–1943 and the base value to 10. All the S&P series were again changed significantly on July 1, 1976, when the stocks consid-ered were changed from 425 industrials, 60 utilities, and 15 rails to 400 indus-trials, 40 utilities, 20 transportation, and 40 financial. A number of stocks added were listed on the OTC which was necessary because, as noted in Chapter 3, most of the major banks and insurance companies have been traded on the OTC market. Therefore, to construct a relevant financial index, it was necessary to break the tradition of only including NYSE-listed stocks.[6] In addition to their

---

[6] For a further discussion of the specific changes see *S&P 500 Stock Index Adds Financial, Transportation Groups* (New York: Standard & Poor's Corporation, 1976). For a detailed discussion of the computation of all the series and all the potential adjustments, see *Trade and Securities Statistics* (New York: Standard & Poor's Corp., 1983).

TABLE 5.3
Example of Value-Weighted Index

Stock	Share Price	Number of Shares	Market Value
December 31, 1982			
A	$10.00	1,000,000	$ 10,000,000
B	15.00	6,000,000	90,000,000
C	20.00	5,000,000	100,000,000
Total			$200,000,000 — Base Value Equal to an Index of 100
December 31, 1983			
A	$12.00	1,000,000	$ 12,000,000
B	10.00	12,000,000[a]	120,000,000
C	20.00	5,500,000[b]	110,000,000
Total			$242,000,000

$$\text{New Index Value} = \frac{\text{Current Market Value}}{\text{Base Value}} \times \text{Beginning Index Value}$$

$$= \frac{\$242,000,000}{200,000,000} \times 100$$

$$= 1.21 \times 100$$

$$= 121.$$

[a] Stock split 2 for 1 during year.
[b] Company paid 10 percent stock dividend during the year.

major market indicators, S&P has constructed over 90 individual industry series that include from 3 to 11 companies within an industry group. Daily figures for the major S&P indexes are carried in *The Wall Street Journal* and other newspapers, and weekly data are contained in *Barron's*. Standard & Poor's has a weekly publication titled *The Outlook* that contains weekly values for all the industry groups. Extensive historical data on all these indexes and other financial series are contained in Standard & Poor's *Trade and Securities Statistics*.

New York Stock Exchange Index.   In 1966, the NYSE derived five market value indexes (industrial, utility, transportation, financial, and composite, which contains the other four) with figures available back to 1940. (The December 31, 1965, figures are equal to 50.) In contrast to other indexes, the various NYSE series are not based upon a sample of stocks but include all stocks listed on the Exchange. Therefore, questions about the number of stocks in the sample or the breadth of the sample do not arise. However, because the index is value-weighted, the issues of large companies still control major movements in the index. For example, the 500 stocks in the Standard & Poor's Composite Index represent 74 percent of the market value of all stocks on the Exchange although they are only about 28 percent of Exchange listings in terms of numbers.[7]

[7] For a detailed discussion of the index, written shortly after its creation and including a historical chart, see Stan West and Norman Miller, "Why the New NYSE Common Stock Indexes?" *Financial Analysts Journal* 23 no. 3 (May–June 1967): 49–54.

128 NASDAQ Series.   These constitute a comprehensive set of price indicator series for the OTC market developed by the National Association of Securities Dealers (NASD). The NASDAQ – OTC Price Indicator Series were released to the public on May 17, 1971, with figures available from February 5, 1971. (The index value was 100 as of February 5.) Through NASDAQ, the NASD provides daily, weekly, and monthly sets of stock price indicators for OTC securities in different industry categories. All domestic OTC common stocks listed on NASDAQ are included in the indexes, and new stocks are included when they are added to the system. The 2,337 issues contained in the NASDAQ – OTC Price Indexes have been divided into seven categories:[8]

1. Composite (2,337 issues)
2. Industrials (1,584 issues)
3. Banks (53 issues)
4. Insurance (125 issues)
5. Other finance (449 issues)
6. Transportation (51 issues)
7. Utilities (75 issues).

The indexes are value-weighted series similar to the S&P series and the NYSE series. Because they are value weighted, they are heavily influenced by the largest 100 stocks on the NASDAQ system. The NASDAQ series differs from the NQB – OTC series in terms of size of the samples (35 blue-chip stocks versus over 2,000 issues) and method of computation.

Most of the NASDAQ series are reported daily in *The Wall Street Journal* and are contained in *Barron's* on a weekly basis.

American Stock Exchange.   The ASE developed a market indicator series in 1966. As originally developed, it was a price-change series in which the price changes during a given day were added and then divided by the number of issues on the exchange. This average price change was then added to or subtracted from the previous day's index to arrive at a new index value.[9] As pointed out in two studies published in *Barron's,* this procedure eventually caused a substantial distortion in the value of the series.[10] Because of criticism of the series, the ASE subsequently commissioned the creation of a value-weighted series similar to that used by the NYSE and the NASD. This new series was released in October 1973 with figures available back to 1969.

Wilshire 5000 Equity Index.   This is a value-weighted index published by Wilshire Associates (Santa Monica, California) which derives the dollar value of 5,000 common stocks, including all NYSE and ASE issues plus the most active stocks on the OTC market. Because of its sample, one would expect this index to

---

[8] Securities on the NASDAQ system not included in any of the indexes are warrants, preferred stocks, foreign stocks, and common stocks that are listed on an exchange but traded OTC (third market stocks).

[9] An extended discussion of the original series, including a historical chart, is contained in B. Alva Schoomer, Jr., "The American Stock Exchange Index System," *Financial Analysts Journal* 23 no. 3 (May–June 1967): 57–61.

[10] S. C. Leuthold and C. E. Gordon II, "Margin for Error," *Barron's,* March 1, 1971, p. 9; and S. C. Leuthold and K. F. Blaich, "Warped Yardstick," *Barron's,* September 18, 1972, p. 9.

be a weighted composite of the NYSE composite series, the ASE market value series, and the NASDAQ composite, with the NYSE having the greatest influence because of the higher market value of its stocks. Weekly figures for this series are available in *Barron's.*

Unweighted Price Indicator Series

In an unweighted index, all stocks carry equal weight regardless of their price and/or their value. A $20 stock is as important as a $40 stock, and the total market value of the company is not important. Such an index can be used by an individual who randomly selects stocks for his portfolio. One way to visualize an unweighted series is to assume that equal dollar amounts are invested in each stock in the portfolio (e.g., an equal $1000 investment in each stock). Therefore, the investor would own 50 shares of a $20 stock, 100 shares of a $10 stock, and 10 shares of a $100 stock.

The best known unweighted (or equal-weighted) stock market series are those constructed by Lawrence Fisher at the University of Chicago.[11] These series were constructed in the course of studies conducted by Fisher and James Lorie that examined the performance of stocks on the NYSE assuming that an investor bought equal amounts of each stock on the exchange.[12] These series are updated periodically and have been used extensively in empirical studies.

Another unweighted price-indicator series that has gained in prominence is the *Indicator Digest* index of all stocks on the NYSE. It is contended that compared to value-weighted series that are heavily influenced by large firms, the *Indicator Digest* series is more representative of all stocks on the exchange. In several instances, the *Indicator Digest* series reached a trough earlier than other indicator series and continued to be depressed after some of the "popular" market indicator series resumed rising during a bull market. Such a difference indicates that the market increase only included the large, popular stocks contained in the DJIA or the Standard & Poor's market indicator series.[13]

COMPARISON OF INDICATOR SERIES CHANGES OVER TIME

In this section we will discuss price movements in the different series with an emphasis on the *source* of the samples as opposed to size or selection process. We will also consider price movements for the series in the short run (daily) and over more extended periods (yearly). Our emphasis will be on the difference in results for segments of the total equity market, the NYSE, the ASE, and OTC.

---

[11] Lawrence Fisher, "Some New Stock Market Indexes," *Journal of Business* 39 no. 1, Part II (January 1966 Supplement): 191–225.

[12] Lawrence Fisher and James H. Lorie, "Rates of Return on Investments in Common Stock," *Journal of Business* 37 no. 1 (January 1964): 1–21; L. Fisher and J. H. Lorie, "Rates of Return on Investments in Common Stock: The Year-By-Year Record, 1926–1965," *Journal of Business* 41 no. 3 (July 1968): 291–316; Lawrence Fisher, "Outcomes for 'Random' Investments in Common Stock Listed on the New York Stock Exchange," *Journal of Business* 38 no. 2 (April 1965): 149–161.

[13] Carol J. Loomis, "How the Terrible Two-Tier Market Came to Wall Street," *Fortune* (July 1973): 82–89.

TABLE 5.4
Correlation Coefficients between Daily Percentage of Price Changes for Alternative
Market Indicator Series January 4, 1972 – December 31, 1983 (3,013 Observations)

	DJIA	S&P 400	S&P 500	NYSE Composite	ASE Value Index	NASDAQ Industrials	NASDAQ Composite
DJIA	—						
S&P	.944	—					
S&P 500	.933	.965	—				
NYSE Composite	.881	.912	.901	—			
ASE Value Index	.707	.746	.745	.732	—		
NASDAQ Industrials	.672	.694	.692	.678	.708	—	
NASDAQ Composite	.766	.788	.788	.775	.790	.825	—

Daily Percentage of Changes

Table 5.4 contains a matrix of the correlation coefficients of the daily percentage
of price changes for alternative market indicator series during the period January
4, 1972 through December 31, 1983 (3,013 observations). This recent twelve-
year period was selected because data were available for all the major series
including the new ASE market value series and the NASDAQ series initiated in
February 1971.

The results are notable because *almost all of the differences in the correlations of daily percentages of price changes are apparently attributable to differences in the sample of stocks,* i.e., differences in the types of firms listed. All the
major series except the DJIA are now total market value indexes that include a
large number of stocks. Therefore, the computational procedure is the same for
each, the sample sizes are all quite large (from 400 to 2,400), and the samples
represent either a large segment of the total population in terms of value or all
members of the population. Thus, the only notable difference between several
of the series is the members of the population; i.e., the stocks are from different
segments of the aggregate stock market.

The results reported in Table 5.4 indicate that there is *very high positive
correlation* between the alternative series that include almost all NYSE stocks
(the DJIA, S&P 400, S&P 500, and the NYSE composite). Although there has been
criticism of the DJIA because of its sample size and weighting, its correlation
with the other major NYSE series ranged from about 0.88 to 0.94. This indicates
that, on a short-run basis, the DJIA is a very adequate indicator of price movements on the Exchange.

In contrast, there is a significantly lower correlation between each of these
NYSE series and the ASE series, from an average of about 0.67 to 0.77. These
results indicate the possibility that the market is segmented between the two
exchanges (segmentation being indicated by significant differences in stock
price movements).[14]

The average correlation of the NYSE series with the NASDAQ industrial
index is about 0.68, which likewise is significantly lower than the correlation

---

[14] For a study which considers this notion, see Frank K. Reilly, "Evidence Regarding a Segmented Stock
Market," *Journal of Finance* 27 no. 3 (June 1972): 607 – 625.

among alternative NYSE series. In addition, the relationship between the NASDAQ and the ASE series is about the same as it is with any of the NYSE series.

There is likewise a fairly strong correlation between the NASDAQ composite index and the alternative NYSE series. One might question this because of the difference in the sample for the two series. The NASDAQ composite series, as of 1984, contained 753 nonindustrial stocks, which obviously have a substantial impact on the composite index because they make up one-third of the sample in terms of number of issues, but have a much greater effect because of size. The NASDAQ series are value weighted and some of the very largest OTC companies are insurance and finance firms in the nonindustrial group. These insurance and financial firms obviously have a large impact on the NASDAQ composite series and are, in many cases, similar to NYSE-listed companies.

Annual Price Changes

The annual percentage of price changes for the alternative price indicator series are contained in Table 5.5 on page 132. The comparison between market segments cannot be made for all years from 1965 through 1983 because the series for the ASE is not available before 1969, while the OTC series was not available prior to February 1971. The four NYSE series, however, can be analyzed for a full 19-year period.

One would expect the DJIA series to be generally less volatile and also to experience lower average returns. The average returns were basically consistent with expectations because the returns for the DJIA were lower than they were for the other three NYSE series. In contrast, all the standard deviations were similar with a tendency for the DJIA to be the largest.

For the 15-year period 1969–1983 it is possible to compare the results for the NYSE series to the ASE series. One would expect a higher return and a higher risk for the ASE series because of the smaller, more volatile companies listed on this exchange. The total period returns confirmed this, because the risk was higher, as indicated by a higher standard deviation of annual changes. The average price changes were also larger, as expected.

The results for the 12-year period 1972–1983 included all three market segments. The risk-measure results were consistent with expectations; the four NYSE series all had lower standard deviations than either the ASE or the OTC market. Further, the ASE series was *more* volatile than the NASDAQ series. This difference can be explained by the types of companies on the ASE (especially compared to the NASDAQ composite), and by the fact that there are more companies in the NASDAQ series.

The average of the annual changes was consistent with risk: the DJIA had the lowest price changes, followed by the other NYSE series, followed by the NASDAQ series. Finally, the ASE series experienced the highest average price change. The average price changes were generally consistent with the standard deviations for the various series.[15]

[15] For two studies that examined this relationship in more detail, see Frank K. Reilly, "Price Changes in NYSE, AMEX, and OTC Stocks Compared," *Financial Analysts Journal* 27 no. 2 (March–April 1971): 54–59; Arthur A. Eubank, Jr., "Risk-Return Contrasts: NYSE, AMEX, and OTC," *Journal of Portfolio Management* 3 no. 4 (Summer 1977): 25–30.

132

TABLE 5.5
Percentage Changes in Stock Price Indicator Series 1965–1983

Year	DJIA	S&P[a] 400	S&P 500	NYSE Composite	ASE[b] Value Index	NASDAQ[c] Industrials	NASDAQ[c] Composite
1965	10.88	9.88	9.06	9.53			
1966	−18.94	−13.60	−13.09	−12.56			
1967	15.20	23.53	20.09	23.10			
1968	5.24	8.47	7.66	10.39			
1969	−15.19	−10.20	−11.36	−12.51	−28.98		
1970	4.82	−0.58	.10	−2.52	−18.00		
1971	6.11	11.71	10.79	12.34	18.86		
1972	14.58	16.10	15.63	14.27	10.33	13.63	17.18
1973	−16.58	−17.38	−17.37	−19.63	−30.00	−36.88	−31.06
1974	−27.57	−29.93	−29.72	−30.28	−33.22	−32.44	−35.11
1975	38.34	31.92	31.55	31.86	38.40	43.38	29.76
1976	17.86	18.42	19.15	21.50	31.58	23.68	26.10
1977	−17.27	−12.35	−11.50	−9.30	16.43	9.30	7.33
1978	−3.15	2.39	1.06	2.13	17.73	15.92	12.31
1979	4.19	12.88	12.31	15.54	64.10	38.10	28.11
1980	14.93	27.62	25.77	25.68	41.25	49.19	33.88
1981	−9.23	−11.22	−9.73	−8.67	−8.13	−12.27	−3.21
1982	19.60	14.95	14.76	13.95	6.23	19.32	18.67
1983	20.27	18.16	17.27	17.46	30.95	18.31	19.87

Average of Annual Changes (arithmetic mean)

Year	DJIA	S&P 400	S&P 500	NYSE Composite	ASE Value Index	NASDAQ Industrials	NASDAQ Composite
1965–1983	3.37	5.30	4.86	5.38	—	—	—
1969–1983	3.45	4.83	4.58	4.79	10.50	—	—
1972–1983	4.66	5.96	5.77	6.21	15.47	12.44	10.32

Standard Deviation of Annual Changes

Year	DJIA	S&P 400	S&P 500	NYSE Composite	ASE Value Index	NASDAQ Industrials	NASDAQ Composite
1965–1983	16.66	16.54	16.00	16.55	—	—	—
1969–1983	17.47	17.27	16.90	17.36	28.17	—	—
1972–1983	18.72	18.61	18.15	18.46	27.64	26.23	21.75

Average Annual Compound Rate of Change (geometric mean)

Year	DJIA	S&P 400	S&P 500	NYSE Composite	ASE Value Index	NASDAQ Industrials	NASDAQ Composite
1965–1983	1.99	3.92	3.57	3.99	—	—	—
1969–1983	1.94	3.32	3.13	3.25	6.68	—	—
1972–1983	2.93	4.19	4.08	4.45	11.80	8.89	7.72

[a] S&P 425 prior to July 1976.
[b] Market-value index started on August 31, 1973, with data back to January 1, 1969.
[c] Index started on February 5, 1971, with no previous data available.

SUMMARY

Given the several uses of stock market indicator series, it is important to know how they are constructed and the differences among them in terms of computational and sampling procedures. Because new series for the ASE and OTC have been introduced, the computational differences are slight. A comparison of short-run and long-run price changes for the alternative series indicates that the computational differences are not nearly as important as the differences in the sample of stocks used; i.e., whether the stocks are from the NYSE, the ASE, or the

OTC market. Finally, the results were generally consistent with expectations regarding risk and return. The ASE and OTC typically had higher risk (more volatility) and higher returns (larger negative and positive price changes).

QUESTIONS

1. Set forth and discuss briefly the several uses that can be made of stock market indicator series.
2. What are the major factors that must be considered when constructing a market indicator series? Put another way, what characteristics differentiate indicator series?
3. What is meant when it is stated that a market indicator series is price weighted? In such a case, would you expect a $100 stock to be more important than a $25 stock? Why?
4. What are the major criticisms made of the Dow-Jones Industrial Average?
5. Describe the procedure used in computing a value-weighted series.
6. Describe how a price-weighted series adjusts for stock splits. How does a value-weighted series adjust for splits?
7. What is meant by an unweighted price-indicator series? How would you construct such a series? Assume a 10 percent price change in IBM and Coors Brewing; which change will have the greater impact on such an indicator series? Why?
8. If you correlated percentage changes in the Wilshire 5000 equity index with percentage changes in the NYSE composite, the ASE index, and the NASDAQ composite index, would you expect a difference in the results? Why or why not?
9. The correlation results between the daily percentage of price changes for the alternative NYSE price indicator series indicated substantial correlation among series. What would explain this similarity: size of sample, source of sample, or method of computation?
10. Regarding daily percentage of price changes, what would explain the significantly lower correlation between price changes for the NASDAQ industrial index and the various NYSE series? Would it be size of sample, source of sample, or method of construction?
11. Why is the relationship of the NASDAQ composite results and the NYSE series much better than between the NASDAQ industrial results and the NYSE series?
12. Regarding the historical annual price movements for the various NYSE price/indicator series, how did they differ in terms of annual price changes and variability of annual price changes? Were the differences generally consistent with what you would expect based upon economic theory? Discuss.
13. Compare indicator series for all three market segments for the period 1972–1983. During this period, were the results in terms of return (price change) and risk (variability of returns) consistent with expectations based upon economic theory? Discuss specifically why or why not.

REFERENCES

"Amex Introduces New Market Value Index System." *American Investor* September 1973.

Butler, H. L., Jr., and Allen, J. D. "The Dow-Jones Industrial Average Re-Reexamined." *Financial Analysts Journal* 35 no. 6 (November–December 1979).

Butler, H. L., Jr., and Decker, M. G. "A Security Check on the Dow-Jones Industrial Average." *Financial Analysts Journal* 9 no. 1 (February 1953).

Carter, E. E., and Cohen, K. J. "Bias in the DJIA Caused by Stock Splits." *Financial Analysts Journal* 22 no. 6 (November–December 1966).

Carter, E. E., and Cohen, K. J. "Stock Average, Stock Splits, and Bias." *Financial Analysts Journal* 23 no. 3 (May–June 1967).

Cootner, Paul. "Stock Market Indexes—Fallacies and Illusions." *Commercial and Financial Chronicle* (September 29, 1966).

Eubank, Arthur A., Jr. "Risk-Return Contrasts: NYSE, AMEX, and OTC." *Journal of Portfolio Management* 3 no. 4 (Summer 1977).

Fisher, Lawrence. "Outcomes for 'Random' Investments in Common Stock Listed on the New York Stock Exchange." *Journal of Business* 38 no. 2 (April 1965).

Fisher, Lawrence. "Some New Stock Market Indexes." *Journal of Business* 39 no. 1, Part II (January 1966 Supplement).

Jessup, Paul F., and Upson, Roger B. "Opportunities in Regional Markets." *Financial Analysts Journal* 26 no. 2 (March–April 1970).

Jessup, Paul F., and Upson, Roger B. *Returns in Over-the-Counter Stock Markets.* Minneapolis: University of Minnesota Press, 1973.

Latane, Henry A., Tuttle, Donald L., and Jones, Charles P. *Security Analysis and Portfolio Management,* 2nd ed. New York: The Ronald Press Company, 1975, Chapter 25.

Latane, Henry A., Tuttle, Donald L., and Young, William E. "Market Indexes and Their Implications for Portfolio Management." *Financial Analysts Journal* 27 no. 5 (September–October 1971).

Lorie, James H., and Hamilton, Mary T. *The Stock Market: Theories and Evidence.* Homewood, Ill.: Richard D. Irwin, 1973, Chapters 2 and 3.

Milne, P. D. "The Dow-Jones Industrial Average Re-examined." *Financial Analysts Journal* 22 no. 6 (November–December 1966).

Molodovsky, Nicholas. "Building a Stock Market Measure—A Case Story." *Financial Analysts Journal* 23 no. 3 (May–June 1967).

Reilly, Frank K. "Evidence Regarding a Segmented Stock Market." *Journal of Finance* 27 no. 3 (June 1972).

Reilly, Frank K. "Price Changes in NYSE, AMEX and OTC Stocks Compared." *Financial Analysts Journal* 27 no. 2 (March–April 1971).

Rudd, Andrew T. "The Revised Dow-Jones Industrial Average: New Wine in Old Bottles?" *Financial Analysts Journal* 35 no. 6 (November–December 1979).

Schellbach, Lewis L. "When Did the DJIA Top 1200?" *Financial Analysts Journal* 23 no. 3 (May–June 1967).

Schoomer, B. Alva, Jr. "The American Stock Exchange Index System." *Financial Analysts Journal* 23 no. 3 (May–June 1967).

Senchack, Andrew J., Jr., and Beedles, William L. "Price Behavior in a Regional Over-the-Counter Securities Market." *Journal of Financial Research* 2 no. 2 (Fall 1979).

Shaw, R. B. "The Dow-Jones Industrials vs. the Dow-Jones Industrial Average." *Financial Analysts Journal* 11 no. 5 (November 1955).

Upson, Roger B., and Jessup, Paul F. "Risk-Return Relationships in Regional Securities Markets." *Journal of Financial and Quantitative Analysis* 4 no. 1 (January 1970).

West, Stan, and Miller, Norman. "Why the New NYSE Common Stock Indexes?" *Financial Analysts Journal* 23 no. 3 (May–June 1967).

Chapter 6   *Sources of Information on Investments*

I n the chapters that follow, we will discuss the factors that influence aggregate security prices, the prices for securities issued by various industries, and the unique factors that influence the returns on individual securities. It is important for the reader to know where to get relevant information to carry out these analyses. This chapter briefly describes some of the major sources of information needed for aggregate economic and market analysis, industry analysis, and individual firm analysis. The outline of the presentation is as follows:

— Aggregate economic analysis
    Government sources
    Bank publications
— Aggregate stock market analysis
    Government publications
    Commercial publications
    Brokerage firm reports
— Industry analysis
    S&P Industry Survey
    Trade associations
    Industry magazines
— Individual stock analysis
    Company-generated information
    Commercial publications
    Brokerage firm reports
    Investment magazines
    Academic journals
    Computerized data sources.

SOURCES FOR AGGREGATE ECONOMIC ANALYSIS

This section is concerned with data used in estimating overall economic changes as contrasted to data regarding the aggregate securities markets (stocks, bonds, etc.).

138 Government Sources

It should come as no surprise that the main source of information on the economy is the federal government, which issues a variety of publications on the topic.

Federal Reserve Bulletin.   This is a monthly publication issued by the Board of Governors of the Federal Reserve System. The magazine contains extensive economic data with thorough coverage of such areas of monetary concern as: monetary aggregates; factors affecting member bank reserves; member bank reserve requirements; Federal Reserve open market transactions; and loans and investments of all commercial banks. It is the primary source for almost all monetary data. In addition, it contains figures on financial markets, including interest rates and some stock market statistics; data for corporate finance including profits, assets, and liabilities of corporations; extensive nonfinancial statistics on output, the labor force, and the GNP; and an extensive section on international finance.

Survey of Current Business.   A monthly publication issued by the U.S. Department of Commerce that gives details on national income and production figures. It is probably the best source for current, detailed information on all segments of the gross national product and national income. It also contains an extensive listing of industrial production for numerous segments of the economy. The survey is an excellent secondary source for labor statistics (employment and wages), interest rates, and statistics on foreign economic development.

Economic Indicators.   A monthly publication prepared for the Joint Economic Committee by the Council of Economic Advisers, it contains monthly and annual data on output, income, spending, employment, production, prices, money and credit, federal finance, and the international economic situation.

Business Conditions Digest (BCD).   A monthly publication issued by the Department of Commerce's Census Bureau containing data and charts relating to economic indicators derived by the National Bureau of Economic Research (NBER). The NBER has developed a set of economic time series that has consistently indicated future trends in the economy. These series are referred to as *leading indicators.* There is also a set of series that turn with the general economy and are used to define business cycles (referred to as *coincident series*). Finally, there are economic series that tend to turn up or down *after* the general economy does and are referred to as *lagging indicators.*[1] Basic data for the major series and analytical charts are provided in the BCD. In addition, it contains composite and analytical measures such as diffusion indexes and rate of change series.

---

[1] These series are discussed more extensively in Chapter 12 where they are related to stock market movements.

The Quarterly Financial Report (QFR).   The QFR is prepared by the Federal Trade Commission and contains up-to-date aggregate statistics on the financial position of U.S. corporations. Based upon an extensive quarterly sample survey, the QFR presents estimated statements of income and retained earnings, balance sheets, and related financial and operating ratios for all manufacturing corporations. Since the third quarter of 1974, the publication has also included data on mining and trade corporations. The statistical data are classified by industry and, within the manufacturing group, by size.

Business Statistics.   A biennial supplement to the *Survey of Current Business* that contains extensive historical data for about 2,500 series contained in the survey. The historical data is usually monthly and covers the past four or five years and includes quarterly data for the previous ten years. Annual data typically go back to 1947 if available. A notable feature is a section of explanatory notes for each series that describes the series and indicates the original source for the data.

Federal Reserve Monthly Chart Book.   This is a publication of the Federal Reserve Board that presents graphs depicting many of the monetary and economic series contained in the *Federal Reserve Bulletin.* It emphasizes the short-run changes in these series.

Historical Chart Book.   A supplement to the *Federal Reserve Monthly Chart Book* that contains long-range financial and business series not included in the monthly book. At the back of the publication is an excellent section on the various series that indicates the source of the data for further reference.

Economic Report of the President.   Each January, the president of the United States prepares an economic report that he transmits to the Congress indicating what has transpired during the past year and including a discussion of what he considers to be the major economic problems during the coming year.

   This message is published by the federal government, and it also contains an extensive document entitled, "The Annual Report of the Council of Economic Advisers." The report generally runs over 150 pages and contains a detailed discussion of developments in the domestic and international economies gathered by the council (the group that advises the president on economic policy). An appendix contains statistical tables relating to income, employment, and production. Many of the tables provide annual data from the 1940s, in some instances from 1929 to the present.

The Statistical Abstract of the United States.   This book, which has been published annually since 1878, is the standard summary of statistics on the social, political, and economic organization of the United States. Prepared by the Bureau of the Census, it is designed to serve as a convenient statistical reference and as a guide to other statistical publications and sources. This volume, which currently runs over 900 pages, includes a selection of data from many statistical publications both government and private.

140 Bank Publications

In addition to the material issued by the government, there are data and comments on the economy published by a number of banks. Almost all of these appear monthly and are sent free of charge to individuals requesting them. They can be categorized as publications of Federal Reserve Banks or of commercial banks.

Federal Reserve Banks. The Federal Reserve System is divided into 12 Federal Reserve Districts with a major Federal Reserve Bank in each as follows:[2]

1. Boston
2. New York
3. Philadelphia
4. Cleveland
5. Richmond
6. Atlanta
7. Chicago
8. St. Louis
9. Minneapolis
10. Denver
11. Dallas
12. San Francisco.

Each of the Federal Reserve district banks has a research department that issues periodic reports. Although most of the publications generated by the various banks differ, monthly reviews, which are available to interested parties, are published by all district banks. These reviews typically contain one or several articles of interest to those in the region as well as statistics. A major exception is the St. Louis Federal Reserve Bank, which publishes numerous statistical releases weekly, monthly, and quarterly containing extensive national and international data and comments in addition to its monthly review.[3]

Commercial Banks. A number of large banks prepare a weekly or monthly letter that is available to interested individuals. These letters are generally a comment on the current and future outlook of the economy. Therefore, they typically contain only limited data. Some of the banks publishing letters are:

— Chase Manhattan (New York)
— Continental Illinois (Chicago)
— Harris Trust and Savings (Chicago)
— Manufacturers Hanover Trust Company (New York).

AGGREGATE STOCK MARKET ANALYSIS

There are several government publications that provide useful data on the stock market, but the bulk of detailed information is provided by private firms. Several of the government publications discussed earlier *(Federal Reserve Bulletin; Survey of Current Business)* contain financial market data such as interest rates and stock prices.

---

[2] Specific addresses for each of the district banks and names of major personnel are contained in the *Federal Reserve Bulletin,* published monthly by the Board.

[3] An individual can request to be put on the mailing list for any of these publications (free) by writing to: Federal Reserve Bank of St. Louis, P.O. Box 442, St. Louis, MO 63166.

Government Publications

The main source of data in this area is the Securities and Exchange Commission (SEC). The SEC is the federal agency responsible for regulating the operation of the securities markets and collects data in this regard.

Statistical Bulletin.   A monthly publication of the SEC that contains data on securities trading in the United States with an emphasis on common stocks. This includes volume of trading on all exchanges and the OTC market, prices on these exchanges, volatility and liquidity measures, and information on new issue registrations.

Annual Report of the SEC.   This is an annual publication of the SEC for the fiscal year ending in June. In contains a detailed discussion of important developments during the year and comments on the SEC's disclosure system and regulation of the securities markets. Finally, it includes a statistics section containing historical data on many of the items in the *Statistical Bulletin* as well as other annual series.

Commercial Publications

Considering the numerous advisory services in existence, a section dealing with their publications could become voluminous. Therefore, our intent is to list and discuss the *major* services and allow the reader to develop his own list of other available sources. An excellent source of advertisements for these services is *Barron's.*

New York Stock Exchange Fact Book.   An annual publication of the New York Stock Exchange. The book is an outstanding source of current and historical data on activity on the NYSE, but it also contains comparative data on the ASE, the OTC, institutional trading, and investors in general.

Amex Statistical Review.   This is a comparable data book for the American Stock Exchange. The first book (entitled *Amex Databook*), was published in 1969 with subsequent editions in 1971, 1973, and 1976. The title was changed to *Amex Statistical Review* in 1981 and it is now published annually. It contains pertinent information on the exchange, its membership, administration, and trading activities.

Wall Street Journal.   Published by Dow-Jones and Company, it is the only daily national business newspaper in the United States. It is published five days a week and is clearly the most complete source of daily information on companies and security market prices. It contains complete listings for the NYSE, the ASE, the NASDAQ–OTC market, bond markets, options markets, and commodities quotations. It is recognized worldwide as a primary source of financial and business information.[4]

Barron's.   This is a weekly publication of Dow-Jones and Company that typically contains four articles on topics of interest to investors. In addition, this newspaper has the most complete weekly listing of prices and quotes for all financial markets. It provides weekly data on individual stocks and the latest information on earnings and dividends as well as including quotes on commodities, stock options and financial futures. Finally, toward the back (typically the last three pages), there is an extensive statistical section with detailed information on stock market behavior for the past week.[5]

The Dow-Jones Investor's Handbook.   This publication contains the complete DJIA results for each year along with earnings and dividends for the series since 1939. Individual reports on common and preferred stocks and bonds listed on the NYSE and ASE, including high and low prices, volume, dividends, and the year's most active stocks, are also included.[6]

S&P Trade and Security Statistics.   This is a service of Standard & Poor's that includes a basic set of historical data on various economic and security price series and a monthly supplement that updates the series for the recent period. There are two major sets of data: (1) business and financial, and (2) security price index record. Within the business and finance section are long-term statistics on trade, banking, industry, price, agriculture, and financial trends.

The security price index record contains historical data for all of the Standard & Poor's indexes. This includes the 500 stocks broken down into 88 individual groups. The four main groups are composed of the industrial composite, rails, utilities, and the 500 composite are composed. There are also four supplementary group series: capital goods companies, consumer goods, high grade common stocks, and low priced common stocks. In addition to the stock price series, Standard & Poor's has derived a quarterly series of earnings and dividends for each of the four main groups. The earnings series includes data from 1946 to the present.

The booklet also contains data on daily stock sales on the NYSE from 1918 on and historical yields for a number of bond series both corporate and government.

Brokerage Firm Reports

As a means of competing for the investor's business, brokerage firms provide, among other services, information and recommendations on the outlook for

---

[4] A booklet that includes a discussion of many of the features of the *Wall Street Journal* is "A Future Manager's Guide to the *Wall Street Journal*." Copies are available from *The Wall Street Journal,* Educational Service Bureau, P.O. Box 300, Princeton, NJ 08540.

[5] A booklet that discusses many of the features in *Barron's* and how the series are used by technicians is Martin E. Zweig, *Understanding Technical Forecasting.* It is likewise available, free of charge, from the *Wall Street Journal,* Educational Service Bureau, address above.

[6] Prior to 1980 the firm published handbooks on several other topics, including "Barron's Market Laboratory", "The Dow-Jones Commodities Handbook," and "The Dow-Jones Stock Options Handbook."

securities markets (bonds and stocks). These reports are typically prepared monthly and distributed to customers (or potential customers) of the firm free of charge. In the competition for institutional business, some of these firms have generated reports that are quite extensive and sophisticated. Among the brokerages issuing these reports are: Goldman Sachs & Company; Merrill Lynch, Pierce, Fenner & Smith; and Salomon Bros.

INDUSTRY ANALYSIS

There are only a few publications with extensive information on a wide range of industries. The major source of data on various industries is trade associations or industry magazines.

Standard & Poor's Industry Survey.   This is a two-volume reference work that is divided into 34 segments dealing with 69 major domestic industries. Coverage in each area is divided into a current analysis and a basic analysis. The latter begins with an examination of the prospects for that particular industry, followed by an analysis of trends and problems presented in historical perspective. Major segments of the industry are spotlighted, and a comparative analysis of the principal companies in the industry is also included. The current analysis provides information on the latest developments in the industry and available industry, market, and company statistics, along with appraisals of the investment outlook for the specific area covered.

Standard & Poor's Analysts Handbook.   This handbook contains selected income account and balance sheet items and related ratios as applied to the Standard & Poor's industry group stock price indexes from 1949 to date. (The *Handbook* is typically not available until about seven months after year-end.) With these series, it is possible to compare the major factors bearing on group price actions (e.g., sales, profit margins, earnings), as well as the stock price actions themselves. We will use this data extensively in the industry analysis chapter. Figure 6.1 is a sample page from the *Handbook*.

Trade associations.   These are organizations set up by those involved in an industry or a general area of business to provide information for others on such topics as education, advertising, lobbying for legislation, and problem solving. Trade associations gather extensive statistics for the industry. Examples of such organizations include:[7]
— Iron and Steel Institute
— American Railroad Association
— National Consumer Finance Association
— Institute of Life Insurance

[7] For a more extensive list see *Encyclopedia of Associations* (Detroit: Gale Research Company, 1977).

FIGURE 6.1
Sample Page from Standard & Poor's *Analysts Handbook*

Chemicals
Per share data—adjusted to stock price index level. Average of stock price indexes,
1941–1943 = 10

	Sales	Operating Profit	Profit Margin Percent	Depreciation	Income Taxes	Earnings		Dividends	
						Per Share	Percent of Sales	Per Share	Percent of Earnings
1952	12.53	3.58	28.57	0.74	1.84	1.26	10.06	0.91	72.22
1953	13.84	3.92	28.32	0.94	1.88	1.34	9.68	0.95	70.90
1954	13.79	3.73	27.05	1.06	1.35	1.60	11.60	1.16	72.50
1955	16.14	4.77	29.55	1.17	1.82	2.13	13.20	1.39	65.26
1956	16.83	4.44	26.38	1.22	1.62	1.98	11.76	1.38	69.70
1957	17.38	4.44	25.55	1.28	1.59	1.95	11.22	1.43	73.33
1958	16.89	4.01	23.74	1.36	1.25	1.69	10.01	1.36	80.47
1959	19.34	5.16	26.68	1.40	1.90	2.23	11.53	1.47	65.92
1960	19.97	4.82	24.14	1.50	1.65	2.08	10.42	1.46	70.19
1961	20.67	4.96	24.00	1.66	1.64	2.08	10.06	1.55	74.52
1962	23.55	5.92	25.14	1.88	2.01	2.42	10.28	1.67	69.01
1963	26.69	6.60	24.73	2.10	2.22	2.75	10.30	1.83	66.55
1964	31.88	7.99	25.06	2.41	2.58	3.34	10.48	1.99	59.58
1965	34.52	8.59	24.88	2.64	2.55	3.41	9.88	1.89	55.43
1966	38.18	8.97	23.49	2.88	2.58	3.50	9.17	1.94	55.43
1967	38.63	8.12	21.02	3.15	1.99	2.84	7.35	1.87	65.85
1968	43.96	9.37	21.31	3.51	2.56	3.16	7.19	2.00	63.29
1969	47.18	9.55	20.24	3.70	2.52	3.17	6.72	1.94	61.20
1970	47.51	8.89	18.71	3.90	1.95	2.70	5.68	1.90	70.37
1971	49.55	9.36	18.89	3.99	2.07	2.93	5.91	1.90	64.85
1972	54.18	10.77	19.88	4.15	2.66	3.61	6.66	1.97	54.57
1973	64.00	13.54	21.16	4.23	3.91	5.10	7.97	2.08	40.78
1974	85.47	17.01	19.90	4.76	5.10	6.79	7.94	2.21	32.55
1975	80.33	15.24	18.97	4.92	4.18	5.51	6.86	2.18	39.56
1976	91.16	17.47	19.17	5.49	4.52	6.59	7.23	2.48	37.63
R1977	101.01	18.44	18.26	6.37	4.31	6.16	6.10	2.78	45.13
1978	112.76	20.82	18.46	7.21	5.07	7.16	6.35	3.10	43.30
1979	129.30	22.59	17.47	7.51	5.13	9.17	7.09	3.38	36.86
R1980	140.37	20.86	14.86	7.73	4.03	8.07	5.75	3.56	44.11
1981	143.65	21.09	14.68	7.72	R4.79	7.71	5.37	3.37	43.71
1982	159.01	21.85	13.74	9.56	5.52	5.21	3.28	3.57	68.52

Stock price indexes for this group extend back to 1926
'Dow Chemical (7-30-47)
'Du Pont de Nemours (1-16-35)
'Hercules Inc. (9-17-30)
'Monsanto Co. (1-16-35)
'Stauffer Chemical Co. (7-25-79)
'Union Carbide Co. (12-31-25)
Airco Inc. (Formerly Air Reduction) (1-2-18 to 2-5-75)

Allied Chemical Corp. (1-2-18 to 7-25-79)
American Cyanamid (9-17-30 to 7-25-79)
American Potash & Chemical (2-14-62 to 1-3-68)
Atlas Powder (1-16-35 to 7-23-47)
Chemetron Corp. (Formerly Nat'l Cylinder Gas) (4-16-58 to 2-5-75)
Columbian Carbon (12-31-25 to 2-7-62)
Commercial Solvents (12-31-25 to 6-16-65)

SOURCE: *Analysts Handbook*, 1983 edition (New York: Standard & Poor's, Inc.) Reprinted with permission.

(continued)

— American Bankers Association
— Machine Tool Association.

Industry magazines are an excellent source of data and general information.
Depending upon the industry, there can be several publications—the computer

FIGURE 6.1 (continued)

Chemicals

Per share data — adjusted to stock price index level. Average of stock price indexes,
1941 – 1943 = 10

Price		Price/Earning Ratio		Dividend Yields Percent		Book Value			
1941 – 1943 = 10						Per Share	Percent Return	Working Capital	Capital Expenditures
High	Low	High	Low	High	Low				
25.94	22.05	20.59	17.50	4.13	3.51	8.69	14.50	4.01	1.85
26.79	23.35	19.99	17.43	4.07	3.55	9.31	14.39	4.40	1.74
37.44	26.23	23.40	16.39	4.42	3.10	9.91	16.15	4.82	1.36
50.25	35.54	23.59	16.69	3.91	2.77	11.15	19.10	5.13	1.21
52.30	41.55	26.41	20.98	3.32	2.64	12.29	16.11	5.01	1.95
47.21	37.97	24.21	19.47	3.77	3.03	13.11	14.87	5.18	2.36
49.76	38.27	29.44	22.64	3.55	2.73	13.81	12.24	5.14	1.79
61.60	48.57	27.62	21.78	3.03	2.39	14.75	15.12	5.76	1.62
60.80	44.15	29.23	21.23	3.31	2.40	15.79	13.17	5.67	2.29
56.69	47.55	27.25	22.86	3.26	2.73	16.66	12.48	5.68	2.17
54.31	39.16	22.44	16.18	4.26	3.07	17.34	13.96	6.75	2.33
62.36	52.50	22.68	19.09	3.49	2.93	18.61	14.78	7.77	2.71
72.87	62.96	21.82	18.85	3.16	2.73	20.09	16.63	8.99	3.85
76.78	68.78	22.52	20.17	2.75	2.46	21.94	15.54	9.90	4.88
75.38	49.82	21.54	14.23	3.89	2.57	23.51	14.89	9.93	5.41
60.53	50.87	21.31	17.91	3.68	3.09	24.40	11.64	10.21	5.07
61.43	50.20	19.44	15.89	3.98	3.26	26.25	12.04	11.21	4.59
57.95	40.08	18.28	12.64	4.84	3.35	27.17	11.67	11.79	5.40
47.11	36.93	17.45	13.68	5.14	4.03	27.77	9.72	11.75	5.95
58.71	47.56	20.04	16.23	3.99	3.24	29.48	9.94	12.97	5.25
67.13	56.40	18.60	15.62	3.49	2.93	30.64	11.78	14.51	5.00
72.95	55.46	14.30	10.87	3.75	2.85	33.84	15.07	16.39	6.39
68.80	47.20	10.13	6.95	4.68	3.21	38.34	17.71	18.71	10.26
74.63	48.76	13.54	8.85	4.47	2.92	39.26	14.03	17.59	11.95
89.70	67.27	13.61	10.21	3.69	2.76	43.27	15.23	18.93	12.97
72.45	52.70	11.76	8.56	5.28	3.84	46.55	13.23	19.77	12.10
59.62	46.05	8.33	6.43	6.73	5.20	50.65	14.14	22.27	12.13
61.04	51.75	6.66	5.64	6.53	5.54	54.58	16.80	24.87	12.48
64.88	49.70	8.04	6.16	7.16	5.49	60.53	13.33	25.83	15.11
73.84	52.81	9.58	6.85	6.38	4.56	65.84	11.71	29.45	15.26
63.30	45.44	12.15	8.72	7.86	5.64	65.63	7.94	26.03	15.89

GAF Corp. (Formerly General Aniline & Film) (6-16-65 to 2-5-75)
Hooker Chemical (1-3-68 to 7-30-68)
Olin Corp. (1-2-18 to 2-5-75) (Formerly Olin-Mathieson Chemical)
United Carbon (1-16-35 to 7-23-47)
U.S. Industrial Chemicals (5-11-38 to 8-1-51)

industry has spawned at least five such magazines. Examples of industry publications include:

— *Computers*
— *Real Estate Today*
— *Chemical Week*
— *Modern Plastics*
— *Paper Trade Journal*
— *Automotive News.*

INDIVIDUAL STOCKS

Company-Generated Information

An obvious source of information about a company is the company itself. In the case of some small firms, it may be the *only* source of information because there is not enough activity to justify its inclusion in studies issued by commercial services.

Annual Reports.   All firms with publicly traded stock are required to prepare and distribute to their stockholders an annual report of financial operations and current financial position. In addition to basic information, most reports contain a discussion of what happened during the year and some consideration of future prospects. Most firms also publish a *quarterly financial report* that includes a brief income statement for this interim period and, sometimes, a balance sheet. Both of these reports can be obtained directly from the company. To find an address for a company one should consult *Standard & Poor's Register of Corporations, Directors, and Executives.* The register is published in three volumes of which the most useful for the specified purpose is volume one, which contains an alphabetical listing, by business name, of approximately 37,000 corporations.

Security Prospectus.   When a firm wants to sell some securities (bonds, preferred stock, or common stock) in the primary market to raise new capital, the Securities and Exchange Commission (SEC) requires that it file a registration statement describing the securities being offered and containing information on the company. The financial information is more extensive than that required in an annual report. Also, there is a substantial amount of nonfinancial information on the firm's operations and personnel. A condensed version of the registration statement, referred to as a *prospectus,* is published by the underwriting firm and contains most of the relevant information. Copies of a prospectus for a current offering can be obtained from the underwriter or from the company.

Required SEC Reports[8].   In addition to registration statements, the SEC requires three *periodic* statements from publicly held firms. The 8–K form is a report which firms registered with the SEC are required to file each month. In this report, any action that affects the debt, equity, amount of capital assets, voting right, or other changes that would be expected to have a significant impact on the stock is indicated.

The 9–K form is an unaudited report that must be filed every six months containing revenues, expenses, gross sales, and special items. This is typically more extensive than the quarterly statements are.

The 10–K form is an annual version of the 9–K but is even more complete. Recently, the SEC required that firms indicate in their annual reports that a copy of their 10–K is available from the company upon request without charge.

---

[8] For a further discussion of these reports, see Carl W. Schneider, "SEC Filings — Their Use to the Professional," *Financial Analysts Journal* 21 no. 1 (January–February 1965): 33–38.

Commercial Publications

There are numerous firms that sell advisory services supplying information on the aggregate market and individual stocks. Therefore, the following is only a partial discussion of what is available.

Standard & Poor's Corporation Records.   This is currently a set of seven volumes, the first six of which contain basic information on corporations arranged alphabetically and not according to industry type. The volumes are in binders and are updated throughout the year. The seventh volume is a daily news volume that contains recent data on all companies listed in all the volumes.

Standard & Poor's Stock Reports are comprehensive two-page reports on numerous companies with stocks listed on the NYSE, ASE, and traded OTC. They include the near term sales and earnings outlook, recent developments, key income statement and balance sheet items, and a chart of stock price movements. They are in bound volumes by exchange. These reports are revised every three to four months. A sample page is shown in Figure 6.2.

Standard & Poor's Stock Guide is a monthly publication that contains, in compact form, pertinent financial data on more than 5,100 common and preferred stocks. A separate section covers over 380 mutual fund issues. For each stock, the guide contains information on price ranges (historical and recent), dividends, earnings, financial position, institutional holdings, and ranking for earning and dividend stability. It is a very useful quick reference for almost all actively traded stocks, as is shown by the example in Figure 6.3.

Standard & Poor's Bond Guide is likewise published monthly. It contains the most pertinent comparative financial and statistical information on a broad list of bonds including domestic and foreign bonds (about 3,900 issues), 200 foreign government bonds, and about 650 convertible bonds.

The Outlook is a weekly publication of Standard & Poor's Corporation. It contains advice regarding the general market environment and also has features on specific groups of stocks or industries (e.g., high dividend stocks, stocks with low price to earnings ratios, high yielding bonds, stocks likely to increase their dividends, etc.). It also contains weekly figures for 88 industry groups and other market statistics.

Moody's Industrial Manual is similar to the Standard & Poor's service. It is currently published once a year in two bound volumes. It covers industrial companies listed on the NYSE and ASE as well as companies listed on regional exchanges. There is also a section on international industrial firms and an industrial news reports section that contains items occurring after publication of the basic manual.

(continued on page 151)

FIGURE 6.2
Sample Page from Standard & Poor's Stock Reports

Int'l Business Machines   1210

NYSE Symbol IBM   Options on CBOE (Jan-Apr-Jul-Oct)

Price	Range	P-E Ratio	Dividend	Yield	S&P Ranking
Apr. 18'84	1984				
111⅛	125–106½	12	3.80	3.4%	A+

Summary

IBM is the world's largest manufacturer of computers and information processing equipment and systems. Another good earnings gain is expected for 1984, aided by continued strong demand for information processing, greater penetration of the personal computer market, and aggressive product introductions and marketing efforts. A dividend increase of 10%–15% is anticipated.

Current Outlook

Earnings for 1984 are estimated at $10.75 a share, up from 1983's $9.04.

An early increase in the dividend, to $1.05–$1.10 quarterly from the current $0.95, is expected.

Gross income for 1984 is expected to advance on the order of 15%–20%, reflecting continued growth in demand for data processing, and greater penetration of personal computer, mini-computer and telecommunications markets. Margins are expected to be maintained and possibly to widen, given the greater volume and IBM's policy of encouraging sales rather than rentals of equipment. A higher tax rate is anticipated. Longer term, IBM's dominant position in the industry, and its aggressiveness in entering new markets, should enable it to grow at a rate above the industry average.

Gross Income (Billion $)

Quarter:	1984	1983	1982	1981
Mar.	9.59	8.29	7.07	6.46
Jun.	---	9.59	8.05	6.90
Sep.	---	9.41	8.17	6.72
Dec.	---	12.90	11.07	8.99
	---	40.18	34.36	29.08

Gross income for the three months ended March 31, 1984 increased 16%, year to year, on 38% higher sales, 26% lower rental income, and 26% greater service revenues. Operating margins narrowed slightly, but other income (primarily interest) doubled, and pretax income rose 19%. After taxes at 46.1%, versus 47.8%, net income advanced 23%.

TRADING VOLUME
THOUSAND SHARES

1978 1979 1980 1981 1982 1983 1984

Capital Share Earnings ($)

Quarter:	1984	1983	1982	1981
Mar.	1.97	1.62	1.33	1.25
Jun.	E2.68	2.22	1.81	1.37
Sep.	E2.55	2.14	1.75	1.18
Dec.	E3.55	3.06	2.50	1.83
	E10.75	9.04	7.39	5.63

Important Developments

Apr. '84—In its first quarter report IBM said that orders continued to grow at a strong pace across all product lines, and were significantly above 1983 levels. Separately, IBM expanded the text processing capabilities of its PC line, and added videotex capability. In March the company had projected 18% greater shipments of its 308X family of large-scale mainframes.

Next earnings report due in mid-July.

Per Share Data ($)

Yr. End Dec. 31	1983	1982	1981	1980	1979	1978	1977	1976	1975	1974
Book Value	38.02	33.13	30.66	28.18	25.64	23.14	21.39	21.15	19.05	17.05
Earnings	9.04	7.39	5.63	6.10	5.16	5.32	4.58	3.99	3.34	3.12
Dividends	3.71	3.44	3.44	3.44	3.44	2.88	2.50	2.00	1.62½	1.39
Payout Ratio	41%	47%	62%	56%	67%	54%	54%	50%	49%	45%
Prices—High	134¼	98	71½	72¾	80½	77½	71½	72⅛	56⅞	63½
Low	92¼	55⅝	48⅜	50⅜	61⅛	58¾	61⅛	55⅞	39⅜	37⅝
P/E Ratio—	15–10	13–8	13–9	12–8	16–12	15–11	16–13	18–14	17–12	20–12

Data as orig. reptd. Adj. for stk. div(s). of 300% Jun. 1979. E-Estimated.

Standard NYSE Stock Reports
Vol. 51/No. 81/Sec. 14

April 26, 1984
Copyright © 1984 Standard & Poor's Corp. All Rights Reserved

Standard & Poor's Corp.
25 Broadway, NY, NY 10004

(continued)

SOURCE: *Standard & Poor's Stock Reports* (New York: Standard & Poor's Corp., 1984). Reprinted by permission.

FIGURE 6.2 (continued)

1210   International Business Machines Corporation

Income Data (Million $)

Year Ended Dec. 31	Revs.	Oper. Inc.	% Oper. Inc. of Revs.	Cap. Exp.	Depr.	Int. Exp.	Net Bef. Taxes	Eff. Tax Rate	Net Inc.	% Net Inc. of Revs.
1983	40,180	13,262	33.0%	4,930	3,673	[3]390	[2]9,940	44.8%	5,485	13.7%
1982	34,364	11,199	32.6%	6,685	3,143	514	[2]7,930	44.4%	[1]4,409	12.8%
1981	29,070	8,926	30.7%	6,845	2,899	480	[2]5,988	44.8%	3,308	11.4%
1980	26,213	8,102	30.9%	6,592	2,362	[1]325	[2]5,897	39.6%	3,562	13.6%
1979	22,863	7,215	31.6%	5,991	1,970	140	5,553	45.8%	3,011	13.2%
1978	21,076	7,265	34.5%	4,046	1,824	55	5,798	46.3%	3,111	14.8%
1977	18,133	6,657	36.7%	3,395	1,999	40	5,092	46.6%	2,719	15.0%
1976	16,304	5,928	36.4%	2,518	1,858	45	4,519	46.9%	2,398	14.7%
1975	14,437	5,245	36.3%	2,439	1,822	63	3,721	46.5%	1,990	13.8%
1974	12,675	4,871	38.4%	2,913	1,708	69	3,435	46.5%	1,838	14.5%

Balance Sheet Data (Million $)

Dec. 31	Cash	Current Assets	Current Liab.	Ratio	Total Assets	Ret. on Assets	Long Term Debt	Common Equity	Total Cap.	% LT Debt of Cap.	Ret. on Equity
1983	5,536	17,270	9,507	1.8	37,243	15.6%	2,674	23,219	26,606	10.1%	25.2%
1982	3,300	13,014	8,209	1.6	32,541	14.1%	2,851	19,960	23,134	12.3%	22.9%
1981	2,029	10,303	7,320	1.4	29,586	11.7%	2,669	18,161	21,082	12.7%	19.0%
1980	2,112	9,925	6,526	1.5	26,703	13.9%	2,099	16,453	18,734	11.2%	22.7%
1979	3,771	10,851	6,445	1.7	24,530	13.3%	1,589	14,961	16,690	9.5%	21.2%
1978	4,031	10,321	5,810	1.8	20,771	15.7%	286	13,494	13,889	2.1%	24.0%
1977	5,407	10,073	5,209	1.9	18,978	15.0%	256	12,618	12,962	2.0%	21.7%
1976	6,156	9,920	4,082	2.4	17,723	14.4%	275	12,749	13,088	2.1%	19.8%
1975	4,768	8,115	3,363	2.4	15,531	13.4%	295	11,416	11,756	2.5%	18.4%
1974	3,805	7,010	3,210	2.2	14,027	13.9%	336	10,110	10,482	3.2%	19.3%

Data as orig. reptd. 1. Reflects accounting change. 2. Incl. equity in earns. of nonconsol. subs. 3. Net of interest income.

Business Summary

IBM is primarily involved in information-handling systems, equipment and services.

Gross revenues	1983	1982
Processors/peripherals	54%	55%
Office products	20%	19%
Programs/maint./other	23%	24%
Federal systems	3%	2%

Sales provided 58% of revenues in 1983, rentals 23%, and services 19%. Foreign operations contributed 42% of revenues and 39% of profits.

Processors manipulate data through the operation of a stored program. Peripherals include printers, copiers, and storage and telecommunication devices. Office products include small business computers, intelligent workstations and typewriters. IBM provides software, maintenance, data communications, remote computing, consulting, biomedical products, analytical instruments, and robots.

The Federal systems group serves U.S. government space, defense and other agencies.

IBM also provides education and testing materials and services for school and industrial use.

Dividend Data

Dividends have been paid since 1916. A dividend reinvestment plan is available.

Amt. of Divd. $	Date Decl.	Ex-divd. Date	Stock of Record	Payment Date
0.95	Apr. 22	May 5	May 11	Jun. 10'83
0.95	Jul. 26	Aug. 4	Aug. 10	Sep. 10'83
0.95	Oct. 25	Nov. 2	Nov. 9	Dec. 10'83
0.95	Jan. 31	Feb. 3	Feb. 9	Mar. 10'84

Next dividend meetings: Apr. & Jul. '84.

Finances

The company owns a 19% interest in Intel Corp., a major semiconductor maker, and 20% of Rolm Corp., a maker of telecommunications equipment. Agreements permit IBM to raise its holdings of each company to 30%.

Capitalization

Long Term Debt: $2,674,000,000.

Capital Stock: 610,724,641 shs. ($1.25 par). Institutions hold approximately 51%. Shareholders of record: 769,979.

Office—Armonk, New York 10504. Tel—(914) 765-1900. Stockholder Relations Dept—590 Madison Ave., NYC 10022. Tel—(212) 407-4000. Chrmn & CEO—J. R. Opel. Pres—J. F. Akers. Secy—J. H. Grady. Treas—J. W. Rotenstreich. Investor Contact—J. M. Heatley. Dirs—J. F. Akers, S. D. Bechtel, Jr., G. B. Beitzel, H. Brown, J. E. Burke, F. T. Cary, W. T. Coleman, Jr., P. R. Harris. C. A. Hills, A. Houghton, Jr., J. N. Irwin II, N. deB. Katzenbach, R. W. Lyman, J. G. Maisonrouge, M. McK. Moller, W. H. Moore, J. R. Munro, J. R. Opel, D. P. Phypers, P. J. Rizzo, W. W. Scranton, I. S. Shapiro, C. R. Vance, T. J. Watson, Jr. Transfer Agents—Company's NYC & Chicago offices. Registrars—Morgan Guaranty Trust Co., NYC; First National Bank, Chicago. Incorporated in New York in 1911.

Information has been obtained from sources believed to be reliable, but its accuracy and completeness are not guaranteed.   Christopher J. Pauley

FIGURE 6.3
Example from Standard & Poor's Stock Guide

84 Equ-Fal Standard & Poor's Corporation

¶S&P 500 •Options Index	Ticker Symbol	Name of Issue (Call Price of Pfd. Stocks)	Market	Com. Rank. & Pfd. Rating	Par Val.	Inst.Hold Cos	Inst.Hold Shs. (000)	Principal Business	Price Range 1971-82 High	1971-82 Low	1983 High	1983 Low	1984 High	1984 Low	Feb. Sales in 100s	February,1984 Last Sale Or Bid High	Low	Last	%Div. Yield	P-E Ratio
1	EBNC	Equitable Bancorp	OTC	A—	5	11	1179	Multi-bank hldg: Baltimore	18⅛	4¾	21¼	12⅝	19¼	17½	289	19	17½	17½B	s4.3	13
2	EQT	Equitable Gas	NY,B,M,Ph	A	No	55	3475	Nat'l gas dstr in Pa & W.V.	26⅞	4⅝	33⅞	15⅜	33⅞	29⅞	2225	33⅝	29⅞	33¼	4.1	10
3	EQICB	Equitable of Iowa Cl'B'[52]	OTC	B+	1	8	89	Life insurance: dept strs	23⅛	6⅝	28¾	17¼	23¾	21¼	462	21¾	21¼	21½B	6.0	7
4	EQTC	Equitec Fin'l Group	OTC	NR	1¢	6	310	Diversified financial svcs	....	....	32	15	27½	19½	1167	23½	19½	23½B	0.5	10
5	ATF	Equity Income Fund[53]	AS	NR	No	...	....	1st exch series-AT&T shrs	....	....	....	....	64	62⅝	224	64	62⅝	62¾	8.8	..
6	EQTY	Equity Oil	OTC	B+	1	14	2653	Expl & prod crude oil & gas	28⅝	1	12¼	6⅞	9¼	7	2704	9¼	7¼	8⅜B	2.4	17
7	ERB	Erbamont N.V.	NY,M	NR	4	40	3659	Int'l pharmaceutical co.	....	....	25¼	11½	14⅛	10¾	4931	13⅛	10¾	12¾	...	15
8	ERICY	Ericsson(LM)Tel'B'ADR	OTC	NR	j50	51	8476	Worldwide telecommunic'ns	47	16⅜	64	44¾	48⅜	44½	9759	48	44½	44½B	1.9	19
9	ERO	Ero Indus	AS	B—	1	...	....	Outdoor sporting goods	12	½	13½	7⅝	9⅞	8⅝	122	9⅝	8¾	8¾	...	7
¶10	ESM	Esmark Inc	NY,B,C,M,P,Ph	B+	1	147	19589	Food,chem prod:auto rental	30⅜	5¼	44⅜	27½	46	38⅛	17943	44	38⅛	42	2.5	11
11	Pr B	$2.80 cm Cv Cl 2 B Pfd([60]33)	NY	BBB	No	4	26	personal & cosmetic prod	....	....	39	30½	39	34¾	556	37½	34¾	36	7.8	..
12	ESP	Espey Mfg & Electr	AS	B+	33⅓¢	3	31	Electronic pwr supply,syst's	17¼	¾	32½	13	38	27⅜	1136	32¾	27⅜	29⅝	1.1	12
13	ETI	Esprit Systems	AS	NR	1¢	4	325	Mkts video display terminals	....	....	8¾	7	9¼	5¾	478	7¼	5¾	6¼	...	..
14	EE	Esquire Radio & Elec	AS	B+	10¢	2	32	Private brand radios, hi-fi	29	2⅜	29⅛	24¼	28⅜	24⅜	232	28¼	27⅜	27½B	2.6	7
15	ESX	Essex Chemical	NY,M	B+	1	17	445	Chemicals:sealants, coatings	20⅞	1½	25⅞	17¾	21⅞	17	776	19¾	17	17¼	4.6	14
16	ESEX	Essex Corp	OTC	NR	10¢	2	109	Tech svcs to US/state govts	12¼	3⅝	11	4¼	5	4½	348	5	4½	4½B	...	11
17	ESL	Esterline Corp	NY,M	↓B+	20¢	67	3105	Analy/record'g instr:autom'n	39½	1¼	36⅝	20⅝	34⅜	27⅝	2028	31¼	27⅝	28½	2.2	27
18	EY	Ethyl Corp	NY,B,M,P,Ph	A	1	107	15859	Ind'l & petroleum chemicals	18¼	4¾	29⅜	14½	27⅞	20	12331	25¼	20	21	4.0	8
19	Pr	$2.40 cm Cv A 2d Pfd (75)vtg	[1]NY,P	A—	10	3	2	plastics,alum,ins,coal,o/g	92½	26	144½	76	140	140	....	....	....	109¼B	2.2	..
20	ETZ	Etz Lavud Ltd Ord	AS	NR	j8½	...	....	Laminates & wood products	24½	1¼	31⅝	16⅞	34¼	30¾	224	34¼	32⅞	34¼	0.6	11
21	ERC	Evaluation Research	AS	NR	5¢	...	....	Provides engin'g tech svcs	3⅞	3	16¾	3⅝	10	5⅝	1432	8¾	5⅝	6	...	17
¶22	EVY	Evans Products	NY,B,M,P	B—	1	26	7183	Mfr/retail bldg mat'l:transp.	25¾	1⅞	19½	7¾	11	6½	4894	9	6½	6⅞	...	d
23	Pr	$1.40cm JrPfd([65]16.74)	NY	CCC	No	...	....	systems & ind'l equip	15⅝	6⅝	11½	9½	10⅞	8⅞	512	10⅞	8⅞	9½	14.7	..
24	Pr B	$2.10 cm Jr Pfd([66]22.55)	NY	CCC	No	...	....		19¾	10	16¾	13	14½	13¼	46	14½	13½	13½B	15.6	..
25	ESCC	Evans&Sutherl'd Comp	OTC	B+	20¢	61	2769	3d computer graphics sys	48	3⅜	50½	28	31½	16⅞	4935	24	16⅞	19B	...	16
26	EJ.B	Everest/Jennings Intl[67]	AS	B+	1	5	74	Wheelchairs: medical equip	16⅝	1⅛	13½	7¾	10⅝	9⅜	163	10¼	9⅝	9⅞B	1.0	d
27	EJ.A	Class A Lmtd vtg	AS	A—	1	11	2403	metal castings	16	6¼	13¼	7	10½	9⅜	448	10⅛	9⅝	10	2.0	d
¶28	XLO	Ex-Cell-O	NY,B,M,Ph	A	3	96	5920	Precision eq:mchy:aero:auto	36¼	6⅜	44½	25½	41	31⅜	3806	37¼	31⅜	31⅝	5.1	10
29	EIS	Excelsior Inc Shares	NY,M	NR	1¢	3	3	Closed-end investment co	25⅜	12½	16⅞	15	15⅞	15	268	15⅞	15	15¼	†11.9	..
30	EXL	Exolon Co	B	B—	1	3	3	Prod for abrasive purposes	17½	7¼	16¼	8	12¾	11¾	8	12¼	11¾	11¾	3.4	..
31	ESI	Exploration Surveys'A'	AS	NR	10¢	7	432	Geophysical data, oil & gas	8¾	1⅛	4⅜	1¾	4⅛	2⅞	338	3⅞	3	3⅜B	...	d
¶32•[2]	XON	Exxon Corp	NY,B,C,M,P,Ph	A	No	962	264771	World's leading oil co	44⅜	13¾	39¾	28½	40	36⅛	169814	40	36⅛	38½	8.3	7
33	FIT	Fab Indus	AS	B+	20¢	15	1130	Warp knit textile producer	11½	½	19¾	9½	18⅜	15½	340	16½	15½	15¾	2.2	7
¶34	FBG	Faberge Inc[69]	NY,B,M,Ph	B	40¢	12	264	Fragrance,cosmetics,grooming	28½	4¼	28⅜	17⅛	31½	27½	9066	30¾	29½	30⅝	2.0	43
35	FCA	Fabri-Centers Amer	NY,M	B+	No	23	1629	Sells fabric, notions, drapery	21⅛	1⅝	22¾	11¾	13	9⅝	1298	11⅜	9⅝	10½	2.7	11
36	FBRC	Fabric Wholesalers	OTC	B+	No	1	26	Sells fabric,notions,patterns	10½	⅛	13¾	8½	11¼	9½	413	11¼	9½	9½B	1.6	9
37	FCT	Facet Enterprises	NY,M	B—	1	15	579	Auto parts - filters	9⅝	3⅞	15⅞	8⅛	16⅛	10	2110	13	10	11⅜	...	10
38	FAFO	Fafco, Inc	OTC	NR	1¼¢	1	24	Solar heat exch sys-swim pool	10½	2¼	7¼	3	4½	3½	250	3¾	3½	3½B	...	d
39	FAIR	Fair Lanes	OTC	A—	1	7	1106	Bowling ctrs: restaurants	3⅞	½	5⅞	3⅜	6¼	5½	1441	6⅛	5½	5⅞B	2.7	15
40	FEN	Fairchild Indus	NY,B,M,P,Ph	B+	1	48	5148	Mfr comm'l jets, aerospace	33⅞	1½	24⅞	14⅛	19¼	15	5231	18¼	15	16⅞	4.7	11
41	Pr A	$3.60 cm Cv A Pfd([77]46.80)vtg	[3]NY,B	BBB—	No	29	765	precision metal products	53¼	26½	43⅞	31⅝	39	34½	1537	37¾	34½	36⅛	10.0	..
42	FCI	Fairfield Cmnties	NY,M	NR	10¢	36	3089	Home/lot sales,time sharing	10⅛	¼	17 1/16	8¾	15¼	11¼	4324	15¼	11¼	[4]2⅝	1.3	10
43	FMT	Fairmount Chemical	AS	C	1	...	....	Hydrazine:agri,graphic chems	8⅛	1⅛	5⅝	2⅝	3⅝	3	69	3¼	3	3	...	d
44	FFIC	Fairmont Financial	OTC	NR	No	4	235	Ins hldg:workers' compens'n	....	....	10	5¾	7¼	6	1127	6¼	6	6¼B	3.2	d
45	FLCP	Falcon Products	OTC	C	2¢	...	....	Food sv eq:contract furniture	6⅜	1⅛	3¾	1½	2	2	62	2	2	2B	...	d
46	FALCF	Falconbridge Ltd	OTC,To,Mo	C	No	80	1202	Mines nickel, copper, cobalt	156	14½	70½	37½	58¾	48¾	39	54¾	48¾	50½B	...	d

Uniform Footnote Explanations—See Page 1. Other: [1]Ph. [2]CBOE:Cycle 1. [3]M. [51]◎$2.56,'82. [52]Non vtg. [53]Unit Invest't Tr. [54]Fiscal Jan'81 & prior. [55]11 Mo Dec'81. [56]Incl pension & new financing. [57]△$8.41,□$2.68,'80. [58]□$0.10,'81. [59]△$0.21,'82. [60]Fr 10-1-88. [61]17 Wk May'83. [62]Deferred comp. [63]△$0.19,□$0.18,'80. [64]◎$2.56,'83. [65]To 1-31-85,scale to $15.50 in 2000. [66]To 3-30-84,scale to $20.50 in 2003. [67]Cl'B'. [68]△$0.36,'79. [69]McCregor Corp plan mgr, %$32. [70]△$0.32,'79. [71]□$0.91,'81. [72]□$0.15,'82. [73]◎$1.52,'83. [74]□$0.26,'80. [75]□$0.20,'82. [76]△$0.04,'83. [77]Fr 1-1-89 scale to $45 in'94. [78]◎$0.89,'83.

Common and Preferred Stocks **Equ-Fal** 85

Splits ◆ Index	Cash Divs. Ea. Yr. Since	Dividends Latest Payment Per$	Date	Ex. Div.	Total $ So Far 1984	Ind. Rate	Paid 1983	Financial Position Mil-$ Cash& Equiv.	Curr. Assets	Curr. Liab.	Balance Sheet Date	Capitalization Lg Trm Debt Mil-$	Shs. 000 Pfd.	Com.	Earnings $ Per Shr. Years End	1979	1980	1981	1982	1983	Last 12 Mos.	Interim Earnings Period	$ Per Shr. 1982	1983	Index
1◆	1916	5% Stk	5-17-84	4-13	s0.33	0.756	s0.561	Book Value $16.98			12-31-82	p39.3	★1100	p6774	Dc	■1.43	■1.02	▲1.09	■1.46	P1.34	1.34				1
2◆	1950	Q0.340	3-1-84	2-7	0.34	1.360	1.090	5.91	125.	108.	9-30-83	179.	...	11899	Dc	2.18	2.91	3.31	[51]2.81	....	3.27	12 Mo Sep	3.14	▲3.27	2
3◆	1889	Q0.32	3-8-84	2-14	0.32	1.28	1.28	Equity per shr $34.70			9-30-83	21.5	200	±6236	Dc	△3.75	△3.06	△2.09	△1.72	....	2.96	9 Mo Sep	△0.61	△1.85	3
4	1977	0.02¾	3-28-84	3-8	0.02¾	0.11	0.02¾	11.6	15.5	4.49	10-31-83	★21.7	...	2582	Ap	0.27	0.49	0.67	0.88	1.08	2.46	9 Mo Jan△	0.57	1.95	4
5	1983	1.38	2-1-84		1.38	5.52	1.38	...	...	...		....	...	11738	Dc	....	....	....	....	....	....				5
6◆	1948	S0.10	4-9-84	3-12	0.10	0.20	0.20	4.61	10.1	2.72	9-30-83	0.08	...	11784	Dc	0.22	0.42	0.47	0.36	P0.49	0.49				6
7	.....	None Since Public			....	Nil	....	28.0	517.	326.	12-31-82	115.	...	★43627	Dc	....	....	....	0.87	....	0.87				7
8◆	1967	0.849	6-3-83	4-28	....	0.85	0.849	2797	17039	9776	j12-31-82	7230	...	±★36683	Dc	1.46	1.51	2.39	2.30	....	2.30				8
9◆	.....	0.05	1-16-61	12-22	....	Nil	....	0.71	8.86	3.34	9-30-83	0.38	...	899	Dc	d0.37	[54]•0.11	■[55]0.43	1.15	P1.33	1.33				9
10◆	1934	Q0.26	1-1-84	12-13	0.26	1.04	0.92	149.	2051	1407	10-29-83	[56]793.	2601	p40444	Oc	1.35	[57]△1.27	□[58]2.91	△[59]3.18	3.66	3.66				10
11	1983	Q0.70	1-1-84	12-13	0.70	2.80	0.168	Cv into 0.71 shr com				.....	2601	...	Oc	....	....	....	....	b2.44	....	Mand SF 5% fr Oct'94 $33			11
12◆	1977	0.333	11-14-83	10-17	....	0.33	0.333	7.87	9.66	1.76	9-30-83	....	...	1218	Je	0.23	0.28	■0.71	1.71	2.23	2.56	6 Mo Dec	0.98	△1.31	12
13	.....	None Since Public			....	Nil	....	0.85	10.7	2.92	11-30-83	1.00	...	3678	My	....	....	....	[61]■0.12	....	n/a	6 Mo Nov	n/a	0.22	13
14	1976	0.72	4-12-83	3-25	....	0.72	0.72	10.2	32.4	14.6	9-30-83	[62]0.09	...	483	Dc	2.37	3.54	5.51	4.32	....	3.75	9 Mo Sep	2.69	2.12	14
15◆	1975	Q0.20	2-9-84	1-4	0.20	0.80	0.727	4.90	71.3	30.9	9-30-83	63.0	...	3445	Dc	1.39	1.57	▲2.32	1.85	▲P1.20	1.20				15
16	.....	None Since Public			....	Nil	....	0.29	5.96	2.85	9-30-83	0.01	...	1222	Dc	0.18	0.29	0.43	0.43	....	0.41	9 Mo Sep	0.31	0.29	16
17◆	1969	Q0.16	1-31-84	12-27	0.16	0.64	0.64	22.1	121.	42.2	10-31-83	33.0	...	8444	Oc	1.66	2.51	2.32	1.26	0.91	1.07	3 Mo Jan△	0.14	0.30	17
18◆	1957	Q0.21¼	4-1-84	3-12	0.42½	0.85	0.82½	73.0	479.	227.	12-31-83	293.	p418	p40563	Dc	2.47	□[63]△2.23	2.28	▲2.34	P■[64]2.61	2.61				18
19	1967	Q0.60	4-1-84	3-12	1.20	2.40	2.40	Conv into 5.2 com				....	152	....	Dc	b4.48	b5.28	b5.51	b2.99	....	....				19
20	1979	0.20	1-23-84	12-19	0.20	0.20	0.20	1.45	22.0	17.9	3-31-83	2.95	...	1709	Mr	1.39	2.28	2.76	2.85	....	3.10	9 Mo Dec	1.94	2.19	20
21◆	.....	None Since Public			....	Nil	....	3.28	12.0	3.66	9-30-83	0.45	...	2878	Dc	0.27	0.22	0.26	0.35	P0.36	0.36				21
22◆	.....	0.227	2-15-82	1-26	....	Nil	....	14.4	398.	258.	9-30-83	398.	3088	13809	Dc	■4.23	2.66	△0.75	□▲d4.11	Ed2.50	d4.23	9 Mo Sep	▲d1.96	■d2.08	22
23	1977	Q0.35	3-1-84	2-8	0.35	1.40	1.40	...	...	...		....	2712	...	Dc	b2.44	b1.68	b1.13	b0.38	....	....	SF 5% ea Dec 1,$15.50			23
24	1979	Q0.52½	3-1-84	2-8	0.52½	2.10	2.10	...	...	...		....	350	...	Dc	b2.44	b1.68	b1.13	b0.38	....	....				24
25◆	.....	None Since Public			....	Nil	....	33.0	64.6	22.8	9-30-83	4.93	...	8795	Dc	0.32	0.76	1.07	1.10	P1.21	1.21				25
26◆	1971	Q0.02½	4-13-84	3-19	0.05	0.10	0.10	2.60	49.1	16.4	9-23-83	38.4	...	±7781	Dc	■1.24	1.38	0.55	0.45	....	d0.01	9 Mo Sep	0.40	■d0.06	26
27	1980	Q0.05	4-13-84	3-19	0.10	0.20	0.20	...	...	...		....	...	5333	Dc	■1.24	1.38	0.55	0.45	....	d0.01	9 Mo Sep	0.40	■d0.06	27
28◆	1936	Q0.40	4-2-84	3-5	0.80	1.60	1.60	119.	440.	176.	8-31-83	46.3	...	14172	Nv	3.54	3.27	3.71	3.25	P△3.29	3.29				28
29	1973	†0.46	3-30-84	3-12	†0.46	1.81	†1.87	Net Asset Val $16.33			2-24-84	....	...	2217	Dc	§18.13	§16.16	§14.31	§16.76	§16.77	....				29
30	1936	0.20	3-8-84	2-22	0.20	0.40	0.20	0.10	15.2	8.54	9-30-83	5.26	33	499	Dc	2.92	0.60	0.09	d0.97	....	0.42	9 Mo Sep	d1.06	0.33	30
31◆	.....	3% Stk	9-9-81	8-13	....	Nil	....	3.95	5.72	1.34	9-30-83	1.98	...	±2150	Dc	0.10	0.38	0.40	0.07	Pd0.37	d0.37				31
32◆	1882	Q0.80	3-10-84	2-6	0.80	3.20	3.10	3799	19086	15168	9-30-83	4777	...	859347	Dc	△[68]4.51	6.49	6.44	4.82	P5.79	5.79				32
33◆	1976	0.35	1-6-84	12-1	0.35	0.35	0.301	24.3	66.2	13.6	8-27-83	1.65	...	★3824	Nv	2.19	1.98	1.83	1.85	P2.12	2.12				33
34	1960	Q0.15	3-30-83	3-5	0.15	0.60	0.57	8.52	146.	63.7	9-30-83	14.8	...	5619	Dc	△[70]0.95	0.38	□[71]0.96	□[72]1.30	....	0.72	9 Mo Sep	0.94	0.36	34
35◆	1969	Q0.07	3-16-84	2-27	0.07	0.28	0.28	4.38	67.0	25.7	10-29-83	6.21	...	5171	Ja	0.73	0.91	1.22	[73]1.60	....	0.97	9 Mo Oct	1.13	0.50	35
36◆	1975	S0.07½	3-5-84	2-10	0.07½	0.15	0.13¾	0.13	12.9	8.06	9-30-83	0.40	...	1092	Dc	0.19	0.40	0.57	0.95	....	1.07	9 Mo Sep	0.60	0.72	36
37	.....	0.15	1-18-80	12-13	....	Nil	....	2.88	60.9	17.9	12-31-83	25.9	...	2968	Sp	△•Nil	□[74]d2.05	•0.22	□•[75]0.58	△•1.02	1.09	3 Mo Dec	•0.05	•0.12	37
38	.....	None Since Public			....	Nil	....	0.47	2.85	1.40	9-30-83	....	...	2822	Dc	•0.42	•0.54	0.02	d0.66	....	d1.21	9 Mo Sep	d0.28	d0.83	38
39◆	1966	Q0.04	2-15-84	1-19	0.04	0.16	0.134	6.86	12.4	12.8	9-30-83	55.7	...	13084	Je	0.28	0.26	0.29	0.34	[76]0.40	0.38	6 Mo Dec	0.17	•0.15	39
40◆	1966	Q0.20	1-6-84	12-20	0.20	0.80	0.60	9.30	520.	316.	9-30-83	167.	3581	13300	Dc	3.41	4.02	▲3.48	1.90	P1.51	1.51				40
41	1981	Q0.90	1-18-84	12-28	0.90	3.60	3.60	Conv into 1.51 shrs common				.....	3581	...	Dc	....	b3.35	b2.09	b1.55	....	....	Redeem 10% fr'89,$45			41
42◆	1978	Q0.04	2-29-84	2-8	0.04	0.16	0.12	Equity per shr $7.70			11-30-83	p184.	...	p10063	Fb	0.98	0.79	1.00	[78]1.16	....	1.29	9 Mo Nov	0.77	0.90	42
43	.....	0.15	11-27-78	11-6	....	Nil	....	0.20	3.12	3.14	9-30-83	....	...	1250	Dc	0.13	d0.17	d0.49	d1.84	....	d1.95	9 Mo Sep	d0.97	d1.08	43
44	1983	0.10	12-15-83	11-7	....	0.20	0.10	Equity per shr $7.82			9-30-83	0.70	...	2694	Dc	1.05	□1.29	1.18	□0.64	Pd0.45	d0.45				44
45◆	.....	0.045	9-28-79	9-10	....	Nil	....	0.05	12.4	6.10	10-31-83	14.7	...	1594	Oc	0.57	0.51	0.53	d1.97	d2.44	d2.44				45
46	.....	g0.50	9-30-81	9-18	....	Nil	....	298.	562.	134.	j9-30-83	p459.	...	★7256	Dc	•21.01	△13.04	□d0.78	d17.12	P△d2.71	jd2.71				46

◆ **Stock Splits & Divs By Line Reference Index** [1]Adj for 5%,2-for-1,'83. [2]2-for-1,'79:3-for-2,'81,'84. [3]Adj for Cl'A'dstr,'80. [6]4-for-1,'80. [8]3-for-2,'82. [9]5-for-4,'82. [10]5-for-4,'81,'82:2-for-1,'83. [12]3-for-1,'84(wi'83). [15]10% Jan,'81,Nov,'81,'82,'83. [17]3-for-2 twice,'80. [18]2-for-1,'83. [21]5-for-4,'83. [22]10%,'83. [25]2-for-1,'80:3-for-1,'81. [26]7-for-4,'80,2-for-1 dstr in Cl'A','80. [28]3-for-2,'81. [31]Adj to 3%,'81. [32]2-for-1,'81. [33]3-for-2,'79:5-for-3,'83. [35]3-for-2,'82. [36]2-for-1,'83. [39]5-for-4,'82,'83:2-for-1,'84. [40]5-for-4,'79:2-for-1,'80. [42]3-for-2,'83:2-for-1,'83. [45]10%,'80.

SOURCE: *Standard & Poor's Stock Reports* (New York: Standard & Poor's Corp., 1984). Reprinted by permission.

Moody's OTC Industrial Manual is similar to the *Moody's Industrial Manual* of listed firms but is limited to stocks traded on the OTC market. Supplementary volumes containing information on recent developments are also published.

Moody's Public Utility Manual provides information on public utilities including electric and gas, gas transmission, telephone, and water companies. It also contains a news report section.

Moody's Transportation Manual covers the transportation industry including railroads, airlines, steamship companies, electric railway, bus and truck lines, oil pipe lines, bridge companies, and automobile and truck leasing companies. A supplementary transportation news report is also published.

Moody's Bank and Finance Manual is published in two volumes and covers the field of finance represented by banks, savings and loan associations, credit agencies of the U.S. government, all phases of the insurance industry, investment companies, real estate firms, real estate investment trusts, and miscellaneous financial enterprises.

Moody's Municipal and Government Manual is published in two volumes and contains data on the U.S. government, all the states, state agencies, municipalities (over 13,500), foreign governments, and international organizations.

The Value Line Investment Survey is published in two parts. Volume 1 contains basic historic information on about 1,700 companies as well as a number of analytical measures of earnings stability, growth rates, and a common stock safety factor. It also includes extensive two-year *projections* for the given firms and three-year *estimates* of performance. In early 1986 it will include a projection for 1986, 1987, and 1988–1990. The second volume includes a weekly service that provides general investment advice and also recommends individual stocks for purchase or sale. An example of a company report is shown in Figure 6.4 on the next page.

The Value Line OTC Special Situations Service is published 24 times a year for the experienced investor who is willing to accept high risk in the hope of realizing exceptional capital gains. In each issue, past recommendations are discussed and eight to ten new stocks are presented for consideration.

Daily Stock Price Records are published by Standard & Poor's. The bound volumes are published quarterly with individual volumes for the NYSE, the ASE, and the OTC market.

Each quarterly book is divided into two parts. Part 1, "Major Technical Indicators of the Stock Market," is devoted to market indicators widely followed as technical guides to the stock market and includes price indicator series, volume series, and data on odd lots and short sales. Part 2, "Daily and Weekly Stock Action," gives daily high, low, close, and volume information and data on short interest for the stock, insider trading information, a 200-day moving average of

FIGURE 6.4
Sample Listing from Value Line

SEARS, ROEBUCK NYSE-S | RECENT PRICE **41** | P/E RATIO **11.0** (Trailing: 11.8 / Median: 11.0) | EARN'S YLD **9.1 %** | DIV'D YIELD **4.0 %** | **1677**

| High | 37.4 | 38.3 | 52.1 | 59.8 | 61.6 | 45.2 | 37.2 | 39.6 | 34.6 | 28.1 | 21.9 | 19.6 | 20.8 | 32.0 | 45.1 |
| Low | 30.1 | 25.5 | 37.4 | 48.7 | 39.1 | 20.8 | 24.2 | 30.8 | 27.0 | 19.8 | 17.8 | 14.4 | 14.9 | 15.8 | 27.0 |

18.0 x "Cash Flow" p sh
2-for-1 split
Relative Price Strength

Target Price Range
1986 1987 1988 1989
Dec. 9, 1983 Value Line
TIMELINESS 2 Above Average
(Relative Price Performance Next 12 Mos.)
SAFETY 2 Above Average
(Scale: 1 Highest to 5 Lowest)
BETA 1.00 (1.00 = Market)

1986-88 PROJECTIONS
	Price	Gain	Ann'l Total Return
High	80	(+95%)	21%
Low	60	(+45%)	13%
© Value Line, Inc. 86-88E

Insider Decisions 1983
J A S O N D J F M A M J J A S
to Buy   0 0 1 0 0 1 0 0 2 1 4 5 0 1 9
to Sell 1 1 1 0 1 1 0 1 0 0 0 0 0 0 0

Options Trade On CBO

Institutional Decisions
	2Q'82	3Q'82	4Q'82	1Q'83	2Q'83
to Buy	124	140	106	111	132
to Sell	132	124	135	147	131
Hdg's(000)	151521	158726	164256	167459	169764

Percent 3.0
shares 2.0
traded 1.0

1968	1969	1970	1971	1972	1973	1974	1975	1976	1977	1978	1979	1980	1981	1982	1983	1984	1985		86-88E
26.71	28.74	29.98	32.15	35.00	39.12	41.50	43.02	46.86	53.51	55.63	55.19	79.89	78.64	85.43	100.30	109.25		Sales per sh (A)	137.35
1.70	1.78	1.84	2.11	2.34	2.57	2.09	2.17	2.71	3.21	3.51	3.24	2.81	2.72	3.41	4.60	5.25		"Cash Flow" per sh	7.25
1.37	1.44	1.51	1.78	1.97	2.16	1.62	1.65	2.19	2.62	2.86	2.54	1.92	2.06	2.46	3.60	4.20		Earnings per sh (B)	5.75
.65	.68	.68	.75	.81	.88	.93	.80	1.08	1.27	1.28	1.36	1.36	1.36	1.52	1.68		Div'ds Decl'd per sh ■ (C)	2.30
10.34	11.15	12.00	13.05	14.38	15.87	16.60	16.72	18.61	20.27	21.98	23.53	24.38	23.77	25.08	27.25	29.70		Book Value per sh	38.45
306.87	308.37	308.97	311.22	314.02	314.56	315.65	317.09	319.01	321.87	322.63	317.33	315.36	347.89	351.41	354.00	357.00		Common Shs Outst'g	364.00
24.2	23.8	22.1	25.1	29.5	22.1	20.8	20.1	15.5	11.2	8.0	7.6	8.6	8.4	8.8				Avg Ann'l P/E Ratio	12.0
4.1%	4.2%	4.5%	4.0%	3.5%	4.5%	4.8%	5.0%	6.5%	8.9%	12.5%	13.2%	11.6%	11.9%	11.4%	Bold figures are Value Line estimates			Avg Ann'l Earn's Yield	8.3%
2.0%	2.0%	2.0%	1.7%	1.4%	1.8%	2.7%	2.8%	2.4%	3.7%	5.5%	6.7%	8.2%	7.8%	6.3%				Avg Ann'l Div'd Yield	3.3%

CAPITAL STRUCTURE as of 12/31/82
Total Debt $8849.2 mill. Due in 5 Yrs $4178.4 mill.
LT Debt $5816.1 mill. LT Interest $550.0 mill.
Incl. $116.5 mill. capitalized leases.
(LT interest earned: 2.2x; Total interest
coverage: 1.7x) (40% of Cap'l)

Leases, Uncapitalized Annual rentals $212.0 mill.

Pension Liability None vs. $38.7 mill. in '81

Pfd Stock None

Common Stock 351,409,668 shs. (60% of Cap'l)

13101	13640	14950	17224	17946	17514	25195	27357	30020	35500	39000		Sales ($mill) A)	50000
3750	3776	3779	3763	3727	3680	3062	3239	3991	4100	4200		Number of Stores	4600
511.4	522.6	694.5	838.0	921.5	810.1	606.0	650.1	861.2	1270	1500		Net Profit ($mill)	2100
37.3%	42.9%	38.5%	29.8%	27.1%	21.3%	12.3%	1.5%	21.2%	22.0%	25.0%		Income Tax Rate	28.0%
3.9%	3.8%	4.7%	4.9%	5.1%	4.6%	2.4%	2.4%	2.9%	3.6%	3.8%		Net Profit Margin	4.2%
1979.3	1877.6	2215.1	2626.1	2533.4	2651.5	2721.6	3103.1	3146.1	3900	4200		Inventories ($mill) (D)	4800
6.6	7.3	6.8	6.6	7.1	6.6	9.3	8.8	9.5	6.3	6.3		Inventory Turnover (D)	6.5
2352.9	2646.5	3161.8	3582.9	3750.0	3994.4	1174.3	1575.2	1965.9	2150	2300		Working Cap'l ($mill) (D)	3200
1095.1	1326.3	1563.5	1990.3	2040.2	2473.5	2961.9	4779.3	5816.1	6100	6100		Long-Term Debt ($mill)(E)	6500
5241.1	5302.4	5936.9	6524.1	7091.6	7467.2	7688.8	8268.9	8812.4	9650	10600		Net Worth ($mill)	14000
8.6%	8.5%	9.9%	10.7%	11.0%	9.2%	7.0%	7.4%	9.1%	10.0%	10.5%		% Earned Total Cap'l	12.0%
9.8%	9.9%	11.7%	12.8%	13.0%	10.9%	7.9%	7.9%	9.8%	13.0%	14.0%		% Earned Net Worth	15.0%
4.2%	4.3%	7.4%	7.4%	7.2%	5.4%	2.4%	2.9%	4.6%	7.5%	8.5%		% Retained to Comm Eq	9.0%
57%	56%	37%	42%	44%	50%	70%	63%	53%	42%	40%		% All Div'ds to Net Prof	40%

CURRENT POSITION (D)
	1980	1981	12/31/82
Cash Assets	149.4	157.8	177.2
Receivables	221.8	198.5	160.8
Inventory (LIFO)	2604.8	2991.0	3092.2
Other	354.2	468.1	483.7
Current Assets	3330.2	3815.4	3913.9
Accts Payable	954.3	1135.4	1196.9
Debt Due	--	--	--
Other	715.8	726.9	751.1
Current Liab.	1670.1	1862.3	1948.0

ANNUAL RATES
of change (per sh)	Past 10 Yrs	Past 5 Yrs	Est'd '80-'82 to '86-'88
Sales	9.5%	11.0%	9.0%
"Cash Flow"	3.5%	2.0%	16.0%
Earnings	2.0%	0.0%	18.0%
Dividends	6.0%	8.0%	9.0%
Book Value	6.5%	5.5%	9.0%

QUARTERLY SALES ($ mill.) (A)
Cal- endar	Mar. 31	June 30	Sept. 30	Dec. 31	Full Year
1980	5471	6000	6462	7262	25195
1981	5835	6662	6826	8034	27357
1982	6436	7203	7508	8873	30020
1983	(E) 16133	8933	10434	35500
1984	8300	9500	9800	11400	39000

EARNINGS PER SHARE (A)
Cal- endar	Mar. 31	June 30	Sept. 30	Dec. 31	(B) Full Year
1980	.19	.42	.43	.88	1.92
1981	.17	.42	.42	1.05	2.06
1982	.20	.47	.48	1.31	2.46
1983	.47	.87	.81	1.45	3.60
1984	.60	1.00	.90	1.70	4.20

QUARTERLY DIVIDENDS PAID (C)
Cal- endar	Mar. 31	June 30	Sept. 30	Dec. 31	■Full Year
1979	.28	.32	.32	.32	1.24
1980	.32	.34	.34	.34	1.34
1981	.34	.34	.34	.34	1.36
1982	.34	.34	.34	.34	1.36
1983	.34	.38	.38		

BUSINESS: Sears, Roebuck & Co., the world's largest retailer of general merchandise, sells through retail stores, catalog, telephone sales offices, and independent catalog merchants. Credit sales over half of total. Also owns Allstate Insurance Company, a major underwriter. Equity in undistributed earnings of subsidiaries, principally Allstate Insurance, accounts for 51% of income. Acquired Coldwell Banker and Dean Witter in '81. Has 316,800 employees, 350,300 stockholders. Payroll costs: about 23% of sales. Employee pension fund owns 19% of stock; insiders under 1%. Chrmn.: E.R. Telling. Pres.: A.R. Boe. Inc.: New York. Address: Sears Tower, Chicago, Illinois 60684.

Earnings comparisons will be much harder beginning in the current quarter. For a start, there was a large LIFO credit in the final 1982 period due to overaccrual in earlier quarters. We expect a much smaller credit this year. And in late 1982 results started to benefit from much lower short-term interest rates than in the prior year. (Sears is a heavy user of short-term debt the year 'round to carry its inventories and receivables.) We expect such rates will average only a bit lower than a year earlier both in the final quarter and through 1984. In addition, earnings started to soar at the Dean Witter subsidiary a year ago as the bull market was getting underway. The company's ambitious store remodeling program (see below) might also put some pressure on the bottom line.

But they might still remain favorable. In the merchandising area, volume gains in recent months have been the best in a long time. Demand for durable goods, Sears' specialty, may continue strong due to the greater volume of home sales. The company's efforts to improve its merchandising strategy are also helping, we believe.

Financial services might also help the bottom line. Allstate profits should continue to reflect higher investment income. Allstate, Dean Witter, and Coldwell Banker may benefit from the addition of more financial service centers in Sears' stores. This strategy has apparently been successful since its launching in 1982; the number of such centers will be increased rapidly.

The store remodeling program may regain some market share for Sears. The company intends to upgrade most of its larger stores over the next five years to improve merchandise presentation, which might well increase the sales productivity of the chain. Progress in both the merchandising and financial service areas, which will be aided by the company's strong balance sheet and consumer franchise, lead us to project considerably higher share earnings by 1986-88 suggesting a good potential total return from a stock of such high quality. The stock is a good choice for the year ahead, too. M.S./L.K.

Restated Sales (and Pretax Profit Margins) by Business Line
	1980	1981	1982	1983
Merchandising	18579.7 (0.9%)	20091.8 (1.0%)	20549.3 (1.7%)	24500(2.2%)
Insurance	6165.4 (6.9%)	6776.8 (5.6%)	7487.1 (6.3%)	8000(7.0%)
Real Estate	146.3(14.7%)	165.1(51.7%)	530.0 (7.9%)	600(8.0%)
Financial Svcs.	269.6 (1.5%)	323.2(d7.8%)	1453.7 (0.2%)	2400(5.0%)
Company Total	25161.0 (2.4%)	27357.0 (2.4%)	30020.0 (2.9%)	35500(3.6%)

(A) Fiscal yr. ends Jan. 31 of fol. cal. yr. through '80. Calendar yr. thereafter. Incl. discontinued subs. from '80. Incl. Coldwell Banker & Dean Witter from 12/31/81. (B) Avg. shs. Next egs. rep't due late Feb. Est'd current cost egs/sh.: '82, $1.30. (C) Next div'd meet'g about Feb. 7. Goes ex about Feb. 17. Div'd paym't dates: Jan. 3, Apr. 1, July 1, Oct. 1. ■ Div'd reinvest. plan av'ble. (D) Retailing only. (E) 6 mos. Incl. 100% of Seraton Banker.

Company's Financial Strength	A
Stock's Price Stability	80
Price Growth Persistence	5
Earnings Predictability	70

prices, and a weekly relative strength series. The books for the NYSE and ASE are available from 1962 on; the OTC books begin in 1968.

Brokerage Firm Reports.   Many brokerage firms prepare reports on individual firms. In some cases, these are rather objective and only contain basic information, while some contain specific recommendations, usually regarding purchase.

Investment Magazines

Forbes is published twice monthly and contains 12 to 14 articles on individual companies and industries. Several regular columnists who discuss the economy, the aggregate money and stock markets, and the commodity market are also published regularly.

Financial World is likewise published twice a month and generally contains about six articles on companies, industries, and the overall market and a large number of regular features on taxes and options. It also has a section containing market data.

The Wall Street Transcript is a composite of sources of information other than market quotations and the like which is published every Monday. It contains texts of speeches made at analysts' meetings, copies of brokerage house reports on companies and industries, and interviews with corporate officials. It also includes discussions of forthcoming new stock issues.

The Media General Financial Weekly is likewise published every Monday and contains a series of feature articles and columns. Of primary interest is a comprehensive set of financial and statistical information on 3,400 common stocks, including every common stock listed on the NYSE and ASE and over 700 OTC issues. There are also charts on 60 major industry groups.

OTC Review is a monthly publication devoted to the analysis and discussion of stocks traded on the OTC market. It usually contains an analysis of an industry traded by numerous OTC companies and a discussion of three or four individual firms. In addition, extended earnings reports on OTC firms, name changes, stock exchange listings, and statistics on OTC trading (price and volume) are published in the review.

Fortune is published bi-weekly by Time, Inc. It contains extensive articles on the economy, politics, individual companies, securities markets, and personal investing. The magazine is well-known for its annual special report on the *Fortune 500* and also the *Fortune 1000* that contains several financial items for the largest industrial business firms in the country. There is also a listing of large nonindustrial firms and, finally, a listing of major foreign companies.

Money is published monthly by Time, Inc. and deals specifically with topics of interest to individual investors. This includes articles on individual companies and general investment suggestions (e.g., "how to determine your net worth;" "the why and how of investing in foreign securities"). Also, each issue presents an actual financial planning discussion with an individual or couple.

Pension and Investment Age.   This newspaper of corporate and institutional investing is published every other Monday. It is intended for those who are involved in pension investing either as a corporate manager or as a money manager who manages pension funds assets. The emphasis is on stories and interviews related to pension fund management. There is substantial consideration of personnel changes.

Academic Journals.   The material in academic journals differs from that in investment magazines in timeliness and general orientation. Investment magazines are concerned with the *current* investment environment and with providing advice for current action. They are generally nonquantitative. The articles in academic journals are longer, more theoretical and quantitative in approach, and typically not expected to be immediately useful. They deal with long-run implications for investments.

Journal of Finance is a quarterly published by the American Finance Association. The articles are almost all by academicians and rather theoretical and empirical. The typical issue will include 15 articles, notes and comments, and book reviews.

Journal of Financial and Quantitative Analysis is a quarterly published by the Western Finance Association and the University of Washington. It is very similar to the *Journal of Finance* in that almost all articles are by academicians. It differs in that it contains fewer articles in the area of monetary economics.

Journal of Financial Economics was first published in May 1974 by North Holland Publishing Company in collaboration with the Graduate School of Management of the University of Rochester, New York. The intent of the quarterly is to publish academic research in the areas of consumption and investment decisions under uncertainty, portfolio analysis, efficient markets, and the normative theory of financial management.

Financial Analysts Journal is published six times a year by the Financial Analysts Federation. An issue contains six or seven articles of interest to practicing financial analysts and/or portfolio managers, a regular feature on securities regulation, and book reviews.

Institutional Investor is published monthly by Institutional Investors Systems and is aimed at professional investors and portfolio managers with emphasis on what is happening to the investment industry. It is written by a professional staff.

Journal of Portfolio Management is likewise published by Institutional Investors Systems. It is published quarterly with the avowed intent of being a forum for academic research of use to the practicing portfolio manager. Over half the articles are written by academicians but are written to be read by the practitioner.

Financial Management is published quarterly by the Financial Management Association. It is intended for executives and academicians interested in the financial management of a firm, but it also contains investment-related articles on such topics as stock splits, dividend policy, mergers, and stock listings.

The Financial Review is a journal currently published three times a year by the Eastern Finance Association. It is a general finance journal directed at the academic community with about half the articles in a typical issue concerned with investments and portfolio management.

Journal of Financial Research is a joint publication of the Southern Finance Association and the Southwestern Finance Association. It is published three times a year and contains articles on financial management, investments, financial institutions, capital market theory, and portfolio theory.

The C.F.A. Digest is published quarterly by the Institute of Chartered Financial Analysts. Its purpose is to provide, as a service to members of the investment community, abstracts of published articles considered to be of interest to financial analysts and portfolio managers from a wide variety of academic and nonacademic journals.

Other General Business Journals.   There are a number of general business and economics journals that include articles on finance and some specifically on investments. One of the foremost is the *Journal of Business* published by the University of Chicago, which has contained some outstanding articles in the area of investments by members of the university's faculty. Other journals to consider include: *Quarterly Review of Economics and Business* (University of Illinois); *Review of Business and Economic Research* (University of New Orleans); *Journal of Business Research* (North Holland Publishing Co.); *American Economic Review* (American Economic Association); *Journal of Political Economy* (University of Chicago); *Bell Journal of Economics* (American Telephone and Telegraph).

COMPUTERIZED DATA SOURCES

In addition to the numerous published sources of data, some of the financial service firms have developed computerized data sources. Again, owing to space limitations, only the major sources will be discussed.

Compustat.   This is a computerized data bank of financial data developed by Standard & Poor's and currently handled by a subsidiary, Investors Management Services (P.O. Box 239, Denver, CO 80201). The Compustat tapes contain 20 years of data for approximately 2,220 listed industrial companies, 1,000 OTC companies, 175 utilities, 120 banks, and 500 Canadian firms. There are also quarterly tapes that contain 20 years of quarterly financial data for over 2,000 industrial firms and 12 years of quarterly data for banks and utilities. The specific financial data on the annual tapes includes almost every possible item from a firm's balance sheet and income statement as well as stock market data (stock prices and trading volume).

Value Line Data Base.   This contains historical annual and quarterly financial and market data for 1,600 industrial and finance companies. The annual data begins in 1954 and quarterly data starts in 1963. In addition to historical data, there is an estimate of dividend and earnings for the coming year.

University of Chicago Stock Price Tapes.   The Center for Research in Security Prices (CRSP) at the University of Chicago (Graduate School of Business, Chicago, IL 60637) has developed a set of monthly stock price tapes and daily stock prices. The monthly tapes contain month-end prices from January 1926 to the present (updated annually) for every stock listed on the NYSE. Stock prices are adjusted for all stock splits, dividends, and any other capital changes. There is also a daily stock price tape that contains the daily high, low, and close since 1960 for every stock listed on the NYSE.

Media General Data Bank.   This is provided by Media General Financial Services, Inc. (P.O. Box 26991, Richmond, VA 23261). The data bank includes current price and volume data plus major corporate financial data on 2,000 major companies. In addition, extensive daily price and volume history on all NYSE and ASE listed stocks, as well as a large number of major OTC stocks plus comparable data on the principal market indicator series, are included.

ISL Daily Stock Price Tapes.   These are prepared by Interactive Data Corporation (122 E. 42nd St., New York, NY 10017). The tapes are issued quarterly and contain the same information that is contained in the *Daily Stock Price Records* published by Standard & Poor's and discussed earlier in this chapter.

SUMMARY

The intent of this chapter is to introduce the reader to the major sources of information on the economy, the aggregate securities markets, alternative industries, and individual firms. It should be recognized that this is *only a beginning*. It is virtually impossible to discuss all sources without writing a separate book. The reader is advised to use this information as a starting point and attempt to spend time in a university library examining these and the many other sources available. Three books that would help in this regard are:

Paul Wasserman, ed. *Encyclopedia of Business Information Sources.* 3d ed. Detroit: Gale Research Co., 1976.

P. M. Daniells. *Business Information Sources.* Berkeley, CA: University of California Press, 1976.

Sylvia, Michanie. *Course Syllabus for Information Souces of Business and Economics.* Brooklyn, NY: Pratt Institute School of Library and Information Science, 1977.

QUESTIONS

1. Assume that you want information on the gross national product for the past ten years. Name at least *three* sources of such information.
2. Name two sources of information on rates of exchange with major foreign countries.
3. Assume you are interested in the steel and auto industry and want to compare production for these two industries to overall industrial production for the economy. How would you do it? What data would you use? Where would you get the data? Be specific.
4. You are told that there is a relationship between growth in the money supply and stock price movements. Where would you go to get the data to verify this relationship?
5. You are an analyst for Hot Stock Investment Company, and the head of research tells you he just got a tip on the Baron Corporation, a stock that is traded on the OTC. He wants you to gather some data on the company's sales, earnings, and recent stock price movements. Where would you go for this information? Name several sources because the company may not be big enough to be included in some of them.
6. As an individual investor, discuss three publications you believe you should subscribe to (besides *The Wall Street Journal*). In your discussion indicate what is contained in these publications and why it is appropriate for you as an individual investor.
7. As the director of the newly established research department of a bank, discuss the first three investment services that you will subscribe to and indicate why these are first.
8. Select one company from the NYSE, the ASE, and the OTC and look up the name and address of the financial officer you would write to obtain recent financial reports for each firm.

SOURCES OF INVESTMENT INFORMATION

American Stock Exchange, 86 Trinity Place, New York, New York 10006.

Business Statistics may be obtained from Superintendent of Documents, U.S. Government Printing Office, Washington, D.C. 20402. Approximate price, $7.

Dow-Jones & Co., publishers of *The Wall Street Journal* and *Barron's.* Subscriptions office: 200 Burnett Rd., Chicopee, Massachusetts 01021.

Dow-Jones Handbook. The handbook is published annually and can be obtained from Dow-Jones Books, P.O. Box 455, Chicopee, Massachusetts 01021. Approximate cost is $5 a book.

Economic Indicators. Available from the Superintendent of Documents (address as above). Approximate price, $12/year.

Economic Report of the President may be obtained from Superintendent of Documents (address as above). Approximate price, $5.

Federal Reserve Bulletin may be obtained from the Division of Administrative Services, Board of Governors of the Federal Reserve System, Washington, D.C. 20551. Approximate cost, $20/year.

Moody's Investor's Services, Inc., 99 Church Street, New York, New York 10007.

New York Stock Exchange, 11 Wall Street, New York, New York 10005.

Quarterly Financial Report. Available from Superintendent of Documents (address as above). Approximate cost, $12/year.

Standard & Poor's Corporation, 345 Hudson Street, New York, New York 10014.

Statistical Abstract of the United States may be obtained from the Superintendent of Documents. Approximate cost, $12 (cloth); $9 (paper).

Statistical Bulletin may be subscribed to through the Superintendent of Documents. Approximate cost, $20/year.

Survey of Current Business may be obtained from Superintendent of Documents.

Value Line Services. These are published by Arnold Bernhard and Company, Inc., 5 East 44th Street, New York, New York 10017.

Part 2

Modern Developments in Investment Theory

Before any analytical study can be attempted, a theoretical framework must be established. This is as true for the analysis of investments as it is for any other academic discipline. In the area of investments, several major theories that affected the way in which the entire subject is approached have been developed in the last 25 years. It is with these theories that Part 2 is concerned.

In the late 1950s the random walk hypothesis was developed. Most of the research on this theory dealt with price changes over time, reaching the general conclusion that stock price changes were similar to a random series. This early work eventually became part of a much larger theory known as the efficient market hypothesis that considered not only stock price changes alone, but also these changes as they related to different sets of information. Studies related to the efficient market hypothesis (EMH) are important because of what they can tell us about our financial markets. Therefore, in Chapter 7 we will examine the EMH and discuss numerous studies that produced findings in support of various forms of the hypothesis, as well as some studies that have *not* supported it. We will also consider the implications of the hypothesis for various segments of the investment industry. These implications tend to be misunderstood, so you are urged to read the section carefully and keep an open mind.

Another major development in investment theory, which also affected financial management, was the basic portfolio model developed by Harry Markowitz in 1954. Markowitz indicated the importance of diversification in terms of reducing the overall risk of a portfolio and derived a risk measure for individual securities. This basic portfolio model is presented in detail in Chapter 8.

In 1964, William Sharpe extended the basic portfolio model into a general equilibrium model that generated an alternative risk measure for all risky assets. Chapter 9 contains a fairly detailed discussion of these developments and an explanation of the relevant risk measure implied by the Sharpe model, generally referred to as the capital asset pricing model (CAPM). We have introduced the CAPM at this early stage because the risk measure it generates is subsequently used in all analysis.

Chapter 7   Efficient Capital Markets

E fficient capital markets are considered at this point for two reasons. First, since we have already discussed capital markets, it seems natural to consider how efficiently they operate. Second, several *very important implications* for security valuation and portfolio management are derived from the existence of efficient capital markets. Some of these are not very pleasant to accept, so it is crucial for the reader to become aware of them early and avoid "future shock." Also, this knowledge is useful in the subsequent chapters on analysis.

There are four major sections in this chapter. The initial section contains a discussion of why capital markets should be efficient. In the second section we will consider the alternative efficient market hypotheses and the tests of the hypotheses. The results for a number of the studies on this topic are presented and discussed in the third section. The final section deals with the implications of the results for technicians, fundamental security analysts, and portfolio managers.

RATIONALE OF THE EFFICIENT CAPITAL MARKETS THEORY

While the definition of an efficient capital market is relatively straightforward, we often fail to consider *why* capital markets should be expected to be efficient. What conditions do we assume exist in order to have an efficient capital market?

An initial, and very important, premise of an efficient market is that there are a large number of profit-maximizing participants concerned with the analysis and valuation of securities and who operate independently of each other. A second assumption is that *new information regarding securities comes to the market in a random fashion* and the announcements over time are generally independent from one another. The third assumption of an efficient market is especially crucial. *Investors adjust security prices rapidly to reflect the effect of new information.* While the price adjustment made is not always perfect, it is

163

unbiased. (That is, sometimes there is an overadjustment or an underadjustment, but you don't know which it will be.) It is contended that the attempt to adjust the security price takes place rapidly because *the number of profit maximizing investors is large*. The combined effect of (1) information coming in a random, independent fashion, and (2) *numerous* investors who adjust stock prices rapidly to reflect this new information is that *price changes are independent and random*. A crucial point of this discussion is that the adjustment process requires a large number of investors who follow the stock, analyze the impact of new information, and buy or sell the stock to adjust the price to reflect the new information. This implies that efficient markets require some minimum amount of trading and that *more trading should result in more rapid price adjustment*— i.e., more efficiency. We will return to this concept when we discuss some anomalies regarding the efficient market hypothesis.

Finally, because security prices adjust to all new information and, therefore, supposedly reflect all public information at any point in time, *the security prices that prevail at any point in time should be an unbiased reflection of all currently available information*. The price of a security at any point in time is an unbiased estimate of the true intrinsic value of the security at that point in time given all the information available. Based upon the foregoing discussion, *an efficient market is one in which security prices adjust rapidly to the infusion of new information, and current stock prices fully reflect all available information including the risk involved*. Therefore, the returns implicit in the price reflect the risk involved, so *the expected return is consistent with risk*.

ALTERNATIVE EFFICIENT MARKET HYPOTHESES

A great deal of the early work in the area of efficient markets was done under the random walk hypothesis and contained extensive empirical analysis without much theory behind it. The first real attempt to synthesize theory and organize the numerous empirical studies was made by Eugene Fama in a 1970 *Journal of Finance* article,[1] which was the initial presentation of the efficient market theory in terms of the "fair game" model.

Expected Return or Fair Game Model[2]

Unlike work done under the random walk hypothesis, which dealt with price movement over time, the fair game model deals with price at a specified period. It assumes that the price of a security fully reflects all available information at that period. The model requires that the price formation process be specified in enough detail so that it is possible to indicate what is meant by *fully reflect*. Most of the available models of equilibrium prices formulate prices in terms of rates of

[1] Eugene F. Fama, "Efficient Capital Markets: A Review of Theory and Empirical Work," *Journal of Finance* 25 no. 2 (May 1970): 383–417.

[2] This section is drawn heavily from Fama, ibid.

return that are dependent on alternative definitions of risk. All such expected
return theories of price formation can be described notationally as follows:

(7.1) $$E(\tilde{p}_{j,t+1} \mid \phi_t) = [1 + E(\tilde{r}_{j,t+1} \mid \phi_t)]p_{j,t},$$

where:

$E =$ expected value operator

$p_{j,t} =$ price of security j at time t

$p_{j,t+1} =$ price of security j at time $t + 1$

$r_{j,t+1} =$ the one period percent rate of return for security j during period $t + 1$

$\phi_t =$ the set of information that is assumed to be "fully reflected" in the security price at time t.

Equation 7.1 indicates that the expected price of security j, given the full set of information available at time $t(\phi_t)$, is equal to the current price times one plus the expected return on security j, given the set of available information. This expected future return should reflect the set of information available at t, which includes the state of the world at time t, including all current and past values of *any relevant variables* such as earnings, the GNP, etc. In addition, it is assumed that this information set includes knowledge of *all the relevant relationships among variables*—i.e., how alternative economic series relate to each other and how they relate to security prices.

If equilibrium market prices can be stated in terms of expected returns that "fully reflect" the information set ϕ_t, this implies that it is *not possible* to derive trading systems or investment strategies based on this current information set and experience returns beyond what should be expected on the basis of risk. Thus, let us define $x_{j,t+1}$ as the difference between the actual price in $t + 1$ and the expected price in $t + 1$:

(7.2) $$x_{j,t+1} = p_{j,t+1} - E(p_{j,t+1} \mid \phi_t).$$

Equation 7.2 can be described as a definition of *excess market value* for security j, because it is the difference between the *actual* price and the *expected* price projected at t on the basis of the information set ϕ_t. In an efficient market:

(7.3) $$E(\tilde{x}_{j,t+1} \mid \phi_t) = 0.$$

This equation indicates that the market reflects a "fair game" with respect to the information set ϕ. In such a fair game market, investors can acquire the securities at current prices and be confident that these prices fully reflect all available information and are consistent with the risk involved. Fama divided the overall efficient market hypothesis and empirical tests into three categories depending upon the information set involved.

Weak Form Efficient Market Hypothesis

The weak form efficient market hypothesis assumes that current stock prices fully reflect all *stock market* information including the historical sequence of prices, price changes, trading volume, and any other market information such as odd lot transactions. Because current prices already reflect all past price changes and any other stock market information, this hypothesis implies that there should be no relationship between past price changes and future price changes; i.e., price changes are independent. Therefore, any trading rule (i.e., the conditions under which an investor will buy or sell stock) that depends upon past price changes or past market data to predict future price changes should be of little value.

Semistrong Form Efficient Market Hypothesis

The semistrong form efficient market hypothesis asserts that *security prices adjust rapidly to the release of all new public information;* i.e., stock prices fully reflect *all public* information. Obviously the semistrong hypothesis encompasses the weak form hypothesis because all public information includes all market information (stock prices, trading volume, etc.), plus all nonmarket information, such as earnings, stock splits, economic news, political news. A direct implication of this hypothesis is that investors who act on important new information *after* it is public cannot derive above average profits from the transaction, considering the cost of trading, because the security price already reflects the effect of the new public information.

Strong Form Efficient Market Hypothesis

The strong form efficient market hypothesis contends that stock prices fully reflect *all* information (public and otherwise). Hence, it implies that no group of investors has a monopolistic access to information relevant to the formation of prices. Therefore, *no group of investors should be able to consistently derive above average profits.* The strong form hypothesis encompasses *both* the weak and semistrong forms. Further, the strong form hypothesis requires not only efficient markets (where prices adjust rapidly to the release of new public information), but it also requires *perfect* markets in which *all information is available to everyone at the same time.* This form of the EMH contends that because all information is immediately available to everyone and is rapidly discounted by everyone, no group has monopolistic access to important new information and, therefore, *nobody* can derive above average profits.

ALTERNATIVE EFFICIENT MARKET HYPOTHESES: TESTS AND RESULTS

Weak Form Hypothesis

There have been two groups of tests for the weak form efficient market hypothesis. The first category involves statistical tests of independence between stock price changes. The second group entails specific testing of trading rules that attempt to generate investment decisions on the basis of past market information as opposed to a simple buy-and-hold policy (i.e., simply buying stock at the beginning of a test period and holding it to the end).

Statistical Tests of Independence.   As discussed earlier, stock price changes over time should be independent because new information comes to the market in a random, independent fashion, and stock prices adjust rapidly to this new information. Therefore, in an efficient capital market, stock price changes should be independent and random.

Two major statistical tests have been employed to verify this. First were the autocorrelation tests which correlated price changes over time to see if there was independence; i.e., was there significant positive or negative correlation in price changes over time? Is the percentage price change on day t correlated with the percentage price change on day $t-1$, $t-2$, or $t-3$?[3] Those who support the theory of efficient capital markets would expect insignificant correlations between all such combinations.

Analysis of the serial correlations between stock price changes has been done by various authors for several different intervals including one day, four days, nine days, and 16 days.[4] The results consistently indicated *insignificant* correlation in stock price changes over time. The typical range of correlation coefficients was from $+0.10$ to -0.10, but the correlations were typically not statistically significant. Individual stocks had a tendency toward slight negative correlation in stock price changes. In contrast, price changes for aggregate market indicator series tended to have a slight positive correlation. Lawrence Fisher of the University of Chicago has shown that this difference in correlation is probably caused by the fact that the numerous stocks in the market indicator series close at different points in time during a day. Therefore, stocks that close early have some lag in price adjustment to late news that is picked up the following day. In any case, the empirical evidence from serial correlation tests consistently indicated that *stock price changes over time are in general statistically independent.* These results imply that one *cannot* use past price changes alone to project future price changes.

The second statistical test of independence included "runs" tests. Given a series of price changes, each price change is designated a plus $(+)$ if it is an increase or a minus $(-)$ if it is a decrease. The result is a set of pluses and minuses as follows: $+++-+--++--++$. A run occurs when there is no difference between two changes; two or three *consecutive* positive or consecutive negative price changes is one run. When the price change is to a different

---

[3] For a discussion of tests of independence see Ya-lun Chou, *Statistical Analysis,* 2d ed. (New York: Holt Rinehart and Winston, 1975), pp. 540–542.

[4] Sidney S. Alexander, "Price Movements in Speculative Markets: Trends or Random Walks," *Industrial Management Review,* 2 no. 2 (May 1961): 7–26; Eugene F. Fama, "The Behavior of Stock Market Prices," *Journal of Business,* 38 no. 1 (January 1965): 34–105; Maurice G. Kendall, "The Analysis of Economic Time Series," *Journal of the Royal Statistical Society,* 96 (1953): 11–25; Arnold Moore, "A Statistical Analysis of Common Stock Prices," (Ph.D. dissertation, University of Chicago Graduate School of Business, 1962): Eugene Fama and James MacBeth. "Risk, Return and Equilibrium: Empirical Tests," *Journal of Political Economy,* 81 no. 3 (May–June 1973): 607–636.

sign (e.g., a negative price change followed by a positive price change), the run is ended and a new run begins.[5] Even in a series of purely random numbers, one would expect some instances of runs of two, three, or four changes. Therefore, one should not expect the number of runs to equal the number of observations. In fact, the expected number of runs for a random series is $1/3(2n-1)$, where n is the number of observations.[6] If there are too many or too few runs for a given series (the actual number deviates significantly from the expected number noted above), it is probably not a random series, because there is too much correlation in the signs. Specifically, if the actual number of runs is significantly *less* than expected, there is *positive* correlation in successive signs. In contrast, if the actual number of runs is significantly *more* than expected, this implies *negative* correlation in the signs. To test for independence, one calculates the number of runs for a given series and compares this with a table that provides the limits above and below the expected number for a random series of that size.

Tests of stock price runs likewise indicated independence in stock price changes over time. While positive price changes were occasionally followed by positive price changes and vice versa, a number of such cases can be explained by a random model in which you would expect some positive and negative runs. The actual number of runs for stock price series consistently fell into the range expected for a random series. Therefore, these statistical tests likewise supported the notion that stock price changes over time are independent. These statistical tests for independence were repeated on the OTC market and the results likewise supported the EMH.[7]

While the evidence of daily, weekly, and monthly data consistently supported the weak form EMH, the evidence of individual transaction price changes is not supportive. A well-known study by Niederhoffer and Osborn examined price changes in terms of individual transactions on the NYSE and found significant serial correlation.[8] These correlation results were confirmed in a study by Ken Carey.[9] None of the authors attempted to show that the dependence in price movements could be used to derive above average risk-adjusted returns. Therefore, apparently there is some significant correlation among individual transactions caused by the market-making activities of the specialist, but it is highly unlikely that this small imperfection could be used by an investor to derive excess profits after transaction costs.

Tests of Trading Rules.   The second group of tests of the weak form hypothesis were prompted by the assertion of technical analysts that the statistical tests described above were too rigid to pinpoint the very intricate price patterns examined by technical analysts. Supposedly analysts do not believe it is a me-

---

[5] For the details of a runs test see Ya-lun Chou, *Statistical Analysis,* op. cit, pp. 537–539.

[6] Ya-lun Chou, *Statistical Analysis,* 2d ed. (New York: Holt Rinehart and Winston, 1975).

[7] Robert L. Hagerman and Richard D. Richmond, "Random Walks, Martingales and the OTC," *Journal of Finance,* 28 no. 4 (September 1973): 897–909.

[8] Victor Niederhoffer and M. F. Osborn, "Market-Making and Reversal on the Stock Exchange," *Journal of American Statistical Association,* 61 no. 316 (December 1966): 897–916.

[9] Kenneth Carey, "A Model of Individual Transactions Stock Prices," (Ph.D. dissertation, University of Kansas, 1971)

chanical number of positive or negative price changes that signal a move to a new equilibrium, but a general consistency in trend over time that might include both positive and negative changes. Technical analysts believed their trading rules were too sophisticated and complicated to be simulated by a rigid statistical test. Therefore, investigators attempted to examine alternative technical trading rules specifically through simulation. Advocates of an efficient market hypothesized that investors using any technical trading rule that asserted that stock prices moved in trends could not derive above average profits (i.e., rates of return greater than returns from a buy-and-hold policy) *if the trading rule depended solely on past market information* whether it be price data, volume data, or what have you.

The trading rule studies were intended to simulate the conditions under which a specific technical system was used to make decisions based on public market information and to compare the investment results derived from such a simulation, including commission costs, to the results from a simple buy-and-hold policy. Three major pitfalls can negate the results of such studies: (1) *only use data that is publicly available* in the decision rule; e.g., the earnings for a firm as of December 31 may not be *publicly* available until April 1; (2) when determining the returns from a trading rule, be sure to *include all transactions costs* involved in implementing the trading strategy. This is important, because most trading rules involve many more transactions than a simple buy-and-hold policy does; (3) *be sure that the final results are risk-adjusted.* It is possible the trading rule simply helps in the selection of high-risk securities that should experience higher returns.

Two operational problems have been encountered in these tests. First, trading rules require a fair amount of personal interpretation. Therefore, it is often difficult, if not impossible, to simulate a trading rule mechanically. In many cases two technical analysts looking at the same set of data might differ in their projections. Therefore, *it is not possible to test some technical rules.* The second problem is that *there is an almost infinite number of potential trading rules.* Therefore, it is not possible to test all of them. As a result, only a number of the better known technical trading rules that could be simulated have been tested.

Also, the tests may be somewhat biased because the studies have concentrated on the simple trading rules which many technicians contend are rather naive. In addition, the authors almost always employ readily available data from the NYSE. This means the sample is typically biased toward well-known, heavily traded stocks that *should* enjoy efficient markets. Specifically, our initial discussion pointed out that markets *should* be efficient if one assumes a large number of aggressive, profit-maximizing investors who attempt to adjust stock prices to reflect new information. This implies that *efficiency is dependent on trading;* i.e., the more trading in a security, the more efficient the market should be, up to a point. (Beyond some fairly high volume, it would probably be difficult to measure differences in efficiency). Alternatively, in cases where there is very little trading activity, one could envision a lack of complete efficiency because there is not much interest in the security, and, therefore, there is not adequate trading activity to move the security to the new equilibrium price that reflects the new information.

The most popular trading technique has been to use filter rules. (A filter is set for a given stock, which is traded when the price change exceeds the filter specified.) As an example, one might set up a 5 percent filter for a stock based upon past movements. When the stock has risen 5 percent from some base, it is hypothesized by the technical analyst that this movement indicates a "breakout" and that stock prices will continue to rise. Therefore, technical traders using this filter would acquire the stocks and would expect to take advantage of the continued rise. If the stock declines 5 percent from some peak price, technicians would identify this as a breakout on the downside and would expect the price to continue to decline. Therefore, they would sell the stock acquired previously and possibly would sell it short, based upon the expectation of a further price decline.

Studies of this trading rule have used a range of filters from very small (one-half percent) to very large (50 percent), and they have generated consistent results which indicated that by using *small* filters and *not* taking account of trading commission, one *can* derive above average profits. Such results are consistent with the small correlation in price changes discussed earlier, although the use of small filters resulted in numerous trades and substantial commissions. Therefore, when trading commissions were considered, all the trading *profits* turned to *losses*. These conclusions were true for the Alexander studies and also for the Fama and Blume studies.[10]

Trading techniques have been simulated using past market data other than stock prices. Trading rules have been devised that used odd lot figures, advanced-decline ratios, and short sales or short positions. In a few cases there were slight profits, but generally the simulations using these trading rules did *not* outperform a buy-and-hold policy after taking account of commissions. An article by George Pinches reviewed a number of these studies.[11] Based upon this review, Pinches concluded:

> While the results of mechanical trading rules that simulate technical trading rules are not entirely consistent, it appears that these findings could support a very narrow interpretation of the random-walk hypothesis. If mechanical trading rules could be devised that consistently outperformed a random buy-and-hold policy, then substantial proof would exist that the random-walk hypothesis is incorrect. However, with some exceptions, the studies of mechanical trading rules do not indicate that profits can be generated by these rules.[12]

Therefore, it is probably safe to say that the great bulk of the evidence generated by simulating mechanical trading rules supports the weak form of the efficient market hypothesis.

[10] Alexander, "Price Movements in Speculative Markets;" Sidney S. Alexander, "Price Movements in Speculative Markets: Trends or Random Walks, Number 2," *Industrial Management Review,* 5 (Spring 1964): 25–46; Eugene F. Fama and Marshall Blume, "Filter Rules and Stock Market Trading Profits," *Journal of Business,* 39 no. 1 (January 1966 Supplement): 226–241.

[11] George Pinches, "The Random Walk Hypothesis and Technical Analysis," *Financial Analysts Journal,* 26 no. 2 (March–April 1970): 104–110.

[12] Ibid., p. 108.

Semistrong Form Hypothesis

Recall that the semistrong EMH asserts that security prices adjust rapidly to the release of *all new public information;* i.e., stock prices fully reflect all public information. Given the statement of the hypothesis and the direct implication, studies of the semistrong form of the EMH have involved one or both of the following:

1. Examination of price movements around the time of an important announcement in an attempt to see when the expected price adjustment took place: did security prices adjust *before* the announcement was made; did prices adjust *during* the announcement period; or did prices appear to adjust *after* the announcement? The efficient market hypothesis would imply that prices adjust either *before* the announcement, because of news leaks or some such phenomenon, or *during* the period of announcement.

2. Examination of the potential for above average profit assuming an investor acted after the information became public. Specifically, one would assume an investor acquired the security after an announcement was made public and would determine whether such an investor would have enjoyed above average risk-adjusted profits compared to those from a buy-and-hold policy after taking into account transactions costs.

Adjustment for Market Effects.   Whether an analyst is going to use one or both tests of the semistrong EMH, it is necessary to adjust the individual stock price movements (or the security returns) for aggregate price movements (or market returns) during the period considered. The point is, a 5 percent price change in a stock during the period surrounding an announcement is not meaningful until you know what the aggregate stock market did during the same period and how this stock normally acts under such conditions; e.g., if the market experienced a 10 percent change, the 5 percent change may be lower than expected. Authors have generally recognized the need to make such adjustments and typically assumed (pre-1970) that the individual stocks should experience returns or percentage price changes equal to those of the aggregate market. Therefore, the adjustment process simply entailed subtracting the market return from the actual return to derive "abnormal" returns as follows:

(7.4) $$AR_{it} = R_{it} - R_{mt},$$

where:

AR_{it} = the abnormal rate of return on security i during period t

R_{it} = the rate of return on security i during period t

R_{mt} = the rate of return on a market index during period t.

Using the previous example in which the stock experienced a 5 percent price increase and the market increased 10 percent, the abnormal price change would be minus 5 percent.

Fama, Fisher, Jensen, and Roll Study. An alternative adjustment technique was suggested by Fama, Fisher, Jensen, and Roll (FFJR) in a study that examined the impact of stock splits.[13] Based upon work in capital market theory, the study contended that the market adjustment procedure should recognize that each individual security has a unique relationship with the market. A given stock will tend to rise or decline more or less than the market.[14] This unique relationship between a stock and the market can be derived by computing a regression of stock returns and market returns for a period prior to and subsequent to a significant economic event as follows:

$$(7.5) \qquad R_{it} = a_i + \beta_i R_{mt} + \epsilon,$$

R_{it} = the rate of return on security i during period t

a_i = the intercept or constant for security i in the regression

β_i = the regression slope coefficient for security i equal to cov_{im}/σ^2_m

R_{mt} = the rate of return on a market index during period t

ϵ = a random error term that sums to zero.

Given that the deviations from the regression line are random, one would expect them to sum to zero over long periods of time. Given the parameters of this model, the expected return for a stock can be derived for a specified market rate of return. As an example, assume the following values for a sample firm:

$$a_i = -.01$$

$$\beta_i = 1.3.$$

In this instance, if the market return (R_{mt}) during a specified period was 8 percent, the expected return for stock i would be as follows:

$$E(R_{it}) = -.01 + 1.3\,(.08)$$

$$= -.01 + .104$$

$$= .094.$$

In turn, the abnormal return (AR_{it}) would be equal to the *actual* return minus the *expected* return:

$$(7.6) \qquad AR_{it} = R_{it} - E(R_{it}).$$

[13] E. F. Fama, L. Fisher, M. Jensen, and R. Roll, "The Adjustment of Stock Prices to New Information," *International Economic Review,* 10 no. 1 (February 1969): 1–21.

[14] For a discussion of why the response to market changes should be different and the relevance of the difference, see William F. Sharpe, "Capital Asset Prices: A Theory of Market Equilibrium under Conditions of Risk," *Journal of Finance,* 19 no. 3 (September 1964): 425–442. For subsequent analysis of beta coefficient, see Marshall E. Blume, "On the Assessment of Risk," *Journal of Finance,* 26 no. 1 (March 1971): 1–10. This notion is discussed in detail in Chapter 9.

In this example, if the actual return for the stock during this period was 12 percent, the abnormal return would be:

$$AR_{it} = .12 - .094$$
$$= .026.$$

During this period, the stock experienced a rate of return that was 2.6 percent more than expected where expectations were based upon what the aggregate market did and the stock's relationship with the market. The main point of this adjustment technique is that over a long period, these abnormal returns *should cancel out;* i.e., they should sum to zero. Alternatively, if there is significant new information that is positive or negative, it should be reflected in these abnormal returns. Therefore, it is possible to examine the impact of an announcement or event *and its timing* by examining *what happens to these abnormal returns* surrounding the announcement or event.

As an example, if a firm announced a significant increase in earnings, it would not only be possible to determine the impact of this announcement on the security returns, (i.e., were the abnormal returns positive) but also to determine *when* the impact took place. The typical procedure is to examine the abnormal returns during individual periods surrounding an event and to derive a series of *cumulative* abnormal returns to determine the *total* impact of the event.

To summarize, various tests of the semistrong EMH either examine abnormal price changes surrounding the announcements of new information to see when the price adjustment took place, or they examine abnormal rates of return for a period immediately after an announcement to determine whether it would have been possible for an investor to derive above average risk-adjusted rates of return. The numerous studies in this area are best organized in terms of specific events, i.e., announcements of stock splits, exchange listings, accounting changes, etc.

Stock Split Studies.   One of the more popular kinds of information to examine is stock splits. There is a belief that the prices of stocks that split increase in value because the shares are priced lower, which will increase demand for them. In contrast, advocates of efficient markets would not expect a change in value, because all the firm has done is issue additional stock and nothing fundamentally affecting value has occurred.

The first study that one can identify as a test of the semistrong hypothesis is the well-known FFJR.[15] The FFJR study is noteworthy because it made a contribution in three areas. First, it is a very well-regarded and extensive study of the long-run effect of stock splits on returns to stockholders. Second, in dealing with stock splits, the authors provided important evidence on the semistrong efficient market hypothesis because they were concerned with how rapidly stock prices adjusted to this important economic event. Finally, the authors employed a technique to adjust for "market effects" that was based on advances in capital market theory. The market adjustment technique which was discussed in the prior section differed substantially from prior methods and has been used extensively since the original study.

In the study it was hypothesized that stock splits alone do not cause higher rates of return because they add nothing to the value of a firm. Therefore, there should be no significant price change following a split. In addition, one would hypothesize that, in an efficient market, investors would adjust for the forthcoming stock split *prior* to the announcement, because any relevant information that caused the split has already been discounted. It is contended that the stock price increase that leads a company to split its stock is caused by increases in earnings or other important successes, and these bits of information are known and adjusted for *prior* to the split announcement.

Another reason for expecting a price increase is that companies typically raise their dividends when they split their stock. It is contended that the dividend change has an information effect because it indicates that management is confident that it will have a new, higher level of earnings in the future which will justify a higher level of dividends. Therefore, the price increase that accompanies a dividend increase is *not* caused by the dividend itself but by the information transmitted by the increase.

To determine the effect on the stocks, they derived unique parameters for each stock relative to the market and computed abnormal returns for the period 20 months before and after the stock split. It was hypothesized that if there was any abnormal information to be derived from the split, it would show up in the residuals (deviations from the regression line). These residuals were considered abnormal price changes. If there were positive residuals surrounding splits, this would indicate the presence of good information and vice versa. The purpose was to determine *when* the positive effects took place — before or after the split. The authors cumulated the residuals for individual stocks and for all the stocks in the sample over time. To examine the differential effect of dividend increases, the total sample was divided into two groups: stocks that split and also experienced an increase in their dividend rate, and stocks that split but did *not* increase their dividend rate.

The results indicated that both groups of stocks experienced positive abnormal price changes *prior* to the split. Alternatively, stocks that split but did *not* increase their dividend experienced abnormal price *declines* following the split. In fact, within 12 months the no-dividend-increase stocks lost all their accumulated abnormal gains.

In contrast, stocks that split and also increased their dividend experienced no change in their abnormal return pattern after the split; i.e., the abnormal price pattern flattened. This indicated that the full impact of the price changes took place *prior* to the stock split. After the split, stocks with dividend increases were able to maintain their positive abnormal price increase, while stocks that did not increase their dividend, and thereby did not confirm the expectations regarding their favorable outlook, returned to their status prior to the split announcement.

These results were considered substantial evidence that stock splits alone do not result in higher rates of return for stockholders. They also support the semistrong efficient market hypothesis, because they indicate that the price adjustment occurred *prior* to a split.

The authors also considered whether investors could gain from the information on the split after the public announcement. It was argued that investors could *not* have gained by acquiring the stock *after* the split announcement. Although the aggregate results indicated that stocks in general rose prior to the actual split, after the announcement of the split, it was contended that this rising price pattern was due to the aggregation of the returns. The analysis of individual stocks indicated that it would have been impossible to gain from acquiring individual stocks after the stock split was announced.

This conclusion regarding market efficiency surrounding a stock split was confirmed in a subsequent study by Hausman, West, and Largay which specifically examined the profit opportunity question.[16] In contrast, Charest found large positive residuals during the period surrounding the announcement.[17] Finally, Reilly and Drzycimski found strong support for the EMH using daily price and volume data for the period surrounding the announcement.[18]

New Issue Studies.   During the 1960s a number of closely held companies decided to go public by selling some of their common stock. The determination of the appropriate price for a stock that does not have a public market is a difficult task. Because of uncertainty about the price and the risk involved in underwriting such issues, it was hypothesized by some authors that the underwriters would tend to underprice the new issues.[19] The authors therefore hypothesized that investors who acquired the new issues *at the offering price* would tend to receive abnormal profits. There was also a question regarding how fast the market would adjust to the underpricing. To examine the efficiency of the market, the typical test considered the returns to an investor who acquired the new issue *in the after market* (the public price after the offering) and held it for various periods.[20] The

---

[16] W. H. Hausman, R. R. West, and J. A. Largay, "Stock Splits, Price Changes, and Trading Profits: A Synthesis," *Journal of Business,* 44 no. 1 (January 1971): 69–77.

[17] Guy Charest, "Split Information, Stock Returns and Market Efficiency," *Journal of Financial Economics,* 6 no. 2/3 (June–September 1978): 265–296.

[18] Frank K. Reilly and Eugene F. Drzycimski, "Short-Run Profits from Stock Splits," *Financial Management,* 10 no. 3 (Summer 1981): 64–74.

[19] For a discussion of these reasons see Frank K. Reilly and Kenneth Hatfield, "Investor Experience with New Stock Issues," *Financial Analysts Journal,* 25 no. 5 (September–October 1969): 73–80.

[20] Other studies include: Roger G. Ibbotson, "Price Performance of Common Stock New Issues," *Journal of Financial Economics,* 2 no. 3 (September 1975): 235–272; Dennis E. Logue, "On the Pricing of Unseasoned New Issues, 1965–1969," *Journal of Financial and Quantitative Analysis,* 8 no. 1 (January 1973): 91–103; J. G. McDonald and A. K. Fisher, "New-Issue Stock Price Behavior," *Journal of Finance,* 27 no. 1 (March 1972): 97–102; Brian M. Neuberger and Carl T. Hammond, "A Study of Underwriters' Experience with Unseasoned New Issues," *Journal of Financial and Quantitative Analysis,* 9 no. 2 (March 1974): 165–177; Frank K. Reilly, "Further Evidence on Short-Run Results for New Issue Investors," *Journal of Financial and Quantitative Analysis,* 8 no. 1 (January 1973): 83–90; Frank K. Reilly, "New Issues Revisited," *Financial Management,* 6 no. 4 (Winter 1977): 28–42; Hans R. Stoll and Anthony J. Curley, "Small Business and the New Issues Market for Equities," *Journal of Financial and Quantitative Analysis,* 5 no. 3 (September 1970): 309–322; Roger G. Ibbotson and Jeffrey Jaffe, "Hot Issues Markets," *Journal of Finance,* 30 no. 4 (September 1975): 1027–1042; Stanley Block and Marjorie Stanley, "The Financial Characteristics and Price Movement Patterns of Companies Approaching the Unseasoned Securities Market in the Late 1970s," *Financial Management,* 9 no. 4 (Winter 1980): 30–36.

results on the two questions of interest (underpricing and market efficiency) were quite consistent. *All* the studies indicated that, on average, new issues yield abnormally positive short-run returns assuming a purchase *at the offering price*. Most authors attribute these excess returns to underpricing by the underwriters. The results also tended to support the semistrong efficient market hypothesis, because it appears *the market adjusted the prices almost immediately for the underpricing.* The returns from acquiring the new issue shortly after the offering and holding it for various periods either yielded returns consistent with the added risk involved in these new issues, or the returns were actually below expectations. The evidence of rapid price adjustment is most evident in the recent Miller–Reilly study in which it is shown that prices adjust by the day following the offering.[21]

Exchange Listing.   Another economic event that is expected to have a significant impact on a firm and its stock is the decision to become listed on a national exchange or, specifically, to become listed on the NYSE, because it is the largest and most prestigious exchange. It is hypothesized that such a listing will increase the market liquidity of the stock and, possibly, add to the prestige of the firm. There are two questions of interest. First, does listing on a major exchange cause a permanent change in the value of the firm? Second, given the change in expectations or perceptions surrounding the listing, is it possible to derive abnormal returns from investing in the newly listed stock around the time of the listing? A study by Furst examined the effect of listing on price using a multiple regression model which included all the variables that normally influence price (dividends, growth, retention rate, earnings stability, leverage, and corporate size) plus a dummy variable for listing.[22] The results generally indicated that the dummy variable was *not* statistically significant, which led the author to conclude that listing did not have an impact on price.

A study by Van Horne considered price effects and also the ability to profit from these effects.[23] The analysis compared price movements for stocks listed on the NYSE and ASE and similar movements on the S&P 500 Index. The results indicated positive abnormal price changes for the period between four and two months before listing, but, after taking account of transactions costs and certain biases, the average price change after the listing adjusted for industry price movements was not significant. It is concluded:

> On the basis of the studies undertaken, support cannot be marshalled for the hypothesis that market participants can "profit" from buying a stock upon the announcement to list and selling it at the time of listing, nor for the idea that listing is a thing of value.[24]

[21] Robert Miller and Frank K. Reilly, "Initial Public Offerings: An Analysis of Daily Returns," mimeo. (April, 1984).

[22] Richard W. Furst, "Does Listing Increase the Market Price of Common Stock?" *Journal of Business,* 43 no. 2 (April 1970): 174–180.

[23] James C. Van Horne, "New Listings and Their Price Behavior," *Journal of Finance,* 25 no. 4 (September 1970): 783–794.

[24] Ibid., p. 794.

A study by Goulet considered not only price changes, but also the effect on shares outstanding, sales of stock, and the number of stockholders.[25] Typically, there was an increase in the latter variables (shares outstanding and stockholders) but a decrease in stock price after the listing. It is not clear whether an investor could profit from this price change.

Recent Contrary Evidence. Several recent studies provide contrary evidence on this topic. Specifically, Ying, Lewellen, Schlarbaum, and Lease (YLSL) did an extensive analysis of 248 firms that were listed on the NYSE and ASE during 1966–1968.[26] They were specifically concerned with examining the potential for extraordinary profits surrounding the listing event with substantial concern for the risk adjustment of the stocks involved. As a result, they were examining abnormal returns similar to what was discussed earlier, but the derivation of the parameters employed a technique used by Fama and MacBeth.[27] They initially examined abnormal returns surrounding the actual listing date and found positive abnormal returns during all 24 months prior to listing (many of them statistically significant). In contrast, they discovered *negative* abnormal returns during most months after listing.

The public information related to the listing comes with the announcement to *apply* for listing; because almost all firms go through a confidential review prior to applying. As a result, virtually all applications are approved. Therefore, YLSL examined the abnormal returns during the months following the announcement to apply. These results indicated a significant positive abnormal return of 7.54 percent during the application month and a 5.00 percent abnormal return (without commission) during the month *following* the announcement. Such a result would be considered evidence against the semistrong EMH, since it implies that an investor could experience an abnormal risk-adjusted return based upon public information. Even with a reasonable commission, this abnormal return should persist. There were also consistently negative abnormal returns after the listing, but apparently they were not large enough to be profitable for someone willing to sell the stocks short.

A subsequent study by McConnell and Sanger reexamined this question with a different sample and a number of other changes and extensions to ensure that all factors had been considered.[28] In addition to using weekly rather than monthly data, they considered several different models to derive expected returns (i.e., a mean return model, a one-factor market model, and a zero-beta model), and they employed different market indexes and different OTC prices (bid, ask, or the mean of bid and ask). Notably, with all of these additional considerations, the results were very consistent with those of YLSL. Specifically,

---

[25] Waldemar M. Goulet, "Price Changes, Managerial Actions and Insider Trading at the Time of Listing," *Financial Management,* 3 no. 1 (Spring 1974): 30–36.

[26] Louis K. W. Ying, W. G. Lewellen, G. G. Schlarbaum, and R. C. Lease, "Stock Exchange Listings and Securities Returns," *Journal of Financial and Quantitative Analysis,* 12 no. 4 (September 1977): 415–432.

[27] Eugene Fama and J. MacBeth, "Risk Return and Equilibrium, Some Empirical Results," *Journal of Political Economy,* 81 no. 2 (May 1973): 607–636.

[28] John McConnell and Gary C. Sanger, "New Listings on the NYSE: A Reexamination of Some Anomalous Evidence Regarding Market Efficiency," mimeo. (May 13, 1981).

they found significant positive abnormal returns for the five weeks following the public announcement to apply for listing. Subsequently, there was practically no impact from the approval of the application, and there were negative abnormal returns after the actual listing. Again, this is considered evidence against the semistrong EMH, because it appears that investors can derive significant excess returns (adjusted for risk) even after considering a 1 percent commission to buy and sell. (Actually, the allowance for commission in the study is excessive.) While there are negative abnormal returns after the listing, there is no attempt to benefit from the short sale. Apparently, the negative returns are not large enough to cover the commissions involved.

In summary, it appears that the results regarding new listings are mixed related to the semistrong EMH with more recent evidence not providing support. Several studies have also examined the impact of listing on the risk (cost of equity capital) of the stocks involved. These results indicated *no* impact from listing; i.e., there was *no significant change* in systematic risk or cost of equity capital.[29]

Stock Prices and World Events.   Reilly and Dryzcimski examined the adjustment of stock prices to significant world events.[30] In an efficient market, stock prices should adjust rapidly to the new information contained in the announcement of a world event. Therefore, investors should *not* be able to profit from the public information. The analysis covered the announcement of seven unexpected world events. Several stock price series were analyzed prior to the announcement, at the market opening after the announcement, and during the two days following. The results consistently indicated that the major adjustment in stock prices took place during the time interval between the close before the announcement and *before* the market opened after the announcement. While there were some large stock price changes after the opening stock price that followed the announcement, the direction of these changes was not consistent.

On the question of whether investors could have made a profit from investing in stocks at the opening following the announcement, the results consistently indicated that this would not have been possible. Therefore, these tests generally supported the notion that the stock market was semistrong efficient.

Announcements of Accounting Changes.   Numerous studies have analyzed the impact of announcements of accounting changes on stock prices. These studies implicitly contend that the capital markets are relatively efficient. If markets are efficient, and accounting procedures or announcements of account-

---

[29] Frank J. Fabozzi, "Does Listing on the AMEX Increase the Value of Equity?" *Financial Management,* 10 no. 1 (Spring 1981): 43–50; Frank Fabozzi and R. A. Hershkoff, "The Effect of the Decision to List on a Stock's Systematic Risk," *Review of Business and Economic Research,* 14 no. 2 (Spring 1979): 77–82; Susan Phillips and J. R. Zecker, "Exchange Listing and the Cost of Equity Capital," *Capital Market Working Papers,* (Washington, D.C.: Securities and Exchange Commission, March 1982); William Reints and Peter Vanderberg, "The Impact of Changes in Trading Location on a Security's Systematic Risk," *Journal of Financial and Quantitative Analysis,* 10 no. 5 (December 1975): 881–890; Kent Baker and James Spitzfaden, "The Impact of Exchange Listing on the Cost of Equity Capital," *The Financial Review,* 17 no. 3 (September 1982): 128–141.

[30] Frank K. Reilly and Eugene F. Drzycimski, "Tests of Stock Market Efficiency Following Major World Events," *Journal of Business Research,* 1 no. 1 (Summer 1973): 57–72.

ing changes are important, one should be able to substantiate this by examining what happens to stock prices during the time period surrounding the announcement of an accounting change. It is also possible to determine the effect investors expect the accounting change to have, if any. If the accounting change will affect the economic value of the firm, there should be a rapid change in stock prices to reflect this. If the accounting change only affects *reported* earnings but has no economic significance (e.g., a change in the technique used to compute depreciation for bookkeeping purposes), an advocate of an efficient capital market would not expect the announcement to have an impact on stock prices.

Impact of Annual Earnings Reports.   A study by Brown and Ball examined the differential stock price movements for companies that had experienced good earnings reports, and stock price movement of companies that had experienced poor earnings reports.[31] They used the FFJR technique to derive the abnormal price performance of individual stocks, and they related these abnormal price movements to abnormal earnings changes for the companies. They derived the abnormal earnings changes by examining the historical relationship between firm earnings and aggregate earnings. Subsequently, for a given change in the aggregate earnings series, if the firm did not do as well as it had done historically, this was considered a poor earnings year; i.e., earnings were below expectations. The opposite would be true if the firm did better than expected — it would be considered a good earnings year. They divided the sample into companies with good and bad earnings reports, and they examined the abnormal stock price returns for the two samples during the year prior to the earnings report.

The results generally confirmed expectations that companies with abnormally good earnings reports also experienced positive abnormal stock price performance. However, most of the stock price adjustment (about 85 percent) took place prior to year-end and prior to release of the annual report. This indicated that stock prices adjust prior to the new information regarding annual earnings. It is likely that some of the new information was derived from prior quarterly reports.

Effect of Depreciation Changes.   Archibald examined the market reaction to changing the depreciation accounting method from accelerated depreciation to straight–line depreciation for financial statement purposes.[32] Because of the change, all 65 firms in the sample experienced an increase in their reported profits over what they otherwise would have reported. Since this change has no true economic impact, an advocate of an efficient market would hypothesize that no abnormal price changes would accompany the announcement. Those who believe that investors are naive regarding income figures would hypothesize that there would be positive abnormal stock price changes because of higher reported earnings. The results indicated that the majority of abnormal returns

---

[31] Philip Brown and Ray Ball, "An Empirical Evaluation of Accounting Income Numbers," *Journal of Accounting Research,* 6 no. 2 (Autumn 1963): 159–178.

[32] T. Ross Archibald, "Stock Market Reaction to the Depreciation Switch-Back," *Accounting Review,* 47 no. 1 (January 1972): 22–30.

before the accounting change were negative, while the abnormal price changes during the 24 months after accounting change were mixed. Notably, price changes during the initial five months after the announcement were negative. The author believed these results supported the EMH, because stock prices definitely did not increase as expected by those who assume investors are naive, but prices appeared to be reacting to poor earnings performance by these firms.

Kaplan and Roll examined investor reaction to two accounting changes:[33] (1) the switch in 1964 to the flow-through method of reporting investment credit, and (2) the switch back from reporting accelerated depreciation to reporting straight-line depreciation. Both changes affected only financial statements and had no effect on taxes, cash, or any real economic asset or liability. Using the FFJR market model technique, they examined abnormal stock price movements for the 60 weeks surrounding the announcements. The abnormal price movements were generally negative except during the few weeks surrounding the announcements. The authors believed that this indicates that firms making accounting changes are typically performing poorly, as shown by the negative abnormal price changes prior to the announcement. There apparently is some temporary benefit from the accounting change and the resulting higher reported earnings, as shown during the few weeks around the time of the announcement. However, the benefit is temporary, and the average negative price changes resumed shortly thereafter and continued to the end of the test period. Apparently, such practices are *unsuccessful in permanently affecting stock prices,* as one should expect in an efficient capital market.

Effect of Inventory Changes.   Two studies have examined the effect on stock prices of changes in inventory valuation methods from FIFO (first-in, first out) to LIFO (last-in, first-out) or vice versa during periods of significant inflation. An extensive study by Sunder examined 126 firms that changed to LIFO and 29 firms that changed to FIFO during the 21-year period 1946–1966.[34] Two alternative hypotheses were suggested regarding what should happen to stock prices in the period surrounding the announcement of the changes. The naive investor view is that investors rely on reported earnings and, because a change to LIFO will result in a decrease in earnings, stock prices should *decline.* In contrast, if one believes that investors rely on the economic value of the firm, stock prices should *increase* after the change because it causes an increase in cash flow (i.e., lower reported earnings cause a reduction in taxes payable, and, therefore, higher cash flow). The expectations were opposite for firms that changed to the FIFO method.

The abnormal price change results derived from a market model indicated that the price changes were generally positive prior to the announcement of a change from FIFO to LIFO and slightly negative after the announcement. The abnormal price changes for the total period were consistantly positive. Price

---

[33] Robert S. Kaplan and Richard Roll, "Investor Evaluation of Accounting Information: Some Empirical Evidence," *Journal of Business,* 45 no. 2 (April 1972): 225–257.

[34] Shyam Sunder, "Stock Price and Risk Related to Accounting Changes in Inventory Valuation," *The Accounting Review,* 50 no. 2 (April 1975): 305–315.

changes for firms that changed from LIFO to FIFO were very close to zero. The author believed that these results supported the hypotheses that changes in stock prices are associated with changes in the economic value of the firms rather than with changes in reported earnings.

A study by Reilly, Smith, and Hurt tested the same hypotheses for a sample of 32 firms that changed from FIFO to LIFO during the period 1972–1974.[35] The averages of the abnormal stock price changes for each of the six months prior to the announcements were *always positive.* The averages of the abnormal price changes during the announcement month and the two subsequent months were positive. The results for the following months were generally small negative values. It was concluded that the results supported the efficient market hypothesis because positive price changes are consistent with increases in economic value. In contrast, there is almost no support for the naive reported income hypothesis of negative abnormal price changes.

Some Anomalies

While the majority of evidence supports the semistrong EMH, there have likewise been several studies that have provided evidence that is inconsistent with this hypothesis. In this section we discuss a number of these studies with anomalous evidence and also consider a pattern that might explain most of the results.

Quarterly Earnings Reports.   A major set of studies consistently did *not* support the semistrong EMH related to the usefulness of quarterly earning reports. Most studies in this area have been carried out for a number of years by Latané and associates and deal with the usefulness of stock selection models that employed available quarterly data.[36] Although all of these studies suggested that the market is not completely semistrong efficient as related to quarterly earnings announcements, each of them had a small shortcoming which was overcome in a study by Joy, Litzenberger, and McEnally (JLM).[37] Therefore, the subsequent discussion concentrates on the JLM study.

Prior studies on the price adjustment to quarterly earnings announcements had typically simply ranked stocks on the basis of their earnings to price ratio (*E/P*) where *E* was the latest quarterly earnings and *P* was the stock price two months after the quarter ended. It was assumed that an investor acquired the stocks with the highest E/P ratio and sold the stocks with the lowest E/P ratio.

[35] Frank K. Reilly, Ralph E. Smith, and Ron Hurt, "Stock Market Reaction to Changes in Inventory Valuation Methods," Financial Management Association Meeting, Kansas City, Mo. (October 1975).

[36] Representative studies in the area are H. A. Latané, D. L. Tuttle, and C. P. Jones, "Quarterly Data: E/P Ratios vs. Changes in Earnings in Forecasting Future Price Changes," *Financial Analysts Journal,* 25 no. 1 (January–February 1969): 117–120, 123; H. A. Latané, O. Maurice Joy, and Charles P. Jones, "Quarterly Data, Sort-Rank Routines, and Security Evaluation," *Journal of Business,* 43 no. 4 (October 1970): 427–438; C. Jones and R. Litzenberger, "Quarterly Earnings Reports and Intermediate Stock Price Trends," *Journal of Finance,* 25 no. 1 (March 1970): 143–148; H. A. Latané, Charles P. Jones, and Robert Rieke, "Quarterly Earnings Reports and Subsequent Holding Period Return," *Journal of Business Research,* 2 no. 2 (April 1974): 119–132.

[37] O. Maurice Joy, Robert H. Litzenberger, and Richard W. McEnally, "The Adjustment of Stock Prices to Announcements of Unanticipated Changes in Quarterly Earnings," *Journal of Accounting Research,* 15 no. 2 (Autumn 1977): 207–225.

Analysis of stock price movements over the subsequent six months typically indicated the high E/P ratio portfolio did better than the market, while the low E/P ratio portfolio experienced inferior performance. Most of these studies did not adjust the results for possible risk differences.

In the study by JLM, the authors selected firms that experienced unanticipated changes in quarterly earnings similar to those Ball and Brown used in their annual earnings study, but they also considered different degrees of good and bad earnings. Three categories were established depending on the deviation from expectations—i.e., (1) any deviation from expectations, (2) the deviation must be plus or minus 20 percent, and (3) the deviation must be 40 percent. The abnormal price changes for the period, from 13 weeks prior to the announcement to 26 weeks following it, were analyzed using the FFJR technique with some modifications to adjust for differential risk relative to the market. Given the adjusted FFJR model, they examined the API (abnormal performance index) during the period before and after the announcement.

The results for the "any deviation" category indicated that the abnormal price movement for the *good* earnings companies was about 1 – 2 percent during the period. When this is compared to transactions costs of 2 – 3 percent, it indicates that no trading profits are available.

The models with the 20 and 40 percent deviation requirement generated much better results. For the 20 percent above expectations category the postannouncement gain was about 4 percent, compared to 5 – 6 percent gains for the sample that experienced earnings increases 40 percent above expectations. These abnormal returns would be adequate without information and distribution costs. The price adjustment to unfavorable earnings performance was more rapid, and there were no abnormal returns for any category.

An analysis of the cumulative abnormal price index indicated that the postannouncement change was statistically significant for the models using 20 and 40 percent deviations. Such results suggest that favorable information contained in quarterly earnings reports are not instantaneously reflected in stock prices. Finally, the authors examined whether there is a significant relationship between the size of the unexpected earnings performance and the postannouncement stock price change. The results supported the notion that the price change is influenced by the size of the favorable earnings change.

There have been two review articles that considered a number of studies in this area. An article by Joy and Jones considered several of the earlier studies and noted problems, but it also reviewed some of the more recent studies where they believed that the weaknesses have been remedied.[38] While they acknowledged that there is some possibility of debate on minor points, they stated:

> We conclude from the array of studies we have reviewed that market inefficiencies exist with respect to earnings reports.[39]

---

[38] O. Maurice Joy and Charles P. Jones, "Earnings Reports and Market Efficiencies: An Analysis of Contrary Evidence." *Journal of Financial Research,* 2 no. 1 (Spring 1979): 51 – 63.

[39] Ibid, p. 62.

An article by Ball in the *Journal of Financial Economics* was devoted to anomalous evidence regarding market efficiency. He reviewed 20 studies of price reaction to earnings announcements and found that the postannouncement risk-adjusted abnormal returns are consistently positive, which is inconsistent with market efficiency. In contrast to Joy and Jones, he contended that the abnormal returns are because of problems with the two parameter asset pricing model used to derive expected returns, not because of market inefficiencies.[40]

An article by Watts found significant abnormal returns even after making all the adjustments suggested by Ball.[41] He explicitly showed that the abnormal returns were due to market inefficiencies rather than the two parameter market model. However, the abnormal returns were small and were not completely consistent over time.

In summary, the evidence from studies on quarterly earnings announcements generally are not consistent with semistrong market efficiency, although there might be some continuing consideration of the size of the excess returns and consistency over time.

Price-Earnings Ratios and Returns. A study by Basu tested the EMH by examining the relationship between the price-earnings ratios for stocks and the returns on the stocks.[42] Some observers contend that stocks with low price-earnings ratios (p/e ratios) will tend to outperform stocks with high p/e ratios. Apparently, there is no well-developed reasoning behind this hypothesis but a belief that growth companies enjoy high p/e ratios consistent with that growth; possibly the market overestimates growth potential and, therefore, overvalues the stocks of these growth companies. One might speculate that the market has a tendency to undervalue low growth firms that have low p/e ratios. The Basu study empirically examined whether the investment performance of common stocks is related to their p/e ratios. If there was a definite relationship between the historical p/e ratio of a stock and its subsequent market performance, this would constitute evidence against the semistrong efficient market hypothesis, because it would imply that investors could use available public information (historical p/e ratios) to generate abnormal returns.

The general methodology was to rank stocks on the basis of their historical p/e ratios and to determine the risk and return for portfolios containing high p/e ratio stocks compared to portfolios with low p/e ratio stocks. The stocks were divided into five p/e ratio classes, and returns and alternative measures of risk were computed for each class. The average annual rates of return were substantially different—i.e., 9 percent for high p/e ratio stocks, 16 percent for the low

[40] Ray Ball, "Anomalies in Relationships between Securities' Yields and Yield-Surrogates," *Journal of Financial Economics,* 6 no. 2/3 (June–September 1978): 103–126.

[41] Ross L. Watts, "Systematic 'Abnormal' Returns after Quarterly Earnings Announcements," *Journal of Financial Economics,* 6 no. 2/3 (June–September 1978): 127–150.

[42] S. Basu, "Investment Performance of Common Stocks in Relation to Their Price-Earnings Ratios: A Test of the Efficient Market Hypothesis," *Journal of Finance,* 32 no. 3 (June 1977): 663–682. There is a companion article: S. Basu, "The Information Content of Price-Earnings Ratios," *Financial Management,* 4 no. 2 (Summer 1975): 53–64.

p/e ratio group. An unexpected result was that *the low p/e ratio group also had lower risk.* Obviously, composite performance measures that consider return and risk indicated that low p/e ratio stocks experienced superior results relative to the market, while high p/e ratio stocks had significantly inferior results.[43] Subsequent analysis attempted to avoid any potential bias in the performance measures and also account for taxes, transactions costs, and search costs. Although there was some impact of taxes and transactions costs, the author concluded that publicly available p/e ratios possess valuable information and should be considered by investors. Obviously, these results are not consistent with semistrong efficiency because they indicate that investors can use available public information to derive abnormal risk-adjusted rates of return.

The Size Effect.   Following the Basu studies, two authors did a similar analysis, but they examined the impact of *size* on the risk-adjusted rates of return.[44] Size was measured in terms of the total market value of the firm. In these studies, the authors ranked all the stocks on the NYSE (Banz) or all stocks on the NYSE and the ASE (Reinganum) on the basis of the market value of their stock. The ranked sample was divided into ten portfolios with equal weighting of stocks in the portfolios. Risk was measured in terms of the one-period CAPM — i.e., beta from the basic market model used by FFJR. Given this measure of risk, they derived risk-adjusted abnormal returns for the ten portfolios for extended periods (10–15 years) and found that the *small firms consistently experienced significantly larger risk-adjusted returns than the larger firms.* It is also contended that the p/e ratio results found by Basu were really small firms effects; i.e., it is size, not p/e ratio, that caused the Basu results.

These studies on market efficiency are dual tests of the efficient market hypothesis *and* the capital asset pricing model which is used to derive expected rates of returns. Specifically, the abnormal returns derived from these studies can be because the markets are not efficient, *or* they can be because the market model is not properly specified and, therefore, does not provide correct estimates of expected returns. In the Reinganum article, he contended that the reason for the abnormal returns is not that the market is inefficient, but that the simple one-period CAPM is an inadequate description of the real-world capital markets.[45]

Roll responded to these articles by contending that the results were probably because the riskiness of the small firms was improperly measured.[46] Roll contended that because small firms are traded less frequently, risk measures

---

[43] Composite performance measures are discussed in Chapter 22.

[44] R. W. Banz, "The Relationship between Return and Market Value of Common Stocks," *Journal of Financial Economics,* 9 no. 1 (March 1981): 3–18; and Marc R. Reinganum, "Misspecification of Capital Asset Pricing: Empirical Anomalies Based on Earnings Yield and Market Values," *Journal of Financial Economics,* 9 no. 1 (March 1981): 19–46: Marc R. Reinganum, "Abnormal Returns in Small Firm Portfolios," *Financial Analysts Journal,* 37 no. 2 (March–April 1981): 52–57.

[45] Marc R. Reinganum, "Abnormal Returns in Small Firm Portfolios," *Financial Analysts Journal,* 37 no. 2 (March–April 1981): 52–57.

[46] Richard Roll, "A Possible Explanation of the Small Firm Effect," *Journal of Finance,* 36 no. 4 (September 1981): 879–888.

obtained from short interval returns data (such as daily) seriously *understate* the actual risk from holding a small firm portfolio. With infrequent trading there may be instances where there is little or no trading. This infrequent trading will cause an increase in serial correlation of prices over time and a decrease in the variance of returns over time. Either or both of these results will mean that gross measures of risk are reduced and the covariance of returns for the stock with the market portfolio will be reduced; i.e., the stock's beta will be lower. This phenomenon was noted earlier by Dimson, who suggested adding lagged and leading market returns to the market model and summing the coefficients to arrive at the beta for infrequently traded stocks.[47] Reinganum responded to this suggestion by examining a number of portfolios ranked by size and computing betas for each market value portfolio by the standard ordinary least squares (OLS) model and the Dimson aggregated coefficients model.[48] Notably, there was a substantial difference in the beta estimates using the two methods; e.g., the beta for the smallest firm portfolio was 0.75 using OLS and 1.69 using the aggregated coefficients method. The difference narrowed with size until the largest firm portfolio beta was 0.98 with OLS and 0.97 with aggregated coefficients. The results clearly supported the basic contention by Dimson and Roll regarding the underestimation of risk for small firms. To test whether these new betas could explain the large differences in rates of return for the different portfolios, the author related the returns to the betas and firm size. The firm size coefficients are generally significant and the author contended:

> For the overall period, market capitalizations exhibit a statistically significant negative relationship to portfolio returns . . . Thus, after controlling the size effects, differences in Dimson betas seem to explain only a small portion of the differences in average portfolio returns.[49]

Overall, the author acknowledged that the new estimation procedure indicated that risk for small firms is underestimated, but he also contended that the difference in beta still did not account for the very large difference in rates of return:

> Thus, one can conclude with confidence that the small firm effect is still a significant economic and empirical anomaly.[50]

A study by Stoll and Whaley contended that the differential impact of transaction costs on small and large firms has not been given adequate attention.[51] They confirmed that the total market value of common stock equity varies inversely with risk-adjusted returns. Also, there is a strong positive correlation between

---

[47] Elroy Dimson, "Risk Measurement when Shares Are Subject to Infrequent Trading," *Journal of Financial Economics,* 7 no. 2 (June 1979): 197–226.

[48] Marc R. Reinganum, "A Direct Test of Roll's Conjecture on the Firm Size Effect," *Journal of Finance,* 37 no. 1 (March 1982): 27–35.

[49] Ibid, p. 33.

[50] Ibid, p. 35.

[51] Hans R. Stoll and Robert E. Whaley, "Transactions Costs and the Small Firm Effect," *Journal of Financial Economics,* 12 no. 1 (June 1983): 57–80.

average price per share and market value; i.e., firms with small market value have low stock prices. Because it has been shown that transaction costs vary inversely with price per share, it is contended that transaction costs must be considered when examining the small firm effect. Transaction costs include both the dealer's bid-ask spread and the broker's commission. Specifically, when you buy or sell stock on an exchange, there is a market quote that is relevant if you use a market buy or sell order; i.e., you would buy at the ask price and sell at the bid price. In addition, once you get the price from the specialist, you have a broker's commission on the transaction. Both of these components vary with price — i.e., the proportional bid-ask spread varies inversely with price,[52] and the percentage of commission (i.e., the commission as a proportion of price) is a decreasing function of price per share. Based upon some sample stocks, it is shown that the proportional bid-ask spread varies from 2.93 percent for small value stocks to 0.69 percent for large value stocks. In addition, the total commission to buy and sell stock was 3.84 percent for small firms and 2.02 percent for large firms. This indicates a total difference in transaction cost of 4.06 percent between large and small firms — i.e., a combined cost of 2.93 plus 3.84 (6.77 percent) for small firms and 0.69 plus 2.02 (2.71 percent) for large firms. Given this differential in transaction cost, if there is frequent trading, it can have a significant impact on the results. It is shown that, assuming *daily* transactions, the original small firm effects are reversed. As you assume less trading, the original abnormal return for small firms reoccurs, but it is not statistically significant at one year. The point is, there is a definite difference in transaction costs for small, lower-priced stocks and large, higher-priced stocks. Therefore, subsequent studies on differential performance must consider these transactions costs explicitly and specify realistic holding period assumptions.

Impact of Annual Rebalancing.   A subsequent study of Reinganum considered the holding period assumption when he investigated whether strategies that buy and hold securities for longer periods of time are capable of yielding results similar to the results by using daily trading strategies.[53] The author constructed ten portfolios that included all securities traded on the NYSE and ASE at the end of each year based on year-end market capitalizations. The initial analysis indicated that the rates of return for the various portfolios differed systematically depending on market capitalizations: the smaller the capitalization, the greater the return for the period 1963–1980. As an example, the average annual return for the portfolio with the smallest firms was 32.77 percent compared to 9.47 percent for the portfolio with the largest firms. Consistent with the Stoll and Whaley study, the average share price was positively correlated with size of firm. Risk was measured using the Dimson aggregated coefficients estimator, and it varied from 1.58 for the smallest firm portfolio to 0.96 for the largest firm portfolio. Reinganum contended that this differential is not enough to explain the

[52] Seha M. Tinic, "The Economics of Liquidity Service," *Quarterly Journal of Economics,* 86 no. 1 (February 1972): 79–93; George Benston and R. Hagerman, "Determinants of Bid-Ask Spreads in the Over-the-Counter Market," *Journal of Financial Economics,* 1 no. 4. (December 1974): 353–364.

[53] Marc R. Reinganum, "Portfolio Strategies Based on Market Capitalization," *Journal of Portfolio Management,* 9 no. 2 (Winter 1983): 29–36.

difference based on the analysis of his earlier article. He pointed out that the differential would require a market risk premium of over 37 percent, which is clearly excessive.

Two holding period strategies were considered: a one-year holding period, which assumed rebalancing every year, and a buy-and-hold strategy, which assumed an investor held the original portfolios derived at the beginning of 1963 through 1980. The results with the active strategy (annual rebalancing) were striking. With the small portfolio, $1 in 1963 grew to over $46 without commissions, while $1 in the largest firm portfolio grew to about $4. The results were monotonic across portfolios with one exception, and they were typically consistent over time. Most of the very small firms came from the ASE.

The results with the passive strategy (no rebalancing) still indicated the superiority of small firms. A dollar in the small firm portfolio grew to about $11, while $1 in the large firm portfolio grew to over $4 (about the same as annual rebalancing). Still, it was clear that the returns to annual rebalancing would be substantial. There was no explicit consideration of transaction costs. It was pointed out that because the differential returns were large, it was unlikely that any reasonable difference in transaction costs could overcome this return superiority for small firms. Finally, there was an analysis of the distribution of individual security returns. The results indicated that the distributions were generally non-normal and the small firm distributions were substantially different from the large firm distributions in terms of skewness and kurtosis. Specifically, the small firm distribution was very positively skewed, which indicates a higher than expected number of large positive observations. Following the analysis of these distributions, the author stated:

> Over time, the returns of the big winners more than offset the losses within the small firm portfolio, and these extremely large returns apparently account for the superior performance of the small capitalization companies over the large ones.[54]

In summary, the author contended that small firms outperform large firms even after considering risk and transaction costs assuming annual rebalancing, which he strongly recommended. Notably, the consideration of risk and transaction costs was more indirect; i.e., in both instances, the unadjusted rates of return were so different that neither risk nor transaction cost (considered individually) could account for the difference.

Impact of Trading Activity.   Arbel and Strebel contended that there is an additional influence beyond size — attention or neglect.[55] They measured attention in terms of the number of analysts who regularly follow a stock, and they divided the stocks into three groups: (1) highly followed, (2) moderately followed, (3) neglected. They measured risk using the standard single factor CAPM (rather than the Dimson method) and also considered total risk. While they

---

[54] Ibid, p. 36.

[55] Arner Arbel and Paul Strebel, "Pay Attention to Neglected Firms!" *Journal of Portfolio Management,* 9 no. 2 (Winter 1983): 37 – 42.

confirmed the small firm effect, they contended that the neglected firm effect persists beyond this impact. They reasoned that this effect is due to the lack of information on these firms and limited institutional interest. Because the neglected firm concept applied across size classes, institutions can invest in medium-sized neglected firms, while individuals can look for small neglected firms and can derive maximum benefits recognizing the information problems and the need for diversification. A major problem with the study was the risk measure used, which did not consider infrequent trading that could affect the beta risk measure.

Peavy and Goodman examined the p/e ratio question with adjustments for firm size, industry effects, and infrequent trading.[56] They attempted to eliminate the size problem by considering only firms with a market value above $100 million and to control the industry effect by examining only firms within three industries (electronics, paper/container, and food). They attempted to overcome the infrequent trading problem by using quarterly intervals and by including only stocks which had an average monthly trading volume exceeding 25,000 shares. Given these adjustments, they found that the risk-adjusted returns for stocks in the lowest p/e ratio quintile for all three industries were superior to those in the highest p/e ratio quintile. The lingering questions are: were the risk measures adequate even with the sample selection criteria? Was the size differential compensated for by limiting the sample to stocks over $100 million?

A study by James and Edmister examined the impact of trading volume on this question by considering the relationship between returns, market volume, and trading activity.[57] They initially examined the basic relationship between size and rates of return and confirmed prior results that there is a significant inverse relationship between size and risk-adjusted rates of return, even using the aggregate coefficients technique intended to take account of infrequent trading. They also considered the impact of trading volume as an alternative explanation for these results, since there is a strong positive correlation between size and trading activity. Firm size was hypothesized to be a proxy for trading activity; trading activity was the relevant factor. This is an appealing argument, because one could then justify the excess return for these stocks on the basis of a liquidity premium—i.e., an added return because of poor market liquidity.

The results did *not* support the hypothesis regarding trading activity; i.e., there was no significant difference between the mean returns of the highest and lowest trading activity portfolios, nor was there any evidence of an inverse relationship between trading activity and mean daily returns. They also tested this hypothesis by examining whether the firm size effect existed among firms of roughly equivalent trading activity. The results indicated the existence of a size effect; i.e., a pattern of increasing mean daily returns as firm size declined was observable in most trading volume and trading day groups. In summary, these results indicated that the size anomaly cannot be explained by differential trading activity (i.e., market liquidity).

---

[56] John W. Peavy, III and David A. Goodman, "The Significance of P/Es for Portfolios Returns," *Journal of Portfolio Management,* 9 no. 2 (Winter 1983): 43–47.

[57] Christopher James and Robert Edmister, "The Relation between Common Stock Returns, Trading Activity, and Market Value," *Journal of Finance,* 38, no. 4 (September 1983): 1075–1086.

In summary, the firm size effect on rates of return has emerged as a major anomaly in the efficient markets literature. Following the initial findings by Banz and Reinganum, there have been numerous attempts to explain the anomaly in terms of superior risk measurements, transaction costs, analysts attention, and trading activity. In general, no single study has been able to explain these very unusual results. Apparently, the two strongest explanations are the risk measurements that consider the significant impact of infrequent trading and the clear differential in transaction costs. Depending on the frequency of trading (i.e., the investment horizon), the *combination* of these two factors may account for most of the differential.

The January Anomaly.   Several years ago Branch proposed a unique trading rule for those interested in taking advantage of tax selling.[58] The basic idea was that investors tend to engage in tax selling toward the end of the year to establish losses on stocks that have declined during the current year or prior years. Subsequently, right after the new year, there is a tendency to reacquire some of these stocks or simply reinvest the proceeds from the prior tax sale. Based on this scenario, one would expect downward pressure on stock prices in late November and December and a positive impact in early January. Efficient market advocates would not expect such a seasonal pattern to persist; it should be eliminated by arbitrageurs or speculators who would buy in December and would be prepared to sell in early January.

There is also support for the existence of tax selling in an article by Dyl. He found that trading volume was abnormally high during December for stocks that had experienced large losses during the previous year, and volume was abnormally low for stocks that had experienced large gains.[59] He also reported significant abnormal returns during January for stocks that had experienced losses during the prior year.

A study by Roll considered this January anomaly along with the small firm effect.[60] After providing support for the existence of the price pattern on the last day of December and the first four days of January, he discussed some potential causes and dismissed all of them. He also confirmed that stocks with negative returns over the entire preceding year had higher returns around January 1. A major question considered was whether the entire year-end return is caused by tax selling or whether size has an additional effect. The results indicated that *smallness had an effect beyond that attributable to volatility and tax selling.*

Returning to why the seasonal tax selling pattern is not eliminated by arbitrage, Roll considered the impact of transaction costs. A simple trading rule generated strong returns from buying on the second-to-last day of the year and selling on the fourth day of the new year—6.89 percent for the NYSE; 14.2 percent for the ASE. Applying the commissions estimated by Stoll and Whaley (6.77 percent commission to buy and sell for small firms), they still had excess

[58] Ben Branch, "A Tax Loss Trading Rule," *Journal of Business,* 50 no. 2 (April 1977): 198–207.

[59] Edward A. Dyl, "Capital Gains Taxation and Year-End Stock Market Behavior," *Journal of Finance,* 32 no. 1 (March 1977): 165–175.

[60] Richard Roll, "Vas Ist Das?" *Journal of Portfolio Management,* 9 no. 2 (Winter 1983): 18–28.

returns of 3.94 percent for the NYSE and 10.3 percent for the ASE. Finally, as an extreme estimate of the spread, Roll assumed an investor bought at the high price for the second-to-last trading day and sold at the low price on the fourth day of the new year. Under these assumptions and also adding commissions, there was no profit on the NYSE, but there was still an excess on the ASE. Based upon this, Roll contended that it is entirely possible that, because of transaction costs, arbitrageurs do not eliminate the January tax selling anomaly. Finally, he discussed some problems with estimating an appropriate long-run risk measure that would explain both the seasonal phenomenon and the remaining small firm effect.

In summary, there appears to be a strong January anomaly that is clearly attributable to tax selling of stocks that experienced losses during the previous year. At least part of the reason this tax anomaly is not arbitraged away is the high transaction costs for small firms. Notably, the small firm effect is present in addition to this January anomaly.

Summary Regarding Semistrong EMH.   The evidence regarding the semistrong EMH is best described as mixed. A number of studies dealing with specific events (e.g., stock splits, world events, accounting changes) consistently support the semistrong hypothesis, because they indicate that security prices react very rapidly to new information and investors generally cannot derive abnormal returns by acting after the announcement of the event.

In contrast, evidence regarding the reporting of quarterly earnings does not support the hypothesis. In addition, a substantial amount of research on the alternative returns available for large and small firms (measured by market value) has indicated that small firms consistently experience superior abnormal risk-adjusted returns. Several studies have attempted to explain these small firm results in terms of the measures of risk, trading volume, and transaction costs. While the standard measure of risk is inadequate for small firms, the higher risk does not fully explain the significant differences in rates of return. Alternatively, there are significant higher transaction costs for small firms, but this would only equalize returns for investors who do a lot of short-term trading. Therefore, for short-term investors, it appears that a combination of risk and transaction costs would equalize risk-adjusted returns. Investors with annual investment horizons could still experience superior abnormal risk-adjusted returns by investing in small firms. Such results would not support the semistrong EMH. Finally, there appears to be a January anomaly due to tax selling that is partially neutralized if one assumes very heavy transaction costs.

Strong Form Hypothesis Test Results

The strong form efficient market hypothesis contends that stock prices fully reflect *all* information (public and private). Therefore, no group of investors possesses information such that they could consistently generate above average profits. As stated, this hypothesis is extremely rigid and requires not only that stock prices must adjust rapidly to new public information, but *also* that no group has monopoly access to specific information. The strong form hypothesis requires that the market adjusts rapidly to new information, but it also implies that *all* information is readily available to *all* investors *at the same time.*

The tests of this hypothesis have examined the performance of alternative groups of investors to determine whether any identifiable group has consistently experienced above average risk-adjusted returns. If any group did consistently receive such returns, this would indicate that either they had monopolistic access to important information or they consistently had the ability to act on public information before other investors could, so the market was not adjusting stock prices to *all* new information rapidly.

There have been three major groups of investors examined in this regard. First, several studies have analyzed the returns of those possessing inside information by examining the returns experienced by *corporate insiders* in their stock trading. Another group of studies analyzed the returns available to *stock exchange specialists.* The third group of tests examined the overall performance of *professional money managers,* with emphasis on returns generated by mutual funds because of the availability of data.

Corporate Insider Trading. Securities laws require that individuals defined as *corporate insiders* report their transactions (purchases or sales) in the stock of the firm for which they are insiders to the SEC each month. Insiders are typically defined as major corporate officers, members of the board of directors, and major stockholders of the firm. About six weeks after the reporting period, this insider trading information is made public by the SEC.

Given this information, it has been possible to identify how corporate insiders traded over a period of time and determine whether their transactions were generally profitable; i.e., did they buy on balance before abnormally good price movements and sell on balance before poor market periods for their stock? The results of these studies have generally indicated that *corporate insiders consistently enjoyed profits that were significantly above average.*[61] Corporate insiders consistently had inside information and were able to use this information to derive above average returns on investments in their companies' stocks. These results would be considered evidence against the strong form efficient market hypothesis, which requires that all investors have equal access to information. It appears that corporate insiders have access to valuable information and are able to use it to generate above average profits. The only justification for this finding is that the strong form hypothesis requires more than an efficient market; it requires a *perfect* market in which all participants have equal access to all information. Therefore, this hypothesis requires a perfect *information-generating process* and a perfect *information-processing* market. In the case of corporate insiders, one would say that insiders have access to valuable information before the public does, and when they act upon this information, they are

[61] The major studies on this topic are: James H. Lorie and Victor Niederhoffer, "Predictive and Statistical Properties of Insider Trading," *Journal of Law and Economics,* 11 (April 1968): 35–53; Shannon P. Pratt and Charles W. DeVere, "Relationship between Insider Trading and Rates of Return for NYSE Common Stocks, 1960–1966," included in James Lorie and Richard Brealey, eds. *Modern Developments in Investment Management,* (New York: Praeger Publishers, 1972): 268–279; Jeffrey Jaffe, "Special Information and Insider Trading," *Journal of Business,* 47 no. 3 (July 1974): 410–428; Joseph E. Finnerty, "Insiders and Market Efficiency," *Journal of Finance,* 31 no. 4 (September 1976): 1141–1148; Joseph E. Finnerty, "Insiders Activity and Inside Information: A Multivariate Analysis," *Journal of Financial and Quantitative Analysis,* 11 no. 2 (June 1976): 205–215.

able to generate above average profits. This is as one would expect in a competitive environment.

In addition to these findings, there is evidence that public investors who consistently traded with the insiders based upon announced insider transactions would have enjoyed returns (after commissions) in excess of those from a simple buy-and-hold policy. This is shown in the Pratt–DeVere study (cited above) in which the authors show results assuming a purchase one, two, three, and four months after the period in which insiders bought or sold. In all cases the returns were superior to market returns. These results are noteworthy, because they constitute evidence against the semistrong efficient market hypothesis. They imply that investors should be able to derive above average returns by simply trading on the basis of available public information (insider transactions).

Stock Exchange Specialists.   Several studies have examined the function of the stock exchange specialist. They have determined that specialists have monopolistic access to certain very important information about unfilled limit orders. Therefore, one would expect specialists to derive above average returns from this information. An SEC study found that typically the specialist sells above his last purchase on 83 percent of all his sales and buys below his last sale on 81 percent of all his purchases.[62] One would expect such activity to provide above average returns.

Niederhoffer and Osborn conducted an extensive analysis of individual transaction data on the NYSE and pointed out that specialists apparently use their access to information about unfilled limit orders to generate excess profits.[63] Further, the extensive Institutional Investor Study (IIS) likewise indicated that the returns derived by specialists were substantially above what one should expect based upon the risk involved.[64] The study indicated that the average return on capital exceeded 100 percent. A study by Reilly and Drzycimski indicated that, following major unexpected world announcements, the typical stock exchange specialist, acting *as he is directed,* would have consistently made profits on the trades following such announcements.[65] Assume a specialist bought stocks at the opening following an unfavorable announcement, which would cause most investors to sell, and subsequently sold this accumulation. The specialist consistently would have made a profit on these purchases. He likewise would have made money when he sold stock following favorable announcements.

Performance of Professional Money Managers.   The tests of the strong form efficient market hypothesis discussed thus far have been concerned with two

---

[62] *Report of the Special Study of the Security Markets* (Washington, D.C.: Securities and Exchange Commission, 1963): Part 2, 54.

[63] Victor Niederhoffer and M. F. M. Osborne, "Market-Making and Reversal on the Stock Exchange," *Journal of American Statistical Association,* 61 no. 316 (December 1966): 897–916.

[64] U.S. Securities and Exchange Commission, *Institutional Investor Study Report,* 92nd Congress, 1st Session, House Document No. 92–64 (Washington, D.C.: U.S. Government Printing Office, 1971).

[65] Frank K. Reilly and Eugene F. Drzycimski, "The Stock Exchange Specialist and the Market Impact of Major World Events," *Financial Analysts Journal,* 31 no. 4 (July–August 1975): 27–32.

small, unique groups of investors who consistently have been able to derive above average returns *because they have monopolistic access to important information and take advantage of it.* The studies dealing with the third group, professional money managers, are more realistic because one would not expect these investors to have monopolistic access to important new information on a consistent basis. The reasoning behind these studies is that these are highly trained professionals who work full time at investment management, and if any "normal" investors should be able to derive above average profits without inside information, it should be this group. Also, one might speculate that if any noninsider should be able to derive inside information, professional money managers should because they do extensive management interviews.

While investigators would ideally like to examine the performance of a wide range of money managers, most of the studies have been limited to those involved with mutual funds because data is readily available. Only recently have data been available for bank trust departments, insurance companies, and investment advisers.

Several studies have examined the performance of a number of mutual funds over extended periods.[66] The results indicated that the majority of the funds were *not* able to match the performance of a buy-and-hold policy. When a large sample of mutual funds was examined in terms of their risk-adjusted rates of return without considering commission costs, slightly more than half did better than the overall market. When commission costs, load fees, and management costs were considered, approximately two thirds of the mutual funds generally did *not* match the performance of the overall market. In addition, it was found that funds were *not* consistent in their performance. A fund that did well one year could do well the next year, but it was just as likely to be a poor performer. A fund that did better than average two years in a row was no more likely to do well three years in a row than one would expect on the basis of a random chance model. Assuming a 0.50 probability of doing better than the market, one should expect 25 percent of the funds to outperform the market two years in a row $(.50 \times .50)$, and 0.125 of the funds to do better three years in a row $(.50^3)$, etc. This progression is similar to actual findings. A study by Klemkosky examined the consistency in the risk-adjusted performance of a sample of 158 mutual funds at two and four year intervals during the eight-year period 1968–1975.[67] Following his analysis he concluded:

> The results of this study indicate that investors should exercise caution in using past relative risk-adjusted performance to predict future relative performance. This is true whether performance was measured relative to other funds or the market. As the evaluation was expanded, risk-adjusted performance became

---

[66] Notable studies in this area include: William F. Sharpe, "Mutual Fund Performance," *Journal of Business,* 39 no. 1 (January 1966 Supplement): 119–139; Michael Jensen, "The Performance of Mutual Funds in the Period 1945–1964," *Journal of Finance,* 23 no. 2 (May 1968): 389–416; Jack L. Treynor, "How to Rate Management of Investment Funds," *Harvard Business Review,* 43 no. 1 (January–February 1965): 63–75. There is a review of these studies in Chapter 26.

[67] Robert C. Klemkosky, "How Consistently Do Managers Manage?" *Journal of Portfolio Management,* 3 no. 2 (Winter 1977): 11–15.

more consistent. However, the relationships were still not strong enough to make relative predictions with a high degree of certainty.[68]

Therefore, the performance of mutual fund managers supported the strong form efficient market hypothesis. The results indicated that most mutual fund managers, using publicly available information (and anything else available), could not consistently outperform a buy-and-hold policy.

Recently, some firms have been collecting performance figures for other institutional investors and the results have generally been consistent with the mutual fund results. Notably, it is not possible to compare these results directly to the mutual fund results because the multi-institution figures generally *do not consider measures of risk*—i.e., they only report annualized rates of return. One of the most well-recognized firms that collects and reports these data is the Frank Russell Co., a Tacoma, Washington, firm that is involved in evaluating investment results for institutions. Table 7.1 contains the mean rates of return for several investment groups for six time periods compared to the Standard & Poor's 500 Index and 91-day U.S. T-Bills.

With one exception, the banks never experienced returns above the Standard & Poor's 500. In contrast, the equity-oriented separate accounts consistently did better in terms of rates of return.[69] Similarly, the insurance companies and the growth mutual funds did better for the longer time periods. Finally, the results for the balanced and income funds were mixed. Again, it should be remembered that these results are not adjusted for risk and this could impact upon the results for the separate accounts and especially the growth mutual funds.

The tests of the strong form efficient market hypothesis generated mixed results, but the bulk of relevant evidence supported the strong form hypothesis. The results for two unique groups of investors (corporate insiders and stock exchange specialists) definitely did not support the hypothesis, because both groups apparently have monopolistic access to important information and they use it to derive above average returns. Analysis of performance by professional money managers definitely *supported* the strong form hypothesis. Numerous studies have indicated that these highly trained, full-time investors could not consistently outperform a simple buy-and-hold policy on a risk-adjusted basis.[70] Because this last group is similar to the bulk of investors who do not have consistent access to inside information, their results are considered most relevant to the hypothesis. Therefore, there is substantial support for the strong form hypothesis as applied to most investors.

IMPLICATIONS OF EFFICIENT CAPITAL MARKETS

Overall, it is safe to conclude that the equity market is generally efficient for the great majority of investors. Because of the substantial and consistent empirical

---

[68] Ibid., p. 14.

[69] It is pointed out that the results for these individual accounts have an upward bias because they only consider accounts retained—i.e., if a firm or bank does a poor job on an account and the client leaves, it is not included.

[70] These studies on mutual fund performance are discussed in detail in Chapter 26.

TABLE 7.1
Annual Rates of Return During Alternative Periods Ending December 31, 1983

	1 Year	2 Years	4 Years	6 Years	8 Years	10 Years
Standard & Poor's 500	22.5	22.0	17.0	15.4	13.3	10.6
91 T-Bills	8.7	9.6	11.2	10.3	9.0	8.5
Bank I[1]-Equity Pooled Accounts	19.8	21.3	16.9	15.7	13.0	9.7
Bank II[2]-Equity Pooled Accounts	16.7	19.8	16.3	15.0	12.8	9.6
Equity Oriented Separate Accounts[3]	21.1	23.3	19.4	18.5	16.7	13.2
Insurance Comp-Equity Pooled Accounts	21.6	21.7	17.3	15.9	13.9	11.1
Growth Mutual Funds	20.5	22.0	18.2	20.0	18.0	13.8
Balanced and Income Mutual Funds	18.6	22.9	16.7	15.3	14.2	11.8

[1]Bank I are large banks (trust assets over $ Billion).
[2]Bank II are smaller banks.
[3]As contrasted to pooled accounts, these are individual accounts for specific clients.
SOURCE: Frank Russell Co. Reprinted with permission.

results indicating an efficient market, one who assumes otherwise does so at great risk. This evidence supporting the existence of an efficient equity market makes it important to consider the implication of such a market for those most affected by this efficiency—investment analysts and portfolio managers.

Efficient Markets and Technical Analysis

It is widely recognized that a belief in technical analysis and the notion of efficient markets are directly opposed. A basic premise of technical analysis is that *stock prices move in trends that persist.*[71] Expectations for such a pattern of price movements is based upon the belief that when new information comes to the market, it is *not* immediately available to everyone. Instead, those who advocate technical analysis contend that new information is typically disseminated from the informed professional to the aggressive investing public and then to the great bulk of investors. Also, it is believed that analysis of the information and subsequent action by the various groups is *not* immediate but is spread over time. Given this gradual dissemination of information and gradual analysis and action, it is hypothesized that the movement of stock prices to a new equilibrium following the release of new information does not occur rapidly but takes place *over a period of time.* As a result, there are *trends in stock price movements that persist for a period of time.* Technical analysts believe that nimble traders can develop "systems" that help them to detect the beginning of a movement to a new equilibrium. Given some signal indicating the beginning of a movement to a new equilibrium (a *breakout*), the technical analyst attempts to buy or sell the stock immediately and thereby take advantage of the remaining price adjustment.

The belief in such a pattern of events is in direct contrast to the efficient market hypothesis, which contends that the information dissemination process

---

[71] There is an extensive discussion of technical analysis in Chapter 15. The reader is also referred to E. W. Tabell and A. W. Tabell, "The Case for Technical Analysis," *Financial Analysts Journal,* 20 no. 2 (March–April 1964): 67–76; and Robert A. Levy "Conceptual Foundations of Technical Analysis," *Financial Analysts Journal,* 22 no. 4 (July–August 1966): 83–89.

is quite rapid, and, therefore, most interested investors receive new information at about the same time. Advocates of an efficient market contend that the adjustment of security prices to the new information is *very rapid.* It is *not,* however, contended that the price adjustment is perfect. In some cases there will be an overadjustment or an underadjustment. Still, because there is nothing certain about whether the market will over- or underadjust, it is not possible to derive abnormal profits consistently from the adjustment process.

If the capital market is efficient and prices fully reflect all relevant information, any technical trading system that depends only upon past trading data *cannot be of any value* because, by the time the information is public, the price adjustment has taken place. Therefore, a purchase or sale using a technical trading rule after information becomes public and after the rapid adjustment in stock prices takes place should *not* generate above average returns after taking account of commissions.

Efficient Markets and Fundamental Analysis

Advocates of fundamental analysis believe that, at any point in time, there is a basic intrinsic value for the aggregate stock market, for alternative industries and for individual securities; this value depends upon underlying economic values. The way to determine the intrinsic value is to examine the variables that are supposed to determine value (i.e., current and future earnings and risk variables) and, based upon these variables, derive an estimate of intrinsic value for the aggregate stock market, an industry, or a company. If the prevailing market price differs substantially from instrinsic value (enough to cover transaction costs), appropriate action should be taken: buy if the market price is substantially below the intrinsic value and vice versa. Advocates of fundamental analysis believe that there are instances in which the market price and intrinsic value differ, but they also believe that eventually the market will recognize the discrepancy and correct it. Therefore, if an analyst can do a superior job of *estimating* intrinsic value, he can consistently acquire undervalued securities and derive above average returns. The following sections deal with the implications of efficient markets on various subcategories of fundamental analysis: aggregate market analysis, industry analysis, company analysis, and portfolio management.

Efficient Markets and Economic Market Analysis. Based upon the work done by King and others, it is possible to make a fairly strong case that intrinsic value analysis should begin with a consideration of aggregate market analysis.[72] At the same time, the efficient markets hypothesis implies that if analysis is limited to individual *past* economic events, it is unlikely the analyst will be able to beat a buy-and-hold policy. This is supported by the findings of the Reilly–Drzycimski study on world events which indicated that the market adjusts very rapidly to

[72] Benjamin F. King, "Market and Industry Factors in Stock Price Behavior," *Journal of Business,* 39 no. 1 (January 1966 Supplement): 139–190. Such an approach is also advocated in Frank K. Reilly, "Our Misdirected Emphasis in Security Valuation," *Financial Analysts Journal,* 29 no. 1 (January–February 1973): 54–57. There is a detailed discussion of this approach in Chapter 10.

individual world events.[73] Still, there is evidence that stock prices experience long-run movements over time.[74] The fact that these trends exist makes any attempt to project them worthwhile. The efficient market hypothesis indicates that the projection cannot depend only upon past data; there must be a *projection* of the variables that influence the overall economy and the aggregate stock market. An investment based upon a model using only available economic data should not do better than a buy-and-hold policy.

Hence, aggregate market analysis is important and can be financially rewarding, but *it is not easy.* Successful market projections require knowledge of the important variables that affect market movements, and a superior *projection* of movements of the crucial variables.

Efficient Markets and Industry and Security Analysis. An examination of alternative industry returns or returns on individual stocks indicates a wide distribution. Therefore, industry and stock analysis should be of value, because it is important to separate industries and stocks that are in the upper portion of the distribution of returns from those in the lower segment.[75] Again, though, the EMH implies that it is necessary to understand the variables that determine stock prices, but it is also mandatory to *project* movements in these valuation variables. A study by Malkiel and Cragg developed a model that did an excellent job of explaining past stock price movements for individual stocks employing past company data.[76] However, when they attempted to employ this model to project future stock price changes, still using past company data, the results were consistently inferior to results from a buy-and-hold policy. This implies that, even with a properly specified valuation model, *it is not possible to select stocks using only past data.*

Another bit of evidence regarding the necessity for accurately projecting future earnings is derived from a study by Niederhoffer and Regan.[77] They showed that the crucial difference between the stocks that enjoyed the best price performance during a given year and the stocks that experienced the worst price performance was the relationship between *estimated* earnings and *actual* earnings. The stock with the best price performance had actual earnings results substantially above the estimated earnings, while the stocks with the worst price performance were companies for which the earnings estimates were substantially above actual earnings. Therefore, if an analyst can do a superior job of *projecting* earnings that are significantly different from general expectations, he

[73] Frank K. Reilly and Eugene F. Drzycimski, "Tests of Stock Market Efficiency Following Major World Events," *Journal of Business Research,* 1 no. 1 (Summer 1973): 57–72.

[74] Julius Shiskin, "Systematic Aspects of Stock Price Fluctuations," James Lorie and Richard Brealey, eds., *Modern Developments in Investment Management* (New York: Praeger Publishers, 1972), 670–688.

[75] A study that examines the distribution of industry returns and reviews past studies is Frank K. Reilly and Eugene F. Drzycimski, "Alternative Industry Performance and Risk," *Journal of Financial and Quantitative Analysis,* 9 no. 3 (June 1974): 423–446.

[76] Burton G. Malkiel and John G. Cragg, "Expectations and the Structure of Share Prices," *American Economic Review,* 60 no. 4 (September 1970): 601–617.

[77] Victor Niederhoffer and Patrick J. Regan, "Earnings Changes, Analysts Forecast, and Stock Prices," *Financial Analysts Journal,* 28 no. 3 (May–June 1972): 65–71.

can likely achieve a superior stock selection record. Hence, this study indicates that an important factor is the ability to estimate earnings and also to estimate future changes in the stock's earnings multiple.

Theory and evidence both indicate that it is not impossible to be a superior analyst, but it is *very difficult* to be consistently superior.[78] An analyst must understand what variables are relevant for changes in valuation and must be able to estimate future values consistently for these variables to be consistently superior. Most analysts can recognize the relevant variables for an individual stock, and most can estimate future values for *some* of these variables for *some* stocks *some* of the time. The difficulty comes in doing this consistently for a number of different stocks. These requirements led Fama to suggest a system for evaluating the performance of analysts.[79]

Evaluating the Performance of Analysts.   A survey of practicing security analysts would probably indicate that about 98 percent of them believe that they are superior, while the other 2 percent believe they are about average. Not everyone can be superior, as the empirical results for professional money managers discussed earlier show. To determine who the superior analysts are, the following relatively simple evaluation system was suggested. Examine the performance of numerous buy and sell recommendations made by an analyst over time relative to the performance of randomly selected stocks *of the same risk class.* The test is whether an analyst can outperform random selection consistently. If the analyst produces results that are *consistently* better than those produced by random selection, he is a superior analyst. The consistency requirement is crucial because one would expect securities chosen by random selection to outperform the market about half the time.

A text on security valuation can indicate the relevant variables to analyze, why these variables are relevant, and point out the important techniques to consider when attempting to project the relevant valuation variables, but the task of deriving the actual estimate is as much an art as it is a science. If the estimates of valuation variables were mechanical, it would be possible to program a computer to carry out the function and there would be no need for analysts. Therefore, the superior analyst must understand what is important and have the ability to *estimate* these variables.

Efficient Markets and Portfolio Analysis

Prior studies indicated consistently that the performance of professional money managers does not consistently exceed a simple buy-and-hold policy on a risk-

---

[78] A much harder line in this regard is taken in Fischer Black, "Implications of the Random Walk Hypothesis for Portfolio Management," *Financial Analysts Journal,* 27 no. 2 (March–April 1971): 16–22. Black contends that it is virtually impossible to consistently do better than buy-and-hold, especially if one considers the cost of research.

[79] Eugene F. Fama, "Random Walks in Stock Market Prices," *Financial Analysts Journal,* 21 no. 5 (September–October 1965): 55–58.

adjusted basis. One explanation is that there are no superior analysts and the cost of research produces these inferior results. Another explanation (favored by the author with no empirical support) is that institutions employ superior and inferior analysts. In turn, the average or inferior performance is because the recommendations of the few superior analysts are offset by the costs and recommendations of the inferior analysts.

Portfolio Management without Superior Analysts. Recent work in the area of portfolio management has shown that there are ways of increasing profits within a given portfolio even though a manager is dependent upon nonsuperior analysts. The area of portfolio analysis has experienced several significant advances that have been heavily dependent upon the existence of efficient capital markets.[80] An especially notable study for our purposes is by Sharpe and Cooper. It indicated that there was a good relationship between the returns for a portfolio of stocks in period *t*, and risk measures in the prior period.[81] These findings indicate that it is possible to build a portfolio of stocks that will conform to the risk preferences of a portfolio manager's clientele *using available historical risk information.* In addition, one should expect to receive a rate of return that is fairly consistent with the risk level specified. This selection process does not appear to require extensive research efforts. Therefore, assuming that a portfolio manager recognized that he did not have any superior analysts, one can conceive of how the portfolio should be managed in a world with efficient capital markets to provide maximum risk-adjusted returns for the client.

The major points of this process have been outlined by Lorie and Hamilton.[82] First, the major efforts of the portfolio manager should be directed toward determining and attempting to measure the risk preferences of his clientele. Managers tend to transmit their risk preferences to the clients without recognizing that the existence of other investments by the client may influence the client's preferences for a particular portfolio. Therefore, subjective discussions of risk must be transformed into useful quantitative measures which can be used to determine a client's risk preference in terms of the capital asset pricing model (i.e., a model used to measure the risk of an asset based on its covariance with the market portfolio of risky assets).

Once the client's risk preferences are quantified, the second function is to derive a given risk portfolio by investing a certain proportion of the wealth available into a well-diversified portfolio of risky assets and the rest into a risk-free asset.[83] Therefore, the second task of the portfolio manager is to construct a portfolio that conforms to the client's quantified risk preferences by combining a portfolio of risk-free assets with a diversified portfolio of risky assets.

The third task is to ensure that the risk asset portfolio is *completely diversified* so that it moves consistently with the aggregate market. The need for com-

[80] There is a detailed discussion of these developments in Chapters 8, 9, and 20.

[81] William F. Sharpe and Guy M. Cooper, "Risk-Return Classes of New York Stock Exchange Common Stocks, 1931–1967," *Financial Analysts Journal,* 28 no. 2 (March–April 1972): 46–54, 81.

[82] James Lorie and Mary T. Hamilton, *The Stock Market* (Homewood, Ill.: Richard D. Irwin, 1973), 105–108.

[83] There is a detailed discussion of this in Chapters 8 and 9.

plete diversification has been emphasized in an article by Lorie that points out the uncertainty present when there is only 90–95 percent diversification.[84]

If one assumes that the portfolio manager is not capable of predicting future market movements, the fourth task is to *maintain the specified risk level* rather than attempting to change the risk of the portfolio based upon market expectations, i.e., shift to a high risk portfolio during a period when a bull market is projected or change to a defensive portfolio if a bear market is expected. Because of changing market values there will be some change in the risk of a portfolio, so it is necessary to trade occasionally to return to the desired balance.

Finally, it is important to *minimize transaction costs.* Assuming that the portfolio is completely diversified and that past relations between risk and return hold over the long run, a major deterrent to the client receiving the expected return would be excessive transaction costs that do not generate added returns. There are three factors involved in minimizing total transaction costs.[85] One is *minimizing taxes* for the client. How this is accomplished will vary, but it should be given prime consideration when carrying out transactions. The second factor seems rather obvious: *reduce trading turnover to the level necessitated by liquidity needs and risk control* (trades needed to maintain a given risk level). Finally, when trades are made, the portfolio manager should attempt to *minimize the liquidity costs of the trade.* There will typically be a number of stocks available that will accomplish the goal. The stocks used should be those that have low trading costs, but that are also relatively *liquid* so that the trade will have little effect on the price of the stock. To accomplish this, orders to buy or to sell several stocks should be submitted at net prices that approximate the specialist's quote (i.e., limit order to buy at bid or sell at ask). The stock that is bought or is sold first is the one that meets your criteria, and all other orders are withdrawn.

If a portfolio manager does not have any superior analysts, he should do the following:

1. Determine the risk preferences of his client and quantify these preferences to be consistent with the capital asset pricing model.
2. Given the risk preferences of the client, construct the appropriate portfolio by dividing the total portfolio between a portfolio of risk-free assets and one of risky assets.
3. Be sure the portfolio of risk assets is completely diversified so that returns are closely related to returns for a market portfolio of risky assets.
4. Maintain the specified risk level rather than attempting to shift the risk to conform to expected market movements.
5. Minimize total transactions costs by:
   a. Minimizing taxes
   b. Reducing turnover; only trade for liquidity and to maintain the desired risk level
   c. Minimizing liquidity costs by buying and selling currently liquid stocks as determined by the market.

[84] James H. Lorie, "Diversification: Old and New," *The Journal of Portfolio Management,* 1 no. 2 (Winter 1975): 25–28.

[85] These factors are discussed in Fischer Black, "Can Portfolio Managers Outrun the Random Walkers?" *Journal of Portfolio Management,* 1 no. 1 (Fall 1974): 32–36.

TABLE 7.2
Quarterly Returns for Index Funds and Standard & Poor's 500: 1975–1983

Quarter/ Year	American National Bank	Batterymarch Financial	Wells Fargo	Standard & Poor's 500
1/75	23.40	21.30	22.56	22.90
2/75	15.67	14.90	15.24	15.31
3/75	−11.12	−11.00	−10.95	−10.93
4/75	8.64	8.70	8.76	8.64
Year	37.65	34.80	36.36	36.92
1/76	14.89	14.80	14.82	14.96
2/76	2.67	2.80	2.53	2.44
3/76	2.06	1.80	1.71	1.89
4/76	2.11	2.20	3.24	3.18
Year	22.93	22.80	23.63	23.64
1/77	−8.16	−8.30	−7.50	−7.44
2/77	3.07	3.00	3.31	3.28
3/77	−2.88	−2.50	−2.77	−2.79
4/77	−.09	−.15	−.11	−.13
Year	−8.15	−8.05	−7.19	−7.19
1/78	−4.98	−5.50	−4.99	−4.95
2/78	8.62	8.00	8.42	8.52
3/78	8.88	8.10	8.70	8.66
4/78	−5.16	−4.20	−4.97	−4.95
Year	6.58	5.69	6.41	6.53
1/79	6.91	6.40	7.70	7.06
2/79	2.62	2.30	2.69	2.70
3/79	7.46	7.10	7.59	7.62
4/79	.10	−.10	.16	.10
Year	17.92	16.46	18.49	18.45
1/80	−4.05	−3.30	−4.00	−4.07
2/80	13.40	12.50	13.38	13.43
3/80	11.03	10.00	11.13	11.19
4/80	9.46	9.50	9.54	9.47
Year	32.24	31.00	32.50	32.45
1/81	1.34	4.70	1.37	1.34
2/81	−2.25	−2.73	−2.24	−2.29
3/81	−10.01	−9.78	−9.95	−10.17
4/81	6.99	7.12	6.89	6.94
Year	−4.62	−1.58	−4.62	−4.88
1/82	−7.21	−7.27	−7.18	−7.28
2/82	−.59	−.51	−.59	−.53
3/82	11.52	11.17	11.52	11.44
4/82	18.13	17.67	18.09	18.21
Year	21.52	20.68	21.52	21.50
1/83	10.07	9.94	10.06	9.98
2/83	10.91	10.94	11.00	11.07
3/83	−.15	−.03	−.12	−.15
4/83	.35	.23	.28	.40
Year	22.32	22.21	22.37	22.46

202   **Index Funds.**   The discussion above indicates that, if one assumes that there
are efficient capital markets and only a limited number of truly superior analysts,
a large amount of money should be managed so that the performance simply
matches that achieved by the aggregate market and costs are minimized so they
do not drop below the market. In response to such an apparent need, three
institutions instigated *market funds,* also referred to as *index funds,* during the
early 1970s. Index funds are security portfolios specially designed to duplicate
the performance of the overall security market as represented by some selected
market index series. Three major funds were started in the early 1970s: (1)
American National Bank and Trust Company of Chicago, (2) Batterymarch Financial Management Corporation of Boston, and (3) Wells Fargo Investment
Advisors, a division of Wells Fargo Bank in San Francisco. In all cases, these
equity portfolios were designed to match the performance of the S&P 500 Index.

Initially the funds experienced slow growth and limited attention. However,
as the result of a number of articles describing the reasoning behind index funds
and the justification for their existence, client demand grew, and a number of
financial institutions established their own index funds.[86] In fact, at present it is
not a matter of institutions having index funds, but of their attempting to develop
a "better" index fund.[87]

The ability of the three major index funds to match the market can be seen
from the figures in Table 7.2. These quarterly figures for the period 1975–1983
for the major funds indicate that the correlation of quarterly rates of return for the
index funds and the S&P 500 generally exceeded 0.98. Therefore, it appears that
the funds generally are able to fulfill their stated goal of matching market performance.

Portfolio Management with Superior Analysts.   If a portfolio manager has
superior security analysts with unique insights and analytical ability, they should
obviously be utilized. The problem is recognizing the superior analysts and
utilizing them while being able to avoid the costs entailed by using inferior
analysts. The system suggested earlier should be utilized to determine the truly
superior analysts and should be updated to ensure that they continue to be
superior. Assuming that several superior analysts are present, the portfolio manager would allow each of them to make investment recommendations for a
certain proportion of the portfolio, ensuring that their recommendations are
implemented in a way that maintains the risk preferences of the client. Also,
superior analysts should be encouraged to *concentrate their efforts in the second
tier of stocks.* Recall that, in Chapter 4 there was reference to the three tier market
created by the need of institutions for large liquid securities. The article by Reilly
suggested that the tiered market could be divided into three tiers as follows:[88]

[86] A. F. Ehrbar, "Index Funds–An Idea whose Time Is Coming," *Fortune* (June 1976), 145–148. John H.
Langbein and Richard A. Posner, "Market Funds and Trust-Investment Law," *American Bar Foundation
Research Journal,* 1976 no. 1: 1–34; John H. Langbein and Richard A. Posner, "Market Funds and Trust-
Investment Law II" *American Bar Foundation Research Journal,* 1977 no. 1: 1–27.

[87] "Here Come the 'Super' Indexers," *Institutional Investor,* 12 no. 11 (November 1978): 109–112.

[88] Frank K. Reilly, "A Three Tier Stock Market and Corporate Finance," *Financial Management,* 4 no. 3
(Autumn 1975): 7–15.

1. Top tier. Companies large enough to accommodate *all* institutions wishing to establish a meaningful position and yet retain liquidity. Assuming it was necessary to have a market value of $400 million or more to be in this tier, approximately 400 firms would meet this criterion.
2. Middle tier. Companies large enough to be acquired by most institutions and large investors, although probably *not* the largest 25–30 institutions. This tier required a market value of $200 million, and an additional 300 companies were estimated to be in this tier.
3. Bottom tier. All remaining companies not large enough to be considered by institutions. The total number of public companies in this tier is at least 5,000 and could be over 8,000.

Analysts should be encouraged to concentrate their analytical skills on middle-tier firms because these stocks probably possess the required liquidity, but they do not receive the attention given the top-tier stocks, so the markets may not be as efficient. Recall that, in the initial discussion of why one should expect markets to be efficient, it was contended that prices would fully reflect all information because many investors were receiving the news and analyzing the effect of the new information on security values. If there is a difference in the number of analysts following a stock, one could conceive of differences in the efficiency of the markets. In the case of top-tier stocks, all new information regarding the stock is well publicized and numerous analysts evaluate the effect. Therefore, one should expect the price to adjust rapidly and fully reflect the information. News about middle-tier firms is not as well publicized, and few analysts follow some of these firms. Therefore, prices may not adjust as rapidly to new information, and it would be worthwhile to concentrate analytical skills on these stocks for which the probabilities of finding a temporarily undervalued security are greater. Empirical support for this concept is contained in the article discussed earlier by Arbel and Strebel, which indicates superior returns for stocks followed by fewer analysts.[89]

SUMMARY

It is necessary to consider efficient capital markets at this point because there are several very important implications of such markets that have a direct bearing on security analysis and portfolio management. Capital markets are expected to be efficient because there is a large number of rational, profit-maximizing investors who react quickly to the release of new information. Because investors adjust prices rapidly to reflect new information, stock prices at any point in time are unbiased estimates of the securities' true, intrinsic value; consequently, there is a consistent relationship between the return on an investment and the risk it involves.

Because of the voluminous research that has been done on the EMH, the overall hypothesis has been divided into three segments and each has been tested separately. The weak form EMH states that stock prices fully reflect all *market* information, so any trading rule that uses past market data to predict

[89] Arner Arbel and Paul Strebel, "Pay Attention to Neglected Firms!" *Journal of Portfolio Management,* 9 no. 2 (Winter 1983): 37–42.

future returns should not be of value. The methods employed to test this hypothesis are pure statistical tests of independence (serial correlation tests and "runs" tests) and specific tests of various technical trading rules compared to buy-and-hold policies. The results consistently supported the weak form EMH.

The semistrong EMH asserts that security prices adjust rapidly to the release of *all public* information, and, therefore, prevailing prices fully reflect all such information. The tests of this hypothesis involve detailed examination of abnormal price movements surrounding the announcement of important new information and an analysis of whether investors could derive above average returns from trading on the basis of public information. The results for a number of studies related to significant economic events such as stock splits consistently supported the semistrong hypothesis. In contrast, some recent studies that examined the reaction to quarterly earning announcements and the differential returns to small firms did not support the hypothesis. Therefore, at this point it is appropriate to conclude that most studies support the hypothesis, but there are clearly some well-documented anomalies.

The strong form efficient market hypothesis states that security prices reflect *all* information. No groups of investors has monopolistic access to important information, and, therefore, no group should be able to derive above average returns consistently. The analysis of returns to corporate insiders and stock exchange specialists did not support the strong form hypothesis. In contrast, an analysis of results achieved by professional money managers supported the hypothesis, because their performance was typically inferior to those achieved with buy-and-hold policies.

The implications for a number of major participants in the equity market, including technical analysts, fundamental analysts, and portfolio managers, were discussed. The EMH indicates that technical analysis should be of no value. All forms of fundamental analysis are useful but difficult to implement because they involve the ability to *estimate future values* for relevant economic variables. It *is* possible to be a superior analyst, but it is *very difficult* because it requires the ability to consistently make projections that are superior to those made by other analysts.

Portfolio managers should constantly evaluate analysts to determine whether their performance is superior. If you do not have superior analysts, the portfolio should be run like an index fund. If you have superior analysts, allow them to make decisions for some part of the portfolio and concentrate on middle-tier firms where there is a higher probability of discovering misvalued stocks.

There is some good news and some bad news. The good news is that the practice of security analysis and portfolio management is not an art that has been lost to the great computer in the sky. These are still viable professions for those willing to extend the effort and able to accept the pressures.

The bad news is that, because of many bright, hardworking people with extensive resources, the game is not easy. In fact, the aforementioned competitors have created a very efficient capital market in which it is very difficult to be superior.

QUESTIONS

1. Discuss the rationale for expecting the existence of an efficient capital market.
2. Based upon the factors that contribute to an efficient market, what would you look for to differentiate the market for two alternative stocks; i.e., why should there be a difference between the markets for the stocks?
3. Define and discuss the weak form efficient market hypothesis (EMH).
4. Describe the two sets of tests used to examine the weak form efficient market hypothesis.
5. Define and discuss the semistrong efficient market hypothesis.
6. Describe the two general tests used to examine the semistrong EMH. Would you expect the results from the two different tests to be consistent? Why?
7. Using the standard one-factor CAPM, describe how you would derive abnormal risk-adjusted returns for a stock during a period surrounding a significant economic event. Give an example.
8. It is contended that many tests of the semistrong EMH are a *joint* test of the capital asset pricing model *and* the efficient market hypothesis. Explain this contention and discuss its impact in the small firm studies.
9. When testing the EMH using alternative trading rules versus a buy-and-hold policy, there are three common mistakes that can bias the results against the EMH. Discuss each individually and explain why it would cause a bias.
10. Describe the results of a study that supported the semistrong EMH and specifically discuss why the results supported the hypothesis.
11. Describe the results of a study that did *not* support the semistrong EMH and specifically discuss why the results did not support the hypothesis.
12. Define and discuss the strong form EMH. Why do some observers contend that the strong form hypothesis really requires a perfect market in addition to efficient markets? Be specific.
13. Discuss in general terms how one would go about testing the strong form EMH. Consider why these tests are relevant. Give a brief example.
14. Describe the results of a study that does *not* support the strong form EMH. Discuss specifically why these results do not support the hypothesis.
15. Describe the results of a study that indicates support for the strong form EMH. Discuss specifically why these results support the hypothesis.
16. What are the implications of the EMH for the use of technical analysis?
17. What are the implications of the EMH for fundamental analysis? Be specific and discuss what the EMH does and does not imply.
18. In a world with efficient capital markets, what is required to be a superior analyst? Be specific.
19. How would you determine whether an analyst is truly superior? Be very specific in discussing the test.
20. What are the implications of an efficient market for a portfolio manager without any superior analysts? Specifically, how should he run his portfolio?
21. Describe an index fund. What are its purposes? How is such a fund run?
22. You are told that the great majority of banks rejected the idea of index funds until forced into them by their clients. Does this surprise you? How would you explain this attitude?
23. Some observers contend that index funds are the ultimate answer in a world with

efficient capital markets. Discuss the purpose of index funds and what they do that is correct in a world with efficient capital markets.

24. At a social gathering you meet the portfolio manager for the trust department of a local bank. He confides to you that he has been following the recommendations of his six analysts for an extended period and has found that two are superior, two are average, and two are clearly inferior. What would you recommend that he do in terms of running his portfolio? Be specific.

25. Do you think the development of a tiered market has any implications for the discussion of efficient capital markets? If so, what are they?

REFERENCES

Alexander, Sidney S. "Price Movements in Speculative Markets: Trends or Random Walks." *Industrial Management Review.* 2 no 2. (May 1961).

Alexander, Sidney S. "Price Movements in Speculative Markets: Trends or Random Walks, Number 2." *Industrial Management Review.* 5 no. 2. (Spring 1964).

Arbel, Arner, and Strebel, Paul. "Pay Attention to Neglected Firms!" *Journal of Portfolio Management.* 9 no. 2 (Winter 1983).

Archibald, T. Ross. "Stock Market Reaction to the Depreciation Switch-Back." *Accounting Review.* 47 no. 1 (January 1972).

Ball, Ray. "Anomalies in Relationships between Securities' Yields and Yield-Surrogates." *Journal of Financial Economics.* 6 no. 2/3 (June–September 1978).

Ball, Ray. "Changes in Accounting Techniques and Stock Prices." *Empirical Research in Accounting.* (Supplement to *Journal of Accounting Research*) 10 (1972).

Ball, Ray. "Risk, Return, and Disequilibrium—An Application to Changes in Accounting Techniques." *Journal of Finance.* 27 no. 2 (May 1972).

Banz, R. W. "The Relationship between Return and Market Value of Common Stocks." *Journal of Financial Economics.* 9 no. 1 (March 1981).

Bar-Yosef, Sasson, and Brown, Lawrence. "A Reexamination of Stock Splits Using Moving Betas." *Journal of Finance.* 32 no. 4 (September 1977).

Basu, S. "The Information Content of Price-Earnings Ratios." *Financial Management.* 4 no. 2 (Summer 1975).

Basu, S. "Investment Performance of Common Stocks in Relation to Their Price-Earnings Ratios: A Test of the Efficient Market Hypothesis." *Journal of Finance.* 32 no. 3 (June 1977).

Black, Fischer. "Can Portfolio Managers Outrun the Random Walkers?" *Journal of Portfolio Management.* 1 no. 1 (Fall 1974).

Black, Fischer. "Implications of the Random Walk Hypothesis for Portfolio Management." *Financial Analysts Journal.* 27 no. 2 (March–April 1971).

Block, Stanley, and Stanley, Marjorie. "The Financial Characteristics and Price Movement Patterns of Companies Approaching the Unseasoned Securities Market in the Late 1970s." *Financial Management.* 9 no. 4 (Winter 1980).

Branch, Ben. "A Tax Loss Trading Rule." *Journal of Business.* 50 no. 2 (April 1977).

Brenner, Menachem. The Effect of Model Misspecification on Tests of the Efficient Market Hypothesis." *Journal of Finance.* 32 no. 1 (March 1977).

Brown, Phillip, and Ball, Ray. "An Empirical Evaluation of Accounting Income Numbers." *Journal of Accounting Research.* 6 no. 2. (Autumn 1963).

Brown, Stewart L. "Earnings Changes, Stock Prices, and Market Efficiency." *Journal of Finance.* 33 no. 1 (March 1978).

Carey, Kenneth. "A Model of Individual Transactions Stock Prices." Ph.D. dissertation. University of Kansas, 1971.

Carey, Kenneth. "Non-Random Price Changes in Association with Trading in Large Blocks." *Journal of Business.* 50 no. 4 (October 1977).

Charest, Guy. "Split Information, Stock Returns and Market Efficiency." *Journal of Financial Economics.* 6 no. 2/3 (June–September 1978).

Dann, Larry, Mayers, David, and Raab, Robert. "Trading Rules, Large Blocks, and the Speed of Price Adjustment." *Journal of Financial Economics.* 4 no. 1 (January 1977).

Dimson, Elroy. "Risk Measurement when Shares Are Subject to Infrequent Trading." *Journal of Financial Economics.* 7 no. 2 (June 1979).

Dodd, Peter, and Ruback, Richard. "Tender Offers and Stockholders Returns." *Journal of Financial Economics.* 5 no. 3 (December 1977).

Dyl, Edward A. "Capital Gains Taxation and Year-End Stock Market Behavior." *Journal of Finance.* 32 no. 1 (March 1977).

Ehrbar, A. F. "Index Funds—An Idea Whose Timing is Coming." *Fortune.* (June 1976).

Elia, Charles J. "Most Professionals Lagged Market Averages in Past Two Years, Study of Pooled Funds." *Wall Street Journal.* February 28, 1977.

Eskew, Robert, and Wright, William. "An Empirical Analysis of Differential Capital Market Reactions to Extraordinary Accounting Items." *Journal of Finance.* 41 no. 2 (May 1976).

Fama, Eugene F. "The Behavior of Stock Prices." *Journal of Business.* 38 no. 1 (January 1965).

Fama, Eugene F. "Efficient Capital Markets: A Review of Theory and Empirical Work." *Journal of Finance.* 25 no. 2 (May 1970).

Fama, Eugene, F. "Random Walks in Stock Market Prices." *Financial Analysts Journal.* 21 no. 5 (September–October 1965).

Fama, Eugene F., and MacBeth, J. "Risk Return and Equilibrium, Some Empirical Results." *Journal of Political Economy.* 81 no. 2 (May 1973).

Fama, Eugene F., Fisher, L., Jensen, M., and Roll, R. "The Adjustment of Stock Prices to New Information." *International Economic Review.* 10 no. 1 (February 1969).

Fama, Eugene F., and Blume, Marshall. "Filter Rules and Stock Market Trading Profits." *Journal of Business.* 39 no. 1 (January 1966 Supplement).

Finnerty, Joseph E. "Insiders Activity and Inside Information: A Multivariate Analysis." *Journal of Financial and Quantitative Analysis.* 11 no. 2 (June 1976).

Finnerty, Joseph E. "Insiders and Market Efficiency." *Journal of Finance.* 31 no. 4 (September 1976).

Firth, Michael. "The Impact of Earnings Announcements on the Share Price Behavior of Similar Type Firms." *The Economic Journal.* (June 1976).

Foster, G. "Stock Market Reaction to Estimates of Earnings Per Share by Company Officials." *Journal of Accounting Research.* 11 no. 1 (Spring 1973).

Furst, Richard W. "Does Listing Increase the Market Price of Common Stocks?" *Journal of Business.* 43 no. 2 (April 1970).

Goulet, Waldemar M. "Price Changes, Managerial Actions and Insider Trading at the Time of Listing." *Financial Management.* 3 no. 1 (Spring 1974).

Grier, Paul, and Albin, Peter. "Non-Random Price Changes in Association with Trading in Large Blocks." *Journal of Business.* 46 no. 3 (July 1973).

Hagerman, Robert L., and Richmond, Richard D. "Random Walk Martingales and the OTC." *Journal of Finance.* 28 no. 4 (September 1973).

Hausman, W. H., West, R. R., and Largay, J. A. "Stock Splits, Price Changes, and Trading Profits: A Synthesis." *Journal of Business.* 44 no. 1 (January 1971).

Ibbotson, Roger G. and Jaffe, Jeffrey. "Hot Issues Markets." *Journal of Finance.* 30 no. 4 (September 1975).

Ibbotson, Roger G. "Price Performance of Common Stock New Issues." *Journal of Financial Economics.* 2 no. 3 (September 1975).

Jaffe, Jeffrey. "Special Information and Insider Trading." *Journal of Business.* 47 no. 3 (July 1974).

James, Christopher, and Edmister, Robert. "The Relation between Common Stock Returns, Trading Activity and Market Value." *Journal of Finance* 38 no. 4 (September, 1983).

Jensen, Michael. "The Performance of Mutual Funds in the Period 1945–1964." *Journal of Finance.* 23 no. 2 (May 1968).

Jones, C., and Litzenberger, R. "Quarterly Earnings Reports and Intermediate Stock Price Trends." *Journal of Finance.* 25 no. 1 (March 1970).

Jordan, Ronald J. "An Empirical Investigation of the Adjustment of Stock Prices to New Quarterly Earnings Information." *Journal of Financial and Quantitative Analysis.* 8 no. 4 (September 1973).

Joy, O. Maurice, Litzenberger, Robert H., and McEnally, Richard W. "The Adjustment of Stock Prices to the Announcements of Unanticipated Changes in Quarterly Earnings." *Journal of Accounting Research.* 15 no. 2 (Autumn 1977).

Joy, O. Maurice, and Jones, Charles P. "Earnings Reports and Market Efficiencies: An Analysis of Contrary Evidence." *Journal of Financial Research.* 2 no. 1 (Spring 1979).

Kaplan, Robert S., and Roll, Richard. "Investor Evaluation of Accounting Information: Some Empirical Evidence." *Journal of Business.* 45 no. 2 (April 1972).

Katz, Steven. "The Price Adjustment Process of Bonds to Rating Reclassifications: A Test of Bond Market Efficiency." *Journal of Finance.* 26 no. 2 (May 1974).

Kendall, Maurice G. "The Analysis of Economic Time Series." *Journal of the Royal Statistical Society.* 96 (1953).

Kiger, J. E. "An Empirical Investigation of NYSE Volume and Price Reactions to the Announcement of Quarterly Earnings," *Journal of Accounting Research.* 10 no. 1 (Spring 1972).

Langbein, John H., and Posner, Richard A. "Market Funds and Trust-Investment Law." *American Bar Foundation Research Journal.* 1976 no. 1.

Latane, H. A., Joy, O. Maurice, and Jones, Charles P. "Quarterly Data Sort-Rank Routines and Security Evaluation." *Journal of Business.* 43 no. 4 (October 1970).

Latane H. A., Tuttle, D. L., and Jones, C. P. "Quarterly Data: E/P Ratios vs. Changes in Earnings in Forecasting Future Price Changes." *Financial Analysts Journal.* 25 no. 1 (January–February 1969).

Loque, Dennis E. "On the Pricing of Unseasoned New Issues, 1965–1969." *Journal of Financial and Quantitative Analysis.* 8 no. 1 (January 1973).

Lorie, James H., and Niederhoffer, Victor. "Predictive and Statistical Properties of Insider Trading." *Journal of Law and Economics.* 11 (April 1968).

McConnell, John, and Sanger, Gary C. "New Listings on the NYSE: A Reexamination of Some Anomalous Evidence Regarding Market Efficiency." mimeo. (May 13, 1981).

McDonald, J. G., and Fisher, A. K. "New Issue Stock Price Behavior." *Journal of Finance.* 27 no. 1 (March 1972).

Miller, Robert, and Reilly, Frank K. "Initial Public Offerings: An Analysis of Daily Returns." mimeo. (April 1984).

Moore, Arnold. "A Statistical Analysis of Common Stock Prices." Ph.D. dissertation. University of Chicago, Graduate School of Business. 1962.

Neuberger, Brian M., and Hammond, Carl T. "A Study of Underwriters' Experience with Unseasoned New Issues." *Journal of Financial and Quantitative Analysis* 9 no. 2 (March 1974).

Niederhoffer, Victor, and Osborne, M. F. M. "Market Making and Reversal on the Stock Exchange." *Journal of American Statistical Association.* 61 no. 316 (December 1966).

Peavy, John W. III, and Goodman, David A. "The Significance of P/Es for Portfolio Returns." *Journal of Portfolio Management.* 9 no. 2 (Winter 1983).

210

Pettit, R. Richardson. "Dividend Announcements, Security Performance, and Capital Market Efficiency." *Journal of Finance.* 27 no. 5 (December 1972).

Pinches, George. "The Random Walk Hypothesis and Technical Analysis." *Financial Analysts Journal.* 26 no. 2 (March–April 1970).

Pinches, George, and Singleton, J. Clay. "The Adjustment of Stock Prices to Bond Rating Changes." *Journal of Finance.* 33 no. 1 (March 1978).

Pratt, Shannon P., and DeVere, Charles W. "Relationship between Insider Trading and Rates of Return on NYSE Common Stocks, 1960–66." James Lorie and Robert Brealey, eds. *Modern Developments in Investment Management.* New York: Praeger Publishers, 1972.

Reilly, Frank K. "Further Evidence on Short-Run Results for New Issue Investors." *Journal of Financial and Quantitative Analysis.* 8 no. 1 (January 1973).

Reilly, Frank K. "New Issues Revisited." *Financial Management.* 6 no. 4 (Winter 1977).

Reilly, Frank K., and Drzycimski, Eugene F. "Short-Run Profits from Stock Splits." *Financial Management.* 10 no. 3 (Summer 1981).

Reilly, Frank K., and Drzycimski, Eugene F. "The Stock Exchange Specialist and the Market Impact of Major World Events." *Financial Analysts Journal.* 31 no. 4 (July–August 1975).

Reilly, Frank K., and Drzycimski, Eugene F. "Tests of Stock Market Efficiency Following Major World Events." *Journal of Business Research.* 1 no. 1 (Summer 1973).

Reilly, Frank K., and Hatfield, Kenneth. "Investor Experience with New Stock Issues." *Financial Analysts Journal.* 25 no. 5 (September–October 1969).

Reilly, Frank K., Smith, Ralph E., and Hurt, Ron. "Stock Market Reaction to Changes in Inventory Valuation Methods." Financial Management Association Meeting, Kansas City, Mo. (October 1975).

Reinganum, Marc R. "Abnormal Returns in Small Firm Portfolios." *Financial Analysts Journal.* 37 no. 2 (March–April 1981).

Reinganum, Marc R. "A Direct Test of Roll's Conjecture on the Firm Size Effect." *Journal of Finance.* 37 no. 1 (March 1982).

Reinganum, Marc R. "Portfolio Strategies Based on Market Capitalization." *Journal of Portfolio Management.* 9 no. 2. (Winter 1983).

Reinganum, Marc R. "Misspecification of Capital Asset Pricing: Empirical Anomalies Based on Earnings Yield and Market Values." *Journal of Financial Economics.* 9 no. 1 (March 1981).

Roll, Richard. "A Possible Explanation of the Small Firm Effect." *Journal of Finance.* 36 no. 4 (September 1981).

Roll, Richard. "Vas Ist Das?" *Journal of Portfolio Management.* 9 no. 2 (Winter 1983).

Samuelson, Paul A. "Challenge to Judgement." *Journal of Portfolio Management.* 1 no. 1 (Fall 1974).

Samuelson, Paul A. "Proof that Properly Anticipated Prices Fluctuate Randomly." *Industrial Management Review.* 6 (1965).

Scholes, Myron, and Williams, Joseph. "Estimating Betas from Nonsynchronous Data." *Journal of Financial Economics.* 5 no. 3 (December 1977).

Sharpe, William F. "Mutual Fund Performance." *Journal of Business.* 39 no. 1 (January 1966 Supplement).

Stoll, Hans R., and Curley, Anthony J. "Small Business and the New Issues Market for Equities." *Journal of Financial and Quantitative Analysis.* 5 no. 3 (September 1970).

Stoll, Hans R., and Whaley, Robert E. "Transactions Costs and the Small Firm Effect." *Journal of Financial Economics.* forthcoming.

Sunder, Shyam. "Stock Price and Risk Related to Accounting Changes in Inventory Valuation." *The Accounting Review.* 50 no. 2 (April 1975).

U.S. Congress, Securities and Exchange Commission, *Institutional Investor Study Report,* 92nd Congress, 1st Session, Howe Document No. 92–64. Washington, D.C.: U.S. Government Printing Office, 1971.

Watts, Ross L. "Systematic 'Abnormal' Returns after Quarterly Earnings Announcements." *Journal of Financial Economics.* 6 no. 2/3 (June–September 1978).

Ying, Louis K. W., Lewellen, W. G., Schlarbaum, G. G., and Lease, R. C. "Stock Exchange Listings and Securities Returns." *Journal of Financial and Quantitative Analysis.* 12 no. 4 (September 1977).

Chapter 8   *An Introduction to Portfolio Management*

T he study of portfolio theory and capital market theory is generally placed near the end of a text on investments because it is considered necessary to deal with the analysis of individual securities before you consider how to combine these securities into a portfolio. Unfortunately, such a sequence creates a problem in analyzing individual industries and stocks because capital market theory has generated a risk variable that is very important for such an analysis. Work done in these areas has indicated an important measure of risk for an individual asset in a world in which investors attempt to derive optimum returns from their portfolios. In other words, there is a general principle of risk derived from portfolio theory which must be understood before any attempt to deal with individual securities is made. Therefore, this chapter is an introduction to the basic concepts of portfolio theory. In the following chapter, we will introduce capital market theory with an emphasis on the risk measure for individual assets.

The purpose of this chapter is to explain portfolio theory step by step so that you understand the basic portfolio risk formula and recognize what is important when you combine different assets.

AN OPTIMUM PORTFOLIO

One basic assumption of portfolio theory is that any investor wishes to maximize the returns from his investments. In order to adequately deal with such an assumption, certain ground rules must be laid. The first of these is that the portfolio being considered by an individual should include all of his assets and liabilities, not only stocks or even only marketable securities, but also such items as the investor's car, house, and less marketable assets like coins, stamps, antiques, furniture, etc. The full spectrum of assets must be considered because the returns from all of these assets interact and *this interaction is important.* Hence, a good portfolio is *not* simply a collection of individually good assets.

An Assumption — Risk Aversion

It is also assumed that *investors are basically risk averse,* which simply means that, given a choice between two assets with equal rates of return, an investor will select the asset with the lower level of risk. Evidence that most investors are risk averse is provided by the fact that they purchase various types of insurance, including life insurance, car insurance, and hospital and accident insurance. Insurance is basically a current certain outlay of a given amount to guard against an uncertain—possibly larger—outlay in the future. People who purchase insurance are willing to pay to avoid the uncertainty of the future regarding these items. In other words, they want to avoid the risk of a potentially large future loss. Further evidence of risk aversion is the difference in promised yield for different grades of bonds that are supposedly of different risk classes; i.e., the required rate of return (promised yield) increases as you go from AAA (the lowest risk class) to AA to A, etc. This means that investors require a higher rate of return in order to accept higher risk.

The foregoing does not imply that everybody is risk averse, or that investors are completely risk averse regarding all financial commitments. Not everybody buys insurance for everything. There are some people who have no insurance against anything, either by choice or because they can't afford it. In addition, some individuals buy insurance and also gamble at race tracks or in Las Vegas where it is known that the expected returns are negative, which means that participants are willing to pay for the excitement of the risk involved. This combination of risk preference and risk aversion can be explained by a utility function that is not completely concave or convex, but it is a combination of the two that depends upon the amount of money involved. Friedman and Savage speculate that such is the case for people who like to gamble for small amounts (in lotteries or nickel slot machines) but insure themselves against large losses like fire or accidents.[1]

However, most investors committing large sums of money to developing a portfolio of earning assets are risk averse. This means that there should be a positive relationship between expected return and expected risk.

Definition of Risk

While there is a difference in the specific definitions of risk and uncertainty, for our purposes and in most financial literature the two terms are used interchangeably. In fact, one way to define risk is as *the uncertainty of future outcomes.* An alternative definition might be as *the probability of an adverse outcome.*

MARKOWITZ PORTFOLIO THEORY

In the 1950s and early 1960s a large segment of the investment community talked about risk, but there was no measurable specification for the term. One aspect of the portfolio model is that it required investors to quantify their risk variable. The

[1] Milton Friedman and Leonard J. Savage, "The Utility Analysis of Choices Involving Risk," *Journal of Political Economy,* 56 no. 3 (August 1948): 279–304.

basic portfolio model, developed by Harry Markowitz, derived the expected rate of return for a portfolio of assets and an expected risk measure.[2] Markowitz showed that the variance of the rate of return was a meaningful measure of risk under a reasonable set of assumptions and derived the formulas for computing the variance of the portfolio. This portfolio variance formulation indicated the importance of diversification for reducing risk and showed how to properly diversify. The Markowitz model is based on several assumptions regarding investor behavior:

1. Investors consider each investment alternative as being represented by a probability distribution of expected returns over some holding period.
2. Investors maximize one period expected utility and possess utility curves that demonstrate diminishing marginal utility of wealth.
3. Individuals estimate risk on the basis of the variability of expected returns.
4. Investors base decisions solely on expected return and risk; i.e., their utility curves are a function of expected return and variance (or standard deviation) of returns only.
5. For a given risk level, investors prefer higher returns to lower returns. Similarly, for a given level of expected return, investors prefer less risk to more risk.

Under these assumptions, *a single asset or portfolio of assets is considered to be efficient if no other asset or portfolio of assets offers higher expected return with the same (or lower) risk, or lower risk with the same (or higher) expected return.*

One of the best known measures of risk is the *variance or standard deviation of expected returns.* It is a statistical measure of the dispersion of returns around the expected value; i.e., a larger value indicates greater dispersion, all other factors being equal. The idea is that the more disperse the returns, the greater the uncertainty of those returns in any future period. Another measure of risk is the *range of returns* based upon the assumption that a larger range of returns, from the lowest to the highest, means greater uncertainty regarding future expected returns.

In contrast to using measures that analyze any deviation from expectations, some believe that the investor should only be concerned with *returns below expectations*—deviations below the mean value. A measure that only considers such adverse deviations is the semivariance. An extension of this measure would be *deviations below zero* or negative returns. Both measures implicitly assume that investors want to minimize their regret from below average returns. It is implicit that investors would welcome positive returns or returns above expectations, so these are not considered when measuring risk. Similarly, Zinbarg proposed the use of *negative opportunity returns* as a measure of risk. Negative opportunity returns are returns below the risk-free rate of return.[3]

Although there are numerous potential measures of risk, we begin with the variance or standard deviation of returns, because this measure is somewhat intuitive, and it is a correct risk measure for most investors.

[2] Harry Markowitz, "Portfolio Selection," *Journal of Finance,* 7 no. 1 (March 1952): 77–91; and *Portfolio Selection—Efficient Diversification of Investments* (New Haven, Conn.: Yale University Press, 1959).

[3] Edward D. Zinbarg, "Modern Approach to Investment Risk," *Financial Executive,* 41 no. 2 (February 1973): 44–48.

Portfolio Return

The expected rate of return for a portfolio of assets is simply the weighted average of the expected rates of return for the individual assets in the portfolio. The weights are the proportion of total value for the asset. The expected return for a hypothetical individual asset is computed as shown in Table 8.1. In this example, we assume that we have estimated equal probabilities for all the potential returns.

The expected return for *an individual asset* with the set of potential returns and probabilities used in the example would be 11 percent. The expected return for a hypothetical four-asset *portfolio* is shown in Table 8.2.

The expected return for the total portfolio would be 11.5 percent. The effect of adding or dropping any security from the portfolio would be easy to determine, given the new weights based on value and the expected returns for each of the assets. This computation of the expected return for the portfolio can be generalized as follows:

$$E(R_{port}) = \sum_{i=1}^{n} W_i R_i .$$

Variance (Standard Deviation) of Returns. It was mentioned earlier that we would be using the variance, or the standard deviation of returns, as the measure of risk. (The reader will recall that the standard deviation is the square root of the variance.) Therefore, at this point we will demonstrate the computation of the standard deviation of returns for an individual asset. Subsequently, after a discussion of some other statistical concepts, we will consider the determination of the standard deviation for a *portfolio* of assets.

The variance or standard deviation is a measure of the variation of possible rates of return (R_i) from the expected rate of return $[E(R_i)]$ as follows:

$$\text{Variance } (\sigma^2) = \sum_{i=1}^{n} [R_i - E(R_i)]^2 P_i ,$$

where P_i is the probability of the possible rate of return (R_i).

$$\text{Standard Deviation } (\sigma) = \sqrt{\sum_{i=1}^{n} [R_i - E(R_i)]^2 P_i} .$$

The computation of the variance and standard deviation for the individual risky asset in Table 8.1 is set forth in Table 8.3.

Prior to discussing the derivation of the risk of the portfolio, it is necessary to understand two basic concepts in statistics: covariance and correlation.

Covariance of Returns — Discussion and Example. Covariance is a measure of the degree to which two variables "move together" over time. In portfolio analysis, we usually are concerned with the covariance of *returns* rather than that

TABLE 8.1
Computation of Expected Return for Individual Risky Asset

Probability	Potential Return (Percent)	Expected Return (Percent)
.25	.08	.0200
.25	.10	.0250
.25	.12	.0300
.25	.14	.0350
		$E(R) = .1100$

TABLE 8.2
Computation of the Expected Return for a Portfolio of Risky Assets

Weight (W_1) (Percent of Portfolio)	Expected Security Return R_i	Expected Portfolio Return ($W_i \times R_i$)
.20	.10	.0200
.30	.11	.0330
.30	.12	.0360
.20	.13	.0260
		$E(R_{port}) = .1150$

TABLE 8.3
Computation of the Variance for an Individual Risky Asset

Potential Return (R_i)	Expected Return $E(R_i)$	$R_i - E(R_i)$	$[R_i - E(R_i)]^2$	P_i	$[R_i - E(R_i)^2 P_i$
.08	.11	−.03	.0009	.25	.000225
.10	.11	−.01	.0001	.25	.000025
.12	.11	.01	.0001	.25	.000025
.14	.11	.03	.0009	.25	.000225
					.000500

Variance (σ^2) = .00050
Standard Deviation (σ) = .02236

of prices or some other variable.[4] If the covariance between the returns for two assets is positive, this indicates that the returns tend to move in the same direction at the same time; if the covariance is negative, it indicates that the returns tend to move in opposite directions. The *magnitude* of the covariance depends

---

[4] Returns, of course, can be measured in a variety of ways, depending upon the type of asset being considered. The reader will recall that we defined returns in Chapter 1 as

$$R_t = \frac{EV - BV + CF}{BV},$$

where *EV* is ending value, *BV* is beginning value, and *CF* is the cash flow during the period.

TABLE 8.4
Computation of Monthly Rates of Return

	Avon			IBM		
	Closing Price	Dividend	Rate of Return (Percent)	Closing Price	Dividend	Rate of Return (Percent)
12/81	30	—	—	56 7/8	—	—
1/82	30 3/8	—	1.25	63 5/8	—	11.87
2/82	25 1/2	—	(16.05)	61 7/8	—	(2.75)
3/82	24	.75	(2.94)	59 3/4	.86	(2.04)
4/82	25 1/4	—	5.21	64 1/4	—	7.53
5/82	24 1/2	—	(3.92)	61 1/2	—	(4.28)
6/82	23 1/2	.75	(1.02)	60 5/8	.86	(0.02)
7/82	20 5/8	—	(12.23)	65 5/8	—	8.25
8/82	25	—	21.21	70 1/2	—	7.43
9/82	22 7/8	.50	(6.50)	73 3/8	.86	5.30
10/82	25 1/8	—	9.84	79 7/8	—	8.86
11/82	27 3/4	—	10.45	86 1/2	—	8.29
12/82	26 3/4	.50	(1.80)	96 1/4	.86	12.27
			$\overline{R}_{Avon} = .29$			$\overline{R}_{IBM} = 5.06$

upon the variances of the individual return series, as well as on the relationship between the series.

Table 8.4 contains the monthly closing prices and dividends for Avon and IBM. Given this data it is possible to compute monthly rates of return for these two stocks during 1982.

Figure 8.1 and 8.2 contain a time-series plot of the monthly rates for the two stocks. Although it appears that the two return series moved together during some months, in other months it appears that the returns moved in opposite directions. The purpose of the covariance measure is to provide an *absolute* measure of their movement together over time.

For two assets, i and j, the covariance of monthly rates of return is defined as:

$$Cov_{ij} = E\{[R_i - E(R_i)][R_j - E(R_j)]\}$$
$$= \frac{1}{12} \sum_{i=1}^{12} [R_i - E(R_i)][R_j - E(R_j)].$$

As can be seen, if the rates of return for one stock are above its mean during a given period, and the returns for the other stock are likewise above its mean during this same period, then the *product* of these deviations from the mean will be positive (i.e., the covariance will be some large positive value). In contrast, if, during a given month, the return on Avon was above its mean and the return on the IBM stock was below its mean, the product of these deviations would be negative. If this contrary movement happened consistently, the covariance between the rates of return would be a large negative value.

As an example, Table 8.5 contains the monthly rates of return during 1982 for Avon and IBM as computed in Table 8.4. Without looking one might expect the returns for the two stocks to have reasonably low covariance because of the

FIGURE 8.1
Time Series of Returns for Avon

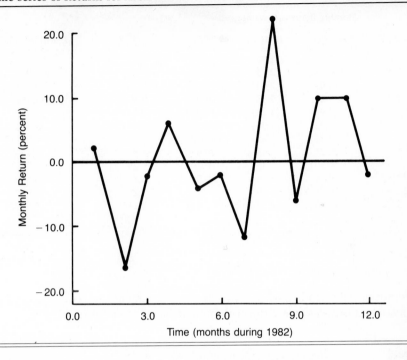

FIGURE 8.2
Time Series of Returns for IBM

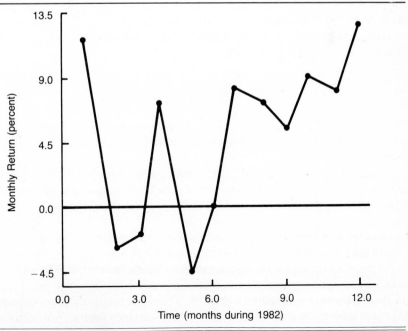

TABLE 8.5
Computation of Covariance of Returns for Avon and IBM

Month/Year	Monthly Return (Percent)		$R_i - E(R_i)$	$R_j - E(R_j)$	$[R_i - E(R_i)][R_j - E(R_j)]$
	Avon (R_i)	IBM(R_j)			
1/82	1.25	11.87	.96	6.81	6.538
2/82	(16.05)	(2.75)	(16.34)	(7.81)	127.615
3/82	(2.94)	(2.04)	(3.23)	(7.10)	22.933
4/82	5.21	7.53	4.92	2.47	12.152
5/82	(3.92)	(4.28)	(4.21)	(9.34)	39.321
6/82	(1.02)	(.02)	(1.31)	(5.04)	6.602
7/82	(12.23)	8.25	(12.52)	3.19	(39.939)
8/82	21.21	7.43	20.92	2.37	49.580
9/82	(6.50)	5.30	(6.79)	.24	(1.630)
10/82	9.84	8.86	9.55	3.80	36.290
11/82	10.45	8.29	10.16	3.23	32.817
12/82	(1.80)	12.27	(2.09)	7.21	(15.069)
					$\Sigma = 277.21$

differences in the products these firms produce (cosmetics and computers). The expected returns $E(R)$ were the arithmetic mean of the monthly returns:

$$E(R_i) = 1/12 \sum_{t=1}^{12} R_{it} \text{ and } E(R_j) = 1/12 \sum_{t=1}^{12} R_{jt}.$$

All figures (except those in the last column) were rounded to the nearest tenth of one percent. As shown, the average monthly return on Avon was 0.29 percent and the average monthly return on IBM stock was 5.06 percent. From the results of the last column, we can derive the covariance between these two stocks as follows:

$$Cov_{ij} = \frac{1}{12}(277.21) = 23.10.$$

Interpretation of a number like 23.10 is difficult; i.e., is 23 high or low for covariance? We know the relationship is generally positive, but it is not possible to be more specific.

Figure 8.3 shows a scatter diagram with paired values of R_{it} and R_{jt} plotted against each other. This plot demonstrates the linear nature and strength of the relationship.

Covariance and Correlation.   Covariance is affected by the variability of the two return series. Therefore, interpreting a number such as the 23.10 computed in the previous section is difficult because, if the two individual series were very volatile, 23 might not indicate a very strong positive relationship. In contrast, if the two series were very stable, a value of 23 could be relatively large. Obviously, what you want to do is to "standardize" this covariance for the individual varia-

FIGURE 8.3
Scatter Plot of Monthly Returns during 1982: Avon vs. IBM

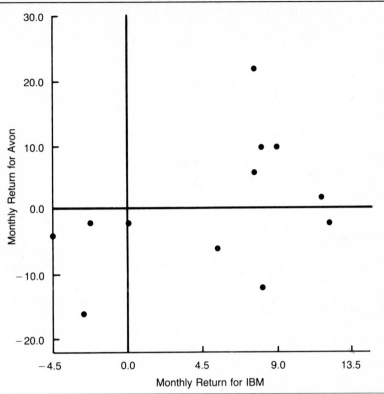

bility of the two return series. This is done in the following relationship:

$$r_{ij} = \frac{Cov_{ij}}{\sigma_i \sigma_j},$$

where:

r_{ij} = the correlation coefficient of returns

σ_i = the standard deviation of R_{it}

σ_j = the standard deviation of R_{jt}.

$$\sigma_i^2 = E\{[R_{it} - E(R_i)]^2\} = \sum_{t=1}^{N} [R_{it} - E(R_i)]^2 \frac{1}{N}$$

$$\sigma_j^2 = E\{[R_{jt} - E(R_j)]^2\} = \sum_{t=1}^{N} [R_{jt} - E(R_j)]^2 \frac{1}{N}.$$

As shown, when we standardize the covariance by the individual standard deviations, we derive the correlation coefficient (r_{ij}) which can only vary in the range

TABLE 8.6
Computation of Standard Deviation of Returns for Avon and IBM

	$R_{it} - E(R_i)$	$[R_{it} - E(R_i)]^2$	$R_{jt} - E(R_j)$	$[R_{jt} - E(R_j)]^2$
1/82	.96	.92	6.81	46.39
2/82	(16.34)	267.06	(7.81)	61.00
3/82	(2.65)	7.01	(7.10)	50.41
4/82	4.92	24.19	2.47	6.10
5/82	(4.21)	17.74	9.34	87.24
6/82	1.31	1.72	(5.04)	25.40
7/82	(12.52)	156.80	3.19	10.18
8/82	20.92	437.56	2.37	5.62
9/82	(6.79)	46.13	.24	.06
10/82	9.55	91.16	3.80	14.44
11/82	10.16	103.18	3.23	10.43
12/82	(2.09)	4.38	7.21	51.98
		$\Sigma = 1157.86$		$\Sigma = 369.24$

-1 to $+1$. A value of $+1$ would indicate a perfect positive linear relationship between R_i and R_j; i.e., the returns for the two stocks would move together in a completely linear manner.

To derive this standardized measure of the relationship, it is necessary to compute the standard deviation for the two individual series. We already have the values for $R_{it} - E(R_i)$ and $R_{jt} - E(R_j)$ in Table 8.5. We can square each of these values and sum them as is done in Table 8.6.

Thus:

$$\sigma_i^2 = \frac{1}{12}(1157.86) = 96.488$$

and

$$\sigma_j^2 = \frac{1}{12}(369.24) = 30.770.$$

Therefore:

$$\sigma_i = \sqrt{96.488} = 9.823\%$$
$$\sigma_j = \sqrt{30.770} = 5.547\%.$$

Thus, the correlation coefficient between returns for Avon and IBM is:

$$r_{ij} = \frac{Cov_{ij}}{\sigma_i \sigma_j} = \frac{23.10}{(9.823)(5.547)} = .42.$$

As noted, a correlation of $+1.0$ would indicate perfect positive correlation, a value of -1.0 would mean that the returns moved in a completely opposite direction, while a value of zero would mean that there is no linear relationship between the returns. That is, they are uncorrelated from a statistical standpoint; this does not mean that they are independent. The value of $r_{ij} = 0.42$ is significant but not very high compared to the correlation between some stocks within industries where the correlations exceed 0.85.

Given this understanding of the concepts of covariance and correlation, it is now possible to consider the formula for computing the standard deviation of returns for a portfolio of assets. It is necessary to be able to compute the standard deviation because this is the measure of risk we will use. As noted, the derivation of the formula for computing the standard deviation of a portfolio of assets was accomplished by Harry Markowitz.[5]

Standard Deviation of a Portfolio.   Earlier we set forth the formula for the expected return for a portfolio of assets and showed that the expected return of the portfolio was simply the weighted average of the expected returns for the individual assets in the portfolio; the weights were the percentage of value of the portfolio. (See the example in Table 8.2.) Under such conditions, it is very easy to see the impact on the portfolio's expected return of adding or deleting an asset. Based upon this, one might assume that it is possible to derive the standard deviation of the portfolio in the same manner, i.e, by computing the weighted average of the standard deviations for the individual assets. The fact is, this is *not* correct! When Markowitz derived the general formula for the standard deviation of a portfolio it was as follows:[6]

$$\sigma_{port} = \sqrt{\sum_{i=1}^{N} W_i^2 \sigma_i^2 + 2 \sum_{\substack{i=1 \\ i \neq j}}^{N} \sum_{j=1}^{N} W_i W_j Cov_{ij}}$$

where

σ_{port} = the standard deviation of the portfolio

W_i^2 = the weights of the individual assets in the portfolio, where weights are determined by the proportion of value in the portfolio

σ_i^2 = the variance of asset i

Cov_{ij} = the covariance between the returns for assets i and j.

In words, this formula indicates that the standard deviation for the portfolio is a function of the weighted average of the individual variances (where the weights are squared), plus two times *the weighted covariances between all the assets in the portfolio.* The point is, the standard deviation for the portfolio encompasses not only the variances, but *also* the covariances between pairs of individual securities. Further, it can be shown that, in a portfolio with a large number of securities, this formula can be stated as the summation of weighted covariances.

---

[5] Markowitz, "Portfolio Section," *Journal of Finance,* 7 no. 1 (March 1952): 77–91; and *Portfolio Selection — Efficient Diversification of Investments* (New Haven, Conn.: Yale University Press, 1959).

[6] For the detailed derivation of this formula, the reader is referred to Markowitz, *Portfolio Selection: Efficient Diversification.*

This means that the important factor to consider when adding an asset to a portfolio with a number of other assets is *not* the individual asset's variance, but *its average covariance with all the other assets in the portfolio.* In the following examples we will consider the simple case of a two-asset portfolio. It is important to see the impact of different covariances on the total risk (standard deviation) of the portfolio.

The Two-Asset Portfolio

Examining the simplest case, in which only two assets are combined to form a portfolio, serves to illustrate the computations involved and helps to explain the characteristic shape of the efficient frontier. Because the Markowitz model assumes that any asset or portfolio of assets can be described by only two parameters, the expected return and expected standard deviation of returns, the following could be applied to two *individual* assets with the indicated parameters and correlation coefficients, or to two *portfolios* of assets with the same indicated parameters and correlation coefficients.

Equal Risk and Return — Changing Correlations.   Consider first the case in which both assets have the same expected return and expected standard deviation of return. As an example, let us assume:

$$E(R_1) = .20 \qquad E(\sigma_1) = .10$$
$$E(R_2) = .20 \qquad E(\sigma_2) = .10$$

To see the effect of different covariances (i.e., we assume different levels of correlation between the two assets), consider the following set of examples where the two assets have equal weights in the portfolio (i.e., $W_1 = .50$; $W_2 = .50$). Therefore, the only value that will change in each example is the correlation between the returns for the two assets. Recall that:

$$Cov_{ij} = r_{ij}\sigma_i\sigma_j.$$

Thus, consider the following alternative correlation coefficients and attendant covariances. The covariance will be equal to: $(r_{1,2})(.10)(.10)$ because both standard deviations are 0.10.

a. $r_{1,2} = 1.00 \qquad Cov_{1,2} = (1.00)(.10)(.10) = .01$
b. $r_{1,2} = .50 \qquad Cov_{1,2} = .005$
c. $r_{1,2} = .00 \qquad Cov_{1,2} = .000$
d. $r_{1,2} = -.50 \qquad Cov_{1,2} = -.005$
e. $r_{1,2} = -1.00 \qquad Cov_{1,2} = -.01.$

Now let us see what happens to the standard deviation of the portfolio under these five conditions. Recall that:

$$\sigma_{port} = \sqrt{\sum_{i=1}^{N} W_i^2\sigma_i^2 + 2\sum_{i=1}^{N}\sum_{\substack{j=1 \\ i \neq j}}^{N} W_iW_jCov_{ij}}$$

Thus in Case a:

$$\sigma_{port(a)} = \sqrt{(.5)^2(.10)^2 + (.5)^2(.10)^2 + 2(.5)(.5)(.01)}$$
$$= \sqrt{(.25)(.01) + (.25)(.01) + 2(.25)(.01)}$$
$$= \sqrt{(.0025) + (.0025) + (.50)(.01)}$$
$$= \sqrt{(.0050) + (.0050)}$$
$$= \sqrt{.01}$$
$$= .10.$$

As shown, in this case the returns for the two assets are perfectly positively correlated, so the standard deviation for the portfolio *is* the weighted average of the individual standard deviations, and *there is no real benefit to combining the two assets;* they are like one asset already because their returns move together. Now consider Case b where $r_{1,2}$ equals 0.50.

$$\sigma_{port(b)} = \sqrt{(.5)^2(.10)^2 + (.5)^2(.10)^2 + 2(.5)(.5)(.005)}$$
$$= \sqrt{(.0025) + (.0025) + (.50)(.005)}$$
$$= \sqrt{(.0050) + (.0025)}$$
$$= \sqrt{.0075}$$
$$= .0866.$$

As can be seen by comparison to the previous example, Case a, the only term that changed in the computation was the last term (i.e., $Cov_{1,2}$), which changed from 0.01 to 0.005. The ultimate result was that the standard deviation declined by about 13 percent from 0.10 to 0.0866. Note that *the expected return did not change* because it is simply the weighted average of the individual expected returns; i.e., it is equal to 0.20 in both cases.

The reader should be able to confirm that the standard deviations for Portfolios c and d are as follows:

c.   .0707
d.   .50.

The final case where the correlation between the two assets is -1.00 indicates the ultimate benefits of diversification.

$$\sigma_{port(e)} = \sqrt{(.5)^2(.10)^2 + (.5)^2(.10)^2 + 2(.5)(.5)(-.01)}$$
$$= \sqrt{(.0025) + (.0025) + (.0025) + (.5)(-.01)}$$
$$= \sqrt{(.0050) + (-.0050)}$$
$$= \sqrt{0}$$
$$= 0.$$

FIGURE 8.4

Time Pattern of Returns for Two Assets with Perfect Negative Correlation

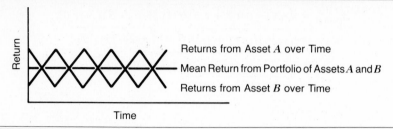

In this final case, the covariance term exactly offsets the individual variance terms, and so the overall standard deviation of the portfolio is zero. *This would be a risk-free portfolio.* A graph of such a pattern is contained in Figure 8.4.

The result of perfect negative correlation is that the mean return for the two securities combined over time is equal to the mean for each of them, and there is no variability of returns for the portfolio. Returns above and below the mean for each of the assets are *completely offset* by the return for the other asset, so there is no variability in total returns for the portfolio; it is a riskless portfolio because there is no uncertainty of returns. The combination of two assets that are completely negatively correlated provides the maximum benefits of diversification — it eliminates risk.

The graph in Figure 8.5 shows the difference in the risk-return posture for these five cases. As noted, the only impact of the change in correlation is the change in the standard deviation of a portfolio that contains the two assets. As we combine assets that are not perfectly correlated, we do *not* affect the expected return of the portfolio, but we are able to *reduce the risk* of the portfolio (its standard deviation) until we reach the ultimate combination in which there is perfect negative correlation and we *eliminate* risk.

Combining Stocks with Different Returns and Risk.   The previous discussion indicated what happens when we combined two assets with the same ex-

FIGURE 8.5

Plot of Risk-Return for Portfolios with Different Correlations

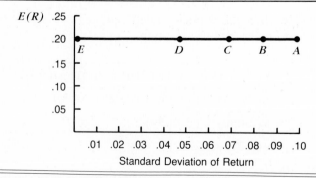

pected return and standard deviation, and the only difference was the correlation coefficient (covariance) between the assets. In this section we will consider two assets (or portfolios) that have different expected rates of return and individual standard deviations and show what happens when we vary the correlations between them. We will assume the following:

Stock	$E(R_i)$	W_i	σ_i^2	σ_i
1	.10	.50	.0049	.07
2	.20	.50	.0100	.10

We will briefly consider the same set of correlation coefficients as previously, with a different set of covariances as follows:

Case	Correlation Coefficient	Covariance $(r_{ij}\sigma_i\sigma_j)$
a	+1.00	.0070
b	+0.50	.0035
c	0.00	.0000
d	−0.50	−.0035
e	−1.00	−.0070

Because we are assuming that the proportion (weights) in all cases is the same (.50−.50), the expected return in *all* instances will be:

$$E(R_{port}) = .5(.10) + .5(.20)$$

$$= .15.$$

The standard deviation for Case a will be:

$$\sigma_{port(a)} = \sqrt{(.5)^2(.07)^2 + (.5)^2(.10)^2 + 2(.5)(.5)(.0070)}$$
$$= \sqrt{(.25)(.0049) + (.25)(.01) + (.5)(.0070)}$$
$$= \sqrt{.007225}$$
$$= .085.$$

Again it is shown that *in case of perfect positive correlation, the standard deviation of the portfolio is the weighted average of the standard deviations of the individual assets:*

$$(.5)(.07) + (.5)(.10) = .085.$$

Obviously, as we changed the weights, the standard deviation would change in a linear fashion. This property is emphasized because it is important in the discussion of the capital asset pricing model (CAPM) in the following chapter.

For Cases b, c, d, and e, the standard deviation for the portfolio would be as follows:[7]

$$\sigma_{port(b)} = \sqrt{(.001225) + (.0025) + (.5)(.0035)}$$
$$= \sqrt{.005475}$$
$$= .07399$$

$$\sigma_{port(c)} = \sqrt{(.001225) + (.0025) + (.5)(.00)}$$
$$= \sqrt{.003725}$$
$$= .0610$$

$$\sigma_{port(d)} = \sqrt{(.001225) + (.0025) + (.5)(-.0035)}$$
$$= \sqrt{.0019755}$$
$$= .0444$$

$$\sigma_{port(e)} = \sqrt{(.003725) + .5(-.00700)}$$
$$= \sqrt{.000225}$$
$$= .015$$

Note that in this set of examples, with perfect negative correlation the standard deviation of the portfolio is not zero. This is because the different examples have equal weights, but the individual standard deviations are not equal.[8]

Figure 8.6 shows the results for the two individual assets and the portfolio of the two assets under the assumption of different correlation coefficients as set forth in Cases a through e. As before, the expected return does not change because the proportions are all set at .50—.50, so all the portfolios lie along the horizontal line at the return $R = .15$.

Changing Weights.   If we changed the weights of the two assets for a given correlation coefficient, we would derive a set of combinations which trace out an ellipse that would start at stock two, go through the .50—.50 point and end at stock one. To show this, consider Case c in which the correlation coefficient is zero (this eases the computation), and we change the weights as follows:

Case	W_1	W_2	$E(R_i)$
f	.20	.80	.18
g	.40	.60	.16
h	.50	.50	.15
i	.60	.40	.14
j	.80	.20	.12

[7] In all of the following examples, we will skip some steps because the reader is aware that only the last term changes. The reader is encouraged to work out the individual steps to ensure understanding of the computational procedure.

[8] The two appendices to this chapter show proofs for equal weights with equal variances and the appropriate weights when standard deviations are not equal.

FIGURE 8.6
Plot of Risk-Return for Portfolios with Different Correlations

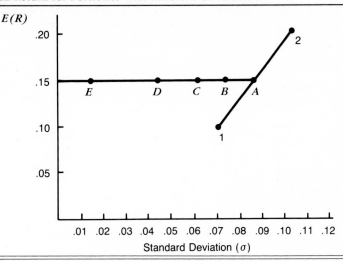

In Cases f, g, i, and j the standard deviations would be (we already know the σ for Portfolio h):[9]

$$\sigma_{port(f)} = \sqrt{(.20)^2(.07)^2 + (.80)^2(.10)^2 + 2(.20)(.80)(.000)}$$

$$= \sqrt{(.04)(.0049) + (.64)(.01) + (0)}$$

$$= \sqrt{.006596}$$

$$= .0812$$

$$\sigma_{port(g)} = \sqrt{(.40)^2(.07)^2 + (.60)^2(.10)^2 + 2(.40)(.60)(.00)}$$

$$= \sqrt{.004384}$$

$$= .0662$$

$$\sigma_{port(i)} = \sqrt{(.60)^2(.07)^2 + (.40)^2(.10)^2 + 2(.60)(.40)(.00)}$$

$$= \sqrt{.003364}$$

$$= .0580$$

$$\sigma_{port(j)} = \sqrt{(.80)^2(.07)^2 + (.20)^2(.10)^2 + 2(.80)(.20)(.00)}$$

$$= \sqrt{.003536}$$

$$= .0595.$$

Therefore, the alternative weights, assuming the same correlations, indicate the following risk-return combinations:

---

[9] Again, the reader is encouraged to fill in the steps we skipped in the computations.

FIGURE 8.7

Plot of Portfolio Risk Return for Different Weights When $r_\pi = 0.00$.

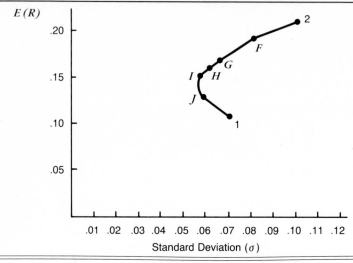

Case	W_1	W_2	$E(R_i)$	$E(\sigma_{port})$
f	.20	.80	.18	.0812
g	.40	.60	.16	.0662
h	.50	.50	.15	.0610
i	.60	.40	.14	.0580
j	.80	.20	.12	.0595

A graph of what these combinations provide in terms of return and risk is con-tained in Figure 8.7. It would be possible to derive a complete curve by simply varying the weights by small increments.

As noted, the amount of curvature in the graph will depend upon the corre-lation between the two assets or portfolios. In the case where $r_{ij} + 1.00$, the combinations would lie along a straight line between the two assets. If we draw the possible combinations when we assumed that $r_{ij} = -1.00$, the graph would be more curved than the one in Figure 8.7, and would actually touch the vertical line with some combination (i.e., the risk would be zero).

If we examined a number of assets and derived the curves assuming all the possible weights, we would have a graph as shown in Figure 8.8, if we only considered combinations of two assets and portfolios.

The envelope curve that contains the best of all these possible combinations is referred to as the *efficient frontier*. Specifically, *the efficient frontier is that set of portfolios that has the maximum return for every given level of risk, or the minimum risk for every level of return.* An example of such a frontier is con-tained in Figure 8.9. As can be seen, the set of portfolios on the efficient frontier dominates all the portfolios *beneath* the frontier. Specifically, every portfolio *on* the frontier has either higher return for equal risk or lower risk for equal return than some portfolio beneath the frontier. As an example, Portfolio a dominates Portfolio c because it has an equal return but substantially less risk. Portfolio b

FIGURE 8.8
Graph of Numerous Portfolio Combinations from Set of Available Assets

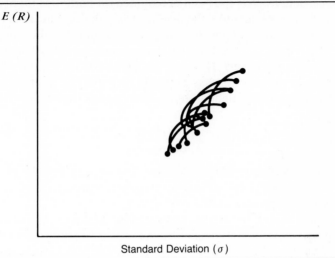

dominates Portfolio c because it has equal risk but a higher expected rate of return. Because of the benefits of diversification among assets that are not perfectly correlated, we would expect the efficient frontier to be made up of *portfolios,* with the possible exception of the two end points (i.e., the highest return asset and the lowest risk asset).

It was postulated that investors would determine where they wanted to be along the frontier based upon their utility function and attitude toward risk. They would select some portfolio on the efficient frontier based upon their risk preferences. No portfolio on the efficient frontier is dominated by any other portfolio on the efficient frontier. They all have different return and risk measures, and returns increase with risk.

FIGURE 8.9
Efficient Frontier for Alternative Portfolios

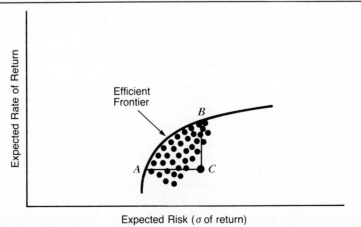

The Efficient Frontier and Investor Utility

Once the efficient frontier has been determined for portfolios formed from the securities under consideration, the investor has a choice to make. The efficient frontier will show him the portfolio that offers the highest attainable expected return for each attainable risk level (or the lowest attainable risk for each attainable expected return level). However, as Figure 8.9 shows, the shape of the efficient frontier for risky assets is generally such that one has to tolerate more and more risk to achieve higher returns. The slope of the efficient frontier

$$\frac{\Delta E(R_{port})}{\Delta E(\sigma_{port})}$$

decreases steadily as you move up the curve. This implies that taking on the same amount of added risk, as you move up the efficient frontier, will add progressively *less* of an increment in expected return.

The utility curves for an individual specify the trade-offs he is willing to make between expected return and risk. An investor's utility curves are used in conjunction with the efficient frontier to determine which *particular* efficient portfolio is the best, given these risk-return preferences. Two investors will not choose the same portfolio from the efficient set unless their utility curves are identical. In Figure 8.10, two sets of utility curves have been drawn, along with the efficient frontier. The curves labeled U_1 are for a very risk-averse investor

FIGURE 8.10
Choice of the Optimal Risky Portfolio

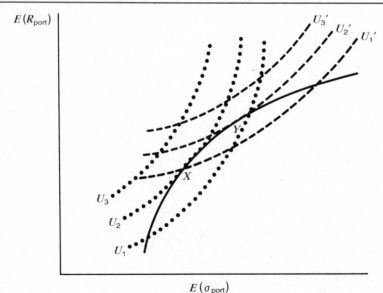

(with $U_3 > U_2 > U_1$). These curves are quite "steep," indicating that the investor will not tolerate much additional risk to obtain additional returns. The investor is indifferent to any $E(R), E(\sigma)$ combinations along a specific utility curve (e.g., U_1).

The curves labeled $U_1'(U_3' > U_2' > U_1')$ are for a less risk-averse investor. He is willing to tolerate a bit more risk to get a higher expected return; thus, he will choose a portfolio with higher risk and expected return than will the investor whose preferences are described by U_1, U_2, and U_3.

The *optimal portfolio* is the efficient portfolio with the highest utility. This will be found at *the point of tangency between the efficient frontier and the curve with the highest possible utility for a given investor.* For the more conservative investor, the highest utility is at the point where the curve U_2 just touches the efficient frontier, X in Figure 8.10. The other investor, because he is less risk averse, would choose Portfolio Y, which has both higher expected returns and higher risk than Portfolio X. Thus, given their respective attitudes toward risk and return, it is perfectly logical that these two investors will choose different portfolios from the efficient set.

SUMMARY

The purpose of this chapter has been to present the basic Markowitz portfolio model in detail. Initially, we considered the assumption that investors are risk averse, followed by a consideration of alternative measures of risk and the observation that, at this point, the preferred measure of risk is the standard deviation of expected return. It was shown that the expected return of a portfolio was simply the weighted average of the expected return for the individual assets in the portfolio. After a detailed discussion and demonstration of the concept of covariance and correlation, it was shown that the standard deviation of a portfolio was a function not only of the individual standard deviations, but *also* of the covariance between all the pairs of assets in the portfolio. The impact of different correlation coefficients was shown with a series of examples using two assets that had equal return and risk and also for a series where the assets had different returns and risk. It was also possible to show how different weights would yield a curve of potential combinations.

Assuming a number of available assets and a multitude of combination curves, it was shown that the efficient frontier is the envelope curve that encompasses all of the best combinations; i.e., the efficient frontier is that set of portfolios that has the highest expected return for each given level of risk, or the minimum risk for each given level of return. Finally, given this set of dominant portfolios, the investor is expected to select a specific portfolio based upon the point of tangency between the efficient frontier and his highest utility curve. Because alternative investors have different utility functions in terms of their trade-off between return and risk, they will have different points of tangency and, therefore, they can logically select different portfolios.

Given this understanding of basic portfolio theory, it is possible to consider the capital asset pricing model (CAPM), which is an extension of portfolio theory. The CAPM is an equilibrium asset pricing model. Consideration of the CAPM is the subject of the following chapter.

QUESTIONS

1. Why do most investors hold diversified portfolios?
2. What is covariance and why is it important in portfolio theory?
3. Why do most assets of the same type show positive covariances of returns with each other? Would you expect this to be true of covariances of returns between *different* types of assets (e.g., returns on treasury bills, General Motors common stock or commercial real estate)? Why or why not?
4. What is the relationship between the covariance and the correlation coefficient? Why is the correlation coefficient considered more useful?
5. Given the monthly rates of return for Anheuser-Busch and General Motors during a six-month period, *compute* the covariance between the returns and the correlation coefficient ($r_{1,2}$). What level of correlation did you expect? How did this compare to the computed correlation?

Month	Anheuser Busch	General Motors
1	.04	.07
2	.03	−.02
3	−.07	−.10
4	.12	.15
5	−.02	−.06
6	.05	.02

6. You are considering two assets with the following characteristics:
   $E(R_1) = .15$ $E(\sigma_1) = .10$ $W_1 = .5$
   $E(R_2) = .20$ $E(\sigma_2) = .20$ $W_2 = .5$
   Compute the mean and standard deviation of two portfolios if $r_{1,2} = .40; −.60$. Plot the two portfolios on a risk-return graph.
7. Explain why the efficient frontier takes its characteristic shape.
8. Draw a properly labeled graph of the Markowitz efficient frontier. Describe in exact terms what the efficient frontier is. Discuss the concept of dominant portfolios.
9. Assume you want to run a computer program to derive the efficient frontier for your feasible set of stocks. What information must you provide for the program; i.e., what are your inputs?
10. Why are investor's utility curves important in portfolio theory?
11. Explain how the optimal portfolio for a given investor is chosen. Will it always be a diversified portfolio, or could it be a single asset? Explain your answer.

REFERENCES

Blume, Marshall E. "Portfolio Theory: A Step towards Its Practical Application." *Journal of Business.* 43 no. 2 (April 1970).

Cohen, Kalmen J., and Pogue, Gerald A. "An Empirical Evaluation of Alternative Portfolio Selection Models." *Journal of Business.* 40 no. 2 (April 1967).

Elton, Edwin, Gruber, Martin J., and Padberg, Manfred W. "Optimal Portfolios from Simple Ranking Devices." *Journal of Portfolio Management.* 4 no. 3 (Spring 1978).

Evans, John L., and Archer, Stephen H. "Diversification and the Reduction of Dispersion: An Empirical Analysis." *Journal of Finance.* 24 no. 1 (December 1968).

Farrell, James L. Jr. "Homogeneous Stock Groupings: Implications for Portfolio Management." *Financial Analysts Journal.* 31 no. 3 (May–June 1975).

Farrell, James L. Jr. *Guide to Portfolio Management.* New York: McGraw-Hill, 1983.

Fisher, Lawrence. "Using Portfolio Theory to Maintain an Efficiently Diversified Portfolio." *Financial Analysts Journal.* 31 no. 3 (May–June 1975).

Francis, Jack C., and Archer, Stephen H. *Portfolio Analysis,* 2d ed. Englewood Cliffs, N. J.: Prentice-Hall, 1979.

Friedman, Milton, and Savage, Leonard J. "The Utility Analysis of Choices Involving Risk." *Journal of Political Economy.* 56 no. 3 (August 1948).

Gaumnitz, Jack E. "Maximal Gains from Diversification and Implications for Portfolio Management." *Mississippi Valley Journal of Business and Economics.* 6 no. 3 (Spring 1971).

Hagin, Robert. *Modern Portfolio Theory.* Homewood, Ill. Dow Jones-Irwin, 1979.

Hakansson, Nils H. "Capital Growth and the Mean-Variance Approach to Portfolio Selection." *Journal of Financial and Quantitative Analysis.* 6 no. 1 (January 1971).

Hodges, Stewart D., and Brealey, Richard A. "Portfolio Selection in a Dynamic and Uncertain World." *Financial Analysts Journal.* 29 no. 2 (March–April 1973).

Markowitz, Harry. "The Optimization of Quadratic Function Subject to Linear Constraints." *Naval Research Logistics Quarterly.* 3 (March–June 1956).

Markowitz, Harry. "Portfolio Selection." *Journal of Finance.* 3 no. 1 (March 1952).

Markowitz, Harry. *Portfolio Selection: Diversification of Investments.* New York: John Wiley and Sons, 1959.

Martin, A. D., Jr. "Mathematical Programming of Portfolio Selections." *Management Science.* 1 no. 2 (January 1955).

Modigliani, Franco, and Pogue, Gerald. "An Introduction to Risk and Return." *Financial Analysts Journal.* 30 no. 2 (March–April 1974).

Sharpe, William F. "Linear Programming Algorithms for Mutual Fund Portfolio Selection." *Management Science.* 13 no. 7 (March 1967).

Sharpe, William F. *Portfolio Theory and Capital Markets.* New York: McGraw-Hill, 1970.

Proof That Minimum Portfolio Variance Occurs with Equal Weights When Securities Have Equal Variance

When $E(\sigma_i) = E(\sigma_2)$, we have:

$$
\begin{aligned}
E(\sigma_{port}^2) &= W_1{}^2 E(\sigma_1)^2 + (1 - W_1)^2 E(\sigma_1)^2 + 2W_1(1 - W_1)r_{12}E(\sigma_1)^2 \\
&= E(\sigma_1)^2[W_1{}^2 + 1 - 2W_1 + W_1{}^2 + 2W_1 r_{12} - 2W_1^2 r_{12}] \\
&= E(\sigma_1)^2[2W_1{}^2 + 1 - 2W_1 + 2W_1 r_{12} - 2W_1{}^2 r_{12}].
\end{aligned}
$$

For this to be a minimum:

$$
\frac{\partial E(\sigma_{port}^2)}{\partial W_1} = 0 = E(\sigma_1)^2[4W_1 - 2 + 2r_{12} - 4W_1 r_{12}].
$$

assuming $E(\sigma_1)^2 > 0$, this implies:

$$
4W_1 - 2 + 2r_{12} - 4W_1 r_{12} = 0
$$

$$
4W_1(1 - r_{12}) - 2(1 - r_{12}) = 0
$$

from which:

$$
W_1 = \frac{2(1 - r_{12})}{4(1 - r_{12})} = \frac{1}{2},
$$

regardless of r_{12}. Thus, if $E(\sigma_1) = E(\sigma_2)$, $E(\sigma_{port}^2)$ will *always* be minimized by choosing $W_1 = W_2 = 1/2$, regardless of the value of r_{12}, except when $r_{12} = +1$ (in which case $E(\sigma_{port}) = E(\sigma_1) = E(\sigma_2)$). This can be verified by checking the second order condition

$$
\frac{\partial^2 E(\sigma_{port}^2)}{\partial W_1{}^2} > 0.
$$

Appendix 8B

Derivation of Weights That Will Give Zero Variance When Correlation Equals −1.00

$$E(\sigma_{port}^2) = W_1{}^2 E(\sigma_1)^2 + (1 - W_1)^2 E(\sigma_2)^2 + 2W_1(1 - W_1)r_{12}E(\sigma_1)E(\sigma_2)$$
$$= W_1{}^2 E(\sigma_1)^2 + E(\sigma_2)^2 - 2W_1 E(\sigma_2) + W_1{}^2 E(\sigma_2)^2$$
$$+ 2W_1 r_{12}E(\sigma_1)E(\sigma_2) - 2W_1{}^2 r_{12}E(\sigma_1)E(\sigma_2).$$

If $r_{12} = -1$, this can be rearranged and expressed as:

$$E(\sigma_{port}^2) = W_1{}^2[E(\sigma_1)^2 + 2E(\sigma_1)E(\sigma_2) + E(\sigma_2)^2]$$
$$- 2W_1[E(\sigma_2)^2 + E(\sigma_1)E(\sigma_2)] + E(\sigma_2)^2$$
$$= W_1{}^2[E(\sigma_1) + E(\sigma_2)]^2 - 2W_1 E(\sigma_2)$$
$$[E(\sigma_1) + E(\sigma_2)] + E(\sigma_2)^2$$
$$= \{W_1[E(\sigma_1) + E(\sigma_2)] - E(\sigma_2)\}^2.$$

We want to find the weight, W_1, which will reduce $E(\sigma_{port}^2)$ to *zero*, therefore:

$$W_1[E(\sigma_1) + E(\sigma_2)] - E(\sigma_2) = 0,$$

which yields:

$$W_1 = \frac{E(\sigma_2)}{E(\sigma_1) + E(\sigma_2)}, \text{ and } W_2 = 1 - W_1 = \frac{E(\sigma_1)}{E(\sigma_1) + E(\sigma_2)}.$$

Derivation of Weights That Will Give Zero Variance When Correlation Equals −1.00

Chapter 9

An Introduction to Capital Market Theory

C apital market theory builds on portfolio theory, and so, in this chapter, we will basically begin where the Markowitz efficient frontier ended. It is assumed that the set of risk assets has been examined, and that the aggregate efficient frontier has been derived. Further, it is assumed that you and all other investors want to maximize your utility, so you will choose a portfolio of risky assets on the efficient frontier at a point where your utility map is tangent to the frontier as shown in Figure 8.10. When you act in this manner, you are referred to as a Markowitz efficient investor. The purpose of capital market theory is to extend portfolio theory to a model that can be used to price all risky assets. The final product is the capital asset pricing model (CAPM) that will indicate how you determine the required rate of return for all risky assets.

In this chapter, we will initially consider some of the assumptions required to derive the model. Subsequently we will discuss the concept of a risk-free asset, its properties relative to a portfolio of risk assets, and how this allows us to derive a linear relationship between the expected return on an asset and the risk involved. This analysis also implies the existence of a simple, unique risk measure for all risky assets. We will show in detail how this risk measure is computed for an individual asset, and how this model can be used to select undervalued, overvalued, and properly valued securities.

ASSUMPTIONS OF CAPITAL MARKET THEORY

Because capital market theory builds upon the Markowitz portfolio model, this theory requires all of the assumptions discussed in relation to the Markowitz model, but they are expanded as follows:

1. *All investors are Markowitz efficient investors who want to be somewhere on the efficient frontier.* The exact location on the efficient frontier will depend upon the risk-return function of the investor and will differ among investors.
2. *It is possible for investors to borrow or lend any amount of money at the*

risk-free rate of return (RFR). Clearly, it is always possible to lend money at the nominal risk-free rate by buying risk-free securities such as government T-bills. It is not always possible to borrow at this risk-free rate, but we will see that assuming a higher borrowing rate does not change the results very much.

3. *All investors have homogeneous expectations; i.e., all investors estimate identical probability distributions for future rates of return.* Again, this assumption can be relaxed, and, as long as expectations are not vastly different, the effect is minor.

4. *All investors have the same one-period time horizon, e.g., one month, six months, one year.* The model will be developed for one hypothetical period, but it is acknowledged that the results could be affected by a different assumption, and an investor would have to derive risk measures that are consistent with his horizon.

5. *All investments are infinitely divisible; i.e., it is possible to buy or sell fractional shares of any asset or portfolio.* This assumption simply allows us to discuss the various investment alternatives as continuous curves. Changing this assumption would have little impact on the theory.

6. *There are no taxes or transaction costs involved in buying or selling assets.* This is a reasonable assumption in a number of instances. Specifically, there are many investors who do not have to pay taxes (e.g., pension funds, religious groups), and the transactions costs for most financial institutions is less than 1 percent on most financial instruments. Again, the relaxation of this assumption modifies the results, but it does not change the basic thrust.

7. *There is no inflation or change in interest rates, or inflation is fully anticipated.* This is a reasonable initial assumption and can be modified.

8. *Capital markets are in equilibrium.* This means that we begin from a state in which all assets are properly priced in terms of the risk involved.

You may believe that some of these assumptions are unrealistic and wonder how useful a theory can be that is based on them. In this regard, two points are important. First, as discussed above, we will see that many of these assumptions can be relaxed with minor impact on the model and no change in the main implications or conclusions. Second, a theory should *not* be judged on the basis of the assumptions it involves, but on *how well it explains and helps us predict behavior in the real world.* Specifically, if we can develop a model that includes these assumptions, and the model helps us explain the rates of return on a wide variety of risky assets, the theory is very useful. Put another way, the important test of the model is *how well it works.* If the model works with these unrealistic assumptions, it simply means that the factors assumed away were really not very important in attaining the ultimate objective — determining the required rate of return for risky assets. In this regard, after presenting the model, we will briefly review some of the studies that have empirically tested the model.

THE INITIAL DEVELOPMENT

The major factor in developing capital market theory was the introduction of the concept of a risk-free asset. Specifically, following the development of the Markowitz portfolio model, several authors considered what would happen if we assumed the existence of a risk-free asset that, by definition, would have zero variance. It will be shown that such an asset would have zero correlation with all other risky assets. Such an asset would yield the risk-free rate of return (RFR) and would be on the vertical axis of a portfolio graph. Assuming the existence of a risk-free asset made it possible to extend the Markowitz portfolio theory and to derive a generalized theory of capital asset pricing under conditions of uncertainty. This development has generally been attributed to William Sharpe, but similar independent derivations were made by Lintner and Mossin.[1] (Because of this parallel development, the reader may see the reference to the Sharpe-Lintner-Mossin (SLM) capital asset pricing model). Given its importance to the model, we will begin with a discussion of the risk-free asset, and consider the effect of combining a risk-free asset with other risky assets.

Risk-Free Asset

We have defined a *risky* asset as one about which *there is uncertainty regarding the future return.* Further, we have measured this uncertainty by the variance or standard deviation of returns. A *risk-free asset is one for which there is no uncertainty regarding the expected rate of return;* i.e., the standard deviation of returns is equal to zero ($\sigma_{RF} = 0$). Such an asset should provide a rate of return that is consistent with this characteristic, and this return should be equal to the long-run growth rate of the economy with short-run liquidity having some effect. In other words, the RFR is approximately equal to the long-run real growth rate of the economy.

Covariance with the Risk-Free Asset. The reader will recall that the covariance between two sets of returns is equal to:

$$Cov_{ij} = \sum_{i=1}^{n} ((R_i - E(R_i)) \ (R_j - E(R_j)))/n.$$

Because the returns for the risk-free asset are certain, $\sigma_{RF} = 0$, which means $R_i = E(R_i)$ during all periods. Consequently, when computing the covariance of the risk-free asset with that of *any* risky asset or portfolio of assets, the expression for the risk-free asset will always be equal to zero (i.e., $R_i - E(R_i) = 0$) and the product will equal zero. Therefore, *the covariance between any risky asset or portfolio of risky assets and a risk-free asset is zero.*

Combining the Risk-Free Asset and a Risky Portfolio. At this point, an important question to consider is, what happens to the average rate of return and standard deviation when a risk-free asset is combined with a portfolio of risky assets such as exists on the Markowitz efficient frontier?

---

[1] William F. Sharpe, "Capital Asset Prices: A Theory of Market Equilibrium under Conditions of Risk," *Journal of Finance,* 19 no. 3 (September 1964): 425–442; John Lintner, "Security Prices, Risk and Maximal Gains from Diversification," *Journal of Finance,* 20 no. 4 (December 1965): 587–615; and J. Mossin, "Equilibrium in a Capital Asset Market," *Econometrica,* 34, no. 4 (October 1966): 768–783.

Expected Return. Similar to the expected return for a portfolio of two risky assets, *the expected return is the weighted average of the two returns* as follows:

$$E(R_{port}) = W_{RF}(RFR) + (1 - W_{RF})E(R_i)$$

where:

W_{RF} = the proportion of the portfolio invested in a risk-free asset

$E(R_i)$ = the expected rate of return on risky Portfolio i.

Standard Deviation. Recall from Chapter 8 that the expected variance for a two-asset portfolio is:

$$E(\sigma^2_{port}) = W_1^2\sigma_1^2 + W_2^2\sigma_2^2 + 2W_1 W_2 r_{1,2}\sigma_1\sigma_2.$$

Substituting the risk-free asset for security one, and the risky asset portfolio for security two, this formula would become:

$$E(\sigma^2_{port}) = W_{RF}^2\sigma_{RF}^2 + (1 - W_{RF})^2\sigma_i^2 + 2W_{RF}(1 - W_{RF})r_{RFi}\sigma_{RF}\sigma_i.$$

We know that the variance of the risk-free asset is zero (i.e., $\sigma_{RF}^2 = 0$) and the correlation between the risk-free asset and any risky asset, *i*, is also zero (i.e., $r_{RF,i} = 0$). Therefore, any component of the formula that has either of these terms will equal zero and the formula will become:

$$E(\sigma^2_{port}) = (1 - W_{RF})^2\sigma_i^2.$$

The standard deviation is:

$$E(\sigma_{port}) = \sqrt{(1 - W_{RF})^2\sigma_i^2}$$
$$= (1 - W_{RF})\sigma_i.$$

Therefore, the standard deviation of a portfolio that combines the risk-free asset and a portfolio of risky assets is *the linear proportion of the standard deviation of the risky asset portfolio.*

And, *both* the expected return *and* the standard deviation of return for such a portfolio are *linear* combinations, which means the alternative portfolio returns and risks are represented by a *straight line* between the two assets. A graph depicting portfolio possibilities when the risk-free asset is combined with alternative risky portfolios on the Markowitz efficient frontier is contained in Figure 9.1.

It is possible to attain any point along the straight line *RFR-A* by investing some portion of your portfolio in the risk-free asset (W_{RF}) and the remainder $(1 - W_{RF})$ in the risky asset portfolio at Point A on the efficient frontier. This set of portfolio possibilities dominates all risky asset portfolios below Point A because there is a portfolio along the Line *RFR-A* that has equal variance but a higher rate of return than the portfolio on the original efficient frontier. Likewise, it is possible to attain any point along the Line *RFR-B* by investing in some combination of the risk-free asset and the risky asset portfolio at Point B. Again, these

FIGURE 9.1

Portfolio Possibilities Combining the Risk-Free Asset and Risky Portfolios on Efficient Frontier

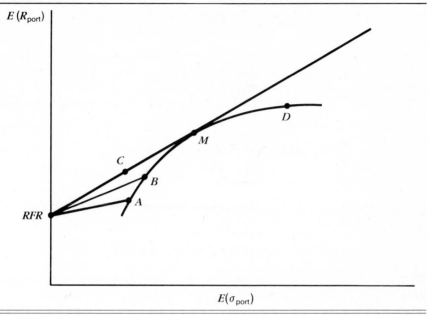

combinations dominate all portfolio possibilities below Point B (including Line *RFR-A*).

It is possible to draw further lines from the RFR to the efficient frontier at higher and higher points until you reach the point of tangency which is set at Point M. The set of portfolio possibilities along Line *RFR-M* dominates *all* portfolios below Point M. You could attain a risk and return combination at Point C (which is midway between the RFR and Point M) by investing one half of your portfolio in the risk-free asset (lending money at the RFR) and the other half in the risky portfolio at Point M.

A Leveraged Portfolio

An investor may want to attain a higher expected return than is available at Point M and also be willing to accept higher risk. One alternative would be to invest in one of the risky asset portfolios on the efficient frontier beyond Point M, e.g., the portfolio at Point D. A second alternative is to add *leverage* to the portfolio by *borrowing* money at the risk-free rate and investing the proceeds in the risky asset portfolio at Point M. Assuming an investor does this, what effect will it have on the return and risk for the portfolio? If the investor *borrows* an amount equal to *50 percent* of his original wealth, W_{RF} will not be a positive fraction, but a negative 50 percent (i.e., $W_{RF} = -.50$). The effect on the expected return for the portfolio is as follows:

$$E(R_{port}) = W_{RF}(RFR) + (1 - W_{RF})E(R_m)$$
$$= -.50(RFR) + (1 - (-.50))E(R_m)$$
$$= -.50(RFR) + 1.50E(R_m).$$

As shown, the return will increase in a *linear* fashion along the Line *RFR-M*, because the gross return increases by 50 percent, but it is necessary to pay interest (at the RFR) on the money borrowed. As an example, assume that the $E(RFR) = .06$ and $E(R_m) = .12$, then the return to the leveraged portfolio would be:

$$E(R_{port}) = -.50(.06) + 1.5(.12)$$
$$= -.03 + .18$$
$$= .15.$$

The effect on the standard deviation of the leveraged portfolio is similar.

$$E(\sigma_{port}) = (1 - W_{RF})\sigma_m$$
$$= (1 - (-.50))\sigma_m = 1.50\sigma_m.$$

Therefore, *both return and risk increase in a linear fashion along the original Line RFR-M,* and this extension dominates everything below the line on the original efficient frontier. Thus, this "new" efficient frontier is the straight line from the *RFR* tangent to Point M. This line is referred to as the *capital market line (CML)* and is shown in Figure 9.2.

As was shown in the discussion of portfolio theory, when two assets were *perfectly correlated,* the set of portfolio possibilities between them was on a *straight line.* Therefore, because it is a straight line, *all the portfolios on the CML are perfectly positively correlated.* This positive correlation is also intuitive because, as shown, all the portfolio possibilities on the CML are a combination of risky Portfolio M and either borrowing or lending at the risk-free rate, so all

FIGURE 9.2
Derivation of Capital Market Line Assuming Lending or Borrowing at the Risk-Free Rate

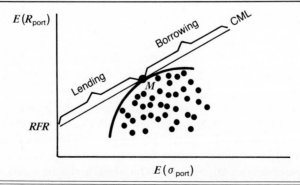

variability is caused by the variability of the M portfolio. The only difference is the *magnitude* of the variability because of the proportion of the risky asset in the total portfolio.

The Market Portfolio

Because Portfolio M is the tangent portfolio that gives the highest portfolio possibility line, everybody will want to invest in this risky asset portfolio and borrow or lend to be somewhere on the CML. Because *all* investors want this portfolio of risky assets as part of their total portfolio, *all* risky assets *must* be in this portfolio. If a risky asset were not in this portfolio, it would have no demand and, therefore, no value. Because the market is in equilibrium, *all assets are included in this portfolio in proportion to their market value.* If this were not true, prices would adjust until the value of the asset was consistent with its proportion in Portfolio M. If a higher proportion of an asset than was justified by its value was included in Portfolio M for any reason, the excess demand for this asset would cause an increase in its price until its value was consistent with the proportion. This portfolio of all risky assets is referred to as the *market portfolio.*

The market portfolio does *not* include only common stocks, but *all* risky assets, such as bonds, options, real estate, coins, stamps, etc. Since the market portfolio contains *all* risky assets, it is a *completely diversified* portfolio. Because of this, all unsystematic risk of individual assets in the portfolio is diversified away in the M portfolio; i.e., the "unique" risk of one asset is offset by the "unique" variability of the other assets in the portfolio. The only risk is the systematic risk caused by macroeconomic variables that influence all risky assets. This systematic risk is measured by the standard deviation of returns of the market portfolio. This market variability (systematic risk) can change over time as the macroeconomic variables that affect the valuation of risky assets change.[2]

Measure of Diversification. All portfolios on the CML are perfectly positively correlated, which means that all portfolios on the CML are perfectly correlated with the market portfolio. This implies a *measure of complete diversification.*[3] Specifically, a portfolio that is completely diversified will be perfectly correlated with the market portfolio (i.e., $R^2 = +1.00$). This is also logical because *complete diversification requires the elimination of all unsystematic risk,* and if all that is left is systematic risk, such a completely diversified portfolio should be perfectly correlated with the market portfolio that only has systematic risk.

Diversification and Unsystematic Risk. As discussed in Chapter 8, the purpose of diversification is to reduce the standard deviation of the total portfolio.

[2] For an analysis of changes in stock price volatility see, Dennis W. Logue, "Are Stock Markets Becoming Riskier?" *Journal of Portfolio Management,* 2 no. 3 (Spring 1976): 13–19; R. R. Officer, "The Variability of the Market Factor of the New York Stock Exchange," *The Journal of Business,* 46 no. 3 (July 1973): 434–453; John M. Wachowicz and Frank K. Reilly, "An Analysis of Changes in Aggregate Stock Market Volatility," Paper presented at Midwest Finance Association (April 1979).

[3] James Lorie, "Diversification: Old and New," *Journal of Portfolio Management,* 1 no. 2 (Winter 1975): 25–28.

To do this you should find securities that have very low covariance (ideally negative) with the other securities in the portfolio. Ideally, as you add securities, the average covariance declines. An important question is, what is the impact of the number of securities in the portfolio? About how many securities must be included in a completely diversified portfolio? Several studies have examined the question, and the results are interesting and important for the practice of portfolio management.[4]

The discussion in Chapter 8 indicated that if you can find securities with perfect negative correlation, it is possible to eliminate risk. Alternatively, it can be shown that if there is *zero* correlation between various assets, you can eventually eliminate risk by having a large enough sample. The important question is, what happens as you increase the sample size for securities that generally have some level of positive correlation? The typical correlation between U.S. securities is about 0.5 to 0.6. The studies attempted to answer this question by examining the average standard deviation for a number of portfolios of different size. Specifically, they determined what is the average standard deviation for a sample of 100 one-stock portfolios, 100 two-stock portfolios, 100 eight-stock portfolios, up to 100 128-stock portfolios. The results indicated that the initial impact was quite large; i.e., *there was a large reduction in the average standard deviation for portfolios of two or four stocks compared to portfolios of single stocks.* At the same time, *the major benefits of diversification were achieved rather quickly;* i.e., about 90 percent of the maximum benefit was derived with portfolios of 12–18 stocks. Figure 9.3 is a graph of the effect.

FIGURE 9.3
Impact of Number of Stocks in a Portfolio on the
Standard Deviation of Portfolio Return

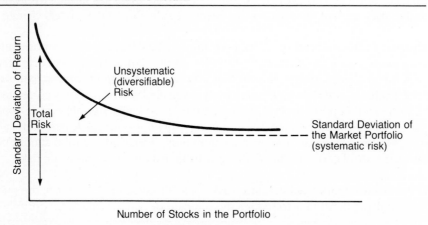

[4] Lawrence Fisher and James H. Lorie, "Some Studies of Variability of Returns on Investments in Common Stock," *Journal of Business,* 43 no. 2 (April 1970): 99–134; John L. Evans and Stephen H. Archer, "Diversification and the Reduction of Dispersion: An Empirical Analysis," *Journal of Finance,* 23 no. 5 (December 1968): 761–767; Jack E. Gaumnitz, "Investment Diversification under Uncertainty: An Examination of the Number of Securities in a Diversified Portfolio," (Ph.D. dissertation, Stanford University, 1967); Thomas M. Tole, "You Can't Diversify without Diversifying," *Journal of Portfolio Management,* 8 no. 2 (Winter 1982): 5–11.

The point is, by adding stocks to the portfolio that are not perfectly corre-lated, you can *reduce* the overall standard deviation of the portfolio, but you *cannot eliminate it.* The standard deviation will eventually reach the level of the market portfolio, which means you have eliminated all unsystematic risk that is due to unique factors. At this point, you are completely diversified. At the same time, you are left with *market risk,* also referred to as *systematic risk,* which is due to aggregate market factors that cannot be eliminated.

Separation Theorem.   Given the existence of the CML, everyone should in-vest in the *same* risky asset portfolio, the M portfolio. The only difference among individual investors should be in the *financing* decision they make, which de-pends upon their risk preferences. If you are relatively risk averse, you will lend some part of your portfolio at the RFR (i.e., you will buy some risk-free securi-ties) and invest the remainder in the market portfolio. For example, you might invest in the portfolio combination at Point A in Figure 9.4. In contrast, if you prefer more risk, you will borrow funds at the RFR and invest everything in the market portfolio. As a result, you will invest in a portfolio combination such as the one at Point B, which provides more risk and greater return than the market portfolio. The CML becomes the efficient frontier of portfolios, and investors decide where they want to be along this efficient frontier, as shown in Figure 9.4. This division of the *investment decision and the financing decision* is referred to as the separation theorem and was developed by James Tobin.[5] Specifically, to

FIGURE 9.4
Choice of Optimal Portfolio Combinations on the CML

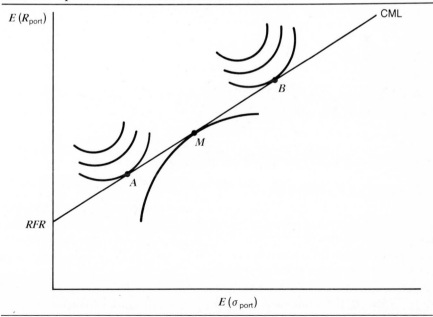

[5] James Tobin, "Liquidity Preference as Behavior towards Risk," *Review of Economic Studies,* 25 no. 2 (February 1958): 65 – 85.

be somewhere on this CML, which is the efficient frontier, you initially make an investment decision to invest in the market portfolio, M. Subsequently, based upon your risk preferences, you make a separate financing decision (i.e., whether to borrow or lend) to attain the preferred point on the CML (e.g., A or B).

Risk in a CML World.   The relevant risk measure for risky assets is *their covariance with the M portfolio.* This covariance with the market portfolio is referred to as the stock's *systematic risk.* One can see why this covariance is important if one considers the following:

1.   In the Markowitz portfolio discussion, it was noted that the relevant risk consideration for a security being added to a portfolio is its average covariance with all other assets in the portfolio. Because the only relevant portfolio is the M portfolio, the only important consideration for any individual risky asset is its average covariance with all the stocks in the M portfolio, or simply, *the asset's covariance with the market portfolio.* This, then, is the relevant risk measure for an individual risky asset.

2.   Alternatively, because all individual risky assets are a part of the M portfolio, one can describe individual asset returns in relation to the returns for the M portfolio with the following linear model:

$$R_{it} = a_i + b_i R_{mt} + \epsilon,$$

where:

R_{it} = return for asset i during period t

a_i = constant term for asset i

b_i = slope coefficient for asset i

R_{mt} = return for M portfolio during period t

ϵ = random error term.

Its variance of returns could be described as:

$$\begin{aligned} Var(R_{it}) &= Var(a_i + b_i R_{mt} + \epsilon) \\ &= Var(a_i) + Var(b_i R_{mt}) + Var(\epsilon) \\ &= 0 + Var(b_i R_{mt}) + Var(\epsilon), \end{aligned}$$

but $Var(b_i R_{mt})$ is the variance due to the variance of the market return, which is referred to as *systematic variance.* $Var(\epsilon)$ is the residual variance, which is the variance of return for the individual asset that is *not* related to the market portfolio. It is also referred to as *unsystematic variance* or *unique variance,* because it is caused by the unique features of the asset. Therefore:

$$Var(R_{it}) = (\text{Systematic Variance}) + (\text{Unsystematic Variance}).$$

We know that all unsystematic variance is *eliminated* in a completely diversified portfolio such as the market portfolio. Therefore, *the unsystematic variance is*

FIGURE 9.5
Graph of Security Market Line

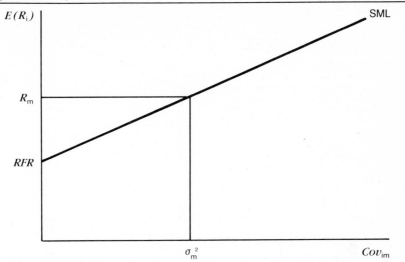

not relevant to investors, and they should not expect to receive added returns for assuming this risk. *The only variance that is relevant is the systematic variance* that *cannot* be diversified away, because it is attributable to macroeconomic factors that affect *all* risky assets.

Security Market Line.   Because the relevant risk measure for an individual risky asset is its covariance with the market portfolio (Cov_{im}), we can draw the risk-return relationship as shown in Figure 9.5

The market return (R_m) should be consistent with its own risk, which is the covariance of the market with itself. The reader will recall that the covariance of any asset with itself is its variance: $Cov_{ii} = \sigma_i^2$. Therefore, the covariance of the market with itself is the variance of the market rate of return (i.e., $Cov_{mm} = \sigma_m^2$). The equation for this line is:

$$E(R_i) = RFR + \frac{R_m - RFR}{\sigma_m^2}(Cov_{im})$$

$$= RFR + \frac{Cov_{im}}{\sigma_m^2}(R_m - RFR),$$

but $Cov_{im}/\sigma_m^2 =$ beta (β_i), so this can be stated:

$$E(R_i) = RFR + \beta_i(R_m - RFR).$$

Beta is a *normalized* measure of systematic risk; the covariance of any asset *i* with the market portfolio (Cov_{im}) is normalized by the market portfolio covariance. Therefore, if β_1 is above 1.0, the asset has higher risk than the market has. Now the SML graph can be expressed as shown in Figure 9.6.

FIGURE 9.6
Graph of Security Market Line with Normalized Systematic Risk

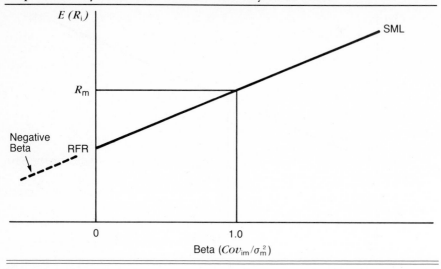

Determining Expected Return.   Therefore, the expected rate of return for a risky asset is determined by the RFR plus a risk premium that is a function of the *systematic risk* of the asset (β_i), and the prevailing market risk premium ($R_m - RFR$). Consider the following example stocks:

Stock	Beta
A	.70
B	1.00
C	1.15
D	1.40
E	−.30

If we expect the economy's RFR to be 0.08 and the expected market return (R_m) to be 0.14, the expected return for these five stocks would be:

$$E(R_i) = RFR + \beta_i(R_m - RFR)$$

$$E(R_a) = .08 + 0.70\,(.14 - .08)$$
$$= .122 = 12.2 \text{ percent.}$$

$$E(R_b) = .08 + 1.00\,(.14 - .08)$$
$$= .14 = 14 \text{ percent.}$$

$$E(R_c) = .08 + 1.15\,(.14 - .08)$$
$$= .149 = 14.9 \text{ percent.}$$

$$E(R_d) = .08 + 1.40\,(.14 - .08)$$
$$= .164 = 16.4 \text{ percent.}$$

$$E(R_e) = .08 + (-0.30)\,(.14 - .08)$$
$$= .08 - .018$$
$$= .062 = 6.2 \text{ percent.}$$

As stated, these are the expected (required) rates of return that these stocks should provide based upon the systematic risk of each stock. Stock A has lower risk than the aggregate market, so an investor should not expect (require) a return from it as high as the return on the market portfolio of risky assets. In this instance, one should expect a return of 12.2 percent. In Case B, the stock has systematic risk equal to the market (beta = 1.00), so the rate of return expected should likewise be equal to the expected market return (0.14). Stocks C and D have systematic risk greater than the market and are expected to provide returns consistent with this risk. Finally, Stock E is an asset that not only has systematic risk that is below the market risk, but has a *negative* beta (which is quite rare in practice). As a result, the expected return on this stock is *below* the RFR.

In equilibrium, *all* assets and *all* portfolios of assets should plot on the SML. That is, all assets should be priced such that their expected (required) rates of return are consistent with their systematic risk. Any security that plots *above* the SML would be considered *underpriced,* because its estimated return would be above what is required in terms of its systematic risk. In contrast, assets that plot *below* the SML would be considered *overpriced,* because their estimated return is below the return required for an asset having that expected systematic risk. In a market that is completely efficient and in equilibrium, one would not expect to find any assets that plot off the SML. Alternatively, if the market is generally efficient but not completely efficient, it might be possible to find certain assets that are somewhat mispriced, because not *everyone* is aware of *all* the relevant information for the asset. As discussed in Chapter 7 (the efficient markets chapter), the function of a superior analyst is to derive estimates of value and rates of return that are consistently superior to the aggregate market's evaluation and also different from the consensus estimate, so that the returns derived will be above average on a risk-adjusted basis.

Determination of Undervalued and Overvalued Assets. Now that we have determined the rate of return that an investor should expect or require for a specific risky asset using the SML, it is possible to compare this required return to the rate of return that is projected over some future investment horizon to determine whether we should invest in a given asset or not. Such an evaluation requires an *independent* estimate of the return outlook for the security using either fundamental or technical analysis techniques. To understand what is involved in such a determination, let us consider the following example for the five assets discussed in the previous section.

Assume that there are five stocks being followed by analysts in a major trust department. Based upon extensive fundamental analysis, such as will be discussed, the analysts report the following price and dividend outlooks for the stocks:

Stock	Current Price (P_t)	Expected Price (P_{t+1})	Expected Dividend (D_{t+1})	Estimated Future Rate of Return (percent)
A	25	27	1.00	12.0
B	40	42	1.25	8.1
C	33	40	1.00	24.2
D	64	65	2.40	5.3
E	50	55	—	10.0

TABLE 9.1
Comparison of Required Rate of Return to Estimated Rate of Return

Stock	Beta	$E(R_i)$	Estimated Return	Estimated Return minus $E(R_i)$	Evaluation
A	.70	12.2	12.0	−.2	Properly Valued
B	1.00	14.0	8.1	−5.9	Overvalued
C	1.15	14.9	24.2	9.3	Undervalued
D	1.40	16.4	5.3	−11.1	Overvalued
E	−.30	6.2	10.0	3.8	Undervalued

Table 9.1 summarizes the relationship between the *required* rates of return based on systematic risk and the estimated future rate of return based upon the current price, the future price, and the dividend outlook.

When these values are plotted on the SML, they would appear as shown in Figure 9.7. As shown, Stock A is almost exactly on the line and so is considered properly valued. Alternatively, Stocks B and D are considered overvalued, because you would not expect to receive a rate of return during the coming period that is consistent with the risk involved. Therefore, they both plot below the SML. In contrast, Stocks C and E are expected to provide rates of return greater than what is required based upon their systematic risk; i.e., both stocks plot above the SML.

Assuming that you had faith in the ability of your analyst to forecast estimated values and, therefore, estimated returns, you would buy Stocks C and E and you would sell Stocks B and D, possibly selling them short if you are aggressive in this regard. Finally, you would probably take no action on Stock A, because it is expected to provide a return about in line with its systematic risk.

FIGURE 9.7
Plot of Estimated Returns on SML Graph

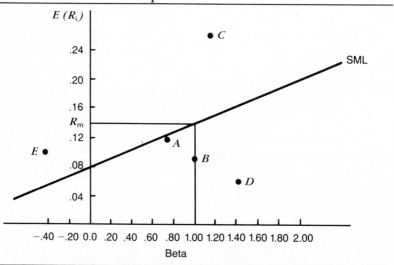

The Characteristic Line

How do you compute the systematic risk for an asset? The systematic risk input for an individual asset is derived from the following regression model that is referred to as the asset's characteristic line with the market portfolio:

$$R_{it} = a_i + B_i R_{mt} + \epsilon$$

where:

R_{it} = the rate of return for asset i during period t

R_{mt} = the rate of return for the market portfolio during period t

a_i = the constant term or intercept of the regression which equals $\overline{R}_i - B_i\overline{R}_m$

B_i = the slope coefficient for the regression which is equal to Cov_{im}/σ^2_m

ϵ = the random error term

The characteristic line is the line of best fit through a scatter plot of rates of return for the individual risky asset and for the market portfolio of risky assets over some designated past period, as shown in Figure 9.8.

In practice the number of observations used and the time interval employed varies. As an example, Value Line Investment Services derives the characteristic line for stocks using the most recent five years of *weekly* rates of return (i.e., 260 weekly observations). Alternatively, Merrill Lynch, Pierce, Fenner & Smith provides betas based upon the recent five-year period using *monthly* rates of return.[6] The point is, there is no theoretically correct time interval and period of analysis. It becomes a trade-off between using enough observations to eliminate the impact of random rates of return, and yet not going so far back in time (e.g., 15 or 20 years) that the subject company may have changed dramatically in the interim. It is important to remember that you are using the historical data to help you estimate the *future* beta for the asset.

FIGURE 9.8
Scatter Plot of Rates of Return

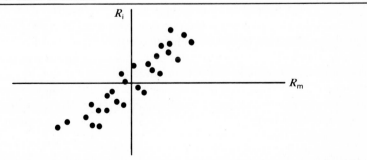

---

[6] A comparison of the estimates in Meir Statman, "Betas Compared: Merrill Lynch vs. Value Line," *Journal of Portfolio Management*, 7 no. 2 (Winter 1981): 41–44. The author does not find a bias, but the coefficient of determination for 195 large firms was only 0.55. The relationship between portfolio betas was about the same.

TABLE 9.2
Computation of Covariance of IBM and the Standard & Poor's 500 during 1982

Month/ Year	Month-End Price S&P 500	R_{mt}	$R_{IBM_t}{}^a$	$R_{mt} - \overline{R_m}$	$R_{IBM_t} - \overline{R_{IBM^a}}$	$(R_{mt} - \overline{R_m})(R_{IBM_t} - \overline{R_{IBM}})$
12/81	122.55	—	—	—	—	—
1/82	120.40	(1.75)	11.87	(3.04)	7.14	(21.71)
2/82	113.11	(6.05)	(2.75)	(7.34)	(7.48)	54.90
3/82	111.96	(1.02)	(3.43)	(2.31)	(8.16)	18.85
4/82	116.44	4.00	7.53	2.71	2.80	7.59
5/82	111.88	(3.92)	(4.28)	(5.21)	(9.01)	46.94
6/82	109.61	(2.03)	(1.42)	(3.32)	(6.15)	20.42
7/82	107.09	(2.30)	8.25	(3.59)	3.52	(12.64)
8/82	119.51	11.60	7.43	10.31	2.70	27.84
9/82	120.42	.76	4.08	(.53)	(.65)	.34
10/82	133.71	11.04	8.86	9.75	4.13	40.27
11/82	138.54	3.61	8.29	2.32	3.56	8.26
12/82	140.64	1.52	11.27	.23	7.54	1.73
$E(R)$		1.29	4.73			$\Sigma = 192.79$
σ		5.28	5.82			

^{a} These are percent price changes as contained in Table 8.4.

Also, there is no obviously available portfolio series that contains all the risky assets in the economy. Therefore, most investigators use the Standard & Poor's 500 Composite Index as a proxy for the market portfolio. The stocks in this index have a large proportion at the total market value of stocks, and it is a value-weighted series.[7]

An Example Computation. To demonstrate how one goes about deriving the characteristic line for a specific risky asset, consider the following computation of the characteristic line for IBM based upon the monthly rates of return during 1982.[8] Twelve is probably not enough observations, but it should provide a good example. As is often done, we will use the S&P 500 Index as a proxy for the market portfolio.

The actual monthly price changes for IBM and the S&P 500 Index during 1982 are computed using the closing prices for the last day of each month; e.g., the return for January 1982 is the percentage change from the closing price on December 30, 1981, to the closing price on January 30, 1982. These data are contained in Table 9.2. A scatter plot of the rates of return is contained in Figure 9.9. During most months, IBM had returns that were generally consistent with the aggregate market returns. As shown in Table 9.2, there were only three instances in which one series experienced a return above or below its mean while the other series was not likewise above or below its mean. As a result,

---

[7] There has been substantial discussion of the market index used and its impact on the empirical results and usefulness of the CAPM. This controversy and the empirical tests of the CAPM are discussed at length in Chapter 20.

[8] This beta is computed using only monthly price changes for both IBM and the S&P 500 (i.e., dividends are not included). This is for simplicity, but it is also based upon a study by Sharpe and Cooper, which indicated that betas with and without dividends are correlated 0.99.

almost all the products are positive, and the covariance between IBM and the market is positive. To derive an index of systematic risk, we compare this covariance to the market portfolio's covariance with itself, i.e., the market portfolio's variance of return. The results indicate a ratio less than one. The covariance divided by the market variance is equal to 0.58 which means that IBM's systematic risk index (beta) is less than one. This implies that based upon this analysis for a limited period, IBM is less risky than the aggregate market is.

$$Cov_{IBM,M} = 192.79/12 = 16.07$$

$$\sigma_M^2 = \Sigma(R_{mt} - R_m)^2/N$$
$$= 333.93/12 = 27.83$$

$$\beta_{IBM} = 16.07/27.83 = .58$$

$$\sigma_M = \sqrt{27.83} = 5.28.$$

$$r_{IBM,M} = \frac{Cov_{IBM,M}}{\sigma_{IBM}\sigma_M} = \frac{16.07}{(5.82)\,(5.28)} = \frac{16.07}{30.73} = .52$$

$$\alpha = \bar{R}_{IBM} - \beta_{IBM}\bar{R}_M$$
$$= 4.73 - (.58)\,(1.29)$$
$$= 4.73 - .75$$
$$= 3.98.$$

The intercept for the characteristic line is computed using the formula set forth before. When this characteristic line is drawn on Figure 9.9 most of the

FIGURE 9.9
Scatter Plot of IBM and Standard & Poor's 500 with Characteristic Line for IBM

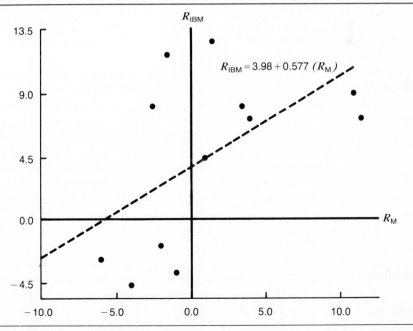

scatter plots fall fairly close to the characteristic line which is consistent with the correlation coefficient of 0.52.

Some Remaining Questions

As indicated by the chapter title, this has been an introduction to capital market theory. The intent has been to provide the basic concepts and theory in order that you can appreciate the justification for using systematic risk (beta) as the relevant measure of risk for individual securities and for portfolios of securities. It is important that you have this understanding when we discuss valuation theory. On the other hand, because it has only been an introduction, we have not considered a number of questions regarding the theory as it applies to the real world. The questions include:

— What do you use as a proxy for the market portfolio of risky assets, and what is the effect if this is not a good proxy?
— Assuming that you cannot borrow and lend at the risk-free rate, how does this affect the CML and SML?
— Assuming you are not allowed to borrow, how can you attain a high risk portfolio?
— How stable is the systematic risk (beta) for individual stocks and for portfolios?
— What is the empirical relationship between the rates of return and systematic risk; i.e., how good is the CAPM as a predictive model?

All of these questions, and others as they relate to the CAPM will be discussed in Chapter 20.

SUMMARY

Following a consideration of the assumptions of capital market theory, we defined a risk-free asset and showed that the correlation and covariance of any asset with the risk-free asset is zero. Given this relationship, it was demonstrated that any combination of an asset or portfolio with the risk-free asset generated a linear return and risk function. Therefore, when you combine the risk-free asset with any risk asset on the Markowitz efficient frontier, you derive a set of straight-line portfolio possibilities with the dominant line the one that is tangent to the efficient frontier. This dominant line is referred to as the capital market line (CML), and all investors should want to be somewhere along this line depending upon their risk preferences. Because all investors want to invest in the risky portfolio at the point of tangency, this portfolio, referred to as the market portfolio, must contain all risky assets in proportion to their relative values. Moreover, the investment decision and the financing decision can be separated, because while everyone will want to invest in the market portfolio, each will differ in financing decisions (i.e., lending or borrowing), which are based upon risk preferences.

Given the CML and the dominance of the market portfolio, it was shown that the relevant risk measure for an individual risk asset is its covariance with the market portfolio, i.e., its systematic risk. When this covariance is normalized by the covariance for the market portfolio, we can derive the well-known beta measure of systematic risk. With the beta coefficient, it is possible to construct a security market line (SML) that relates expected return to beta. All individual securities and portfolios should plot on this SML. This means one can determine the expected (required) return on a security based upon its systematic risk. Alternatively, assuming markets for all securities are not completely efficient, we demonstrated how undervalued and overvalued securities can be identified. We included an example of how to calculate the characteristic line for an individual risky asset and thereby compute its beta coefficient. We concluded with a listing of some remaining questions regarding the CAPM and its application in the real world. These questions will be considered in Chapter 20 when we return to the CAPM after a discussion of valuation. At this point it is important to be aware of the theoretical justification for using systematic risk (beta) as the risk measure in valuation.

QUESTIONS

1. Define a risk-free asset.
2. What is the covariance between a risk-free asset and a portfolio of risky assets? Explain your answer.
3. Why is the set of points between the risk-free asset and a portfolio on the Markowitz efficient frontier a straight line? Explain.
4. What happens to the Markowitz efficient frontier when you assume the existence of a risk-free asset and combine this with alternative risky asset portfolios on the Markowitz efficient frontier? Draw a graph to show this and explain it.
5. Explain why the line from the RFR that is tangent to the efficient frontier is the dominant set of portfolio possibilities. Demonstrate it graphically.
6. It has been shown that the Sharpe capital market line (CML) is tangent to one portfolio on the Markowitz efficient frontier. This portfolio at the point of tangency is referred to as Portfolio M. What stocks are in this portfolio and why are they in it? Be precise in your discussion.
7. Discuss leverage and indicate what it does to the CML.
8. Why is the CML considered the "new" efficient frontier?
9. Define complete diversification in terms of capital market theory.
10. How would you *measure* the extent of diversification of a portfolio? Discuss the rationale for this answer.
11. In terms of the standard deviation for a portfolio of stocks, discuss what change you would expect between 4 and 10 stocks; between 10 and 20 stocks; and between 50 and 100 stocks.
12. Discuss why, in a world with a CML, the investment decision and the financing are separate.
13. Given the Sharpe capital market line, what is the relevant measure of risk for an individual security? Why is this the relevant risk measure? Be very precise and complete in your discussion.
14. It is contended that the total variance of returns for a security can be broken down into systematic variance and unsystematic or unique variance. Describe what is meant by each of these terms.

15. In a capital asset pricing model (CAPM) there is systematic and unsystematic risk for an individual security. Which is the relevant risk variable in a CAPM framework and why is it relevant? Why is the other risk variable not relevant?

16. Draw a properly labeled graph of the security market line (SML) and explain it. How does the SML differ from the CML?

17. a. Assume that you expect the economy's rate of inflation to be 3 percent and, in line with this, you expect the RFR to be 0.06 and the market return (R_m) to be 0.12. Draw the SML.

    b. Now assume that you expect an increase in the rate of inflation from 3 percent to 6 percent. What effect would you expect this to have on your RFR and R_m? Draw another SML on the same graph used for Part a.

    c. Draw the SML on the same graph if you expect the RFR to be 0.09 and the R_m to be 0.17. How does this SML differ from that derived in Part b? Explain what has transpired.

18. You expect the RFR to be 0.10 and the market return (R_m) to be 0.14. Compute the expected return for the following stocks, and plot these on an SML graph.

Stock	Beta	$E(R_i)$
U	.85	
N	1.25	
D	−.20	

19. You ask a stockbroker what his firm's research department expects for these three stocks. The broker responds with the following information:

Stock	Current Price	Expected Price	Expected Dividend
U	22	24	.75
N	48	51	2.00
D	37	40	1.25

Plot your estimated returns on the graph from Question 18 and indicate what action you would take with regard to these stocks. Discuss your decision.

20. Select a stock from the NYSE and collect the month-end prices for the latest 13 months in order to compute 12 monthly percentages of price changes (ignore dividends). Do the same for the S&P 500 series. Plot these on a graph and draw a *visual* characteristic line of best fit (the line which minimizes the deviations from the line). Compute the slope of this line *from the graph.*

21. Given the returns derived in Question 20, compute the beta coefficient using the formula and techniques employed in Table 9.2. How many negative products did you have for the covariance? How does this computed beta compare to the visual beta derived in Question 20?

22. Select a stock that is listed on the ASE and plot the returns during the last 12 months relative to the S&P 500. In general, would you expect this stock to have a higher or lower beta than the NYSE stock? Explain your answer.

23. Given the returns for the ASE stock in Question 22, plot the stock returns relative to monthly rates of return for the ASE index and draw a *visual* line of best fit. Does the slope of this line differ from that derived in Question 22? If so, how can you explain this? Hint: Consider the formula for the beta coefficient and what changes between Question 22 and 23.

REFERENCES

Blume, Marshall E. "On the Assessment of Risk." *Journal of Finance.* 27 no. 1 (March 1972).

Fuller, Russell Jr. "Capital Asset Pricing Theories — Evolution and New Frontiers." Monograph no. 12. *Financial Analysts Research Foundation,* Charlottesville, Va., 1981.

Gaumnitz, Jack E. "Investment Diversification under Uncertainty: An Examination of the Number of Securities in a Diversified Portfolio." Ph.D. dissertation, Stanford University, 1967.

Hagin, Robert. *Modern Portfolio Theory.* Homewood, Ill. Dow-Jones-Irwin, 1979.

Jensen, Michael C. "Capital Markets: Theory and Evidence." *Bell Journal of Economics and Management Science.* 3 no. 2 (Autumn 1972).

Jensen, Michael C. ed. *Studies in the Theory of Capital Markets.* New York: Praeger Publishers, 1972.

Klemkosky, Robert C., and John D. Martin. "The Effect of Market Risk on Portfolio Diversification." *Journal of Finance.* 30 no. 1 (March 1975).

Lindahl-Stevens, Mary. "Some Popular Uses and Abuses of Beta." *Journal of Portfolio Management.* 4 no. 2 (Winter 1978).

Lintner, John. "The Valuation of Risk Assets and the Selection of Risky Investments in Stock Portfolios and Capital Budgets." *Review of Economics and Statistics.* 47 no. 2 (February 1965).

Lintner, John. "Security Prices, Risk, and Maximal Gains from Diversification." *Journal of Finance.* 20 no. 12 (December 1965).

Modligliani, Franco, and Gerald Pogue. "An Introduction to Risk and Return." *Financial Analysts Journal.* 30 no. 2 (March-April 1974).

Mossin, Jan, "Equilibrium in a Capital Asset Market." *Econometrica.* 34 no. 10 (October 1966).

Rosenberg, Barr. "The Capital Asset Pricing Model and the Market Model." *Journal of Portfolio Management.* 5 no. 1 (Winter 1981).

Rosenberg, Barr. "Extra Market Components of Covariance among Security Prices." *Journal of Financial and Quantitative Analysis.* 9 no. 2 (March 1974).

Rosenberg, Barr, and Marathe, Vinay. "Prediction of Investment Risk: Systematic and Residual Risk." *Proceedings of the Seminar on the Analysis of Security Prices.* 20 no. 1 University of Chicago (November 1975).

Ross, Stephen A. "The Current Status of the Capital Asset Pricing Model (CAPM)." *Journal of Finance.* 33 no. 3 (June 1978).

Sharpe, William F. "A Simplified Model for Portfolio Analysis." *Management Science.* 9 no. 2 (January 1963).

Sharpe, William F. "Capital Asset Prices: A Theory of Market Equilibrium under Conditions of Risk." *Journal of Finance.* 19 no. 3 (September 1964).

260

Sharpe, William F. "Risk, Market Sensitivity and Diversification." *Financial Analysts Journal.* 28 no. 1 (January-February 1972).

Sharpe, William F., and Cooper, Guy M. "Risk-Return Classes of New York Stock Exchange Common Stocks." *Financial Analysts Journal.* 28 no. 2 (March-April 1972).

Tobin, James. "Liquidity Preference as Behavior towards Risk." *Review of Economic Studies.* 25 no. 2 (February 1958).

Tole, Thomas M. "You Can't Diversify without Diversifying." *Journal of Portfolio Management.* 8 no. 2 (Winter 1982).

Vasicek, O. A., and McQuown, J. A. "The Efficient Market Model." *Financial Analysts Journal.* 28 no. 5 (September-October 1972).

Wagner, W. H., and Lau, S. C. "The Effect of Diversification on Risk." *Financial Analysts Journal.* 27 no. 6 (November-December 1971).

Part 3

Analysis and Valuation of Equity Securities

In order to properly evaluate an investment vehicle, several analyses must be carried out, beginning with a valuation of the aggregate market and progressing through the examination of various industries, to a consideration of an individual company and its stock. The techniques used for such valuations are dealt with in this section. Chapter 10 contains a discussion of why our initial and major analysis is of the aggregate securities market, followed by industry and company analysis. There is also a basic presentation of the theory of valuation and its application to bonds, preferred stock, and common stock.

Because the main source of information for major business decisions is the financial statements of individual companies, it is essential that you understand what statements are available, what they contain, and how to analyze them in order to answer some significant questions. Chapter 11 provides this background.

Chapter 12 is concerned with the analysis of the aggregate stock market including specific estimation procedures. Chapter 13 deals with industry analysis and employs the same micro technique (i.e., the dividend valuation model) used in market analysis but applies it to a specific industry. The company analysis in Chapter 14 likewise uses this approach for the valuation of a company in the industry analyzed in Chapter 13. The overall goal is to select one of the best companies in a superior industry during a favorable market environment.

Chapter 15 is a separate discussion of the analysis of growth companies because the technique employed in Chapters 10–14 is not applicable to true growth companies given their high current growth rate that cannot be sustained for a long period. Therefore, it is necessary to employ different valuation models to allow for this. Several models are presented and applied to growth company examples.

Throughout this section, we refer to the semistrong efficient market hypothesis. You must realize, however, that while many studies have supported this hypothesis, not all have. Therefore, the idea is to present a valuation technique that is consistent and justifiable. You should always remember that the output of the valuation models is only as good as the *estimated* inputs, and the superior analyst is the one who provides the best *estimates.*

The final chapter in this section deals with technical analysis, an alternative to the fundamental analysis approach discussed in prior chapters. Rather than attempting to estimate value based upon numerous external variables, the technical analyst contends that the market is its own best estimator. Therefore, he believes it is possible to project future stock price movements based upon past stock price changes or other stock market data. A number of techniques used by technical analysts are discussed and demonstrated.

Chapter 10
The Process and Theory of Valuation

A s noted previously, investments constitute the commitment of funds for a period of time to derive a rate of return that compensates the investor for the time during which the funds are invested and for the uncertainty involved. Obviously, before an individual makes an investment, he must determine the required rate of return and how much he should pay for a particular investment to get this required return. The determination of how much to pay for an investment is really a determination of the value of the asset. This chapter is involved with the basic background required to *value* alternative investments. The first section is an overview of the valuation *process*. The second section contains a consideration of the *theory of valuation* including the specific determinants of value; in the third section, these concepts are applied to the valuation of different assets, i.e., bonds, preferred stock, and common stock. In the final section, the determinants of the required rate of return and the expected growth rate of dividends are dealt with.

AN OVERVIEW OF THE VALUATION PROCESS

The valuation process is much like the problem of the chicken and the egg. Do you first deal with individual securities and gradually build up to an analysis of the entire economy or vice versa? It is our contention that the discussion should first center on the analysis of the aggregate economy and the overall securities markets. Only after this is done can different industries be considered. Finally, following the industry analysis, one should consider the securities issued by various firms within the better industries. Therefore, the analysis should follow

265

the three-step process schematized as follows:

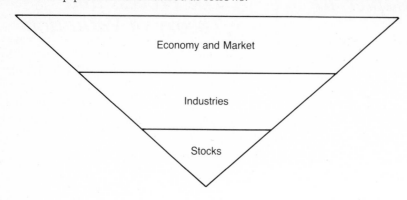

WHY A THREE-STEP PROCESS?

General Economic Influences

It is well recognized that various agencies of the federal government have a major impact on the aggregate economy because they control monetary and fiscal policy. These basic economic forces exert an influence on all industries and all companies in the economy. Fiscal policy can do such things as encourage spending (through investment credits) or discourage spending (through taxes on gasoline). Increases or decreases in spending on defense, unemployment, or highways also influence the general economic picture. All such changes have a major impact on those directly affected by the changes, but there is also a *multi-plier* effect on those who supply goods and services to those directly affected.

The same overall impact can result from a significant change in monetary policy. A restrictive monetary policy that produces a decline in the growth rate of the money supply reduces the supply of funds available to all businesses for working capital and expansion, and of funds available to individuals for acquiring goods and services. Monetary policy affects *all* segments of the economy.

Another overall economic variable that must be considered is *inflation,* because it has a major impact on interest rates and on how consumers and corporations save and spend their money.

In addition to domestic monetary and fiscal actions, other occurrences such as war, political upheavals in foreign countries, or international monetary devaluations influence the aggregate economy. Therefore, it is difficult to conceive of any industry or company that will not be affected in some way by macroeconomic developments that affect the total economy.

Because events influencing the aggregate economy also have such a profound effect on all industries and all companies within these industries, *these macroeconomic factors must be considered before industries can be analyzed.*[1]

---

[1] There is an interesting discussion of an overall investment philosophy for a given economic environment contained in, James H. Gipson, "Investing in a Zero Sum Economy," *Journal of Portfolio Management,* 7 no. 4 (Summer 1981): 15–16.

If the economic outlook indicates a recession that will have an impact on all industries and all companies, it must be expected that all security prices will also be affected. Under such economic conditions, an analyst will probably be extremely apprehensive about recommending an industry. The best recommendation would probably be high portfolio liquidity. In contrast, assume that the economic and stock market outlook is bullish. Under such conditions, the analyst would look for an outstanding industry. This industry search would be enhanced by economic analysis, because, typically, the future performance of an industry depends upon the economic outlook and the particular industry's expected relationship to the economy.

Industry Influences

Because of the importance of the general economic outlook, one should only consider investing in alternative industries *after* it has been decided that the general outlook is favorable. Assuming that it is, the question then becomes one of deciding on the industry or industries to be considered. The industry outlook is determined by the general economic outlook and special industry factors that are generally national in scope but have their greatest influence on one or several industries. Examples of industry influence are an industry-wide strike, import or export quotas or taxes, or government-imposed regulations.

In addition, industries feel the influence of an economic change at different points in the business cycle. Construction typically lags the business cycle and, therefore, this industry is only affected toward the end of a cycle. Finally, different industries respond differently to the business cycle. As an example, cyclical industries (e.g., steel, autos) typically do much better than the aggregate economy during expansions, but they suffer more during contractions. Because of this differential performance it is important to analyze the industry *before* analyzing individual companies within the industry. It is unusual for a company to perform well in a poor industry. (Even the best company in a poor industry will suffer.)

Because of the significance and pervasiveness of industry influences, *an industry evaluation should be conducted prior to analyzing any individual firm.* If the industry outlook is negative, an analyst should not spend a great deal of time on individual firms in the industry. If the industry outlook is good, the prior industry analysis would be useful, because a major component of firm analysis is a comparison of individual firms to the entire industry in terms of relevant financial ratios. In fact, many of the ratios employed in security analysis are only valid when viewed in terms of the entire industry.

EMPIRICAL SUPPORT FOR THE THREE-STEP PROCESS

While the foregoing discussion may appear logical, one may ask whether the implied importance of economic and industry analysis is empirically supported. Is there a relationship between the *earnings* of the aggregate economy, alternative industries, and individual firms? Is there a relationship among the *rates of return* for the aggregate stock market, the stocks in alternative industries, and individual stocks that would indicate that there is value in market and industry analysis?

Association among Corporate Earnings

It was just such a relationship that was examined by Brown and Ball. The authors dealt with the degree of association between the earnings of an individual firm, the earnings of other firms in the industry, and the earnings of all firms in the economy.[2] Brown and Ball examined the earnings of 316 firms for the 19-year period 1947–1965 using six alternative measures of earnings. Employing a linear correlation model, the earnings for individual firms during the period were related to the earnings of all firms except the individual firm being examined. In addition, they related individual firm earnings to the earnings of all other firms in the particular industry.

The results indicated that, on the average, approximately 30–40 percent of the variability of a firm's annual earnings was associated with the variability of earnings averaged for all firms. Also on average, an additional 10–15 percent of the firm's earnings was associated with the earnings for the industry. Further tests on industry relations indicated that the industries were reasonably well defined and that the firms were well classified by industry.

These results indicate that approximately 45–55 percent of a firm's total variability in annual earnings can be explained by the overall economy and a firm's industry with the economic factor being of greater importance.

While these average results clearly confirm the importance of economic and industry analysis, *there is variation among firms.* On the one hand, a highly diversified industrial firm could have earnings that are more closely related to the economy than these results imply; i.e., earnings might be almost perfectly related to the total economy, because in terms of composition the firm may be an image of the economy. In contrast, only a small portion of the earnings of many small firms with a unique product and clientele can be explained by the behavior of the economy or the firm's industry.

Systematic Stock Price Fluctuations

To justify aggregate market analysis it is necessary to determine whether there is a cyclical pattern in stock prices. A detailed analysis of market movements by Shiskin used the techniques employed by the National Bureau of Economic Research to break the stock price series down into several components: seasonal, irregular, and trend cycle.[3] For short-run intervals, the irregular component was dominant. *As the interval was increased to three months or longer the cyclical component became dominant.* An analysis of the duration of monthly runs

---

[2] Philip Brown and Ray Ball, "Some Preliminary Findings on the Association between the Earnings of a Firm, Its Industry, and the Economy," *Empirical Research in Accounting, Selected Studies, 1967,* Supplement to vol. 5, *Journal of Accounting Research:* 55–77.

[3] Julius Shiskin, "Systematic Aspects of Stock Price Fluctuations," reprinted in James Lorie and Richard Brealey, *Modern Developments in Investment Management,* 2d ed. (Hinsdale, Ill.: The Dryden Press, 1978), 640–658.

indicated that the average duration of run for monthly and quarterly stock prices was clearly more than expected for a random series. Diffusion indexes for stock prices using 80 industries indicated the proportion of industries that were rising at a point in time. Using a short time span, the diffusion indexes acted like a random series. *As the span of comparison was extended to 9 or 12 months, a clear cyclical pattern emerged and the diffusion indexes definitely led the stock price series.* Finally, Shiskin examined the relationship between the stock price series and a number of other economic series (employment, income, production). The results indicated that stock prices consistently conform to economic expansions and contractions, but *stock prices clearly lead the general economy.* Although some suggestions were made, prediction of these stock price fluctuations was acknowledged as being difficult because the fluctuations vary in amplitude, pattern, and duration. Therefore, there *is* a cycle in stock prices, and it may be useful to predict the cycle if it can be shown to relate to individual stock price returns.

Market and Industry Effect

A study by King examined the relationship between market returns, industry returns, and the returns on individual stocks.[4] The object of the study was to determine how much of the total price movement for a given stock over time was attributable to overall market factors, how much was due to industry influences, and how much could be ascribed to a stock's "unique" component. To do this, King examined the price behavior of 63 securities listed on the New York Stock Exchange over a total period of 403 months from June 1927 through December 1960, and over four subperiods within this time frame. The variable examined was monthly percentages of change in price. The 63 securities were from the following six industries (number of companies in the industry shown in parentheses): tobacco products (11), petroleum products (11), metals (ferrous and nonferrous) (11), railroads (10), utilities (10), and retail stores (10).

King employed factor analysis, which breaks down the variability of each security's price change into that part attributable to common factors (*communality*) and the part due to a stock's unique factor. The total communality is the percentage of the stock's total price variance attributable to all the other 62 securities, i.e., an overall market factor, and/or an industry factor. The mean communality for the overall time period was 0.72, which indicates that the unique component, on the average, was only 0.28 for the full time period. However, the total communality factor declined during the four subperiods.

King attempted to determine how much of the variability was attributable to overall market movement and how much could be traced to industry factors. For the overall period, King concluded that *about half the variance* (52 percent) in the typical stock for the time period considered was explained by the whole market.[5]

[4] Benjamin F. King, "Market and Industry Factors in Stock Price Behavior," *Journal of Business,* 39 no. 1, Part 2 (January 1966): 139–190.

[5] Ibid., p. 151.

An analysis of the net price changes after the market effect was removed indicated that *almost all of the large positive correlations among individual stocks corresponded to industry groupings* and that all large negative correlations were with stocks in other industries.[6] King employed cluster analysis to group stocks with the highest correlation in a step-by-step procedure until all the stocks were combined. The results supported an industry influence, since the comovement of price changes, after removing the market effect, corresponded to the typical industry classifications. The application of multiple factory analysis and a modified principal components analysis confirmed these results.

These tests indicated that, on average for the total period, more than 10 percent of the total variation in the stock's price could be attributed to the industry influence. Therefore, for King's sample and time period, about 62 percent of the security price changes was explained by a combination of market and industry components.

Again, the importance of the market factor tended to decline over time, and there was a clear difference in the importance of the market factor for alternative stocks. For some stocks, the market factor explained over 70 percent of the variance, while in other instances the proportion was less than 25 percent.

More on the Market and Industry Factor.   A study by Meyers confirmed King's findings regarding market influence but questioned some of his results in the area of the importance of the industry factor.[7] Meyers selected a sample similar to King's and added a second sample of 5 stocks from each of 12 industries (a total of 60). Principal components analysis was performed on samples for the same periods studied by King and for the seven-year period from January 1961 through December 1967. The results for both samples were consistent with those reported earlier by King. *The percentage of variance explained by the market factor declined from more than 55 percent prior to 1944 to less than 35 percent for the period 1952–1967.* Meyers analyzed the importance of the industry factors using a cluster analysis similar to that employed by King and a somewhat different principal components analysis. The analysis for the same six industries and time period used by King gave quite similar results. However, the figures for the period *after* 1952 indicated a weakening of the industry affiliation. Analysis of the 12 new industries confirmed the expectation that *industry clustering was less dominant for a sample that included less homogeneous and distinct industry groups.* The principal components analysis provided considerably less convincing evidence of an industry relationship than had King's analysis.

Therefore, these results confirm the importance of market analysis even with the decline in explanatory power over time. They also confirm the importance of industry analysis, but they indicate that *the importance of the industry component varies across industries.* A study by Livingston confirms the overall importance of industry analysis, but likewise suggests that the relative importance varies across industries.[8]

---

[6] Ibid., p. 153.

[7] Stephen L. Meyers, "A Re-Examination of Market and Industry Factors in Stock Price Behavior," *Journal of Finance,* 28 no. 3 (June 1973): 695–705.

[8] Miles Livingston, "Industry Movements of Common Stocks," *Journal of Finance,* 32 no. 2 (June 1977): 861–874.

TABLE 10.1
Summary of Beta Results for Stocks on NYSE

Time Period	Number of Companies	Mean Beta	Coefficient of Determination (R^2)
7/26–6/33	415	1.051	.51
7/33–6/40	604	1.036	.49
7/40–6/47	731	.990	.36
7/47–6/54	870	1.010	.32
7/54–6/61	890	.998	.25
7/61–6/68	847	.962	.28

SOURCE: Adapted from Marshall E. Blume, "On the Assessment of Risk," *Journal of Finance*, 26 no. 1 (March 1971): 1–10. Reprinted by permission.

A widely read study by Blume likewise contains evidence of the relative importance of the market factor.[9] Following a discussion that justified the use of beta as a measure of risk, Blume derived the beta coefficient for all NYSE stocks that had adequate data for several subperiods from July 1926 through June 1968. A summary of these results contained in Table 10.1 document the importance of the market factor, since they indicate that, even after a decline, aggregate market behavior explains almost 30 percent of the variance for individual securities. The discussion of empirical studies points toward the following generalizations:

1. The market factor was very important prior to 1940 and has declined so that it currently accounts for about 25–30 percent of individual stock price variance.

2. Even after the decline, the market still accounts for a significant part of the variance in individual securities such that market analysis is important.

3. The importance of the market factor in explaining individual price variance fluctuates among securities, ranging from over 50 percent to below 5 percent.

4. When using time intervals exceeding three months, there definitely are cycles in stock price movements, which means it is feasible and practical to project market movements; (i.e., over longer intervals, the market is *not* a random walk). Therefore, market analysis is not only justified but also feasible because of the existence of cycles.

These generalizations confirm the statement made at the beginning—the most important decision is the first decision: *whether to be in common stocks at all!*

An Alternative View.   An article by Sharpe questioned the value of attempting to predict market movements and generally argues against the practice.[10] Sharpe pointed out that, if one assumes the existence of an efficient market, such information cannot be used to achieve superior returns. Likewise, one should not expect to be able to derive superior results from engaging in aggregate market predictions and investing in stocks during good market periods and T-bills during poor market periods. He pointed out that, because T-bills yield less than

---

[9] Marshall E. Blume, "On the Assessment of Risk," *Journal of Finance*, 26 no. 1 (March 1971): 1–10.

[10] William F. Sharpe, "Likely Gains from Market Timing," *Financial Analysts Journal*, 31 no. 2 (March–April 1975): 60–69.

stocks do, if you miss a few turns of the market, you will be at a disadvantage; this loss, along with transactions costs, will yield a return below that from a buy-and-hold policy.

Sharpe analyzed results that could be produced by predicting market returns under three assumptions. First, the differential average annual capital growth from a buy-and-hold policy was compared to the growth derived from perfect foresight (timing) regarding annual peaks and troughs. Second, he assumed that, for each calendar year, a prediction is made as to whether the year will be a good market year (returns on stocks above the returns on cash equivalent T-bills) or a bad market year (return on cash equivalents above return on stocks). The returns from perfect foresight regarding good and bad market years and a buy-and-hold stock policy were compared in this context. It was assumed that, with perfect foresight, the investor will invest in T-bills during bad market years and in stocks during good market years. Third, a comparison was made of returns from a buy-and-hold policy and returns with less than perfect timing. The first two comparisons were done for three time periods: 1929–1972, 1934–1972, and 1946–1972. The final analysis considered only 1934–1972.

The results assuming perfect timing of peaks and troughs indicated substantial returns would be obtained by an individual with the ability to project the absolute peaks and troughs in the market (about 4 percent for buy-and-hold versus 20 percent for perfect timing). While these results are not surprising, it is also clearly not realistic to expect such ability on a consistent basis. The analysis of results assuming the ability to predict good and bad years compared to a buy-and-hold policy or holding only T-bills likewise indicated superior returns were achieved with the former. Even assuming 2 percent trading commissions were paid, the timing-ability portfolio had higher returns and lower risk (standard deviation of returns). The final analysis derived the returns from alternative decisions and examined these returns assuming the investor predicted correctly from 50 percent of the time (no real insight) to 100 percent of the time (perfect foresight). The returns were negative at 50 percent and improved and became positive at 74 percent. This implies that if you had predicted the behavior of the market correctly 74 percent of the time, you would derive superior returns compared to those for a buy-and-hold policy. Based upon these results, Sharpe concluded that, unless a portfolio manager is quite good at predicting where the market is going each year, he should not attempt to engage in market timing.

One might question some of Sharpe's conclusions for several reasons. First his assumption of a 2 percent commission on T-bill shifts is unnecessary, and he does not consider the discounting on commissions since May Day (May 1, 1975). Also, because the study stopped in 1972, it missed several major swings that would have been very profitable to anyone with forecasting ability. Further, it seems that Sharpe underestimated the impact of small differences in returns on long-run wealth positions—e.g., a 2 percent difference for 25 years on a initial portfolio of $10,000 is about $64,000 in the ending wealth position. However, his finding that an investor must be correct about seven times out of ten regarding market turns is important. Similar to other findings and our discussion in Chapter 7 (the efficient markets chapter), it implies that it *is possible* to be a superior portfolio manager, but that it is *not easy*. Even so, it is worth the time and effort, because as discussed previously, these market movements have a significant impact on the returns for individual stocks.

THEORY OF VALUATION

Given an understanding that the valuation process should proceed from the market to the individual stock, this section considers the specific factors that determine value. We will subsequently apply these valuation concepts to alternative types of investments (bonds, preferred stocks, and common stocks). In later chapters we will use the common stock valuation model to analyze the aggregate stock market, alternative industries, and individual common stocks. We will also use the bond valuation model in the chapters dealing with bond analysis and portfolio management.

The reader may recall from accounting, economics, or corporate finance courses that *the value of an asset is the present value of the expected returns from the asset during the holding period.* Specifically, an investment is expected to provide a stream of returns during the holding period, and it is necessary to discount this stream of expected returns at the investor's required rate of return to determine the value of the asset. Therefore, to derive a value for an asset it is necessary to estimate: (1) the stream of expected returns, and (2) the required rate of return on the investment.

Streams of Returns.   An estimate of the future returns expected from an investment encompasses the *size* of the returns, the *form* of the returns, the *time pattern* of returns, and the *uncertainty* of returns.

Form of Return.   Returns from an investment can take many forms including earnings, dividends, interest payments, or capital gains based upon an increase in value during a period. A major question in valuation theory as applied to common stocks has been whether the appropriate form of returns to consider should be the *earnings* of the firm or the *dividends* of the firm. These can differ over time depending on whether a firm retains earnings for reinvestment. In such a case, the firm would have high earnings but would pay small dividends. Fortunately, it has been shown by Miller and Modigliani that this is an unnecessary controversy because, if one makes proper allowance for the investment decisions made by the issuing firm, the two are equivalent.[11] Later in this chapter we will set forth the dividend valuation model for common stocks, because this model is quite intuitive and is very useful if one makes some simplifying assumptions. The point is, returns can come in many forms and it is necessary to consider all of them.

Time Pattern of Returns.   In addition, it is important to estimate *when* the returns will be received because money has a time value. (A dollar of income today is worth more than a dollar of income received a year from now.) There-

---

[11] Merton H. Miller and Franco Modigliani, "Dividend Policy, Growth, and the Valuation of Shares," *Journal of Business,* 34 no. 4 (October 1961): 411–433.

fore, it is necessary to know the time pattern of returns from an investment so that the stream can be properly valued relative to alternative investments.

Required Rate of Return.   The reader will recall from Chapter 1 that the required rate of return on an investment is determined by: (1) the economy's real risk-free rate of return, plus (2) the expected rate of inflation during the holding period, plus (3) a risk premium. *All* investments are affected by the risk-free rate and inflation (i.e., the nominal risk-free rate); the differentiating factor is the risk premium for alternative assets. In turn, this risk premium is a function of the uncertainty of returns on the assets.

The uncertainty of returns and what affects this can be considered in terms of the *internal* characteristics of the asset or in terms of *market-determined* factors. Earlier we subdivided the internal characteristics into: business risk (BR), financial risk (FR), and liquidity risk (LR). Alternatively, in Chapter 9 we considered developments in capital market theory which indicated that the relevant risk measure is the systematic risk of the asset, i.e., variability in an asset's returns that is due to variability in aggregate market returns (the asset's covariance with the market portfolio). When this systematic market risk is normalized relative to market variance, the result is a measure referred to as *beta*.

Summary: Determinants of Value

To derive the value of an asset it is necessary to estimate the following:
1. The expected stream of returns. This includes the size and the form of the returns, which can be earnings, dividends, interest, or change in price.
2. The time pattern of expected returns. Because money has a time value it is necessary to consider alternative time streams for the returns and discount the streams to the present using an appropriate discount rate (i.e., the investor's required rate of return).
3. The required rate of return on the investment which is determined by the uncertainty of returns. Uncertainty can be examined in terms of internal characteristics or in terms of a market-determined measure of risk derived from capital asset pricing theory. One would expect these alternative approaches to the analysis of uncertainty to provide consistent results — i.e., assets that have high levels of internal risk should have large betas. This consistency between internal risk characteristics and market measures of risk has generally been supported by numerous empirical studies.[12]

INVESTMENTS: COMPARISON OF VALUE AND PRICE

On several occasions it has been stated that an investment is the commitment of funds for a period of time to derive a rate of return that compensates the investor for the time during which the funds are given up and the uncertainty (risk) involved. As noted in the chapter introduction, in order to ensure that you are

---

[12] A summary of the major studies is contained in, Donald J. Thompson II, "Sources of Systematic Risk in Common Stocks," *Journal of Business*, 49 no. 2 (April 1976): 173–188.

going to get your required return on an investment, it is necessary to *determine the value of the asset at your required rate of return* and then compare this value to the *prevailing market price of the asset.* The point of investments is that you should *buy assets where the market price of the asset is equal to or less than the value you have estimated.* Alternatively, you should *not* buy an asset if the market price *exceeds* your estimated value. The point made throughout this book is that if the asset's market price exceeds your estimated value, you will not receive your required rate of return on the investment. In summary:

If Estimated Value ≥ Market Price→Buy

If Estimated Value < Market Price→Don't Buy.

VALUATION OF ALTERNATIVE INVESTMENTS

Valuation of Bonds

It is relatively easy to determine the value of bonds because the size and time pattern of the returns from the bond over its life are known. Specifically, a bond promises:
1. Interest payments every six months equal to one half the coupon rate times the face value of the bond[13] and
2. The payment of the principal (also referred to a *face value*) at the maturity of the bond.

As an example, in 1985, a $10,000 bond due in 2000 with a 10 percent coupon will pay $500 every six months for the life of the bond (the next 15 years). In addition, there is a promise to pay the $10,000 principal at maturity in 2000. Therefore, assuming the borrower does not default, the investor knows *what* payments will be made and *when* they will be made.

Recalling the specification that the value of any asset is the present value of the returns from an asset, the value of the bond is the present value of the interest payments (i.e., an annuity of $500 every six months for 15 years) and the present value of the principal payment. The only unknown for this asset (assuming the borrower does not default) is the rate of return that should be used to discount the expected stream of payments. Assuming that the prevailing nominal risk-free rate is 9 percent and the investor requires a 1 percent risk premium on this bond (because there is some probability of default), the required rate of return would be 10 percent.

The present value of the interest payments is an annuity for 30 periods (15 years every six months) at one half the required return (5 percent).[14]

$500 × 15.3725 = $7,686 (present value of interest at 10 percent).

---

[13] The coupon rate is the annual dollar interest payment, which is expressed as a percentage of the bond's face value. In turn, the face value appears on the face of the bond and is the repayment due at the maturity of the bond. This face value is also referred to as the *par value* or *principal* of the bond.

[14] The annuity factors and present value factors are contained in Appendix A, at the end of the book.

The present value of the principal is likewise discounted at 5 percent for 30 periods[15]

$$\$10,000 \times .2314 = \$2,314.$$

Present value of interest payments	$ 7,686
Present value of principal payment	2,314
Value of bond at 10 percent	$10,000

This is the amount that an investor should be willing to pay for this bond assuming that his required rate of return on a bond of this risk class was 10 percent. If the bond is selling for less than this in the market, this would clearly be acceptable. If the market price is above this value, an investor should not buy it because his promised yield to maturity will be less than his required rate of return.

Alternatively, if the investor wants a 12 percent return on this bond, the value would be as follows:

$$\$500 \times 13.7648 = \$6,882$$
$$10,000 \times \quad .1741 = \underline{\quad 1,741}$$
$$\$8,623$$

This example shows that if you want a higher rate of return you will not pay as much for an asset—i.e., a given stream of returns has a lower value to you. As before, you would compare this computed value to the market price of the bond to determine whether you would invest in it.[16]

Valuation of Preferred Stock

Preferred stock involves a promise to pay a stated dividend, usually each quarter, for an infinite period; i.e., there is no maturity. As was true with a bond, stated payments are to be made on specified dates. However, preferred stock does not entail the same *legal* obligation to pay as bonds do, and payments are made only *after* bond interest payments are met, so the uncertainty of payments is greater. This increased uncertainty implies that a higher rate of return should be required on a firm's preferred stock than is required on a firm's debentures. While this differential should exist in theory, it has not existed in practice for a number of years because of the tax treatment accorded dividends paid to corporations. As noted in Chapter 2, dividends received by corporations from other corporations are 85 percent tax-exempt, so the effective tax on dividends would be about 6.9 percent, assuming a corporate tax rate of 46 percent. As a result, there is a great demand for preferred stocks, and the yield on them has generally been below that on AAA (the highest grade) corporate bonds.

---

[15] If annual compounding were assumed, this would be 0.239 rather than 0.2314. Semiannual compounding is used because it is consistent with the interest payments and is also used in practice.

[16] The reader should check that if the required rate of return was 8 percent, the value of this bond would be $11,729.

Because preferred stock is a perpetuity, the value is simply the stated annual dividend divided by the required rate of return on the asset as follows:[17]

$$V = \frac{\text{Dividend}}{i}.$$

As an example, assume that a preferred stock has a $100 par value and a dividend of $8 a year. At the present time, assume that AAA corporate bonds are yielding 10 percent and, because of the uncertainty involved and the tax advantage of this preferred stock issue to you as a corporate investor, the required rate of return is 9 percent. Therefore, the value of this preferred stock to you is:

$$V = \frac{\$8}{.09}$$
$$= \$88.89.$$

Also, given the price of preferred stock, it is possible to derive the promised yield on this investment:

$$i = \frac{\text{Dividend}}{\text{Price}}.$$

Valuation of Common Stocks

The valuation of common stocks is definitely more difficult than that of bonds or preferred stock because almost all the required inputs are unknown. Recall that in the case of a bond, the periodic interest payments are known, and we also know the final payment at maturity. The only unknown is the discount rate, which is calculated from the prevailing nominal RFR plus a risk premium that is dependent upon the uncertainty of the interest payment. Similarly, for preferred stock the only unknown is the required rate of return on the stock. In contrast, in the case of common stock, an investor is uncertain about the size of the returns, the time pattern of returns, *and* the required rate of return. In addition, as mentioned earlier, there is a question of what stream of returns should be discounted (earnings or dividends). Because it has been shown that the two approaches are equivalent if comparable assumptions are made, the approach used is a matter of choice. Some observers prefer to use earnings because they are the source of dividends. Alternatively, it is contended that investors discount that which they receive—dividends. In this discussion we will use the dividend model, because it is intuitively appealing and because it has been used extensively by others, so the reader may be familiar with the reduced form of the valuation model that will be derived later. Basically, the dividend model in-

---

[17] For a sophisticated valuation model for preferred stock based upon the option-hedging methodology of Black-Scholes, see David Emanuel, "A Theoretical Model for Valuing Preferred Stock," *Journal of Finance,* 38, no. 4 (September, 1983): 1133–1155.

volves the assumption that the value of a share of common stock is the present value of all future dividends as follows:[18]

$$V_j = \frac{D_1}{(1+i)} + \frac{D_2}{(1+i)^2} + \frac{D_3}{(1+i)^3} + \cdots \frac{D_\infty}{(1+i)^\infty}$$

$$= \sum_{t=1}^{\infty} \frac{D_t}{(1+i)^t}$$

where:

V_j = value of the common stock j

D_t = dividend during period t

i = required rate of return on stock j.

An obvious question is, what happens in the case where the stock is not held for an infinite period? Assume a sale of the stock at the end of Year 2. In such an instance the formulation would be as follows:

$$V_j = \frac{D_1}{(1+i)} + \frac{D_2}{(1+i)^2} + \frac{SP_{j2}}{(1+i)^2}.$$

where: SP_{j2} = the sale price of stock j at the end of year 2.

The value is the two dividend payments during Years 1 and 2 and the sale price (SP) for the stock at the end of Year 2. Regarding the selling price of the stock at the end of Year 2, it is simply *the value of all remaining dividend payments* as follows:

$$SP_{j2} = \frac{D_3}{(1+i)} + \frac{D_4}{(1+i)^2} + \cdots \frac{D_\infty}{(1+i)^\infty}.$$

Given that SP_{j2} is discounted back to the present by $1/(1+i)^2$, this expression becomes:

$$\frac{\dfrac{D_3}{(1+i)} + \dfrac{D_4}{(1+1)^2} + \cdots \dfrac{D_\infty}{(1+i)^\infty}}{(1+i)^2}$$

$$= \frac{D_3}{(1+i)^3} + \frac{D_4}{(1+i)^4} + \cdots \frac{D_\infty}{(1+i)^\infty},$$

which is simply an extension of the original equation. The point is, whenever the stock is sold, its value (sale price) will be the present value of all future dividends. When this ending value is discounted back to the present, you are back to the basic formulation.

What about stocks that do not pay dividends? Again, the concept is the same

---

[18] This model was initially set forth in J. B. Williams, *The Theory of Investment Value* (Cambridge, Mass.: Harvard, 1938). It was subsequently reintroduced and expanded by Myron J. Gordon, *The Investment, Financing and Valuation of the Corporation* (Homewood, Ill.: Richard D. Irwin, 1962).

except that some of the near-term dividend payments are zero. Notably, there are expectations that at some point the firm *will* pay dividends. If there was not such an expectation, an investor would never expect any cash flows, and nobody would be willing to buy such a security. With a nondividend paying stock the firm is not paying anything now, but reinvesting capital so that it will grow faster in the future. The formulation is as follows:

$$V_j = \frac{D_1}{(1+i)} + \frac{D_2}{(1+i)^2} + \frac{D_3}{(1+i)^3} + \cdots \frac{D_\infty}{(1+i)^\infty}$$

where:

$$D_1 = 0$$

$$D_2 = 0.$$

The expectation is that, when the firm starts paying dividends in D_3, they will grow faster. The stock has value because of these *future* dividends. This model will be best understood if it is applied to several cases involving different holding periods ranging from short periods to longer intervals.

One-Year Holding Period.   In this example, it is assumed that the investor wants to buy the stock, hold it for one year, and sell it at the end of the year. As noted, to determine the value of the stock (i.e., how much the investor should pay for it) the dividend to be received during the period, the expected price at the end of the holding period, and the required rate of return on this stock must be estimated.

The estimate of the dividend for the coming year will probably be based upon the current dividend and expectations regarding changes during the year. Assume that the company earned $2.50 a share last year and paid a dividend of $1 a share (a 40 percent payout which has been fairly consistent over time). Further, the firm is expected to earn about $2.75 during the coming year and to raise the dividend to $1.10 per share.

A crucial estimate is the expected price for the stock that will prevail a year from now. There are three alternative estimation procedures that one could employ. The first is a direct application of the dividend discount model — i.e., attempt to estimate the specific dividend payments for a number of years into the future and derive a value based on these estimates. The second is to use the earnings multiplier approach wherein you multiply the future expected earnings for the stock by an earnings multiple figure to derive an expected price.[19] Finally, you can estimate what you think will be the dividend yield for this stock one year from now and apply this to the expected dividend to derive the future price.

For now, let us assume that you prefer the dividend yield approach. You expect the dividend yield on this stock to be 5 percent. Given the expected dividend of $1.10 per share, this implies a future stock price of $22 (1.10/.05).

Finally, it is necessary to determine the required rate of return on this stock investment. Naturally, this rate will be influenced by the fact that there are other

---

[19] The earnings multiplier approach will be discussed in detail in a later section of this chapter.

potential investments entailing less risk, approximately equal risk, and more risk. Again, we will discuss the determination of this estimate for the aggregate market, industries, and companies in more detail in subsequent chapters. For the moment, assume that long-term AAA bonds are yielding 10 percent, and you believe that a 4 percent risk premium over the yield of these bonds is appropriate for the stock. Thus, you specify a required rate of return of 14 percent.

In summary, you have estimated the dividend at $1.10 (payable at year end), the ending price at $22, and the required rate of return at 14 percent. Given these inputs, the value of this asset to you is as follows:

$$V_i = \frac{\$1.10}{(1+.14)} + \frac{\$22.00}{(1+.14)}$$
$$= \frac{1.10}{1.14} + \frac{22.00}{1.14}$$
$$= .96 + 19.30$$
$$= \$20.26.$$

Note that there has been no mention of the current price of the stock. This is because the current market price is *not* relevant to the investor until after he has derived an *independent* value based on *his* estimates of the relevant variables. *After* a value has been derived, it is necessary to consider the market price. The decision to acquire the stock is dependent upon whether the *computed* value is equal to or above the *market* price. Obviously, if the market price is above the derived value, you would not want to acquire the stock, because by definition the stock will cost more than it is worth and you won't receive your required rate of return.

Multiple-Year Holding Period.   In this instance it is assumed that you are considering acquiring the stock now and anticipate holding the stock for several years and then selling it. The decision to hold the stock for several years complicates the valuation procedure, because it is necessary to estimate *several* future dividend payments and also to estimate the value of the stock for a number of years in the future.

The difficulty with estimating future dividend payments is that the future stream can have numerous forms. The exact estimate depends on your outlook for earnings growth, because earnings are the source of dividends' and the firm's dividend policy (i.e., does it make a constant payout each year, which implies a change in dividend each year, or does the firm follow a step pattern). The easiest case to analyze is one in which the firm considered enjoys a constant rate of growth in earnings and also maintains a constant dividend payout. In this instance, the dividend stream will have a constant growth rate equal to the earnings growth rate. Alternatively, a firm could increase the dividend rate by a constant dollar amount each year or change the rate by a given dollar amount every two or three years (i.e., a step pattern).

In the current example, assume the expected holding period is three years

and you estimate the following dividend payments at the end of each year:
— Year 1 — $1.10/share
— Year 2 — $1.20/share
— Year 3 — $1.35/share.

The next estimate to be made is the expected ending price for the stock three years in the future. Again, if we want to use the dividend yield approach, it is necessary to project the dividend yield on this stock three years from now. Assume that you think rates will be lower than your previous estimate for one year; i.e., you estimate a dividend yield of 4 percent. Given the $1.35 dividend payment, this implies an ending price of $33.75 ($1.35/.04).

The final estimate is the required rate of return on this stock during this period. Assuming that the 14 percent desired rate is still appropriate for this period, the value of this stock is as follows:

$$
\begin{aligned}
V_i &= \frac{1.10}{(1+.14)} + \frac{1.20}{(1+.14)^2} + \frac{1.35}{(1+.14)^3} + \frac{33.75}{(1+.14)^3} \\
&= \frac{1.10}{(1.14)} + \frac{1.20}{(1.30)} + \frac{1.35}{(1.4815)} + \frac{33.75}{(1.4815)} \\
&= .96 + .92 + .91 + 22.78 \\
&= \$25.57.
\end{aligned}
$$

Again, at this point you would compare this derived value for the stock to its market price to determine whether you should buy the stock or not.

At this point the reader should recognize that the procedure of valuation being discussed is very similar to that followed in corporate finance when making investment decisions, but the cash flows we are concerned with are from dividends. Rather than estimating the scrap value or salvage value of a corporate asset, we are estimating the ending sales price for the stock. Finally, rather than cost of capital, we estimate our required rate of return for the individual investor. In both cases we are looking for excess present value, which means the present value of expected cash inflows (i.e., the value of the asset) exceeds the present value of cash outflows (i.e., the cost of the asset).

Infinite Period Model.   It would certainly be possible to extend the discussion of the multi-period model by considering longer holding periods (e.g., 5, 10, or 15 years). It is believed that the benefits to be derived from the extensions would be minimal and the boredom factor would quickly dominate. Therefore, at this point we will consider the very popular infinite period model.

This model assumes that investors estimate future dividend payments from the present to perpetuity. Needless to say, this is a formidable task! To allow mortal investors to carry out this valuation, it is necessary to make some simplifying assumptions about this future stream of dividends. The easiest assumption is that *the future dividend stream grows at a constant rate for the infinite period.* As we will discuss, this is a rather heroic assumption in many instances, but it allows us to derive a model that is very useful in valuing the aggregate market, alternative industries, and even some individual stocks. This model is specified as follows:

$$V_j = \frac{D_0(1+g)}{(1+i)} + \frac{D_0(1+g)^2}{(1+i)^2} + \cdots \frac{D_0(1+g)^n}{(1+i)^n}$$

where:

V_j = the value of stock j

D_0 = the dividend payment in the current period

g = the constant growth rate of dividends

i = the required rate of return on stock j

n = the number of periods, which is assumed to be infinite.

In the appendix to this chapter it is shown that this formulation can be simplified to the following expression:

$$V_j = \frac{D_1}{i-g}.$$

The reader will probably recognize this formula as one that is widely used in corporate finance to derive the cost of equity capital for the firm. In many cases, rather than V_j, the expression is written:

$$P_j = \frac{D_1}{i-g}.$$

Given this model, the major estimates to be made are: (1) the required rate of return (i), and (2) the expected growth rate of dividends (g). After estimating g, it is a simple matter to estimate D_1, because it is the current dividend (D_0) times $(1+g)$.

Consider the example of a stock with a current dividend of $1 a share, which you expect to rise to $1.09 next year. Upon reflection you believe that, over the long run, this company's earnings and dividends will continue to grow at 9 percent; i.e., your estimate of g is 0.09.

Regarding the required rate of return, for the near term you believe 14 percent was appropriate due to a high current rate of inflation. For the long run, you expect the rate of inflation to decline and believe that your long-run required rate of return on this stock should be 13 percent; your estimate of i is 0.13. Therefore, the relevant variables are:

$$g = .09$$

$$i = .13$$

$$D_1 = 1.09(\$1.00 \times 1.09)$$

$$P = \frac{1.09}{.13 - .09}$$

$$= \frac{1.09}{.04}$$

$$= \$27.25.$$

A small change in any of the original estimates will have a large impact, as can be shown by the following examples:

1. $g = .09$; $i = .14$; $D_1 = \$1.09$ (We assume an increase in i.)

$$P = \frac{\$1.09}{.14 - .09}$$

$$= \frac{\$1.09}{.05}$$

$$= \$21.80.$$

2. $g = .10$; $i = .13$; $D_1 = \$1.10$ (We assume an increase in g.)

$$P = \frac{\$1.10}{13 - .10}$$

$$= \frac{\$1.10}{.03}$$

$$= \$36.67.$$

Obviously, a 1 percent change in either g or i has a major impact on the computed price of the stock. The crucial relationship *is the spread between the required rate of return and the expected growth rate.* Anything that causes a *decline* in the spread will cause an *increase* in prices, while any change that results in an *increase* in the spread will cause a *decline* in stock prices.

Infinite Growth Model and Growth Companies.   It is essential that you recall the restrictive assumptions of the infinite dividend growth model if this model is used to determine the value for growth companies. Recall that the three major assumptions of the growth model are:

1. A *constant* rate of growth.
2. The constant growth rate will continue for an *infinite* period.
3. The required rate of return (i) *is greater than the infinite growth rate* (g). If it is not, the model explodes and gives meaningless results—i.e., the denominator becomes a negative value.

Growth companies are firms that have the opportunities and the abilities to earn rates of return on investments that are consistently above the firm's required rate of return.[20] As a result of these outstanding investments, these firms generally retain a high percent of earnings for reinvestment, and the earnings for these firms grow faster than the typical firm. Examples of such firms include IBM, Xerox, McDonald's, and Apple Computer. An important point is, the earnings growth pattern for these firms is *not* consistent with the assumption of the infinite growth model. First, it is not feasible for these firms to grow constantly at these above average rates; e.g., for a period, IBM's earnings were growing at 30–40 percent a year; currently they are growing at 15–20 percent a year. There-

---

[20] Outstanding discussions of growth companies are contained in Ezra Salomon, *The Theory of Financial Management,* (New York: Columbia University Press, 1963). Merton Miller and Franco Modigliani, "Dividend Policy, Growth, and the Valuation of Shares," *Journal of Business,* 34 no. 4 (October 1961): 411–433.

fore, while the growth is still above average, it is almost certain that these firms *cannot* continue such abnormal growth for an infinite period. Finally, it is very likely that during this period of abnormal growth the *current* rate of growth will exceed the required rate of return; e.g., during its period of superior growth, IBM's required rate of return was very likely not 30 or 40 percent.

In summary, some firms experience finite periods of abnormally high growth rates. During these periods, it is not possible to use the infinite growth model for valuing the stock, because these temporary conditions are not consistent with the assumptions of the infinite growth model. Following Chapter 14 on the valuation of companies, Chapter 15 is devoted to models used to derive the value of growth companies.

Pragmatic Multiplier Approach

Rather than concentrate on dividends alone, many investors prefer to derive value based upon an earnings multiplier approach. The basic rationale for this approach is that assets are the capitalized value of future earnings, which implies that investors derive value by determining how many dollars they are willing to pay for a dollar of expected earnings (typically earnings during the next 12-month period). As an example, if investors are supposedly willing to pay 10 times expected earnings, a stock that is expected to earn $2 a share will sell for $20. This multiplier, also referred to as the *price-earnings (P/E) ratio,* is derived as follows:

$$\text{Earnings Multiplier} = \text{Price Earnings Ratio} = \frac{\text{Current Price}}{\text{Next 12 Month Earnings}}.$$

The important question to consider is which factors influence the earnings multiplier (P/E ratio) over time? In the forthcoming chapter on aggregate market valuation (Chapter 12), it is shown that the P/E ratio for the stock market has varied from about 6 times earnings to over 20 times earnings.[21] Again, we will see that the present-value-of-dividend model can be used to indicate the relevant variables. Specifically, the basic dividend valuation model is as follows:

$$P_i = \frac{D_1}{i - g}.$$

If we divide both sides of the equation by E_1 (expected earnings during the next 12 months):

$$\frac{P_1}{E_1} = \frac{D_1/E_1}{i - g}.$$

Thus, the P/E ratio is determined by:
1. The expected dividend payout ratio (dividends divided by earnings)

---

[21] When computing historical P/E ratios, the practice is to use earnings for the *last* 12 months rather than expected earnings. Although this will influence the level, it should not affect the changes over time.

2. The required rate of return on the stock
3. The expected growth rate of dividends for the stock.

As an example, if we assume that a stock under consideration has an expected dividend payout of 50 percent (i.e., the firm generally pays out 50 percent of its earnings in dividends), a required rate of return of 13 percent, and an expected growth rate for dividends of 9 percent, we would have the following:

$$D/E = .50; \ i = .13; \ g = .09$$

$$P/E = \frac{.50}{.13 - .09}$$

$$= \frac{.50}{.04}$$

$$= 12.5.$$

Again, a small change in either *i* or *g* will have a large impact on the multiplier, as shown in the following examples:

1. $D/E = .50; \ i = .14; \ g = .09$ (We assume an increase in *i*.)

$$P/E = \frac{.50}{.14 - .09}$$

$$= \frac{.50}{.05}$$

$$= 10.$$

2. $D/E = .50; \ i = .13; \ g = .10$ (We assume an increase in *g*.)

$$P/E = \frac{.50}{.13 - .10}$$

$$= \frac{.50}{.03}$$

$$= 16.7.$$

As before, the crucial factor is the spread between *i* and *g*. While the dividend payout ratio obviously has an impact, this ratio typically is a rather stable variable and so would not be very important in projecting year-to-year changes in security values.

The Pragmatic Multiplier and Growth Companies.   Again, one might wonder how this pragmatic multiplier can be used to derive a value for growth companies. The answer is the same as it was for the infinite growth model—it *cannot* be used because it is derived from this model. Specifically, in many cases growth firms pay no dividends so the D/E ratio would be zero. Similarly, there would either be no growth rate of dividends and/or the growth rate of the earnings or dividends would exceed the required rate of return, which is unacceptable for the model. As before, it is necessary to use P/E models specifically derived for the valuation of growth companies. These specialized models will be considered in Chapter 15.

Thus far, we have considered the estimates (future stream of flows and required rate of return) that are required and, given these estimates, how one determines the value of bonds, preferred stock, and common stock under several investment horizons. In the final section we will deal with the determinants of the required rate of return and the expected growth rate. In subsequent chapters we consider how an investor goes about estimating these determinants of value for the aggregate securities market, alternative industries, and individual firms.

DETERMINANTS OF THE REQUIRED RATE OF RETURN AND THE EXPECTED GROWTH RATE OF DIVIDENDS

The Required Rate of Return

This discussion is basically a brief review of the presentation in Chapters 1 and 9 dealing with the determinants of the required rate of return on an investment. There are basically three major factors:
1. The economy's "real" risk-free rate (RFR)
2. The expected rare of inflation (I)
3. A risk premium (RP).

The Risk-Free Rate.   This rate reflects the basic time value of money assuming no probability of default. It is a function of the underlying investment opportunities in the economy, which are determined by *the real growth rate of the economy*. In turn, the real growth rate for the economy is a function of: (a) the growth of the labor force; (b) the growth in number of hours worked per week; and (c) the growth in labor productivity.

As noted earlier, the average real growth rate for the U.S. economy has generally ranged from 2.5 percent to 3.5 percent a year, with the recent rate closer to 2.5 percent due to a decline in the growth of productivity during the late 1960s and the 1970s. It is also important to note that this basic determinant of the required rate of return is quite stable over any short-run or intermediate time period, i.e., one or two years. This stability is because the basic factors that influence the real growth in the economy are very slow to change.

The Expected Rate of Inflation.   This rate is important, because investors are interested in "real" rates of return that will allow them to increase their rate of consumption. Therefore, if investors expect a given rate of inflation, they will increase their "nominal" required rate of return to reflect this expectation as follows:

$$\text{Nominal } RFR = [1 + RFR][1 + E(I)] - 1.$$

As an example, if the real RFR is 3 percent and the expected rate of inflation $[E(I)]$ during the coming year is 8 percent, an investor should require a nominal rate of return of approximately 11 percent on a risk-free one-year security as follows:

$$(1 + .03)(1 + .08) = 1.1124 - 1 = .1124.$$

The typical example of a risk-free security would be a one-year government bond. Given the basic stability of the real RFR, it is clear that changes in the expected rate of inflation have caused the *nominal* promised yield on government bonds (i.e., the nominal RFR) to fluctuate between 5 percent and 14 percent during the period 1974–1984.

Note that the two factors that determine the nominal RFR should affect *all* investments from U.S. government securities to highly speculative land deals. This is why the estimation of the expected rate of inflation is such a crucial part of the valuation process.

The Risk Premium.   This causes a *difference* in required rates of return for alternative investments, e.g., for government bonds, corporate bonds, and common stocks. It also explains the difference in the expected return for various grades of corporate bonds (AAA vs. AA vs. A)[22] and different common stocks.

In Chapter 1 we discussed the notion that investors demand a risk premium because of the *uncertainty* of returns expected from an investment. Further, we pointed out that this uncertainty of returns was indicated by the *dispersion of expected returns*. In turn, this dispersion could be measured in terms of such factors as range, variance, standard deviation, or semivariance. Because the theoretical work in this area has generally used the variance or standard deviation, this was the one we generally employed. Subsequently, in Chapter 9 the discussion on the capital asset pricing model indicated that the relevant risk measure should be systematic risk which is the covariance of the asset's rate of return over time with the returns for the market portfolio or the normalized systematic covariance, beta. Combining the discussions from Chapter 1, where we considered the factors that influenced the variability of returns, with the discussion in Chapter 9, we see that it is possible to evaluate the risk of an asset on the basis of: (1) *internal* factors (business risk, financial risk, and liquidity risk), or (2) via *market-determined* risk measures (beta).

Business risk (BR) is the uncertainty due to a firm's sales volatility, which is generally related to the characteristics of the firm's industry. In addition, the variability of the firm's operating earnings is affected by the firm's production function (i.e., the mix of fixed and variable costs), which is indicated by its operating leverage.

Financial risk (FR) is the additional uncertainty (variability) caused by the method of financing an investment. This financial risk is typically an integral part of the investment, e.g., the stock of a firm that has fixed debt in its capital structure. Because as a stockholder, you are an owner of the firm, the fact that the firm has debt means that you implicitly share the risk. Therefore, the variability of stock returns is affected by the firm's financing decisions. Alternatively, an investor can explicitly add financial risk to an investment by borrowing money on his own to finance the acquisition, such as by buying stock on margin or by borrowing money to buy real estate. In either case, the variability of expected returns increases and the investor's required rate of return should also increase.

[22] As will be discussed in detail in Chapter 16, corporate bonds are rated by investment services based upon their risk of default. In this regard, AAA is very low risk and A would be higher risk.

Liquidity risk (LR) is uncertainty caused by the inability to buy or sell an asset quickly with little price change assuming no new information. This specification of liquidity has two components—the time involved to complete the transaction and the price change. The lack of either a quick transaction or a small price change means that you are less certain of your ultimate return and you should be compensated for this added uncertainty.

As an alternative to the internal risk factors, *systematic risk (beta)* is a measure of the variability of returns over time for an individual asset related to the variability of returns for the aggregate market portfolio of risky assets. You will recall that it is *not* total risk (total variance) that is important, because the unsystematic (unique) variance can be eliminated by diversification. Therefore, *the relevant risk is the systematic risk that cannot be eliminated.*

As indicated earlier, a number of studies have examined the relationship between the internal risk factors and the systematic risk measures.[23] The typical analysis involves a large cross section of stocks during some specified period. For each company, the authors would compute a beta and a number of internal risk measures, such as variability of operating earnings, variability of return on assets or return on equity, debt-equity ratio, current ratio, interest coverage ratio, degree of operating leverage, and stock trading activity. Given these variables, the intent is to see if these internal risk variables have a significant relationship to the measures of systematic risk. In addition, there have been attempts to see if these internal variables are useful in predicting the systematic risk for securities compared to a naive estimate of no change in beta.

While the specific internal risk variables used in the studies have differed, the great majority of the results have indicated that *there is a significant relationship between the internal risk variables and the systematic market measures.* Therefore, the two approaches for measuring and evaluating risk are *not* competitive but *complementary,* and both should be used as confirmation. Specifically, when examining a firm, we will examine both the internal risk variables *and* compute the systematic risk measure. Based upon these studies, we would expect the risk estimation results to be consistent; i.e., a firm that has above average internal risk characteristics should have above average systematic risk (a beta greater than one). In instances where the risk indicators are not consistent, it will be necessary to try to reconcile the difference.

The other major factor in the valuation of common stocks is the estimation of the growth rate of dividends. The relevant factors are presented in the following section.

Expected Growth Rate of Dividends

The growth rate of dividends is influenced by the basic growth rate of earnings and the proportion of earnings paid out in dividends (i.e., the payout ratio). For

[23] Studies in this area include, William Beaver, Paul Kettler, and Myron Scholes, "The Association Between Market-Determined and Accounting-Determined Risk Measures," *Accounting Review,* 45, no. 2 (October 1970): 654–682 Robert G. Bowman, "The Theoretical Relationship Between Systematic Risk and Financial (Accounting) Variables," *Journal of Finance,* 34 no. 3 (June 1979): 617–630; Donald J. Thompson II, "Sources of Systematic Risk in Common Stock," *Journal of Business,* 49, no. 2 (April 1976): 173–188.

short-run periods, it is possible that dividends can grow faster or slower than earnings do if the economic unit changes its payout ratio. Specifically, if a firm's earnings are growing at 6 percent a year and the firm always pays out exactly 50 percent of earnings in dividends, then the firm's dividends will likewise grow at 6 percent a year. Alternatively, if the firm's earnings are growing at 6 percent a year, and, during a three-year period, the firm *increases* its payout from 50 percent of earnings to 65 percent of earnings, while the payout ratio is increasing, the dividends will increase by more than the earnings; the growth rate of dividends will be above 6 percent (e.g., 8 or 9 percent). In contrast, if the firm reduced its payout ratio, dividends would grow at a lower rate than earnings for a period of time. Clearly, there is a limit to how long this difference can continue, because the payout cannot exceed 100 percent or be less than zero.[24] We will also see that this payout ratio has an inverse relationship to the basic growth rate of earnings. Still, for long-run analysis, the typical assumption is that the dividend payout ratio is relatively stable. Thus, the analysis of what determines the growth rate of dividends is really an analysis of what factors determine the growth rate of equity earnings.

The internal growth rate of an economic unit, whether it is an industry or a company, is basically a function of what resources are retained and reinvested in the unit and of the rate of return derived from these internal investments. Generally, a firm retains some proportion of current earnings and acquires additional assets (e.g., inventory, fixed plant, machinery). Assuming the firm is able to derive some positive rate of return on these additional assets, the total earnings of the firm will increase simply because the firm has a larger asset base. Clearly, how much the earnings will increase depends upon: (1) how much is retained and reinvested in new assets, and (2) the rate of return that is earned on these new assets. More specifically, it can be shown that the growth rate of equity earnings (i.e., earnings per share) without any external financing is equal to the proportion of net earnings retained (1 − payout ratio) times the rate of return on equity capital.

$$g = (\text{Retention Rate}) \times (\text{Return on Equity})$$
$$= RR \times ROE.$$

Therefore, a firm can increase its growth rate by increasing its rate of earnings retention and can continue to invest these added funds at the same rate as before. Alternatively, the firm can maintain the same rate of reinvestment but can increase its rate of return on these investments. As an example, if a firm retains 50 percent of net earnings, reinvests these funds and consistently derives a 10 percent rate of return on these investments, the net earnings for the firm will grow at the rate of 5 percent a year as follows:

$$g = RR \times ROE$$
$$= .50 \times .10$$
$$= .05.$$

---

[24] This is generally true, but public utilities have paid dividends in excess of periodic earnings which is a form of liquidating dividends, and is treated as a return of capital by the IRS.

Alternatively, if the firm increases its retention rate to 75 percent and continues to invest these funds at 10 percent, the firm's growth rate will increase to 7.5 percent as follows:

$$g = .75 \times .10$$
$$= .075.$$

Alternatively, if the firm continues to reinvest 50 percent of its earnings but is able to derive a higher rate of return on these investments (e.g., 15 percent), the firm can likewise increase its growth rate as follows:

$$g = .50 \times .15$$
$$= .075.$$

Breakdown of ROE. While the retention rate is basically a management decision, changes in the return on equity require basic changes in operating performance. As a means of seeing what is required in this respect, it is useful to break the ROE ratio into components. One alternative breakdown is as follows:

$$ROE = \frac{\text{Net Income}}{\text{Equity}}$$
$$= \frac{\text{Net Income}}{\text{Sales}} \times \frac{\text{Sales}}{\text{Equity}}$$
$$= (\text{Profit Margin}) \times (\text{Equity Turnover}).$$

This breakdown (which is really an identity) indicates that the return on equity depends upon how efficiently the firm operates in terms of generating sales from equity capital (equity turnover), but it also depends upon how profitable these sales are, as indicated by the firm's profit margin. The point is, a firm can improve its ROE by increasing either of these components — generating additional sales per dollar of equity at a constant profit margin or increasing the profit margin on the current level of sales.

It is also possible to increase the equity turnover by changing the firm's financial structure. Specifically, if the firm increases its asset base by borrowing (i.e., issuing debt securities), sales will increase because the asset base is larger; but if equity was not used to finance the acquisition of assets, the equity turnover will increase. The effect of this change in financial structure can be examined using the following breakdown of ROE:

$$ROE = \frac{\text{Net Income}}{\text{Equity}}$$
$$= \frac{\text{Net Income}}{\text{Sales}} \times \frac{\text{Sales}}{\text{Equity}}$$
$$= \frac{\text{Net Income}}{\text{Sales}} \times \frac{\text{Sales}}{\text{Total Assets}} \times \frac{\text{Total Assets}}{\text{Equity}}$$
$$= (\text{Profit Margin}) \times (\text{Total Asset Turnover}) \times (\text{Leverage}).$$

The ratio of total assets to equity is a measure of leverage, because it indicates the relationship of total assets to equity. The higher this ratio, the more total assets are financed with nonequity capital (i.e., debt). As an example, if this ratio is two, it means that 50 percent of the firm's assets are financed with equity and 50 percent with debt. Alternatively, a ratio of three means that only 33 percent is financed with equity and two-thirds is debt. Over time, what you would look for is a change in this ratio that would signal a change in the firm's capital structure and, therefore, its financial risk.

By breaking down the equity turnover into total asset turnover and a measure of leverage (total assets/equity) it is possible to determine whether a firm is really operating efficiently (total asset turnover) or whether a change in financial structure (leverage) caused the change in equity turnover. The point is, if total assets increase by a larger proportion than equity, it means that more of these assets are being financed by debt securities. This does not mean that it is wrong to increase ROE by increasing financial leverage. Rather, it is important to recognize that the increase in ROE is not due to an increase in profitability or higher operating efficiency, but it was caused by a change in the firm's capital structure.

SUMMARY

This chapter has three major parts. The first part contained an overview of the valuation process including the overall procedure that should be followed. Specifically, market analysis and industry analysis should be considered prior to company and stock analysis. Besides having intuitive appeal (the economy affects all industries and industry performance influences all firms in the industry), there is substantial empirical support for this three-step process. When markets are efficient, it is not easy to be a superior market analyst, but the potential rewards from correct estimates make the attempt worthwhile.

The second part of the chapter discussed the basic concept of value as the present value of future expected returns and considered the variables that must be estimated in the valuation process. Assuming knowledge of these variables, we discussed the specific valuation of bonds, preferred stock, and common stock under several different holding periods, from one year to perpetuity. It was shown that, with the constant growth model, the crucial factor determining the value of common stock and *changes* in common stock value is the spread between the required rate of return and the expected rate of growth. The infinite growth model cannot be used in the valuation of significant growth companies because these firms do not conform to the basic assumptions of the model.

The final part of the chapter dealt with the specific factors that determine the two major elements of value: the required rate of return and the expected rate of growth. The discussion of the required rate of return was basically a review of the presentation in Chapters 1 and 9. The elements of expected growth can be summarized as follows:

A.	Rate of earnings retention (RR)	Profit margin
B.	Rate of return on equity (ROE)	Equity turnover
		or
		Profit margin
		Total asset turnover
		Leverage

Given this background on the procedure and determinants of value, in the following chapters we will apply these concepts to the valuation of the aggregate stock market, alternative industries, and finally individual firms within industries.

QUESTIONS

1. Discuss why it is contended that market analysis and industry analysis should come before individual security analysis.
2. Discuss briefly the empirical evidence given by King that supports the above contention.
3. Would you expect all industries to have a similar relationship to the economy? Why or why not? Give an example.
4. Would you expect all individual stocks to have a similar relation to the aggregate stock market? What factors would contribute to any differences?
5. What "batting average" is required to be superior in terms of predicting market turns? Does it seem to be worthwhile to spend time attempting to predict aggregate market turns? Why or why not?
6. Given an efficient stock market, what do you believe is necessary to make such predictions? Of what value is past information regarding market performance? Discuss.
7. What is the value to you of a 12 percent coupon bond with a par value of $10,000 that matures in 12 years if you want a 10 percent return on the bond? Use semiannual compounding.
8. What would the value of the bond in Question 7 have to be if you wanted a 14 percent rate of return on this bond?
9. The preferred stock of the Raymond Engineering Company has a par value of $100 and an $11 coupon. You require a 9 percent yield on this stock. What is the maximum price you would pay for it?
10. The Bourke Basketball Company (BBC) earned $5 a share last year and paid a dividend of $3 a share. Next year you expect the company to earn $5.50 and continue their payout ratio. Assuming you expect a 5 percent dividend yield a year from now when you anticipate selling the stock, if you require 12 percent on this stock, how much would you be willing to pay for it?
11. Given the expected earnings and dividend payments in Question 10 if you expected a 4 percent dividend yield, but decided you wanted a 14 percent return on this investment, what would you pay for the BBC stock?
12. Over the very long run you expect dividends for BBC to grow at a 10 percent rate and you require 14 percent on the stock. Using the dividend model that assumes a perpetuity, how much would you pay for this stock?

13. Based upon new information regarding the popularity of basketball, you revise your growth estimate to 9 percent. What is the maximum P/E ratio you will apply to BBC and what is the price you will pay for the stock?

14. The Baron Dogfood Company (BDC) has consistently paid out 30 percent of its earnings in dividends. The company's return on equity is 15 percent. What would you estimate as its growth rate of dividends?

15. Given the low risk in dog food, your required rate of return on BDC is 12 percent. What P/E ratio would you apply to the firm's earnings?

16. What P/E ratio would you apply if you understood that Baron had decided to increase its payout to 40 percent?

17. Discuss three ways a firm can increase its ROE. Make up an example to illustrate your discussion.

18. It is widely known that grocery chains have very low profit margins (e.g., about 1 percent). How would you explain the fact that their ROE is about 12 percent? Does this seem logical?

19. Compute a recent five-year average of the following ratios for three companies of your choice (attempt to select diverse firms):
   a. Retention rate   d. Total asset turnover
   b. Net profit margin e. Total assets/equity.
   c. Equity turnover

   Based upon these ratios, discuss which firm you would expect to have the highest growth rate of earnings and justify your answer.

20. You have been reading about the Pear Computer Co. that is currently retaining 90 percent of its earnings ($3 a share this year) and experiencing an ROE of almost 40 percent. Assuming a market return (Rm) of 12 percent, an RFR of 6 percent, and a beta of 1.60, how much would you pay for Pear on the basis of the pragmatic multiplier approach? Discuss in detail the reason for your answer. What would you pay if the retention rate was 70 percent and the Roe was 20 percent? Show all your work.

REFERENCES

Ahearn, Daniel S. "Investment Management and Economic Research." *Financial Analysts Journal.* 20 no. 1 (January–February 1964).

Arditti, Fred D. "Risk and the Required Return on Equity." *Journal of Finance.* 22 no. 1 (March 1967).

Beaver, William, Paul Kettler, and Myron Scholes. "The Association between Market Determined and Accounting-Determined Risk Measures." *Accounting Review.* 45 no. 4 (October 1970).

Beaver, William, and James Manegold. "The Association between Market-Determined and Accounting-Determined Measures of Systematic Risk: Some Further Evidence." *Journal of Financial and Quantitative Analysis.* 10 no. 2 (June 1975).

Bower, R. S., and D. H. Bower. "Risk and the Valuation of Common Stock." *Journal of Political Economy.* 77 no. 3 (May–June 1969).

Ben-Zion, Uri, and Sol. S. Shalit. "Size, Leverage and Dividend Record as Determinants of Equity Risk." *Journal of Finance.* 20 no. 4 (September 1975).

Blume, Marshall E. "On the Assessment of Risk." *Journal of Finance.* 26 no. 1 (March 1971).

Bowman, Robert G. "The Theoretical Relationship Between Systematic Risk and Financial (Accounting) Variables" *Journal of Finance,* 34, no. 3 (June 1979).

Brown, Philip, and Ray Ball. "Some Preliminary Findings on the Association between the Earnings of a Firm, Its Industry, and the Economy." *Empirical Research in Accounting: Selected Studies 1967,* supplement to vol. 5. *Journal of Accounting Research.*

Emanuel, David. "A Theoretical Model for Valuing Preferred Stock" *Journal of Finance,* 38, no. 4 (September 1983).

Farretti, Andrew P. "The Economist Role in the Stock Market." *Business Economics.* 4 no. 1 (January 1969).

Fisher, Lawrence. "Determinants of Risk Premiums on Corporate Bonds." *Journal of Political Economy.* 67 no. 3 (June 1959).

Fouse, William L. "Risk and Liquidity: The Keys to Stock Price Behavior." *Financial Analysts Journal.* 32 no. 3 (May–June 1976).

Fouse, William L. "Risk and Liquidity Revisited." *Financial Analysts Journal.* 33 no. 1 (January–February 1977).

Hamada, Robert. "The Effect of the Firm's Capital Structure on the Systematic Risk of Common Stocks." *Journal of Finance.* 27 no. 2 (May 1972).

King, Benjamin F. "Market and Industry Factors in Stock Price Behavior." *Journal of Business.* 39 no. 1 part II (January 1966).

Lev, Baruch, "On the Association between Operating Leverage and Risk." *Journal of Financial and Quantitative Analysis.* 9 no. 2 (June 1974).

Mennis, Edmund A. "Economics and Investment Management." *Financial Analysts Journal.* 22 no. 6 (November–December 1966).

Meyers, Stephen L. "A Re-Examination of Market and Industry Factors in Stock Price Behavior." Journal of Finance. 28 no. 3 (June 1973).

Reilly, Frank K. "The Misdirected Emphasis in Security Valuation." *Financial Analysts Journal.* 29 no. 1 (January–February 1973).

Reints, William, and Reteo Vanderberg. "The Impact of Changes in Trading Location on a Security's Systematic Risk." *Journal of Financial and Quantitative Analysis.* 10 no. 5 (December 1975).

Robichek, Alexander, and Richard Cohn. "The Economic Determinants of Systematic Risk. *Journal of Finance.* 29 no. 2 (May 1974).

Robichek, Alexander A. "Risk and the Value of Securities." *Journal of Financial and Quantitative Analysis.* 4 no. 5 (December 1969).

Rosenberg, Barr, and Walt McKibbon. "The Prediction of Systematic and Specific Risk in Common Stocks." *Journal of Financial and Quantitative Analysis.* 8 no. 1 (March 1973).

Rosenberg, Barr, and James Guy. "Prediction of Beta from Investment Fundamentals." *Financial Analysts Journal.* 32 no. 3 (May-June 1976).

Sharpe, William F. "Likely Gains from Market Timing." *Financial Analysts Journal.* 31 no. 2 (March–April 1975).

Shiskin, Julius. "Systematic Aspects of Stock Price Fluctuations." Reprinted in James Lorie and Richard Brealey, *Modern Developments in Investment Management.* 2d ed. Hinsdale, Ill.: The Dryden Press, 1978.

Thompson, Donald J., II. "Sources of Systematic Risk in Common Stocks." *Journal of Business.* 49 no. 2 (April 1976).

Appendix 10A

Derivation of Constant Growth Dividend Model

The basic model is:

$$P_0 = \frac{D_1}{(1 + i_j)^1} + \frac{D_2}{(1 + i_j)^2} + \frac{D_3}{(1 + i_j)^3} + \cdots \frac{D_n}{(1 + i_j)^n}$$

where:

P_0 = Current price

D_i = Expected dividend in period i

i_j = Required rate of return on asset j.

If growth rate (g) is constant:

$$P_0 = \frac{D_0(1 + g)^1}{(1 + i)^1} + \frac{D_0(1 + g)^2}{(1 + i)^2} + \cdots \frac{D_0(1 + g)^n}{(1 + i)^n}.$$

This can be written:

(10A.1)

$$P_0 = D_0 \left[\frac{1 + g}{1 + i} + \frac{(1 + g)^2}{(1 + i)^2} + \frac{(1 + g)^3}{(1 + i)^3} + \cdots \frac{(1 + g)^n}{(1 + i)^n} \right].$$

Multiply both sides of Equation 10A.1 by $\dfrac{1 + i}{1 + g}$:

(10A.2)

$$\left[\frac{(1 + i)}{(1 + g)} \right] P_0 = D_0 \left[1 + \frac{(1 + g)}{(1 + i)} + \frac{(1 + g)^2}{(1 + i)^2} + \cdots \frac{(1 + g)^{n-1}}{(1 + i)^{n-1}} \right]$$

Subtract Equation 10A.1 from Equation 10A.2:

$$\left[\frac{(1+i)}{(1+g)} - 1\right]P_0 = D_0\left[1 - \frac{(1+g)^n}{(1+i)^n}\right]$$

$$\left[\frac{(1+i) - (1+g)}{(1+g)}\right]P_0 = D_0\left[1 - \frac{(1+g)^n}{(1+i)^n}\right]$$

Assuming $i > g$, as $N \rightarrow \infty$ the term in brackets on the right side of the equation goes to 1 leaving:

$$\left[\frac{(1+i) - (1+g)}{(1+g)}\right]P_0 = D_0.$$

This simplies to:

$$\left[\frac{1+i-1-g}{(1+g)}\right]P_0 = D_0$$

which equals:

$$\left[\frac{i-g}{(1+g)}\right]P_0 = D_0.$$

This equals:

$$(i-g)P_0 = D_0(1+g) \text{ but } D_0(1+g) = D_1$$

so:

$$(i-g)P_0 = D_1$$

$$P_0 = \frac{D_1}{i-g}.$$

Remember this model assumes:
— A constant growth rate
— An infinite time period
— The required return on the investment (i) is greater than the expected growth rate (g).

Chapter 11

Analysis of Financial Statements

INTRODUCTION

The main source of information for major business decisions is the financial statements of individual firms. The potential decisions include whether to lend money to a firm, whether to invest in the preferred or common stock of a firm, or whether to acquire a firm. To properly make such decisions it is necessary to understand what financial statements are available and what information is included in each of the alternative financial statements. More importantly, you must know how to analyze this financial information to arrive at a rational decision. To help you derive this understanding and knowledge, this chapter has four parts. The first part briefly presents the major financial statements for an example corporation that we will use throughout this chapter. The second part contains a discussion of why financial ratios are useful and in what context they should be analyzed. The third section involves a detailed discussion of the major financial ratios used to analyze various characteristics of firms and the computation of these ratios for our example firm. The final section discusses four major areas in investments where financial ratios have been employed extensively and have been found very useful.

The example company that will be used is Deere & Co., a leading manufacturer and distributor of farm equipment, industrial equipment, and consumer outdoor work and leisure power equipment.

MAJOR FINANCIAL STATEMENTS

The underlying purpose of financial statements is to provide information to interested parties regarding the resources available to management, how these resources were financed, and what was accomplished with these resources. This information is contained in three financial statements—the balance sheet, the income statement, and the sources and uses statement, which reconciles changes in the other two financial reports.

The Balance Sheet

This financial report indicates what are the resources (assets) controlled by the firm and how these assets have been financed. Specifically, it indicates *at a point in time* (usually the end of the fiscal year or the end of a quarter) the current and fixed assets available to the firm. Typically, these assets are owned by the firm,

EXHIBIT 11.1

Deere & Co. Consolidated Balance Sheet Year Ended October 31 ($000 omitted)

Assets	1982	1981	1980
Current Assets			
Cash	48,101	57,213	69,089
Due from J.D. Credit Co.	215,934	236,428	292,904
Short-Term Investments	4,268	10,998	512
Tax Claim	75,204	13,437	—
Net Receivables	2,660,897	2,374,393	2,093,272
Inventory	760,945	872,045	877,465
Total Current Assets	3,765,349	3,564,514	3,404,291
Fixed Assets			
Gross Property, etc.	2,525,951	2,446,359	2,093,671
Accumulated Depreciation	1,197,891	1,038,021	844,835
Net Property, etc.	1,328,060	1,408,338	1,248,836
Investment in J.D. Credit Co.	781,233	657,884	497,664
Other Assets	16,812	18,323	14,196
Deferred Charges	44,225	34,818	37,437
Total Fixed Assets	2,170,330	2,119,363	1,798,133
Total Assets	5,935,679	5,683,877	5,202,424
Liabilities and Equity			
Current Liabilities			
Notes Payable	969,754	693,344	741,684
Accounts Payable	1,104,011	1,286,409	1,143,944
Dividends Payable	16,919	33,754	29,693
Accrued Taxes	304,886	291,001	232,005
Total Current Liabilities	2,395,570	2,304,508	2,147,326
Long-Term Liabilities			
Long-Term Debt	897,682	676,147	702,335
Capital Lease Obligations	16,296	20,409	22,074
Pension, etc. Reserves	52,950	63,359	55,987
Deferred Income Taxes	184,985	169,868	127,397
Minority Interest	—	—	6,239
Total Long-Term Liabilities	1,151,913	929,783	914,032
Stockholders' Equity			
Common Stock, $1 par	67,852	67,724	62,727
Capital Surplus	418,101	414,709	221,064
Earned Surplus	1,904,968	1,970,508	1,860,630
Reacquired Stock	(2,725)	(3,355)	(3,355)
Net Stockholders' Equity	2,388,196	2,449,586	2,141,066
Total Liabilities and Equity	5,935,679	5,683,877	5,202,424

but with recent changes in accounting procedures, some of these assets may be leased to the firm on a long-term basis.

Beyond knowing what resources are available, it is important to know how these assets were acquired—i.e., how they were financed. This information is likewise indicated in the balance sheet in terms of current liabilities (typically used to finance current assets, such as inventory), long-term liabilities (fixed debt), and owner's equity, which includes preferred stock, common stock, and retained earnings.

The balance sheet for Deere & Co. is contained in Exhibit 11.1. Note that the information on the balance sheet represents the *stock* of assets and financing alternatives for the firm *at a point in time.* Because Deere & Co's year end is October 31, it is as of October 31, 1980, 1981, and 1982.

The Income Statement

This statement contains information on the efficiency, control, and profitability of management during some specified period of time (a quarter or a year). Specifically, efficiency is indicated by the sales generated during the period, while expenses indicate control, and the earnings derived from these sales indicates the profitability. In contrast to the stock concept in the balance sheet, the income statement indicates the *flow* of sales, expenses, and earnings during a period of time. The income statement for Deere & Co. for the years 1980, 1981, and 1982 is contained in Exhibit 11.2.

The Sources and Uses Statement

This financial statement is especially useful since it integrates the two prior statements. Specifically, for a given period the sources and uses statement indi-

EXHIBIT 11.2
Deere & Co. Consolidated Income Statement Year Ended October 31 ($000 omitted)

	1982	1981	1980
Net Sales	4,608,226	5,446,720	5,469,825
Cost of Sales	3,821,761	4,274,040	4,342,402
Gross Profit	786,465	1,172,680	1,127,423
Selling & General Expense	511,512	515,184	495,428
Research & Development	242,459	239,960	231,195
Operating Profit	32,494	417,536	400,800
Financial, Interest & Miscellaneous Income	115,446	112,321	82,202
Foreign Exchange Gain (Loss)	46,870	61,789	10,717
Other Deductions	8,501	79,241[a]	4,286
Earnings before Interest & Taxes	186,309	512,405	489,433
Interest Expense	266,581	232,042	189,696
Net before Taxes	(80,272)	280,363	299,737
Income Taxes	(40,821)	119,909	115,658
Equity Income	92,349	90,540	44,192
Net Income	52,898	250,994	228,271

[a] Includes $74,000,000 in financial support to Deere Credit Co.

EXHIBIT 11.3
Deere & Co. Sources and Uses Statement Year Ended October 31 ($000 omitted)

Sources of Funds	1982	1981	1980
From Operations:			
Net Income	52,898	250,994	228,271
Nonfund Transactions:			
Depreciation expense	208,808	185,425	147,735
Increase in Deferred Income Taxes	15,117	42,471	53,372
Undistributed Earnings of Unconsolidated Subsidiary	(83,202)	(89,374)	(140,785)
Other—Net	(12,908)	975	890
Additions to Long-Term Debt	65,000	15,935	149,625
Deferred Income Taxes, Reclassified & Related to losses	830	—	60,802
Proceeds from Stock Options (incl. tax benefit)	—	2,919	3,880
Conversion of Converted Debentures: New Shares,			—
Treasury Shares	3,300	29,577	50,829
Sale of New Stock	—	165,791	—
Total Sources	249,843	588,780	654,619
Use of Funds			
Net Additions to Property & Equipment	149,454	344,929	407,730
Cash Dividends Declared	135,236	133,055	116,004
Decrease in Long-Term Debt and Capital Lease Obligation	36,686	28,030	65,565
Increase in Investment in Unconsolidated Retail Finance Subsidiary	⎰ 8,720	(17,045)	40,494
Increase in Investment in Other Unconsolidated Subsidiaries	⎱	21,958	44,851
Other	(20,363)	1,231	4,546
Total Uses	309,733	512,158	679,190
Increase (Decrease) in Working Capital			
Cash and Short-Term Investments	(15,842)	(1,390)	11,242
Refundable Income Taxes	61,767	(57,612)	71,049
Receivables from Unconsolidated Subsidiaries	—	9,457	(105,471)
Trade Receivables—Net	303,199	281,121	691,657
Inventories	(92,251)	(5,420)	(8,138)
Notes Payable	(474,025)	45,413	(543,968)
Accounts Payable	171,445	(127,757)	(115,279)
Accrued Taxes	—	(66,056)	(32,505)
Other Changes—Net	(43,483)	(1,134)	1,842
Net Decrease in Working Capital	(59,890)	76,622	(24,571)

cates how alternative items on the balance sheet changed by examining the beginning and ending balance sheet and likewise shows the impact of relevant items from the income statement. It is extremely helpful in determining where funds are coming from for expansion and other requirements, such as stock acquisition or debt retirement.[1] The sources and uses statement for Deere & Co. for 1980, 1981, and 1982 is contained in Exhibit 11.3.

---

[1] A complete discussion of this statement and its preparation is contained in Erich Helfert, *Techniques of Financial Analysis,* 5th ed., (Homewood, Ill.: Richard D. Irwin, 1982).

Purpose of Financial Statement Analysis. *The underlying purpose of finan-*
cial statement analysis is to aid in the evaluation of management performance
in a number of areas. Specifically, the analysis is intended to help evaluate past
management performance regarding *profitability, efficiency,* and *risk.* More important than the historical analysis is *the projection of future management performance* based upon the analysis of the historical results. The expected future
performance will influence the decision whether to lend money to or invest in
the firm.

ANALYSIS OF FINANCIAL RATIOS

Why Ratios?

Analysts employ financial ratios because *numbers in isolation are typically of
little value;* e.g., what information is there in knowing that the net income for a
firm was $100,000? Given an income number, an analyst would want to know the
sales figure that generated this income ($1 million or $10 million) and the assets
or capital employed in generating these sales or this income. Therefore, *ratios
are used to provide meaningful relationships between individual values in the
financial statements.*[2] Because there are numerous individual items in the major
financial statements, there is a substantial number of potential combinations.
Therefore, the analyst must limit the examination to the *relevant* ratios and
categorize the ratios into groups that provide information on alternative economic aspects of the firm's operation. Prior to discussing specific areas of analysis and the relevant ratios, we should consider the importance of *relative* analysis.

All Ratios Should Be Relative

More to the point, *only relative financial ratios are relevant!* Just as a single
number from a financial statement is not of value, an individual financial ratio is
of little value until it is placed in perspective relative to other ratios. The impor-
tant comparisons are *relative* to:
— The aggregate economy
— The company's industry or industries
— The firm's major competitor within the industry
— The firm's own past performances.
 The comparison to the aggregate economy is important because the economy has consistently experienced business cycles and almost all firms are influenced by the business cycle — i.e., an expansion or a contraction (recession).
As an example, it is not reasonable to expect an increase in the profit margin for a
firm during a recession. Alternatively, a small increase in a firm's margin during a
major business expansion may be considered a sign of weakness. An analysis
relative to the economy will help you to understand how a firm reacts to the
business cycle. In turn, this analysis will indicate the firm's relative business risk

---

[2] For a discussion of the history of ratio analysis, see James O. Horrigan, "A Short History of Financial Ratio
Analysis," *Accounting Review* 43 no. 2 (April 1968): 284–294.

and will help in projecting the firm's future performance during subsequent business cycles.

Probably the most popular comparison is a firm's performance relative to its industry.[3] This comparison is essential because of the strong impact an industry has on the firms within the industry. This influence will vary by industry and is strongest within industries with a homogenous product—e.g., steel, rubber, glass, wood products. In these instances, there is typically a common demand for the homogenous product and all firms within the industry experience relatively common shifts in demand. In addition, the technology and production process for companies within these industries are fairly similar. Under such conditions, analyzing an individual firm within the industry without considering the overall industry trend or cycle is meaningless because of the strong industry impact; e.g., even the best managed steel firm is going to experience a decline in profit margins during a recession. In line with the prior discussion, it is generally useful to examine an industry's performance relative to aggregate economic activity to understanding the relative cyclicality of the industry; e.g., how does this industry respond to the business cycle?

A major problem when comparing a firm to its industry is that the analyst may not feel comfortable with the measure of central tendency used for the industry. Specifically, the average (mean) value may not be a very useful measure because of the wide dispersion of values for the individual firms within the industry. Alternatively, the analyst might believe that the firm being analyzed is not typical; i.e., it has a strong unique component. If either of these conditions are present, it might be preferable to compare the firm to one or several individual firms within the industry that are comparable in size or clientele to the firm being analyzed. As an example, within the computer industry it might be preferable to compare IBM to certain individual firms within the industry (e.g., Burroughs; Control Data) rather than some total industry data which includes numerous small firms that serve unique components of the industry. Another example might be found in the utility industry where an analyst would probably want to limit the industry comparison to a comparable utility; e.g., compare an electric utility to other electric utilities versus gas and water utilities. Even within the electric utility segment you would probably consider electric utility firms from the same geographical area (e.g., south, midwest) and those with a comparable mix of residential, commercial, and industrial customers.

Finally, it is important to *examine a firm's performance over time* to determine if the firm is progressing or regressing over time by comparing its profit margins or return on equity to past periods. This time series analysis is crucial when attempting to estimate *future* performance. Too often we consider the average for a five- or ten-year period without considering the trend. For example, it is possible to have an average rate of return of 10 percent based upon rates of return going from 5 percent to 15 percent over time or based upon a series that begins at 15 percent and declines to 5 percent. Obviously, the difference in the time series trend would have a major impact on what you would estimate for the future.

---

[3] An excellent source of comparative ratios for alternative lines of business is, *Industry Norms and Key Business Ratios,* Dun and Bradstreet, Inc., 99 Church Street, New York, New York 10007. Robert Morris Associates also provides comparative ratios by industry.

In summary, financial ratios can be a very valuable tool in the analysis of financial statements. However, in order to derive maximum benefit it is important to remember *only relative financial ratios are relevant.*

COMPUTATION OF FINANCIAL RATIOS

Ratio Categories

The ratios discussed are divided into five major categories based upon alternative economic aspects of a firm:
1. Internal liquidity (solvency)
2. Operating performance
3. Risk analysis
4. Growth analysis
5. External liquidity (marketability).

Internal Liquidity Ratios

These solvency ratios are intended to indicate the ability of the firm to meet future short-term financial obligations. As such, the idea is to match the potential near-term obligations, such as accounts payable, with current assets that will be available on a short notice to meet these obligations.

Current ratio. Clearly the most-well known liquidity measure is the current ratio which examines the relationship between current assets and current liabilities as follows:

$$\text{Current Ratio} = \frac{\text{Current Assets}}{\text{Current Liabilities}}.$$

For Deere & Co. the current ratios were:

— 1982: $\dfrac{3,765,349}{2,395,570} = 1.57$

— 1981: $\dfrac{3,564,514}{2,304,508} = 1.55$

— 1980: $\dfrac{3,404,291}{2,147,326} = 1.59.$

While the ratios appear adequate, it would be necessary to compare these values to comparable figures for the firm's total industry and its major competitors. The major concern is the substantial decline in the ratio relative to the period prior to 1980 when it exceeded 2.0. Also, it is recognized that the ratio can be manipulated.[4]

Quick ratio. Some observers believe that *total* current assets are not a very conservative estimate of assets available to meet current obligations since inventories are generally not a very liquid asset. Because of this, they prefer to use the quick ratio which relates current liabilities to the most liquid current assets as

---

[4] In this regard, see Kenneth W. Lemke, "The Evaluation of Liquidity: An Analytical Study," *Journal of Accounting Research* 8 no. 1 (Spring 1970): 47–77.

follows:

$$\text{Quick Ratio} = \frac{\text{Cash} + \text{Receivables}}{\text{Current Liabilities}}.$$

This ratio is intended to indicate the amount of very liquid assets available to pay near-term liabilities. For Deere & Co. the quick ratios were:

— 1982:

$$\frac{3,004,404}{2,395,570} = 1.25$$

— 1981:

$$\frac{2,692,469}{2,304,508} = 1.17$$

— 1980:

$$\frac{2,526,826}{2,147,326} = 1.18.$$

In this case, we used all current assets (including tax claims) except inventories as quick assets. One might envision cases where some of these assets might not be included because further analysis would indicate the assets were not as liquid as desired. Again, all the ratios are adequate, but one would naturally be concerned about the decline relative to before 1980 and would want to know whether this is related to the economy or to industry trends.

Receivables turnover.   In addition to looking at supposedly liquid assets relative to near-term liabilities, some analysts attempt to analyze the quality of the receivables by examining how often they turn over, which can be used to determine the average collection period. Put another way, the intent is to determine the liquidity of these current assets. The receivables turnover is computed as follows:

$$\text{Receivables Turnover} = \frac{\text{Net Annual Sales}}{\text{Average Receivables}}.$$

The average receivables is typically the beginning figure plus the ending value divided by two. Deere & Co.'s receivable turnover figures were:

— 1982:

$$\frac{4,608,226}{(2,660,897 + 2,374,393)/2} = 1.83$$

— 1981:

$$\frac{5,446,720}{(2,374,393 + 2,093,272)/2} = 2.44.$$

It is not possible to compute a turnover value for 1980, because there is no beginning receivables figure for 1980 (i.e., the ending figure for 1979).

Given this annual turnover figure, one can compute an average collection period as follows:

$$\text{Average Collection Period} = \frac{365}{\text{Annual Turnover}}.$$

— 1982:

$$\frac{365}{1.83} = 199.5 \text{ days}$$

— 1981: $$\frac{365}{2.44} = 149.6 \text{ days.}$$

This indicates that receivables are generally collected in almost 200 days which is double what it was in 1980. To determine whether this is good or bad it should be related to the firm's credit policy and to a comparable number for other firms in the industry. Obviously, relative to the firm's prior performance, this low turnover and long collection period is quite poor.

Some analysts also compute an inventory turnover figure to determine the liquidity of the firm's inventory. For our purposes, this inventory ratio is considered in the operating performance category.

OPERATING PERFORMANCE

The ratios that indicate how well the management is operating the business are typically divided into two subcategories: (1) efficiency ratios, and (2) profitability ratios. The efficiency ratios examine how the management uses the assets and capital at its disposal. The use of assets and capital is mainly measured in terms of the dollar of sales generated by various asset categories or capital categories. In turn, the profitability ratios analyze the profits earned on these sales and also on the assets and capital employed.

Analysis of Efficiency

Total asset turnover.   This ratio is intended to indicate the use of the firm's total asset base (net assets equal gross assets minus depreciation on fixed assets). It is computed as follows:

$$\text{Total Asset Turnover} = \frac{\text{Net Sales}}{\text{Average Total Net Assets}}.$$

Deere & Co.'s asset turnover values were:

— 1982: $$\frac{4,608,226}{(5,935,679 + 5,683,877)/2} = 0.79$$

— 1981: $$\frac{5,446,720}{(5,683,877 + 5,202,424)/2} = 1.00.$$

This ratio should be compared to other firms in an industry since it varies substantially between industries. As an example, it will range from about one for large capital firms (e.g., steel companies) to over ten for many retailing operations. It is also affected by the use of leased facilities. One should consider a *range* of turnover values, since in many instances it is poor management to have too few assets for the potential business (sales), just as it is poor judgment to have an excess.

Beyond the analysis of the total asset base, it is insightful to examine the utilization of some specific assets, such as inventories and fixed assets.

Inventory turnover. This ratio should indicate the utilization of inventory by the management. It is computed as follows:

$$\text{Inventory Turnover} = \frac{\text{Net Sales}}{\text{Average Inventory}}$$

or

$$= \frac{\text{Cost of Sales}}{\text{Average Inventory}}.$$

It is preferable to compute the turnover using the cost of sales figure because inventory is at cost. Historically, the net sales figure was used because firms often did not report cost of sales. Currently, firms are *required* to report the cost of sales, so it is possible to compute the turnover using this value. The inventory turnover ratios for Deere & Co. were:

— 1982: $\dfrac{3,821,761}{(760,945 + 872,045)/2} = 4.68$

— 1981: $\dfrac{4,274,040}{(872,045 + 877,465)/2} = 4.89$

Again, it is crucial that the emphasis be on the firm's performance *relative* to the industry since the appropriate values vary widely. Also, it is important to consider the range, because a value that is too low *or* too high is not good. Too low an inventory turnover ratio means excess inventory and possibly some obsolete inventory. In contrast, while a high inventory turnover ratio may indicate efficiency, if it gets *too* high, it can indicate inadequate inventory that can lead to shortages and eventually a loss of sales.

Net fixed asset turnover. This ratio provides information on the firm's utilization of fixed assets. It is computed as follows:

$$\text{Fixed Asset Turnover} = \frac{\text{Net Sales}}{\text{Average Net Fixed Assets}}.$$

Deere & Co.'s fixed asset turnover ratios were:

— 1982: $\dfrac{4,608,226}{(2,170,330 + 2,119,363)/2} = 2.15$

— 1981: $\dfrac{5,446,720}{(2,119,363 + 1,798,133)/2} = 2.78.$

It is important to examine this turnover relative to comparable firms in the same industry and to take into account the impact of leased assets. Also remember that a very high asset turnover ratio can be due to the use of old, fully depreciated equipment that may be obsolete.

Equity turnover.   In addition to specific asset turnover ratios, it is useful to examine the turnover for alternative capital components. One of the most important in this regard is the equity turnover, which is computed as follows:

$$\text{Equity Turnover} = \frac{\text{Net Sales}}{\text{Average Equity}}.$$

Equity includes common stock, paid-in capital and total retained earnings.[5] The purpose of this ratio is to determine the dollar of sales generated per dollar of equity capital. The difference between this ratio and the total asset turnover is that the capital provided from current liabilities, long-term debt, and preferred stock is not considered. Therefore, when examining the trend for this series, it is important to be aware of the capital ratios for the firm, because it is possible to show improvements in the equity turnover ratio by increasing the firm's proportion of debt capital (i.e., its debt/equity ratio). Deere & Co.'s equity turnover ratios were:

— 1982:
$$\frac{4,608,226}{(2,388,196 + 2,449,586)/2} = 1.91$$

— 1981:
$$\frac{5,446,720}{(2,449,586 + 2,141,066)/2} = 2.37.$$

Now that we have some idea of the firm's relative ability to generate sales from the assets and capital at their disposal, the next step is to determine the profitability of the sales.

Analysis of Profitability.   The ratios in this category indicate the rate of profit on sales and ultimately the percent return on the capital employed.

Gross profit margin.   Gross profit is equal to net sales minus the cost of goods sold. The gross profit margin is computed as:

$$\text{Gross Profit Margin} = \frac{\text{Gross Profit}}{\text{Net Sales}}.$$

The gross profit margins for Deere & Co. were:

— 1982:
$$\frac{786,465}{4,608,226} = 17.06\%$$

— 1981:
$$\frac{1,172,680}{5,446,720} = 21.53\%$$

— 1980:
$$\frac{1,127,423}{5,469,825} = 20.61\%.$$

[5] The reader will note that the equity figure used does *not* include the preferred stock, which is considered equity by accountants. This author's preference is to only consider *owner's* equity, which would not include preferred stock.

This ratio should indicate the basic cost structure of the firm. An analysis of this margin over time relative to the industry figure is a prime indicator of the cost-price position of the firm. Given the substantial decline in 1982 and the overall decline relative to pre-1980 ratios for Deere and Co., such a comparison would be very important.

Operating profit margin.   Operating profit is gross profit minus sales, general, and administrative expenses (S.G. + A.). The operating profit margin is equal to:

$$\text{Operating Profit Margin} = \frac{\text{Operating Profit}}{\text{Net Sales}}.$$

For Deere & Co. the operating profit margins were:

— 1982: $\dfrac{32{,}494}{4{,}608{,}226} = .71\%$

— 1981: $\dfrac{417{,}536}{5{,}446{,}720} = 7.67\%$

— 1980: $\dfrac{400{,}800}{5{,}469{,}825} = 7.32\%.$

The variability of this profit margin over time is a prime indicator of the business risk for a firm. If the firm has other income or expenses like Deere & Co., these are considered before arriving at the earnings before interest and taxes. In the case of Deere & Co., the other income is fairly substantial while the other costs are small. The major concern is the sharp decline in the operating profit margin during 1982. Prior to 1980 this margin exceeded 10 percent. Much of this decline in the operating profit margin is a result of the decline in the gross profit margin.

In some instances you might want to add back depreciation and compute a profit margin that is earnings before depreciation, interest, and taxes as a percentage of sales. This is considered an alternative operating profit margin that reflects all controllable expenses.

Net profit margin.   Net income is earnings after taxes but before dividends on preferred and common stock. This margin is equal to:

$$\text{Net Profit Margin} = \frac{\text{Net Income}}{\text{Net Sales}}.$$

For Deere & Co. the net profit margins were:

— 1982: $\dfrac{52{,}898}{4{,}608{,}226} = 1.15\%$

— 1981: $\dfrac{250{,}994}{5{,}446{,}720} = 4.61\%$

— 1980: $\dfrac{228{,}271}{5{,}469{,}825} = 4.17\%.$

Common size income statement.   Beyond the analysis of these ratios that
examine various income figures, an additional technique is to prepare a common
size income statement, which examines all expense and income items as a
percentage of sales. The analysis of such a statement for several years (five at
least) indicates the trend in cost figures and profit margins. A common size
statement for Deere & Co. for three years is shown in Exhibit 11.4. As noted, the
greatest value comes from a detailed analysis of various cost and margin figures
over time relative to other firms in the industry.

For Deere & Co. this statement indicates the steady increase in cost of goods
and the resultant decline in the gross profit margin. Likewise, selling and general
expense increased as a percentage of sales. Other negative factors are the increase in research and development (which may be good for the long run) and
the substantial rise in interest expense in absolute dollars and as a percentage of
sales.

Beyond the analysis of earnings on sales, the ultimate determination of the
success of management is the rate of return earned on the assets of the firm or the
capital committed to the enterprise.

Return on total capital.   This ratio indicates the earnings available for all the
capital involved in the enterprise (debt, preferred stock, and common stock).
Therefore, the earnings figure used is the net income (before any dividends)
plus the interest paid on debt.

$$\text{Return on Total Capital} = \frac{\text{Net Income} + \text{Interest}}{\text{Average Total Capital}}.$$

For Deere & Co., the only interest is for long-term debt. Thus the rate of return on
total capital was:

— 1982: $\dfrac{52,898 + 266,581}{(5,935,679 + 5,683,877)/2} = 5.50\%$

— 1981: $\dfrac{250,994 + 232,042}{(5,683,877 + 5,202,424)/2} = 8.87\%.$

Again, it is not possible to compute a comparable rate of return for 1980 since we
cannot derive an average total capital figure from the statements included. This
ratio indicates the overall return earned on all the capital employed by the firm,
and it should be compared to other firms in the industry and to the general
economy. Obviously, if this rate of return is not commensurate with the perceived risk of the firm, one should question if the entity should continue to exist,
since the capital could be used more productively elsewhere in the economy.

Return on owner's equity.   Again, this rate of return ratio is extremely important to the owner of the enterprise (the common stockholder), since it indicates what rate of return the manager earns on the capital provided by the owner

Exhibit 11.4
Deere & Co. Common Size Income Statement

	1982		1981		1980	
	$000	Percent	$000	Percent	$000	Percent
Net Sales	4,608,226	100.00	5,446,720	100.00	5,469,825	100.00
Cost of Goods	3,821,761	82.93	4,274,040	78.47	4,342,402	79.39
Gross Profit	786,465	17.07	1,172,680	21.53	1,127,423	20.61
Selling & General Expense	511,512	11.10	515,184	9.46	495,428	9.06
Research & Development	242,459	5.26	239,960	4.41	231,195	4.23
Operating Profit	32,494	0.71	417,536	7.67	400,800	7.33
Finance, Interest and Miscellaneous Income	115,446	2.51	112,321	2.06	82,202	1.50
Foreign Exchange Gain (Loss)	46,870	1.02	61,789	1.13	10,717	.20
Other Deductions	8,501	.18	79,241	1.45	4,286	.08
Earnings before Interest & Taxes	186,309	4.04	512,405	9.41	489,433	8.95
Interest Expense	266,581	5.78	232,042	4.26	189,696	3.47
Net before Taxes	(80,272)	(1.74)	280,363	5.15	299,737	5.48
Income Taxes	(40,821)	(.89)	119,909	2.20	115,658	2.11
Equity Income	92,349	2.00	90,540	1.67	44,192	.81
Net Income	52,898	1.15	250,994	4.61	228,271	4.17

after accounting for payments to all other capital suppliers. If one were to consider *all* equity (including preferred stock), this would equal:

$$\text{Return on Total Equity} = \frac{\text{Net Income}}{\text{Average Total Equity}}.$$

If one is only concerned with owner's equity (i.e., common equity), the ratio would be:

$$\text{Return on Common Equity} = \frac{\text{Net Income} - \text{Preferred Dividend}}{\text{Average Common Equity}}.$$

In the case of Deere & Co., it is not necessary to make the distinction because the firm does not have any preferred stock outstanding. Therefore, the Deere & Co. return on equity figures are:

— 1982: $\dfrac{52,898}{(2,388,196 + 2,449,584)/2} = 2.19\%$

— 1981: $\dfrac{250,994}{(2,449,586 + 2,141,066)/2} = 10.94\%.$

This ratio reflects the rate of return on the equity capital provided by the owners. As such, it should reflect not only the overall business risk involved, but also the additional *financial* risk assumed by the common stockholder because of the prior claim of the firm's debt. Notably, this return on equity ratio can be broken down into two of the prior ratios discussed.

$$\frac{\text{Sales}}{\text{Equity}} \times \frac{\text{Net Income}}{\text{Sales}} = \frac{\text{Net Income}}{\text{Equity}}$$

Equity Turnover × Net Profit Margin = Return on Equity.

Therefore, a firm's return on equity can be improved by either using the equity more efficiently (i.e., increasing the firm's equity turnover) *or* by increasing the firm's net profit margin. As will be discussed later, it is possible to increase the firm's equity turnover by employing more debt capital. While such a change in capital structure (i.e., an increase in the proportion of debt capital) will increase the equity turnover, it will also increase the financial risk of the firm, which in turn should increase the required rate of return on equity.

RISK ANALYSIS

The purpose of risk analysis is to determine the uncertainty of income flows for the total firm and for individual capital sources (i.e., debt, preferred stock, and common stock). Specifically, one can derive an estimate of the uncertainty of flows to the various sources of capital by examining the uncertainty of flows to the firm. In turn, the typical approach is to consider the major factors that cause uncertain flows to the firm where uncertainty is measured in terms of the variability of returns over time; i.e., the more variable the income flows, the greater the uncertainty or risk facing the investor. In this regard, the total risk of the firm is generally divided into: (1) business risk, and (2) financial risk.

Business Risk[6]

Business risk is the uncertainty of income that is due to the firm's industry (i.e., variability of sales due to its products and customers) and the way it produces its products (i.e., its production function). Specifically a firm's earnings vary over time because its sales and production costs vary. As an example, one would expect the earnings for a steel firm to vary more than for a grocery chain, because steel sales are more volatile than grocery sales over a business cycle. Also, because the steel firm has more fixed production costs, its earnings vary more than its sales.

Business risk is generally measured by *the variability of the firm's operating income over time.* A more volatile earnings series means that an investor/lender will be more uncertain regarding future earnings; i.e., a more volatile earnings series indicates greater business risk. The earnings volatility is generally computed in terms of the standard deviation of the historical earnings series. Because the standard deviation of a series is influenced by the size of the numbers, analysts have attempted to normalize this measure by dividing the standard deviation by the mean value for the series. The resulting ratio of the standard deviation of operating earnings divided by the average operating earnings is the coefficient of variation (CV). Thus:

$$\text{Business Risk} = f(\text{Coefficient of Variation of Operating Earnings})$$

$$= \frac{\text{Standard Deviation of Operating Earnings } (OE)}{\text{Mean Operating Earnings}}$$

$$= \frac{\sqrt{\sum_{i=1}^{n}(OE_t - \overline{OE})^2/N}}{\sum_{i=1}^{n} OE_t/N}.$$

The coefficient of variation of operating earnings has a great advantage: you can compare these normalized measures of variability for firms of different size — e.g., duPont compared to a smaller chemical firm. The computation of the CV of operating earnings generally covers a minimum of five years up to about ten years. Less than five years is not very meaningful, while much more than ten years can involve data that could be out of date. It is not possible to compute the CV of operating earnings for Deere & Co. since we only have provided data for three years.

In addition to an overall measure of business risk, one should attempt to determine the components that contribute to this variability — i.e., what causes the variability of operating earnings. In general, there are two components: (1) sales variability, and (2) operating leverage.

[6] For a further discussion on this general topic, see Stephen H. Archer, G. Marc Choate, and George Racette, *Financial Management: An Introduction* (New York: John Wiley and Sons, 1979), 46–56; Eugene Brigham, *Financial Management Theory and Practice* 3d ed.(Hinsdale, Ill.: The Dryden Press), 1982, 596–602.

Sales volatility.   This is the prime determinant of earnings volatility, since operating earnings volatility cannot be lower than sales volatility; i.e., operating leverage can only increase earnings volatility from the level derived from sales volatility. To understand this, conceive of a case where all costs for the firm were variable costs. In this instance, the relative sales volatility and the earnings volatility for the firm would be equal. When we introduce fixed production costs, we know that earnings will be *more* volatile than sales on a relative basis. Also, sales volatility is *basically outside of the control of management.* The sales volatility for a firm is a function of the aggregate economic environment and the particular industry involved. As an example, a firm in a cyclical industry (e.g., automobiles or steel) will have a very volatile sales pattern over the business cycle compared to a firm in a noncyclical industry, such as hospital supplies. The sales volatility for a firm is typically measured by the coefficient of variation of sales during some specified time period (e.g., most recent five to ten years). The coefficient of variation (CV) is equal to the standard deviation of sales divided by the mean sales for the period.

$$\text{Sales Volatility} = f(\text{Coefficient of Variation of Sales})$$

$$= \frac{\text{Standard Deviation of Sales } (S)}{\text{Mean Sales}}$$

$$= \frac{\sqrt{\sum_{i=1}^{n}(S_i - \bar{S})^2/N}}{\sum_{i=1}^{n} S_i/N} \ .$$

Operating leverage.   In addition to sales volatility, the variability of a firm's operating earnings is also affected by the production function of the firm; i.e., what mixture of costs are involved in producing the goods and services sold? As mentioned, if a firm does not have any fixed production costs, then total production costs would vary directly with sales and operating profits would be a constant proportion of sales; i.e., the operating profit margin would be constant. Under these conditions, the operating profit series would have the same relative volatility as sales. Realistically, firms almost always have some fixed production costs (e.g., buildings, machinery), or they employ some relatively permanent personnel (supervisors, foremen, etc.). The existence of fixed production costs means that *operating profits will vary more than sales vary over the business cycle.* During slow periods, profits will decline by a larger percentage than the percentage sales decline. In contrast, during periods of economic expansion, profits will increase by a larger percentage than the percentage that sales increase. The employment of fixed production costs is referred to as *operating leverage.* Clearly, *the greater the firm's operating leverage, the more volatile the operating earnings series will be relative to the sales series.*[7] Given this basic relationship between operating profit and sales, operating leverage is measured as the percentage change in operating earnings relative to a percentage change

---

[7] For a further treatment of this area, see James C. Van Horne, *Financial Management and Policy,* 6th ed. (Englewood Cliffs, N.J.: Prentice-Hall, 1983), Chapter 27; O. Maurice Joy, *Introduction to Financial Management,* 3rd ed. (Homewood, Ill.: Richard D. Irwin, 1983), Chapter 20.

in sales during several recent years as follows:

$$\text{Operating Leverage} = \sum_{i=1}^{n} \left| \frac{\%\Delta OE}{\%\Delta S} \right| \bigg/ N.$$

The absolute value of the changes are considered, because it is possible for the two series to move in opposite directions. It is not the direction that is important — only the relative size of the change. The more volatile the operating earnings are compared to sales, the greater the operating leverage.

In summary, business risk is measured by the relative variability of operating earnings for a firm over time. In turn, the variability of operating earnings is caused by sales volatility and the amount of operating leverage employed by the firm.

Financial Risk

Financial risk is the additional uncertainty of returns faced by equity holders because a firm uses fixed obligation debt securities. This financial uncertainty is *in addition* to the business risk discussed above. Specifically, if the firm did not derive any of its capital from debt obligations (i.e., it was an all equity firm), the only uncertainty for the owner would be that due to sales volatility and operating leverage (i.e., business risk). With only business risk, the earnings available to the common stockholder would have the same volatility as the operating earnings. The point is, when a firm derives some of its capital from debt securities, the payments on this capital come prior to the common stock earnings, and it is a *fixed* obligation. Therefore, similar to the effect of operating leverage, during good times the earnings on equity will experience a larger percentage *increase* than operating earnings, while during a period of adverse business the earnings available to equity holders will experience a larger percentage *decline* than operating earnings. Put another way, because of the use of fixed debt obligations, the relative volatility of earnings available for equity is greater than the relative volatility of operating earnings.[8] There are two sets of ratios used to measure financial risk. The first set indicates the proportion of capital derived from debt securities. The second set considers the coverage of earnings available to pay the fixed obligations.

Proportion of Debt Ratios.   These ratios indicate what proportion of the firm's capital is derived from long-term debt compared to other sources of capital, such as preferred stock and common equity. Clearly, the higher the proportion of debt compared to other sources, the more volatile the earnings available to common stock will be and also the higher the probability of the firm defaulting on the bonds. Therefore, *higher debt ratios indicate greater financial risk.* Also, the acceptable level of financial risk depends upon the firm's business risk.

---

[8] This relationship is referred to as *financial leverage* and is discussed in Steven E. Bolten and Robert L. Conn, *Essentials of Managerial Finance,* (Boston, Mass.: Houghton Mifflin Co., 1981), Chapter 10, and also in, Sol S. Shalit, "On the Mathematics of Financial Leverage," *Financial Management* 4 no. 1 (Spring 1975): 57–66.

If the firm has lower business risk, investors are willing to accept higher financial risk. An example is public utilities which typically have rather stable operating earnings streams that allow them to have heavy debt capital structures (higher financial risk).

Debt-equity ratio. This ratio is equal to:

$$\text{Debt-Equity Ratio} = \frac{\text{Total Long-Term Debt}}{\text{Total Equity}}.$$

The debt would include all long-term fixed obligations including subordinated convertible bonds. The equity is typically the book value of equity and includes preferred stock, common stock, and retained earnings. In some cases the analyst may want to exclude preferred stock and only consider common equity. The total equity figure is probably preferable if some firms being analyzed have preferred stock and some do not. Alternatively, if you consider the preferred stock dividend akin to an interest payment, you might want to derive a ratio of debt plus preferred stock relative to common equity. In the case of Deere & Co., it is not necessary to select an alternative because the firm does not have preferred stock. Moreover, it seems appropriate to consider all long-term liabilities. Thus, the debt-equity ratios for Deere & Co. were:

— 1982: $\frac{1,151,913}{2,388,196} = 48.23\%$

— 1981: $\frac{929,783}{2,449,586} = 37.96\%$

— 1980: $\frac{914,032}{2,141,066} = 42.69\%$.

Debt-total capital ratio. This ratio indicates what proportion of long-term capital is derived from debt capital. It is computed as:

$$\text{Debt to Capital Ratio} = \frac{\text{Total Long-Term Debt}}{\text{Total Long-Term Capital}}.$$

The long-term capital would include all debt, any preferred stock, and the total equity. While this ratio is completely consistent with the debt–equity ratio, it is somewhat more intuitive; it indicates what percentage of long-term capital is fixed debt. The debt-total capital ratios for Deere & Co. were:

— 1982: $\frac{1,151,913}{3,540,109} = 32.54\%$

— 1981: $\frac{929,783}{3,379,369} = 27.51\%$

— 1980: $\frac{914,032}{3,055,098} = 29.92\%$.

In some cases it is useful to examine *total* debt (current liabilities plus long-term liabilities) to total capital if a firm derives substantial funds from short-term borrowing. This seems to apply to Deere & Co., because it has sub-stantial current liabilities in general but also experienced a major increase in notes payable during 1980 and 1982. Therefore, the total debt to total capital ratios for Deere & Co. were:

— 1982: $\dfrac{3,547,483}{5,935,679} = 59.77\%$

— 1981: $\dfrac{3,234,291}{5,683,877} = 56.90\%$

— 1980: $\dfrac{3,061,358}{5,202,424} = 58.84\%.$

As always, it would be necessary to compare these ratios to other companies in the industry to see if they are consistent with the business risk of this industry. Note that, although all the ratios increased from 1980 to 1982, none of the changes would be considered dramatic.

Coverage Ratios.   In addition to the balance sheet ratios that indicate the *stock* of debt, analysts also employ ratios that relate the *flow* of funds from earnings that are available to meet debt obligations to the required fixed debt payments. In this case, the *higher* the value (i.e., the greater the coverage), the *less* the finan-cial risk.

Interest coverage.   It is computed as follows:

$$\text{Interest Coverage} = \frac{\text{Income before Interest and Taxes}}{\text{Debt Interest Changes}}.$$

This ratio indicates how many times the fixed interest charges are earned based upon the earnings available to pay these charges. Alternatively one minus the reciprocal of the coverage ratio indicates how much earnings could decline before it would be impossible to pay the fixed financial charges; i.e., a coverage ratio of five means earnings could decline by 80 percent (1 minus 1/5) and the firm could still pay the fixed financial charges. The interest coverage ratios for Deere & Co. were:

— 1982: $\dfrac{186,309}{266,581} = .70$

— 1981: $\dfrac{512,405}{232,042} = 2.21$

— 1980: $\dfrac{489,433}{189,696} = 2.58.$

The coverage ratios prior to 1980 were quite good—i.e., in excess of five. The significant decline in 1980 was a result of lower earnings, but more importantly, a substantial rise in interest expense due to higher interest rates and the increase in notes payable pointed out previously. The major decline in 1982 was mainly a function of much lower earnings with some further increase in interest charges. Clearly, these coverage ratios indicate a dramatic increase in the financial leverage and financial risk for Deere & Co. This differs from the slight change in the proportion of debt ratios.

Total fixed charge coverages. Alternatively, an analyst might want to determine the coverage for fixed financial charges including preferred dividends. For this we must recognize that preferred dividends are paid out of earnings *after* taxes. Thus it is necessary to determine the pretax earnings required for these payments as follows:

$$\text{Fixed Charge Coverage} = \frac{\text{Income before Interest and Taxes}}{\text{Debt Interest} + (\text{Preferred Dividend} / 1\text{-Tax Rate})}.$$

GROWTH ANALYSIS

Importance of Growth Analysis

The purpose of growth analysis is to examine specific ratios that indicate how fast a firm should grow. Such analysis is important for both lenders and owners. The rationale for owners analyzing growth potential is obvious, since the future value of the firm is heavily dependent on the future growth in earnings and dividends. The reader will recall the standard dividend valuation model discussed in Chapter 10, which showed that the value of the firm is a function of dividends in Period 1, the required rate of return for the stock (i), and the expected growth rate of dividends for the firm (g_i). Therefore, an estimation of *expected* growth of earnings and dividends on the basis of the variables that influence growth is obviously crucial. An analysis of past values for these growth determinants should be helpful in the estimation process.

A firm's growth potential is also important to creditors, since the major factor that determines the firm's ability to pay an obligation is the firm's future success, which in turn is influenced by its growth. Many financial ratios employed in credit analysis tend to emphasize the amount of assets covering the financial obligations. These ratios imply that it is possible to liquidate these assets to pay off the loan in case of default. In fact, using these assets for such a purpose is extremely questionable since the usual payoff on assets sold in a forced liquidation is about 10–15 cents on the dollar. Clearly, the more relevant analysis is the ability of the firm to pay off the obligations as an *ongoing* enterprise. In this regard, the analysis of growth potential indicates the future status of the firm as an ongoing enterprise.

Determinants of Growth

The growth of a business firm is similar to the growth of any economic entity including the aggregate economy. Specifically, the rate of growth depends on:

1. The amount of resources retained and reinvested in the entity
2. The rate of return that is earned on the resources retained

Obviously, the more a firm reinvests, the faster it will grow. Alternatively, for a given level of reinvestment, a firm will grow faster if it is able to earn a higher rate of return on the resources reinvested.

For both lenders and owners, the growth *of net earnings available to the owners* is of prime importance. This variable is obviously important for the equity holders, but it is also important for the lender, because a growing stream of earnings protects the debtholder and determines the overall health of the enterprise. Therefore, we concentrate on the growth of equity earnings. In turn, the growth rate of equity earnings is a function of two variables: (1) the percentage of net earnings retained (i.e., the retention rate), and (2) the rate of return on the firm's equity capital (ROE). These ratios flow directly from the discussion above. The retention rate $(1 -$ the percentage of payout) indicates what proportion of earnings are retained for reinvestment. The return on equity (ROE) indicates the rate of return earned on these retained earnings, because when earnings are retained they become equity. Specifically:

$$g = \text{(Percentage of Earnings Retained)} \times \text{(Return on Equity)}$$
$$= RR \times ROE.$$

The retention rate is a decision by the board of directors based upon the investment opportunities available to the firm. Theory would indicate that the firm should retain earnings and should reinvest them as long as the expected rate of return on the investment exceeds the firm's cost of capital.

As discussed in the profitability section, it is possible to examine the firm's ROE in terms of two components:

$$\text{ROE} = \frac{\text{Sales}}{\text{Equity}} \times \frac{\text{Income}}{\text{Sales}} = \text{(Equity Turnover)} \times \text{(Net Profit Margin)}.$$

Therefore, it is possible for a firm to improve its ROE either by becoming more efficient in the use of its equity capital (increase its equity turnover) *or* by increasing its profitability—i.e., its profit margin on sales. When examining the equity turnover, it is important to examine the debt-equity ratio to ensure that an increase in the equity turnover is not attributable to a change in the capital structure. An increase in equity turnover accompanied by an increase in the debt-equity ratio would cause a faster rate of growth in equity earnings, but it also would cause an increase in financial risk, which in turn would cause equity holders to increase their required rate of return on the stock.

It is possible to derive a more specific idea of any change in financial leverage by breaking the equity turnover ratio into two components, as follows:

$$\frac{\text{Sales}}{\text{Equity}} = \frac{\text{Sales}}{\text{Total Assets}} \times \frac{\text{Total Assets}}{\text{Equity}}.$$

The total assets/equity ratio is an indicator of *financial leverage.* Given that assets are financed by either debt or equity, the higher the ratio of total assets to equity, the greater the proportion of assets financed by debt and the higher the financial leverage. This specification shows that equity turnover can be changed by either a change in total asset turnover or a change in the proportion of total assets financed by equity (i.e., a change in capital structure).

By substituting this into the prior equation, we have the following relationship:

$$ROE = \frac{Sales}{Total\ Assets} \times \frac{Total\ Assets}{Equity} \times \frac{Income}{Sales}$$

$$= (Total\ Asset\ Turnover) \times (Financial\ Leverage)$$
$$\times (Net\ Profit\ Margin).$$

This equation shows very clearly that the ROE can be increased by becoming more efficient with your assets (increasing the total asset turnover), by changing your capital structure (increasing your financial leverage), or by increasing your profitability (raising your profit margin).

Alternatively, it is possible to divide the ROE into four components, two of which are operating factors and two that are nonoperating as follows:

$$\overbrace{\frac{Pretax\ Income}{Sales} \times \frac{Sales}{Total\ Assets}}^{Operating\ Factors} = \frac{Pretax\ Income}{Total\ Assets} \times \overbrace{\frac{Total\ Assets}{Equity} = \frac{Pretax\ Income}{Equity} \times \frac{Tax\ Retention\ Rate:(1-T)}{}}^{Nonoperating\ Factors} = \frac{Net\ Income}{Equity}$$

With this breakdown one can see that it is possible to increase the ROE as follows: (1) increase the pretax profit margin, (2) increase the total asset turnover, (3) increase the firm's financial leverage, or (4) increase the tax retention rate (i.e., reduce T, the tax rate). Obviously, as an analyst you would prefer the increases to come in the operating variables (profit margin and asset turnover) rather than the nonoperating variables. The important part of the analysis is to examine each of the components over time in order to arrive at a *projection* for ROE. Using the three-component breakdown, let us examine the sustainable growth outlook for Deere & Co.

The earnings retention rate (RR) for Deere & Co. was:

$$Retention\ Rate = 1 - \frac{Dividends\ Declared}{Net\ Income}$$

— 1982: $1 - \dfrac{118,401}{52,898} = 1 - 2.238 = -1.238$

— 1981: $1 - \dfrac{133,055}{250,994} = 1 - .530 = .470$

— 1980: $1 - \dfrac{116,004}{228,271} = 1 - .508 = .492.$

These results indicate a major change for Deere & Co. Prior to 1980 the firm's retention rate was more than 65 percent. As shown, it declined to about 50 percent in 1980 and 1981 and to a negative value in 1982, which implies a partial liquidation of the firm—i.e., the firm is paying out more than it earns.

The total asset turnover was computed earlier as:
— 1982: .79
— 1981: 1.00
— 1980: 1.05.

The total asset to equity ratio (financial leverage) for Deere & Co. was as follows:

— 1982: $\dfrac{5,935,679}{2,388,196} = 2.49$

— 1981: $\dfrac{5,683,877}{2,449,586} = 2.32$

— 1980: $\dfrac{5,202,424}{2,141,066} = 2.43$.

As noted earlier, while this ratio indicates an increase in financial leverage, it understates the increase in financial risk implied by the significant decline in interest coverage ratios.

The net profit margins computed earlier were:
— 1982: 1.15%
— 1981: 4.61%
— 1980: 4.17%.

Therefore, the implied ROE was:

— 1982: $0.79 \times 2.49 \times 1.15\% = 2.26\%$

— 1981: $1.00 \times 2.32 \times 4.61\% = 10.70\%$

— 1980: $1.05 \times 2.43 \times 4.17\% = 10.64\%$.

In the case of Deere & Co., although the firm experienced an increase in financial leverage during 1982, the ROE declined because of the decline in total asset turnover and a substantial drop in the net profit margin.

Finally, the implied sustainable growth rates were:

— 1982: $2.26\% \times -1.238 = -2.80\%$

— 1981: $10.70\% \times .470 = 5.03\%$

— 1980: $10.64\% \times .492 = 5.23\%$.

Similar to prior ratios, these results indicate substantial deterioration in the operations of Deere & Co. Before 1980, the sustained growth rate was over 10 percent based upon a ROE of over 15 percent and a retention rate of over 65 percent. In contrast, by 1982 the sustained growth rate was a negative value, which implies a liquidation of the firm based upon a negative retention rate.

This analysis indicates that the important consideration in estimating growth is not the one-year performance, but the *long-run* outlook for the components of sustainable growth. Specifically, the results prior to 1980 were probably too optimistic regarding the outlook for Deere & Co. growth, while the results for 1982 are clearly too pessimistic regarding the long-run growth for Deere & Co. Given this background, it is the function of the analyst to derive a reasonable set of estimates for the relevant variables.

As pointed out in a private memo by Lempereur, the important consideration when relating ROE to expected growth is the relationship of the *expected* ROE to the current ROE.[9] Specifically, if the expected ROE is *above* the current ROE, then the actual future growth will *exceed* the growth implied by the model. In contrast, if the expected ROE is *below* the current ROE, the actual growth will *not* be as high as that implied by the model. Therefore, when using these relationships, you want to *project* each of the components and derive an estimate of the *expected* ROE to use in the growth model.

EXTERNAL MARKET LIQUIDITY

Market Liquidity Defined

Market liquidity is the ability to buy or sell an asset *quickly* with *little price change* from a prior transaction assuming no new information. In order to determine how liquid an asset is, one should ask two questions: (1) how long will it take to buy or sell the asset? (2) what will be the purchase or selling price compared to recent transaction prices? In the case of a liquid asset, you should be able to buy or sell it very quickly (in less than an hour) at a price close to the prior transaction price. (For example, if the last sale on the stock was at $30 a share, you might be able to sell your stock at $29 7/8 or even $30.) Examples of liquid common stocks are AT&T and IBM, because you can sell large amounts of these stocks very quickly with very little price change from the prior trade. In the case of an illiquid stock, you might be able to sell it quickly, but the price would be significantly different from the prior price (e.g., a quick sale at $28 for a stock that sold recently for $30). Alternatively, the broker might be able to get $30 a share, but it could take several days.

Determinants of Market Liquidity

Investors should know the liquidity characteristics of securities they currently own or want to own because they may want to change the composition of their portfolio. While the major factors that indicate market liquidity are derived from market trading data, there are several internal corporate variables that are good proxies for these market variables. Specifically, the most important determinant of external market liquidity is the number of shares traded in the security and/or

---

[9] Douglas R. Lampereur, "Projected Growth Calculations: Impact of Changes in Projected ROE," Standish, Ayer, & Wood, Inc. (memorandum), 1981.

the dollar value of shares traded (which adjusts for different price levels of alternative securities). It is reasoned that with more trading activity, there is a greater probability that when you decide to buy or sell a stock there will be someone available to take the other side of the transaction. Another variable that has been widely used as an indicator of market liquidity is the bid-ask spread — i.e., the difference between the market-maker's bid price and his asking price on a security. Fortunately, there are some internal corporate variables that are typically highly correlated with these market trading variables. Specifically, they are:

1. Total market value of outstanding securities (number of common shares outstanding times the market price per share)
2. Number of security owners.

Numerous studies have shown that the main determinant of the market spread (besides price) is the dollar value of trading.[10] In turn, the value of trading is highly correlated with the market value of the outstanding securities and the number of security holders. The intuitive explanation for this relationship is that, with more shares outstanding, there will be more stockholders and at any point in time some of these security holders will be buying or selling for a variety of purposes. It is the existence of numerous buyers and sellers that provides liquidity.

For Deere & Co. one can derive an estimate of the market value of outstanding stock by using the number of shares outstanding at the year end times the average market price for the year (defined as the high price plus the low price divided by two) as follows:

— 1982: $67,852,221 \times \{(22.00 + 36.88)/2\} = \$1,997,569,386$

— 1981: $67,723,864 \times \{(32.13 + 40.38)/2\} = \$2,455,328,689$

— 1980: $62,727,000 \times \{(49.75 + 28.50)/2\} = \$2,454,193,800.$

The number of stockholders is 31,418 including institutions that own 39,302,142 shares (approximately 63 percent of the outstanding stock). Clearly all of these values are quite substantial, and they indicate that there should be significant trading activity in the common stock of Deere & Co., which would provide a *very liquid market* for the stock.

The point is, it is important to be aware of the prevailing market liquidity for your securities and it is possible to derive some indication of this liquidity by comparing companies in an industry using the two variables suggested.

USES OF FINANCIAL RATIOS

We have discussed some general uses of financial ratios as related to credit analysis and security valuation. Beyond this, several studies have employed specific financial ratios to aid in valuation and other financial decisions. One can

---

[10] Studies on this topic include, Harold Demsetz, "The Cost of Transacting," *Quarterly Journal of Economics* 82 no. 1 (February 1968); Seha M. Tinic, "The Economics of Liquidity Services," *Quarterly Journal of Economics* 86 no. 1 (February 1972); Seha M. Tinic and Richard R. West, "Competition and the Pricing of Dealer Services in the Over-the-Counter Stock Market," *Journal of Financial and Quantitative Analysis* 7 no. 3 (June 1972): 1707–1727.

conceive of four major areas related to investments where financial ratios have been used: (1) stock valuation, (2) the identification of internal corporate variables affecting a stock's systematic risk (beta), (3) assigning quality ratings on bonds, and (4) predicting insolvency (bankruptcy) of firms.

Stock Valuation Models

The purpose of most valuation models is to derive an appropriate price-earnings ratio for a stock—i.e., an earnings multiple as discussed in Chapter 10. You will recall that the earnings multiple should be influenced by the expected growth rate of earnings and dividends and the required rate of return on the stock. Clearly, financial ratios can help in both estimates. The growth rate estimate employs the ratios discussed in the growth analysis section—i.e., the retention rate and the return on equity ratios along with the components of ROE, which help to determine if the current ROE can be sustained.

When attempting to determine an appropriate required rate of return (i), the required rate of return depends on the risk premium for the security, which was a function of business risk and financial risk. Business risk is typically measured in terms of earnings variability, while financial risk is identified by either the debt proportion ratios or the interest coverage ratios.

The typical empirical valuation model has examined a cross section of companies and used a multiple regression model that relates the price-earnings ratios for the sample firms to some of the following corporate variables:[11]

1. Operating earnings variability (last five years)
2. Average debt-equity ratio (last three, five, or ten years)
3. Average interest coverage ratio
4. Stock's systematic risk (beta) during last five years
5. Average dividend payout ratio
6. Average rate of growth of earnings during last five or ten years
7. Average return on equity last five years.

Financial Ratios and Systematic Risk

Prior to the widespread acceptance of the capital asset pricing model (CAPM), the analysis of risk factors concentrated on the business and financial risk factors considered in this chapter. As discussed in Chapter 9, the CAPM implied that the relevant risk variable for an investor building a diversified portfolio should be the systematic risk of the asset—i.e., its beta coefficient related to the market portfolio of all risky assets. Initially, it appeared that there might be some conflict between the two approaches—i.e., fundamental risk variables and market-determined risk measures. Upon reflection, such a conflict would be inconsistent with efficient capital markets where stock prices are expected to reflect all relevant information for the security. Specifically, in efficient markets one would expect a significant relationship between internal corporate risk variables and market-determined risk variables. The first study on this topic was by Beaver,

---

[11] A list of studies that have used financial ratios in valuation models appears in the reference section at the end of the chapter.

Kettler, and Scholes.[12] This was followed by numerous studies that examined other variables intended to reflect business risk and financial risk.[13] Some of the variables that were consistently used and were found to be significant included the following:

Financial ratios (typically five-year average)
1.   Dividend payout ratio
2.   Total debt to total assets
3.   Cash flow to total debt
4.   Interest coverage
5.   Working capital to total assets
6.   Current ratio.

Variability measures (latest five years)
1   Variance of earnings multiple
2.   Coefficient of variation of operating earnings
3.   Operating earnings beta (company earnings related to aggregate earnings).

Nonratio variables
1.   Asset size
2.   Market volume of trading in stock.

Financial Ratios and Bond Ratings

As discussed in Chapter 16, there are four financial services that assign quality ratings to bonds on the basis of the issuing company's ability to meet all the obligations of the bond. A triple A rating (AAA) indicates very high quality and almost no chance of default, while a C rating indicates the bond is already in default. Because it is important to understand the variables used by these rating services, authors of a number of studies have attempted to build models that use financial ratios to predict what rating will be assigned to a bond.[14] The major financial ratios used have been those concerned with internal liquidity and financial risk as follows:

Financial ratios (typically five-year average)
1.   Long-term debt/total assets
2.   Net income plus depreciation (cash flow)/long-term senior debt
3.   Net income plus interest/interest expense (fixed charge coverage)
4.   Market value of stock/par value of bonds
5.   Net operating profit/sales
6.   Net income/total assets
7.   Working capital/sales
8.   Sales/net worth (equity turnover).

---

[12] William H. Beaver, Paul Kettler, and Myron Scholes, "The Association between Market-Determined and Accounting-Determined Risk Measures," *Accounting Review* 45 no. 4 (October 1970): 654–682.

[13] A list of other studies in this area appears in the reference section at the end of the chapter.

[14] A list of studies in this area is in the reference section at the end of the chapter.

Variability Measures (latest five years)
1. Coefficient of variation (CV) of net earnings (CV = Standard Deviation/ Mean)
2. Coefficient of variation of return on assets.

Nonratio variables
1. Subordination of the issue
2. Size of the firm (total assets)
3. Issue size
4. Par value of all publicly traded bonds of the firm.

Financial Ratios and Insolvency (Bankruptcy)

The financial insolvency of a firm is an event that has substantial implications for those who lend it money or invest in it. Obviously, there is interest in determining which financial ratios might be useful in identifying firms that might default on a loan or declare bankruptcy. In response to this interest, a number of studies have examined various financial ratios as predictors of bankruptcy for a number of years prior to the declaration.[15] The typical test design is to derive a sample of firms that have declared bankruptcy (i.e., failed) and also to select a matched sample of firms in the same industry and of comparable size that have not failed. The analysis involves examining a number of financial ratios expected to reflect declining liquidity for several years prior to the declaration of bankruptcy (usually five years) to determine which ratios or set of ratios provide the best predictions. Most studies have used discriminant analysis, where the criteria is which financial ratios or set of financial ratios give the fewest misclassifications. Some of the multiple discriminant analysis models (MDA) are able to properly classify over 90 percent of the firms the year prior to failure and there are reasonably high classification results three to five years before failure. The financial ratios that have typically provided the best results include the following:
1. Cash flow/total debt
2. Net income/total assets
3. Total debt/total assets
4. Working capital/total assets
5. Current ratio
6. Cash/current liabilities
7. Working capital/sales.

Limitations of Financial Ratios

In addition to the earlier point that you should always consider *relative* financial ratios, there are other limitations of financial ratios that you should keep in mind.
1. Is the accounting treatment used by alternative firms comparable? It is well recognized that there are several generally accepted methods for treating various accounting items, and the alternatives can cause a difference in

---

[15] A list of studies on this topic is in the reference section at the end of the chapter.

results for the same event. Therefore, it is necessary to check on the accounting treatment of significant items and to adjust for major differences.

2. How homogeneous is the firm? Many companies have several divisions that operate in different industries. This may make it difficult to derive comparable industry ratios.

3. Are the implied results consistent? It is important that you develop a *total profile* on the firm and not depend on only one set of ratios (e.g., internal liquidity ratios). As an example, it may be that the firm is having short-term liquidity problems, but the firm is very profitable, which will eventually alleviate the short-run liquidity problem.

4. Is the ratio within a reasonable range for the industry? As noted on several occasions, typically you are looking for a *range* of values for the ratio because a value that is too high or too low can be a cause for concern; e.g., a low current ratio may indicate a liquidity problem, while a very high current ratio would indicate excessive liquidity, which means the firm is underutilizing its assets.

SUMMARY

This chapter was concerned with the purposes and uses of financial statement analysis. Because the overall purpose is to help you make decisions on investing in a firm's bonds or stocks, we initially considered why financial ratios are important and how these ratios should be examined (i.e., relative to the economy, the industry, the firm's main competitors, and the firm's past ratios).

The specific ratios considered were divided into five categories depending upon the purpose of the analysis (i.e., internal liquidity, operating performance, risk analysis, growth analysis, and external market liquidity). You should recognize that the ratios presented are not exhaustive, but they are the most widely used ratios for the purposes specified. Following a presentation and application of the principal ratios we discussed four major uses of financial ratios. This presentation indicated the broad uses of ratios and the specific ratios that are most important for these purposes. We concluded with a brief discussion of some limitations of financial ratios and some questions you should ask during an analysis.

A final caveat; it is clearly possible to envision a very large number of potential ratios that will examine almost every possible relationship. Therefore, the trick is not to come up with more ratios, but to attempt to *limit* the number of ratios and to *examine them in a meaningful way*. This entails an analysis of the time series properties of the ratios *relative* to the economy, the industry, or the past. Any additional effort should be spent on deriving better comparisons for a limited number of ratios.

QUESTIONS

1. What is the overall purpose of financial statements?
2. Discuss briefly some of the decisions that require the analysis of financial statements.

3. Why do analysts employ financial ratios rather than the absolute numbers?
4. The Geno Company, which produces Polish sausage, earned 12 percent on their equity last year. What does this indicate about the management of Geno's? Is there any other information you want? What is it and why do you want it?
5. Besides comparing a company's performance to its total industry, what other comparisons should be considered *within* the industry? What is the justification for this comparison?
6. What is the purpose of the internal liquidity ratios? What information are they intended to provide? Who would be most interested in this information?
7. What are the components of operating performance? Discuss each of them and indicate the purpose of the ratios involved.
8. In terms of asset turnover and profit margin, how do a jewelry store and a grocery store differ? Would you expect their return on equity to differ assuming equal risk? Discuss.
9. Describe the components of business risk and discuss how the components affect the variability of operating earnings.
10. Would you expect a steel firm or a utility to have greater business risk? Discuss your reasoning for this expectation in terms of the components of business risk.
11. When examining a firm's financial structure, would you be concerned with the firm's business risk? Why or why not?
12. How does the fixed charge coverage ratio differ from the debt-equity ratio? Which would you prefer and why?
13. Why is growth analysis important to the common stockholder? Why is it important to the debtholder?
14. In a general sense, what are the factors that determine the rate of growth of *any* economic unit? Discuss each of the factors.
15. IBM pays out about 40 percent of its earnings in dividends and earns about 18 percent on equity. What is its expected growth rate under these conditions?
16. If a firm is earning 20 percent on equity and has low risk, would you expect it to have a high or low retention rate? Discuss why.
17. The ND Company earned 18 percent on equity while the MSU Company only earned 14 percent on equity. Does this mean that ND is better then MSU? If not, what else do you want to consider?
18. Briefly discuss the two components of external market liquidity.
19. Given the components of market liquidity, why do people consider real estate to be a relatively illiquid asset? Be specific.
20. What internal factors about a company would indicate its market liquidity? Discuss why these variables are potentially useful as indicators of external liquidity.
21. Select one of the four uses of financial ratios and discuss how you would use financial ratios to help you as an analyst.

REFERENCES

General

Bernstein, Leopold A. *Financial Statement Analysis: Theory Application, and Interpretation.* rev. ed. Homewood, Ill.: Richard D. Irwin, 1978.

Foster, George. *Financial Statement Analysis.* Englewood Cliffs, N.J.: Prentice-Hall, 1978.

Foulke, R. A. *Practical Financial Statement Analysis.* 6th ed. Highstown, N.J.: McGraw-Hill, 1968.

Helfert, Erich, A. *Techniques of Financial Analysis.* 5th ed. Homewood, Ill.: Richard D. Irwin, 1982.

Horrigan, James D. "A Short History of Financial Ratio Analysis." *Accounting Review.* 43 no. 2 (April 1968).

Jaedicke, Robert K., and Robert T. Sprouse. *Accounting Flows: Income, Funds, and Cash.* Englewood Cliffs, N.J.: Prentice-Hall, 1965.

Lev, Baruch. *Financial Statement Analysis: A New Approach.* Englewood Cliffs, N.J.: Prentice-Hall, 1974.

Seitz, Neil. *Financial Analysis: A Programmed Approach.* Reston, Va.: Reston Publishing Company, 1976.

Sprouse, R. T., and R. J. Swieringa. *Essentials of Financial Statement Analysis.* Reading, Mass.: Addison-Wesley, 1972.

Viscione, Jerry A. *Financial Analysis: Principles and Procedures.* Boston, Mass.: Houghton Mifflin Co., 1977.

Financial Ratios and Stock Valuation Models

Arditti, Fred D. "Risk and the Required Return on Equity." *Journal of Finance.* 22 no. 1 (March 1967).

Babcock, Guilford. "The Concept of Sustainable Growth." *Financial Analysts Journal.* 26 no. 3 (May–June 1970).

Bower, Dorothy, and Richard S. Bower. "Test of the Stock Evaluation Model." *Journal of Finance.* 25 no. 2 (May 1970).

Bower, Richard S., and Dorothy Bower. "Risk and the Valuation of Common Stock." *Journal of Political Economy.* 83 no. 2 (May–June 1969).

Eiteman, David K. "A Computer Program for Common Stock Valuation." *Financial Analysts Journal.* 24 no. 4 (July–August 1968).

Foster, Earl M. "The Price-Earnings Ratio and Growth." *Financial Analysts Journal.* 26 no. 1 (January–February 1970).

Litner, John. "Dividends, Earnings, Leverage, Stock Prices and the Supply of Capital to Corporations." *Review of Economics and Statistics.* 34 no. 3 (August 1962).

Malkiel, Burton G., and John G. Cragg. "Expectations and the Structure of Share Prices." *American Economic Review.* 60 no. 4 (September 1970).

McKibben, Walt. "Econometric Forecasting of Common Stock Investment Returns: A New Methodology Using Fundamental Operating Data." *Journal of Finance.* 27 no. 2 (May 1972).

Whitbeck, Volkert S., and Manown Kisor. "A New Tool in Investment Decision Making." *Financial Analysts Journal.* 19 no. 3 (May–June 1963).

Financial Ratios and Systematic Risk (Beta)

Beaver, William H., Paul Kettler, and Myron Scholes. "The Association Between Market-Determined and Accounting-Determined Risk Measures." *Accounting Review.* 45 no. 4 (October 1970).

Breen, William J., and Eugene M. Lerner. "Corporate Financial Strategies and Market Measures of Risk and Return." *Journal of Finance.* 28 no. 2 (May 1973).

Gonedes, Nicholas J. "Evidence on the Information Content of Accounting Numbers: Accounting-Based and Market-Based Estimates of Systematic Risk." *Journal of Financial and Quantitative Analysis.* 8 no. 2 (June 1973).

Hamada, Robert S. 'The Effect of the Firm's Capital Structure on the Systematic Risk of Common Stocks." *Journal of Finance* 27 no. 2 (May 1972).

Lev, Baruch. "On The Association between Operating Leverge and Risk." *Journal of Financial and Quantitative Analysis.* 9 no. 3 (September 1974).

Logue, Dennis, and Larry J. Merville. "Financial Policy and Market Expectations." *Financial Management.* 1 no. 2 (Summer 1972).

Melicher, Ronald W. "Financial Factors which Influence Beta Variations within an Homogeneous Industry Environment." *Journal of Financial and Quantitative Analysis.* 9 no. 1 (March 1974).

Rosenberg, Barr, and Walt McKibben. "The Prediction of Systematic and Specific Risk in Common Stocks." *Journal of Financial and Quantitative Analysis.* 8 no. 2 (March 1973).

Thompson, Donald J. II. "Sources of Systematic Risk in Common Stocks." *Journal of Business.* 49 no. 2 (April 1976).

Financial Ratios and Bond Ratings

Ang, James S., and A. Kiritkumar. "Bond Rating Methods: Comparison and Validation." *Journal of Finance.* 30 no. 2 (May 1975).

Atkinson, Thomas R., and Elizabeth T. Simpson. *Trends in Corporate Bond Quality.* New York: National Bureau of Economic Research, 1967.

Bullington, Robert A. "How Corporate Debt Issues Are Rated." *Financial Executive.* 42 no. 9 (September 1978).

Edelman, Richard B. "A New Approach to Ratings on Utility Bonds." *Journal of Portfolio Management.* 5 no. 3 (Spring 1979).

Ferri, Michael G., and Charles G. Martin. "The Cyclical Pattern in Corporate Bond Quality." *Journal of Portfolio Management.* 6 no. 2 (Winter 1980).

Fisher, Lawrence. "Determinants of Risk Premiums on Corporate Bonds." *Journal of Political Economy.* 67 no. 3 (June 1959).

Fraser, H. Russell. "Utility Bond and Commercial Paper Ratings." *Public Utilities Fortnightly.* September 27, 1973.

Hickman, W. Braddock. "Corporate Bonds: Quality and Investment." New York:

332

National Bureau of Economic Research (Princeton University Press). volume 1–4, 1958–60.

Horrigan, James O., "The Determination of Long-Term Credit Standing with Financial Ratios." *Empirical Research in Accounting: Selected Studies, 1966.* Supplement to vol. 4, *Journal of Accounting Research.*

Kaplan, Robert S., and Gabriel Urwitz. "Statistical Models of Bond Ratings: A Methodological Inquiry." *Journal of Business.* 52 no. 2 (April 1979).

Long, Hugh III. *An Analysis of the Determinants and Predictability of Agency Ratings of Domestic Utility Bond Quality,* Ph.D. dissertation, Stanford University, Stanford, Calif., 1973.

Pinches, George E., and Kent A. Mingo. "A Multivariate Analysis of Industrial Bond Ratings." *Journal of Finance.* 28 no. 1 (March 1973).

Pinches, George E., and Kent A. Mingo. "The Role of Subordination and Industrial Bond Ratings." *Journal of Finance.* 30 no. 1 (March 1975).

Pogue, Thomas F., and Robert M. Soldofsky. "What's in a Bond Rating?" *Journal of Financial and Quantitative Analysis.* 4 no. 2 (June 1969).

Pye, Gordon. "Gauging the Default Premium." *Financial Analysts Journal.* 30 no. 1 (January–February 1974).

Rating Electric Utility Bonds. New York: Moody's Investor Service, 1975.

Ross, Irwin. "Higher Stakes in the Bond Rating Game." *Fortune.* (April 1976).

Shapiro, Harvey D. "How Corporations are Trying to Improve Their Credit Ratings." *Institutional Investor.* 10 no. 1 (January 1976).

Standard and Poor's Corporation. "Corporation Bond Ratings: An Overview." 1978.

West, Richard R. "An Alternative Approach to Predicting Bond Ratings." *Journal of Accounting Research.* 8 no. 1 (Spring 1970).

Financial Ratios and Corporate Bankruptcy

Altman, Edward I. "Financial Ratios, Discriminant Analysis and the Prediction of Corporate Bankruptcy." *Journal of Finance.* 23 no. 4 (September 1968).

Altman, Edward I. "Corporate Bankruptcy Potential, Stockholder Returns and Share Valuation." *Journal of Finance.* 24 no. 5 (December 1969).

Altman, Edward I. *Corporate Financial Distress* (New York: John Wiley & Sons, 1983).

Altman, Edward I., Robert G. Haldeman, and P. Narayanan. "Zeta Analysis: A New Model to Identify Bankruptcy Risk of Corporations." *Journal of Banking and Finance.* 1 no. 2 (June 1977).

Beaver, William H. "Financial Ratios as Predictors of Failure." *Empirical Research in Accounting: Selected Studies,* 1966 Supplement to vol. 4 *Journal of Accounting Research.*

Beaver, William H. "Market Prices, Financial Ratios, and the Prediction of Failure." *Journal of Accounting Research.* 6 no. 2 (Autumn 1968).

Beaver, William H. "Alternative Accounting Measures as Predictors of Failure." *The Accounting Review.* 43 no. 1 (January 1968).

Blum, Marc. "Failing Company Discriminant Analysis." *Journal of Accounting Research.* 12 no. 1 (Spring 1974).

Deakin, Edward B. "A Discriminant Analysis of Predictors of Business Failure." *Journal of Accounting Research.* 10 no. 1 (Spring 1972).

Edmister, Robert O. "An Empirical Test of Financial Ratio Analysis for Small Business Failure Prediction." *Journal of Financial and Quantitative Analysis.* 7 no. 2 (March 1972).

Gentry, James A., Paul Newbold, and David T. Whitford. "Comparing Funds Flow Components to Financial Ratios as Predictors of Bankruptcy." University of Illinois. mimeo (March 1984).

Johnson, Craig G. "Ratio Analysis and the Prediction of Firm Failure." *Journal of Finance.* 25 no. 5 (December 1970).

Moyer, R. Charles. "Forecasting Financial Failure: A Re-Examination." *Financial Management.* 6 no. 1 (Spring 1977).

Wilcox, Jarrod W. "A Simple Theory of Financial Ratios as Predictors of Failure." *Journal of Accounting Research.* 9 no. 2 (Autumn 1971).

Wilcox, Jarrod W. "A Prediction of Business Failure Using Accounting Data." *Empirical Research in Accounting: Selected Studies,* 1973, supplement to *Journal of Accounting Research.* vol. 11 (1973).

Chapter 12

Aggregate Stock Market Analysis

I n Chapter 10 we discussed the importance of attempting to estimate future aggregate stock market values which, in turn, indicate future return from investing in common stocks. It was pointed out that such an analysis should be done before an industry analysis or a company analysis is attempted. Consequently, investors should become familiar with the major techniques available for estimating future market values or changes in market values. There are basically three techniques employed in this regard. The first is a *macroeconomic* approach, which is based upon the underlying relationship between the aggregate economy and the securities markets. The second technique is the *present value of dividends* approach which follows directly from the valuation theory discussed in Chapter 10. Specifically, the idea is to apply the basic dividend valuation model to the aggregate stock market. The third is the *technical analysis* approach, which assumes that the best way to determine *future* changes in stock market values is to examine *past* movements in security prices and other market variables.

In this chapter we consider the macroeconomic approach, the microeconomic analysis, and the value of dividends approach. The technical analysis approach is discussed in Chapter 16.

THE STOCK MARKET AND THE ECONOMY

It is widely accepted that there is a strong relationship between the aggregate economy and the stock market. This is not surprising if you consider that the price of a given stock reflects investor expectations as to how the issuing firm will perform, and that performance is, in turn, affected by the overall performance of the economy. There is substantial empirical support for the existence of this relationship, most of it derived by the National Bureau of Economic Research (NBER) in connection with the Bureau's work on business cycles. Based on the relationship of alternative economic series to the behavior of the entire economy, the NBER has classified numerous economic series into three groups: leading, coincident, and lagging. Based upon extensive analysis, it has been shown that stock prices are one of the better leading series in terms of consistency and stability.

The evidence clearly indicates not only a relationship between stock prices and the economy, but also indicates that stock prices consistently turn *before* the economy does; i.e., stock prices turn down prior to a peak in the economy and start rising before the economy begins its recovery from a recession. There are two possible reasons for this phenomenon. One is that stock prices reflect *expectations* of earnings and dividends, and thus they react to investor perceptions of *future* earnings and dividends. Hence, because investors attempt to estimate *future* earnings, stock prices are based upon *future* economic activity not on current activity. A second possible reason is that the stock market reacts to various economic series, but the series considered most important by equity investors are *leading indicator* series of the economy. In this regard, the economic series mentioned most often as important to stock prices are corporate earnings, corporate profit margins, and changes in the growth rate of the money supply. Therefore, because analysts and portfolio managers analyze economic series that lead the economy and adjust stock prices rapidly to changes in these relevant economic series, stock prices become a leading series.

Because stock prices turn before the aggregate economy does, it is difficult to use economic behavior in predicting fluctuations in stock prices, although there are ways of doing so:

1. Estimate aggregate economic activity *very far* into the future. Assuming the average lead of stock prices is about nine months, this would indicate that it is necessary to project changes in the aggregate economy close to one year in advance.
2. Analyze other economic series that also lead the economy. The ideal would be to find a series that leads the economy by *more* than stock prices do, i.e., a series that typically leads by more than nine months.
3. Attempt to project the behavior of economic series that do not lead the economy by as much as stock prices do. An example would be a series that leads the economy by six months; the analyst would project fluctuations in this leading series for four or more months ahead.

Given that stock prices lead the aggregate economy, our macroeconomic approach to market analysis will concentrate on economic series that likewise lead the economy—hopefully by more than stock prices do. The initial discussion considers the cyclical indicator approach of the National Bureau of Economic Research (NBER) with specific reference to leading economic indicators and their relationship to stock prices. The subsequent discussion considers a very popular leading series, the money supply, and how growth in the money supply relates to stock prices.

CYCLICAL INDICATOR APPROACH

The cyclical indicator approach to economic forecasting is based on the belief that the economy experiences discernible periods of expansion and contraction.

This view has been investigated by the NBER, a nonprofit organization that attempts to ascertain and to present important economic facts and interpret them scientifically and impartially. The NBER explains the business cycle as follows:

> The "business cycle" concept has been developed from the sequence of events discerned in the historical study of the movements of economic activity. Though there are many cross-currents and variations in the pace of business activity, periods of business expansion appear to cumulate to peaks. As they cumulate, contrary forces tend to gain strength bringing about a reversal in business activity and the onset of a recession. As a recession continues, forces making for expansion gradually emerge until they become dominant and a recovery begins. . . .[1]

This explanation emphasizes the *cumulative* aspects of the process and indicates that there are certain events that regularly take place during the various phases of the business cycle.

Based upon an examination of the behavior of hundreds of economic time series in relation to past business cycles, the NBER grouped various economic series into three major categories in terms of this relationship. The inital list was compiled in 1938 and it has undergone numerous revisions over the years. The most recent revision was by Zarnowitz and Boschan.[2]

Indicator Categories

The first category is the *leading indicators* and includes those economic time series that have usually reached peaks or troughs before the corresponding points in aggregate economic activity were reached. The group currently includes the 12 series shown in Table 12.1. The table indicates the median lead or lag for each economic series relative to business cycle peaks or troughs. The bureau also graded each economic series in terms of several characteristics considered important, and these scores are also included. A high score for a series indicates that it should be a useful series in the analysis of cyclical movements. One of the 12 leading series is common stock prices, which has a median lead of nine months at peaks and four months at troughs.[3] Another leading series is the money supply in constant dollars, which has a median lead of ten months at peaks and eight months at troughs.

The second category is *coincident indicators,* which consist of those economic time series in which the peaks and troughs of the series roughly coincide with the peaks and troughs in the business cycle. Many of the economic time series in this category are employed by the Bureau to help define the different phases of the cycle.

[1] Julius Shiskin, "Business Cycle Indicators: The Known and the Unknown," *Review of the International Statistical Institute* 31 no. 3 (1963): 361–383.

[2] Victor Zarnowitz and C. Boschan, "Cyclical Indicators: An Evaluation and New Leading Index," *Business Conditions Digest* (May 1975): V–XXII, and "New Composite Indexes of Coincident and Lagging Indicators," *Business Conditions Digest* (November 1975): V–XXIV.

[3] A detailed analysis of this relationship is contained in Geoffrey H. Moore, "Stock Prices and the Business Cycle," *Journal of Portfolio Management* 1 no. 3 (Spring 1975): 59–64.

TABLE 12.1
Economic Series in NBER Leading Indicator Group

Series	Median Lead (−) or Lag (+) in Months			Scores						
	Peaks	Troughs	All Turns	Economic Significance	Statistical Adequacy	Timing	Conformity	Smoothness	Currency	Total
1. Average Work Week of Production Worker—Manufacturing	−12	−2	−5	70	80	81	60	60	80	73
2. Index of New Business Formations	−11	−2	−3	80	61	78	59	80	80	73
3. Index of Stock Prices: 500 Common Stocks	−9	−4	−5½	80	85	89	51	80	100	80
4. Index of New Building Permits	−13	−8	−9½	90	70	80	55	80	80	76
5. Layoff Rate—Manufacturing	−11	−1	−6½	70	80	79	80	60	80	76
6. New Orders—Consumer Goods (1967 dollars)	−6	−1	−4½	80	75	76	70	60	80	74
7. Contracts & Orders for Plant & Equipment (1967 dollars)	−9	−2	−5½	90	50	87	72	40	80	72
8. Net Change in Inventory (1967 dollars)	−5	−4	−4½	90	53	83	60	80	40	71
9. Net Change in Sensitive Prices	−15	−5	−5½	70	80	82	60	60	66	72
10. Vendor Performance	−6	−5	−6	70	75	79	46	60	80	69
11. Money Balance (M1)—(1967 dollars)	−10	−8	−9	90	85	80	41	100	80	79
12. Percentage Change in Total Liquid Assets	−6½	−6	−6	90	81	84	41	80	66	75

SOURCE: Victor Zarnowitz and Charlotte Boschan, "Cyclical Indicators: An Evaluation and New Leading Indexes," *Business Conditions Digest*, May 1975, pp. 5–22.

TABLE 12.2
Economic Series in NBER Coincident and Lagging Indicator Group

Series	Median Lead (−) or Lag (+) in Months			Scores						
	Peaks	Troughs	All Turns	Economic Significance	Statistical Adequacy	Timing	Conformity	Smoothness	Currency	Total
Coincident										
1. Number of Employees on Nonagricultural Payrolls	−2	0	0	100	78	89	80	100	80	88
2. Index of Industrial Production	−3	0	− ½	90	72	90	85	100	80	86
3. Personal Income, Less Transfers (deflated by PEE)	0	− 1	− ½	90	70	74	64	100	80	78
4. Manufacturing & Trade Sales, Deflated	−3	0	− ½	90	65	90	75	80	53	78
Lagging										
1. Average Duration of Employment	+1	+ 8	+ 3½	90	78	89	95	80	80	86
2. Manufacturing & Trade Inventories (1967 dollars)	+2½	+ 3	+ 3	90	70	89	64	100	53	80
3. Labor Cost Per Unit Output, Manufacturing	+8½	+11	+10	80	55	87	51	80	80	73
4. Commercial & Industrial Loans Outstanding, Weekly Representative Banks	+1½	+ 5	+ 3½	80	60	86	81	100	100	83
5. Ratio of Consumer Installment Debt to Personal Income	+6½	+ 7	+ 7	80	70	87	44	100	53	74
6. Average Prime Rate Charged by Banks	+3½	+14	+ 4	90	95	85	62	100	100	87

SOURCE: Victor Zarnowitz and Charlotte Boschan, "New Composite Indexes of Coincident and Lagging Indicators," *Business Conditions Digest*, November 1975, pp. 5–24.

The third category is *lagging indicators,* which includes series that have experienced their peaks and troughs after peaks and troughs occur in the aggregate economy. Timing and scores for the coincident and lagging series are contained in Table 12.2.

A final category is titled *other selected series* and includes series that are expected to influence aggregate economic activity but that cannot be neatly categorized in one of the three main groups. This includes such series as U.S. balance of payments, federal surplus or deficit, and military contract awards.

Analytical Measures

When examining a given economic series for predictive purposes, it is important to consider more than simply the behavior of the series overall. The NBER has devised certain analytical measures for examining behavior within a series.

Diffusion indexes. As the name implies, these indexes indicate how pervasive a given movement is in a series. They are used to specify *the percentage of reporting units in a series indicating a given result.* If there are 100 companies that constitute the sample reporting new orders for equipment, the diffusion index for this series would indicate what proportion of the 100 companies was reporting higher orders during an expansion. In addition to knowing that aggregate new orders are increasing, it is helpful to know whether 55 percent of the companies in the sample are reporting higher orders or whether 95 percent are. Such information helps the analyst project the future length and strength of an expansion. It is also helpful to know past diffusion index values to determine whether a trend exists. The existence of a trend is important, because it has been shown that *the diffusion indexes for a series almost always reach their peak or trough before the peak or trough in the corresponding aggregate series.* Therefore, it is possible to use the diffusion index of a series to predict the behavior of the series itself. As an example, assume that you are interested in the leading series, New Orders—Consumer Goods. It is possible to derive an early indication of weakening in this series by observing the diffusion index. If the diffusion index goes from 85 percent to 75 percent and then to 70 percent, it indicates widespread receipt of new orders but also indicates *weakening* in terms of the breadth of the increase and possibly an impending decline in the series itself.

Besides creating diffusion indexes for individual series, the Bureau has derived such indexes for the 12 leading indicators that show the percentage of the indicators that are rising or falling during a given period.

Rates of change. Somewhat similar to the diffusion index is the rate of change measure for the series. It is one thing to know that there has been an increase in a series, but quite another to know that it is a 10 percent increase as compared to a 7 percent increase the previous month. Like the diffusion index, the rate of change values for a series reach a peak or trough prior to the peak or trough in the aggregate series.

Direction of change.   These tables show at a glance which series went up or down (plus or minus) during the period and how long the movement in this direction has persisted.

Comparison with previous cycles.   These tables show the movements of individual series over previous business cycles. Current movements are then compared to previous cycles for the same economic series. This comparison indicates how this series is acting in the current expansion or contraction: is it slower or faster, stronger or weaker than it was during the last cycle? This information can be useful because, typically, movements in the *initial* months of an expansion or contraction indicate the *ultimate* length and strength of the expansion or contraction.[4]

Limitations of the Indicator Approach.   The NBER has consistently attempted to improve the usefulness of the indicator approach while acknowledging some very definite limitations. The most obvious limitation is false signals; i.e., past patterns suggest that the indicators are currently signaling a contraction, but they turn up again and nullify previous signals.

A similar problem occurs when the indicators do not point toward a definite change in direction but experience a period of hesitancy which is difficult to interpret. These problems are likewise caused by another limitation, the *variability* of the leads and lags. While a given economic series may *on the average* lead the peak or trough in the business cycle by five or six months, the range of leads over the years may have varied from one to ten months. This variability means that the analyst is not able to act with complete confidence based upon short-run signals.

There are also problems both gathering the data (getting the original data as soon as possible) and revising it. Many of the series are seasonally adjusted, and there may be subsequent adjustments to the seasonal adjustment factors. Finally, the NBER points out that there are numerous political or international developments which significantly influence the economy but which cannot be encompassed in a statistical system.

Leading Indicators and Stock Prices

Because of the relationship between leading indicators and the economy, some authors have suggested that one might be able to use leading indicators to predict stock prices. A study by Heathcotte and Apilado examined this relationship using the 1966 short list of leading economic series and a stock price series (the S&P 500).[5] The authors derived a three-month moving average of the diffusion index and used the moving average of these diffusion indexes with different filter rules to construct an investment policy. That is, if the index increased by some specified percentage, they would buy and hold until the index declined by

---

[4] Monthly presentations of all the series and analytical measures are contained in U.S. Department of Commerce, *Business Conditions Digest* (Washington, D.C.: U.S. Government Printing Office).

[5] Bryan Heathcotte and Vincent P. Apilado, "The Predictive Content of Some Leading Economic Indicators for Future Stock Prices," *Journal of Financial and Quantitative Analysis* 9 no. 2 (March 1974): 247–258.

some percentage. The authors compared their investment results to those for a buy-and-hold policy and found that, as long as they had perfect foresight regarding the correct filters to use, they beat a buy-and-hold policy. When the authors used the trading rule without foresight as to the best filter (they merely used the previous best filter), the results were very mixed.

From this, it appears that several of the leading series do lead stock prices and that a diffusion index of these series could be useful if one could determine an appropriate filter. Without such foresight these series do not appear to be able to beat a buy-and-hold policy when one takes commissions into account.

MONETARY VARIABLES AND STOCK PRICES

One of the economic factors assumed to be most closely related to stock prices is monetary policy. The best-known monetary variable in this regard is the money supply. In actuality, the influence of the money supply on stock prices is an offshoot of its influence on the aggregate economy. Friedman and Schwartz have thoroughly documented the historical record of the empirical relationship that exists between changes in the growth rate of the stock of money and subsequent changes in aggregate economic activity.[6] Their research indicated that, during the period 1867–1960, declines in the rate of growth of the money supply preceded business contraction by an average of 20 months.[7] Expansions in the growth rate of the money supply, on average, preceded expansions in the business activity by about eight months. The timing of the relationship was highly variable, but its existence was consistent; every major contraction or expansion during the period 1867–1960 was preceded by a contraction or expansion in the growth rate of the money supply. In addition, Friedman specified the transmission mechanism through which changes in the growth rate of the money supply affect the aggregate economy, and this work led several authors to specifically examine the relationship between alternative monetary variables (typically the MI money supply) and stock prices. According to the hypothesis, when the Federal Reserve buys or sells bonds to adjust bank reserves and, eventually, the money supply, the initial impact is on the government bond market, then on corporate bonds, then on common stocks, and subsequently on the real goods market.[8] This means that the initial effect is on financial markets and only subsequently on the aggregate economy. In terms of the securities market, this would indicate that there should be a relationship between changes in the growth rate of the money supply and changes in stock prices; i.e., changes in the growth rate of the money supply should *precede* changes in the level of stock prices.

Several studies have examined the empirical evidence supporting this hypothesized relationship. Some of the earliest and most widely read research on

---

[6] Milton Friedman and Anna J. Schwartz, "Money and Business Cycles," *Review of Economics and Statistics* supplement vol. 45 no. 1, part 2 (February 1963): 32–78, reprinted in Milton Friedman, *The Optimum Quantity of Money and Other Essays* (Chicago: Aldine Publishing Co., 1969), 189–235.

[7] In the Friedman-Schwartz study money supply was defined as bank demand deposits and time deposits plus currency in the hands of the public (M2). Business cycle expansions and contractions were used as defined by the National Bureau of Economic Research.

[8] Leonall C. Anderson and Jerry L. Jordan, "Money in a Modern Quantity Theory Framework," Federal Reserve Bank of St. Louis *Review,* 49 no. 12 (December 1967): 4–5.

this topic was carried out by Sprinkel, who examined a six-month moving average of the growth rate of the money supply and the S&P 425 stock price series for the period 1918–1963 and, subsequently, 1970.[9] Based upon a visual analysis of the two series, Sprinkel generally concluded that there was a relationship between them, but that the timing was not always consistent and the lead appeared to be getting shorter. A subsequent study by Palmer examined the relationship between the growth rate of the money supply and a moving average of percentage changes in stock prices for the period 1959–1969.[10] The author concluded that there was a consistent relationship between the two series and that changes in the money supply generally led stock price changes. Keran developed a model intended to explain the level of stock prices that included money supply growth as one of the affecting factors.[11] While the overall results were quite good and the money supply variable was statistically significant, the impact of the money supply appeared to be slight. Homa and Jaffee (HJ) employed a regression model that used the level of money supply and the rate of growth of the money supply to predict the level of stock prices.[12] The results were supportive of the hypothesis because an investment policy assuming perfect foresight regarding the money supply outperformed a buy-and-hold policy. The investment results without foresight were mixed. Hamburger and Kochin tested the hypothesis that the money supply had a direct effect on the stock market and also considered the impact of the money supply on common stock risk.[13] They concluded that changes in the money supply have a direct effect on the level of stock prices and that the volatility of the money supply had an impact on common stock risk.

All of these studies indicated a strong relationship between money supply changes and stock prices. Beyond this, some of the studies indicated that money supply changes *preceded* stock price changes, which would indicate that the money supply could be used as an indicator of stock price changes.

In contrast, there have been studies that questioned these findings in terms of the statistical techniques used and the conclusions reached. Miller questioned the Keran and the Hamburger-Kochin studies on statistical grounds.[14] Pesando, likewise, discussed some potential empirical problems in the Keran, Hamburger-Kochin, and Homa-Jaffee studies.[15] After reestimating the models and

---

[9] The original work is contained in Beryl W. Sprinkel, *Money and Stock Prices* (Homewood, Ill.: Richard D. Irwin, 1964). The update is in, Beryl W. Sprinkel, *Money and Markets: A Monetarist View* (Homewood, Ill.: Richard D. Irwin, 1971).

[10] Michael Palmer, "Money Supply, Portfolio Adjustments and Stock Prices," *Financial Analysts Journal,* 26 no. 4 (July–August 1970): 19–22.

[11] Michael W. Keran, "Expectations, Money and the Stock Market," Federal Reserve Bank of St. Louis *Review,* 53 no. 1 (January 1971): 16–31.

[12] Kenneth E. Homa and Dwight A. Jaffee, "The Study of Money and Common Stock Prices," *Journal of Finance,* 26 no. 5 (December 1971): 1045–1066.

[13] Michael J. Hamburger and Levis A. Kochin, "Money and Stock Prices: The Channels of Influence," *Journal of Finance,* 27 no. 2 (May 1972): 231–249.

[14] Merton H. Miller, "Discussion of Hamburger and Kochin, 'Money and Stock Prices. . . ,'" *Journal of Finance,* 27 no. 2 (May 1972): 294–298.

[15] James E. Pesando, "The Supply of Money and Common Stock Prices: Further Observations on the Econometric Evidence," *Journal of Finance,* 29 no. 3 (June 1974): 909–921.

running them with Canadian data, Pesando concluded that, "one should not place undue confidence in the quantitative estimates of the impact of fluctuations in the money supply on common stock prices.[16]

Cooper examined the relationship between money supply and stock prices in terms of the efficient market hypothesis.[17] He discussed the simple quantity theory of money concept (SQ) and the efficient market hypothesis (EMH) that contends one should not be able to use past data to forecast price changes. His combined theory (SQ-EMH) states that money supply may influence the market rate of return, but that because of the existence of aggressive investors who attempt to forecast important variables, market returns may actually *lead* money changes. Test results indicated a definite relationship between the money supply and stock prices, but the analysis of the lead-lag relationship indicated that the money supply appeared to *lag* stock returns by about one to three months on a relatively consistent basis. Based upon further tests, Cooper concluded that money supply changes appear to have an important effect on stock returns, but evidence indicated that stock returns *lead* money supply changes.

A study by Auerbach likewise questioned the Keran and Homa-Jaffee findings for statistical reasons.[18] He noted that it is necessary to take account of common long-run trends and cycles in variables that are related and demonstrated that this could have been a problem with previous studies. Auerbach removed the trend and cyclical components of the money and stock prices series and correlated the adjusted series. The results indicated that past changes in the M1 money supply were *not* related to future stock price changes, but that stock returns *were* related to current and *future* changes in the M1 money supply series, although the relationship was weak. He concluded that his results are consistent with the efficient market hypothesis, which contends that historical information is not of value in predicting future stock prices.

Two studies by Rozeff also raised doubts about the usefulness of the money supply in predicting stock price changes.[19] The author reexamined the returns achieved using the trading rule reported in Sprinkel's first book and using more realistic assumptions, derived returns below those from a buy-and-hold policy. Using regression analysis, Rozeff found a very weak relationship when money supply led stock prices. There was an increase in explanatory power when contemporaneous money supply changes were taken into account, and there was a significant increase in the correlation when *future* money supply changes were included. These regression results were confirmed with trading rule tests. It was concluded that money supply changes are important, but the timing relationship indicates that stock prices *lead* the money supply.

[16] Ibid., p. 921.

[17] Richard V. L. Cooper, "Efficient Capital Markets and the Quantity Theory of Money," *Journal of Finance,* 29 no. 3 (June 1974): 887–908.

[18] Robert D. Auerbach, "Money and Stock Prices," Federal Reserve Bank of Kansas City *Monthly Review* (September–October 1976): 3–11.

[19] M. S. Rozeff, "Money and Stock Prices: Market Efficiency and the Lag Effect of Monetary Policy," *Journal of Financial Economics,* 1 no. 3 (September 1974): 245–302; M. S. Rozeff, "The Money Supply and the Stock Market," *Financial Analysts Journal,* 31 no. 5 (September–October 1975): 18–26.

Summary of Money Supply Studies.   The early work done by Sprinkel indicated that, on average, there was a lead of money over stock prices, but the relationship was variable and the lead declined during the 1960s. This was generally confirmed in studies by Palmer, Keran, Homa-Jaffee, and Hamburger-Kochin, although Miller and Pesando questioned some of the methodology.

Studies by Cooper, Rozeff, and Auerbach contended that with efficient capital markets one should not expect changes in monetary growth to precede stock price changes. The recent empirical results have generally supported the efficient market hypothesis. All of these studies have basically concluded that, although there *is* a relationship between money supply growth and stock prices, it is not possible to use the relationship to derive above average returns, because the stock market *anticipates* changes in monetary growth.

Summary of Macroeconomic Analysis

This discussion of aggregate market analysis using macroeconomic variables indicates ample evidence of a strong and consistent relationship between activity in the overall economy and in the stock market. At the same time, it has been shown that stock prices consistently turn from four to nine months *before* the economy does. This means it is necessary to either forecast economic activity 12 months ahead or examine indicator series that lead the economy by more than stock prices do.[20] The subsequent discussion examined two sets of series that possibly lead the economy by more than stock prices do, the NBER leading indicator series and money supply.

Following a description of the leading indicator approach and the specific series available, there was a discussion of a study that attempted to use the leading indicators to time investment decisions. The results indicated that, if the investigator had *perfect foresight* regarding the appropriate filter to use with a diffusion index of leading series, the investment results would clearly be superior to those achieved with a buy-and-hold policy. If the investor attempted to invest using *past* filters as a guide, the results were mixed.

There was an extensive discussion of the expected relationship between the money supply and stock prices, which is an outgrowth of the quantity theory of money. Interestingly, the empirical results have changed over time. The early work indicated that money supply was important and that it could be used in making investment decisions, while contrary evidence began to appear in 1974. However, all of the studies acknowledge that *there is a significant relationship between money supply and stock prices.* Unfortunately, for those looking for a mechanical trading device, recent rigorous research indicates that *monetary growth and stock prices generally turn at about the same point in time or that stock prices turn before the money supply does.* Therefore, it is *not* possible to

---

[20] A paper by Davidson and Froyen examined the relationship during the recent period and generally confirmed the efficient market's point of view. See, Lawrence S. Davidson and Richard T. Froyen, "Monetary Policy and Stock Returns: Are Stock Markets Efficient?" Federal Reserve Bank of St. Louis *Review*, 64 no. 3 (March, 1982): 3–12.

use the monetary series to develop a mechanical trading rule that will outperform a buy-and-hold policy, because the market reacts very quickly to relevant information.

MICRO ANALYSIS OF THE STOCK MARKET

The determination of the future value of the aggregate stock market employing microeconomic techniques is simply the application of basic valuation theory to the aggregate stock market. Therefore, our initial discussion recalls what is involved in the derivation of a valuation model for common stocks. Given the model, it will be shown that the valuation process can be divided into two main parts. Subsequently, we will discuss how this valuation process is applied to an aggregate stock market series.

Determinants of Value

The reader will remember that in Chapter 10 we discussed the basic determinants of value for any earning asset (e.g., bonds, stock, real estate, etc.) Valuation required the analyst to estimate the following:
1. The stream of expected returns
2. The time pattern of expected returns, and
3. The required rate of return on the investment.

Given this background, we considered the application of these concepts to the valuation of bonds, preferred stock, and common stock under several different assumptions regarding the holding period and the stream of future dividends. Specifically, we assumed a one-year holding period, a multiple-year holding period, and finally an infinite holding period. In the case of the infinite holding period model, we also assumed a constant growth rate. The specific model derived from this set of assumptions was as follows:

$$V_j = \frac{D_0(1+g)}{(1+i)} + \frac{D_0(1+g)^2}{(1+i)^2} + \cdots \cdots \frac{D_0(1+g)^\infty}{(1+i)^\infty}$$

where:

V_j = the value of stock j

D_0 = the dividend payment in the current period

g = the constant growth rate of dividends

i = the required rate of return on stock j

∞ = the number of periods, which is assumed to be infinite.

It was shown in the appendix to Chapter 10 that this information could be simplified to the following expression:

$$V_j = \frac{D_1}{i-g} \quad \text{or} \quad P_j = \frac{D_1}{i-g}$$

where:

$$P_j = \text{the price of stock } j.$$

Given this model, the parameters to be estimated are: (1) the required rate of return (i), and (2) the expected growth rate of dividends (g). After estimating g, it is a simple matter to estimate D_1, because it is the current dividend (D_0) times $(1 + g)$.

After deriving the basic valuation model, it was shown that it is possible to transform this into a pragmatic earnings multiplier model as follows:

$$\frac{P_j}{E_1} = \frac{\dfrac{D_1}{E_1}}{i - g}.$$

Thus, the P/E ratio (the earnings multiplier) is determined by:
1. The expected dividend payout ratio (D_1/E_1),
2. The required rate of return on the stock (i), and
3. The expected growth rate of dividends for the stock (g).

It was shown that the difficult parameters to estimate are i and g, or more specifically, the *spread* between i and g. It was demonstrated that very small changes in either of these can affect the spread and change the value substantially.

Two-Part Valuation Procedure

We will be using the earnings multiplier version of the valuation model to generate an estimate of the future value for the stock market for several reasons: it is more commonly used in practice; it is the more extensive model; and once the earnings multiplier model is grasped, understanding the dividend model becomes rather straightforward. Finally, before a future dividend figure or dividend growth estimate can be derived, it is necessary to determine the growth of earnings.

The ultimate objective is to estimate the future market value for some major stock market series, such as the DJIA or the S&P 400. This estimation process is a two-step procedure:
1. Estimating the future earnings value, and
2. Estimating a future earnings multiplier for the series.[21]

Some studies have tended to concentrate on estimating earnings for these series but have generally ignored changes in the earnings multiplier. The implicit assumption is that the earnings multiplier is relatively constant over time, so that stock prices would generally move in line with earnings. The fallacy of such an assumption and the incomplete procedure it implies is obvious when one examines what transpired during the period since 1960, as shown in Table 12.3.

---

[21] In line with the efficient market hypothesis, our emphasis will be on *estimating future* values. The intent is to show the relevant variables and provide a procedural framework. The final estimate depends upon the ability of the analyst.

TABLE 12.3

Annual Changes in Corporate Earnings, the Earnings Multiplier, and Stock Prices:
The Standard & Poor's 400, 1960–1982

Year	Earnings per Share	Percentage Change	Year-End Earnings Multiple	Percentage Change	Year-End Stock Prices	Percentage Change
1960	3.40	—	18.09	—	61.49	—
1961	3.37	− .9	22.49	24.4	75.72	23.11
1962	3.83	13.6	17.23	−23.4	66.0	−12.8
1963	4.24	10.7	18.69	8.5	79.25	20.1
1964	4.85	14.4	18.48	− 1.1	89.62	13.1
1965	5.50	13.4	17.90	− 3.1	98.47	9.9
1966	5.87	6.7	14.52	−18.9	85.24	−13.4
1967	5.62	− 4.3	18.70	28.8	105.11	23.3
1968	6.16	9.6	18.35	− 1.9	113.02	7.5
1969	6.13	− .5	16.56	− 9.8	101.49	−10.2
1970	5.41	−11.7	18.65	12.6	100.90	− .6
1971	5.97	10.4	18.88	1.2	112.72	11.7
1972	6.83	13.9	19.31	2.3	131.87	17.0
1973	8.89	30.9	12.28	−36.4	109.14	−17.2
1974	9.61	8.9	7.96	−35.2	76.47	−29.9
1975	8.58	−10.7	11.62	46.0	100.88	31.9
1976	10.69	24.6	11.17	− 3.9	119.46	18.4
1977	11.45	7.1	9.14	−18.8	104.71	−12.4
1978	13.04	13.9	8.22	−10.1	107.21	2.4
1979	16.29	24.9	7.43	− 9.6	121.02	12.9
1980	16.12	− 1.0	9.58	28.9	154.45	27.6
1981	16.74	3.8	8.19	−14.5	137.12	−11.2
1982	13.18	−21.3	11.96	46.0	157.62	15.0

With Signs:

Mean	—	7.10	—	.57	—	5.70
Standard Deviation	—	12.16	—	22.41	—	16.43
Coefficient of Variability	—	1.71	—	39.32	—	2.88

Without Signs:

Mean	—	11.70	—	17.50	—	15.50
Standard Deviation	—	7.86	—	14.03	—	7.86
Coefficient of Variability	—	.67	—	.80	—	.51

SOURCE: *Analysts Handbook* (New York: Standard & Poor's): Various issues.

Examples where stock prices moved counter to earnings changes are numerous and striking. Specifically:

— 1973 Profits *increased* by 30 percent, stock prices *declined* by 17 percent.
— 1974 Profits *increased* by 9 percent, stock prices *declined* by 30 percent.
— 1975 Profits *declined* by 10 percent, stock prices *increased* by 30 percent.
— 1977 Profits *increased* by 8 percent, stock prices *declined* by 12 percent.
— 1980 Profits *decreased* by 1 percent, stock prices *increased* by 27 percent.
— 1982 Profits *decreased* by 21 percent, stock prices *increased* by 15 percent.

FIGURE 12.1
Time Series Plot of Year-End Earnings Multipliers Standard & Poor's 400
Industrial Index 1960–1982

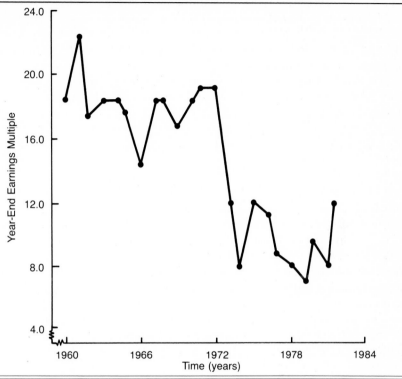

SOURCE: *Analyst's Handbook* (New York: Standard & Poor's): Various issues.

During each of these years, the major factor that influenced stock price movements was changes in the multiplier. The consistency of large changes in the multiplier can be seen from the summary figures at the bottom of Table 12.3 and from the time series plot in Figure 12.1. As shown, the standard deviation of the annual changes for the earnings multipler series is much larger than the standard deviation of earnings changes. Also, if you consider the mean of the series without sign, the multiple series has a larger mean value and a larger standard deviation.

Further evidence of the importance of changes in the multiple affecting stock prices can be derived from correlation analysis of annual percentage changes in the three series for the period 1960–1982. The simple correlation between percentage changes in earnings and stock prices was -0.27, while the correlation between the multiple and stock prices was 0.84. The regression equation relating both variables to stock prices was as follows:

$$\%\Delta \text{ Stock Prices} = -2.15 + 1.03 \ (\%\Delta \text{ Multiple}) + 1.02 \ (\%\Delta \text{ Earnings})$$
$$(t \text{ value}) \qquad\qquad (24.36) \qquad\qquad\qquad (13.12)$$
$$R^2 = .971.$$

While both coefficients were positive and very significant, it is notable that the multiple variable was more significant.

The intent is not to reduce the importance of the earnings estimate, but simply to *increase the awareness* of the importance of the earnings multiple. Therefore, we will initially consider the procedure for estimating aggregate earnings, but we will likewise discuss in detail the procedure for estimating the aggregate market earnings multiple.

We will initially derive an estimate of expected earnings for the market series for the coming year based upon the outlook for the aggregate economy and for the corporate sector. The second major step is deriving an expected earnings multiplier for the stock market series based upon the current earnings multiplier and projected changes in the variables that affect the earnings multiplier.

Estimate of expected earnings.   There are several distinct steps involved in estimating expected earnings for an aggregate stock market series, beginning with an estimate of sales for the stock market series.[22] In turn, this sales estimate involves estimating gross national product (GNP) and relating the sales for the stock market series to this measure of aggregate economic production. Given a sales estimate, the next step is to estimate the expected gross profit margin for the stock market series. This estimate involves consideration of a number of factors that affect the profit margin for industrial firms. When this estimated gross profit margin is applied to the sales estimate, it provides the estimate of gross earnings per share for the upcoming year. We conclude with an estimate of depreciation and a tax rate.

Estimating Gross National Product.   Because GNP is a basic measure of aggregate economic sales, one would expect aggregate *corporate* sales to be related to GNP. Hence, an earnings projection begins with an estimate of nominal GNP, which can be obtained from one of several banks or financial services that regularly publish such estimates for public distribution.[23]

After the analyst has derived a reasonable estimate of nominal GNP from one of several public sources, the next step is to estimate corporate sales relative to aggregate economic sales (GNP).[24]

Corporate Sales Relative to GNP.   To derive an estimate of earnings for an aggregate stock market series, it is best to use sales figures for such a series if they are available. Fortunately, there is a sales series for the S&P 400 industrial series

---

[22] An alternative approach for estimating corporate profits is set forth in, Edmund A. Mennis, "New Tools for Profit Analysis," and Grace Wickersham, "The Latest Tools for Profit Analysis," paper presented at National Association of Business Economists (October 1979). A general view of corporate profitability is contained in, Richard D. Rippe, "Corporate Profitability: The Record and the Prospect," Dean Witter Reynolds, New York, 1981.

[23] This would include, "Business and Money," Harris Trust and Savings Bank, 111 West Monroe Street, Chicago, Ill 60690, and projections by Standard & Poor's appearing late in the year in *The Outlook*.

[24] For an extended discussion of the GNP and its components, the reader is referred to any one of several macroeconomics texts.

TABLE 12.4
Nominal GNP and Standard & Poor's Industrial Sales per Share: 1960–1982

Year	Nominal GNP (billions of $)	Percentage Change	S&P 400 Sales (dollar sales per share)	Percentage Change
1960	506.0	—	59.47	—
1961	523.3	3.4	59.51	.1
1962	563.8	7.7	64.63	8.6
1963	594.7	5.5	68.50	6.0
1964	635.7	6.9	73.19	6.8
1965	688.1	8.2	80.69	10.2
1966	753.0	9.4	88.46	9.6
1967	796.3	5.8	91.86	3.8
1968	868.5	9.1	101.49	10.5
1969	935.5	7.7	108.53	6.9
1970	982.4	5.0	109.85	1.2
1971	1,063.4	8.2	118.23	7.6
1972	1,171.1	10.1	128.79	8.9
1973	1,306.6	11.6	149.22	15.9
1974	1,413.2	8.2	182.10	22.0
1975	1,516.3	7.3	185.16	1.7
1976	1,692.4	11.6	202.66	9.5
1977	1,887.2	11.5	224.24	10.6
1978	2,106.6	11.6	251.32	12.1
1979	2,413.9	14.6	292.38	16.3
1980	2,626.1	8.8	327.36	12.0
1981	2,954.1	12.5	344.31	5.2
1982	3,073.0	4.0	333.32	− 3.2
Average:	—	8.6	—	8.3

SOURCE: Reprinted by permission of Standard & Poor's.

on a per share basis.[25] The S&P sales and nominal GNP figures for the recent period are contained in Table 12.4, and a scatter plot for the figures is contained in Figure 12.2. The plot indicates a very close relationship between the two series with only a few years (most notably 1974) in which the difference was substantial. The equation for the least square regression line relating annual percentage changes (%Δ) in the two series for the period 1960–1982 is:

$$\%\Delta \text{ S + P 400 Sales}_t = -2.00 + 1.32 \ (\%\Delta \text{ in Nominal GNP})_t$$
$$R^2 = 0.44 \qquad SEE = 4.40 \qquad F(1, 21) = 15.67$$

These results indicate that about 44 percent of the variance in percentage changes in S&P 400 sales can be explained by percentage changes in the nominal GNP. Given the linear regression model results and an estimate of the expected percentage of change in the nominal GNP for the forthcoming year, it should be

[25] The figures are available back to 1945 in Standard & Poor's *Analysts Handbook* (New York: Standard & Poor's Corporation). The book is updated annually and some series are updated quarterly in a monthly supplement.

FIGURE 12.2
Scatter Plot of Annual Percentage Change in Sales: Standard & Poor's 400 vs. Gross National Product

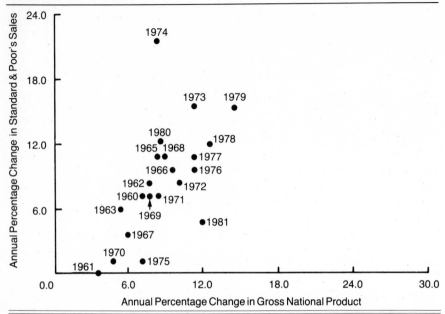

possible to derive a fairly good estimate of the percentage change in sales for the S&P 400 series and, therefore, an estimate of the dollar value for sales per share. Assume that the most likely estimate of nominal GNP for the next year is an 11 percent increase (6 percent real plus 5 percent inflation). Given the regression results this implies the following:

$$\%\Delta \text{ S} + \text{P } 400 \text{ Sales} = -2.00 + 1.32 \ (11.0)$$
$$= -2.00 + 14.52$$
$$= 12.52$$

Alternative Estimates of Corporate Net Profits. Once sales per share for the market series has been estimated, the difficult estimate is that of after-tax profits as a percentage of sales—i.e., the net profit margin—for industrial corporations. There are three procedures suggested, all of which are similar but depend upon further aggregation.

The first is the direct estimation of the *net* profit margin based upon recent trends. As shown in Table 12.5, this net income margin series has been quite volatile over time because of the effect of changes in depreciation as a percentage of sales and of changes in the tax rate over time. Obviously, going directly to the bottom line is the most uncertain approach, but should be attempted as a check on other techniques.

The second estimate is derived from a separate analysis of the net before tax (NBT) profit margin and an estimate of the expected tax rate. The NBT profit

TABLE 12.5
Profit Margins for Standard & Poor's Industrial Index: Net Income; Net before Tax; and
Net before Taxes and Depreciation, 1960–1982

Year	Net Income	Percentage of Sales	NBT	Percentage of Sales	Depreciation	NBT + Depreciation	Percentage of Sales
1960	3.40	5.72	6.27	10.54	2.56	8.83	14.85
1961	3.37	5.66	6.17	10.37	2.66	8.83	14.84
1962	3.83	5.93	6.99	10.82	2.89	9.88	15.29
1963	4.24	6.19	7.75	11.31	3.04	10.79	15.75
1964	4.85	6.63	8.55	11.68	3.24	11.79	16.11
1965	5.50	6.82	9.64	11.95	3.52	13.16	16.31
1966	5.87	6.64	10.22	11.55	3.87	14.09	15.93
1967	5.62	6.12	9.73	10.59	4.25	13.98	15.22
1968	6.16	6.07	11.30	11.13	4.56	15.86	15.63
1969	6.13	5.65	11.27	10.38	4.87	16.14	14.87
1970	5.41	4.92	9.64	8.78	5.17	14.81	13.48
1971	5.97	5.04	10.95	9.26	5.45	16.40	13.87
1972	6.83	5.30	12.71	9.87	5.76	18.47	14.34
1973	8.89	5.96	16.48	11.04	6.25	22.73	15.23
1974	9.61	5.28	19.83	10.89	6.86	26.69	14.66
1975	8.58	4.63	17.98	9.71	7.36	25.44	13.69
1976	10.69	5.27	20.90	10.31	7.58	28.48	14.05
1977	11.45	5.11	22.59	10.07	8.53	31.12	13.88
1978	13.04	5.19	25.18	10.02	9.64	34.82	13.85
1979	16.29	5.57	30.31	10.37	10.82	41.13	14.07
1980	16.12	4.92	29.79	9.10	12.37	42.16	12.88
1981	16.74	4.86	29.69	8.62	13.82	43.51	12.64
1982	13.18	3.95	24.07	7.22	15.19	39.26	11.78

SOURCE: Reprinted by permission of Standard & Poor's.

margin is less volatile than the net profit margin because it is not affected by changes in the tax rate over time. As such the NBT margin should be easier to estimate. Once this is derived, a separate estimate of the tax rate is obtained based upon recent rates and current government tax pronouncements.

The third method begins with an estimate of the *gross* profit margin, i.e., income before taxes and depreciation as a percentage of sales. Because the cash flow as a percentage of sales is not influenced by changes in depreciation allowances or tax rates, it should be a relatively stable value over time. This stability can be seen from the data in Table 12.5. It is clear that the gross profit margin series is the least volatile series in terms of relative variability. The figures in Table 12.6 on means, standard deviations, and coefficients of variation likewise make this point. As shown, the coefficient of variation, which is a *relative* measure of variability, indicates that the net profit margin is the most volatile series. In the next section, we will discuss the factors influencing the gross profit margin. For the time being, once the analyst has derived an estimate of this gross profit margin, he will multiply this by the estimate of sales to derive *a dollar value of earnings before depreciation and taxes (EBDT)*. The second step is to derive a separate estimate of *aggregate depreciation* for the year. This depreciation estimate is then subtracted from the EBDT figure to arrive at earnings before taxes (EBT). Finally, there should be a separate estimate of the expected tax rate

TABLE 12.6
Summary Data: 1960–1982 Standard & Poor's 400

	Mean	Standard Deviation	Coefficient Variation[a]
Net Profit Margin	5.54	.69	.125
NBT Margin	10.24	1.08	.105
NBT & Depreciation Margin	14.49	1.14	.079

[a] Coefficient of variation = Std. Deviation/Mean.

SOURCE: Reprinted by permission of Standard & Poor's.

based upon the recent trend and current government policy. The estimated tax rate applied to the earnings before tax (EBT) figure indicates the estimated taxes. Subtracting estimated taxes from the NBT figure gives the net income estimate for the coming year.

Hopefully the three estimates will generally confirm one another and thereby allow a consensus estimate of corporate profits. The following sections discuss the details of estimating the earnings per share figure, beginning with the gross profit margin.

Determinants of Aggregate Gross Profit Margin

As pointed out in a study by Finkel and Tuttle (FT), there has been a great deal of analysis of factors that influence the profit margins of individual firms, but there has been limited analysis of what determines the aggregate profit margin.[26] The variables suggested and tested by Finkel and Tuttle to obtain this aggregate were:

1. Utilization rate of existing industrial capacity (proportion of capacity being used)
2. Unit labor costs of production
3. The rate of inflation
4. The level of foreign competition
5. The unemployment rate.

Utilization rate.   The relationship between the utilization rate and the profit margin is quite straightforward. If production increases as a proportion of total capacity, there is a decrease in the fixed production costs per unit of output because more units are being produced in the given plant capacity. In addition, fixed *financial* costs per unit decline. Therefore, one should expect a *positive* relationship between the aggregate utilization rate and the aggregate profit margin. The relationship may not be completely linear at very high rates of utilization, because operating diseconomies are introduced as firms are forced to employ marginal labor and/or use older plant and equipment to reach the higher capacity. The figures in Table 12.7 indicate that capacity utilization reached a peak of over 91 percent in 1966 and a low point of less than 70 percent during the recession of 1982.

[26] Sidney R. Finkel and Donald L. Tuttle, "Determinants of the Aggregate Profits Margin," *Journal of Finance,* 26 no. 5 (December 1971): pp 1067–1075.

TABLE 12.7
Variables that Affect the Aggregate Profit Margin: Utilization Rate, Compensation, Productivity and Unit Labor Cost: 1960–1984

Year	Utilization Rate	Compensation/Work Hours[a]		Output/Work Hours[a]		Unit Labor Cost[a]	
		Index	Percentage Change	Index	Percentage Change	Index	Percentage Change
1960	80.2	35.7	4.4	68.3	.8	52.3	3.5
1961	77.4	36.8	3.1	70.3	2.9	52.4	.3
1962	81.6	38.3	4.1	72.8	3.6	52.6	.4
1963	83.5	39.6	3.4	75.2	3.2	52.7	.2
1964	85.6	41.4	4.5	78.1	3.9	53.1	.6
1965	89.6	42.8	3.4	80.5	3.1	53.2	.3
1966	91.1	45.4	6.1	82.5	2.5	55.0	3.4
1967	86.9	47.9	5.5	84.1	1.9	57.0	3.6
1968	87.2	51.5	7.5	86.8	3.3	59.3	4.0
1969	86.3	54.9	6.5	86.6	-.3	63.4	6.9
1970	79.5	58.7	7.0	86.8	.3	67.6	6.6
1971	78.5	62.5	6.5	89.7	3.3	69.7	3.1
1972	83.5	66.7	6.7	93.0	3.7	71.7	2.9
1973	87.6	71.8	7.6	95.3	2.4	75.3	5.0
1974	83.7	78.5	9.4	92.9	-2.5	84.5	12.2
1975	72.9	86.1	9.6	94.8	2.0	90.8	7.5
1976	79.6	93.0	8.1	97.8	3.2	95.1	4.7
1977	82.2	100.0	7.5	100.0	2.2	100.0	5.2
1978	84.7	108.6	8.6	100.6	.6	108.0	8.0
1979	86.0	118.4	9.0	99.0	-1.5	119.5	10.7
1980	79.6	130.6	10.3	98.3	-.7	132.8	11.1
1981	79.4	143.1	9.6	99.8	1.5	143.5	8.0
1982	71.1	154.5	8.0	100.0	.2	154.5	7.7
1983	75.2	162.0	4.9	103.4	3.4	156.6	1.4
1984(p)	81.7	169.5	4.6	106.6	3.1	158.9	1.5

[a] Private nonfarm business, 1977 = 100: Source: Department of Labor, Bureau of Labor Statistics.
SOURCE: Federal Reserve Board Series, "Total Manufacturing," contained in Economic Report of the President, 1983 (Washington, D.C.: U.S. Government Printing Office).

Unit labor cost.   The change in unit labor costs is really a compound effect of two individual factors: (1) changes in wages per hour, and (2) changes in worker productivity. Wage costs per hour typically increase every year by varying amounts depending upon the economic environment. The figures in Table 12.7 indicate that the annual percentage increase in wages varied from 3.1 percent to about 10.2 percent. If workers did not become more productive, this increase in per hour wage costs would be the increase in per unit labor cost. Fortunately, because of advances in technology and greater mechanization, the units of output produced by the individual laborer per hour have increased over time — the laborer has become *more productive.* If wages per hour increase by 5 percent and labor productivity increases by 5 percent, there would be *no* increase in unit labor costs because the workers would *offset* the wage increase by producing more. Therefore, the increase in *per unit labor cost* is a function of the percentage change in hourly wages minus the increase in productivity during the period. The actual relationship is typically not this exact because of measurement problems, but it is quite close as indicated by the figures in Table 12.7. As shown, during the early 1960s productivity increased by as much or more than the hourly compensation did, and the result was very small changes in unit labor cost. In 1974, wage rates increased by 9.5 percent, productivity actually *declined* by 2.1 percent because of the recession and, therefore, unit labor costs increased by over 12 percent. Because unit labor is the major variable cost of a firm, one would expect a *negative* relationship between the aggregate profit margin and percentage changes in unit labor cost.

Inflation.   The precise effect of inflation on the aggregate profit margin is unresolved. In the Finkel–Tuttle article it was hypothesized that there is a positive relationship between inflation and the aggregate profit margin for several reasons. First, it was contended that an increase in the level of inflation increases the ability of firms to pass increasing service costs on to the consumer and thereby increase their profit margin.[27] Second, if the inflation were the classical demand-pull type, the increase would indicate an increase in general economic activity and would be encouraging. Finally, an increase in the rate of inflation might stimulate consumption as individuals attempt to shift their holdings from financial assets to real assets.

The alternative effect of inflation on profit margins is supported by those who doubt the ability of all businesses to consistently increase prices in line with rising costs. Assume a 5 percent increase in the rate of inflation and that the costs of labor and material generally increase by this rate. The question is whether all firms are able to *completely* pass these cost increases along to their customers. If a firm is able to pass cost increases along *completely* in terms of selling price, the result will be a *constant* profit margin *not* an increase. *Only* if a firm can increase prices by *more* than the increase in costs can the firm increase its margin. Many firms will probably not be able to raise prices in line with increased costs be-

---

[27] This assumes either that there is a wage lag or that the demand curve facing the firm is inelastic so that it can raise prices.

cause of the elasticity of demand for their products.[28] In these cases, the profit margin will *decline.* Given the three alternatives, it is hard to imagine most firms increasing their profit margins or even holding them constant. Many firms will suffer declines in their profit margins during periods of inflation, which means that the *aggregate* profit margin will be constant or probably will decline with an increase in the rate of inflation. Therefore, there are alternative arguments regarding the relationship, and only empirical evidence will show how inflation has tended to affect the aggregate margin.

Foreign competition. Some observers contend that export markets are more competitive than domestic markets and, therefore, export sales are made at a lower margin.[29] A reduction in the trade surplus, due to a reduction in exports by the United States, would have a positive effect on profit margins, because a lower proportion of sales would be made at the lower margin. This line of reasoning was challenged by Gray, who contended that undue emphasis was placed on the fact that exports increased less than imports did.[30] Gray believed that only exports made at arm's length (i.e., by two independent firms) should be considered and they should be examined relative to total output exported. Further, he contended that imports could have an important negative impact on the margin because they influence the selling price of all competing domestic products. Therefore, one may likewise question the ultimate effect of the trade surplus variable and examine the empirical results for support of the alternative views.

The unemployment rate. This variable is of potential interest but, as with the others, a case can be made for either a positive or negative relationship. On the one hand, a high rate of unemployment would indicate the existence of excess labor and should cause a low rate of increase in unit labor cost and, therefore, a higher profit margin, all other factors being equal. Thus, a positive relation would result. In contrast, one might argue that a high unemployment rate would be related to a period of economic recession and low utilization of capacity; therefore, it would result in a low profit margin. This line of reasoning would indicate a negative relationship.

Empirical Evidence of Determinants of Profit Margins. The FT study indicated the following relationships between variables and the profit margin:[31]
— Trade surplus — negative and significant at 0.01 level
— Inflation — positive and significant at 0.05 level
— Utilization rate — positive and significant at 0.10 level

---

[28] An extreme example of this inability is regulated industries that may not be able to raise prices at all until after lengthy hearings before regulatory agencies. Even then the increase may still not match the cost increases.

[29] This is the reasoning by Sidney R. Finkel and Donald L. Tuttle, "Determinants of the Aggregate Profits Margin," *Journal of Finance,* 26 no. 5 (December 1971): 1071.

[30] H. Peter Gray, "Determinants of the Aggregate Profit Margin: A Comment," *Journal of Finance,* 31 no. 1 (March 1976): 163–165.

[31] Finkel and Tuttle, "Determinants of the Aggregate Profits Margin."

— Unit labor cost—negative and significant at 0.01 level
— Unemployment rate—not significant.

These results were derived using quarterly data for the period 1955–1967. They also attempted to use the model to estimate the aggregate margin during the period from 1968 to the second quarter of 1970. The difference between the estimates and actual results was not significant.

In his comment, Gray attempted to replicate the FT results with special emphasis on the trade surplus.[32] The results indicated a negative coefficient for the trade surplus variable, but it was not statistically significant. Also, there was a very high correlation between the GNP deflator (the measure of inflation) and the unit labor cost variable.

Some work by this author using annual data for the period 1947–1974 confirmed the importance of the utilization rate and unit labor cost. The relationship between the profit margin and the utilization rate was always significant and positive. In contrast, the relationship between percentage changes in unit labor cost and the profit margin was always negative and significant. Finally, the inflation rate was never significant in the multiple regression. Further, the simple correlations between the profit margin and inflation were consistently *negative*.

There is consistent strong support for a positive relationship between profit margins and the utilization rate and also for a negative relation between the margin and unit labor cost. Unfortunately, it is not possible to derive an independent effect for inflation, but the simple correlation indicates a *negative* relationship. Finally, the effect of a trade surplus is unresolved at this point. Therefore, when attempting to estimate the gross profit margin, you should pay particular attention to estimates of changes in the utilization rate for the economy and the rate of change in unit labor cost. When the utilization rate is expected to increase by several percentage points and only small increases are expected in unit labor costs, one might expect a healthy increase in the profit margin. One should also be aware of changes in the rate of inflation and the foreign trade environment, but these variables should receive less emphasis because of the mixed empirical evidence concerning their effect.

After estimating the gross profit margin, one can derive the dollar value of earnings before depreciation and taxes (EBDT) by applying this gross margin estimate to the previously estimated sales figure. The next step is to estimate aggregate depreciation.

Estimating Depreciation.   As shown in Table 12.8, the depreciation series has not experienced a decline since 1960. (Actually it has not declined since 1946.) This is not too surprising because depreciation expense is by definition a fixed cost related to the total amount of fixed assets in the economy which increases over time. Therefore, the relevant question for an analyst estimating depreciation is *not* whether it will increase or decrease, but by *how much will depreciation expense increase?*

One can use the recent *absolute* change or the recent *percentage* of change

[32] Gray, "Determinants of the Aggregate Profit Margin: A Comment," *Journal of Finance,* 31 no. 1 (March 1976): 163–165.

TABLE 12.8
Percentage Changes in Depreciation and Tax Rate for Standard & Poor's
Industrial Index, 1960–1982

Year	Depreciation	Percentage Change	NBT[a]	Income Taxes	Tax Rate
1960	2.56	—	6.27	2.87	45.8
1961	2.66	3.9	6.17	2.80	45.4
1962	2.89	8.6	6.99	3.16	45.2
1963	3.04	5.2	7.75	3.51	45.3
1964	3.24	6.6	8.55	3.70	43.3
1965	3.52	8.6	9.64	4.14	42.9
1966	3.87	9.9	10.22	4.35	42.6
1967	4.25	9.8	9.73	4.11	42.2
1968	4.56	7.3	11.30	5.14	45.5
1969	4.87	6.8	11.27	5.14	45.6
1970	5.17	6.2	9.64	4.23	43.9
1971	5.45	5.4	10.95	4.98	45.5
1972	5.76	5.7	12.71	5.90	46.4
1973	6.25	8.5	16.48	7.59	46.1
1974	6.86	9.8	19.83	10.22	51.5
1975	7.36	7.3	17.98	9.40	52.3
1976	7.58	3.0	20.90	10.21	48.9
1977	8.53	12.5	22.59	11.14	49.3
1978	9.64	13.0	25.18	12.14	48.2
1979	10.82	12.2	30.31	14.02	46.3
1980	12.37	14.3	29.79	13.67	45.9
1981	13.82	11.7	29.69	12.95	43.6
1982	15.19	9.9	24.07	10.89	45.2
Average	—	8.5	—	—	46.0

[a] NBT = net before tax

SOURCE: Reprinted by permission of Standard & Poor's.

as a guide to the future increase. Probably the biggest factor that could influence the series is recent capital expenditures, i.e., expenditures during year $t-1$ and $t-2$, because with accelerated depreciation these recent expenditures become dominant. The data in Table 12.8 indicate that the average percentage of increase in depreciation expense has been almost 9 percent, with most recent years falling in the 10 to 12 percent range.

After the analyst has estimated depreciation, the figure obtained is subtracted from the gross profit estimate. The result is a net earnings before taxes estimate.

Expected Tax Rate.   The annual tax rates are contained in Table 12.8. The tax rate series was steady during the initial years, declined during 1964–1967, and then returned to the 45–46 percent range in the early 1970s. In the mid 1970s, the rate increased to over 50 percent but has subsequently declined to the mid 40 percent range.

Estimating the future tax rate is difficult because it is heavily influenced by political action. Therefore, it is necessary to consider the current tax rate but also to evaluate recent tax legislation affecting business firms (e.g., tax credits, etc.).

Given an estimate of the tax rate, one minus this figure times the net before tax earnings estimate indicates the estimated net income for industrial corporations. This earnings per share is subsequently used with an earnings multiplier to arrive at an estimate of the future value for the aggregate market.

A Sample Estimate

This attempt at estimating earnings per share for the year is best described as casual since it is meant as an example of the procedure. The reader is welcome to check the figures for accuracy as an exercise in data gathering. The major steps are as follows:

1. Estimate the nominal GNP for 1984
2. Estimate sales for the S&P 400 Index based upon the GNP estimate
3. Estimate the gross profit margin for the S&P series, i.e., the profit margin before taxes and depreciation. This is based upon estimates of:
   a. Utilization rate in 1984 versus 1983
   b. Percentage of change in unit labor cost
   c. Change in the rate of inflation in 1984 over 1983
   d. Foreign trade as a percentage of GNP
4. Estimate depreciation for 1984
5. Estimate the average corporate tax rate for 1984.

Nominal GNP for 1984 is based upon an estimate for 1983 of approximately $3,311 billion. In 1984 the economy will be in its second year of expansion. Most economists expect the real GNP to increase by about 6 percent and the economy to experience a rate of inflation of approximately 5 percent. Therefore, nominal GNP is estimated to increase by about 11 percent in 1984 to $3,675 billion.

Corporate sales have typically followed nominal GNP as shown in Figure 12.1. During 1983, when nominal GNP increased by about 8 percent, S&P sales rose by about 10 percent to $366 per share. In 1984, with GNP rising 11 percent, one might estimate an increase in corporate sales of about 13 percent to $414 per share.

The gross profit margin increased to about 12 percent in 1983 compared to 11.78 percent in 1982. This increase was a function of an increase in the utilization rate from 69.8 in 1982 to over 75 percent during 1983, a lower rate of increase in unit labor cost (6.5 percent in 1983 versus 7.0 percent during 1982), and a lower rate of inflation of about 3.5 percent. For 1984 the outlook is for a further increase in the gross profit margin. There should be another increase in the utilization rate to about 83 percent. The outlook for the unit labor cost is moderate. Compensation per hour will increase, but gains in productivity are expected to be a little lower this late in the business expansion. Therefore, the outlook for unit labor cost is for an increase of about 7 percent. Finally, the average rate of inflation will probably increase from the low 1983 rate on a continual basis throughout the year. Therefore, the overall outlook is for a small increase in the gross profit margin from 12 percent in 1983 to 12.5 percent in 1984. Applying a 12.5 percent gross profit margin to the per share sales figure ($414) results in a net before taxes and depreciation of $51.75 (.125 × $414).

Depreciation during 1983 was approximately $16.50 per share. Because the utilization rate continues to increase, the outlook is for an increase in capital expenditures of about 10 percent during 1984 and, therefore, a further increase in depreciation of 9 percent to $17.98. Thus the estimated net before taxes is $33.77 ($51.75 − $17.98).

The corporate tax rate during 1983 was apparently slightly higher than it was during 1982. Because no major corporate tax legislation is pending, the outlook for 1984 is for a 46 percent tax rate. Applying a 46 percent rate to the NBT figure of $33.77 indicates that net income will be approximately $18.24 during 1984. Because the estimating procedure is admittedly casual, the figure used in future discussions is $18.25 a share.

ESTIMATING THE EARNINGS MULTIPLE FOR THE AGGREGATE STOCK MARKET

Many analysts, when attempting to estimate the future value of the aggregate stock market, concentrate their efforts on the earnings estimate, thereby implicitly assuming that the value of the market will move with the earnings changes (i.e., the aggregate earnings multiple is constant over time). Reilly and Drzycimski contended that it is incorrect to assume that the multiple is stable because there has been *more volatility* in the *earnings multiple series* over time than in the earnings series.[33] The evidence also indicated that the multiple series turned *before* the earnings series did. Therefore, it is obviously important to consider the variables that influence the earnings multiple and to attempt to project them.

Determinants of the Market Earnings Multiple

The factors that influence the earnings multiple depend upon the earnings figure used. If the earnings multiple is being applied to the true *expected* earnings figure that takes into account *all future earnings growth,* then the earnings multiple is only a function of the required rate of return on the investment. In the more typical real world situation, investors apply an earnings multiple to near-term future earnings (earnings for the following year). In the latter case, it is necessary to adjust the earnings multiple to take into account long-run future growth expectations.

Multiplier Determinants without Growth.   Assume that no growth opportunities exist or that all future growth expectations have been included in the

---

[33] Frank K. Reilly and Eugene F. Drzycimski, ''Aggregate Market Earnings Multiples over Stock Market Cycles and Business Cycles,'' *Mississippi Valley Journal of Business and Economics,* 10 no. 2 (Winter 1974/75): 14 – 36. Recent evidence of this greater volatility is contained in Table 12.1.

expected earnings figure. Under these assumptions the earnings multiplier, given an infinite time horizon, becomes $1/i$, where i is the total required return on the investment. The multiplier is inversely related to the required rate of return; the higher the required rate of return an investor wants, the less he will pay for current and future earnings. On several previous occasions (in Chapters 1 and 10) we discussed the factors that determine the required rate of return on an investment: (1) the economy's risk-free rate (RFR); (2) the expected rate of inflation during the period of investment (I); and (3) the risk premium (RP) for the specific investment being considered. The reader will recall that we combined the first two factors (the RFR and I) into a *nominal risk-free rate* which affects *all* investments. In turn the "real" RFR rate is influenced for short periods, by liquidity in the capital markets but is determined in the long run by the real growth rate of the economy.

Obviously the major factor that has caused and that will continue to cause changes in the nominal RFR is changes in the rate of inflation. Because investors forgo current consumption to increase future consumption by some rate (i.e., the real RFR), they are looking for increases in *real* goods. Therefore, if there is a change in the rate of inflation, investors should increase their nominal rate of return by the same amount. Actually, the nominal RFR should equal:

$$\text{Nominal RFR} = (1 + \text{Real } RFR)(1 + I) - 1 .$$

As an example, if the real RFR were 3 percent and you expected the rate of inflation during your period of investment to be 8 percent, your nominal rate of return would be 11.24 percent $[(1.03)(1.08)] - 1$.[34] A good proxy for the nominal risk-free rate is the current promised yield to maturity of a government bond that has a maturity equal to your investment horizon. For example, if you had a short horizon, you could use the rate on treasury bills, while you would use the long-term government bond rate if your horizon extended over several years.

The major factor causing differences in required return for alternative investments is the risk premium. In the valuation of common stocks, it is necessary to consider the "normal" risk premium for stocks and then to determine whether current conditions are such that the normal premium should prevail. This analysis should indicate the current risk premium. Given this current premium, it is necessary to determine whether the risk premium will change during the subsequent period.

Regarding the normal risk premium for common stocks, a study by Ibbotson and Sinquefield estimated the equity risk premium as the difference in annual rates of return from common stocks and treasury bills.[35] They found that the geometric mean of this risk premium for the period 1926–1981 was 6.1 percent. Given this long-run historical estimate, it is possible to determine what the normal expected return should be by combining this premium with the nominal RFR. As an example, assume that the current yield on government bonds with the appropriate maturity is 10 percent. If you consider the current equity-market

---

[34] The appendix to this chapter contains an extensive discussion of common stocks and inflation.

[35] Roger G. Ibbotson and Rex A. Sinquefield, *Stocks, Bonds, Bills, and Inflation: The Past and The Future* (Charlottesville, Va.: Financial Analysts Research Foundation, 1982).

environment normal, you would estimate the current required return on common stock to be about 16 percent. Obviously, the important question is whether the expected rate of inflation or the risk premium on common stock will change during the investment horizon so as to change the required returns.

You will recall that in Chapters 1 and 10 we discussed the factors that influence the risk premium on investments from a fundamental point of view and also considered a market-derived risk variable. Specifically, the intrinsic determinants of the risk premium were business risk (BR), financial risk (FR), and liquidity risk (LR). Alternatively, as shown in Chapter 9, one can derive a market measure of risk that was shown to be the covariance of an asset with the market portfolio of risky assets. Because a stock market index is typically used as the market portfolio, *the relevant measure of market risk is the variance of returns for stocks.* Therefore, when there is a change in the variability of stock prices, one would expect a change in the risk premiums on stocks.

The required return on common stocks can therefore be stated as:

$$i_{cs} = f(RFR, I, BR, FR, LR)$$

or

$$i_{cs} = f(RFR, I, \sigma_m^2) \ ,$$

where:

i_{cs} = the required return on common stocks

RFR = the economy's risk-free rate of return

I = the expected rate of inflation

BR = aggregate corporate business risk

FR = aggregate corporate financial risk

LR = aggregate stock market liquidity risk

σ_m^2 = market risk for common stocks measured as the variance of returns.

Multiple Determinants with Growth.　In the more realistic situation in which the earning and dividend streams are growing, and/or investors do not fully adjust the expected earnings figure for all future growth, the earnings multiple must take into account the expected growth rate $(\bar{g})$ for the common stock earnings stream.[36] There is a positive relationship between the earnings multiplier and the rate of growth; i.e., the higher the expected growth rate, the higher the multiple. It is important, when attempting to estimate an earnings multiplier for the aggregate market, to consider the expected rate of growth during the investment horizon period and estimate any *changes* in the rate. Such changes

---

[36] The reader will recognize that the g in the valuation model is the expected growth rate for dividends. In most of the present discussion it is assumed that there is a relatively constant dividend payout ratio (dividend/earnings), so the growth of dividends is dependent on the growth in earnings and the growth rates are approximately equal.

364

will indicate a change in the relationship between i and g and will have a profound effect on market value.

A firm's growth rate has been shown to be a function of: (1) the proportion of earnings retained and reinvested by the firm, and (2) the rate of return earned on investments.[37] In fact, assuming an all-equity firm, it can be shown that the expected growth rate (g) is equal to the product of the retention rate expressed as a percentage (b), times the rate of return on equity investments (ROE). The multiplier should be positively related to both of these variables, because an increase in either or both of them causes an increase in the growth rate and an increase in the multiplier. Therefore, the growth rate can be stated as:

$$g = f(b, ROE)$$

where:

g = expected growth rate

b = the expected retention rate equal to $1 - \dfrac{D}{E}$

ROE = the expected return on equity investments.

Because the multipler (M) is a function of i and g, this can be summarized as:

$$M = f(RFR, I, BR, FR, LR, b, ROE)$$

or

$$M = f(RFR, I, \sigma^2, b, ROE).$$

Estimating Changes in the Growth Rate

When attempting to estimate changes in the growth rate, it is necessary to examine the basic factors that determine this rate. Recall that the growth rate (g) was a function of the retention rate (b), and the return on equity (ROE): $g = f(b, ROE)$. Therefore, you must first estimate changes in the aggregate retention rate. The figures in Table 12.9 indicate that this series was relatively constant in the 45–50 percent range prior to an increase in 1972–1974 that accompanied large earnings increases. It remained around 56–60 percent until 1982. Because the valuation model is a long-run model, it is important to consider only changes that are relatively permanent, although short-run changes can affect expectations.

The second variable of interest is changes in the return on equity (ROE)

[37] For an excellent discussion of alternative growth models, see Ezra Solomon, *The Theory of Financial Management* (New York: Columbia University Press, 1963), 55–68. A further discussion of growth models, with consideration of outside financing, is contained in Merton Miller and Franco Modigliani, "Dividend Policy, Growth, and the Valuation of Shares," *Journal of Business*, 34 no. 4 (October 1966): 411–433. Also, see Manown Kisor, Jr., "The Financial Aspects of Growth," *Financial Analysts Journal*, 20 no. 2 (March–April 1964) and Guilford Babcock, "The Concept of Sustainable Growth," *Financial Analysts Journal*, 26 no. 3 (May–June 1970).

TABLE 12.9
Factors Influencing the Aggregate Growth Rate of Corporate Earnings per Share
Standard and Poor's 400 Index, 1960–1982

Year	Dividend per Share	Percentage Change	Retention Rate	Equity Turnover	Net Profit Margin	Return on Equity
1960	2.00	—	41.2	1.76	5.72	10.08
1961	2.07	3.5	38.6	1.71	5.66	9.67
1962	2.20	6.2	42.6	1.78	5.93	10.53
1963	2.36	7.2	44.3	1.79	6.19	11.11
1964	2.58	9.3	46.8	1.82	6.63	12.06
1965	2.82	9.3	48.7	1.85	6.82	12.64
1966	2.95	4.6	49.7	1.94	6.64	12.88
1967	2.97	.7	47.1	1.92	6.12	11.76
1968	3.16	6.4	48.7	2.02	6.07	12.27
1969	3.25	2.8	47.0	2.10	5.65	11.86
1970	3.20	−1.5	41.8	2.09	4.92	10.28
1971	3.16	−1.2	47.1	2.14	5.04	10.80
1972	3.22	1.9	52.9	2.21	5.30	11.71
1973	3.46	7.5	61.1	2.37	5.96	14.15
1974	3.71	7.2	61.4	2.69	5.28	14.17
1975	3.72	.3	56.6	2.61	4.63	12.11
1976	4.22	13.4	60.5	2.66	5.27	14.02
1977	4.95	17.3	56.8	2.73	5.11	13.93
1978	5.37	8.5	58.8	2.81	5.19	14.60
1979	5.92	10.2	63.7	2.96	5.57	16.50
1980	6.49	9.6	59.7	3.02	4.92	14.88
1981	7.01	8.0	58.1	2.97	4.86	14.42
1982	7.13	1.7	45.9	2.82	3.95	11.16
Average	—	6.0	51.3	2.29	5.54	12.50

SOURCE: Reprinted by permission of Standard & Poor's.

defined as:

$$ROE = \frac{\text{Net Income}}{\text{Equity}}.$$

This return can be broken down into components as follows:

$$\frac{\text{Net Income}}{\text{Equity}} = \frac{\text{Sales}}{\text{Equity}} \times \frac{\text{Net Income}}{\text{Sales}} = \left(\frac{\text{Equity}}{\text{Turnover}}\right) \times \left(\frac{\text{Net Profit}}{\text{Margin}}\right).$$

This identity indicates that the two factors affecting the return on equity are the
equity turnover and the *net profit margin* on sales. A firm, or the aggregate
economy, can improve its return on equity and, thereby, its growth rate by *either*
increasing its equity turnover or increasing its net profit margin. The figures in
Table 12.9 and the time series plot in Figure 12.3 indicate that the aggregate
return on equity for the S&P 400 index increased from about 10 percent to over
fifteen percent prior to a decline in 1982. The increase is *completely* attributable

FIGURE 12.3
Time Series Plot on Return on Equity for Standard & Poor's 400 Index, 1960–1982.

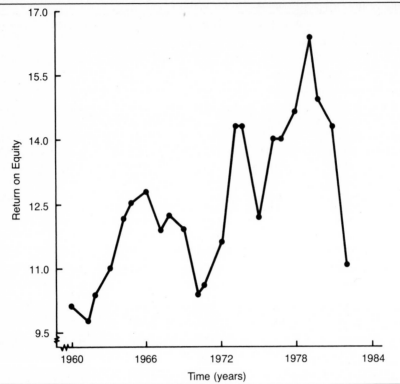

to the increase in the equity turnover from about 1.7 to almost 3.0, which more than offset the overall *decline* in the net profit margin during this period. One must ask what caused the increases in equity turnover and whether the increases can continue. To derive some understanding in this regard, it is useful to break the equity turnover into its components as follows:

$$\frac{\text{Sales}}{\text{Equity}} = \frac{\text{Sales}}{\text{Total Assets}} \times \frac{\text{Total Assets}}{\text{Equity}}$$

$$= (\text{Total Asset Turnover}) \times (\text{Financial Leverage}).$$

Again, this is an identity and indicates that one can increase the equity turnover by increasing the total asset turnover and/or by increasing financial leverage. The point is, it is entirely possible to have no increase in operating efficiency, as shown by an increase in total asset turnover, but to experience an increase in equity turnover simply by increasing the proportion of total assets financed with debt. In other words, because assets must be financed by either debt or equity, if the ratio of total assets to equity increases, the proportion financed with debt must have increased.

During a period of inflation, it is possible that both of the components increase and contribute to the higher equity turnover. Total asset turnover has an upward bias, because sales will be influenced more by inflation than the book value of total assets will. Unfortunately, the data provided on the S&P 400 series does not include information on total assets, so it is not possible to examine this breakdown between total asset turnover and financial leverage, but other sources indicate a secular increase in financial leverage since the 1960s.

A noteworthy point in this context is that return on equity has increased due to an increase in equity turnover. Therefore, it is important to understand the factors contributing to that increase and the consequent growth.

Summary of Microeconomic Multiple Estimate.   Such an estimate is begun with the current multiple and the direction and extent of the change is estimated based on expectations for the variables that influence the aggregate *i* and *g*. The *direction* of the change is probably more important than the extent of the change is. The overall estimate requires that an estimate be derived for each of the following component variables:

1. Dividend-payout ratio defined as dividend/earnings
2. Real RFR
3. Expected rate of inflation
4. Risk premium for common stock
5. Retention rate
6. Return on equity:
    a. Net profit margin
    b. Equity turnover.

As noted, in addition to estimating the level for each of these variables, the important thing to forecast is what *changes* will occur during the investment period. As stated previously, the crucial change is in *the size of the spread between* i *and* g. Note that it is possible to derive an estimate of the size of the spread as follows:

$$P = \frac{D_1}{i - g}$$

$$\frac{P}{D_1} = \frac{1}{i - g}$$

$$\frac{D_1}{P} = i - g.$$

Therefore, the prevailing dividend yield (using an estimate of the dividend for next year) is an estimate of the spread. Note that this does not indicate the two factors that determine the spread (i.e., the actual value of *i* and *g*), but it tells you the approximate difference between them.

Empirical Analysis of Determinants

A study by Reilly, Griggs, and Wong specified empirical proxies for the several variables in the equations above and analyzed the relationship during the period

1962–1980.[38] The earnings multiple series employed was the price-earnings ratio for the S&P 400 series. The P/E ratio was obtained by dividing the end of the period stock price index by the seasonally adjusted annual rate of earnings for the corresponding quarter.

The authors considered a dividend-payout ratio for the S&P 400 using actual dividends and earnings during the prior 12 months. The real RFR used was the Standard & Poor's average yield on AAA corporate bonds adjusted for inflation. The rate of inflation proxy was percentage changes in the CPI (all items). The rate of inflation was also included as a separate variable. There was no operating earnings series available, so the seasonally adjusted net income figure for the S&P 400 series was used. A 20 quarter moving coefficient of variation series was derived as a measure of business risk. On a macroeconomic basis there are no debt/total asset ratios or interest coverage figures. There were three financial risk proxies available: (1) a current ratio series from the *Federal Reserve Bulletin* (subsequently deleted based on initial analysis), (2) the failure rate per 10,000 U.S. firms, and (3) a debt-equity ratio series published by the Federal Trade Commission (FTC) for all industrial corporations. There was also a direct measure of the risk premium—i.e., the yield spread between BBB corporate bonds and AAA corporate bonds. They considered the absolute spread and the percentage spread.

Rather than examining the components of growth (*b* and ROE), a direct measure of actual growth in earnings per share during alternative past periods was employed similar to the variables used in several previous studies of individual firm P/E ratios.[39] The earnings per share figure employed was the S&P 400 index (seasonally adjusted quarterly figures). For each year, an average of the four quarters was derived and the percentage of change was computed. Average growth rates were derived for one-, three-, and five-year periods by computing the average percentage of change for each period on a moving basis.

The model included *percentages of change* for all variables, since the major questions of interest were what changes occurred in the earnings multiple and what variables influenced these changes.

In summary, the analysis considered:
- *M*   The earnings multiple for the S&P 400.
- *GR*   The growth rate in EPS for the S&P 400: *GR1*—one year; *GR3*—three years; *GR5*—five years.
- *RFR* The yield on Standard & Poor's AAA corporate bond series adjusted for inflation.
- *I*   The annualized rate of inflation as indicated by percentage changes in the CPI.
- *CV*   The coefficient of variation of EPS during the most recent 20 quarters.

[38] Frank K. Reilly, Frank T. Griggs, and Wenchi Wong, "Determinants of the Aggregate Stock Market Earnings Multiple," *Journal of Portfolio Management*, 10 no. 1 (Fall 1983): 36–45.

[39] Burton Malkiel, "Equity Yields, Growth, and the Structure of Share Prices," *American Economic Review*, 53 no. 5 (December 1963): 834–850; Burton Malkiel and John Cragg, "Expectations and the Structure of Share Prices," *American Economic Review*, 60 no. 4 (September 1970): 601–617; V. S. Whitbeck and M. Kisor, "A New Tool in Investment Decision-Making," *Financial Analysts Journal*, 19 no. 3 (May–June 1963): 55–62.

— *POR* The dividend-payout ratio for the S&P 400.
— *D/E* The debt-equity ratio for all industrial firms.
— *FLR* The failure rate per thousand firms as measured by the Department of Commerce.
— *YS1* The difference in yield to maturity for the S&P BBB corporate bond series and the S&P AAA corporate bond series.
— *YS2* The *ratio* of yield to maturity for the S&P BBB bond series to the S&P AAA corporate bond series.

The authors considered a coincident relationship among the variables and also a lagged model that considered the multiple in period *t* and the independent variables in period *t*-1. The lagged model is obviously more useful for predictive purposes. The best regression model using lagged variables had an R^2 of 0.25 and five variables had significant coefficients at the 10 percent level or better: (1) one-year growth, (2) payout ratio, (3) real risk-free rate, (4) inflation, and (5) failure rate. All coefficients had the expected sign except the failure rate. The results were similar with a multiple discriminant analysis model (MDA).

An analysis of the ability of the lagged model (with the coefficient of variability of earnings and the debt-equity ratio added) to predict the direction of change for the earnings multiple indicated that the model provided correct predictions during 24 of 32 quarters. (The best MDA model had 23 of 32.) When this predictive model was used to make investment decisions (i.e., buy stocks or T-bills) compared to a buy-and-hold portfolio, the results were clearly superior after commissions: a 9.83 percent annual rate of return for the predicting model versus 1.85 percent for the buy-and-hold strategy. The standard deviation for the predictive model portfolio was *lower*. The predicting model also had a higher rate of return than T-bills but also higher risk.

It was concluded that it is possible to specify macroeconomic variables that influence changes in the aggregate stock market earnings multiple and a fairly simple multiple regression model generates strong correlations. Notably, the success of the predicting model was very encouraging and generated risk-adjusted returns in an investment simulation that were clearly superior to buy and hold.

Estimating the Multiple.   It is possible, therefore, to conceive of two approaches to estimating an aggregate stock market earnings multiple: (1) a macro approach using the variables suggested in the Reilly, Griggs, and Wong study, or (2) a micro approach in which you consider the specific variables that influence *i* and *g* and attempt to estimate whether the spread between *i* and *g* will increase or decline in the future.

The idea is to begin with the current multiple and estimate the *direction* and extent of the change based on expectations for either the macro variables or the micro variables that influence the aggregate *i* and *g*. The direction of the change is probably more important than the extent of the change.

The macro approach.   The major variables that must be estimated are:
1.   Changes in the growth rate of earnings
2.   Changes in the dividend-payout ratio

3. Changes in the real risk-free interest rate as represented by a high-grade corporate bond series.
4. Changes in the rate of inflation
5. Changes in the failure rate for U.S. corporations.

During 1984, the economy will be in its second full year of an expansion. Although it will only be in its second year, some of the changes will be adverse *relative* to the initial year of the expansion, 1983. The growth rate of earnings will be quite respectable and will exceed the growth during 1983 which approximated 12 percent. Likewise, although there will be a healthy increase in dividend payments, the increase may not match the increase in earnings gains. Therefore, the dividend-payout ratio will probably decline slightly. The real risk-free interest rate will be under some pressure to increase due to higher productivity. The rate of inflation peaked in 1981, dropped sharply in 1982, and declined further during 1983 to about 3.2 percent. The inflationary outlook for 1984 is for an increase to about 5 percent as the expansion continues. Finally, the failure rate should be declining due to the economic expansion. In summary:

— The one-year growth rate will increase relative to 1983
— The dividend-payout ratio will decline
— The real risk-free interest rate will increase
— The inflation rate will increase
— The failure rate will decline.

Overall, the consensus would be for a decline in the earnings multiple relative to 1983. This is not very surprising when one considers what happened to the multiple during 1982 and 1983 relative to 1981. At the end of 1981 the multiple was about 8, and it increased to almost 12 in 1982 and was about the same at the end of 1983. This represents a 50 percent increase in just two years. Therefore, assuming a multiple of about 12 at the end of 1983, one might expect the multiple at the end of 1984 to be about 10.5.

The micro approach.   The major variables that must be estimated are:
1. Changes in the dividend-payout ratio
2. Changes in the real RFR
3. Changes in the market risk premium
4. Changes in the rate of inflation
5. Changes in the retention rate
6. Changes in the return on equity.

As indicated in the macro discussion, the dividend-payout ratio will be stable or will decline. The next three variables deal with the required rate of return. As discussed above, there will be an increase in the real RFR due to higher real growth. Likewise, the rate of inflation will increase. Finally, the risk premium should be relatively stable during this phase of the cycle. Therefore, there should be an increase in i during 1984.

The last two factors relate to the growth rate. Because we expect a decline in the payout rate, this implies an increase in the retention rate. The outlook for the ROE during 1984 is for an increase since it is a function of the profit margin and equity turnover. The profit margin in 1984 will increase relative to 1983. There should also be a higher equity turnover ratio. Therefore, the outlook is for an increase in the growth rate. In summary:

— A decline in the payout ratio
— A clear increase in the required return, *i*
— A small increase in the growth rate.

Overall, this would imply a decline in the earnings multiple. This is consistent with the macro estimate.

Based upon this background, consider the following estimate using the dividend-growth model version of the multiple:

$$P/E = \frac{D/E}{i - g}$$

As indicated earlier, the retention rate has fluctuated between 55 and 60 percent during the past five years (except for 1982). Therefore, a reasonable dividend-payout ratio (*D/E*) would be 45 percent.

An empirical estimate for the required return (*i*) can be derived from knowledge of the interest rate on long-term goverment bonds plus an estimate of the risk premium for common stocks. An approximate rate on long-term government bonds during the initial months of 1984 was 12 percent. In turn, an appropriate risk premium could range from 3 percent to 6 percent. The 6 percent is the long-term average risk premium as indicated by the Ibbotson-Sinquefield study for the period 1926–1981. Notably, during the recent period (1975–1981), the risk premium has been more in the range of 2.5–3.5 percent. Therefore, the required return (*i*) should be in the range of 15–18 percent (i.e., 12 percent plus 3 or 6 percent risk premium).

The estimate of growth should be based upon the current and expected return on equity (ROE) and the rate of retention. As shown by the data in Table 12.9, the ROE for the Standard & Poor's 400 was in the 14–16 percent range during the period 1976–1981, prior to a decline in 1982. Assuming that 1984 is part of an economic expansion, a figure of 14–15 percent seems appropriate. As indicated earlier, the retention rate has been between 55 and 60 percent. Therefore, a lower figure would combine the 55 percent retention rate and 14 percent: $.55 \times .14 = .077$. An upper estimate would combine the 60 percent retention rate and a 15 percent ROE: $.60 \times .15 = .09$. To summarize:

> *D/E* = .40 to .45
> L. t. govt. bonds   .12
> Equity risk premium   .03 to .06
> Required return (*i*)   .15 to .18
> ROE   .14 to .15
> Sustainable growth   .077 to .09

By combining the most optimistic figures we can derive a reasonably generous estimate. Alternatively, we can derive a relatively low estimate using the lower estimates. Notably, the *D/E* figure should be consistent with the retention rate.

High Estimate: $D/E = .40$

$$i = .15$$

$$g = .09 \ (.60 \times .15 \ \text{ROE})$$

$$P/E = \frac{.40}{.15 - .09} = \frac{.40}{.06} = 6.67$$

If we had used a payout of .45, it would have been:

$$.45/.06 = 7.5$$

Low estimate: $D/E = .45$

$$i = .18$$

$$g = .077 \ (.55 \times .14)$$

$$P/E = \frac{.45}{.18 - .077} = \frac{.45}{.103} = 4.37$$

Therefore, these data imply a range of earnings multiples from about 4.5 to 7.5. These are definitely below that estimated using the macro approach.

Putting It Together.   Previously, we derived an estimate of earnings per share for the Standard & Poor's 400 of $18.25. Clearly, it would have been possible to derive several additional estimates in addition to this point estimate.

Our prior discussion has generated several estimates for the price earnings multiple that vary from about 4.5 to 7.5 to 10.5. Combining these indicates the following estimates for the Standard & Poor's 400 market series:

$$4.5 \times \$18.25 = 82.125$$

$$7.5 \times \$18.25 = 136.875$$

$$10.5 \times \$18.25 = 191.625$$

These estimates are intended to help you understand the procedure. The estimation of the relevant variables was very casual and certainly was not as extensive as one would like in practice. In addition, this was a point estimate for earnings rather than a range of estimates (pessimistic, optimistic, most likely) which would be preferable in this instance. The important point is to understand *what the relevant variables are* and *how these variables relate to either corporate earnings or the earnings multiple.*

SUMMARY

In earlier chapters we emphasized the importance of analyzing the aggregate stock market before an industry or a company analysis. It is very important to determine whether the market outlook justifies investing in stock at all before you consider the best industry or company to invest in. The purpose of this chapter was to present techniques that will assist you in making that decision.

The techniques can be described as either macro techniques, which are based upon the strong relationship between the aggregate economy and the stock market, or micro techniques, which attempt to determine future market values by applying basic valuation models to the aggregate stock market.

The discussion indicated that there is a strong, consistent relationship between the behavior of the aggregate economy and that of the stock market, but it also noted that the stock market generally turned before the economy did. Therefore, the macro techniques emphasized using series that likewise led the economy and possibly the stock market. We discussed the NBER leading indicator series (which includes stock prices) and a study that specifically used a composite of the leading series to predict stock prices. It was shown that the NBER leading indicator series could be useful if the analyst could choose an appropriate filter. Unfortunately, without this ability, the investment results were similar to those from a buy-and-hold policy.

The second macro technique considered was using the money supply to predict aggregate market behavior. Extensive research has indicated that changes in the growth rate of the money supply lead the economy by several months, and the average lead appeared to be even longer than the lead of stock prices relative to the economy. In addition, theoretically, monetary changes should have an impact on financial markets. A review of the numerous empirical studies in this area indicated that these assumptions may be in error. Specifically, the earlier studies indicated a strong relationship between money supply and stock prices and indicated that money supply changes generally *led* stock prices. In contrast, more recent studies confirmed the link between money supply and stock prices, but they generally indicated that stock prices turned coincidentally with or before money supply changes, as one might expect in a world with efficient capital markets. These later results imply that money supply changes have an important impact on stock prices, but it is not possible to use the money supply in a mechanical way to predict stock price changes.

The micro technique involved applying the basic dividend valuation model discussed in Chapter 10 to the aggregate stock market. We discussed how to derive an estimate of earnings per share for a market series and an estimate of an earnings multiplier. Given these two components, it is possible to compute an estimate of the future value for the market and to derive an expected return for common stocks during the period. It is important to recognize that the procedure generated only a best estimate, and it is appropriate to make several estimates that reflect various possible conditions. This micro technique is best summarized by outlining the steps used in the earnings multiple approach as outlined below.

Outline of Earnings Multiple Approach to Projecting Aggregate Stock Market Values

I. Estimate Expected Earnings

A.   Estimate nominal GNP for year
  1.   Estimate real GNP
  2.   Estimate inflation rate.

B. Estimate corporate sales based upon relationship to GNP
C. Estimate aggregate operating profit margin (NBDT/sales)
   1. Utilization rate
   2. Unit labor cost
     a. Wage/hour increases
     b. Productivity changes
   3. Inflation
   4. Trade surplus.
D. Estimate net profits
   1. Compute operating profits (operating profit margin times sales)
   2. Subtract estimated depreciation
   3. Estimate taxes (tax rate times NBT)
   4. Subtract taxes.

II. Estimate the Expected Earnings Multiple

A. Estimate changes in the required return (i)
   1. Changes in the risk-free rate (ΔRFR)
   2. Changes in the risk premium (ΔRP)
     a. Changes in business risk
     b. Changes in financial risk
     c. Changes in liquidity risk, or
     d. Changes in stock price volatility
   3. Changes in the expected rate of inflation (ΔI).
B. Estimate changes in the expected growth rate (Δg)
   1. Changes in the aggregate earnings retention rate
   2. Changes in the return on equity
     a. Changes in equity turnover
     b. Changes in profit margin
C. Estimate changes in the spread between i and g

III. Estimate Market Value

A. Estimated earnings times estimated earnings multiple.

Following this aggregate market analysis, you are ready to make a decision as to whether to commit part of your portfolio to stocks during the forthcoming investment period. If the answer is affirmative, the next step in the analysis procedure is industry analysis, which is considered in the following chapter.

QUESTIONS

1. Why would you expect there to be a relationship between economic activity and stock price movements?
2. While at a social gathering you discuss the reason for the relationship between the economy and the stock market, but one of the listeners points out that stock prices typically turn *before* the economy does. How would you explain this phenomenon?

3. Define leading, lagging, and coincident indicators. Give an example of each and discuss why you think it is classified as such, i.e., the economic reasons for a relationship between this series and the economy.

4. Discuss a diffusion index of leading series and why you might expect it to be useful in predicting stock market movements.

5. Assuming that changes in monetary growth *should* effect stock price movements, what argument would an advocate of the efficient market hypothesis set forth regarding use of the monetary series to predict stock price changes?

6. Is it a contradiction to say that there is a strong, consistent relationship between money supply changes and stock prices and yet also say that money supply changes cannot be used to predict price movements?

7. At a social gathering you are talking to another investor who contends that the stock market will experience a substantial increase next year because it is estimated that corporate earnings are going to rise by at least 12 percent. Would you agree or disagree with the investor? Why or why not?

8. Go the the library and find at least *three sources* of *historical* information on nominal and real GNP. Attempt to find two sources that provide an *estimate* of nominal GNP for the coming year or that gave one for the previous year.

9. Prepare a table for the last ten years showing the percentage of change each year in: (a) consumer price index (all items); (b) nominal GNP; (c) real GNP (in constant dollars); (d) the GNP deflator. Discuss what proportion of nominal growth was due to real growth and what part to inflation. Is the outlook for the coming year any different from that for last year? Discuss.

10. You are told that nominal GNP will increase by about 8 percent next year. Using Figure 12.2, what would you estimate to be the most likely increase in corporate sales? What would be your most optimistic estimate? Most pessimistic estimate?

11. Given that you eventually want to arrive at an estimate of the *net profit margin,* why do you spend time estimating the gross margin and working down?

12. The long-run trend for all the margins in Table 12.5 is downward. How would you explain this? What factors might account for the trend?

13. Compute the ratio of depreciation as a percentage of sales for the last ten years. What has been the trend in this series? What does this tell you about fixed costs per unit?

14. You are convinced that capacity utilization next year will decline from 91 percent to about 89 percent. What would you expect the effect of this to be on the gross profit margin? Explain your reasoning.

15. There are contrary arguments regarding the expected relationship between inflation and the aggregate profit margin. Briefly discuss the alternative arguments.

16. There are well-regarded estimates that hourly wage rates will increase by about 6 percent next year. How does this affect your estimate of the aggregate profit margin? Is there any other information you need to use this information? What is it and why do you need it?

17. It is estimated that hourly wage rates will increase by 7 percent and that productivity will increase by 5 percent. Approximately what would you expect to happen to unit labor cost? How would this estimate influence your estimate of the aggregate profit margin? Discuss.

18. There has generally been a strong cyclical pattern to productivity changes. Specifically, following a cyclical trough the gains in productivity are substantial,

while immediately following a peak the productivity gains are very slight or in some instances productivity declines. Discuss this phenomenon and why it occurs.

19. What is meant by this statement: "The factors that influence the earnings multiplier depends upon the earnings figure used."

20. Assuming no growth in earnings or that the earnings figure used is long-run expected earnings, what factors influence the earnings multiplier? Discuss each of the variables and indicate *how* and *why* they influence the multiplier.

21. In a CAPM world, a risky asset's *systematic* risk is supposed to be the relevant risk variable. How does this apply to the aggregate stock market? What should the measure be? Because of the measurement problems, what is the most likely measure?

22. Assume a growing earnings stream; what additional variables besides those concerned with required return must be considered to determine changes in the earnings multiplier? Discuss each of them.

23. Assume each of the following changes are independent and, except for this change, all other factors remain unchanged. In each case, indicate *what* will happen to the earnings multiplier and discuss *why* it should happen.
    a. There is an increase in the return on equity
    b. There is an increase in stock price volatility
    c. The aggregate debt-equity ratio increases
    d. The overall productivity of capital increases.

24. Currently, the dividend-payout ratio (D/E) for the aggregate market is 55 percent, the required return (i) is 14 percent, and the expected growth rate for dividends (g) is 9 percent:
    a. Compute the current earnings multiplier.
    b. You expect the D/E ratio to decline to 45 percent, but you assume there will be no other changes. What will be the P/E?
    c. Starting with the initial conditions, you expect the dividend-payout ratio to be constant but expect the rate of inflation to increase by 3 percent, while growth will increase by 2 percent. Compute the expected P/E.
    d. Starting with the initial conditions, you expect the dividend-payout ratio to be constant but expect the rate of inflation to decline by 3 percent, while growth will decline by 2 percent. Compute the expected P/E.

25. *CFA Examination I* (June 1983) There has been considerable growth in recent years in the use of economic analysis in investment management. Further significant expansion may lie ahead as financial analysts develop greater skills in economic analysis and these analyses are integrated more into the investment decision making process.

    The following questions address the use of economic analysis in the investment decision making process:
    a. 1. **Differentiate** among a leading, lagging, and coincident indicator of economic activity, and **give** an example of each.
        2. **Indicate** whether the leading indicators are one of the best tools for achieving above-average investment results. **Briefly justify** your conclusion.

(8 minutes)

b. Interest rate projections are used in investment management for a variety of purposes. **Identify** *three* significant reasons why interest rate forecasts may be important in reaching investment conclusions.

(6 minutes)

c. Assume you are a fundamental research analyst following the automobile industry for a large brokerage firm. **Identify** and **briefly explain** the relevance of *three* major economic time series, economic indicators, or economic data items that would be significant to automotive industry and company research.

(6 minutes)

REFERENCES

Andersen, Leonall C., and Jerry L. Jordan. "Money in a Modern Quantity Theory Framework." Federal Reserve Bank of St. Louis *Review.* 49 no. 12 (December 1967).

Auerbach, Robert D. "Money and Stock Prices." Federal Reserve Bank of Kansas City *Monthly Review.* (September–October 1976).

Auerbach, Robert D., and Jack L. Rutner. "Money and Income: Is There a Simple Relationship?" Federal Reserve Bank of Kansas City *Monthly Review.* (May 1975).

Arditti, Fred D. "Risk and the Required Return on Equity." *Journal of Finance.* 22 no. 1 (March 1967).

Babcock, Guilford. "The Concept of Sustainable Growth." *Financial Analysts Journal.* 26 no. 3 (May–June 1970).

Bolton, A. H. *Money and Investment Profits.* Homewood, Ill., Dow Jones-Irwin, 1967.

Butler, William F., Robert A. Kavesh, and Robert B. Platt, eds. *Methods and Techniques of Business Forecasting,* Englewood Cliffs, N. J.: Prentice-Hall, 1974.

Cooper, Richard V. L. "Efficient Capital Markets and the Quantity Theory of Money." *Journal of Finance.* 29 no. 3 (June 1974).

Finkel, Sidney R., and Donald L. Tuttle. "Determinants of the Aggregate Profits Margin." *Journal of Finance.* 26 no. 5 (December 1971).

Fisher, Lawrence. "Determinants of Risk Premiums on Corporate Bonds." *Journal of Political Economy.* 67 no. 3 (June 1959).

Fouse, William L. "Risk and Liquidity: The Keys to Stock Price Behavior." *Financial Analysts Journal.* 32 no. 3 (May–June 1976).

Friedman, Milton J. *The Optimum Quantity of Money and Other Essays.* Chicago: Aldine Publishing Co., 1969.

Friedman, Milton J., and Anna J. Schwartz. "Money and Business Cycles." *Review of Economics and Statistics.* 45 no. 1 Supplement (February 1963).

Gibson, W. E. "Interest Rates and Inflationary Expectations: New Evidence." *American Economic Review.* 62 no. 5 (December 1972).

Gibson, W. E. "Price-Expectations Effects on Interest Rates." *Journal of Finance.* 25 no. 1 (March 1970).

Gray, H. Peter. "Determinants of the Aggregate Profit Margin: Comment." *Journal of Finance.* 31 no. 1 (March 1976).

Gray, William S. III. "Developing a Long-Term Outlook for the U. S. Economy and the Stock Market." *Financial Analysts Journal.* 35 no. 4 (July–August 1979).

Gupta, Manak C. "Money Supply and Stock Prices: A Probabalistic Approach." *Journal of Financial and Quantitative Analysis.* 9 no. 1 (January 1974).

Hamburger, Michael J., and Lewis A. Kochin. "Money and Stock Prices: The Channels of Influence." *Journal of Finance.* 27 no. 2 (May 1972).

Harris, Maury, and Deborah Jamroz. "Evaluating the Leading Indicators." Federal Reserve Bank of New York *Monthly Review* (June 1976).

Heathcotte, Bryan, and Vincent P. Apilado. "The Predictive Content of Some Leading Economic Indicators for Future Stock Prices." *Journal of Financial and Quantitative Analysis.* 9 no. 1 (March 1974).

Hirsch, Michael D. "Liquidity Filters: Tools for Better Performance." *Journal of Portfolio Management.* 1 no. 1 (Fall 1975).

Homa, Kenneth E., and Dwight M. Jaffee. "The Supply of Money and Common Stock Prices." *Journal of Finance.* 26 no. 5 (December 1971).

Keran, Michael W. "Expectations, Money and the Stock Market." Federal Reserve Bank of St. Louis *Review.* 53 no. 1 (January 1971).

Kisor, Manown. "The Financial Aspects of Growth." *Financial Analysts Journal.* 20 no. 2 (March–April 1964).

The Liquidity Report (monthly). New York: Amivest Corporation.

Mabert, Vincent A., and Robert C. Radcliffe. "Forecasting—A Systematic Modeling Methodology." *Financial Management.* 3 no. 3 (Autumn 1974).

Malkiel, Burton. "Equity Yields, Growth, and the Structure of Share Prices." *American Economic Review.* 53 no. 5 (December 1963).

Malkiel, Burton G., and John G. Cragg. "Expectations and the Structure of Share Prices." *American Economic Review.* 60 no. 4 (September 1970).

Martin, Peter. "Analysis of the Impact of Competitive Rates on the Liquidity of NYSE Stocks." Economic staff paper 75 no. 3 Office of Economic Research, Securities and Exchange Commission (July 1975).

Meigs, A. James. *Money Matters.* New York: Harper & Row, 1972.

Miller, Merton, and Franco Modigliani. "Dividend Policy, Growth and the Valuation of Shares." *Journal of Business.* 34 no. 4 (October 1966).

Miller, Merton H. "Money and Stock Prices: The Channels of Influence, Discussion." *Journal of Finance.* 27 no. 2 (May 1972).

Moore, Geoffrey H. ed. *Business Cycle Indicators.* Princeton, N.J.: Princeton University Press, National Bureau of Economic Research, 1961.

Moore, Geoffrey H. "Stock Prices and the Business Cycle." *Journal of Portfolio Management.* 1 no. 3 (Spring 1975).

Moore, Geoffrey H., and Julius Shiskin. "Indicators of Business Expansions and Contractions." *Occasional Paper 103.* New York: National Bureau of Economic Research, 1967.

Palmer, Michael. "Money Supply, Portfolio Adjustments and Stock Prices." *Financial Analysts Journal.* 26 no. 4 (July–August 1970).

Pesando, James E. "The Supply of Money and Common Stock Prices: Further Observations on the Econometric Evidence." *Journal of Finance.* 29 no. 3 (June 1974).

Reilly, Frank K. "Companies and Common Stocks as Inflation Hedges." New York University Graduate School of Business, Center for the Study of Financial Institutions, *Bulletin.* (April 1975).

Reilly, Frank K., Frank T. Griggs, and Wenchi Wong. "Determinants of the Aggregate Stock Market Earnings Multiple." *Journal of Portfolio Management.* 10 no. 1 (Fall 1983).

Reilly, Frank K., and David Wright. "An Analysis of Aggregate Stock Market Liquidity." Paper presented at Eastern Finance Association Meeting, Boston, Mass. (April 1977).

Reilly, Frank K., and Eugene F. Drzycimski. "Aggregate Market Earnings Multiples over Stock Market Cycles and Business Cycles." *Mississippi Valley of Business and Economics.* 10 no. 2 (Winter 1974/1975).

Rogalski, R., and J. Vinco. "Stock Returns, Money Supply, and the Direction of Causality." *Journal of Finance.* 32 no. 4 (September 1977).

Rozeff, M. S. "Money and Stock Prices: Market Efficiency and the Lag Effect of Monetary Policy." *Journal of Financial Economics.* 1 no. 3 (September 1974).

Rozeff, M. S. "The Money Supply and the Stock Market." *Financial Analysts Journal.* 31 no. 5 (September–October 1975).

Seligman, Daniel. "A Bad New Era for Common Stocks." *Fortune.* (October 1971).

Shiskin, Julius. "Business Cycle Indicators: The Known and the Unknown." *Review of the International Statistical Institute.* 31 no. 3 (1963).

Solomon, Ezra. *The Theory of Financial Management.* New York: Columbia University Press, 1963.

Sprinkel, Beryl W. *Money and Markets: A Monetarist View.* Homewood, Ill.: Richard D. Irwin, 1971.

Sprinkel, Beryl W. *Money and Stock Prices.* Homewood, Ill.: Richard D. Irwin, 1964.

Standard & Poor's. *Analysts Handbook.* New York: Standard & Poor's Corporation, annually.

Suits, Daniel B. "Forecasting and Analysis with an Econometric Model." *American Economic Review.* 52 no. 1 (March 1962).

Whitbeck, V. S., and M. Kisor. "A New Tool in Investment Decision-Making." *Financial Analysts Journal.* 19 no. 3 (May–June 1963).

Yohe, W. P., and D. S. Karnosky. "Interest Rates and Price Level Changes, 1952–1969." Federal Reserve Bank of St. Louis *Review.* 51 no. 12 (December 1969).

Zarnowitz, Victor, and C. Boschan. "Cyclical Indicators: An Evaluation and New Leading Index." *Business Conditions Digest.* (May 1975).

Zarnowitz, Victor, and C. Boschan. "New Composite Indexes of Coincident and Lagging Indicators." *Business Conditions Digest.* (November 1975).

Common Stocks as an Inflation Hedge

One of the most pervasive bits of folklore on Wall Street prior to the 1970s was that common stocks were a good hedge against inflation. This assumption was called into question during the 1970s when very consistent empirical evidence indicated that common stocks had done very poorly during the periods of high inflation since 1966. In addition, several studies examined the long-run evidence and generally indicated that recent experience was not unique and that common stocks have consistently *not* been good inflation hedges. The purpose of this appendix is to explain under what conditions one might expect common stocks to be an inflation hedge, and to analyze the variables that determine whether stocks should be a hedge. Finally, we review some of the studies that examined the performance of common stocks as hedges during periods of significant inflation.

THE DIVIDEND VALUATION MODEL AND INFLATION

The reader is familiar with the following dividend valuation model:

$$P_i = \frac{D_1}{i_i - g_i}$$

where:

P_i = price of stock i

D_1 = expected dividend in period 1

i_i = the required rate of return on stock i

g_i = the expected growth rate of dividends for stock i

Using this simplified version of the model, it is possible to consider what will happen as a result of a change in expectations regarding inflation and what must happen in order for common stocks to be a complete hedge against inflation.

Complete Inflation Hedge Defined

A hedge is a transaction intended to safeguard against loss on another investment. A hedge against inflation then, is the acquisition of an asset that would be a safeguard against an increase in the general price level. It is an asset that generates a return equal to the increase in the general price level. Unfortunately, the traditional definition of an inflation hedge is incomplete when applied to common stock investments because it overlooks the *normal* required rate of return on an investment in common stocks *regardless* of the current rate of inflation.

Investors normally require a rate of return in line with the economy's risk-free rate of interest, as well as a return commensurate with the business and financial risks involved, or an added return for the stock's systematic market risk. The "normal" required rate does not take inflation into account; it is an inflation-free rate of return. Therefore, *in order for a stock to be a complete inflation hedge, its "real" rate of return must be equal to or greater than its normal required rate of return.* This can be represented as follows:

$$r' \geq i$$

where:

$r' =$ "real" rate of return. The "real" rate of return is the nominal rate of return during a period (r), adjusted for the rate of inflation during the period (I). Specifically:

$$= \frac{1 + \text{nominal rate of return}}{1 + \text{rate of inflation}} - 1$$

$$= \frac{1 + r}{1 + I} - 1$$

$i =$ normal rate of return for the risk class of stock assuming a zero rate of inflation

Assume that investors in common stock have a normal required return of 8 percent ($i = .08$); that the general price level is increasing at 4 percent ($I = .04$); and the nominal return from common stocks is 10 percent ($r = .10$). Under these conditions the "real" rate of return is 5.8 percent

$$(r' = \frac{1.10}{1.04} - 1 = .058).$$

When the real rate of return (.058) is compared to the normal required rate of return (.08) it is seen that the real rate is *below* the required rate and therefore, common stocks were *not* a complete inflation hedge during the period. If the nominal return had been 14.0 percent, the real return would have been 9.6 percent which, compared to the 8 percent normally required, would indicate that common stocks were a complete inflation hedge.

Therefore, when there is a change in the expected rate of inflation, *i will increase by this amount.* Given a change in the required return, the crucial question becomes *what will happen to the value of the asset* so that the investor will receive his required return? One possibility is that *nothing else will change* and the stock price will decline so that *i* will increase as follows:

$$\text{If } P = \frac{D_1}{i - g}$$

then,

$$i = \frac{D_1}{P} + g.$$

If nothing else changes, the *P must decline* until there is an increase in the D_1/P term to compensate for the increase in the required return. Clearly, during this period of adjustment the stockholder will experience negative returns.

Another possibility is that *the growth rate of dividends* (g) *will increase by the rate of inflation.* If this occurs, the stock price will not change because *the spread between* i *and* g *will not change. i* is still equal to:

$$i = \frac{D_1}{P} + g$$

The difference is that the dividend yield does *not* change because *P* does not change, but the growth rate has increased. Therefore, the return (*i*) has increased and the stock will be a complete inflation hedge. *g must increase by the change in the rate of inflation if the stock is to be a complete inflation hedge without the stock price declining.* This is the implicit assumption made by many who contend that common stocks will be an inflation hedge. An example is found in an article by Jahnke that employs the dividend model to explain changes in stock prices based upon changes in the spread between *i* and *g.*[1] He states, "Thus common stocks should serve as a hedge against inflation to the extent that changes in the rate of inflation are mirrored in the dividend growth rate."[2] The question then becomes, under what conditions will the growth rate increase in line with the rate of inflation?

Inflation and the Growth Rate

As discussed in Chapters 9 and 10, a firm's dividend growth rate is directly related to the firm's earnings growth rate. In turn, the earnings growth rate is a function

---

[1] William W. Jahnke, "What's Behind Stock Prices?" *Financial Analysts Journal,* 31 no. 5 (September–October, 1975), pp. 69–76.

[2] Ibid., p. 71.

of the retention rate (*RR*) and the return on equity (ROE) as follows:

$$g = RR \times \text{ROE}$$

Further, you will recall that it was shown that the ROE is composed of the equity turnover and the net profit margin as follows:

$$\text{ROE} = \frac{\text{Net Income}}{\text{Equity}} = \frac{\text{Sales}}{\text{Equity}} \times \frac{\text{Net Income}}{\text{Sales}}$$

$$= (\text{Equity Turnover}) \times (\text{Net Profit Margin})$$

Therefore, the growth rate will increase if there is an appropriate increase in one or several of the following variables:

1. the retention rate
2. the equity turnover
3. the net profit margin

You should probably not expect a major impact from changes in the retention rate because an analysis of the historical series indicates that this rate changes slowly over time. As shown in Table 12A.1, the retention rate was about 47–50 percent from 1965 to 1971. Beginning in 1973, it increased to the 60 percent range except for a drop in 1982. It can be shown that it would require a significant change in this rate to have the desired impact. Therefore, although you might hope for an increase in the retention rate during periods of inflation, it is clear that the major impact on the growth rate must come from an increase in the ROE.

As noted, the ROE is equal to the equity turnover times the net profit margin. During a period of inflation, there is a natural tendency (bias) for the equity turnover to increase because sales should be directly and quickly influenced by inflation, while changes in the level of equity capital will be slower to respond since it is composed of the historical equity figure plus changes due to earnings (minus dividends) and stock sales. This tendency for equity turnover to rise is reflected in the figures in Table 12A.1 which show an increase in equity turnover from about 2.0 during the period 1965–1970 to about 3.0 for the period 1979–1982 — i.e., on average the equity turnover increased by about 50 percent during this period. Therefore, this turnover variable would support a higher ROE.

The final variable required to change is the net profit margin. As a minimum we would want the profit margin to remain constant. In this instance, if sales increased in line with the rate of inflation and the profit margin was constant, net earnings would increase by the rate of inflation. Alternatively, it would be very desirable for the profit margin to increase since it would make a positive contribution to the ROE and growth in earnings. Unfortunately, the figures in Table 12A.1 do not provide support for either of these scenarios. As shown, the net profit margin has *declined* substantially from almost 7 percent in 1965–1966 to less than 5 percent in 1980–1981 and 4 percent in 1982. While the 1982 results are considered below normal, it is still clear that overall the trend in the net profit margin has been down.[3] Following, is a discussion of the *a priori* reasons for expecting stability or an increase in the profit margin.

---

[3] A study that considers a similar approach with modifications is Russell J. Fuller and Glenn H. Petry, "Inflation, Return on Equity, and Stock Prices," *Journal of Portfolio Management,* 7 no. 4 (Summer 1981): 19–25.

TABLE 12A.1
Annual Return on Equity for Standard & Poor's 400 with Components of ROE

Year	Retention Rate	Equity Turnover	Net Profit Margin	Return on Equity
1965	48.7	1.85	6.82	12.64
1966	49.7	1.94	6.64	12.88
1967	47.1	1.92	6.12	11.76
1968	48.7	2.02	6.07	12.27
1969	47.0	2.10	5.65	11.86
1970	41.8	2.09	4.92	10.28
1971	47.1	2.14	5.04	10.80
1972	52.9	2.21	5.30	11.71
1973	61.1	2.37	5.96	14.15
1974	61.4	2.69	5.28	14.17
1975	56.6	2.61	4.63	12.11
1976	60.5	2.66	5.27	14.02
1977	56.8	2.73	5.11	13.93
1978	58.8	2.81	5.19	14.60
1979	63.7	2.96	5.57	16.50
1980	59.7	3.02	4.92	14.88
1981	58.1	2.97	4.86	14.42
1982	45.9	2.82	3.95	11.16

SOURCE: Standard & Poor's *Analysts Handbook*.

Profit Margins and Inflation. Most literature dealing with the ability of corporations to hedge against inflation has considered the factors that influence the profit margin. There are three hypotheses offered to explain why given firms might be able to gain during periods of inflation: (1) the wage-lag hypothesis, (2) the net debtor hypothesis, and (3) fixed operating assets or raw materials.

The wage-lag hypothesis contends that sales prices can be raised immediately in response to an increase in the rate of inflation while wage rate increases lag because they are generally negotiated at yearly intervals. During the lag period, there is a shift in wealth from wage earners to firms, i.e., profit margins increase at the expense of labor. This effect should be relatively short-term because, eventually, the wage earners should gain during negotiations.

A second possibility is the net debtor-creditor hypothesis which contends that, during periods of inflation, there is a transfer of wealth from creditors to debtors because the money received by a creditor is reduced in value while a debtor pays off his obligation in lower valued money. Given the fixed nature of the obligations, the net debtor firm (i.e., monetary liabilities exceed monetary assets) will enjoy lower capital costs during the period of inflation. Assuming that the prices of products increase in line with the inflation, and that costs other than capital costs increase in line with inflation, the firm's average costs (including capital costs), will *not* increase in line with inflation. Hence, there will be *an increase in the firm's profit margin,* and the company's nominal earnings will increase by more than the rate of inflation.

Finally, one would expect an increase in relative profits when firms have significant operating assets or raw materials acquired prior to the period of inflation that will last throughout the period. Examples could be drawn from capital intensive firms or natural resource firms (e.g., coal, lumber, oil). In these cases, if the prices of products increase in line with inflation, and major material costs are constant, *the firm's profit margin will increase* and nominal earnings will rise at a rate in *excess* of the rate of inflation. In all cases in which a firm gains during a period of inflation this shows up as an *increase in the profit margin during the period.*

Empirical evidence regarding wage-lag hypothesis.   Kessel and Alchian reviewed past studies of this hypothesis and provided new evidence on the topic.[4] They disagreed with most evidence that supported the hypothesis because: (1) prior authors did not consider factors other than wages and prices; (2) the data was possibly inadequate; or (3) the beginning and ending points of the study caused biases. They tested the hypothesis by examining the proposition that firms with large annual wage bills would experience a greater increase in profits and stock prices than would firms with smaller wage bills, using data from the total period 1939–1952. The results did not support the hypothesis because they indicated that the average increase in equity was greater for firms with lower wage ratios. A multiple correlation analysis including the net debtor position also did not support the wage-lag hypothesis.

Cargill examined numerous wage and price series using spectral analysis to determine whether there was a consistent lead-lag relationship in the United States and England.[5] For the United States there was no particular wage-price relationship. In England the long-run intervals indicated evidence of a wage lag, while there was no relationship, for short-run intervals.

A study by Reilly that examined earnings and prices during the period 1947–1973 hypothesized that the wage-lag would be short-run because labor would eventually require compensation.[6] The analysis indicated that, with one exception, at peaks and troughs *the price series either turned ahead of or coincidentally with the wage series.* It was concluded that prices tended to turn before wages, but the wage-lag was generally short-lived.

Empirical evidence regarding net debtor hypothesis.   Kessel pointed out that net debtor firms would gain during a period of unanticipated inflation relative to creditor firms and that *large* debtors should gain more than small debtors should, while large creditors would lose more than small creditors would.[7] An analysis of bank shares and randomly selected industrial firms consistently sup-

---

[4] Reuben A. Kessel and Armen A. Alchian, "The Meaning and Validity of the Inflation-Induced Lag of Wages Behind Prices," *American Economic Review,* 50 no. 1 (March 1960): 43–66.

[5] Thomas F. Cargill, "An Empirical Investigation of the Wage-Lag Hypothesis," *American Economic Review,* 59 no. 5 (December, 1969): 806–816.

[6] Frank K. Reilly, "Companies and Common Stocks as Inflation Hedges," New York University Graduate School of Business, Center for the Study of Financial Institutions, *Bulletin* (April, 1975).

[7] Reuben A. Kessel, "Inflation-Caused Wealth Redistribution: A Test of a Hypothesis," *American Economic Review,* 46 no. 1 (March 1956): 128–141.

ported the hypothesis that, during periods of significant inflation, the stocks of debtor firms gained, while the stocks of creditor firms gained during periods of significant deflation.

DeAlessi employed five independent tests to determine whether net debtor firms in the United Kingdom gained during periods of unanticipated inflation during the years 1948–1957.[8] The results differed somewhat depending upon the sample and the definitions used for wealth and a firm's monetary position. Still, the overall test results *consistently supported the debtor-creditor hypothesis* during the years of significant inflation (i.e., 1949–1952 and 1956–1957).

Before one can judge the impact of the net debtor hypothesis on the aggregate market, it is necessary to determine the number of net debtor firms. DeAlessi examined the proportion of such firms in the U.S. and the U.K.[9] For the U.S., the data indicated that, from the mid-1930s through the mid-1950s, the proportion of net debtor firms was about 55 percent. Broussalian found a 50–50 split during the period 1948–1956.[10]

The studies supported the net debtor hypothesis during periods of significant unanticipated inflation but because only about half of U.S. firms are net debtors, the overall impact is probably minimal.

Empirical evidence on profit margins during inflation.   The discussion of the alternative theories indicates one might expect a positive relationship between profit margins and inflation, but the arguments are not overpowering because one would expect the wage-lag effect to be short-run and the net debtor effect will probably be minimal for the U.S. economy because only about half the firms are net debtors.

The prior discussion in this appendix on the profit margin series was not very encouraging based upon the long-run trend for the series. To completely document the relationship, the author examined the direct relationship between the level of the profit margin for the S&P 400 series and the rate of inflation (CPI) for the period 1960–1982. The correlation was -0.60. We also considered the annual percentage changes in the two series and the correlation was -0.11. These results confirm that profit margins do *not* increase during periods of inflation, and generally do not even remain stable, but in fact, appear to decline. Given the impact of the profit margin on ROE and the effect of ROE on growth, these results would not be very encouraging for those who expect common stocks to be inflation hedges.

EMPIRICAL EVIDENCE ON COMMON STOCKS AS INFLATION HEDGES

Analyzing common stocks in terms of their use as an inflation hedge presents several problems in terms of methodology, as previous studies have shown.

---

[8] Louis DeAlessi, "The Redistribution of Wealth by Inflation: An Empirical Test with United Kingdom Data," *The Southern Economic Journal,* 30 no. 4 (October 1963): 113–127.

[9] Louis DeAlessi, "Do Business Firms Gain from Inflation?" *Journal of Business,* 37 no. 2 (April 1964): 162–166.

[10] J. V. Broussalian, "Unanticipated Inflation: A Test of the Debtor-Creditor Hypothesis," Ph.D. dissertation, University of California, Los Angeles, 1961.

388

Before we attempt our own analysis, we would be well advised to examine some of them.

Problems in Inflation Hedge Analysis

The first problem is the fact that common stocks have been examined over extremely long time periods that include significant inflation, deflation, and relative price stability. This is a mistake because one would expect investors to periodically review their portfolio based upon new expectations so they are only interested in whether an investment is an inflation hedge during periods of significant inflation. They should not care about how common stocks perform as an inflation hedge during periods of price stability or price deflation. When one examines stock performance over an extended period, one finds that common stock prices increase faster than consumer prices during the *total* period. An analysis of common stocks during periods of *differential* price change indicates that common stocks do quite well during periods of price stability and this admirable performance offsets their very poor performance during most periods of significant inflation. However, *it is only the performance of common stocks during periods of significant inflation that is important to the investor looking for an inflation hedge.*

The second problem is that *an investor's normal required rate of return during a period of noninflation has generally been ignored.* Previous analyses implicitly assumed that returns on common stock only had to exceed the rate of inflation to be considered a good hedge. However, investors have a "normal" required rate of return on common stocks. Therefore, when inflation occurs, investors increase their required return by the rate of inflation. To determine whether common stocks have been a complete inflation hedge during a period of significant inflation, it is necessary to compare the "real" return on the stock (r') to the investor's normal required return (i). A good proxy for the long-run required return on common stocks is provided in the study by Ibbotson and Sinquefield.[11] They found that the nominal return on common stocks during the period 1926–1981 was 11.4 percent. When this nominal return is adjusted for the average rate of inflation of 3.1 percent, the estimated "real" rate of return was 8.1 percent.

RJS Studies.   Several studies by Reilly, Johnson, and Smith (RJS) considered whether common stocks have been complete inflation hedges during periods of significant inflation (annual rate above 3 percent). They divided the total time period into periods of significant inflation, relative noninflation, and deflation and determined what happened to stock prices during the periods of significant inflation. The results for several well-known stock price series during the period 1937–1973 indicated that during most of the periods of significant inflation, *real*

[11] Roger G. Ibbotson and Rex A. Sinquefield, *Stocks, Bonds, Bills and Inflation: The Past and Future,* 1982 ed. (Financial Analysts Research Foundation, Charlottesville, Va., 1982).

rates of return were negative even before allowing for a "normal" rate of return.[12] Based upon these results and subsequent analysis, the authors concluded that common stocks have generally *not* been a complete inflation hedge. A later study considered the tax effects and confirmed the prior results.[13] An analysis of total "real" rates of return on common stocks indicated that the worst results were derived during periods of significant inflation, while encouraging results were experienced during periods of price stability.[14] In addition, the authors examined the performance of a sample of individual stocks and the results were very consistent with the aggregate market results.[15]

Further Studies. A study by Oudet indicated that, during the total period 1953–1970, the rates of return on common stock were highest during the periods of least inflation and lowest during periods of high inflation.[16] As a crude confirmation of this phenomenon, the current author divided all years from 1916 to 1974 into years of significant inflation (over 3 percent increase in prices), years of deflation (over one percent decrease in prices), and years of relative price stability (between 3 percent increase and one percent decrease). The average of the annual changes in the S&P 500 during periods of significant inflation was −0.25 percent; the average change during years of price stability was +12.31 percent, while the average change during years of deflation was −0.34 percent.

Some studies examined international stock price series as inflation hedges. Branch examined stock price indexes, inflation rates, and industrial production rates for 22 industrialized countries for the total period 1953–1969 and concluded that stocks were a partial inflation hedge.[17] Unfortunately, during most of this period there was price stability, which means the results are not indicative of performance during significant inflation. Further, if one eliminates Chile (which had very inconsistent results) and divides the rest of the countries into those with low inflation (under 3 percent) and high inflation (over 3 percent), the results indicate that the average rate of stock price increase was 1.96 percent for the high inflation countries, and 7.16 percent for the low inflation countries. Apparently, investors were better off investing in low inflation countries.

[12] These results were contained in Frank K. Reilly, Glenn L. Johnson, and Ralph E. Smith, "Inflation, Inflation Hedges, and Common Stocks," *Financial Analysts Journal,* 26 no. 1 (January–February 1970): 104–110. The results were updated in, Frank K. Reilly, "Companies and Common Stocks as Inflation Hedges," New York University, Center for the Study of Financial Institutions, *Bulletin* (April 1975).

[13] Frank K. Reilly, Glenn L. Johnson, and Ralph E. Smith, "A Note on Common Stocks as Inflation Hedges — the After Tax Case," *Southern Journal of Business,* 7 no. 4 (November 1972): 101–106.

[14] Ralph E. Smith, Glenn L. Johnson, and Frank K. Reilly, "A Year-by-Year Analysis of 'Real' Rates of Return on Common Stocks," *Quarterly Review of Economics and Business,* 14 no. 1 (Spring 1974): 79–88.

[15] G. L. Johnson, F. K. Reilly, and R. E. Smith, "Individual Common Stocks as Inflation Hedges," *Journal of Financial and Quantitative Analysis,* 6 no. 3 (June 1971): 1015–1024; F. K. Reilly, G. L. Johnson, and R. E. Smith, "A Correction and Update Regarding Individual Common Stocks as Inflation Hedges," *Journal of Financial and Quantitative Analysis,* 10 no. 5 (December 1975): 871–880.

[16] Bruno A. Oudet, "The Variation of the Return on Stocks in Periods of Inflation," *Journal of Financial and Quantitative Analysis,* 8 no. 2 (March 1973): 247–258.

[17] Ben Branch, "Common Stock Performance and Inflation: An International Comparison," *Journal of Business,* 47 no. 1 (January 1974): 48–52.

A study by Cagan dealt with long-run returns from stocks for alternative countries.[18] He considered a combination of price change periods and, assuming that investors held common stocks through all periods, concluded that common stocks were a good inflation hedge in the long-run. A careful reading of the results indicates that stocks apparently did not do well during the periods of inflation, but eventually made up for the loss after the inflation was over.

Townsend analyzed the performance of stocks from 15 industries and 474 companies during the period 1965–1974.[19] He concluded that his results provided overwhelming evidence of the inability of all the selected industries and most of the individual companies (95 percent) to protect against declining purchasing power during the period 1965–1974.

A study by Jaffe and Mandelker examined the question by analyzing a series of regressions between rates of return on common stocks and the rate of inflation.[20] The results using monthly data for the period January 1953 to December 1971 consistently indicated a *significant negative* relationship for contemporaneous data or using data with various leads or lags. Somewhat different results were generated using annual data for the period 1875 to 1970 — i.e., the coefficients were positive but not statistically significant which implies no relationship. Overall these results indicate that common stocks are either a very poor hedge (negative) or simply not a positive hedge.

Nelson's study was very similar to Jaffe and Mandelker's since the major analysis involved the correlation of the monthly rates of return on common stocks and the rates of inflation using the CPI during the period 1953–1974.[21] Again, there were a number of leads and lags employed because of how the CPI is constructed (it is not a discrete series at two points in time, but derived on the basis of prices collected throughout the month), and because it is interesting to consider how investors react to old information and future expectations. Overall, the results indicated uniformly *negative and significant coefficients*. Such results are clearly not consistent with stocks as an inflation hedge. The author also examined market returns against a measure of "unanticipated" inflation. Again, the results indicated a negative impact of inflation on stock returns. Finally, because of the lagged effect of inflation on stock returns the author devised several prediction tests. The results indicated positive returns using the predicting models relative to buy-and-hold and other strategies, but transaction costs were not considered.

In the paper by Bodie, the author measures the effectiveness of common stocks as an inflation hedge as the proportional reduction in that variance attainable by combining a "representative" well-diversified portfolio of common

[18] Phillip Cagan, "Common Stock Values and Inflation—The Historical Record of Many Countries," *National Bureau Report Supplement* (New York: National Bureau of Economic Research, Inc., March 1974).

[19] James E. Townsend, "Relative Strengths of Common Stocks of Various Industries to Serve as Inflation Hedges," paper presented at Southwestern Finance Association Meeting, Houston, Texas, (March 1975).

[20] Jeffrey F. Jaffe and Gershon Mandelker, "The 'Fisher Effect' for Risky Assets: An Empirical Investigation," *Journal of Finance,* 31 no. 2 (May 1976): 447–458.

[21] Charles R. Nelson, "Inflation and Rates of Return on Common Stocks," *Journal of Finance,* 31 no. 2 (May 1976): 471–483.

stocks and a nominal bond in their variance minimizing proportions.[22] The tests include an analysis of the relationship between the real rate of return on equity and various specifications of inflation (i.e., anticipated; unanticipated). The results consistently indicated that there was a negative correlation between the real return on equity and both unanticipated and anticipated inflation. The author concluded:

> . . . the estimates seem to indicate that, contrary to a commonly held belief among economists, the real return on equity is negatively related to both anticipated and unanticipated inflation, at least in the short-run. This negative correlation leads to the surprising and somewhat disturbing conclusion that to use common stocks as a hedge against inflation one must sell them short.[23]

A more recent study by Gultekin is more encouraging using *forecasts* of inflation.[24] In contrast to earlier research, this study uses data from the Livingston survey of inflation expectations to test the effect of inflation in a pure form which relates *expected* stock returns to *expected* inflation. The results support the "Fisher Effect" which implies that rates of return on financial assets increase with the rate of inflation. Specifically, there was a strong positive relationship between expected stock market returns and expected inflation rates. He also derived a series of expected real returns on common stocks and found that this series is definitely not constant. Again, he found a positive correlation between expected inflation and the expected real return on common stocks.

It appears, then, that with one exception, the empirical studies indicate that common stocks have *not* been complete inflation hedges. They have generally been rather *poor investments* during periods of significant inflation. Apparently this poor performance for common stocks is because the growth rate in dividends has *not* kept up with the increases in the rate of inflation. In turn, the growth rate has not increased because profit margins have declined.

Effect on Industries and Companies

The foregoing has emphasized the necessity of examining the factors that should cause stocks to be inflation hedges. This is especially important when analyzing individual industries and companies because, although common stocks *in the aggregate* are not good inflation hedges, this does *not* mean that some individual industries or stocks cannot be. The analyst must examine alternative industries and companies within the industry to determine how the industry or company growth rate will be affected by inflation. Inflation will have different effects due to differences in the elasticity of demand, the wage component, the net debtor position, and the cost components of the industry or company.

---

[22] Zvi Bodie, "Common Stocks as a Hedge Against Inflation," *Journal of Finance,* 31 no. 2 (May 1976): 459–470.

[23] *Ibid.,* p. 470.

[24] N. Bulent Gultekin, "Stock Market Returns and Inflation Forecasts," *Journal of Finance,* 38 no. 3 (June 1983): 663–673.

392 QUESTION

CFA Examination III (June 1982) As an investment adviser you have just made a presentation to the investment committee of a large endowment fund. One of the members of the committee makes the following remarks to you.

"Bob, that was an interesting presentation that you made to our committee. I think I understand your expectation that a decline in the rate of inflation will be good for stocks. I still have some questions about how this will impact the required rate of return for stocks."

a. "Treasury bill rates have been dropping the past few weeks. Will this affect the required rate of return?" **Explain**.

b. "Some of the corporations we have been investing in have had their troubles with inflation. Would a reduction in the rate of inflation eventually change the required rate of return on stocks generally—as well as help the prices of those stocks directly benefited?" **Explain**.

c. "What will lower inflation rates do for the balance sheets of corporations and for the required rate of return?" **Explain**.

d. "How will a decline in inflation affect the stock market liquidity risk?" **Explain**.

(20 minutes)

Chapter 13   *Industry Analysis*

A sk an analyst what he does and he will typically reply that he is an oil analyst, a retail analyst, or a business machine analyst. Portfolio managers talk about being in or out of the oils, the autos, or the utilities. This is because most practitioners in the securities markets are extremely conscious of alternative industries and organize their analyses and portfolio decisions according to industry groups. In contrast, the results of academic research have been mixed in terms of indicating the usefulness of industry analysis. There have been several studies that have important implications for industry analysis, and we will begin our discussion with these studies of industry performance and risk. Subsequently, we will discuss what should be considered when analyzing alternative industries and how industries should be analyzed.

PREVIOUS STUDIES OF INDUSTRY ANALYSIS

Cross-Sectional Return Performance

Several studies have examined the performance of alternative industries during a specific period of time; e.g., how did different industries perform during 1984? Such studies have major implications for industry analysis, because if there is complete consistency over time for different industries, it would indicate that industry analysis is not necessary once a market analysis has been completed. Assume that, during 1984, the aggregate market rose by 10 percent and *all* industry returns were bunched between 9 and 11 percent. Under these conditions, one might ask how much it would be worth to find an industry that will return 11 percent when random selection would provide about 10 percent (the average return).

One of the first studies of industry performance was done by Latané and Tuttle, who examined the long-run price performance of 59 industries listed in the Standard & Poor's *Analysts Handbook* for the years 1950 and 1958 and for the month of October 1967.[1] The results indicated that, between 1950 and 1967, the aggregate market had increased by a factor greater than five times, but that *the difference between alternative industries was substantial,* ranging from a decline for one industry (brewing) to an increase of almost 40 times (office and business equipment). They also found that the wide dispersion between industries did not decline over time even with the growth of conglomerates.

These findings were confirmed in a study done by Brigham and Pappas of rates of return for 658 industrial and utility firms during the period 1946–1965.[2] After dividing the sample into 103 standard industrial classifications and examining the difference between industries, they concluded that, "an aggregate rate of return is by no means representative of all industries in the sample."[3]

Reilly and Drzycimski examined the performance of the 30 *Barron's* industry averages for the total period 1958–1970 and during selected subperiods.[4] The authors concluded that there was substantial divergence in relative performance among industries during any given time period.

There is consistent empirical evidence that industries do *not* perform in the same way over a long time period or over selected shorter subperiods.[5] This would imply that *industry analysis is a very necessary part of the valuation and portfolio management process.* It is clearly worthwhile to attempt to determine the differences in performance that can be expected for various industries.

Time Series Return Performance

This discussion naturally leads to our next question, whether industry performance is consistent over time. Do industries that perform well in one time period continue to perform well or at least continue to outperform the aggregate market? Latané and Tuttle examined the performance of individual industries and found *almost no association in industry performance over time.*[6] These results are confirmed in the Reilly–Drzycimski study that analyzed the relative performance of alternative industries for different types of market periods. They concluded that there was a *very low correlation* in industry performance over sequential rising or falling markets or over sequential periods irrespective of market behavior.[7] Tysseland examined the performance of 40 major industries

---

[1] Henry A. Latané and Donald L. Tuttle, "Framework for Forming Probability Beliefs," *Financial Analysts Journal,* 24 no. 4 (July–August 1968): 51–61.

[2] Eugene F. Brigham and James L. Pappas, "Rates of Return on Common Stock," *Journal of Business,* 42 no. 3 (July 1969): 302–316.

[3] Ibid., p. 311.

[4] Frank K. Reilly and Eugene Drzycimski, "Alternative Industry Performance and Risk," *Journal of Financial and Quantitative Analysis,* 9 no. 3 (June 1974): 423–446.

[5] Various financial services provide graphs of *annual* rates of return for alternative industries. Again, these indicate the substantial variance between industries.

[6] Latané and Tuttle, "Framework for Forming Probability Beliefs," *Financial Analysts Journal,* (July–August 1968).

[7] Reilly and Drzycimski, "Alternative Industry Performance and Risk," *Journal of Financial and Quantitative Analysis* (June 1974).

over the period 1949–1966 inclusive.[8] Rank correlations were used to test for the consistency of industry returns over successive time periods (one-, three-, six-, and nine-year periods). He found significant and positive results for short-run periods but negative results (with few exceptions) for longer periods of time.

These studies imply that it is not possible to use past performance to project future performance for an industry. Although this conclusion is consistent with the weak form efficient market hypothesis, it does *not* negate the usefulness of industry analysis. Such findings mean that it is not possible to simply extrapolate past performance and, therefore, it is necessary to *project* future industry performance on the basis of *future estimates* of the relevant variables.

Performance within Industries

The final relevant question with regard to industry performance is whether there is consistency *within* an industry. Do the firms within an industry experience similar performance during a specified time period? If the distribution of returns was consistent within an industry, it would reduce the need for company analysis since, once the industry analysis was complete, one could expect all the firms in the industry to perform similarly.

A detailed discussion of 14 firms in the paper industry, done by Brigham and Pappas, indicated *a wide range of returns* for alternative firms, leading the authors to state: "A further examination of the data revealed that the volatility found in the paper industry is not atypical."[9]

Tysseland also contended that there is variability *within* industries, but there are no figures supporting his contention.[10] A study by Cheney examined percentage of price changes during 1964 and 1965 for a sample of eight industries and 227 stocks.[11] He examined both growth and nongrowth industries to determine the amount of cohesion within these two types of industry. He found a definite central tendency for the food industry, "some" central tendency for the building, paper, and steel industries, and no central tendency for the growth industries. It was concluded:

> This study of industry cohesiveness does little to reassure the investor that he can expect individual stocks to follow the industry trend, as exposed by the industry index, over the short and intermediate term.[12]

Several other studies have implicitly considered the relationship between a company and its industry by examining the relationship of returns over time for a group of stocks relative to the aggregate market and other stocks. The best

---

[8] Milford S. Tysseland, "Further Tests of the Validity of the Industry Approach to Investment Analysis," *Journal of Financial and Quantitative Analysis,* 6 no. 2 (March 1971): 835–847.

[9] Brigham and Pappas, "Rates of Return on Common Stock," *Journal of Business,* p. 311.

[10] Tysseland, "Further Tests," p. 840.

[11] Harlan L. Cheney, "The Value of Industry Forecasting as an Aid to Portfolio Management," *Appalachian Financial Review,* 1 no. 5 (Spring 1970): 331–339.

[12] Ibid., p. 335.

known study was done by King.[13] The reader will recall that King found, on average, about 52 percent of the variance of individual stocks was attributable to the market and an additional 10 percent was related to the industry component. King clearly believed that there was an industry influence after taking account of the market.

Gaumnitz used cluster analysis to detect the impact of the industry component on stock price movements.[14] The Gaumnitz sample was selected on the basis of size and included 140 stocks from every industrial classification except the air transport industry. He concluded that there was a clustering of *some* stocks along industry lines, but for the majority of stocks, the clusters had little correspondence to the initial industrial classifications.

Meyers modified King's statistical techniques and looked at an expanded sample of industries over a longer period, including the years 1961–1967. Meyers came to conclusions similar to those reached by Gaumnitz.[15] The results for the overlapping industries and periods were consistent with King's but they showed some weakening in the relationship after 1960. The results for six new industries that were not as homogeneous as King's indicated that industry clustering was not as dominant as it was in the original six, especially during the most recent period, 1961–1967.

The studies by Gaumnitz and Meyers indicate that there is a strong comovement for companies within some industries, but the pattern is clearly not universal. For most industries, there is not a strong relationship between returns for different companies within the industry.

Livingston analyzed the industry effect after removing the market effect using regression analysis rather than factor analysis.[16] The author compared 734 companies from over 100 industries of varying size to a broad market index. Each security's monthly rate of return was regressed against the S&P composite index for the period January 1966 through June 1970. The purpose was to analyze the residuals from this market regression to determine the market correlation between the residuals of different companies in a specified industry (within industry effect) and for different companies in different industries (the cross-industry effect). It was concluded that there is very strong evidence of positive correlation within industries after the market effect is removed. Also, while the *average* within industry correlation was significant, it was definitely *not* universal for all industries.

Livingston suggested that *each industry be examined to determine the importance of residual industry comovement.* He estimated the proportion of total variance explained by the industry effect to be about 18 percent. A table that listed the values indicated a wide range from 0.15 to 0.75. Those industries that

---

[13] Benjamin F. King, "Market and Industry Factors in Stock Price Behavior," *Journal of Business,* 39 no. 1 Part 2 (January 1966): 139–190.

[14] Jack E. Gaumnitz, "Influence of Industry Factors in Stock Price Movements," paper presented at Southern Finance Association Meeting, October 1970.

[15] Stephen L. Meyers, "A Re-Examination of Market and Industry Factors in Stock Price Behavior," *Journal of Finance,* 28 no. 3 (June 1973): 695–705.

[16] Miles Livingston, "Industry Movements of Common Stocks," *Journal of Finance,* 32 no. 2 (June 1977): 861–874.

had the lowest correlations with the aggregate market had the strongest industry factors. Examples of cohesive industries are gold mining, agricultural machinery, department stores, meat packers, and vegetable oil companies. The author concluded that the results supported the concept of industry analysis and also implied that alternative industries should be considered when diversifying one's portfolio.

Implications of Intra-Industry Dispersion.   Some observers have contended that, because all firms in an industry do not move together, industry analysis is useless. Such a contention is wrong because it requires too much from industry analysis. It would be desirable if all firms in an industry were tightly bunched around some mean value because then, after analyzing the industry, it would not be necessary to do a company analysis. Dispersion may be caused by the fact that different companies have different industry betas; i.e., they have a different relationship to the industry in the same way that they have a different relationship to the market. Assuming that a firm does have a different industry beta, if the relationship (industry beta) is stable, it would be a valuable piece of information. For industries in which there is a strong, consistent industry component, such as gold, steel, tobacco, railroads, etc., one can possibly reduce the emphasis on company analysis once the industry analysis is complete. For most industries in which the industry component is not so strong, *the analyst's job is not as easy as it might be, because company analysis is necessary.* Even for the nonhomogeneous industries, industry analysis is valuable, because it is much easier to select a superior company from a good industry than to find a good company in an industry expected to experience inferior performance. It seems likely that one of the *worst* companies in a *good* industry will outperform the *better* companies in one of the *poor* industries. Therefore, after completing the industry analysis, you have a *substantially higher probability* of selecting a high return stock. Once you have selected the best stock or stocks within an industry with good expectations, the chances are *substantially less* that your good company analysis will be negated by poor industry performance. In addition, the disperion of results for individual firms indicates that industry analysis alone will not suffice. Company analysis *is* necessary.

Analysis of Differential Industry Risk

In contrast to studies done on industry return performance, there have been few done on industry *risk* measures. The Reilly–Drzycimski study (RD) referred to earlier contained an analysis of industry risk in terms of the beta coefficient derived from the CAPM.[17] The authors derived the systematic risk for the 30 *Barron's* industry groups using weekly data for the period January 1958 through December 1970 and for several subperiods that conformed to alternative market periods.

There were two questions of interest: (1) what was the difference in risk for

[17] Reilly and Drzycimski, ''Alternative Industry Performance and Risk,'' *Journal of Financial and Quantitative Analysis,* 9 no. 3 (June 1974): 423–446.

alternative industries during a given time period; and (2) how stable was the industry risk measure over time?

The analysis of the beta coefficients during specified time periods indicated *a wide range of systematic risk.* The systematic risk for the total period ranged from 1.426 (air transportation) to −0.002 for gold mining. If gold mining is eliminated, the low value was 0.662 for grocery chains. The range between industries was typically larger for successive rising and falling markets. These results indicate that it is important to consider the differences in risk for the various industries.

The authors examined the persistence of the risk measures by correlating the beta values for the first seven years with those for the last six years, during the nine sequential subperiods, and between alternative periods of rising and falling stock prices. The correlations indicated a *reasonably stable relationship* between the beta coefficients for alternate periods. There was stability during the last ten years with the best results derived during the final five years. The correlation coefficient between the betas for the sixth and seventh alternative periods was +0.657; the coefficient for the seventh and eighth periods was +0.731; and for the eighth and ninth periods, +0.732. The results indicated a large measure of correspondence and agreed substantially with those obtained by Blume and Levy for portfolios of stocks, which is what an industry can be considered.[18]

Therefore, regarding industry risk, there is some bad news and some good news. The bad news is that there is substantial dispersion in the risk for alternative industries, which means that this risk must be considered in analyzing industries. The good news is that there is a fair amount of stability in the risk measure over time, which means that the past risk analysis for alternative industries can be of some benefit in analyzing future risk.

ESTIMATING INDUSTRY RETURNS

The Overall Procedure

The procedure for estimating the expected returns for alternative industries is similar to that employed in aggregate market analysis. It is a two-step process in which the initial phase involves estimating the expected earnings per share for an industry and then estimating the future industry earnings multiple.

Estimating Earnings per Share.   This involves several phases, the first of which is deriving an estimate of sales per share based upon an analysis of the relationship between sales of the given industry and aggregate sales for some relevant economic series; e.g., automobile sales are influenced by aggregate GNP or national income, but they are typically more closely related to disposable personal income. Having derived a relationship to some economic variables, the next step is to estimate the future performance of these independent variables

[18] Marshall E. Blume, "On the Assessment of Risk, *Journal of Finance,* 26 no. 1 (March 1971): 1–10; Robert A. Levy, "On the Short-Term Stationarity of Beta Coefficients," *Financial Analysts Journal,* 27 no. 6 (November–December 1971): 55–62.

for the next year and thereby to derive an estimate of sales per share for the industry.

If this analysis is meant to generate a long-run estimate of the sales outlook rather than a one-year projection, input-output analysis should be used to indicate the long-run relationship between industries. Such an analysis indicates which other industries supply the inputs for the industry of interest and who gets the output. Knowing this, it is a matter of determining the long-run outlook for both suppliers and major customers. For an explanation of input-output analysis, the reader is referred to several articles on the topic.[19]

The second step is to derive an estimate of the profit margin for the industry. As before, one can consider the gross margin (net before taxes and depreciation), the net before tax margin (NBT), or the net margin. The gross margin is preferred because it should be relatively less volatile. The depreciation and tax rate figures must then be estimated to derive a net income estimate.

An Industry Example

To demonstrate the analysis procedure, we will use the information in Standard & Poor's composite retail store index. This composite index contains four subindustries: (1) department stores, (2) retail stores (drugs), (3) food chains, and (4) general merchandise chains. The reader is probably familiar with a number of the companies included in these categories. The department store group includes eight companies:

— Allied Stores   — Associated Dry Goods
— Carter Hawley Hales Stores   — Dayton Hudson
— Federated Department Stores   — R. H. Macy
— May Department Stores   — Mercantile Stores.

The retail drug stores index was started in 1970 and includes:

— Eckerd (Jack)   — Revco D. S. Incorporated
— Rite Aid   — Walgreen Co.

The retail food chain group includes:

— American Stores   — Lucky Stores
— Great Atlantic and Pacific   — Safeway Stores
— Jewel Company   — Winn-Dixie Stores.
— Kroger Company

Finally, the general merchandise chains index was started in 1970 and includes:

— Kmart   — Wal-Mart Stores
— J. C. Penney Company   — F. W. Woolworth Company.
— Sears Roebuck & Company

Given the companies involved and the wide spectrum of stores, this industry group involves a fairly diversified portfolio.

Sales Forecast.   The sales forecast for the retail store industry involves an analysis of the relationship between sales for the industry and some aggregate

[19] D. A. Hodes, "Input-Output Analysis: An Illustrative Example," *Business Economics,* 1 (Summer 1965): 35 – 37; Howard B. Bonham, Jr., "The Use of Input-Output Economics in Common Stock Analysis," *Financial Analysts Journal,* 23 no. 1 (January – February 1967): 27 – 31.

TABLE 13.1
S&P Composite Retail Store Sales and Various Economic Series 1960–1982

| | | | | Per Capita | |
| | | | | --- | --- |
Year	Composite Retail Stores	Disposable Personal Income	Personal Consumption Expenditures	Disposable Personal Income	Personal Consumption Expenditures
1960	122.65	352.0	324.9	1947	1797
1961	127.04	365.8	335.0	1991	1823
1962	134.34	386.8	355.2	2073	1904
1963	140.75	405.9	374.6	2144	1979
1964	147.58	440.6	400.5	2296	2087
1965	156.75	475.8	430.4	2448	2241
1966	169.68	513.7	465.1	2613	2366
1967	179.15	547.9	490.3	2757	2467
1968	198.39	593.4	536.9	2956	2674
1969	214.75	638.9	581.8	3152	2870
1970	224.38	695.3	621.7	3390	3031
1971	239.11	751.8	672.2	3620	3237
1972	263.04	810.3	737.1	3860	3511
1973	284.72	914.5	812.0	4315	3831
1974	311.56	998.3	888.1	4667	4152
1975	315.80	1096.1	976.4	5075	4521
1976	342.01	1194.4	1084.3	5477	4972
1977	374.47	1314.0	1204.4	5965	5468
1978	397.53	1474.0	1346.5	6621	6048
1979	418.67	1650.2	1507.2	7331	6695
1980	484.43	1824.1	1667.2	8012	7323
1981	521.52	2029.1	1843.2	8827	8018
1982	510.32	2172.5	1972.0	9362	8498

SOURCE: *Analysts Handbook* (New York: Standard & Poor's Corp., 1983). *Economic Report of the President* (Washington, D.C.: U.S. Government Printing Office, 1983). Reprinted by permission of Standard & Poor's.

economic series that is related to the goods and services produced by the industry. The products of the retail store industry range from a basic necessity (food) to general merchandise, such as that sold by Sears, Roebuck, to an equally varied range of products sold in department stores like R. H. Macy. Therefore, the economic series should be fairly broad to reflect the demand for these products. The primary economic series considered are disposable personal income (DPI) and personal consumption expenditures (PCE). Table 13.1 contains the aggregate and the per capita values for the two series.

The scatter plot of retail sales versus the two economic series contained in Figure 13.1 indicates *a strong linear relationship between retail sales per share and these economic series.* Retail sales appear to be strongly related to either disposable personal income or personal consumption expenditures. Therefore, if one can do a good job of estimating changes in either of these series, one should derive a good estimate of expected changes in sales per share for a composite of retail stores. This close relationship with an aggregate economic series is not too surprising given the number of retail stores involved and the

FIGURE 13.1
Scatter Plot of Retail Store Sales and Disposable Personal Income and Retail Store
Sales and Personal Consumption Expenditures 1960–1982

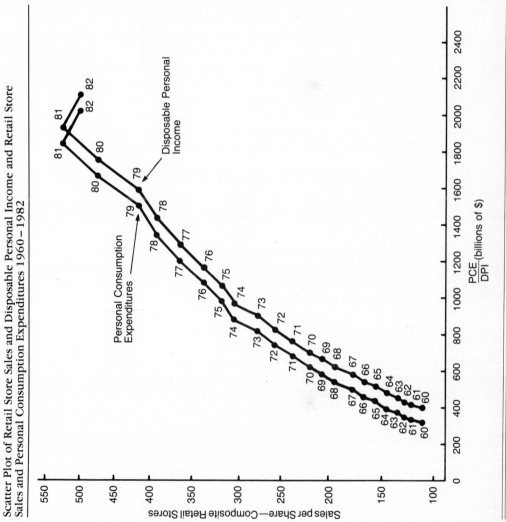

diverse nature of these stores, which means they would be a good reflection of aggregate retail sales. If the intent is to project sales for one of the component groups, such as food chains, it would be preferable to consider a subset of consumer expenditures, such as expenditures for nondurables. *As the industry becomes more specialized and unique, it is necessary to find a more unique economic series that reflects the demand for the industry's product.*

One might also consider *per capita* disposable personal income. Although aggregate DPI increases each year, there is also an increase in the aggregate population, so the increase in the DPI per capita (the average DPI for each adult and child) will typically be less than the increase in the aggregate series. During 1982 aggregate DPI increased about 7 percent, but per capita DPI only increased 6 percent. Because the per capita series may have a closer relationship to the retail sales series in some instances, it should be considered. Finally, it is often useful to analyze the relationship between *changes* in the economic variable and changes in industry sales. Such an analysis will indicate how the two series move together but will also highlight any changes in the relationship. Using percentage of changes, it is possible to derive the following regression model:

$$\%\Delta \text{ Industry Sales} = \alpha_i + \beta_i (\%\Delta \text{ in Economic Series}).$$

The size of the β_i coefficient should indicate how closely the two series move together. Assuming the intercept (α_i) is close to zero, a slope (β_i) value of 1.00 would indicate relatively equal percentage of change (e.g. a 10 percent increase in DPI is typically related to a 10 percent increase in industry sales). A β_i of less than unity would imply that industry sales are not growing as fast as the economy is. This analysis would help the analyst find the series that most closely reflects the demand for the industry's products *and* would indicate the form of the relationship.[20]

Table 13.2 contains the results for several of the regressions discussed. The regressions that relate the level of sales to the level of DPI and PCE confirm the close relationship, but these results also indicate that the long-run trend in the alternative series is a strong factor. The more sensitive percentage of change regressions (whether absolute or per capita) indicate that percentages of change in retail sales are more closely related to percentages of change in the PCE than they are to percentages of change in the DPI. The slope coefficients (β_i) are less than one, which indicates that retail sales are less volatile than the aggregate economy is. Consider the percentage of change regression relating industry sales to PCE. The equation is as follows:

$$\%\Delta \text{Industry Sales}_t = .88 + .69(\%\Delta PCE).$$

Because the intercept (.88) is not considered significant, it should not be included in the estimate. Assuming that economists estimate that the PCE will increase by 11 percent next year, the analyst using this regression will estimate that retail store sales would increase by 7.6 percent (.69 × 11.0). Because the

[20] A similar approach is advocated in Gary M. Wenglowski, "Industry Profit Analysis—A Progress Report and Some Predictions," Paper presented at I.C.F.A./F.A.R.F. Seminar (March 1975). Institute of Chartered Financial Analysts, Financial Analyst Research Foundation.

TABLE 13.2
Results for Regressions Relating Retail Store Sales to Aggregate Economic Series (DPI and PCE) 1960–1982

Variable		α	β	R^2	S.E.	F	D.W.
Dependent	Independent	(*t*)	(*t*)				
Industry Sales	DPI (levels)	59.63 (9.01)	.23 (37.31)	.99	15.96	1392.22	.74
Industry Sales (%Δ)	DPI (%Δ)	2.52 (.85)	.49 (1.47)	.10	3.47	2.16	2.08
Industry Sales	PCE (levels)	60.78 (8.73)	.25 (35.30)	.98	16.85	1246.29	.62
Industry Sales (%Δ)	PCE (%Δ)	.88 (.33)	.69 (2.25)	.20	3.27	5.07	1.91
Industry Sales	DPI per capita (levels)	31.08 (4.73)	.06 (41.42)	.99	14.40	1715.63	.86
Industry Sales (%Δ)	DPI per capita (%Δ)	3.31 (1.34)	.46 (1.46)	.10	3.48	2.14	2.07
Industry Sales	PCE per capita (levels)	32.41 (4.61)	.06 (38.49)	.99	15.48	1481.22	.69
Industry Sales (%Δ)	PCE per capita (%Δ)	6.67 (3.83)	.00 (.05)	.00	3.66	.00	1.80

slope is less than one, sales will not increase as much as the economy will during expansions, but it also will not decline as much as the economy will during recessions.

Industry Profit Margin Forecast.   The next step is to estimate the profit margin that will apply to this sales figure. Although it is possible to consider the *gross* profit margin (earnings before taxes and depreciation), the net before tax profit margin, or the net profit margin, the net profit margin is the most volatile and the hardest to estimate directly. An alternative is to begin with the gross profit margin and to progress to an estimate of depreciation and the tax rate. Therefore, the initial step involves an estimate of the gross profit margin for the industry.

Estimating the industry's gross profit margin.   It is natural to expect that the estimate of the industry gross profit margin will be done in a manner similar to that used in market analysis. Recall that the market analysis specified the factors that should influence the economy's margin, including capacity utilization, unit labor cost, inflation, and net exports and then analyzed the relative effect of each. The most important variables were capacity utilization and the unit labor cost. It is not possible to conduct such an analysis for individual industries because the relevant variables are not available on an industry basis, except in rare cases.[21]

---

[21] Again, this is used in Wenglowski, "Industry Profit Analysis—A Progress Report and Some Predictions," paper presented at ICFA/FARF seminar (March 1975).

FIGURE 13.2
Scatter Plot of Gross Profit Margin (GPM) for Standard & Poor's 400 and Standard &
Poor's Composite Retail Stores

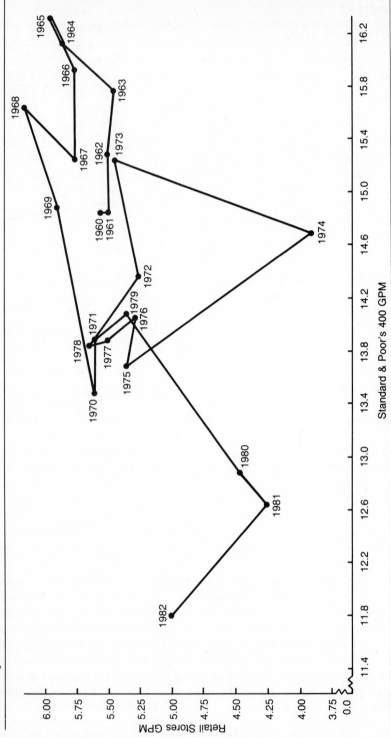

SOURCE: Reprinted by permission of Standard & Poor's.

Although it is not possible to derive these figures, one might assume that movements in these variables affecting the industry profit margin are related to movements in similar variables for the aggregate economy. As an example, when there is an increase in capacity utilization for the aggregate economy, there is probably a comparable increase in utilization for the auto industry or the chemical industry. The same could be true for unit labor cost and exports. *If there is some generally stable relationship between these variables for the industry and the economy, one should expect a relationship to exist between the profit margin for the industry and the profit margin for the economy.* It is not necessary that the relationship be completely linear with a slope of one. The most important characteristic is a generally stable relationship.

To demonstrate such a comparison, the gross profit margin for the S&P 400 industrial index and the S&P composite retail store index is contained in Table 13.3 and a scatter plot is contained in Figure 13.2. As shown in the plot, except for 1974, the relationship was quite consistent. One could derive a more detailed estimate of the relation by computing a regression line for the plot. It is wise to exclude 1974 since the inclusion of figures for this year would cause a major change in the coefficients and the figures apparently represent a random event that probably will not be repeated.

One might also consider analyzing *percentages of change* in the profit margins for each year to determine how sensitive the industry is to aggregate changes. Again, in the current case one would probably ignore 1974. The form of the regression would be:

$$\%\Delta\text{Industry Profit Margin} = \alpha + \beta_i(\%\Delta\text{Aggregate Profit Margin}).$$

The slope coefficient (β_i) indicates how sensitive the industry's profit margin is to economic changes. If the industry is relatively stable (as retail stores are), one would expect this slope coefficient to be less than one, which would indicate that the industry profit margin does not increase or decrease as much as the economy's profit margin does.

Table 13.4 contains the results for several regressions that related the GPM for the retail store industry and the GPM for the S&P 400 index. Note that the exclusion of 1974 has a significant positive impact on the levels regressions. The most useful regression is the levels model, excluding 1974 figures. The intercept is about 1.50 and almost significant, and the slope coefficient indicates that the retail store margin is about one-fourth the level of the aggregate market GPM. If the market analyst estimated a small increase in the GPM for the aggregate market, you would expect the following for the GPM for retail stores. Assume a market GPM of 12 percent, and an estimate of an increase in the market GPM from 12 percent to 13 percent. Given the intercept of 1.49 and the slope coefficient of 0.27, you would expect the gross profit margin for retail stores to be: 1.49 + 0.27 (13.0) = 5.00.

This analysis can be a very useful tool, but the technique should *not* be applied mechanically. You should be aware of any unique factors affecting the specific industry such as price wars, contract negotiations, or building plans. These unique events should be considered as adjustment factors when estimat-

TABLE 13.3
Profit Margins for Standard & Poor's 400 Industrial Index and Standard & Poor's Composite Retail Store Index 1960–1982

Year	Gross Profit Margin		Depreciation		NBT Margin		Tax Rate		Net Profit Margin	
	S&P 400	Composite Retail Store	S&P 400	Composite Retail Store	S&P 400	Composite Retail Store	S&P 400	Composite Retail Store	S&P 400	Composite Retail Store
1960	14.85	5.52	2.56	1.30	10.54	4.46	45.8	49.9	5.72	2.23
1961	14.84	5.57	2.66	1.38	10.37	4.48	45.4	49.4	5.66	2.27
1962	15.29	5.52	2.89	1.51	10.82	4.40	45.2	49.4	5.93	2.23
1963	15.75	5.43	3.04	1.61	11.31	4.28	45.3	47.4	6.19	2.25
1964	16.11	5.85	3.24	1.71	11.68	4.69	43.3	45.5	6.63	2.55
1965	16.31	5.96	3.52	1.83	11.95	4.79	42.9	44.6	6.82	2.65
1966	15.93	5.76	3.87	2.04	11.55	4.56	42.6	44.4	6.64	2.53
1967	15.22	5.75	4.25	2.21	10.59	4.52	42.2	44.3	6.12	2.52
1968	15.63	6.15	4.56	2.57	11.13	4.85	45.5	49.1	6.07	2.47
1969	14.87	5.92	4.87	2.52	10.38	4.75	45.6	49.1	5.65	2.42
1970	13.48	5.58	5.17	2.62	8.78	4.41	43.9	47.0	4.92	2.34
1971	13.87	5.60	5.45	2.82	9.26	4.42	45.5	45.1	5.04	2.43
1972	14.36	5.25	5.76	3.05	9.87	4.09	46.4	43.2	5.30	2.32
1973	15.23	5.43	6.25	3.24	11.04	4.30	46.1	44.0	5.96	2.41
1974	14.66	3.89	6.86	3.58	10.89	2.74	51.5	47.6	5.28	1.43
1975	13.69	5.35	7.36	3.71	9.71	4.18	52.0	46.5	4.63	2.24
1976	14.05	5.31	7.58	3.79	10.31	4.20	48.9	43.6	5.27	2.37
1977	13.88	5.48	8.53	4.38	10.07	4.31	49.1	42.5	5.11	2.48
1978	13.85	5.65	9.64	5.24	10.02	4.33	48.2	41.9	5.19	2.52
1979	14.07	5.36	10.82	5.66	10.37	4.00	46.3	38.7	5.57	2.46
1980	12.88	4.46	12.37	6.54	9.10	3.11	45.9	36.7	4.92	1.97
1981	12.64	4.25	13.82	7.24	8.62	2.87	43.6	38.3	4.86	1.77
1982	11.78	5.02	15.19	7.27	7.22	3.59	45.2	38.6	3.95	2.20

Gross Profit Margin = Net Before Tax and Depreciation/Sales.

SOURCE: *Analysts Handbook* (New York: Standard & Poor's Corp., 1983). Reprinted by permission of Standard & Poor's.

TABLE 13.4

Results for Regressions Relating the Gross Profit Margin for the Retail Store
Industry to the GPM for the Standard & Poor's 400 Industrial Index 1960–1982

Variables		α	β				
Dependent	Independent	(t)	(t)	R^2	S.E.	F.	D.W.
Industry GPM	S&P GPM (levels)	1.55 (1.27)	.27 (3.16)	.32	.46	9.96	1.60
Industry GPM	S&P 400 GPM (w/o '74) (levels)	1.49 (1.82)	.27 (4.88)	.54	.31	23.77	1.21
Industry GPM ($\%\Delta$)	S&P 400 GPM ($\%\Delta$)	.23 (.08)	−.03 (−.05)	.001	12.48	.00	2.64
Industry GPM ($\%\Delta$)	S&P GPM (w/o '74) ($\%\Delta$)	1.42 (.59)	−.25	.01	10.84	.20	1.71

SOURCE: Reprinted by permission of Standard & Poor's.

ing the final gross profit margin or used in estimating a range of profit margins
(optimistic, pessimistic, most likely) for the industry. Also, for many industries
the percentage change regression results may be more useful.

Estimating industry depreciation.   After estimating the industry's gross
profit margin, the next step is to estimate industry depreciation. This is typically
easier to estimate than other variables are because the series generally is always
increasing; the only question is by how much. As shown in Table 13.3, except for
1969, the depreciation series for retail stores has increased every year since 1960.
The regressions in Table 13.5 relate industry depreciation to depreciation for the
S&P 400 index. The results indicate a strong relationship between levels, with
the retail store depreciation consistently at about 50 percent of that for the
aggregate market. This is true for the total period and for most individual years.
These regressions, along with estimates of market depreciation, should provide
realistic estimates of depreciation for the retail store industry.

When the estimated depreciation is subtracted from the gross profit figure,
the result is the net before tax (NBT) figure. The final step is estimating the tax
rate for the industry and, therefore, the net income profit margin for the industry.

Estimating the industry tax rate.   Although different industries have different tax factors to contend with, one would generally assume that most tax
changes influence all industries in a comparable manner. Therefore, one would
expect a relationship to exist between changes in the aggregate tax rate and
changes in the tax rate for various industries.

The composite retail store industry's tax rate historically moved with the
economy's tax rate. However, recently the tax rate for the industry has changed in
its relationship to the economy. During the early years of the period, the industry
tax rate was *above* the economy's rate and the tax rates almost always moved in
the same direction. In 1971 and 1972, the economy's tax rate increased and the
industry tax rate declined. As a result, the industry tax rate is now *below* the
economy's. This shifting relationship is reflected in the regressions in Table 13.5

TABLE 13.5
Results of Regressions Relating Depreciation and Taxes for the Retail Store Industry
and the Standard & Poor's 400 Industrial 1960–1982

Variables		α	β				
Dependent	Independent	(t)	(t)	R^2	S.E.	F.	D.W.
Industry Depreciation	S&P 400 Depreciation (levels)	0.08 (1.27)	.51 (57.14)	.994	.152	3265.01	1.45
Industry Depreciation	S&P 400 Depreciation (%Δ)	−.54 (−.20)	1.04 (3.39)	.365	4.304	11.49	2.22
Industry Tax Rate	S&P 400 Tax Rate (levels)	41.05 (2.75)	0.08 (.24)	.001	3.970	.06	.23
Industry Tax Rate	S&P 400 Tax Rate (%Δ)	−1.08 (−1.48)	.71 (3.90)	.43	3.420	15.24	2.00

SOURCE: Reprinted by permission of Standard & Poor's.

that relate the industry and the market tax rates (i.e., the levels regression results
are insignificant). The percentage of change results are significant and indicate
that the industry tax rate has not been as volatile as the market rate has been.
Again, given some estimate of a change in the market tax rate, it should be
possible to estimate a tax rate for the retail store industry.

Example of Earnings Estimate

To help the reader understand the procedure discussed, the following is a rough
estimate of the net income for the retail store industry based upon the estimates
for the economy set forth in Chapter 12 and the relationship between the industry and market derived in this chapter. A practicing analyst would use this
example as an *initial* estimate that would be modified based upon his knowledge of the industry and of current events.

Based upon the regression analysis contained in Table 13.2, the best relationship was between percentages of change in retail sales and percentages of
change in PCE. The outlook for PCE during 1984 is for a 10.0 percent increase.[22]
This estimate indicates an increase in retail sales of approximately 6.9 percent
(.69 × 10.0). Therefore, given that retail sales were expected to be $530 in 1983,
the 1984 estimate is about $567 (1.069 × 530).

The GPM for retail stores was 5.02 in 1982. During 1983 aggregate margins
increased and retail store margins probably increased less, to about 5.20. The
aggregate GPM was expected to increase during 1984. Based upon the regression results in Table 13.4, this would indicate that retail store margins should
increase to about 5.40. This indicates that the gross profit per share for the retail
store industry should be $30.62. (5.40 × $567).

Aggregate depreciation for the S&P 400 series during 1984 was estimated to
be $17.98. Assuming the retail store industry will maintain its 50 percent ratio,

[22] Leon Cooperman and Steven G. Einhorn, "Portfolio Strategy" (New York: Goldman Sachs & Co., May, 1984).

this would imply an estimate of about $9.00 depreciation for retail stores and a net before tax earnings of $21.62 ($30.62 − $9.00).

The tax rate for the retail store industry has been lower than the aggregate, which was estimated at 46 percent during 1984. Therefore, a rate of about 39 percent seems appropriate for the retail store industry. This implies that net income should be $13.19 (21.62 − 8.43) per share, indicating a net profit margin of 2.33 percent (13.19/567.00), which is consistent with recent experience.

Therefore, at this point, the analyst has derived an estimate of the industry's net income per share. The next step is to estimate the likely earnings multiple for this industry in the period ahead.

INDUSTRY EARNINGS MULTIPLES

There are two approaches to estimating a multiple for an industry. One is similar to the technique used for estimating the market multiple, i.e., examining the specific variables that influence the earnings multiple—the dividend-payout ratio, the required rate of return (i), and the expected growth rate of earnings and dividends (g). This technique will be referred to as the *micro* approach. On the other hand, one can conceive of a *macro* approach in which the relationship between the industry multiple and the aggregate market multiple is analyzed.

Macro Analysis of Industry Multiples

The macro approach is based on the assumption that several of the major variables influencing the industry multiple are related to similar variables for the aggregate market. It is hypothesized that there is a relationship between changes in i and g for specific industries and comparable changes in i and g for the aggregate market. If these relevant variables are related in their movements (even though they are not the same values), then there will be a relationship between *changes* in the industry multiple and *changes* in the market multiple.

A study by Reilly and Zeller contained an extensive analysis of the relationship between the P/E ratios for 71 Standard & Poor's industries and the P/E ratios for the S&P 400 index during the period 1946–1971.[23] While the study examined both levels and percentages of change, the current discussion is limited to the percentage of change results. The analysis considered four partially overlapping 21-year periods. The slope coefficients varied from about 0.10 to 3.00, and the r^2 averaged about 0.36. About 76 percent of the slope coefficients were statistically significant, which led the authors to contend that, "there was a statistically significant positive relationship between percent changes in earnings multiples for the majority of industries examined.[24] An analysis of the predictive ability of the percentage of change model compared to a naive model that assumed no change indicated that the predictive model was superior during three of the four periods analyzed. Notably, there was a difference between industries in terms of per-

---

[23] Frank K. Reilly and Thomas Zeller, "An Analysis of Relative Industry Price-Earnings Ratios," *The Financial Review* (1974): 17–33.

[24] Ibid., p. 23.

TABLE 13.6
Results of Regressions between Retail Store P/E Ratio and Standard & Poor's 400
Index P/E Ratio

	α (t)	β (t)	R^2	S.E.	F.	D.W.
Levels: 1960–1982	1.12 (.52)	1.08 (7.30)	.72	2.90	53.26	.99
Levels: 1960–1982 w/o 1974	−1.06 (−.68)	1.20 (11.43)	.87	2.00	130.72	.89
Percentage of Change: 1960–1982	−1.20 (−.36)	.31 (1.26)	.07	15.44	1.60	2.38
Percentage of Change: 1960–1982 w/o 1974	−2.01 (−.61)	.48 (1.76)	.14	15.14	3.10	1.96

SOURCE: Reprinted by permission of Standard & Poor's.

formance. Therefore, the industries were judged on the basis of the stability of the slope coefficient and the size of the percentage errors when predicting. Nineteen industries were superior in all the tests, roughly another 20 were superior in one of the tests, and three were seriously inferior in all tests. It was concluded that the results supported the general expectation of a relationship between the earnings multiples for alternative industries and the market, but that *the significant relationship is not universal.* Therefore, *it is necessary to examine the quality of the relationship between an industry and the market before using this technique.*

The results of an analysis of the relationship for the retail store industry during the period 1960–1982 are contained in Table 13.6. They are encouraging since they indicate that most of the coefficients are significant. The best results relate the levels of the P/E ratios during the most recent period, excluding 1974. The percentage of change regressions for the period without 1974 are almost significant and indicate that the industry P/E ratios are less volatile than the market P/E ratios. Therefore, this technique should be considered, but an analyst should also use the micro approach and analyze the multiple on the basis of the variables that determine it.

Micro Analysis of Industry Multiple

The micro analysis examines the three major variables affecting the earnings multiple and compares the industry values to the comparable market values in order to determine how the industry multiple should relate to the market multiple — should it be above, below, or about equal to the market's multiple during the next period. Initially, one should examine the long-run relationship between the industry and market multiple and then look for factors that would cause differences over time.

Industry vs. Market Multiple.   The mean of the high and low multiple for the aggregate market and the composite retail store industry is contained in Table 13.7. The figures indicate that the multiple for retail stores was above the aggre-

TABLE 13.7
Earnings Multiples for the Standard & Poor's 400 Index and the Composite Retail Store Index with Variables that Influence Earnings Multiples 1960–1982

Year	Mean Earnings Multiple		Retention Rate		Return on Equity		Equity Turnover		Net Profit Margin	
	S&P 400	Composite Retail Store	S&P 400	Composite Retail Store	S&P 400	Composite Retail Store	S&P 400	Composite Retail Store	S&P 400	Composite Retail Store
1960	17.70	17.47	41.2	41.2	10.08	9.18	1.76	4.11	5.72	2.23
1961	20.41	21.21	38.6	43.1	9.67	9.46	1.71	4.17	5.66	2.27
1962	16.98	19.82	42.6	40.8	10.53	9.55	1.78	4.29	5.93	2.23
1963	17.07	19.67	44.3	43.2	11.11	9.45	1.79	4.20	6.19	2.25
1964	17.63	20.89	46.8	49.3	12.06	11.18	1.82	4.38	6.63	2.55
1965	16.82	22.05	48.7	50.0	12.64	11.74	1.85	4.42	6.82	2.65
1966	15.20	17.37	49.7	48.6	12.88	11.66	1.94	4.60	6.64	2.53
1967	17.04	16.21	47.1	50.1	11.76	11.13	1.92	4.42	6.12	2.52
1968	17.30	18.66	48.7	51.8	12.27	10.98	2.02	4.44	6.07	2.47
1969	17.46	19.23	47.0	52.8	11.86	11.96	2.10	4.95	5.65	2.42
1970	16.49	17.72	41.8	52.6	10.28	11.33	2.09	4.84	4.92	2.34
1971	18.02	16.66	47.1	54.8	10.80	11.61	2.14	4.79	5.04	2.43
1972	17.95	24.11	52.9	57.3	11.71	11.39	2.21	4.90	5.30	2.32
1973	13.38	19.24	61.1	61.2	14.15	12.11	2.37	5.03	5.96	2.41
1974	9.43	20.63	61.4	38.3	14.17	7.75	2.69	5.40	5.28	1.43
1975	10.79	12.83	56.6	62.0	12.11	11.72	2.61	5.24	4.63	2.24
1976	10.41	13.39	60.5	66.3	14.02	12.45	2.66	5.25	5.27	2.37
1977	9.55	10.50	56.8	63.8	13.93	13.06	2.73	5.28	5.11	2.48
1978	8.21	8.20	58.8	61.4	14.60	13.19	2.81	5.24	5.19	2.52
1979	7.11	7.48	63.7	60.1	16.50	12.85	2.96	5.23	5.57	2.46
1980	8.44	7.40	59.7	53.8	14.88	11.01	3.02	5.60	4.92	1.97
1981	8.45	8.60	58.1	51.5	14.42	10.31	2.97	5.83	4.86	1.77
1982	10.38	9.07	45.9	58.9	11.16	12.47	2.82	5.65	3.95	2.20
Mean[a]	14.22	15.81	50.8	53.4	12.43	11.35	2.28	4.86	5.55	2.35

[a] 1974 not included.

SOURCE: Reprinted by permission of Standard & Poor's.

gate market multiple prior to 1978. Since then, the relationship has been mixed. This observation is also supported by the average multiples for the period (14.22 for the market compared to 15.81 for the composite retail store index). *Why do the multiples differ over time?* Why have investors been willing to pay more for a dollar of earnings from retail stores than for a dollar of earnings from the aggregate market? Also, why has this changed? An analysis of the factors that determine the earnings multiple should indicate the cause for this difference.

Dividend payout.   As shown in Table 13.7, the retention rates were typically similar prior to the 1970s (usually within 2 percentage points). Since then there have been major differences on a yearly basis and numerous changes in relative position (i.e., which was larger). Still, the overall averages indicate a higher retention rate for the retail stores (53.4 vs. 50.8) and this long-term result is confirmed by the more recent experience. Specifically, the retention rates since 1975 were 57.5 percent for the S&P 400 and 59.7 percent for retail stores. While the differences are small, they would indicate a higher payout (lower retention) for the S&P 400 which would imply a higher multiple for the S&P 400 on the basis of this particular variable.

Required return.   The required rate of return on *all* investments is influenced by the risk-free rate and the inflation rate, so the *differentiating factor is the risk premium.* The difference in the required return on the aggregate stock market and the required return for composite retail stores is caused by a difference in the risk premium for two indexes. The risk premium is a function of business risk (BR), financial risk (FR), and liquidity risk (LR). In an environment with the capital asset pricing model, the risk premium is a function of the systematic risk of the asset, i.e., its covariance with the market portfolio of risky assets. Therefore, an analyst could measure the BR, FR, and LR for the industry and compare these directly to comparable variables for the aggregate market. The other alternative is to compute the systematic risk for the industry and determine whether the beta is above or below unity.

The business risk for the retail store industry is clearly below average. Business risk is typically considered to be a function of relative sales volatility and operating leverage. Analysis of the percentage of change in retail sales compared to aggregate sales (Table 13.2) indicated that industry sales were only about 69 percent as volatile as overall economy sales were. Analysis of the gross profit margin likewise indicated that the GPM for retail stores was much less volatile than the aggregate market GPM. Therefore, since both sales and the GPM were less volatile, it implies that operating profits are substantially less volatile and *business risk for the retail store industry is below average.*

The financial risk for this industry is difficult to judge because leases on buildings are extensive. Based upon reported liabilities prior to 1977, these firms had low debt-equity ratios and high coverage ratios. When the firms were required to capitalize their lease obligations, the ratios changed drastically. In most cases the debt and interest figures increased by a factor of four or five. If one considers the capitalized leases, the firms in this industry generally have *above average financial risk.*

Based upon an analysis of the Amivest liquidity ratios for a number of companies in the retail store industry, there is substantial variation among the firms which range from Safeway and Sears, Roebuck, *very* liquid, to American Stores, quite illiquid.[25] Generally, most of the stocks are slightly below average in liquidity. Therefore, retail stores probably have *slightly above average liquidity risk.*

Business risk is definitely below average, financial risk is above average, and liquidity risk is slightly above average for retail stores. Assuming that business risk is the most significant variable, the consensus is that *overall risk is about even with the market or slightly below average* on the basis of internal characteristics.

The systematic risk for the composite retail store industry is computed using the market model as follows:

$$\%\Delta CRS_t = \alpha_i + \beta_i \,(\%\Delta \text{ S\&P } 400_t),$$

where:

$\%\Delta CRS_t$ = percentage price change in composite retail store (CRS) index during month t

α_i = regression intercept for CRS industry

β_i = systematic risk measure for CRS industry equal to $Cov_{i,m}/\theta_m^2$

$\%\Delta \text{ S\&P } 400_t$ = percentage price change in S&P 400 index during month t.

To derive an estimate in the current case, the model specified was run with monthly data for the five-year period 1978–1982. The results for this regression are as follows:

$$\alpha_j = 0.152 \qquad R^2 = .383$$
$$\beta_j = 0.76 \qquad \text{S.E.} = 4.66$$
$$t\text{-value} = 6.00 \qquad F = 35.96$$

The systematic risk for the retail store industry is below unity indicating a lower risk industry (i.e., risk less than the markets). Those results are generally consistent with the evaluation based upon micro internal variables (business risk, financial risk, and liquidity risk). It was generally concluded that the industry risk was slightly *below* average because of the dominant effect of lower business risk.

Translating this systematic risk into a required return figure (i) calls for using the security market line which is specified as follows:

$$i_j = RFR + \beta_j(R_m - RFR).$$

Assuming a nominal risk-free rate during this period of 10 percent (.10), a market return (R_m) of 15 percent, and a beta for the industry of 0.76 yields the following:

$$i_j = .10 + 0.76(.15 - .10)$$
$$= .10 + .038$$
$$= .138.$$

---

[25] Amivest Corporation, *The Liquidity Report,* 12 no. 10 (August 1983).

Based upon a micro estimate of risk slightly *below* average and a market risk estimate likewise below average, one should probably assume a consensus risk below market risk. This would imply an earnings multiple for this industry above the market multiple, all other factors being equal.

Expected Growth

The prime determinants of earnings and dividend growth are the retention rate and the return on equity investments; i.e., how much is put back into investments and what is the return on these investments:

$$g = f(\text{Retention Rate; Return on Equity}).$$

Return on equity can be broken down into equity turnover and net profit margin as follows:

$$\text{Net Income/Equity} = \frac{\text{Sales}}{\text{Equity}} \times \frac{\text{Net Income}}{\text{Sales}}$$

Therefore, it is necessary to examine each of these variables to determine whether there is any factor that would imply a difference in expected growth for the composite retail trade as compared to expected growth for the aggregate market. The data for the series involved are contained in Table 13.7.

Retention rate.   The retention rate is simply one minus the dividend-payout rate discussed earlier. The two series were quite similar, with the S&P 400 series having a slightly higher payout rate, which means that the composite retail store industry has a slightly higher retention rate (53.4 percent versus 50.8 percent). The small difference indicated a higher growth rate for the composite retail store industry.

Return on equity.   Because the return on equity is a function of the equity turnover and profit margin, these two variables are examined individually.

A comparison of the equity turnover indicates that both series experienced a substantial increase over time and that the CRS series has consistently been higher. The S&P 400 series turnover increased from 1.76 in 1960 to about 3.00 in 1982, a 70 percent increase. Concurrently, the CRS industry turnover went from 4.11 to about 5.7, a 40 percent increase. The average for the period was 2.28 for the S&P 400 versus 4.86 for CRS. Therefore, *the average equity turnover for the CRS industry was more than double that for the aggregate market.*

A comparison of the net profit margin tells a different story. *The profit margin for the S&P 400 was consistently higher than the margin for the CRS industry, typically more than double.* Both series declined during the total period. The higher profit margin for the market offset the higher turnover in the CRS industry. This is a prime example of what can be done to generate high returns on investment. One can either have a low turnover but a high profit margin, or accept a lower profit margin but have rapid turnover of assets and equity.

Combining the two factors, the return on equity for the two groups is reasonably close, with the S&P 400 being higher for almost every individual year and on average (12.43 percent versus 11.35 percent). These average percentages are quite consistent with what would be derived from multiplying the components as follows:

$$\text{Turnover} \times \text{Profit Margin} = \text{Return on Equity}$$

S&P 400: 2.28 $\times$ 5.55 $= 12.65$

CRS: 4.86 $\times$ 2.35 $= 11.42.$

Estimating Growth.   The growth rate is a function of the retention rate times the return on equity. The CRS industry has a slightly higher retention rate (53.4 versus 50.8), while the S&P 400 has a slightly higher return on equity (12.43 versus 11.35). When these are combined, the estimated long-run growth rate is as follows:

$$\text{S\&P 400: } 50.8 \times 12.43 = 6.31\%$$

$$\text{CRS: } \quad 53.4 \times 11.35 = 6.06\%$$

Clearly, *the expected growth rates for the two series based upon the historical values are very similar.* Therefore, the difference in past earnings multiples probably cannot be explained on the basis of a difference in the growth rates. Notably, the difference that does exist favors the S&P 400 series.

Why the Difference?

Based upon the dividend growth model, it was noted that the earnings multiple was a function of (1) the dividend-payout ratio, (2) the required rate of return, and (3) the expected growth rate. Any differences in earning multiples should likewise be explained in terms of differences in one or several of these variables.

Our initial analysis indicated that the earnings multiple for the combined retail store industry was historically higher than the multiple for the S&P 400, but in recent years there was little difference. The question then became: why has the CRS industry historically enjoyed this premium in terms of its multiple? There was almost no difference in the payout ratio for the two series, and the difference that did exist favored the S&P 400 series. The analysis of risk in terms of internal characteristics and a market measure of risk concluded that the CRS industry risk was lower than the market risk.

Finally, an analysis of the growth characteristics of the two series indicated differences in equity turnover and profit margin but relatively similar return on equity figures. When the return on equity figures was combined with offsetting retention rates, the implied growth rates were almost identical.

Therefore, although the historical record indicated that the CRS multiple was consistently higher, an analysis of historical values for the relevant variables did not support this relationship. Almost all the variables were identical with some offset between dividend payout and risk. This would indicate that the earnings multiple for the CRS industry should be quite similar to the market multiple. Notably, this is exactly what has happened since 1978—they are similar with changes in position over time.

Estimating the Future

The purpose of our discussion up to this point was to demonstrate a technique and to indicate the relationships that should exist between an industry and the market so that you will be aware of the variables that are important to the analysis. At the same time, it should never be forgotten that *the past alone is of little value in projecting the future,* because past relationships may not hold in the future, *especially in the short run.* For the analyst attempting to *project* the earnings multiple for the CRS industry, it is necessary to have an estimate of the market multiple and then to determine whether the CRS multiple will be above or below the market multiple based upon estimates of the expected relevant variables. Our previous discussion indicated the relevant variables to consider and how these variables are related to each other and to the multiple. Your function as an analyst is to determine the future values for these relevant variables based upon your unique knowledge of the industry. The analyst who does a better job of *estimating* the payout, risk, and growth for the industry will derive a better estimate of the industry earnings multiple relative to the market multiple and a better estimate of returns for the industry.

Example of Multiple Estimate.   Ideally one would like to apply both techniques (macro and micro) to estimate the earnings multiple and produce estimates that are reasonably consistent. In the current case, the macro approach was supported by the significance of the relationship, but the results were discouraging because the percentage of change coefficients were not stable. The results indicate that the retail store P/E is *less* volatile than the market P/E. In Chapter 12 it was estimated that the market multiple would decline in 1984 from about 11 to about 9. Therefore, one would expect a small percent decline for the retail industry. Note that the beginning value for the CRS industry is also lower. Therefore, a reasonable estimate for the CRS industry multiple on the basis of the macro relationships is for a P/E of about 8.0.

The analysis of individual components generally indicated that there should be little difference in the multiple for the market and the retail store industry because almost all of the components were very similar. The only clear difference was the risk factor for retail stores was lower. Assuming a slight premium for retail stores would imply a multiple of about 9.2 for the retail stores versus a multiple of about 9.0 for the market.

In summary, the P/E estimate on the basis of the macro relationships of the industry with the aggregate market is for an earnings multiple of about 8.0. Alternatively, the micro analysis indicates that a multiple of about 9.2 would be reasonable. While it is certainly acceptable and desirable to have several estimates, for the purposes of the example we will use the mean value of these two estimates (8.6).

The Total Estimate. The net earnings estimate was for $13.19 a share during 1984. This, coupled with a multiple estimate of 8.6, implied an index value estimate of 113.43 at the end of 1984. Given this index value, it is possible to derive the return you expect based upon the current value of the index and the expected dividend as follows:

$$R_{crs} = \frac{113.43 - \text{Index (current)} + \text{Dividend}}{\text{Index (Current)}}$$

SUMMARY

This chapter has two major parts. In the first, a number of studies dealing with cross-section industry performance and risk and time series measures of industry performance were discussed. The studies generally showed that there was wide dispersion in the performance of alternative industries during specified time periods, which implies that industry analysis would be of value. It was also shown that the performance of specific industries over time was *not* consistent, which means past performance is not of value in projecting future performance. Also, performance within industries is not very consistent for many industries, which means that individual companies must be analyzed after an industry analysis is done. The analysis of industry *risk* indicated wide dispersion between industries but a fair amount of consistency over time for individual industries. This implies that risk analysis is important but also that past values may be of some use.

The second section discussed the procedure for analyzing an industry using the dividend growth model. This procedure involves estimating sales based upon the relationship of the industry to some economic variables. Then the net profit margin was derived based upon an estimate of the gross profit margin, depreciation, and the industry tax rate. The second half of the procedure involves estimating the earnings multiple for the industry using either a macro or micro approach.

Because of the dispersion of industry performance and its volatility over time, it seems clear that industry analysis is both necessary and can be very lucrative. The function of a good analyst is to estimate the relevant variables. As always, the superior analyst will be the one who does the best job of *estimating* based upon knowledge of the industry and insights regarding relevant information.

QUESTIONS

1. Several studies have examined differences in the performance of alternative industries over specific time periods. Briefly describe the results of these cross-sectional studies and discuss their implications for industry analysis.
2. A number of studies have considered the time series of industry performance. Briefly describe the empirical results of these studies and discuss their implications for those who are involved in industry analysis. Do these results imply that industry analysis is easier or harder?

3. You are told that all the firms in a particular industry have consistently experienced rates of return *very similar* to the results for the aggregate industry. What does this imply regarding the importance of industry analysis for this industry? What does it imply regarding the importance of individual company analysis for this industry? Discuss.

4. Some authors contend that, because there is a great deal of dispersion in the performance of different firms in an industry, industry analysis is of little value. Would you agree or disagree with this contention? Why?

5. What are some factors that might cause different companies in a given industry to experience some similarity in their operating results? Discuss several of these briefly.

6. Would you expect there to be a difference in the industry influence on rates of return for companies in different industries? What is the empirical evidence on this question? Describe it briefly.

7. There has been an analysis of the difference in the risk for alternative industries during a specified time period. Describe the results of this analysis briefly and discuss their implications for the practice of industry analysis.

8. What were the results when the risk for alternative industries was examined during successive time periods? Describe the results and discuss the implications for those involved in industry analysis.

9. Select three industries from the S&P *Analysts Handbook* with different characteristics in terms of demand. Indicate what economic time series you would use in the analysis of the sales growth for each industry. What is the source of the economic time series? *Why* is this series relevant for this industry?

10. Prepare a scatter plot of industry sales and economic values over the last ten years using information available in the *Analysts Handbook* for one of the three industries selected in Question 9. Discuss the results of scatter plot; do you think the economic series was very closely related to industry sales?

11. If you could derive the data, what would you examine to determine future values of the gross profit margin for an industry?

12. Why is it contended that one should expect a relationship between the profit margin for a given industry and the aggregate profit margin?

13. Prepare a scatter plot of the profit margin for a selected industry and the aggregate profit margin for the S&P 400 index for the most recent ten years. How close is the relationship? What factors would make this industry's margin different?

14. Prepare a time series plot of the annual mean price-earnings ratio (highest ratio + lowest ratio/2) for an industry and the S&P 400 for the most recent ten years available. Has the relationship between the two series been consistent over time?

15. Prepare a table that contains the relevant variables that influence the earnings multiple for your industry and the S&P 400 series for the most recent ten years.

   a. Does the average dividend-payout ratio differ? How should the dividend payout influence the difference between the multiples?

   b. Would you expect the systematic risk for this industry to differ from that for the market? In what direction and why? What effect will this difference have on the industry multiple relative to the market multiple?

   c. Analyze the different components of growth (retention rate, equity turnover, and profit margin) for your industry and the S&P 400 during the most recent ten years and discuss each of the components. On the basis of this discussion, would you expect the growth rate for your industry to be above or below the growth rate for the S&P 400? How would this difference in growth affect the difference between the multiples?

419

d. Given the conclusions reached in a, b, and c above, is the difference in the industry multiple found in Question 14 logical and justified?

REFERENCES

Abernathy, William J., and Kenneth Wayne. "The Limits of the Learning Curve." *Harvard Business Review*. 52 no. 5 (September–October 1974).

Bonham, Howard B. Jr. "The Use of Input-Output Economics in Common Stock Analysis." *Financial Analysts Journal*. 23 no. 1 (January–February 1967).

Brigham, Eugene F., and James L. Pappas. "Rates of Return on Common Stock." *Journal of Business*. 42 no. 3 (July 1969).

Cheney, Harlan L. "The Value of Industry Forecasting as an Aid to Portfolio Management." *Appalachian Financial Review*. 1 no. 5 (Spring 1970).

Fruhan, William E. Jr. *Financial Strategy*. Homewood, Ill.: Richard D. Irwin, 1979.

Gaumnitz, Jack E. "The Influence of Industry Factors in Stock Price Movements." Paper presented at Southern Finance Association Meeting, October 1970. Subsequently released as University of Kansas School of Business working paper no. 42 (June 1971).

Hodes, D. A. "Input-Output Analysis: An Illustrative Example." *Business Economics*. 1 no. 3 (Summer 1965).

King, Benjamin F. "Market and Industry Factors in Stock Price Behavior." *Journal of Business*. 39 no. 1, part 2 (January 1966).

Latané, Henry A., and Donald L. Tuttle. "Framework for Forming Probability Beliefs." *Financial Analysts Journal*. 24 no. 4 (July–August 1968).

Livingston, Miles. "Industry Movements of Common Stocks." *Journal of Finance*. 32 no. 3 (June 1977).

Meyers, Stephen L. "A Re-Examination of Market and Industry Factors in Stock Price Behavior." *Journal of Finance*. 32 no. 3 (June 1973).

Porter, Michael E. "Industry Structure and Competitive Strategy: Key to Profitability." *Financial Analysts Journal*. 36 no. 4 (July–August 1980).

Porter, Michael E. *Competitive Strategies: Techniques for Analyzing Industries and Competitors*. New York: The Free Press, 1980.

Reilly, Frank K., and Eugene Drzycimski. "Alternative Industry Performance and Risk." *Journal of Financial and Quantitative Analysis*. 9 no. 3 (June 1974).

Reilly, Frank K., and Thomas Zeller. "An Analysis of Relative Industry Price-Earnings Ratios." *The Financial Review*. 1974.

Tysseland, Milford S. "Further Tests of the Validity of the Industry Approach to Investment Analysis." *Journal of Financial and Quantitative Analysis*. 6 no. 2 (March 1971).

Appendix 13A

Preparing an Industry Analysis

Studies of the price movements of individual stocks have indicated that basic market trends over the short to intermediate term are more influential than any other factor. Industry trends are the second most important influence on a stock's price followed by those elements peculiar to the company itself. It is very important, therefore, to study industry characteristics and trends before projecting the outlook for individual issues. Here are some guidelines for preparing an industry appraisal.

WHAT IS AN INDUSTRY?*

Identifying the one industry into which a company can be classified may be difficult in today's business world. Airlines, railroads, and utilities are easy to categorize. But what of manufacturing companies with three different divisions, none of them dominant, for example? Some diversified companies may not be comparable to any other, but these are rare exceptions. Perhaps the best way to test whether a company you are studying fits into an industry grouping is to compare their numbers. You will soon learn if it fits. Thus, for purposes of this study, an industry may be defined as a group of companies with similar characteristics.

Characteristics to Study

1. Price history reveals valuable long-term relationships
   a. Price-earnings ratios
   b. Common stock yields
   c. Price-book ratios.
2. Operating data shows comparisons of
   a. Return on total investment (ROI)

---

*Reprinted with permission of Stanley D. Ryals, CFA

    b. Return on equity (ROE)
    c. Sales growth
    d. Net earnings growth
    e. Book value growth
    f. Earnings per share growth
    g. Profit margin trends.
3. Comparative results of industries
    a. Effect of business cycles on each industry group
    b. Secular trends affecting results
    c. The industry as compared to other industries as to growth
    d. Regulatory changes
    e. Importance of overseas operations.

Factors in Industry Analysis

Markets for products

1. Trends in the markets for the industry's major products, historical and projected
2. Industry growth relative to GNP; possible changes from past trends
3. Shares of markets for major products among domestic producers; changes in market shares in recent years; outlook
4. Effect of imports on their markets; share of market taken by imports; price and margin changes caused by imports.

Financial

1. Capitalization ratios; ability to raise new capital; earnings retention
2. Ratio of fixed assets to capital invested; depreciation policies; capital turnover
3. Return on total capital; return on equity capital
4. Return on foreign investments; need for foreign capital.

Operations

1. Degrees of integration; cost advantages of integration; major supply contracts
2. Operating rates as a percentage of capacity; backlogs; new order trends
3. Trends of industry consolidation
4. New product development; research and development budgets in both dollars and percentage of sales
5. Diversification; comparability of product lines; trends toward or away from major products.

Management

1. Management depth and ability to develop from within; board of directors; organizational structure
2. Flexibility to deal with product demand changes; weeding out losing operations

3. Record and outlook of labor relations
4. Dividend progression.

Sources of Industry Information.   For information on industries, check the library or these sources:
1. Recognized and independent industry journals
2. Industry and trade associations
3. Government reports and statistics
4. Independent research organizations
5. Brokerage house research.

Chapter 14   *Company Analysis*

A   t this point it is assumed that you have made two decisions. First, after an extensive analysis of the economy and aggregate stock market, you have decided that some portion of your portfolio should be in common stocks. Second, after an extensive analysis of a number of industries, you determined that certain industries will experience above average risk-adjusted performance over the relevant investment horizon. The question you now face is, *which companies within these desirable industries are best?* In this chapter we will discuss the procedure for analyzing the companies in an industry. Although in the discussion we will only consider one firm, *the same procedure should be applied for all firms in the industry to derive a ranking of firms.* Our ultimate objective is to select the best firms in the better industries and invest in them.

Before we discuss company analysis, we must consider the differences between types of companies and types of stocks.

TYPES OF COMPANIES AND TYPES OF STOCK[1]

The label given to a company is principally determined *internally* by the investment decisions of the firm (what assets they own) and by the operating and financial philosophy of the firm's management. When a company invests in assets (whether human or physical), it thereby determines its characteristics and accepts the accompanying risks and opportunities. At the same time, two different sets of management personnel can obtain substantially different results with the same set of assets. Management's operating and financial decisions can influence not only the expected flow of earnings, but also the *risk* inherent in it. Therefore, it is necessary to consider the assets of the firm, what the corporate management is capable of doing with these assets, and what they intend to do

---

[1] The discussion in this section draws heavily on Frank K. Reilly, "A Differentiation between Types of Companies and Types of Stock," *Mississippi Valley Journal of Business and Economics,* 7 no. 1 (Fall 1971): 35–43.

with them. Finally, these company factors should be compared to similar factors for all other companies to determine the firm's *relative* position in the universe of all companies.

The type of stock is determined by comparing the expected value of the security as shown with the market and alternative industries. The risk for a stock can be determined by internal characteristics or measured in terms of the stock's systematic risk.

The major point of the ensuing discussion is that the type of *company* and the type of *stock* is *not* necessarily the same; e.g., the stock of a growth company is *not* necessarily a growth stock. The recognition of this difference is very important for successful investing.

Growth Companies and Stocks

Growth companies have historically been defined in terms of results rather than causes. They are companies that consistently experience above average growth in sales and earnings. Unfortunately, such a definition means that many firms qualify on the basis of results that are not internally generated but that are the consequence of certain accounting procedures introduced in the course of mergers or other factors not indicative of superior markets or superior managements.

Currently, as a result of the writings of Solomon, Miller and Modigliani, and others, it has become generally accepted that *a true growth company is a firm with the management ability and the opportunities to invest in projects that yield returns greater than the firm's required rate of return* (i.e., its average cost of capital).[2] A growth company would be one that has the ability to acquire capital at an average cost of, say, 10 percent and yet has the management ability and the opportunity to invest those funds (whether internally generated or externally acquired) at rates of return in excess of 10 percent. As a result, the firm enjoys profits and earnings growth greater than that experienced by other firms in a similar risk category.

The result of being a true growth company (above average investment opportunities) is that the firm should, and typically does, retain a large portion of its earnings to invest in above average investment alternatives. Sales and earnings of the true growth firm grow faster than they do for average firms or for the overall economy. Given these expected results, the search for growth firms *ex post* typically involves examining a large cross section of firms to find companies that retain a substantial portion of earnings and that also consistently experienced above average increases in earnings. This method allows growth companies to be identified by *results* in contrast to the suggested definition that concentrates on *causes*. Searching for results means that the growth firm can be identified only after the fact. Examining firms in terms of causes may make it possible to identify a firm *before* it has exhibited superior growth or at least *while* it is in the early stages of growth.

---

[2] Ezra Solomon, *The Theory of Financial Management* (New York: Columbia University Press, 1963), 55–68; M. Miller and F. Modigliani, "Dividend Policy, Growth, and the Valuation of Shares," *Journal of Business,* 34 no. 4 (October 1961): 411–433.

A growth stock is a stock possessing superior return capabilities when compared to other stocks in the market with similar risk characteristics. This superior return potential is due to the fact that the stock *is undervalued* at a given point in time relative to other stocks in the market. In a strong form efficient market with perfect information, all firms would generate rates of return consistent with the systematic risk involved, and there would never be any growth stocks.[3] While the stock market is relatively efficient in adjusting stock prices to new information, it is also very likely that the information is not perfect or complete.[4] This means that at any point in time, owing to imperfect information or the lack of information, a given stock may be undervalued or overvalued.[5] If it is undervalued, the stock price should increase to reflect its value when the correct information becomes available. During the period in which the stock changes from an undervalued security to a properly valued security, the realized returns will exceed the required returns for a stock with its risk, and the stock will be considered a growth stock.

A future growth stock is basically a currently undervalued stock that has a high probability of being properly valued in the near term. This means that *growth stocks are not necessarily limited to growth companies.* If investors recognize a growth firm and discount the future earnings stream properly, the current market price will reflect the future growing earnings stream. The investor who acquires the stock of the growth company at this "correct" market price will receive only the market rate of return, even when the superior earnings growth is attained. If investors *overprice* the stock of a growth company and an investor pays the inflated price, the realized returns will be below the risk-adjusted normal return. A future growth stock can be issued by any type of company; it is only necessary that the stock has not been properly valued by the market at a given point in time.

As with a growth company, the search for a growth stock after the fact is relatively easy since it is necessary only to examine past returns relative to the risk involved. The search for *future* growth stocks is the function of a securities analyst. The ability to uncover such stocks *consistently* is, by definition, the description of a superior analyst.[6]

Defensive Companies and Stocks

A defensive company possesses assets and management such that there is a high probability that future earnings will withstand an economic downturn. Typical

---

[3] For a discussion of the relationship and a summary of some empirical evidence on the subject, see Richard A. Brealey, *An Introduction to Risk and Return from Common Stocks* (Cambridge, Mass.: The MIT Press, 1969), 47–54.

[4] For a discussion of price adjustment to new information, see Eugene F. Fama, "Efficient Capital Markets: Review of Theory and Empirical Work," *Journal of Finance,* 25 no. 2 (May 1970): 383–417. For a discussion of recent evidence, see Chapter 7.

[5] As noted in Chapter 7, an analyst is more likely to find such stocks outside the top tier of companies that is already being scrutinized by numerous analysts.

[6] See Eugene F. Fama, "Random Walks in Stock Market Prices," *Financial Analysts Journal,* 21 no. 5 (September-October 1965): 55–58. Also, the discussion in Chapter 7 on "Evaluating the Performance of Analysts."

examples of defensive firms are public utilities or grocery chains. They supply basic consumer necessities; therefore, they should not suffer a decline in sales and earnings during a period of reduced economic activity.

There are two concepts of a defensive stock. The first is consistent with the specification of a defensive company, while the second is derived from the statistical portfolio model. The first definition states that a defensive stock *is a stock that is not expected to experience a reduced rate of return during an overall market decline or that will experience significantly better performance than the market will during market declines.*

In contrast to a definition that is concerned only with the stock's rate of return during overall market *declines,* the second definition considers a stock's total price performance. In the discussion of portfolio theory it was noted that, in a state of equilibrium, the relevant risk measure for any risky asset is its covariance with the market portfolio of risky assets, i.e., its systematic risk. A stock with *low systematic risk* (a small beta) would be considered a defensive stock according to this theory. Because there are two definitions, it will be necessary, in the search for a defensive stock, to specify the definition being employed.

Cyclical Companies and Stocks

A cyclical company is one whose future earnings will be heavily influenced by aggregate business activity. In turn, this volatile net earnings pattern is a function of the firm's business risk and financial risk.

A cyclical stock is expected to experience changes in rates of return as great as or greater than changes in overall market rates of return. As was true of the growth company–growth stock relationship, the stock of a cyclical company is not necessarily cyclical. If investors recognize a company as cyclical and discount future earnings accordingly, it is possible that the rates of return on the stock of a cyclical company may hold up substantially better than aggregate market rates of return during a market decline. A cyclical stock could be the stock of a cyclical company or any company stock which has a price that is more volatile than overall market prices.[7] In terms of the CAPM, these *cyclical stocks would have high beta values.*

Speculative Companies and Stocks

A speculative company is one whose assets involve great risk; it offers a relatively large chance for a loss and a small chance for a large gain. The returns from the assets of a speculative firm have a great risk connected with them. There is a high probability that the returns to the firm will be either very low, nonexistent, or

---

[7] For a discussion of why the stocks of growth companies will decline more during periods of declining markets, see Burton Malkiel, "Equity Yields, Growth, and the Structure of Share Prices," *American Economic Review,* 53 no. 5 (December 1963): 1004–1031. Other articles have discussed the fact that growth stocks have longer *duration* than other stocks and this makes them more volatile. For this discussion, see Robert A. Hangen and Dean W. Wichern, "The Elasticity of Financial Assets," *Journal of Finance,* 29 no. 4 (September 1974): 1229–1240; John A. Boquist, George A. Racette, and Gary G. Schlarbaum, "Duration and Risk Assessment for Bonds and Common Stocks," *Journal of Finance,* 30 no. 5 (December 1975): pp 1360–1365; Frank K. Reilly and Rupinder S. Sidhu, "The Many Uses of Bond Duration," *Financial Analysts Journal,* 36 no. 4 (July–August 1980): 58–72.

negative. Typically, there is also a small probability of very substantial returns. A good example of a speculative firm is one involved in oil exploration.

A speculative stock is one that possesses a high probability of low or negative rates of return during a given period and a low probability of normal or high rates of return. There are two types of speculative stocks. The first is closely akin to the speculative company and is typified by the penny mining stock. There is a high probability that there will be no return on the stock during a given period, and most likely there will be a complete loss. At the same time, there is some small probability of very substantial gains.

The second type of speculative stock is almost the opposite of a growth stock. A growth stock is undervalued at the present time. In contrast, the second type of speculative stock is overpriced; therefore, there is a high probability that, in the future, during the period when the market adjusts the stock price to its true value, there will be either very low or possibly negative rates of return on it. This might be the case for an excellent growth *company* which has stock selling at an extremely high price-earnings ratio. In such a case the current stock price is reflecting a belief that outstanding growth will continue for a substantial period in the future.[8] If there is any reduction in the growth pattern or any disruption in growth, this price-earnings ratio can drop rapidly and substantially. The level of the current price-earnings ratio indicates that there is a very strong likelihood of a substantial price decline if everything does not conform to the most optimistic expectations. Therefore, *an overpriced stock is considered speculative.*

COMPANY ANALYSIS PROCEDURE

Analyzing an individual firm involves examining the internal characteristics of the firm and its relationship to its industry and to the economy. Based upon such an examination, an analyst should have some very strong convictions regarding the firm in terms of the time pattern of its earnings stream and its financial characteristics. This includes knowing something about the firm's sales volatility and operating leverage and, therefore, its *business risk.* Based upon an analysis of the firm's capital structure, it is possible to derive some estimates of its *financial risk.* The analyst should have an opinion about the *type of company* he is dealing with — is it a cyclical company, a defensive company, a speculative company, or a growth company?

After analyzing the company, it is necessary to consider the characteristics of the firm's common stock. *The type of company and the type of stock may not necessarily be the same!* As mentioned, the stock of a cyclical company may not be cyclical.

An Example

To demonstrate the procedure, we will analyze Safeway Stores, one of the firms in the retail food chain industry. For purposes of comparison with the industry

---

[8] For a method of measuring the implied period of growth, see Charles C. Holt, "The Influence of Growth Duration on Share Prices," *Journal of Finance,* 17 no. 3 (September 1962): 465–475. Other models for analyzing the stocks of growth companies are discussed in Chapter 15.

analysis, using a firm within the composite retail store group seemed appropriate. Unfortunately, it was not possible to examine any companies in the retail drug or the general merchandise group, because the industry indexes for both of these were started in 1970. We wanted specific industry data available since 1960 to allow reasonable historical analysis.

Safeway Stores is the largest grocery store chain in the United States. As of January 1984, the firm operated over 2,400 stores: about 2,100 in the U.S., the remainder in Canada, the United Kingdom, Australia, and West Germany. Of the stores in the U.S., the vast majority (about 90 percent) are located west of the Mississippi River.

You have decided to invest in equities, and you predict that the retail food chain industry should experience above average performance during the relevant investment horizon. Therefore, your company analysis involves examining all of the firms in the retail food chain industry to determine which stocks should experience the best performance within the industry. The objective is to estimate the expected return and risk for all the individual firms over the investment horizon. These values are then used by the portfolio manager as inputs into the portfolio model.

Estimating Expected Return

The analyst estimates the expected return for the investment by estimating the future value for the security, which indicates the expected capital gain or loss and, when combined with the expected dividend yield, indicates the expected return. The future value of the security is estimated using the dividend growth model to predict expected earnings and the expected earnings multiple for the stock. In turn, expected earnings is a function of the sales forecast and the estimated profit margin for the firm.

Sales Forecast.   The sales forecast includes an analysis of the relationship of company sales to various economic series that should influence the demand for the firm's products and a comparison of the firm's sales to the sales for the company's industry. Such an analysis is supported by the sales forecast derived in the industry analysis. This company–industry analysis indicates how the company is performing in relation to its most immediate competition.

Table 14.1 contains data on sales for Safeway Stores, sales per share for the retail food store industry, and several personal consumption expenditure (PCE) series. The most relevant is the personal consumption expenditure for food (PCE–food), which has comprised between 20 and 25 percent of total PCE. The scatter plot of Safeway sales and the PCE–food expenditures contained in Figure 14.1 indicates a good linear relationship. It also indicates that Safeway sales have been growing at a faster rate than the PCE for food has. During the period 1960–1982 Safeway sales increased by about 614 percent compared to an increase in PCE–food of 390 percent. In addition, Safeway sales grew from about 3.0 percent of the total PCE for food to over 4.4 percent. The first two regressions in Table 14.2 that relate Safeway sales to PCE–food support the relationship of levels and percentages of change. The percentage of change results reflect a

TABLE 14.1
Sales for Safeway Stores, the Retail Food Store Industry, and Various Economic Series, 1960–1982

Year	Safeway Stores (millions of $)	Retail Stores Food Industry (sales per share)	Personal Consumption Expenditures (PCE) (billions of $)	PCE per Capita ($)	PCE–Food (billions of $)	PCE: Food/Total Percentage
1960	2,469.0	293.76	324.9	1,797	81.1	25.0
1961	2,538.0	302.82	335.0	1,823	83.2	24.8
1962	2,509.6	311.17	355.2	1,904	85.5	24.1
1963	2,649.7	318.81	374.6	1,979	87.8	23.4
1964	2,817.6	331.89	400.5	2,087	92.7	23.2
1965	2,939.0	339.20	430.4	2,214	98.9	23.0
1966	3,345.2	367.21	465.1	2,366	106.6	22.9
1967	3,360.9	377.07	490.3	2,467	109.6	22.3
1968	3,685.7	399.19	536.9	2,674	118.7	22.1
1969	4,099.6	439.97	581.8	2,870	127.5	21.9
1970	4,860.2	464.40	621.7	3,031	138.9	22.3
1971	5,358.8	482.38	672.2	3,237	144.2	21.5
1972	6,057.6	526.29	737.1	3,511	154.9	21.0
1973	6,773.7	563.16	812.0	3,831	172.1	21.2
1974	8,185.2	588.26	888.1	4,152	193.7	21.8
1975	9,716.9	637.67	976.4	4,521	213.6	21.9
1976	10,442.5	619.07	1,084.3	4,972	230.6	21.3
1977	11,249.4	667.55	1,204.4	5,468	249.8	20.7
1978	12,550.6	690.69	1,346.5	6,048	275.9	20.5
1979	13,717.9	714.74	1,507.2	6,695	311.6	20.7
1980	15,102.7	808.53	1,667.2	7,323	343.7	20.6
1981	16,580.3	871.91	1,843.2	8,018	375.3	20.4
1982	17,632.8	904.98	1,972.0	8,498	397.8	20.2

SOURCE: Reprinted by permission of Standard & Poor's

FIGURE 14.1
Scatter Plot of Safeway Sales and Personal Consumption Expenditures for Food:
1960–1982 (billions of $)

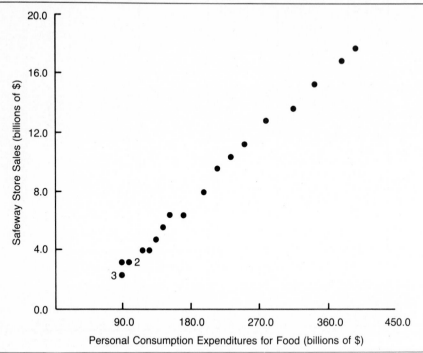

significant relationship and indicate that Safeway sales are more volatile than the PCE is because they are growing faster than the PCE for food is.

The figures in the last column of Table 14.1 indicate that, during this period, the proportion of PCE allocated to food went from 25 percent in 1960 to only 20.2 percent in 1982. Therefore, Safeway derived an increasing share of these expenditures. The declining proportion of PCE spent on food, especially at retail food chains, apparently is a function of the changing lifestyle of consumers. With an increase in disposable income, less of it is spent on necessities such as food and shelter. In addition, an increasing proportion of meals are consumed outside the home, so a larger percentage of food expenditures is spent at restaurants and fast-food outlets.

Regarding the relationship between Safeway sales and the total PCE, Safeway grew faster than the total, 614 percent for Safeway versus 507 percent for total PCE. Most of Safeway's growth has been internal, since the number of common shares outstanding during this period has only gone from about 25 million (adjusted for a split) in 1960 to about 26 million at the end of 1982. In turn, internal growth has been a function of a small increase in the number of stores, from 2,207 in 1960 to 2,454 in 1982. *The more important change has been a major increase in the annual sales per store because of the upgrading of stores.* The net number of stores has increased by about 250, which includes the con-

TABLE 14.2

Results for Regressions Between Safeway Sales and Various Economic and
Industry Series

Dependent Variable	Independent Variable	α (t value)	β (t value)	R^2	S.E.	F.	D.W.
Safeway Sales (levels)	PCE – Food (levels)	−1785.53 + (−10.49)	50.00 (60.74)	.99	385.05	3689.85	.36
Safeway Sales (%Δ)	PCE – Food (%Δ)	− .06 + (−.03)	1.27 (4.65)	.52	3.95	3.95	1.45
Safeway Sales (levels)	PCE (levels)	− 999.42 + (−5.17)	9.76 (49.95)	.99	467.62	2495.10	.38
Safeway Sales (%Δ)	PCE (%Δ)	− .15 + (− .04)	1.12 (2.40)	.22	5.02	5.77	1.58
Safeway Sales (levels)	PCE per Capita (levels)	−2108.16 + (−10.95)	2.37 (55.20)	.99	423.49	3046.74	.43
Safeway Sales (%Δ)	PCE per Capita (%Δ)	1.34 + (.40)	1.11 (2.53)	.24	4.96	6.41	1.61
Safeway Sales (levels)	Retail Food Stores Sales (levels)	−6234.48 + (−11.76)	25.96 (27.15)	.97	851.99	736.96	.34
Safeway Sales (%Δ)	Retail Food Stores Sales (%Δ)	5.75 + (2.83)	.70 (2.18)	.19	5.12	4.73	1.32

struction of a number of new, large stores and the closing of many smaller stores in declining areas.

The regressions in Table 14.2 confirm that there is a significant relationship between sales and total PCE. Notably, the relationship is not as strong as the one with PCE–food, and the coefficients that are greater than one indicate the large percentages of change in Safeway sales relative to the PCE series.

The relationship between sales for the Safeway Stores and sales per share for the retail food store industry is not as consistent as the prior economic analysis, but it is impressive in terms of the performance by Safeway. Again, for the total period, Safeway sales increased by 614 percent compared to an increase for the industry of only 216 percent. Because industry figures are sales per share, this could make some difference, but it would have little effect on Safeway because total outstanding shares have only increased by about 4 percent during the 22 years being considered.

This performance by Safeway is not very surprising given the previous analysis. Safeway sales grew faster than the total PCE, and the total PCE has grown faster than PCE–food. Finally, the sales growth for the retail food store index has been smaller than the growth in PCE–food. The industry index grew about 216 percent during the period 1960–1982 as compared to PCE–food growth of 390 percent.

The last two regressions in Table 14.2 confirm that there is a relationship between Safeway sales and retail food industry sales, but, again, the relationship is not as strong as the one with the aggregate series is. The slope of the percentage of change regression is not as large as one might expect, but the intercept, at almost 6 percent, is significant. This would indicate an average long-term growth of 6 percent in Safeway sales *in addition* to the growth in aggregate retail sales.

Sample Estimate of Safeway Sales.   Based on this, an analyst would likely concentrate on the regressions that relate Safeway sales to PCE – food. To estimate PCE – food it would be preferable to initially estimate total PCE and then to estimate the food component. Economists were generally forecasting an increase in PCE of 10 percent during 1984. Given a 1983 preliminary figure of $2135 billion, this implies a 1984 figure of $2348 billion ($2135 × 1.10). Regarding how much of this PCE will be spent on food, the data indicate a consistent decline to 20.2 percent in 1983. Assuming a further decline to 20.0 percent, this indicates an estimate of PCE – food of $470 billion in 1984 (.200 × $2348) which is a 9.0 percent increase from 1983 (470/431).

Using the second regression in Table 14.2, which has a coefficient of 1.27, this implies an 11.4 percent increase in Safeway sales (1.27 × 9.0). Admittedly, this appears to be a generous estimate following several years with increases between 6 and 10 percent.

Because other estimates with the regressions would generally confirm this estimate, they are not considered. An alternative estimate can be derived using company data on stores, square footage, sales per store, and sales per square foot. The figures are contained in Table 14.3. The data confirm the earlier discussion which noted that Safeway had experienced substantial increases in sales with a relatively small increase in the net number of stores. In general, the company has closed smaller stores and has built a number of very large stores that sell a variety of higher priced items. The result has been a consistent increase in total store area *and* an increase in sales per 1,000 square feet. The store area has generally increased by 2,000,000 square feet per year. Assuming such an increase in 1984, total area would be about 70,000,000 square feet. Sales per square feet have likewise increased and, assuming a further increase to $285,000, this would imply a sales forecast of about $20,000 million for 1984, which is a 7.5 percent increase over 1983 sales of $18,600 million.

Given the two estimates, the preference is for the lower figure with an upward adjustment to 9.5 percent. Therefore the final sales forecast for 1984 is *$20,400 million.*

The next step is to derive an estimate of the net profit margin for the firm.

Estimating the Profit Margin.   Analysis of the firm's profit margin should consider two general areas: the firm's internal performance and any changes that have occurred, and the firm's relationship to its industry. The initial analysis should indicate general trends for the firm and should point out areas of concern. When company performance is related to the industry, the analysis should indicate whether the company's performance (good or bad) is attributable to the industry or is unique to the firm. Profit margin figures for Safeway and the retail food industry are in Table 14.4 on page 434. The figures on the net before tax margin for Safeway and the retail food industry indicate a relatively steady decline for both series. This indicates that Safeway experienced a decline in its profit margin over the past 22 years and that part of this decline is related to a similar phenomenon in the total industry. The analyst should understand the reason for the industry decline and also what added factors contributed to Safeway's performance.

TABLE 14.3
Data on Number of Stores, Store Area and Sales for Safeway 1967–1982

Year	Number of Stores	Sales per Store	Store Area (1,000 sq. ft)	Sales per 1,000 sq ft.
1967	2,237	$1,502,405	37,850	$ 88,795
1968	2,241	1,644,663	39,033	94,425
1969	2,260	1,784,783	40,169	102,060
1970	2,297	2,115,876	41,769	116,358
1971	2,283	2,347,279	42,752	125,347
1972	2,331	2,258,727	44,844	135,082
1973	2,364	2,865,350	46,480	145,733
1974	2,426	3,373,945	50,159	163,185
1975	2,451	3,964,459	51,854	187,398
1976	2,438	4,283,237	53,223	196,203
1977	2,428	4,633,195	55,184	203,853
1978	2,436	5,152,122	57,461	218,419
1979	2,425	5,656,850	59,470	230,669
1980	2,416	6,251,106	62,069	243,321
1981	2,477	6,693,709	65,483	253,200
1982	2,454	7,185,339	66,816	263,901

Industry Factors. The major factors influencing the decline in industry profit margins over the past two decades have been the increased cost of advertising and other promotional drives and, more important, a number of price wars among the large chains.[9] Because of some overbuilding of stores during the 1950s, the chains engaged in heavy promotion and advertising during the 1960s in an attempt to hold their share of the market or even to increase it. In the early 1970s there were numerous price wars as A&P (The Great Atlantic and Pacific Tea Company), owing to its decline in volume, introduced price cuts to become competitive. These price wars continued sporadically for several years and seriously affected profit margins for several of the chains. The outlook is for more price stability and some improvement in the industry margins.

Company Factors. The major factor that affected Safeway's profit margin during the last several years has been the sporadic outbreak of price wars. The effect on Safeway was more intense, because the conflict was especially heavy in California where Safeway is highly concentrated. The general outlook for profit margins is good because of the continued building of larger stores that contain more nonfood items and high margin facilities, such as delicatessens.

Specific estimates for Safeway should probably begin with an analysis of the relationship between the firm's margin and the food chain industry margin as specified by the linear correlation model on the next page.[10]

[9] For a more complete discussion see "Retailing–Food," *Standard and Poor's Industry Surveys* (New York: Standard & Poor's Corp., 1983).

[10] Both the operating margin and the net before tax margin were analyzed, but the results indicated that the net profit margins yielded the best relationships.

TABLE 14.4
Profit Margins for Safeway Stores and the Retail Food Industry 1960–1982

Year	Safeway Stores						Retail Food Store Index[b]		
	Earnings after Costs & Expenses[a] (millions of $)	Percentage of Sales	Income Before Taxes (millions of $)	Percentage of Sales	Net Income	Percentage of Sales	Operating Profit Margin	NBT Margin	Net Profit Margin
1960	76.9	3.11	75.2	3.05	34.8	1.41	3.61	2.70	1.29
1961	81.1	3.20	78.6	3.10	36.6	1.44	3.54	2.59	1.25
1962	85.7	3.41	83.3	3.32	39.3	1.57	3.58	2.56	1.23
1963	95.9	3.62	94.7	3.57	44.8	1.69	3.41	2.40	1.19
1964	101.9	3.62	97.9	3.47	50.0	1.77	3.45	2.39	1.24
1965	99.1	3.37	95.1	3.24	48.2	1.64	3.33	2.28	1.23
1966	121.2	3.62	117.8	3.52	59.7	1.78	3.28	2.22	1.20
1967	103.4	3.08	100.2	2.98	50.9	1.51	3.08	2.07	1.10
1968	118.5	3.21	115.5	3.13	55.1	1.49	3.19	2.11	1.07
1969	112.9	2.75	108.9	2.66	51.3	1.25	3.18	2.13	1.07
1970	146.1	3.01	140.7	2.89	68.9	1.41	3.19	2.14	1.10
1971	158.4	2.96	155.3	2.90	80.2	1.50	2.77	1.69	.92
1972	176.3	2.91	168.6	2.78	91.1	1.50	1.90	.86	.53
1973	166.6	2.46	157.5	2.33	86.3	1.27	2.48	1.35	.78
1974	156.2	1.91	140.8	1.72	79.2	.97	2.58	.85	.27
1975	287.9	2.96	275.3	2.83	148.6	1.53	2.53	1.59	.90
1976	196.9	1.89	191.3	1.83	105.6	1.01	2.53	1.57	.87
1977	250.4	2.22	184.2	1.64	102.3	.91	2.76	1.47	.82
1978[c]	352.8	2.81	289.6	2.31	159.0	1.27	3.25	1.79	.93
1979	306.6	2.23	229.2	1.67	147.7	1.08	3.22	1.78	1.05
1980	286.8	1.90	203.7	1.35	129.1	.86	2.90	1.44	.83
1981	270.9	1.63	166.3	1.00	108.3	.65	2.96	1.19	.58
1982	351.2	1.99	248.3	1.41	159.7	.91	3.33	1.82	1.10

[a] Costs and expenses include cost of sales and selling, general, and administrative expenses.

[b] SOURCE: Standard & Poor's, *Analysts Handbook* (New York: Standard & Poor's Corp., 1983). Reprinted by permission.

[c] The figures for 1978 onward are adjusted for a change in the method of accounting for translation of foreign currencies to conform with the Statement of Financial Accounting Standards No. 52. The change was made in 1982 with prior figures adjusted to reflect the change.

Safeway Net Proft Margin$_t$ = a_t + b_t (Retail Food Chain Net Profit Margin$_t$).

The results of such a model for the period 1960–1982 indicated the following:

$$a_t = 0.626 \qquad b_t = 0.711 \qquad R^2 = .343$$
$$(t) = 3.31 \qquad F = 10.98.$$

These correlation results, along with the estimate of the food chain profit margin for the subsequent year, would imply one estimate. As always, you should consider any unique factors that would cause this long-run relationship to deviate from expectations this coming year — e.g., foreign exchange charges; an abnormal number of store openings — any expectations regarding price wars that would affect Safeway more or less than the average.

You might also want to consider the relationship between percentages of change (%Δ) in the profit margins as follows:

%Δ Safeway Net Profit Margin$_t$ = a_t + b_t (%Δ Retail Food Chain Industry Net Profit Margin$_t$),

where:

$$a_t = -2.180 \qquad b_t = 0.274 \qquad R^2 = .497$$
$$(t) = 4.44 \qquad F = 19.77.$$

Again, following the industry analysis you would have an estimate of the percentage of change in the industry profit margin. Using this long-run relationship, you can derive another estimate for Safeway that should be adjusted for any unique expectations.

In addition, the investor should analyze the firm's income statement for a number of years on the basis of a 100 percent breakdown (also referred to as a *common size statement*). The extent of the breakdown depends upon the consistent detail provided by the firm. As an example, Table 14.5 contains a common size statement for the period 1977–1982. The main items of interest would be cost of goods sold and operating and administrative expense. An analysis of these items for Safeway is both encouraging and discouraging. The cost of goods figure has been under control and was at its lowest point in 1982. In contrast, the firm's operating and administrative expense (O&A) has grown steadily over time and has increased by more than sales have. As a result, the O&A expense has grown steadily from 18.5 percent in 1974 to 20.7 percent in 1982 and more than offset the decline in percentage of cost of goods sold. The firm's interest expense has also increased as the firm added new store leases, but this expense has generally been consistent with growth because the percentage has increased only slightly. The impact of the rising O&A expense can be seen from the net before tax margin that went from 2.3 percent in 1978 to 1.4 percent in 1982. Even with a relatively low tax rate, the net income margin is 0.9 percent.

Net Margin Estimate.   The overall outlook for the industry is encouraging because of a decline in price wars and generally more stable prices. Also, there has been an increase in mechanization within the industry and a continuing tendency to broaden product lines to include high profit items like drugs and

TABLE 14.5
Common Size Income Statement for Safeway Stores 1977–1982[a]

	1982		1981		1980	
	$(000)	Percentage	$(000)	Percentage	$(000)	Percentage
Sales	17,632,821	100.0	16,580,318	100.0	15,102,673	100.00
Cost of Goods Sold	13,628,052	77.3	12,945,923	78.1	11,816,733	78.2
Gross Profit	4,004,769	22.7	3,634,395	21.9	3,285,940	21.8
Operating & Administrative Expense	3,653,561	20.7	3,363,478	20.3	2,999,130	19.9
Interest Expense	129,484	.7	120,393	.7	99,614	.7
Other Income–Net	(26,536)		(15,822)		(16,486)	
Net before Taxes	248,260	1.4	166,346	1.0	203,682	1.3
Income Taxes	88,600	.5	58,062	.3	74,544	.4
Net Income	159,660	.9	108,284	.7	129,138	.9
Tax Rate	35.7%		34.9%		36.6%	

[a] Figures for 1978–1982 reflect a change in accounting for translation of foreign currencies to conform with Statement of Financial Accounting Standards No. 52.
SOURCE: Safeway *Annual Report,* 1982, Safeway Stores, Inc.

cosmetics. Therefore, the industry margin should increase during 1984 and, given the relationship of Safeway to the industry, the firm should likewise show an increase. In addition, it is believed that Safeway should be able to reduce the rate of increase in the O&A expense, and any improvement in this area will be reflected in the margin. Therefore, the estimate for Safeway's net margin in 1984 is 1.03 percent.

This margin estimate combined with the prior sales estimate of $20,400 million indicates net income of *$210 million.* Assuming about 54 million common shares outstanding after the 2-for-1 stock split in 1983, this implies earnings of about *$3.90 per share* for 1984. This constitutes an increase of about 20 percent over the earnings of $3.26 per share in 1983. The next step is to estimate the earnings multiple for Safeway.

Estimating the Earnings Multiple

Similar to the procedure for the industry multiple, this analysis involves the macro relationships between the company multiple and the industry and market multiples and a micro analysis of the individual variables that affect a firm's multiple.

Macro Analysis of Earnings Multiple.   Table 14.6 contains the mean earnings multiple for the company, the retail food store industry, and the aggregate market for each year from 1960–1982. In general, the earnings multiple for Safeway has been lower than the multiple for either the retail food industry or the aggregate market. This is true for almost all the individual years and on average. The regression relationship of Safeway's multiple to its industry and the market is shown in Table 14.7. All the regressions indicate that the relationships are significant, and the levels results confirm that the Safeway multiple has been smaller

1979		1978		1977	
$(000)	Percentage	$(000)	Percentage	$(000)	Percentage
13,717,861	100.0	12,550,569	100.0	11,249,398	100.0
10,793,570	78.7	9,828,391	78.3	8,916,719	79.3
2,924,291	21.3	2,722,178	21.7	2,332,679	20.7
2,617,697	19.1	2,369,324	18.9	2,082,246	18.5
91,276	.7	74,110	.6	70,104	.6
(13,865)		10,826		(3,918)	
229,183	1.7	289,570	2.3	184,247	1.6
81,456	.6	130,600	1.0	81,942	.7
147,727	1.1	158,970	1.3	102,305	.9
35.5%		45.1%		44.5%	

TABLE 14.6
Average Earnings Multiple for Safeway, the Retail Food Store Industry, and the Standard & Poor's 400 1960–1982

		Safeway				Retail Food Stores			S&P 400
		Price[a]			Mean		Mean	Mean	Mean
Year	EPS[a]	High	Low	Mean	P/E	EPS	Price	P/E	P/E
1960	1.36	20.25	16.25	18.25	13.42	3.78	55.45	14.67	17.70
1961	1.42	31.87	18.33	25.11	17.68	3.78	74.09	19.60	20.41
1962	1.53	30.18	18.12	24.15	15.79	3.83	67.33	17.58	16.98
1963	1.75	32.37	22.68	27.53	15.73	3.79	64.73	17.08	17.07
1964	1.94	37.75	28.00	32.88	16.95	4.13	68.81	16.66	17.63
1965	1.89	42.25	30.12	36.19	19.15	4.16	73.51	17.67	16.82
1966	2.35	31.50	23.67	27.38	11.65	4.39	59.31	13.51	15.20
1967	2.00	28.12	21.37	24.75	12.38	4.13	53.44	12.94	17.04
1968	2.16	31.25	23.25	27.25	12.62	4.29	61.52	14.34	17.30
1969	2.01	30.25	23.50	26.88	13.37	4.76	61.66	13.12	17.46
1970	2.70	34.37	22.12	28.25	10.46	5.09	49.50	11.69	16.49
1971	3.08	40.25	32.12	36.19	11.75	4.44	69.18	15.58	18.02
1972	3.48	44.25	34.00	39.13	11.24	2.80	61.63	22.01	17.95
1973	3.28	44.12	27.25	35.69	10.88	4.37	55.67	12.74	13.38
1974	2.98	43.87	29.62	36.75	12.33	1.61	50.18	31.17	9.43
1975	5.64	52.62	34.12	43.37	7.69	5.71	52.19	9.14	10.79
1976	3.89	50.25	39.25	44.75	11.50	5.41	57.40	10.61	10.45
1977	3.93	50.38	39.00	44.69	11.37	5.49	57.12	10.40	9.48
1978	6.10	46.00	35.38	40.69	6.67	6.42	55.80	8.69	8.19
1979	5.66	44.00	33.62	38.81	6.86	7.47	58.88	7.88	7.11
1980	4.94	36.25	26.00	31.12	6.30	6.71	52.32	7.80	8.44
1981	4.15	37.75	24.25	31.00	7.47	5.08	56.53	11.13	8.45
1982	6.11	50.25	26.25	38.25	6.26	9.98	70.78	7.09	10.39
Mean[b]	—	—	—	—	11.69	—	—	13.27	14.22

[a] Adjusted for 2 for 1 split in 1964.
[b] Excluding 1974.
SOURCE: Reprinted by permission of Standard & Poor's.

TABLE 14.7
Results of Regressions between Safeway Multiple and Multiple for the Industry and the Market 1960–1982 (excluding 1974)

Dependent Variable	Independent Variable	α	β	R^2	S.E.	F.	D.W.
Safeway P/E	Retail Food Store P/E (levels)	1.66 (.98)	+ 0.76 (6.16)	.65	2.29	37.91	1.27
Safeway P/E (%Δ)	Retail Food Store P/E (%Δ)	− .19 (−0.05)	+ .53 (3.85)	.44	17.04	14.84	2.43
Safeway P/E (levels)	S&P 400 P/E (levels)	1.26 (.70)	+ .73 (6.03)	.65	2.32	36.41	1.05
Safeway P/E (%Δ)	S&P 400 P/E (%Δ)	−1.60 (− .32)	+ .23 (.57)	.02	22.55	.33	2.75

than the industry or market multiple. Further, the percentage of change regression indicates that Safeway's multiple is less volatile than the industry multiple (0.53) and the market multiple (0.23). The better relationship in terms of explanatory power (R^2) was with the industry multiple.

Micro Analysis of Earnings Multiple. The variables that should influence the multiple are the dividend-payout ratio, the risk for the security, and the expected growth rate for the firm, which, in turn, is a function of the retention rate and the return on equity. The historical data for these series are contained in Table 14.8. The relevant questions are: why has the Safeway multiple been consistently below the market multiple? Would we expect this relationship to persist based upon the relationship of the relevant variables?

Dividend-payout ratio. The dividend-payout ratio for Safeway compared to its industry indicates that the payout for Safeway has been lower than that of its industry, as reflected in the average for the period. The relationship between the Safeway payout and the market payout is less consistent. The overall relationship is for Safeway to have a similar payout. Taken by themselves, these results would indicate that the Safeway multiple should be *below* the multiple for the industry and about equal to the aggregate market.

Required rate of return (i). This analysis should consider the firm's internal risk characteristics (BR, FR, LR), and the stock's systematic market risk (beta). One would expect Safeway to have relatively low business risk because of its sales growth, which has been more stable than that of both its industry and the aggregate economy (in terms of food expenditure). Unfortunately, over the long run the firm has experienced a relatively high level of operating leverage because of the price wars discussed earlier. As a result, the operating profit figures for Safeway have been quite volatile. In fact, the firm's coefficient of variation (CV) of operating earnings during the last five- and ten-year periods has been

TABLE 14.8
Variables that Influence the Earnings Multiple for Safeway, Retail Food Chains, and the Standard & Poor's 400 1960–1982

Year	Safeway				Retail Food Chains				S&P 400			
	Dividends/Earnings	Equity Turnover	Profit Margin	ROE	Dividends/Earnings	Equity Turnover	Profit Margin	ROE	Dividends/Earnings	Equity Turnover	Profit Margin	ROE
1960	50.77	10.63	1.41	15.00	48.94	10.02	1.29	12.89	58.82	1.76	5.72	10.08
1961	52.03	10.11	1.44	14.58	52.12	9.67	1.25	12.07	61.42	1.71	5.66	9.67
1962	51.06	9.29	1.57	14.54	59.27	9.45	1.23	11.63	57.44	1.78	5.93	10.53
1963	46.24	9.00	1.69	15.22	59.37	9.30	1.19	11.06	55.66	1.79	6.19	11.11
1964	46.75	8.74	1.77	15.51	57.14	9.15	1.24	11.39	53.20	1.82	6.63	12.06
1965	52.66	8.49	1.64	13.92	58.89	9.06	1.23	11.11	51.27	1.85	6.82	12.64
1966	43.58	8.74	1.78	15.60	57.63	9.28	1.20	11.10	50.26	1.94	6.64	12.88
1967	54.97	8.34	1.51	12.63	63.20	9.18	1.10	10.05	52.85	1.92	6.12	11.76
1968	50.92	8.58	1.49	12.82	58.04	9.27	1.07	9.96	51.30	2.02	6.07	12.27
1969	54.65	8.99	1.25	11.25	54.04	9.54	1.07	10.19	53.02	2.10	5.65	11.86
1970	42.55	9.78	1.41	13.86	50.29	9.67	1.10	10.60	59.15	2.09	4.92	10.28
1971	42.21	10.49	1.47	15.42	59.91	9.63	.92	8.86	52.93	2.14	5.04	10.80
1972	38.79	10.63	1.47	15.63	75.36	10.44	.53	5.55	47.14	2.21	5.30	11.71
1973	45.73	10.97	1.25	13.71	41.88	10.75	.78	8.34	38.92	2.37	5.96	14.15
1974	57.05	12.54	.94	11.79	133.54	12.27	.27	3.36	38.61	2.69	5.28	14.17
1975	33.69	12.93	1.51	19.52	36.43	12.60	.90	11.28	43.36	2.63	4.63	12.11
1976	52.70	13.01	.97	12.62	41.22	12.87	.87	11.25	39.47	2.66	5.27	14.02
1977	55.09	13.26	.91	12.07	45.36	13.30	.82	10.94	43.23	2.73	5.11	13.93
1978	37.70	13.90	1.27	17.65	41.74	13.63	.93	12.66	41.18	2.81	5.19	14.60
1979	45.94	13.79	1.08	14.89	40.56	13.76	1.05	14.38	36.34	2.96	5.57	16.50
1980	52.63	14.31	.86	12.31	48.29	16.21	.83	12.29	40.26	3.02	4.92	14.88
1981	62.65	15.42	.65	10.02	69.88	15.39	.58	8.97	41.88	2.97	4.86	14.42
1982	43.37	15.51	.91	14.04	39.48	14.87	1.10	16.40	54.10	2.82	3.95	11.16
Mean[a]	49.29	11.19	1.32	14.11	52.68	11.17	1.01	11.05	49.24	2.28	5.55	12.43

[a] Excluding 1974.

SOURCE: Reprinted by permission of Standard & Poor's.

TABLE 14.9
Coefficient of Variation of Operating Earnings: Safeway; Retail Food Stores; S&P 400

	Safeway	Retail Food Store	S&P 400
5 Year (1978–1982)	.106	.107	.068
10 Year (1973–1982)	.253	.249	.213
10 Year around Trend	.080	.079	.067

SOURCE: Reprinted by permission of Standard & Poor's.

above comparable figures for the industry and for the S&P 400. As shown in Table 14.9, the firm's five-year CV was about 50 percent above that for the S&P 400, and the ten-year comparison was also higher. Because the ten-year figure could have been influenced by growth,[11] the analysis was repeated computing the deviation from a trend line that adjusted for growth. The result was a smaller CV for Safeway, but it still exceeded the CV for the industry and the market. Therefore, one would have to conclude that Safeway has experienced *higher business risk* than its industry or the market has experienced.

The firm's financial risk is comparable to that of its industry and somewhat above that of the aggregate market, after considering the effect of capitalizing leases. When they were not required to capitalize leases, retail firms had only minimal debt on their balance sheet. After capitalizing leases and adjusting the interest charges, Safeway had an interest coverage ratio of less than 3.0 and a debt to total capital ratio of over 50 percent. These ratios are about equal to those for other retail firms after capitalizing leases. The interest coverage ratio is a little below the aggregate market average of about 3.5, and the debt/total capital ratio is above the overall average of approximately 45 percent. Therefore, one would probably conclude that Safeway's *financial risk is somewhat above average.*

The firm's external market *liquidity risk* is quite low compared to that for its industry and substantially below the figure for the average firm in the aggregate. The factors generally indicating market liquidity are: (1) the number of stockholders, (2) the number of shares outstanding, (3) the number of shares traded, and (4) institutional interest in the stock as indicated by the number of institutions that own the stock and the proportion of stock owned by institutions. As of January 1, 1984, the firm had 57,619 holders of common stock compared to the NYSE requirement of only 2,000 round lot owners (i.e., owners of 100 shares or more). In terms of its ranking among all firms on the NYSE, it is almost certain that this number would place Safeway in the top 150 or better. As of the end of 1983, following a 2 for 1 split there were over 53,000,000 common shares outstanding with a market value of *over $1.3 billion.* Clearly Safeway would qualify as an investment for those institutions that require firms with large market value (recall that the limit was set at between $200 and $400 million to be in the top

---

[11] The standard deviation is adversely affected by a strong growth trend because the deviations are computed from the overall mean. Therefore, high growth firms will have a higher standard deviation just because of growth.

tier). The percentage of shares traded averages about 2 percent per month, which would indicate monthly volume of over 1 million and annual turnover of 24 percent, somewhat above the NYSE average of 20–21 percent. All of these characteristics are apparently appreciated by financial institutions since they own about 7 million shares of Safeway, constituting about 27 percent of the outstanding shares. Finally, if one considers the *Amivest Liquidity Ratio* a useful measure of market liquidity, as of August 1983 the three-month average ratio for Safeway was 903, which ranked it 153 among all stocks on the NYSE and ASE. This compares to an Amivest value of 124 for A&P (ranked 724) and 157 for Jewel (which was ranked 662). In fact, the food store chain closest to Safeway was Kroger with an Amivest ratio of 790 and a rank of 185. The overall average for 35 food chains was 101. Therefore, based upon almost any measure of external market liquidity, *Safeway has the lowest liquidity risk in its industry.* The firm's liquidity relative to the aggregate market is also quite good, as indicated by its rank of 153 on the NYSE. This is further confirmed by comparing Safeway's Amivest ratio of 903 to an average for all NYSE stocks of 427, which indicates that Safeway has about twice as much liquidity as the average stock on the exchange has. Therefore, Safeway has *much lower liquidity risk* than the aggregate market does.

It appears, then, that Safeway has above average business risk and somewhat above average financial risk. It is clear that Safeway's common stock has a below average liquidity risk. Because of the overriding importance of business and financial risk, one would probably conclude that the overall risk for Safeway is above the average for the market.

The systematic risk for Safeway is derived using the linear regression model that relates rates of return for Safeway to comparable rates of return for the S&P 500 series. According to a June 1983 *Value Line* report on Safeway, the firm's historical beta was 0.80, which would indicate a below average market risk.

The overall consensus probably indicates risk about equal to that of the aggregate market with a tendency toward above average risk. This would suggest a multiple equal to or slightly below the market multiple.

Expected Growth Rate (g).   The expected growth rate of dividends is dependent on the expected growth rate of earnings, which is a function of the retention rate and the return on equity (ROE). Based upon our discussion of the dividend-payout ratio, we know that, generally, Safeway has had a lower payout than either the industry or the aggregate market had, which implies a slightly higher retention rate.

We know that the firm's ROE is a function of the equity turnover and the profit margin. The figures in Table 14.8 indicate that the equity turnover for Safeway has been typically similar to what it has been for the overall industry, as shown by the average values (11.19 vs. 11.17). The yearly and average turnover for Safeway is substantially larger than that for the aggregate market, as one would expect given the nature of the retail industry. This turnover comparison would indicate that the industry should grow at the same rate that Safeway will.

The profit margin results indicate that Safeway does better than the industry overall. The profit margin for Safeway is almost always larger than that for the industry. The average margin for Safeway is more than 30 percent larger than the industry margin (1.32 vs. 1.01), but notably, the industry was above Safeway in 1982. Again, as expected, the Safeway margin is always lower than the aggregate margin.

The combined effect of turnover and profit margin indicates an ROE for Safeway that is substantially higher than the industry figure (14.11 vs. 11.05) and also higher than the aggregate market figure (14.11 vs. 12.43). The computed ROE figures implied by the equity turnovers and margin figures are very close to the long-run average figures, as one would expect.

	Equity Turnover	Profit Margin	Expected ROE	Average ROE
Safeway	11.19	1.32	14.77	14.11
Industry	11.17	1.01	11.28	11.05
S&P 400	2.28	5.55	12.65	12.43

SOURCE: Reprinted by permission of Standard & Poor's.

These results for ROE, combined with the results for the retention rate, imply a higher growth rate for Safeway than will be experienced by the industry or the economy. The derived figures are shown below.

	Retention Rate	ROE	Expected Growth Rate
Safeway	.507	14.11	7.15
Retail Food Chain Industry	.473	11.05	5.23
S&P 400	.508	12.43	6.31

SOURCE: Reprinted by permission of Standard & Poor's.

These results indicate a higher growth rate for Safeway and, other things being equal, a higher multiple.

The combined effect.   The overall effect of the three variables indicates that the earnings multiple for Safeway should be about equal to, or slightly below that for its industry and the market. The payout indicates a lower multiple, and the risk likewise indicates a lower multiple for Safeway. In contrast, the growth rate for Safeway has been above that of the industry and the market, but it is necessary to discount this historical growth because of the weakness in the profit margin.

An Example of a Multiple Estimate.   The macro analysis indicated that Safeway's multiple was below that of the industry and less volatile. Alternatively, it indicated percentages of change comparable to those occurring in the market. The micro analysis indicated a multiple comparable to the market's or slightly below it. It was estimated that the market multiple would be about 9.0 and the retail store multiple would be about 8.6. Based upon the foregoing, the multiple for Safeway should be between 8.0 and 8.4.

Price estimate.   In the earnings section, we estimated earnings for Safeway of $3.90 per share. Assuming a multiple of 8.0 implies a year-end price of about $31.00 (8.0 × $3.90). Using a multiple of 8.4 implies a price of about $32.75 (8.4 × $3.90).

ALTERNATIVE EARNINGS MULTIPLE MODELS

In contrast to the approach in which individual components of the multiple are examined in relation to the industry and market, several authors have analyzed a large cross section of stocks using regression analysis. The best-known study was done by Whitbeck and Kisor who examined the estimated earnings multiple for a cross section of stocks. The multiple was computed as the current price for the stock divided by the normalized earnings for the company as estimated by the analysts at a New York bank.[12] The estimated multiple was regressed against three variables that intuitively seemed related to the multiple. Although there was no formal model used, the variables selected were quite consistent with those derived from the dividend growth model: the dividend-payout ratio, an earnings variability measure to reflect business risk, and an earnings growth variable.

The results indicated that all the variables had the expected sign and apparently were significant (although no standard errors were reported). The empirical regression results were as follows for the historical period:

Theoretical P/E Ratio
$$= 8.2 + 1.5 \text{ (Growth Rate)} + 6.7 \text{ (Payout)} - .2 \text{ (Standard Deviation)}.$$

The authors then tested the usefulness of the model in stock selection. For each of the 135 stocks in their sample, they computed the theoretical P/E ratio based upon their *projected* payout, earnings variability, and growth, and compared this theoretical P/E ratio value to the prevailing value. Stocks that had an actual P/E ratio 15 percent below the theoretical P/E ratio were considered undervalued, while stocks with a P/E ratio 15 percent above the theoretical value were considered overvalued. An analysis of the two groups indicated that the undervalued group consistently outperformed the S&P 500 on the basis of rate of return during the four individual quarters. The overvalued group consistently underperformed the S&P 500.

While these results are quite encouraging, it should be recognized that they contain a great deal of nonhistorical information. The P/E ratio is not historical but is equal to price over earnings normalized by an analyst. Further, all the explanatory variables are estimates generated using historical data adjusted by an analyst to take account of current and projected events.

Numerous papers on the same general topic followed, but one of the most complete and informative for practical purposes was done by Malkiel and

---

[12] V. Whitbeck and M. Kisor, "A New Tool in Investment Decision Making," *Financial Analysts Journal*, 19 no. 3 (May–June 1963): 55–62.

444   Cragg.[13] After developing a dividend growth valuation model, the authors employed the following empirical variables:
— The dividend-payout ratio
— The variance of earnings
— A systematic market risk variable (beta)
— A financial risk variable
— Short-term and long-term growth variables.

The model was tested using *historical* financial measures and *expected* values for each of the variables (including normalized earnings) as estimated by analysts at 17 investment firms.

The initial results considered regressions using historical variables for growth, instability, and payout, and comparable regressions using expectational variables. The regression results using expectational data were clearly superior to the historical data results. (r^2 was approximately 0.50 with historical data versus 0.75 with expectations data.) Using beta as the risk measure typically gave superior results. Regressions that employed a combination of expectations and historic data generated very good results (r^2 from 0.78 to 0.85). The growth variables were most important and the financial risk variable was also significant. The dominance of the growth variable was apparent in additional regressions with only expectation variables.

The authors also considered changes in the valuation relationship over time. This is very important for the long-run use of the models because if the variable coefficients change each year, the usefulness of the coefficients in estimating future earnings multiple values is reduced substantially. The authors state:

An inspection . . . indicates that *the coefficients of our equation change considerably from year to year* and in a manner that is consistent with the changing standards of value in vogue at the time.[14] (emphasis added)

Finally, they considered whether the models could be used to select securities by comparing the actual market P/E ratios to the normal P/E ratio predicted by the valuation equation. As did Whitbeck and Kisor, the authors assumed that, if the actual P/E ratio was below the normal P/E ratio, the stock was underpriced and vice versa. Malkiel and Cragg did not limit their discussion to those stocks 15 percent above or below their theoretical P/E ratio but included all stocks. The test related the percentage of under- or overpricing to the return on the stock; i.e., a stock that is heavily underpriced should have a large positive return during the subsequent year. Based upon the results for five individual years, it was stated:

. . . in only three of the five years for which this experiment was performed was the relationship negative, and the degree of association was extremely low. In the other two years, there was either a positive or zero relationship.[15]

---

[13] Burton G. Malkiel and John G. Cragg, "Expectations and the Structure of Share Prices," *American Economic Review,* 60 no. 4 (September 1970): 601–617.

[14] Ibid., p. 613. This instability of coefficients was evident in *all* tables in the article.

[15] Ibid., p. 615.

Discussion of the reasons for the poor results with the predictive model indicated that better results were derived assuming perfect foresight rather than only using historical data, and even better results could be derived assuming knowledge of future expectations. Therefore, *although the models were quite good in explaining past variance in price-earnings ratios, the analysis was not successful in isolating underpriced securities.*

This lack of success appears to have been caused by a lack of stability in the variable coefficients. Therefore, although it is possible to explain past results with these models, it is *not* possible to use them to select stocks if only historical information is taken into acccount. Such results are obviously consistent with the semistrong efficient market hypothesis.

An article by Beaver and Morse offers a somewhat different view of what affects P/E ratios based upon an analysis of portfolios of stocks.[16] There is a consideration of the basic dividend valuation model which implies the expected importance of risk and growth in explaining differential price-earnings ratios. For the sample of stocks with the required data, they computed the P/E ratios (December 31 price dividend by earnings per share for the year), ranked the P/E ratios and divided them into 25 equal-sized portfolios. They compared the median P/E ratio for each portfolio during its base year with the median realized one year growth in earnings per share, and the median risk (measured by the portfolio beta during the subsequent five years).

The results indicated strong correlation in the P/E ratios over time—i.e., a 0.74 correlation after 10 years. This implied a long-term persistence in the portfolio P/E ratios. To test the impact of growth, they correlated the P/E ratios during a year to individual year growth rates. The correlation during the year of formation was −0.28, which implied that low growth caused a high P/E ratio. It was contended that this was because investors were cognizant of a transitory component of earnings. The correlation during the next year was a respectable 0.53 followed by 0.25 in Year 2. While it was not possible to determine the impact of past earnings growth because they were not considered, these results implied that investors consider short-run future growth—i.e., they only go out two years. The authors contended that these results indicated that a difference in P/E ratios exists which is not explained by earnings growth. They likewise examined the relationship between the P/E ratio and risk *subsequent* to the year of formation. The results were generally discouraging since there was not a consistent relationship. Multiple regressions that consider risk and growth were reasonably good with R^2 that ranged from 0.185 to 0.783 with a median of 0.505.

The authors did not consider these prior results very good. Without any formal testing, they suggested that the accounting methods used by the firm were an alternative factor that could explain the difference. Specifically, they contended that the P/E ratio will be influenced by the effect on earnings of differing accounting methods. For example, a firm with conservative accounting methods will have a higher P/E ratio that holds the effect of risk and growth constant. There were some brief tests of this idea in a prior article that examined

[16] William Beaver and Dale Morse, ''What Determines Price-Earnings Ratios?'' *Financial Analysts Journal,* 34 no. 4 (July–August 1978): pp. 65–76.

the difference in P/E ratio for firms that used straight-line versus accelerated depreciation.[17]

Summary of P/E Studies.   These and a myriad of studies have considered the variables that affect a stock's P/E ratio and indicate the following:

A stock's P/E ratio is generally positively related to its growth rate of earnings, but it is necessary to be able to *predict* the future growth rate during the next two or three years. Past growth rates may explain past P/E ratios, but they are *not* very good at predicting future P/E ratios. Also, numerous studies have indicated that growth rates in general are *not* correlated over time, so it is not possible to simply extrapolate past growth rates.[18] A stock's P/E ratio is generally negatively related to alternative measures of risk. The typical internal risk measures are business risk (variability of earnings) and financial risk (financial leverage ratios). Alternatively, some studies have used the stock's systematic risk (beta). The specific risk measure that is superior varies by the studies and the time period considered.

A study by Beaver and Morse did not consider a cross section of individual stocks but a cross section of portfolios of stocks. The analysis of growth and risk only considered future values. Even so, growth was significant during the first and second year after formation, and multiple regression models with growth and risk were significant. The authors did not believe that the results were as strong as expected and suggested that the P/E ratios were also influenced by the accounting methods employed—i.e., a firm with conservative accounting methods would have a higher P/E ratio.

SUMMARY

This chapter dealt with the procedure for evaluating individual common stocks using the dividend growth model. The analyst should be aware that there are several different types of companies and types of common stocks, and there is a high probability that the two are *not* the same—e.g., the stock of a growth company may not be a growth stock. The procedure for company analysis was demonstrated using Safeway Stores as an example. The earnings estimate was derived based upon an analysis of the sales performance of Safeway in relation to the performance of its industry and of an aggregate economic series. The profit margin estimate considered the firm's relationship to its industry and any unique features.

The comparison of the earnings multiple for Safeway to the figure for its industry and the market indicated that the Safeway multiple was consistently below the others. Each of the components that influence the multiple was ana-

---

[17] William Beaver and R. Dukes, "Delta-Depreciation Methods: Some Empirical Results," *Accounting Review,* 47 no. 2 (April 1972): 320–332.

[18] S. Little, "Higgledy Piggledy Growth," Institute of Statistics, Oxford (November 1962); Ray Ball and Ross Watts, "Some Time Series Properties of Accounting Earnings Numbers," *Journal of Finance,* 27 no. 3 (June 1972): 663–682; J. Cragg and Burton Malkiel, "The Consensus and Accuracy of Some Predictions of the Growth of Corporate Earnings," *Journal of Finance,* 18 no. 1 (March 1963): 67–84; J. Murphy, "Relative Growth in Earnings per Share—Past and Future," *Financial Analysts Journal,* 22 no. 6 (November–December 1966): 63–76.

lyzed indicating that, on balance, the Safeway multiple should have been below that for the industry or the market based upon these historical results.

The final section discussed three studies dealing with the cross-sectional analysis of earnings multiples and internal corporate variables. Such models are helpful in explaining past multiples, but they are *not* useful in selecting under-priced securities.

QUESTIONS

1. Define a growth company and a speculative stock.
2. Give an example of a growth *company* and discuss why you would expect it to be considered a growth company. Be specific.
3. Give an example of a cyclical *stock* and discuss why you have designated it as such a stock. Is it also issued by a cyclical company?
4. You are told that a computer technology firm is growing at a compound rate of 22 percent a year. (Its ROE is over 30 percent and it retains about 70 percent of its earnings.) The stock of this company is currently priced at 74 times next year's earnings. Discuss why this is or is not a growth company. Is it a growth stock? Why or why not?
5. Select a company outside the retail store industry and indicate what economic series you would use for a sales projection. Discuss why this is a relevant series.
6. Select a company outside the retail store industry and indicate what *industry* series you would use in an industry analysis. (Try to use one of the industry groups designated by Standard & Poor's.) Discuss why this series is most appropriate and whether there were several possible alternatives.
7. Taking the company and industry selected in Question 5, examine the operating profit margin for the company as it relates to the operating margin for the industry. Discuss the annual results in terms of levels and percentage changes and the long-run averages for the latest ten-year period.
8. Compute the average earnings multiple for a company for each of the last ten years and relate this to a comparable multiple for the market (consider using the high + low/2, in which case some of the market figures are included in Table 14.6). Discuss the short-run and long-run differences.
9. Compare your average company multiple to a similar industry multiple for the last ten years. Discuss the short-run and long-run differences.
10. Assume that there is some difference between your company and its industry. What are the three major variables that could account for this difference? Discuss each individually and indicate what difference in each (holding everything else constant) would explain it. (For example, the company multiple is higher because variable A is lower and this influences the multiple in the following way.)
11. *Case Project*—Collect the data for your company and your industry. Analyze all the variables that should affect the multiple to determine whether the historical differences are consistent with the historical relationship between the multiples; i.e., can you explain why the average company multiple is higher or lower than the industry multiple?
12. *CFA Examination II (June 1981):* The value of an asset is the present value of the expected returns from the asset during the holding period. An investment will provide a stream of returns during this period, and it is necessary to discount this

stream of returns at an appropriate rate to determine the asset's present value. A dividend valuation model such as the following is frequently used.

$$P_i = \frac{D_i}{(K_i - g_i)}$$

P_i = current price of common stock i

D_1 = expected dividend in period 1

K_i = required rate of return on stock i

g_i = expected constant growth rate of dividends for stock i

A. *Identify* the three factors that must be estimated for any valuation model and *explain* why these estimates are more difficult to derive for common stocks than for bonds.

(9 minutes)

B. *Explain* the principal problem involved in using a dividend valuation model to value:
    (1) Companies whose operations are closely correlated with economic cycles
    (2) Companies that are of giant size and are maturing
    (3) Companies that are of small size and are growing rapidly
    (Assume all companies pay dividends)

(6 minutes)

REFERENCES

Arditti, Fred D. "Risk and the Required Return on Equity." *Journal of Finance.* 22 no. 1 (March 1967).

Babcock, Guilford C. "The Concept of Sustainable Growth." *Financial Analysts Journal.* 26 no. 3 (May–June 1970).

Ball, Ray, and Ross Watts. "Some Time Series Properties of Accounting Earnings Numbers." *Journal of Finance.* 27 no. 3 (June 1972).

Beaver, William, and Dale Morse. "What Determines Price-Earnings Ratios?" *Financial Analysts Journal.* 34 no. 4 (July–August 1978).

Benishay, Haskell. "Variability in Earnings-Price Ratios of Corporate Equities." *American Economic Review.* 51 no. 1 (March 1961).

Black, Fischer, and Myron Scholes. "The Effects of Dividend Yield and Dividend Policy on Common Stock Prices and Return." *Journal of Financial Economics.* 1 no. 1 (May 1974).

Boquist, John A., George Racette, and Gary G. Schlarbaum. "Duration and Risk Assessment for Bonds and Common Stocks." *Journal of Finance.* 30 no. 5 (December 1975).

Bower, Richard S., and D. H. Bower. "Risk and the Valuation of Common Stock." *Journal of Political Economy.* 77 no. 3 (May–June 1969).

Bower, Dorothy H., and R. S. Bower. "Test of a Stock Valuation Model." *Journal of Finance.* 25 no. 2 (May 1970).

Cragg, John G., and Burton G. Malkiel. "The Consensus and Accuracy of Some Predictions of the Growth of Corporate Earnings." *Journal of Finance.* 23 no. 1 (March 1968).

Foster, Earl M. "The Price-Earnings Ratio and Growth." *Financial Analysts Journal.* 26 no. 1 (January–February 1970).

Friend, Irwin, and M. Puckett. "Dividends and Stock Prices." *American Economic Review.* 54 no. 4 (September 1964).

Gordon, Myron J. *The Investment, Financing, and Valuation of the Corporation.* Homewood, Ill.: Richard D. Irwin, 1962.

Graham, Benjamin, D. L. Dodd, and S. Cottle. *Security Analysis, Principles and Techniques.* 4th ed. New York: McGraw-Hill, 1962.

Lintner, John. "The Valuation of Risk Assets and the Selection of Risky Investments in Stock Portfolios and Capital Budgets." *Review of Economics and Statistics.* 47 no. 1 (February 1965).

Lintner, John, and Robert Glauber. "Higgledy Piggledy Growth in America." James Lorie and Richard Brealey, eds. *Modern Developments in Investment Management.* New York: Praeger Publishers, 1972.

Malkiel, Burton G., and John Cragg. "Expectations and the Structure of Share Prices." *American Economic Review.* 60 no. 4 (September 1970).

Miller, Merton, and Franco Modigliani. "Dividend Policy, Growth, and the Valuation of Shares." *Journal of Business.* 34 no. 4 (October 1961).

Mossin, Jan. "Equilibrium in a Capital Asset Market." *Econometrica.* 34 no. 4 (October 1966).

Murphy, J. "Relative Growth in Earnings per Share—Past and Future." *Financial Analysts Journal.* 22 no. 6 (November–December 1966).

Nicholson, S. F. "Price-Earnings Ratios." *Financial Analysts Journal.* 26 no. 4 (July–August 1970).

Niederhoffer, Victor, and Patrick J. Regan. "Earnings Changes, Analysts' Forecasts, and Stock Prices." *Financial Analysts Journal.* 28 no. 3 (May–June 1972).

Pratt, J. W. "Risk Aversion in the Small and in the Large." *Econometrica.* 32 no. 1 (January–February 1964).

Reilly, Frank K. "A Differentiation between Types of Companies and Types of Stock." *Mississippi Valley Journal of Business and Economics.* 7 no. 1 (Fall 1971).

Whitbeck, V., and M. Kisor. "A New Tool in Investment Decision Making." *Financial Analysts Journal.* 19 no. 3 (May–June 1963).

Chapter 15

Analysis of Growth Companies

I nvestment literature contains numerous accounts of the rapid rise of growth companies, such as IBM, Xerox, and Hewlett Packard, and stories about investors who became wealthy because of timely acquisitions of these stocks. Given such increases in value, it is clear that the proper valuation of true growth companies can be extremely rewarding. At the same time, for every IBM or Xerox that became successful, there are numerous firms that did not survive. Further, there are instances in which the stock price of a true growth company became overvalued and the subsequent returns were clearly below expectations. As stated — the common stock of a growth company is *not* always a growth stock!

By now, the reader should be aware of the dividend valuation model, of the important factors in valuation, and of the basic assumption of the model, i.e., that dividends are expected to grow at a *constant rate for an infinite time period*. As noted, these assumptions are reasonable when evaluating the aggregate market and some large industries, but they become more tenuous when analyzing individual securities. The point of this chapter is that *these assumptions are extremely questionable for a growth company*.

DEFINITION

A growth company is defined as a firm that has the opportunities and ability to invest capital in projects that generate returns greater than the firm's cost of capital. Such a condition is considered to be *clearly temporary*. In a competitive economy, all firms are expected to produce at the point where marginal revenue equals marginal cost, and under such conditions, the returns to the producer will exactly compensate for the risks involved. If the returns are below what is expected for the risk involved, the producer will leave the industry. In contrast, if the investment returns for a given industry exceed the returns expected based upon the risk involved, other investors will enter the industry, will increase the supply, and will drive the prices down until the returns *are* consistent with the inherent risk, resulting in a state of equilibrium.

Actual Returns above Expected Returns

The notion of consistently earning returns above the expected rate requires elaboration. Firms are engaged in business ventures that offer opportunities for investment of corporate capital, and these investments entail some uncertainty or risk. Investors determine their required return for owning this firm based upon the risk of the investments made by the firm compared to the risk of other firms. Take a firm that is involved in producing and selling medical equipment and assume perfect capital markets. There is some uncertainty about the sales of this equipment and about the ultimate profit that will be derived from these sales. Comparing this composite uncertainty to the uncertainty involved in other investments and the rates of returns expected from the other investments, one can estimate the return investors should require from an investment in the production and sale of medical equipment. Based upon the CAPM, one would expect the difference in the required rate of return to be a function of the difference in the systematic risk for the firm's investments which affect the stock's systematic risk.

Investors derive a required return for investing in a firm based upon the systematic risk of the investments made by the firm. *This required rate of return is referred to as the firm's cost of capital.* In a perfect market in a state of equilibrium, one would expect *these two rates of return to be equal.* The return derived from risky investments by the firm would equal the return required by investors. Any returns earned by the firm above those required for the systematic risk involved are referred to as *pure profits.* One of the costs of production is the cost of the capital employed. Therefore, in a purely competitive environment, marginal revenue should equal marginal costs (including capital costs) and there are no excess returns or pure profits.[1] Such excess profits are only possible in a noncompetitive environment. Assume that the medical equipment firm is able to earn 20 percent on its capital, while investors only require 15 percent on such investments, given the systematic risk involved. The extra 5 percent is defined as pure profit. In a totally competitive environment, numerous companies would enter the medical equipment field in order to enjoy the excess profits available. These competitors would increase the supply of equipment and would reduce price until the marginal returns equaled the marginal costs.

The fact that a number of firms have been able to derive excess profits for a number of years indicates that these excess returns are probably not due to a temporary disequilibrium, but are due to some noncompetitive factors that are allowed to exist in our capitalistic economy, such as patent or copyright laws that provide a firm or person with monopoly rights to a process or a manuscript for a specified period of time. During this period of protection from competition, the firm has the ability to derive above normal returns without fear of competition.

---

[1] For a further discussion of profits, see George J. Stigler, *The Theory of Price* (revised ed.), (New York: The Macmillan Co., 1952), 180–182.

Also one can conceive of a firm possessing special management skills that provide added profits (e.g., a unique marketing technique or other organizational characteristic). Finally, in some instances the capital required to enter an industry can be a barrier (e.g., the auto industry).

In a purely competitive economy with no frictions, there should be no such thing as a true growth company because competition would negate such growth. As it is, our economy is not a perfect competitive model (although this is probably the best model to use in most cases), and there are a number of real world frictions that restrict competition. Therefore, it is possible to envision the *temporary* existence of true growth companies in our economy. The question is — how long can they last?

Growth Companies and Growth Stocks

In many instances the characteristics of a company and those of its stock are distinct. At this point it is appropriate to briefly recall the definitions of a growth company and a growth stock to ensure that the reader does not assume that the two are synonymous.

A growth *company* has the opportunities and ability to consistently invest capital in projects that generate rates of return greater than the firm's cost of capital. A growth *stock* is a security that is expected to experience above average risk-adjusted rates of return during some future period. This definition of a growth stock means that *any* stock that is currently undervalued can be a growth stock regardless of the type of company issuing it. The securities of growth *companies* that have become temporarily overvalued could be speculative stocks because the probability of deriving below normal returns from them would be very high. A major intent of this analysis of growth companies is to present models that will help you evaluate the *unique* earnings stream of a growth company and thereby devise a better estimate of the value of the growth firm and its stock. The result should be superior judgment regarding whether the *stock* of the growth *company* is: (1) a growth stock, (2) simply a properly valued stock, or (3) a speculative stock.

Growth Companies and the Dividend Model

The dividend model assumes a *constant rate of growth for an infinite time period.* It should be clear that it is *impossible* for a true growth firm to exist for an infinite time period in a purely competitive economy. Further, even in a competitive economy with some noncompetitive factors, *a true growth firm cannot exist for very long.* Patents and copyrights run out, unusual management practices can eventually be copied, and large amounts of capital can be accumulated. Therefore, the dividend growth model is *not* appropriate for the valuation of growth companies, and it is necessary to consider special valuation models that allow for finite periods of abnormal growth and for the possibility of different rates of growth. The rest of the chapter deals with models that can be used in the valuation of growth companies.

454   ALTERNATIVE GROWTH MODELS[2]

In this section we will consider the full range of growth models, from no growth and negative growth to dynamic true growth. Knowledge of the full range will help the reader understand why the dividend growth model used extensively in financial literature is unrealistic and is not applicable to true growth firms. This background will also be useful in understanding growth company valuation models. Each model assumes that the company is an all-equity firm in order to simplify the computations.

No Growth Firm

The no growth firm is that mythical company that is established with a specified portfolio of investments that generate a constant stream of earnings (E) equal to r times the value of assets. Earnings are calculated after allowing for deprecia-tion to maintain the assets at their original value. Therefore:

$$E = r \times \text{Assets}.$$

It is also assumed that *all earnings of the firm are paid out in dividends;* i.e., if b is the rate of retention, $b = 0$. Hence:

$$E = r \times \text{Assets} = \text{Dividends}.$$

Under these assumptions, the value of the firm is the discounted value of the perpetual stream of earnings (E). The discount rate (the required rate of return) is specified as i. In this case, it is assumed that $r = i$. The firm's *rate of return on assets is exactly equal to the required rate of return.* The value of the firm is:

$$V = \frac{E}{i} = \frac{(1-b)E}{i}.$$

In the no growth case, the earnings stream never changes because the asset base never changes and the rate of return on the assets never changes. Therefore, the value of the firm never changes and investors continue to receive i on their investment.

$$i = E/V.$$

Long-Run Growth Models

These models differ from the models for a no growth firm because *they assume some of the earnings are reinvested.* We will begin with the case in which a firm

---

[2] The discussion in this section is drawn to a great extent from Ezra Solomon, *The Theory of Financial Management* (New York: Columbia University Press, 1963), 55–63. Another article in which the value for true growth companies is derived is M. Miller and F. Modigliani, "Dividend Policy, Growth and the Valuation of Shares," *Journal of Business,* 34 no. 4 (October 1961): 411–433. This latter article is heavily involved in discussing the importance of dividends in valuation.

retains a *constant dollar amount of earnings* and reinvests these retained earnings in assets that obtain a rate of return above the required rate.

In all cases it is postulated that the market value (V) of an all-equity firm is the capitalized value of three component forms of returns discounted at the rate i:

E = the level of (constant) net earnings expected from existing assets, without further net investments

G = the gross present value of capital gains expected from reinvested funds. The return on reinvested funds is equal to r which equals mi. If m is equal to one, then $r = i$. If m is greater than one, then these are considered true growth investments ($r > i$). If m is less than one, the investments are generating returns (r) below the cost of capital ($r < i$).

R = the reinvestment of net earnings is equal to bE, where b is a percent between zero (no reinvestment) and unity (total reinvestment; no dividends).

Simple Growth Model.   It is assumed that the firm has investment opportunities that provide rates of return equal to r, where r is greater than i (m is above one). Further, it is assumed that these opportunities allow the firm to invest R dollars a year at these rates and that $R = bE$; R is a *constant dollar amount* because E is the constant earnings at the beginning of the period.

The value of G, the capital gain component, is computed as follows: the first investment of bE dollars yields a stream of earnings equal to bEr dollars, and this is repeated every year. Each of these earnings streams has a present value, as of the year it begins, of bEr/i, which is the present value of a constant perpetual stream discounted at a rate consistent with the risk involved. Assuming the firm does this every year, it has a *series* of investments, each of which has a present value of bEr/i. The present value of *all* these series is $(bEr/i)/i$ which equals bEr/i^2. But because $r = mi$, this becomes:

$$(15.1) \qquad \frac{bEmi}{i^2} = \frac{bEm}{i} \quad \begin{array}{l}\text{(Gross present value of} \\ \text{growth investments).}\end{array}$$

In order to derive these flows, it was necessary to invest bE dollars each year. The present value of these annual investments is equal to bE/i. Therefore, the *net* present value of growth investments is equal to:

$$(15.2) \qquad \frac{bEm}{i} - \frac{bE}{i} \quad \begin{array}{l}\text{(Net present value of} \\ \text{growth investments).}\end{array}$$

The important variable is the value of m, which indicates the relationship of r to i. Combining this growth component with the capitalized value of the constant earnings stream indicates the value of the firm is:

$$(15.3) \qquad V = \frac{E}{i} + \frac{bEm}{i} - \frac{bE}{i}.$$

This equation indicates that the value of the firm is equal to the constant earnings stream plus a growth component equal to the *net* present value of reinvestment in growth projects. By combining the first and third terms in Equation 15.3, this becomes:

(15.4)
$$V = \frac{E(1 - b)}{i} + \frac{bEm}{i}.$$

Because $E(1 - b)$ is the dividend, this model becomes:

(15.5)
$$V = \frac{D}{i} + \frac{bEm}{i} \quad \text{(Present value of constant dividend plus the present value of growth investments).}$$

It can be stated as earnings only by rearranging Equation (15.3).

(15.6)
$$V = \frac{E}{i} + \frac{bE(m - 1)}{i} \quad \text{(Present value of constant earnings plus present value of excess earnings from growth investments).}$$

Expansion Model.   The expansion model assumes a firm retains earnings to reinvest, but only gets a rate of return equal to the cost of capital ($m = 1$, so $r = i$). The effect of such a change can be seen in Equation 15.2 where the net present value of growth investments would be zero. Therefore, Equation 15.3 would become:

(15.7)
$$V = \frac{E}{i}.$$

It would still be possible to have equations comparable to 15.4, but it would become:

(15.8)
$$V = \frac{E(1 - b)}{i} + \frac{bE}{i} = \frac{E}{i}.$$

Equation 15.5 is still valid, but the present value of the growth investment component would be smaller because m would be equal to one. Finally, the last term in Equation 15.6 would disappear.

This indicates that, simply because a firm retains earnings and reinvests them, it is not necessarily of benefit to the stockholder *unless the reinvestment rate is above the required rate* ($r > i$). Otherwise, the investor would be as well off with all earnings paid out in dividends.

Negative Growth Model.   The negative growth model applies to a firm that retains earnings ($b > 0$), and reinvests these funds in projects that generate rates of return *below* the firm's cost of capital ($r < i$ or $m < 1$). The effect of such a practice on the value of the firm can be seen from an examination of Equation 15.2, which indicates that with $m < 1$, the net present value of the growth invest- ments would be *negative*. This implies that the value of the firm in Equation 15.3 would be *less* than the value of a no growth firm or an expansion firm. This can also be seen by examining the effect of $m < 1$ in Equation 15.6. The firm is withholding funds from the investor and investing them in projects that generate returns less than those available from comparable risk investments.

Such poor performance may be difficult to uncover because the asset base of the firm and the earnings of the firm *will increase* if it earns *any positive rate of return* on the new assets. The crucial point is *the earnings will not grow by as much as they should,* so the value of the firm will decline when investors dis- count this reinvestment stream.

What Determines Capital Gain Component?   These equations highlight the factors that influence the capital gain component. All the equations beginning with 15.1 suggest that the gross present value of the growth investments is equal to:

$$bEm/i.$$

This indicates that three factors are important to the size of this term. The first is the size of *b, the percentage of earnings retained for reinvestment.* The greater the proportion of earnings retained, the larger the capital gain component. The second is the value of *m, which indicates the relationship between the firm's rate of return on investments and the firm's required rate of return (i.e., its cost of capital).* A value of one indicates that the firm is only earning its required return. A firm with an *m* greater than one is a true growth company. The important question is, how much greater than one is the return? The final factor of impor- tance is *the time period for the superior investments.* This is easily overlooked because, throughout the discussion, we assume an infinite horizon to simplify the computations. However, when analyzing growth companies, the length of time a firm can continue to invest large amounts of funds at superior rates in a relatively competitive environment is clearly a major consideration. The three factors that influence the capital gain component are:
1.   The amount of capital invested in growth investments
2.   The rate of return earned on the funds retained relative to the required rate of return
3.   The time horizon in which these growth investments will be available.

Dynamic True Growth Model

This model applies to a firm that invests a constant *percentage* of current earn- ings in projects that generate rates of return above the firm's required rate ($r > i$, $m > 1$). The effect of this is that the firm's earnings and dividends will grow at a *constant rate* that is equal to *br* (the percentage of earnings retained times the return on investments). In the current model, this would equal *bmi,* where *m* is

TABLE 15.1
Summary of Company Descriptions

	Retention	Return on Investments
No Growth Company	$b = 0$	$r = i$
Long-Run Growth (assumes reinvestment)		
Negative Growth	$b > 0$	$r < i$
Expansion	$b > 0$	$r = i$
Simple Long-Run Growth	$b > 0$ (constant $)	$r > i$
Dynamic Long-Run Growth	$b > 0$ (constant %)	$r > i$

greater than one. Given these assumptions, the dynamic growth model for an infinite time period would be the dividend valuation model derived in the Appendix to Chapter 12:

$$V = \frac{D}{i - g}.$$

This model applied to the true growth company means that earnings and dividends are growing at a constant rate and *the firm is investing larger and larger dollar amounts in projects that generate returns greater than i.* Moreover, it is implicitly assumed that the firm can continue to do this *for an infinite time period.* If the growth rate (g) is greater than i, the model blows up and indicates that the firm should have an infinite value. Because of this possibility, Durand basically concluded that, although many firms had current growth rates above the normal required rates of return, very few of their stocks were selling for infinite values.[3] He believed that the best explanation for this phenomenon was the expectation that the reinvestment rate would decline or that the investment opportunities would not be available for an infinite time period.

The Real World

All of these models are simplified to allow the development of a range of alternatives. As a result, several of the models are extremely unrealistic. *The real world is composed of companies that are a combination of these models.* Unfortunately, most firms have made some investments where $r < i$, and many firms invest in projects that generate returns about equal to the cost of capital. Finally, almost all firms have the opportunity to invest in some projects that provide rates of return above the firm's cost of capital ($r > i$). *How much* is invested in these growth projects and *how long* these opportunities last are crucial considerations.

[3] David Durand, "Growth Stocks and the Petersburg Paradox," *Journal of Finance,* 12 no. 3 (September 1957): 348–363.

In the remainder of this chapter we will discuss various models that concentrate on these questions to help you derive better estimates of the value of the growth company.

GROWTH DURATION

The earnings multiple for a stock (the P/E ratio multiple) is a function of: (1) the firm's expected rate of growth in terms of earnings per share, (2) the required rate of return on the security based upon its systematic risk, and (3) the firm's dividend-payout ratio. If one assumes that the risk for different firms is similar and also assumes no significant difference in the payout ratio for different firms, then the principal variable affecting the earnings multiple is the difference in the growth estimate. Further, the growth estimate must be considered in terms of the *rate of growth and the duration* of expected growth. No company can continue to grow indefinitely at a rate substantially above normal. IBM cannot continue to grow at 20 percent a year for an extended period or it will eventually become the entire economy. IBM or any similar growth firm will run out of high profit investment projects. Continued growth at a sustained rate requires that larger and larger amounts of money be invested in high return projects. Eventually competition will encroach upon these high return investments, and the firm's growth rate will decline to a rate consistent with the rate for the overall economy. Ascertaining the duration of the high growth period therefore becomes significant.

Computation of Growth Duration

The growth duration concept was originally derived by Holt,[4] who showed that, if risk between a given security and a market security (he used the Dow-Jones Industrial Average as the market security) is assumed to be constant, it is possible to examine the differential past growth rates for the market and for the growth firm. Then, given the alternative P/E ratios, one can compute the market's *implied growth duration* for the growth firm. If $E'(0)$ is the firm's current earnings, then $E'(t)$ is earnings in period t according to the expression:

(15.9) $$E'(t) = E'(0)(1 + G)^t,$$

where G is the annual percentage growth rate for earnings. To adjust for dividend payments, it was assumed that all such payments are used to purchase further shares of the stock. This means the number of shares (N) will grow at the dividend rate (D). Therefore:

(15.10) $$N(t) = N(0)(1 + D)^t.$$

---

[4] Charles C. Holt, "The Influence of Growth Duration on Share Prices," *Journal of Finance,* 17 no. 3 (September 1962): 465–475. The discussion in this section draws on the original article. A subsequent article that rediscovered the concept is Robert M. Baylis and Suresh L. Bhirud, "Growth Stock Analysis: A New Approach," *Financial Analysts Journal,* 29 no. 4 (July–August 1973): 63–70.

To derive the total earnings for a firm $E(t)$, the growth rate in per share earnings and the growth in shares are combined as follows:

$$(15.11) \qquad E(t) = E'(t)N(t) = E'(0)[(1 + G)(1 + D)]^t.$$

Because G and D are small, this expression can be approximated by:

$$(15.12) \qquad E(t) \cong E'(0)(1 + G + D)^t.$$

Assuming that the general characteristics of the growth stock (g) and the non-growth stock (a) are the same (similar risk and payout), one would expect the market to value the shares of the two stocks in direct proportion to their earnings in year T, where T is the investor's horizon. In other words, *current prices should be in direct proportion to the expected future earnings ratio in year T.* This can be stated:

$$(15.13) \qquad \left(\frac{Pg(0)}{Pa(0)}\right) \cong \left(\frac{Eg(0)(1 + G_g + Dg)^T}{Ea(0)(1 + G_a + D_a)^T}\right)$$

or

$$(15.14) \qquad \left(\frac{Pg(0)/Eg(0)}{P_a(0)/E_a(0)}\right) \cong \left(\frac{1 + G_g + Dg}{1 + G_a + D_a}\right)^T.$$

The result is that *the P/E ratios of the two stocks are in direct proportion to the ratio of composite growth rates raised to the Tth power.* It is possible to solve for T by taking the log of both sides as follows:

$$(15.15) \qquad ln\left(\frac{Pg(0)/Eg(0)}{P_a(0)/E_a(0)}\right) \cong T \, ln\left(\frac{1 + G_g + Dg}{1 + G_a + D_a}\right).$$

The growth duration model answers the question: how long must the earnings of the growth stock grow at the past rate, relative to the nongrowth stock, to justify its current premium in P/E ratio relative to the nongrowth stock? It is the function of the analyst to determine whether the *implied* duration estimate is reasonable in terms of his analysis of the company's potential.

Consider the following example. The stock of a well-known growth company is currently selling for $63 a share with expected per share earnings of $3.50 (its earnings multiple is 18). The firm's average growth rate in earnings per share during the past five- and ten-year periods has been 15 percent a year, and the dividend yield has averaged 3 percent. In contrast, the S&P 400 industrial index has a current P/E ratio of 10, an average dividend yield of 5 percent, and an average growth rate of 6 percent. Therefore, the comparison looks as follows:

	S&P 400	Growth Company
P/E Ratios (Current Price ÷ Expected Earnings)	10.00	18.00
Average Growth Rate	.0600	.1500
Dividend Yield	.0500	.0300

Inserting these values into Equation 15.15:

$$ln\left(\frac{18.00}{10.00}\right) \cong T \, ln\left(\frac{1 + .1500 + .0300}{1 + .0600 + .0500}\right)$$

$$ln\,(1.800) \cong T\,ln\left(\frac{1.1800}{1.1100}\right)$$

$$ln(1.800) \cong T\,ln(1.063)$$

$$T = ln\,(1.800)/ln(1.063)$$
$$= .255273/.026533 \text{ (log base 10)}$$
$$= 9.62 \text{ years}.$$

These results indicate that the market is implicitly assuming that the growth company can continue to grow at this composite rate (18 percent) for almost ten more years, after which it is assumed that the growth company will grow at the same rate as the aggregate market, as represented by the S&P 400, will. The question the analyst must ask at this points is, can this growth rate be sustained for at least this period? If the implied growth duration is greater than the analyst believes is reasonable, he will likely discourage purchase of the stock. If it is below his expectations, he will likely recommend the purchase.

Intra-Industry Analysis

Besides using the growth duration to compare a company to some market base, it is possible to use this technique for a direct comparison of two firms. When doing an intercompany analysis, it is best to consider firms in the same industry because then it is likely that one of the assumptions of the growth duration technique — equal risk — is valid.

Consider the following example from the cosmetics industry:

	Company A	Company B
P/E Ratios	21.00	15.00
Average Annual Growth Rate	.1700	.1200
Dividend Yield	.0250	.0300
Growth Rate plus Dividend Yield	.1950	.1500
Estimate of T^a	8.79 years	

[a] The reader should check to see that he gets the same answer.

These results imply that the market expects Company A to grow at a total rate of almost 20 percent for about nine years followed by a decrease to the same rate of growth as Company B will experience. The analyst must decide whether he agrees with this implicit market valuation. If he believes the implied duration is too long, he will prefer Company B; if he believes it is reasonable or low, he will recommend Company A.

An Alternative Use of T

Instead of solving for T and then deciding whether the figure derived is reasonable, it is also possible to use this formulation to derive a reasonable earnings multiple for a security relative to the aggregate market (or another stock) if the implicit assumptions are reasonable for the stock involved. Assume that you have been analyzing a growth company and you estimate that its composite growth will be about 20 percent a year compared to the market growth of 11 percent. Further, you believe that this firm can maintain such superiority for about seven years. Using Equation 15.15, this becomes:

$$ ln(X) = 7 \cdot ln \frac{1.20}{1.11} $$
$$ = 7 \cdot ln\ (1.081) $$
$$ = 7 \cdot (.033826) $$
$$ = .236782. $$

To determine what the P/E ratio should be, it is necessary to derive the antilog of 0.236782, which is approximately 1.725. Therefore, assuming the market multiple is 10.00, the earnings multiple for this growth company should be about 1.725 times the market P/E ratio or 17.25.

Alternatively, if you expect that the firm can only maintain this differential growth for five years, you would derive the antilog for 0.16913 ($5 \times .033826$). The answer is 1.4761 which implies that you should use a P/E ratio of 14.76 for the stock.

Factors to Consider

When employing this tool, the following major factors should be recognized. First, the technique assumes *equal risk* between the securities compared. Although this assumption may be acceptable when comparing two large, well-established firms (e.g., General Motors and Standard Oil), it is very likely *not* true when comparing a small firm to the aggregate market.

Another problem is deciding *which growth estimate to use.* In the typical case, historical growth rates used are for five- and ten-year periods. Which time interval is most relevant? Which does the market employ? What about using the expected rate of growth?

Third, *the technique assumes that the stock with higher P/E ratio has the higher growth rate.* In numerous instances, the stock with the higher P/E ratio did not have a higher historical growth rate. In these cases, the formulation generates a negative growth duration value which is of no use to the analyst. Inconsistency between growth and the P/E ratio could be attributed to one of four factors:

1.   A major difference in the risk involved
2.   Inaccurate growth rate estimates. Possibly the firm with the higher P/E ratio is expected to grow at a higher rate in the future than it did in the past. It is important to consider the growth rate figures employed and whether any changes in the rate are expected.

3. An underevaluation of a stock with a low P/E ratio relative to its growth rate. (Before this is accepted, the first two alternatives should be considered.)
4. An overvaluation of a stock with a high P/E ratio and low growth rate. (Before this is accepted, consider Alternative 2 above.)

The growth duration concept is valid, *given the assumptions made,* and can be useful in evaluating investments. It is by no means universally valid, because it generates an answer that is only as good as the data inputs (relative growth rates) and the applicability of the assumptions. The answer must be evaluated on the basis of the analysts's knowledge. The technique is probably most useful for spotting clearly overvalued growth stocks when the multiple exceeds 30 or 40. In such a case, this technique will indicate that it is necessary for the company to continue to grow at some very high rate for an extended period of time (e.g., 15–20 years) to justify such a multiple. Also, it is very helpful in deciding between two growth companies in the same industry.

A FLEXIBLE GROWTH STOCK VALUATION MODEL

Several years ago, Mao developed an investment opportunities growth model that incorporated some of the previous work on growth stock valuation.[5] Mao noted that the earlier studies done by Solomon, and Miller and Modigliani had recognized the true nature of a growth firm — i.e., one that had opportunities to consistently invest funds at rates of return greater than the firm's required rate of return. However, in order to simplify the exposition, these authors assumed the existence of infinite growth horizons which do not exist in a competitive environment. Therefore, while their presentations have been extremely useful in developing an understanding of valuation, the models have not been applicable to practical problems because their assumptions concerning the growth period are unrealistic.[6] To alleviate this problem, Mao developed a three-stage model of valuation that applied the investment opportunities approach of Solomon and Miller and Modigliani, and he also recognized the finite growth pattern of firms. The Mao model took into account: (1) *a dynamic growth period* during which it is assumed that the firm invests a constant percentage of current earnings in growth projects, (2) *a simple growth period* during which it is assumed that the firm invests a constant dollar amount in growth opportunities, and finally, (3) *a declining growth period* during which the amount invested in growth investments declines to zero. The result was a theoretically correct and realistic model, but, unfortunately, it was rather difficult to use because of the computations required. In addition, the model was somewhat rigid in its assumptions about the parameters b (the retention rate), r (the return on growth investments), and i (the required rate of return on the stock). Because of these problems, the model has not been applied as widely as one might expect. In this section we will

---

[5] James C. T. Mao, "The Valuation of Growth Stocks: The Investment Opportunities Approach," *Journal of Finance,* 21 no. 1 (March 1966): 95–102.

[6] As noted previously, the Holt growth duration model assumed away other facets of the growth model and concentrated on the duration of growth problem. Still, the Holt model ignored risk differences and alternative growth patterns.

discuss the basics of the flexible growth model more thoroughly, will apply it to a growth company, and will discuss the effects of varying the parameters.

The Valuation Model

Mao assumed that the price of the stock is equal to: (1) the present value of current earnings, E, discounted to infinity at the required rate of return, i, ($P = E/i$) plus (2) the net present value of growth opportunities. The difference between Mao and previous authors is that he allowed for three stages of growth.

The first stage in Mao's three-stage model is a period of dynamic growth that lasts for n_1 years. During this period, it is assumed that each year the firm has opportunities to invest a given percentage of current earnings in projects that generate returns equal to r, and that r is greater than i ($r > i$). Since b is a constant percentage of current earnings, and current earnings are growing each year, the dollar amount invested in these growth projects is growing at an exponential rate. The value of the dynamic investments is given by:

$$(15.16) \qquad \left(\frac{r-i}{i}\right)(bE) \sum_{t=1}^{n_1} \frac{(1+br)^{t-1}}{(1+i)^t} \text{ (Value of dynamic growth opportunities).}$$

The second stage is a period Solomon referred to as simple growth that lasts for n_2 years. During this period, it is assumed that the firm still has opportunities to invest in growth projects ($r > i$), but the amount to be invested in these growth projects is a *constant dollar amount* (bE). The value of these projects is given by:

$$(15.17) \qquad \left(\frac{r-i}{i}\right)(bE) \sum_{t=1}^{n_2} \frac{1}{(1+i)^t} \text{ (Value of simple growth opportunities).}$$

During the final period of declining growth (which lasts n_3 years), it is still assumed that the firm has opportunities to invest funds in growth projects, but the dollar amount that can be invested at $r > i$ *declines* steadily from bE to zero. The amount of the decline is steady at $1/n_3$ each year. If bE equals \$100,000 and n_3 is 20, then the amount invested in growth projects would decline by \$5,000 a year. The value of this component is:

$$(15.18) \qquad \left(\frac{r-i}{i}\right)(bE) \sum_{t=1}^{n_3} \frac{(n_3 - t + 1)}{n_3(1+i)^t} \text{ (Value of declining growth opportunities).}$$

The complete model is then simply a combination of the no growth component (E/i) plus the three growth factors. If A stands for the final summation term in Equation 15.16, B stands for the summation in Equation 15.17, and C stands for the summation term in Equation 15.18, this formulation can be written as follows:

$$(15.19) \qquad P = \frac{E}{i} + \left(\frac{r-i}{i}\right)(bE)\left[A + \frac{(1+br)^{n_1-1}}{(1+i)^{n_1}} B + \frac{(1+br)^{n_1-1}}{(1+i)^{n_1+n_2}} C\right].$$

Mao provided some tables that contained limited values for A and C (B is the present value of an annuity). Even with the tables and no change in the parameters, the computation of a single value is rather tedious.

Flexible Parameters.   In the Mao model, it is assumed that, irrespective of the firm's stage of growth, there is no change in the required rate of return (i); the firm always gets the same rate of return on growth projects (r); and it always retains the same percentage of earnings (b) during different periods of growth. The assumption of constant parameters was probably made to avoid complicating a technique that already involved fairly extensive computations. Also, many analysts may agree with these assumptions. However, there is some work which indicates that investors probably change their required return (i) on stocks during different phases of the firm's life cycle. Malkiel has shown that it is logical to require a higher return on high growth stocks because the stream of returns is such that they are inherently longer duration securities.[7] At the other end of the spectrum, a firm during its declining years may be more subject to cyclical variations that would indicate more business risk. Such an assumption would imply an increase in the required rate of return.

Regarding the return on investments (r), it could be considered rather optimistic to assume that, during the period of simple growth, the firm can continue to earn very high rates even on a stable dollar amount. Many analysts would probably prefer to use a large n_2 and assume a somewhat smaller r.

Finally, is it realistic to assume that a firm will retain the same percentage of earnings (b) over its life cycle? It seems more logical to expect a high retention rate during the early years when opportunities for growth investment are abundant and capital is scarce, and a lower rate during the later years when growth investment opportunities are limited, the level of earnings is high, and outside capital is available.

In any case, the model should be more useful if flexibility is possible in these parameters. For the analyst not interested in changing them, it is possible to simply repeat the original values.

Application of the Model.   Mao applied the investment opportunities technique to a valuation of the Polaroid Corporation using several tables to aid in determining the dynamic growth value and declining growth value. The simple growth value was derived using a standard annuity table. Given a computer program, it is only necessary to prepare three statements for each case. Because of the ease of application, you should consider several alternative sets of parameters, including most pessimistic, most optimistic, and most likely. In the case of a stock with a very high earnings multiple, you should determine the alternative sets of estimates that *would be required* to justify the prevailing market price.

In applying this technique to the evaluation of growth companies, the following suggestions might prove useful.

---

[7] Burton G. Malkiel, "Equity Yields, Growth, and the Structure of Share Prices," *American Economic Review,* 53 no. 5 (December 1963): 1004–1031.

1. The earnings figure (E) is assumed to be the figure for the coming year. It can be crudely estimated as the actual earnings for the most recent year times the long-run growth rate for the past five or ten years.

2. The retention rate (b) can be estimated as the average percentage of earnings retained for the last several years, assuming that this is a relatively stable decision by management.

3. The estimate of the return on investment (r) is obviously crucial.[8] One means of deriving it is to ascertain the average return on equity during the recent period. Another is to separately estimate the two factors that should influence this ratio, the equity turnover and the profit margin, and use the product of these two estimates. Finally, Mao suggested using the return on recently retained earnings by computing the *increase* in earnings per share during some period divided by the amount of earnings retained over a comparable period with a one-year lag, e.g., the increase in earnings per share for the period 1983–1987 divided by the retained earnings for the period 1982–1986. This computation attempts to estimate what rate of return the firm is currently deriving from retained earnings. The typical estimate of return on equity is current net earnings divided by current equity. Note that this is an average figure that can be heavily influenced by past performance. Also, this latter method uses historical equity, which can become seriously distorted over time. The estimate suggested by Mao is current and more in the nature of a marginal return on equity.

4. The required return estimate (i) could be the actual return derived from all common stocks during some recent period or even the return from the specific stock during the recent period. Such an estimating procedure would likely suggest a rate in the range of 9–12 percent for most periods. Because *the model is extremely sensitive to changes in i,* it is strongly suggested that you consider a full range of alternative i's from *about 8 percent to 16 percent.*

An Example

Assume the following about a firm that you consider to be a true growth company:

— Earnings: 1986	$2.50
1987 (Estimated)	2.88 ($2.50 × 1.15)
— Annual Growth Rate in EPS (1982–1986)	.15
— Retention Rate (1982–1986)	.65
— Average Return on Equity (1982–1986)	.24
— Marginal Return on Equity (1982–1986)	.26
— Estimated r for Analysis	.25.

Given these estimates of the major parameters, it is possible to derive a number of stock price values by simply changing the values for the three n's (n_1, n_2, n_3) and the required returns. It is possible to change the values for each of these

---

[8] An article that discusses in detail the components of growth is, Guilford C. Babcock, "The Concept of Sustainable Growth," *Financial Analysts Journal,* 26 no. 3 (May–June 1970): 236–242.

TABLE 15.2
Estimated Values for Stock Assuming Alternative Time Periods and Required Rates of Return ($E = \$2.88$; $b = .65$; $r = .25$)

N_1	N_2	N_3	.08	.10	.12	.14	.16
5	5	10	117.91	81.71	59.60	45.14	35.22
5	10	15	126.33	84.89	60.47	45.00	34.66
10	10	15	170.08	105.76	70.22	49.06	35.73
15	15	20	252.06	142.07	86.78	56.54	38.89

parameters for each growth period, but it will simplify the analysis to hold them constant at these historical values. Subsequent estimates should consider alternative parameters.

For the example, the initial estimates of the n's are relatively conservative (5, 5, 10) and are changed to more liberal estimates as follows:

A. $n_1 = 5$, $n_2 = 5$, $n_3 = 10$
B. $n_1 = 5$, $n_2 = 10$, $n_3 = 15$
C. $n_1 = 10$, $n_2 = 10$, $n_3 = 15$
D. $n_1 = 15$, $n_2 = 15$, $n_3 = 20$.

The i's considered ranged from 8 percent to 16 percent in increments of 2 percent (8, 10, 12, 14, 16). The results are contained in Table 15.2. These results clearly indicate a wide range of values for the example. The function of the analyst at this point is to select the best estimate of the three periods and, most important, *the superior estimate of the required return for this stock* based upon its systematic risk and the expected security market line (SML). Because almost all growth companies have above average systematic risk (i.e., betas above 1.00), the required return will typically exceed the expected market return.

Assume the following estimates regarding the SML: $RFR = .08$; $Rm = .12$. Further assume that the company has a beta of 1.5. Then the estimate of required return would be:

$$i = RFR + B_i (Rm - RFR)$$
$$i = .08 + 1.5 (.12 - .08)$$
$$i = .14.$$

This would indicate further consideration of the 0.14 column and possibly the adjoining columns. A comparison of these prices with the prevailing market prices will indicate whether the stock should be considered for inclusion in the portfolio.

It is also possible to draw a graph of the values for the stock for a given set of n values and different i's. If this is done for the several sets of n's, one will derive a set of curves sloping downward to the right as shown in Figure 15.1. Given this graph, there are two ways of examining the results of the model. First, compare the prevailing market price or range of recent prices to the range of computed values. Beyond expecting the prevailing price to be somewhere within the total range, one might also get an indication of relative undervaluation or overvaluation depending upon whether the current market price is toward the upper or

FIGURE 15.1
Plot of Values for Flexible Growth Model

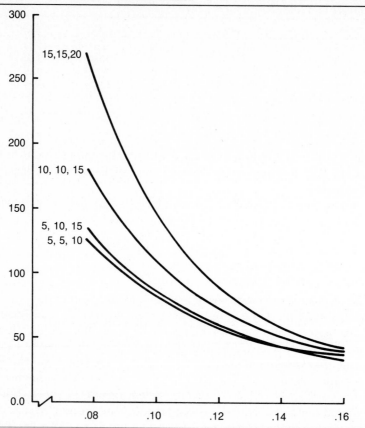

lower end of the range. Second, examine the market price in terms of the implied rate of return. This can be done by drawing the current market price horizontally across the valuation curves. Assuming that the valuation curves generally represent the full range of feasible parameters, the intersection of the price line with the curve to the right indicates the highest *i* that can be expected with the most liberal parameters if you acquire the stock at the current market price. The curve to the left indicates the lowest *i* possible if you acquire the stock at the price indicated.[9]

SUMMARY

This chapter demonstrated the impossibility of employing standard valuation models when analyzing true growth companies. The reason is the standard models assume constant growth for long periods of time, and true growth companies, which, by definition, are able to earn above normal profits on their investments, cannot continue to grow abnormally for indefinite periods.

[9] A program for an alternative valuation model is set forth in, Russell J. Fuller, "Programming the Three-Phase Dividend Discount Model," *Journal of Portfolio Management,* 5 no. 4 (Summer 1979): 28–32.

The second section reviewed the full range of growth company models from negative growth to dynamic true growth. The final section discussed two models that should be of help in the valuation of growth companies. The growth duration model should assist the analyst in concentrating on the major question of concern with true growth companies: how long will this superior growth last and is it consistent with the implied duration?

A flexible model by Mao concentrates on the relevant variables that affect growth. The three-stage model was presented and explained. Use of the model was demonstrated with an example, and it was shown that there are several uses for the set of values derived from the model.

Because of the potential rewards possible from the analysis of growth companies, one should expect strong competition in the valuation process. The models discussed in this chapter and the techniques presented should give the analyst an edge. As always, although models can help derive a value for a firm, *it is the estimated inputs that are crucial.* The superior analyst will be the one who consistently derives the best estimates.

QUESTIONS

1. What are the basic assumptions of the dividend growth model?
2. What is the definition of a true growth company? Be very specific.
3. You are told that a company retains 80 percent of its earnings, and its earnings are growing at a rate of about 8 percent a year versus an average of 6 percent for all firms. Is this a growth company?
4. It is contended by some that, in a completely competitive economy, there would never be a true growth company. Discuss the line of reasoning behind such a contention.
5. Why is it not feasible to use the dividend growth model in the valuation of true growth companies?
6. Assume a firm has an expected dividend of $2.00 a share, a required rate of return of 0.10, and a growth rate of 0.08. What is its value? What is the value if the required return is only 0.07? Show all computations and discuss your results.
7. What are the major assumptions of the growth duration model? Discuss each assumption and why it could present a problem.
8. You are told that a growth company has a P/E ratio of 10 times and a growth rate of 15 percent compared to the market growth rate of 10 percent. The market has a P/E ratio of 11 times. What does this comparison imply regarding the growth company? What else do you need to know to properly compare the growth company to the aggregate market?
9. You are given the following information about two computer firms and the S&P 400:

	Co. A	Co. B	S&P 400
P/E Ratio	24.0	20.0	12.0
Average Annual Growth Rate	.18	.15	.07
Dividend Yield	.02	.03	.05

    a.   Compute the growth duration of each company stock relative to the S&P 400.

    b.   Compute the growth duration of Co. A relative to Co. B.

    c.   Given these durations, what must you decide in order to make an investment decision?

10. Define the following:

    a.   A negative growth company

    b.   An expanding company

    c.   A simple growth company

    d.   A dynamic growth company.

11. Given the terms listed in Question 10, which label would you give IBM? Why?

12. What label would you give U.S. Steel? Why?

13. When using the flexible growth valuation model, what are the most important variables that must be estimated?

REFERENCES

Babcock, Guilford C. "The Concept of Sustainable Growth." *Financial Analysts Journal.* 26 no. 3 (May–June 1970).

Benishay, Haskel. "Variability in Earnings–Price Ratios of Corporate Equities." *American Economic Review.* 51 no. 1 (March 1961).

Bernstein, Peter L. "Growth Companies vs. Growth Stocks." *Harvard Business Review.* 34 no. 5 (September–October 1956).

Brigham, Eugene F., and James L. Pappas. "Duration of Growth, Change in Growth Rates, and Corporate Share Prices." *Financial Analysts Journal.* 22 no. 3 (May–June 1966).

Durand, David. "Growth Stocks and the Petersburg Paradox." *Journal of Finance.* 12 no. 3 (September 1957).

Fuller, Russell J. "*Programming* the Three-Phase Dividend Discount Model." *Journal of Portfolio Management.* 5 no. 4 (Summer 1979).

Holt, Charles C. "The Influence of Growth Duration on Share Prices." *Journal of Finance.* 17 no. 3 (September 1962).

Kisor, Manown, Jr. "The Financial Aspects of Growth." *Financial Analysts Journal.* 20 no. 2 (March–April 1964).

Malkiel, Burton G. "Equity Yields, Growth, and the Structure of Share Prices." *American Economic Review.* 53 no. 5 (December 1963).

Malkiel, Burton G., and John G. Cragg. "Expectations and the Structure of Share Prices." *American Economic Review.* 60 no. 4 (September 1970).

Mao, James C. T. "The Valuation of Growth Stocks: The Investments Opportunity Approach." *Journal of Finance.* 21 no. 1 (March 1966).

Miller, Merton, and Franco Modigliani. "Dividend Policy, Growth, and the Valuation of Shares." *Journal of Business.* 34 no. 4 (October 1966).

Molodovsky, Nicholas, C. May, and S. Chottiner. "Common Stock Valuation: Theory and Tables." *Financial Analysts Journal.* 20 no. 2 (March–April 1965).

Nerlove, Marc. "Factors Affecting Differences among Rates of Return on Investments in Individual Common Stocks." *Review of Economics and Statistics.* 50 no. 3 (August 1968).

Niederhoffer, Victor, and Patrick J. Regan. "Earnings Changes, Analysts Forecasts, and Stock Prices." *Financial Analysts Journal.* 28 no. 3 (May–June 1972).

Reilly, Frank K. "Differentiation between Types of Companies and Types of Stocks." *Mississippi Valley Journal of Business and Economics.* 7 no. 1 (Fall 1971).

Soldofsky, Robert M., and James T. Murphy. *Growth Yield on Common Stocks: Theory and Tables* (revised ed.). Iowa City: State University of Iowa, Bureau of Business and Economics Research, 1964.

Solomon, Ezra. *The Theory of Financial Management.* New York: Columbia University Press, 1963.

Wendt, Paul F. "Current Growth Stock Valuation Methods." *Financial Analysts Journal.* 21 no. 2 (March–April 1965).

Chapter 16 Technical Analysis

"The market reacted yesterday to the report of a large increase in the short interest on the NYSE."

"Although the market declined today it was not considered bearish because there was very light volume."

"The market declined today after three days of increases due to profit taking by investors."

These and similar statements appear almost daily in the financial news as commentators attempt to explain stock market changes. All of these statements have as their rationale one of numerous technical trading rules. This chapter explains the reasoning behind technical analysis and discusses many of the trading rules.

Prior to the development of the efficient market theory, investors were generally divided into two groups—"fundamentalists" and "technicians." Fundamental analysts contend that the price of a security is determined by basic underlying economic factors, such as expected return and risk considerations. To arrive at estimates of these return and risk expectations for a security, an analyst should examine the underlying factors from the economy, to the industry, and then to the company. After extensive analysis, the analyst derives an estimate of the intrinsic value of the security, which is then compared to its market price. If the value exceeds the market price, the security should be acquired and vice versa. The fundamentalist attempts to derive value and compare it to market price and acts based upon the implicit assumption that the market price for the security should approach the intrinsic value in the future.

Technicians contend that it is *not* necessary to study economic fundamentals in order to know where the price of a security is going, because past price movements will indicate future price movements. In the first section of this chapter, we will examine the basic philosophy underlying all technical approaches to market analysis and the assumptions of these approaches. The next section contains a discussion of the supposed advantages of the technical approach and some problems in this area of analysis. The remaining sections discuss alternative technical trading rules.

BASIC PHILOSOPHY AND ASSUMPTIONS OF TECHNICAL ANALYSIS

The basic philosophy and assumptions of technical analysis are well summarized in an article by Robert A. Levy:

1. Market value is determined solely by the interaction of supply and demand.
2. Supply and demand are governed by numerous factors, both rational and irrational. Included in these factors are those relied upon by the fundamentalist, as well as opinions, moods, guesses, and blind necessities. The market weighs all of these factors continually and automatically.
3. Disregarding minor fluctuations in the market, *stock prices tend to move in trends which persist for an appreciable length of time.* (Emphasis added.)
4. Changes in trend are caused by the shifts in supply and demand relationships. These shifts, no matter why they occur, *can be detected sooner or later in the action of the market itself.*[1] (Emphasis added.)

The emphasis is added to highlight those aspects of the technical approach that differ from the belief of fundamentalists and advocates of an efficient market. The two initial statements are almost universally accepted by technicians and nontechnicians alike. Almost anyone who has had a basic course in economics would agree that, at any point in time, the price of a security (or any good or service) should be determined by the interaction of supply and demand. In addition, most observers would acknowledge that supply and demand are governed by a multitude of variables. The only difference might be that some observers would expect the irrational factors to be rather transitory and that, therefore, the rational factors would prevail in the long run. Finally, everyone would expect the market to weigh and evaluate these factors continuously.

A difference of opinion begins to become apparent in the third statement because it implies something about the *speed of adjustment* of stock prices to changes in supply and demand factors. *Technicians expect stock prices to move in trends which persist for long periods.* This is based upon a belief that new information causing a change in the relationship between supply and demand does *not* come to the market at one point in time, but comes over a period of time, because there are alternative sources of information or because certain investors receive the information earlier than others and analyze the effect before others do. As various groups (insiders, well-informed professionals, the average investor) receive the information and invest or disinvest accordingly, the price is *partially* adjusted toward the new equilibrium. Therefore, technicians believe the price adjustment is *not* abrupt because there is a *gradual* flow of information from insiders, to high-powered analysts, and eventually to the mass of investors. As a result, the pattern of price adjustment involves a *gradual* movement to the new equilibrium price. Figure 16.1 shows what technicians

---

[1] Robert A. Levy, "Conceptual Foundations of Technical Analysis," *Financial Analysts Journal,* 22 no. 4 (July–August 1966): 83.

FIGURE 16.1
Technicians' View of Price Adjustment to New Information

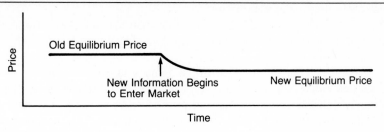

contend happens when new information causing a decrease in the equilibrium price for a security begins to enter the market. The price adjusts, but the implied adjustment is not very rapid. Therefore, *during the adjustment period,* prices tend to move in one direction (i.e., in a trend) that persists until the stock reaches its new equilibrium. Given this *gradual* adjustment in price, the point follows: *when the change occurs, the shift to a new equilibrium can be detected in the market itself.* Therefore, the task of the technical analyst is to derive a system that allows him to detect the *beginning* of a movement from one equilibrium value to a higher or lower equilibrium value in a stock (or in the aggregate market). Technical analysts are not concerned with why the change in equilibrium value occurred, but only with the fact that there is a definite movement and that they can take advantage of this change in equilibrium value to derive above average returns. Technicians emphasize *detecting the start of a change* in the supply-demand relationship. You want to get on the bandwagon early and to benefit from the ride to a new equilibrium. If the adjustment process was very rapid, the ride would be very short and would not be worth the effort; i.e., the ride would be over before you could get on the bandwagon.

ADVANTAGES OF TECHNICAL ANALYSIS

Most technical analysts would probably admit that a fundamental analyst with good information and good analytical ability should be able to do better than a technician, but that is a qualified statement. *If* the analyst can get the new information before other investors can, and *if* he has the ability to process it correctly and quickly, *then* he should be able to derive returns above what a technical analyst can expect. The point is, because the technician must wait until the price movement is underway, he misses part of the potential return. However, *technical analysts do not believe that it is possible to consistently get good information and process it quickly.* Therefore, our discussion of the advantages of technical analysis will be basically concerned with the limitations of fundamental analysis.

A major advantage claimed for technical analysis is that it is not heavily dependent on financial accounting statements, which are a major source of information about the past performance of a firm or industry. The fundamentalist uses them to evaluate past performance and thereby to project future returns and risk characteristics. The technician is quick to point out several major problems with published financial statements.

1. They do not contain a great deal of the information that is desired by analysts, such as details on sales and general expenses or sales and earnings by product line and customers.

2. There are several ways of reporting expenses, assets, or liabilities that can give vastly different results and, typically, several of these alternatives are equally acceptable for accounting purposes. As a result, it is difficult to compare the statements of two firms in the same industry, much less firms in different industries.

3. Many psychological factors and other nonquantitative variables are not included in financial statements. Examples would include employee training and loyalty, customer goodwill, and general investor attitude toward an industry (e.g., tobacco companies).

Technicians are somewhat suspicious of financial statements and consider it an advantage that they generally are not dependent upon them. As our later discussion will show, most of the data used by technicians is derived from the stock market itself.

Once a fundamental analyst has some new information, it is necessary to process this data *correctly* and *very quickly* to derive a new value before the competition can. The technician asks how many analysts can do this consistently and remain ahead of the competition. Technicians contend that they do not have to be the first to see the impact, but only be quick to recognize a movement to a new equilibrium value *for whatever reason.*

Finally, assume an analyst has determined that a given security is under- or overvalued a long time before the competition has. This can present the problem of determining *when* to make the purchase or sale. Ideally, an investor would like to buy or sell a stock just before the change in market value occurs. Because a technician doesn't invest until the move to the new equilibrium is under way, he is not likely to purchase a stock that must be held for a long period of time before it is revalued.

DISADVANTAGES OF TECHNICAL ANALYSIS

The major problem with technical analysis stems from the efficient market hypothesis. The problems considered here are in addition to this.

An obvious problem is that the past price patterns may not be repeated in the future. As a result, there will be instances in which a technique that worked for some period of time misses later market turns. Because of this attribute, almost all technicians follow several trading rules and attempt to arrive at a consensus. In addition, many price patterns may become self-fulfilling prophecies because everyone believes in them. Assume that a stock is selling at $40 a share and it is widely recognized that, if it breaks out of a trading channel at $45, it will be expected to go to $50 or more. If it does get to $45, a number of technicians will buy and the price will probably go to $50, which is exactly what was predicted. In fact, some technicians may place a stop-buy order at such a breakout point.

Under such conditions, the increase will probably only be temporary and the price will return to its true equilibrium.

Also, the success of a trading rule will encourage competition, which will eventually neutralize the value of the technique. If a large number of investors are using a given rule, some of them will eventually attempt to anticipate what will happen and either ruin the expected price pattern or take the profits away from most users of the rule. As an example, assume it becomes known that technicians who have been investing on the basis of odd-lot data have been enjoying very high rates of return. You would expect that other technicians will start using these data and affect the stock price pattern following odd-lot changes so that the rule that worked previously may no longer work or will only work for the first few investors who react.

Finally, as will be discussed later, all of the rules or techniques imply a great deal of subjective judgment. In some cases, two technical analysts looking at the same price pattern will arrive at widely different interpretations and investment decisions. This implies that the use of various techniques is neither completely mechanical nor easy. Also, as will be discussed in connection with several trading rules, the standard values that signal investment action can change over time. Therefore, it is necessary to change the trading rule over time to conform to the new environment.

TECHNICAL TRADING RULES

There are numerous technical rules and a large number of interpretations for each of them. Almost all technical analysts use more than one rule, and some watch many alternatives. This section contains a discussion of most of the well-known techniques, but certainly does not attempt to be all-inclusive.

Contrary Opinion Rules

One set of technical trading rules contends that the majority of investors are wrong most of the time or at least they are wrong at peaks and troughs. Therefore, the idea is to determine when the majority is either very bullish or very bearish and trade in the opposite direction.

The Odd-Lot Theory.   This contends that, although the small investor is generally correct, he or she is almost always wrong at the peaks and troughs. To determine what the small investor is doing, you should watch the odd-lot transactions (i.e., transactions involving less than a round lot, which is usually 100 shares of stock) reported daily in the financial press. In contrast to other trading reports, the figures on odd lots indicate how many shares were purchased and how many were sold, and the two figures obviously do not have to match. Using these figures, technicians develop a ratio of purchases to sales and examine the trend of this ratio, trading when it becomes very bullish or bearish. Historically, the purchase to sales ratio has fluctuated between 0.60 (very strong sales ratio) to about 1.35 (high proportion of purchases). Therefore, when the ratio approaches the low end of this range (e.g., below 0.65 or 0.70), the contrary technician would contend that the odd lotter is very bearish and it is time for a market trough and subsequent rally. In contrast, when the ratio approached the upper end of the range (e.g., above 1.25), this would indicate that the small investor was extremely bullish, and the follower of this ratio would expect the market to peak in the very near future. A major problem with this ratio is that individual investors have been net sellers of common stocks (i.e., selling more than they buy) since the later 1960s, so that the ratio is biased downward by this trend. This makes the range of values change over time; therefore, the purchase/sales ratio values that are considered extreme must be adjusted. The required data for this technique is contained in the *Wall Street Journal* daily and in *Barron's* on a weekly basis.[2]

The Odd-Lot Short-Sales Theory.   This is an extension of the general odd-lot theory. The use of short sales is generally considered bearish because it is based upon an expectation of declining stock prices. It is also considered to be a fairly high-risk form of investing. Most small investors are optimists and would consider short selling too risky. Therefore, they do not get involved in it except when they feel especially bearish. Therefore, the technical rule contends that a relatively high rate (3 percent or more) of odd-lot short sales as a percentage of total odd-lot sales is an indication of a very bearish attitude by small investors. Contrary opinion would consider this bearish attitude by small investors an indicator of a near-term trough, and technicians following this rule would become bullish. Alternatively, when the ratio declines to below 1 percent, it would indicate that small investors are very bullish and would cause the contrarian to become bearish. Notably, recent figures for this ratio suggest that it may be necessary to change the action percentages.

Mutual Fund Cash Positions.   This is considered a contrary tool by some technical analysts. Mutual funds report the ratio of cash as a percentage of total assets in their portfolios over time, and this ratio typically varies from a low point of less than 5 percent to a high point in excess of 15 percent. The contrary opinion technicians consider the mutual funds the odd lotters of the institutional investor group and contend that mutual funds are usually wrong at the peaks and troughs. They expect mutual funds to have heavy cash positions (a high ratio of cash) near the trough of a market cycle. This would indicate that the mutual funds are very bearish exactly at the time that they should be fully invested to take advantage of the impending market rise. At the peak, the technicians expect mutual funds to be almost fully invested (a low ratio of cash), indicating a bullish outlook at a point where the funds should have liquidated part of their portfolios. Therefore, these technicians watch for the mutual fund cash position to be at one of the extremes and act contrary to mutual funds behavior; i.e., they would invest when the cash ratio exceeds 12–13 percent and would sell when the cash ratio approaches 5 percent.

---

[2] *Barron's* is a prime source for numerous technical indicators. For a readable discussion of this data and its use, see Martin E. Zweig, *Understanding Technical Forecasting* (New York: Dow-Jones & Co., 1978). Complimentary copies are available from Dow-Jones & Co. A test of this technique is contained in Stanley Kaish, "Odd-Lot Profit and Loss Performance," *Financial Analysts Journal,* 25 no. 2 (March–April 1969):83–89.

Heavy mutual fund cash positions are also considered bullish because they are potential buying power. Whether the cash balances have built up because of the previous sale of stocks in the portfolio or because of purchases of the fund by investors, technicians believe these funds will eventually be invested and will cause an increase in stock prices. Obviously, a low cash ratio would indicate a low level of potential buying power.

A study by Massey examines the ratio of liquid assets to total assets and also the components of the ratio and contends that the ratio is not as strong a predictor as one would expect.[3] He contends that the significant relationship is between total assets and stock prices although he does not examine the results with a trading rule.

Credit Balances. These result when investors sell stocks and leave the proceeds with their brokers because they expect to reinvest them shortly. These credit balances are reported by the SEC and the NYSE and are contained in *Barron's*. A declining level of credit balances is subject to two interpretations. One is that these funds are considered to be a pool of potential purchasing power, so a decline in this pool would be considered bearish, i.e., the market is approaching a peak. The other interpretation of some contrary opinion technicians is that these balances are maintained by small investors, and they are drawn down just before peaks because of the enthusiasm of this group, which is typically wrong.[4]

Notably, the decision rule is stated in terms of a rising or declining series rather than relative to some other base series. This assumption of an absolute trend could make interpretation difficult as market levels change.

Investment Advisory Opinions. An analysis of these opinions is another contrary opinion technique. The idea is that when a large proportion of investment advisory services become bearish, this signals the approach of a market trough and it is time to become bullish. The specific ratio examined is the number of advisory services that are bearish as a ratio of the number of services expressing an opinion. When this "Bearish Sentiment Index" reaches 60 percent, it indicates a pervasive bearish attitude and is considered bullish for contrarians. In contrast, when this Bearish Sentiment Index ratio declines to 10 percent, this indicates a pervasive optimistic attitude by investment services, and the followers of this index would become bearish. An analysis of this index made by *Investors Intelligence* indicated that it has been a useful series.[5]

Follow the Smart Money

An alternative set of rules for technical analysts involves determining what smart, sophisticated investors are doing and following them.

---

[3] Paul H. Massey, "The Mutual Fund Liquidity Ratio: A Trap for the Unwary," *Journal of Portfolio Management*, 5 no. 2 (Winter 1979): 18–21. There are similar results in, R. David Ranson and William G. Shipman, "Institutional Buying Power and the Stock Market," *Financial Analysts Journal*, 37, no. 5 (September–October 1981): 62–68.

[4] This series is discussed in, Martin E. Zweig, "New Sell Signal?" *Barron's* (October 13, 1975), p. 4.

[5] A. W. Cohen, "A Contrary Opinion Indicator," *Investors Intelligence* (October 23, 1975), p. 1.

The Confidence Index.   This is published by *Barron's* and is the ratio of *Barron's* average yield on 10 top-grade corporate bonds to the yield on the Dow-Jones average of 40 bonds, indicating the difference in yield spread between high-grade bonds and a large sample of bonds.[6] (The differences in grades of bonds will be dealt with fully in the next chapter.) One would expect the yield on high-grade bonds to be lower than that on a large cross section of bonds, so the ratio should never exceed 100.

The theory behind the ratio is that, during periods of high confidence, investors invest more in lower quality bonds for the added yield. This increased demand for lower quality bonds should cause a decrease in the yield on a large cross section of bonds relative to the yield on high-grade bonds. Therefore, the ratio of yields will increase (the Confidence Index increases). When investors are pessimistic, they avoid the low-quality bonds and increase their investments in high-grade bonds, which increases the yield differential between the two groups and the Confidence Index declines.

A major problem with the concept has been that it is basically demand-oriented. It assumes that changes in the yield spread are almost wholly caused by changes in investor demand for different quality bonds. There have been several instances in which the yield differences have changed because of an increased *supply* of bonds in one of the groups or in a related group (e.g., government bonds). A large issue of high-grade AT&T bonds could cause a temporary increase in yields on all high-grade bonds, which would cause an increase in the Confidence Index although investors' attitudes did not change. In other words, the change was supply-oriented. Under such conditions, the series gives a false signal of a change in confidence. Advocates of the index believe that it can be used as an indicator of future stock-price movements, although one may ask why investors in bonds would change their attitude before equity investors do. Several studies that have examined its usefulness for predicting stock-price movements have not been very supportive regarding the predictive ability of the series as related to common stock.

Short Sales by Specialists.   These are regularly reported by the NYSE and the SEC. It will come as no surprise that technicians who want to follow the smart money attempt to determine what the specialist is doing and act accordingly. Specialists regularly engage in short selling as a part of their market-making function, but they also have some discretion when they feel strongly about market changes. The normal ratio of specialists' short sales to the total amount of short sales on the exchange has been about 55 percent. When this ratio declines much *below 40 percent* it is considered a sign that specialists are generally *bullish* and are attempting to avoid short selling. When the ratio *exceeds 65 percent,* it is contended that specialists are generally *bearish* and are attempting to do as much short selling as possible. Two points should be noted regarding this ratio. First, you should not expect it to be a long-run indicator; given the nature of the specialists' portfolio, it will probably serve only in the short run.

---

[6] Historical data for this series is contained in Maurice L. Farrell, ed., *The Dow-Jones Investor's Handbook* (Princeton, NJ: Dow-Jones Books, annual).

Second, there is a two-week lag in the reporting of this data; e.g., the data for a week ending April 14 would be contained in *Barron's* dated May 1. A study by Reilly and Whitford indicated some support for the ratio as a buying signal based on graphical analysis.[7] In contrast, the examination of profit potential from alternative trading rules indicated insignificant excess returns even prior to risk adjustment. Therefore, the results generally supported the weak form efficient markets hypothesis.

Debit Balances in Brokerage Accounts.   These are considered indicative of the attitude of a sophisticated group of investors because debit balances represent borrowing by knowledgeable investors from their brokers, i.e., margin purchases. Therefore, an increase in these balances indicates an increase in purchasing by this astute group and would be a bullish sign. There can be problems in using this series because it does not include borrowing from other sources (banks, etc.). In addition, an increase in debit balances is considered bullish because it is a source of increased demand for stocks. In contrast, a decline in debit balances would indicate an increase in the supply of stocks as these investors liquidate their positions.

Other Techniques

Breadth of Market.   This is a measure of the number of issues that have increased each day and the number of issues that have declined. Everyone is aware of the direction of change in a composite market indicator series like the DJIA or the S&P 400 Index, but they may not be aware of what caused the change. Most of the popular stock market indicator series are either confined to large, well-known stocks or are heavily influenced by the stocks of large firms because most indicator series are value weighted. On occasion composite market indicator series may go up, but the majority of individual issues are not increasing, which is cause for concern. Such a situation can be detected by examining the advance-decline figures along with the composite series.

The advance-decline series is a cumulative series of net advances or net declines. Each day major newspapers publish figures on the number of issues on the NYSE that advanced, the number of issues that declined, and the number that were unchanged. The figures for a five-day sample, as reported in *Barron's,* are shown in Table 16.1. These figures, along with the market indicator figures at the bottom of the table, indicate a strong market advance. Not only was the DJIA increasing, but there was a strong net advance figure, which indicates that the increase was broadly based; i.e., most individual stocks were increasing. Even the results on Day 3, when the market declined 5 points, were somewhat encouraging because there was a very small net decline figure of 41. The market average was down, but individual stocks were split just about 50-50.

The usefulness of the advance-decline series is supposedly greatest at market peaks and troughs because, at such times, the composite value-weighted

[7] Frank K. Reilly and David Whitford, "A Test of the Specialists' Short Sale Ratio," *Journal of Portfolio Management,* 8 no. 2 (Winter 1982): 12–18.

TABLE 16.1
Daily Advances and Declines on New York Stock Exchange

Day	1	2	3	4	5
Issues Traded	1,908	1,941	1,959	1,951	1,912
Advances	1,110	1,050	708	1,061	1,125
Declines	409	450	749	433	394
Unchanged	389	441	502	457	393
Net Advances (advances minus declines)	+701	+600	−41	+628	+731
Cumulative Net Advances	+701	+1,301	+1,260	+1,888	+2,619
Changes in DJIA	+10.47	+3.99	−5.15	+4.16	+5.56

SOURCE: Reprinted by permission of the New York Stock Exchange.

market series might be moving either up or down, but the advance or decline would *not* be broadly based and the majority of individual stocks might be moving in the opposite direction. Near a peak, the DJIA would be increasing, but the net advance-decline ratio for individual days would become negative and the cumulative series would begin to decline. The *divergence* between the aggregate market indicator series and the cumulative advance-decline series is a signal for a market peak. At the trough, the composite series would be declining, but the advance-decline ratio would become positive and the cumulative series would turn up before the aggregate market series did.

The principle behind the advance-decline ratio is somewhat akin to the notion of the diffusion index used by the National Bureau of Economic Research. A diffusion index for a given economic series, such as new orders for durable goods, indicates how many of the reporting units show an increase in new orders; i.e., a diffusion index of 60 means 60 percent of the sample report an increase in new orders. During a period of rapid expansion, the diffusion index would be high, and the composite series would be increasing rapidly. Near the peak of an economic expansion, the diffusion index would turn down (e.g., from 90 to 70), but the composite would continue to increase. Therefore, the diffusion index turns *before* the composite series does. Similarly, a technician would expect the net advance-decline series and the cumulative advance-decline series to turn before the composite stock market series.

Short Interest.   This is the ratio between the number of shares sold short and not covered and the average daily volume on the exchange. The interpretation of this ratio by technicians is probably contrary to your initial intuition. Because short sales are made by investors who expect stock prices to decline, one would typically expect an increase in the short-interest ratio to be bearish. On the contrary, technicians consider a high short-interest ratio *bullish* because it indicates *potential demand* for stock by those who sold short. It is reasoned that short sellers will have to buy the stock in the future to cover their outstanding short position. The ratio has generally fluctuated between 1.00 and 1.75. A ratio of 1.00 means that the outstanding short interest on the NYSE is equal to about one day's trading volume.) The short interest position is calculated as of the twentieth of each month and is reported about two days later in the *Wall Street Journal.* As the short-interest ratio approaches 1.75, it would be considered very bullish, while a decline toward 1.00 would be bearish.

The results of a number of studies on the usefulness of the short-interest series as a predictor of stock-price movements have been extremely mixed. For every study that supported the technique, another indicated that it should be rejected.[8]

Stock Price and Volume Techniques

Most technicians also use trading rules for the market and individual stocks that are based upon stock price and volume movements. Technicians believe that prices move in trends that persist so they contend that it is therefore possible to determine *future* price trends from an astute analysis of *past* price and volume trends. Technicians contend that *price alone is somewhat inadequate* and investors should also examine the volume of trading that accompanies price changes.

The Dow Theory.   Any discussion of technical analysis using price and volume must begin with a consideration of the Dow Theory developed by Charles Dow, publisher of the *Wall Street Journal,* during the late 1800s.[9] Dow contended that stock prices moved in trends that were analogous to the movement of water. There were three types of price movements that should be analyzed over time: (1) major trends that are like tides in the ocean; (2) intermediate trends that are similar to waves; and (3) short-run movements that are like ripples. The idea is to detect which way the major price trend (tide) is going, recognizing that there will be intermediate movements (waves) in the opposite direction. A major market advance does not go straight up, but is accompanied by small price declines as some investors decide to take profits. The typical bullish pattern is portrayed in Figure 16.2. The technician would look for every recovery to reach a high point above the prior peak with heavy trading volume, while each reversal should have a trough above the prior trough and volume should be relatively light during the reversals. When this no longer happens, the major trend (tide) may be ready for a permanent reversal.

Support and Resistance Levels.   A *support level* is the price range at which the analyst would expect a considerable increase in the demand for a stock. Gener-

[8] Barton M. Biggs, "The Short Interest —A False Proverb," *Financial Analysts Journal,* 22 no. 4 (July – August 1966): 111 – 116. Joseph J. Seneca, "Short Interest: Bearish or Bullish?" *Journal of Finance,* 22 no. 1 (March 1967): 67 – 70. Thomas H. Mayor, "Short Trading Activities and the Price of Equities: Some Simulation and Regression Results," *Journal of Financial and Quantitative Analysis,* 3 no. 3 (September 1968): 283 – 298. Randall Smith, "Short Interest and Stock Market Prices," *Financial Analysts Journal,* 24 no. 6 (November – December 1968): 151 – 154. Thomas J. Kerrigan, "The Short Interest Ratio and Its Component Parts," *Financial Analysts Journal,* 32 no. 6 (November – December 1974): 45 – 49. William Goff, "Letter to the Editor," *Financial Analysts Journal,* (March – April 1975): pp. 8 – 10.

[9] An extensive discussion of the Dow Theory is contained in George W. Bishop, Jr. "Evolution of the Dow Theory," *Financial Analysts Journal,* 17 no. 5 (September – October 1961): 23 – 36. A study by Glickstein and Wubbels discusses the theory and provides results supportive of the theory, David A. Glickstein and Rolf E. Wubbels, "Dow Theory is Alive and Well," *Journal of Portfolio Management,* 9 no. 3 (Spring 1983): 28 – 32.

FIGURE 16.2
An Example of a Bullish Price Pattern

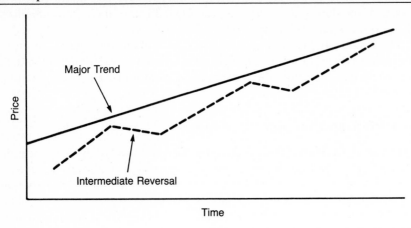

ally, a support level will develop after the price has increased and the stock has begun to experience a reversal because of profit taking. At some price there are other investors who did not buy during the first rally and have been waiting for a small reversal to get into the stock. When the price reaches the point at which they want to buy, there is an increase in demand and the price begins to increase again.

A *resistance level* is the price range at which the analyst would expect the supply of stock to increase substantially and any price rise to be abruptly reversed. A resistance level tends to develop after a stock has experienced a steady decline from a higher price level. Because of the decline, investors who acquired the stock at a higher price are waiting for an opportunity to sell it and get out at about their breakeven point. Therefore, this supply of stock is overhanging the market and, when the price rebounds to the target price set by these investors, the supply increases dramatically and the price increase is reversed.

Importance of Volume.   Technicians are clearly not only concerned with price movements, but they also watch volume changes as an indicator of changes in supply and demand for a stock or for stocks in general. A price movement in one direction indicates that the *net* effect is in that direction but does not indicate how *widespread* the excess demand or supply is at that time. A price increase of a half point on volume of 1,000 shares indicates excess demand but not much overall interest. In contrast, a one-point increase on volume of 20,000 shares indicates a large demand. Therefore, it is not only a price increase, but also heavy volume relative to the stock's normal trading volume that interests the technician. Following the same line of reasoning, a price decline with heavy volume is very bearish because it means strong and widespread desire to sell the stock. A generally bullish pattern is a price increase on heavy volume and a price reversal with light trading volume indicating only limited desire to sell and take profits.

Moving-Average Line.   Technicians are constantly looking for ways of detecting changes in major price trends for an individual stock or for the aggregate market. One relatively popular tool is constructing a moving average of past stock prices as an indicator of the long-run trend and examining current prices in terms of this trend to see whether the relationship between current prices and the long-term trend signals a change. The number of days used in computing the moving average is a matter of judgment, but a *200-day moving average* is a relatively popular measure for the aggregate market. If the overall trend has been down, the moving-average line would generally be above the current individual prices. If prices reverse and *break through the moving-average line from below on heavy volume,* a technician might speculate that the declining trend has been reversed. In contrast, given a rising trend, the moving-average line would be rising and would be below the current prices. If current prices broke through the moving-average line from above on heavy volume, this would be a bearish indication of a reversal of the long-run rising trend.[10]

Relative Strength.   Technicians believe that, once a trend is initiated, it will continue until some major event causes a change in direction. This is also true of *relative* performance. If a stock is outperforming the market, technicians believe it will continue to outperform the market. To detect this relative performance, technicians compute relative-strength ratios for individual stocks in terms of some aggregate market series on a weekly or monthly basis. This is simply a ratio of the stock price to the value for some market series like the DJIA or the S&P 400. If the ratio increases over time, the stock is outperforming the market and it is believed that this superior performance will continue for a time. The relative-strength ratios work during declining and rising markets. (If the stock does not decline as much as the market does, the relative-strength ratio will continue to rise.) It is believed that, if the ratio holds up or increases during a bear market, the stock should do very well during the ensuing bull market. These ratios are used for industry analysis as well as for company analysis.[11]

Bar Charting.   The basic chart used in technical analysis is one on which the time series of prices for specified time intervals (daily, weekly, monthly) are plotted. For a given interval, the technical analyst will plot the high and low price

[10] A test of this technique is contained in F. E. James, Jr., "Monthly Moving Averages—An Effective Investment Tool?" *Journal of Financial and Quantitative Analysis,* 3 no. 2 (June 1968): 315–326; and in J. C. Van Horne and G. C. Parker, "The Random Walk Theory: An Empirical Test," *Financial Analysts Journal,* 23 no. 6 (November–December 1967): 57–64.

[11] For further discussion of this technique by a leading advocate, see Robert A. Levy, "Relative Strength as a Criterion for Investment Selection," *Journal of Finance,* 23 no. 5 (December 1967): 595–610; and Robert A. Levy and Spero L. Kripotos, "Sources of Relative Price Strength," *Financial Analysts Journal,* 25 no. 6 (November–December 1969): 60, 62, 64; Robert A. Levy, *The Relative Strength Concept of Common Stock Price Forecasting* (Larchmont, N.Y.: Investors Intelligence, 1968). Studies that support the technique are, Charles A. Akemann and Werner E. Keller, "Relative Strength Does Persist!" *Journal of Portfolio Management,* 4 no. 1 (Fall 1977): 38–45 and James Bohan, "Relative Strength: Further Positive Evidence," *Journal of Portfolio Management,* 7 no 1 (Fall 1981): 39–46. A study that rejects the technique: Robert D. Arnott, "Relative Strength Revisited," *Journal of Portfolio Management,* 6 no 3 (Spring 1979): 19–23. Finally, a study that combines it with modern portfolio theory is, John S. Brush and Keith Boles, "The Predictive Power in Relative Strength and CAPM," *Journal of Portfolio Management,* 9 no 4 (Summer 1983): 20–23.

486

FIGURE 16.3
A Typical Bar Chart

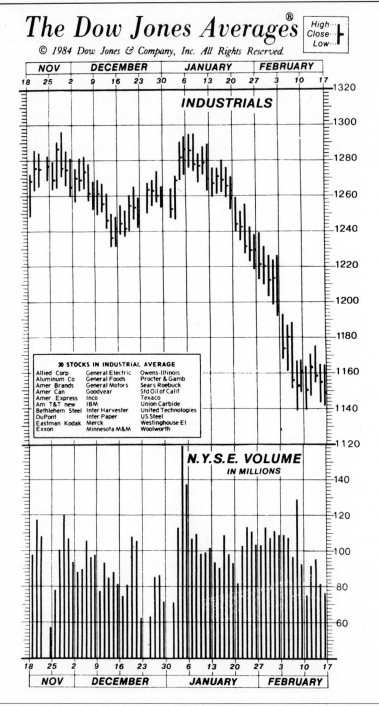

The Dow Jones Averages®

© 1984 Dow Jones & Company, Inc. All Rights Reserved.

High···
Close···
Low···

INDUSTRIALS

30 STOCKS IN INDUSTRIAL AVERAGE

Allied Corp	General Electric	Owens-Illinois
Aluminum Co	General Foods	Procter & Gamb
Amer Brands	General Motors	Sears Roebuck
Amer Can	Goodyear	Std Oil of Calif
Amer Express	Inco	Texaco
Am T&T new	IBM	Union Carbide
Bethlehem Steel	Inter Harvester	United Technologies
DuPont	Inter Paper	US Steel
Eastman Kodak	Merck	Westinghouse El
Exxon	Minnesota M&M	Woolworth

N.Y.S.E. VOLUME
IN MILLIONS

SOURCE: *Wall Street Journal*, February 20, 1984. Reprinted with permission of the *The Wall Street Journal*, © Dow Jones & Company, Inc., 1984. All rights reserved.

and connect the two points to form a bar. Typically, he will also draw a small horizontal line across it to indicate the closing price. Finally, almost all bar charts include the volume of trading at the bottom of the chart so that the analyst can relate the price and volume movements. An example is given in Figure 16.3, which is the bar chart for the DJIA from *The Wall Street Journal* along with the volume figures for the NYSE.

The technical analyst might also include a 200-day moving average for the series and possible resistance and support levels based upon past patterns. Finally, if it is a bar chart for an individual stock, it could contain a relative-strength line. Most technicians include as many price and volume series as is reasonable on one chart and attempt to arrive at a consensus concerning future movement for the stock based upon the performance of several technical indicators.

Point-and-Figure Charts. Another popular device used by technicians is called point-and figure charting.[12] As is true of all other technical tools, its purpose is to detect changes in the supply and demand for a particular security. In contrast to the bar chart that typically includes all ending prices and volume for purposes of detecting a trend, the point-and-figure chart only includes significant price changes regardless of the time interval involved. The analyst determines which significant price changes will be recorded (one point, two points, etc.) and when a price reversal will be recorded. The following example should make this clear. Assume that you want to chart a stock that is currently selling for $40 a share and is quite volatile (beta of 1.60). Because of its volatility, you believe that anything less than a two-point price change is not relevant. Also, you consider anything less than a four-point reversal quite minor. Therefore, you would set up a chart similar to the one in Figure 16.4 (page 488) that starts at 40 and progresses in two-point increments. If the stock moves to 42, you place an *X* in the box above 40 and do nothing else until the stock rises to 44 or drops to 38 (a four-point reversal from its high of 42). If it drops to 38, you move over a column to the right and begin again at 38 (fill in boxes at 42 and 40). Assuming the stock price drops to 34, you would enter an *X* at 36 and another at 34. If the stock then rises to 38 (another four-point reversal), you move to the next column and begin at 38 going up (fill in 34 and 36). Assuming the stock then goes to 46, you would fill in as shown and wait for further increases or a reversal.

Depending upon how fast the prices rise and fall, this process may have taken anywhere from two to six months. Given these figures, the analyst would attempt to determine trends in the same manner as he did with the bar chart.

As always, you are looking for breakouts to either higher or lower price levels.[13] A long sideways movement in which there are many reversals but no major shifts in any direction would be considered a period of consolidation as the stock is moving from one group to another with no strong consensus of direction. Once the stock breaks out and moves up or down after a period of consolidation, it is assumed that this is a major move because of the previous

[12] Daniel Seligman, "The Mystique of Point-and-Figure," *Fortune* (March 1962): 113–115.

[13] A study that examined the usefulness of various price patterns is Robert A. Levy, "The Predictive Significance of Five Point Chart Patterns," *Journal of Business,* 44 no. 3(July 1971): 316–323. The results were not encouraging for the technician.

FIGURE 16.4
Example of a Point-and-Figure Chart

```
50 |     |   |     |   |     |     |
48 |     |   |     |   |     |     |
46 |     |   |  X  |   |     |     |
44 |     |   |  X  |   |     |     |
42 |  X  | X |  X  |   |     |     |
40 |  X  | X |  X  |   |     |     |
38 |     | X |  X  |   |     |     |
36 |     | X |  X  |   |     |     |
34 |     | X |  X  |   |     |     |
32 |     |   |     |   |     |     |
30 |     |   |     |   |     |     |
```

trading that set the stage for it. The difference between point-and-figure and bar charts is that with the former you have a compact record of movements because only those price changes considered relevant for the particular stock analyzed are recorded. Therefore, it is easier to work with and to use in visualizing movements.

SUMMARY

This chapter introduced the reader to *what* technical analysts do, *why* they do it, and *how* they do it. Our initial discussion considered the basic rationale behind technical analysis and how it differed from the practices of those who believe in an efficient stock market. The main differences relate to the information dissemination process (does everybody get the information at about the same time?) and to how quickly investors adjust stock prices to reflect this new information. Because technical analysts believe that the information dissemination process is not the same for everyone and that price adjustment is not instantaneous, they contend that *stock prices move in trends that persist* and, therefore, that you can use past price trends to determine future price trends.

Subsequently we discussed the advantages and disadvantages of technical analysis. The rest of the chapter discussed specific technical trading rules under four general categories: contrary opinion rules, follow the smart money, other trading rules, and stock price and volume techniques. Most technicians use several rules at any one point in time and attempt to derive a consensus decision which can be buy, sell, or do nothing.[14] According to many technicians, their conclusion on many occasions is to do nothing.

QUESTIONS

1. The basic belief of technical analysts is that it is possible to use past price changes to predict future price changes. What is the principal contention that makes this basic belief possible?

---

[14] A discussion of the results for a well-known advocate of employing numerous indicators is contained in Jerome Baesel, George Shows, and Edward Thorp, "Can Joe Granville Time the Market?" *Journal of Portfolio Management*, 8 no. 3 (Spring 1982): 5–9.

2. Technicians contend that stock prices move in trends that persist for a long time. What is there about the real world that causes those trends? Put another way, what do technicians believe happens in the real world that would cause stock prices to move in trends?

3. Briefly discuss the problems involved with fundamental analysis that are considered to be advantages for technical analysis.

4. What are some of the disadvantages of technical analysis?

5. The odd-lot purchase/sales ratio reaches 1.40. What would this indicate to a contrary opinion technician? What is the reasoning behind this?

6. The mutual fund cash position increases to 13 percent; is this bullish or bearish? Why? Give two reasons for your position.

7. There is a strong decline in credit balances at brokerage firms. Give two reasons why this is considered bearish.

8. The Bearish Sentiment Index of advisory service opinions increases to 61 percent; is this bullish or bearish? Discuss the concept and indicate why this figure is bullish or bearish.

9. Define the Confidence Index and describe the reasoning behind it. Discuss why the fact that the Confidence Index is demand-oriented is a problem.

10. The ratio of specialists' short sales to total short sales increases to 70 percent. As a technician would you consider this bullish or bearish and why?

11. The odd-lot short-sales ratio increases to 3 percent. As a technician, what would you do and why would you do it? Does your reasoning in this case differ from your reasoning in Question 10? Why or why not?

12. Why is an increase in debit balances considered bullish? What problems are involved with using this series as a technical tool?

13. Describe the Dow theory and its three components. Which component is most important?

14. Why is volume important to a technician? Describe a bearish price and volume pattern and discuss why it is bearish.

15. Describe the computation of the breadth of market index. How is it used to confirm an important peak in stock prices?

16. During a ten-day trading period, the cumulative net advance series goes from 1,752 to 1,253. During this same period of time, the DJIA goes from 1,157 to 1,192. As a technician, what would you say about this set of events? Discuss your reasoning.

17. Describe a support and a resistance level and explain why they are expected to occur.

18. What is the purpose of computing a moving-average line for a stock? Describe a bullish pattern using a moving-average line and discuss why it is considered bullish.

19. How would you construct a relative-strength series for a stock? What do you mean when you say a stock had good relative strength during a bear market?

20. Select a stock on the NYSE and construct a daily high, low, and close bar chart for the stock that includes volume for ten trading days.

21. Compute the relative-strength ratio for the stock in Question 20 relative to the S&P 500 Index and prepare a table that includes all the data and indicates the computations as follows:

Day	Closing Price		Stock Price/S&P 500
	Stock	S&P 500	

22. Plot the relative-strength ratio computed in Question 21 on your bar chart and discuss whether the stock's relative strength is bullish or bearish.

23. Construct a one-point interval point-and-figure chart and use a two-point reversal rule for a stock selling at $25 a share. Fill in the chart for the following closing prices: 24,22,21,24,26,28,29,27,24,22,20,19.

24. Most technicians follow several technical rules and attempt to derive a consensus. What is the reason for this?

REFERENCES

Akeman, Charles A., and Werner E. Keller. "Relative Strength Does Persist!" *Journal of Portfolio Management.* 5 no. 3 (Spring 1979).

Arnott, Robert D. "Relative Strength Revisited." *Journal of Portfolio Management.* 5 no. 3 (Spring 1979).

Baesel, Jerome, George Shows, and Edward Thorp. "Can Joe Granville Time the Market?" *Journal of Portfolio Management.* 8 no. 3 (Spring 1982).

Biggs, Barton M. "The Short Interest–A False Proverb." *Financial Analysts Journal.* 22 no. 4 (July–August 1966).

Bishop, George W. Jr. "Evolution of the Dow Theory." *Financial Analysts Journal.* 17 no. 5 (September–October 1961).

Bishop, George W. Jr. *Charles H. Dow and the Dow Theory.* (New York: Appleton Century Crofts, 1960), 23.

Bohan, James. "Relative Strength: Further Positive Evidence." *Journal of Portfolio Management.* 7 no. 1 (Fall 1981).

Branch, Ben. "The Predictive Power of Stock Market Indicators." *Journal of Financial and Quantitative Analysis.* 11 no. 2 (June 1976).

Brush, John and Keith Boles. "The Predictive Power in Relative Strength and CAPM." *Journal of Portfolio Management.* 9 no. 4 (Summer 1983).

Croach, Robert L. "Market Volume and Price Changes." *Financial Analysts Journal.* 26 no. 4 (July–August 1970).

Dines, James. *How the Average Investor Can Use Technical Analysis for Stock Profits.* New York: Dines Chart Corporation, 1974.

Drew, Garfield A. "A Clarification of the Odd Lot Theory." *Financial Analysts Journal.* 23 no. 5 (September–October 1967).

Edwards, R. D., and John Magee Jr. *Technical Analysis of Stock Trends.* Springfield, Md.: Stock Trend Service, 1966.

Ehrbar, A. F. "Technical Analysts Refuse to Die." *Fortune,* August 1975.

Encyclopedia of Stock Market Techniques. Larchmont, N.Y., Investor's Intelligence, 1971.

Garbisch, Michael W., and Gordon T. Alexander. "Is Standard and Poor's Master List Worthless?" *Journal of Portfolio Management.* 4 no. 1 (Fall 1977).

Glickstein, David A. and Rolf E. Wubbels. "Dow Theory is Alive and Well." *Journal of Portfolio Management.* 9 no. 3 (Spring 1983).

Gould, Alex and Maurice Buchsbaum. "A Filter Approach to Stock Selection." *Financial Analysts Journal.* 25 no. 6 (November–December 1969).

Grant, Dwight. "Market Timing: Strategies to Consider." *Journal of Portfolio Management.* 5 no. 4 (Summer 1979).

Hardy, C. Colburn. *Investor's Guide to Technical Analysis.* New York: McGraw-Hill, 1978.

James, F. E., Jr. "Monthly Moving Averages—An Effective Investment Tool?" *Journal of Financial and Quantitative Analysis.* 3 no. 2 (June 1968).

Jiler, William L. *How Charts Can Help You in the Stock Market.* New York: Commodity Research Publications Corp., 1967.

Kaish, Stanley. "Odd Lot Profit and Loss Performance." *Financial Analysts Journal.* 25 no. 5 (September–October 1969).

Kaish, Stanley, "Odd Lotter Trading of High and Low Quality Stocks." *Financial Analysts Journal.* 25 no. 2(March–April 1969).

Kerr, H. S. "The Battle of Insider Trading vs. Market Efficiency." *Journal of Portfolio Management.* 6 no. 4 (Summer 1980).

Kerrigan, Thomas J. "The Short Interest Ratio and Its Component Parts." *Financial Analysts Journal.* 32 no. 6 (November–December 1974).

Levy, Robert A. "Conceptual Foundations of Technical Analysis." *Financial Analysts Journal.* 22 no. 4 (July–August 1966).

Levy, Robert A. "The Predictive Significance of Five Point Chart Patterns." *Journal of Business.* 44 no. 3 (July 1971).

Levy, Robert A. *The Relative Strength Concept of Common Stock Price Forecasting.* Larchmont, N.Y.: Investors Intelligence, 1968.

Levy, Robert A. "Random Walks: Reality or Myth." *Financial Analysts Journal.* 23 no. 6 (November–December 1967).

Levy, Robert A. "Relative Strength as a Criterion for Investment Selection." *Journal of Finance.* 22 no. 5 (December, 1967).

Levy, Robert A., and Spero L. Kripotos. "Sources of Relative Price Strength." *Financial Analysts Journal.* 25 no. 6 (November–December 1969).

Massey, Paul F. "The Mutual Fund Liquidity Ratio: A Trap for the Unwary." *Journal of Portfolio Management.* 5 no. 2 (Winter 1979).

Pinches, George F. "The Random Walk Hypothesis and Technical Analysis." *Financial Analysts Journal.* 26 no. 5 (March–April 1970).

Ranson, R. David and William G. Shipman. "Institutional Buying Power and the Stock Market." *Financial Analysts Journal.* 37 no. 5 (September–October 1981).

Reilly, Frank K. and David T. Whitford. "The Stock Specialists Short Sale Ratio as an Investment Tool." *Journal of Portfolio Management.* 8 no. 2 (Winter 1982).

492

Seligman, Daniel. "The Mystique of Point-and-Figure." *Fortune.* (March 1962).

Seneca, Joseph J. "Short Interest: Bearish or Bullish?" *Journal of Finance.* 22 no. 1 (March 1967).

Shaw, Alan R. "Technical Analysis." *Financial Analysts Handbook.* Sumner N. Levine (ed.) Vol. 1 Homewood Il.: Dow Jones-Irwin, 1975.

Smith, Randall. "Short Interest and Stock Market Price." *Financial Analysts Journal.* 24 no. 6 (November–December 1968).

Tabell, Edmund W., and Anthony W. Tabell. "The Case for Technical Analysis." *Financial Analysts Journal.* 20 no. 2 (March–April 1964).

VanHorne, James C., and G. C. Parker. "The Random Walk Theory: An Empirical Test." *Financial Analysts Journal.* 23 no. 6 (November–December 1967).

Ying, Charles C. "Stock Market Prices and Volume of Sales." *Econometrica.* 34 no. 3 (July 1966).

Zweig, Martin E. "New Sell Signal?" *Barron's* (October 13, 1975).

Zweig, Martin E. *Understanding Technical Forecasting,* New York: Dow Jones & Co., 1978.

Part 4

Analysis and Management of Bonds

As an investment vehicle, bonds have undergone several cycles of popularity during the twentieth century. In the early decades, bonds were the major investment instrument. This changed during the "Roaring Twenties" when the stock market became the favorite of investors who thought they could become wealthy overnight by investing in common stock purchased on large margins. This dream ended with the stock market crash in 1929. In reaction to the crash there was increased interest in bonds because of the safety involved. During the "Flying Fifties" and "Soaring Sixties" the pendulum again swung in favor of common stocks, and it was generally believed that the only investors interested in bonds were those on pensions or those who did not recognize the excitement and advantages of common stock. Toward the end of this period (about 1965), even the large financial institutions drastically changed their portfolio mix toward common stocks. Finally, since the onset of significant inflation in 1966, it became clear that common stocks have not performed very well and investors recognized the fact that common stocks are *not* a good hedge during periods of significant inflation. After about a decade of poor performance by common stocks and reasonably good returns from bonds, beginning in about 1975 the pendulum began swinging back rather strongly toward a renewed interest in bonds. In contrast to past periods, the current interest is more balanced and rational, which is partially attributable to the recognition that bonds contribute to a well-diversified portfolio. Also, investors realize that superior returns can be derived from a certain amount of trading in bonds. Moreover, capital markets are experiencing the highest interest rates in recorded history and extreme interest rate volatility. This combination of factors is leading to the consideration of portfolio strategies with a premium on risk control and also the creation of new investment instruments that contribute to this control.

Because of this strong and continuing interest in bonds, the purpose of the three chapters in this section is to provide you with a thorough background on bonds. Chapter 17 discusses the attributes of bonds. Chapter 18 concerns the valuation of bonds and considers several factors that influence bond value and price movements. Finally, Chapter 19 discusses trading strategies that can be used by bond investors who want to increase their returns while controlling risk. There is also a consideration of alternative portfolio management policies and how they are implemented.

Chapter 17   *Bond Fundamentals*

T he market for fixed income securities is large and diverse, and it represents an exciting and profitable outlet for investment. This chapter is primarily concerned with publicly issued, long-term, nonconvertible, straight-debt obligations of both public and private issuers. In later chapters, we will consider other fixed income securities, such as preferred stock and convertible bonds. An understanding of bonds is helpful in an efficient market because bonds and other forms of fixed income securities increase the universe of investing options necessary for diversification.[1]

In this chapter we will discuss bond fundamentals including a review of some basic features of bonds, an extensive examination of the fixed income securities market structure, and a look at alternative fixed income investment vehicles. The chapter ends with a brief review of the data requirements of bond investors and the sources of such information.

BASIC FEATURES OF A BOND

Essentially, bonds are the long-term, public debt of an issuer that has been marketed in a convenient and affordable denomination. They differ from other forms of debt, such as mortgages and privately placed obligations, because they have been placed in the hands of numerous public investors rather than channeled directly to a single lender. Bond issues are considered fixed-income securities because the debt-service obligations of the issuer are fixed. Specifically, the issuer agrees to:

1. Pay a fixed amount of periodic *interest* to the holder of record, and
2. Repay a fixed amount of *principal* at the date of maturity.

Normally, interest on bonds is paid every six months. Occasionally, how-

---

[1] William F. Sharpe, "Bonds Versus Stocks: Some Lessons from Capital Market Theory," *Financial Analysts Journal,* 28 no. 6 (November–December 1973): 73–79.

ever, a bond issue may carry provisions to pay interest in intervals as short as a month or as long as a year. The principal is due at maturity; this is the *par value* of the issue. The par value of most debt issues is fairly substantial, very rarely less than $1,000 and often more.

Another important dimension of bonds is their term to maturity or the life of issue. The public debt market is often divided into three time segments defined in terms of an issue's original maturity as follows:

1. Short-Term — instruments with maturities of one year or less. This segment is commonly known as the *money market.*
2. Intermediate — involves issues with maturities in excess of one year but less than seven to ten years. These are known as *notes.*
3. Long-Term — includes obligations with maturities in excess of seven to ten years. These are referred to as *bonds.*

The lives of debt obligations, however, are constantly changing as the issues progress toward maturity. Thus, seasoned issues (i.e., those that have been outstanding in the secondary market for any period of time) move from one maturity segment to shorter segments. As an example, a bond issued in 1985 with a maturity in 2010 will originally be a long-term bond, but eventually it will become an intermediate-term security when it has less than ten years to maturity; finally it will be a short-term security when there is less than a year to maturity. This movement is important, because the price volatility of a debt obligation is affected by, among other things, the prevailing maturity of the issue. Thus, a 3-year obligation, other things being equal, will have less price volatility than, say, a 25-year obligation has. The fact that the 3-year bond was originally a 25-year bond would have absolutely no effect on its *current* price behavior.

Bond Characteristics

One can characterize a bond in many different ways. Each bond has intrinsic features that relate to the issue itself. There are different types of bonds, and there are various indenture provisions that can affect the yield and/or price behavior.

Intrinsic Characteristics.   There are several intrinsic features that are important: coupon, maturity, the principal value of the issue, and finally, the type of bond ownership. The coupon indicates the income that the bond investor will receive over the life (or holding period) of the issue, and is known as *interest income, coupon income,* or *nominal yield.*

The maturity of an issue specifies the date at which the bond will mature (or expire), and is referrred to as *term to maturity.* Two important types of bonds can be distinguished on the basis of maturity, a term bond and a serial issue. A *term bond* has a single maturity date specified in the issue and is the most common type of corporate or government bond. A *serial obligation* actually involves a series of maturity dates. Thus, a single 25-year issue, for example, may possess 20 or 25 different maturity dates. Each maturity, although a subset of the total issue, is really a small bond issue in itself with a different maturity and, generally, a different coupon. Municipalities are the biggest issuers of serial bonds.

The principal, or par value, of the issue represents the original principal value of the obligation and is generally stated in $1,000 increments. While $1,000 is a popular principal value, there are many issues with denominations that go much higher, to $25,000 or more. Principal value is *not* necessarily the same as the market value. It is not uncommon to find issues traded at market values that are substantially above or below their original principal value. Such price behavior is the result of a difference between the coupon of the obligation and the prevailing market rate of interest. When market rates go up, lower coupon issues decline in value to a market price below par. If the issue carries a coupon comparable to the market interest rate, its market value will correspond to its original principal value.

The final intrinsic provision is whether the issue is a bearer bond or a registered issue. With the former type, the holder, or *bearer,* is the owner. The issuer keeps no account of transfers in ownership, and interest is obtained by clipping coupons and sending them to the issuer for payment. Such payment is usually handled through local commercial banks in a routine, systematic manner. The issuers of registered bonds keep track of owners of record and, at the time of principal or interest payment, simply pay the owner of record by check.

Types of Issues. In contrast to common stock, issuers of bonds can have many different types outstanding at a single point in time. Generally, one type of bond is differentiated from another by the type of collateral behind the issue. Bonds can be distinguished as either senior or junior securities. The former are generally thought of as secured bonds; that is, they are backed by a legal claim on some specified property of the issuer. For example, mortgage bonds are secured by real assets, and equipment trust certificates, which are popular with railroads and airlines, indicate a senior claim on the equipment of the railroad or airline.

Unsecured (junior) bonds are issues backed only by the promise of the issuer to pay interest and principal on a timely basis. There are several classes of unsecured bonds. One is a debenture, which is simply a bond secured by the general credit of the issuer. In addition, there are subordinated debentures that represent a claim on income that is subordinated (or secondary) to the claim of another debenture bond. Income issues represent the most junior type because interest on these need to be paid only to the extent to which income is earned. They entail no legally binding requirement to pay interest on a periodic basis. While they are unusual in the corporate sector, they are a very popular municipal issue and are referred to as *revenue bonds.*

Finally, an issue could be a refunding type, which means one bond is prematurely retired by paying off its principal from the proceeds of the sale of another issue. The second issue remains outstanding after the refunding operation. Thus, such terms as *first* and *refunding* refer to refunding obligations. A refunding bond can take either a junior or senior position depending upon whether it is secured or not. The type of issue has only a marginal effect on comparative yield because it is the credibility of the issuer that basically determines the quality of the obligation. In fact, a study of corporate bond price behavior found that the collateral of the obligation, or lack of it, did not become important until the issue approached default.[2] Usually, collateral and security only influence yield differentials when such senior/junior positions affect the quality ratings given to a bond by agencies such as Moody's, Standard & Poor's, Duff and Phelps, or Fitch.

Indenture Provisions.   The indenture is the contract between the issuer and the bondholder specifying the legal conditions that must be met by the issuer. Most of the provisions are of little interest to bond investors because the trustee (i.e., the organization or institution acting in behalf of the bondholders) sees to it that all of the provisions are met, including the timely and orderly distribution of interest and principal.

However, investors should be aware of a few popular indenture provisions, especially the *call features.* There are three types of call provisions: (1) the bond can be freely callable, which means that the issuer can retire the bond at any time within its life given a notification period of, usually, 30 to 60 days; (2) the obligation can be noncallable, which means that the issuer *cannot* retire the bond prior to its maturity; and (3) it may have a deferred call feature stipulating that the obligation cannot be called for a certain length of time after the date of issue. (Recently the most popular time period has been between five and ten years.) At the end of the deferred call period, the issue becomes freely callable. The investor should also be aware of the call premium—the added cost the issuer must pay to the bondholder for prematurely retiring the bond.

In lieu of a call feature, a bond may contain a refunding provision which is exactly like the call feature *except that* it only prohibits (or allows) one thing: the retirement of an issue from the proceeds of a lower coupon refunding bond. This means that the obligation can still be called and prematurely retired for any reason other than refunding! If a firm has excess cash, for example, the issue could carry a nonrefunding provision but still be retired prior to maturity. In fact, during 1975 this occurred when many issuers did not refund their obligations but, instead, simply retired these costly high-coupon issues early because they had the cash and viewed the action as a viable investment opportunity.

Another important provision is the sinking fund feature which specifies how the bond will be amortized (or repaid) over its life. While most issues require some form of sinking fund provisions, a number of industrial obligations and government issues do not. In these cases, all or most of the issue is payable at maturity, and no attempt is made to systematically retire these obligations over their life. Such provisions have an effect on comparative yields at date of issue but little subsequent effect on differential price behavior.

There are many different types of sinking fund provisions. For example, utility issuers often employ provisions actually giving them the right to use the periodic sinking fund to either acquire outstanding bonds *or to increase the capital assets of the firm.* This is known as an *improvement fund* and requires an annual sinking fund of at least one percent of the *total* bonds outstanding. The

[2] W. Braddock Hickman, *Corporate Bond Quality and Investor Experience* (Princeton, N.J.: Princeton University Press, 1958).

size of the sinking fund can be a percentage of a given issue or of the *total* debt outstanding. Moreover, it can be a fixed or variable sum stated on a dollar or percentage basis. The amount of the issue that must be repaid before maturity ranges from a nominal sum to 100 percent; the payments may commence at the end of the first year or may be deferred for as long as five to ten years from date of the issue.

Like a call or refunding provision, the sinking fund feature also carries a nominal call premium, perhaps one percent or less. Unlike call or refunding features, however, a sinking fund provision must be carried out regardless of interest rate behavior or other market conditions. Therefore, a potential small risk for investors in a bond with a sinking fund is that the bond issue could be called on a random basis. Basically, that is one way that sinking fund provisions are enforced—the bonds are simply called randomly by lot. Such public calls have been fairly rare since most bonds have been trading at a discount (i.e., at a price below par) and are retired for sinking fund purposes through direct negotiations with institutional holders. Essentially, the issuer or trustee negotiates with a big institutional holder, usually an insurance company or pension fund, to buy back the necessary amount of bonds at a price slightly above the current market price.

Bond Rates of Return

The rate of return on a bond is computed in the same way as the rate of return on stock or any asset; it is determined by the beginning and ending price and the cash flows during the holding period. The major difference between stocks and bonds is that the interim cash flows (i.e., the interest) are specified for bonds, while the dividends on stock are not contractual. Therefore, the rate of return for a bond will be:

$$R_{i,t} = \frac{P_{i,t+1} - P_{i,t} + Int_{i,t}}{P_{i,t}},$$

where:

$R_{i,t}$ = the rate of return for bond i during period t

$P_{i,t+1}$ = the market price of bond i at the end of period t

$P_{i,t}$ = the market price of bond i at the beginning of period t

$Int_{i,t}$ = the interest payments on bond i during period t.

It is important to recognize that the only fixed and known factor is the interest payments which are specified by contract. The beginning price will be determined by market forces, which we will discuss. The ending price will likewise be determined by market forces prevailing at the time of sale unless the bond is held to maturity, in which case the investor will receive the par value. The point is, there can be large price variations in bonds which provide opportunities for an investor in bonds to experience capital gains or losses during different holding periods. Because of substantial interest rate volatility since the 1960s, there have been large price fluctuations in bonds. As a result, the capital gain or loss segment of the total return has been the major factor determining the rates of return on bonds.

Determination of Bond Price.   The price of a bond is determined by the coupon that the issue carries, the length of its term to maturity, and the prevailing market interest rate on the bond, referred to as its *yield.* While the next chapter contains the detailed mathematics of bond price behavior, it is important at this point to gain a basic understanding of how the price of bonds is determined. As we will show, given the coupon and maturity for a bond, the price is determined by the market interest rate on the bond (i.e., by the yield required). Therefore, bond price behavior over time is determined by how market interest rates change over time.

As discussed in Chapter 10, the price (value) of a bond is determined like that of any other financial asset; it is the present value of the expected cash flows from the asset. In the case of a bond, we know what the promised cash flows are, so the only unknown is the required rate of return. As an example, assume you want to determine the price of a $1,000 par value bond with a 10 percent coupon that matures in ten years. Assuming annual interest payments are made, this implies that the expected cash flows will be $100 a year (0.10 times $1,000) for ten years and $1,000 at the end of ten years. Given this information, it is necessary to know the required market yield on this bond. Assume the required yield is 12 percent. As discussed in Chapter 10, the value of the bond is:

$100 × 5.650 (the present value of a ten-year   = $565.00
annuity at 12 percent)

$1,000 × .322 (the present value factor for ten   = $\underline{\ \ 322.00}$
years at 12 percent)

Total Present Value $887.00

Therefore, the market price for this bond should be $887.00 or 88.7 percent of par. Obviously, because the market yield on this bond is above its coupon rate, the bond is selling at a discount from par.

Assume that over the next year, market interest rates decline and the market yield on this bond declines to 8 percent. At this point it is a nine-year bond (nine years to maturity) and the market price would be as follows:

$100 × 6.247 (the present value of a nine-year   = $624.70
annuity at 8 percent)

$1,000 × .500 (the present value factor for nine   = $\underline{\ \ 500.00}$
years at 8 percent)

Total Present Value $1,124.70

Therefore, the market price for this bond would be $1,124.70 or 112.47 percent of par. Because the market yield is below the coupon rate, the bond is selling at a premium relative to its par value. The rate of return for an investor who owned the bond during this year was as follows:

$$R_{i,t} = \frac{\$1,124.70 - 887.00 + 100.00}{887.00}$$

$$= \frac{237.70 + 100.0}{887.00}$$

$$= \frac{337.70}{887.00}$$

$$= .3807 = 38.07\%.$$

Two important points regarding this example:
1. There was a substantial price change because of the change in market interest rates which affected the required market yield on this bond.
2. The rate of return received by the investor who held the bond during this year was mainly due to the change in price that occurred during the holding period.

Because bonds are so closely tied to market interest rates, the price of an issue actually depends on its prevailing *yield.* In practice, therefore, the yield of an issue is determined *first,* and then the dollar price of the obligation is derived. This is because a wide diversity of coupons and maturities exist in the market at any point in time, and the yield based computation serves as an effective equalizer, allowing market-makers to systematically account for variations in coupon and/or maturity in the pricing of an issue. To appreciate the complexity of trying to directly price issues with different coupons and maturities, all one has to do is quickly glance at the bond quote page of the *Wall Street Journal* or *Barron's* and observe the myriad different combinations of coupons and maturities.

While bond price volatility is directly affected by the magnitude of movement in interest rates, price is more than a simple function of interest rates, because different bonds react differently to changes in these rates. Specifically, for a given change in market rates, a bond's price will vary according to the coupon and maturity of the issue. Bonds with longer maturities and/or lower coupons will respond most vigorously to a given change.[3] Other factors likewise cause differences in price volatility, including the call feature, but they are typically much less important. Even so, to the extent that they affect comparative rates of return, such factors certainly should not be ignored.

Bond Yields.   Because the concept of yield is critical to the mechanics of bond pricing, it is important to differentiate among the types of yields. In the simplest sense, there are two: current yield and promised yield to maturity, or what is commonly known as *promised yield.* Current yield is the amount of current income that a bond provides (annual interest) relative to its prevailing market price. It is to a bond what dividend yield is to common stocks and has very little use in the bond valuation process. Promised yield, in contrast, is very important

---

[3] This relationship among bond price volatility and maturity and coupon is discussed in detail in Chapter 18.

and is the yield upon which all bond prices are based! It encompasses interest income and price appreciation (or depreciation) in the valuation process, and total cash flow received over the life of the issue. Because it entails cash flow timing, the promised yield computation is based on the present value concept. Indeed, it is the same mathematical process as *internal rate of return* considered in the study of basic corporation finance. In discussing yield, the percentage point has been broken into 100 parts with each part being called a *basis point.* Thus, a basis point is 1/100th of one percent and is a convenient means of depicting changes in yield or yield comparisons; e.g., a decline in yield from 8.5 percent to 8.0 percent is a 50 basis point decline.

AN OVERVIEW OF BOND MARKET STRUCTURE

The market for fixed-income securities is gigantic and literally dwarfs the listed equity exchanges (NYSE, ASE, etc.). One reason is that corporations tend to issue bonds rather than common stock. Federal Reserve figures indicate that, during 1982, out of $84.2 billion in new corporate security issues, only about $30.6 billion (approximately 36 percent) were equity, which included preferred as well as common stock. Corporations do not issue common or preferred stock more frequently because the major source of equity financing for a firm is internally generated funds. Also, unlike the equity market, which is strictly corporations, the bond market has three substantial noncorporate sectors: the U.S. Treasury, several U.S. government agencies, and state and local governments. Federal Reserve figures reveal that, while recent corporate bond issues have been substantial, such volume has accounted for only 15 to 18 percent of *total* new bond issues! In 1982 the face value of corporate bonds issued was approximately $54 billion, whereas the noncorporate sector added over $350 billion in bonds to the market. Further evidence of the economic dimensions of the bond market can be gleaned from Table 17.1 which lists the dollar par value outstanding for different types of bonds.

The Participants

There are five different types of issuers: (1) the U.S. Treasury, (2) various agencies of the U.S. government, (3) various state and local political subdivisions (known as municipalities), (4) corporations, and (5) institutional issuers.

U.S. Treasury.   The market for treasuries is the largest and the best known; it involves bonds, notes, and other debt instruments issued as a means of meeting the burgeoning needs of the U.S. government. These different types of debt instruments, along with obligations of several other issuers, will be reviewed in detail in the following section of this chapter.

Government Agencies.   An important issuer, which has experienced the most rapid increase in size, is the U.S. government through various agencies. These agencies represent political subdivisions of the government although the securities are *not* direct obligations of the treasury. The agency market is composed of

TABLE 17.1
Total Amounts Outstanding (in billions of dollars at year end)

	1974	1975	1976	1977	1978	1979	1980	1981	1982	1983
U.S. Treasury Obligations:										
Bills	119.70	157.50	164.00	161.10	161.70	172.60	216.10	245.00	311.80	343.80
Notes	129.80	167.10	216.70	251.80	265.80	283.40	321.60	375.30	465.00	573.40
Bonds	33.40	38.60	40.60	47.00	60.00	74.70	85.40	99.90	104.60	133.70
Total—Marketable Issues	282.90	363.20	421.30	459.90	487.50	530.70	623.20	720.30	881.50	1,050.90
Total—Nonmarketable Issues[a]	208.70	212.50	231.20	255.30	294.80	313.20	305.70	307.00	314.00	350.00
Grand Total	491.60	575.70	652.50	715.20	782.30	843.90	928.90	1,027.30	1,195.50	1,400.90
Corporates:										
Total	261.52	293.41	323.29	345.92	364.85e	385.10e	421.72e	445.62e	474.32e	506.02e
Municipals:										
Long Term	179.20	196.10	213.90	232.90	250.70e	269.40e	322.30e	351.30e	405.30e	454.30e
Agency Issues:										
Federal Agencies[b]	12.72	19.05	22.42	22.76	23.49	24.72	28.61	31.81	33.06	33.94
Federally Sponsored[c]	76.66	78.63	81.43	89.71	113.58	138.58	160.06	190.14	204.03	205.78
Federal Financing Bank[d]	4.47	17.15	28.71	38.58	51.30	67.38	87.46	110.70	126.42	135.79
Total	93.85	114.83	132.04	151.05	188.37	230.68	276.13	332.65	363.51	375.51

[a] Includes: Securities issued to the Rural Electrification Administration and to state and local governments, depository bonds, retirement plan bonds, and individual retirement bonds.

[b] Includes: Defense Department, Export-Import Bank, FHA, GNMA, Postal Service, TVA, and U.S. Railway Association.

[c] Includes: Federal Home Loan Banks, Federal Home Loan Mortgage Corp., FNMA, federal intermediate credit banks, banks for cooperatives, Student Loan Marketing Association, and Farm Credit Banks.

[d] The FFB, which began operations in 1974, is authorized to purchase or to sell obligations issued, sold, or guaranteed by other federal agencies. Because FFB incurs debt solely for the purpose of lending to other agencies, its debt is not included in the main portion of the table in order to avoid double counting.

e estimated

SOURCE: *Federal Reserve Bulletin*, various issues.

two types of issuers: government-sponsored enterprises and federal agencies. Similar to treasuries, these securities are issued under the authority of an act of Congress, and the proceeds are used to finance many of the legislative mandates of that body. A number of these obligations carry guarantees of the U.S. government, and, therefore, effectively represent the full faith and credit of the U.S. Treasury although they are not direct obligations of the government. Moreover, some have unusual interest payment provisions and tax features. But, in general, tax exposure of agencies is like that of treasury issues; while they are subject to the usual IRS federal tax provisions on interest and capital gains, the interest income is *free* from state and local levies. This is an important feature to investors, because it can obviously increase the net return. Finally, another important feature is that the market yield of agency obligations is generally above that attainable from treasuries. Therefore, agencies represent a way to increase returns with only marginal differences in risk.

Corporations.   The major nongovernmental issuer of debt is, of course, the corporate sector. Corporate bonds represent obligations of firms domiciled in the United States, Canada, and a few foreign countries. The market for corporate bonds is commonly subdivided into several segments: *industrials* (the most heterogeneous of the groups), *public utilities* (the dominant group in terms of volume of new issues), *rails and transportation* bonds, and *financial* issues (including those issued by banks, finance companies, and holding companies). The corporate sector probably provides the greatest diversity in types of issues and quality. In effect, the issuer can range from the highest investment-grade firm, such as American Telephone and Telegraph or IBM, to a high-risk firm that is relatively new or one that has experienced a default on its debt securities.

Municipalities.   This debt issue is unlike any of the preceding three sectors. The major difference is that *interest income* on municipal obligations (which includes the issues of states, school districts, cities, or any other type of political subdivision such as a state university) is not subject to federal income tax. In contrast, however, *capital gains* on these issues based on price changes after the original issue are subject to normal federal income taxes. Moreover, with the exception of Puerto Rican issues, the obligations enjoy exemption from state and local taxes *when they are issues of the state or locality in which the investor resides.* That is, while a California issue would not be taxed in California, its interest income would be subject to state tax if the investor happens to reside in New York. The interest income of Puerto Rican issues enjoys total immunity from federal, state, and local taxes. Another distinguishing feature of municipal bonds is that the issues typically are serial obligations. Finally, while revenue obligations are rare in other sectors of the market, they are popular with some municipal issuers and account for a substantial portion of the municipal market.

Institutions.   The final group are institutional obligations which are marketed by a variety of private, nonprofit institutions like schools, hospitals, and churches. These securities represent only a minute segment of the market, although they have some features that many investors would find fairly attractive.

Unfortunately, because of the small size of these issues and the fact that the issuers are local there is a very thin, almost nonexistent, secondary market for these issues. Hence, most of the activity in the institutional segment of the market is centered in new issues. Many of the issuers are affiliated with a religious order (Roman Catholic-affiliated organizations have traditionally dominated the market). Likewise, hospital issues have been the preponderant type of obligation. These issues are sometimes referred to as *heart bonds* because of their emotional appeal, and some investors consider these investments charitable activities in support of a church or local hospital. However, the credit ratings on most of these issues is quite high because there have been very few defaults. At the same time, the yields have been above those on comparable corporate obligations, which makes them attractive investments for those willing to accept the low liquidity characteristic.

Participating Investors

All sorts of individual and institutional investors, with myriad investment objectives, participate in the fixed-income security market, because they believe that these securities yield competitive risk-adjusted rates of return. While numerous wealthy individual investors participate in this market, they still represent a relatively minor portion. Most individuals are discouraged by the sophistication required and the minimum denominations of most issues. Institutional investors dominate the bond market, typically accounting for 90–95 percent of the trading.[4] Of course, different segments of the market are more institutionalized than others. For example, the agency market is heavily institutional, whereas individuals play a significant role in the municipal sector. Institutions have a substantial influence on the behavior of market yields because of the magnitude of their involvement. The size of their transactions is fairly substantial, often millions of dollars. It is not unusual for a few institutions (three or four) to acquire 70–80 percent of a $50–$100 million new issue. In contrast, large financial institutions have almost no interest in institutional bonds because of their lack of liquidity. These institutional bonds are typically acquired by individuals and local banks with an interest in the community.

A variety of different institutions regularly invest a substantial proportion of their resources in the bond market. *Life insurance companies* are heavy investors in corporate bonds and, to a lesser extent, in treasury and agency securities; *commercial banks* invest substantial sums in the municipal market, as well as in government and agency issues; *property and liability insurance companies* are heavy investors in municipal obligations, as well as in treasuries; *private and government retirement and pension funds* are heavily committed to corporates and also invest in treasuries and agencies. Finally *mutual funds*, because of their traditional equity orientation, have seldom considered bonds and fixed-income securities as an investment outlet, though attitudes are changing as various types of bond mutual funds attract the investing public. As the above review suggests,

---

[4] Sidney Homer, "The Historical Evolution of Today's Bond Market," *Journal of Portfolio Management,* 1 no. 3 (Spring 1975): 6–11.

certain types of institutions tend to favor certain types of issues. There are two factors affecting these preferences: (1) the tax liability of the investing institution, and (2) the nature of the liability that the institution assumes in relation to its depositors or clients. For example, commercial banks are subject to normal taxation and have fairly short-term liability structures. As a result, they favor short- to intermediate-term municipals. Life insurance companies and pension funds are virtually tax-free institutions with long-term commitments, so they prefer high-yielding, long-term corporate bonds. Such institutional investment practices affect the supply of loanable funds and interest rate changes over short-run periods.

Investment and Trading Opportunities

Fixed-income securities are useful for investors who require current income, although an investor with a more speculative, shorter-term investment horizon can also find abundant trading opportunities. An important dimension of recent bond investment has been high interest rates that provide attractive competitive returns, while the volatility of yields presents capital gains opportunities.

In contrast to the equity market, the bond market is primarily a new-issue (primary) market. As a result, the secondary market for seasoned securities is relatively thin and lacking in trading activity. Fortunately, some segments have fairly active secondary markets, including the treasury market, which does provide liquidity. Likewise, agencies are fairly actively traded in the secondary market, as are public utilities within the corporate market. In contrast, the municipal and institutional bond secondary markets are much less active. In fact, it is almost impossible for individual investors without access to specialized institutional publications to keep abreast of the price activity of municipal holdings because quotes do not appear regularly in the popular financial media. The cause of this illiquidity is that new municipal issues are relatively small with total par values of less than $15–$20 million. In addition, because most municipals are serial obligations, the total issue is actually subdivided into a series of smaller issues, which compounds the size problem.

The trading of bonds is also unlike equity shares, which are mainly traded on organized exchanges (i.e., the NYSE, the ASE, etc.). For example, commercial banks are popular dealers in government, agency, and municipal securities. Moreover, the trust departments of large commercial banks often act as secondary market dealers in the corporate OTC sector. While national and regional brokerage firms are active in marketing new issues, they only trade listed bond issues in the secondary market, and the listed issues only represent a small portion of total activity. Thus, there are few transactions in the secondary bond market because order placement and execution are carried out by specialized investment houses.

Because of the generally low level of liquidity, care must be exercised by trading-oriented investors to ensure that a substantial purchase or sale order can be executed rapidly. An investor who wishes to buy 50 bonds of a particular corporate issue (and this is certainly not a large order) may discover that normal volume in this issue amounts to fewer than ten bonds a week. Clearly, it would be very time consuming to fill the order and probably equally time consuming to dispose of the position at the end of the investment horizon. With this time lag, substantial changes in yield and price could occur. Because such changes may seriously alter holding-period returns, you should consider an issue's trading volume before investing in it.

Bond Ratings

Agency ratings are an integral part of the bond market. Most fixed-income securities in the corporate, municipal, and institutional markets are regularly evaluated and rated by one or more agencies. The exceptions are bonds considered too small to rate and certain industry categories like bank issues (known as *nonrated bonds*). There are four major rating agencies: (1) Duff and Phelps, (2) Fitch Investors Service, (3) Moody's, and (4) Standard & Poor's.

Bond ratings are a very important service in the market for fixed-income securities because they provide the fundamental analysis for thousands of issues.[5] The rating agencies conduct extensive analyses of the intrinsic characteristics of the issuing organization and of the issue to determine the default risk for the investor and to inform the market of their analysis through their ratings. Thus, in contrast to the situation with common stock, with bonds, the rating agencies have performed the fundamental analysis for the investor. Given the large, highly qualified staffs of the rating agencies, the general consensus is that additional analysis would only yield marginal insight regarding the intrinsic value or strength of an issue.

The primary question in bond analysis is not necessarily the growth prospect of the firm, but, rather, the ability of the firm to service a fixed amount of debt over the life of a given issue. Such an emphasis requires less attention be paid to highly uncertain expectations and forecasts and more concern with available data regarding the historical and current financial position of the company. Fortunately, the agencies have done an admirable job, although rare mistakes happen.[6] If anything, the rating services tend to be overly conservative, as indicated by a study which suggests that risk of default has actually been *overestimated* by the market and has resulted in unnecessarily high risk premiums given the default possibility.[7]

Because investors rely so heavily on agency ratings, it follows that there should be some concrete evidence to support the relationship between bond ratings and the quality of the issue. A study by Horrigan[8] concluded that the

---

[5] Irwin Ross, "Higher Stakes in the Bond-Rating Game," *Fortune* (April 1976): 132–140.

[6] W. Braddock Hickman, *Corporate Bond Quality and Investor Experience* (Princeton, N.J.: Princeton University Press, 1958).

[7] Gordon Pye, "Gauging the Default Premium," *Financial Analysts Journal,* 30 no. 1 (January–February 1974): 49–52.

[8] James O. Horrigan, "The Determination of Long-Term Credit Standing with Financial Ratios," *Empirical Research in Accounting: Selected Studies* Supplement to *Journal of Accounting Research,* 4 1966: 44–62.

510

TABLE 17.2
Bond Ratings

	Duff and Phelps	Fitch	Moody's	Standard & Poor's	Definition
High Grade	1	AAA	Aaa	AAA	The highest rating assigned to a debt instrument indicating an extremely strong capacity to pay principal and interest. Bonds in this category are often referred to as *gilt edge securities.*
	2–4	AA	Aa	AA	High-quality bonds by all standards with strong capacity to pay principal and interest. These bonds are rated lower primarily because the margins of protection are not as strong as those for Aaa and AAA.
Medium Grade	5–7	A	A	A	These bonds possess many favorable investment attributes, but elements may be present which suggest a susceptibility to impairment given adverse economic changes.
	8–10	BBB	Baa	BBB	Bonds regarded as having adequate capacity to pay principal and interest, but certain protective elements may be lacking in the event of adverse economic conditions which could lead to a weakened capacity for payment.
Speculative	11–13	BB	Ba	BB	Bonds regarded as having only moderate protection of principal and interest payments during both good and bad times.
	14	B	B	B	Bonds that generally lack characteristics of other desirable investments. Assurance of interest and principal payments over any long period of time may be small.
Default	15	CCC	Caa	CCC	Poor quality issues that may be in default or in danger of default.
	16	CC	Ca	CC	Highly speculative issues that are often in default or possessing other marked shortcomings.

TABLE 17.2   *(cont.)*

	Duff and Phelps	Fitch	Moody's	Standard & Poor's	Definition
Default	17		C		The lowest rated class of bonds. These issues can be regarded as extremely poor in investment quality.
		C		C	Rating given to income bonds on which no interest is being paid.
		DDD, DD,D		D	Issues in default with principal and/or interest payments in arrears. Such bonds are extremely speculative and should be valued only on the basis of their value in liquidation or reorganization.

Adapted from: *Bond Guide* (New York: Standard & Poor's Corporation, monthly); *Bond Record* (New York: Moody's Investors Services, Inc., monthly); *Rating Register* (New York: Fitch Investors Service, Inc., monthly) Reprinted by permission.

accounting data and financial ratios of the firm were, indeed, imbedded in corporate bond ratings. A subsequent study[9] found that bond ratings tend to vary directly with profitability, size, and earnings coverage, while they move inversely with financial leverage and earnings instability. The results of these and other empirical studies[10] clearly demonstrate that agency ratings are far more than the qualitative judgments of analysts.

The ratings assigned to bonds at the time of issue are important in terms of the marketability and effective interest rate of the issue. Generally, the four agencies will give a particular bond approximately the same rating. However, there can be *split ratings*, i.e., different ratings from each service for one bond. Seasoned issues are also regularly reviewed to ensure that the assigned rating is still valid. While most issues will carry a given rating for an extended period of time (often over the life of the issue), it is not uncommon for some issues to experience revisions in their assigned ratings. Revisions can be either upward or downward and are usually done in increments of one rating grade.[11] The ratings are based upon the company *and* the issue. After an overall evaluation of the creditworthiness of the total company, a company rating is applied to the most

[9] Thomas F. Pogue and Robert M. Soldofsky, "What's in a Bond Rating?" *Journal of Financial and Quantitative Analysis,* 4 no. 2 (June 1969): 201–208.

[10] See for example: Richard R. West, "An Alternative Approach to Predicting Corporate Bond Ratings," *Journal of Accounting Research,* 8 no. 1 (Spring 1970): 118–125; and George E. Pinches and Kent A. Mingo, "A Multivariate Analysis of Industrial Bond Ratings," *Journal of Finance,* 28 no. 1 (March 1973): 1–18; James S. Ang and K. A. Patel, "Bond Rating Methods: Comparison and Validation," *Journal of Finance,* 30 no. 2 (May 1975): 631–640; Richard B. Edelman, "A New Approach to Ratings on Utility Bonds," *Journal of Portfolio Management,* 5 no. 3 (Spring 1979): 63–68; Robert S. Kaplan and Gabriel Urwitz, "Statistical Models of Bond Ratings: A Methodological Inquiry," *Journal of Business,* 52 no. 2 (April 1979): 231–262.

[11] Bond rating changes and bond market efficiency are discussed in Chapter 19.

senior unsecured issue outstanding. All junior obligations then receive lower ratings, but the difference in rating could be minimal depending on the indenture specifications. Also, some issues could receive a *higher* rating than the general credit of the company would justify because of credit enhancement devices such as the attachment of bank letters of credit, surety or indemnification bonds from insurance companies.

The agencies assign letter ratings, depicting what they view as the risk of default of an obligation. Letter ratings range from AAA to D. Table 17.2 on page 510 specifies the various ratings that can be assigned to issues by the major services. Except for the slight variation in designations, the meaning and interpretation is basically the same. In addition to the letter designations by the three agencies, they further modify the ratings with + and − signs (Fitch and S&P) or numbers (1-2-3) for Moody's. As an example, an A+ bond is at the top of the A rated group. The top four ratings are generally considered to be investment-grade securities. The next level of securities is known as *speculatives* and include the BB and B rated obligations.[12] The last group is the C and D categories, which are generally either income obligations or revenue bonds, many of which are trading flat. (They are in arrears with regard to interest payments.) In the case of DDD- through D-rated obligations, the issues are in outright default and the ratings indicate the bond's relative salvage value. Moody's also identifies the better quality *municipals* within the A and Baa categories as A1 and Baa1, respectively.

Market Rates of Return

Interest rate behavior is probably the most important variable to the investment-grade bond investor. Figures 17.1 and 17.2 illustrate different important characteristics of bond market interest rates. The first shows comparative yields in different market sectors and indicates that *there is not a single market rate* applicable to all segments of the bond market. Each segment of the market has its own, somewhat unique, level. Those shown are just three of the many different rates that exist in the market at any given point in time. For example, the corporate rate could be broken down into different segments of the corporate market (such as industrials, public utilities, and rails), and each of these could be further subdivided according to different quality levels (AAA through BBB). Observe that, generally, the various market segments tend to move together, a common characteristic in investment-grade securities. In fact, previous studies have indicated that correlations *within* a wide variety of short-, intermediate-, and long-term yield series nearly always exceeded 90 percent.[13]

Another important aspect to bond investors is how interest rates have performed historically, as shown in Figure 17.2. The data span more than 50 years

---

[12] Michael D. Joehnk and James F. Nielsen, "Risk Return Characteristics of Speculative Grade Bonds." *Quarterly Review of Economics and Business,* 15 no. 1 (Spring 1975): 35–43. Increased interest in these bonds is discussed in, Ben Weberman, "The King of the BBs," *Forbes* (December 5, 1983): 112, 114 and Steven Solomon, "The Art of Managing Junk Bonds," *Institutional Investor,* 18 no. 5 (May 1984): 127, 128, 135.

[13] Michael D. Joehnk and James F. Nielsen, "Risk Return Characteristics of Speculative Grade Bonds," *Quarterly Review of Economics and Business,* 15 no. 1 (Spring 1975): 35–45.

FIGURE 17.1
Comparative Bond Yield Behavior

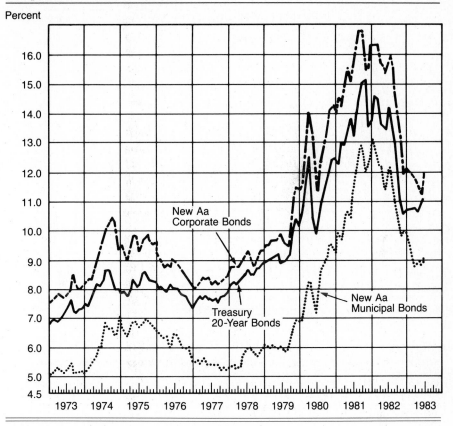

SOURCE: *Treasury Bulletin* (Summer Issue, Third Quarter, 1983).

and include the average behavior of one representative segment of the market: corporate investment-grade securities. Behavior in the first half of the period differs significantly from that in the second half and indicates why investors have recently found the bond market to be an attractive investment outlet. Prior to the mid-1960s, the bond market was fairly stable, and there were few opportunities for aggressive investing. After the mid-1960s, interest rates moved to highly competitive levels, and the substantial swings in interest rates have provided opportunities for capital gains-oriented investors. This increased volatility has also increased the risk in bond portfolio management.[14]

Bond Investment Risks.   The typical bond investor is exposed to the same risk that any other investor faces. The important risks for bondholders include: (1)

---

[14] In this regard, see Daniel Hertzberg, "Bond Market Becomes Increasingly Volatile, with Some Big Losses," *Wall Street Journal*, February 21, 1980, p. 1; and idem, "Bond Trading Has Been Basically Changed by Inflation, Price Volatility, Experts Say," *Wall Street Journal*, November 7, 1980, p. 46.

FIGURE 17.2
Corporate Bond Yields by Ratings

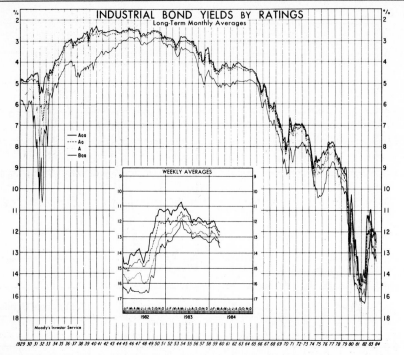

NOTE: As of December 1976, railroad bonds were removed from the combined Corporate Averages, retroactive to January 1974. This adjustment was necessary because of a lack of comparability to the Industrial and Public Utility averages, reflecting the limited availability of reasonably current coupon railroad bonds.

SOURCE: *Bond Record* (New York: Moody's Investors Services), April, 1984. Reprinted by permission.

interest rate, (2) purchasing power, (3) liquidity or marketability, and (4) business.

The most important of these is interest rate risk, which is a function of the variability of bond returns (prices) caused by changes in the level of interest rates. Because of the relationship between bond prices and interest rates, no segment of the market, except perhaps for the highly speculative issues, is free of this important and powerful force. The price stability of investment-grade securities is mainly a function of interest rate stability and, therefore, interest rate risk.[15]

Purchasing power risk is linked to inflation and the loss of purchasing power over time. While purchasing power may decline over time with a given level of inflation, what is important to bond investors is the effect of inflation on yields and prices. While the level of inflation affects the promised yield, changes in the

[15] Frank K. Reilly and Michael D. Joehnk, "Association between Market-Determined Risk Measures for Bonds and Bond Ratings," *Journal of Finance,* 31 no. 5 (December 1976): 1387–1403.

rate of inflation (or inflation expectations) lead to changes in the level of interest rates and thereby to changes in the prices of seasoned issues.

Marketability risk has to do with the liquidity of the obligation and the ease with which an issue can be sold at the prevailing market price. Smaller issues and those with inactive secondary markets will often experience marketability difficulties and are, therefore, subject to such risk.

Finally, business risk is the risk of default because of the financial and operating risks of the issuer. Such risks are only relevant for corporate, municipal, and institutional obligations. Generally, the ratings assigned by the various agencies reflect differences in business risk, and the ratings, in turn, influence the promised yields (the lower the default risk, the higher the agency rating and the lower the prevailing yield to maturity).

Default risk and marketability risk have an insignificant effect on price behavior because they only affect prevailing *levels* of yields. In contrast, interest rate risk and purchasing power risk can have dramatic effects on the price behavior of an obligation over time.

ALTERNATIVE INVESTMENT VEHICLES

Numerous sectors that exist within the bond market are characterized by fundamentally different issuers, the major categories of which include: the U.S. Treasury and government agencies, municipalities, corporations, and institutions. This section is a brief review of some of the popular issues available in these market sectors.

Treasury and Agency Issues

The dominant fixed-income market is that for U.S. Treasury obligations. Acting on behalf of the U.S. government, and with the backing of its full faith and credit, the U.S. Treasury issues treasury bills (T-bills), which are for less than one year. The treasury also issues long-term obligations in one of two forms: government notes, which have maturities of ten years or less; and treasury bonds, with maturities of more than ten years (current maximum maturities go to about 25 years).

Treasury obligations come in denominations of $1,000 and $10,000, although a few older issues carry $500 par values, and are either in registered or bearer form. The interest income from the U.S. government securities is subject to federal income tax but *exempt* from state and local levies. Such obligations are popular with individual and institutional investors because they possess substantial liquidity.

Short-term T-bills differ from notes and bonds in terms of how the payments are made. Treasury bills are sold at a discount from par to provide the desired yield (they are the same as zero coupon bonds since the return is the difference between the purchase price and the par at maturity). In contrast, government notes and bonds carry semiannual coupons (similar to those on almost all other bonds) that specify the nominal yield of the obligation.

While government notes and bonds are similar to other straight-debt issues in most respects, they do have some unusual features. First, the deferred call

516   features on treasury issues is unusually long and is generally measured relative to the *maturity* date of the issue rather than from date of issue. For example, many treasury issues carry a deferment feature that expires five years *prior* to the *final* maturity date.

Also, certain government issues provide a tax break to investors because they can be used, at par, to pay federal estate taxes. It is possible, therefore, for an investor to acquire a treasury bond at a substantial discount which his estate can subsequently use at par to pay estate taxes. Such bonds have been given a nickname — *flower bonds*. Although *new* flower bonds can no longer be issued, there are still approximately nine such issues available in the market. Most of these carry 2 3/4 – 4 1/2 percent coupons and have maturities that range between 1985 and 1998. This is advantageous to the investor because the lower the coupon, the better the price discount, and the more assurance of price appreciation at "time of departure." Recent revisions in estate tax laws that increased the size of an estate exempt from taxes have reduced the demand for such issues. At the same time, the available supply has declined because, as these flower bonds are used, they are retired by the government. Therefore, prices have been maintained, and the yields on these bonds are consistently below those of other treasury issues of comparable maturity. As an example during 1984 when most Treasury bonds were yielding between 12.5 percent and 13.5 percent, these flower bonds were yielding about 5.5 percent to 6.5 percent.

Government Agency Issues

Agency issues are obligations issued by the U.S. government through some political subdivisions, such as a government agency or a government-sponsored corporation. While there are only six government-sponsored enterprises, there are over two dozen federal agencies. Table 17.3 lists selected characteristics of the more popular government-sponsored and federal agency obligations. It includes recent size of the market, typical minimum denominations, tax features, and the availability of bond quotes. (The issues in the table are only meant to be representative of the wide variety of different obligations available to the investor and not an exhaustive list.) Generally, agency issues are similar to those of other issuers.[16] Interest is usually paid semiannually, principal is due in full at maturity, and the minimum denominations vary between $1,000 and $10,000, although there are exceptions. These obligations are unusual because they are *not* direct issues of the treasury, yet they carry the full faith and credit of the U.S. government. Moreover, unlike government obligations, some of the issues are subject to state and local income tax, while some are specifically exempt from such levies.[17]

Except for the fact that they are of high quality and involve special tax provisions, agency obligations are not unique. However, one agency issue offers

---

[16] For expository purposes, we will no longer distinguish between federal agency and government-sponsored obligations; instead, the term *agency* shall apply to either type of issue.

[17] Federal National Mortgage Association (Fannie Mae) debentures, for example, are subject to state and local income tax, whereas the interest income from Federal Home Loan Bank bonds is exempt. In fact, a few issues are even exempt from *federal* income tax as well, e.g., Public Housing bonds.

particularly attractive investment opportunities: GNMA *(Ginnie Mae)* pass-through certificates, which are obligations of the Government National Mortgage Association.[18] These bonds represent an undivided interest in a pool of federally insured mortgages. The bondholders receive monthly, rather than semiannual, payments from Ginnie Mae, and these payments include both principal and interest because they represent a pass through of the mortgage payments made by the original borrower (the mortgagee) to Ginnie Mae. This is why the bond has come to be known as a *pass-through obligation.*

The pass throughs carry coupons that are somewhat related to the interest charged on the pool of mortgages. Also, since part of the cash flow represents return of capital (i.e., the principal part of payment), that portion is tax-free. The interest income is subject to federal, state, and local taxes. The issues are marketed in minimum denominations of $25,000, which eliminates some individual investors from this market. They come with maturities of 25 to 30 years but generally have an average life of only 12 years because, as pooled mortgages are paid off, payments and prepayments are passed through to the investor. This also implies, however, that unlike the case with other issues, the monthly payment is *not* fixed.

Another important feature of these securities is that they are modified pass throughs since the bonds are the obligation of the issuing body, the Government National Mortgage Association, and *not* the ultimate borrower, who is the home owner making the mortgage payment. Thus, the cash flow to the mortgage pool is quite distinct from the obligation of Ginnie Mae and is totally separate from the cash flow to the bond investor. Moreover, the rates of return are relatively attractive compared to those for corporates. Most of the return is tax-free, at least in the early life of the obligation. A major disadvantage of GNMA issues, however, is that they tend to be self-depletive. Because the monthly cash flow represents interest and a return of capital the obligation does not have a maturity value in the normal sense of the word.

Municipal Obligations

Municipal bonds are issued by states, counties, cities, and other political subdivisions. Basically, municipalities issue two distinct types of bonds: (1) general obligation bonds, and (2) revenue issues. General obligation bonds (GOs) are essentially backed by the full faith and credit of the issuer and its taxing power. Revenue bonds, in turn, are serviced by the income generated from specific revenue producing projects of the municipality, for example, bridges, toll roads, municipal coliseums, public utility and water works, etc. As might be expected, revenue bonds generally provide higher returns to investors than GOs do, because the default risk inherent in the former obligations is greater. A revenue bond is like a general obligation bond except that, should a municipality fail to

---

[18] For a more extensive discussion of mortgage-backed securities, see: "Mortgage Securities Make It Big on Wall Street," *Savings and Loan News,* 98 (1977): 33–35; and Donald Moffitt, "Ginnie Mae Pass-Throughs Offer High Yields Plus Safety for Cautious Savers," *Wall Street Journal,* September 18, 1978, p. 38; *Mortgage-Backed Bond and Pass-Through Symposium,* Financial Analysts Research Foundation, Charlottesville, Va. 1980.

TABLE 17.3
Agency Issues: Selected Characteristics

Type of Security	Minimum Denomination	Form	Life of Issue	Tax Status		How Interest Is Earned
Government Sponsored:						
Banks for Cooperatives (coops)	$5,000	Bearer	6 Months to (currently) 3 1/2 Years	Fed.: State: Local:	Taxable Exempt Exempt	Interest Bearing: 360-Day Year
Federal Intermediate Credit Banks (FICBs)	$5,000	Bearer	9 Months to 4 Years	Fed.: State: Local:	Taxable Exempt Exempt	Interest Bearing: 360-Day Year
Federal Home Loan Bank	$10,000	Bearer	1 to 20 Years	Fed.: State: Local:	Taxable Exempt Exempt	Semiannual Interest Payments
Federal Home Loan— Mortgage-Backed Bonds	$25,000	Registered or Bearer	12 to 25 Years	Fed.: State: Local:	Taxable Taxable Taxable	Semiannual Interest Payments
Mortgage Corporation— Participation Certificates (FHLMC)	$100,000	Registered	15 to 30 Years	Fed.: State: Local:	Taxable Taxable Taxable	Monthly Interest Payments
Federal Land Banks (FLBs)	$1,000	Bearer	1 to 10 Years	Fed.: State: Local:	Taxable Exempt Exempt	Semiannual Interest Payments
Federal National Mortgage Association (FNMA) — Discount Notes	$5,000[a]	Bearer	30 to 270 Days	Fed.: State: Local:	Taxable Taxable Taxable	Discounted 360-Day Year
Secondary-Market Notes and Debentures	$10,000	Registered and Bearer	3 to 25 Years	Fed.: State: Local:	Taxable Taxable Taxable	Semiannual Interest Payments

TABLE 17.3 *(Cont.)*

Federal Agencies:

	Minimum	Registration	Maturity	Tax Status	Interest
Export-Import Bank (Exim Bank)	$5,000	Registered or Bearer	3 to 7 Years	Fed.: Taxable State: Taxable Local: Taxable	Semiannual Interest Payments
Farmers Home Administration (FHDA) (notes)	$25,000	Registered or Bearer	4 to 15 Years	Fed.: Taxable State: Taxable Local: Taxable	Annual Interest Payments
Federal Housing Administration (FHA)	$50,000	Registered	1 to 40 Years	Fed.: Taxable State: Taxable Local: Taxable	Semiannual Interest Payments
Government National Mortgage Association Mortgage Backed and Participation	$25,000	Registered or Bearer	1 to 25 Years	Fed.: Taxable State: Taxable Local: Taxable	Semiannual Interest Payments
(GNMA) Modified Pass Through	$25,000	Registered	1 to 25 Years (12-Year Average)	Fed.: Taxable State: Taxable Local: Taxable	Monthly Interest Payments
Tennessee Valley Authority (TVA)	$1,000	Registered or Bearer	3 to 25 Years	Fed.: Taxable State: Exempt Local: Exempt	Semiannual Interest Payments
U.S. Postal Service	$10,000	Registered or Bearer	25 Years	Fed.: Taxable State: Exempt Local: Exempt	Semiannual Interest Payments
Other Federal Financing Bank	$10,000	Registered or Bearer	1 to 20 Years	Fed.: Taxable State: Exempt Local: Exempt	Semiannual Interest Payments

[a] Minimum Purchase Requirement of $50,000.

SOURCE: Adapted from: David M. Darst, *The Complete Bond Book* (New York: McGraw-Hill, 1975), pp. 274–283. Copyright © 1975 by McGraw-Hill, Inc. Reprinted by permission.

generate sufficient income from a project used to secure a revenue bond, it has *no* legal debt service obligation until the income becomes sufficient.

Another feature of municipal bonds, particularly the general obligations, is that they tend to be issued on a serial basis. Most general obligations are set up this way so that the issuer's cash flow requirements will be steady over the life of the obligation. Therefore, the principal portion of the total debt service requirement generally begins at a fairly low level and builds up over the life of the obligation. In contrast, revenue obligations are mostly term issues, so the major portion of the issue's total principal value is not due until the final maturity date or last few dates. In fact, even if a revenue issue is serial, it is generally set up so that the serial portion amortizes a relatively small amount of the bond (perhaps 10–25 percent) with the majority of the obligation due at or near final maturity. As an example, see the issue in Figure 17.3.

The most important feature of municipal obligations is, of course, that the interest payments are exempt from federal income tax, as well as taxes in the locality and state in which the obligation was issued. This means that people in different income brackets find municipal bonds to be of varying attractiveness. The investor can convert the *tax-free yield* of a municipal to an equivalent *taxable* yield using the following equation:

$$TY = \frac{i}{(1 - t)},$$

where:

TY = equivalent taxable yield

i = coupon rate of the municipal obligations

t = marginal tax rate of the investor.

(Note that *TY* can also be used to find the yield of treasury and/or agency obligations whenever state and local taxes are an issue.) An investor in the 35 percent marginal tax bracket would find that a 7 percent municipal yield is equivalent to a 10.77 percent fully taxable yield according to the following calculations:

$$TY = \frac{.07}{(1 - .35)} = .1077.$$

This conversion is essential since the tax-free yield is presumed to be the major motive for investing in municipal bonds. As a result, an investor's marginal tax rate is a *primary* concern in determining whether municipals are a viable investment vehicle. As a rough rule of thumb, an investor must be in the 30–35 percent tax bracket before municipal bonds offer yields that are competitive with those from fully taxable bonds, because before tax municipal yields are substantially *lower* than returns available from fully taxable issues, such as corporates. However, only the interest is tax-free; any capital gains are treated in the normal way.

Pollution Control Revenue Bonds.   Most issues of municipal bonds are fairly standard and, as a result, seldom offer issue-oriented opportunities. One notable exception falls within the revenue category. Specifically, pollution control

FIGURE 17.3
An Example of a Municipal Bond Offering

In the opinion of counsel, interest on the Bonds is exempt from federal income taxes under existing statutes and court decisions.

NEW ISSUE

Ratings: Moody's: Aa
Standard & Poor's: AA—

$75,000,000

State of Connecticut

General Obligation Bonds

Dated: April 1, 1984

Due: April 1, as shown below

The Bonds will bear interest from April 1, 1984, payable on October 1, 1984 and semiannually thereafter on April 1 and October 1 in each year until maturity, will be issued in fully registered form and will be in the denomination of $5,000 each or a whole multiple thereof. Principal on the Bonds will be payable at the principal office of The Connecticut National Bank, in Hartford, Connecticut, or the Hartford Trust Company of New York (A Limited Purpose Trust Company) in the Borough of Manhattan, City and State of New York (the "Paying Agent"), and interest will be payable to the registered owner as of the close of business on the fifteenth day of the calendar month next preceding each interest payment date by check mailed to such registered owner at his address as shown on the registration books kept by The Connecticut National Bank (the "Registrar and Transfer Agent").

The Bonds are subject to redemption as described in the Official Statement.

Amount	Due	Rate	Yield	Amount	Due	Rate	Price or Yield
$3,750,000	1985	8.80%	5.50%	$3,750,000	1995	8.80%	100%
3,750,000	1986	8.80	6.00	3,750,000	1996	9.00	100
3,750,000	1987	8.80	6.50	3,750,000	1997	9.00	9.15
3,750,000	1988	8.80	7.00	3,750,000	1998	9.00	9.25
3,750,000	1989	8.80	7.30	3,750,000	1999	9.00	9.35
3,750,000	1990	8.80	7.60	3,750,000	2000	9.10	9.40
3,750,000	1991	8.80	7.90	3,750,000	2001	9.10	9.45
3,750,000	1992	8.80	8.20	3,750,000	2002	9.10	9.50
3,750,000	1993	8.80	8.40	3,750,000	2003	9.10	9.50
3,750,000	1994	8.80	8.60	3,750,000	2004	9.10	9.50

(Plus accrued interest)

Bonds of particular maturities may or may not be available from the undersigned or others at the above prices on or after the date of this announcement.

The Bonds are offered for delivery when, as and if issued subject to the approval of legality by Bond Counsel. It is anticipated that the Bonds in definitive form will be available for delivery in New York, New York, on or about April 26, 1984. The offering of these Bonds, is made only by means of the Official Statement, copies of which may be obtained in jurisdictions in which this announcement is circulated from such of the undersigned or other brokers or dealers as may lawfully offer these securities in such jurisdiction.

Merrill Lynch Capital Markets

Morgan Guaranty Trust Company of New York

Salomon Brothers Inc

Bank of America, N.T. & S.A.

Connecticut National Bank

E. A. Moos & Co.
Incorporated

Herzog, Heine, Geduld, Inc.

April 12, 1984

SOURCE: *Wall Street Journal*, April 13, 1984. Reprinted by permission of *The Wall Street Journal*, © Dow Jones & Company, Inc., 1984. All Rights Reserved.

revenue bonds are actually disguised forms of *corporate* obligations which derive their debt service funds through leases or other similar payment pledges made between a municipality and a business firm, such as a public utility. To illustrate, in December 1977, Marshall County, West Virginia, issued $50 million of term revenue bonds, due 2007, secured with a long-term payment pledge from the Ohio Power Company. Congress maintained that our environment has to be cleaned up, and this financing vehicle was provided as a means to help corporations meet the gigantic expense and also to encourage industrial development in smaller communities.[19]

Municipal Bond Guarantees.   These are another unusual and growing feature of the municipal bond market. They provide the bondholder with the assurance of a third party *other than the issuer* that the principal and interest payments will be promptly made. The third party provides an additional source of collateral. The guarantees are actually a form of insurance placed on the bond at date of issue and are *irrevocable* over the life of the issue. The issuer purchases the insurance for the benefit of the investor, and the municipality benefits from the lower issue costs and increased marketability.

In 1975, four states and two private organizations provided municipal bond guarantees. The states included: California, which guarantees certain forms of health facilities; New Hampshire, which guarantees school and sewage bonds; Minnesota, which guarantees any general obligations; and Michigan, which guarantees GO school bonds. There are two private guarantors that provide bond insurance throughout the country rather than within a particular state. The first is a consortium of four large insurance companies that market their product under the name of Municipal Bond Insurance Association (MBIA). The second is a subsidiary of a large Milwaukee-based private insurer known as American Municipal Bond Insurance Corporation (AMBAC). Both of the private guarantors will insure either general obligation or revenue bonds issued for any purpose. To qualify for private bond insurance, the issue must carry an S&P rating of BBB or better. Because MBIA enjoyed a AAA rating from Standard & Poor's, it initially captured more of the market than AMBAC did. In late 1979, AMBAC signed a reinsurance agreement with 14 large insurance companies. Standard & Poor's indicated that they will now automatically give an AAA rating to any bond insured by AMBAC. This feature is expected to help AMBAC.[20] A purported effect of the private guarantee is that such issues enjoy a more active secondary market and, therefore, greater liquidity, although such claims have not been documented.

Corporate Bonds

Corporate bonds are one of two categories of *private* issues and represent the most significant segment.[21] Utilities dominate the corporate market. The other

---

[19] These bonds are not to be confused with industrial development revenue bonds, which became so popular that there was some pressure to restrict their use by limiting the amount a community could issue.

[20] For a discussion of this feature and the bond insurance industry, see Maureen Bailey, "Triple-A Rating," *Barron's* (December 31, 1979): 13–15.

[21] The other category is institutional bonds issued by hospitals, churches, etc. They will be discussed in the following section.

important segments include industrials (which rank second to utilities and include everything from mining firms to multinational oils to retail concerns), rail and transportation issues, and financial issues. This market includes debentures, first-mortgage issues, convertible obligations, bonds with warrants, subordinated debenture bonds, income bonds (similar to municipal revenue bonds), collateral trust bonds (typically backed by financial assets), equipment trust certificates, and mortgage-backed bonds.

If we ignore equity-related securities, equipment trust certificates, and mortgage-backed bonds, the above list of obligations varies essentially according to the type of collateral behind the bond. Most issues have semiannual interest payments, sinking funds, and a single maturity date. Maturities range from 25 to 40 years with public utilities generally on the longer end and industrials preferring the 25- to 30-year range. Nearly all corporate bonds carry deferred call provisions that range from 5 to 20 years. The length of the deferment tends to vary directly with the level of the interest rates (i.e., the higher the prevailing interest rate level, the more likely an issue will carry a seven- to ten-year deferment). On the other hand, *corporate notes*, which normally carry maturities of from five to seven years, are generally noncallable. Notes are popular with virtually all issuers, and they tend to increase in popularity during periods of higher interest rates because issuers prefer to *avoid* long-term obligations during such periods.

Generally, the average yields for industrial bonds will be the lowest of the three major sectors, followed by utility returns, with yields on rail and transportation bonds generally being the highest. The differential in yield between utilities and industrials is simply a matter of demand for loanable funds. Because utilities dominate the market in terms of the supply of bonds, yields on these securities must rise to attract the necessary demand.

Corporate issues are popular with individual and institutional investors because of the availability of such issues and their relatively attractive yields. *Established* firms have very low default records, leading many investors to consider corporate bonds a means of attaining higher returns without assuming abnormal risk.

Equipment Trust Certificates.   Several corporate issues contain unusual features. One is the equipment trust certificate issued by railroads (which are the biggest issuers of these obligations), airlines, and other transportation concerns. The proceeds are used to purchase equipment (freight cars, railroad engines, and airplanes) that serves as collateral for the equipment trust issue. Equipment trust issues generally carry maturities that range from one year to a maximum that seldom exceeds 15 to 17 years. The fairly short maximum maturities are popular because of the nature of the collateral. Equipment is subject to substantial wear and tear and tends to deteriorate rapidly.

Equipment trust certificates appeal to investors because of their *attractive yields* and because they have a record of very few defaults. Equipment trust certificates do not enjoy the same visibility and acceptance that other forms of corporate bonds do, but they have active secondary markets and attractive liquidity.

Mortgage-Backed Bonds.   Another unusual form of corporate debt initiated in September 1977 is the mortgage-backed bond. These issues are marketed by commercial banks, savings and loan associations, and mortgage lenders, and are exactly like the GNMA pass-through certificates. They are backed by a pool of mortgages which provide the collateral for the bonds. These securities differ because they are *not* backed by the full faith and credit of the U.S. government; instead, they carry the insurance of a third party, usually a private mortgage insurance company, that provides insurance against defaults on the mortgages in the pool. The biggest private mortgage insurer for these bonds is the MGIC Investment Corporation.[22]

Variable-Rates Notes.   These were available in Europe for decades but were not introduced in this country until the summer of 1974. They became popular while interest rates were high. The typical variable-rate note possesses two unique features:

1. After the first 6–18 months of the issue's life, during which a minimum rate is often guaranteed, the coupon rate floats, so that every 6 months it is pegged at a certain amount, usually one percentage above a stipulated short-term rate (normally defined as the preceding three week's average 90-day T-bill rate).

2. After the first year or two, the notes are redeemable at par, at the *holder's* option, usually at six-month intervals.

    Thus, such notes represent a long-term commitment on the part of the borrower, yet provide the lender with all the markings of a short-term obligation. Such obligations are available to investors in minimum denominations of $1,000. Because of the unusual features of such obligations, variable-rate notes could be attractive to yield-conscious, liquidity-oriented investors. However, although the six-month redemption feature provides liquidity, the variable rates can subject the issue to wide swings in semiannual coupons.[23]

Zero Coupon and Deep Discount Bonds.   The typical corporate long-term bond has a coupon and maturity, and the value of the bond is the present value of the stream of cash flows (interest and principal) discounted at the required yield to maturity (YTM). Alternatively, one can conceive of a fixed-income security that does not have any coupons or has coupons that are below the market rate at the time of issue. Such securities are referred to as *zero coupon bonds* or *mini-coupon, original issue, deep discount bonds*. A zero coupon discount bond promises to pay a stipulated amount at a future maturity date, but it does *not* promise to make any interim interest payments. Therefore, the investor pays the present value of the principal payment at the maturity date, and the return on the bond is the difference between what is paid at the time of issuance and the principal payment at maturity.

---

[22] A conference on these bonds was held by the Boston Society of Security Analysts in December 1979. For a copy of the proceedings contact Institute of Chartered Financial Analysts, University of Virginia, P.O. Box 3665, Charlottesville, VA 22903. Also see Richard G. Marcis, "Mortgage-Backed Securities," *Federal Home Loan Bank Board Journal*, November 1978.

[23] See Jill Bettner, "Once Stodgy Municipal Bonds, Going Modern, Now Offer Flexible Yields, Shorter Maturities," *Wall Street Journal* (December 8, 1980): 44.

An example of such a bond would be a $10,000 par value bond, due to mature in 20 years with a zero coupon (i.e., no interim interest payments). The price of the bond at the time of issuance would be the present value of the $10,000 par value to be paid in 20 years at the current market discount rate. The crucial variable in the valuation would be the required market rate of return on the bond. As an example, assume that when the bond is issued, the required rate of return on bonds of equal maturity and quality is 8 percent. Assuming semiannual discounting, the initial selling price of a 20-year bond would be $2,082.89, since the present value factor at 8 percent compounded semiannually for 20 years is 0.208289. The point is, $2,082.89 compounded semiannually at 8 percent for 20 years would grow to $10,000. Notably, during the period from the time of purchase to the point of maturity, *the investor would not receive any cash flow from the firm.* For tax purposes the investor must pay taxes on the *implied* interest on the bond, although no cash is received. This means that an investor subject to taxes would experience severe negative cash flows during the life of the bond. Therefore, these bonds are primarily of interest to investment accounts not subject to taxes such as pensions or for use in IRA or Keough accounts for individuals.[24]

A modified form of these bonds is the original issue deep discount bond. In this instance, there is a coupon, but the coupon is set substantially below the prevailing market rate (e.g., a 5 percent coupon on a bond when market rates are 12 percent). As a result, the bond will be issued at a deep discount from par value.

Institutional Bonds

By far the smallest sector of the bond market is that for institutional issues such as hospital bonds. Even though these obligations have a virtually spotless default record, they offer returns of 100–150 basis points above comparably rated corporates, because most institutional obligations do *not* enjoy an active secondary market! Offsetting such a handicap are many benefits in addition to the extra returns. For example, the obligations are issued on a serial basis with relatively short maximum maturities (seldom exceeding 15 to 18 years). Unlike most other serial bonds, institutional obligations generally call for *semiannual* maturities within the serial structure. Finally, they typically have deferred call features.

OBTAINING INFORMATION ON BONDS

As might be expected, the data needs of bond investors are considerably different from those of stockholders. For one thing, fundamental intrinsic analysis is far less important because of the widespread reliance on rating agencies for in-depth analysis of the risk of default. In fact, except in the case of speculative-grade bonds and questionable revenue obligations, most fixed-income investors rely on the rating agencies to determine the default risk of an obligation. Some very large institutions employ in-house analysts to confirm assigned agency

---

[24] These bonds will be discussed further in Chapter 19 in the section on duration and immunization. A discussion of the price volatility of these bonds in IRA accounts is contained in, Randall Smith, "Zero Coupon Bonds' Price Swings Jolt Investors Looking for Security," *Wall Street Journal* (June 1, 1984): 19.

ratings or to uncover marginal incremental return opportunities. Given the vast resources that these institutions invest each year, the rewards of only a few more basis points can be substantial, and the institutions enjoy economies of scale in research. Finally, because of an increasing demand for an independent appraisal of bond ratings, several private firms have established research houses that concentrate on bonds.[25]

So what type of information do bond investors require? In addition to information on risk of default, they need: (1) information on market and economic conditions, and (2) information on intrinsic bond features. Market and economic information allows investors to stay abreast of the general tone of the market, overall interest rate developments, and yield-spread behavior between different market sectors. Bond investors also require information on certain bond characteristics, such as call features and sinking-fund provisions, that can affect comparative yield and price behavior.

Where do bondholders find such information? Some is readily available in such popular publications as *The Wall Street Journal, Barron's, Business Week, Fortune*, and *Forbes*, which were discussed in Chapter 6. In addition, bond investors are regular users of other publications, many specifically dealing with bonds. We will deal with some of the more representative ones but *not* with the numerous financial services that are available at varying costs. Two popular sources of bond data are the *Federal Reserve Bulletin* and the *Survey of Current Business*, which were also described in Chapter 6.

Treasury Bulletin.   This includes average yields on long-term treasury, corporate, and municipal bonds as well as graphs of monthly average yields on new AA corporate bonds, treasury bonds, and municipal bonds. The bulletin is published monthly.

The Standard & Poor's Bond Guide.   This is published monthly and presents a condensed review of pertinent financial and statistical information. This was likewise described in Chapter 6. Moody's has a comparable publication available to investors titled *Moody's Bond Record.* (Nearly all bond publications produced by Standard & Poor's have counterparts marketed by Moody's.)

Moody's Bond Survey.   This is published weekly and provides information on current conditions in the economy and their possible effects on bond markets. Recent and prospective taxable bond offerings are listed along with information such as assigned agency rating, offering date, amount of offer, name and type of issue, call price, re-offering price and yield, and recent bid price and yield. For each of the *major* government, agency, corporate, and municipal obligations coming to the market, *detailed* information is provided on bond features, indenture provisions, and corporate or municipal finances. This is a valuable source of information to bond investors because it provides information

---

[25] Reba White, "Is Credit Analysis a Growth Industry?" *Institutional Investor,* 10 no. 1 (January 1976): 57–58; Robert J. Cirino, "Building a Fixed-Income Boutique," *Institutional Investor,* 12 no. 3 (March 1978): 35–36.

on all three categories of bonds. Standard & Poor's has a similar publication titled *Credit Week*, while Duff and Phelps has one entitled *Credit Decisions*.

527

Moody's Manuals. These include the *Municipal and Government Manual, The Bank and Financial Manual, Industrial Manual, OTC Industrial Manual, Transportation Manual*, and *Public Utility Manual*. These publications were described in Chapter 6 and are a primary source of fundamental information pertaining to the risk of default. They also contain data on various features of each outstanding issue.

Fitch Investors Service. Fitch publishes the following services:
Fitch Rating Register is a monthly publication featuring all ratings published by Fitch for corporate, municipal and health care bond issuers including pollution control and industrial development revenue bond issues, commercial paper and preferred stock. It includes a summary indicating all new ratings and rating changes by month for each of the preceding twelve months. *Fitch Corporate Credit Analysis* are research reports on issuers of bonds, preferred stock and commercial paper. They contain verbal discussion and a statistical summary of financial statements and ratio analysis. Each report begins with a "Rating Comment" summarizing the reason for the ratings. *Fitch Municipal Credit Analysis* are research reports on issuers of tax-exempt commercial paper, notes, enterprise and general obligation bonds. Likewise, they contain verbal discussion and statistical background and ratio analysis.

Investment Dealers Digest. This provides extensive information on new issues and new issue market activity, sections dealing with reviews of various segments of the bond market, and the market outlook. Detailed new issue information is published weekly including extensive data on the features of bond issues currently in underwriting. The digest also contains the most extensive list of pending and recent issues available, which gives insight into future demand for loanable funds and the effects of such demand on interest rates.

The Bond Buyer. This is a daily publication dealing with the municipal bond market. In addition to articles of general interest to municipal bond investors, there is a complete listing of all proposed municipal bond issues, redemption notices, and statistics in the government bond market. *Credit Markets* is a weekly publication by the same publisher (The Bond Buyer) that contains a recap of relevant news for the week relating to the total bond market (municipals, governments, corporates, etc.) along with columns discussing the market outlook.

Sources of Bond Quotes

The above list includes sources intended to fill three needs of investors: evaluating risk of default, staying abreast of market and interest rate conditions, and obtaining information on specific bonds. Another important data need is *current* market information, i.e., bond quotes and prices. Unfortunately, many of the prime sources are simply not widely distributed. For example, *Bank and Quota-*

tion Record is a valuable, though not widely circulated, source that provides a summary of price information on a monthly basis for government and agency bonds, a large number of listed and OTC corporate issues, municipals, and many money-market instruments. Quotes on municipal bonds are only available through a fairly costly publication, used by many financial institutions, titled *The Blue List.* It contains over 100 pages of price quotes for municipal bonds, municipal notes, and industrial development and pollution-control revenue bonds. Daily information on all publicly traded treasury issues, most important agency obligations, and many corporate issues is published in *The Wall Street Journal.* Similar data is available on a weekly basis in *Barron's.* While the list is fairly extensive for treasury and agency obligations, corporate bond quotes in *The Wall Street Journal* and *Barron's* include only listed obligations which represent a minor portion of the total market. In addition to these published sources, major market dealers maintain firm quotes on a variety of issues that are available to clients and/or cooperating institutions.

Interpreting Bond Quotes

Essentially, all bonds are either quoted on the basis of yield or price. When they are quoted on the basis of price, the quote is always interpreted as a *percentage of par.* For example, a quote of 98 1/2 is not interpreted as $98.50, but 98 1/2 percent of par. The dollar price can then be derived from the quote, given the par value. If par is $5,000 on a particular municipal bond, then the price of an issue quoted at 98 1/2 would be $4,925. Actually, the market follows three systems of bond pricing: one system for corporates, another for governments (this includes both treasuries and agency obligations), and a third for municipals.

Corporate Bond Quotes.   Figure 17.4 is a listing of corporate bond quotes and NYSE bond quotes which appeared in *The Wall Street Journal* of Tuesday, February 21, 1984. The data pertains to trading activity on February 17. Several quotes have been designated for illustrative purposes. The first is an AT&T (American Telephone and Telegraph) issue and is representative of most corporate prices. In particular, the "7 1/8s03" indicates the coupon and maturity of the obligation; in this case, the AT&T issue carries a 7 1/8 percent coupon and matures in 2003. The small *s* between the coupon and maturity is interpreted as *series* and has no real meaning. The next column provides the *current* yield of the obligation and is found by comparing the coupon to the current market price; e.g., a bond with a 7 1/8 percent coupon selling for 61 5/8 would have a 12 percent current yield. The next column is the volume of $1,000 par value bonds traded that day. The next columns indicate the high, low, and closing quote, which is followed by the net change in the closing price from the last day the issue was traded. In this case, the issue went down by 1/2 of a point or $5.00 (since that is 1/2 of one percent of $1,000). The second quote, for the Bldw U (Baldwin United) bond, has one unique feature that makes a very significant difference. A small letter *f* follows the maturity date of the obligation; this means that the issue is trading *flat.* Simply stated, the issuer is not meeting interest payments on the obligation. Therefore, the coupon of the obligation may be inconsequential. The third bond is

FIGURE 17.4   Sample Bond Quotations

CORPORATION BONDS
Volume, $28,000,000

New York Exchange Bonds

Friday, February 17, 1984

Total Volume $28,510,000

	Domestic		All Issues	
	Fri.	Thu.	Fri.	Thu.
Issues traded	947	929	955	940
Advances	252	343	255	347
Declines	482	379	484	381
Unchanged	213	207	216	212
New highs	14	15	14	17
New lows	23	16	23	16

SALES SINCE JANUARY 1

1984	1983	1982
$923,886,000	$1,240,921,000	$686,022,000

Dow Jones Bond Averages

| | —1982— | —1983— | —1984— | | | —————Friday————— | | |
	High Low	High Low	High Low			—1984—	—1983—	—1982—
20 Bonds	71.52 55.67	77.84 69.35	71.75 69.62			71.05 – .13	71.49 + .34	56.11 + .30
10 Utilities	72.71 53.80	78.88 65.76	69.31 66.07			67.95 – .21	70.93 + .52	54.55 + .54
10 Industrial	71.23 57.36	77.13 71.51	74.37 73.17			74.15 – .05	72.05 + .15	57.67 + .06

SOURCE: *The Wall Street Journal,* February 21, 1984. Reprinted by permission of *The Wall Street Journal.* © Dow Jones & Company, Inc., 1984. All rights reserved.

Bkam zr 92s which refers to a Bank of America zero coupon bond (zr) due in 1992. As discussed, these securities do not pay interest, but are redeemed at par at maturity. Because there is no coupon they do not report a current yield. The fourth bond in column three is a *registered* (r) bond for Consolidated Edison with a 4 5/8 coupon due in 1991. Recall that registered bonds are recorded with the firm and interest checks sent to the holder rather than clipping coupons. Finally, bond number 5 that is also in column 3, is both a deep discount bond (d) and convertible (cv) from Dana. Deep discount means that the original coupon was set clearly below the going rate at the time of issue — e.g., a 5 7/8 coupon when market rates were 9 or 10 percent. As a result, the firm expects the bond to sell at a big discount from par during its life. The conversion feature means that the bond is convertible into the common stock of the Company.

All fixed-income obligations, with the exception of preferred stock, are traded on an *accrued interest basis.* The prices pertain to principal value only and exclude interest that has accrued to the holder since the last interest payment date. The actual price of the bond will exceed the quote listed because accrued interest must be added. With the AT&T 7 1/8 percent issue, if two months have elapsed since interest was paid, then the current holder of the bond is entitled to 2/6 (or 1/3) of the normal semiannual interest payment. More specifically, the 7 1/8 percent coupon provides semiannual interest income of $35.625. The investor who held the obligation for two months beyond the last interest payment date is entitled to 1/3 of that $35.625 in the form of accrued interest. To the price of $616.25 (61 5/8) an accrued interest value of $11.87 will be added.

Treasury and Agency Bond Quotes. Figure 17.5 illustrates the quote system used with treasury and agency issues. These quotes are like those customarily used for other over-the-counter securities because they contain both bid and ask prices, rather than high, low, and close. Looking first at the U.S. Treasury bond quotes, observe the small *n* behind the maturity date indicating that the obligation in question is actually a treasury *note.* All other obligations in this section are, of course, treasury bonds. The first quote selected for discussion is the 7 percent issue. The security identification is slightly different from that used with corporates because it is not necessary to list the issuer. Instead, the usual listing indicates the coupon, the year of maturity, the *month* of maturity, and any information on the call feature of the obligation. For example, the 7 percent issue carries a maturity of 1993–1998; this means that the issue has a deferred call feature until 1993 (and is thereafter freely callable), and a (final) maturity date of 1998. The bid–ask figures are then provided and are also stated as a percentage of par. Unlike the current-yield figure used with corporate issues, yield to maturity or *promised* yield is used with these issues including treasuries, agencies, and municipals.

Quote 2 is an 8 3/8 percent obligation of 1995–2000 which demonstrates the basic difference in the price system of governments (i.e., treasuries and agencies). The bid quote is 74.24 and the ask is 75. Governments are traded in thirty-seconds of a point (rather than eighths), and the figures to the right of the decimal indicate the number of thirty-seconds in the fractional bid or ask. The bid price is actually 74 24/32 percent of par.

FIGURE 17.5 Sample Quotes for Treasury and Agency Issues

Treasury Issues

* * *

Bonds, Notes & Bills

Friday, February 17, 1984

Representative mid-afternoon Over-the-Counter quotations supplied by the Federal Reserve Bank of New York City, based on transactions of $1 million or more.

Decimals in bid-and-asked and bid changes represent 32nds; 101.1 means 101 1/32. a-Plus 1/64. b-Yield to call date. d-Minus 1/64. n-Treasury notes.

Treasury Bonds and Notes

Rate	Mat. Date		Bid	Asked	Bid Chg.	Yld.
15 1/8s,	1984	Feb n	100.5	100.9	- .1	0.00
14 1/8s,	1984	Mar n	100.13	100.17	- .1	8.49
14 1/4s,	1984	Mar n	100.14	100.18	- .1	8.31
13 7/8s,	1984	Apr n	100.25	100.29	- .1	8.57
9 1/4s,	1984	May n	99.28	100	- .1	9.02
13 1/4s,	1984	May n	100.25	100.29	- .1	8.87
13 3/4s,	1984	May n	101.2	101.6	- .1	8.97
15 3/4s,	1984	May n	101.11	101.15	- .1	8.80
8 7/8s,	1984	Jun n	99.21	99.25	- .1	9.39
14 3/8s,	1984	Jun n	101.17	101.21	- .1	9.35
13 1/8s,	1984	Jul	101.13	101.17	- .1	9.42
6 3/8s,	1984	Aug	98.16	99.16	....	7.44
7 1/4s,	1984	Aug n	98.29	99.1	....	9.34
11 5/8s,	1984	Aug n	100.28	101	- .1	9.61
13 1/4s,	1984	Aug n	101.19	101.23	- .1	9.49
12 1/8s,	1984	Sep n	101.7	101.11	- .1	9.79
9 3/4s,	1984	Oct	99.28	99.30	- .1	9.85
9 7/8s,	1984	Nov n	99.29	100.1	- .1	9.83
14 3/8s,	1984	Nov n	103	103.4	- .4	9.84
16s,	1984	Nov n	104.5	104.9	- .2	9.79
9 3/8s,	1984	Dec n	99.15	99.19	- .1	9.88
14s,	1984	Dec n	103.5	103.13	- .2	9.76
9 1/4s,	1985	Jan n	99.9	99.13	- .2	9.93
8s,	1985	Feb n	98.12	98.20	- .1	9.50
9 5/8s,	1985	Feb n	99.16	99.24	- .1	9.89
14 5/8s,	1985	Feb n	104.6	104.14	- .2	9.77
9 5/8s,	1985	Mar	99.11	99.19	- .2	10.02
13 3/8s,	1985	Mar n	103.7	103.15	- .2	9.98
9 1/2s,	1985	Apr n	99.6	99.10	- .2	10.13
3 1/4s,	1985	May	93.7	94.7	....	8.29
4 1/4s,	1975-85	May	93.17	94.17	+ .1	9.05
9 7/8s,	1985	May n	99.15	99.19	- .2	10.22
9s,	1994	Feb	83.23	83.31	- .10	11.77
4 1/8s,	1989-94	May	91.10	91.26	- .4	5.16
8 3/4s,	1994	Aug	81.18	81.26	- .17	11.82
10 1/8s,	1994	Nov	90.1	90.9	- .17	11.75
3s,	1995	Feb	91.6	92.6	+ .10	3.87
10 1/2s,	1995	Feb	91.21	91.29	- .14	11.83
10 3/8s,	1995	May	90.31	91.7	- .8	11.81
12 5/8s,	1995	May	104.16	104.24	- .11	11.85
11 1/2s,	1995	Nov	97.25	98.1	- .11	11.82
1 → 7s,	1993-98	May	68.12	68.28	- .16	11.40
3 1/2s,	1998	Nov	91.4	92.4	- .6	4.23
8 1/2s,	1994-99	May	76.25	77.1	- .3	11.78
7 7/8s,	1995-00	Feb	71.20	71.28	- .9	11.84
2 → 8 3/8s,	1995-00	Aug	74.24	75	- .10	11.87
11 3/4s,	2001	Feb	98.19	98.27	- .12	11.91
13 1/8s,	2001	May	108.9	108.17	- .14	11.95
8s,	1996-01	Aug	72.6	72.14	- .6	11.74
13 3/8s,	2001	Aug	110.10	110.18	- .7	11.93
15 3/4s,	2001	Nov	129.28	130.4	- .7	11.69
14 1/4s,	2002	Feb	117.3	117.11	- .7	11.89
11 5/8s,	2002	Nov	97.3	97.11	- .8	11.99
10 3/4s,	2003	Feb	90.18	90.26	- .8	11.98
10 3/4s,	2003	May	9.18	90.26	- .8	11.99
11 1/8s,	2003	Aug	93.8	93.16	- .10	12.00
11 7/8s,	2003	Nov	98.18	98.22	- .19	12.05
8 1/4s,	2000-05	May	72.28	73.4	- .16	11.69
7 5/8s,	2002-07	Feb	67.11	67.19	- .13	11.73
7 7/8s,	2002-07	Nov	69.4	69.12	- .10	11.72
8 3/8s,	2003-08	Aug	72.28	73.4	- .8	11.73
8 3/4s,	2003-08	Nov	74.31	75.7	- .15	11.88
9 1/8s,	2004-09	May	77.28	78.4	- .12	11.87
10 3/8s,	2004-09	Nov	87.12	87.20	- .16	11.93
11 3/4s,	2005-10	Feb	98.17	98.25	- .17	11.01
10s,	2005-10	May	84.15	84.23	- .16	11.91
12 3/4s,	2005-10	Nov	105.23	105.31	- .16	11.98
13 7/8s,	2006-11	May	114.20	114.28	- .19	11.94
14s,	2006-11	Nov	115.26	116.2	- .18	11.96
10 3/8s,	2007-12	Nov	87.14	87.22	- .18	11.90
12s,	2008-13	Aug	99.25	99.29	- .23	12.01

U.S. Treas. Bills

Mat. date	Bid (Discount)	Asked (Discount)	Yield	Mat. date	Bid (Discount)	Asked (Discount)	Yield
-1984-				6-14	9.19	9.13	9.56
2-23	9.14	9.06	9.23	6-21	9.25	9.19	9.64
3- 1	8.78	8.68	8.84	6-28	9.28	9.22	9.69
3- 8	8.92	8.84	9.02	7- 5	9.29	9.23	9.72
3-15	8.87	8.79	8.99	7-12	9.28	9.22	9.73
3-22	9.01	8.95	9.17	7-19	9.31	9.25	9.78
3-29	8.95	8.89	9.12	7-26	9.32	9.26	9.81
4- 5	8.99	8.93	9.18	8- 2	9.33	9.27	9.84
4-12	9.01	8.95	9.21	8- 9	9.33	9.29	9.88
4-19	9.16	9.10	9.39	8-16	9.32	9.30	9.91
4-26	9.15	9.09	9.39	9- 6	9.30	9.24	9.86
5- 3	9.17	9.11	9.43	10- 4	9.32	9.26	9.90
5-10	9.17	9.11	9.45	11- 1	9.34	9.28	9.96
5-17	9.17	9.15	9.51	11-29	9.34	9.28	10.00
5-24	9.17	9.11	9.48	12-27	9.33	9.27	10.03
5-31	9.17	9.11	9.50	-1985-			
6- 7	9.18	9.12	9.53	1-24	9.28	9.24	10.05

SOURCE: *The Wall Street Journal,* February 21, 1984. Reprinted by permission of *The Wall Street Journal.* © Dow Jones & Company, Inc., 1984. All rights reserved.

The securities listed below the treasury bond section are for U.S. treasury bills. Notice that there are only dates reported and no coupons. This is because these are pure discount securities — i.e., the return is the difference between the price you pay and par at maturity.[26]

Municipal Bond Quotes. The final illustration, Figure 17.6, pertains to municipal bond quotes and is drawn from *The Blue List of Current Municipal Offerings* for Friday, June 1, 1984. As can be seen, *The Blue List* provides daily quotes on municipal bonds ordered according to states and alphabetically within states. The information provided for each issue is: the amount of bonds being offered (in thousands of dollars), the name of the security, the coupon rate, the maturity (which includes month, day, and year), and the yield or price, and finally, the dealer offering the bonds. Bond quote 1 is 280 bonds ($280,000) of Hendry County, Florida, Public Improvement Revenue Bonds. The AMBAC/MGIC indicates that the bonds are guaranteed by both of these firms as described earlier. The bonds have a 10 percent coupon and are due June 1, 2000. In this instance, the yield to maturity is given (10.40 percent). To determine the price you would either compute or look up in a yield book the price of a 10 percent coupon bond, due in six years to yield 10.40 percent. The dealer offering the bonds is Houghwme. A list in the back of the publication indicates that this is the Wm. R. Hough & Co. (syndicate) and gives the firm's phone number.

The second bond is 50 Hillsborough County Aviation Authority bonds with a 5.875 percent coupon. This is somewhat unique in that there is a price on the bond rather than the current yield to maturity — i.e., the bond is selling for 80 which is 80 percent of par. These are called *dollar bonds*.

The third bond is 15 Hillsborough County Aviation Authority bonds that are *registered* (*REG*) and callable at 103. The C91 likewise indicates that they are callable and it is necessary to contact the dealer (FMS-First Miami Securities, Inc.) for details.

The + in the far left column indicates that this is a new item since the prior issue of *The Blue List.* A * in the column prior to the yield to maturity or the price indicates that the price or yield has changed since the last issue. In all instances it is necessary to call the dealer to determine the current yield/price since these quotes are necessarily at least one day old when they are published.

SUMMARY

This chapter dealt with the fundamental aspects of bonds necessary to provide background for discussing bond valuation and investment strategies. We initially looked at the basic features of bonds with respect to interest, principal, and maturity.

Several key relationships were discussed in regard to price behavior. First, price is essentially a function of coupon, maturity, and prevailing market interest rates. Second, bond price volatility depends on coupon and maturity. In general,

---

[26] For a discussion on calculating yields, see Bruce D. Fielitz, "Calculating the Bond Equivalent Yield for T-Bills," *Journal of Portfolio Management,* 9, no. 3 (Spring 1983): 58–60.

FIGURE 17.6
Quotes for Municipals

```
                        FLORIDA-CONTINUED

        230 HENDRY CO.PUB.IMP.RV. AMBAC/MGIC  9.90    6/ 1/98          10.10 HOUGHWME
        160 HENDRY CO.PUB.IMP.RV. AMBAC/MGIC 10       6/ 1/99          10.20 HOUGHWME
  1 ──→ 280 HENDRY CO.PUB.IMP.RV. AMBAC/MGIC 10       6/ 1/00          10.40 HOUGHWME
        315 HENDRY CO.PUB.IMP.RV.            10.25    6/ 1/05          10.50 HOUGHWME
         65 HERNANDO CO.HLTH.FAC.AU.ESC/MAT  10.50   10/ 1/06     *      100 DUNCANWM
            (LYKES HOSPITAL)
  +      20 HIALEAH HOSP.REV.      ESC/MAT   12.25   10/ 1/87           8.00 MILLSCHR
        100 HIALEAH HOSP.REV.                12       2/ 1/14     *       98 BEARSATL
        400 HIGHLANDS CO.HLTH.FAC.AU.        13       3/ 1/14            100 BUCHANAN
            (BRETHREN HOME)

        100 HIGHLANDS CO.HLTH.FAC.AU.        13       3/ 1/14            100 HENDATL
            (BRETHREN HOME)
        100 HIGHLANDS CO.HLTH.FAC.AU.        13       3/ 1/14         97 1/4 NORRISHI
            (BRETHERN HOME)
         75 HIGHLANDS CO.HLTH.FAC.AU.        13       3/ 1/14             97 JURANMOF
          5 HILLSBOROUGH CO.        L.T.      5.50    8/ 1/95           9.75 FIRSEMOB
        485 HILLSBOROUGH CO.        ESC/MAT   6.40    4/ 1/02          10.50 MATTHEWS
         50 HILLSBOROUGH CO.AVIA.AU.          5.875  10/ 1/99             79 BARRBROS
  2 ──→  50 HILLSBOROUGH CO.AVIA.AU.          5.875  10/ 1/99             80 BEARSTER
         25 HILLSBOROUGH CO.AVIA.AU.          5.875  10/ 1/99             76 TRANSGLF

         25 HILLSBOROUGH CO.AVIA.AU.          6      10/ 1/99             77 TRANSGLF
  3 ──→  15 HILLSBOROUGH CO.AVIA.*REG*       10.875  10/ 1/09 C91      10.40 FMS
            (CA @ 103)(AMBAC/MGIC)
          5 HILLSBOROUGH CO.AVIA.AU.         10      10/ 1/11          10.75 HOUGHWMC
         40 HILLSBOROUGH CO.AVIA.AU.         10      10/ 1/11          10.75 STOEVERG
            (TAMPA INTERNATIONAL AIRPORT)
         60 HILLSBOROUGH CO.AVIA.AU BEARER   11.25   12/ 1/12          11.00 THOMSNSP
            (DELTA AIRLINES)
         50 HILLSBOROUGH CO.HOSP.AU.         11.25   10/ 1/12     *       85 HUTTONMI
            (TAMPA GENERAL)

         40 HILLSBOROUGH CO.HOSP.AU.         11.25   10/ 1/12             85 HOUGHWMF
        100 HILLSBOROUGH CO.HOSP.AU.         11.25   10/ 1/12         85 1/2 MILLERSE
        100 HILLSBOROUGH CO.HOSP.AU.         11.25   10/ 1/12         84 1/2 PAINEWPB
            (TAMPA GENERAL HOSPITAL)
        100 HILLSBOROUGH CO.HOSP.AU.         11.25   10/ 1/12 C92          88 TUCKRAN
            (TAMPA GENERAL)
         45 HILLSBOROUGH CO.I.D.R.            7.75   12/ 1/94           9.50 HOUGHWMC
         15 HILLSBOROUGH CO.I.D.R.            8.25   12/ 1/04          10.50 HOUGHWMC
         40 HILLSBOROUGH CO.I.D.R.           11.875   8/ 1/11          10.75 HOUGHWMC
         15 HILLSBOROUGH CO.I.D.R.           12.625   5/ 1/12          10.75 HOUGHWMC

         85 HILLSBOROUGH CO.I.D.R.BEARER     12.625   5/ 1/12 C92      10.75 STJOHNS
            (P/C @ 103)
         25 HILLSBOROUGH CO.PCR  (TAMPA EL)  12.625   5/ 1/12 C92      10.85 BRSFL
            (CA @ 103)
         20 HILLSBOROUGH CO.PT.DST.RV.        6.25   12/ 1/00           9.00 STRAHSME
            (ESC/MAT)
         10 HILLSBOROUGH CO.PT.DST.RV.        8       8/ 1/06          11.00 STRAHSME
            (TAMPA SHIP BUILDING)
         20 HILLSBOROUGH CO.PT.DST.RV.        8       8/ 1/06          11.25 WILLIAMJ
          5 HILLSBOROUGH CO.SCH.BD.           5.90    5/ 1/91          10.25 HOUGHWMC

        125 HILLSBOROUGH CO.UTIL.*REG*  MBIA  9.15   12/ 1/96           9.90 DREXLAUD
         20 HOLLYWOOD                         5       7/ 1/93           9.60 HOUGHWMC
          5 HOLLYWOOD UTIL.TAX RV.            3.40    4/ 1/91           9.75 BRSFL
         15 JACKSON CO.SCH.BD. -       MBIA   6.25   12/ 1/85           7.00 RODMANIN
        255 JACKSONVILLE ARPT.RV.             4       8/ 1/98          10.75 HOUGHWMF
        500 JACKSONVILLE EL. REV.             8      10/ 1/85           7.25 MARONNUG
       1085 JACKSONVILLE EL. REV.             6.75   10/ 1/86           7.25 HOUGHWMC
  +     250 JACKSONVILLE FL. REV.             6.75   10/ 1/86           7.25 DWRSTP

        PAGE 24A                   FRIDAY JUNE 01, 1984
```

SOURCE: *The Blue List of Current Municipal Offerings,* June 1, 1984. The Blue List, Division of Standard & Poor's. Reprinted by permission.

bonds with longer maturities and/or lower coupons respond most vigorously to a given change in market rates. Finally, other factors, including intrinsic characteristics, type of issue, and indenture provisions, must be considered.

Major benefits to investors included: high returns for nominal risk, potential for capital gains, certain tax advantages, and the opportunity for additional returns based on aggressive trading of bonds. Major concerns for the aggressive bond investor include secondary-market activity, investment risks, and interest rate behavior.

Several popular issues available in the various market sectors were reviewed with consideration given to liquidity, yield spreads, tax implications, and special features unique to each sector. The final section discussed the information needs of investors. In terms of default risk, most bond investors rely on agency ratings as their source of information. For additional information on market and economic conditions and information on intrinsic bond features, individual and institutional investors rely on a host of readily available publications. Various examples of typical issue quotes were given with accompanying explanations.

QUESTIONS

1. How does a bond differ from other types of debt instruments?
2. Explain the difference between calling a bond and bond refunding.
3. Identify the three most important factors in determining the price of a bond. Describe the effect of each.
4. Given a change in the level of interest rates, what are the two major factors that will influence the relative change in price for individual bonds? What is their impact?
5. Define two different types of bond yields.
6. What factors determine whether a bond is senior or junior? Give examples of each type of bond.
7. What is a bond indenture?
8. Explain the differences in taxation of income from municipal bonds as opposed to U.S. treasury bonds and corporate bonds.
9. List several types of institutional participants in the bond market and explain what types of bond they are likely to purchase and why they purchase them.
10. Why should an investor be aware of the trading volume for a particular bond in which he is interested?
11. What is the purpose of bond ratings? What are they supposed to indicate?
12. What part does a bond's rating play in the evaluation of a bond for investment?
13. Demonstrate through an example the effects of interest rate risk on the price of a bond.
14. An investor in the 35 percent tax bracket is trying to decide which of two bonds to purchase. One is a corporate bond carrying an 8 percent coupon and selling at par. The other is a municipal bond with a 5 1/2 percent coupon, and it, too, sells at par. Assuming all other relevant factors are equal, which bond should the investor select?
15. Compare and contrast a corporate mortgage-backed bond with a Ginnie Mae pass-through certificate.
16. What would be the initial offering price for the following bonds (assume semiannual compounding):
    a. A 15-year zero coupon bond with a yield to maturity (YTM) of 12 percent.
    b. A 20-year zero coupon bond with a YTM of 10 percent.
    c. A 20-year 6 percent coupon bond with a YTM of 12 percent.

17. In the latter part of this chapter, a large number of sources of information on bonds were described and their contents discussed. Yet the statement was made earlier that "it is almost impossible for individual investors . . . to keep abreast of the price activity of municipal holdings." Discuss this apparent paradox, explaining how such a condition might exist.
18. Using various sources of information described in the chapter, name at least five bonds, rated B or better, that have split ratings.
19. Using various sources of information, select five bonds from those firms listed on the NYSE. Prepare a brief description of each bond, including such factors as its rating, call features, collateral (if any), interest dates, and refunding provisions.

REFERENCES

Ahearn, Daniel S. "The Strategic Role of Fixed Income Securities." *The Journal of Portfolio Management.* 1 no. 3 (Spring 1975).

Altman, Edward I., and S. Katz. "Statistical Bond Ratings Classification Using Financial and Accounting Data." In *Proceedings of the Conference on Topical Research in Accountancy.* Michael Schiff and George Sorter (eds.). New York University School of Business, 1976.

Ang, James S., and K. A. Patel. "Bond Rating Methods: Comparison and Validation." *Journal of Finance.* 30 no. 2 (May 1975).

Baskin, Elba F., and Gary M. Crooch. "Historical Rates of Return on Investments in Flat Bonds." *Financial Analysts Journal.* 24 no. 6 (November–December 1968).

Belkaoui, Ahmed. "Industrial Bond Ratings: A New Look," *Financial Mangement.* 9 no. 3 (Autumn 1980).

Bierman, Harold, and Jerome Hass. "An Analytical Model of Bond Risk Differentials." *Journal of Financial and Quantitative Analysis.* 10 no. 5 (December 1975).

Brimmer, Andrew F. "Credit Conditions and Price Determination in the Corporate Bond Market." *Journal of Finance.* 15 no. 3 (September 1960).

Bullington, Robert A. "How Corporate Debt Issues Are Rated." *Financial Executive.* 42 no. 9 (September 1974).

Darst, David M. *The Complete Bond Book.* New York: McGraw-Hill, 1975.

Edelman, Richard B. "A New Approach to Ratings on Utility Bonds." *Journal of Portfolio Management.* 5 no. 3 (Spring 1979).

Fabozzi, Frank J., and Irving M. Pollack. (eds.) *The Handbook of Fixed Income Securities.* Homewood, Ill.: Dow Jones-Irwin, 1983.

Fisher, Lawrence. "Determinants of Risk Premiums on Corporate Bonds." *Journal of Political Economy.* 67 no. 3 (June 1959).

Greenbaum, Mary. "Sorting Out the Floating Rate Issues." *Fortune.* (December 17, 1979).

Hickman, W. Braddock. *Corporate Bond Quality and Investor Experience.* Princeton, N.J.: Princeton University Press, 1958.

Homer, Sidney. "The Historical Evolution of Today's Bond Market." *The Journal of Portfolio Management.* 1 no. 3 (Spring 1975).

Horrigan, James O. "The Determination of Long-Term Credit Standing with Financial Ratios." *Empirical Research in Accounting: Selected Studies.* Supplement to *Journal of Accounting Research* 4, 1966.

Joehnk, Michael D., and James F. Nielsen. "Return Risk Characteristics of Speculative Grade Bonds." *Quarterly Review of Economics and Business.* 15 no. 1 (Spring 1975).

Kaplan, Mortimer. "Yields on Recently Issued Corporate Bonds: A New Index." *Journal of Finance.* 17 no. 1 (March 1962).

Kaplan, Robert S., and Gabriel Urwitz. "Statistical Models of Bond Ratings: A Methodological Inquiry." *Journal of Business.* 52 no. 2 (April 1979).

Landsea, William F. "Agency Bonds in Liquidity Portfolios." *Mississippi Valley Journal of Business and Economics.* 7 no. 2 (Winter 1971–1972).

Lindvall, John R. "New Issue Corporate Bonds, Seasoned Market Efficiency and Yield Spreads." *Journal of Finance.* 32 no. 4 (September 1977).

Meyer, Kenneth, R. "The Dividends from Active Bond Management." *The Journal of Portfolio Management.* 1 no. 3 (Spring 1975).

Pinches, George E., and Kent A. Mingo. "A Multivariate Analysis of Industrial Bond Ratings." *Journal of Finance.* 28 no. 1 (March 1973).

Pinches, George, and K. Mingo. "A Note on the Role of Subordination in Determining Industrial Bond Ratings." *Journal of Finance.* 30 no. 1 (March 1975).

Pogue, Thomas F., and Robert M. Soldofsky. "What's in a Bond Rating?" *Journal of Financial and Quantitative Analysis.* 4 no. 2 (June 1969).

Pye, Gordon. "Gauging the Default Premium." *Financial Analysts Journal.* 30 no. 1 (January–February 1974).

Reilly, Frank K., and Michael D. Joehnk. "Association between Market Determined Risk Measures for Bonds and Bond Ratings." *Journal of Finance.* 31 no. 5 (December 1976).

Ross, Irwin. "Higher Stakes in the Bond-Rating Game." *Fortune.* (April 1976).

"Say Hello to Tax-Free Bond Funds." *Savings and Loan News.* 98 no. 2 (February 1977).

Sharpe, William F. "Bonds Versus Stocks: Some Lessons from Capital Market Theory." *Financial Analysts Journal.* 29 no. 6 (November–December 1973).

Thygerson, Kenneth J., and Thomas J. Parliment. "Mortgage Securities Make It Big on Wall Street." *Savings and Loan News.* 98 no. 12 (December 1977).

Van Horne, James C. *Financial Market Rates and Flows.* 2nd ed. Englewood Cliffs, N.J.: Prentice-Hall, 1984.

Weil, Roman. "Realized Interest Rates and Bondholder's Returns." *American Economic Review.* 60 no. 3 (June 1970).

West, Richard R. "An Alternative Approach to Predicting Corporate Bond Ratings." *Journal of Accounting Research.* 8 no. 1 (Spring 1970).

West, Richard R. "Bond Ratings, Bond Yields and Financial Regulation: Some Findings." *Journal of Law and Economics.* 15 no. 1 (April 1973).

Chapter 18   *Principles of Bond Valuation*

L ike any long-term investment, fixed-income securities are valued on the basis of their future stream of income. Periodic interest income, along with payment of principal at maturity, are the two fundamental sources of return to bondholders. The basic problem of bond valuation revolves about the specification, at desired levels of certainty, of the various components of the future cash flow to be realized by the bond investor, especially the size of capital recovery (i.e., payment of principal).

The purpose of this chapter is to explore the valuation process and to identify the important determinants that affect bond price and yield. It represents an extension of the preceding chapter since it explicitly demonstrates how many of the important variables introduced there can affect promised yield and realized return. Initially there is an overview of the general concepts and fundamental dimensions of the bond valuation process. The arithmetic of bond prices and bond yields will then be examined and the mathematics of tax-exempt issues will be addressed. The role of interest rates in affecting bond yields and prices will then be explored, as will the determinants of interest rates and yield spreads. Finally, there is an analysis of the causes and effects of variations in bond price volatility including a consideration of the important concept of bond duration.

FUNDAMENTALS OF THE BOND VALUATION PROCESS

Present Value Model

Basically, the bond valuation process is similar to the procedures used with equity securities since the value of a bond is equal to the present value of expected cash flows. The only real difference is that the cash flow involved is the periodic interest payments and capital recovery. In a theoretical framework, the basic principles of bond valuation can be described in the following present value model:

(18.1)
$$P = \sum_{t=1}^{n} C_t \frac{1}{(1 + i)^t},$$

where:

n = the number of periods in the investment horizon, or what is more popularly known as *term to maturity*

C_t = the cash flow (periodic interest income and principal) received in period t

i = the rate of discount (or market yield) for the issue.

Essentially, any fixed income security can be valued on the basis of Equation 18.1, which provides an indication of what the investor expects to realize by holding the issue over a given investment horizon. In most cases, the holding period is equal to the term to maturity of the obligation and, as a result, the rate of discount represents the *promised yield to maturity* that can be earned by purchasing the obligation and holding it to its expiration date. Aggressive bond investors, however, normally do not hold obligations to maturity. Rather, the intent is to buy and subsequently sell the security prior to that point. Under such conditions, *realized yield* is a more important description of performance. In such a case, Equation 18.1 would represent an expected yield rather than promised return.

The present value model is attractive because it incorporates several important aspects of bond yields and prices. Current income is a facet of coupon receipts and is included in C_t. More important, we know that interest rate behavior is a critical aspect of bond yield and bond price performance. The effect of interest rates is incorporated in i, where the discount rate is interpreted as the prevailing bond yield (described as promised yield to maturity) at a given point in time. Another important dimension is *changes* in interest rates because it affects the level of capital gains (or losses) that would be realized by an investor who buys and sells an issue prior to maturity.[1] The capital gain or loss is incorporated into the model within the cash flow component, C_t.

Because the present value model is a valuation procedure applicable to individual securities, another important factor that impacts on the capital gain or loss component is the effect of changes in *yield spreads* over the investment horizon. These spreads are simply differences in yields that exist between different market sectors or types of issues (e.g., the difference in yields for long treasuries and long corporate bonds). Yield spreads account for the subtle differences in performance because of differential risk, call feature, variations in coupons and maturities, etc.

The bond valuation framework rests on an evaluation of interest receipts, interest rates, changes in interest rates, and yield spreads. *The major problem facing the bond analyst is to determine the extent of interest rate changes and*

---

[1] Indeed, for many aggressive investors, it is *the* major facet because their major objective is attractive capital gains.

yield spread behavior. The definition of coupon income and par value is not a significant problem since it is specified and fixed. The only real concern is determining the risk of default, and much of that is handled by agency ratings. Moreover, if an investor is examining an obligation solely on the basis of promised yield, then prevailing available market rates define *i*. In contrast, the computation of *realized* yield assumes that the investment horizon is less than term to maturity and is directly related to the possibility of capital gains or losses. Further, the potential capital gains or losses depend upon changes in interest rates and yield spreads.

The investor must not only understand those forces which affect the *level* of interest rates in order to judge current market rates, but also he must be able to project future interest rates. Once interest rate levels have been evaluated and anticipated *changes* in rates have been formulated, attention shifts to the more specific consideration of differential market rates, and that implies examination of yield spreads. That is, an evaluation of the yield spread behavior over the holding period will indicate that certain segments of the market will be more attractive because of their relative yield performance. In effect, yield spread analysis is the application of interest rate behavior to specific segments of the market.

Finally, there is a considerable difference in the valuation process when an investor follows a buy-and-hold approach versus a trading strategy. In the latter case, there is considerable risk and uncertainty surrounding future bond prices and expected capital gains opportunities. After the formulation of future price behavior through the evaluation of interest rates and yield spreads, it is necessary to select the appropriate coupon, maturity, call feature, etc. in order to procure the desired performance.

Buy-and-hold investors deal with similar estimates, although their magnitude is *substantially* less than that for the investor with a trading strategy. For example, the buy-and-hold investor must consider the technical dimensions of bond valuation, such as maturity, coupon, and call features, to determine how such features might affect investment objectives. The buy-and-hold investor is working with *known* information and the only uncertainty is whether it is the appropriate time to buy or sell. His uncertainty over interest rates is nominal compared to that assumed by aggressive capital gains-oriented bond investors, because *failure to formulate interest rates correctly* has much *less* impact on the realized gains of the buy-and-hold investor; at the worst, it means not realizing quite as much as hoped. For the aggressive capital gains-oriented investors such errors can mean not only reduced profit, but *substantial losses* as well!

The subsequent discussion of the valuation process pertains to investment-grade securities which possess acceptable levels of interest sensitivity. Essentially, speculative-grade securities are *less* sensitive to interest rates. Therefore, given the importance of interest rates in the bond valuation process, the framework specified would be inappropriate for bonds that are not interest sensitive.[2]

[2] For a more detailed discussion of the determinants of speculative-grade bond yields and price behavior, see Michael D. Joehnk and James F. Nielsen, "Return and Risk Characteristics of Speculative Grade Bonds," *Quarterly Review of Economics & Business,* 15 no. 1 (Spring 1975): 35 – 43 and Elba F. Baskin and Gary M. Crooch, "Historical Rates of Return on Investments in Flat Bonds," *Financial Analysts Journal,* 24 no. 6 (November – December 1968): 95 – 97.

542   THE MATHEMATICS OF BOND PRICING AND YIELDS

Basically there are five types of yields in bond market trading vernacular: nominal yield, current yield, promised yield, yield to call, and realized yield. Nominal yield is the coupon rate a particular issue carries. A bond with an 8 percent coupon would have an 8 percent nominal yield. It has practical significance only to the extent that it provides a convenient way of describing the coupon characteristics of an issue.

Current yield is to bonds what dividend yield is to stocks, and is computed as:

(18.2)
$$CY = c_t / P_m,$$

where:

c_t = the annual coupon payment of the obligation, and

P_m = the current market price of the issue.

This yield indicates the relative level of current income provided by the obligation and is important to income-oriented investors. Unfortunately, it excludes an important component in the bond valuation process, capital recovery (i.e., the potential for capital gain or loss).

Promised Yield

Promised yield is *the* most important and widely used bond valuation model! Essentially, promised yield indicates the fully compounded rate of return offered to the investor at prevailing prices, assuming the investor *holds the obligation to maturity.* Also known as *yield to maturity,* it excludes any trading possibilities. The concept simply involves prevailing market prices, periodic coupon income, and par value (which, when related to prevailing market price, accounts for capital appreciation or depreciation). Then, assuming the investor buys and holds the bond to maturity, the computation indicates the issue's yield to maturity.

Like any present value based computation, promised yield has important reinvestment implications. In particular, the promised yield is the required reinvestment rate that the investor must subsequently earn on each of the interim cash flows (coupon receipts) in order to realize a return equal to, or greater than, promised yield. This is directly related to compound value and is also known as *interest-on-interest.*[3] The yield to maturity figure is the return promised so long as the issuer meets all interest and principal obligations on a timely basis *and the investor reinvests coupon income to maturity at an average rate equal to the computed promised yield.* If a bond promises an 8 percent yield to maturity, the investor must reinvest coupon income at a rate equal to 8 percent in order to realize that promised return. If coupons are not reinvested, or if future invest-

---

[3] Sidney Homer and Martin L. Leibowitz, *Inside the Yield Book* (Englewood Cliffs, N.J.: Prentice-Hall, 1972), Chapter 1.

FIGURE 18.1
The Effect of Interest-on-Interest on Total Realized Return

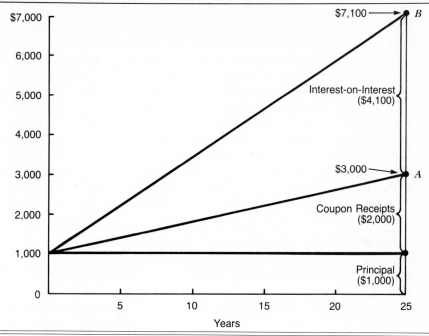

Promised yield at time of purchase	8.00%
Realized yield over the 25-year investment horizon with no coupon reinvestment (*A*)	4.50%
Realized yield over the 25-year horizon with coupons reinvested at 8% (*B*)	8.00%

ment rates during the life of the issue are less than the promised yield at purchase, then the *realized* yield earned will be *less* than promised yield to maturity.

This important and often overlooked concept is fully developed in the excellent book by Homer and Leibowitz.[4] The importance of interest-on-interest varies directly with coupon and maturity; the higher the coupon and/or the longer the term to maturity, the more important is reinvestment. Figure 18.1 depicts the concept and the impact of interest-on-interest assuming an 8 percent, 25-year bond was bought at par to yield 8 percent. This chart shows that if you invested $1,000 today at a rate of 8 percent for 25 years and all the income were reinvested at 8 percent, you would have approximately $7,100 at the end of 25 years. To prove this, look up the compound value for 8 percent for 25 years (which is 6.8493) or 4 percent for 50 periods (this assumes semiannual compounding), which is 7.1073. The chart shows that this $7,100 is made up of $1,000 principal return, $2,000 of coupon payments over the 25 years ($80 a year for 25 years), and the rest ($4,100) is interest earned on the coupon payments at 8 percent. If you had never reinvested any of the coupon payments, you would

---

[4] Ibid.

only have an ending wealth value of $3,000. This ending wealth value relative to the beginning investment of $1,000 implies a *realized* yield of 4.5 percent (i.e., 4.5 percent is the rate that will discount $3,000 back to $1,000 in 25 years). If you had reinvested the coupon payments at some rate between 0 and 8 percent, your ending wealth position would have been above $3,000 and below $7,100; therefore, your realized return would be somewhere between 4.5 percent and 8 percent. Alternatively, if you were able to reinvest the coupon payments consistently at rates above 8 percent, your ending wealth position would be above $7,100 and your realized return would be above 8 percent.

Interestingly, during periods of very high interest rates, you will often hear investors talk about *locking in* high yields. In many instances they do not realize that they are subject to *yield illusion* because they don't realize that to attain the high promised yield, they must reinvest all the coupon payments at the *very high yields that currently exist*. As an example, if you buy a 20-year bond with a promised yield to maturity of 15 percent, to *realize* the 15 percent yield you must be able to reinvest all the coupon payments at 15 percent over the next 20 years.

Approximate Promised Yield. Depending upon the accuracy desired, there are several procedures that can be used to compute promised yield. (Although the initial discussion assumes that the yield computations are executed on interest payment dates, this unrealistic assumption will be relaxed later). The promised yield can be computed on the basis of approximate yield, or, for slightly more accuracy, it can be measured on the basis of present value using annual compounding. Finally, promised yield can be computed in terms of semiannual compounding, which is the most precise procedure and is used in the marketplace.

Looking first at the approximate promised yield (APY), the mechanics of this measure are relatively straightforward as seen in Equation 18.3:

(18.3)
$$APY = \frac{c_t + \dfrac{P_p - P_m}{n}}{\dfrac{P_p + P_m}{2}},$$

where:

P_p = par value of the obligation

n = number of years to maturity

c_t = the *annual* coupon value of the obligation

P_m = the current market price of the issue.

APY is an approximate estimate of the promised yield of an obligation that assumes interest is compounded annually. It is useful because, unlike present value computations, it does not require iteration.

Assume that we want to determine the approximate promised yield of an 8

percent bond with 20 years remaining to maturity and a current price of $900.
The approximate yield of this bond is 8.95 percent:

$$APY = \frac{80 + \dfrac{1000 - 900}{20}}{\dfrac{1000 + 900}{2}}$$

$$= 8.95\%.$$

For even more accuracy, promised yield can also be computed using the present
value model and annual compounding. Equation 18.4 shows this version of the
promised yield valuation model:

(18.4)
$$P_m = \sum_{t=1}^{n} \frac{c_t}{(1+i)^t} + \frac{P_p}{(1+i)^n},$$

where all variables are as described on page 544. This model is more accurate,
but it is also more complex because iteration must be employed to arrive at a
solution. It is a variation of internal rate of return (IRR) and involves the determination of that discount rate, i, which will equate the present value of the stream of
coupon receipts (c_t) and principal value (P_p) with the current market price of the
obligation (P_m). Using the same illustration as above (the 8 percent, 20-year
bond, priced at $900), we can see that promised yield now amounts to 9.11
percent:[5]

$$900 = 80 \sum_{t=1}^{20} \frac{1}{(1.0911)^t} + 1000 \frac{1}{(1.0911)^{20}}$$
$$= 80 \, (9.0625) + 1000 \, (.1750)$$
$$= 900.$$

(In the above illustration, the values for $\dfrac{1}{1+i}$ were obtained from present value
interest factor tables.)

A comparison of the results from Equation 18.4 with those obtained from the
approximate promised yield computation indicates a variation of 16 basis points
in computed promised yield. As a rule, approximate yield tends to *understate*
actual promised yield for issues trading at a discount, and the size of the differential varies directly with the length of the holding period; i.e., the greater n is, the
bigger the difference will be. With APY, the *ranking* of yields based on Equation
18.3 will generally be identical to the rankings determined by more precise
methods.

For maximum accuracy, semiannual, rather than annual, compounding
should be used since the cash flow from bonds is semiannual. Even in those

[5] You will recall from corporate finance that you would start with one rate (e.g., 9 percent) and compute the
value of the stream. In this example, the value would exceed $900, so you would select another higher rate
until you had a value of less than $900. Given the rates above and below the true rate, you would iterate or
interpolate to the correct rate.

situations in which the cash flow occurs over something other than six-month intervals (for example, GNMA pass throughs), semiannual compounding is still employed as a basis for yield valuation. Semiannual compounding can be calculated by altering Equation 18.4 as follows:

$$(18.5) \qquad P_m = \sum_{t=1}^{2n} \frac{c_t/2}{(1 + i/2)^t} + \frac{P_p}{(1 + i/2)^{2n}},$$

where all the variables are as described on page 544. The major adjustments include doubling the number of periods within the investment horizon, since each now covers six months rather than one year. Since coupons are received every six months, the value of c_t is halved. The promised yield with this method amounts to 9.09 percent. The mechanics of the calculation are identical to those in Equation 18.4, so an illustration is unnecessary. The student can, instead, test his skills by using Equation 18.5 to arrive at the indicated yield.

Clearly, the improvement in accuracy (two basis points) is nowhere near as great as it was when we moved from approximate yield to Equation 18.4. Such improved accuracy would be necessary only for large investment sums and large bond portfolios. Notably, Equation 18.5 is the procedure used to determine published bond quotes.

Given prevailing market prices for issues with different coupons and maturities, the investor would use Equations 18.3, 18.4, or 18.5 to select the obligation which provided the most attractive yield opportunities. Determining promised yield and evaluating the return opportunities relative to perceived risk should provide you with insight into the investment merits and attractiveness of competing obligations.

Yield to Call

While promised yield to maturity is used most often, it is occasionally necessary to estimate return on the basis of promised yield to call. Whenever a *premium bond* is quoted at a value equal to or greater than par plus one year's interest, yield to call should be computed in place of yield to maturity, because the marketplace bases its pricing on the most conservative (i.e., lowest) yield measure. Therefore, when bonds are trading at or above a certain dollar value, the *crossover point* (which approximates par plus one year's interest) yield to call will normally provide the lowest yield measure.[6] At this price above par, the implied yield is low enough that it would be profitable for the firm to call the issue when allowed to and refund it with a new issue. Therefore, at a price above this crossover point, it is assumed that the obligation will not remain outstanding to maturity, but instead it will be retired at the end of the deferred call period. Thus, it is the promised yield based on an investment horizon extending only to the call date. Yield to call has become a particularly important measure recently

[6] For an extended discussion of the derivation of the crossover point, see Homer and Leibowitz, *Inside the Yield Book,* (Englewood Cliffs, N.J.: Prentice-Hall, 1972), Chapter 4.

because of the many high yielding, high coupon obligations that have been issued which possess substantial levels of call risk.[7]

Yield to call is calculated by using variations of Equations 18.3, 18.4, or 18.5. If the approximate yield to call (AYC) was desired, then the investor would use the following variation of the approximate promised yield computation:

$$(18.6) \qquad AYC = \frac{c_t + \dfrac{P_c - P_m}{nc}}{\dfrac{P_c + P_m}{2}},$$

where:

P_c = the call price of the obligation (as noted, this is generally equal to par value plus one year's interest)

nc = the number of years to first call date.

All other variables in the model are as defined on page 544. Observe that this model is comparable to approximate yield to maturity, except that P_c has replaced P_p in Equation 18.3 and nc has replaced n.

As an illustration, consider a 12 percent, 20-year bond that is trading at 115 ($1150) and has five years remaining to first call at a price of 112 ($1120). Using Equation 18.6, we see that:

$$AYC = \frac{120 + \dfrac{1120 - 1150}{5}}{\dfrac{1120 + 1150}{2}} = 10.04\%.$$

The approximate yield to call of the obligation is 10.04 percent and is derived under the assumption that the issue will be prematurely retired after five years at the call price of 112. You can compute the approximate promised yield to maturity of this issue to confirm that yield to call is the more conservative value. (Promised yield based on Equation 18.3 will equal 10.47 percent).

Similar simple adjustments can be made in present value models (Equations 18.4 and 18.5). For the annual compounding approach, yield to call would appear as follows:

$$(18.7) \qquad P_m = \sum_{t=1}^{nc} \frac{c_t}{(1 + i)^t} + \frac{P_c}{(1 + i)^{nc}},$$

---

[7] There is an extensive literature on the refunding of bond issues including: W. M. Boyce and A. J. Kalotay, "Optimum Bond Calling and Refunding," *Interfaces* (November 1979): 36–49; R. S. Harris, "The Refunding of Discounted Debt: An Adjusted Present Value Analysis," *Financial Management*, 9 no. 4 (Winter 1980): 7–12; A. J. Kalotay, "On the Structure and Valuation of Debt Refundings," *Financial Management*, 11 no. 1 (Spring 1982): 41–42; and John D. Finnerty, "Evaluating the Economics of Refunding High-Coupon Sinking-Fund Debt," *Financial Management*, 12 no. 1 (Spring 1983): 5–10.

where all the variables are described as previously. For the semiannual approach to bond valuation, yield to call can be determined using the following model:

$$(18.8) \qquad P_m = \sum_{t=1}^{2nc} \frac{c_t/2}{(1 + i/2)^t} + \frac{P_c}{(1 + i/2)^{2nc}},$$

where all the variables are described as previously. The same two changes that were noted with the approximate method are used with the present value methods; i.e., P_p (par value) is replaced with the call price of the issue (P_c), and the remaining life of the obligation is no longer considered term to maturity (n) but, instead, is the number of years or semiannual periods to call (nc).

Finally, note that the return measures determined via the approximate and annual compounding methods are more precise under yield to call situations since they deal with considerably shorter investment horizons. Using the annual compounding procedure (Equation 18.7), the yield to call for our 12 percent, 20-year bond amounts to 9.96 percent. The difference from approximate yield to call (10.04 percent) is only eight basis points, although it is in the *opposite* direction than the promised yield comparison—a common relationship with premium bonds. It is normal to expect approximate yield figures to exceed more precise compounding results for *premium* bonds.

Realized Yield

The final measure is realized yield. Rather than assuming that the issue is bought and held to maturity (or first call), realized yield assumes that the investor is taking a trading position and intends to liquidate the bond prior to maturity (or first call) date. In essence, the investor has a holding period (hp) which is less than n (or nc). Realized yield determines the level of return attainable from trading bonds over relatively short investment horizons. Such information is used to compare realized yield performance in order to select the most promising issue or issues. The evaluation process considers the forecasted value of the bond at the expected date of liquidation, which is, of course, subject to uncertainty. (It is also possible to use this procedure to measure *actual* realized yield earned in a completed buy-and-sell transaction.)

The measure of realized yield is based on the basic promised yield valuation models (Equations 18.3, 18.4, and 18.5). The approximate realized yield (ARY) is given in Equation 18.9:

$$(18.9) \qquad ARY = \frac{c_t + \dfrac{P_f - P_m}{hp}}{\dfrac{P_f + P_m}{2}},$$

where:

P_f = the future (selling) price of the issue

hp = the holding period of the issue in years.

All other variables are as defined previously. Again, the same two variables change: the holding period (hp) is used instead of n and P_f is used in lieu of P_p. Also note that P_f is a *computed value* rather than a given contractual value. It is calculated through use of promised yield by defining the years remaining to maturity as $n - hp$ and by stipulating a forecasted future market yield, i. The computation of future price will be more fully explored in the section below.

Once hp and P_f are determined, approximate realized yield can be calculated. Using an 8 percent, 20-year bond as a basis of illustration, consider a situation in which an investor buys the issue at $750 and anticipates selling it two years later, after interest rates have, hopefully, experienced a substantial decline, at a price of $900. The realized yield of this example would be:

$$ARY = \frac{80 + \dfrac{900 - 750}{2}}{\dfrac{900 + 750}{2}} = 18.79\%.$$

The high return is the result of the expected realization of a substantial capital gains in a fairly short period of time.

In a comparable manner, the introduction of P_f and hp into the annual and semiannual compounding versions of yield provides the respective present value versions of realized yield:

(18.10)
$$P_m = \sum_{t=1}^{hp} \frac{c_t}{(1+i)^t} + \frac{P_f}{(1+i)^{hp}}$$

and

(18.11)
$$P_m = \sum_{t=1}^{2hp} \frac{c_t/2}{(1+i/2)^t} + \frac{P_f}{(1+i/2)^{2hp}}.$$

Because of the usually small number of periods in hp, the added accuracy of these measures is somewhat marginal. In fact, it could be argued that, to the extent that realized yield measures are based on expected price performance, and given the uncertainty inherent in such forecasts, there is ample justification for using either the approximate or annual compounding methods. Surely they would provide more than adequate levels of accuracy under most circumstances. In contrast, if *actual* realized yield is being measured for performance purposes, there is justification for using the more accurate semiannual basis of compounding.

Bond Prices

There are two conditions under which bond dollar prices are important. The first is with regard to realized yield, i.e., the determination of the future price of an issue (P_f). The second condition is when issues are quoted on a (promised) yield basis, as with municipals.

Depending upon the accuracy desired and whether the analyst wishes to work with annual or semiannual compounding, the conversion of a yield-based quote to a dollar price can be readily accomplished using Equations 18.4 or 18.5. Using 18.5 as a basis for discussion, it can be seen that the mechanics are simple and no longer involve iteration. Instead, the analyst need only solve the equation for P_m. Coupon (c_t) is given, as is par value (P_p), and market yield (i), which is used as the discount rate. Consider a 10 percent bond with 25 years remaining to maturity that is quoted to yield 12 percent. Using the semiannual version of the model to price this issue:

$$P_m = 100/2 \sum_{t=1}^{50} \frac{1}{\left(1 + \frac{.120}{2}\right)} + 1000 \frac{1}{\left(1 + \frac{.120}{2}\right)^{50}}$$

$$= 50(15.7619) + 1000(.0543)$$
$$= \$788.10 + 54.30$$
$$= \$842.40.$$

In contrast to current market price, anticipated future price (P_f) is computed when bond traders attempt to establish the expected realized yield performance of alternative issues. Portfolio managers with relatively short investment horizons who trade bonds on a regular basis for the capital gains consider expected realized yield, rather than promised yield, to be critical to the investment decision. Again, depending on whether annual or semiannual compounding is desired, P_f can be determined by using the following variations of the realized yield models (Equations 18.10 and 18.11):

(18.12)
$$P_f = \sum_{t=1}^{n-bp} \frac{c_t}{(1 + i)^t} + \frac{P_p}{(1 + i)^{n-bp}}$$

and

(18.13)
$$P_f = \sum_{t=1}^{n-2bp} \frac{c_t/2}{(1 + i/2)^t} + \frac{P_p}{(1 + i/2)^{2n-2bp}}$$

where all of the variables are as previously defined.

Observe that Equations 18.12 and 18.13 are simply versions of promised yield: derived measures which, in turn, are based on expected price performance at the *end* of the holding period (hp). Essentially, $n - hp$ defines the remaining term to maturity of the issue at the end of the investor's holding period, i.e., the number of years (or six-month periods) remaining at the date the issue is to be sold. The determination of P_f is based on coupon (c_t) and par value (P_p), both of which are given. In contrast, the length of the holding period, and, therefore, the number of years remaining to maturity at date of sale ($n - hp$), and the expected prevailing market yield at time of sale (i) must be forecast by the analyst. Once this information is obtained/generated, the future price of the obligation can be determined. The real difficulty (and potential source of error) in specifying P_f lies in formulating hp and i.

As an example, consider the 10 percent, 25-year bond just discussed. Assume that you bought this bond at about $842, which implies a yield to maturity of 12 percent. Based upon extensive analysis, you expect the market yield on this bond to decline to 8 percent in two years. Therefore, at this point you want to compute what the future price (P_f) will be of the bond to estimate your expected rate of return if you are correct. As noted, the two estimates you make are the holding period (2 years), which implies that the remaining life of the bond is 23 years, and the market yield of 8 percent. Using an annual model, the future price is:

$$P_f = 100 \sum_{t=1}^{23} \frac{1}{(1.08)} + 1000 \frac{1}{(1.08)^{23}}$$
$$= 100(10.3711) + 1000(.1703)$$
$$= \$1,037.11 + 170.30$$
$$= \$1,207.41.$$

Further, your approximate annual return on this investment would be:

$$APY = \frac{100 + \dfrac{1,207 - 842}{2}}{\dfrac{1,207 + 842}{2}}$$
$$= \frac{100 + 182.50}{1,024.50}$$
$$= 27.57\%.$$

Price and Yield Determination on Noninterest Dates

So far, in the bond valuation process we have assumed that the investor buys (or sells) an obligation precisely on the date that interest is due. As a result, the measures are only accurate when issues are traded exactly on coupon payment dates. If approximate yield or the annual compounding version of the present value based model is used, sufficient accuracy is normally obtained by simply employing the computed values, or, perhaps, by roughly extrapolating for transactions that take place on noninterest payment dates. The investor would be dealing with varying degrees of approximation as it is, and certainly a bit more will not upset matters.

However, when the semiannual version of the models is employed, and when high degrees of accuracy are necessary, another version of the price and yield model must be employed for transactions that occur on noninterest payment dates. Fortunately, to do this the basic models presented thus far need be extended only one more step, since, even in practice, the value of an issue that trades X years, Y months, and so many days from maturity is found by extrapolating the bond value (price or yield) for the month before and the month after the day of transaction. Thus, the valuation process involves full months to maturity rather than years or semiannual periods.[8]

Bond valuation on a noncoupon payment date involves the following simple algorithm:

1. Determine the price of the issue via the standard semiannual compounding model for the *next* coupon payment date.
2. Add the coupon payment to be received at the *next* coupon date (since it is not included in Step 1).
3. Discount this sum, which is equivalent to the value of the bond on the next coupon payment date, to its present value.
4. Adjust the computed value for the accrued interest.

This can be shown as:

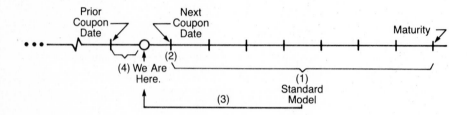

Essentially, we find the value of the bond on the next coupon date (Step 1), add the interest payment to be received on the next coupon date (Step 2), discount the sum of these back to the present (Step 3), and finally, net out accrued interest (Step 4). This can conveniently be put in equation form as follows:

$$(18.14) \qquad P_m = \left[\frac{\sum_{t=1}^{2n} \frac{c_t/2}{(1 + i/2)^t} + \frac{P_p}{(1 + i/2)^{2n}} + \frac{c_t}{2}}{(1 + i/2)^{m/6}} \right] - \frac{c_t}{2}\left(1 - \frac{m}{6}\right),$$

where:

m = the number of months to the next coupon payment date

n = the number of annual periods to maturity *after* the next coupon payment date, and all other variables are as defined previously.

An examination of Equation 18.14 quickly reveals the four steps in the algorithm. It is a suprisingly simple procedure and does not involve extensive computational complexity. This can be used to determine *yield* by solving for i (through iteration) or, when given a market yield, can also be used to determine *price* by solving for P_m. In addition, with slight variations of this basic (promised yield to maturity) model, yield to call and expected realized yield can be readily computed.

---

[8] Note that for corporate, agency, and municipal markets, a month is described as a 30-day period, regardless of the number of days actually in the month. In contrast, treasury obligations use a 365- (or 366-) day calendar and actually count the number of days in the month. For our purposes, we will assume that the standard 30-day month prevails.

To demonstrate the application of the model, consider the following example. Assume we want to find the price, on an accrued interest basis, of a $1,000, 10 percent bond with 12 years and 3 months remaining to maturity that is being traded to yield 8 percent. Using Equation 18.14, we can determine its price as follows:

$$P_m = \left[\frac{\sum\limits_{t=1}^{24} \dfrac{100/2}{(1.04)^t} + \dfrac{1.000}{(1.04)^{24}} + \dfrac{100}{2}}{(1.04)^{3/6}} \right] - \frac{100}{2}\left(1 - \frac{3}{6}\right)$$

$$= \left[\frac{50(15.247) + 1000(.3901) + 50}{1.01980} \right] - 50(.5)$$

$$= \left[\frac{1202.45}{1.01980} \right] - 25 = \$1,154.10.$$

This procedure is universal in finding the price or yield of an obligation that trades on any date other than the interest payment date. For those situations in which the issue trades within the month, Equation 18.14 is used to find the price (or yield) at full monthly intervals on both sides of the purchase date. To find the price of an issue that has 12 years, 3 months, and 15 days to maturity, one would value the obligation (in full monthly increments) on both sides of the 15 days; i.e., find the price with 12 years and 3 months to maturity, and with 12 years and 4 months to maturity. The value at 12 years, 3 months was determined above. What is lacking is the price figure for 12 years, 4 months (which, of course, is also computed via Equation 18.14). Once the investor has these two values, he would simply use extrapolation to determine the price or yield of the obligation.

Tax-Exempt Issues

Municipal bonds, treasury issues, and many agency obligations possess one common characteristic: their interest income is partially or fully tax-exempt. Recall that treasury and federal agency obligations are exempt from state and local taxation. In fact, some agencies are even free from federal income taxes (HUD project notes, for example). And, of course, the interest income on municipal obligations is exempt from federal and local levies.

Using promised yield as a basis of discussion, the tax status of an issue (including its ordinary income and capital gains tax liability) can be included in the valuation model as follows:

(18.15) $$P_m = \sum_{t=1}^{2n} \frac{C_t/2\ (1 - \tau)}{(1 + i/2)^t} + \frac{P_p - k\ (P_p - P_m)}{(1 + i/2)^{2n}},$$

where:

τ = the investor's marginal tax liability on ordinary income

k = the investor's capital gains tax rate, and the other terms are as defined above.

While Equation 18.15 provides a measure of *after-tax* promised yield, it follows that, with slight variations, yield to call and realized yield can also be modified to readily accommodate the various tax effects and transactions that occur on non-interest payments dates.

In addition, the tax-adjusted models can be used when some of the issues are subject to normal taxation and others are totally tax-free. The valuation process itself adjusts for the specific tax liability of the obligation in generating after-tax yield (or price), because the specification of τ and k in Equation 18.15 does not define the source or extent of tax liability. As a result, these variables should include appropriate federal, state, and/or local tax rates (depending, of course, on the exposure of the specific issue). For example, τ would equal 0 for a person holding a municipal bond in the state of Texas, since Texas has no state or local income taxes. Likewise, it would be 0 for a California resident holding a California issue. In contrast, however, that same California issue would require a $\tau > 0$ for a person living in New York City, as the issue would not be tax-exempt for residents of New York, and residents of that city are subject to state and local income taxes.

Place of residency is, of course, totally irrelevant in the case of capital gains. Since the mechanics of yield and price valuation for the tax-adjusted models are no different than those for other approximate yield and present value based models, it is unnecessary to provide a detailed illustration of computational techniques. Instead, if you want to try your hand, consider the following example. Assume a resident of Texas (with $\tau = 0$) is considering the purchase of a 5 percent, 25-year municipal obligation that is currently priced at \$3,827. (Remember par value with municipals is normally \$5,000). The investor has a 20 percent capital gains tax rate and wants to determine the after-tax promised yield of the issue.[9]

Undoubtedly the most popular and one of the most often cited measures of performance for municipal issues is the *fully taxable equivalent yield* (FTEY). This is a simple adjustment for computing promised yields for those issues with tax-exempt features. The process involves determining promised yield using any of the variations presented above. The computed promised yield figure is then adjusted to reflect the rate of return that must be earned on fully taxable issues, such as corporates, in order to provide a yield equivalent to the fully or partially tax-exempt obligation. It is measured as:

(18.16)
$$FTEY = \frac{i}{1 - T},$$

where:

i = promised yield

T = the amount and type of tax *exemption* provided by the issue in question, and all other terms are as defined earlier.

A caveat is in order, however. This simple computation *is applicable only to par bonds or current coupon obligations*, such as new issues. In other words, the

---

[9] Using Equation 18.15, the answer is 6.91 percent.

measure considers only interest income and, by ignoring capital gains, is inappropriate for issues trading at significant variation from par value. Like τ in the after-tax promised yield model (Equation 18.15), T in the fully taxable equivalent yield computation includes any applicable federal, state, or local income taxes. Rather than dealing with an issue's tax liability, as was done with Equation 18.15, T is concerned with the extent of tax *exemption* provided by the bond.

Bond Yield Books

Bond value tables, commonly known as *bond books* or *yield books* are available to eliminate much of the mathematics from bond valuation. An illustration of a page from a yield book is provided in Figure 18.2. It is like a present value

FIGURE 18.2
A Yield Book

A — YEARS and MONTHS — 8%

Yield	14-6	15-0	15-6	16-0	16-6	17-0	17-6	18-0
4.00	143.69	144.79	145.88	146.94	147.98	149.00	150.00	150.98
4.20	140.96	141.97	142.97	143.95	144.91	145.84	146.76	147.66
4.40	138.29	139.23	140.14	141.04	141.92	142.78	143.62	144.44
4.60	135.69	136.55	137.39	138.21	139.01	139.80	140.56	141.31
4.80	133.15	133.94	134.71	135.46	136.19	136.90	137.60	138.28
5.00	130.68	131.40	132.09	132.77	133.44	134.09	134.72	135.33
5.20	128.27	128.92	129.55	130.16	130.76	131.35	131.92	132.47
5.40	125.91	126.50	127.07	127.62	128.16	128.69	129.20	129.70
5.60	123.62	124.14	124.65	125.15	125.63	126.10	126.55	127.00
5.80	121.38	121.84	122.30	122.74	123.16	123.58	123.98	124.38
6.00	119.19	119.60	120.00	120.39	120.77	121.13	121.49	121.83
6.10	118.11	118.50	118.87	119.24	119.59	119.93	120.26	120.59
6.20	117.05	117.41	117.76	118.10	118.43	118.75	119.06	119.36
6.30	116.01	116.34	116.67	116.98	117.29	117.58	117.87	118.15
6.40	114.97	115.28	115.58	115.88	116.16	116.43	116.70	116.96
6.50	113.95	114.24	114.51	114.78	115.05	115.30	115.54	115.78
6.60	112.94	113.20	113.46	113.71	113.95	114.18	114.40	114.62
6.70	111.94	112.18	112.42	112.64	112.86	113.07	113.28	113.48
6.80	110.95	111.17	111.39	111.59	111.79	111.99	112.17	112.35
6.90	109.98	110.18	110.37	110.56	110.74	110.91	111.08	111.24
7.00	109.02	109.20	109.37	109.53	109.70	109.85	110.00	110.15
7.10	108.07	108.22	108.38	108.52	108.67	108.80	108.94	109.07
7.20	107.13	107.27	107.40	107.53	107.65	107.77	107.89	108.00
7.30	106.20	106.32	106.43	106.54	106.65	106.75	106.85	106.95
7.40	105.28	105.38	105.48	105.57	105.66	105.75	105.83	105.92
7.50	104.37	104.46	104.54	104.61	104.69	104.76	104.83	104.90
7.60	103.48	103.54	103.61	103.67	103.73	103.78	103.84	103.89
7.70	102.59	102.64	102.69	102.73	102.78	102.82	102.86	102.90
7.80	101.72	101.75	101.78	101.81	101.84	101.87	101.89	101.92
7.90	100.85	100.87	100.88	100.90	100.91	100.93	100.94	100.95
8.00	100.00	100.00	100.00	100.00	100.00	100.00	100.00	100.00
8.10	99.16	99.14	99.13	99.11	99.10	99.09	99.07	99.06
8.20	98.32	98.29	98.26	98.24	98.21	98.18	98.16	98.14
8.30	97.50	97.45	97.41	97.37	97.33	97.29	97.26	97.22
8.40	96.68	96.62	96.57	96.51	96.46	96.41	96.37	96.32
8.50	95.88	95.81	95.74	95.67	95.61	95.55	95.49	95.43
8.60	95.08	95.00	94.91	94.84	94.76	94.69	94.62	94.56
8.70	94.29	94.20	94.10	94.01	93.93	93.85	93.77	93.69
8.80	93.52	93.41	93.30	93.20	93.10	93.01	92.92	92.84
8.90	92.75	92.63	92.51	92.40	92.29	92.19	92.09	92.00
9.00	91.99	91.86	91.73	91.61	91.49	91.38	91.27	91.17
9.10	91.24	91.09	90.96	90.82	90.70	90.57	90.46	90.35
9.20	90.50	90.34	90.19	90.05	89.91	89.78	89.66	89.54
9.30	89.76	89.60	89.44	89.29	89.14	89.00	88.87	88.74
9.40	89.04	88.86	88.69	88.53	88.38	88.23	88.09	87.96
9.50	88.32	88.13	87.96	87.79	87.62	87.47	87.32	87.18
9.60	87.61	87.42	87.23	87.05	86.88	86.72	86.56	86.42
9.70	86.91	86.71	86.51	86.32	86.15	85.98	85.81	85.66
9.80	86.22	86.01	85.80	85.61	85.42	85.24	85.08	84.91
9.90	85.54	85.31	85.10	84.90	84.70	84.52	84.35	84.18
10.00	84.86	84.63	84.41	84.20	84.00	83.81	83.61	83.45
10.20	83.53	83.28	83.05	82.82	82.61	82.41	82.21	82.03
10.40	82.23	81.97	81.72	81.48	81.25	81.04	80.84	80.64
10.60	80.96	80.68	80.42	80.17	79.93	79.71	79.50	79.29
10.80	79.72	79.43	79.15	78.89	78.64	78.41	78.19	77.98
11.00	78.50	78.20	77.91	77.64	77.39	77.14	76.91	76.70
11.20	77.31	77.00	76.71	76.43	76.16	75.91	75.67	75.45
11.40	76.15	75.83	75.52	75.24	74.96	74.70	74.46	74.23
11.60	75.02	74.68	74.37	74.07	73.79	73.53	73.28	73.04
11.80	73.90	73.56	73.24	72.94	72.65	72.38	72.13	71.89
12.00	72.82	72.47	72.14	71.83	71.54	71.26	71.00	70.76

8% — YEARS and MONTHS — B

Yield	18-6	19-0	19-6	20-0	20-6	21-0	21-6	22-0
4.00	151.94	152.88	153.81	154.71	155.60	156.47	157.32	158.16
4.20	148.54	149.40	150.25	151.08	151.89	152.68	153.46	154.22
4.40	145.24	146.03	146.80	147.56	148.29	149.02	149.72	150.41
4.60	142.05	142.76	143.46	144.15	144.82	145.47	146.11	146.74
4.80	138.95	139.60	140.23	140.85	141.45	142.05	142.62	143.19
5.00	135.94	136.52	137.10	137.65	138.20	138.73	139.25	139.76
5.20	133.02	133.54	134.06	134.56	135.05	135.52	135.99	136.44
5.40	130.18	130.65	131.11	131.56	132.00	132.42	132.84	133.24
5.60	127.43	127.85	128.26	128.66	129.04	129.42	129.79	130.14
5.80	124.76	125.13	125.49	125.84	126.18	126.51	126.84	127.15
6.00	122.17	122.49	122.81	123.11	123.41	123.70	123.98	124.25
6.10	120.90	121.20	121.50	121.78	122.06	122.33	122.59	122.84
6.20	119.65	119.93	120.21	120.47	120.73	120.98	121.22	121.46
6.30	118.42	118.68	118.93	119.18	119.42	119.65	119.87	120.09
6.40	117.21	117.45	117.68	117.91	118.13	118.34	118.55	118.75
6.50	116.01	116.23	116.45	116.66	116.86	117.05	117.24	117.43
6.60	114.83	115.04	115.23	115.42	115.61	115.79	115.96	116.13
6.70	113.67	113.86	114.04	114.21	114.38	114.54	114.70	114.85
6.80	112.53	112.69	112.86	113.01	113.17	113.31	113.46	113.59
6.90	111.40	111.55	111.70	111.84	111.97	112.11	112.23	112.36
7.00	110.29	110.42	110.55	110.68	110.80	110.92	111.03	111.14
7.10	109.19	109.31	109.42	109.54	109.64	109.75	109.85	109.94
7.20	108.11	108.21	108.31	108.41	108.50	108.59	108.68	108.77
7.30	107.04	107.13	107.22	107.30	107.38	107.46	107.54	107.61
7.40	105.99	106.07	106.14	106.21	106.28	106.35	106.41	106.47
7.50	104.96	105.02	105.08	105.14	105.19	105.25	105.30	105.35
7.60	103.94	103.99	104.04	104.08	104.12	104.16	104.20	104.24
7.70	102.93	102.97	103.00	103.04	103.07	103.10	103.13	103.16
7.80	101.94	101.96	101.99	102.01	102.03	102.05	102.07	102.09
7.90	100.96	100.98	100.99	101.00	101.01	101.02	101.03	101.04
8.00	100.00	100.00	100.00	100.00	100.00	100.00	100.00	100.00
8.10	99.05	99.04	99.03	99.02	99.01	99.00	98.99	98.98
8.20	98.11	98.09	98.07	98.05	98.03	98.01	97.99	97.98
8.30	97.19	97.16	97.13	97.10	97.07	97.04	97.01	96.99
8.40	96.28	96.24	96.20	96.16	96.12	96.08	96.05	96.02
8.50	95.38	95.33	95.28	95.23	95.19	95.14	95.10	95.06
8.60	94.49	94.43	94.37	94.32	94.26	94.21	94.16	94.12
8.70	93.62	93.55	93.48	93.42	93.36	93.30	93.24	93.19
8.80	92.76	92.68	92.60	92.53	92.46	92.40	92.34	92.28
8.90	91.91	91.82	91.74	91.66	91.58	91.51	91.44	91.38
9.00	91.07	90.98	90.89	90.80	90.72	90.64	90.56	90.49
9.10	90.24	90.14	90.04	89.95	89.86	89.78	89.70	89.62
9.20	89.43	89.32	89.21	89.11	89.02	88.93	88.84	88.76
9.30	88.62	88.51	88.40	88.29	88.19	88.09	88.00	87.91
9.40	87.83	87.71	87.59	87.48	87.37	87.27	87.17	87.08
9.50	87.05	86.92	86.79	86.68	86.57	86.46	86.36	86.26
9.60	86.27	86.14	86.01	85.89	85.77	85.66	85.55	85.45
9.70	85.51	85.37	85.24	85.11	84.99	84.87	84.76	84.66
9.80	84.76	84.62	84.48	84.34	84.22	84.10	83.98	83.87
9.90	84.02	83.87	83.72	83.59	83.46	83.33	83.21	83.10
10.00	83.29	83.13	82.98	82.84	82.71	82.58	82.45	82.34
10.20	81.86	81.69	81.53	81.38	81.24	81.10	80.97	80.85
10.40	80.46	80.28	80.12	79.96	79.81	79.67	79.53	79.40
10.60	79.10	78.92	78.74	78.58	78.42	78.28	78.13	78.00
10.80	77.78	77.59	77.41	77.24	77.08	76.92	76.78	76.64
11.00	76.49	76.29	76.11	75.93	75.76	75.60	75.45	75.31
11.20	75.23	75.03	74.84	74.66	74.49	74.33	74.17	74.03
11.40	74.01	73.80	73.61	73.42	73.25	73.08	72.93	72.78
11.60	72.82	72.61	72.41	72.22	72.04	71.87	71.71	71.56
11.80	71.66	71.44	71.24	71.05	70.87	70.70	70.53	70.38
12.00	70.53	70.31	70.10	69.91	69.72	69.55	69.39	69.23

SOURCE: Reproduced with permission from Expanded Bond Values Publication #83, pp. 879–880, copyright 1970 Financial Publishing Co., Boston, Mass.

interest factor table to the extent that a matrix of bond prices is provided relative to a stated coupon rate, various terms to maturity (on the horizontal axis), and promised yields (on the vertical axis). Such a table allows the user to readily determine either promised yield or price. Observe in Situation A that a 17 1/2-year, 8 percent bond yielding 10 percent would carry a price of 83.63. Likewise, in Situation B, a 20-year issue which is priced at 109.54 would yield 7.10 percent. As might be expected, access to computers via office and portable terminals has substantially reduced the need for and use of yield books. For our purposes though, it is essential that the detailed mechanics and subtleties of the various yield and price models be fully understood in order to appreciate the dimensions of promised yield, yield to call, realized yield, and bond prices.

DETERMINANTS OF BOND YIELDS AND YIELD SPREADS

The value of a bond is equal to the present value of its future cash flow stream. An important dimension of the bond valuation model is the rate at which the future cash flows are discounted. In the promised yield version of the model, this rate reflects prevailing market interest rates and indicates the importance of interest rates in the bond valuation process. Because the prices of both new and seasoned issues are closely related to interest behavior, they are stated in terms of economic cost, *bond yields* or *interest rates*. Thus, market interest rates are reflected in bond yields which, in turn, influence the cost of funds to issuers in the new issues market, the return to investors in the new and seasoned issues segments of the market, and the price behavior of obligations in the secondary market. It follows that bond managers must constantly evaluate the current level of market interest rates and expected changes in these rates.

This book takes a practical view of the role of interest rates in the bond investment decision. We maintain that the assessment of interest rates is absolutely essential to the attainment of attractive bond portfolio returns. But the assessment of interest rates and the development of interest rate formulations are complex economic matters which often involve extensive econometric modeling, a task we shall leave to the professional economist. Instead, our goal as bond investors and bond portfolio managers should be to continually monitor current and expected interest rate behavior. This can be done informally if attention is paid to the determinants of interest rates. A bond portfolio manager can assess the *major* dimensions of interest rate behavior on his own and rely on economic service bureaus for more detailed insight into the structure and behavior of market rates. This is precisely the way many bond houses and large bond portfolio management firms operate.

Fundamental Determinants of Interest Rates

According to published market sources, average interest rates for long-term corporate bonds during 1981 amounted to over 16 percent. By early 1984 the same average corporate bond rate had dropped to 11 percent. A primary concern to the bond investor is *why* interest rates behave this way. Obviously, bond prices rose dramatically during the period when market interest rates dropped and very attractive returns were obtained by aggressive, knowledgeable bond investors. Although this is only a single case in point, it indicates the need for monitoring interest rates. Essentially, interest rates (r) can be specified according to the following conceptual model:

$$(18.17) \qquad r = RFR + RP + I,$$

where:

$$RFR = \text{the risk-free rate of interest}$$

$$RP = \text{the risk premium}$$

$$I = \text{expected inflation.}$$

While Equation 18.17 appears deceptively simple, it is a complete statement of the complex nature of interest rate behavior. The difficult part is the specification of *future* behavior with regard to such aspects as inflation, default, and other economic considerations. In this regard, interest rates are not unlike stock prices since they are extremely difficult to forecast with any degree of accuracy.[10]

In essence, interest rates can be viewed as being related to economic and issue characteristics:

$$r = f \text{ (Economic Forces + Issue Characteristics)}$$

$$= (RFR + I) + RP.$$

This is nothing more than a rearranged version of Equation 18.17, but it facilitates a more thorough discussion of the fundamental determinants of interest rates.[11]

The pure rate of interest (RFR) is the economic cost of money, and it represents the opportunity cost necessary to compensate individuals for foregoing consumption. The pure rate of interest is some interest rate level below which investors would be indifferent to holding either cash or a financial asset like bonds. The pure rate is that fairly stable marginal rate of return which must be offered in order to induce individuals to save or invest.

Inflation is the other economic dimension of interest rates. The *level of inflation* (I) is added to the risk-free rate (RFR) in order to specify a general *market based* level of interest. For example, if the *RFR* is 3 percent, and expected inflation (I) is 6 percent, then it follows that the market based (nominal) risk-free rate of interest (r) would equal approximately 9 percent. Given the stability of the RFR, it is clear that *the wide swings in* r *experienced in the past decade or so can largely be attributable to swings in real or perceived inflation.*[12]

---

[10] Oswald D. Bowlin and John D. Martin, "Extrapolations of Yields over the Short Run; Forecast or Folly?" *Journal of Monetary Economics,* 1 (1975): 275–488; and Stephen F. Leroy, "Interest Rates and the Inflation Premium," Federal Reserve Bank of Kansas City Monthly *Review* (May 1973): 11–18.

[11] For an excellent and extensive exploration of interest rates and interest rate behavior, see James C. Van Horne, *Financial Market Rates and Flows,* 2nd ed. (Englewood Cliffs, N.J.: Prentice-Hall, 1984).

[12] In this regard, see R. W. Hafer, "Inflation: Assessing Its Recent Behavior and Future Prospects," Federal Reserve Bank of St. Louis *Review,* 65 no. 7 (August/September 1983): 36–41; Milton Friedman and Anna J. Schwartz, *Monetary Trends in the United States and the United Kingdom: Their Relation to Income, Prices, and Interest Rates, 1867–1975* (University of Chicago Press, 1982).

Supply and demand for loanable funds are the fundamental variables within the economic dimensions of r. For example, as the supply of loanable funds increases, the level of interest rates declines, other things being equal; the opposite effect, of course, holds when the demand for loanable funds increases. On the *supply side*, the actions of the Federal Reserve Open Market Committee have a definite influence on the cost of funds because they affect the supply of money. In addition, the supply of loanable funds is influenced by institutional investment policies. The technical side of the market, including such things as the unsold inventory of new issues held by underwriters and the new issue calendar, also affects supply.

Affecting demand are the capital and operating needs of the U.S. government, federal agencies, state and local governments, corporations, and institutions.[13] Essentially, the *net* intensity of demand varies according to requirements in each of the sectors. The taxation and expenditures policy (fiscal policy) of the federal government often leads to deficit budgets and increases demand for loanable funds from the treasury. Likewise, the level of consumer demand, along with the amount of internally generated funds (net of dividend payouts) will help determine corporate needs to raise capital.

An article by Feldstein and Eckstein (FE)[14] described the fundamental determinants of interest rates using many of the same economic variables noted above. They attempted to define the determinants of yield on seasoned long-term Moody's AAA-rated corporate bonds over the 62 quarters from 1954 through 1969. FE found that bond yields were inversely related to money supply and directly related to the level of real personal income (used as a proxy for economic activity), the demand for loanable funds (from the treasury), the level of inflation, and changes in short-run interest rate expectations (included as a psychological facet of market behavior). The r^2 value of their model was a hefty 99.2 percent. Variable relationships with interest rates were as expected, and many of the economic variables noted above were significant determinants. Such findings imply that because of the importance of interest rates in yield and price behavior, investors should monitor such economic factors as the supply and demand for loanable funds, Federal Reserve policy, fiscal policy, and prices.

Interest rates (r) are also influenced by issue characteristics. The *risk premium* (RP) component of r is directly associated with the characteristics of the issue and issuer. Whereas the economic forces (the risk-free rate and inflation) reflect a market- or systemwide level of interest rates, issue characteristics are unique to individual securities or market sectors. Thus, the differences in the yields of corporate and treasury issues are *not* caused by economic forces but by differential issue characteristics, i.e., differences in the risk premium.

There are three major components within the risk premium that should be considered by bond investors and portfolio managers:

---

[13] William C. Freund and Edward D. Zinbarg, "Application of Flow of Funds to Interest Rate Forecasting," *The Journal of Finance*, 13 no. 2 (May 1963): 231–248; and Edmund A. Mennis, "Aggregate Measures of Corporate Profits," *Financial Analysts Journal*, 20 no. 1 (January–February 1964): 30–31.

[14] Martin Feldstein and Otto Eckstein, "The Fundamental Determinants of the Interest Rate," *The Review of Economics and Statistics*, 52 no. 4 (November 1970): 363–375.

1. Quality differentials (or risk of default)
2. Term to maturity, which can affect rate uncertainty as well as yield and price volatility
3. Indenture provisions (including collateral, call features, and sinking fund provisions).

Of the three, quality and maturity considerations are the most important and dominate the risk premium.

Quality considerations reflect the risk of default. These are largely captured in agency ratings. The matter of quality is primarily the ability of the issuer to service outstanding debt obligations. The greater the ability of the issuer to service the debt, the lower the risk of default. Quality considerations mean yield differentials will exist not only between differently rated issues, but also between different market segments. For example, AAA-rated obligations possess lower risk of default than, say, BBB obligations do and, therefore, provide lower yield.

There is substantial empirical support for the position that quality derived risk premiums are largely dependent upon the intrinsic characteristics of the issuer.[15] However, quality based yield premiums are, at times, also closely related to prevailing economic conditions. When the economy becomes depressed and activity begins to slacken, the desire for quality increases, and higher quality issues are bid up in price as investors abandon low quality obligations to seek the security of higher rated bonds. Except in these times of depressed economic activity (when quality derived yield spreads are abnormally wide), the default risk component of the risk premium is fairly stable and tends to vary inversely with the quality of the issue.

Maturity is also an important determinant of the risk premium, because it affects the level of uncertainty assumed by the investor as well as price and yield volatility. While this component will be discussed in the section dealing with the term structure, it should be clear that, other things being equal, there is generally a positive relationship between the term to maturity of an issue and the level of interest rates.

Bond indenture provisions are the final risk premium determinant. Relevant aspects include the amount of collateral provided, the call feature, and sinking fund provisions. Collateral provides capital protection to the investor on those rare occasions of corporate insolvency and forced liquidation,[16] and it is the

---

[15] See for example: Lawrence Fisher, "Determinants of Risk Premiums on Corporate Bonds," *Journal of Political Economy*, 67 no. 3 (June 1959): 217; Larry K. Hastie, "Determinants of Municipal Bond Yields," *Journal of Financial and Quantitative Analysis*, 7 no. 3 (June 1972): 1729–1748; and Joseph J. Horton, Jr., "Statistical Classification of Municipal Bonds," *Journal of Bank Research* (Autumn 1970): 29–40. These are in addition to the numerous studies that examined the relationship between bond quality ratings and internal firm characteristics as discussed in Chapter 9.

[16] Harold G. Fraine and Robert H. Mills, "Effect of Defaults and Credit Determination on Yields of Corporate Bonds," *Journal of Finance*, 16 no. 3 (September 1961): 423–434.

factor that distinguishes a mortgage bond from a debenture obligation. Because it influences the quality of an issue, collateral is often an aspect of an agency rating. However, differences of several basis points are common for comparably rated issues which differ only in terms of collateral provisions.

The call feature is perhaps the most influential bond indenture provision. Other things being equal, the greater the call risk protection provided, the lower the market yield of the obligation, particularly for new issues and current coupon obligations.[17] Clearly, a ten-year deferred call feature provides more call risk protection than, say, a freely callable provision does and, therefore, should logically result in lower yield. This call protection becomes especially important and valuable during a period of high interest rates.

The final indenture provision affecting the risk premium is the sinking fund feature. This has a fairly nominal effect, and its main influence is felt in the new issues market. The sinking fund provision is normally a means of reducing the investor's risk and, therefore, should result in lower yield for two major reasons. First, a sinking fund reduces default risk by providing for orderly debt service and systematic reduction of outstanding principle. Second, purchases for a sinking fund are viewed as providing support for the bond because of added demand and also a more liquid secondary market because of the increased trading. In fact, Jen and Wert[18] demonstrated that the lower yields on sinking fund issues can be explained in terms of the term structure of interest rates. Since sinking fund provisions result in reduced average maturity, their effect is to reduce the risk premium component of interest rates much like a shorter maturity would reduce yield.[19]

Thus, such issue characteristics as sinking funds, call features, and collateral, along with term to maturity and risk of default, should be carefully evaluated in order to fully appreciate current and expected levels of market yield on *competitive* fixed income securities.

Term Structure of Interest Rates

The term structure of interest rates has long intrigued theoreticians, academicians, and practitioners. As a result, this concept has been the subject of consider-

[17] Frank C. Jen and James E. Wert, "The Value of the Deferred Call Privilege," *National Banking Review*, 3 no. 1 (March 1966): 369–378; and Michael D. Joehnk and James E. Wert, "The Call-Risk Performance of the Discounted Seasoned Issue," *Mississippi Valley Journal of Business and Economics,* 9 no. 2 (Winter 1973–1974): 1–15, William Marshall and Jess B. Yawitz, "Optimal Terms of the Call Provision on a Corporate Bond," *Journal of Financial Research*, 3 no. 3 (Fall, 1980): 203–211. Michael G. Ferri, "Systematic Return Risk and the Call Risk of Corporate Debt Instruments," *Journal of Financial Research*, 1 no. 1 (Winter 1978): 1–13. For an analysis of the profitability of refunding by the borrower, see Oswald D. Bowlin, "The Refunding Decision: Another Special Case in Capital Budgeting," *Journal of Finance*, 21 no. 1 (March 1966): 55–68; and Aharon R. Ofer and Robert A. Taggart, Jr., "Bond Refunding: A Clarifying Analysis," *Journal of Finance*, 32 no. 1 (March 1977): 21–30; Jess B. Yawitz and James A. Anderson, "The Effect of Bond Refunding on Shareholder Wealth," *Journal of Finance*, 32 no. 5 (December 1977): 1738–46; and W. M. Boyce and A. J. Kalotay, "Optimum Bond Calling and Refunding," *Interfaces, The Institute of Management Science,* 9 no. 4 (November 1979): 36–49.

[18] Jen and Wert, "The Value of the Deferred Call Privilege."

[19] For a further discussion of sinking funds, see Edward A. Dyl and Michael D. Joehnk, "Sinking Funds and the Cost of Corporate Debt," *Journal of Finance,* 34 no. 4 (September 1979): 887–893; A. J. Kalotay, "On the Management of Sinking Funds," *Financial Management*, 10 no. 2 (Summer 1981): 34–40; A. J. Kalotay, "Sinking Funds and the Realized Cost of Debt," *Financial Management*, 11 no. 1 (Spring 1982): 43–54.

FIGURE 18.3
Construction of a Yield Curve

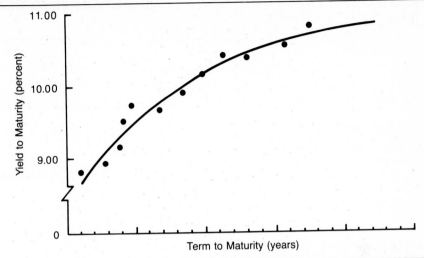

able theoretical and empirical work.[20] Burton Malkiel notes in one of his works:

> . . . indeed the major reasons for differences in bond yields may be unrelated to the maturity of the securities involved. Nevertheless, one of the most intriguing differences among market interest rates concerns the relationship among the yield of high grade securities that differ only in their term to maturity . . .[21]

The term structure of interest rates (or the *yield curve* as it is more popularly known) is a static function which relates *term* to maturity to *yield* to maturity at *a given point in time.* Thus, it represents a cross section of yields for a category of bonds that *are comparable in all respects but maturity.* The quality of the issues must be held constant, as should coupon, call feature, and perhaps even industry category. One can derive different yield curves for treasury issues, government agencies, prime grade municipals, AAA utilities, and so on.

As an example, consider Figure 18.3. The yield curve is constructed for a sample of U.S. Treasury obligations. Yield to maturity information on a variety of comparable treasury issues was obtained from *The Wall Street Journal.* These promised yields are represented on the graph by the several plotted points. After the yields are plotted, the yield curve itself is drawn.

---

[20] See, for example: J. Huston McCulloch, "Measuring the Term Structure of Interest Rates," *Journal of Business,* 44 no. 1 (January 1971): 19–31; William T. Carleton and Ian A. Cooper, "Estimation and Uses of the Term Structure of Interest Rates," *Journal of Finance,* 31 no. 4 (September 1976): 1067–1084; Burton G. Malkiel, *The Term Structure of Interest Rates* (Princeton, N.J.: Princeton University Press, 1966); David Meiselman, *The Term Structure of Interest Rates* (Englewood Cliffs, N.J.: Prentice-Hall, 1962); and Martin E. Ecols and Jan W. Elliott, "A Quantitative Yield Curve Model of Estimating the Term Structure of Interest Rates," *Journal of Financial and Quantitative Analysis,* 11 no. 1 (March 1976): 80–90.

[21] Burton G. Malkiel, *The Term Structure of Interest Rates: Theory, Empirical Evidence, and Applications* (New York: The McCaleb–Seiler Publishing Company, 1970), 12.

FIGURE 18.4
Types of Yield Curves

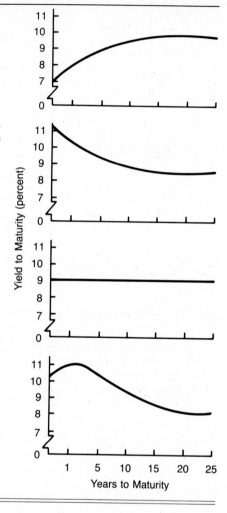

A Rising Yield Curve is formed when the yields on short-term issues are low and rise consistently with longer maturities and flatten out at the extremes.

A Declining Yield Curve is formed when the yields on short-term issues are high and yields on subsequently longer maturities decline consistently.

A Flat Yield Curve has approximately equal yields on short-term and long-term issues.

A Humped Yield Curve is formed when yields on intermediate-term issues are above those on short-term issues; and the rates on long-term issues decline to levels below those for the short-term and then level out.

All yield curves, of course, do not have the same shape as Figure 18.3. Quite the contrary, for, while yield curves per se are static in nature, *their behavior over time is quite fluid!* As a result, the shape of the yield curve can undergo dramatic alterations. In particular, it can follow one of the four patterns shown in Figure 18.4. The ascending curve is the most common and tends to prevail when interest rates are at low or modest levels. The declining yield curve is relatively common and tends to exist when rates are at relatively high levels. The humped yield curve occurs when interest rates are extremely high and about to retreat to more normal levels. Finally, there is the flat yield curve which rarely exists for any period of time. In all of the yield curve illustrations, the slope of the line tends to level off after 15 years. This is common market behavior. After a point ($\cong 15$ years), promised yield differentials which exist with longer maturities tend to be rather insignificant, especially relative to the spreads that occur at the shorter end.

While the effects of term to maturity on comparative promised yield (r) are obvious from examining the various shapes of the term structure, it is *not* equally clear why the term structure assumes different shapes. Fortunately, there is an extensive body of theoretical and empirical literature available to help explain the shape of yield curves. Three major theories are available: the expectations hypothesis, the liquidity preference hypothesis, and the segmented market hypothesis.[22]

Expectations Hypothesis.   According to this theory, the shape of the term structure is explained by the interest rate expectations of market participants. More specifically, *any long-term rate is simply the geometric mean of current and future one-year rates expected to prevail over the horizon of the issue.*

In essence, a series of intermediate and long-term rates are part of the term structure, each of which, in turn, is a reflection of the geometric average of current and expected one-year rates. Under such conditions, the equilibrium long-term rate is clearly that which the long-term investor would expect to earn through successive investments in short-term securities over an investment horizon equal to the term to maturity of the longer-term issue. This relationship can be formalized in a general manner as follows:

(18.18) $(1 + {_t}R_N) = [(1 + {_t}R_1)(1 + {_{t+1}}r_1) \cdots (1 + {_{t+n-1}}r_1)]^{1/N}$

where:

R_N = actual long-term rate

N = term to maturity (in years) of long issue

R = current one-year rate

${_{t+i}}r_1$ = expected one-year yield during some future period, $t + i$.

As a practical approximation of Equation 18.18, it is, of course, possible to use the *arithmetic* average of one-year rates to generate long-term yields.

The expectations theory can account for any shape of yield curve. If short-term rates are expected to rise in the future, then the yield curve will be ascending; if short-term rates are expected to fall, then the long-term rates will lie below the short-term rates and the term structure will descend. Similar explanation can be made for flat and humped yield curves. Consider the following example of how the expectations hypothesis can explain the shape of the term structure of interest rates. Given:

$${_t}R_1 = 5\ 1/2\% \qquad {_{t+1}}r_1 = 6\% \qquad {_{t+2}}r_1 = 7\ 1/2\% \qquad {_{t+3}}r_1 = 8\ 1/2\%$$

---

[22] For a more extensive discussion of the alternative theories of the term structure of interest rates, see Malkiel, *Term Structure of Interest Rates: Theory, Empirical Evidence and Applications* and James C. Van Horne, *Financial Markets Rate and Flows* 2nd ed.

and also that:

$$_tR_1 = 5.50\% \text{ (given)}$$

$$_tR_2 = (.055 + .06)/2 = 5.75\%$$

$$_tR_3 = (.055 + .06 + .075)/3 = 6.33\%$$

$$_tR_4 = (.055 + .06 + .075 + .085)/4 = 6.88\%.$$

In the above illustration (which uses the arithmetic average as an approximation of the geometric mean), the yield curve is upward sloping because investors currently expect future short-term rates to be above current short-term rates. This is not how the term structure is formally constructed. It is constructed as demonstrated in Figure 18.3 by using prevailing promised yields for issues with different maturities. Rather, what the expectations hypothesis attempts to explain is *why* the yield curve is upward sloping, downward sloping, humped, or flat. It attempts to explain the type of expectations implicit in various term structures. The evidence is fairly substantial (and convincing) that the expectations hypothesis is a workable and (somewhat) practical explanation of the term structure.[23]

The implications of the expectations hypothesis are, of course, quite clear. If, for example, lower rates are more likely to occur in the future than high yields are, then the term structure should be descending. This expectation would suggest that long-term bonds may be attractive investments, because the investor would want to lock in prevailing higher yields (which should decline in the future) and/or capture the capital gains potential that should accompany a decline in rates. Such expectations based action on the part of investors will only reinforce the descending shape of the yield curve as long maturities are bid up (and yields decline) and short issues are avoided (so yields rise). These shifts between long- and short-term maturities will continue until equilibrium occurs or expectations are revised. Similarly, an ascending yield curve indicates that investors expect rates to rise. Under such conditions, investors would prefer shorter maturity securities, because the decline would not be as severe when rates rise and the shorter maturities can be rolled over (sold) and the proceeds used to invest in higher yielding securities when rates rise. Again, this preference will accentuate the rising curve as investors switch out of long-term securities into short-term securities.

Because of its documentation, relative simplicity, and intuitive appeal, the expectations hypothesis of the term structure of interest rates is widely accepted in both academia and in the market.

---

[23] See for example David Meiselman, *The Term Structure of Interest Rates* (Englewood Cliffs, N.J.: Prentice-Hall, 1962); Franco Modigliani and Richard Sutch, "Innovations in Interest Rate Policy," *American Economic Review: Papers and Proceedings,* 56 no. 2 (May 1966): 178–197; and Anthony M. Santomero, "The Error-Learning Hypothesis and the Term Structure of Interest Rates in Eurodollars," *Journal of Finance,* 30 no. 3 (June 1975): 773–784; Thomas F. Cargill, "The Term Structure of Interest Rates: A Test of the Expectations Hypothesis," *Journal of Finance,* 30 no. 3 (June 1975): 761–772; James Van Horne, "Interest Rate Risk and the Term Structure of Interest Rates," *Journal of Political Economy,* 73 no. 3 (August 1965): 344–351. For some alternate evidence, see J. A. Grant, "Meiselman on the Structure of Interest Rates: A British Test," *Economica,* 37 no. 1 (February 1967): 184–196; A. Buse, "Interest Rates, The Meiselman Model and Random Numbers," *Journal of Political Economy,* 75 no. 1 (February 1967): 132–138.

Liquidity Preference. This theory holds that long-term securities should provide higher returns than short-term obligations do, since rational investors are willing to pay a price premium (i.e., accept lower yields) on short maturity obligations to avoid the risk of principal volatility, which is an intrinsic aspect of the long maturity obligation. The liquidity preference theory is the product of an important criticism leveled at the expectations hypothesis; i.e., one of the important (and questionable) assumptions of the latter hypothesis is that bond investors possess perfect certainty and perfect foresight. Given the uncertainty which exists in the real world, it follows that short-term issues should be more desirable than longer maturities because they can easily be converted into cash should unforeseen events occur. As noted by Malkiel, "the crux of the liquidity preference theory is that long term bonds, because of their greater potential price volatility, ought to offer the investor a larger return than the short term securities."[24]

The liquidity preference theory argues that, in the absence of market anomalies, the yield curve should be upward sloping and any other shape should be viewed as a temporary aberration. While this theory is an outgrowth of a major criticism leveled at the expectations hypothesis, it is also an extension of the same hypothesis. In particular, the formal liquidity preference position contends that the liquidity premium inherent in longer yields is formally expressed as an amount to be added to the expected future rate in arriving at long-term yields. Thus, because the liquidity premium (L) is provided to compensate the long-term investor, the general liquidity preference model is simply a variation of Equation 18.18 and may be stated as follows:

$$(1 + {_t}R_N) = [(1 + {_t}R_1)(1 + {_{t+1}}r_1 + L_2) \cdots$$
$$(1 + {_{t+N-1}}r_1 + L_N)]^{1/N}.$$

Like the expectations hypothesis, the liquidity preference theory has been subjected to empirical testing and found to possess considerable validity.[25] Available evidence indicates that expectations alone are not the unique determinant of the term structure because the yield curve shows a definite upward bias, which implies that a combination of the two theories is probably preferable to either alone.

Segmented Market Theory. The segmented market theory is a simple, yet interesting, variation of the theory of the term structure of interest rates. Unfortunately, the empirical evidence offered in support of this theory has been meager

---

[24] Burton Malkiel, *Term Structure of Interest Rates: Theory, Empirical Evidence and Applications*, (New York: The McCaleb–Seiler Publishing Company, 1970): 13.

[25] See Reuben A. Kessel, "The Cyclical Behavior of the Term Structure of Interest Rates," Occasional Paper 91, National Bureau of Economic Research, 1965; Phillip Cagan, *Essays on Interest Rates* (New York: Columbia University Press for the National Bureau of Economic Research, 1969); R. H. Scott, "A Liquidity Factor Contributing to Those Downward Sloping Yield Curves: 1900–1916," *Review of Economics and Statistics,* 45 no. 3 (August 1963): 328–329; and Jean M. Gray," New Evidence on the Term Structure of Interest Rates, 1884–1900," *Journal of Finance,* 28 no. 3 (June 1973): 635–646; Benjamin M. Friedman, "Interest Rate Expectations versus Forward Rates: Evidence from an Expectations Survey," *Journal of Finance,* 34 no. 4 (September 1979): 965–973; J. Huston McCulloch, "An Estimate of the Liquidity Premium," *Journal of Political Economy,* 83 no. 1 (January–February 1975): 95–119.

566

and rather inconclusive. Nonetheless, it still enjoys wide acceptance among market practitioners. The segmented market theory—also known as *preferred habitat*, the *institutional theory*, or the *hedging pressure theory*—asserts that different groups of institutional investors have different maturity needs which lead them to confine their security selections to specific maturity segments of the term structure. Thus, it is argued that the term structure is ultimately a function of the investment policies of major financial institutions.

Financial institutions tend to structure their investment policies in line with such things as their tax liability, liability structure, and the level of earnings demanded by savers and depositors. Therefore, because commercial banks, for example, are subject to normal corporate tax rates, and because their liability is generally short to intermediate in length (due to the short-term nature of time and demand deposits), we find commercial banks consistently invest in short- to intermediate-term municipals. In a like manner, because life insurance companies have little tax exposure and long-term obligations/liabilities, they tend to seek out high yielding, long-term corporate bonds. Therefore, the segmented market theoretician contends that these forces, along with legal and regulatory limitations, tend to coerce or to prompt alternative financial institutions into consistently allocating their resources to particular types and maturity segments of the market. In fact, in its strongest form, the segmented market theory holds that the maturity preferences of different investors and borrowers are so strong that they would *never* purchase securities outside of their preferred maturity range to take advantage of yield differentials. As a result, advocates of this hypothesis argue that the short and long maturity markets are effectively segmented, and yields are determined solely by supply and demand *within* each market maturity segment.

A study by Kane and Malkeil provide support for this theory based upon a survey of banks and insurance firms.[26] In contrast, some results are not supportive of a preferred habitat concept.[27]

Trading Implications of the Term Structure.   Information on maturity behavior can be used to formulate yield expectations by simply observing the shape of the term structure; e.g., if the shape is humped, then historical evidence suggests that the odds are fairly good that interest rates are about to undergo a broad based decline. Ardent expectations theorists would suggest that one need *only* examine the prevailing yield curve to obtain some idea of what interest rates should do in the future.

A more significant use of the term structure is in predicting future movements. In effect, it is essential to formulate predictions of the future shape of the term structure, along with interest rates, in order to assess yield volatility by maturity sector. Such an analysis allows those maturity segments which offer the greatest yield and, therefore, potential price appreciation to be identified.

[26] Edward J. Kane and Burton G. Malkiel, "The Term Structure of Interest Rates: An Analysis of a Survey of Interest Rate Expectations," *Review of Economics and Statistics*, 49 no. 3 (August 1967): 350–356.

[27] Franco Modigliani and Richard Sutch, "Innovations in Interest Rate Policy," *American Economic Review*, 56 no. 2 (May 1966): 178–197; S. W. Dobson, R. C. Sutch and D. E. Vanderford, "An Evaluation of Alternative Empirical Models of the Term Structure of Interest Rates," *Journal of Finance*, 31 no. 4 (September 1976): 1035–1065.

A final, albeit less important, use of the term structure is to identify under- or overpriced issues. Figure 18.3 contained a yield curve based on observations of individual promised yields prevailing at a given date. Since the issues are supposedly comparable in all respects but maturity, if an issue (whose yield is indicated by one of the plotted points on the graph) offers a promised yield substantially above the yield curve line, such an obligation is apparently providing an unusually high yield and, therefore, is underpriced. As a result, the issue should be viewed as one which offers a temporary investment opportunity. Likewise, issues that plot substantially below the yield curve provide abnormally low yields, are apparently overpriced, and may be good sell candidates. If the issues in the yield curve are really comparable, then one should assume that the chance of issue anomalies is remote and the under- or overpriced issues are a temporary market phenomenon. Of course, the higher the quality of the obligation, the more faith we can place in such an assumption. However, when dealing with rated obligations, such as corporates and municipals, it should be remembered that this behavior may not necessarily be an aberration so much as a rational market perception of differential quality *within* a rating class.

Yield Spreads

Another important dimension of interest rate behavior is yield spreads. Basically, *a yield spread is a difference in promised yield, which exists at any given point in time, between different bond issues or segments of the market*. These differences are issue or market specific and, thus, are additive to the rates determined by economic forces (RFR + I). Yield spreads are caused by quality differentials, different maturities, and unique call features. These variables lead to different promised yields for different types of securities.[28]

A yield spread may be either positive or negative depending upon whether a particular bond provides a promised yield to maturity in excess of (or less than) that offered on an alternative issue. Moreover, *the magnitude or direction of these yield spreads changes over time*. A yield spread narrows whenever the differences in yield become smaller, and it widens as the difference becomes greater.

Table 18.1 (page 568) provides average data on a variety of past yield spreads. Yield spreads change due to changing levels of interest rates and variations in investor perceptions of risk. Four major factors account for the existence of various yield differentials:

1. Different *segments* of the bond market (e.g., government vs. agencies, or governments vs. corporates)
2. Different *sectors* of the same market segment (e.g., prime-grade municipals vs. good-grade municipals, or AA utilities vs. BAA utilities, or AAA industrials vs. AAA public utilities)

[28] Michael D. Joehnk, "The Effects of Yield Spreads on Comparative Bond Price Behavior," *The Financial Planner,* 6 no. 4 (April 1977): 34–40; Dwight M. Jaffe, "Cyclical Variations in the Risk Structure of Interest Rates," *Journal of Monetary Economics,* 1 no. 3 (July, 1975): 309–325; Timothy Q. Cook and Patric H. Hendershott, "The Impact of Taxes, Risk and Relative Security Supplies on Interest Rate Differentials," *Journal of Finance,* 33 no. 4 (September, 1978): 1173–1186

TABLE 18.1
Selected Mean Yield Spreads (reported in basis points)

Comparisons	1977	1978	1979	1980	1981	1982
1. Short Governments: Long Governments	+148	+22	−62	−19	−81	−69
2. Long Governments: Long Aaa Corporates	+33	+27	+36	+72	+97	+154
3. Long Municipals: Long Aaa Corporates	+246	+283	+324	+343	+294	+213
4. Long Aaa Municipals: Long Baa Municipals	+92	+75	+81	+116	+133	+160
5. AA Utilities: BBB Utilities	+42	+42	+72	+130	+130	+138
6. AA Utilities: AA Industrials	−21	+84	−34	−48	−71	−76

SOURCE: *Federal Reserve Bulletin,* various issues; Standard & Poor's Statistical Service.

1. Median yield to maturity of a varying number of bonds with 2–4 years maturity and more than 10 years, respectively.
2. Long Aaa corporates based on yields to maturity on selected long-term bonds.
3. Long-term municipal issues based on a representative list of high-quality municipal bonds with a 20-year period to maturity being maintained.
4. General obligation municipal bonds only.
5. & 6. Based on a changing list of representative issues.

3.   Different *coupons* within a given market segment/sector (e.g., current coupon governments vs. deep discount governments, or new AA industrials vs. seasoned AA industrials), and

4.   Different *maturities* within a given market segment/sector (e.g., short agencies vs. long agencies, or 3-year prime municipals vs. 25-year prime municipals).

Whether yield spreads are a result of segment, sector, coupon, and/or maturity differences, they exist because there are different market rates associated with different types of bonds. A bond investor should evaluate yield spread *changes* because they influence price behavior and comparative realized yield performance over a given investment horizon. If (in the absence of yield spreads) two issues undergo an identical 150-basis-point change in yield over an equal investment horizon, then, other things being equal, there would be nothing to make one preferable to the other as an investment. In contrast, if the yield spread change over time is greater for one than for the other, then the issue that enjoyed the larger drop in yield would provide the superior realized yield (because of its greater price volatility).

There are three important types of yield spread conditions in the market: (1) a normal beginning yield spread which is expected to become *abnormal* (i.e., the spread is expected to move to an abnormally wide or narrow position); (2) a beginning yield spread that is abnormally wide or narrow but is expected to become *normal;* and (3) a normal beginning yield spread that is expected to change, but remains normal, with an anticipated *major swing* in market interest rates. Economic and market analysis would be necessary in order to arrive at any of these expectations. Each of the conditions possesses one common denominator: *the potential for yield spreads to undergo substantial change.*

Having identified the market conditions which can result in differences in investment returns, let us discuss the types of anticipated yield spread behavior. Since each of the three conditions is based on the premise that a normal or abnormal yield spread exists initially, it is necessary to consider both the initial yield spread and the expected change in spread, even though the change is far more important. Other things being equal, when a positive (+) beginning yield spread exists and is expected to narrow (−) over time, the *higher* yielding issue would provide the greatest return. If a negative yield spread (−) exists initially and is expected to widen (+), the *lower* yielding bond would be the superior investment. This applies for any of the three market conditions and in any interest rate environment. Actually, having ascertained future market conditions, the investor would know which type of yield spread behavior to anticipate and, using the procedure discussed, could identify the issue with the greatest potential. Assume that a negative yield spread is abnormally narrow but is expected to move to its normal relationship. This implies that the negative (−) spread should widen (+) so the lower yielding bond would be selected.

Such analysis should enable the investor to capitalize on temporary yield spread anomalies and allow him to gain the most from anticipated major swings in market rates.

BOND PRICE VOLATILITY

Numerous variables can affect yield behavior and are, therefore, important to price-conscious bond investors. Price volatility, however, is not linked solely to yield behavior. So what causes the variations in price? Malkiel used the bond valuation model to demonstrate that the market price of a fixed-income security is ultimately a function of four factors: (1) the par value of an obligation, (2) the issue's coupon, (3) its years to maturity, and (4) the prevailing market rate.[29] Using these variables in the context of the basic bond valuation model, Malkiel showed (with mathematical proofs) that the following relationships (theorems) exist between yield changes and bond price behavior:

1. Bond prices move inversely to bond yields.
2. For a given change in market yield, changes in bond prices are greater for longer-term maturities; i.e., bond price volatility is *directly* related to term to maturity.
3. The amount of maturity derived price volatility (percentage of price change) increases at a diminishing rate as term to maturity increases.
4. Price movements resulting from equal absolute increases or decreases in yield are not symmetrical since a decrease in yield raises bond prices by more than a corresponding increase in yield lowers prices.
5. The higher the coupon of the issue, the smaller the percentage of price

---

[29] Burton G. Malkiel, "Expectations, Bond Prices, and the Term Structure of Interest Rates," *Quarterly Journal of Economics,* 76 no. 2 (May 1962): 197–218.

fluctuation will be for a given change in yield; i.e., bond price volatility is *inversely* related to coupon.[30]

Homer and Leibowitz[31] showed that the absolute level of market yields significantly affects bond price volatility, i.e., the higher the level of prevailing yields, the greater the price volatility of bonds. They showed that yield swings are greatest when prevailing interest rates are also greatest (and therefore so, too, is price volatility).

Thus, price volatility is a function of the percentage of change in yield, the issue's coupon, the term to maturity of the obligation, the level of yields, and the direction of yield change. However, while both the level and direction of change in yields may be interesting variables to consider, they do not provide concrete trading strategies. This is not true of the other variables. Any time price volatility is sought (or avoided), the percentage of change in yield must be of paramount importance. Attention can then shift to the two variables within the selection process over which investors have control: *coupon and maturity*. As yields change, these two variables have a dramatic effect on comparative bond price volatility.

The Concept of Duration

Because the price volatility of a bond varies inversely with the coupon and directly with the term to maturity, it can be difficult to balance these two factors when selecting bonds. It would obviously be desirable to have a composite measure that considered both of these factors. Fortunately, such a measure was developed almost 50 years ago by Macaulay[32] and is known as the *duration* of a security. Macaulay showed that duration was a more appropriate measure of the time element of a bond than term to maturity because it takes into account not only the ultimate recovery of capital at maturity, but also the size and timing of coupon payments that occur prior to final maturity. Duration is defined as *the weighted average time to full recovery of principal and interest payments.* Using annual compounding, we can define duration (D) as:

$$(18.20) \qquad D = \frac{\displaystyle\sum_{t=1}^{n} \frac{C_t(t)}{(1 + i)^t}}{\displaystyle\sum_{t=1}^{n} \frac{C_t}{(1 + i)^t}},$$

[30] Some empirical evidence demonstrates that the lowest coupon bond does not always provide maximum price volatility when interest rates decline; however, this evidence does not negate the *general* implications of Theorem 5. See Michael D. Joehnk, H. Russell Fogler, and Charles D. Bradley, "The Price Elasticity of Discounted Bonds: Some Empirical Evidence," *Journal of Financial and Quantitative Analysis,* 13 no. 3 (September 1978): 559–566.

[31] Sidney Homer and Martin L. Leibowitz, *Inside the Yield Book* (Englewood Cliffs, N. J.: Prentice-Hall, 1972).

[32] Frederick R. Macaulay, *Some Theoretical Problems Suggested by the Movements of Interest Rates, Bond Yields, and Stock Prices in the United States Since 1856* (New York: National Bureau of Economic Research, 1938).

where:

t = the time period in which the coupon and/or principal payment occurs

C_t = the interest and/or principal payment that occurs in period t

i = the market yield on the bond.

The denominator in Equation 18.20 is the price of an issue as determined by the present value model. The numerator is the present value of all cash flows weighted according to the length of time to receipt.

At first glance, this formula for computing duration may look rather forbidding. The following example, which sets forth the specific computations for two bonds, indicates the procedure and also will highlight some of the properties of duration. Consider the following two sample bonds:

	Bond A	Bond B
Face Value	$1,000	$1,000
Maturity	10 yrs.	10 yrs.
Coupon	4%	8%

Assuming annual interest payments and an 8 percent market yield on the bonds, duration is computed as shown in Table 18.2 on the next page. This example indicates the following characteristics of duration:

1. When a bond has coupons, the duration of the bond will always be less than the term to maturity because duration gives weight to these interim payments.
2. A bond with a *larger* coupon will have a *shorter* duration because more of the total cash flows come earlier in the form of interest payments; i.e., the 8 percent bond has a shorter duration than the 4 percent bond.
3. A bond with no coupon payments (i.e., a pure discount bond like a treasury bill) will have duration *equal* to term to maturity. In this case, the only payment is made at maturity, so the only flow is at maturity.
4. There is generally a positive relationship between term to maturity and duration; i.e., all else the same, *a bond with longer term to maturity will almost always have a higher duration.* Note that the relationship is not direct because, as maturity increases, the present value of the principal declines in value. As shown in Figure 18.5 on page 573, the shape of the curve depends upon the coupon and the market yield—i.e., a low coupon bond selling at a deep discount will have a curve that turns down at long maturities.
5. All else the same, *the higher the market yield, the lower the duration.* As an example, in Table 18.2, if the market yield had been 12 percent rather than 8 percent, the durations would have been about 7.75 and 6.80 rather than 8.12 and 7.25.[33]

---

[33] These properties are discussed and demonstrated in Frank K. Reilly and Rupinder Sidhu, "The Many Uses of Bond Duration," *Financial Analysts Journal,* 36 no. 4 (July–August 1980): 58–72; and Richard W. McEnally, "Duration as a Practical Tool for Bond Management," *Journal of Portfolio Management,* 3 no. 4 (Summer 1977): 53–57.

TABLE 18.2
Computation of Duration (assuming 8 percent market yield)

			Bond A		
(1) Year	(2) Cash Flow	(3) PV at 8%	(4) PV of Flow	(5) PV as % of Price	(6) (1) × (5)
1	$ 40	.9259	$ 37.04	.0506	.0506
2	40	.8573	34.29	.0469	.0938
3	40	.7938	31.75	.0434	.1302
4	40	.7350	29.40	.0402	.1608
5	40	.6806	27.22	.0372	.1860
6	40	.6302	25.21	.0345	.2070
7	40	.5835	23.34	.0319	.2233
8	40	.5403	21.61	.0295	.2360
9	40	.5002	20.01	.0274	.2466
10	1,040	.4632	481.73	.6585	6.5850
Sum			$731.58	1.0000	8.1193

Duration = 8.12 Years

			Bond B		
1	$ 80	.9259	$ 74.07	.0741	.0741
2	80	.8573	68.59	.0686	.1372
3	80	.7938	63.50	.0635	.1906
4	80	.7350	58.80	.0588	.1906
5	80	.6806	54.44	.0544	.2720
6	80	.6302	50.42	.0504	.3024
7	80	.5835	46.68	.0467	.3269
8	80	.5403	43.22	.0432	.3456
9	80	.5002	40.02	.0400	.3600
10	1,080	.4632	500.26	.5003	5.0030
Sum			$1000.00	1.0000	7.2470

Duration = 7.25 Years

This concept of duration can be very useful to you in bond portfolio management because it combines the properties of maturity and coupon mentioned earlier. Duration is positively related to term to maturity and inversely related to coupon. It has been shown, both theoretically and empirically, that bond price movements *will vary proportionally* with duration. *The percentage of change in bond price is equal to the change in yield times adjusted duration.*[34] As an example, if yields decline by one percent (100 basis points), a bond with an adjusted duration of ten years will increase in price by approximately 10 percent. Thus, *maximum price variation* is achieved with the *longest* duration.[35] These and other characteristics of duration are shown in Table 18.3 on page 574.

---

[34] Adjusted duration is equal to the Macaulay duration, computed in Table 18.2, divided by one plus the current market yield. As an example, a bond with a Macaulay duration of 10 years and market yield of 9 percent will have an adjusted duration of 9.17 (10/1.09).

[35] A generalized proof of this is contained in Michael H. Hopewell and George Kaufman, "Bond Price Volatility and Term to Maturity: A Generalized Respecification," *American Economic Review*, 63 no. 4 (September 1973): 749–753.

FIGURE 18.5
Duration vs. Maturity

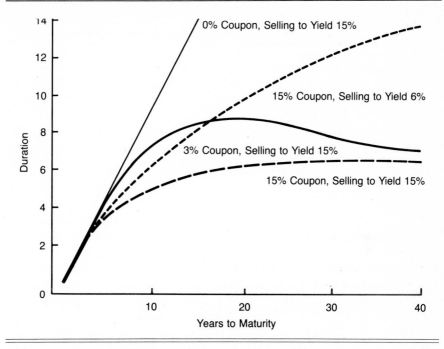

SOURCE: William L. Nemerever, C.F.A. "Managing Bond Portfolios through Immunization Strategies," *The Revolution in Techniques for Managing Bond Portfolios* (Charlottesville, Va.: The Institute of Chartered Financial Analysts, 1983), p. 42.

While bond price variation tends to move proportionally with duration, Table 18.3 demonstrates that there are numerous ways to achieve a given duration measure. Thus, if you anticipate a decline in interest rates and want to capture maximum gains by increasing the duration of your bond portfolio, there are several maturity/coupon combinations that would provide the desired price performance. The duration concept has become increasingly popular because it is the convenient way of incorporating the time element of a security in terms of *both* coupon and term to maturity, and it is useful for the active bond trader in structuring his portfolio to take advantage of changes in market yields. For example, if you expect a decline in market yields, you should increase the average duration of your bond portfolio to experience maximum price volatility and vice versa.

Portfolio Immunization. In contrast to an investor who wants to maximize the return from his bond portfolio by changing duration in anticipation of changes in market interest rates, there are some investors who do not want to play the trading game but simply want to be assured of a specified return for a predetermined investment period, e.g., a 10 percent annual return over the next

TABLE 18.3
Bond Duration in Years for Bond Yielding 6 Percent under Different Terms

Years to Maturity	Various Coupon Rates			
	.02	.04	.06	.08
1	.995	.990	.985	.981
5	4.756	4.558	4.393	4.254
10	8.891	8.169	7.662	7.286
20	14.981	12.980	11.904	11.232
50	19.452	17.129	16.273	15.829
100	17.567	17.232	17.120	17.064
∞	17.167	17.167	17.167	17.167

SOURCE: L. Fisher and R. L. Weil, "Coping with the Risk of Interest Rate Fluctuations: Returns to Bondholders from Naive and Optimal Strategies," *Journal of Business*, 44 no. 4 (October 1971): 418. Copyright © 1971 by The University of Chicago Press. Reprinted by permission of The University of Chicago Press.

five years. The problem in this regard is that as market interest rates change, this can influence the *price* of your securities, and these changes also affect your *reinvestment rates.* Fortunately, these two risks work in opposite directions: when interest rates decline, there are *positive* price effects (bond prices increase) but *negative* reinvestment effects (your reinvestment rate declines).

Because of the conflict between price and reinvestment risk, it is maintained that, to immunize fixed-income investments to subsequent changes in market rates, these two risks must be balanced so that they completely offset one another. Balancing occurs only when an investment horizon is equal to a bond's measure of duration. *When duration equals the planning period, interest rate risk is minimized.* Thus, an investor with a five-year horizon should not necessarily seek an issue with five years to maturity, but he should seek issues with maturity/coupon combinations that provide a *duration* of approximately 5.0.[36]

The use of bond portfolio immunization and further extensions of the concept will be discussed in detail in Chapter 19 when we consider alternative bond portfolio management techniques.

In summary, the concept of duration has implications for both aggressive and conservative bond investors. It is an important idea that conveniently encompasses the coupon *and* maturity dimensions of bond price behavior.[37]

SUMMARY

The concept of bond valuation is essentially the same as that for equity pricing, i.e., the present value of all future cash flows accruing to the investor. Cash flows

[36] For a detailed derivation and test of this concept, see Lawrence Fisher and Roman L. Weil, "Coping with the Risk of Interest-Rate Fluctuations: Returns to Bondholders from Naive and Optimal Strategies," *Journal of Business,* 44 no. 4 (October 1971): 408–431; and G. O. Bierwag and George C. Kaufman, "Coping with the Risk of Interest Rate Fluctuations: A Note," *Journal of Business,* 50 no. 3 (July 1977): 364–370.

[37] Following the rediscovery of duration, it has been found to be of value in other areas beyond bond analysis and portfolio management. In this regard, see John A. Boquist, George A. Racette, and Gary G. Schlarbaum, "Duration and Risk Assessment for Bonds and Common Stocks," *Journal of Finance,* 30 no. 5 (December 1975): 1360–1365; and Edward Blocker and Clyde Stickney, "Duration and Risk Assessments in Capital Budgeting," *The Accounting Review,* 54 no. 1 (January 1979): 180–188.

for the bond investor include periodic interest payments and capital recovery. The present value model incorporated several important dimensions of bond yields and prices, including coupon receipts, interest rates, interest rate changes, and yield spread changes. *The major problem facing the bond analyst is estimating expected changes in interest rate and yield spread behavior.* Once these factors have been evaluated, the next step is to select the coupon, maturity, call feature, etc., that best captures the performance sought by the investor. Errors in estimating interest rates and yield changes can, however, lead to substantial losses for the aggressive investor and reduced return for the buy-and-hold strategist.

The next part of the chapter reviewed the mathematics of bond pricing and bond yields. We looked at the five basic types of yields including: nominal yield, current yield, promised yield, yield to call, and realized yield. The concept of interest-on-interest, or coupon reinvestment, was discovered to be an extremely important factor in calculating realized yield.

Because an important aspect of bond pricing is the rate at which future cash flows are discounted, we examined the fundamental determinants of interest rates. They were seen to be a function of the risk-free rate, a risk premium, and an inflation premium. Consideration was then given to the term structure of interest rates, i.e., yield curve analysis. The four basic patterns of yield curves were examined, and theoretical explanations were given for the different shapes of yield curves based on the expectations hypothesis, the liquidity preference hypothesis, and the segmented market hypothesis. Trading strategies were developed using yield curve analysis and related changes in the yield curve.

In the final section of the chapter, we saw that bond price volatility was a function of the percentage of change in yield, the coupon of the issue, the term to maturity, the level of yields, and the direction of yield changes. In developing trading strategies based on price volatility, emphasis is placed on the percentage of yield change with consideration given to coupon and maturity. The concept of duration was developed to incorporate both of these variables in one measure that indicates the response of bond price to a change in interest rates. Beyond discussing the properties of duration, we introduced its use as a means to immunize a portfolio from interest rate changes.

QUESTIONS

(Note: In all bond valuation problems, assume a par value of $1000.)

1. Why does the present value equation appear to be more useful for the bond investor than for the common stock investor?
2. What is the most crucial assumption the investor makes when he calculates promised yield? Why is it crucial to the computation?
3. An investor purchases a bond with a nominal yield of 6 percent for $800. If the bond has 20 years to maturity, find promised yield by:
   a. The approximation method
   b. Present value method, assuming annual interest payments
   c. Present value method, assuming semiannual interest payments.

4. A bond is currently quoted at $1100 and has a current yield of 6.36 percent. The remaining life of the bond is 15 years, but it has three years remaining on a deferred call feature.
  a. Calculate promised yield using:
    (1) Approximation method
    (2) Present value method, assuming annual payments.
  b. Calculate yield to call, assuming a call premium equal to one year's interest, using:
    (1) Approximation method
    (2) Present value method, assuming annual payments.

5. An investor purchases a bond during a period of high yields. He pays $800 for a 7¾ percent bond, expecting rates to drop over the next three years to the point at which the value of the bond would increase to $1050. However, interest rates edge slightly upward, so that when he sells the bond three years later, he actually receives $750 for it.
  a. Calculate the realized yield the investor anticipated using the approximation method.
  b. Calculate the actual yield he realized using the present value method and assuming semiannual receipts.

6. A bond with a 7 percent coupon and 10 years to maturity is selling to yield 9 percent. What is its price?

7. A speculator has decided that, because of anticipated declines in interest rates, a given bond should be selling for $950 two years from now. It carries a 10 percent coupon, but because of capital gains, he figures that he could make 15 percent if he could buy it at a certain price. What is the price, assuming semiannual payments?

8. A new 20-year bond with an 8 percent nominal yield and paying an annual coupon is priced to yield 10 percent. An investor purchasing the bond expects that, two years from now, yields on comparable bonds will have declined to 9 percent. Calculate his realized yield if he expects to sell the bond in two years.

9. A bond carrying a 6 percent coupon has eight years and seven months to maturity.
  a. What would its price be if similar bonds yield 8 percent? Assume semiannual coupon payments.
  b. Find the price if the term to maturity were 8 years, 7 months, and 15 days.

10. a. Define the variables included in the following model:

$$r = (RFR,\ RP,\ I).$$

  b. Comment on the appropriateness of the model, given the information that the firm whose bonds you are considering is not expected to break even this year.

11. The following exercise deals with the problem of differing reinvestment rates. An investor purchases a bond for $900 with a 7 percent coupon which matures in five years. Find the promised yield, assuming annual payments and that:
  a. Interest payments are reinvested in more of the same bonds at the same promised yield
  b. Interest payments are reinvested in a Mexican bank savings account at 12 percent
  c. Interest payments are not reinvested at all but are spent as they arrive.

12. Using the most current information available, construct a graph depicting the term structure of interest rates for Aaa-rated corporate bonds. (See Figure 18.3 for example.)

13. Of the three hypotheses mentioned in the text, which one do you think best explains the reasons for a yield curve? Defend your choice.

14. Construct a chart demonstrating current ranges of yields for bonds of various ratings. For example, you might want to randomly select three or four bonds in each rating category and show the average yield on each group, as well as the spread for each group.

15. You are given two 8 percent coupon bonds, one with a term to maturity of five years, the second with a term to maturity of 20 years. Assuming that market interest rates go from 8 percent to 12 percent, compute the prices of the two bonds before and after the rate change and discuss the differential percentage price change.

16. Consider two bonds with term to maturity of ten years, one with a 4 percent coupon, the second with a 10 percent coupon. Assuming that market interest rates go from 10 percent to 6 percent, compute the prices of the two bonds before and after the rate change and discuss the differential percentage price change.

17. Compute the duration of a 5-year bond with a 7 percent coupon (annual payments) yielding 8 percent. Show all work.

18. What will happen to the duration of the bond in Question 17 if:
    a. The coupon is 12 percent rather than 7 percent?
    b. The market rate is 4 percent rather than 8 percent?

19. You own a bond with a Macauley duration of 8 years. If market rates are 8 percent, what is the adjusted duration of this bond? If market rates decline by 2 percent (200 basis points), what will be the percentage change in price for this bond?

20. *CFA Examination I (June 1982)*
    a. ***Explain*** what is meant by the term structure of interest rates. ***Explain*** the theoretical basis of an upward sloping yield curve.

    (8 minutes)

    b. ***Explain*** the economic circumstances under which you would expect to see the inverted yield curve prevail.

    (7 minutes)

    c. ***Define*** "real" rate of interest.

    (2 minutes)

    d. ***Discuss*** the characteristics of the market for U.S. Treasury securities. ***Compare*** it to the market for AAA-corporate bonds. ***Discuss*** the opportunities which may exist in bond markets that are less than efficient.

    (8 minutes)

    e. Over the past several years, fairly wide yield spreads between AAA-corporates and treasuries have occasionally prevailed. ***Discuss*** the possible reasons why this occurred.

    (5 minutes)

21. *CFA Examination III (June, 1982)* As the portfolio manager for a large pension fund, you are offered the following bonds:

	Coupon	Maturity	Price	Call Price	Yield to Maturity
Edgar Corp. (new issue)	14.00%	2002	$101.3/4	$114	13.75%
Edgar Corp. (new issue)	6.00	2002	48.1/8	103	13.60
Edgar Corp. (1972 issue)	6.00	2002	48.7/8	103	13.40

Assuming that you expect a decline in interest rates over the next three years, **identify** and **justify** which of these bonds you would select.

(10 minutes)

REFERENCES

Axilrod, Stephen A., and Ralph A. Young. "Interest Rates and Monetary Policy." *Federal Reserve Bulletin.* 43 no. 3 (September 1962).

Baskin, Elba F., and Gary M. Crooch. "Historical Rates of Return on Investments in Flat Bonds." *Financial Analysts Journal.* 24 no. 6 (November–December 1968).

Bierwag, G. O. and George G. Kaufman. "Coping with the Risk of Interest Rate Fluctuations: A Note." *Journal of Business.* 50 no. 3 (July 1977).

Bierwag, G. O. "Immunization, Duration, and the Term Structure of Interest Rates." *Journal of Financial and Quantitative Analysis.* 12 no. 5 (December 1977).

Bierwag, G. O., and George G. Kaufman. "Bond Portfolio Strategy Simulations: A Critique." *Journal of Financial and Quantitative Analysis.* 13 no. 3 (September 1978).

Bierwag, G. O., George G. Kaufman and Chulsoon Khang. "Duration and Bond Portfolio Analysis: An Overview." *Journal of Financial and Quantitative Analysis.* Forthcoming.

Blocher, Edward, and Clyde Stickney. "Duration and Risk Assessments in Capital Budgeting." *The Accounting Review.* 54 no. 1 (January 1979).

Boquist, John A., George A. Racette, and Gary G. Schlarbaum. "Duration and Risk Assessment for Bonds and Common Stocks." *Journal of Finance.* 30 no. 5 (December 1975).

Bowlin, Oswald D., and John D. Martin. "Explorations of Yields over the Short Run; Forecast or Folly?" *Journal of Monetary Economics.* 1 (1975).

Burton, John S., and John R. Toth. "Forecasting Secular Trends in Long-Term Interest Rates." *Financial Analysts Journal.* 30 no. 5 (September–October 1974).

Cagan, Phillip. ed. *Essays on Interest Rates* (New York: Columbia University Press for the National Bureau of Economic Research, 1969).

Caks, John. "The Coupon Effect on Yield to Maturity." *Journal of Finance.* 32 no. 1 (March 1977).

Conard, Joseph W., and Mark W. Frankena. "The Yield Spread between New and Seasoned Corporate Bonds." *Essays on Interest Rates.* 1 (1969).

Durand, David. "Payout Period, Time Spread, and Duration: Aids to Judgment in Capital Budgeting." *Journal of Bank Research.* 4 no. 1 (Spring 1974).

Ederington, Louis H. "The Yield Spread on New Issues of Corporate Bonds." *Journal of Finance.* 27 no. 5 (December 1974).

Feldstein, Martin, and Otto Eckstein, "The Fundamental Determinants of the Interest Rate." *The Review of Economics and Statistics.* 52 no. 4 (November 1970).

Ferri, Michael G. "Systematic Return and the Call Risk of Corporate Debt Instruments," *Journal of Financial Research* 1 no. 1 (Winter 1978).

Finnerty, John D. "Evaluating the Economics of Refunding High-Coupon Sinking-Fund Debt." *Financial Management.* 12 no. 1 (Spring 1983).

Fisher, Lawrence. "Determinants of Risk Premiums on Corporate Bonds." *Journal of Political Economy.* 67 no. 3 (June 1959).

Fisher, Lawrence, and Roman L. Weil. "Coping with the Risk of Interest-Rate Fluctuations: Returns to Bondholders from Naive and Optimal Strategies." *Journal of Business.* 44 no. 4 (October 1971).

Freund, William C., and Edward D. Zinbarg. "Application of Flow of Fund to Interest Rate Forecasting." *Journal of Finance.* 13 no. 2 (May 1963).

Gibson, William E. "Interest Rates and Inflationary Expectations: New Evidence." *American Economic Review.* 62 no. 5 (December 1972).

Grove, Myron A. "On Duration and the Optimal Maturity Structure of the Balance Sheet." *Bell Journal of Economics and Management Science.* 5 no. 2 (Autumn 1974).

Hastie, Larry K. "Determinants of Municipal Bond Yields." *Journal of Financial and Quantitative Analysis.* 7 no. 3 (June 1972).

Haugen, Robert A., and Dean W. Wichern. "The Elasticity of Financial Assets." *Journal of Finance.* 29 no. 4 (September 1974).

Homer, Sidney, and Martin L. Leibowitz. *Inside the Yield Book.* Englewood Cliffs, N.J.: Prentice-Hall, 1972.

Hopewell, Michael H., and George G. Kaufman. "Bond Price Volatility and Term to Maturity: A Generalized Respecification." *American Economic Review.* 63 no. 4 (September 1973).

Jen, Frank C., and James E. Wert. "The Value of the Deferred Call Privilege." *National Banking Review.* 3 no. 1 (March 1966).

Joehnk, Michael D., and James F. Nielsen. "Return and Risk Characteristics of Speculative Grade Bonds." *Quarterly Review of Economics & Business.* 15 no. 1 (Spring 1975).

Joehnk, Michael D., and James C. Wert. "The Call-Risk Performance of the Discounted Seasoned Issue." *Mississippi Valley Journal of Business and Economics.* 9 no. 2 (Winter 1973–1974).

Johannesen, Richard I., Jr. "The Effect of Coupon on Bond Price Fluctuations." *Financial Analysts Journal.* 24 no. 5 (September–October 1968).

Johnson, Ramon E. "Term Structure of Corporate Bond Yields as a Function of Risk of Default." *Journal of Finance.* 22 no. 2 (May 1967).

Kalotay, A. J. "On the Structure and Valuation of Debt Refundings." *Financial Management.* 11 no. 1 (Spring 1982).

Kalotay, A. J. "On the Management of Sinking Funds." *Financial Management.* 10 no. 2 (Summer 1981).

Kalotay, A. J. "Sinking Funds and the Realized Cost of Debt," *Financial Management.* 11 no. 1 (Spring 1982).

Kane, Edward J., and Burton G. Malkiel. "The Term Structure of Interest Rates: An Analysis of a Survey of Interest Rate Expectations." *Review of Economics and Statistics.* 49 no. 3 (August 1967).

Kaufman, George G. "Measuring Risk and Return for Bonds: A New Approach." *Journal of Bank Research.* 9 no. 2 (Summer 1978).

Kessel, Reuben A. "The Cyclical Behavior of the Term Structure of Interest Rates." Occasional Paper 91 National Bureau of Economic Research, 1965.

Lindvall, John R. "New Issue Corporate Bonds, Seasoned Market Efficiency and Yield Spreads." *Journal of Finance.* 32 no. 4 (September 1977).

Livingston, Miles, and John Caks, "A 'Duration' Fallacy." *Joural of Finance.* 32 no. 1 (March 1977).

Livingston, Miles. "Duration and Risk Assessment for Bonds and Common Stock: A Comment." *Journal of Finance.* 33 no. 1 (March 1978).

Macaulay, Frederick R. *Some Theoretical Problems Suggested by the Movements of Interest Rates, Bond Yields, and Stock Prices in the United States Since 1865.* New York: National Bureau of Economic Research, 1938.

Malkiel, Burton G. "Expectations, Bond Prices, and the Term Structure of Interest Rates." *Quarterly Journal of Economics.* 76 no. 2 (May 1962).

Malkiel, Burton G. *The Term Structure of Interest Rates: Theory, Empirical Evidence, and Applications.* New York: The McCaleb–Seiler Publishing Company, 1970.

McEnally, Richard W. "Duration as a Practical Tool in Bond Management." *Journal of Portfolio Management.* 3 no. 4 (Summer 1977).

Meiselman, David. *The Term Structure of Interest Rates.* Englewood Cliffs, N.J.: Prentice-Hall, 1962.

Modigliani, Franco, and Richard Sutch. "Innovations in Interest Rate Policy." *American Economic Review Papers and Proceedings.* 56 no. 2 (May 1966).

Reilly, Frank K., and Rupinder Sidhu. "The Many Uses of Bond Duration." *Financial Analysts Journal.* 36 no. 4 (July–August 1980).

Santomero, Anthony M. "The Error-Learning Hypothesis and the Term Structure of Interest Rates in Eurodollars." *Journal of Finance.* 30 no. 3 (June 1975).

Van Horne, James C. *Financial Market Rates and Flows.* 2nd ed. Englewood Cliffs, N.J.: Prentice-Hall, 1984.

Van Horne, James C. "Interest Rate Risk and the Term Structure of Interest Rates." *Journal of Political Economy.* 73 no. 3 (August 1965).

Van Horne, James C. "Called Bonds: How Does the Investor Fare? " *Journal of Portfolio Management.* 6 no. 4 (Summer 1980).

Weil, Roman L. "Macaulay's Duration: An Appreciation." *Journal of Business.* 46 no. 4 (October 1973).

Whittaker, John. "The Relevance of Duration." *Journal of Business Finance.* 2 (Spring 1970).

Yawitz, Jess. "The Relative Importance of Duration and Yield Volatility on Bond Price Volatility." *Journal of Money, Credit and Banking.* 9 no. 1 (February 1977).

Yohe, William P., and Denis S. Karnosky. "Interest Rates and Price Level Changes, 1952–1969." Federal Reserve Bank of St. Louis *Review.* (December 1966).

Chapter 19   *Bond Portfolio Management Strategies*

S uccessful bond investment involves far more than mastering myriad technical aspects. Investors and portfolio managers use such information, in combination with economic and market data, to formulate viable portfolio policies and investment strategies. Technical information is only useful if it can help investors generate higher risk-adjusted returns. In this chapter, we shift attention from the technical dimensions to the equally important question of bond portfolio management strategies.

ALTERNATIVE BOND PORTFOLIO STRATEGIES

Bond portfolio management strategies can be divided into three groups:
1. Buy and Hold
2. Active Management Strategies
   a. Interest rate anticipation
   b. Valuation analysis
   c. Credit analysis
   d. Spread analysis
   e. Bond swaps.
3. Immunization Strategies
   a. Classical immunization
   b. Contingent immunization.

We will discuss each of these alternatives because they are all viable and acceptable for alternative portfolios with different needs and risk profiles. Notably, prior to the 1960s, only the first two groups were available and most portfolios were managed on the basis of buy and hold. During the 1960s and early 1970s, there was growing interest in the alternative active management strategies. The investment environment since the late 1970s has been characterized by record-breaking inflation and interest rates, extremely volatile markets, and the introduction of new financial instruments in response to volatility and the

584

emerging needs of institutional clients. About this same time, the rediscovery of duration that occurred in the early 1970s was being recognized and implemented by practitioners. This rediscovery allowed the introduction of an important bond portfolio management strategy that responded to the needs of institutional clients to control risk. As briefly discussed in Chapter 18, this strategy is referred to as *bond portfolio immunization* which attempts to assure the attainment of a target rate of return during a specified time horizon by eliminating interest rate risk. Subsequently, a modification of this strategy (now called *classical immunization*) has been developed which is referred to as *contingent immunization*.

Following discussion of the alternative strategies, we will consider the role of bonds in a total portfolio context—i.e., how bonds fit into a total portfolio management framework in light of the work in capital asset pricing theory. We conclude with a brief discussion of bond market efficiency.

Investment Strategies

Understanding bond portfolio management requires knowledge of the various bond portfolio management techniques: buy and hold, active management strategies, and immunization strategies.

BUY-AND-HOLD STRATEGY

This is the simplest strategy and is obviously not unique to bond investors. It involves finding issues with desired quality, coupon levels, term to maturity, and important indenture provisions, such as call feature. The buy-and-hold-investor does not consider trading in and out of positions to achieve attractive returns. Rather, because of his risk-return preferences, he seeks modest returns with little risk. Buy-and-hold investors also tend to look for vehicles whose maturities (or duration) approximate their stipulated investment horizon in order to reduce price and reinvestment risk.

Many successful bond investors and portfolio managers (particularly institutional managers) follow a *modified* version of the buy-and-hold strategy. The approach is similar to strict buy and hold in the sense that investment is made in an issue with the intention of holding it until the end of the investment horizon. However, such investors actively look for opportunities to trade into more desirable positions.[1]

Whether the investor follows a strict or a modified buy-and-hold approach, the key ingredient is finding investment vehicles that possess attractive maturity and yield features. The strategy does not restrict the investor to accept whatever the market has to offer, nor does it imply that selectivity is unimportant. Attractive high yielding issues with desirable features and quality standards are actively sought. The buy-and-hold investor is aware that buying agency issues will provide him with attractive incremental returns relative to treasuries with little sacrifice in quality, and that utilities provide higher returns than comparably

---

[1] Obviously, if the strategy becomes too modified, it would become one of the active strategies.

rated industrials, and that various call features affect not only the risk of an issue, but realized yield as well.

Thus, the successful buy-and-hold investor actively evaluates investment outlets and uses his knowledge of markets and issue characteristics to seek out attractive yields. Aggressive buy-and-hold investors will incorporate timing considerations into their investment decisions. Given their knowledge of market rates and expectations, if they do not like prevailing returns, they can always wait for higher yields by "sitting on the sidelines" in cash or very short-term money market investments.

ACTIVE MANAGEMENT STRATEGIES[2]

Interest Rate Anticipation

This approach to bond investment is perhaps the riskiest strategy, because it involves relying on uncertain forecasts of future interest rate behavior as a guide to restructuring a bond portfolio. This strategy entails preserving capital when an increase in interest rates is anticipated and achieving attractive capital gains when interest rates are expected to decline. Such objectives are usually attained by altering the maturity structure of the portfolio, i.e., shortening the maturity (duration) of the bonds in the portfolio when interest rates are expected to increase and lengthening the average maturity when a decline in yields is anticipated.

The risk in such portfolio restructuring is largely a function of maturity alterations. When the portfolio manager shortens his maturities to preserve capital, he could sacrifice substantial income and the opportunity for capital gains. Similarly, when the investor anticipates a decline in rates, his risk is great because the coupon at this point in the interest rate cycle is normally reduced as maturity increases. Therefore, the investor is sacrificing current income (by investing in lower coupon bonds) and exposing the portfolio to substantial price volatility (with an unexpected increase in yields). Comparatively speaking, an anticipated increase in rates involves less risk since it involves less chance of an absolute capital loss. Therefore, the worst that can happen is interest income is reduced and/or capital gains forgone (opportunity cost) by shortening maturities.

Once future (expected) interest rates have been determined, the procedure relies largely on technical matters. Assume that an investor anticipates an increase in interest rates and wants to preserve his capital by reducing maturities as much as possible. Most bond portfolio managers would look for high yielding, short-term obligations such as treasury bills. While a primary goal is preservation of capital, the question of *income* is not totally ignored. Therefore, the investor would look for the best return possible given the maturity constraint. *Liquidity* is also important since an investor who is maintaining this posture involving yield sacrifice would only want to sit on the sidelines when rates were drifting upward.

[2] The discussion in this subsection benefited from H. Gifford Fong, "Active Strategies for Managing Bond Portfolios," *The Revolution in Techniques for Managing Bond Portfolios* (Charlottesville, Va. The Institute of Chartered Financial Analysts, 1983), 21–38.

When rates were either level or declining, the investor would want to shift positions *quickly* in order to seize the opportunity for higher income and/or capital gains.

One way to shorten maturities is to use a cushion bond, which is a very high yielding, long-term obligation. Such a bond carries a coupon substantially above the current market rate and has a current call feature. Because of its call price ceiling, its actual market price is below what it should be given current market yields. With the price of the issue being held back because of its call exposure, its yield is higher than normal. Knowledgeable bond investors look for cushion bonds when a *modest* increase in rates is anticipated since such an issue provides attractive current income and protection against capital loss. The issue gives capital loss protection because it is trading at an abnormally high yield; market rates would have to *rise to its level* before its price would react. The investor who anticipates an increase in interest rates, therefore, has two simple strategies available: either shorten the duration of the portfolio or select an attractive cushion bond. In either case, a very liquid issue is sought.[3]

A totally different posture is assumed by investors anticipating a *decline* in interest rates. Although there are substantial risks involved in restructuring a portfolio to take advantage of a decline, substantial capital gains and holding period returns can be realized. When investors anticipate a decline in interest rates, the basic rule is to *lengthen maturities* (duration) because the longer the duration, the greater the price volatility. *Liquidity* is also important because the investor wants to be able to close out the position *quickly* when the drop in rates has been completed.

Given the constraints of duration and liquidity, the investor attempts to determine the most attractive market segments and issues. The object is to find the market segment which promises the greatest price reaction to the decline in interest rates.

Generally, one would expect investors who anticipate rate declines to look for *long maturities and low coupons* (i.e., long duration). An exception might be when only a *modest* decrease in yields is anticipated. Under such circumstances, a portfolio manager might consider a *current coupon obligation*, since such issues are more interest sensitive than deep discounted bonds are and, therefore, they react to small changes in yield. Of course, long maturity would still be important.

In any investment strategy based on a decline in interest rates, *interest sensitivity* is critical so high grade securities (e.g., Baa through Aaa) should be used. Likewise treasuries and agencies might be attractive since they are also very interest sensitive. In fact, the higher the quality of the obligation, the more sensitive it is to interest rate behavior.

Valuation Analysis

With this strategy, the portfolio manager attempts to select bonds based upon the intrinsic value of the securities and considers the specific characteristics of the

---

[3] For an extended discussion of cushion bonds, see Sidney Homer and Martin L. Leibowitz, *Inside the Yield Book* (Englewood Cliffs, N.J.: Prentice-Hall, 1972), Chapter 5.

particular bond. The normal value of each characteristic of the bond is deter-mined based upon the characteristics's average value in the market place. As an example, long maturity might be worth an added 60 basis points relative to short maturity; a given deferred call feature might require a higher or lower yield; a specified sinking fund would likewise mean higher or lower required yields. Given all the characteristics and their normal cost, you would arrive at a required normal return for alternative bonds. Given this required yield, you determine the implied intrinsic value for the bond and compare this derived value to the pre-vailing market price to determine if the bond is under or overvalued. Obviously, based upon the talent of the individual assigning the normal costs of the charac-teristics, you would buy issues judged undervalued and would ignore or sell overvalued issues.

Credit Analysis

Using credit analysis as the principal portfolio management strategy involves detailed analysis of the bond issuer to determine expected changes in its default risk. You can conceive of this as attempting to project changes in the quality ratings assigned to bonds by the four rating agencies discussed in Chapter 17. These rating changes are affected by internal changes in the entity (e.g., changes in important financial ratios) and also by changes in the external environment (i.e., changes in the economy). During periods of strong economic expansion, even financially weak firms may be able to exist and prosper. In contrast, during severe economic contractions, even strong firms may experience changes in their ability to meet financial obligations. Therefore, there is a strong cyclical pattern to rating changes—i.e., an increase in downgradings during economic contractions and vice versa.

Assuming a portfolio manager wants to employ credit analysis as a manage-ment strategy, it is necessary to project rating changes *prior* to the actual an-nouncement by the rating agencies. As the subsequent discussion on bond market efficiency will note, the market adjusts rather quickly to rating changes — especially downgradings. Therefore, the idea would be to acquire issues that you *expect* to experience upgradings and to sell or avoid issues expected to be downgraded by one of the agencies.

Spread Analysis

As discussed in Chapter 18, spread analysis assumes there are normal relation-ships between the yields for bonds in alternative sectors — e.g., high grade vs. low-grade industrial or utility bonds. Therefore, the idea is to monitor these relationships and when an abnormal relationship occurs, various sector swaps can be undertaken. The crucial factor is the background to know the normal relationship and the liquidity necessary to buy or sell the required issues *quickly* to take advantage of the supposedly *temporary* abnormality.

Bond Swaps

This is perhaps the most intriguing of the various investment strategies. *Bond swaps involve liquidating a current position and (simultaneously) buying a different issue in its place.* An investor holds a particular bond in his portfolio and is offered another bond with similar attributes except that it offers the chance for improved return. Many large portfolio managers employ this strategy to attain substantial portfolio returns.

Swaps can be executed to increase current yield, to increase yield to maturity, to take advantage of shifts in interest rates or realignments of yield spreads, to improve the quality of a portfolio, or for tax purposes. Some swaps are highly sophisticated and require a computer to comprehend the details fully. Most, however, are fairly simple transactions, with obvious goals and chances of risk. They go by such names as *profit take outs, substitution swaps, intermarket spread swaps,* or *tax swaps.* While many of these swaps involve low risk (such as the pure yield pick-up swap), others entail substantial risk (the rate anticipation swap). Regardless of the risk involved or the swap used, all swaps are employed for one basic reason: *as a means to portfolio improvement.*

Most swaps involve several different types of risk. One obvious risk is that the market will move against you while the swap is outstanding. Interest rates may move up over the holding period and may cause the investor to incur a loss. Another risk is that such things as yield spreads may fail to respond as anticipated, thus offsetting the benefits of the bond swap. The new bond may not, in fact, be a true substitute; even if our expectations and interest rate formulations are correct, the swap may be unsatisfactory because the *wrong* issue was selected. Finally, if the work-out time is longer than anticipated, the realized yield might be less than expected or a loss may result.

These risks will become more obvious as we examine several types of popular bond swaps. Such risk is accepted by the investor in order to realize portfolio improvements through improved yield. Three of the more popular potential bond swaps will be briefly reviewed below.[4]

The Pure Yield Pick-Up Swap. A yield pick-up swap is basically long term and involves little or no estimation of market rates. You would swap out of a low coupon bond into a comparable higher coupon bond to realize an automatic and instantaneous increase in current yield and yield to maturity. Your risks are that the market will move against you and, possibly, that the issue may not be a viable swap candidate. Also, because you are moving to a higher coupon obligation, there is greater call risk.

An example of a pure yield pick-up swap begins with an investor who currently holds a 30-year, Aa-rated 10 percent issue that is trading at 11.50 percent. Assume that the investor is offered a comparable 30-year, Aa-rated obligation bearing a 12 percent coupon priced to yield 12 percent. The investor would report (and realize) some book loss if he had acquired the original issue at par, but he is also able to improve current yield and yield to maturity simultaneously

[4] For additional information on these and other types of bond swaps, the reader is directed to: Sidney Homer and Martin L. Leibowitz, *Inside the Yield Book* (Englewood Cliffs, N.J.: Prentice-Hall, 1972); and Martin L. Leibowitz, "How Swaps Can Pay Off," *Institutional Investor,* 7 no. 8 (August 1973): 49ff.

TABLE 19.1
A Pure Yield Pick-Up Swap

Pure Yield Pick-Up Swap: A bond swap involving a switch from a low coupon bond to a higher coupon bond of similar quality and maturity in order to pick up higher current yield and a better yield to maturity.

Example: Currently Hold: 30-yr., 10.0% coupon priced at 874.12 to yield 11.5%.
Swap Candidate: 30-yr., Aa 12% coupon priced at $1000 to yield 12.0%.

	Current Bond	Candidate Bond
Dollar Investment	$874.12	$1,000.00[a]
Coupon	100.00	120.00
i on One Coupon (12.0% for 6 mos.)	3.000	3.600
Principal Value at Year End	874.66	1,000.00
Total Accrued	977.66	1,123.60
Realized Compound Yield	11.514%	12.0%

Value of Swap: 48.6 basis points in one year (assuming a 12.0% reinvestment rate).

---

[a] Obviously the investor can invest $874.12, the amount obtained from the sale of the bond currently held, and still obtain a realized compound yield of 12.0%.

The rewards for a pure yield pick-up swap are automatic and instantaneous in that both a higher coupon yield and a higher yield to maturity are realized from the swap.

Other advantages include:
1.   No specific work-out period needed since the investor is assumed to hold the new bond to maturity
2.   No need for interest rate speculation
3.   No need to analyze prices for overvaluation or undervaluation.

A major disadvantage of the pure yield pick-up swap is the book loss involved in the swap. In this example, if the current bond were bought at par the book loss would be: ($1,000 − 874.12) $125.88.

Other risks involved in the pure yield pick-up swap include:
1.   Increased risk of call in the event interest rates decline
2.   Reinvestment risk is greater at higher coupon rates.

Swap evaluation procedure is patterned after technique suggested by Sidney Homer and Martin L. Leibowitz. SOURCE: Adapted from the book *Inside the Yield Book* by Sidney Homer and Martin L. Leibowitz, Ph.D. © 1972 by Prentice-Hall. Published by Prentice-Hall, Englewood Cliffs, N.J. 07632.

if the new obligation is held to maturity. An explanation of this swap is contained in Table 19.1.

The investor need not predict rate changes, and the swap is not based on any imbalance in yield spread. You are simply seeking higher yields through a bond swap. Quality and maturity stay the same, as do all other factors *except coupon*. The major risk is that future reinvestment rates may not be as high as expected and, therefore, the total terminal value of the investment (capital recovery, coupon receipts, and interest-on-interest) may not be as high as expected or comparable to the original obligation. This reinvestment risk can be evaluated by analyzing the results with a number of rates to determine the minimum reinvestment rate that must prevail before the swap becomes unacceptable.

Substitution Swap.   In contrast to our previous illustration, the substitution swap is generally short term, relies heavily on interest rate expectations, and is subject to considerably more risk. The procedure rests on the existence of a short-term imbalance in yield spreads which is expected to be corrected in the near future. Moreover, it is assumed that the yield spread imbalance exists in issues which are perfect substitutes for each other. The investor might hold a 30-year, 12 percent issue that is yielding 12 percent and be offered comparable 30-year, 12 percent bonds that are yielding 12.20 percent. The issue offered will trade at a price less than $1000. Thus, for every issue sold, the investor can buy more than one of the offered obligations.

The expectation is that the yield spread imbalance will be corrected because the yield on the offering bond will *decline* to the level of the issue that you currently hold. Thus, you would realize capital gains by switching out of your current position into the higher yielding obligation. This swap is described in Table 19.2.

While there are only modest differential rewards in *current* income, it is clear that, as the yield imbalance is corrected, attractive capital gains can be earned causing a handsome differential in *realized* yield. The work-out time is important in order to realize as high a differential return as possible. Note that, even if the yield is not corrected until maturity, 30 years hence, you will still attain minor improvement in realized yield (less than 10 basis points). In contrast, if the correction takes place in one year, the differential return is much greater, as shown in Table 19.2.

At the end of the work-out time, you would have additional capital available for a subsequent swap or investment transactions. Of course, there are risks in this swap. In addition to the pressure of work-out time, the market could move *against* you, the yield spread may *not* be temporary, and the issue may *not* be a viable swap candidate if the spread exists because the issue is of a lower quality.

Tax Swap.   The tax swap is the most popular swap with individual bond investors. It is a relatively simple procedure that involves no projections and few risks. The concept rests on the existence of tax laws and of *realized capital gains* in some other part of the portfolio. Assume you held $100,000 worth of corporate bonds for a period of two years and sold the securities for $150,000. As a result, you have a capital gain of $50,000. One way to eliminate the tax liability of that capital gain is to review the portfolio for any issues that may have comparable long-term capital losses.[5] If you found another long-term investment of $100,000 that presently has a current market value of $50,000, you could execute a tax swap to establish the $50,000 capital loss. By offsetting this capital loss and the comparable capital gain, you would enjoy *reduced income taxes.*

Municipal bonds are considered particularly attractive tax swap candidates since an investor can *increase his tax-free income* and still use the capital loss (which is subject to normal federal and state taxation) to *reduce capital gains tax liability.* To continue our illustration, assume that you own $100,000 worth of

---

[5] While this discussion deals with tax swaps that involve bonds, comparable strategies could be used with other types of investments.

TABLE 19.2
A Substitution Swap

Substitution Swap: A swap executed to take advantage of temporary market anomalies in yield spreads between issues that are equivalent with respect to coupon, quality, and maturity.

Example: Currently Hold: 30-yr., Aa 12.0% coupon priced at $1,000 to yield 12.0%
          Swap Candidate: 30-yr., Aa 12.0% coupon priced at $984.08 to yield 12.2%
          Assumed work-out period: 1 year
          Reinvested at 12.0%

	Current Bond	Candidate Bond
Dollar Investment	$1,000.00	$ 984.08
Coupon	120.00	120.00
i on One Coupon (12.0% for 6 mos.)	3.60	3.60
Principal Value at Year End (12.0% YTM)	1,000.00	1,000.00
Total Accrued	1,123.60	1,123.60
Total Gain	123.60	139.52
Gain per Invested Dollar	.1236	.1418
Realized Compound Yield	12.00%	13.71%

Value of Swap: 171 basis points in one year.

The rewards for the substitution swap are realized in terms of additional basis point pick-ups for YTM and realized compound yield and in capital gains that accrue when the anomaly in yield corrects itself.

In the substitution swap, it is important for you to realize that any basis point pick-up (171 points in this example) will be realized only during the work-out period. Thus, in our example, in order to obtain the 171 basis point increase in realized compound yield, you must swap an average of once each year and pick up an average of 20 basis points in yield to maturity on each swap.

Potential risks associated with the substitution swap include:
1. A yield spread thought to be temporary may, in fact, be permanent, thus reducing capital gains advantages.
2. The market rate may change adversely.

Swap evaluation procedure is patterned after a technique suggested by Sidney Homer and Martin L. Leibowitz.
SOURCE: Adapted from the book *Inside the Yield Book* by Sidney Homer and Martin L. Leibowitz, Ph.D. © 1972 by Prentice-Hall. Published by Prentice-Hall, Englewood Cliffs, N.J. 07632.

New York City, 20-year, 7 percent bonds which presently have a market value of $50,000. You, therefore, have a tax loss; now all that is needed is a comparable bond swap candidate. Suppose you are offered (or find) a New York City bond of comparable maturity which carries a 7.1 percent coupon and also has a market value of 50. By selling your New York 7's and instantaneously reinvesting in a comparable amount of New York 7.1's, you would totally eliminate any capital gains tax liability from the corporate bond transaction. In effect, you have $50,000 of capital gains tax-free, and you can increase your current tax-free yield. Of course, the money saved by eliminating the tax liability can then be used for investment purposes to increase the yield on the portfolio. This is shown in Table 19.3.

TABLE 19.3
A Tax Swap

Tax Swap: A swap undertaken in a situation when you wish to offset capital gains in other securities through the sale of a bond currently held and selling at a discount from the price paid at purchase. By swapping into a bond with as nearly identical features as possible, you can use the capital loss on the sale of the bond for tax purposes and still maintain your current position in the market.

Example: Currently Hold: $100,000 worth of corporate bonds with current market value of $150,000 *and* $100,000 in N.Y., 20-year, 7% bonds with current market value of $50,000.
　　　　Swap Candidate: $50,000 in N.Y., 20-year, 7.1% bonds,

A.	Corporate Bonds Sold and Long-Term Capital Gains Profit Established	$50,000	
	Capital Gains Tax Liability (Assume you have 20% capital gains tax rate.) ($50,000 × .20)		$10,000
B.	N.Y. 7's Sold and Long-Term Capital *Loss* Established	$50,000	
	Reduction in Capital Gains Tax Liability ($50,000 × .20)		($10,000)
	Net Capital Gains Tax Liability		0
	Tax *Savings* Realized		$10,000
C.	Complete Tax Swap by Buying N.Y. 7.1's from Proceeds of N.Y. 7's Sale (Therefore, amount invested remains largely the *same*.)[a]		
	Annual Tax Free Interest Income — N.Y. 7's	$ 7,000	
	Annual Tax Free Interest Income — N.Y. 7.1's	$ 7,100	
	Net *Increase* in *Annual* Tax-Free Interest Income	$ 100	

[a] N.Y. 7.1's will result in substantial capital gains when liquidated at maturity (since they were bought at deep discounts) and, therefore, will be subject to future capital gains tax liability. The swap is designed to use the capital loss resulting from the swap to offset capital gains from other investments. At the same time, your funds remain in a security almost identical to your previous holding while you receive a slight increase in both current income and YTM.

Since the tax swap involves no projections in terms of work-out period, interest rate changes, etc., the risks involved are minimal. Your major concern should be to avoid potential wash sales.

The only caveat is that you cannot swap *identical* issues. In other words, you could not sell the New York 7's to establish a loss and then instantaneously buy back the same New York 7's. If it is not a different issue, the IRS considers such a transaction a *wash sale* and does not allow the loss to be claimed. It is easier to avoid wash sales in the bond market than it is in the stock market because every bond issue, even though it might have identical coupons and maturities, is considered distinct. Likewise, it is easier to find comparable issues in the bond market that have only modest differences in coupon, maturity, quality, etc. Such tax swap transactions are common at year end as investors establish capital losses. Also remember that the capital loss *must* occur in the *same taxable year* as the capital gain does.

This procedure is slightly different from other swap transactions since it does not rest upon temporary market anomalies. Rather, it exists solely because of tax statutes.

IMMUNIZATION STRATEGIES

As noted, in contrast to a buy-and-hold strategy or one of the several active strategies, a portfolio manager, after consulting with his client, may decide that the optimal strategy is to immunize the portfolio. The purpose of this strategy is to derive a specified rate of return (quite close to the current market rate) during a given investment horizon regardless of what happens to market interest rates; i.e., you are attempting to immunize the portfolio from interest rate changes.

In this section we will consider how and why immunization works and the practical requirements for it. We will also discuss contingent immunization that is an extension of classical immunization. *Contingent immunization* allows a portfolio manager some opportunities to engage in active bond portfolio management while retaining a safety net of classical immunization.

Components of Interest Rate Risk

A major problem encountered in bond portfolio management is deriving a given rate of return to satisfy an ending wealth requirement at a future specific date — i.e., the investment horizon. If the term structure of interest rates were flat and the level of market rates never changed between time of purchase and the future specific date when funds were required, it would be possible to acquire a bond with a term to maturity equal to the desired investment horizon, and the ending wealth from the bond purchase would equal the *promised* wealth position implied by the promised yield to maturity. Specifically, the ending wealth position would be the beginning wealth times the compound value of a dollar at the promised yield to maturity. Unfortunately, in the real world, the term structure of interest rates is not typically flat and the level of interest rates is constantly changing.

Because of changes in the shape of the term structure and changes in the interest rate levels, the bond portfolio manager faces what is referred to as *interest rate risk* between the time of investment and the future target date. Specifically, *interest rate risk can be defined as the uncertainty regarding ending wealth position due to changes in market interest rates between the time of purchase and the target date.* In turn, interest rate risk is composed of two risks: *price risk* and *coupon reinvestment risk.* The price risk occurs because if interest rates change before the target date and the bond is sold before maturity, the market price for the bond (i.e., the *realized price*) will differ from the *expected price* assuming there was no change in rates. If rates increased since the time of purchase, the realized price for the bond in the secondary market would be below expectations, while if interest rates declined, the realized price would be above expectations.

The coupon reinvestment risk arises because the yield to maturity computation implicitly assumes that all coupon flows will be reinvested to yield the promised yield to maturity.[6] If, after the purchase of the bond, interest rates

---

[6] This point was discussed in detail in Chapter 17 and also in Sidney Homer and Martin L. Leibowitz, *Inside the Yield Book* (Englewood Cliffs, N.J.: Prentice-Hall, 1972), Chapter 1.

decline, it will not be possible to reinvest the coupon cash flows at the promised yield to maturity; they will be reinvested at lower rates and the ending wealth would be below expectations. In contrast, if interest rates increase, the interim cash flows will be reinvested at rates above expectations, and ending wealth would be above expectations.

Classical Immunization and Interest Rate Risk

Note that the price risk and the reinvestment risk derived from a change in interest rates *have an opposite effect on the investor's ending wealth position.* Specifically, an *increase* in the level of market interest rates will cause an ending price that is *below* expectations, but the reinvestment of interim cash flows will be at a rate *above* expectations. In contrast, a *decline* in market interest rates will provide a *higher* than expected ending price but *lower* than expected ending wealth from the reinvestment of interim cash flows. It is clearly important to a bond portfolio manager with a specific target date (i.e., known holding period) to attempt to eliminate these two risks derived from changing interest rates. The elimination of these risks from a bond portfolio is referred to as *immunization.* This concept is discussed by Redington,[7] and it is defined by Fisher and Weil as follows:

> A portfolio of investments in bonds is *immunized* for a holding period if its value at the end of the holding period, regardless of the course of interest rates during the holding period, must be at least as large as it would have been had the interest-rate function been constant throughout the holding period.
>
> If the realized return on an investment in bonds is sure to be at least as large as the appropriately computed yield to the horizon, then that investment is immunized.[8]

The Fisher and Weil study analyzed the *promised* yields on bonds for the period 1925–1968 compared to the *realized* returns on bonds. The significant difference between these yields indicated the importance of being able to immunize a bond portfolio. They showed that it is possible to immunize a bond portfolio if you can make one assumption. The required assumption is: *if the interest rate function shifts, the change in interest rates is the same for all future rates.* Somewhat more technically, the assumption says that if forward interest rates change, all rates change by the same amount. Given this assumption, Fisher and Weil proved that *a portfolio of bonds is immunized from the interest rate risk if the duration of the portfolio is equal to the desired investment horizon.* As an example, if the desired holding period of a bond portfolio is eight years, in order to immunize the portfolio, the *duration* of the bond portfolio should equal eight years. In order to have a portfolio with a given duration, the weighted average duration (with weights equal to the proportion of value) is set at the desired

---

[7] F. M. Redington, "Review of the Principles of Life – Office Valuations," *Journal of the Institute of Actuaries,* 78 (1952) 286–340.

[8] Lawrence Fisher and Roman L. Weil, "Coping with the Risk of Interest Rate Fluctuations: Returns to Bond-holders from Naive and Optimal Strategies," *Journal of Business,* 44 no. 4 (October 1971): 408–431.

length following an interest payment, and all subsequent cash flows are invested in securities to keep the portfolio duration equal to the remaining horizon value.

The immunization theorem by Fisher and Weil showed that the two risks discussed (price risk and reinvestment rate risk) are affected differently by a change in market rates; i.e., when the price change is positive, the reinvestment change will be negative and vice versa. The crucial question regarding immunization is: when will these two components of interest rate risk be equal so that they offset each other? Fisher and Weil proved that *duration was the time period at which the price risk and the coupon reinvestment risk of a bond portfolio are of equal magnitude but opposite in direction.*[9]

Application of the Immunization Principle

Subsequently, Fisher and Weil simulated the effects of applying the immunization concept in the real world compared to a naive portfolio strategy where the portfolio's maturity was equal to the investment horizon; i.e., if the investment horizon was eight years, the average term to maturity of the portfolio would be eight years. Clearly, the duration of the portfolio of coupon bonds with an average maturity of eight years would be shorter than eight years. The simulation computed the ending wealth ratios for alternative investment horizons (5, 10, and 20 years) assuming: (1) the expected yield was realized (the yield curve never shifted), (2) the portfolio was constructed so that the *duration* was equal to the investment horizon (i.e., the duration strategy), and (3) the portfolio's *maturity* was equal to the investment horizon (i.e., the naive maturity strategy). They compared the ending wealth ratio for the duration and naive strategy portfolios to the wealth ratio, assuming no change in the interest rate structure. The point is, if a portfolio was perfectly immunized, the *actual* ending wealth should equal the *expected* ending wealth implied by the promised yield. Therefore, these comparisons should indicate which portfolio strategy does a superior job of immunization. It was shown that *the duration strategy results were consistently closer to the expected promised yield results,* although the results were not perfect (i.e., the duration portfolio was not perfectly immunized). The difference was because the basic assumption was not always true; when interest rates changed, all interest rates did *not* change by the same amount. The authors concluded that the naive maturity strategy removes most of the uncertainty of the expected wealth ratio from a long-term bond portfolio, and much of the remaining uncertainty is removed when the duration strategy is employed.

Bierwag and Kaufman[10] pointed out that there are several specifications of the duration measure. The duration measure derived by Macauley,[11] which is

---

[9] This is also noted and discussed in G. O. Bierwag and George G. Kaufman, "Coping with the Risk of Interest Rate Fluctuations: A Note," *Journal of Business,* 50 no. 3 (July 1977): 364–370; and G. O. Bierwag, "Immunization, Duration, and the Term Structure of Interest Rates," *Journal of Financial and Quantitative Analysis,* 12 no. 5 (December 1977): 725–742.

[10] Bierwag and Kaufman, "Coping with the Risk of Interest Rate Fluctuations: A. Note," pp. 364–370.

[11] Frederick R. Macauley, *Some Theoretical Problems Suggested by the Movements of Interest Rates, Bond Yields, and Stock Prices in the United States Since 1865* (New York: National Bureau of Economic Research, 1938).

used throughout this book, discounts all flows by the prevailing average yield to maturity on the bond being measured. Alternatively, Fisher and Weil[12] defined duration using future one period discount rates (forward rates) to discount the future flows. Depending upon the shape of the yield curve, the two definitions could give different answers. If all forward rates are equal so that the yield curve is flat, the two definitions will compute equal durations. After similarly demonstrating that the way to immunize a portfolio is to match duration and the investment horizon, Bierwag and Kaufman noted that *the definition of duration used should be a function of the nature of the shock to the interest rate structure.* Specifically, it is possible to conceive of an *additive* shock to interest rates where all interest rates are changed by the same nominal amount (e.g., 50 basis points). Alternatively, the interest rate shock could be multiplicative where all interest rates change by the same percent (e.g., all rates decline by 10 percent). It was proven in Bierwag[13] that the optimal definition of duration used to immunize a portfolio perfectly depends upon the nature of the shock to the interest rate structure. In the case of an additive shock the Fisher and Weil definition is best, while a third definition of duration is best if the shock is multiplicative. Bierwag and Kaufman computed the duration for a set of bonds using the three definitions of duration (D_1 = Macauley, D_2 = Fisher-Weil, D_3 = Bierwag-Kaufman) and concluded:

> Except at high coupons and long maturities, the values of the three definitions do not vary greatly. Thus, D_1 may be used as a first approximation for D_2 and D_3. The expression for D_1 has the additional advantage of being a function of the yield to maturity of the bond. As a result, neither a forecast of the stream of one-period forward rates over the maturity of the bond nor a specific assumption about the nature of the random shocks is required.[14]

Example of Classical Immunization.   Table 19.4 shows the effect of attempting to immunize a portfolio by matching the investment horizon and the duration of a bond portfolio using a single bond. The portfolio manager's investment horizon is eight years, and the current yield to maturity for eight-year bonds is 8 percent. Therefore, the ending wealth ratio for an investor should be $1.8509[(1.08)^8]$, which should be the ending wealth ratio for a completely immunized portfolio. The example considers two portfolio strategies—the maturity strategy where the term to maturity is set at eight years, and the duration strategy where the duration is set at eight years. For the maturity strategy, the portfolio manager acquires an eight-year, 8 percent bond. In contrast, for the duration strategy, the portfolio manager acquires a *ten*-year, 8 percent bond which has approximately an eight-year duration (8.12 years), assuming an 8 percent yield to maturity (see Table 18.2). It is assumed there is a single shock to the interest rate structure at the end of Year 4, and the market yield goes from 8 percent to 6 percent and remains at 6 percent through Year 8.

---

[12] Fisher and Weil, "Coping with the Risk of Interest Rate Fluctuations: Returns to Bondholders from Naive and Optimal Strategies," *Journal of Business,* 44 no. 4 (October 1971): 408–431.

[13] Bierwag, "Immunization, Duration, and the Term Structure of Interest Rates," pp. 725–742.

[14] Bierwag-Kaufman, "Coping with the Risk of Interest Rate Fluctuations: A Note," p. 367.

TABLE 19.4

An Example of the Effect of a Change in Market Rates on a Bond (Portfolio) that Uses the Maturity Strategy Versus the Duration Strategy

	Results with Maturity Strategy			Results with Duration Strategy		
Year	Cash Flow	Reinvestment Rate	End Value	Cash Flow	Reinvestment Rate	End Value
1	$ 80	.08	$ 80.00	$ 80	.08	$ 80.00
2	80	.08	166.40	80	.08	166.40
3	80	.08	259.71	80	.08	259.71
4	80	.08	360.49	80	.08	360.49
5	80	.06	462.12	80	.06	462.12
6	80	.06	596.85	80	.06	596.85
7	80	.06	684.04	80	.06	684.04
8	$1080	.06	$1805.08	$1120.64[a]	.06	$1845.72

Expected Wealth Ratio = 1.8509 or $1850.90.

[a] The bond could be sold at its market value of $1,040.64, which is the value for an 8 percent bond with two years to maturity priced to yield 6 percent.

As shown, due to the interest rate change, the wealth ratio for the maturity strategy bond is *below* the desired wealth ratio because of the shortfall in the reinvestment cash flow after Year 4. (That is, the interim coupon cash flow is reinvested at 6 percent rather than 8 percent.) Note that *the maturity strategy eliminated the price risk* because the bond matured at the end of Year 8. Alternatively, the duration strategy portfolio likewise suffered a shortfall in reinvestment cash flow because of the change in market rates. Notably, this shortfall due to the reinvestment risk is offset by an *increase* in the ending value for the bond due to the decline in market rates. The bond is sold at the end of Year 8 at 104.06 because it is an 8 percent coupon bond with two years to maturity selling to yield 6 percent.

If market interest rates had increased during this period, the maturity strategy portfolio would have experienced an *excess* of reinvestment income compared to the expected cash flow, and the wealth ratio for this strategy would have been above expectations. In contrast, in the duration portfolio, the excess cash flow from reinvestment under this assumption would have been *offset* by a decline in the ending price for the bond. While under these latter assumptions the maturity strategy would have provided a higher than expected ending value, the whole purpose of immunization was to *eliminate uncertainty* (i.e., have the *realized* wealth position equal the *expected* wealth position) which is what is accomplished with the duration strategy.

Application of Classical Immunization.   Once you understand the reasoning behind immunization (i.e., that it is meant to offset components of interest rate risk) and the general principle (match duration and the investment horizon), it could be tempting to conclude that this strategy is fairly simple to apply. One might even consider that it is a passive strategy; i.e., simply match duration and the investment horizon and you can ignore the portfolio until the end of the horizon period. The fact is *the application of immunization is neither simple,* *nor is it a passive strategy.* The following discussion indicates why immunization cannot be considered a passive strategy, and the implied requirements for properly implementing immunization makes it very clear that it is not simple.

The point is, except for the case of a zero coupon bond, *an immunized portfolio requires frequent rebalancing.* The zero coupon bond is unique because it is a pure discount bond. As such, there is *no reinvestment risk* because the discounting assumes that the value of the bond will grow at the discount rate. For example, if you discount a future value at 10 percent, the present value factor assumes that the value will grow at a compound rate of 10 percent to maturity. Also, there is *no price risk* if you set the duration at your time horizon because you will receive the face value of the bond at maturity. Also, recall that *the duration of a zero coupon bond is always equal to its term to maturity.*

As noted, except for a zero coupon bond, it is necessary for the portfolio manager to rebalance the portfolio frequently. The reason is simply that in order for the immunization concept to work, *the duration of the portfolio should always be equal to the remaining time horizon.* It is *not* possible to set a duration that is equal to the remaining horizon at the initiation of the portfolio and ignore it thereafter.

There are several characteristics of duration that dictate rebalancing. First, *duration declines slower than term to maturity assuming no change in market interest rates.* As an example, assume you have a security with a computed duration of five years at a 10 percent market yield. A year later, you compute the duration of the security at 10 percent to find that it has a duration of approximately 4.2 years; i.e., while the term to maturity has declined by a year, the duration has only declined by 0.8 years. This means that, assuming *no* changes in market rates, the portfolio manager must *rebalance* the portfolio to *reduce* its duration to four years. Typically, this is not too difficult because cash flows from the portfolio can be invested in short-term T-bills if necessary.

A second consideration is the property that *duration changes with a change in market interest rates.* Recall the discussion in Chapter 18 of the inverse relationship between market rates and duration: for a given bond, with *higher* market rates there will be *lower* duration and vice versa. This means that a portfolio with the required duration can have its duration changed immediately if market rates change. The portfolio manager would have to rebalance the portfolio if the deviation becomes too large.

Another factor is *the assumption that when market rates change, they will change by the same amount and in the same direction.* Clearly, if this does not happen, it will affect the performance of a portfolio of diffuse bonds. As an example, consider a portfolio of long- and short-term bonds that average out to 6-year duration (e.g., two-year duration bonds and ten-year duration bonds). Assume that the term structure curve changes such that short-term rates decline and long-term rates rise. In this instance, you would experience a major price decline *and* also would be penalized on reinvestment, assuming you generally reinvest the cash flow in short-term securities. This potential problem suggests that you should attempt to bunch your portfolio selections close to the desired duration. For example, an 8-year duration portfolio should be made up of 7–9-year duration securities to avoid this problem.

   Finally, there can always be a problem of acquiring the bonds you want in the market. For instance, can you buy long duration bonds at the price you consider acceptable?

   In summary, immunization can be a very desirable portfolio strategy for specified portfolios. At the same time, it is important to recognize that it is *not a passive strategy* and *it is not without potential problems.*[15]

Contingent Immunization

Subsequent to the development and application of classical immunization, Leibowitz and Weinberger initiated a technique referred to as *contingent immunization.*[16] Basically, contingent immunization allows a bond portfolio manager to pursue the highest returns available through active strategies while relying on classical bond immunization techniques to ensure the portfolio achieves a given minimal return over the investment horizon. Put another way, it allows active portfolio management with a safety net provided by classical immunization.

   To understand contingent immunization it is necessary to consider classical immunization from a slightly different perspective. Remember the ultimate objective of immunization is for the ending value of the portfolio to equal what it would be with no change in market rates. The earlier discussion centered on the fact that immunization worked because for changes in interest rates, there were opposite impacts on price and on reinvestment risk; these two impacts were equal when the duration of the portfolio was equal to the investment horizon. In other words, when the portfolio has the appropriate duration (equal to the investment horizon), *its price sensitivity ensures that for any change in interest rates, the dollar value of the portfolio changes such that the new asset value compounded at the new market rate equals the desired ending value.*

   Consider the following example of a portfolio with an initial value of $10 million. If you were to immunize it at 10 percent for a five-year period, you would expect an ending wealth value of:

$$\$10 \text{ million} \times 1.6105 \ (1.10^5 = 1.6105) = \$16,105,000.$$

   The point is, if interest rates decline, you would expect the value of the portfolio to increase such that, even at the lower rate of return, the ending value of the portfolio would be $16,105,000. To continue the example, assume that at the end of Year 1, when the value was $11 million (one year at 10 percent), market rates suddenly declined to 8 percent. Because of the decline in market interest rates, there would be an increase in the value of the portfolio in line with its current duration and the change in yield, to $11,837,558. This new higher

[15] Several of these problems were discussed in William L. Nemerever, "Managing Bond Portfolios through Immunization Strategies," *The Revolution in Techniques for Managing Bond Portfolios* (Charlottesville, Va.: The Institute of Chartered Financial Analysts, 1983), 39–65.

[16] Martin L. Leibowitz and Alfred Weinberger, "Contingent Immunization — Part I: Risk Control Procedures," *Financial Analysts Journal,* 38 no. 6 (November–December 1982): 17–32; Martin L. Leibowitz and Alfred Weinberger, "Contingent Immunization — Part II: Problem Areas," *Financial Analysts Journal,* 29 no. 1 (January–February 1983): 35–50. This section draws heavily from these articles.

FIGURE 19.1
Classical Immunization

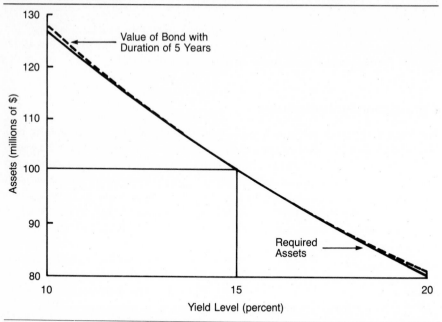

SOURCE: Martin L. Leibowitz and Alfred Weinberger, "Contingent Immunization — Part I: Risk Control Procedures," *Financial Analysts Journal*, 38 no. 6 (November–December 1982): 17–32.

value of the portfolio compounded at 8 percent would provide the desired ending wealth position as follows:

$$\$11,837,558 \times 1.3605 = \$16,104,997 \ (1.08^4 = 1.3605).$$

As noted, the purpose of immunization is to have the value of the portfolio change with a change in market interest rates so that the ending wealth value will equal the target value at the new interest rate. The crucial point is: *this required change in value only occurs when the duration of the portfolio is equal to the remaining time horizon.* The portfolio will have the necessary price sensitivity if duration equals the horizon. That is why it is so important that the duration be maintained at this value.

Figure 19.1 shows an example of the required assets for five years beginning at 15 percent. With five years left at 15 percent you need $100 million of assets, with lower rates you need more assets, and with higher rates you need less assets. The dotted line indicates that the price sensitivity of a portfolio with a duration of five years will have almost exactly the price sensitivity required.

The idea of contingent immunization is that if you are willing to accept a potential return below the current market return, this *cushion spread* (i.e., the difference between the current market return and some floor rate) will provide a great deal of flexibility for the manager to engage in active portfolio strategies. As

FIGURE 19.2
Price Behavior Required for Floor Return

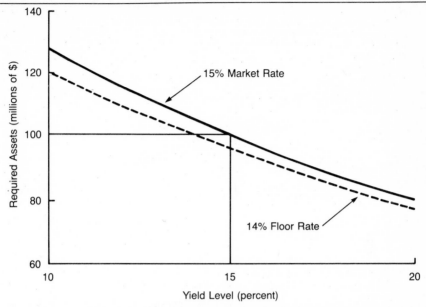

SOURCE: Martin L. Leibowitz and Alfred Weinberger, "Contingent Immunization— Part I: Risk Control Procedures," *Financial Analysts Journal,* 38 no 6 (November–December 1982): 17–32.

an example, if current market rates are 15 percent, a manager and the client might be willing to accept a floor rate of 14 percent, because it is still a very good rate and the acceptance of this lower rate will mean that the portfolio manager does not have the same ending asset requirements. Because of this lower floor rate, it is possible to allow some value declines while attempting to do better than the market through active management strategies.

Figure 19.2 shows that the required value of assets at 14 percent is below that for 15 percent. The portfolio manager can engage in various strategies to increase the value of the portfolio above that required at 14 percent. As an example, assume that the portfolio manager believes that market rates will decline and would like to acquire a 30-year bond which has a duration greater than the investment horizon of five years. In such a case, the bond has greater price sensitivity to changes in market rates; i.e., if rates decline as expected, the value of the portfolio will rise above the value stipulated initially. In contrast, if rates increase, the value of the portfolio will decline rapidly. Depending upon how high rates go, the value of the portfolio could decline to a figure clearly below that needed to reach the desired ending wealth value at 14 percent. Figure 19.3 shows that if rates decline from 15 percent, the portfolio would experience a large increase in value and develop a safety margin (i.e., a portfolio value above the required value). In contrast, if rates increase, the value of the portfolio will decline until you reach the asset value required at 14 percent. When the portfolio

FIGURE 19.3
Safety Margin for a Portfolio of 30-Year Bonds

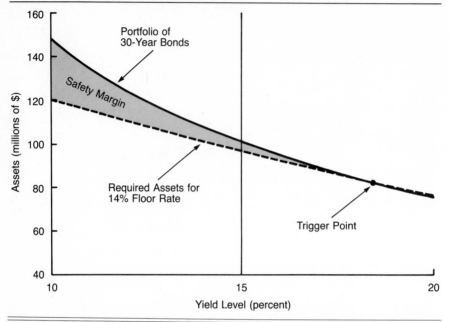

SOURCE: Martin L. Leibowitz and Alfred Weinberger, "Contingent Immunization — Part I: Risk Control Procedures," *Financial Analysts Journal,* 38 no 6 (November–December 1982): 17–32.

value reaches this point of minimum return (referred to as a *trigger point*), it is necessary to stop active portfolio management and use classical immunization with the remaining assets to ensure the desired ending assets at the lower rate.

Potential Return.   The concept of potential return is helpful in understanding the objective of contingent immunization. Specifically, *potential return is the return the portfolio would achieve over the entire investment horizon if, at any point, the assets in hand were immunized at the then-current market rate.*

Figure 19.4 contains the various points on Figure 19.3. If the portfolio were immediately immunized when market rates were 15 percent, it would naturally earn the 15 percent market rate; i.e., its potential return would be 15 percent. Alternatively, if yields declined instantaneously to 10 percent, the portfolio's asset value would increase to $147 million (see Figure 19.3). If this $147 million portfolio were then immunized at the market rate of 10 percent over the remaining five-year period, the resulting portfolio would grow to a total value of $239 million. This ending value of $239 million represents an 18.25 percent rate of return on the original $100 million portfolio. Consequently, as shown in Figure 19.4, the portfolio's potential return would be 18.25 percent. That is, if rates decline by 5 percent, the potential return at this point in time is 18.25 percent.)

In contrast, if interest rates rose, the asset value would decline substantially

FIGURE 19.4
The Potential Return Concept

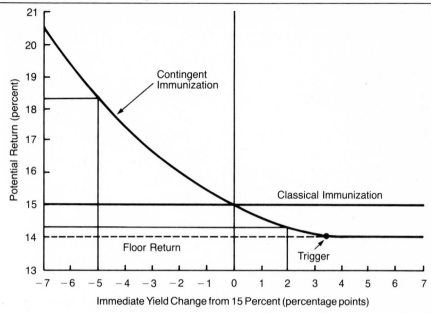

SOURCE: Martin L. Leibowitz and Alfred Weinberger, "Contingent Immunization — Part I: Risk Control Procedures," *Financial Analysts Journal,* 38 no. 6 (November–December 1982): 17–32.

and the potential return would decline. For example, if market rates rose to 17 percent (i.e., a yield change of 2 percent), the asset value of the 30-year par bond portfolio would decline to $88 million (see Figure 19.3). If this portfolio of $88 million were immunized for the remaining five years at 17 percent, the ending value would be $199 million at the investment horizon. This ending value corresponds to a potential return of 14.32 percent for the total period.

As Figure 19.3 shows, if rates rose to the 18.50 percent interest rate level, the 30-year bonds would decline to a value of $81 million. At this value, the portfolio would have to be immunized. Obviously, at this point, assuming the remaining assets of $81 million were invested at 18.50 percent, the potential return for the portfolio would be exactly 14 percent. Regardless of what happens to subsequent market rates, the portfolio has been immunized at 14 percent. That is a major characteristic of the immunized portfolio; if there is proper monitoring, you can be assured of the minimum return specified.

Monitoring the Immunized Portfolio.   Clearly, a crucial factor in the contingent immunized portfolio is monitoring it to ensure that if the asset value falls to the trigger point, it is detected and the appropriate action is taken to ensure the portfolio is immunized at the floor-level rate. This can be done using a chart as in Figure 19.5. The top line is the current value of the portfolio over time. The

FIGURE 19.5
Contingent Immunization over Time

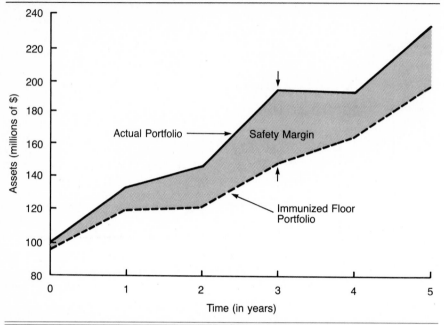

SOURCE: Martin L. Leibowitz and Alfred Weinberger, "Contingent Immunization — Part I: Risk Control Proce-dures," *Financial Analysts Journal,* 38 no.6 (November–December 1982): 17–32.

bottom line is the required value of the immunized floor portfolio. Specifically, the bottom line is *the required value needed if we were to immunize at today's rates to attain the necessary ending wealth value.*

As an example of how this floor portfolio would be constructed, consider the original 14 percent value which we indicated would imply an ending wealth value of about $196 million. If, one year after the initiation of the portfolio, market rates were 10 percent, you would need a minimum of approximately $132.65 million to get to $196 million in four years. This is $196 million times the present value factor for 10 percent for four years, assuming semiannual com-pounding. Put another way, $132.65 invested at 10 percent for four years equals $196 million. The point is, if the active manager had predicted correctly and had a long duration portfolio under these conditions of declining market rates, the actual value would be much higher than the required value, and you would have a safety margin. Another year later, you would determine the assets needed at the new rate. Assuming the rates had increased to 12 percent, you could determine that you would need a floor portfolio of about $138.18 million, because this is the present value of the $196 million for three years at 12 percent (assuming semian-nual compounding). Again, you would expect the actual value of the portfolio to be greater than this, so you still have a safety margin. If you ever reach the point where the actual value of the portfolio is equal to the required floor value, you

FIGURE 19.6
Comparison of Return Distributions

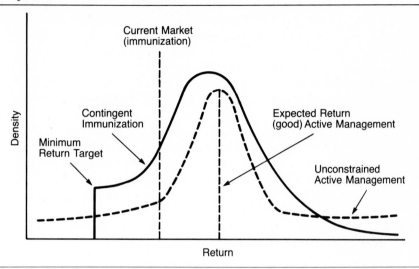

SOURCE: Martin L. Leibowitz and Alfred Weinberger, "Contingent Immunization — Part II: Problem Areas," *Financial Analysts Journal,* 39 no. 1 (January – February 1983): 35 – 50.

must stop the active management and immunize what is left *at the current market rate* to ensure the end value is $196 million.

In summary, contingent immunization strategy encompasses the opportunity to engage in active portfolio management *if* you are willing to accept a floor return below what is currently available. You can achieve this minimum level return through the use of classical immunization *if* it becomes necessary. Put another way, you are willing to accept a minimum return below what is currently available with classical immunization for the opportunity to try for returns that are greater than what is currently available through classical immunization. A graph that describes these trade-offs is in Figure 19.6.

PORTFOLIO IMPLICATIONS

The high level of interest rates that has prevailed since the latter part of the 1960s has provided increasingly attractive returns to bond investors, while the wide *swings* in interest rates that have accompanied the high levels of market yield have provided capital gains opportunities for the more aggressive portfolio managers. It might be argued that this recent performance of fixed-income securities is not out of the ordinary. In fact, it may be substandard when compared to performance of other investment vehicles, which may raise questions about the place of these securities in a *total* portfolio. An important consideration for portfolio managers, therefore, is the proper role of fixed-income securities in an efficient market.

Bonds in a Total Portfolio Context

A more attractive market environment, along with more aggressive and sophisticated management tactics, has enhanced the investment role of fixed-income securities. When viewed in an efficient market context, the performance of fixed-income securities has improved even more than indicated by returns alone because bonds offer substantial diversification benefits in fully managed portfolios. In an efficient market, neither stocks nor bonds should dominate a portfolio. Instead, some combination of stocks and bonds should provide a superior risk-adjusted return compared to one composed solely of either taken alone, assuming low correlation between stocks and bonds. Such was the theme of an article by Sharpe.[17] Sharpe confirmed that stock returns were superior to bond yields over his test period of 1938–1971. However, when bonds were viewed in the context of a financial portfolio, his results showed that, due to the favorable covariance between bonds and equities, the addition of fixed-income securities to an equity portfolio vastly improved the return per unit of variability measure. Therefore, the diversification attributes of fixed-income securities should be fully appreciated by investors and portfolio managers.

Bonds and Capital Market Theory

Modern capital market theory contends that, when the universe of financial assets is evaluated in terms of risk-return characteristics, an upward sloping market line will occur; i.e., greater return is accompanied by greater risk. Financial assets which characteristically exhibit high levels of return logically possess higher levels of risk. Compared to other market vehicles, fixed-income securities have traditionally been viewed as low risk, and, therefore, the rates of return demanded by investors have been correspondingly modest.

A brief review of historical bond yields will quickly confirm this. In the absence of abnormal inflation (in the late 1950s and early 1960s), the returns from fixed-income securities were low. Since the late '60s, however, when the inflation rate increased, the level of bond yields likewise increased. In periods of high economic uncertainty, such as the recession of 1974, yields on low rated bonds (Baa obligations) moved to levels that *greatly* exceeded those on comparable higher rated obligations; i.e., the risk premiums on bonds increased substantially. This is rather common during periods of economic stress, and it points out the effect of perceived risk of default on investor returns. Because the risk of default for low rated obligations is naturally thought to increase during economic recessions, the yield on such obligations moves up accordingly.[18]

Clearly the risk-return behavior of fixed-income securities, in terms of yield for bonds of different quality, is compatible with traditional capital market theory. Capital market theory, however, also relates the risk-return behavior of

---

[17] William F. Sharpe, "Bonds vs. Stocks: Some Lessons from Capital Market Theory," *Financial Analysts Journal*, 29 no. 6 (November–December 1973): 74–80.

[18] For a detailed discussion on this topic that considers several studies on the subject, see James C. Van Horne, *Financial Market Rates and Flows* 2nd ed.(Englewood Cliffs, N.J.: Prentice-Hall, 1984), Chapter 6.

FIGURE 19.7
Risk Premium Curve,[a] 1950–1966

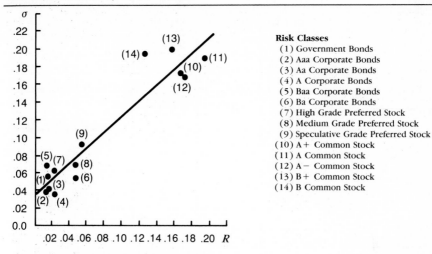

Risk Classes
(1) Government Bonds
(2) Aaa Corporate Bonds
(3) Aa Corporate Bonds
(4) A Corporate Bonds
(5) Baa Corporate Bonds
(6) Ba Corporate Bonds
(7) High Grade Preferred Stock
(8) Medium Grade Preferred Stock
(9) Speculative Grade Preferred Stock
(10) A + Common Stock
(11) A Common Stock
(12) A − Common Stock
(13) B + Common Stock
(14) B Common Stock

[a] Minimum term to maturity on bonds is 15 years.
Equation for least squares regression line is $y = .035 + .8783 \times R^2 = .90992$.

SOURCE: Robert M. Soldofsky and Roger L. Miller, "Risk Premium Curves for Different Classes of Long-Term Securities, 1950–1966," *Journal of Finance* (June 1969) 4 No. 2. Reprinted by permission.

fixed-income securities to *other* types of financial assets. Because fixed-income securities are considered to be relatively conservative investments, we would expect long-term bonds to be on the lower end of the capital market line.

Numerous tests have been conducted on capital market behavior, and one of the earlier studies examined the comparative risk-return characteristics of 14 classes of long-term securities.[19] Government bonds, various grades of corporate bonds, preferred stock, and common stock were compared in terms of their risk premium behavior. Figure 19.7 shows the basic findings of the study and confirms the a priori expectations since bonds behaved in line with capital market theory. More recent results of a study comparing corporate and government bonds to common stocks and treasury bill obligations were similar. Figure 19.8 indicates that the long-run risk-return behavior was as expected. Treasury bills have the least amount of risk and, therefore, provide the lowest risk-return profile, followed by government bonds, corporates, and finally, the most risky alternative, common stocks.[20]

Of course, such behavior is the reason for the diversification benefits of fixed-income securities. Because bonds have risk-return profiles that are different from those of equity securities, they provide viable diversification opportunities for portfolio managers. As Sharpe noted, while there is some correlation in

[19] Robert M. Soldofsky and Roger L. Miller, "Risk Premium Curves for Different Classes of Long-Term Securities, 1950–1966," *Journal of Finance,* 24 no. 2 (June 1969): 429–446.

[20] Roger G. Ibbotson and Rex A. Sinquefield, *Stocks, Bonds, Bills and Inflation: The Past and the Future* 1982 ed. (Charlottesville, Va.: The Financial Analysts Research Foundation, 1982).

FIGURE 19.8
Basic Series: Total Annual Returns, 1926–1981

Series	Geometric Mean (percent)	Arithmetic Mean (percent)	Standard Deviation (percent)	Distribution
Common Stocks	9.1	11.4	21.9	
Small Stocks	12.1	18.1	37.3	
Long-Term Corporate Bonds	3.6	3.7	5.6	
Long-Term Government Bonds	3.0	3.1	5.7	
U.S. Treasury Bills	3.0	3.1	3.1	
Inflation	3.0	3.1	5.1	

−90%   0%   +90%

SOURCE: Roger G. Ibbotson and Rex A. Sinquefield, *Stocks, Bills, and Inflation: The Past and the Future* (Financial Analysts Research Foundation, 1982). Reprinted by permission.

the return behavior of stocks and bonds, the "amount of such correlation by no means eliminates the advantages to be obtained from holding both types of investments."[21]

Bond Price Behavior in a CAPM Framework

The capital asset pricing model (CAPM) provides an excellent framework for explaining security returns as a function of risk. Typically security returns are defined as *ex post* holding period returns; therefore, rather than examining promised yield behavior, attention is directed toward *realized* yields.

When dealing with the CAPM, we are considering nondiversifiable market risk. It is logical to expect the returns from bonds to be linked directly to risk of default and interest rate risk. Certainly, interest rate risk should be nondiversifiable, but what about the risk of default? Some evidence suggests that default risk is also largely nondiversifiable because default experience is closely related to the business cycle.[22] Thus, the major bond risks are largely nondiversifiable; therefore, we should be able to define bond returns in the context of CAPM.

[21] William F. Sharpe, "Bonds vs. Stocks: Some Lessons from Capital Market Theory," *Financial Analysts Journal* 29, no. 6 (November–December 1973): 77. Sharpe's analysis of market behavior also uncovered similar risk-return behavior for stocks vs. bonds as observed in Figure 19.7 and Figure 19.8.

[22] Hickman, *Corporate Bond Quality*, and T. R. Atkinson, *Trends in Corporate Bond Quality* (New York: National Bureau of Economic Research, 1967).

Because of data collection problems, relatively few studies have examined bond price behavior in a CAPM framework. An early study that addressed this problem only showed a *modest* effect of beta on bond returns.[23] Using a population of 175 bonds, and a bond portfolio as the measure of market return, betas were computed and used to explain realized returns. Beta was found to have a small (the regression coefficient equaled 0.00983), although significant, effect on return within a multiple regression model. However, when beta was examined as a function of bond and issuer characteristics, it was found that bond betas were more responsive to the intrinsic characteristics of the issue than of the issuer. This indicates that the price behavior of an issue is intimately linked to such features as coupon, maturity (duration), and other characteristics that are influenced by the market behavior of interest rates.

There were similar default risk results in a study on bond betas.[24] The study dealt with the relationship between market risk and bond ratings and found that *average bond betas had no significant and consistent relationships with agency rating.* The explanation offered was that, since the data base involved only investment-grade securities, bond prices were reacting to interest rate movements *across* ratings. Thus, since the study dealt with interest-sensitive securities, interest rate risk, which is a market-related risk, has an overpowering effect on price performance and largely negated the effects of differential default risk (a company specific risk), which is reflected in comparative agency ratings. This is certainly compatible with our previous discussion, which indicates that the general movement in interest rates is more powerful than yield spreads and the differential bond yields that exist as a result of differential risk of default and agency ratings.

A subsequent study by Alexander examined some of the assumptions of the market model as related to bonds.[25] The results indicated two major factors that could cause problems in this area. First, the bond betas and the properties of the regression results were sensitive to the market index used.[26] Specifically, when he considered a pure stock index, a pure bond index, or a composite stock-bond index, there were clearly different results, and the pure bond index had the biggest problems. Second, the results also tended to be sensitive to the time period used; i.e., the bond betas tended to increase during periods when bond yields were abnormally high. The author concluded that one must be very cautious when interpreting results for bonds in the market model context.

A study by Weinstein computed betas for bonds also using several market series and related the betas to term to maturity, coupon, and bond ratings.[27] The

[23] John Percival, "Corporate Bonds in a Market Model Context," *Journal of Business Research,* 2 no. 4 (October 1974): 461–467.

[24] Frank K. Reilly and Michael D. Joehnk, "The Association between Market-Determined Risk Measures for Bonds and Bond Ratings," *Journal of Finance,* 31 no. 5 (December 1976): 1387–1403.

[25] Gordon J. Alexander, "Applying the Market Model to Long-Term Corporate Bonds," *Journal of Financial and Quantitative Analysis,* 15 no. 5 (December 1980): 1063–1080.

[26] Note that this is similar to the well-known work by Roll on market series, which will be discussed further in Chapter 20.

[27] Mark I. Weinstein, "The Systematic Risk of Corporate Bonds," *Journal of Financial and Quantitative Analysis,* 16 no. 3 (September 1981): 157–278.

results for beta using alternative market indexes (pure stock, pure bond, combined) indicated a very strong correlation between betas from the stock and the combined indexes, a fairly strong relationship between the betas from the bond and the combined indexes, and a weak relationship between the betas from stock and bond indexes. Because of some perceived problems of using duration, he examined maturity and coupon separately. The results were as you would expect knowing the impact of each of these variables on duration—there was a positive relationship between beta and term to maturity and a weak negative relationship between the coupon and beta. On the question of the relationship between beta and bond rating, there was no significant relationship for the top four classes of ratings (similar to Reilly and Joehnk), but there was a weak relationship when the top six ratings were included. The author postulated a nonlinear relationship where the risk of default only becomes significant for low ratings.

A more recent study by Weinstein employed the same sample, used the combined stock-bond index to compute the bond betas, and examined their stability over time.[28] He employed a model that assumed the bond betas are constant compared to a model that allowed the systematic risk to vary consistently with the Black-Scholes-Merton options pricing model. The results indicated definite instability in the risk measure; i.e., a model which assumes the bond betas change over time has more explanatory power than one which assumes constant risk. Also, the variation in systematic risk was found to be related to firm characteristics (e.g., debt/equity ratios, variance of rate of return on assets) and bond characteristics (coupon, term to maturity).

In summary, evidence on the usefulness of the CAPM as related to the bond market is mixed. First, there are obvious problems regarding the application in terms of the appropriate market index to use and the apparent lack of stability of the systematic risk measure. Further, there is some question as to the risk-return relationship, especially for the higher rated securities. The good news is that there appears to be a relationship between the systematic risk measure (however measured) and some characteristics of the firm and the bond.

Bond Market Efficiency

The efficient capital market hypothesis contends that market prices fully reflect all information so that consistently superior performance on the part of investors is largely unattainable. No institution or body of investors can command a superior investment position based on public information and/or timing advantages. Two versions of the efficient market hypothesis are examined in the context of fixed-income securities, the weak and the semistrong theories.

The weak form assumes that security prices fully reflect all market information and maintains that price movements are independent events; therefore, *historical* price information is largely useless in predicting *future* price behavior. There has not been an abundance of empirical research on the question of

---

[28] Mark I. Weinstein, "Bond Systematic Risk and the Option Pricing Model," *Journal of Finance*, 38 no. 5 (December 1983): 1415–1429.

bond market efficiency. However, the studies that considered the weak form of bond market efficiency have provided convincing evidence of price efficiency.

The vehicle for studying the weak form efficiency of bond prices has been the ability of investors to *forecast interest rates.* Such studies are logical because of the effects that interest rates have on price behavior and the prominent position that interest rate expectations occupy in bond portfolio management. If interest rates can be forecast with a high degree of certainty so, too, can future price behavior. Several studies[29] reached the same conclusion; interest rate behavior *cannot* be consistently forecast with a high degree of accuracy! In fact, one study goes so far as to suggest that the best forecast is no forecast at all. In these studies, the models developed ranged from the naive approach to fairly sophisticated techniques; some models used historical information and some ignored it. One study incorporated the interest rate expectations of acknowledged experts. The results were always the same since *the most naive model, or no forecast at all, provided the most successful measure of future interest rate behavior.* Thus, it is clear that, if interest rates cannot be forecast, then neither can bond prices using historical prices, which supports the weak form efficient market hypothesis.

The semistrong efficient market hypothesis has only recently been subject to empirical documentation in the bond market. This version of the hypothesis asserts that current prices fully reflect *all public knowledge* and efforts to obtain and evaluate such information are largely unproductive. Three studies on the information content of *bond ratings* are worth noting in this context.[30] The studies did not question the accuracy of agency ratings in reflecting the financial strength of the issuers, but they were directed toward examining the informational value of bond rating *changes.* Efficient market proponents contend that a rating change should have no effect on bond prices, since the information is not new but is already a factor in the current price of the issue. The results of the semistrong form of bond market efficiency are mixed but generally *supportive.* Some studies have indicated that the market fully anticipated bond rating changes, while others provide evidence that indicates no anticipation prior to public announcement of reclassification.

It has also been suggested that industrial bonds are more efficient than public utility bonds are in anticipating rating changes. As an aside, the major reason cited for the possible lack of market efficiency is the domination of the bond markets by institutions that are unable to buy and sell large positions and

---

[29] See, for example: Michael J. Prell, "How Well Do the Experts Forecast Interest Rates?" Federal Reserve Bank of Kansas City *Monthly Review* (September–October 1973): 3–13; Oswald D. Bowlin and John D. Martin, "Extrapolations of Yields over the Short Run: Forecast or Folly? *Journal of Monetary Economics,* 1 (1975): 275–288; R. Roll, *The Behavior of Interest Rates* (New York: Basic Books, 1970); William A. Bomberger and W. J. Frazer, "Interest Rates, Uncertainty, and the Livingston Data," *Journal of Finance,* 36 no. 3 (June 1981): 661–675; Stephen K. McNees, "The Recent Record of Thirteen Forecasters," Federal Reserve Bank of Boston *New England Economic Review* (September–October 1981); and Adrian W. Throop, "Interest Rate Forecasts and Market Efficiency," Federal Reserve Bank of San Francisco *Economic Review* (Spring 1981): 29–43.

[30] Steven Katz, "The Price Adjustment Process of Bonds to Rating Reclassifications: A Test of Bond Market Efficiency," *Journal of Finance,* 29 no. 2 (May 1974): 551–559; George W. Hettenhouse and William L. Sartoris, "An Analysis of the Informational Value of Bond-Rating Changes," *Quarterly Review of Economics and Business,* 16 no. 2 (Summer 1976): 65–78; George E. Pinches and Clay Singleton, "The Adjustment of Stock Prices to Bond Rating Changes," *Journal of Finance,* 33 no. 1 (March 1978): 29–44.

612

the generally low level of trading in the secondary market. Thus, from a semi-strong perspective, it is suggested by Pinches and Singleton,[31] that the bond market is, indeed, less efficient than the stock market is.

What does market efficiency imply regarding specific bond market strategies, such as bond swaps and yield spreads? By their very nature, bond swaps suggest the existence of some degree of market inefficiency. If temporary anomalies exist within or between market segments, then such occurrences afford alert investors the opportunity for extraordinary returns. Numerous profitable swap opportunities suggest that underlying price irregularities are neither rare nor random events. An increase in yield through a quality bond swap that results in a lower agency rating does *not* imply any market inefficiency, since the change is totally compatible with efficient market theories; i.e., the greater the risk, the greater the return. However, to derive improved return through a swap based on temporary price anomalies, as in a substitution swap, does imply some degree of market inefficiency.

Such opportunities may be caused by the *institutional* nature of the market and the resulting *market segmentation.* In effect, it may be largely artificial constraints, regulations, and statutes that lead to the opportunity to execute profitable bond swaps.

Yield spreads, on the other hand, are indications of high degrees of market efficiency, because they reflect equilibrium yield rates that are based on differential standards of risk, quality, and other issue characteristics. In effect, their existence is totally rational. A AAA corporate *should* yield less than an A-rated obligation does because it possesses a different risk-return profile. Moreover, the magnitude of such spreads can be traced (theoretically) to comparative equilibrium realized yields, and this is additional evidence (or confirmation) of market efficiency. The existence of yield spreads is rational, and the sizes of such spreads are determined in a highly efficient manner.

SUMMARY

This chapter discussed the range of bond portfolio management strategies from the simplistic buy-and-hold strategy, through several alternative active portfolio strategies, to the recently conceived immunization strategy based upon duration, finally to the notion of contingent immunization, which combines the characteristics of active portfolio management and classical immunization. At this point, you should understand the alternatives available and how to implement them. The choice of strategy is based upon the needs and desires of the client and the background and talents of the portfolio manager.

The concluding sections considered the overall view of bonds as part of the total portfolio. This discussion considered how bonds fit into the total mix of all assets and their impact on the total portfolio. It was shown that bond performance relative to other financial assets has generally been as expected in terms of risk and return. Further, bonds have been important additions to portfolios because of their low covariance with other financial assets. Regarding the applica-

---

[31] Pinches and Singleton, "The Adjustment of Stock Prices to Bond Rating Changes."

tion of CAPM concepts to bonds, the results thus far have been mixed, since it has been difficult to derive completely acceptable measures of systematic risk, and there has been a lack of stability for the risk measures derived. Also, the relationship between these risk measures and other variables have not always been consistent with expectations.

We concluded the chapter with a consideration of efficiency in the bond market. The evidence related to weak form efficiency was generally supportive. In contrast, the evidence for semistrong efficiency has been mixed and not very supportive for the few studies. The reason suggested for this lack of efficiency has been the relatively inactive secondary markets for most corporate bonds compared to the very active markets for equities.

QUESTIONS

1. Explain the difference between a pure buy-and-hold strategy and a modified buy-and-hold strategy.
2. Using Moody's, Standard and Poor's, etc., find five cushion bonds. To what level would interest rates have to rise before the price would be affected?
3. Briefly define the following bond swaps: pure yield pick-up swap, substitution swap, and tax swap.
4. What are two primary reasons for investing in deep discounted bonds?
5. Briefly describe three techniques that are considered active bond portfolio management strategies.
6. What are the two components of interest rate risk? Describe each of these components.
7. What is meant by bond portfolio immunization?
8. If the yield curve was flat and did not change, how would you immunize your portfolio?
9. Assume you have a 5-year investment horizon and current market rates are 12 percent. If you immunize and assume semiannual compounding, what will be your ending portfolio wealth assuming an initial value of $150 million?
10. You have a portfolio with a market value of $50 million and a Macauley duration of 7 years (assuming a market interest rate of 10 percent). If interest rates jump to 12 percent, what will be the value of your portfolio? Show all work.
11. At the initiation of an investment account, the market value of the portfolio is $200 million. You immunize the portfolio at 12 percent for six years. During the first year, interest rates are constant at 12 percent.
    a. What is the market value of the portfolio at the end of Year 1?
    b. Assume that immediately after the end of the year, interest rates *declined* to 10 percent. What will be the new value of the portfolio assuming the portfolio manager had been conscious of the required rebalancing?
    c. Assume that immediately after the end of Year 1, interest rates had *risen* to 14 percent. What would be the *required* value of the portfolio if it were to be immunized assuming semiannual compounding?
    d. Given the assumptions in Part c, what would be the new value of the portfolio assuming the portfolio manager had rebalanced the portfolio as required?
    e. Discuss the answer to Parts c and d in light of the purpose of immunization.

12. Compute the Macauley duration under the following conditions:
    a. A bond with a five-year term to maturity, a 12 percent coupon (annual payments), and a market yield of 10 percent
    b. A bond with a four-year term to maturity, a 12 percent coupon (annual payments), and a market yield of 10 percent
    c. Compare your answers to Parts a and b and discuss the implications of this for classical immunization.

13. Compute the Macauley duration under the following conditions:
    a. A bond with a four-year term to maturity, a 10 percent coupon (annual payments), and a market yield of 8 percent
    b. A bond with a three-year term to maturity, a 10 percent coupon (annual payments), and a market yield of 12 percent
    c. Compare your answers to Parts a and b and discuss the implications of this comparison for classical immunization
    d. Without computing duration, discuss what would have happened if the market yield in Part b had declined to 5 percent. What would have been the impact on a manager attempting to immunize?

14. You begin with an investment horizon of four years and a portfolio duration of four years with a market interest rate of 10 percent. A year later, what is your investment horizon? Assuming no change in interest rates, what is the duration of your portfolio relative to your investment horizon? What does this imply about your ability to immunize your portfolio?

15. Assume a zero coupon bond with a term to maturity at issue of 10 years (assume semiannual compounding):
    a. What is the duration of the bond at issue assuming a market yield of 10 percent? What is its duration if the market yield is 14 percent? Discuss these two answers.
    b. What is the initial issue price of this bond at a market yield of 12 percent?
    c. What is the initial issue price of this bond at a market yield of 8 percent?
    d. A year after issue, the bond in Part c is selling to yield 12 percent, what is its current market price? Assuming you owned this bond during this year, what was your rate of return?

16. It has been contended that a zero coupon bond is the ideal financial instrument to use for immunizing a portfolio. Discuss the reasoning for this statement in terms of the objective of immunization (i.e., the elimination of interest rate risk).

17. During a conference with a client, the subject of classical immunization is introduced. The client questions the fee charged for developing and managing an immunized portfolio. It is her understanding that it is basically a passive investment strategy so the management fee should be substantially lower. What would you tell the client to show that it is *not* a passive policy and that it actually requires more time and talent than a buy-and-hold policy?

18. Describe the concept of contingent immunization. What do you give up with this, and what do you gain?

19. A major requirement in running a contingent immunization portfolio policy is the need to monitor the relationship between the current market value of the portfolio and the required value of the floor portfolio. In this regard, assume a $200 million portfolio with a horizon of six years. The available market rate at the initiation of the portfolio is 12 percent, but the client is willing to accept 10 percent as a floor rate to allow you to use active management strategies. The

current market values and current market rates at the end of Year 1, 2, and 3 are as follows:

	Market Value	Market Yield	Required Floor Portfolio	Safety Margin (deficiency)
1	235.70	.10		
2	280.60	.08		
3	255.80	.12		

   a. What is the required ending wealth value for this portfolio?

   b. What is the value of the required floor portfolio at the end of Years 1, 2, and 3?

   c. Compute the safety margin or deficiency at the end of Years 1, 2, and 3.

20. *CFA Examination III (June 1983)* The ability to *immunize* a bond portfolio is very desirable for bond portfolio managers in some instances.

   a. **Discuss** the components of interest rate risk—i.e., assuming a change in interest rates over time, **explain** the two risks faced by the holder of a bond.

   b. **Define** immunization and **discuss** why a bond manager would immunize his portfolio.

   c. **Explain** why a duration-matching strategy is a superior technique to a maturity-matching strategy for the minimization of interest rate risk.

   d. **Explain** in specific terms how you would use a zero coupon bond to immunize a bond portfolio. **Discuss** why a zero coupon bond is an ideal instrument in this regard.

   e. **Explain** how *contingent immunization,* another bond portfolio management technique, differs from *classical immunization.* **Discuss** why a bond portfolio manager would engage in *contingent immunization.*

(35 minutes)

REFERENCES

Ahearn, Daniel S. "The Strategic Role of Fixed Income Securities." *Journal of Portfolio Management.* 1 no. 3 (Spring 1975).

Alexander, Gordon J. "Applying the Market Model to Long-Term Corporate Bonds." *Journal of Financial and Quantitative Analysis.* 15 no. 5 (December 1980).

Bierwag, G. O., and George G. Kaufman. "Coping with the Risk of Interest Rate Fluctuations: A Note." *Journal of Business.* 50 no. 3 (July 1977).

Bierwag, G. O. "Immunization, Duration, and the Term Structure of Interest Rates." *Journal of Financial and Quantitative Analysis.* 12 no. 5 (December 1977).

Bierwag, G. O., and George G. Kaufman. "Bond Portfolio Strategy Simulations: A Critique." *Journal of Financial and Quantitative Analysis.* 13 no. 3 (September 1978).

Bierwag, G. O., George G. Kaufman, and Alden Toevs. "Single Factor Duration Models in a General Equilibrium Framework." *Journal of Finance.* 37 no. 2 (May 1982).

616

Bierwag, G. O., George G. Kaufman, and Alden Toevs. eds. *Innovations in Bond Portfolio Management: Duration Analysis and Immunization.* Greenwich, Conn.: JAI Press, 1983.

Bierwag, G. O., George G. Kaufman, and Alden Toevs. "Duration: Its Development and Use in Bond Portfolio Management." *Financial Analysts Journal.* 39 no. 4 (July–August 1983).

Bierwag, G. O., George G. Kaufman, and Chulsoon Khang. "Duration and Bond Portfolio Analysis: An Overview." *Journal of Financial and Quantitative Analysis.* 13 no. 5 (November 1978).

Bierwag, G. O., George G. Kaufman, and Alden Toevs. "Immunizing Strategies for Funding Multiple Liabilities." *Journal of Financial and Quantitative Analysis.* 18 no. 1 (March 1983).

Bierwag, G. O., George G. Kaufman, Robert L. Schwitzer, and Alden Toevs. "The Art of Risk Management in Bond Portfolios." *Journal of Portfolio Management.* 7 no. 3 (Spring 1981).

Bowlin, Oswald D., and John D. Martin. "Extrapolations of Yields over the Short Run: Forecast or Folly?" *Journal of Monetary Economics.* 1 (1975).

Carter, Andrew M. "Value Judgments in Bond Management." *Bond Analysis and Selection.* Financial Analysts Research Foundation, 1977.

Cox, John, Jonathon E. Ingersoll, and Stephen A. Ross. "Duration and Measurement of Basis Risk." *Journal of Business.* 52 no. 1 (January 1979).

Fabozzi, Frank J., and Irvins M. Pollack, eds. *The Handbook of Fixed Income Securities.* Homewood, Ill.: Dow Jones-Irwin, 1983.

Fisher, Lawrence, and James H. Lorie. "Rates of Return on Investments in Common Stock: The Year-by-Year Record, 1926–1965." *Journal of Business.* 41 no. 3 (July 1968).

Fisher, Lawrence, and Roman L. Weil. "Coping with the Risk of Interest-Rate Fluctuations: Returns to Bondholders from Naive and Optimal Strategies." *Journal of Business.* 44 no. 4 (October 1971).

Friend, Irwin, Randolph Westerfield, and Michael Granito, "New Evidence on the Capital Asset Pricing Model." *Journal of Finance.* 33 no. 3 (June 1978).

Hawawini, Gabriel A. ed. *Bond Duration and Immunization: Early Developments and Recent Contributions.* New York: Garland Publishing, 1982.

Hickman, W. Braddock. *Corporate Bond Quality and Investor Experience.* A study by the National Bureau of Economic Research. Princeton, N.J.: Princeton University Press, 1958.

Homer, Sidney, and Martin L. Leibowitz. *Inside the Yield Book.* Englewood Cliffs, N.J.: Prentice-Hall, 1972.

Ibbotson, Roger G., and Rex A. Sinquefield. *Stocks, Bonds, Bills and Inflation: The Past and the Future.* Financial Analysts Research Foundation, 1982.

Ingersoll, Jonathon E., Jeffrey Skelton, and Roman L. Weil. "Duration: Forty Years Later." *Journal of Financial and Quantitative Analysis.* 13 no. 5 (November 1978).

Katz, Steven. "The Price Adjustment Process of Bonds to Rating Reclassifications: A Test of Bond Market Efficiency." *Journal of Finance.* 29 no. 2 (May 1974).

Lanstein, Ronald, and William F. Sharpe. "Duration and Systematic Risk." *Journal of Financial and Quantitative Analysis.* 13 no. 5 (November 1978).

Leibowitz, Martin L. "How Swaps Can Pay Off." *Institutional Investor.* 7 no. 8 (August 1973).

Leibowitz, Martin L., and Alfred Weinberger. "Contingent Immunization – Part I: Risk Control Procedures." *Financial Analysts Journal.* 38 no. 6 (November – December 1982).

Leibowitz, Martin L., and Alfred Weinberger. "Contingent Immunization – Part II: Problem Areas." *Financial Analysts Journal.* 39 no. 1 (January – February 1983).

Leibowitz, Martin L., and Alfred Weinberger. "The Uses of Contingent Immunization." *Journal of Portfolio Management.* 8 no. 1 (Fall 1981).

Percival, John. "Corporate Bonds in a Market Model Context." *Journal of Business Research.* 2 no. 4 (October 1974).

Pinches, George E., and Clay Singleton. "The Adjustment of Stock Prices to Bond Rating Changes." *Journal of Finance.* 33 no. 1 (March 1978).

Prell, Michael J. "How Well Do the Experts Forecast Interest Rates?" Federal Reserve Bank of Kansas City *Monthly Review* (September – October 1973).

Redington, F. M. "Review of the Principle of Life Office Valuations." *Journal of the Institute of Actuaries.* 78 (1952).

Reilly, Frank K., and Rupinder Sidhu. "The Many Uses of Bond Duration." *Financial Analysts Journal.* 36 no. 4 (July – August 1980).

Reilly, Frank K., and Michael D. Joehnk. "The Association between Market-Determined Risk Measures for Bonds and Bond Ratings." *Journal of Finance.* 31 no. 5 (December 1976).

Roll, R. *The Behavior of Interest Rates.* New York: Basic Books, 1970.

Sharpe, William F. "Bonds vs. Stocks: Some Lessons from Capital Market Theory." *Financial Analysts Journal.* 29 no. 6 (November – December 1973).

Soldofsky, Robert M., and Roger L. Miller. "Risk Premium Curves for Different Classes of Long-Term Securities, 1950 – 1966." *Journal of Finance.* 24 no. 2 (June 1969).

Tuttle, Donald. ed. *The Revolution in Techniques for Managing Bond Portfolios.* Charlottesville, Va.: The Institute of Chartered Financial Analysts, 1983.

Van Horne, James. *Financial Market Rates and Flows.* 2nd. ed. Englewood Cliffs, N.J.: Prentice-Hall, 1984.

618

Warner, Jerold B. "Bankruptcy, Absolute Priority, and the Pricing of Risky Debt Claims." *Journal of Financial Economics*. 4 no. 3 (May 1977).

Weil, Roman L. "Macauley's Duration: An Appreciation." *Journal of Business*. 46 no. 4 (October 1973).

Weinstein, Mark I. "The Effect of a Rating Change Announcement on Bond Price." *Journal of Financial Economics*. 5 no. 3 (December 1977).

Weinstein, Mark I. "The Systematic Risk of Corporate Bonds." *Journal of Financial and Quantitative Analysis*. 16 no. 3 (September 1981).

Weinstein, Mark I. "Bond Systematic Risk and the Option Pricing Model." *Journal of Finance*. 38 no. 5 (December 1983).

Part 5

Extensions and Application of Asset Pricing and Portfolio Theory

The chapters in this section are intended to extend and apply earlier material dealing with portfolio theory and asset pricing theories. While Chapters 8 and 9 contained a detailed introduction to portfolio theory and the capital asset pricing model, Chapter 20 considers several extensions of these models including the effect of relaxing some of the major assumptions. In addition, there is a discussion of the results of numerous studies that have empirically tested the CAPM. Finally, we consider an alternative asset pricing theory referred to as the arbitrage pricing theory (APT).

Chapter 21 considers one of the most important applications of portfolio theory—i.e., the implication that investors should give serious consideration to engaging in international diversification. The discussion considers several studies that contain strong evidence in support of this concept. There is also consideration of the problems inherent in implementing the idea, and finally suggestions of how an individual can do it.

The final chapter in this section deals with the very important question about how one goes about evaluating the performance of portfolio managers. While there are two sets of techniques considered for equities and fixed-income securities, an overall consideration is that the techniques allow you to evaluate the risk-adjusted performance of your portfolio managers. Further, while several techniques are presented, they should not be considered as alternatives, but combinations to be used together because various techniques generally provide different insights into performance.

Chapter 20

Extensions and Testing of Asset Pricing Theories

C hapters 8 and 9 contained a detailed introduction to both Markowitz portfolio theory and the capital asset pricing model (CAPM). These introductions were intended to provide the basic understanding of the concepts so they could be used in the subsequent valuation chapters. In turn, this chapter considers several extensions of the CAPM and relaxes some of the assumptions and examines the impact of this on the model. More important, it is necessary to examine the empirical tests of the theory. These test results clearly indicate some support for the theory in terms of its predictive ability, but they also indicate that there are some problems and questions regarding the model, including a contention by Roll that it is not possible to test the model. We conclude the chapter with a discussion of an alternative asset pricing model referred to as *arbitrage pricing theory*. This theory developed by Stephen Ross does not require the extensive assumptions of the CAPM.

RELAXING THE ASSUMPTIONS

In Chapter 9 several assumptions were set forth related to the CAPM. In this section, we discuss the impact on the capital market line (CML) and the security market line (SML) when we relax several of these assumptions.

Differential Borrowing and Lending Rates

One of the first assumptions of the CAPM was that investors could borrow and lend any amount of money at the risk-free rate. As noted, it is reasonable to assume that an investor can always *lend* as much as desired at the risk-free rate by buying government securities (e.g., T-bills). In contrast, one may question the ability of investors to borrow unlimited amounts at the T-bill rate, because this rate is usually lower than the prime rate and most investors must pay a premium relative to the prime rate when they borrow money. For example, when T-bill

623

FIGURE 20.1

Investment Alternatives When the Cost of Borrowing is Higher than the Cost of Lending

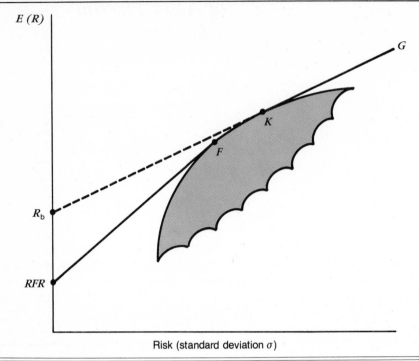

rates are about 9 percent, the prime rate will probably be about 11 percent; most individuals would have to pay about 12 percent to borrow at the bank.

The effect of this differential is that there will be two different lines going to the Markowitz efficient frontier as shown in Figure 20.1. There is a segment $RFR-F$ which indicates the investment opportunities available from some combination of investing in risk-free assets (i.e., lending at the RFR) and Portfolio F on the Markowitz efficient frontier. It is not possible to extend this line any further because it is assumed that you cannot borrow at this risk-free rate to acquire further units of Portfolio F. If you borrow at R_b, you would find the point of tangency on the curve at point K. This indicates that you could borrow at R_b and could invest in Portfolio K to extend the CML to G. Therefore, the CML is made up of $RFR-F-K-G$—that is, a line segment ($RFR-F$), a curb segment ($F-K$), and another line segment ($K-G$). This implies that you can either lend or borrow, but obviously the borrowing portfolios are not as profitable as when it was assumed that you could borrow at the RFR. In this instance, because you must pay a rate to borrow that is higher than the RFR, your net return is less—i.e., the slope of the line is below that for $RFR-F$.

FIGURE 20.2
Security Market Line with Zero Beta Portfolio

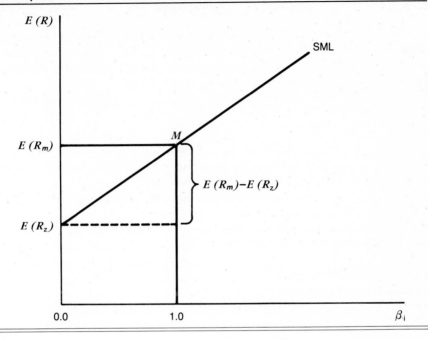

Zero-Beta Model

If the market portfolio (*M*) is mean-variance efficient (i.e., it has the lowest risk for a given level of return among the attainable set of portfolios), Black derived an alternative model that does not require a risk-free asset.[1] Specifically, within the set of feasible alternative portfolios, there will be several portfolios where the returns are completely uncorrelated with the market portfolio; i.e., the beta of these portfolios with the market portfolio is zero. From among the several portfolios that have this property, you would select the one with minimum variance. While the availability of this zero-beta portfolio will not affect the CML, it will allow construction of a linear SML as shown in Figure 20.2. In the model, the intercept is the expected return for the zero-beta portfolio rather than a risk-free asset. Similar to the proof in Chapter 9, the combinations of this zero-beta portfolio and the market portfolio will be a linear relationship in return and risk; i.e., again the covariance between the zero-beta portfolio (R_z) and the market portfolio is zero. Assuming that the return for the zero-beta portfolio is greater than that for a risk-free asset, the slope of the line through the market

[1] Fischer Black, "Capital Market Equilibrium with Restricted Borrowing," *Journal of Business,* 45 no. 3 (July 1972): 444–445.

portfolio would not be as steep. The equation for this line would be:

$$E(Ri) = E(R_z) + Bi[E(Rm) - E(R_z)].$$

Obviously, the risk premiums would be a function of the beta for the individual security and the market risk premium: $[E(Rm) - E(R_z)]$. Some of the empirical results discussed in the next section indicate that this model with its higher intercept and flatter slope is supported by those studies.

Transaction Costs

The basic assumption is that there are no transaction costs so that investors will buy or sell mispriced securities until they again plot on the SML. For instance, if a stock plots above the SML, it is underpriced (i.e. its $E(R)$ is greater than justified by its risk level) so investors should buy it and bid up its price until its $E(R)$ is in line with its risk—i.e., it will plot on the SML. The point is, with transaction costs, investors will not correct all mispricing because, in some instances, the cost of buying and selling the security will offset any potential excess return. Therefore, securities will plot very close to the SML but not exactly on it; i.e., the SML will be a band of securities, as shown in Figure 20.3, rather than a single line. Obviously, the width of the band is a function of the size of the transaction costs. In a world with a large proportion of purchases and sales by institutions that trade at pennies per share and with discount brokers for individuals, the band should be quite narrow.

The existence of transaction costs also will affect the extent of diversification by investors. In Chapter 9, there was a discussion of the relationship between the number of stocks in a portfolio and the variance of the portfolio (see Figure 9.3). You will recall that initially the variance declined rapidly and approached about 90 percent of complete diversification with about 15–18 securities. An important question is how many more securities must be added to derive the last 10 percent. Clearly, the existence of transaction costs would indicate that, at some point, the trade-off of diversification would not be worth the cost for most investors, especially if there were also costs of monitoring and analyzing the added securities.

Heterogeneous Expectations and Planning Periods

If all investors have different expectations about risk and return, each investor would have a unique CML and/or SML, and the composite would be a set of lines as broad as expectations differed. If all investors had about the same information and background, the band would be reasonably narrow, compared to an environment with widely different information sources and points of reference.

The impact of *planning periods* is similar. Recall that the CAPM is a one period model. Therefore, the period employed must be the planning period for the individual investor; i.e., if you are thinking in terms of a one-year planning period, your CML and SML could differ from mine assuming my planning period is one month.

FIGURE 20.3
Security Market Line with Transaction Costs

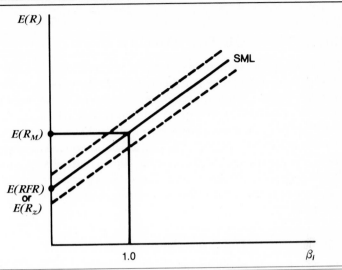

Taxes

The rates of return that we normally record and that were used throughout the model were pretax returns. In fact, the actual returns for most investors are impacted as follows:

$$E(R_i) = \frac{(P_e - P_b) + (Div)}{P_b} \text{ (pretax rate of return)},$$

where:

P_e = ending price

P_b = beginning price

Div = dividend paid during period.

$$E(R_i^*) = \frac{[(P_e - P_b) \times (1 - T_{cg})] + [(Div) \times (1 - T_i)]}{P_b},$$

R_i^* = after tax rate of return

T_{cg} = tax on capital gain or loss

T_i = tax on ordinary income.

Clearly, the tax rates differ between individuals and also institutions. Hence, for many institutions that don't pay taxes, the original pre-tax model is correctly specified. Alternatively, if investors have heavy tax burdens, this could cause major differences.[2]

EMPIRICAL TESTS OF THE THEORY

In the discussion of the assumptions of capital market theory, it was pointed out that a theory should not be judged on the basis of its assumptions but on *how well it explains the relationships that exist in the real world*. While there have been numerous tests of the CAPM, two major questions should concern us. The first involves the stability of the measure of systematic risk, i.e., *the stability of beta*. Given that beta is our principal risk measure, it is important to know whether past betas can be used as estimates of future betas. The second question is basic to the theory: *is there a positive linear relationship as hypothesized between beta and the rate of return on risky assets?* More specifically, how well do returns conform to the SML equation:

$$E(R_i) = RFR + B_i (Rm - RFR)?$$

Some specific questions might include:
— Does the intercept approximate the RFR that prevailed during the period?
— Was the slope of the line positive? Was it consistent with that implied by the risk premium $(Rm - RFR)$ during that period?

Stability of Beta

Numerous studies have considered the question of the stability of beta and generally reached similar conclusions. A study by Levy examined weekly rates of return for 500 stocks on the NYSE during the period 1960–1970.[3] The author concluded that the risk measure was not stable for individual stocks over fairly short periods (52 weeks). Alternatively, when stocks were put into portfolios, the stability of the portfolio betas increased dramatically. Further, the larger the portfolio (e.g., 25 or 50 stocks) and the longer the period (over 26 weeks), the more stable the beta of the portfolio. Specifically, the correlation of 25- and 50-stock portfolio betas over 26-week periods averaged above 0.91. He also noted a tendency for the betas to regress toward the mean; high-beta portfolios had a tendency to decline over time toward unity (1.00), while low-beta portfolios tended to increase over time toward unity.

A study by Blume likewise examined the stability of beta for all common stocks listed on the NYSE over the period January 1926 through June 1968.[4] Besides providing some very interesting descriptive statistics on beta, he carried

[2] For a detailed consideration of this, see Robert Litzenberger and K. Ramaswamy, "The Effect of Personal Taxes and Dividends on Capital Asset Prices: Theory and Empirical Evidence," *Journal of Financial Economics,* 7 no. 2 (June 1979): 163–196.

[3] Robert A. Levy, "On the Short-Term Stationarity of Beta Coefficients," *Financial Analysts Journal,* 27 no. 6 (November–December 1971): 55–62.

[4] Marshall E. Blume, "On the Assessment of Risk," *Journal of Finance,* 26 no. 1 (March 1971): 1–10.

out an extensive analysis of the stability of beta. The correlation of beta for individual stocks during adjoining periods was quite good, 0.60 to 0.73. Similar to Levy's findings, the stability was shown to increase substantially for portfolios of 20 or more stocks, i.e., the correlation of the betas over time ranged from 0.93 to 0.98. He also found a tendency for a regression of the betas toward one.

Fielitz examined the ability of individual investors to carry out their own diversification rather than use mutual funds.[5] As part of the analysis, he considered the impact of the number of securities on the undiversifiable risk of the portfolio. (The stocks were selected randomly.) He concluded that there was a need to increase the number of stocks in the portfolio, but there was substantial stability of risk with eight securities.

Porter and Ezzell derived a different conclusion based upon a random assignment of stocks to alternative portfolios and examined the correlation coefficient of average betas over contingent periods. Their test results indicated that the correlation coefficients for portfolio betas did *not* increase as the average size of the portfolio increased.[6]

Tole contended that the appropriate way to assign stocks to portfolios was randomly rather than ranking stocks by the size of the beta.[7] He also differed in terms of the test for beta stability. Whereas all prior studies examined the *relative* stability (i.e., the size of the correlation coefficient), he considered absolute measures—i.e., the size of the standard deviation of the betas for portfolios of different sizes. After examining portfolios of 1, 3, 5, 10, 25, 50, 75, 100, 250, and 500 stocks, he concluded there is substantially greater stability in beta as the portfolio size is increased. While confirming the overall conclusion of most prior studies, he differed in contending that the benefit of larger portfolios extends beyond 10 or 25 stocks. In fact, for some tests the benefits go beyond 100 stocks in the portfolio.

In addition to examining the number of stocks in a portfolio, another factor that apparently has an impact on the stability of beta is the estimating period—i.e., how many months are used to estimate the original beta and the test beta. Baesel varied the estimation period from 12 months to 108 months.[8] The results indicated that the stability of the individual betas increased as the length of the estimation period increased. Altman, Jacquillat, and Levasseur found similar results to those derived by Baesel using French data.[9]

Roenfeldt, Griepentrog, and Pflamm (RGP) reexamined the Baesel conclusions which were based upon using the same base period and test period; i.e., if the base period used to estimate the beta was 108 months, the test period was

---

[5] Bruce Fielitz, "Indirect versus Direct Diversification," *Financial Management,* 3 no. 4 (Winter 1974): 54–62.

[6] R. Burr Porter and John R. Ezzell, "A Note on the Predictive Ability of Beta Coefficients," *Journal of Business Research,* 3 no. 4 (October 1975): 365–372.

[7] Thomas M. Tole, "How to Maximize Stationarity of Beta," *Journal of Portfolio Management,* 7 no. 2 (Winter 1981): 45–49.

[8] Jerome B. Baesel, "On the Assessment of Risk: Some Further Considerations," *Journal of Finance,* 29 no. 5, (December 1974): 1491–1494.

[9] Edward Altman, B. Jacquillat, and M. Levasseur, "Comparative Analysis of Risk Measures: France and the United States," *Journal of Financial and Quantitative Analysis,* 13 no. 1 (March 1978): 117–121.

likewise 108 months.[10] RGP contended that, in many instances, investors want to use the estimate for a much shorter period. For instance, you may want to use the base period estimate of beta for a shorter period. (You want an estimate of beta to cover your investment horizon of 24 months.) The analysis used betas derived from 48 months of data and compared these betas to subsequent betas for 12, 24, 36, and 48 months. While the base period betas were not good for estimating subsequent 12-month betas, they were quite good for estimating 24, 36, and 48-month betas.

A paper by Theobald derived a set of analytical expressions that explain how and why the Baesel empirical results occur.[11] While it is shown that the stationarity of beta will increase with the length of the calendar period examined, it is demonstrated that the stationarity will not increase indefinitely; i.e., the beta must remain stationary over the longer period. He also partially explained the findings of RGP regarding the improved stability as you lengthen the period used to derive the test beta. It was suggested that the optimal length could be in excess of 120 months, but it was acknowledged that this assumed that the beta within the period had not shifted — if it had, shorter beta sets were necessary. A paper by Chen likewise contained an analytical analysis of the relationship between the variability of the beta coefficients and the residual risks for portfolios.[12] The ordinary least square (OLS) estimate would be biased if the betas for individual stocks were unstable. He suggested employing a Bayesian approach to estimate these time varying betas.

In addition to examining the impact of the number of stocks in a portfolio or the length of the examination period, Carpenter and Upton considered the influence of the trading volume on beta stability.[13] They examined the betas for various firms during alternative periods of high volume, low volume, and average volume. They contended there was some small difference in the betas derived and that the predictions of betas were slightly better using the volume adjusted betas. This impact of volume on the estimation of beta is related to the discussion in Chapter 7, where it was noted that the estimated beta for securities with limited trading was biased downward (i.e., see the discussion of the small firm effect).

To summarize the stability of beta studies, the results indicated that individual betas are generally *not* stable, but portfolios of stocks have stable betas. In addition, it is important to examine a long period and also be conscious of volume.

Comparability of Published Estimates of Beta

In contrast to deriving your own estimate of beta for a stock, there may be instances when you want to use a published source for speed or convenience.

[10] Rodney L. Roenfeldt, Gary L. Griepentrog, and Christopher C. Pflamm, "Further Evidence on the Stationarity of Beta Coefficients," *Journal of Financial and Quantitative Analysis,* 13 no. 1 (March 1978): 117–121.

[11] Michael Theobald, "Beta Stationarity and Estimation Period: Some Analytical Results," *Journal of Financial and Quantitative Analysis,* 16 no. 5 (December 1981): 747–757.

[12] Son-Nan Chen, "Beta Nonstationarity, Portfolio Residual Risk and Diversification," *Journal of Financial and Quantitative Analysis,* 16 no. 1 (March 1981): 95–111.

[13] Michael D. Carpenter and David E. Upton, "Trading Volume and Beta Stability," *Journal of Portfolio Management,* 7 no. 2 (Winter 1981): 60–64.

The two major sources of published betas are: (1) Merrill Lynch *Security Risk Evaluation Report,* and (2) *Value Line Investment Survey.* The Merrill Lynch *Report* is done monthly and distributed to institutional clients. The *Value Line* estimates are a part of their *survey* reports that are generally available in most libraries that carry investment services. Therefore, the *Value Line* estimate is probably the most convenient source.

A major question regarding these two estimates is how do the beta estimates differ since the methods of computation differ? While both services use the same market model equation ($R_i = RFR + B_i\ R_m + \epsilon_i$), they differ in the data employed. Specifically, the Merrill Lynch estimates use *60 monthly observations,* while the Value Line estimate uses *260 weekly observations.* They likewise both use an adjustment process because of the regression tendencies reported by Blume.[14] Again, the adjustment equations differ as follows:

Merrill Lynch: Adjusted Beta = .33743 + .66257 (beta)
Value Line: Adjusted Beta = 0.35 + 0.67 (beta).

Given these relatively minor differences, one would probably expect the published betas to be quite comparable. A study by Statman examined the betas for the 195 firms with the largest market value for a comparable five-year period ending September 1978.[15] The following equation indicates the relationship between the adjusted betas for the 195 securities:

Merrill Lynch Adjusted Beta = 0.127 + 0.879 Value Line Adjusted Beta.

While both the intercept and slope are significant, there did not appear to be any systematic bias in the differences. Also, for betas close to one, the differences were very small. Since there was no systematic bias and a partial sample confirmed this, one would expect that the differences would disappear for portfolios. The fact is, for 19 portfolios of ten stocks, the coefficient of determination was almost the same as for individual stocks. Unfortunately, while Statman considered portfolios of less than ten stocks (three to nine), he did not examine portfolios greater than ten where one would expect much better results. In summary, there appears to be a small but significant difference in the estimates of beta that could be partially explained by the adjustment equation employed. Obviously, the remaining difference in measured beta is due to the difference in data used (monthly versus weekly), but there is not a consistent bias, which means the estimates should be fairly comparable for large portfolios of stocks.

RELATIONSHIP BETWEEN SYSTEMATIC RISK AND RETURN

The ultimate question regarding the CAPM is whether it is useful in explaining the return on risky assets. Specifically, is there a positive linear relationship between the systematic risk of risky assets and the rates of return on these assets?

---

[14] Marshall Blume, "On the Assessment of Risk," *Journal of Finance,* 26 no. 1 (March 1971): 1–10.

[15] Meir Statman, "Betas Compared: Merrill Lynch vs. Value Line," *Journal of Portfolio Management,* 7 no. 2 (Winter 1981): 41–44.

A study by Sharpe and Cooper generally provided support for a positive relationship between return and risk, although it was not completely linear.[16] Specifically, they put stocks into risk classes based upon their systematic risk (beta) and examined the average rates of the return for each of the risk classes. The returns increased with risk class except for the very highest risk classes where there was a tendency for the returns to level off and decline slightly. They also showed that the betas for portfolios were stable. Therefore, it was possible to derive the average beta for a portfolio based upon historical betas, and the return during a subsequent period was generally consistent with the risk.

A study by Douglas examined the relationship between rate of return and several risk measures for individual stocks.[17] Specifically, he studied over 600 stocks during alternative five-year periods between 1926 and 1960. In addition to considering a systematic risk variable, he also included a variance of return measure and examined both risk measures relative to return. The results were clearly not consistent with expectations. The intercepts were a little larger than expected based upon the prevailing risk-free rates. More important, the coefficient for the variance risk variable (i.e., total risk) was generally significant, which is certainly not consistent with the CAPM. Further, the coefficients for the systematic risk variables were typically *not* significant.

A subsequent study by Miller and Scholes discussed some potential statistical problems with the Douglas study.[18] They contended that the results derived by Douglas could be caused by measurement errors in estimating the betas for individual stocks and the fact that unsystematic risk and betas are highly correlated. They also noted that the distribution of returns for the stocks were very skewed and this could make a difference. Even with these problems, it was not possible to fully explain the Douglas results.

Because of the potential statistical problems with individual stocks, a study by Black, Jensen and Scholes (BJS) considered the risk and return for *portfolios* of stocks.[19] All NYSE stocks listed between 1931–1965 were placed into ten portfolios on the basis of their betas. The analysis of the relationship between monthly excess return and portfolio beta indicated a positive linear relationship, although the intercept was higher than expected. (That is, it should have been zero.) A copy of some of the charts from the BJS study is contained in Figure 20.4. As shown, while almost all the measured SMLs have a positive slope, the slopes change, the intercepts are not zero, and they likewise change.

A study by Fama and MacBeth examined the relationship between the rates

---

[16] William F. Sharpe and Guy M. Cooper, "Risk-Return Classes of New York Stock Exchange Common Stocks: 1931–1967," *Financial Analysts Journal*, 28 no. 2 (March–April 1972): 46–54. A subsequent study concentrated on the impact of yield tilting portfolios, but also confirmed many of these results. See, William F. Sharpe and Howard B. Sosin, "Risk, Return and Yield: New York Stock Exchange Common Stocks: 1928–1969," *Financial Analysts Journal*, 32 no. 2 (March–April 1976): 33–42.

[17] G. W. Douglas, "Risk in the Equity Markets: An Empirical Appraisal of Market Efficiency," *Yale Economic Essays*, 9 no. 1 (1969): 3–48.

[18] Merton H. Miller and Myron Scholes, "Rates of Return in Relation to Risk: A Re-Examination of Some Recent Findings," in *Studies in the Theory of Capital Markets*. Michael Jensen (ed.) (New York: Praeger Publishers, 1976).

[19] Fischer Black, Michael Jensen, and Myron Scholes, "The Capital Asset Pricing Model: Some Empirical Tests," in *Studies in the Theory of Capital Markets*. Michael Jensen (ed.) (New York: Praeger, 1970).

FIGURE 20.4
Average Excess Monthly Rates of Return Compared to Systematic Risk During
Alternative Time Periods

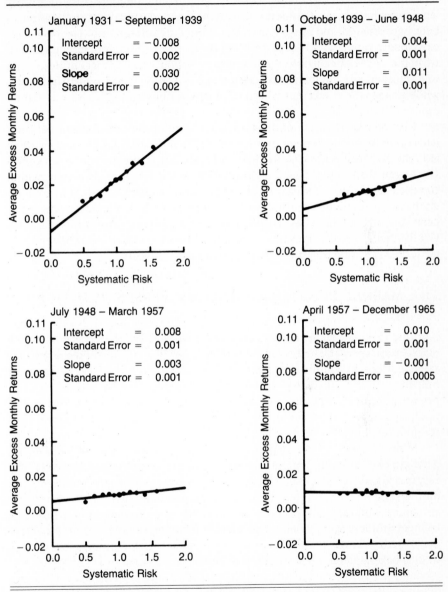

SOURCE: Fischer Black, Michael Jensen, and Myron Scholes, "The Capital Asset Pricing Model: Some Empirical
Tests," in *Studies in the Theory of Capital Markets,* Michael Jensen (ed.) (New York: Praeger, 1970).

of return and betas for portfolios during each month from 1935 to 1968.[20] In addition, they also considered a beta-squared variable (to test for linearity) and a measure of unsystematic risk. Notably, all the independent variables were lagged one month; i.e., the model related the return during the current month to beta, beta squared, and unsystematic risk during the prior month. The results for each month varied widely over time, but the overall results were rather supportive of the CAPM. Specifically, the intercept was about equal to that implied by the *RFR*. Further, the coefficient for systematic risk was positive and significant, while neither the coefficient for beta squared nor unsystematic risk was significant.

In summary, the bulk of the evidence regarding the relationship between rates of return and systematic risk for portfolios indicate support for the CAPM. Still, the evidence is not without question. Specifically, the intercepts are generally higher than implied by the risk-free rate. This is either consistent with a zero-beta model or the existence of a higher borrowing rate. Also, the few studies that have examined the risk-return relationship for individual stocks have not been supportive, which has caused most studies to employ portfolios of stocks. Finally, beta generally does better than other measures of risk and better when the tests cover long time periods (i.e., more than 10 years).

THE MARKET PORTFOLIO: THEORY VERSUS PRACTICE

Throughout our presentation of the basic model, it was noted that the market portfolio included *all* the risky assets in the economy. In fact, it was pointed out that all assets had to be in this most desirable portfolio or they would not have any value. Further, in equilibrium, the various assets would be included in the portfolio in the proportion of their market value. Therefore, one should envision this market portfolio containing not only stocks and bonds, but also real estate, options, stamps, coins, foreign securities, etc. All of these assets should have weights equal to their relative market value.

While this concept of a market portfolio is reasonable in theory, it is difficult, if not impossible, to implement in practice when testing or using the CAPM. The easy part is getting a stock series for the NYSE and the ASE. There are stock series for the OTC market, too, but these series are generally incomplete. There are also some well-regarded bond series available (e.g., from Salomon Brothers, Lehman Brothers, Kuhn Loeb). The difficult, if not impossible, requirement is to derive series for the numerous other assets mentioned. Further, most tests or studies have generally been limited to *only* using a stock or bond series. It is probably safe to say that the vast majority of studies have used the S & P 500 series or some other stock series limited to the NYSE. The implied assumption of such a practice is that this particular series is highly correlated with the true market portfolio.

While most academicians generally recognized this potential problem, they assumed that the deficiency was not serious. A series of articles by Roll examined

---

[20] Eugene Fama and R. MacBeth, ''Risk, Return and Equilibrium: Empirical Tests,'' *Journal of Political Economy,* 81 no. 2 (May–June 1973): 453–474.

FIGURE 20.5
Differential Performance Based upon an Error in Estimating Systematic Risk

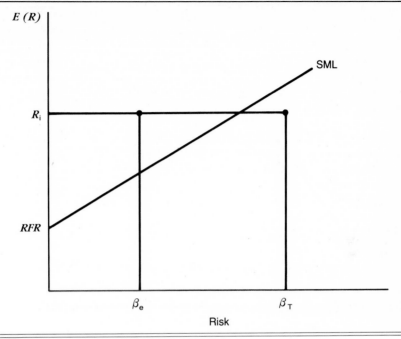

the problem in detail and concluded that it was clearly not a trivial matter but had very serious implications for all prior tests of the model, especially for use in evaluating portfolio performance.[21] Roll referred to it as a *benchmark error,* because the practice is to compare the performance of a portfolio manager to the return of an unmanaged portfolio of equal risk. In the CAPM, the unmanaged portfolio is the market portfolio adjusted for risk. Clearly, if the benchmark is mistakenly specified, it is not possible to measure the performance of portfolio managers properly. A mistakenly specified market portfolio can have two effects. The first is that the beta computed for alternative portfolios would be wrong because the market portfolio is wrong. Second, the supposed SML is wrong because it goes from the *RFR* through the *M* portfolio. Figure 20.5 shows an instance where the true risk of the portfolio being evaluated is underestimated, possibly because of the market portfolio used in computing the beta. As shown, the portfolio may appear to be above the SML and thus reflect superior management. If in fact, the true risk is greater, the portfolio will shift to the right and be below the SML, which indicates inferior performance.

---

[21] Richard Roll, "A Critique of the Asset Pricing Theory's Tests," *Journal of Financial Economics,* 4 no. 4, (March 1977): 129–176; Richard Roll, "Ambiguity when Performance is Measured by the Securities Market Line," *Journal of Finance,* 33 no. 4 (September 1978): 1051–1069; Richard Roll, "Performance Evaluation and Benchmark Error I," *Journal of Portfolio Mangement,* 6 no. 4 (Summer 1980): 5–12; Richard Roll, "Performance Evaluation and Benchmark Error II," *Journal of Portfolio Management,* 7 no. 2 (Winter 1981): 17–22. This discussion draws heavily from these articles.

FIGURE 20.6

Differential SML Based upon Measured Risk-Free Asset and Proxy Market Portfolio

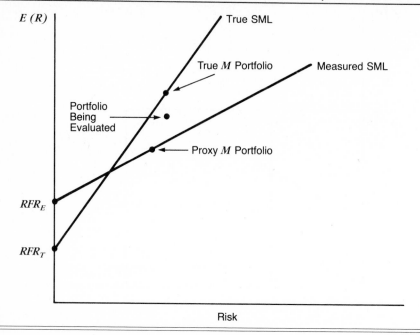

Figure 20.6 indicates what can happen to the SML if there is an error in selecting a proper risk-free asset *and* if the market portfolio selected is not the correct mean-variance efficient portfolio. In this instance, the intercept *and* the slope will differ. Obviously, it is very possible that, under these conditions, a portfolio judged to be superior relative to the first SML (above the measured SML), could be inferior relative to the true SML (below the true SML).

The point Roll made is that when we enter into a test of the CAPM, an inherent part of the test is whether the market portfolio proxy used is mean-variance efficient (on the Markowitz efficient frontier) *and* if it is the true optimum market portfolio. Roll showed that, if the proxy market portfolio selected (e.g., the S & P 500 index) is mean-variance efficient, it is mathematically possible to show a linear relationship between returns and betas derived with this portfolio; however, this is not a true test of CAPM because you are not working with the true SML, as shown in Figure 20.7.

In summary, the points Roll made are concerned with the market proxy used and the impact of using a proxy that is not the true *M* portfolio. This will affect the risk measures derived (i.e., the betas) and the position and slope of the SML that is used to evaluate the performance of portfolio managers. In general, the errors will tend to overestimate the performance of portfolio managers, because the proxy market portfolio employed is probably not as efficient as the true market portfolio, which means the slope of the SML is underestimated.

Figure 20.7
Differential SML Using Market Proxy that Is Mean-Variance Efficient

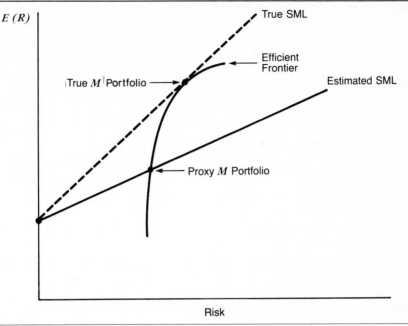

An important point is that the benchmark problems that Roll analyzed do *not* negate the value of the CAPM in terms of its usefulness as *a normative model of asset pricing.* The theory is still viable; the problem is in *measurement* when attempting to test the theory and to implement it for evaluating the performance of portfolio managers. (We will discuss this further in Chapter 22, on evaluating performance.) It is necessary to work toward a better market portfolio proxy or to adjust the performance measures for this potential problem.

ARBITRAGE PRICING THEORY

At this point we have discussed the CAPM in terms of the basic theory and the impact of changing some of its major assumptions. In addition to these assumptions, the model also assumes that investors have quadratic utility functions and that the distribution of security prices is normal—i.e., symmetrically distributed with a variance term that can be estimated. Also the CAPM is heavily dependent on the existence of a market portfolio of all risky assets.

The review of empirical tests of the CAPM indicated that the beta coefficients for individual securities were definitely not stable, but the betas for the portfolios of stocks were generally stable assuming long enough sample periods and adequate trading volume. There was also support for a positive linear relationship between rates of return and systematic risk for portfolios of stock, although again, this did not hold for individual stocks.

While the empirical results generally provided support for the theory, a set of papers by Roll criticized the tests and the usefulness of the model because of its dependence on a true market portfolio of risky assets that almost certainly is not actually available. If the proxy for the market portfolio is mean-variance efficient, the risk-return results are shown to be a mathematical result. In addition, when the CAPM is used to evaluate portfolio performance, the market portfolio proxy is used as a benchmark for performance. It is demonstrated that the performance results can be changed because the computed betas relative to the market portfolio could be wrong and the slope of the SML could change dramatically, depending on the location of the true market portfolio relative to the proxy used.

Given these questions and criticisms, it is not surprising that the academic community has considered an alternative asset pricing theory that is reasonably intuitive and also requires only limited assumptions. Specifically, the arbitrage pricing theory (APT) was developed by Ross in the early 1970s and initially published in 1976.[22] The APT has three major assumptions:
1. Capital markets are perfectly competitive.
2. Investors always prefer more wealth to less wealth with certainty.
3. The stochastic process generating asset returns can be represented as a K factor model (to be described).

There are several major assumptions that are *not* required. Specifically, this theory does not require that investors have a quadratic utility function, that security returns be normally distributed, nor that there be a market portfolio which contains all risky assets and is mean-variance efficient. Obviously, if such a theory is able to explain differential security prices, it would be considered a superior theory because it is simpler (i.e., it requires fewer assumptions).

As noted, the theory assumes that the stochastic process generating asset returns can be represented as a K factor model of the form:

$$R_i = E_i + b_{i1}\delta_1 + b_{i2}\delta_2 + \ldots + b_{ik}\delta_k + \epsilon_i \text{ for } i = 1 \text{ to } N$$

where:

R_i = return on asset i during a specified time period

E_i = expected return for asset i

b_{ik} = reaction in asset i's returns to movements in the common factor δk

k = a common factor with a zero mean that influences the returns on all assets

ϵ_i = a unique effect on asset i's return which, by assumption, is completely diversifiable in large portfolios and has a mean of zero

N = number of assets.

---

[22] Stephen Ross, "The Arbitrage Theory of Capital Asset Pricing," *Journal of Economic Theory*, 13 no. 2 (December 1976): 341–360; Stephen Ross, "Return, Risk, and Arbitrage," in I. Friend and J. Bicksler (eds.) *Risk and Return in Finance* (Cambridge: Ballinger, 1977): 189–218.

Two terms require elaboration: δk and b. As indicated, the δk terms are the *multiple* factors that are expected to have an impact on the returns of *all* assets. Examples might include inflation, growth in GNP, major political upheavals, or changes in interest rates. The point is the APT contends there are a *number* of such factors that influence returns. This is in contrast to the CAPM, where the only variable of importance is the covariance of the asset with the market portfolio.

Given these common factors, the b_{ik}'s determine how each asset reacts to this common factor. To extend the earlier example, while all assets may be affected by growth in GNP, the impact will differ between assets; e.g., stocks of cyclical firms will have larger b_{ik}'s for this common factor than noncyclical firms, such as grocery chains. Likewise, you will hear discussions about interest-sensitive stocks: all stocks are affected by changes in interest rates, but some stocks experience larger impacts. The theory contends that there are common factors and we can envision some likely examples of common factors, such as inflation, etc. Still, in the application of the theory, *the factors are not identified.* As we will see when we discuss the empirical studies, there will be an identification of three, four, or five factors that affect security returns, but *there is no indication of what these factors represent.*

Similar to the CAPM model, it is assumed that the unique effects (E_i's) are independent and, therefore, that they will be diversified away in a large portfolio.

The APT assumes that, in equilibrium, the return on a zero-investment, zero systematic-risk portfolio is zero when the unique effects are diversified away. This assumption and some theory from linear algebra implies that the expected return on any asset i (E_i) can be expressed as:

$$E_i = \lambda_o + \lambda_1 b_{i1}, + \lambda_2 b_{i2} + \ldots + \lambda_k b_{ik}$$

where

λ_o = the expected return on an asset with zero systematic risk where $\lambda_o = E_o$

λ_i = the risk premium related to each of the common factors—e.g., the risk premium related to interest rate risk ($\lambda_i = E_i - E_o$)

b_i = the pricing relationship between the risk premium and asset i—i.e., how responsive asset i is to this common factor K.

Consider the following example of two stocks and a two factor model.

K_1 = changes in the rate of inflation. The risk premium related to this factor is one percent for every one percent change in the rate ($\lambda_1 = .01$).

K_2 = percent growth in real GNP. The average risk premium related to this factor is two percent for every one percent change in the rate ($\lambda_2 = .02$).

λ_o = the rate of return on a zero systematic risk (zero beta: $b_{oj} = 0$) asset is three percent ($\lambda_o = .03$).

The two assets (X, Y) have the following response coefficients to these factors:

b_{x1} = the response of asset X to changes in the rate of inflation is 0.50 (b_{x1} = .50). This asset is not very responsive to changes in the rate of inflation.

b_{y1} = the response of asset Y to changes in the rate of inflation is 2.00 (b_{y1} = 2.00).

b_{x2} = the response of asset X to changes in the growth rate of real GNP is 1.50 (b_{x2} = 1.50).

b_{y2} = the response of asset Y to changes in the growth rate of real GNP is 1.75 (b_{y2} = 1.75).

These response coefficients indicate that if these are the major factors influencing asset returns, overall asset Y is a higher risk asset and, therefore, the expected return should be greater, as shown below:

$$E_i = \lambda_o + \lambda_1 b_{i1} + \lambda_2 b_{i2}$$
$$= .03 + (.01) b_{i1} + (.02) b_{i2}.$$

Therefore:

$$E_x = .03 + (.01)(0.50) + (.02)(1.50)$$
$$= .065 = 6.5\%$$

$$E_y = .03 + (.01)(2.00) + (.02)(1.75)$$
$$= .085 = 8.5\%.$$

Given these expected returns, if the prices of the assets do not reflect these returns, we would expect investors to enter into arbitrage arrangements whereby they would sell overpriced assets short. With the proceeds they would purchase the underpriced assets until the relevant prices were corrected. The point is, given these linear relationships, it should be possible to find an asset or a combination of assets with equal risk to the mispriced asset.

Empirical Tests of the APT

Because the APT is relatively new (any academic theory less than ten years old is considered new), there have only been a few empirical studies of this theory. This is not unusual, since it typically requires several years before the theory is generally accepted as potentially valid then several more years before other academicians can conceive of and carry out empirical tests. The discussion of the empirical tests will be fairly extensive because it is important that you understand the procedure for testing this new theory as well as the results. Because of its growing acceptance, there will be numerous tests forthcoming on the APT.

Roll-Ross Study

The empirical test by Roll and Ross followed a two-step procedure:[23]
1. Estimate the expected returns and the factor coefficients from times series data on individual asset returns.
2. Use these estimates to test the basic cross-sectional pricing conclusion implied by the APT—i.e., are the expected returns for these assets consistent with the common factors derived in Step 1?

The basic hypothesis they tested is the pricing relationship:

H_o: There exists nonzero constants $(E_o, \lambda_1, \ldots \lambda_k)$ such that:

$$E_i - E_o = \lambda_1 b_{i1} + \lambda_2 b_{i2} + \ldots + \lambda_k b_{ik}.$$

The specific b coefficients were estimated using factor analysis. The authors pointed out that, while the estimation procedure is a maximum likelihood procedure assuming a multivariate normal distribution whereby the estimates will be asymptotically consistent, there is very little known about the small sample properties of the results. Therefore, they emphasize the tentative nature of the conclusions from this first try.

The data file was daily returns contained in the Center for Research Security Prices (CRSP) files from the University of Chicago for the period July 1962 through December 1972. Stocks were put into 42 portfolios of 30 stocks each by alphabetical order (1,260 stocks). Most of the groups had a minimum of 2,400 observations of a total potential of 2,619 daily observations.

The estimation of the factor model indicated that the maximum reasonable number of factors was five. The intent was to err on the high side because subsequent steps could limit the factors considered if they were not significant. While the factors were derived using the first portfolio, they were applied to all 42 portfolios with the realization that the importance of the various factors might differ between portfolios; i.e., the first factor in Portfolio A might not be first in Portfolio B.

Assuming a risk-free rate of 6 percent ($\lambda_o = .06$), the subsequent analysis of the model indicated that at least three factors were important for pricing, but it was unlikely that there were more than four. Further analysis showed that the weight on the first two factors was quite heavy with changes in relative weights for the remaining three factors. When they allowed the model to estimate the risk-free rate (λ_o), only two factors were consistently significant, which indicated that the three factors implied by the earlier model may have been an overestimate.

Beyond the analysis which indicated there were multiple factors that affected security returns (between two and four), a subsequent test examined such a model against an alternative specification wherein individual returns are related to a security's own variance. The point is, the total variance of a security should not affect expected return if the APT is valid, because its diversifiable

[23] Richard Roll and Stephen A. Ross, "An Empirical Investigation of the Arbitrage Pricing Theory," *Journal of Finance*, 35 no. 5 (December 1980): 1073–1103.

component would be eliminated by diversification, and the nondiversifiable component should be explained by the factor loadings. The test involved a cross-sectional analysis of individual returns against the five factors *and* the security's own standard deviation. The results indicated that the security's own standard deviation had significant explanatory power which would be evidence against the APT. A possible source of spurious effect of the security's own variance is skewness in the distribution of returns. That is, positive skewness can create positive dependence between the mean and the standard deviation. To eliminate this problem, they estimated the various parameters (return, factor loadings, and own standard deviation) with a different set of observations. With this procedure, the standard deviation is only significant in nine of 42 portfolios when one day is skipped and seven of 42 portfolios when three days are skipped. At the same time, the impact of the factor loadings increased slightly. Using a test employed by Fama and MacBeth, the standard deviation variable was significant in only three of 42 portfolios. Therefore, they contended that when they adjusted for effect of skewness, the security's own standard deviation was not significant, and this supported the APT.

A final test was to determine if the factor structure across groups was similar. For instance, are the three or four factors that affect Group A the same as the factors that affect Group B? While it is not possible to test for the equivalence of the factors, it is possible to test cross-sectional consistency by examining whether the λ_o's for the 42 groups are similar. The results indicated no evidence that the intercept terms were different, although the test was admittedly weak.

In conclusion, the authors believed that the evidence generally supported the APT but acknowledged that the tests were only a first try and somewhat weak. They suggested other questions to be examined and pointed out that the relevant question is how this theory performs relative to alternative theories in explaining security returns.

Subsequent Extensions of RR Tests

A subsequent paper by Cho, Elton, and Gruber provided further evidence related to the Roll and Ross (RR) study by examining the number of factors in the return generating process that were priced.[24] Specifically, it is noted that the APT model contends that there are more factors that affect stock returns than implied by the CAPM. In this article they analyze the results using the RR procedure for different sets of data to determine the impact on the number of factors priced in the model. You will recall that prior studies found between three and five factors that were significant which is beyond what is implied in the CAPM.

The authors generated simulated returns using the zero beta CAPM with betas derived from Wilshire's fundamental betas and also with betas derived from historical data. They used the same factor analytic procedures as RR to determine the number of factors that were implied. The results with actual rates of return indicated that five factors were required which is more than RR indi-

---

[24] D. Chinhyung Cho, Edwin J. Elton, and Martin J. Gruber, "On the Robustness of the Roll and Ross Arbitrage Pricing Theory," *Journal of Financial and Quantitative Analysis,* 19 no. 1 (March 1984): 1–10.

cated. The results using historical betas implied six factors were necessary, while the Wilshire fundamental betas pointed toward three factors.

Following further tests of specific groups, the authors conclude that there appears to be more than two factors in the market that influence the equilibrium returns. Even when returns are generated by a two factor model, two or three factors are required to explain the returns. These results would support the use of the APT model since it allows for the consideration of these additional factors which is not possible with the classical CAPM.

Dhrymes, Friend, and Gultekin (DFG) reexamine the techniques used by Roll and Ross (RR) in their original study and most subsequent studies, and contend that these techniques have several major limitations.[25] The initial criticism is that RR divided the total sample of stocks into numerous portfolios of 30 stocks. This division is typically necessary because of the limitations of the computer to conduct the extensive analysis for a much larger sample. While recognizing this practical constraint, DFG contend that the results for this limited portfolio differ from comparable results for a larger sample and especially for the total sample of over 1,000 stocks. Specifically, they find *no relationship* between the "factor loading" for groups of 30 stocks and a group of 240 stocks. They also contend that there is some loss of information because of the test procedure.

The second major limitation noted by DFG is that it is not possible to identify the actual number of factors that characterize the return generating process. When they apply the model to portfolios of different size, they determine that the number of factors change—for example, for 15 securities it is a two factor model; for 30 securities there is a three factor model; for 45, a four factor model; for 60, a six factor model and for 90 securities, a nine factor model. There is also a companion problem with the multiple factors—which of the factors are priced? Put another way, given the multiple factors, which of them are significant in explaining returns?

Roll and Ross provide a nontechnical reply to the criticisms.[26] Regarding the point that the factors differ with 30 stocks versus 240, they acknowledge that this would occur and pointed this out in their article. Still, the important consideration is whether the resulting estimates are *consistent,* since it is not feasible to consider all of the stocks together. They felt that they tested for consistency and it was generally supported.

Regarding the question of the number of factors, RR initially point out that the number of factors included is a secondary issue—the important consideration is how well the model explains the return generating process compared to alternative models. In addition, they contend that one would *expect* the number of factors to increase with the sample size because you would expect more potential relationships to arise (e.g., industries, etc.). The important consideration is how many are priced (i.e., are significant) in a diversified portfolio.

---

[25] Phoebus J. Dhrymes, Irwin Friend, and N. Bulent Gultekin, "A Critical Reexamination of the Empirical Evidence on the Arbitrage Pricing Theory," *Journal of Finance,* 39 no. 2 (June 1984): 323–346.

[26] Richard Roll and Stephen Ross, "A Critical Reexamination of the Empirical Evidence on the Arbitrage Pricing Theory: A Reply," *Journal of Finance,* 39 no. 2 (June 1984): 347–350.

Although RR disagree with some of the comments by DFG, they conclude with the observation that their initial study was a first step in testing the APT and it will be improved by constructive suggestions by others.

Reinganum Study[27]

The specific purpose of the study was to determine whether an arbitrage pricing model with limited assumptions can account for the differences in average returns between small firms and large firms. You will recall from Chapter 7 on efficient capital markets that a major anomaly related to the efficient markets hypothesis was that small firms consistently experienced significantly larger risk-adjusted rates of return than large firms. This was true even after special adjustments to the beta coefficients for the small firms. Reinganum contended that this anomaly could not be explained by the CAPM and it should be explained by the APT *if* it is to be considered a superior theory or a theory capable of properly explaining asset prices — i.e., if the APT is to be considered an empirical replacement for the CAPM.

The test is conducted in two stages:

1. During Year Y – 1, factor loadings are estimated for all securities, and securities with similar factor loadings are put into common control portfolios. The securities in each control portfolio are expected to have similar risk characteristics. (The author derives models with three, four, and five factors and all models are tested.) During Year Y, excess security returns are computed for each stock by subtracting the average daily returns for the control portfolio from the daily returns for each of the individual stocks in the portfolio. Assuming that all stocks within a control portfolio have equal risk according to the APT, they should have similar average returns, and the average excess return for stocks in a control portfolio should be zero.

2. Given the excess returns during Year Y, all the stocks were ranked on the basis of their market value at the end of Year Y – 1, and the excess returns of the firms in the bottom 10 percent of the size distribution were combined (equal weights) to form the average excess returns for Portfolio MV1. Similarly, nine other portfolios were formed with MV10 containing excess returns for the largest firms.

Under the null hypothesis, *the ten portfolio should possess identical average excess returns which should be insignificantly different from zero.* If the ten portfolios do not have identical average excess returns, this evidence would be *inconsistent* with the APT.

The sample was drawn from stocks on the University of Chicago daily Center for Research in Security Prices (CRSP) tapes and included firms with certain minimum data availability. The number ranged from 1,457 in 1963 to over 2,500 during the mid-1970s. The ranking procedure, as described in Step 2 above, was carried out for each year. This is necessary because the market values change and firms are added and deleted. As stated, if the average excess returns for the ten portfolios equal zero, then the evidence supports the APT.

---

[27] Marc R. Reinganum, "The Arbitrage Pricing Theory: Some Empirical Results." *Journal of Finance,* 36 no. 2 (May 1981): 313–321.

The results of the tests are *clearly inconsistent with the APT.* Specifically:

> The average excess returns of the ten portfolios are clearly not equal to zero, regardless of whether a three, four, or five factor model is employed to account for APT risk. The small firm portfolio, MV1, possesses a positive and statistically significant average excess return. On the other hand, the large firm portfolio, MV10, is characterized by a negative, but statistically significant, average excess return . . . a conservative estimate of the mean difference in excess returns between the small and large firms might be about twenty-five (250 × .1%) on an annual basis. . . . the point estimates of the mean excess portfolio returns of MV1 through MV10 are perfectly ordered with firm size. That is, the rank correlation between average portfolio excess returns and medium stock values within a portfolio is exactly −1.0.[28]

The author subsequently tested for significant differences between the returns for individual portfolios and also examined the difference between the high and low portfolio on a year-by-year basis. Both tests confirmed the overall conclusions that the low market value portfolios outperformed the high market value portfolios regardless of whether excess returns are derived from the three, four, or five factor model. The author concluded that the APT is *not* supported by the results of this study, although it was acknowledged that the test was a joint test of several hypothesis implicit in the theory and it was not possible to pinpoint the error.

Chen Study

A subsequent study by Chen was not only very supportive of the APT model compared to the CAPM, but also had results related to the small firm effect that were contrary to those generated by Reinganum.[29] Prior to discussing the tests, the problems with limited sample and multiple factors is considered. It is noted that these problems are related to the *testing* of the theory and should not reflect on the theory itself.

The author used 180 stocks which was the limit of the computer available. Based upon prior studies, the author selected five factors. A major consideration was a comparison of the cross sectional results using the APT versus the CAPM. While the first factor was highly correlated with the beta, the subsequent direct tests clearly favored the APT over the CAPM. Chen also considered performance measurement with the two models. It is noted that if the CAPM is misspecified and does not capture all the information related to returns, this remaining information will show up in the residual series and it is possible to see if the APT can provide further factors to explain these residual returns. If so, the APT would be considered superior. Based upon the results, the author concludes that the CAPM is misspecified and the missing price information was picked up by the APT.

---

[28] Ibid., p. 317.

[29] Nai-fu Chen. "Some Empirical Tests of the Theory of Arbitrage Pricing," *Journal of Finance,* 38 no. 5 (December 1983): 1393–1414.

The final tests were concerned with determining whether some major variables have explanatory power after the factor loadings (FL) from the APT model. Specifically, are any variables priced *after* the factor loadings are accounted for? If so, this would cause one to reject the APT. The two variables considered in this regard are: (1) own variance, and (2) firm size. Both of these have been found to be important in prior CAPM studies. Regarding the own variance test the author concluded:

> ". . . we cannot reject the null hypothesis that the APT is correct, and the own variance has no explanatory power net of FL."[30]

The results for tests related to firm size divided the sample by size and formed portfolios with the same factor loadings. The results again led the author to conclude that the firm size had no explanatory power after adjusting for risk by the factor loadings. As noted earlier, these results are in contrast to the earlier results by Reinganum.

The APT and Inflation

In addition to these specific tests of the theory, a paper by Elton, Gruber, and Rentzler extended the APT to consider the impact of inflation on the return for assets.[31] They derived an equilibrium model of real returns assuming an impact of inflation. Subsequently, assuming the inflation factor is not priced, they employed the arbitrage pricing model. They showed that it can be made equivalent to the mean-variance model, and this specification was compared to prior CAPM models that considered inflation. They also thought that it was important to develop APT models with factors that were not only statistically identifiable (i.e., factors derived from a factor analysis model), but which had economic meaning. (That is, it should be possible to identify what specific economic variable affects prices—e.g., inflation, growth in real GNP., etc.)

Further Discussion of Empirical Tests

Clearly, a less supportive paper by Shanken challenged whether the APT can be empirically verified at all.[32] Rather than any concern with the specific tests or methods used in prior empirical tests of the APT, the author considered the fundamental question of what it means to test the APT and questioned whether, in fact, the APT is more susceptible to testing than the CAPM. Shanken pointed out that the usual empirical formulation of the test is to determine that the set of asset returns conforms to a *K* factor model derived from factor analysis. Part of the problem is that, if returns are not explained by such a model, it is not

---

[30] *Ibid.,* 1406.

[31] Edwin Elton, Martin Gruber, and Joel Rentzler, "The Arbitrage Pricing Model and Returns on Assets under Uncertain Inflation," *Journal of Finance,* 38 no. 2 (May 1983): 525–537.

[32] Jay Shanken, "The Arbitrage Pricing Theory: Is It Testable?" *Journal of Finance,* 37 no. 5 (December 1982): 1129–1140.

considered a rejection of the model; however, if the factors do explain returns, it is considered support. It was also contended that there is a real problem with the supposed advantage that the factors need not be observable. It was shown that, under such conditions, equivalent sets of securities may conform to different factor structures, and the empirical formulation of the APT then may yield different implications regarding the expected returns for a given set of securities.

This implies that the theory is not capable of explaining differential returns between securities. In order to explain differential returns, it is necessary to identify the relevant factor structure that will help explain the differential returns, but the factor analysis model is not capable of doing this. This need to identify the relevant factor structure that affects asset returns is similar to the problem with the CAPM of identifying the true market portfolio. Therefore, there is a similar problem with testing the theory: i.e., before you can test the CAPM properly, you must identify and use the true market portfolio, while you must identify the relevant factor structure that affects security returns before you can test the APT.

In addition to this article that expresses a concern with prior tests, there have been two articles that have proposed other statistical techniques for testing the APT model. Jobson proposes that the APT can be tested by using a multivariate linear regression model.[33] Following a general development of the test, it is shown that it can be carried out using univariate multiple regression software. He also shows how this test is related to the Sharpe measure of portfolio performance.

Brown and Weinstein (BW) propose a new approach to estimating and testing asset pricing models employing a bilinear paradigm.[34] Specifically, they contend that the economic content of any equilibrium asset pricing model contains potentially refutable constraints on the set of parameters of the return generating process. Given a set of characteristics that are specific to a security, there is a linear relationship for all securities that relates expected returns to these characteristics. The coefficients in the linear model represent the prices of the alternative characteristics. An important point is that all asset pricing models require that *the market price of each characteristic that is priced be common to all securities.* BW propose a simple test of this bilinear model constraint which can be applied to many well-known asset pricing models. In this paper they apply it to the arbitrage pricing model (APM).

When they implemented the test using RR data, the results appeared to conflict with the APM at standard levels of significance. When they adjusted the test to recognize the large sample size, the results were consistent with a three factor APM, but tended to reject the five and seven factor model. Based upon several variations of factors, they concluded that there were few rather than many factors. Note that this implication is consistent with the majority of prior studies which suggest between three and five factors.

[33] J. D. Jobson, "A Multivariate Linear Regression Test for the Arbitrage Pricing Theory," *Journal of Finance,* 37 no. 4 (September 1982): 1037–1042.

[34] Stephen J. Brown and Mark I. Weinstein, "A New Approach to Testing Asset Pricing Models: The Bilinear Paradigm," *Journal of Finance,* 38 no. 3 (June 1983): 711–743.

648   SUMMARY

This chapter contained four major parts: (1) a discussion of the impact on the CAPM when we relaxed some of the major assumptions of the model; (2) a presentation of empirical studies related to major questions for the CAPM (i.e., the stability of beta and the relationship between systematic risk and return); (3) a presentation and discussion of a major alternative theory of capital asset pricing, the arbitrage pricing theory (APT), and (4) a fairly detailed discussion of some of the major empirical studies related to this emerging theory.

It was shown that, when we relaxed several of the major assumptions of the CAPM, generally the required modifications were reasonably minor and did not change the overall concept of the model. The empirical studies indicated that the betas for portfolios were quite stable, especially if enough observations were used to derive the betas and if there was adequate volume. Further, the majority of tests confirmed the expected relationship between returns and systematic risk with allowance for the zero-beta model. Still, papers by Roll indicated that, because it is basically not possible to empirically derive a true market portfolio, it is not possible to test the model properly or to use it to evaluate portfolio performance.

Coincident with this background of questions, an alternative asset pricing model was proposed by Ross which has fewer assumptions and does not require a true market portfolio. The empirical tests of the APT have thus far been preliminary, and the results are the best described as mixed. The nature of the tests currently conducted are such that it is impossible to derive evidence to reject the theory.

In conclusion, it is probably safe to assume that both the CAPM and APT will continue to exist and will be used to price capital assets. Coincident with this, there will be further empirical tests of both theories, and the ultimate goal will be to determine which theory does the best job of explaining current and future returns.

QUESTIONS

1. In the empirical testing of the CAPM, what are two major questions of concern? Why are they important?
2. Briefly discuss why it is important for beta coefficients to be stationary over time.
3. Discuss the empirical results relative to beta stability for individual stocks and portfolios of stocks.
4. Why is the stability of beta for portfolios of stocks considered more relevant?
5. In the tests of the relationship between systematic risk (beta) and return, what are the major factors being considered? That is, what are you looking for?
6. Draw an ideal SML. Based upon the discussion of the empirical results, what did the actual relationship look like relative to the ideal relationship implied by the CAPM?
7. According to the theory, what assets are included in the market portfolio, and what are the relative weightings? In empirical studies, what are the typical proxies used for the market portfolio?

8. Assuming the empirical proxy for the market portfolio is not a good proxy, what factors related to the CAPM will be affected?

9. Given the following results, indicate what will happen to the beta for Stock W relative to the market proxy compared to the beta relative to the true market portfolio:

<table>
<tr><th></th><th colspan="3">Yearly Rates of Return</th></tr>
<tr><th>Year</th><th>Stock
W
(percent)</th><th>Market
Proxy
(percent)</th><th>True
Market
(percent)</th></tr>
<tr><td>1</td><td>10</td><td>8</td><td>6</td></tr>
<tr><td>2</td><td>20</td><td>14</td><td>11</td></tr>
<tr><td>3</td><td>-14</td><td>-10</td><td>-7</td></tr>
<tr><td>4</td><td>-20</td><td>-18</td><td>-12</td></tr>
<tr><td>5</td><td>15</td><td>12</td><td>10</td></tr>
</table>

Discuss the reason for the differences in measured beta. Does the relationship suggested appear reasonable? Why or why not?

10. Draw the implied SMLs for the following two sets of conditions:
   1. $RFR = .07$; $Rm(S + P\ 500) = .16$
   2. $Rz = .09$; $Rm(True) = .18$

   Under which set of conditions would it be more difficult for a portfolio manager to be superior?

11. Using the graph and equations from Question 10, which of the following portfolios would be superior?
   a. $Ra = 11\%$; $\beta = .09$
   b. $Rb = 14\%$; $\beta = 1.00$
   c. $Rc = 12\%$; $\beta = -.40$
   d. $Rd = 20\%$; $\beta = 1.10$

   Does it matter which SML you use?

12. What are the major assumptions required by the APT? What are some critical assumptions of the CAPM that are *not* required by the APT?

13. Under the following conditions, what are the expected returns for Stocks M and N?
   — $\lambda_0 = .05$ $b_{M1} = 0.70$
   — $K_1 = .02$ $b_{M2} = 1.30$
   — $K_2 = .04$ $b_{N1} = 1.50$
   $b_{N2} = 2.20$

14. Briefly discuss why Reinganum's study does not support the APT.

REFERENCES

Altman, Edward, B. Jacquillet, and M. Levasseur. "Comparative Analysis of Risk Measures — France and the United States." *Journal of Financial and Quantitative Analysis.* 13 no. 1 (March 1978).

Baesel, Jerome B. "On the Assessment of Risk: Some Further Considerations." *Journal of Finance.* 29 no. 5 (December 1974).

Black, Fischer, Michael Jensen, and Myron Scholes. "The Capital Asset Pricing

Model: Some Empirical Tests." in *Studies in the Theory of Capital Markets.* Michael Jensen ed. New York: Praeger Publishers, 1976.

Black, Fischer. "Capital Market Equilibrium with Restricted Borrowing." *Journal of Business.* 45 no. 3 (July 1972).

Blume, Marshall E. "On the Assessment of Risk." *Journal of Finance.* 26 no. 1 (March 1971).

Brown, Stephen J. and Mark I. Weinstein, "A New Approach to Testing Asset Pricing Models: The Bilinear Paradigm," *Journal of Finance.* 38 no. 3 (June, 1983).

Carpenter, Michael, and David E. Upton. "Trading Volume and Beta Stability." *Journal of Portfolio Management.* 7 no. 2 (Winter 1981).

Chen, Son-Nan. "Beta Nonstationarity, Portfolio Residual Risk and Diversification." *Journal of Financial and Quantitative Analysis.* 16 no. 1 (March 1981).

Cho, D. Chinhyung, Edwin J. Elton and Martin J. Gruber. "On the Robustness of the Roll and Ross Arbitrage Pricing Theory." *Journal of Financial and Quantitative Analysis.* 19 no. 1 (March 1984).

Dhen, Nai-Fu. "Some Empirical Tests of the Theory of Arbitrage Pricing." *Journal of Finance.* 38 no. 5 (December 1983).

Dhrymes, Phoebus J., Irwin Friend and N. Bulent Gultekin, "A Critical Reexamination of the Empirical Evidence on the Arbitrage Pricing Theory." *Journal of Finance.* 39 no 2 (June, 1984).

Douglas, G. W. "Risk in the Equity Markets: An Empirical Appraisal of Market Efficiency." *Yale Economic Essays.* 9 no. 1 (1969).

Elton, Edwin, Martin Gruber and Joel Rentzler. "The Arbitrage Pricing Model and Returns on Assets under Uncertain Inflation." *Journal of Finance.* 38 no. 2 (May 1983).

Fama, Eugene, and R. MacBeth. "Risk, Return and Equilibrium: Empirical Tests." *Journal of Political Economy.* 81 no. 2 (May–June 1973).

Fielitz, Bruce. "Indirect Versus Direct Diversification." *Financial Management.* 3 no. 4 (Winter 1974).

Huberman, Gur. "Arbitrage Pricing Theory: A Simple Approach," *Journal of Economic Theory.* 28 no. 1 (October 1982).

Jobson, J. D. "A Multivariate Linear Regression Test for the Arbitrage Pricing Theory." *Journal of Finance.* 37 no. 4 (September 1982).

Levy, Robert A. "On the Short-Run Stationarity of Beta Coefficients." *Financial Analysts Journal.* 27 no. 6 (November–December 1971).

Litzenberger, Robert, and K. Ramaswamy. "The Effect of Personal Taxes and Dividends on Capital Asset Prices." *Journal of Financial Economics.* 6 no. 2 (June 1979).

Miller, Morton H., and Myron Scholes. "Rates of Return in Relation to Risk: A Re-Examination of Some Recent Findings." in *Studies in the Theory of Capital Markets.* Michael Jensen ed. New York: Praeger Publishers, 1976.

Porter, R. Burr, and John R. Ezzell. "A Note on the Predictive Ability of Beta Coefficients." *Journal of Business Research.* 3 no. 4 (October 1975).

Reinganum, Marc R. "The Arbitrage Pricing Theory: Some Empirical Results." *Journal of Finance.* 36 no. 2 (May 1981).

Rosenfeldt, Rodney L., Gary L., Griepentrog, and Christopher C. Pflamm. "Further Evidence on the Stationarity of Beta Coefficients." *Journal of Financial and Quantitative Analysis.* 13 no. 1 (March 1978).

Roll, Richard. "Ambiguity when Performance is Measured by the Securities Market Line." *Journal of Finance.* 33 no. 4 (September 1978).

Roll, Richard. "A Critique of the Asset Pricing Theory's Tests." *Journal of Financial Economics.* 4 no. 4 (March 1977).

Roll, Richard. "Performance Evaluation and Benchmark Error I." *Journal of Portfolio Management.* 6 no. 4 (Summer 1980).

Roll, Richard. "Performance Evaluation and Benchmark Error II." *Journal of Portfolio Management.* 7 no. 2 (Winter 1981).

Roll, Richard, and Stephen A. Ross. "An Empirical Investigation of the Arbitrage Pricing Theory." *Journal of Finance.* 35 no. 5 (December 1980).

Roll, Richard and Stephen A. Ross. "A Critical Reexamination of the Empirical Evidence on the Arbitrage Pricing Theory: A Reply," *Journal of Finance.* 39 no. 2 (June 1984).

Ross, Stephen A. "The Arbitrage Theory of Capital Asset Pricing." *Journal of Economic Theory.* 13 no. 2 (December 1976).

Ross, Stephen A. "Risk, Return and Arbitrage," in *Risk and Return in Finance.* I. Friend and J. Bicksler eds. Cambridge: Ballinger, 1977.

Shanken, Jay. "The Arbitrage Pricing Theory: Is It Testable?" *Journal of Finance.* 37 no. 5 (December 1982).

Sharpe, William F., and Cooper, Gary M. "Risk–Return Classes of New York Stock Exchange Common Stocks: 1931–1976." *Financial Analysts Journal.* 28 no. 2 (March–April 1972).

Statman, Meir. "Betas Compared: Merrill Lynch vs. Value Line." *Journal of Portfolio Management.* 7 no. 2 (Winter 1981).

Theobald, Michael. "Beta Stationarity and Estimation Period: Some Analytical Results." *Journal of Financial and Quantitative Analysis.* 16 no. 5 (December 1981).

Tole, Thomas M. "How to Maximize Stationarity of Beta." *Journal of Portfolio Management.* 7 no. 2 (Winter 1981).

Chapter 21

International Diversification

T he reader is fully aware of the importance of diversification for reducing the risk of the portfolio. He or she also knows that the important factor when selecting an asset for diversification purposes is the covariance of the asset with all other assets in the portfolio. Further, with the CAPM it is shown that the relevant covariance is that between the asset and the market portfolio of *all risky assets in the economy.* In the search for investment assets that have low covariance with the market portfolio, increasing attention has been paid to international capital markets because of the a priori expectation that the covariance between international securities and United States securities should be very low. Hence, one should consider adding such investments to a portfolio composed of domestic stocks.

Because of the growing importance of international investments to individuals and institutions, this chapter deals with the topic in some detail. Initially, we will consider *why* international diversification should be beneficial; i.e., what is the rationale for expecting significant benefits from international diversification? Subsequently, we will discuss the results of several studies that have examined the historical relationships between the returns for U.S. securities and foreign securities. The results of these studies will indicate whether international diversification would have been useful for a U.S. investor.

Given the apparent benefits of international diversification, it is important to consider some of the obstacles involved. The chapter concludes with a consideration of available mutual funds that invest specifically in foreign securities. There are a variety of readily available investments that provide the benefits of international diversification.

WHY INTERNATIONAL DIVERSIFICATION?

Because the objective of any diversification is to reduce the overall variance of a portfolio, one must ask why foreign securities should be expected to have low covariance with a portfolio of U.S. risky assets. Although the market portfolio used in the CAPM is *theoretically* supposed to contain all risky assets available, the investor is typically concerned with risky assets in the United States. Further, it has been noted on several occasions that almost all empirical studies of the CAPM have used the Standard & Poor's 500 composite index as a proxy for the market portfolio. As discussed in Chapter 20, this is a gross understatement of the market portfolio, since the S&P 500 Index only includes common stocks and almost all of them are stocks listed on the NYSE. Given this orientation, it is important to demonstrate that foreign securities *should* be included in domestic portfolios. The true market portfolio should be a *total world portfolio* to derive the maximum benefits of diversification.

This discussion leads us back to our assumption of low covariance between the returns for domestic and foreign securities. To see why this expectation is reasonable, one should consider the basic dividend valuation formula:

$$P = \frac{D_1}{i - g}.$$

The relevant variables are expected dividend (D_1), the required rate of return (i), and the expected growth rate for dividends (g). It is contended that these variables differ significantly between countries and for different securities in the various countries. Because i and g are the most important variables, we will concentrate on them.

Differences in Required Return (i)

i is a function of the economy's risk-free rate of return, the expected inflation in the economy, and a risk premium for the uncertainty involved. Therefore, let us consider each of these components in terms of how they would differ for a foreign country compared to those for the U.S.

The Risk-Free Rate. It has been shown that the risk-free rate is basically determined by the real growth rate in the economy and, in the short run, by tightness or ease in the capital markets. Different countries have experienced different rates of growth during the past several decades. Examples include the high rate of growth in Japan and Germany. The point is these rates of growth in different countries are *not synchronized.* Further, there are differences in the short-run ease or tightness in the capital markets in different countries. Therefore, one would expect differences in the *level* of the RFR and also somewhat independent *changes* in the RFR for various countries.

Differences in the Rates of Inflation. We have talked extensively about the impact of the rate of inflation on the required rate of return on all assets and specifically about how inflation has affected securities in the U.S. In fact, it is probably safe to say that inflation has been the most important variable influencing asset valuation during the last decade. The crucial question in terms of international diversification is whether the level of inflation is generally the same around the world, and more importantly, whether *changes* in the rate of inflation are correlated. If these changes are correlated, then required rates of return would generally move together and security prices would be related. Obviously, such a scenario would reduce the utility of international diversification. In contrast, if changes in rates of inflation are typically unique, then returns for securities in various countries would not be correlated, and international diversification would be useful.

To get a feeling for whether rates of inflation should be related, it is necessary to consider the factors that cause inflation. Specifically, inflation is generally described as either demand-pull (excess demand) or cost-push. In turn there is some controversy regarding whether excess demand inflation is fueled by monetary policy or fiscal policy. Without entering into this discussion, it is enough to recognize that generally *both* the monetary policy and the fiscal policy of a country are determined by internal factors; therefore, the specification and implementation of policy directives should typically be independent among countries. Further, the impact of any monetary or fiscal stimulus will differ between countries depending upon the current state of the country's economy in terms of unemployment, etc. Regarding cost-push inflation, again the impact will depend upon the state of the economy and the power of various economic units, e.g., unions. Again, this inflationary impact will differ between countries.[1]

The point is, while the basic causes of inflation may be reasonably universal, there are major differences in these causes in alternative countries. Therefore, one should expect differences in the level of inflation and relatively independent *changes* in the rate of inflation for different countries. Because of the major impact that inflation has on the required rate of return, this discussion would imply substantial independence in i and consequent *independence* in security returns due to changes in i.

Differences in risk premiums. The risk premium can either be estimated using internal characteristics (business risk, financial risk, and liquidity risk) or external market risk (covariance with the market portfolio). Because this discussion is concerned with why the covariance with the market portfolio should be low, it is appropriate to consider the relationship among the internal characteristics. Because we are interested in *changes* in stock prices, (as they affect rates of return) we will consider whether *changes* in the relevant risk variables are independent.

Recall that business risk is a function of sales volatility and operating leverage. One would therefore generally expect *changes* in business risk for firms in different countries to be unique because the factors that affect domestic sales, such as fiscal policy and monetary policy, are independent; therefore, changes in sales volatility should also be relatively independent. Similarly, the degree of operating leverage (DOL) is a function of how close a firm is operating to its breakeven point. Again, because sales are generally independent, the DOL will be unique and changes in this variable for firms in different countries should not

---

[1] In this regard see Beryl W. Sprinkel, *Money and Markets* (Homewood, Ill.: Richard D. Irwin, 1971), Chapter 7; and Dallas S. Batten and R. W. Hafer, "The Relative Impact of Monetary and Fiscal Actions on Economic Activity: A Cross Country Comparison," Federal Reserve Bank of St. Louis *Review,* 65 no. 1 (January 1983): 5–12.

be consistently related. Therefore, because changes in sales volatility and changes in operating leverage are not related, you should *not* expect changes in business risk to be related.

Financial risk is a function of the proportion of debt in the financial structure and is typically measured in terms of the debt/total capital ratio or interest coverage. Firms within an economy typically determine how much debt to employ based upon the tax laws (the higher the corporate tax rate, the greater the tax advantage of debt versus equity), earnings stability (with greater stability it is possible to employ more debt), and the expected rate of inflation (a higher rate of inflation would prompt more firms to become net debtors). These factors that determine the desired level of financial leverage are generally independent, and *changes* in these factors are unique. Therefore, *changes* in the level of financial risk for different countries should be relatively independent.

Liquidity risk is the uncertainty regarding the ability to buy or sell an asset quickly at a known price. The liquidity of an asset is a function of the number of investors who own and trade the asset, i.e., the volume of trading in the asset. In turn, the amount of trading in common stocks or other financial assets is influenced by the general economic climate in a country, and, again, one would not expect consistency between countries. This expectation is borne out by differences in trading volume on different national exchanges. For example, there have been instances in which trading in Japan was extremely heavy while volume on U.S. exchanges was relatively light. Therefore, because trading-volume changes are unique, we should expect changes in liquidity risk to be independent for different countries.

Summary Regarding Required Rate of Return.   As noted, there are three determinants of the required rate of return on securities: the economy's risk-free rate, the expected rate of inflation, and the risk premium for alternative assets. A specific analysis of each of these factors indicated that *changes* in each of these variables in different countries were generally determined by internal factors that were *independent* between countries. Therefore, one can conclude that *changes in the required rate of return for securities in various countries will not be highly correlated, and, in many cases, the changes could be relatively independent.* If other factors are held constant, and the required rate of return on foreign securities experiences changes that are independent of changes in the required return on U.S. securities, then the resulting rates of return on U.S. and foreign securities should have small covariance or correlation.

The level of covariance between two countries will depend upon the relationship between the economies involved. As an example, one would probably expect a fairly high correlation between U.S. and Canadian securities because the economies are highly related. In contrast, the U.S. economy has a very weak relationship to those of some third world countries, so one would expect a weak correlation between stock returns.

Independent Changes in the Growth Rate

It can similarly be argued that the major factors determining the growth rate (g) are generally independent between countries. You will recall that the growth rate is a function of the retention rate and the return on equity. One would expect changes in the retention rate to vary between countries based upon differences in their tax structure, the investment opportunities in the country, and the availability of external capital in the country's capital markets. Because all of these factors differ between countries and change independently, changes in the retention rate should be unique to a given nation. The return on equity (ROE) is determined by equity turnover and the profit margin. The equity turnover, in turn, is heavily influenced by sales growth, retention policy, and changes in the debt-equity financing ratio. All of these factors differ between countries. The profit margin depends upon such factors as capacity utilization, unit labor cost, inflation, exports, and imports. Again, the two major factors are capacity utilization and unit labor cost, and both of these are clearly variables that are internal to the economy. Therefore, changes in these variables for alternative nations should be relatively independent.

Therefore, almost all of the determinants of growth are unique and differ for different countries. Moreover, *changes* in these variables are generally determined by internal conditions, and these conditions are expected to be independent. Similar to the changes in i, the degree of independence in these growth factors will vary depending upon the economic ties between the countries. Because changes in these growth variables cause changes in security prices, the resultant price changes should likewise be relatively independent.

Summary Regarding Independent Changes.   In this section we employed the basic dividend valuation model to help us determine whether international diversification makes sense. An analysis of the two major determinants of value (i and g) indicated that both variables are heavily influenced by the macroeconomic organization and management of the economy. Moreover, the major decisions that generally affect a country's economy are made by an internal group concerned with a country's well-being. As such, most of the decisions are independent of circumstances in other countries. Therefore, changes in both i and g should be independent between countries or have low correlation. As a result, price changes should be relatively independent, and the covariance between returns for securities in *different* countries should be much lower than the covariance of returns for securities *within* a country.

EMPIRICAL STUDIES OF INTERNATIONAL DIVERSIFICATION

A number of studies have examined the effect of international diversification empirically and attempted to answer questions regarding the real benefits of such diversification.

Grubel Studies.   One of the first studies by Grubel[2] showed the benefits of international diversification by analyzing monthly rates of return (adjusted for changes in the exchange rate) for major countries during the period 1959–1966.

[2] Herbert G. Grubel, "Internationally Diversified Portfolios: Welfare Gains and Capital Flows," *American Economic Review,* 58 no 5 (December 1968): 1299–1314.

TABLE 21.1
Rates of Return and Standard Deviation from Investing in Foreign Capital Market
Averages, 1959–1966

	Percent Per Annum (1)	Standard Deviation (σ) (2)	Correlation (R) with USA (3)
USA	7.54	47.26	1.0000
Canada	5.95	41.19	.7025[a]
United Kingdom	9.59	65.28	.2414[a]
West Germany	7.32	94.69	.3008[a]
France	4.27	49.60	.1938[a]
Italy	8.12	103.33	.1465
Belgium	1.09	37.56	.1080
Netherlands	5.14	86.34	.2107[a]
Japan	16.54	92.52	.1149
Australia	9.44	34.87	.0585
South Africa	8.47	61.92	−.1620

[a] Statistically siginificant at the 5 percent level.
SOURCE: Herbert G. Grubel, "Internationally Diversified Portfolios: Welfare Gains and Capital Flows,"
American Economic Review, 58 no. 5 (December 1968), p. 1304. Reprinted by permission.

The rates of return, standard deviation, and correlation with the U.S. index are
shown in Table 21.1.

Japan had the highest rate of return during the period but also had one of the
largest standard deviations. More importantly, this index had very low correlation with the U.S. index (0.1149) indicating that securities from Japan would be a
good addition to a portfolio composed of U.S. securities. Australia had the lowest
correlation (0.0585) with the U.S. index, and the South African index had a
negative correlation (−0.1620). This negative correlation is probably caused by
heavy involvement in gold mining. You will recall from Chapter 13 that the gold
mining industry was the only one with a negative beta. One would expect all of
these foreign indexes to be excellent additions to a domestic portfolio.

Grubel derived hypothetical portfolios using all 11 countries and using only
the eight in the Atlantic community. The results clearly showed that *diversification among the assets from the 11 countries permitted investors to attain higher
rates of return or lower variance than would be attained with a portfolio of only
U.S. stocks.* Also, if an investor limited himself to investments in securities from
the Atlantic community countries and thereby ignored Japan, South Africa, and
Australia, his opportunities for gains from diversification were reduced considerably.

A subsequent study by Grubel and Fadner was concerned with three questions regarding international diversification.[3] The first involved an analysis of
international diversification as compared to intranational diversification; the second, the effect of holding periods on the correlations, and the third, the effect of
fluctuations in the exchange rate on the variance of returns. The analysis in-

[3] Herbert G. Grubel and Kenneth Fadner, "The Interdependence of International Equity Markets," *Journal of
Finance,* 26 no. 1 (March 1971): 89–94.

volved 51 U.S. industry stock price indexes, 28 industry indexes from the U.K., and 28 West German indexes using weekly data for the period from January 1, 1965 to June 30, 1967.

The initial correlations involved percentages of price changes adjusted for changes in exchange rates. The effect of inter- and intranational diversification was initially examined in terms of the average correlation coefficient between all pairs *within* a country compared to all pairs *between* countries. For weekly and monthly holding periods, the differences were quite dramatic and definitely significant. For monthly data, the average correlation *within* the countries was about 0.50, while the average correlation *between* the countries was about 0.12. They also examined the correlation among pairs of identical industries from the three countries. It was hypothesized that the correlations would be proportional to the amount of importing and exporting done. The results indicated that correlations between identical industries in the U.S. and the U.K. were generally higher than similar correlations between industries in the U.S. and West Germany. The U.S.–U.K. correlations were larger in 13 of the 18 comparisons, and the average U.S.–U.K. correlation was 0.49 compared to an average correlation for the U.S.–West German industries of 0.32. There was also support for the hypothesis that the correlations were influenced by the proportion of importing and exporting done by the industry.

The effect of different holding periods was examined by analyzing the differences in correlations for weekly rates of returns, monthly returns, and quarterly returns. It was hypothesized that the correlation would be positively related to the holding period, since, in the long-run, some unique characteristics briefly affecting returns would be overpowered by the underlying real valuation factors, such as growth and profits. The results strongly supported the hypothesis since the average intranational correlations increased from 0.40 for weekly periods to 0.57 for quarterly holding period returns, while the international correlations went from about 0.06 for weekly holding periods to 0.32 for quarterly holding periods. These results imply some reduction in the benefits of international diversification with longer holding periods.

Finally, the effect of fluctuations in the exchange rate on return variability was examined by comparing the correlation of returns with and without adjustments for exchange rates. During the relatively short period of analysis, there were only small changes in exchange rates, so the fact that there were *no* significant differences caused by exchange rates is not too surprising.

Levy–Sarnat Study[4]

A study by Levy and Sarnat examined the potential gains from international diversification for the period 1951–1967 employing annual returns for 28 countries. An analysis of returns adjusted for exchange rate changes produced a wide range of mean returns (+17.8% to −1.5%) and standard deviations. After deriving the efficient set of portfolios, they utilized a market opportunity line and

---

[4] Haim Levy and Marshall Sarnat, "International Diversification of Investment Portfolios," *American Economic Review,* 60 no. 4 (September 1970): 668–675.

FIGURE 21.1

Alternative Efficient Frontiers When Stocks from Different Countries Are Considered

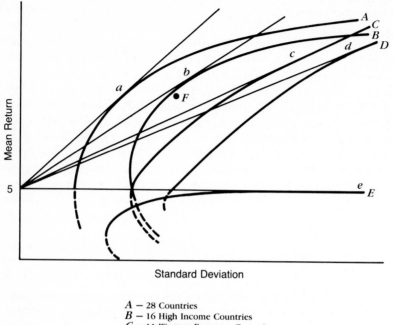

Standard Deviation

A — 28 Countries
B — 16 High Income Countries
C — 11 Western European Countries
D — 5 Common Market Countries
E — 9 Developing Countries
F — United States

SOURCE: Haim Levy and Marshall Sarnat, "International Diversification of Investment Portfolios," *American Economic Review*, 60 no. 4 (September 1979): 673. Reprinted by permission.

employed four borrowing and lending rates (2, 3, 4, and 6 percent), to generate four optimal portfolios. Although 28 countries were considered, only 9 were included in at least one of the optimal portfolios. Investments in the U.S. and Japan accounted for 50–70 percent of the optimal portfolios, with additional investments in developing or borderline countries, such as Venezuela, South Africa, New Zealand, and Mexico. Most of these were included because of the *low or negative correlation* they had with other countries in the sample.

The benefits to American investors of alternative diversification schemes were shown by deriving efficient frontiers using selected samples. As shown in Figure 21.1, if you invested in only developing countries, only common market countries, or only Western European countries, there is a *loss* relative to investing solely in the U.S. When Japan and South Africa are included, there is a significant improvement; i.e., there is a continuous reduction in variance as the opportunity set is broadened until the best frontier is derived *when all 28 countries are considered.* Canada was not included in any of the optimal portfolios because of its high correlation with the U.S. and its low rate of return. It was pointed out that, in a truly perfect capital market, an optimal portfolio would contain some of every country's stock. If it did not, the price of the omitted stock should decline until it entered at least one portfolio. Since this does not happen, it was surmised that restrictions on international trade and capital flows make a difference.

Agmon Studies

The first article by Agmon dealing with international diversification considered whether international stock markets were segmented, as suggested by previous authors, or whether there was support for the notion of one multinational perfect capital market.[5] The author initially argued that earlier studies which simply examined correlations were insufficient, and it would be preferable to use the capital asset pricing model, in which the marginal contribution made by an additional asset is considered, to determine the benefits of diversification. Agmon also argued against the use of composite market indicator series since he contended that whether they represent *all* possible combinations of investments is not certain. While true in theory, it is unlikely that the market indicator series are so poor that they would account for the substantial differences in returns found by other authors.

An analysis of the relationship between monthly returns for the United Kingdom, Germany, Japan, and the United States had significant slopes, but the r^2 were consistently very low. That is, U.S.–U.K. was 0.03; U.S.–Japan was 0.009. The results when the author related rates of return to the beta with the U.S. market was *not* supportive of a one country hypothesis—the slopes were insignificant and/or negative. Finally, he examined the simultaneity of price changes. Unfortunately, he used monthly data which precluded finding major lead-lag relationships for daily data.

A subsequent paper by Agmon examined individual stock price fluctuations unique to a stock's country or origin.[6] The sample included 145 stocks from the United Kingdom, Germany, and Japan during the 55 months from July 1961 to January 1966. While the stocks generally had a stronger relationship with the U.S. than any other foreign index, an analysis of the relationship with the U.S. versus their own country indicated a stronger relationship with their own country. A subsequent test indicated that the major factor explaining price measurements was the stocks *own country factor,* followed by a U.S. factor that was insignificant in two of three instances, and finally a unique factor that was insignificant.

The final question concerned the country factor and the potential benefits of international diversification. Agmon demonstrated that *different countries had unique country risks and that these unique risks were generally independent.* This independence was demonstrated again when the author showed that the country factors (the residuals) have either very low positive correlations (0.04 and 0.07), or negative correlation (−0.15). This indicated that the country factors are generally independent of each other, which implied that the potential gains from international diversification should be substantial.

---

[5] Tamir Agmon, "The Relations among Equity Markets: A Study of Share Price Co-Movements in the United States, United Kingdom, Germany and Japan," *Journal of Finance,* 27 no. 4 (September 1972): 839–855.

[6] Tamir Agmon, "Country Risk: The Significance of the Country Factor for Share Price Movements in the United Kingdom, Germany and Japan," *Journal of Business,* 46 no. 1 (January 1973): 24–32.

Lessard Study[7]

In this study, the sample was limited to four countries at approximately the same level of economic development (Columbia, Chile, Argentina, and Brazil). While, in general, one would expect stocks within a country to move together, Lessard contended that this comovement should be *stronger* in less developed countries because of their unique problems. Also, the common movements of different countries are probably unrelated to each other, because the problems and events in a given country would outweigh any common events of importance between the countries. This notion of independence of unique country returns was supported by the Agmon Study.[8] The Lessard study was concerned with three specific questions: (1) how strong were the common elements for stocks within these four countries? (2) were the individual common elements for each of the countries related or independent? (3) what were the specific benefits of international diversification compared to diversification within countries? The sample consisted of quarterly returns on 110 common stocks from the four countries for the period December 1958 to December 1968.

To derive the common element of variance and the independence of the common elements, the author employed factor analysis. The extent to which returns in individual countries move together was determined by principal component analysis applied to the four samples for three different time periods. In all cases, the proportions of total variance explained by the first component of returns for each of the countries was *larger* than generally found in the United States, ranging from 0.40 to 0.73 compared to an average of about 30 percent in the U.S. This indicated that *stocks within an undeveloped capital market have a large common component.* Further analysis implied that there was no systematic relationship between the major movements in the various stock markets.

Subsequent results confirmed that the returns in each country could be explained by a market factor, and *the market factors were independent of each other.* Of the 110 stocks, only six were closely related to another country's market factor, and all 110 were related to their own country factor.

Given the strong country factors and the independence of the country factors, it was contended that potentially large gains could be derived from international diversification. To estimate the gains, Lessard compared the return and variance of returns for intranational portfolios to the returns and variances possible from international portfolios. When naively diversified portfolios were constructed (equal amounts of each stock), the four nation portfolio dominated all single country portfolios with few exceptions. Assuming a risk-free rate of less than 6 percent, *the four nation portfolio was dominant.*

When efficient portfolios were constructed using past data, the international portfolio dominated all except Brazil and, again assuming almost any reasonable risk-free rate (below 13 percent), *the international portfolio was best.* In sum-

[7] Donald R. Lessard, "International Portfolio Diversification: A Multivariate Analysis for a Group of Latin American Countries," *Journal of Finance,* 38 no. 3 (June 1973): 619–633.

[8] Tamir Agmon, "Country Risk: The Significance of the Country Factor for Share Price Movements in the United Kingdom, Germany, and Japan," *Journal of Business,* 46 no. 1 (January 1973): 24–32.

mary, the results indicated that international diversification is beneficial even among developing countries in a single geographical area.

French Mutual Funds[9]

McDonald examined the investment performance of internationally diversified portfolios by analyzing the performance of French mutual funds for the period 1964–1969. The reason French funds were analyzed is that they typically represent investment in both domestic French stocks and foreign stocks, with the bulk of the latter being securities listed on the NYSE. Also, the funds are typically managed by French banks that have superior access to company information. The results supported the concept of international diversification, since the Sharpe reward-to-variability measure indicated that the all-French fund had the lowest performance ratio, while the fund with the *most* international diversification had the highest performance ratio. Other measures of performance gave about the same relative rankings of performance.

Joy et al. Study[10]

A study by Joy and others considered the fundamental structure of comovements in the returns in major international equity markets and also analyzed *changes* in these relationships over time. The authors examined weekly stock market index levels for 12 countries over the period 1963–1972 inclusive. The countries included were: Australia, France, Switzerland, Austria, Italy, the United Kingdom, Belgium, Japan, the United States, Canada, the Netherlands, and West Germany.

Adjusted and unadjusted rates of return were computed. The correlation matrix of weekly index rates of return for the entire ten-year period is shown in Table 21.2. The top half contains the correlation among unadjusted returns, while the bottom half contains the correlation among adjusted returns. Although there are a few significant positive correlations, *most of the correlations are very low,* as shown by the average correlations between rates of return for all 66 pairs of countries of only 0.139 and 0.133 for unadjusted and adjusted rates respectively. This supports the previous studies, which contended that *there are substantial risk reduction possibilities through international diversification.* Also there was little difference between the results with adjusted and unadjusted rates of return.

The authors used analysis of variance (ANOVA) to test the time effect (do the correlations change over time?) and the country effect (are the correlations between various pairs of countries different?). The results indicated that *both the time and country effects were significant.* Since there are different correlations between countries, it is important to determine the specific relationship with the

---

[9] John G. McDonald, "French Mutual Fund Performance: Evaluation of Internationally Diversified Portfolios," *Journal of Finance,* 28 no. 5 (December 1973): 1161–1180.

[10] O. Maurice Joy, Don B. Panton, Frank K. Reilly, and Stanley A. Martin, "Co–movements of Major International Equity Markets," *The Financial Review* (1976): 1–20.

TABLE 21.2
Ten Year Correlations of Weekly Rates of Return of 12 Major International Equity Markets

	Australia	Austria	Belgium	Canada	France	Italy	Japan	Netherlands	Switzerland	U.K.	W. Germany	U.S.
Australia		−.022	.112	.147	.062	.018	.062	.127	.173	.173	.091	.161
Austria	.013		.044	.026	.061	.050	.024	.058	.038	.081	.102	.020
Belgium	.117	.044		.229	.241	.073	.101	.270	.221	.128	.216	.232
Canada	.167	.058	.179		.150	.061	.180	.369	.278	.162	.226	.643
France	.082	.069	.177	.163		.030	.083	.158	.144	.037	.177	.097
Italy	.022	.011	.079	.060	.012		.129	.119	.155	.074	.066	.021
Japan	.086	.071	.086	.192	.106	.102		.176	.143	.080	.128	.076
Netherlands	.134	.038	.232	.361	.158	.098	.167		.283	.157	.342	.349
Switzerland	.173	.045	.164	.289	.148	.174	.192	.293		.067	.243	.245
U.K.	.171	.034	.093	.146	.039	.078	.110	.131	.002		.030	.125
W. Germany	.106	.072	.186	.201	.153	.050	.113	.357	.207	.035		.171
U.S.	.137	.027	.205	.634	.107	.002	.092	.344	.242	.096	.163	

Adjusted Rates of Returns

SOURCE: O. Maurice Joy, Don B. Panton, Frank K. Reilly, and Stanley A. Martin, "Comovements of International Equity Markets," *The Financial Review* (1976), p. 5. Reprinted by permission.

TABLE 21.3
Mean Correlations of Weekly Rates of Return for the Indices of 12 Major Equity
Markets, 1963–1972

	1963	1964	1965	1966	1967	1968	1969	1970	1971	1972
$\bar{\theta}_t$ (adjusted)	.066	.115	.121	.115	.070	.121	.177	.280	.130	.135
$\bar{\theta}_t$ (unadjusted)	.081	.113	.188	.115	.068	.125	.215	.271	.126	.151

SOURCE: O. Maurice Joy, Don B. Panton, Frank K. Reilly, and Stanley A. Martin, "Comovements of International Equity Markets," *The Financial Review* (1976), p. 11. Reprinted by permission.

country being considered. The significant time effect indicates that the relationships change over time. Therefore, the *ex post* correlation coefficients may not be as useful as one would like in developing portfolios, and it may be necessary to readjust the portfolios over time.[11] A test of whether the correlations change over rising and declining U.S. stock market periods likewise indicated significant differences, which implied that international diversification possibilities are *not* the same during different market periods.

The final analysis examined the possible existence of time trends in the relationships (i.e., have the correlations increased over time?). The mean correlations between the 66 pairs of countries during each of the years is shown in Table 21.3. The analysis tended to support the notion of a significant positive trend in the correlations. The results from a nonparametric ANOVA test were even more supportive of *a significant positive trend*. These results also affirm the conclusion that international equity market comovement was increasing during the period 1963–1972. The study also analyzed the trend in individual pairs of countries. The yearly correlations for the U.S. adjusted returns and those of the other 11 countries are contained in Table 21.4. The results for all the countries indicated that significantly more than half the trends were positive (about 70 percent), but only a few (seven out of 66) were statistically significant. For the U.S., five of the trends were negative while six were positive, but only one of the positive trends was significant. Therefore, it appears that the possibility of reducing portfolio risk through international diversification has been declining over time, *but the trend is very gradual.*

Morgan Guaranty Analysis

A presentation by Swanson for Morgan Guaranty Trust Company contains data for some major countries during the period 1969–1978.[12] Table 21.5 on page 667 contains the total rates of return, standard deviations, and correlation coefficients for these countries and the S & P 500.

As shown, the rates of return from foreign securities were often higher than those from U.S. portfolios. At the same time, the standard deviation of the U.S.

---

[11] A study by Maldonado and Saunders documented this instability in detail and showed that there is reasonable stability for short periods (six months), but the relationship is almost a random walk for longer periods. In this regard, see Rita Maldonado and Anthony Saunders, "International Portfolio Diversification and the Inter-Temporal Stability of International Stock Market Relationships, 1957–1978," *Financial Management*, 10 no. 4 (Autumn 1981): 54–63.

[12] Joel Swanson, *Investing Internationally to Reduce Risk and Enhance Return* (New York: Morgan Guaranty Trust Company, 1979).

TABLE 21.4
Observed Correlations between Adjusted Weekly Rates of Return of the United States (Dow-Jones Industrial Average) and Adjusted Weekly Rates of Return for 11 Major Equity Markets, 1963–1972

	1963	1964	1965	1966	1967	1968	1969	1970	1971	1972	$\overline{Q}_t$
U.S.–Australia	.080	.090	.037	.323	.095	.122	.036	.213	.193	.178	.137
U.S.–Austria	.088	.309	.044	−.001	−.077	−.057	.022	−.124	−.038	.100	.027
U.S.–Belgium	.370	.328	.502	.276	−.001	.131	.168	.455	.032	−.211	.205
U.S.–Canada	.649	.563	.727	.761	.687	.668	.429	.760	.440	.651	.634
U.S.–France	.068	.007	.185	.243	.108	.071	.181	.071	.001	.137	.107
U.S.–Italy	−.024	−.116	−.104	−.006	−.128	−.025	−.020	.183	.254	.005	.002
U.S.–Japan	.203	.029	.033	−.189	−.053	.208	.232	.353	−.059	.164	.092
U.S.–Netherlands	.165	.227	.359	.403	.492	.467	.197	.439	.396	.294	.344
U.S.–Switzerland	.080	.233	.201	.282	.099	.299	.233	.556	.269	.172	.242
U.S.–United Kingdom	.022	−.040	.043	.124	−.078	.091	−.007	.417	.087	.297	.096
U.S.–W. Germany	.188	.125	.420	.049	−.030	.169	.154	.462	.053	.041	.163

SOURCE: O. Maurice Joy, Don B. Panton, Frank K. Reilly, and Stanley A. Martin, "Comovements of International Equity Markets," *The Financial Review* (1976), p. 14. Reprinted by permission.

TABLE 21.5
Rates of Return, Standard Deviations, and Correlation Coefficient for Foreign
Countries and Standard & Poor's 500, 1969–1978

Country	Total Rates of Return (adjusted)	Standard Deviation of Rates of Return	Correlation Coefficient with U.S.
France	2.5	24.8	.37
Germany	11.8	19.1	.30
Japan	18.1	25.0	.28
Switzerland	11.1	22.5	.45
United Kingdom	.7	32.0	.44
United States	2.1	16.9	—

SOURCE: Joel Swanson, *Investing Internationally to Reduce Risk and Enhance Return* (New York: Morgan
Guaranty Trust Company, 1979).

portfolio was consistently lowest. Still, because of the relatively low correlations,
the impact of diversification on a *world portfolio* is quite positive, as shown in
Table 21.6.

As shown, during this period, the world index provided not only a *higher*
rate of return, but also a *lower* level of risk. This would imply that, with international diversification, the efficient frontier would not only move to the left to
reflect lower risk, but also move up due to the higher return.

A study by Bergstrom reviewed some prior studies and provided compound
annual return data for 20 countries including the U.S.[13] For the 16 1/2-year period ending June 30, 1975, the U.S. ranked 17 out of 20 in return, and there is a
discussion of the reason for this inferior performance. He also provided a summary of the results achieved by Putnam Management Company with international investments for the period March 1971–June 1975. It indicates superior
returns for these international investments and low risk relative to the U.S.
market.

Another study by Lessard considered the impact of a world portfolio, a
country index, and industry indexes on the returns for individual securities.[14]
The results indicate that a fairly low proportion of total variance is explained by a
world portfolio and a high proportion is explained by the stock's own country
effect. This implies strong benefits from international diversification. A major
determinant of how effective the diversification will be depends upon whether
the markets for the countries are segmented or integrated. Obviously, from the
view of diversification, it is preferable if the markets are segmented. It is concluded that actual returns are more consistent with a segmented market than an
integrated market, which is encouraging for international investing.

Conclusions and Implications of Studies

Based upon the results of the studies discussed, it is possible to derive several major conclusions regarding the usefulness of international diversifi-

[13] Gary L. Bergstrom, "A New Route to Higher Returns and Lower Risks," *Journal of Portfolio Management*, 2
no. 1 (Fall 1975): 30–38.

[14] Donald R. Lessard, "World, Country, and Industry Relationships in Equity Returns," *Financial Analysts
Journal*, 32 no. 1 (January–February 1976): 32–38.

TABLE 21.6
Differential Return and Risk from Domestic Versus World Portfolios

	1969–1973	1974–1978
Rates of Return (price only)		
U.S. Index	3.34	3.56
World Index	6.40	5.14
Standard Deviation of Return		
U.S. Index	13.9	17.6
World Index	13.4	14.9

SOURCE: Joel Swanson, *Investing Internationally to Reduce Risk and Enhance Return* (New York: Morgan Guaranty Trust Company, 1979).

cation and to derive some implications of these findings for the portfolio manager.

Level of correlation.   The results consistently indicate a *much lower* level of correlation between the stocks of *different* countries than for stocks *within* a country. This implies that there are substantial benefits to be derived from international diversification, as was demonstrated in several of the articles discussed.

It was also shown that *the correlation differs between countries* depending upon their level of development and the level of interdependence of their economies. The relationship between less developed countries and highly developed countries is clearly less than average simply because the undeveloped countries have unique economic problems so that their economies do not move together and the rates of return on their stocks are not associated. Therefore, for purposes of diversification, such undeveloped countries are excellent candidates for investment. The correlations were *not stable over time,* so it is *not* possible to simply use past correlations to develop future portfolios. It will also be necessary to adjust the portfolios over time to reflect expected changes in the relationships.

Finally, there have been results that indicate a positive trend in some of the correlations. This would imply that there will be less benefit derived from international diversification in the future. The trend is gradual and is not positive for all combinations. A portfolio manager should examine each country on an individual basis and make an appropriate decision based upon the past relationship, recent trends, and his assessment of the future relation between the countries involved.

Given a desire to derive the benefits from international diversification, one might consider the alternative of doing so by acquiring U.S. multinational firms rather than pure foreign securities. A study by Jacquillat and Solnik provided evidence that this is clearly a poor alternative.[15] It is shown that the stock prices of multinationals are too highly correlated with purely domestic stocks and have very low correlation with foreign market indicators. This is true even for the countries where they have substantial activities.

---

[15] Bertrand Jacquillat and Bruno Solnik, "Multinationals Are Poor Tools for Diversification," *Journal of Portfolio Management,* 4 no. 2 (Winter 1978): 8–12.

Assuming that you would consider international diversification on a direct basis, there is some question regarding how to do it. A paper by Solnik and Noetzlin examined the risk-reward characteristics during a 10-year period for stocks, bonds, cash, gold, and currencies for six countries.[16] The results when they applied optimal asset allocation strategies to these assets suggested that active investment strategies were worthwhile. Notably, while the rates of return were erratic, the risk measures were relatively stable.

In contrast, Logue reported on an experiment that compared passively managed internationally diversified portfolios to some mechanistic active management rules.[17] A major finding is the active management is likely to generate huge transactions costs, and these costs could easily offset any benefit.

OBSTACLES TO INTERNATIONAL DIVERSIFICATION

Previous studies have generally indicated that the benefit of international diversification stems from the low correlation between foreign and domestic stocks. Even though international investment may involve some problems owing to the instability of relationships between the securities, these are relatively minor and no more of a problem than dealing with unstable betas for individual U.S. stocks. Therefore, given the clear advantages of international diversification and the limited theoretical problems, why do individuals and institutions in the U.S. not invest more in foreign securities? This section discusses the reasons.

The chief obstacle is the fact that international capital markets are clearly not perfect. The major characteristics of perfect markets are complete and costless information, zero transaction costs, and complete liquidity.

Availability of Information. This general heading deals with a *set* of obstacles to foreign investment. The first is the *availability of information* on individual companies, industries, and economies. American investors take for granted an enormous set of data that is simply not available in many other countries, especially in some less developed nations. The numerous sources of economic data, organizations like the Federal Reserve System and the Commerce Department, simply do not exist. Further, we have a number of private sources of industry data, companies like Standard & Poor's, Moody's, Value Line, and industry trade associations, that do not exist elsewhere. Finally, analysts in the U.S. are almost overwhelmed each year by annual reports, quarterly reports, and 10 K reports required by the SEC. Again, *almost none* of this is available in *most* foreign countries. For analysts and portfolio managers accustomed to a plethora of information, it is difficult to make decisions under the conditions noted above.

There is a further problem of *interpretation of the data* received because reporting standards in many countries are different from those used here. Investors often complain about the different accounting techniques used by American

---

[16] Bruno Solnik and Bernard Noetzlin, "Optimal International Asset Allocation," *Journal of Portfolio Management,* 9 no. 1 (Fall 1982): 11–21.

[17] Dennis E. Logue, "An Experiment in International Diversification," *Journal of Portfolio Management,* 9 no. 1 (Fall 1982): 22–27.

firms, techniques that can seriously affect reported income. These differences are minor compared to the variations employed in many foreign countries. What, then, does the analyst do with the Japanese or German earnings figure to make it comparable to a U.S. figure?

Finally, there are timing problems because of *reporting lags.* How long will it take until figures are publicly available? In many instances, the lag is substantial compared to what it is in the U.S. Further, once figures are available, it may be a while until they are reported in the U.S. Clearly, this lag could be very important in the price adjustment process.

Liquidity.   Liquidity is generally defined as the ability to buy or sell an asset quickly without the price changing significantly from what it was during a previous transaction, assuming no new information has entered the market. In earlier chapters we have discussed this concept extensively as it relates to the notion of a tiered market and the effect of liquidity on an investment's required rate of return. Liquidity is important for any investment, and it is especially crucial to large institutional investors who need to establish major positions in an investment if it is going to be worthwhile. As noted, because of this need for liquidity, a tiered market does exist within the U.S. and probably will continue to exist. Unfortunately, the liquidity of most foreign stocks is *substantially below* that of most U.S. stocks listed on an exchange. Although there are some stocks with good trading volume and liquidity, *the great majority of foreign stocks experience only limited trading and substantial volatility.* Therefore, it is conceivable that a number of foreign stocks could be acquired by individuals. In contrast, only a *limited* number of foreign stocks have the necessary liquidity to be considered by institutional investors.

Transaction Costs.   One must also consider the above average transaction costs involved in a foreign trade. These include commission costs (that will probably be above average), transfer taxes, and all the other costs involved in placing the order and securing the certificate.[18]

Notably, there has been a major change in the attitude of U.S. pension funds toward foreign investing. While they generally recognize the problems involved, they believe that the potential benefits in terms of higher returns and lower risk through diversification are worth the effort.[19]

Alternatives to Direct Investment

Assume that an investor acknowledges that it is a good idea to invest in foreign securities and yet is also aware of the problems; what alternatives are available?

---

[18] An article by Anna Marjos indicated that many of these problems have declined in recent years with the growth of American Depository Receipts (ADRs). See Anna Marjos, "How to Invest Abroad," *Barron's* (July 24, 1978), p. 9. An article that discusses the concept of international investing and considers all aspects of the process including sources of information is Roger H. Cass, "A Global Approach to Portfolio Management," *Journal of Portfolio Management,* 1 no. 2 (Winter 1975): 40–48.

[19] See Lawrence Rout, "Many Pension Funds Are Looking Overseas for New Investments," *Wall Street Journal,* May 24, 1979, p. 1; and Daniel Hertzberg, "Pension Managers Invest More Overseas, Aware of Risks but Hopeful about Profits," *Wall Street Journal,* July 2, 1981, p. 36.

For an individual investor, an obvious solution would be to purchase shares in an investment company that specializes in foreign securities.[20] This would solve the problem of lack of information because the professionals involved are familiar with the countries and their markets. This does not mean that the funds will do above average relative to an index for these countries, but they should do about average, and the investor should still derive the benefits of diversification. This approach should also reduce the liquidity problem because many of the funds available are open-end funds that will reacquire shares at their net asset value. The few closed-end funds appear to enjoy relatively active markets on exchanges. (For instance, the Japan Fund is listed on the NYSE).

The following section is a listing of most of the mutual funds investing in foreign securities. This brief description should not be construed as a recommendation, but it is set forth as an aid to the reader interested in this aspect of investment. In all cases, there is an address you can write for the latest prospectus and other information. Note that almost all of these international funds concentrate their portfolios in one country or geographic area. However, several of them are almost wholly concerned with gold or other precious metals. Therefore, it might be necessary to invest in *several* of these international funds to derive the full benefits of world diversification.[21]

Canadian Fund, Inc.
One Wall Street
New York, NY 10005
This is an *open-end* fund that seeks long-term capital growth by investing in companies expected to benefit from any growth or development in Canada. It is a *load* fund.

International Investors Incorporated
122 East 42nd Street
New York, NY 10168
This is an *open-end* fund that has concentrated its investments in gold mining shares. Under normal conditions, the company expects to have at least two thirds of the value of its assets in foreign securities. It is a *load* fund.

The Japan Fund, Inc.
One Rockefeller Plaza
New York, NY 10020
This is a *closed-end* fund that invests primarily (i.e., about 80 percent) in a diversified portfolio of common stocks of leading Japanese companies. Shares of this fund are listed on the New York Stock Exchange and may be bought or sold like any other stock. The commission would be the standard commission for any purchase on the NYSE.

---

[20] For a discussion of the attraction to individuals, see Jill Bettner, "Foreign Stocks Catch on with Small Investors; Gains Are Bigger Lure than Diversification," *Wall Street Journal,* April 20, 1981, p. 36. For a discussion of international funds, see Laurie Cohen, "International Stock Funds Attracting American Investors," *Chicago Tribune,* May 19, 1981, p. 3.

[21] For a discussion of the idea and some of these funds, see Lynn Asinof, "International Mutual Funds Attract Favor as Economies Recover in Europe, Far East," *Wall Street Journal,* January 9, 1984, p. 17.

Kemper International Fund, Inc.
120 South LaSalle Street
Chicago, IL 60603

This is an *open-end* fund that typically invests more than 80 percent of its funds in non-United States issuers. It is a *load* fund. At the end of 1983, major countries represented: Japan (32 percent), United Kingdom (14 percent), Netherlands (12 percent), Switzerland (10 percent), and Sweden (6 percent).

Merrill Lynch Pacific Funds, Inc.
633 Third Avenue
New York, NY 10017

This is an *open-end* fund that primarily invests in equities of corporations in the Far East or Western Pacific countries including Japan, Australia, Hong Kong, Singapore, and the Phillipines. At the end of 1983, the fund had holdings approximately as follows: Japan (65 percent), Australia (18 percent), Hong Kong (6 percent), and Singapore (2 percent). This is a *load* fund.

G. T. Pacific Fund, Inc.
601 Montgomery Street
Suite 1400
San Francisco, CA 94111

This is an *open-end* fund that invests principally in the common stock of Far Eastern issuers. Under normal conditions, at least 80 percent of the fund's assets will be in equity securities of corporations in Japan, Hong Kong, Singapore, Malaysia, the Phillipines, Australia, and New Zealand. It is a *no-load* fund.

Putnam International Equities Fund, Inc.
One Post Office Square
Boston, MA 02109

This is an *open-end* fund that invests up to 70 percent of its assets in securities traded in *several foreign markets.* It is a *load* fund.

Research Capital Fund, Inc.
155 Bovet Road
San Mateo, CA 94402

This is an *open-end* fund that concentrates in securities of issuers engaged in *mining, processing, or dealing in gold or other precious metals.* The fund invests a substantial portion of its assets in securities issued by companies domiciled and operating outside the U.S. It is a *load* fund.

Scudder International Fund, Inc.
345 Park Avenue at 51st Street
New York, NY 10154

This is an *open-end* fund that invests in equity securities in established *companies outside the U.S. and in economies with growth prospects.* The companies represented as of 1983 were: Japan (21 percent), Netherlands (8 percent), Switzerland (7 percent), Hong Kong (7 percent), and Belgium (7 percent). It is a *no load* fund.

So Gen International Fund, Inc.
630 Fifth Avenue
New York, NY 10111

This is an *open-end* fund that invests in U.S. and foreign securities. The investment objective is long-term capital growth. It is a *load* fund.

Strategic Investments Fund, Inc.
10110 Crestover Drive
P. O. Box 20066
Dallas, TX 75220

This is an *open-end* fund that invests in the equity securities of established companies engaged in the *exploration, processing, fabrication, and distribution of natural resources.* As of early 1984, management expected that most assets would be invested in *gold mining companies.* This is a *load* fund.

Templeton Growth Fund, Ltd.
44 Victoria Street
Toronto, Ontario M5C 1Y2
Canada

This is an *open-end* fund that seeks long-term growth through investments in stocks and debt obligations of companies and governments of *any* nation. As of early 1984, the fund held securities from seven different nations as follows: United States, Canada, Japan, Australia, Netherlands, South Africa, Hong Kong, and Sweden. It is a *load* fund.

Templeton World Fund, Inc.
405 Central Avenue
P. O. Box 3942
St. Petersburg, FL 33731

This is an *open-end* fund that seeks long-term growth by investing in companies and governments of *any* nation. As of early 1984, the fund held securities from five different nations as follows: United States, Canada, Australia, Japan, and the Netherlands. This is a *load* fund.

United Services Gold Shares, Inc.
15748 IH 10W at Loop 1604
San Antonio, TX 78249

This is an *open-end* fund that invests virtually all of its funds in foreign precious metals stocks, mainly gold mining stocks. Most of the fund's assets were invested in foreign securities. This is a *no load* fund.

Transatlantic Fund, Inc.
100 Wall Street
New York, NY 10005

This is an *open-end* fund that pursues long-term capital growth, primarily by investing in the common stock of corporations outside the U.S. At the close of 1983, the fund had investments in Japan (28 percent), Germany (8 percent), Australia (7 percent), Netherlands (7 percent), and Hong Kong (6 percent). The balance was invested in Western Europe, the Far East, Southeast Asia, Canada, and Mexico. This is a *no load* fund.

SUMMARY

This chapter analyzed some of the benefits and potential problems involved in international diversification. Our initial discussion considered the reasons that there should be a relatively low level of correlation between securities from different countries based upon the dividend valuation model. Because almost all of the relevant valuation variables are not related, one should not expect the rates of return to be correlated.

The subsequent section contained a discussion of a number of studies that empirically examined the concept. The results consistently indicated that international diversification should be beneficial, although the correlations between countries change over time. There was also some evidence of an increase in the correlations among securities from various countries, but the trend was small and did not apply to all countries.

Although there are theoretical and empirical reasons for international diversification, it is clear that it is not without problems. The main obstacles are the availability of information, the reliability of the information received, the time lag in getting the information, a substantial liquidity problem with many securities, and higher transaction costs.

An alternative to direct investment by individuals is acquiring shares of an investment company that concentrates in foreign stocks. To aid readers, a number of funds that invest in foreign securities were listed and were briefly discussed. Most of these funds either concentrated in a geographical area or were basically concerned with gold and precious metals. Therefore, to derive a truly international portfolio, it may be necessary to acquire shares in several of these funds.

QUESTIONS

1. What is the purpose of international diversification? Why should portfolio managers invest in foreign securities?
2. Discuss in some detail why international diversification should work. Specifically, why would you *expect* low correlation in the rates of return for domestic and foreign securities?
3. Would you expect a *difference* in the correlation of returns between U.S. and various foreign securities? Why? Be specific.
4. Using a source of international statistics, compare the percentage change in the following economic data for Japan, West Germany, Italy, Canada, and the U.S. for a recent year:
   a. Aggregate output (GNP)
   b. Inflation
   c. Corporate earnings
   d. Money supply growth.
   What were the differences, and which country or countries differed most from the U.S.?
5. Using a recent edition of *Barron's,* examine the weekly percentages of change in the stock price indexes for Japan, West Germany, Italy, Canada, and the U.S. For

each of three weeks, which foreign series moved most closely with the U.S. series? Which series was most divergent from the U.S. series? What would this indicate to you regarding international diversification?

6. What were the empirical findings regarding changes in the correlations *over time* between the stock price series for various countries? What are the implications of these results for a portfolio manager interested in international diversification?

7. Would you expect there to be a trend in the correlations between U.S. stock price series and the stock price series for different countries? Why or why not, and what would influence such a trend?

8. Assuming you are told that there has been a small increase in the correlations between the securities market in the U.S. and other countries, what does this mean to you as a portfolio manager?

9. Briefly discuss the major problems involved in international diversification. Which of the problems is greatest for individuals? Which is most important to institutions? Why?

10. Aside from direct investment in foreign stocks, what alternatives are available?

11. Select two of the mutual funds discussed in the chapter and look them up in the Weisenberger *Investment Company* book. During the past five years, how have they done on a year-to-year basis compared to the DJIA?

REFERENCES

Agmon, Tamir. "Country Risk: The Significance of the Country Factor for Share Price Movements in the United Kingdom, Germany and Japan." *Journal of Business.* 46 no. 1 (January 1973).

Agmon, Tamir. "The Relations among Equity Markets: A Study of Share Price Co-Movements in the United States, United Kingdom, Germany and Japan." *Journal of Finance.* 27 no. 4 (September 1972).

Bergstrom, Gary L. "A New Route to Higher Returns and Lower Risks." *Journal of Portfolio Management.* 2 no. 1 (Fall 1975).

Cass, Roger H. "A Global Approach to Portfolio Management." *Journal of Portfolio Management.* 1 no. 2 (Winter 1975).

Garrone, Francois, and Bruno Solnik. "A Global Approach to Money Management." *Journal of Portfolio Management.* 2 no. 4 (Summer 1976).

Grubel, Herbert G. "Internationally Diversified Portfolios: Welfare Gains and Capital Flows." *American Economic Review.* 58 no. 5 (December 1968).

Grubel, Herbert G., and Kenneth Fadner. "The Interdependence of International Equity Markets." *Journal of Finance.* 26 no. 1 (March 1971).

Jacquillat, Bertrand, and Bruno Solnik. "Multinationals Are Poor Tools for Diversification." *Journal of Portfolio Management.* 4 no. 2 (Winter 1978).

Joy, O. Maurice, Don Panton, Frank K. Reilly, and Steve Martin. "Co-Movements of Major International Equity Markets." *The Financial Review.* (1976).

Lessard, Donald R. "International Portfolio Diversification: A Multivariate Analysis for a Group of Latin American Countries." *Journal of Finance.* 28 no. 3 (June 1973).

Lessard, Donald R. "World, National and Industry Factors in Equity Returns." *Journal of Finance.* 29 no. 2 (May 1974).

Lessard, Donald R. "World, Country, and Industry Relationships in Equity Returns." *Financial Analysts Journal.* 32 no. 1 (January–February 1976).

Levy, Haim, and Marshall Sarnat. "International Diversification of Investment Portfolios." *American Economic Review.* 60 no. 4 (September 1970).

Logue, Dennis E. "An Experiment in International Diversification." *Journal of Portfolio Management.* 9 no. 1 (Fall 1982).

Maldonado, Rita, and Anthony Saunders. "International Portfolio Diversification and the Inter-Temporal Stability of International Stock Market Relationships, 1957–1978." *Financial Management.* 10 no. 4 (Autumn 1981).

McDonald, John G. "French Mutual Fund Performance: Evaluation of Internationally Diversified Portfolios." *Journal of Finance.* 28 no. 5 (December 1973).

Solnik, Bruno H. "The International Pricing of Risk: An Empirical Investigation of the World Capital Market Structure." *Journal of Finance.* 29 no. 2 (May 1974).

Solnik, Bruno H. "Why Not Diversify Internationally Rather than Domestically?" *Financial Analysts Journal.* 30 no. 4 (July–August 1974).

Solnik, Bruno, and Bernard Noetzlin. "Optimal International Asset Allocation." *Journal of Portfolio Management.* 9 no. 1 (Fall 1982).

Swanson, Joel. *Investing Internationally to Reduce Risk and Enhance Return.* New York: Morgan Guaranty Trust Company, 1979.

Chapter 22   Evaluation of Portfolio Performance

Investors have always been interested in evaluating the performance of their portfolios. Even if they do their own analysis, it is both expensive and time consuming to analyze and select stocks for a portfolio, so the individual must determine whether the time and effort were well spent. For an individual or company paying a professional money manager, it is imperative to be able to evaluate the performance and determine whether the results justify the cost of the service. Given the obvious importance of the topic, it is noteworthy that there was little rigorous work in the area prior to the mid-1960s.

This chapter outlines the evaluation of a portfolio. Initially we consider what is required of a portfolio manager and discuss how performance was evaluated before portfolio theory and the CAPM were developed. This is followed by a discussion of three major portfolio performance evaluation techniques that consider return and risk (referred to as *composite performance measures*), including applications of these techniques to determine the performance of mutual funds. Some observers have examined these three composite measures of performance and risk and presented evidence that the measures were biased in favor of low risk portfolios. These findings are not universally accepted and, therefore, we examine the alternative arguments. We will also briefly review the discussion by Roll that questions any performance technique that depends upon the CAPM and its implied use of a market portfolio. We also consider an article by Fama that proposed a technique that examines performance in greater detail. Beyond these techniques that generally concentrate on equity portfolios, there has been some recent work on evaluation models for fixed-income portfolios, and these will be discussed.

WHAT IS REQUIRED OF A PORTFOLIO MANAGER?

When evaluating the performance of a portfolio manager, two major factors should be considered:
1.   The ability to derive above average returns for a given risk class

2.   The ability to diversify (eliminate all unsystematic risk from the portfolio).

In terms of return, the first requirement is obvious, but the necessity of considering *risk* in this context was not always immediately apparent. Risk was typically not dealt with prior to the 1960s, when work in portfolio theory showed its significance. In terms of modern theory, superior risk-adjusted return can be derived *either* through superior timing or superior stock selection. If a portfolio manager can do a superior job of predicting market turns, he can change his portfolio composition to anticipate the market, investing in a completely diversified portfolio of high-beta stocks during a rising market, and in a portfolio of low-beta stocks during a declining market, thereby deriving above average risk-adjusted returns. If a portfolio manager and his analysts are able to consistently select undervalued securities for a given risk class, he would also be able to derive above average risk-adjusted returns.

The second factor to consider in evaluating a portfolio manager is his ability to diversify completely. The market only pays returns on the basis of systematic (market) risk. Therefore, investors should not expect to receive returns for assuming unsystematic risk, because this nonmarket risk can be eliminated in a diversified market portfolio of risky assets. Investors consequently want their portfolios to be completely diversified, which means eliminating unsystematic risk. The level of diversification can be judged on the basis of the correlation between the portfolio returns and the returns for a market portfolio. Specifically, a completely diversified portfolio is perfectly correlated with the completely diversified market portfolio.

It is important to be constantly aware of these two requirements of a portfolio manager, because some portfolio evaluation techniques take into account one requirement and not the other, and one evaluation technique implicitly takes both into account, but does not differentiate between them.

COMPOSITE PERFORMANCE MEASURES

Initially investors evaluated portfolios almost entirely on the basis of the rate of return. They were aware of risk and uncertainty, but did not know how to quantify risk, so they could not consider it explicitly. Developments in portfolio theory in the early 1960s enabled investors to quantify risk in terms of the variability of returns, but there was still no composite measure; it was necessary to consider both factors separately. This is basically the approach used in several early studies.[1] The idea was to put portfolios into similar risk classes based upon some measure of risk, such as variance of return, and then to compare the rates of return for alternative portfolios directly *within* a risk class.

The Treynor Measure

The first composite measure of portfolio performance (including risk) was developed by Treynor in an article in the *Harvard Business Review*.[2] Treynor

---

[1] Irwin Friend, Marshall Blume, and Jean Crockett, *Mutual Funds and Other Institutional Investors* (New York: McGraw-Hill, 1970).

[2] Jack L. Treynor, "How to Rate Management of Investment Funds," *Harvard Business Review*, 43 no. 1 (January–February 1965): 63–75.

recognized that one of the major problems in evaluating portfolio managers was deriving a means of measuring the risk for a portfolio, in the case he dealt with, mutual funds. He contended that there were two components of risk: risk produced by general market fluctuations and risk resulting from unique fluctuations in the particular securities in the portfolio. To identify the first risk (market fluctuations as related to the portfolio), Treynor introduced the *characteristic line,* which defines the relationship between the rates of return for a portfolio over time and the rates of return for an appropriate market portfolio. After discussing some scatter plots of rates of return, he noted that the *slope* of the characteristic line measures the *relative volatility* of the fund's returns in relation to aggregate market returns. In current terms, this slope is the fund's beta coefficient. The higher the slope, the more sensitive the fund is to market returns and the greater its market risk.

The deviations from the characteristic line indicate *unique* returns for the fund relative to the market. These unique portfolio returns are attributable to the unique returns on individual stocks in the portfolio. *If* the fund is properly diversified, these unique returns for individual stocks should *cancel out.* Therefore, deviations from the characteristic line are an indication of the ability of the portfolio manager to diversify properly. *The higher the correlation of the fund with the market, the less the unique risk and the better diversified is the portfolio.* Because Treynor was not interested in this aspect of portfolio performance, there was no further consideration of the measure of diversification.

Measure of Performance. Treynor was interested in generating a measure of performance that would apply to all investors regardless of their risk preferences. Based upon developments in capital market theory, he introduced the notion of a risk-free asset that could be acquired by all investors, and he argued that this risk-free asset could be combined with different funds to form a straight *portfolio possibility line.* In a graph, he showed that rational, *risk-averse investors would always prefer portfolio possibility lines that have a larger slope* because such high slope lines would place the investor on a higher indifference curve. It was shown that the slope of the *portfolio possibility line* (designated T) is equal to:[3]

$$T = \frac{R_i - RFR}{B_i},$$

where:

R_i = the average rate of return for portfolio i during a specified time period

RFR = the average rate of return on a risk-free investment during the time period

B_i = the slope of the fund's characteristic line computed during the time period which indicates the fund's relative volatility.

With this specification, the larger the T value, the larger the slope and the more preferable the fund is for *all* investors, regardless of their risk preferences.

[3] The terms used in the formula differ from those used by Treynor but are consistent with our earlier discussion.

One can view the numerator of this ratio ($Ri - RFR$) as the *risk premium* and the denominator as the measure of risk. Therefore, the total expression indicates the fund's *return per unit of risk* and, obviously, all risk-averse investors would prefer to maximize this value. The risk variable is *systematic risk* and, as such, indicates nothing about diversification. In fact, this formulation implicitly assumes that the portfolios are perfectly diversified so that systematic risk is the relevant risk measure. When this *T* value for a fund is compared to a similar measure for the aggregate market (i.e., the market portfolio), this measure indicates whether the fund would plot above the SML.

Treynor points out that this measure of performance is *not* affected by changing the *RFR*. The *T* values may change, but the *ranking* of funds will *not* change. It is possible to have negative *T* values if the fund has a return below the *RFR* and a positive beta. Such a value would simply indicate extremely poor management. Alternatively, there has been an instance in which the *T* value was negative because the *beta* was negative and the numerator was not negative.[4] This was an indication of *very good* performance. Normally one would expect a fund with a negative beta to experience a rate of return below the *RFR*, so the numerator *and* the denominator would be negative and the *T* value would be positive.

The Sharpe Measure[5]

The Sharpe composite measure of portfolio performance follows closely from his earlier work on the capital asset pricing model (CAPM).[6] He assumed that all investors are able to borrow or lend at the risk-free rate, and that all investors share the same set of expectations. Under these conditions, all *efficient* portfolios will fall along a straight line of the form:

$$ER_i = RFR + b\sigma_i,$$

where:

ER_i = the expected rate of return on portfolio i

RFR = the risk-free rate of return

b = the risk premium which will be positive since investors are assumed to be risk averse

σ_i = the standard deviation of returns for portfolio i.

Given this capital market line (CML) and the assumption that investors can borrow or lend at the risk-free rate, an investor can attain any point on the line:

---

[4] The instance was the performance by an international mutual fund heavily involved with gold stocks.

[5] William F. Sharpe, "Mutual Fund Performance," *Journal of Business,* 39 no. 1, Part 2 (January 1966): 119–138.

[6] William F. Sharpe, "Capital Asset Prices: A Theory of Market Equilibrium under Conditions of Risk," *Journal of Finance,* 19 no. 4 (September 1964): 425–442.

$$ER = RFR + \left(\frac{ER_i - RFR}{\sigma_i} \right).$$

This means that any portfolio will give rise to a complete linear set of E, σ combinations, as shown in the capital asset discussion. In such a case, the best portfolio will be the one giving the best boundary, which is the portfolio with the highest ratio of $(ER_i - RFR)/\sigma_i$. If another portfolio is efficient, it must lie along the common line and give the same ratio. In order to use this theory to test *ex post* returns, it is necessary to progress from expectations to average rates of return and the actual standard deviation of returns for alternative portfolios. Therefore, in practice, the Sharpe measure (designated S) is stated as follows:

$$S = \frac{R_i - RFR}{V_i},$$

where:

R_i = the average rate of return for portfolio i during a specified time period

RFR = the average risk-free rate that prevailed during the time period

V_i = the standard deviation of the rate of return during the time period.

This measure can be used to rank the performance of mutual funds or other portfolios. Again this ranking will *not* be affected by changes in the *RFR* since they will affect all values. Also, by computing the measure for the aggregate market, this measure can likewise be used to examine the performance of portfolios relative to the aggregate market.

Treynor Versus Shape Measure

The Sharpe measure uses the standard deviation of returns as the measure of risk, while the Treynor measure employs beta (systematic risk). The Sharpe measure, therefore, implicitly evaluates the portfolio manager on the basis of return performance, but it *also* takes into account how well diversified the portfolio was during this period. If a portfolio is perfectly diversified (does not contain any unsystematic risk), the two measures would give identical rankings because the total variance of the portfolio would be the systematic variance. If a portfolio is poorly diversified, it is possible for it to have a high ranking on the basis of the Treynor measures but a much lower ranking on the basis of the Sharpe measure. Any difference should be directly attributable to the poor diversification of the portfolio. Therefore, the two measures provide *complementary* but *different* information, and *both measures should be derived*. As Sharpe pointed out, if one is dealing with a well-diversified group of portfolios, such as mutual funds, the two measures will provide very similar rankings. Because Sharpe thought the variability due to unsystematic risk was probably transitory, he believed that the Treynor measure might be a better measure for predicting future performance, and his results generally confirmed this expectation.

The Jensen Measure[7]

The Jensen measure is similar to the measures already discussed in that it is based upon the CAPM. All versions of the CAPM indicate the following expression for the expected one-period return on any security or portfolio:

$$E(R_j) = RFR + B_j[E(R_m) - RFR],$$

where:

$E(R_j)$ = the expected return on security or portfolio j

RFR = the one-period risk-free interest rate

B_j = the systematic risk for security or portfolio j

$E(R_m)$ = the expected return on the market portfolio of risky assets.

It has been shown that the single period models can be extended to a multiperiod world in which investors have heterogeneous horizons and trading takes place continuously.[8] Therefore, the equation above can be generalized as follows:

$$E(R_{jt}) = RFR_t + B_j[E(R_{mt}) - RFR_t].$$

Each of the expected returns and the risk-free return are different for different periods. Therefore, we are concerned with the time series of expected rates of return for security j or portfolio j. Moreover, assuming that the asset pricing model is empirically valid, it is possible to express the expectations formula in terms of *realized* rates of return as follows:

$$R_{jt} = RFR_t + B_j[R_{mt} - RFR_t] + U_{jt}.$$

This indicates that the *realized* rate of return on a security or portfolio should be a linear function of the risk-free rate of return during the period, plus some risk premium that is a function of the security's systematic risk during the period, plus a random error term.

If the risk-free return is subtracted from both sides, we have:

$$R_{jt} - RFR_t = B_j[R_{mt} - RFR_t] + U_{jt}.$$

This indicates that the risk premium earned on the jth security or portfolio is equal to B_j times a market risk premium plus a random error term. In this form, one would not expect an intercept for the regression if all assets and portfolios were in equilibrium. If a portfolio manager is a superior forecaster, he will consistently select undervalued securities and his risk premiums will therefore

---

[7] Michael C. Jensen, "The Performance of Mutual Funds in the Period 1945–1964," *Journal of Finance,* 23 no. 2 (May 1968): 389–416.

[8] Michael C. Jensen, "Risk, The Pricing of Capital Assets, and the Evaluation of Investment Portfolios," *Journal of Business,* 42 no. 2 (April 1969): 167–247.

exceed those implied by the market; i.e., he will have consistently positive random errors. To detect such superior performance, it is necessary that the regression not be constrained to go through the intercept (i.e., force it to be zero). If we allow for a possible nonzero constant, this equation becomes:

$$R_{jt} - RFR_t = \alpha_j + B_j[R_{mt} - RFR_t] + U_{jt}.$$

Given this equation, the α_j indicates whether the portfolio manager is superior or inferior in market timing or stock selection. If he is superior, the α will be a *significant positive value;* if he is inferior, α will be a *significant negative value,* indicating that the manager consistently underperformed the market. Finally, if the portfolio manager has no forecasting ability, which means his performance is equal to a naive buy-and-hold policy, the α will be insignificantly different from zero.

This measure is very useful because it allows the investigator to determine whether the abnormal returns are *statistically significant* (positive or negative). Also, the α represents the average incremental rate of return on the portfolio per unit of time which is attributable to the manager's ability to derive above average returns *adjusted for risk.* These superior risk-adjusted returns can be caused by the fact that the manager is good at predicting market turns, or because he has the ability to forecast the behavior of prices of individual issues in the portfolio.

The Jensen formulation requires a different *RFR* to be used for each time interval during the sample period. If one is examining the performance of a fund manager over a ten-year period using yearly intervals, it is necessary to examine the annual returns for the fund for each year, less the return on risk-free assets for each year, and to relate this to the annual return on the market portfolio less the same risk-free rate. This contrasts with other techniques that examine *the average returns for the total period* for all variables (the fund, the market, and the risk-free asset). Also, the Jensen measure, like the Treynor measure, does *not* evaluate the ability of the portfolio manager to diversify, because it only examines risk premiums in terms of *systematic* risk. When evaluating the performance of a group of well-diversified portfolios like mutual funds, this is probably a fairly legitimate assumption. In Jensen's analysis of mutual fund performance, it was shown that assuming complete diversification was valid since the correlations of the funds with the market typically exceeded 0.90.

Application of Performance Measures

In order to demonstrate how one applies these measures, we selected 20 open-end mutual funds for which data was available for the 15-year period 1968–1982. The specific results for the first fund (Affiliated Fund, Inc.) are contained in Table 22.1. The returns are the total returns for each year computed as follows:

$$R_{it} = \frac{EP_{it} + Div_{it} + Cap.\ Dist._{it} - BP_{it}}{BP_{it}}$$

TABLE 22.1
Example of Computation of Portfolio Evaluation Measures Using Affiliated Fund, Inc.

Year	R_{it}	R_{mt}	RFR_t	$R_{it} - RFR_t$	$R_{mt} - RFR_t$
1968	17.1	10.8	5.4	11.7	5.4
1969	−14.6	−8.3	6.7	−21.3	−15.0
1970	1.7	3.5	6.5	−4.8	−3.0
1971	8.0	14.1	4.3	3.7	9.8
1972	11.5	18.7	4.1	7.4	14.6
1973	−5.8	−14.5	7.0	−12.8	−21.5
1974	−15.6	−26.0	7.9	−23.5	−33.9
1975	38.5	36.9	5.8	32.7	31.3
1976	33.2	23.6	5.0	28.2	18.6
1977	−7.0	−7.2	5.3	−12.3	−12.5
1978	2.9	6.4	7.2	−4.3	−.8
1979	27.4	18.2	10.0	17.4	8.2
1980	23.0	31.5	11.4	11.6	20.1
1981	−.6	−4.9	14.1	−14.7	−19.0
1982	21.4	20.4	10.7	10.7	9.7

$\overline{R}_i = 9.40 \quad \sigma_i = 16.98 \quad \overline{B}_i = .889 \quad R^2_{im} = .861 \quad \overline{R}_m = 8.22 \quad \sigma_m = 17.72 \quad \overline{RFR} = 7.43$

$$S_i = \frac{9.40 - 7.43}{16.98} = .116 \qquad T_m = \frac{8.22 - 7.43}{1.00} = .79 \qquad T_i = \frac{9.40 - 7.43}{.889} = 2.216$$

$$S_m = \frac{8.22 - 7.43}{17.72} = .045 \qquad R_{it} - RFR_t = 2.097 + .889(R_{mt} - RFR_t).$$

where:

$$R_{it} = \text{total return on fund } i \text{ during year } t$$

$$EP_{it} = \text{ending price for fund } i \text{ during year } t$$

$$Cap.\ Dist._{it} = \text{capital gain distributions made by fund } i \text{ during year } t$$

$$Div_{it} = \text{dividend payment made by fund } i \text{ during year } t$$

$$BP_{it} = \text{beginning price for fund } i \text{ during year } t.$$

As computed, these returns do not take into account any sales charge by the funds. Given the fund's results for each year, and the aggregate market (represented by the S&P 500), it is possible to compute the composite measures presented at the bottom of the table. As shown, the arithmetic average annual rate of return for Affiliated was above that for the market (9.40 vs. 8.22), and the fund's beta was below 1.00 (0.889). Therefore, the Treynor measure for the fund was *above* the same measure for the market (2.216 vs. 0.790). Likewise, the standard deviation of returns was below the market's (16.98 vs. 17.72), so the Sharpe measure for the fund was also above the measure for the market (.116 vs. 0.045). Finally, the regression of the fund's annual risk premium ($R_{it} - RFR_t$) and the market's annual risk premium ($R_{mt} - RFR_t$) indicated a positive intercept (constant) value of 2.097 that was not statistically significant. If the value was significant, it would have indicated that Affiliated, on average, earned a risk-adjusted annual rate of return that was about two percent above the market average.

Overall results.   An analysis of the overall results in Table 22.2 indicates that they are generally consistent with the findings of earlier studies, although our sample selection was rather casual because it was only made for demonstration purposes. The mean return for all the funds was quite close to the market return (7.72 vs. 8.22). If *only* the rate of return was considered, 8 of the 20 funds performed better than the market did.

The R^2 for a portfolio with the market fund can be used as a measure of diversification, and the closer it is to 1.00, the more perfectly diversified it is. Although the average R^2 is reasonably good at 0.831, the range is quite large, from 0.582 to 0.956. This indicates that a number of funds are not well diversified.

The two risk measures (standard deviation and beta) likewise show a wide range but are generally consistent with expectations. Specifically, 12 of the 20 funds had a standard deviation that was larger than the market's, and the mean was also larger (19.36 vs. 17.72). This larger standard deviation is consistent with the lack of complete diversification. Only seven of the funds had a beta above 1.00, and the average beta was below one (0.986).

The performance of individual funds was very consistent for alternative measures. Using the Sharpe measure, seven of the 20 funds had a higher value than the market did; using the Treynor measure, eight of the 20 funds were above the market, while the Jensen measure indicated that eight of the 20 had positive intercepts, but only four of the positive intercepts were statistically significant. The mean values for all of the composite measures were below the figure for the aggregate market. These results indicate that, on average, this sample of funds did not perform as well as the market did.

Finally, an analysis of the ranks of the funds, using the alternative measures, indicates *almost identical rankings,* as shown by the ranks in parentheses. The specific rank correlations are:
—   Sharpe–Treynor: .992
—   Sharpe–Jensen: .994
—   Treynor–Jensen: .990

An analysis of the individual funds is left to the reader, but it should include a consideration of each of the components: return, risk (both standard deviation and beta), and the R^2 as a measure of diversification. One might expect the best performance to be generated by funds with low diversification since these funds are apparently attempting to beat the market by being unique in their selection or timing.

Potential Bias of One-Parameter Measure.   A study done by Friend and Blume reviewed the various one-parameter measures and indicated to what extent they were consistent with the CAPM.[9] They pointed out that, theoretically, the three one-parameter measures of performance should be independent of corresponding measures of risk because the performance measures specifically consider

---

[9] Irwin Friend and Marshall Blume, "Measurement of Portfolio Performance under Uncertainty," *American Economic Review,* 60 no. 4 (September 1970): 561–575.

TABLE 22.2
Performance Measures for 20 Selected Mutual Funds, 1968–1982

	Return	σ	Beta (β)	R^2	Sharpe	Treynor	Jensen
1. Affiliated Fund, Inc.	9.40	16.98	.889	.861	.116(3)	2.216(3)	2.097(2)[a]
2. Anchor Growth Fund, Inc.	1.95	20.03	.983	.819	−.274(20)	−5.575(20)	−6.313(20)[a]
3. Dividend Shares, Inc.	7.09	15.33	.846	.956	−.022(12)	−.402(13)	−1.010(13)
4. Energy Fund, Inc.	8.81	20.56	.954	.676	.067(5)	1.447(5)	.634(6)
5. Fidelity Fund, Inc.	8.08	16.03	.875	.935	.041(9)	.743(10)	−.038(10)
6. Fundamental Investors, Inc.	5.61	17.68	.930	.869	−.103(19)	−1.957(19)	−2.545(19)[a]
7. Guardian Mutual Fund	11.57	18.33	.971	.881	.226(1)	4.264(1)	3.375(1)
8. Istel Fund, Inc.	7.86	15.46	.666	.582	.028(11)	.646(11)	−.102(12)
9. Lexington Research Fund, Inc.	6.89	18.26	.921	.800	−.030(15)	−.586(15)	−1.274(15)
10. Massachusetts Investors Growth Stock Fund	6.97	19.96	1.017	.815	−.023(14)	−.452(14)	−1.245(14)
11. Oppenheimer Fund, Inc.	6.13	20.73	1.056	.814	−.063(16)	−1.231(16)	−2.128(17)
12. Philadelphia Fund, Inc.	10.02	19.16	.997	.850	.135(2)	2.598(2)	1.793(3)[a]
13. T. Rowe Price Growth Stock Fund	5.97	19.54	1.004	.830	−.075(17)	−1.454(17)	−2.274(18)
14. The Putnam Growth Fund, Inc.	8.12	17.01	.926	.930	.041(9)	.745(9)	−.049(11)
15. Scudder Special Fund, Inc.	8.41	22.92	1.169	.816	.043(8)	.838(8)	.062(9)
16. Security Equity Fund, Inc.	9.05	24.04	1.226	.816	.067(5)	1.321(6)	.657(5)
17. Sigma Investment Shares, Inc.	7.67	17.19	.941	.942	.014(13)	.255(12)	.499(8)
18. Technology Fund, Inc.	9.54	20.86	1.088	.855	.101(4)	1.939(4)	1.258(4)[a]
19. Value Line Special Situations Fund	6.18	13.76	.743	.916	−.091(18)	−1.682(18)	−1.832(16)
20. Wellington Fund, Inc.	9.12	33.40	1.527	.656	.051(7)	1.107(7)	.523(7)
Means	7.72	19.36	.986	.831	.012	.239	−.437
S&P 500	8.22	17.72	1.000	1.000	.045	.790	0
90-Day T-Bill Rate	7.43						

[a] Significant at .05 level.

Rank in parentheses.

risk; i.e., they are *risk-adjusted* measures. This may *not* be true if one or more of the following conditions pertain:

1. The assumptions underlying the market line theory are invalid.
2. The actual distributions of return and risk differ substantially from *ex ante* expectations.
3. Measurement errors caused biased estimates of the relation between risk and return.
4. There are real systematic differences among the risk-adjusted performances of portfolios.

The authors analyzed the relationship between the one-parameter measures of performance and risk by examining the performance and risk measures for 200 random portfolios. These portfolios were selected from among 788 common stocks listed on the New York Stock Exchange during the period January 1960 through June 1968. The 200 random portfolios included 50 individual portfolios consisting of 25 securities, and 50 portfolios consisting of 50, 75, and 100 stocks respectively. An equal investment in each stock was assumed. The three composite performance measures were computed for each of the 200 random portfolios, and these performance measures were regressed against two measures of portfolio risk. The two measures of risk were the beta coefficients for the portfolios and the standard deviation of portfolio returns. *In all cases, the risk-adjusted performance measure was highly correlated with risk.* There was a significant *inverse* relationship between the performance measure and the risk measure (the risk-adjusted performance of low risk portfolios was better than the comparable performance for high risk portfolios). The results of the comparison with the Jensen performance measure are contained in the scatter plot in Figure 22.1.

The authors concluded that improved measures of portfolio performance could be obtained by adjusting the various measures for the potential bias that existed during that particular period. However, even this assumption would give somewhat uncertain results, and Friend and Blume contended that it is probably preferable, given the present stage of knowledge, to use the traditional two separate parameters (the rate of return and the risk) to measure portfolio performance, rather than the more elegant, but possibly more dangerous, composite measures.

Alternative View Regarding Bias.   A later paper by Klemkosky considered this bias and tested it on a number of actual portfolios.[10] The Klemkosky study examined the relationship between composite performance measures and risk measures using *actual* mutual fund data for the period 1966–1971, in contrast to the *random* portfolio data used by Friend and Blume. The data consisted of quarterly rates of return for 40 mutual funds during the 24-quarter period 1966–1971. The author derived the three composite measures as developed by Sharpe, Treynor, and Jensen, but he also added two measures that computed the excess return above the risk-free rate similar to those used by Sharpe and Treynor but

---

[10] Robert C. Klemkosky, "The Bias in Composite Performance Measures," *Journal of Financial and Quantitative Analysis,* 8 no. 3 (June 1973): 505–514.

FIGURE 22.1

Scatter Diagram of Jensen's Performance Measure[a] on Risk January 1960–June 1968

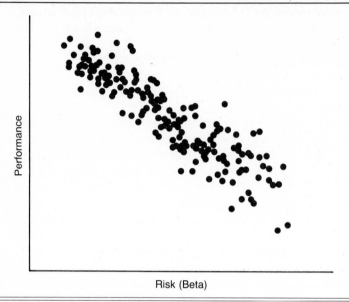

Performance

Risk (Beta)

[a] Using log relatives.

SOURCE: Irwin Friend and Marshall Blume, "Measurement of Portfolio Performance under Uncertainty," *American Economic Review,* 60 no. 4 (September 1970), p. 567. Reprinted by permission.

which utilized as risk proxies the semistandard deviation and the mean absolute deviation.

The results indicated that the composite performance measures were biased in a *positive* direction. There was a *positive* relationship between the performance derived by the mutual funds and the risk involved. This was especially true for the Treynor and Jensen measures. The performance measures incorporating the mean absolute deviation and the semistandard deviation as risk proxies were less biased than the three measures derived from the capital asset pricing model were. Because the time period for this study included a very strong bear market in 1969–1970 and a declining market in 1971, it is unlikely that the *ex post* returns were higher than *ex ante* expectations, or that *ex post* risk was lower than *ex ante* values. It was concluded that the normal bias may *not* be an inverse relationship between the composite performance measures and the risk measures, but that, in fact, there might be a positive relationship.

Comment on Jensen Study.   An article by Mains commented on Jensen's study of mutual fund performance.[11] Mains was concerned with biases introduced because of the way Jensen computed rates of return for the mutual funds and the

[11] Norman E. Mains, "Risk, the Pricing of Capital Assets, and the Evaluation of Investment Portfolios: Comment," *Journal of Business,* 50 no. 3 (July 1977): 371–384.

measures of risk used in the study. There was *no criticism* of Jensen's general methodology for evaluating portfolio performance. The only concern was with the empirical estimates used to evaluate mutual fund performance.

Components of Investment Performance

In addition to the performance measures developed by Treynor, Sharpe, and Jensen, Fama suggested a somewhat finer breakdown of performance.[12] As is true with earlier measures, the underlying philosophy of Fama's evaluation was that the returns on managed portfolios can be judged relative to those of naively selected portfolios with similar levels of risk. The technique begins by using the simple one-period version of the two-parameter model and all the perfect market assumptions. The author briefly derived the *ex ante* market line which indicates that the equilibrium relationship between expected return and risk for any security *j* is:

$$E(\tilde{R}_j) = R_f + \left[\frac{E(\tilde{R}_m) - R_f}{\sigma(\tilde{R}_m)} \right] \frac{\text{Cov.}(\tilde{R}_j, \tilde{R}_m)}{\sigma(\tilde{R}_m)}.$$

$\text{Cov.}(R_j, R_m)$ is the covariance between the returns for security *j* and the return on the market portfolio. According to this equation, the expected return on security *j* is the riskless rate of interest, R_f, plus a risk premium that is $[E(\tilde{R}_m) - R_f]/\sigma(\tilde{R}_m)$, called the *market price per unit of risk*, times the risk of asset *j* which is $[\text{cov.}(\tilde{R}_j, \tilde{R}_m)]/\sigma(\tilde{R}_m)$.

This market line relationship should hold for portfolios as well as for individual assets. This *ex ante* model assumes completely efficient markets in which prices fully reflect all available information. Assuming a portfolio manager believes that the market is not completely efficient and that he can make better judgments than the market can, then an *ex post* version of this market line can provide a benchmark for the manager's performance. Given that the risk variable, $\text{cov.}(R_j, R_m)/\sigma(R_m)$, can be denoted B_j, the *ex post* market line is as follows:

$$R_x = R_f + \left(\frac{R_m - R_f}{\sigma(R_m)} \right) B_x.$$

This *ex post* market line provides the benchmark used to evaluate managed portfolios in a sequence of more complex measures.

Evaluating selectivity.   Assuming R_a is the return on the portfolio being evaluated and $R_x(B_a)$ is the return on the combination of the riskless asset *f* and the market portfolio *m* that has risk B_x equal to B_a, the risk of the portfolio being evaluated, the performance is as follows:

$$\text{Selectivity} = R_a - R_x(B_a).$$

[12] Eugene F. Fama, "Components of Investment Performance," *Journal of Finance,* 27 no. 3 (June 1972): 551–567.

FIGURE 22.2
An Illustration of the Performance Measures

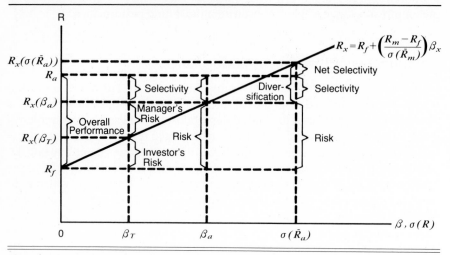

SOURCE: Eugene F. Fama, "Components of Investment Performance," *Journal of Finance,* 27 no. 3 (June 1972), p. 588. Reprinted by permission.

As shown in Figure 22.2, selectivity is a measure of how well the chosen portfolio did relative to a naively selected portfolio of equal risk. This measure indicates any difference from the *ex post* market line and is similar to the other measures, most specifically Treynor's.

It is also possible to examine *overall performance* in terms of selectivity, considered above, and the returns from assuming risk, as follows:

$$
\begin{array}{ccc}
\text{Overall} & & \\
\text{Performance} = & \text{Selectivity} + & \text{Risk} \\
[R_a - R_f] & = [R_a - R_x(B_a)] + & [R_x(B_a) - R_f].
\end{array}
$$

As shown in Figure 22.2, overall performance is the total return above the risk-free return and includes the return that *should* have been received for accepting the portfolio risk (B_a). This expected return is equal to $[R_x(B_a) - R_f]$. Any excess over this expected return is due to selectivity.

Evaluating diversification.   The difference between the Treynor and Sharpe measures is that the former uses systematic risk (B_i), and the latter, total risk (σ_i). If a portfolio is *completely* diversified and, therefore, (by definition) does not have any unsystematic risk remaining, then its *total* risk will equal its systematic risk and the two techniques will give equal rankings. However, if a portfolio manager attempts to select undervalued stocks and, in the process, gives up some diversification, it is possible to generate another measure of the added return that will be necessary to justify this decision. The portfolio's selectivity is made up of *net selectivity* plus diversification as follows:

$$\underset{\text{Selectivity}}{[R_a - R_x(B_a)]} = \text{Net Selectivity} + \underset{\text{Diversification}}{[R_x(\sigma(R_a)) - R_x(B_a)]}$$

or

$$\text{Net Selectivity} = \underset{\text{Selectivity}}{[R_a - R_x(B_a)]} - \underset{\text{Diversification}}{[R_x(\sigma(R_a)) - R_x(B_a)]}$$
$$= R_a - R_x[\sigma(R_a)],$$

where $R_x[\sigma(R_a)]$ is the return on the combination of the riskless asset f and the market portfolio m that has return dispersion equivalent to that of the portfolio being evaluated. Therefore, the diversification measure indicates the *added* return that must be derived to justify any loss of diversification in the portfolio. The term emphasizes the fact that diversification is the elimination of all unsystematic variability. If the portfolio is completely diversified so that total risk (σ) is equal to systematic risk (β), then the $R_x(\sigma(R_a))$ would be the same as $R_x(B_a)$, and the diversification term would equal zero. A comparison of the added return because of poor diversification and the R^2 for the funds with the market should confirm the use of the R^2 as a measure of diversification. The *higher* the R^2, the better diversified the portfolio and the *lower* the added required return to compensate for poor diversification. Because the diversification measure is always positive, net selectivity will always be equal to or less than selectivity. (They will be equal when the portfolio is completely diversified.) There may be cases in which the investor is not concerned with diversification of the portfolio being evaluated, so this particular breakdown will not be important and only gross selectivity will be considered.

Evaluating risk.   It is possible to evaluate risk if it is assumed that the investor has a target level of risk for his portfolio equal to B_T. Under such an assumption, the overall performance due to risk (the total return above the risk-free return) can be assessed as follows:

$$\underset{\text{Risk}}{[R_x(B_a) - R_f]} = \underset{\text{Manager's Risk}}{[R_x(B_a) - R_x(B_T)]} + \underset{\text{Investor's Risk}}{[R_x(B_T) - R_f]}.$$

$R_x(B_T)$ is the return on the naively selected portfolio with the target level of market risk (B_T). If the portfolio risk is equal to the target risk ($B_a = B_T$), then there is no manager's risk. If there is a difference between B_a and B_T, then the manager's risk is the return the manager must earn due to his decision to accept risk (B_a), which is different from the risk desired by the investor (B_T). The investor's risk is the return expected because the investor stipulated some positive level of risk. This evaluation can be done only if the client has specified his desired level of market risk, which is usually the case with pensions and profit sharing plans. Unfortunately, it is not possible to apply the measure for *ex post* evaluations, because the desired risk level is typically not available.

Fama made some further breakdowns in terms of timing ability, but these require an estimate of the expected market return during the period which is usually not available. Therefore, we will not discuss these measures but, if market return estimates are available, it is suggested that they be considered.

Application of Fama Measures.   Several of the components of performance suggested by Fama can be used in *ex post* evaluation, as shown in Table 22.3. Overall performance is the excess return derived above the risk-free return (i.e., the return above 7.43 percent). All but two of the mutual funds considered experienced positive overall performance. The next step is to determine how much the portfolio (fund) should receive for the systematic risk that it contained, using the following expected return equation for this period:

$$E(R_i) = 7.43 + \beta_i(8.22 - 7.43)$$
$$= 7.43 + \beta_i(0.79).$$

The required return for risk is simply the latter expression: $B_i(0.79)$. The required return for risk for Affiliated Fund was: $0.889(0.79) = 0.70$ percent. *The return for selectivity is the difference between overall performance and the required return for risk.* If the overall performance exceeds the required return for risk, the portfolio has experienced a positive return for selectivity. The results indicate that Affiliated had an average annual return of 1.28 percent for selectivity $(1.98 - 0.70)$. A total of eight funds had positive returns for selectivity. Although some funds had positive overall performance, their required return for risk exceeded this figure, giving them negative returns for selectivity.

The next three columns indicate the effect of diversification on performance. The diversification term indicates the required return for not being completely diversified (i.e., total risk above systematic risk). If a fund's total risk is equal to its systematic risk, then the ratio of its total risk to the market's total risk will equal its beta; if this is not the case, then the ratio of total risk will be greater than the beta and will indicate the added return required because of incomplete diversification. In the case of Affiliated, the ratio of total risk was:

$$\frac{\sigma_t}{\sigma_m} = \frac{16.98}{17.72} = .958.$$

This compares to the fund's beta of 0.889, indicating that the fund is not completely diversified, which is consistent with the R^2 of 0.861 (see Table 22.2). The fund's required return given its standard deviation is:

$$Ri = 7.43 + .958(.79)$$
$$= 8.19.$$

Their required return for *systematic* risk was 8.13 [$7.43 + .889(0.79)$]. The difference of 0.06 $(8.19 - 8.13)$ is the added return required because of less than perfect diversification. In contrast to this small required return for diversification is Wellington Fund, Inc., which has an R^2 with the market of 0.656 and a required return for diversification of 0.29 percent. This required diversification return is

TABLE 22.3
Components of Performance for 20 Selected Mutual Funds, 1968–1982

	Overall Performance	Selectivity	Risk	Net Selectivity	Selectivity	Diversification
1. Affiliated Fund, Inc.	1.98	1.28	.70	1.22	1.28	.06
2. Anchor Growth Fund, Inc.	−5.47	−6.26	.79	−6.37	−6.26	.12
3. Dividend Shares, Inc.	−.33	−1.01	.68	−1.02	−1.01	.02
4. Energy Fund, Inc.	1.39	.63	.76	.46	.63	.17
5. Fidelity Fund, Inc.	.66	.04	.70	−.06	−.04	.02
6. Fundamental Investors, Inc.	−1.81	−2.55	.74	−2.61	−2.55	.05
7. Guardian Mutual Fund	4.15	3.37	.78	3.32	3.37	.05
8. Istel Fund, Inc.	.44	−.09	.53	−.26	−.09	.17
9. Lexington Research Fund, Inc.	−.53	−1.27	.74	−1.35	−1.27	.09
10. Massachusetts Investors Growth Stock Fund	−.45	−1.26	.81	−1.35	−1.26	.09
11. Oppenheimer Fund, Inc.	−1.29	−2.13	.84	−2.23	−2.13	.09
12. Philadelphia Fund, Inc.	2.60	1.80	.80	1.73	1.80	.07
13. T. Rowe Price Growth Stock Fund	−1.45	−2.25	.80	−2.33	−2.25	.08
14. The Putnam Growth Fund, Inc.	.70	.04	.74	−.07	−.04	.03
15. Scudder Special Fund, Inc.	.99	.05	.94	−.04	.05	.10
16. Security Equity Fund, Inc.	1.63	.65	.98	.54	.65	.10
17. Sigma Investment Shares, Inc.	.25	−.50	.75	−.53	−.50	.02
18. Technology Fund, Inc.	2.12	1.25	.87	1.18	1.25	.07
19. Value Line Special Situations Fund	−1.24	−1.83	.59	−1.86	−1.83	.03
20. Wellington Fund, Inc.	1.70	.48	1.22	.19	.48	.29

694

subtracted from the selectivity return to arrive at *net* selectivity. Affiliated had a gross selectivity of 1.22, which would indicate that, even accounting for the added cost of not being completely diversified, the Fund's performance was above the market line. Wellington Fund, Inc., on the other hand, obviously decided against diversification in favor of specific selections. Even after a required return for not being diversified (0.29), its return for net selectivity was 0.19 percent. Seven funds had positive net selectivity returns.

Application of Evaluation Techniques

The answers generated using these performance measures are only as good as the data inputs. Therefore it is necessary to be careful in computing the rates of return and to take proper account of all inflows and outflows. More important, it is necessary to use judgment in the evaluation process. Just as Rome was not built in a day, it is not possible to properly evaluate a portfolio manager on the basis of performance during a quarter or even a year. The evaluation should extend over a number of years and should cover *at least* a full market cycle. This will make it possible to determine whether there is any difference in performance during rising or declining markets.[13]

MEASUREMENT PROBLEMS

While there was a discussion in Chapter 20 of the measurement problem set forth by Roll, it is important to recall the problem at this point and to attempt to put it in perspective.

As noted earlier in this chapter, all the equity portfolio performance measures are derived from the CAPM. As such, they depend upon the notion of a market portfolio that is the point of tangency on the Markowitz efficient frontier. Obviously, this implies that the market portfolio is an efficient portfolio which contains all risky assets in the economy and that it is a completely diversified portfolio. The problem arises in finding a real world *proxy* for this theoretical market portfolio. The typical proxy used is the Standard & Poor's 500 index because it is a fairly diversified portfolio of stocks and the sample is market-value weighted, which is how a true market portfolio should be. The assets included in the S&P 500 portfolio are *only* common stocks and most of them are from the NYSE. It does not include the many other risky assets that theoretically should be considered (e.g., bonds, real estate, coins, stamps, antiques, etc.).

This lack of completeness was recognized but not highlighted until several articles by Roll recognized the problem with the market portfolio proxy.[14] Roll referred to this as a *benchmark error;* i.e., when evaluating portfolio perform-

---

[13] In this regard, see Robert C. Kirby, "You Need More than Numbers to Measure Performance," (paper presented at Institute of Chartered Financial Analysts Seminar, Chicago, April 2, 1976).

[14] Richard Roll, "A Critique of the Asset Pricing Theory's Tests," *Journal of Financial Economics,* 4 no. 4 (March 1977): 129–176; Richard Roll, "Ambiguity When Performance is Measured by the Securities Market Line," *Journal of Finance,* 33 no. 4 (September 1978): 1051–1069; Richard Roll, "Performance Evaluation and Benchmark Error I," *Journal of Portfolio Management,* 6 no. 4 (Summer 1980): 5–12; Richard Roll, "Performance Evaluation and Benchmark Error II," *Journal of Portfolio Management,* 7 no. 2 (Winter 1981): 17–22.

ance, various techniques employ the market portfolio as the benchmark in determining superior or inferior performance. We also use this proxy of the market portfolio to derive beta measures which are used as risk measures. As shown in Chapter 20, if the proxy used for the true market portfolio is not a truly efficient portfolio, then the betas derived are not true betas, and the security market line that is derived may not be the true SML—i.e., it could have a higher slope. Therefore, a portfolio which is above the SML when using a poor benchmark (market portfolio proxy) could actually plot below the true SML derived by using the true market portfolio. A shift of a portfolio based upon a change in its beta against the true market portfolio could also occur.

It is important to consider several significant points regarding this criticism. First, the benchmark problems that Roll analyzed do *not* negate the value of the CAPM in terms of its usefulness as a *normative* model of equilibrium pricing. The theory is still correct and viable; the problem is one of *measurement* when attempting to implement the theory in measuring portfolio performance. This problem simply means it is necessary to find a better proxy for the market portfolio or be aware that it is necessary to adjust measured performance for these benchmark errors. In fact, in one of his later articles, Roll made several suggestions in this regard.[15]

Alternatively, one might consider giving greater weight to a portfolio performance measure that does not depend so heavily on the market portfolio—i.e., the Sharpe measure. Recall that this measure relates the excess return to the *standard deviation* of return—i.e., total risk. While the measure still uses a benchmark portfolio that is supposedly available as an unmanaged portfolio, the risk measure does not directly depend upon a market portfolio. While this Sharpe performance measure does not use a systematic risk measure, it is notable that the rank correlation among these alternative performance measures is very high (i.e., typically in excess of 0.98).

EVALUATION OF BOND PORTFOLIO PERFORMANCE

As discussed, the analysis of risk-adjusted performance for equity portfolios did not occur until the late 1960s following the prior development of portfolio theory and the capital asset pricing model (CAPM). Following these developments, several authors (Treynor, Sharpe, Jensen, and Fama) derived performance measures based upon this asset pricing model. Notably, the risk measures used for common stocks has been fairly simple—i.e., either total risk (standard deviation of return) or systematic risk (beta). In contrast, there generally has not been a similar development in the fixed-income area where the factors that can influence the required return are much more complex; i.e., there are several factors that can affect the risk dimension of a fixed-income security. There are two reasons for this lack of development of bond portfolio performance measures. The first is that prior to the 1970s the vast majority of bond portfolios were basically buy-and-hold portfolios. Given this practice, it is unlikely that the per-

---

[15] Richard Roll, "Performance Evaluation and Benchmark Error II," *Journal of Portfolio Management,* 7 no. 2 (Winter 1981): 17–22.

formance for alternative portfolio managers would differ and there was little reason for differences. Second, interest rates were very stable so there was not much to be gained by those who might attempt to be active.

In this section, we present several recent attempts to develop bond portfolio performance systems that consider these multirisk factors.

A Bond Market Line

One of the first attempts to apply modern asset pricing techniques to bond portfolios was done by Wagner and Tito.[16] A prime factor needed to evaluate performance properly is a measure of risk similar to the beta coefficient for equities. It is generally not possible to derive comparable measures for bonds because the maturity factor and coupon has such a significant effect on the relative volatility of bond prices. As you might expect based upon the material in Chapter 19, it is postulated that an appropriate composite risk measure that indicates the relative price volatility for a bond compared to interest rate changes is the bond's *duration*.

Given this proposed risk measure, the authors suggested that it is possible to derive a bond market line which is comparable to the stock market line; i.e., it is the same except that duration replaces beta as the risk variable and the return line is drawn from treasury bills and the Lehman Brothers Kuhn Loeb bond index, which is used rather than the S&P 500 index. The bond market line looks like the graph in Figure 22.3. The return for the Lehman Kuhn Loeb index is the rate of return during some common period and the duration for the index is the value-weighted duration for all the individual bonds used in the index.

Given the bond market line, this technique divides the return on a portfolio that differs from the return on the Lehman Kuhn Loeb market index into four components: (1) a policy effect, (2) a rate anticipation effect, (3) an analysis effect, and (4) a trading effect. When the latter three effects are combined, they are referred to as the *management effect*. These effects are portrayed in Figure 22.4 on page 698.

The *policy effect* measures the difference in the expected return for this portfolio manager because of a difference in the duration of the portfolio manager's long-term portfolio and the duration of the Lehman Kuhn Loeb index. The idea is that the duration of an unmanaged portfolio would be equal to the Lehman Kuhn Loeb index. If the duration for this manager's portfolio generally differs from the index duration, this indicates a basic policy decision regarding relative risk (measured by duration), and there should be a difference in expected return consistent with this risk policy decision. As an example, assume that the duration-return for the Lehman Kuhn Loeb index is 9.0 years and 8.25 percent. The duration for your portfolio manager's long-run portfolio is 9.5 years, and the expected return for this duration according to the prevailing bond market line is 8.60 percent. In this example, the policy effect would be 0.5 years

[16] Wayne H. Wagner and Dennis A. Tito, "Definitive New Measures of Bond Performance and Risk," *Pension World* (May 1977): 17–26, and Dennis A. Tito and Wayne H. Wagner, "Is Your Bond Manager Skillful?" *Pension World* (June 1977): 10–16.

FIGURE 22.3
Specification of Bond Market Line Using Lehman Kuhn Loeb Bond Index

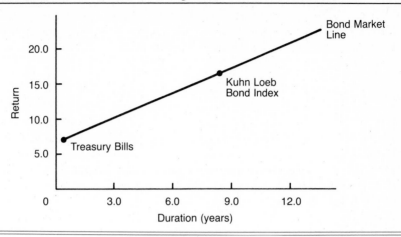

and 0.35 percent (35 basis points); i.e., the higher duration implies that your portfolio manager should have a higher average return of 0.35 percent.

Given the expected return and duration for this long-term portfolio, all deviations from the index portfolio are referred to as *management effects,* which is composed of: (1) interest-rate anticipation effect, (2) an analysis effect, and (3) a trading effect.

The interest-rate anticipation effect attempts to measure the differential return from changing the duration during this period compared to the portfolio's long-term duration. You would hope that the manager would increase the duration of the portfolio during periods of declining interest rates and *vice versa.* Therefore, you would determine the duration of the *actual* portfolio during the period and compare this to the duration of the long-term portfolio. Given this difference in duration, determine the difference in expected return for these two durations using the bond market line. As an example, assume the duration for the long-term portfolio is 9.5 years and 8.60 percent, while the duration for the current actual portfolio is 11.0 years, which implies an expected return of 9.75 percent using the bond market line. Therefore, the rate anticipation effect during this period is 1.15 percent (9.75 − 8.60).

The difference between this expected return taking account of duration and the actual return for the portfolio during this period is a combination of an analysis effect and a trading effect. *The analysis effect* is the differential return attributable to acquiring bonds that are temporarily mispriced relative to their risk. To measure this, compare the *expected* return for the portfolio held at the beginning of the period (using the bond market line) to the *actual* return of this portfolio. Obviously, if the actual return is greater than the expected return, it implies that the portfolio manager acquired some underpriced issues that became properly priced and provided excess returns during the period. If the

FIGURE 22.4
Graphic Display of Bond Portfolio Performance Breakdown

Management effect is the improvement in investment performance of a passive strategy through active bond management. It is the difference between total bond portfolio return and the expected return at the long-term average duration.

Trading effect is the result of the current quarter's trading, either through effective trade-desk operation or short-term selection abilities. It is the difference between total management effect and the effects attributable to analysis and interest rate anticipation.

Analysis effect, attributable to the selection of issues with better than average long-term prospects, is the difference between the actual return of the buy-and-hold portfolio at the beginning of the quarter and the expected return of that buy-and-hold portfolio.

Interest rate anticipation effect is attributable to changes in portfolio duration resulting from attempts to profit from and ability to predict bond market movements. It is the difference between the expected return at the actual portfolio duration and the expected return at the long-term duration.

Policy effect is the difference between long-term duration of a bond portfolio and the duration of a bond market index resulting from long-term investment policy, measured as the return at the long-term average less the return on the Kuhn Loeb Index.

Bond market line is a straight line drawn through the return/duration of treasury bills and the return/duration of the Kuhn Loeb Index.

Buy-and-hold portfolio is the composition of the portfolio at the beginning of the quarter. Used to differentiate between trading gains secured within a quarter and long-term analysis gains.

Duration, a measure of the average time to receipt of cash flows from an investment. It is a measure of the sensitivity of a bond's price to changes in interest rates.

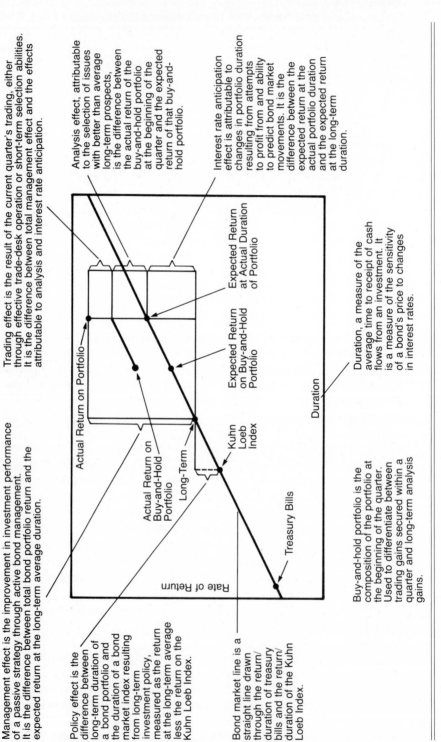

Actual Return on Portfolio

Actual Return on Buy-and-Hold Portfolio

Long-Term

Kuhn Loeb Index

Treasury Bills

Expected Return on Buy-and-Hold Portfolio

Expected Return at Actual Duration of Portfolio

Rate of Return

Duration

SOURCE: Dennis A. Tito and Wayne H. Wagner, "Definitive New Measures of Bond Performance and Risk," *Pension World* (June 1977).

portfolio at the beginning of the period had a duration of ten years, this might indicate an expected return of 9.00 percent for the period. In turn, if the actual return for this buy-and-hold portfolio was 9.40 percent, it would indicate an analysis effect of +0.40 percent (40 basis points).

Finally, *the trading effect* is what happens because of short-run changes in the portfolio during the period. It is measured as the residual after taking account of the analysis effect from the total excess return based upon duration. As an example, the total actual return is 10.50 percent with a duration of 11.0 years. We know that the expected return for a portfolio of 11 years duration given the prevailing bond market line is 9.75 percent. Thus, the combination of the analysis and trading effect is 0.75 percent (10.50 − 9.75). Previously we determined that the analysis effect was 0.40 percent, so the trading effect must be 0.35 percent (0.75 − 0.40).

In summary, for this portfolio manager, the actual return was 10.50 percent compared to a return for the Lehman Kuhn Loeb index of 8.25 percent. This overall excess 2.25 percent would be divided as follows:

— 0.35 percent Policy effect due to higher long-term duration
— 0.15 percent Interest-rate anticipation effect due to increasing the duration of the current portfolio above the long-term portfolio duration
— 0.40 percent Analysis effect. The impact of superior selection of individual issues in the beginning portfolio.
— 0.35 percent Trading effect. The impact of trading of the issues *during* the period.

This technique appears very useful in breaking down the return based upon the duration as a comprehensive risk measure. The only concern is that *it does not consider differences in the risk of default.* Specifically, the technique does not appear to differentiate between a AAA bond with a duration of eight years and a BAA bond with the same duration. This could clearly affect the performance— i.e., a portfolio manager that invested in BAA bonds could experience a very positive analysis effect simply because the bonds were lower quality than the average quality implicit in the Lehman Kuhn Loeb index. The only way to avoid this would be to construct differential market lines for alternative ratings.[17] Alternatively, the subsequent techniques consider this factor.

Decomposing Portfolio Returns

A paper by Dietz, Fogler, and Hardy set forth a technique to decompose the bond portfolio returns into maturity, sector and quality effects.[18] The total return for a bond during a period of time is composed of a known income effect, which is due to normal yield to maturity factors, and an unknown price change effect that is due to several factors (i.e., interest rate effect, sector/quality effect, and a

[17] This problem is briefly discussed in Frank K. Reilly and Rupinder Sidhu, "The Many Uses of Bond Duration," *Financial Analysts Journal,* 36 no. 4 (July/August 1980): 58–72.

[18] Peter O. Dietz, H. Russell Fogler, and Donald J. Hardy, "The Challenge of Analyzing Bond Portfolio Returns," *Journal of Portfolio Management,* 6 no. 3 (Spring 1980): 53–58.

residual effect). It is graphed as follows:

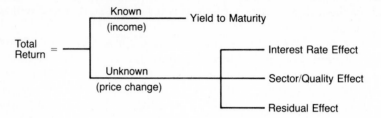

The yield-to-maturity effect is the return if nothing had happened during the period regarding the yield curve. That is, the investor would receive the interest income, the price change relative to par, and any price change due to the shape of the yield curve.

The *interest rate effect* measures what happened to each issue because of changes in the term structure of interest rates during the period. Each bond is valued based upon the treasury yield curve at its maturity and takes account of its normal premium relative to treasuries yields. Assume there is a normal premium of 30 basis points and that treasury bonds with the maturity of a portfolio bond go from 8.50 percent to 9.25 percent. To determine the interest rate effect you would compute the value of your bond at 8.80 percent (8.50 + 0.30) and 9.55 percent (9.25 + 0.30) and compute the price change. This is the price change and the return change caused by a change in market interest rates.

The *sector/quality effect* measures the expected impact on the returns because of the sector of the bonds (e.g., corporates, utilities, financial, GNMA, etc.), and also the quality of the bonds (i.e., Aaa, Aa, A, Baa). The authors determined the average impact of these sets of variables by deriving a matrix of sector/quality returns for all bonds on the Telstat pricing tapes as follows (i.e. one would fill in this table with the appropriate yields):

	Sector/Quality Returns (value-weighted)			
	Aaa	Aa	A	Baa
Corporates				
Utilities				
Financial				
Telephone				
Foreign				
GNMA				
Agencies				

Given this matrix, it is possible to determine what happened to bonds in each cell after taking account of the yield to maturity and the interest rate effect. As an example, during a given period you might find that an average Aa utility had negative excess returns of −0.50 percent after taking account of the yield to maturity and the interest rate effect, while an A corporate bond experienced a comparable excess return of 0.30 percent. Therefore, the sector/quality effect would be −0.50 and 0.30 for these sets of bonds.

The *residual effect* is what remains after taking account of the three prior factors — yield to maturity, interest rate effect, and the sector/quality effect. It is computed as follows:

$$\begin{array}{c} \text{Total} \\ \text{Return} \end{array} = \begin{array}{c} \text{Yield to} \\ \text{Maturity} \end{array} + \begin{array}{c} \text{Interest} \\ \text{Rate Effect} \end{array} + \begin{array}{c} \text{Sector/Quality} \\ \text{Effect} \end{array} + \text{Residual.}$$

Clearly, the presence of a consistently large positive residual would indicate superior selection capabilities. Specifically, such a residual indicates that after taking account of all market effects from interest rate changes and sector/quality, it is still possible to have some remaining positive returns due to selection. Alternatively, strong positive interest rate effects during periods of declining rates and small negative interest rate effects during periods of rising rates would indicate good skills at interest rate anticipation. Consistently positive sector/quality effects would indicate the ability to make proper allocations and to anticipate shifts in this area over time. For a given portfolio, it is suggested that you prepare a time series plot of these alternative effects to determine the strengths and weaknesses of your manager. The authors also suggested that these results be compared to the results for a static portfolio (i.e., buy and hold the beginning portfolio) and also compared to the overall performance of the Russell universe of bonds index which is considered an unmanaged portfolio.

Analyzing Sources of Return

A paper by Fong, Pearson, and Vasicek proposed a performance evaluation technique that also breaks the total returns down into the several components that affect bond returns.[19] The authors indicated that the intent is to provide a precise and comprehensive structure for the measurement of total realized return and for the attribution of the return to its sources (i.e., what factors contributed to the total return?).

The first breakdown divides the total return (R) between the effect of the external interest rate environment (I) which is beyond the control of the portfolio manager, and the impact of the management process (C). Thus:

$$R = I + C.$$

In turn, I is broken down into two parts. The first is the *expected* rate of return (E) on a portfolio of default-free securities assuming *no change* in forward rates (i.e., no change in future one-period rates). This expected return is also referred to as the *market's implicit forecast.* The second component of I is the return attributable to the *actual* change in forward rates (U). The component U is the *unexpected* part of the actual return on the treasury index and this is due to changes in forward rates. Thus:

$$I = E + U.$$

---

[19] Gifford Fong, Charles Pearson, and Oldrich Vasicek, "Bond Performance: Analyzing Sources of Return," *Journal of Portfolio Management,* 9 no. 3 (Spring 1983): 46–50.

As an example, assume that at the beginning of a quarter the expected return on a portfolio of treasury bonds during the coming year is 11 percent. (This expected return assumes no change in the term structure of bonds during this year.) At the end of the year, if you calculate the *actual* return in this portfolio of treasury bonds, you determine that it was 11.75 percent. This would imply an *E* of 11 percent and a *U* of .75 percent.

In turn, *C* (the management contribution) is composed of three factors:

M = Return from maturity management

S = Return from spread/quality management

B = Return attributable to the selection of specific securities.

$$C = M + S + B.$$

The return from *maturity management* (M) should be a function of how well the portfolio manager is able to change maturity (duration) in anticipation of interest rate changes. The component is measured by computing the default-free price of every security (at the beginning and end of the period) based on its maturity using the spot rates for each maturity as indicated by the treasury bond yield curve. The total return over the evaluation period is derived from these prices, while maintaining all actual trading activity. Given this total return based upon maturity yields, subtract the actual treasury index return to arrive at the maturity return. As an example, if the total return based upon the pricing computations was 12.25 percent, the maturity return would be 0.50 percent assuming (as above) a total return on treasury bonds of 11.75 percent.

The *spread/quality management component* indicates what is the effect on return because of the manager's selection of bonds from various sectors and quality. It is measured by pricing each bond at the beginning and end of the period on the basis of its specific sector and quality and then computing the rate of return given these prices. This total return less the return for treasury bonds and for maturity indicates the return for the sector/quality. Assuming this pricing indicates a total return of 12.0 percent, it would imply a negative 0.25 percent for sector/quality (12.00 − 12.25).

The *selectivity component* (B) is the remaining return. It is based upon the selection of specific bonds beyond the maturity or sector/quality decisions — i.e., what bonds you select to carry out these decisions. It is measured as the difference between the actual total return on the portfolio and the prior total return that considered maturity and sector/quality. Continuing our example, if the actual total return was 13.00, the selectivity component would be 1.00 percent since the return for maturity and sector/quality above was 12.00 percent. To summarize the results:

$$R = \underbrace{E + U}_{I} + \underbrace{M + S + B}_{C}$$
$$= 11.00 + 0.75 + 0.50 + (-0.25) + 1.00$$
$$= 13.00.$$

This analysis would indicate that the portfolio manager was quite good at maturity (duration) decisions and at selecting individual bonds, but did not do well in terms of sector/quality decisions.

As before, it seems appropriate to do a similar breakdown for some market index series in order to have a basis of comparison to an unmanaged portfolio. Also, you should examine these components over time to determine any consistent strengths or weaknesses.

Consistency of Performance

Numerous investigators have examined performance consistency for managers of equity portfolios and typically have found that they have generally *not* been very consistent. (These studies are discussed in detail in Chapter 26.) A study by Kritzman examined the ranking for 32 bond managers employed by AT&T.[20] He divided a ten-year period into two five-year periods, determined each manager's percentile ranking in each period, and correlated the rankings. The results appeared to be quite similar to what one would expect if there were *no relationship* between performance in the two periods. Another test of continuations in relative performance indicated that it was *uncorrelated over time;* i.e., there was *no relationship between past and future performance* even among the best and worst performers.

Based upon these results, Kritzman concluded that it would be necessary to examine something besides past performance to determine superior managers. Also, these results would support the strong form efficient market hypothesis.

SUMMARY

This chapter discussed portfolio performance evaluation and the several techniques that can be used in making such an evaluation. The first major goal of portfolio management is to derive rates of returns that equal or exceed the returns on a naively selected portfolio with equal risk. The second goal is to attain complete diversification. Prior to the development of capital market theory, portfolio managers were only judged on the basis of the rate of return they achieved with no consideration of risk. Risk was later considered but in a not very rigorous manner. Since 1965, three major techniques have been derived, based upon the capital asset pricing model, which provide a *composite* measure of performance. The first was developed by Treynor to measure the excess returns earned per unit of *systematic* risk. The Sharpe measure indicates the excess return per unit of *total* risk. The third technique, developed by Jensen, likewise is used to evaluate performance in terms of the systematic risk involved, but the measure also makes it possible to determine whether the difference in risk-adjusted performance (good or bad) is statistically significant.

The application of the evaluation techniques to a selected sample of 20 mutual funds indicated the importance of considering both risk and return be-

[20] Mark Kritzman, "Can Bond Managers Perform Consistently?" *Journal of Portfolio Management,* 9 no. 4 (Summer 1983): 54–56.

cause the different funds presented a wise range of total risk and systematic risk. We also discussed how differences in diversification could influence the rankings generated using different performance measures. The rank correlations among the alternative measures were extremely high, about 0.99.

A paper by Friend and Blume contended that the various composite measures provided biased results; i.e., there was an inverse relationship between the risk of the portfolio and its composite performance. A subsequent paper by Klemkosky indicated a completely different bias. Therefore, it appears that there may be some biases but the direction is unknown. More important, the biases probably would seldom change the ranking. A paper by Mains commented on the empirical results derived by Jensen but was not concerned with flaws in his theory.

In addition to the three composite measures, a paper by Fama discussed ways to break down the composite return and to derive measures related to risk and diversification in addition to measuring overall performance. An analysis of 20 mutual funds, using the component breakdown, showed how much of a fund's overall performance was due to accepting higher risk and how much (positive or negative) was attributable to selection. It was also possible to pinpoint the added return required for loss of diversification, and this coincided with the correlation coefficient discussed earlier.

While the techniques for evaluating equity portfolio performance have been in existence for about 20 years, there have not been comparable techniques for properly examining the performance of bond portfolio management until about six years ago. The difficulty in deriving such an evaluation model for bonds is that there are several important decision variables related to bonds that should be considered separately—the overall market factor, the impact of duration decisions, the influence of sector and quality factors, and the impact of individual bond selection. Alternative models that consider several or all these factors were presented. This chapter ended with discussion of a study that considered the performance consistency for alternative bond portfolio managers and concluded there was not any consistency over time for a sample of managers.

It is important for investors to evaluate their own performance and the performance of hired managers. The various techniques discussed here provide theoretically justifiable measures, but they all differ slightly. *All the measures should be used* in the evaluation process because they provide different information. An evaluation of a portfolio manager should also be done *a number of times* over *different market environments* before a final judgment is reached.

QUESTIONS

1. Assuming you are managing your own portfolio, do you think you should evaluate your own performance? Why or why not? What would you compare your performance against?
2. What are the two major factors that should be considered when evaluating a portfolio manager? What should the portfolio manager be trying to do?
3. What can a portfolio manager do to try do derive superior risk-adjusted returns?

4. What is the purpose of diversification according to the CAPM? How can you measure whether a portfolio is completely diversified? Explain why this measure makes sense.

5. Prior to the development of composite portfolio performance measures, how could you evaluate portfolio performance taking risk into consideration?

6. Define the Treynor measure of portfolio performance. Discuss this measure in terms of what it indicates. (What does it measure?)

7. Assume that during the past ten-year period the risk-free rate was 8 percent and three portfolios had the following characteristics:

Portfolio	Return	Beta
A	.13	1.10
B	.11	.90
C	.17	1.20

Compute the T value for each portfolio and indicate which portfolio had the best performance. Assume you are told that the market return during this period was 12 percent; how did these managers fare relative to the market?

8. Define the Sharpe measure of performance and discuss what it tells.

9. Assume the three portfolios in Question 7 have standard deviations of 0.14, 0.10, and 0.20 respectively. Compute the Sharpe measure of performance. Is there any difference in the ranking achieved using the Treynor versus the Sharpe measure? Discuss the probable cause.

10. Why is it suggested that both the Treynor and Sharpe measures of performance be employed? What additional information is provided by a comparison of the rankings achieved using the two measures?

11. Define the Jensen measure of performance and indicate whether it should produce results similiar to those produced using the Treynor or Sharpe methods. Why?

12. Define overall performance. Assume that you are told a fund had an overall performance figure of five percent. Does that mean the manager is superior? Why or why not? Discuss.

13. You are told that a fund had an overall performance of -0.50 percent. Could the manager of this fund have a positive selectivity value? Why or why not? If so, under what conditions?

14. Define the diversification term. Under what conditions will this term equal zero?

15. Define net selectivity. If a portfolio had a negative selectivity value, could it have a positive net selectivity measure? Under what conditions?

16. You are told that a portfolio has an R^2 with the market of 0.95, and a selectivity value of 2.5 percent. Would you expect the portfolio to have a positive net selectivity value? Discuss why.

17. Assuming that the proxy used for the market portfolio is not a good proxy, discuss the potential problem with the measurement of beta. Show by an example the effect if the measured beta is significantly lower than the true beta.

18. Assuming that the market proxy is a poor proxy, show an example of the potential impact on the security market line (SML) and demonstrate with an example how a portfolio that was superior to the proxy SML line could be inferior when compared to the true SML.

19. It is contended that the derivation of an appropriate model for evaluating the performance of a bond portfolio manager is more difficult than an equity model

because there are more decisions required. Discuss some of the specific decisions that are necessary when evaluating a bond portfolio manager.

20. Briefly describe what you are trying to measure in the following cases:
    a. The interest rate effect (i.e., market effect)
    b. The maturity effect (duration)
    c. The sector/quality effect.
    d. The selection effect.

21. Which of the effects in Question 20 are under the control of the bond portfolio manager?

CFA Examination III (June, 1981) Richard Roll, in an article on using the Capital Asset Pricing Model (CAPM) to evaluate portfolio performance, indicated that it may not be possible to evaluate portfolio management ability if there is an error in the benchmark used.

A. In evaluating portfolio performance, *describe* the general procedure, with emphasis on the benchmark employed.

(5 minutes)

B. **Explain** what Roll meant by the benchmark error and **identify** the specific problem with this benchmark.

(5 minutes)

C. **Draw** a graph that shows how a portfolio that has been judged as superior relative to a "measured" Security Market Line (SML) can be inferior relative to the "true" SML.

(10 minutes)

D. Assume that you are informed that a given portfolio manager has been evaluated as superior when compared to the DJIA, the S&P 500, and the NYSE Composite Index. *Explain* whether this consensus would make you feel more comfortable regarding the portfolio manager's true ability.

(5 minutes)

E. While conceding the possible problem with benchmark errors as set forth by Roll, some contend this does not mean the CAPM is incorrect, but only that there is a measurement problem when implementing the theory. Others contend that because of benchmark errors, the whole technique should be scrapped. *Take* and *defend* one of these positions.

(5 minutes)

CFA Examination III (June, 1982)

During a quarterly review session, a client of Fixed Income Investors, a pension fund advisory firm, asks Fred Raymond, the portfolio manager for the company's account, if he could provide a more detailed analysis of their portfolio performance than simply total return. Specifically, the client had recently seen a copy of an article by Deitz, Fogler and Hardy on the analysis of bond portfolio returns that attempted to decompose the total return into the following four components:

    A. Yield to maturity
    B. Interest rate effect
    C. Sector/quality effect
    D. Residual

While he does not expect you to be able to provide such an analysis this year, he asks you to explain each of these components to him so he will be better prepared to understand such an analysis when you do it for his company's portfolio next year. *Explain* each of these components.

(20 minutes)

REFERENCES

Blume, Marshall, "The Assessment of Portfolio Performance." Ph.D. dissertation, University of Chicago, 1968.

Carlson, Robert S. "Aggregate Performance of Mutual Funds, 1948–1967." *Journal of Financial and Quantitative Analysis.* 5 no. 1 (March 1970).

Dietz, Peter O., H. Russell Fogler, and Donald J. Hardy. "The Challenge of Analyzing Bond Portfolio Returns." *Journal of Portfolio Management.* 6, no. 3 (Spring 1980).

Dietz, Peter O., H. Russell Fogler, and Anthony U. Rivers. "Duration, Nonlinearity, and Bond Portfolio Performance." *Journal of Portfolio Management.* 7 no. 3 (Spring 1981).

Evaluation and Measurement of Investment Performance. Seminars on Portfolio Management. Financial Analysts Research Foundation, Charlottesville, Va., 1977.

Fama, Eugene. "Components of Investment Performance." *Journal of Finance.* 27 no. 3 (June 1972).

Fama, Eugene. "Risk, Return, and Equilibrium." *Journal of Political Economy.* 79 no, 1 (January–February 1971).

Fong, Gifford, Charles Pearson, and Oldrich Vasicek. "Bond Performance: Analyzing Sources of Return." *Journal of Portfolio Management.* 9 no. 3 (Spring 1983).

Friend, Irwin and Marshall Blume. "Measurement of Portfolio Performance Under Uncertainty." *American Economic Review.* 60 no. 4 (September 1970).

Friend, Irwin, Marshall Blume, and Jean Crocket. *Mutual Funds and Other Institutional Investors.* New York: McGraw-Hill, 1970.

Horowitz, Ira. "The 'Reward-to-Variability' Ratio and Mutual Fund Performance." *Journal of Business.* 39 no. 4 (October 1966).

Jensen, Michael C. "The Performance of Mutual Funds in the Period 1945–1964." *Journal of Finance.* 23 no. 2 (May 1968).

Jensen, Michael C. "Risk, the Pricing of Capital Assets, and the Evaluation of Investment Portfolios." *Journal of Business.* 42 no. 2 (April 1969).

Klemkosky, Robert C. "The Bias in Composite Performance Measures." *Journal of Financial and Quantitative Analysis.* 8 no. 3 (June 1973).

Klemkosky, Robert C. "How Consistently Do Managers Manage?" *Journal of Portfolio Management.* 3 no. 2 (Winter 1977).

Kritzman, Mark. "Can Bond Managers Perform Consistently?" *Journal of Portfolio Management.* 9 no. 4 (Summer 1983).

Mains, Norman E. "Risk, the Pricing of Capital Assets, and the Evaluation of Investment Portfolios: Comment." *Journal of Business.* 50 no. 3 (July 1977).

Measuring the Performance of Pension Funds. Park Ridge, Ill.: Bank Administration Institute, 1968. A supplement, *Risk and the Evaluation of Pension Fund Performance,* was written by Eugene Fama.

Reilly, Frank K., and Rupinder Sidhu. "The Many Uses of Bond Duration." *Financial Analysts Journal.* 36 no. 4 (July–August 1980).

Roll, Richard. "A Critique of the Asset Pricing Theory's Tests." *Journal of Financial Economics.* 4 no. 4 (March 1977).

Roll, Richard. "Ambiguity when Performance Is Measured by the Securities Market Line." *Journal of Finance.* 33 no. 4 (September 1978).

Roll, Richard. "Performance Evaluation and Benchmark Error I." *Journal of Portfolio Management.* 6 no. 4 (Summer 1980).

Roll, Richard. "Performance Evaluation and Benchmark Error II." *Journal of Portfolio Management.* 7 no. 2 (Winter 1981).

Sharpe, William F. "Mutual Fund Performances." *Journal of Business.* 39 no. 1, Part 2 (January 1966).

Smith, Keith V., and Dennis A. Tito. "Risk-Return Measures of Ex-Post Portfolio Performance." *Journal of Financial and Quantitative Analysis.* 4 no. 5 (December 1969).

Tito, Dennis A., and Wayne H. Wagner. "Is Your Bond Manager Skillful?" *Pension World.* (June 1977).

Treynor, Jack L. "How to Rate Management of Investment Funds." *Harvard Business Review.* 43 no. 1 (January–February 1965).

Wagner, Wayne H., and Dennis A. Tito. "Definitive New Measures of Bond Performance and Risk." *Pension World.* (May 1977).

Part 6   *Alternative Investments*

This section only contains four chapters, but it obviously could be a book unto itself. Therefore, it was necessary to select for further discussion those investments that would be of greatest interest to the reader. The first chapter is devoted to stock options, convertibles, and warrants. There has been substantial growth in options since the Chicago Board Options Exchange (CBOE) opened in 1973. The creation of highly marketable put and call options allows investors to develop a wide range of risk-return alternatives that were not possible before. We consider how they evolved, what they are, and how to use them given alternative investment outlooks. Within this chapter we also consider warrants and convertible securities since they are similar option securities; i.e., warrants are options to acquire stock from a firm, while a convertible bond is an option to convert a bond into stock. These securities are very useful in terms of reducing the firm's cost of capital because they are attractive for investors. Warrants appeal to investors because of the leverage involved; convertible securities are desirable because they typically provide downside protection and good upside potential. Besides considering their general attributes, we consider how these securities should be analyzed and when they are optimal investments.

Chapters 24 and 25 contain an extensive discussion of futures. Prior to 1976, such a presentation would have been limited to commodities. In 1976 financial futures were introduced and their development since that time has been nothing short of phenomenal. Therefore, Chapter 24 discusses commodity futures. Chapter 25 considers the similarities and differences between stock markets and futures markets and subsequently deals with the theory and practice of futures markets in commodities, financial instruments, and currencies.

The final chapter, Chapter 26, considers an alternative to analyzing and selecting investments yourself — investment companies. After a basic explanation of the concept of investment companies and a description of the major forms, we examine the many types available, from money market funds that only invest in short-term fixed-income securities to high growth common stock funds and options funds. Almost any investment objective can be met by investing in one or several investment companies. A review of several studies that examined the performance of investment companies indicated that they have generally not performed as well as a naive buy-and-hold policy. Even though the typical investment company does not outperform the market, it is capable of fulfilling a number of other functions that are important to an investor.

Chapter 23

Stock Options, Warrants, and Convertibles

STOCK OPTIONS

Options give the holder the right to buy or sell a security at a specified price during a designated period of time. There are two specific types: *call options* give the owner the right to *purchase* a given number of shares of a stock at a specified price during a given time period (usually from three to nine months); *put options* give the holder the right to *sell* a given number of shares of a security at a specified price during a given time interval. Put and call options have been available to investors on the OTC market for a number of years, but they have only become widely accepted and used as an investment vehicle since the Chicago Board Options Exchange (CBOE) was established. As a result of actions by the CBOE and other exchanges that began to list options, there has been a large volume of options trading by individual and institutional investors. Another major reason for the increased interest in options is that they provide a substantial range of investment alternatives for all types of potential investors from the most speculative to the very conservative.

RECENT HISTORY OF OPTIONS TRADING

For a number of years it has been possible to buy and sell put and call options in the OTC market via individual investment firms that were members of the Put and Call Association. Through the individual firms in this association, investors could negotiate specific put and call options on given shares of stock. The arrangements were very flexible and also somewhat disorganized. An investor who wanted to buy an option would go to one of these dealers and would indicate the stock he wanted to buy and the time period he was interested in. The dealer would find an interested investor and the parties would then negotiate individually on the price of the options. Because the amount of secondary trading was limited, it was usually difficult to sell the call again.

The environment changed dramatically when the CBOE was established on April 26, 1973, and began trading options on 16 stocks. The options exchange made numerous innovations in the trading of options on listed securities, such as:

1. *The creation of a central market place* with regulatory, surveillance, disclosure, and price dissemination capabilities
2. *The introduction of a Clearing Corporation* as the guarantor of every CBOE option. Standing as the opposite party to every trade, by making an offsetting transaction the Clearing Corporation enables buyers and sellers of options to terminate their positions in the market at any time.
3. *The standardization of expiration dates.* (Most CBOE options expire in January, April, July, and October, others in February, May, August, and November.) Also *the standardization of exercise prices* (the price per share at which the stock can be acquired upon exercise of the option).
4. *The creation of a secondary market.* While an option is a contract guaranteeing the buyer the right to purchase stock at the agreed upon price, the majority of option buyers sell their options on the exchange either for a profit or to reduce loss. Before the options exchange was established, the buyers and sellers of OTC options were essentially committed to their positions until the expiration date if the option was not exercised.

OPERATION OF THE CBOE

You are well aware of how a market is made on the New York and other stock exchanges. The specialist is at the center of the stock market and has two functions: (1) as a broker who maintains the limit-order book, and (2) as a market-maker who buys and sells for his own account to ensure the operation of a "fair and orderly" market for investors. Recall the concern that the specialists had monopoly information in the form of the limit order book and also a monopoly position as the sole market-maker in a security. One might therefore expect stock specialists to derive above average returns, which they do.

Apparently the CBOE was aware of the potential problems of the stock exchange arrangement and attempted to avoid them. The limit order book on the CBOE is handled by an individual (a *board broker*) who is *not* a market-marker so the two functions are separate. The board broker handles the limit-order book and accepts *only* public orders on the book. In addition, the limit-order book *is public!* Above the trading post there is a video screen that gives figures for the last trade, the current bid and ask for each of the options, and the limit orders on the book. The other major difference is that *there are competing market-makers for all options.* These members, designated market-makers, can *only* trade for themselves and are not allowed to handle public orders. As an example, there are four members of the CBOE who are specifically designated as primary market-makers for IBM. Each of the market-makers is assigned three or four primary options and another three or four options for which they are secondary market-makers. They are required to concentrate 70 percent of their trading activity in their primary issues. Similar to the stock exchange specialist, they are expected to provide liquidity for individual and institutional investors. Given the existence of several market-makers for each option, one would expect more funds to be available for trading and superior markets because of the added competition.

The third category of CBOE members are floor brokers who execute all types of orders for their customers. These floor brokers are very similar to floor brokers on the stock exchanges.

Volume of Trading

The CBOE started with options on 16 stocks. This number was gradually increased and other exchanges were established during 1975 and 1976 as shown in Table 23.1. As of 1984, the various exchanges combined had call options on almost 400 stocks. Initially, all option trading on the exchanges was in call options. As of June 1, 1977, the SEC allowed each of the exchanges to begin trading in five put options, and there was a freeze on adding any more. The freeze was lifted during 1980 and there are currently puts on all stocks that have calls.

As one might expect, the options are on stocks of large companies that enjoy active secondary markets. In fact, the criterion for listing an option is the trading activity of the underlying stock.

The growth in trading volume has been phenomenal. During the first full month of trading on the CBOE (May 1973), the number of contracts traded totaled about 31,000. By 1984, the total number traded on the four exchanges for each month consistently exceeded 8 million. The annual totals are contained in Table 23.2 as well as a breakdown for the individual exchanges. The figures reflect the larger volume in call options compared to put options. This can be explained by the general tendency of investors to buy long rather than sell short (i.e., the purchase of a call is based upon a bullish outlook, while you would buy a put if you were bearish on a stock).

The exchange breakdown reflects the initial dominance of the CBOE, which has declined, but apparently has stabilized at about 55 percent of call volume after the merger with the Midwest Exchange.

TABLE 23.1
Options Listed on Exchanges (as of June 1984)

Exchange	Starting Date	Number of Stocks Listed
Chicago Board Option Exchange (CBOE)	April 26, 1973	145
American Stock Exchange	January 13, 1975	107
Philadelphia Exchange	June 29, 1975	67
Pacific Exchange	April 9, 1976	78
Midwest Exchange[a]	December 10, 1976	—
	Total	397

[a] Merged with CBOE on June 2, 1980.

TABLE 23.2
Number of Put and Call Contracts Traded and Percent of Contracts Traded on Different Exchanges

A. Call Contracts (thousands)

Year	CBOE Number	CBOE Percent	AMEX Number	AMEX Percent	Philadelphia Number	Philadelphia Percent	Pacific Number	Pacific Percent	Midwest[a] Number	Midwest[a] Percent	Total Number
1977	23,583	63.0	9,655	25.8	2,002	5.3	1,704	4.6	497	1.3	37,441
1978	30,743	58.7	13,644	26.1	3,010	5.7	2,929	5.6	2,041	3.9	52,367
1979	29,918	53.5	16,505	29.5	4,527	8.1	3,118	5.6	1,847	3.3	55,915
1980	42,942	53.5	25,104	31.3	6,686	8.3	4,410	5.5	1,111	1.4	80,252
1981	40,801	50.4	26,430	32.7	8,104	10.0	5,610	6.9	a	a	80,945
1982	50,225	53.2	27,665	29.3	9,880	10.5	6,668	7.1	a	a	94,438
1983	57,858	55.2	26,599	25.4	12,085	11.5	8,255	7.9	a	a	104,797

B. Put Contracts (thousands)

Year	CBOE Number	CBOE Percent	AMEX Number	AMEX Percent	Philadelphia Number	Philadelphia Percent	Pacific Number	Pacific Percent	Midwest[a] Number	Midwest[a] Percent	Total Number
1977	1,257	57.2	423	19.3	192	8.7	222	10.1	103	4.7	2,197
1978	3,979	63.7	841	13.5	296	4.7	640	10.2	489	7.8	6,245
1979	5,250	64.6	964	11.9	423	5.2	736	9.0	762	9.4	8,133
1980	9,975	60.0	4,103	24.7	1,051	6.3	1,076	6.5	408	2.5	16,613
1981	16,783	59.0	8,430	29.6	1,906	6.7	1,343	4.7	a	a	28,462
1982	25,511	60.0	11,102	25.9	3,587	8.4	2,642	6.2	a	a	42,842
1983	24,610	59.1	9,601	23.1	4,522	10.9	2,900	7.0	a	a	41,633

[a] Midwest Options Exchange merged with CBOE on June 2, 1980.
SOURCE: Options Clearing Corporation

Competing Markets for Options

When the ASE established trading in options in January 1975, it was with 15 stocks that *were not* being traded on the CBOE. The point is that originally there was a very conscious effort by the exchanges *not* to establish competing markets, and this practice was continued when the Philadelphia Exchange began trading in options.

This changed late in 1976 when the ASE established a market in MGIC which was then traded on the CBOE. In February 1977, the ASE started a market in National Semiconductor, a very active issue on the CBOE.[1] The response by the CBOE was to begin trading in six ASE issues: Merrill Lynch, Digital Equipment, Burroughs, Disney, du Pont, and Tandy. The competition appeared to reduce the spread for these issues and increase their liquidity. There was a major effort by members of both exchanges to draw volume in the competitive issues, because many brokerage houses did not check both markets when placing an order but would select one of them as the primary exchange for an issue and channel all orders for the issue to this exchange.

There was a freeze on adding new options from 1977 to 1980. When they resumed adding new options in 1980, there were no competing options listed. Also, as of 1984 the NYSE has not established an options market.

Terminology

Given the unique nature of the options market, it is hardly surprising to find that it has developed its own terminology.

The option premium is the price paid for the option itself. It is what a buyer must pay for the ability to acquire the stock at a given price during some period in the future. The average premium on a newly issued option with the market price of the stock in question close to the option price is typically about 10 percent of the value of the stock. The premium on a six-month option to buy a stock for $30, when the stock is selling for about $30, would be about $3.

The exercise price (or striking price) is the price at which the stock can be acquired. If the stock is currently selling for $38 a share, one might specify an exercise price of $40 a share, meaning that the holder of the option can buy the stock for $40 for the duration of the option. The intervals for exercise prices are determined by the price of the stock involved. While there are exceptions, typically for stocks selling under $100, the exercise prices are set at $5 intervals: e.g., $35, $40, $45. For stocks selling for over $100 a share, the intervals are $10, e.g., $120, $130, $140. The initial exercise prices are set at the interval closest to the current market price of the stock. In a case of a stock selling for $43 at the time the option is established, the exercise price would be set at $45. If the stock declines to $41 a share, another option would be established at $40. In contrast, if

---

[1] For an extended discussion of what transpired, see Kevin J. Hamilton, "Options: The Dual Trading War," *Institutional Investor,* 11 no. 6 (June 1977): 30–32; and Jonathon R. Laing and Richard E. Rustin, "Options Trading War May Afford a Preview of a National Market," *Wall Street Journal,* May 27, 1977, p. 1.

the price increased to $48 a share, an option would be established at $50. There-fore, when you look in the paper and a stock has options at numerous prices, it is an indication that the price has moved over a wide range during the recent past.

The expiration date. This is the date on which the option expires or the last date on which the option can be exercised. In July the exchange might establish a September option which means that the holder of this option can purchase the stock at any time between July and September when the option expires. The expiration dates are designated by month, while the actual date of expiration is *the Saturday following the third Friday of each month that is specified.* A Sep-tember option would expire on the close of business on the Saturday following the third Friday in September. Actual trading in the option would cease at the close of the market on the third Friday.

Beyond these basic items of terminology, there are three general phrases used extensively in the trade. One of them is the term *in the money option,* which is an option with a *market price for the stock that is in excess of the exercise price for the option.* Assume that the exercise price of an option was $30 and the stock was currently selling for $34 a share. This would be an in the money option meaning that the market price ($34) exceeded the exercise price ($30) and so the option had an intrinsic value of at least $4 a share. The *out of the money option* has *an exercise price above the market price for the stock.* An example would be an option with an exercise price of $30 for a stock that is currently selling at $22 a share. In this instance, an investor may be willing to pay some-thing for the option based on the *possibility* of the stock price increasing. The option itself has no intrinsic value, because it provides the ability to buy stock for $30 a share at a time when it is possible to buy stock in the open market at only $22. The price you are willing to pay for an out of the money option is referred to as its *time value* because you are paying for the ability to acquire the stock at this price for the remaining time to maturity. Finally, an *at the money option* is one with a striking price approximately equal to the market price for the stock.

Example Quotations. Referring to Figure 23.1, an example of a quote for an in the money option is Bristol Myers (BrisMy) indicated on the Chicago Board of Exchange as (1). The 40 option for March is selling for 3 5/8 which is consistent with the market price of the stock of 43 5/8. In this example, the option price equals the intrinsic value of the option (43 5/8 − 40) because the option allows you to buy the stock at $40 a share when the current market price is $43.625. The March option is selling for its intrinsic value only because it expires on Saturday, March 17, which is one week after the quote. If there had been any trading in longer options (June or September), you would expect these options to sell at a premium over the intrinsic value to reflect the time value.

An example of an out of the money option would be the Beatrice Food (Beat F) 35 call option listed on the ASE when the stock is selling for 32 1/4 [desig-nated by (2)]. In this case, the option has no intrinsic value, because it allows you to buy a stock at $35 a share that is only selling for $32.25. Still, it does have some time value (1/4), and the time value increases as you go from March to June to September (1/4 — 1 3/8 — 2 1/2).

FIGURE 23.1
Listed Options Quotations

Listed Options Quotations

Thursday, March 8, 1984

Closing prices of all options. Sales unit usually is 100 shares. Security description includes exercise price. Stock close is New York or American exchange final price.

Most Active Options

CHICAGO BOARD OPTIONS EXCHANGE

		Sales	Last	Chg.	N.Y. Close
CALLS					
SP100	Mar155	46384	9-16	+ 1-16	152.43
SP100	Mar150	25882	3⅝	+ 7-16	152.43
SP100	Apr155	9240	2⅝	+ 3-16	152.43
SP100	Apr160	7080	15-16	....	152.43
SupOil	Mar40	6024	9-16	− ⅜	37⅝
PUTS					
SP100	Mar155	59657	2¾	− ½	152.43
SP100	Mar150	37564	½	− 3-16	152.43
SP100	Apr150	11463	1 15-16	− 1-16	152.43
SP100	Mar160	9145	7⅝	− ¾	152.43
SP100	Apr155	6917	4¼	− ⅜	152.43

AMERICAN STOCK EXCHANGE

		Sales	Last	Chg.	N.Y. Close
CALLS					
Gulf O	Apr65	8423	7⅞	+ 1	67¾
Gulf O	Apr70	7061	4⅞	+ ¾	67¾
Gulf O	Apr75	4602	2 3-16	+ 5-16	67¾
Ph Mor	Mar60	4250	6½	− 1¼	66⅞
MMIdx	Mar110	3637	2⅛	+ 3-16	111.46
PUTS					
Gulf O	Apr60	3053	2⅝	− 1¼	67¾
Gulf O	Apr55	3041	1 5-16	− 11-16	67¾
MMIdx	Mar110	2784	⅜	− 1-16	111.46
Gulf O	Apr70	2272	6¼	− 1⅞	67¾
Gulf O	Apr65	2158	4¼	− 1¾	67¾

PHILADELPHIA STOCK EXCHANGE

		Sales	Last	Chg.	N.Y. Close
CALLS					
Coleco	Apr15	2154	½	+ ⅛	11½
Coleco	Apr10	1823	2¼	+ ½	11½
AnheusB	Jun60	1203	1⅞	− ¼	56⅛
AnheusB	Mar65	1200	1-16	....	56⅛
FinCp	Mar20	918	⅛	+ 1-16	16¾
PUTS					
Coleco	Apr10	7070	1⅛	− ½	11½
Coleco	Jul10	3174	1⅞	− ⅜	11½
Coleco	Apr15	1716	4⅝	− ⅞	11½
Coleco	Oct10	747	2¼	− ¼	11½
FinCp	Mar15	629	⅛	− ⅛	16¾

PACIFIC STOCK EXCHANGE

		Sales	Last	Chg.	N.Y. Close
CALLS					
HouNG	Apr55	7419	4	− ½	52½
HouNG	Apr50	4908	6⅛	− ⅞	52½
HouNG	Apr60	4492	2⅝	− ¼	52½
HouNG	Apr45	2072	9⅛	− ⅞	52½
HouNG	Apr65	1720	1 3-16	− ⅛	52½
PUTS					
ShellO	May55	691	1½	− ¼	57¼
HouNG	Apr45	471	1⅞	+ ⅜	52½
HouNG	Apr50	405	4⅛	+ ¾	52½
DataGn	Mar45	332	1⅛	− ½	44⅞
Seagrm	May30	320	¼	+ ⅛	34⅝

Chicago Board

Option & NY Close	Strike Price	Calls—Last			Puts—Last		
		Mar	Jun	Sep	Mar	Jun	Sep
Apache	..10	2⅝	3	3⅝	r	r	r
12⅝	...15	1-16	7-16	13-16	2½	r	2½
BrisMy	..35	8¾	r	r	r	⅛	5-16
①→ 43⅝	→ 40	3⅝	r	r	r	⅝	r
43⅝	...45	⅛	1⅞	3⅛	1½	2½	3¼
43⅝	...50	r	½	1¼	r	r	r
Bruns	.27½	r	r	s	r	3⅛	s
25⅛	...25	11-16	2 5-16	3¼	¾	1¾	r
25⅛	...30	1-16	⅜	1½	r	r	r
Celan	65	r	r	r	⅛	1½	r
68¼	...70	⅝	2½	r	r	4	r
68¼	...75	r	r	r	6⅝	r	r
Chamin	.20	3	r	r	r	r	r
23¼	...25	⅛	1⅛	1¾	2	2⅝	r
23¼	...30	1-16	⅛	r	r	r	r
CompSc	.15	1-16	⅞	1½	r	1⅝	r
13½	...20	r	r	½	r	r	r
13½	...25	r	1-16	3-16	r	r	r
Dow Ch	.25	s	r	4⅞	s	⅜	r
29	30	⅛	1 3-16	2	1⅛	2⅛	2¾
29	35	r	¼	r	r	r	r
Esmark	37½	r	r	s	1-16	r	s
40⅝	.42½	⅝	r	s	r	r	s
40⅝	...40	1¼	r	r	⅜	r	r
40⅝	...45	3-16	1¾	2½	r	r	r

American Exchange

Option & NY Close	Strike Price	Calls—Last			Puts—Last		
		Mar	Jun	Sep	Mar	Jun	Sep
Alcan	35	⅛	1⅝	2⅝	2	2¾	r
Amax	...20	r	r	8	r	r	7-16
26⅝	...25	1¾	3⅝	4⅝	⅛	1¼	1¾
26⅝	...30	1-16	1 1-16	1 13-16	3⅝	r	r
AmBrnd	.50	r	r	s	r	5-16	s
55⅛	...55	⅞	2⅝	3	¼	1	r
55⅛	...60	r	13-16	1⅝	4¼	4⅝	r
Asarco	..25	8½	9½	r	r	3-16	r
33¾	...30	3¾	5⅛	5¾	1-16	¾	1¼
33¾	...35	⅜	2¼	3⅜	1½	r	3½
33¾	...40	1-16	13-16	s	r	r	s
33¾	...45	r	7-16	s	r	r	s
Beat F	..25	r	r	7⅞	r	r	r
32¼	...30	2⅝	3⅝	r	⅛	¾	1⅝
② 32¼	→ 35	¼	1⅝	2½	2¾	3⅝	r
32¼	...40	s	½	1	s	r	r
BwnFer	.35	½	r	3	1 1-16	2⅝	3
34¾	...40	r	r	1½	r	r	r
34¾	...45	r	5-16	r	r	r	r
BucyEr	..15	1⅞	2½	3	r	r	⅝
17	20	1-16	½	r	r	r	r
Chase	...45	5	6	r	1-16	⅝	r
50¼	...50	⅞	r	3½	½	2⅝	r
50¼	...55	1-16	1	2 1-16	r	r	r

Philadelphia Exchange

Option & NY Close	Strike Price	Calls—Last			Puts—Last		
		Mar	Jun	Sep	Mar	Jun	Sep
AirPd	...35	s	r	r	s	¾	r
39¾	...40	½	r	r	r	1¾	r
39¾	...45	r	⅝	r	r	r	r
AnheusB	55	s	r	r	s	2	3
56⅛	...60	1-16	1⅞	3⅝	3¾	4¾	5½ ←③
56⅛	...65	1-16	13-16	r	r	8¾	r
56⅛	...70	r	r	15-16	r	r	r
ArchDM	.15	r	5¾	r	r	r	r
20¼	...20	11-16	r	r	½	1⅛	1¾
20¼	...25	r	⅜	r	r	r	r
Avco	20	s	r	8⅛	s	r	r
27⅝	...25	2¾	3¼	4⅝	1-16	r	r
27⅝	...30	1-16	1	1¾	2½	r	r
BecDic	..35	11-16	2	r	1⅛	r	r
34⅛	...40	r	5-16	r	5¾	r	r
Chartr	...10	5-16	1 1-16	1⅝	¼	1	1 5-16
10⅛	...15	r	r	r	5¼	r	r

Pacific Exchange

Option & NY Close	Strike Price	Calls—Last			Puts—Last		
		Apr	Jul	Oct	Apr	Jul	Oct
A M D	27½	2⅛	s	s	1⅝	s	s
27½	.32½	¾	s	s	5¼	s	s
27½	...25	3½	5⅛	r	⅞	1¾	2⅛
27½	...30	1⅛	2 9-16	3⅝	3⅝	4¼	r
27½	...35	5-16	1⅝	r	7½	r	r
27½	...40	⅛	⅝	1¼	r	r	r
Comdis	..10	3¾	4¼	4½	5-16	⅝	r
13⅝	...15	11-16	1⅝	2	2¼	2⅝	2¾
13⅝	...20	⅛	½	¾	r	r	r
Datapd	..20	r	r	r	½	r	r
21⅛	...25	¼	r	r	4	r	r
21⅛	...30	1-16	r	r	r	r	r
DayHud	30	r	2⅝	3¼	⅞	r	r
29⅞	...35	3-16	r	r	5¼	r	r

r—Not traded. s—No option offered. o—Old.
Last is premium (purchase price).

SOURCE: *The Wall Street Journal,* March 9, 1984. Reprinted by permission of *The Wall Street Journal,* Dow Jones & Company, Inc. 1984. All rights reserved.

An example of an in the money put is provided by the Anheuser Busch (Anheus B) options on the Philadelphia Exchange [designated (3)]. There is intrinsic value to the 60 put option since it allows you to *sell* the stock at $60 a share when it is only selling for 56 1/8 on the Exchange. As a result it has an intrinsic value of 3 7/8 (60 − 56 1/8). Again, notice that the price of the options increase as the time goes from March to June to September.

720 ALTERNATIVE TRADING STRATEGIES

With the introduction of put options, the number of strategies available to an investor has become enormous and the range of complexity is substantial. In this section, we will not attempt to cover all the strategies but will limit our discussion to the major alternatives and refer the reader to articles and books that describe the more sophisticated techniques. Most trading involves the strategies discussed in this chapter. Also, in order to understand the more sophisticated strategies, it is necessary to understand the basic techniques because the more advanced methods are based upon these.

Buying Call Options

Investors buy call options because they expect the price of the underlying stock to increase during the period prior to the expiration of the option. Given this expectation, the purchase of an option will yield a large return on a small dollar investment. When considering the purchase of a call option, there are several alternatives available in terms of the exercise price relative to the market price. One can purchase an out of the money option, an at the money option, or an in the money option. The riskiest is probably an out of the money option, because it is clearly possible to lose everything that has been invested if the stock price does not rise enough to equal or exceed the exercise price. At the same time, the rate of return can be very large and the initial investment is the lowest of the three alternatives.

Consider the following example (without taking commissions or taxes into account):

	Call Options		
	April	July	Oct
IBM NYSE Cl. 110	3	6	10
108			

Assume that in March, when IBM is selling for 108, you expect a large price rise over the next four months. As indicated by the quote, you can buy a July 110 call for 6 ($600 for a call on 100 shares). Figure 23.2 indicates your situation. As long as the stock remains below $110, the option has no intrinsic value, but it will rise in a linear fashion beyond this point. For you to recoup the premium you paid, the price must increase to $116. Assume that you are correct and the price of IBM stock when the option expires in July is $122. In this instance, the minimum value for the option would be $12 (122 − 110). During this period, the stock price increased by 13 percent [(122 − 108)/108], while the value of the option increased by 100 percent. While the returns are very good, recall that your break-even point was 116, which required a 7.4 percent rise in the price of IBM stock. If the stock price does not increase, the option would expire without value and you would experience a 100 percent loss on the transaction.

As an alternative to the slightly out of the money option, you could acquire an in the money option—i.e., an IBM 100 July option at 13. In this instance, the

FIGURE 23.2
Profits to Buyer of Call Option

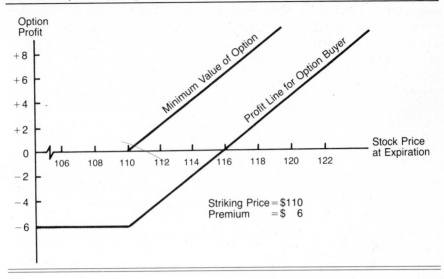

option has an intrinsic value of $8 (108 − 100) and a time value of $5. If the stock price increases to 122, the profit on this option would be about 69 percent [(122 − 113)/13] for the 13 percent stock price increase. While the percent profit is not as much, neither is the required increase to break even—i.e., it is only 4.6 percent [(113 − 108)/108]. Finally, if the stock price does not change from 108, you would lose 38 percent on the investment; i.e., at expiration the value of the option would be 8 compared to your purchase price of 13 [(13 − 8)/13].

Writing Covered Call Options

In contrast to buying call options, which is considered quite speculative, a strategy of writing call options is generally considered to be quite conservative. An option writer enters into a contract to deliver 100 shares of a stock at a predetermined exercise price during some specified time interval. When you enter into such a contract *(sell a call)*, you can either own the stock *(sell a covered option)* or not own the stock *(sell an uncovered, or naked, option)*. The option writer is typically looking for extra income from the stock (the premium received also provides some downside protection). At the same time, the option writer gives *up* a certain amount of upside potential on the stock if it rises above the exercise price and is called away.

Assume that in March you acquired 100 shares of IBM at $108 a share. You could sell an IBM July 110 for about $6 a share (i.e., sell a covered call). This is extra income ($600), or it can be considered downside protection since your *net* price is now $102 (108 − 6) per share.

If the stock does not change price between March and July (approximately four months), you have an additional $600 (a 5.5 percent return during the four-month period). If the stock increases to 11 and is called away, you have sold it at a profit of $3 per share and you still have the premium. Your return (before dividends) during the period was $9 (a $6 premium plus the $3 capital gain), which would be 8.3 percent (9/108) for the four months. As noted, if the stock goes to $120, you give up the gain above $110 because of the option. Therefore, you are protected on the downside by the lower net price but also are restricted on the upside by the exercise price. As an option writer if you want to get out of your contract, you must buy a comparable call option on the exchange and the two contracts cancel each other.

Figure 23.3 indicates the profit potential for the seller of a call option. Note that there is a loss at prices above 116 because this offsets the premium received. In the case of a covered call, it is an opportunity loss, while in the instance of a naked call, it is necessary to go into the market and buy the stock.

There are many other potential transactions for almost any possible set of risk-return desires. This discussion only introduces you to the basic transactions used in other strategies.[2]

Writing Options in Different Markets. Your option writing strategy should differ depending upon the general market environment (stable, rising, declining) and your outlook for the stock. If the market is *very stable,* you would simply continue to sell options over time as a supplement to dividend income. The only unique aspect of this arrangement would be that, if it is an out of the money option or at the money option, you should consider closing out your position (buying an option to offset your written option) prior to expiration so you can sell another one sooner. This is based on the assumption that the option price gets pretty low near its maturity because it has no intrinsic value and its time value declines.

If the market is *declining,* the sale of a call somewhat offsets the decline in price (i.e., the net cost of the stock is lower). After the stock has declined along with the market, the investor must decide whether he still wants to own the stock. If he does, he should write another call at a lower call price. Assume you bought a stock at $58 and sold a 60 call. The stock then declines to 53. If you still want to own the stock, you would sell another call at 55.

Finally, assume that the stock price *increases* because of a market rise or for internal reasons. Again you must decide whether you want to continue to own the stock or let it be called away. Assume you bought the stock at $45, sold a $50 option, and the stock subsequently went to $52. If you are satisfied with the $5 capital gain plus the premium received, you might allow the stock to be called away and put the money into another stock. In contrast, if you think there is further potential in the stock, you could simply buy back your option at $50 and sell another at $55. You would lose on the repurchase of the first option, but you would make it up on the second option and you would still own the stock.

---

[2] For further readable discussion of writing strategies, see *The Merrill Lynch Guide to Writing Options* (New York: Merrill Lynch, Pierce, Fenner & Smith), and *Option Writing Strategies* (Chicago: The Chicago Board Options Exchange).

FIGURE 23.3
Profits to Seller of Call Option

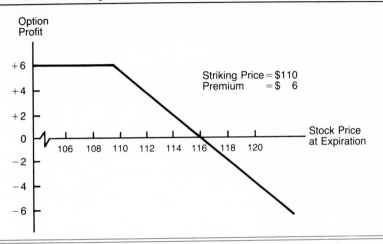

Option Spreads

In contrast to simply buying or selling an option, it is possible to enter into a spread and do both. The purpose is to reduce the risk of a long or short position in the option for a stock. There are two basic types of spread. *A price spread* (or vertical spread) involves buying the call option for a given stock, time, and price, and selling a call option for the same stock and time at a different price, e.g., buy an Avon October 20 and sell an Avon October 30. *A time spread* (or *horizontal spread*) involves buying and selling an option for the same stock and price, but the time differs, e.g., buying an Avon October 30 and selling an Avon January 30.

Bullish Spreads. These are spreads that you would consider if you were bullish on the underlying stock. Assume you are optimistic regarding the outlook for Avon, which is currently selling for 25, and want to enter into a price spread that will reduce the risk of such a transaction. The situation is as follows regarding October options (numbers rounded):

—   Avon 20 October   7
—   Avon 30 October   2

Because you are bullish, you would buy the Avon 20 and sell the Avon 30 for a net cost of 5 ($500) which is also your maximum loss. Assuming you are correct, and the stock goes from 25 to 35, the October 20 would be worth about 15 (only its intrinsic value) and the October 30 would sell for about 6 (a slight premium over intrinsic value). If you closed out both positions, you would obtain the following results:

—   October 20: bought at 7, sold at 15— gain 8
—   October 30: sold at 2, bought at 6 — loss 4
                                          Overall   — gain 4

If the stock had declined dramatically, your maximum loss would have been $500 even though both options were worthless when they expired. Your maximum gain on this transaction is $500. Specifically, at some high stock price, the difference in the value of the options will be 10, which indicates a gross profit of $1,000 less the $500 initial cost.

Bearish Spreads.   If an investor is bearish on a stock or on the market, he would buy the higher priced option and sell the lower priced option. Returning to Avon, you would:

—   Sell October 20 at 7
—   Buy October 30 at 2

This would generate an immediate gain of $500. If you are correct, and the stock declines to below 20, both options will be worthless when they expire and you will have the $500 return. If you were wrong, and the stock goes to 35 as discussed under the bullish spread, you would have the following:

—   October 20: sold at 7; bought at 15— loss 8
—   October 30: bought at 2; sold at 6 — gain 4
                                            Overall   — loss 4

This loss of $400 compares favorably with possible loss of $800 or much more if you did not have some offset from the spread. At some very high price the two options will have a difference of 10, so your maximum loss is $500 ($1000 gross loss less $500 gain on original transaction).

In summary, this discussion of alternative call option investment strategies supports the statement made in the chapter introduction that options provide a wide range of risk-return possibilities.[3] The alternatives can range from very speculative purchases of call options, which involve tremendous leverage and from which your returns can vary from large positive values, to a negative 100 percent (complete loss). Alternatively, option spreads provide definite limits to gains and losses. Finally, an investor who sells covered call options on common stock owned will experience less variability of return on the stock because of the option; i.e., the option premium will offset any loss on the stock and will limit any gain if the stock is called away.

The subsequent discussion of strategies that include put options expands the possibilities even further.

Buying Put Options

There are several major reasons for acquiring a put option on a stock. The most obvious is that you expect a particular stock to decline in price and you want to profit from this decline. As will be shown, the purchase of a put option allows you to do this with the benefits of leverage and yet provides protection, because it limits the potential loss if your expectations regarding a price decline in the stock are wrong. In addition, it will be of benefit if you already own a stock and

---

[3] A more extensive discussion is contained in George M. Frankfurter, Richard Stevenson, and Allan Young, "Option Spreading: Theory and an Illustration," *Journal of Portfolio Management,* 5 no. 4 (Summer 1979): 59–63; M. J. Gombola, R. Rosenfeldt, and Phillip L. Cooley, "Spreading Strategies in CBOE Options: Evidence on Market Performance," *Journal of Financial Research,* 1 no. 1 (Winter 1978): 35–44.

FIGURE 23.4
Profit to Buyer of Put Option

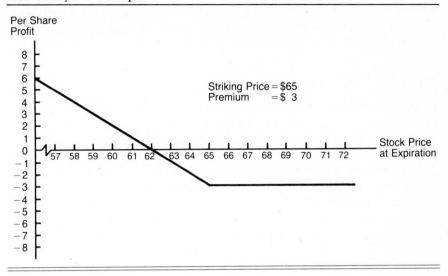

Consider an example of a standard put acquisition. As of April, General
Motors stock is selling for $67 but you think it could decline. An October 65 put
option for GM is selling for $3. Assume you purchase this option and by July GM
stock declines to $59. At this time, your put option will have a minimum value of
$6 ($65 − 59) and probably some value above this because there are still three
months remaining before it expires. Assuming a price of 7, you could sell it and
realize a gain of $4 (before commission), which is a 133 percent return on the
option during a period when the stock declined by 12 percent. Alternatively,
assume that you were wrong and the stock did not decline below 65, or, in fact,
increased in price. In this instance the put option expires worthless and your loss
was limited to the $300 you paid for the option.

do not want to sell it at the present time although you feel it might decline in the
near term. In this case, it is possible to buy a put option on the stock you own as a
hedge against the decline; you will offest the decline in the stock with an increase in the value of the put option. Finally, you might want to acquire a very
volatile stock with a good long-term outlook. While you feel confident of the
long run, you are uncertain about what might happen in the near term. In such a
case, you could acquire the stock and also a put option for the short term. If there
is near-term weakness in the stock, you would make money on the put as an
offset to the stock decline.

Figure 23.4 shows the profit picture for the buyer of a put option (assuming
intrinsic value at expiration). Besides the substantial leverage involved, it is
important to recognize the lower capital commitment and also lower commission for this technique compared to short selling. Also the limited loss characteristic of options is very relevant.

Assume the same set of events except that you owned the stock at $67 and thought the stock might experience some near-term weakness, but you did not want to sell it and then buy it back again. In this instance, if the stock declined to 59, you would have experienced an $800 loss in the value of your stock position, but you would have a gain of $400 on the put option as a partial offset.

Selling Put Options

When you sell (write) a put option you become obligated to buy a stock at a specified price during some time period. For accepting this obligation you receive a premium. An obvious reason for writing such an option is to increase the return on your portfolio during a period when you expect stock prices to rise. As an example, assume that currently Eastman Kodak stock is 67 and you expect the stock price to rise over the next six months. An EK six-month put of 70 is priced at 5. If you sell this put option, you receive $500 premium and, if the stock goes to 75 as you expect, the put option expires worthless and you have the extra $500.

In contrast, if you are wrong and EK declines to 64, the put option may go to about 7, if there is any time left. In this example, you will lose $200 ($700 cost less the $500 premium received) when you buy it back. Alternatively, you may be called upon to actually buy 100 shares of EK at 70 which entails paying $7,000 for stock only worth $6,400 before commissions. Figure 23.5 shows the profits related to this sale of a put option.

Another very interesting strategy that you can use is to sell a put option as a means of acquiring stock that you want at a price below the current market price. Rather than placing a limit buy order below the market, you can sell a put at a striking price below the current market price. As an example, assume you want to buy IBM, but you think it is a little too high at its current price of 108. It is possible for you to sell an IBM 100 put option due in about six months for 2 1/2. If the stock declines (as you expect) to below 100, you will be called upon to buy 100

FIGURE 23.5
Profit to Seller of Put Option

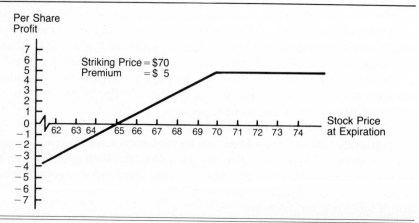

shares at 100, but your effective cost will only be 97 1/2 because of the premium you received. The outcome is that you own IBM as you wanted and at an effective price to you of $10 below the original market price. Alternatively, if the stock increased in price you would miss the profits, but you have the $250 premium.

Again it is possible to see the additional investment opportunities made available by put options. They may be used by a speculative investor who expects a price decline and wants to take advantage of the leverage of the put. Alternatively, they can be used by a very conservative investor who wants to hedge his current stock position. Finally, they can be used as a means to acquire a desirable stock at a lower effective price.

VALUATION OF CALL OPTIONS

There are five figures needed to calculate the value of an American call option,[4] assuming the stock does not pay a dividend. (This assumption will later be dropped.) The five figures are: (1) the stock price, (2) the exercise price, (3) the time to maturity, (4) the interest rate, and (5) the volatility of the underlying stock.

Market price — exercise price.   The relationship between these two prices is obviously important because it determines whether the option is in the money and, therefore, whether the option has an intrinsic value or if it is out of the money and hence has only speculative value. In addition, some of the other variables are influenced by the relationship between the market price and the exercise price.

Time to maturity.   A major component of value of an option is its time to maturity. All other factors being equal, *the longer the time to maturity, the greater the value of the option,* because the span of time during which gains are possible is longer. The longer option allows investors to reap all benefits of a shorter option and also provides added time after the short option has expired. It appears that this time value of the option is greatest when the market price and exercise price are the same. If the market price is below the exercise price (out of the money), it will take some of the time before the market price reaches the exercise price and the option begins to have exchange value. If the option is significantly in the money, for a given increase in the stock price, the percentage of gain would be less than it would be when the market and exercise prices are almost equal. Therefore, an investor who acquires an at the money option pays less than he would for an in the money option and will gain more if the stock price increases.

The interest rate.   When an investor acquires an option, he buys control of the underlying stock for a period of time, but his downside risk is limited to the cost of the option. On the upside, he has the potential to gain at an accelerating

---

[4] An American call option can be exercised at *any time* prior to the expiration date; a European option can only be exercised *on* the expiration date.

rate because of the leverage involved. The option is therefore similar to buying on margin, except there is no explicit interest charge. The higher the market interest rate, the greater the saving from using options, and the greater the value of the option. Therefore, there is a *positive* relationship between the market interest rate and the value of the call option.

Volatility of underlying stock price.   In most cases, one considers a high level of stock price volatility an indication of greater risk and, therefore, this reduces value, all other factors being equal. In the case of call options on a stock, the opposite is true; there is a *positive* relationship between the volatility of the underlying stock and the value of the call option. This is because, with greater volatility, there is greater potential for gain on the upside, and the downside protection of the option is also worth more.

Derivation of Valuation Formula

Black and Scholes developed a formula for deriving the value of American call options in a classic article published in 1973.[5] Merton later refined the Black–Scholes (BS) formula under less restrictive assumptions.[6] The resulting formula is as follows:

$$Po = [P_s][N(d_1)] - [E][\text{anti}ln(-rt)][N(d_2)],$$

where:

   $Po =$ the market value of the option

   $P_s =$ the current market price of the underlying common stock

$N(d_1) =$ the cumulative density function of d_1 as defined below:

   $E =$ the exercise price of the call option

   $r =$ the current annualized market interest rate for prime commercial paper

   $t =$ the time remaining before expiration (in years, e.g., 90 days $= .25$)

$N(d_2) =$ the cumulative density function of d_2 as defined below:

$$d_1 = \left[\frac{ln(P_s/E) + (r + .5\sigma^2)t}{\sigma(t)^{1/2}}\right.$$

$$d_2 = d_1 - [\sigma(t)^{1/2}]$$

---

[5] Fischer Black and Myron Scholes, "The Pricing of Options and Corporate Liabilities," *Journal of Political Economy,* 81 no. 3 (May/June 1973): 637–654.

[6] Robert C. Merton, "The Theory of Rational Option Pricing," *Bell Journal of Economics and Management Science,* 4 no. 1 (Spring 1973): 141–183.

where:

$ln(P_s/E)$ = the natural logarithm of (P_s/E)

σ = the standard deviation of the annual rate of return on the underlying stock.

Implementing the Formula.   Although the formula appears quite forbidding, almost all the required data are observable. The major inputs are: current stock price (P_s), exercise price (E), the market interest rate (r), the time to maturity (t), and the standard deviation of annual returns (σ). The *only* variable that is not observable is the volatility of price changes as measured by the standard deviation of returns (σ). Therefore, this becomes the major factor that must be estimated and is the variable that will cause a difference in the estimated market value for the option. Black, in a subsequent article, made several observations regarding this estimate.[7] First, he noted that knowledge of past price volatility should be helpful, but *more* is needed because *the volatility for individual stocks changes over time.* This should not come as a surprise, because a stock's volatility can change either because the market's volatility changes and the stock's beta is constant, or the market's volatility is constant and the individual stock's beta changes over time. Finally, it is possible for both variables to change. Therefore, given a historical estimate of the stock's volatility, the analyst should concentrate on determining the *direction* of the change; will the stock's volatility increase or decrease during the period prior to expiration? Given the variables determining volatility, one should first consider the future direction of *market* volatility; is there any reason to expect an increase or decrease in market volatility in the short run? Second, what do you expect to happen to the stock's beta in the future? This could be affected by industry factors or internal corporate variables, e.g., any future changes in business risk, or liquidity.

The other variable that requires some attention is the interest rate. The idea is to use a rate that corresponds to the term of the option. The most obvious is the rate on prime commercial paper that is quoted daily in *The Wall Street Journal* for different maturities ranging from 30, 60, and 90 to 240 days.

To demonstrate the formula, consider the following example. All the values except stock price volatility are observable. In the case of volatility, the historical measure is given, but it is also assumed that the analyst expects the stock's volatility to increase.

An Example of Option Valuation Variables

P_s = \$36.00
E = \$40.00
r = .10 (the rate on 90-day prime commercial paper)
t = 90 days — .25 year
Historical σ = .40
Expected σ = .50 (Analysts expect an increase in stock beta because of a new debt issue.)

[7] Fischer Black, "Fact and Fantasy in the Use of Options," *Financial Analysts Journal,* 31 no. 4 (July–August 1975): 36–41 *et. seq.*

TABLE 23.3
Calculation of Option Value ($\sigma = .40$)

$$d_1 = \left[\frac{ln(36/40) + (.10 - .5(.4)^2).25}{.4(.25)^{1/2}}\right]$$

$$= \left[\frac{-.1054 + .045}{.2}\right]$$

$$= -.302$$

$$d_2 = -.302 - [.4(.25)^{1/2}]$$
$$= -.302 - .2$$
$$= -.502$$

$$N(d_1) = .3814$$

$$N(d_2) = .3079$$

$$P_0 = [P_s][N(d_1)] - [E][\text{anti}ln(-rt)][N(d_2)]$$
$$= [36][.3814] - [40][\text{anti}ln(-.025)][.3079]$$
$$= 13.7304 - [40][0.9753][.3079]$$
$$= 13.7304 - 12.0118$$
$$= 1.7186.$$

Table 23.3 contains the detailed calculations for the option assuming the historical volatility ($\sigma = .40$). Table 23.4 contains the same calculations except that we assume volatility is higher ($\sigma = .50$).

These results indicate the importance of estimating stock price volatility; given a 25 percent increase in volatility (0.50 vs. 0.40), there is a 53 percent increase in the value of the option. Because everything else is observable, this is the variable that will differentiate estimates.

Efficiency of Options Market

A study by Galai investigated the pricing mechanism of call options and tested the efficiency of the CBOE shortly after it was established.[8] Efficiency was tested against the Black–Scholes option pricing model and is based on a hedging strategy in which a position in an option is matched with a position in the underlying stock (i.e., a fully covered option) so as to eliminate the risk of the aggregate position. There are two phases to the tests of market efficiency. The first is concerned with whether a specified trading rule can be used to separate profitable from unprofitable investments. Such an analysis indicates the power and accuracy of the trading rule. The second phase determines whether it is possible to use the trading rule to generate above normal risk-adjusted profits *in a real world environment.* It may be possible to use a rule to detect undervalued

[8] Dan Galai, "Tests of Market Efficiency on the Chicago Board Options Exchange," *The Journal of Business,* 50 no. 2 (April 1977): 167–195.

TABLE 23.4
Calculation of Option Value ($\sigma = .50$)

$$d_1 = \left[\frac{ln(36/40) + (.10 + .5(.5)^2).25}{.5(.25)^{1/2}} \right]$$

$$= \frac{-.1054 + .05625}{.25}$$

$$= -.1966$$

$$d_2 = -.1966 - [.5(.25)^{1/2}]$$

$$= -.1966 - .25$$

$$= -.4466$$

$$N(d_1) = .4199$$

$$N(d_2) = .3275$$

$$P_0 = [36][.4199] - [40][anti ln - .025][.3275]$$

$$= 15.1164 - [40][0.9753][.3275]$$

$$= 15.1164 - 12.7764$$

$$= 2.34.$$

securities, but it cannot be used to predict future behavior in an efficient market. The analysis also examines changes in efficiency over time.

The data were daily prices for each option on the CBOE from April 26, 1973 to November 30, 1973 (152 trading days). During this time period, there were 245 options on 32 underlying stocks. Galai used T-bill rates and commercial paper rates as estimates of r. For the estimates of the standard deviation, he used estimates derived by Scholes and two historical series, one for 1972 and another for the last 30 trading days.

The first *ex post* hedging test examined an option on the first day it was available to determine whether it was underpriced or overpriced based upon the relationship of the market price to the price estimated using the BS model. If the option was overpriced (underpriced), it was sold (bought) at the market price, and *this position was maintained for the life of the option.* Each day it was assumed the position was liquidated at the closing price and immediately reestablished. Two versions were considered: one assumed that all prices were those prices estimated by the model; the other used actual closing prices to compute returns. Although none of the returns for any option were significant for the second version, the average returns using the estimated prices were significant.

The second *ex post* test was similar, except that it involved the assumption that the option position could be changed daily depending upon the relationship of the market price and the model price. The average results with this test were much higher than those from the earlier tests and indicated that *the model was able to differentiate quite well between overpriced and underpriced options.* In addition, an analysis of returns over two 75-day trading periods indicated that the profitable opportunities did *not* deteriorate over time.

The tests were later performed with different estimates for the risk-free rate and the variance rate, and it was concluded that the qualitative results were unchanged. The model was also tested using 2, 3, 4, and 5-day holding periods, taking transaction costs into account. Assuming a one percent transaction cost, *all* the *ex post* returns were eliminated.

Earlier tests ignored the dividends on the stocks. When the portfolios were derived based upon the dividend yield, the results indicated superior performance for the low dividend stocks, as compared to the performance of high dividend portfolios, and the excess returns did not decline over time. When the author adapted the option pricing model specifically for dividends using a formula developed by Black, the *ex post* hedge returns were substantially higher. Apparently the dividend correction made the hedging strategy more effective in locating profitable opportunities.

An *ex ante* hedging test was similar to the previous test except that it was applied to past data. Such a test is a better reflection of the *actual* opportunities available to the trader. This test is implemented by lagging the execution of the trading by one day, i.e., based upon the value and price on day t, the option is bought or sold on day $t+1$. The returns were much lower, and the number of options with significant returns declined dramatically. It was concluded that, if the future is like the past, there is less than a 50 percent chance of obtaining a return of more than \$3 per option per day.

An analysis of portfolios based upon dividend yield provided evidence that profit opportunities still might have existed in the CBOE for a market-maker to exploit. Although individual hedges have not yielded significant profits on average, profits were achieved in the portfolio context. *The author concluded that the results of the* ex ante *tests suggest that the CBOE might not have been perfectly efficient during the period investigated and abnormal profit opportunities did exist.* Further, the profits did *not* decline over time.

Because spreading is used extensively by market-makers, Galai tested this strategy. Spreading involves selling the option considered to be overpriced and buying one that is underpriced. The spreading decision is based upon the relative values derived from the BS pricing model. Initially, the author always sold the short maturity and bought the long maturity option. The results indicate small, insignificant average returns, which do not support the general belief that short maturity options are overpriced relative to long maturity prices. Galai then allowed the BS model to determine how the spread should be carried out, and the results were quite good. This indicates that the model was able to differentiate on average between good and bad investments.

The final test is an *ex ante* analysis of the spreading model. Based upon prices and values on day t, a spreading transaction is carried out on day $t+1$. Because so many market-makers use this strategy, it was hypothesized that the returns from this *ex ante* test would be small. The results generally confirmed these expectations; the average returns were reduced by half relative to the *ex post* returns.

Galai's main conclusions were: (1) the trading strategies based on the BS model performed well in the tests when the hedges were based on the model's evaluation of prices versus the market prices; (2) the market did not seem perfectly efficient to market-makers because some of the returns from a realistic trading rule were positive. When transactions costs were considered, almost all positive returns disappeared, which means these above normal returns are *not* available to the public; (3) the dividend adjustment was important; (4) the tests of a time spreading strategy provided results similar to the hedging results; (5) the results did *not* generally indicate that the market became more efficient over time based upon an analysis of the first half of the sample period versus the second half. The whole test was conducted during the period shortly after the establishment of the CBOE, so this conclusion may be somewhat premature.

Analysis of Risks and Returns from Covered Calls

A study by Merton, Scholes, and Gladstein is probably the most complete in terms of results and in relating the results to expectations based upon factors that determine the value of call options.[9] They discussed the determinants of option pricing as related to the Black–Scholes valuation model and showed what returns will be derived from options with different characteristics under varying stock return conditions. The bulk of the paper presented the results of a simulation for a group of 130 stocks that have options traded on the CBOE and the 30 stocks in the Dow-Jones Industrial Average. The simulation involved the risk and returns for a fully covered call option program as compared to returns from owning the stock alone during the period July 1963 to December 1975. The pricing of options was based on the values generated with the Black–Scholes valuation model.

The analysis covered 25 semiannual holding periods during the 12 1/2 years between July 1, 1963 and December 31, 1975. The returns reported are all half-year results and assume dividends are reinvested, but do *not* consider taxes and transaction costs. The portfolios are equal dollar weighted for each stock.

Because several prior studies had confirmed the general accuracy of the valuation model (that was tested again later in the paper), the authors chose to simulate the strategies using option prices generated by the model rather than actual market option prices. This made it possible to consider a period prior to 1973 when the CBOE was founded.

In the simulation it was assumed that all options had six months to expiration and all options were held to expiration. This may not be optimal in many instances because it is often best to exercise an option before the expiration date, but this is offset by a dividend adjustment in the formula. The variance was estimated using the sample variance of the previous six months of daily logarithmic price changes. The article included a plot of the average option premium for different ratios of exercise price to stock price (0.9, 1.0, 1.1, 1.2). The plot indicated that the premiums experienced a fairly strong upward trend. This positive trend was caused by the importance of stock price variance in the for-

---

[9] Robert C. Merton, Myron S. Scholes, and Mathew L. Gladstein, "A Simulation of the Returns and Risk of Alternative Option Portfolio Investment Strategies," *Journal of Business,* 51 no. 2 (April 1978): 183–242.

mula and the increase in return volatility during this period. Also, rising interest rates had an effect.

All the options were for six-month periods. Hence, the simulation covered four strategies with the only difference being the ratio of exercise price (E) to market price of the stock (S). The four E/S ratios are 0.90 (in the money), 1.00 (at the money), 1.1 (out of the money), and 1.2 (deep out of the money). It was assumed that an investor bought 100 shares of the stock and wrote a six-month option on the shares. The option premium was used to reduce the stock investment. The ending value was the stock value plus the dividends received on the stock, less the cost of reacquiring the option if it had any value at the expiration date (i.e., the difference between the exercise price and the market price).

All four strategies were considered bullish because they all gain from an increase in the stock price although the effect differs. Also, the in the money options had the least return volatility (smaller losses on the downside and lower maximum returns on the upside). The large out of the money option had the greatest return volatility of the four option strategies, although the volatility was not as great as it was with the straight stock position. Therefore, it was shown that any *covered call position involves a lower risk than a pure stock position does, and, within the call strategies, an investor writes more out of the money options as he becomes more bullish.* Because of the nature of the return patterns, fully covered option writing will produce results superior to those for the stock during periods of small increases or decreases in the stock price.

Results of Simulation.   In terms of the variability of returns, the results were generally consistent with our previous discussion. The returns from the deep out of the money option strategies were more volatile than those from the other option categories. At the same time, *all option strategies were less volatile than a pure stock position was.* These results, shown in Table 23.5, indicate higher volatility and higher returns for the all-stock portfolio. Apparently, the covered option strategies experience less volatility and higher returns when stock prices either decline or increase by small amounts, but the returns on the option strategy suffer when stock prices increase substantially. Therefore, the returns reflect the strategy employed and also what happened to the underlying stocks during the period. In the simulation, because the stock returns were sufficiently positive, the all-stock portfolio did best, followed by the most bullish option strategy. If the stock returns were different, the rankings would have been different.

An analysis of how sensitive the returns are to deviations in the premium from the value specified by the BS valuation model indicated that such deviations change the *mean* rate of return but not the shape of the distribution. Excessive premiums increase the average returns for an option writing strategy. An analysis of returns from the option strategies, using the *actual* market prices for the options compared to the returns using prices generated by the BS valuation model, indicated how good the valuation model is and, therefore, whether the simulation results are realistic. This comparison was carried out for the period April 1973 to December 1975. Based upon the results, the authors concluded, "While the fully-covered returns are higher using market prices, the

TABLE 23.5
Summary Statistics for Rate-of-Return Simulations, Fully Covered Strategies,
July 1963–December 1975

	Exercise Price = .9 Stock Price	Exercise Price = 1.0 Stock Price	Exercise Price = 1.1 Stock Price	Exercise Price = 1.2 Stock Price	Stock
	136-Stock Sample				
Average Rate of Return (%)	3.3	3.7	4.5	5.3	7.9
Standard Deviation (%)	4.9	7.1	9.3	11.2	16.6
Highest Return (%)	14.6	19.3	24.7	30.4	54.6
Lowest Return (%)	−9.9	−14.4	−17.4	−19.2	−21.0
Average Compound Return (%)	3.0	3.4	4.1	4.7	6.7
Growth of $1,000 ($)	2,171	2,328	2,719	3,162	5,043
Coefficient of Skewness	−.63	−.48	−.26	−.01	.73
	DJ Stock Sample				
Average Rate of Return (%)	2.9	2.9	3.2	3.5	4.1
Standard Deviation (%)	3.7	6.2	8.6	10.4	13.7
Highest Return (%)	12.3	16.9	22.9	29.5	49.1
Lowest Return (%)	−5.4	−9.2	−11.9	−13.8	−16.4
Average Compound Return (%)	2.8	2.7	2.9	3.0	3.3
Growth of $1,000 ($)	1,992	1,942	2,040	2,103	2,226
Coefficient of Skewness	−.22	−.21	.04	.35	1.25

SOURCE: Robert C. Merton, Myron S. Scholes, and Mathew L. Gladstein, "A Simulation of the Returns and Risk of Alternative Option Portfolio Investment Strategies," *Journal of Business,* 51 no. 2 (April 1978): 207. Copyright © 1978 by The University of Chicago Press. Reprinted by permission of The University of Chicago Press.

difference is small." [10] The average percentage premium (i.e., option price to stock price ratio) was 11.7 percent for the market option prices and 11.2 percent for the model-generated prices. For the out of the money options, the average premiums were 7.5 percent for market prices and 7.1 percent for the model-generated prices. These market prices were derived during the early days of the CBOE and, therefore, may have been higher than expected. Because the model appears to derive option prices that are very similar to market prices, the returns estimated from the simulation should be quite similar to the returns that would be derived using actual market prices.

The authors contended that the investor who writes options against a portfolio of stocks will reduce his risk at the expense of also reducing his rate of return. Because the expected value of the option is heavily dependent on the expected volatility of the underlying stock, if an analyst can do a superior job of estimating the return volatility of the stock, then it should be possible to select overpriced options. The returns from consistently selling these overpriced options should be above normal on a risk-adjusted basis. *The crucial talent is the ability to do a superior job of estimating the variance of the individual security.*

[10] Robert C. Merton, Myron S. Scholes, and Mathew L. Gladstein, "A Simulation of the Returns and Risk of Alternative Option Portfolio Investment Strategies," *Journal of Business,* 51 no. 2 (April 1978): 213.

WARRANTS AND CONVERTIBLE SECURITIES

In the rest of this chapter we will consider some other instruments beginning with common stock warrants which, while similar to call options, have some unique features that make them appealing to investors *and* to the companies that issue them. Subsequently, we will discuss convertible securities which are really a hybrid that is essentially a fixed-income security which has an option to convert the security to common stock. Specifically, we will examine convertible bonds that have the characteristics of both bonds and common stocks and convertible preferred stocks, which are a combination of preferred stock and common stock.

Warrants

A warrant is an option to buy a stated number of shares of common stock at a specified price at any time during the life of the warrant. You will probably recognize that this definition is quite similar to the description of a call option. However, there are several important differences. First, the life of a warrant is much longer than the term of a call option. At the time of issue, the typical call option on the CBOE has a term to expiration that ranges from three to nine months. In contrast, a warrant generally has an original term to maturity of at least two years, and many are much longer. (There are a few perpetual warrants.) A second major difference is that *warrants are issued by the company issuing the stock*. As a result, when an investor exercises the warrant and buys stock, the stock involved is acquired *from the company,* and the proceeds from the sale are new capital that goes to the issuing firm.

In general, warrants are used by companies as sweeteners for bond issues or other stock issues, because they are options that could have value if the stock price increases as expected. The price of the stock or bond will be higher because the warrant is attached. At the same time, the warrant can provide a major source of new equity capital for the company. Investors are generally interested in warrants due to leverage possibilities that we will discuss. At the same time, you should recognize that warrants do *not* pay dividends and the holder has *no* voting rights. In addition, the investor must determine that the warrant offers some protection to the warrant holder against dilution in the case of stock dividends or stock splits. In such cases, either the exercise price is reduced or the number of shares that can be acquired is increased.

Example of Warrants.   Consider the following hypothetical example. The Bourke Corporation is going to issue $10 million in bonds but knows that, within the next five years, it will also need an additional $5 million in new external equity (in addition to expected retained earnings). One way to make the bond issue more attractive and also, possibly, to sell the stock, is to attach warrants to the bonds. If Bourke common stock is currently selling at $45 a share, the firm may decide to issue five-year warrants that will allow the holder to acquire the company's common stock at $50 a share. Because it wishes to raise $5 million, it must issue warrants for 100,000 shares ($5 million ÷ $50). Assuming the bonds will have a par value of $1,000, the company will sell 10,000 bonds and each bond will have 10 warrants attached to it. (We are assuming each warrant is for one share.) Assume the company is successful and the market price on the common stock reaches $55 a share over five years. At this point the warrants will have an intrinsic value of $5 each ($55 − $50), and all the warrants should be exercised prior to their expiration. As a result, the company can sell 100,000 shares of common stock at $50 a share. The company pays no explicit commission cost, but it does have administrative costs.

Other actual examples of outstanding warrants are listed in Figure 23.6, which is a page from the *R.H.M. Survey of Warrants, Options & Low-Price Stocks.* For each of the warrants included, there is an indication of the number of shares involved, the exercise terms (price and expiration date), the year of expiration (if the warrant is not perpetual), and the current price of the common stock and the warrant. As an example, consider the American Express Company warrants. As shown, each warrant allows the holder to buy two shares of American Express Company stock for $55.00 (i.e., $27.50 a share) until February 28, 1987 when the warrant expires. There are a million of these warrants outstanding and they are selling for $17.87 each. This price is a function of some intrinsic value because of the difference in the warrant striking price ($27.50) and the current price of the common which is $29.50. The rest of the warrant price is speculative value. We will discuss the specific pricing of the warrant in the following subsection. At this point you should be aware of the numerous firms that have warrants, the many expiration dates, and the wide range of stock prices relative to exercise prices for the warrants.

Valuation of Warrants.   The value of a warrant is determined in a manner similar to that used for call options because the only difference to the investor is the longer term. (An investor does not care whether he has the option to buy the stock from another investor or directly from the firm.) As was true with a call option, you should consider two components of the warrant price: the intrinsic value and the speculative value (sometimes referred to as the *premium*). The latter is based upon the leverage involved and the time value of the warrant. The intrinsic value of the warrant is determined by the difference between the market price of the common stock and the warrant exercise price as follows:

Intrinsic Value = (Market Price of Common Stock − Warrant Exercise Price)
　　　　　　　　× Number of Shares Each Warrant Entitles the Owner to
　　　　　　　　Purchase.

This determines the intrinsic value of a warrant, assuming that the market price exceeds the warrant exercise price. As an example, in Figure 23.6, the Alleghany Corporation warrant has an exercise price of $3.75, and the common stock is currently selling for $72.37. Therefore, this warrant has an intrinsic value of $68.62 (72.37 − 3.75), because it allows the holder to purchase one share of common stock at a price lower than the market price.

Alternatively, if the warrant exercise price exceeds the market price of the common stock, the warrant has zero intrinsic value. (A negative value is meaningless.) An example of this is the Atlas Corp. warrant. In this instance the

FIGURE 23.6
The R.H.M. Survey of Warrants, Options, and Low-Price Stock

THE R·H·M SURVEY
of WARRANTS · OPTIONS & LOW-PRICE STOCKS

VOL. XXXIII, No. 17   **Warrants on Listed Stocks**   May 4, 1984

NAME	EXERCISE TERMS	TDD.	OUTSTG 000	RECOM.	PRICES COM.	WT.
APL Corp '88	14.00 to 12-31-1988	S-O	320		10.25	1.37
Acton Corp '86	1.15 shs at 16.40/sh to 6-2-1986	A-A	387		7.75	2.00
Adams Resources & Energy '88	6.00 to 11-11-1988 F	A-O			3.37	.50
Alleghany Corp	3.75 Perpetual	S-A	42		72.37	67.00
Altex Oil Corp "A"	7.15 to 6-7-1985	A-A	1,100		1.25	.25
Altex Oil Corp "B" '84-Dec.	7.50 to 12-7-1984	A-O	1,089		1.25	.18
American Express Company	2 shs at a total of 55.00 to 2-28-1987 F	S-A	1,000		29.50	17.87
American General Corp '88	24.25 to 1-5-1989	S-S	8,800		22.87	8.12
American Science & Eng. '88	7.50 to 3-17-1988	A-O	936		3.87	.56
Angeles Corp '88	21.00 to 12-1-1988 F	A-A	748		9.37	2.12
Apache Petroleum '86	18.00 to buy 1 APC Unit to 7-15-1986	S-S	4,000		19.12	2.25
Atlas Corp	31.25 Perpetual	S-A	1,000		15.50	3.62
Audiotronics Corp '85	12.42 to 1-21-1985	A-O	350		5.37	.25
Bally Manufacturing '88	40.00 to 1-4-1988 F	S-A	860	Hold	17.75	4.75
Beker Industries '88	10.00 to 7-1-1988 SS	S-O	2,340		8.75	2.93
Beltran Corp	13.92 to 6-1-1986	A-A	208		6.87	2.12
Caesars World '85	24.50 to 8-1-1985 SS	S-O	875	Hold	12.12	1.68
Charter Company	10.00 to 9-1-1988 SS F	S-S	3,358		3.50	1.50
Collins Foods Int'l '88	27.25 to 12-15-1988 F	S-A	960		15.12	3.75
Commonwealth Oil Refining '90	5.50 to 7-24-1990	P-P			.22	.04
Conquest Exploration Co '87	5.26 to 1-15-1987 F	A-A	3,500		10.75	6.87
Consol Oil & Gas '84	30.00 to 6-30-1986 SS F	A-A		Hold	10.12	.56
Custom Energy Svc '85	.5 sh at 14.78/sh to 5-17-84; increases 0.50 each 6 mos thereafter to 11-17-1985	A-O	500		6.37	.62
Damson Oil "O"	14.715 to 3-31-1985 F	A-A	275		7.25	1.87
Digicon Inc '88	16.50 to 6-15-1988 SS	A-A	945		8.50	2.12
Diversified Industries '86	9.25 to 5-14-1986	S-P	603		5.00	1.37
Dome Petroleum '84	18.91 to 12-31-1984	A-O			3.00	.01
Eastern Airlines "A"	16.00 to 10-15-1987 SS F	S-S	5,000		5.50	1.12
Eastern Airlines June '87	10.00 to 6-1-1987	S-O	2,200		5.50	1.62
Eastern Airlines "O"	10.00 to 10-15-1987 SS F	S-S	4,500		5.50	2.87
Elect Mem & Magnetics '88	12.00 to 6-1-1988 SS F	S-O	1,453		7.37	2.00
Evaluation Research '85	4.00 to 12-12-1985	A-O	300		5.50	3.12
Evaluation Research '86	7.625 per .5 sh to 1-2-1986	A-O	1,000	Hold	5.50	.75
FPA Corp '88	12.00 to 8-15-1988 SS F	A-A	1,500		9.25	2.87
Frontier Airlines	9.15 to 3-1-1987 SS (Frontier Holding)	A-A	576		11.87	6.75
Fuqua Industries "1988"	2.290 shs at 13.50/sh to 6-30-1988 SS	S-O	592		26.12	31.00
GTI Corp '86	4.50 to 11-15-1986 F	A-O	400		4.75	2.12
GenCorp Inc '88	39.22 to 3-15-1988 F	S-O	60		29.62	10.50
General Growth Properties	21.00 to 1-4-1985	S-S	1,512		34.62	5.87
Genesco-Feb. '93	8.00 to 2-15-1993 SS F	S-O	1,486	Hold	6.00	2.00
Genesco-Oct. '93	11.75 to 10-15-1993 SS F	S-O	900		6.00	2.12
Geothermal Resources Int'l '88	.5 sh at 13.50/sh to 11-8-1988 F	A-O	300		8.87	2.50
Golden Nugget Inc '88	18.00 to 7-1-1988 SS F	S-S	15,000		10.50	3.62
Golden Nugget Inc '89	5 shs for a total of 25.00 to 7-1-1989 SS F	S-O	260		10.50	41.25
Goldfield Corp '84	1.12 to 12-31-1984	A-O	482		1.37	.50
Goldfield Corp '85	2.33 to 11-7-1985	A-O	2,264		1.37	.37
Grant Industries '86	1.22 shs at 12.06/sh to 7-31-84; 14.07 to 7-28-1986	A-A	500		8.75	1.75

Explanatory Notes—See First Page, "Green Section"

PUBLISHED WEEKLY BY R.H.M. ASSOCIATES, INC.   -785-   172 FOREST AVE., GLEN COVE, NEW YORK 11542

Copyright 1984 R.H.M. Associates $120 PER ANNUM, $68 HALF-YEAR
+Postage   +Postage

SOURCE: Page from *R.H.M. Survey of Warrants, Options and Low-Price Stocks*, May 14, 1984. Reprinted with permission.

exercise price is $31.25, but the stock is only selling for $15.50 in the market. Thus, at this point in time, the Atlas Corp. warrant has no intrinsic value.

In addition, a warrant has speculative value (i.e., premium value) due to its other characteristics. As was the case with a call option, an important feature of a

TABLE 23.6
Differences in Leverage as Shown by Stock Price/Warrant Price Ratio

			Time		
	T	T + 1	T + 2	T + 3	T + 4
Stock Price	$22	$30	$40	$50	$60
Warrant Price	$ 2	$10	$20	$30	$40
Stock Price/Warrant Price Ratio	11	3	2	1.67	1.5
Percentage Change (stock price)		36.4	33.3	25.0	20.0
Percentage Change (warrant price)		400.0	100.0	50.0	33.3

warrant is the *leverage* it provides; i.e., the value of the warrant increases and declines by larger percentages than the value of the underlying stock fluctuates. As an example, assume a stock is selling for $48, and there is a warrant for the stock with an exercise price of $50. Assume the warrant is selling for $3 based upon its speculative value. (This warrant currently has no intrinsic value because the exercise price is above the market price.) If the stock goes to $55 (a 15 percent increase), the warrant will go to *at least* $5 because this is its intrinsic value. Thus, while the stock price increased by about 15 percent (55 − 48/48), the warrant increased by *at least* 67 percent (5 − 3/3). If there were some speculative value (premium), the increase in the price of the warrant would even be larger. Note that an indication of the amount of leverage can be derived by examining the stock price/warrant price relationship (ratio). *The larger this stock price/warrant price ratio, the greater the leverage effect.* The example given in Table 23.6 assumes that the warrant has an exercise price of $20 and sells at its theoretical value over time. The example demonstrates the relationship between the stock price/warrant price ratio and the different percentage changes in stock price and warrant price.

As shown, *the greater the ratio of stock price to warrant price, the greater the leverage of the warrant in terms of the percentage change in the warrant price for a given percentage change in the stock price.* Note that this leverage works both ways; for a given *decline* in the stock price, the warrant price would decline by more. Because investors in warrants typically find this leverage factor a positive attribute, the greater the stock price/warrant price ratio, the greater the speculative value of the warrant.

A major factor determining the price of a warrant, like the price of a call option, is the *length of time to maturity* (the longer the term, the greater the value). Because of their long term to expiration, warrants will typically have value even when they are deep out of the money. For example, a warrant with an exercise price of $50 will have time value even though the stock is selling for $40. As noted, this is a major factor distinguishing warrants from call options, which are typically for less than nine months. As can be seen from Figure 23.6, warrants generally have maturities of 2–5 years, and there are some perpetual warrants.

Another important factor in warrant valuation is the volatility of the stock's price. The more volatile the stock price, the greater the probability of a positive move above the exercise price, and the greater the value of the warrant, as was true with the value of call options. One would not expect this factor to be very important in the valuation of a warrant on AT&T stock, but it could result in a large speculative value for stocks with high price volatility. A warrant would also be adversely affected by the payment of a dividend, because this is subtracted from the total value of a firm, and the warrant holder does not receive the dividend.

Once an investor has analyzed a stock and decided that it could experience an increase in value over the next several years, he should find out whether the firm has any warrants outstanding, because this might allow him to control a large amount of the stock for a fairly long period (possibly several years) for a modest investment.[11]

In summary, the main determinants of the value of a warrant are:

1. The *intrinsic value* of the warrant based upon the difference between the market price of the stock and the exercise price times the number of shares per warrant.
2. The *speculative value* of the warrant (referred to as the *premium value*), which is a function of the following factors:
    a. The potential *leverage* the warrant provides, which is a function of the ratio of the stock price/warrant price. The greater the potential leverage, the larger the premium.
    b. The *length of time to maturity.* The longer the time to maturity, the larger the premium.
    c. The *price volatility* of the underlying stock. The greater the price volatility of the stock, the larger the premium.
    d. The *dividend* paid by the stock. This is an inverse relationship; the larger the dividend, the smaller the premium.

Warrant Strategies.   For the investor who is considering investing in warrants as part of an overall program, the following considerations should be kept in mind:

1. The ultimate success of the warrant depends on *the success of the stock.* Remember that the leverage factor works both ways. Therefore, you should be bullish on the stock and consider the warrant as a means to maximize the return from this stock.
2. *Diversification* is as important with warrants as with other investments. Therefore, if you decide to get involved in warrants, you should probably consider the acquisition of a number of them if they are available on desirable stocks.
3. Given a diversified portfolio of warrants with higher leverage characteris-

[11] For a further discussion on warrant pricing, see John P. Shelton, ''The Relation of the Price of a Warrant to the Price of Its Associated Stock,'' *Financial Analysts Journal,* 23 no. 4 (July–August 1967): 88–99; E. Schwartz, ''The Valuation of Warrants: Implementing a New Approach,'' *Journal of Financial Economics,* 5 no. 1 (January 1977): 79–93; D. Galai and M. Schneller, ''Pricing of Warrants and the Value of the Firm,'' *Journal of Finance,* 33 no. 5 (December 1978): 1333–1342.

tics, it is important to *cut your losses short and let the profits run.* This strategy is used with any leveraged investment, such as options or commodities. Success involves having several *small* losses but a few *very big* winners: three warrants that provide returns in excess of 100 percent can easily compensate for five or six that lose 25–30 percent.

4. The *most desirable warrants* are generally those that have very little intrinsic value so the stock price/warrant price ratio is large and the leverage is high. In addition, you probably want a warrant with a minimum of two years remaining to maturity, preferably three or four years. Also, the more volatile the stock price, the better (i.e., a beta above 1.2). These recommendations presuppose that the warrant has the standard protective features against dilution, call, etc. The final question is whether the speculative premium is reasonable given these characteristics. This can only be determined at a point in time based upon a comparison of alternative warrants as related to the underlying stock. As stated initially, you are ultimately betting on the underlying stock.[12]

5. The search for desirable warrants can take one of two forms. The first is to simply engage in the three-step analysis process and finish with a list of good companies from desirable industries. At this point, given the stock list, check a warrant reference service like the *R.H.M. Survey* to see whether any of these stocks have outstanding warrants that have the desirable characteristics mentioned above. An alternative approach is to initially examine a number of warrants listed in a service such as R.H.M. and select several that apparently have most of the desirable characteristics mentioned above. Given this list of desirable warrants, you must analyze the issuing companies and their industries to see whether the stocks are desirable. The author's implicit preference is for the first approach that simply views warrant selection as part of the total investment process rather than as an end in itself.

CONVERTIBLE SECURITIES

A convertible security is one that gives the holder the right to convert one type of security into a stipulated amount of another type of security at the investor's discretion. Typically, but not invariably, the security is convertible into common stock, but it could be convertible into preferred stock or into a special class of common stock. The most popular convertible securities are convertible bonds and convertible preferred stock.

Convertible Bonds

A convertible bond is usually a subordinated[13] fixed-income security that can be converted into a stated number of shares of common stock of the company that

---

[12] For an analysis of warrant hedging, see Moon K. Kim and Allan Young, "Rewards and Risks from Warrant Hedging," *Journal of Portfolio Management,* 6 no. 4 (Summer 1980): 65–68.

[13] Subordinated means that the claims of the bondholders are junior to the claims of other debenture holders in terms of interest and claims on assets of the firm in the event of default.

issued the bond. The initial conversion price is generally above the current price of the common stock. Assume a company's common stock is selling for $36 a share. The company might decide to sell a subordinated convertible bond that matures in 20 years and is convertible into common stock at $40 a share. If the bonds are $1,000 par value, this would mean the bond is convertible into 25 shares of common stock ($1,000 ÷ $40). Because convertible bonds are generally considered to be an attractive investment (for reasons to be discussed), the interest rate on them is typically below the required return on the firm's straight debentures. In this case, assume an 8 percent coupon.

Advantages to Issuing Firms. Issuing convertible bonds is considered desirable for a company for several reasons. First, as stated, the interest cost is lower than it is on straight debt, and the extent of the saving on interest depends upon the growth prospects of the firm. In most cases, it is a minimum of one-half percent (50 basis points) and can be much higher. This differential in interest cost exists even though convertible bonds are riskier than straight debentures are because they are subordinated. The subordination feature has led bond rating agencies to consistently rate subordinated issues one class lower than a firm's straight debentures.[14] Therefore, the interest rate savings over a comparably rated bond are even more than the 50–100 basis points suggested.

Another advantage is that these bonds are potential common stock. The bondholder may decide to convert on his own, or the firm will make it possible to force conversion in the future by including a call feature on the bonds. This "future common" feature may be desirable for a firm that currently needs equity for an investment but does not want to issue common stock directly because of the potential dilution before the investment begins generating earnings. After the investment generates earnings, the stock price should rise above the conversion value, and the firm can force conversion by calling the bond. To understand how a firm forces conversion, consider the example of the bond convertible into stock at $40 a share (25 shares of common stock). Assume that the bond is callable at 108 percent of par ($1,080), and two years after the issue was sold, the common stock had gone from $36 to $45 a share because earnings have risen. Given the conversion feature, the bond has a *minimum* market value of $1,125 (25 × $45). At this point, if the firm decides that it wants to get the convertible bond off the balance sheet, it would simply issue a call for the bonds at 108 ($1,080). All the bondholders should convert their bonds because the stock they would receive in exchange is worth $1,125.

Advantages to Investor. We have mentioned that convertible bonds have special features that cause them to have coupon rates substantially below what you would expect on the basis of the quality of the issue. The reason for this lower rate is that there are significant advantages to investing in convertible bonds. Specifically, *they provide the upside potential of common stock and the downside protection of a bond.* The upside potential can be seen from the example above. The bond is convertible into 25 shares of common stock, so, as

[14] See George E. Pinches and Kent A. Mingo, "A Multivariate Analysis of Industrial Bond Ratings," *Journal of Finance,* 28 no. 1 (March 1973): 1–18.

soon as the price of the common stock exceeds $40 a share, the price of the bond should move in concert with the price of the common stock because the bond has intrinsic value (conversion value) above its par value.[15] At this point, as long as the stock goes up in value, the price of the bond will increase by *at least* the increase in conversion value. In most cases, the bond price will be above its conversion value because it offers downside protection, and the interest payments on the bond may exceed the dividend payments for the potential common stock (as will be explained shortly).

The convertible bond has downside protection because, regardless of what happens to the stock, the price of the bond will not decline below what it would be worth as a straight bond. To continue our example, assume that this 8 percent subordinated bond is rated A by the rating services. (The company's regular debentures are rated AA.) Also assume that the firm's earnings decline so that the price of common stock declines to $25 a share. At this point, the bond has a conversion value of $625 (25 × $25). Would you expect the bond to decline to $625? The answer is probably no because it still has value as a bond. (This is an example of what is sometimes referred to as a bond's *investment value.*) The bond is an A-rated security with an 8 percent coupon. If we assume that this is an 18-year bond and comparable A-rated bonds are currently selling to yield 9 percent, the price of this bond will decline below par but will *not* decline to $625. In this case, the price will decline to about $938.80 (0.9388 of par.)[16] While the stock price declined about 30 percent (from $36 to $25), the bond price would only decline about 6 percent (from $1,000 to $938.80).

In addition to the upside potential-downside protection they offer, convertible bonds are also desirable because they typically have *higher current returns than common stock does.* Assume that the stock had an annual dividend of $1.50 a share. This would be a 3.75 percent yield on a $40 stock or 4.17 percent on a $36 stock, which is reasonable. Still, the total current income from the potential common shares would be less than what the investor would get from the bond. Total dividends on the 25 shares of stock would be $37.50 a year (25 × $1.50), compared to the interest income of $80 a year from the bond (.08 × $1,000). Obviously, the bond would be preferable until the dividend on the stock was raised to $3.20 a share ($80 ÷ 25). Even then, the bond would probably be preferred because it offers downside protection and because the $80 interest is contractual, while the $80 dividend could be reduced if earnings decline. Therefore, you would probably wait until the common stock dividend reached $3.50 or $4.00 a share before you would convert to take advantage of the higher yield.

An advantage of convertible bonds that has been lost is the potential for leverage on them. Prior to the 1970s, investors could borrow on convertible bonds at about the same rate that they could borrow on straight debentures (about 80 percent). This made it possible to invest in convertibles with little cash and use the interest on the bond to partially offset the interest on the loan. Currently, the margin on convertible bonds is the same as the margin on common stock.

---

[15] The conversion value is equal to the bond's conversion ratio (25 in this example) times the current market price of the stock.

[16] This is the price of an 18-year, 8 percent coupon bond priced to yield 9 percent.

Convertible bonds are, therefore, a desirable investment alternative because they offer upside potential, downside protection, and, typically, higher current income than common stocks offer. This yield advantage is especially true for issues of growth companies that pay low dividends and have substantial potential for price increases. In such cases, institutional investors are willing to accept substantially lower interest on a convertible bond than they accept on straight bonds.

Analysis of Convertible Bonds

Because a convertible bond is actually a hybrid of a bond and common stock, it is necessary to consider both aspects of the security. Specifically, the first part of a valuation analysis should consider the issue as a straight bond; i.e., what should be the yield and implied price of the bond if it were *not* a convertible security? This analysis will indicate your downside risk if the stock declined to the point where the security *only* had value as a straight bond.

As an example, consider the 5 1/2 percent convertible bonds issued by Caterpillar Tractor Company due in 2000. These bonds are A-rated by Standard & Poor's and are convertible into 19.8 shares of common stock until maturity. In terms of the straight bond, it would be necessary to determine what the present going rate would be on an A-rated bond with about 14 years to maturity. If the current yield to maturity on such bonds were about 12 percent, this would imply a straight bond price of approximately $541 (the present value of this bond at 12 percent). You should compare this bond value price to the current market price of the bond to determine the price risk of the bond. If we assume the bond is currently selling for 104 of par based upon its conversion value (which we will discuss shortly), this would imply a 48 percent price risk (1040 − 541/1040). An obvious question you must ask is whether you are willing to accept this much downside risk.

The second part of the analysis is concerned with an evaluation of the bond in terms of its *stock* value, i.e., what is its upside potential due to the conversion factor? This requires that you consider the conversion terms and the conversion parity of the bond compared to the current market price of the stock. The conversion terms indicate how many shares you would receive if you converted the bond into common stock. In the Caterpillar Tractor example, the conversion terms specify that each $1,000 bond can be converted into 19.80 shares of stock. Given this information, you can compute *the conversion parity price of the bond, which is equal to the purchase price of the convertible bond divided by the number of common shares into which it is convertible.* Assuming that the Caterpillar convertible bonds were selling for 95, this would imply a conversion parity price of $47.98 ($950 ÷ 19.8). You should compare this conversion parity price to the current market price of the common stock to determine how much the common stock must increase before the bond must increase. In the case of Caterpillar, assume that when the bond was selling for 95 and had a conversion parity price of $47.98, the common stock was selling for $41 on the NYSE. This indicates a parity price premium over market price of 17 percent. Put another way, the common stock price has to increase 17 percent before the bond price would be justified in terms of its conversion value. Obviously, *the smaller this parity price premium, the more desirable is the bond.*

Beyond considering the current position, you should estimate the future *potential* for the common stock. What do you expect the Caterpillar common stock to sell for during your investment horizon period? If you expect the stock to go to $60 a share, your upside potential is approximately 25 percent. Specifically, if the stock goes to $60 a share, the bond will sell for *at least* $1,188 ($60 × 19.8), which is a 25 percent increase from $950.

Finally, you should consider the differential income from holding the stock compared to the bond. The bond has a 5 1/2 percent coupon which indicates $55 a year interest and a current yield of 5.8 percent at the price of 95 ($55/950). In contrast, the stock is paying a dividend of $2.00 per share, which is a 4.9 percent dividend and indicates a total dividend payment on the 19.8 shares of $39.60. Therefore, at this time, the current income from the bond exceeds the current income from the potential stock.

In summary, the analysis indicates the following characteristics of this bond. First, there is a fairly *large downside risk* on the bond as a straight bond because of its low coupon while interest rates are high. Alternatively, there is a *small premium* of conversion parity price compared to the market price. This means that a reasonable increase in the common stock will be reflected in the price of the convertible bond. Note that you expect about a 25 percent increase in the value of the bond during your investment period. Finally, the yield on the bonds exceeds the dividend yield on the stock. At this point, the investor must decide whether the purchase of the bond is an appropriate way to take advantage of the outlook for the stock. One obvious consideration is the comparative returns on the two alternatives during your investment period. Let us assume this is one year. As stated, the current stock price is $41 and you expect it to go to $60. This information along with the dividend of $2.00 a share implies the following return on the stock:

$$R_{i,t} = \frac{EP - BP + Div}{BP}$$

$$= \frac{60.00 - 41.00 + 2.00}{41.00}$$

$$= \frac{21.00}{51.00}$$

$$= 41.18\%$$

where:

$R_{i,t}$ = the rate of return on security i during period t

EP = ending price

BP = beginning price

Div = dividend paid during the period.

If the stock goes to $60, the conversion value of the bond will be $1,188, and this information, along with the interest of $55, implies the following return on the convertible bond as a minimum:

$$R_{i,t} = \frac{1188 - 950 + 55}{950}$$

$$= \frac{293}{950}$$

$$= 30.84\%$$

As stated, this is a minimum because it assumes that the convertible bond will sell only at its conversion value without a premium. If it maintained its 3 percent premium, it would sell for about $1,224, and the rate of return would be 34.63 percent:

$$R_{i,t} = \frac{1224 - 950 + 55}{950}$$

$$= \frac{329}{950}$$

$$= 34.63\%$$

In this case, it appears that the obvious choice on the basis of the expected returns alone is the common stock. The bond might be considered to have somewhat less downside risk because of the higher yield, but this is not obvious given the low straight-bond value for the security. Note that the reason the straight stock does better for the given increase in the stock price is that the bond has a parity price premium of 17 percent. As discussed, the smaller this is, the better for the investor.

Sources of Information.   A rather complete list of convertible bonds and information regarding these bonds is contained in the convertible bond section of the *Standard & Poor's Bond Guide*. A sample page is contained in Figure 23.7. Another source is *Moody's Bond Record,* which contains a section with information on convertible bonds similar to the one in the *Bond Guide*. A service that provides analysis beyond the statistical information is the *Value Line Options and Convertibles.* This service indicates whether it believes the bond is under- or overvalued and the expected impact on the bond of various changes in the underlying stock, i.e., its upside potential and downside protection.

CONVERTIBLE PREFERRED STOCK

Convertible preferred stock is similar to convertible bonds in that it is a combination of a preferred stock issue and common stock. Beyond the conversion privileges, these issues typically have the following characteristics:
1.   They are cumulative but not participating (i.e., the dividend cumulates if it is not paid, but the holders do not participate in earnings beyond the dividend).

FIGURE 23.7
Sample Page: Standard & Poor's *Bond Guide*

STANDARD & POOR'S CORPORATION

XVI CONVERTIBLE BONDS

Issue, Rate, Interest Dates and Maturity	S&P Quality Rating	Form	Outstdg. Mil.-$	Conv. Expires	Shares per $1,000 Bond	Price per Share	Div. Income per Bond	1984 RANGE Hi	Lo	Curr Bid Sale(s)	Ask(A)	Curr. Return	Yield to Mat	Stock Value of Bond	Conv. Parity	STOCK DATA Curr. Price	P/E Ratio	Yr. End	Earns 1982	1983	Last 12 Mos	1982 Dil.
●White Consol Ind ... 5⅞s ¹ao 1992	BBB	R	3.65	1992	38.87	25.73	58.31	165	132	136	136	4.04	1.11	136	35	·35		11 Dc	2.10	P3.23	3.23	*3.20
●Whittaker Corp ... 4½s iJ 1988	B+	R	4.42	1988	31.28	47.00	34.05	78½	74½	^79	79	5.70	10.6	42¼	37½	·19⅜	6	Oc	3.77	2.55	3.28	n/r
²Wickes³ ... 5¼s iJ 1994	D		11.7	1994	23.12	43.26		54½	53	54½	54	....	Flat	11%	23¾	4.937	d	Ja	d11.9	□d0.22	d0.22	n/r
²Wickes³ ... 9s 1999	D		19.1	1999	46.38	21.56		54½	53	54	54	....	Flat	22%	46½	4.937	d	Ja	d11.9		d0.22	n/r
●Will Ross ... 4⅞s mS 1987	A+	R	3.40	1987	532.22	531.04	16.75	149½	132½	148%	148%	2.86	11.9	148%	46½	·46%	24	Dc	2.77	△1.93	1.93	n/r
●Will Ross ... 5¼s fA 1989	A+	R	11.4	1989	522.75	543.96	11.83	107	102	104%	103	5.01	4.23	104%	46%	·46%	24	Dc	2.77	△1.93	1.93	n/r
●Will Ross ... 4¼s mS 1992	A+	R	21.8	1992	521.82	545.83	11.35	104	98¼	100%	103	4.37	4.07	100%	47%	·46%	24	Dc	2.77	△1.93	1.93	n/r
●Williams Electr ... 12¾s mN 1996	B-	R	22.0	1996	49.58	20.17	13.96	93	81¾	83	83	15.3	15.9	28½	16%	*5%	36	Sp	*2.12	1.31	△0.16	*1.28
◆Wilshire Oil Tex. ... 6s mN 1995	NR	R	1.40	1995	174.52	5.73	9.52	No Sale		170%	170%	3.53	3.53	170%	9%	·9%	30	Dc	p0.25		⁹0.32	0.24
◆Wilson (H.J.) ... 10½s Mn15 2002	BB-	R	20.0	2002	47.62	21.00		101	89¼	89	89	11.8	11.9	60%	18%	12%	20	Ja	0.72		³¹0.62	n/r
Winn Enterprises⁶ ... 8s Ms15 1990	NR	R	6.99	1990	68.17	14.67		64	57½	57%	57%	13.9	20.6	39%	8%	5%	17	Mr	¹²d0.66	¹²d0.43		n/r
●Winners Corp ... 8⅛s iJd 2003	B-	R	25.0	2003	56.34	22.75		100	79	79	79	10.4	10.8	64%	11%	11%	17	Dc	d0.74	▲0.74	P0.65	*0.63
●Witco Chemical ... 4¼s iD15 1993	A-	R	9.46	1993	45.00	22.22	59.40	174	145	141%	88	3.17	13.8	141%	31½	·45%	9	Dc	2.10	P3.60	3.60	*3.47
●Work Wear ... 4¾s mS 1985	NR	R	1.00	1985	⁹183.82	983.82	24.46	91%	90%	88	88	5.40		53%	73¾	·45%	10	Sp	3.43	4.51	4.64	n/r
●Wyle Laboratories ... 5¾s iA 1988	NR	R	9.28	1988	68.68	14.56	16.48	167%	119½	§119%	§119%	4.39		119%	17%	·17%	17	Ja	d0.44	P1.05	1.05	n/r
●Wyly Corp¹⁰ ... 7¾s Ms15 1995	B-	R	13.2	1995	5.52	181.00		62%	60	60	60	12.0	14.6	5	108%	·9%	9	Dc	△d0.04	P0.01	0.01	n/r
●Xerox Corp¹¹ ... 5s AnDc 1988	C	R	73.6	1988	6.76	148.00	20.28	80	78	78	78	6.41	11.0	27¼	67¾	·41%	9	Dc	4.47	P4.42	4.42	n/r
●Xerox Corp ... 6s mN 1995	A+	R	129	1995	10.87	92.00	32.61	76½	71%	s73¾	73¾	8.19	9.92	44¼	23%	·41%	10	Ja	△4.47	P4.42	4.42	n/r
●Zurn Indus ... 5⅞s mN 1994	BBB	R	12.4	1994	35.09	28.50	46.32	104	83	83	83	6.93	8.16	81%	23%	·23%	10	Mr	3.46	P3.46		3.24

Uniform Footnote Explanations—See Page XVI.   Other: ¹Due Oct 23.   ²Filed Bankruptcy Chap 11.   ³Default 5-1-82 int.   ⁴Subsid of & data of Searle (G.D.) & Co.   ⁵Cv into Searle (G.D.).
⁶Was Lincoln Mtg. then Builders Investment Gr.   ⁷Fiscal Sep. '82&prior.   ⁸Assumed by & data of ARA Services.   ⁹Paid int arrears 4-3-78.   ¹¹Offered outside U.S.:P&I pay in U.S.$.

EXPLANATION OF COLUMN HEADINGS AND FOOTNOTES

MARKET: Unlisted except where symbols ● or ◆ are used:
●-New York Stock Exchange ◆-American Stock Exchange
ISSUE TITLE: Name of Bond at time of offering; otherwise issue footnoted with name change of obligor. Minor changes with old title indicated in brackets, i.e. Gen Tel (Corp) & Elec.
#-Prin & int payable in U.S. funds. §Int. and/or prin. in default.
FORM OF BOND: Letters are used to indicate form of bond: C-Coupon only; CR-Coupon or Registered, interchangeable; R-Registered only.
CONVERSION EXPIRES: Footnote keyed to bottom of page when conversion price changes during life of the privilege; also noted on conversion price. ⊕Indicates a change in next 12 months.   a-No fractional shs. issued upon conversion; settlements in cash.
DIVIDEND INCOME PER BOND: If $1,000 Bond were converted, the annual amount of dividends expected to be paid by the company on the stock based on most recent indication of annual rate of payment.
‡-Less than annual rate at origin.   g-In Canadian funds less 15% or 10% non-residence tax.
STOCK VALUE OF BOND: Price at which bond must sell to equal price of stock i.e. number of shares received on conversion times price of the stock.
CONVERSION PARITY: Price at which stock must sell to equal bond price, i.e. price of bond divided by number of shares received on conversion.

P-E RATIO: (Price-Earnings Ratio) Represents market valuation of any $1 of per share earnings i.e., the price of the stock divided by estimated or latest 12 months per share earnings.
EARNINGS, in general, are per share as reported by company. **FOR YEAR INDICATED:** Fiscal years ending prior to March 31 are shown under preceding year. Net operating earnings are shown for banks; net earnings before appropriation to general reserve for savings & loan associations; net investment income for insurance companies; railroads' earnings are reported to ICC. Foreign issues traded ADR are dollars per share, converted at prevailing exchange rate. Specific footnotes used:

△Excl extra-ord income	j-Currency at origin
▲Incl extra-ord income	P-Preliminary
□Excl extra-ord charges	p-Pro forma
■Incl extra-ord charges	b-Before depletion
●Excl tax credits	d-Deficit
‡-Partial Year	E-S&P Estimate
*-New Year Earns	R-Fully diluted
	r/r-Not reported

LAST 12 Mos. indicates earnings through period indicated by superior number preceding figure: for Jan. for Feb., etc. Figure without superior number indicates fiscal year end.
DILUTION: Earnings on a fully diluted basis, as reported in accordance with Accounting Principles Board opinions.

SOURCE: Standard and Poor's Corporation March, 1984. Reprinted with permission.

2. They have no sinking fund or purchase fund.
3. They have fixed conversion rates.
4. There is generally no waiting period before conversion can take place.
5. The conversion privilege does not expire.[17]

As Pinches pointed out, most convertible preferred stock was issued in connection with mergers as a way of providing income and yet not diluting the common equity of the acquiring firm.

Although preferred stock and convertible preferred stock have not been a major source of new financing, there are a number of convertible preferred issues outstanding for the interested investor.

Analysis of Convertible Preferred Stock

Because convertible preferred stock is likewise a hybrid security involving preferred stock and common stock, the valuation analysis, like that of a convertible bond, involves two steps. As an example, consider the FMC Corporation convertible preferred stock issue. This particular cumulative preferred stock issue pays an annual dividend of $2.25 a share. The stock is rated BBB, is listed on the NYSE, and is convertible into 1.25 shares of common stock. As of mid-1984, the common stock was selling for $45 a share and the $2.25 convertible preferred stock was $57 a share.

In terms of a pure preferred stock issue, it would appear to have a fair amount of downside risk. At this time, most straight preferred stock issues were yielding between 10 and 12 percent compared to the yield on the FMC Corp. stock of 3.9 percent. Even using the conservative 10 percent would indicate a straight preferred stock price of $22.50 ($2.25/.10). This represents about a 60 percent decline from the prevailing market price of 57. Obviously, the stock is selling on the basis of its conversion value, which is $56.25 (1.25 × $45).

As for the convertible preferred stock, you can derive a conversion parity value for the stock by dividing the current market price of the preferred stock by the conversion ratio. In this case, the conversion parity is $45.60 ($57/1.25). This indicates a very small difference from the prevailing common stock price of $46. Put another way, the convertible preferred stock is priced almost exactly in terms of its conversion value, which means the convertible preferred stock price will move almost exactly in line with the common stock price.

Given this price relationship, you should examine the income relationship between the common and preferred stock. The common stock was paying an annual dividend of $1.80 a share, which indicates a dividend yield of 4 percent (1.80/45.00). The convertible preferred stock pays an annual dividend of $2.25, which indicates a 3.9 percent yield.

This would indicate that the convertible preferred stock has almost the same downside risk and upside potential as the common stock because it is selling for almost exactly its conversion value, which is substantially above its pure preferred stock value. Similarly, the current yield on the convertible preferred stock is almost equal to the yield on the common stock.

[17] George E. Pinches, "Financing With Convertible Preferred Stock, 1960–1967," *Journal of Finance*, 25 no. 1 (March 1970): 25–36.

SUMMARY

This chapter considered three sets of investments that provide substantial opportunities to an investor beyond what is normally available with only stocks and bonds. Options, warrants, and convertible securities provide an expanded universe of risk and return alternatives.

Our discussion of options began with the recent history of options trading, starting with the establishment of the Chicago Board Options Exchange (CBOE) in April 1973. We reviewed the reasons for the growth and expansion of this market segment, and we discussed the growing competition between exchanges dealing in options. The basic terminology for options and quotations was explained, and we discussed alternative trading strategies, including the purchase and sale of call options under different market conditions, the use of call spreads under various market expectations, and the purchase or sale of put options.

A section on the valuation of call options dealt with major variables that influence the value of a call option. It discussed the direction of the effect and demonstrated the application of a valuation model. This section concluded by studying the efficiency of the options market and the returns and risks involved in option investing. The options market was apparently not completely efficient when first established, but there are indications that this has changed. Recent studies on the return from and risk of selling covered options consistently indicated that returns and risks were lower with options than with pure stock investing; they also emphasized the importance of being able to estimate the variance of the underlying stock.

Subsequently, warrants were described and their major similarities and differences were contrasted with call options. We also discussed factors that influence the valuation of these instruments.

Two types of hybrid securities were considered: convertible bonds and convertible preferred stock. We detailed the advantages of these securities to the issuing corporation and the investor, then we examined the valuation analysis procedure which evaluates both components of these securities: the value of the security as a straight bond or preferred stock, and its conversion value, i.e., its common stock value.

All of these investment instruments provide *additional* opportunities for you *after* you have already evaluated a firm and decided to invest in it. Following such a decision, the question becomes: *how* should I invest in this firm? Clearly, if options, warrants, or convertible securities are available, they should be considered.

QUESTIONS

1. Define a call option; define a put option.
2. How is the CBOE different from the original over-the-counter option market? Discuss the major factors that differentiate them.
3. What are the factors that motivate an exchange to begin trading in an option? Are you surprised that the ASE began to compete with the CBOE on certain options? Why or why not?

4. Define the following terms:
   a. Premium
   b. Exercise price
   c. Expiration date
   d. In the money option
   e. At the money option
   f. Out of the money option.

5. Differentiate between selling a fully covered call and a naked call. Give an example of why the sale of an uncovered call is much riskier.

6. There are five variables that you need to estimate the value of a call option. List and discuss each of them. Indicate *why* each is important and how it influences the value; e.g., when this value increases it causes an increase in the value of the option because. . . .

7. It has been contended that the sale of a fully covered option is a *conservative* investment strategy. Explain why this is so in terms of the possible distribution of returns from such a strategy. Use an example if it will help.

8. Assume you are bullish on the outlook for the stock market. Look up a four- to six-month option that is at the money in *The Wall Street Journal.* Assume the stock increases by 15 percent. Indicate approximately what will happen to your option and compute the percentage return on the option purchase.

9. Describe a time spread and a price spread. Why do investors engage in spreads? Is the risk higher or lower than that for simply writing a call option?

10. Pick out a stock option on the CBOE and discuss what you would do to write a *bullish* price spread.
    a. Describe what will happen if the stock price increases by 20 percent.
    b. Describe what will happen if the stock declines by 20 percent.

11. Select an option listed on the ASE and discuss how you would enter into a price spread assuming you were *bearish* on the stock.
    a. Describe what will happen if the stock price increases by 25 percent.
    b. Describe what will happen if the stock price declines by 30 percent.

12. Assume that you are generally bearish on common stocks so you buy a TBR Corp. six-month put at 50 when the stock is 52. The put contract costs you $200. TBR stock subsequently goes to 55. What is your rate of return? What if TBR stock went to 45?

13. Assume that you want to buy Westman Camera (WC), but think that its current level of 51 is somewhat overpriced. Currently a six-month WC 50 put is selling for $3. Describe how you would use this put to accomplish your goal of buying WC if the stock declined to 45. What would happen if you sold a put and the stock rose to 54?

14. According to the Galai study, how do you test for the efficiency of the options market? Why would this test be considered a semistrong test? Explain.

15. What are two major differences between a warrant and a call option?

16. What advantage does a warrant have over a listed call option from the standpoint of a corporation?

17. What advantage does a warrant have compared to a listed call option for an investor?

18. Define the intrinsic value of a warrant. Give an example of a warrant with positive intrinsic value.

19. Discuss briefly three factors that influence the speculative value of a warrant (i.e., the premium over intrinsic value).

20. As an investor, would you want a high or low stock price/warrant price ratio? Explain why.

21. The Raymond Corporation has a warrant outstanding that allows the holder to acquire two shares of common stock at $15 a share for the next three years. The stock is currently selling for $12 and the warrant is selling for $2.
    a. Compute the intrinsic value of the warrant. What difference does it make that the warrant is for two shares?
    b. Compute the speculative value (premium) of this warrant.
    c. Would you expect the premium to be greater if the stock was selling for $14? Why?

22. The Carson City Corporation (3C) has a warrant that allows the holder to acquire a share of stock for $30 until 1990. The stock is currently selling for $32 and the warrant is selling for $2.
    a. Compute the intrinsic value and the speculative value of this warrant.
    b. What is the leverage factor for this warrant?
    c. Assume the stock increases to $40 a share. What will be the percentage of change in stock price and in warrant price assuming the same premium on the warrant?
    d. Discuss how the answer in Part c relates to your answer to Part b.

23. Find a warrant listed on the American Stock Exchange. (There will be a *wt* after the name.)
    a. From one of several sources determine its exercise terms (price and expiration).
    b. Determine the warrant's intrinsic value and speculative value.
    c. What are its leverage characteristics?

24. Describe how a firm forces conversion of a convertible bond. What conditions must exist?

25. The Baron Corporation debentures are rated Aa by Moody's and are selling to yield 8.75 percent. Their subordinated convertible bonds are rated A by Moody's and are selling to yield 8.40 percent. Explain why this is so.

26. Describe the upside potential of convertible bonds. Why do convertible bonds also provide downside protection?

27. Assume a convertible bond's conversion value is substantially above par. Why would the bondholder continue holding the bond rather than converting?

28. The University Football Corporation (UFC) has outstanding a 6 percent subordinated convertible debenture due in 10 years. The current yield to maturity on this bond, which is rated A, is 5 percent. The current yield on nonconvertible, A-rated bonds is 10 percent. This bond is convertible into 21 shares of common stock and callable at 106 of par, which is $1,000. The company's $10 par-value common stock is currently selling for $54.
    a. What is the straight-debt value of the convertible bond assuming semi-annual interest payments?
    b. What is the conversion value of this bond?
    c. At present, what would you expect the approximate price of the bond to be? Why?
    d. At the present time, could UFC get rid of this convertible debenture? Discuss *specifically* how they would do it.

REFERENCES

Options — Articles and Pamphlets

Are Call Options For You? Chicago: Chicago Board Options Exchange, 1977.

Ball, Clifford, and Walter N. Torous. "The Maximum Likelihood Estimation of Security Price Volatility: Theory, Evidence, and Application to Option Pricing." *Journal of Business.* 57 no. 1 part 1 (January 1984).

Black, Fischer. "Fact and Fantasy in the Use of Options." *Financial Analysts Journal.* 31 no. 4 (July–August 1975).

Black, Fischer, and Myron Scholes. "The Pricing of Options and Corporate Liabilities." *Journal of Political Economy.* 81 no. 2 (May–June 1973).

Black, Fischer, and Myron Scholes. "The Valuation of Option Contracts and a Test of Market Efficiency." *Journal of Finance.* 27 no. 2 (May 1972).

Boness, A. J. "Elements of a Theory of Stock Option Value." *Journal of Political Economy.* 72 no. 2 (April 1964).

Bookstaber, Richard, and Roger Clarke. "Options Can Alter Portfolio Return Distributions." *Journal of Portfolio Management.* 7 no. 3 (Spring 1981).

Boyle, Phelim, and A. I. Ananthanarayanan. "The Impact of Variance Estimation in Option Valuation Models." *Journal of Financial Economics.* 5 no. 3 (December 1977).

Brody, Eugene D. "Options and Mathematics of Defense." *Journal of Portfolio Management.* 1 no. 2 (Winter 1975).

Buying Puts, Straddles and Combinations. Chicago: Chicago Board Options Exchange, 1980.

Chiras, D. P., and S. Manaster. "The Information Content of Option Prices and a Test of Market Efficiency." *Journal of Financial Economics.* 5 no. 2/3 (June–September 1978).

Cox, J. C., S. A. Ross, and M. Rubinstein. "Option Pricing: A Simplified Approach." *Journal of Financial Economics.* 6 no. 3 (September 1979).

Cox, John C., and Stephen A. Ross. "The Valuation of Options for Alternative Stochastic Processes." *Journal of Financial Economics.* 3 no. 1/2 (January–March 1976).

Dawson, Frederic S. "Risks and Returns in Continuous Option Writing." *Journal of Portfolio Management.* 5 no. 2 (Winter 1979).

Finnerty, Joseph. "The Chicago Board Options Exchange and Market Efficiency." *Journal of Financial and Quantitative Analysis.* 13 no. 1 (March 1978).

Frankfurter, George M., Richard Stevenson, and Allan Young. "Options Spreading: Theory and an Illustration." *Journal of Portfolio Management.* 5 no. 4 (Summer 1979).

Galai, Dan. "Tests of Market Efficiency of the Chicago Board Options Exchange." *Journal of Business.* 50 no. 2 (April 1977).

Galai, Dan, and Ronald W. Masulis. "The Option Pricing Model and the Risk Factor of Stock." *Journal of Financial Economics.* 3 no. 2 (June 1976).

Geske, Robert. "The Valuation of Compound Options." *Journal of Financial Economics.* 7 no. 1 (March 1979).

Gombola, M. J., R. Roenfeldt, and P. L. Cooley. "Spreading Strategies in CBOE Options: Evidence on Market Performance." *Journal of Financial Research.* 1 no. 1 (Winter 1978).

Gould, J. P., and D. Galai. "Transaction Costs and the Relationship between Put and Call Prices." *Journal of Financial Economics.* 1 no. 2 (July 1974).

Grube, R. Corwin, Don B. Panton, and J. Michael Terrel. "Risks and Rewards in Covered Call Positions." *Journal of Portfolio Management.* 5 no. 2 (Winter 1979).

Hettenhouse, George W., and Donald Puglisi. "Investor Experience with Put and Call Options." *Financial Analysts Journal.* 31 no. 4 (July–August 1975).

Hsia, Chi-Chang. "On Binomial Option Pricing." *Journal of Financial Research.* 6 no. 1 (Spring 1983).

Kalay, Avner, and M. G. Subrahmanyam. "The Maximum Likelihood Estimation of Security Price Volatility: Theory, Evidence, and Application to Option Pricing." *Journal of Business.* 57 no. 1, part 1 (January 1984).

Klemkosky, Robert C. "The Impact of Option Expirations on Stock Prices." *Journal of Financial and Quantitative Analysis.* 8 no. 3 (September 1978).

Klemkosky, R., and B. Resnick. "Put-Call Parity and Market Efficiency." *Journal of Finance.* 34 no. 5 (December 1979).

Klemkosky, Robert C., and T. Maness. "The Impact of Options on Underlying Securities." *Journal of Portfolio Management.* 6 no. 2 (Winter 1980).

Latane, Henry A., and Richard J. Rendleman, Jr. "Standard Deviation of Stock Price Ratios Implied in Option Prices." *Journal of Finance.* 31 no. 2 (May 1976).

Macbeth, J., and L. J. Merville. "An Empirical Examination of the Black–Scholes Call Option Pricing Model." *Journal of Finance.* 34 no. 5 (December 1979).

Macbeth, J., and L. J. Merville. "Tests of the Black–Scholes and Cox Call Option Valuation Models." *Journal of Finance.* 35 no. 2 (May 1980).

Merton, Robert C. "The Relationship between Put and Call Option Prices: Comment." *Journal of Finance.* 28 no. 1 (March 1973).

Merton, Robert C. "The Impact on Option Pricing of Specification Error when the Underlying Stock Returns Are Discontinuous." *Journal of Financial Economics.* 3 no. 1/3 (January/March 1976).

Merton, Robert C. "The Theory of Rational Option Pricing." *Bell Journal of Economics and Management Science.* 4 no. 3 (August 1973).

Merton, Robert C., Myron S. Scholes and Mathew I. Gladstein. "A Simulation of the Returns and Risk of Alternative Option Portfolio Investment Strategies." *Journal of Business.* 51 no. 2 (April 1978).

754

O'Brien, Thomas, and William Kennedy. "Simultaneous Option and Stock Prices: Another Look at the Black–Scholes Model." *The Financial Review.* 17 no. 4 (November 1982).

Option Spreading. Chicago: Chicago Board Options Exchange, 1982.

Option Writing Strategies. Chicago: Chicago Board Options Exchange, 1982.

Parkinson, Michael. "Option Pricing: The American Put." *Journal of Business.* 50 no. 1 (January 1977).

Pounds, Henry M. "Covered Call Option Writing: Strategies and Results." *Journal of Portfolio Management.* 4 no. 2 (Winter 1978).

Pozen, Robert C. "The Purchase of Protective Puts by Financial Institutions." *Financial Analysts Journal.* 34 no. 4 (July–August 1978).

Puglisi, Donald J. "Rationale for Option Buying Behavior: Theory and Evidence." *Quarterly Review of Economics and Business.* 14 no. 1 (Spring 1974).

Reback, Robert. "Risk and Return in CBOE and AMEX Option Trading." *Financial Analysts Journal.* 31 no. 4 (July–August 1975).

Rendleman, Richard J., Jr. "Optimal Long-Run Option Investment Strategies." *Financial Management.* 10 no. 1 (Spring 1981).

Rogalski, Richard J. "Variances in Option Prices in Theory and Practice." *Journal of Portfolio Management.* 4 no. 2 (Winter 1978).

Roll, Richard. "An Analytic Valuation Formula for Unprotected American Call Options on Stocks with Known Dividends." *Journal of Financial Economics.* 4 no. 4 (November 1977).

Ross, Stephen. "Options and Efficiency." *Quarterly Journal of Economics.* 41 no. 1 (February 1976).

Rubinstein, Mark. "The Valuation of Uncertain Income Streams and the Pricing of Options." *Bell Journal of Economics and Management Science.* 7 no. 3 (August 1976).

Rubinstein, Mark. "Displaced Diffusion Option Pricing." *Journal of Finance.* 38 no. 1 (March 1983).

Schmalensee, Richard, and Robert R. Trippi. "Common Stock Volatility Expectations Implied by Option Premia." *Journal of Finance.* 33 no. 1 (March 1978).

Scholes, Myron. "Taxes and the Pricing of Options." *Journal of Finance.* 31 no. 2 (May 1976).

Slivka, Ronald T. "Call Option Spreading." *Journal of Portfolio Management.* 7 no. 3 (Spring 1981).

Smith, Clifford W., Jr. "Option Pricing: A Review." *Journal of Financial Economics.* 3 no. 1/2 (January–March 1976).

Sterk, William E. "Test of Two Models for Valuing Call Options on Stocks with Dividends." *Journal of Finance.* 37 no. 5 (December 1982).

Stoll, Hans R. "The Relationship between Put and Call Option Prices." *Journal of Finance.* 24 no. 5 (December 1969).

Tax Considerations in Using CBOE Options. Chicago: Chicago Board Options Exchange, 1982.

Understanding Options. Chicago: Chicago Board Options Exchange, 1982.

Weinstein Mark I. "Bond Systematic Risk and the Option Pricing Model." *Journal of Finance.* 38 no. 5 (December 1983).

Options — Books

Auster, Rolf. *Option Writing and Hedging Strategies.* Hicksville, N.Y.: Exposition Press, 1975

Bokron, Nicholas. *How to Use Put and Call Options.* Springfield, Mass.: John Magee, 1975.

Clasing, Henry, Jr. *Dow Jones-Irwin Guide to Put and Call Options,* rev. ed. Homewood, Ill.: Dow Jones-Irwin, 1978.

Cleeton, C. *Strategies for the Option Trader.* New York: John Wiley and Sons, 1979.

Gastineau, Gary. *Stock Options Manual,* 2d ed. New York: McGraw-Hill, 1979.

Gross, LeRoy. *The Stockbroker's Guide to Put and Call Option Strategies.* New York: Institute of Finance, 1974.

Jarrow, Robert A. and Andrew Rudd. *Option Pricing.* Homewood, Ill.: Richard D. Irwin, 1983.

Keynes, Milton. *Put Options.* Englewood Cliffs, N.J.: Cliffs Financial Publishing, 1976.

Malkiel, Burton, and Richard Quandt. *Strategies and Rational Decisions in the Securities Options Market.* Cambridge, Mass.: MIT Press, 1969.

Noddings, Thomas C. *CBOE Call Options: Your Daily Guide to Portfolio Strategy.* Homewood, Ill.: Dow Jones-Irwin, 1975.

Pihlblad, Leslie H. *On Options.* New York: Pershing & Co., 1975.

Rosen, Lawrence R. *How to Trade Put and Call Options.* Homewood, Ill.: Dow Jones-Irwin, 1974.

Rubinstein, Mark and John C. Cox. *Option Markets.* Englewood Cliffs, N.J.: Prentice-Hall, 1980.

Warrants

Galai, D., and M. Schneller. "Pricing of Warrants and the Value of the Firm." *Journal of Finance.* 33 no. 5 (December 1978).

Hilliard, Jimmy E., and Robert N. Leitch. "Analysis of the Warrant Hedge in a Stable Paretian Market." *Journal of Financial and Quantitative Analysis.* 12 no. 1 (March 1977).

Kim, Moon K., and Allan Young. "Rewards and Risks from Warrant Hedging." *Journal of Portfolio Management.* 6 no. 4 (Summer 1980).

Leabo, Dick A., and Richard J. Rogalski. "Warrant Price Movements and the Efficient Market Hypothesis." *Journal of Finance.* 20 no. 1 (March 1975).

Miller, J. D. "Longevity of Stock Purchase Warrants." *Financial Analysts Journal.* 27 no. 6 (November–December 1971).

Parkinson, Michael. "Empirical Warrant-Stock Relationships." *Journal of Business.* 45 no. 4 (October 1972).

Rogalski, Richard J. "Trading in Warrants by Mechanical Systems." *Journal of Finance.* 32 no. 1 (March 1977).

Rush, David F. and Ronald W. Melicher. "An Empirical Examination of Factors Which Influence Warrant Prices." *Journal of Finance.* 19 no. 5 (December 1974).

Samuelson, Paul. "Rational Theory of Warrant Pricing." *Industrial Management Review.* 6 no. 2 (Spring 1965).

Schwartz, E. "The Valuation of Warrants: Implementing a New Approach." *Journal of Financial Economics.* 5 no. 1 (January 1977).

Shelton, John P. "The Relation of the Price of a Warrant to the Price of Its Associated Stock." *Financial Analysts Journal.* 34 no. 3 (May–June 1967).

Sprenkel, Case M. "Warrant Prices as Indicators of Expectations and Preferences." *Yale Economic Essays.* 1 no. 2 (Fall 1961).

Stone, Bernell K. "Warrant Financing" *Journal of Financial and Quantitative Analysis.* 11 no. 1 (March 1976).

Turov, Daniel. "Dividend Paying Stocks and Their Warrants." *Financial Analysts Journal.* 29 no. 2 (March–April 1973).

Turov, Daniel. "Warrants and Options." in *Financial Analysts Handbook.* 1 Homewood, Ill.: Richard D. Irwin, 1975.

VanHorne, James C. "Warrant Valuation in Relation to Volatility and Opportunity Cost." *Industrial Management Review.* 10 no. 3 (Spring 1969).

Yesting, Kenneth L. "CD Warrants." *Financial Analysts Journal.* 26 no. 2 (March–April 1970).

Convertible Securities

Alexander, Gordon J., and Roger D. Hover. "Pricing in the New Issue Convertible Debt Market." *Financial Management.* 6 no. 3 (Fall 1977).

Baumol, William J., Burton G. Malkiel, and R. E. Quandt. "The Valuation of Convertible Securities." *Quarterly Journal of Economics.* 80 no. 1 (February 1966).

Brennan, M. J., and E. S. Schwartz. "Convertible Bonds: Valuation and Optimal Strategies for Call and Conversion." *Journal of Finance.* 32 no. 5 (December 1977).

Brigham, Eugene F. "An Analysis of Convertible Debentures: Theory and Some Empirical Evidence." *Journal of Finance.* 21 no. 1 (March 1966).

Frank, Werner G., and Charles D. Kroncke. "Classifying Conversions on Convertible Debentures over Four Years." *Financial Management.* 3 no. 2 (Summer 1974).

Frank, Werner G., and Jerry J. Weygandt. "A Prediction Model for Convertible Debentures." *Journal of Accounting Research.* 9 no. 1 (Spring 1971).

Frankle, A. W., and C. A. Hawkins. "Beta Coefficients for Convertible Bonds." *Journal of Finance.* 30 no. 1 (March 1975).

Ingersoll, Jonathon E., Jr. "A Contingent-Claims Valuation of Convertible Securities." *Journal of Financial Economics.* 4 no. 3 (May 1977).

Jennings, Edward H. "An Estimate of Convertible Bond Premiums." *Journal of Financial and Quantitative Analysis.* 9 no. 1 (January 1974).

Lewellen, Wilbur G., and George A. Racette. "Convertible Debt Financing." *Journal of Financial and Quantitative Analysis.* 8 no. 5 (December 1973).

Noodings, Thomas C. *The Dow Jones-Irwin Guide to Convertible Securities.* Homewood, Ill.: Richard D. Irwin, 1973.

Pinches, George E. "Financing with Convertible Preferred Stock, 1960–1967." *Journal of Finance.* 25 no. 1 (March 1970).

Poensgen, Otto H. "The Valuation of Convertible Bonds." *Industrial Management Review.* 7 no. 1 (Fall 1965) and 7 no. 2 (Spring 1966).

Soldofsky, Robert M. "Yield-Risk Performance of Convertible Securities." *Financial Analysts Journal.* 27 no. 2 (March–April 1961).

Soldofsky, Robert M. "The Risk Return Performance of Convertibles." *Journal of Portfolio Management.* 7 no. 2 (Winter 1981).

Vinson, Charles E. "Rates of Return on Convertibles: Recent Investor Experience." *Financial Analysts Journal.* 26 no. 4 (July–August 1970).

Vinson, Charles E. "Pricing Practices in the Primary Convertible Bond Market" *Quarterly Review of Economics and Business* 10 no. 2 (Summer 1970).

Walter, James E., and Augustin V. Que. "The Valuation of Convertible Bonds." *Journal of Finance.* 28 no. 3 (June 1973).

Weil, Roman, Joel Segall, and David Green. "Premiums on Convertible Bonds." *Journal of Finance.* 23 no. 2 (June 1968).

Chapter 24   *Commodity Futures*

W hen most individuals consider the subject of investments, they think in terms of securities investments—basically stocks and bonds. While these investment instruments typically constitute the bulk of most investment portfolios, the discussion in Chapter 2 pointed out the importance of considering a wide variety of investment alternatives. Diversification is important to your overall investment objectives, and a knowledge of diverse investments may point toward new opportunities.

Commodities trading meets both of these criteria. As shown in Chapter 2, the correlation between commodity prices and stock and bond prices is quite low, so you could envision commodity trading as a means to further diversify your overall investment portfolio. At the same time, the subsequent discussion will indicate that commodities trading provides a wide range of investment opportunities, from relatively conservative hedging transactions carried out by farmers or food processors, to fairly high-risk speculative transactions from which the short-run returns can be very large positive or negative values.

In this chapter, we will first define the spot, forward, and futures contracts and will point out some basic differences among them. Then we will discuss the similarities and differences between trading in common stocks (and bonds) and trading in futures. This is followed by a description of the organization of future markets and quotations. Further, we will discuss the relationship among spot, forward, and futures prices and will examine whether futures prices are determined efficiently. An interesting issue in this context is the impact of futures trading on spot prices. Finally, we will examine the performance of futures contracts in hedging the price risk of spot assets and in generating speculative profits. The discussion will consider each of the above mentioned issues with respect to commodities in this chapter. We will do the same for interest rate futures, currency futures, stock index futures, and options on index futures contracts in Chapter 25.

760   SPOT, FORWARD, AND FUTURES CONTRACTS

In general, there are four types of contracts for the purchase and sale of assets. A *cash* or *spot contract* is for the immediate delivery of an asset. Transactions in the primary and secondary markets for stocks and bonds are examples of cash contracts. Similarly, if a food processor currently purchases wheat to fill a flour contract, it is a cash or spot market transaction. Often, traders enter into transactions today that call for *deferred* delivery and payment. For instance, a mortgage banker makes a commitment to lend money to a builder in the future but the rate of interest is determined today. Another example is an exporter who agrees to deliver grain in the future for a price agreed upon today. Such deferred delivery contracts can take several forms, such as forward, futures, and options contracts.

A *forward contract* is a contract between two traders for delivery of a specific asset at a fixed time in the future for a price (called the *exercise price*) to be determined today. Transactions by the mortgage banker and the exporter are forward contracts. Here the quality (grade, term to maturity and the coupon on loans), quantity, method and place of delivery, price, and method of settlement are all determined by the two traders. As such, the forward market is a dealer market where transactions are negotiated over the counter. While the buyer of a forward contract knows that the commodity delivered will meet his particular needs, it is necessary to find another trader willing to sell such a contract. Because there is generally not a secondary market for forward contracts, both parties are locked into the contract and subject to the risk of failure to perform on the contract by either party and subsequent price fluctuations.

A *futures contract* overcomes some of the shortcomings of forward contracts. It is a deferred delivery contract between a trader and the clearinghouse of a futures exchange where all terms of trade, except the price and number of contracts, are standardized. Futures contracts are traded in auction markets organized by futures exchanges. The clearinghouse guarantees performance on all contracts. There is a fairly active secondary market for most futures contracts; thus it is possible for traders to close their position prior to the predetermined delivery date by executing a reverse transaction. For example, assume that a mortgage banker makes a commitment to a builder in March to lend money three months later in June at a fixed rate of 14 percent. The banker is exposed to the risk that mortgage rates will increase during the following three months, which would cause a decline in the mortgage price. In arranging this transaction, the banker can use the Government National Mortgage Association (GNMA) futures contract for June delivery which is traded on the Chicago Board of Trade (CBT). First, from today's published quotes on the June contract, the banker can obtain the market consensus forecast of the rate on the GNMA pass-through certificates to prevail at the time of contract delivery in June and could use this information in setting the rate on his forward loan.

Second, the banker can sell an appropriate number of June futures contracts today and subsequently buy them back before delivery. If mortgage rates have increased by June, there will be a loss on the forward commitment to the builder but a gain on the short futures position. On the other hand, if there is a decline in rates from their expected level, this will produce a gain on the forward loan but a loss on the short futures position. Thus, whatever happens to mortgage rates between now and June, the gain/loss on the futures position reduces the variability of the rate of return on the forward loan. Notice that the example does not involve any delivery on the futures contract. This is typical in futures trading; over 95 percent of transactions do *not* involve delivery of the underlying commodity. Therefore, futures contracts are considered temporary (close but imperfect) substitutes for the merchandizing forward contracts. In addition, a <u>futures contract is marked</u> to market at the end of every trading day, while <u>a forward contract *is not*</u>. This means the *gains/losses on futures positions are settled daily*.

The spot, forward, and futures contracts involve an obligation for the buyers and sellers to perform on the contract, i.e., to make and accept delivery and payment. Sometimes traders would like to buy *only* the right to buy or buy *only* the right to sell the underlying asset without incurring the obligation to accept or make delivery. Contracts which involve the exchange of such rights are called *options contracts* and are traded in auction markets (exchange markets) as well as over the counter. As discussed in Chapter 23, a *call option* traded on an exchange is a contract that confers a right on the buyer of the contract to *purchase* (call away) a specified asset from the clearinghouse at a predetermined price (exercise price) during a specified period of time. A *put option* gives the buyer of a contract the right to *sell* to the clearinghouse the underlying asset at a fixed price during a specified period of time. Put and call options traded on exchanges are standardized contracts. The buyer of an option contract is entitled to a right to buy or to sell, but the seller of an option has an obligation to perform when the option is exercised by the buyer. Unlike OTC options, listed options enjoy a fairly active market.

There are other terms and concepts unique to futures trading that are explained in the glossary at the end of this chapter. Given this background, let us consider some specific similarities and differences between stock and futures trading.

Similarities in Stock and Futures Trading Practices

1. There are highly organized exchanges for both areas of investment. This is in contrast to other investment alternatives, such as real estate, coins, or stamps, which have highly fragmented trading markets on a geographical basis.
2. Trading on a given exchange is limited to specified stocks or assets. Just as the New York and American Stock Exchanges only allow trading in listed stocks, the futures exchanges limit trading to specified assets, such as commodity futures, interest rate futures, currency futures, and stock index futures.
3. Only members can trade on an exchange (stock or commodity) for themselves or for others.
4. The mechanics of buying and selling stocks or futures contracts are quite similar. In both cases, you give an order to a local broker who sends it to the floor of the exchange where an exchange member executes the order through the stock specialist or in the appropriate commodities pit.

5. The types of orders on the exchanges are substantially similar. In both areas market orders, stop orders, and limit orders are frequently used.

6. Because they have highly organized exchanges and communication networks, both areas of investment enjoy substantial liquidity. This ability to turn investments into cash very quickly at a fairly certain price contrasts sharply with other investments.

7. In both areas some investors base their decisions on the fundamentals of supply and demand, and there are chartists who mainly depend upon past price movements for indications of future price movements.

Differences in Stock and Futures Trading Practices

1. The buyer of a stock acquires ownership, but the buyer of a futures contract is not entitled to ownership of the underlying asset until he decides to accept delivery at time of final settlement.

2. There is much greater leverage in commodity trading than in stocks. While the current margin requirement on stocks is 50 percent, the requirements on commodity futures range between 10 and 20 percent. Not only is more leverage available for trading futures, but it is also universally used. In stocks leverage is rather limited. In addition, not all common stocks are eligible for margin trading, while it is possible to buy all futures contracts on margin.

3. There are interest charges on money borrowed to acquire stocks, but there are no interest charges on the difference between the total value and the margin for a futures contract. This is because the futures contract is a deferred delivery contract. Therefore, payment of purchase price is deferred until the date the contract is actually scheduled for delivery. In fact, what is referred to as *margin* in futures trading is really a *good faith deposit* to protect the futures broker.

4. While there is a commission charged for purchase and another charged for sale of stocks or bonds, commissions on futures are only paid on a completed contract (purchase and sale). The commissions on futures also tend to be smaller in terms of the total value of the contract.

5. Stock prices are free to fluctuate without limit. In contrast, there is a daily limit on the price change allowed for each future contract. Once a given contract reaches this limit, trading in it cannot take place beyond the limit price.

6. One of the major problems facing the stock market in recent years has been the stock certificate and the stock transfer procedure. This is not a problem in futures trading because there are no certificates and transferring is done through the Commodity Clearing Corporation.

7. In the stock market, there is a clearing corporation but there are also dealers on the buying and the selling side of the trade. In the futures market, the clearing corporation actually takes the other side in all transactions, either buying or selling directly. In commodities, the transaction between two brokers or traders takes place in the pit. After the transaction, each party reports to the clearinghouse which makes sure that the orders match and charges each broker accordingly. Once this is done, the brokers have no

connection to each other but only to the clearing corporation that handles all subsequent closing trades directly and settles with the customer. The clearing corporation eventually records the fact that a sale was offset with a purchase and is thereby closed out.

8. In the stock market, you specifically sell the stock you bought or buy the stock you sold short to complete a transaction. In futures trading, you simply engage in an opposite transaction, and the two individual transactions cancel each other out through the clearing corporation.

9. Although there are organized exchanges in both areas, there are no specialists in futures exchanges. When a trade is desired, a member of the futures exchange simply goes to the appropriate pit, makes it known that he has an order, and all interested traders respond.

10. When an investor wants to sell a stock short, it cannot be done on a down tick (a decrease); he must wait until there is a trade at the previous price or an up tick (an increase). There is no such tick requirement for short selling futures; you simply sell a contract you did not buy previously.

11. Trading in futures is simpler than stock trading because there are no dividends and stock splits. As a result, the price changes reflect all rates of return.

12. About 5 percent of trading in the NYSE is in odd lots (sales or purchases of less than 100 shares). In contrast, there are typically no odd-lot contracts available in futures trading on the major exchanges. Because of the substantial leverage available, it is typically not necessary. Still, there are "mini" contracts on some smaller exchanges.

13. There are differences in sources of information. While the major source of information about a specific firm is the company itself, the principal source of information for major agricultural commodities is the U.S. Department of Agriculture. Because of this, there is less inside information in commodities because the government is scrupulous about any possible leaks.

14. Many of the previously mentioned differences produce a substantially different typical holding period for the two investment alternatives. The holding period for agricultural contracts seldom exceeds 90 days and, generally, cannot exceed a year because the contracts are deliverable within that period. Financial futures, such as GNMA futures and T-bond futures, have delivery periods extending to almost three years, but the volume of trading in the distant delivery contracts is limited. For other financial futures, such as T-bill futures, some delivery periods are longer than the term to maturity of the underlying asset with the result that the spot asset does not exist for distant delivery contracts. In contrast, stocks can be held almost indefinitely, and the average holding period is probably close to a year.

15. There are differences in the normal unit of trading. In stocks, the normal unit of trading is a round lot, which is almost always 100 shares. Futures are traded on the basis of contracts which differ between commodities. As shown in Figure 24.1, the type of contract is listed at the top of each commodity entry; e.g., a wheat contract on the Chicago Board of Trade (CBT) is for 5,000 bushels, a contract of fresh eggs on the Chicago Mercantile Exchange (CME) is 22,500 dozen eggs, and a T-bill futures contract on the International Money Market (IMM) is for a $1 million T-bill.

FIGURE 24.1
Futures Quotations in *The Wall Street Journal,* February 10, 1984.

SOURCE: *The Wall Street Journal,* February 10, 1984. Reprinted by permission of *The Wall Street Journal,*
© Dow Jones & Company, Inc., 1984. All Rights Reserved.

16. There are differences in price volatility and even greater differences in the volatility of rates of return. Agricultural commodity prices are generally more volatile than stock prices because of the nature of the information affecting the price, including the impact of weather and international demand. In addition to basic price volatility, the rates of return will be more volatile due to the substantial leverage caused by buying on margin. That is, the investor is only required to put up a small percentage of the value of the contract as a good faith deposit.

17. Futures contracts have fixed delivery months specified by the sponsoring exchanges. Some contracts, such as GNMA futures and T-bond futures, have quarterly delivery cycles, and many agricultural commodity futures mature at irregular intervals that vary from a month to five months. T-bill futures contracts require delivery during the three business days following the third Monday of the delivery month. The GNMA futures and the T-bond futures permit delivery during the entire delivery month. The futures exchanges also specify the place of delivery. No comparable restrictions on delivery exist in the stock market.

18. As observed earlier, performance on a futures contract — delivery as well as payment — is guaranteed by the clearing corporation for the particular futures contract. In upholding this guarantee, the clearing corporation marks a contract to market at the end of every trading day, thus ensuring that its obligations are limited by the maximum daily price change in the unusual event of default by a member broker and his customer. If the futures price has moved in favor of the customer during the day, his account is credited with the amount of price change. Any unfavorable price change is similarly debited to the customer's account. When the customer opens a futures account he is required to post a minimum amount of margin — the *initial margin* — set by the exchange. While the initial margins vary across commodities, they usually range from 5 to 10 percent of the face value of the contract.

    Subsequently, the customer is required to maintain a minimum amount of margin, called *maintenance margin,* which is typically about 75 percent of the initial margin. While the initial margin can be satisfied by posting interest-bearing securities, the subsequent margin — called the *variable margin* — should be paid in cash. A *margin call* is triggered when the margin in the commodity account falls to the level of the maintenance margin as a result of daily resettlement. On top of the exchange-imposed margins, brokerage houses could ask for additional margins from their clients depending upon the clients' credit worthiness, the volatility of futures prices, and competition.

    Thus the daily mark-to-market practice of futures trading generates many cash flows for futures traders before the contract delivery date. When futures prices rise, the contract buyer accumulates cash in his futures account in the interim, but he will be required to pay a higher price than he originally agreed to at the final settlement of his long position. In contrast, the contract seller experiences many margin calls and cash outflows in the case of rising futures prices. However, he will receive a higher settlement price at the time of closing his short position. Notice that at final settlement the aggregate cash receipt of the seller and net cash payment by the buyer are identical to the originally specified price. The daily mark-to-market practice of futures trading has altered only the timing of these cash flows. Further, the clearinghouse has a zero net position at all times because for every contract buyer there is a seller.

In regular stock trading, there is no daily marking-to-market of customer positions. Even when stocks are traded on margin the positions are not necessarily marked-to-market on a daily basis. Futures margins are good faith deposits, while stock margins represent partial payment of the amount owed to the broker.

19. Open interest in a futures contract represents the number of outstanding contracts at a given time; this differs from the volume of contracts traded and the volume of trading in stocks. When the futures contract holder closes his position by executing a reverse trade, open interest does not change, since the current holder is replaced by another trader, but the volume of trading increases.

20. Trading in stocks is regulated by the SEC, while futures trading is regulated by the Commodity Futures Trading Commission (CFTC). The futures exchanges are required to obtain approval from the CFTC before introducing a new futures contract. For some commodities, the CFTC has placed maximum limits on positions that an individual trader can control. This limitation is intended to prevent possible *corners* and *squeezes*. Further, the CFTC requires larger traders to file periodic reports on their trading activities in regulated commodities.

21. Unlike stock trading, an important motivation for trading futures contracts is hedging. In *hedging,* an investor with a long (short) position in an asset assumes a short (long) position by selling an appropriate number of contracts of a related asset to reduce the variability of expected returns on the uncovered spot position.

22. There are important differences in taxation of profits and losses on stocks and futures positions. A *hedger's* gain or loss on his futures positions is regarded as ordinary income or loss for tax purposes, but profit or loss on a *speculative* futures position is considered a capital asset and is taxed as a long- or short-term capital gain or loss depending upon the length of the holding period. Unlike stocks, most speculative positions in futures are held for a few months and are treated as short-term capital gains or losses.

Futures Quotations

Prior to discussing specific commodity trading procedures, we should briefly consider the information in the futures quotations section of the newspaper. Figure 24.1 is an example of the futures prices section that appears daily in *The Wall Street Journal.* This section lists all the major commodities traded on all the principal exchanges. (The example does not include the full section.) The commodities are divided into the following groups:

1. Grains and feeds
2. Livestock and meat

3. Foods and fiber
4. Metals and petroleum
5. Wood
6. Financial.

For each commodity, the listing indicates where the commodity is traded (e.g., CBT is the Chicago Board of Trade) and the standard contract for the commodity (e.g., the contract for corn on the CBT is for 5,000 bushels). The heading indicates what the quotes are for, e.g., cents per bushel or cents per pound. In the case of wheat, for instance, a quote of 406 means $4.06 per bushel. The left column indicates when the contracts come due, and this obviously differs by commodity depending upon the normal growing season. Naturally, most of the contracts for agricultural commodities are due during the summer months. The subsequent columns indicate the daily movements in the futures contract: the opening transaction, the high and low transaction for the day, and the final transaction *(settle)* of the day. The change column indicates the price change from the previous day's settle price. The season's high and low indicates the range of prices for this contract since it began trading. The open interest is the number of contracts that have not been closed out. At the bottom, there is an estimated volume of trading in all contracts for the day, the total open interest for all months of contracts, and the change in total open interest from the previous day.

SPOT, FORWARD, AND FUTURES PRICE RELATIONSHIPS

Before we examine the economic functions of futures trading, it is essential to consider the relationship among spot, forward, and futures prices. For expository purposes, it is convenient to begin with the price relationships during the delivery period of the futures contract, then investigate the price behavior of these contracts prior to the delivery period of the futures contract.

We observed earlier that a futures contract is a temporary (close but imperfect) substitute for a spot market transaction. To examine this further, assume that the asset underlying the three contracts is *identical* and that the contracts come due for delivery on a date which coincides with the final day of trading. Let $S(T)$ be the spot price per unit of the asset on the last day of trading of the futures contract, T. $F(T,T)$ and $FO(T,T)$ represent the futures price and the forward price, respectively; the first term within the parentheses refers to the date on which the price is observed. Ignoring market imperfections, such as transaction costs, taxes, margins, and units of trading, it is clear that the equilibrium spot and futures prices at T must be equal as dictated by the law of one price:

(24.1)
$$F(T,T) = S(T).$$

If this equilibrium relationship is violated, there would be opportunities for arbitrage between the spot and futures markets. For example, if $F(T,T) > S(T)$, the arbitrageur would sell a futures contract, buy the spot asset, and make delivery on the futures position, thus earning a riskless profit of $F(T,T) - S(T)$. On the other hand, if $F(T,T) < S(T)$, the arbitrageur would buy a futures contract, take delivery, and sell the asset in the spot market. This transaction would yield a riskless profit of $S(T) - F(T,T)$. Obviously, such arbitrage opportunities seldom exist in an efficient auction market with many competing traders.

Further, a forward contract written on the delivery date is indeed a spot contract. Therefore:

$$(24.2) \qquad F(T,T) = FO(T,T) = S(T).$$

Thus, in theory, forward and futures contracts are effectively reduced to a spot contract on the last day of trading, delivery, and settlement.

In reality, however, spot and futures prices at delivery would rarely be identical because of market imperfections, but they would be close to each other. For almost all assets, trading in futures contracts ceases prior to the delivery date. The delivery and settlement process spans several business days, which renders any attempt to arbitrage between the spot and futures markets risky. Further, the specifications of a futures contract permit delivery of varying grades of the underlying asset. It is the *seller* of the futures contract who triggers the delivery process during the delivery month and decides the grade and place of delivery. When the seller gives notice to the clearing corporation of his intention to deliver, the clearing corporation assigns that delivery to the oldest long position. Thus, the *buyer* of a futures contract is uncertain about the time and place of delivery and the grade of the asset until the moment he is notified by the clearing corporation. Because of the delivery privileges enjoyed by the seller of a futures contract, the $F(T,T)$ cannot be greater than the $S(T)$. The uncertainties that the buyer faces as the contract approaches delivery suggest that the $F(T,T)$ would be less than $S(T)$.[1]

Prior to delivery, it is of interest to examine the following price relationships. The notation t refers to the initial period when contracts are opened, and T is the delivery and final settlement date.

1. The relationship between the current spot price, $S(t)$, and the expected future spot price of an asset at the time of delivery of forward and futures contracts written on it, $E_t S(T)$
2. The relationship between the initial forward price, $FO(t,T)$, and $E_t S(T)$
3. The relationship between $FO(t,T)$ and $S(t)$
4. The relationship between the initial futures price, $F(t,T)$, and the current expectation of the spot price at delivery, $E_t S(T)$
5. The relationship between the current futures price, $F(t,T)$, and the current spot price of the underlying asset, $S(t)$
6. The relationship between $F(t,T)$ and $FO(t,T)$
7. The relationship between current prices of futures (and forward) contracts of different delivery months; e.g., current prices of March and June futures contracts: $F(t,March)$ vs $F(t,June)$.

The subject of spot, forward and futures price relationships has been a matter of extended debate. Until the late 1970s, the difference in the cash flow streams of futures and forward contracts (daily vs. maturity payoffs, respectively) was generally ignored and the futures and forward prices were considered equal

[1] John C. Cox, Jonathan E. Ingersoll, Jr., and Stephen A. Ross, "The Relation between Forward Prices and Futures Prices," *Journal of Financial Economics,* 9 no. 4 (December 1981): 321–346.

even *prior* to delivery. Subsequently it was shown that the identity of futures and forward prices would hold *only* when interest rates are deterministic. We shall briefly review the traditional literature and follow with a summary of recent research findings. The initial discussion is concerned with spot prices.

Relationship Between Current and Future Spot Prices

The current spot price of an asset is determined by the current and expected supply and demand conditions. If an excess supply of an asset is expected, that would reduce the inventory of stocks carried and dampen the current spot price. In contrast, if a shortage is expected, there would be larger inventories which would exert upward pressure on spot prices. This means the current spot price, $S(t)$, and the expected future spot price, $E_t[S(t+1)]$, are connected by *the expected cost of carry*, $C(t,t+1)$, and a *risk premium, RP,* for bearing uncertainties about the future spot price. In broad terms:

(24.3) $$E_t[S(t+1)] = S(t) + C(t,t+1) + RP.$$

The cost of carry depends upon the type of asset and includes such items as insurance, spoilage, storage, depreciation, financing costs, convenience yield, and distributions that the asset may generate during the interval $(t,t+1)$. For many commodities, the cost of carry is typically positive. Sometimes, it may be negative because of the convenience yield which represents the benefits of having inventory on hand. Because of a convenience yield, inventory is typically carried even when the expected future spot price is less than the current spot price.[2] For instance, grain merchants and food processors carry stocks from one season to another, even when a bumper crop is expected. They do this to avoid stock-outs and maintain customer goodwill. The convenience yield is inversely related to the size of the inventory. When the current inventories are relatively low, the convenience yield may exceed other (positive) components of the cost of carry and the risk premium. Hence, in such a case, the expected future spot price would be below the current spot price.

The cost of carrying financial assets such as debt instruments and foreign currencies is much lower than that of commodities. It includes the cost of financing and safekeeping. Furthermore, some financial assets, like notes and bonds, may generate cash distributions such as coupon payments during the interval $(t,t+1)$. The net carrying cost is considered fixed over a short period of time, but it becomes stochastic over longer intervals. The last term in Equation 24.1 is the premium for bearing nondiversifiable risk associated with the spot asset. We will discuss the risk premium later.

The Impact of Hedgers and Speculators on Price Relationships

The difference between the current spot price and the current futures price is known as *basis*. In the conventional discussion of futures trading, the market

[2] M.J. Brennan, "The Supply of Storage." *American Economic Review,* 47 no. 1 (March 1958): 50–72; Myron S. Scholes, "The Economics of Hedging and Spreading in Futures Markets," *The Journal of Futures Market,* 1 no. 2 (Summer 1981): 265–286.

participants are classified into two groups: hedgers and speculators. *Hedgers* are those with a long or short position in the spot market (such as a grain elevator company with an inventory of some product or an exporter with a future commitment to deliver at a fixed price) who assume an opposite position in the futures market with a view to reducing the risk of price fluctuations. *Speculators,* in contrast, lack any position in the underlying asset but trade the futures contract with the hope of making a profit because of the additional risk of price changes they assume. Keynes and Hicks[3] argued that the short hedgers generally exceed the long hedgers, so the market is dominated by net short hedgers. In accommodating net short hedgers, long speculators require a premium for bearing the risk of price fluctuation. Thus, the excess supply of the contract by net hedgers and the risk premium demanded by long speculators reduce the current futures price below the current spot price and also the expected future spot price. This specification of the price relationship is known as *normal backwardation.* Under this hypothesis, the current futures price is a downward biased predictor of the expected future spot price at the time of delivery, and the futures price has an upward trend during the life of the contract.

Under the conventional view, the market is characterized as *contango,* which is when long hedgers exceed short hedgers. With net long hedging, there is an excess demand for the futures contract which exerts an upward pressure on the current futures price. To induce speculators to assume short futures positions and supply the contract, the futures price would have to fall on average subsequently. Thus, under contango the current futures price is above the current spot price, and the current futures price is an upward biased predictor of the future spot price expected to prevail at time of delivery. Cootner[4] observed that when there are large inventories immediately after the harvest the net short hedgers dominate the market. In contrast, there is net long hedging at the end of the crop year which causes the current futures price to exceed the prevailing spot price.

Similarly, Working[5] explained the spread between current spot and futures prices in terms of the inventory level of the underlying asset to be carried to the delivery date. He viewed the cash-futures spread as the market-determined cost of storage of stocks and observed that the cost of storage could even be negative because of the convenience yield (i.e., the benefit of having stock on hand).

In contrast to the normal backwardation and contango hypotheses, the *unbiased expectations hypothesis* assumes that speculators are risk neutral. It holds that the current futures price is an unbiased predictor of the future spot price expected to prevail at the time of contract delivery.

Recent Research. The conventional analysis of spot, forward, and futures price relationships ignored the consequences of daily cash settlement of the

---

[3] J. R. Hicks, *Value and Capital* 2nd ed., (Oxford: Oxford University Press, 1946), Chapter 10; John Maynard Keynes, *Treatise on Money,* 2 (London: Macmillan, 1930), 142–144.

[4] Paul H. Cootner, "Speculation and Hedging," *Food Research Institute Studies,* Supplement (Stanford, Calif.: 1967), 65–106.

[5] Holbrook Working, "The Theory of Price of Storage," *American Economic Review,* 39 no. 5 (December 1949): 1254–1262.

futures contract. The modern approach, beginning with a seminal article by Black,[6] explicitly recognized the daily marking-to-market feature of the futures contract.[7] It employed the law of one price to analyze the relationships among spot, forward, and futures prices. According to this principle of pricing, assets (real as well as financial) with identical time patterns of payoffs in the future *must* trade at identical current prices in frictionless markets in order to prevent arbitrage opportunities. This principle showed that the cash flows from the forward and futures contracts can be duplicated by constructing an appropriate portfolio of the underlying asset and default-free discount bonds. Therefore, the current forward and futures prices *must be equal* to the present value of the corresponding portfolios. In reviewing the recent literature, assume that the markets are frictionless and that the underlying asset can be sold short in the spot market.

Relationship Between Spot and Forward Prices

The forward contract provides a mechanism for locking in today the future spot price that is expected to prevail at the time of contract delivery. The forward price, $FO(t,T)$, is fixed today, but the delivery (as well as payment) are deferred until the final settlement date. Hence, the forward contract *eliminates uncertainty* about the future spot price that will prevail at time of delivery. Currently, forward contracts are traded in some treasury securities, GNMA pass-through certificates, and foreign currencies. The actively traded contracts are for standardized terms to maturity. For example, forward contracts in foreign currencies (quoted in *The Wall Street Journal*) are for 30, 90, and 180 days forward delivery. Unlike futures contracts which have standardized delivery months, forward contracts, which are issued on different dates, mature at different points in the future. There is hardly any secondary market activity in forward contracts.

If the storage costs over the life of a forward contract ($T - t$) are *known,* then at the time a forward contract begins trading, the present value of the forward price *must* equal the current spot price of the underlying asset, $S(t)$, plus the present value of the known storage costs, $G(t,T)$:

(24.4) $$FO(t,T) \times B(t,T) = S(t) + G(t,T).$$

The term $B(t,T)$ is the present value of a default-free discount bond, such as a treasury bill, that promises payment of \$1 at T. We need to take the present value of the forward price (which is the exercise price of the contract) since the payment is postponed to time period T. If this condition is violated, one could set up an arbitrage that would produce a certain profit without involving any capital investment by the arbitrageur. For instance, if the present value of the forward

---

[6] Fischer Black, "The Pricing of Commodity Contracts," *Journal of Financial Economics,* 3 no. 1, 2 (January–March 1976): 167–179.

[7] Cox, Ingersoll, Jr., and Ross, "The Relation between Forward Prices and Futures Prices," *Journal of Financial Economics,* 9 no. 4 (December 1981): 321–346; Robert A. Jarrow and George S. Oldfield, "Forward Contracts and Futures Contracts," *Journal of Financial Economics,* 9 no. 4 (December 1981): 373–382; Scott F. Richard and M. Sundaresan, "A Continuous Time Equilibrium Model of Forward Prices and Futures Prices in a Multigood Economy," *Journal of Financial Economics,* 9 no. 4 (December 1981): 347–371.

price exceeds the sum of $S(t)$ and $G(t,T)$, then the following arbitrage could be set up:

At t:

a. Borrow the present value of the forward price, $+FO(t,T)B(t,T)$.
b. Buy and store the underlying asset, $-[S(t) + G(t,T)]$.
c. Sell a forward contract at the exercise price, $FO(t,T)$.
d. Net cash flow $= FO(t,T) \times B(t,T) - S(t) - G(t,T) > 0$.

At T:

a. Deliver the (stored) asset on the forward contract and collect the exercise price, $+FO(t,T)$.
b. Pay off the loan, $-FO(t,T)$.
c. Net cash flow $= FO(t,T) - FO(t,T) = 0$.

Thus, in a frictionless market the arbitrage produces a certain profit at time t equal to the net cash flow. Notice that recognition of frictions in the real-world markets does not invalidate the concept of arbitrage, but it generally implies that the difference between the right and left sides of Equation 24.4 should be large enough to exceed costs due to market frictions. Also, because forward contracts are held over a short period of time (generally a few months), the assumption of known storage costs is not unrealistic. However, if the storage costs are *unknown,* then Equation 24.4 needs to be modified and the arbitrage discussed above would be risky.

In an efficient spot market, the market price of an asset such as a share of stock is the consensus estimate of its value. In contrast, in the forward market the value of the forward *contract* is different from the forward *price.* At the inception of the contract at time t, the market value of the forward contract is zero, because the forward price and the exercise price are identical. Subsequently, the contract acquires a nonzero market value. Assume another forward contract is written on that asset for the same delivery date, T, but at a different exercise price. If a new contract is written at time t^* ($t < t^* < T$) at an exercise price of $FO(t^*,T)$, the value of the outstanding forward contract, $V(t^*,t,T)$, is equal to the present value of the difference between two exercise prices. That is:

(24.5) $$V(t^*,t,T) = [FO(t^*,T) - FO(t,T)]B(t^*,T).$$

If this condition is violated, one could earn arbitrage profits as follows:

At t*:

a. If $FO(t^*,T) > FO(t,T)$, the owner of the outstanding contract could write (sell) the new contract.
b. If $FO(t^*,T) < FO(t,T)$, the seller of the outstanding contract could buy the new contract.
c. These transactions involve no investment of funds.

At T:

a. Take delivery on the long forward contract and redeliver the asset on the short forward contract. The arbitrage profit in either case is equal to the absolute value of the difference between the two exercise prices, $[FO(t^*,T) - FO(t,T)]$.

The market value of a forward contract at the time of delivery is equal to the difference between its exercise price and the current spot price of the underlying asset. That is:

(24.6) $$V(T,t,T) = S(T) - FO(t,T).$$

Clearly, the market value at delivery is equal to the profit or loss on the forward contract. Prior to contract delivery the profit or loss on the contract is not known. The recent research shows that the current forward price, $FO(t,T)$, is a biased estimator of the expected future spot price, $E_t[S(T)]$, and the degree of bias depends upon the covariance between forward profit or loss and the marginal utility of consumption.[8]

Determining the Futures Price

Like the forward contract, the futures contract also provides an opportunity for the mortgage banker or the exporter to lock in today the future spot price of the underlying asset to prevail at the time of delivery. However, *the futures contract is marked-to-market daily.* At the end of every trading day all futures positions are balanced and rewritten by the clearinghouse at the settlement price — a price representative of transaction prices at the close of the day's trading. If the price has moved upward since the previous day's cash settlement, the price gain is credited to long futures positions and debited to short futures positions. Thus the futures contract generates *daily* cash flows. If the upward trend in prices persists until the delivery date, the buyer of the futures contract would accumulate daily cash inflows but would face a higher final settlement price, $F(T,T)$, than the initial futures price $F(t,T)$, called the *exercise price*. The *net* amount the buyer is obliged to pay at final settlement is equal to the initial exercise price, $F(t,T)$. Thus the buyer gets to keep the interest earned on daily cash inflows. Clearly, the cash flows accruing to the seller of the futures contract are just the opposite to those accruing to the buyer.

Again, it is important to note the distinction between the *futures price* and the *value of the futures contract.* At its inception, the value of the futures contract, $Y(t,T)$, is zero because the futures price and the exercise price are identical. During each trading day, the futures contract acquires some value (positive or negative) as the current futures price deviates from the initial futures price. Letting t_1 represent the end of the trading day and $k(t < k < t_1)$ denote any time between the beginning and end of the trading day, the value of the futures

[8] Richard and Sundaresan, "A Continuous Time Equilibrium Model of Forward Prices and Future Prices in a Multigood Economy," *Journal of Financial Economics,* 9 no. 4 (December 1981): 347–371.

contract during the trading day is:

$$(24.7) \qquad\qquad Y(k,T) = F(k,T) - F(t,T).$$

At the end of each trading day, the daily price change on the open futures position is settled and the contract is rewritten at a new exercise price which is equal to the futures settlement price. Thus, the value of the futures contract immediately after it is rewritten is zero.

Equations 24.5 and 24.7 show that the values of the forward and futures contracts written on an identical underlying asset are *not* the same prior to the last day of trading $(T-1)$ because of the difference in the timing of cash flows. Based on arbitrage arguments similar to those used earlier, Cox, Ingersoll and Ross[9] showed that:

1. Prior to the last day of trading $(T-1)$, the current futures price, $F(t,T)$, need not be equal to the current forward price, $FO(t,T)$. Only if interest rates are known (deterministic) is the current futures price equal to the current forward price.
2. The forward price is greater (less) than the futures price if the covariance between the percentage changes in $F(t,T)$ and $B(t,T)$ (the default-free discount bond maturing at T) is positive (negative).
3. Assume that the underlying asset makes no payouts (such as coupon interest during the life of the contract). If the covariance between percentage changes in $S(t)$ and $B(t,T)$ is greater (less) than the variance of percentage changes in $B(t,T)$, the current forward price is greater (less) than the current futures price.
4. The current futures price is greater (less) than the current spot price if the spot interest rate is always greater (less) than the spot rental rate. The spot rental rate is the charge for obtaining the full use of the underlying asset including the right to receive payouts. This would cover the storage costs and coupon interest.
5. Richard and Sundaresan[10] observed that futures and forward contracts provide a mechanism for hedging future consumption and thus serve as insurance against welfare losses. They showed that, in general, the current futures and forward prices are biased predictors of the future spot price expected to prevail at contract delivery. They concluded that normal backwardation was found when futures and forward contracts are *poor consumption hedges* which meant that these contracts are more profitable than average when the marginal utility of consumption is lower than average and vice versa. Alternatively, they contended that contango prevails if forward or futures contracts are good instruments to insure against adverse consumption opportunities. That is, contango exists when futures or forward contracts are more profitable than average and when the marginal utility of consumption is higher than average.

[9] Cox, Ingersoll, and Ross, "The Relation between Forward Prices and Futures Prices," *Journal of Financial Economics*.

[10] Richard and Sundaresan, "A Continuous Time Equilibrium Model of Forward Prices and Futures Prices in a Multigood Economy," *Journal of Financial Economics*.

6. Dusak and Black[11] argued that the capital asset pricing model can be applied to the pricing of commodities as well as futures contracts. Extending this approach, Scholes[12] showed that:

(24.8)
$$E[S(t+1)] = S(t) + S(t) [R_f + C'(t,t+1)] \\ + [E(R_m) - R_f] \beta(S),$$

where:

$E(R_m)$ = the expected return on the market portfolio
$\beta(S)$ = the dollar beta which is a measure of systematic risk of the spot asset
R_f = risk-free rate of return
$C'(t,t+1)$ = cost of carry in percent excluding financing cost.

The term $S(t) [R_f + C'(t,t+1)$ represents the dollar cost of carry including interest charges. It can be assumed to be fixed over a short interval of time, but over longer horizons interest rates and other storage costs are uncertain. $\beta(S)$ is the expected covariance of the change in spot price with the return on the market portfolio divided by the variance of the market return. Under this model, the expected change in the spot price is equal to the dollar cost of carry plus the dollar risk premium.

Likewise, the expected futures price change under the CAPM is:

(24.9)
$$E[F(t+1,T)] - F(t,T) = [E(R_m) - R_f] \beta(F),$$

where:

$\beta(F)$ = the dollar beta of the futures contract.

If the systematic risk of a futures contract is zero, then the expected change in the futures price would be zero.

7. Further, Scholes observed that the current futures price is equal to the current spot price plus the *expected* total cost of carry. That is:

(24.10)
$$F(t,T) = S(t) + C(t,T),$$

where:

$C(t,T)$ = the net dollar cost of carry including interest, storage costs, convenience yields, and distributions by the underlying asset during the life of the futures contract.

Clearly, the cost of carry over the life of the contract is unknown (stochastic). Therefore, the basis (i.e., the difference between the current spot and fu-

[11] Katherine Dusak, "Futures Trading and Investor Returns: An Investigation of Commodity Market Risk Premiums," *Journal of Political Economy*, 81 no. 4 (December 1973): 1387–1406; Fischer Black, "The Pricing of Commodity Contracts," *Journal of Financial Economics*.

[12] Myron S. Scholes, "The Economics of Hedging and Spreading in Futures Markets," *The Journal of Futures Markets*, 1 no. 2 (Summer 1981): 135–144.

tures prices) provides a consensus forecast of the expected cost of carry during the life of the contract. If $F(t,T) > S(t) + C(t,T)$, the holder of the spot asset would expect to gain from selling the futures contract. Conversely, if $F(t,T) < S(t) + C(t,T)$, the spot asset holder would expect to gain by buying the futures contract.

The difference between the current futures prices of two different delivery months, say T and $T'(T' > T)$, is called a *time spread*. It follows from Equation 24.9 that the spread is equal to the change in the expected carrying cost. That is:

(24.11) $$F(t,T') - F(t,T) = C(t,T') - C(t,T).$$

The spread is a market consensus forecast of the expected change in the cost of carry from T to T'.

Empirical Evidence on Price Relationships

Empirical studies have generally addressed the following issues:
1. Is the current futures price an unbiased predictor of the expected future spot price?
2. Does the futures price follow a random walk or exhibit trends?
3. What are the risks and returns to hedgers and speculators in futures markets?

The question of bias in commodity futures prices has been debated for a long time. Rockwell did a comprehensive study of the theory of normal backwardation.[13] A modified version of the theory of normal backwardation assumes that speculators are net long when hedgers are net short and vice versa, that speculators are risk averse, and they are able to forecast prices. These assumptions imply that speculators' profits are a function of the quantity of risk (of price fluctuation) assumed as well as their forecasting abilities. Rockwell examined semimonthly data from 25 commodity futures markets during the 1947–1965 period to determine the proportion of speculators' profits due to normal backwardation and the proportion attributable to their forecasting abilities. The major findings are:

a. The smaller 22 futures markets exhibit no tendency toward normal backwardation whether hedgers are net short or net long. Normal backwardation is characteristic of the three larger markets — wheat, soybeans, and cotton — only when hedgers are net short. This suggests that the current futures price is on average an unbiased estimate of the expected future spot price. However, this conclusion may not hold for all futures markets, or it may not be consistent over all time periods within a market.

b. Speculators' profits are primarily due to their forecasting abilities rather than their risk-bearing function implied in the theory of normal backwardation. Large speculators (professionals) earn substantial and consistent profits. About 75 percent of their profits is due to their ability to forecast short-term price trends; the remaining profit arises from their ability to forecast long-

[13] Charles S. Rockwell, "Normal Backwardation, Forecasting, and the Returns to Commodity Futures Traders," in *Selected Writings on Futures Markets,* Anne E. Peck (ed.) (Chicago: Chicago Board of Trade, 1977), 167–189.

term price trends. Small speculators (nonprofessionals) experience substantial losses net of transactions costs.

Further, numerous studies have examined whether the futures price follows a random walk or exhibits any trend in the short-run. The theory of efficient markets discussed earlier implies that short-term price changes in such markets are independent and randomly distributed, and past price changes are not useful in predicting future price changes. Applying time series analysis to Chicago corn futures daily prices during 1922–1931 and 1949–1958, Larson[14] found a tendency for sudden large price movements to be followed by reversals over short periods and thereafter by weak price trends over longer periods. Smidt[15] reported significant serial dependence among daily price changes in May soybeans during 1952–1961.

Stevenson and Bear[16] examined daily closing prices on July corn and soybeans during the 1951–1968 period. Their major findings are:

a. There is a tendency toward negative serial correlation among price differences for one- and two-day lags.

b. The number of one and two-day runs are slightly more than expected and the number of long runs (five and six or more days) are fewer than expected by pure chance.

c. Application of mechanical trading rules based on filters of different sizes (from 1.5 to 5 percent of price per bushel) produce net profits in excess of that earned on a buy-and-hold strategy. This confirmed the existence of long-term price trends. The authors concluded that the random walk hypothesis does not provide a satisfactory explanation of the behavior of commodity futures prices in the shortrun.

Labys and Granger[17] applied spectral analysis to monthly, weekly, and daily prices of numerous commodity futures covering the period 1950–1965. They found that the price behavior of most of these commodity futures, with the exception of wheat, cotton and cocoa, confirmed the random walk model.

In summary, the survey of empirical evidence indicates a tendency toward negative serial dependence in daily price changes of some commodity futures. The conflicting findings on the existence of price trends should warn speculators to be skeptical in trying to profit from short-term price movements.

ECONOMIC FUNCTIONS OF FUTURES MARKETS

The two primary functions of futures markets are *price discovery* and *hedging.* By price discovery, we mean the forecast of spot price expected at the time of delivery of the futures contract. As observed earlier, recent research indicates that the current futures price is a biased predictor of future spot price. However,

---

[14] Arnold B. Larson, "Measurement of a Random Process in Futures Prices," in *Selected Writings on Futures Markets,* Anne E. Peck (ed.) (Chicago: Chicago Board of Trade, 1977), 295–306.

[15] Seymour Smidt, "A Test of the Serial Independence of Price Changes in Soybean Futures," in *Selected Writings on Futures Markets,* ibid., pp. 257–277.

[16] Richard A. Stevenson and Robert M. Bear, "Commodity Futures: Trends or Random Walk?" *Journal of Finance,* 25 no. 1 (March 1970): 65–81.

[17] Walter C. Labys and C. W. T. Granger, *Speculation, Hedging and Commodity Price Forecasts* (Lexington, Mass.: D.C. Heath and Co., 1970): 66–70.

empirical evidence revealed that for many commodity contracts the bias in the futures price may be small or insignificant. Since futures prices are widely disseminated through daily news media, the market consensus prediction of the expected future spot price of the underlying asset is easily available to anyone interested. The price forecast can be used by the producers to guide production levels and by merchants to manage inventories. For instance, in making planting decisions, a farmer can obtain the market forecast of expected prices at harvest time from the springtime quotes on the July wheat futures contract. Likewise, a corporate treasurer who expects to sell a new issue of bonds in the near future can find the market forecast of long-term interest rates in the current quotes on the near-term treasury bond futures contract.

Futures contracts written on *seasonally* produced, *storable* commodities such as wheat and corn facilitate temporal allocation of inventories. To grain elevators, they provide a consensus forecast of the storage cost between the present and the contract delivery month. This information helps them in inventory-carrying decisions. Commodities such as potatoes and onions (*seasonally* produced) and live beef cattle and eggs (*continuously* produced) are generally regarded as semi- or *nonstorable* products. Futures contracts written on nonstorable commodities provide market forecasts of the prices expected to prevail at the time of delivery. In inventory-carrying markets (i.e., markets in storable commodities), speculators who try to arbitrage between the spot and futures markets strengthen the relationship between the current futures price and the expected future spot price. Does it mean that the current futures price of a nonstorable commodity is not as good a predictor of the future spot price?

To answer this question, Leuthold[18] compared the forecasting performance of corn futures with that of live beef cattle. Recall that at delivery the futures price, $F(T)$, is more or less equal to the spot price, $S(T)$, so we could use $F(T)$ to represent $S(T)$. Using monthly data over 1964 to 1971 covering 36 cattle contracts and 35 corn contracts, Leuthold regressed $F(T)$ against $F(t,T)$ from one to eight months prior to delivery (i.e., $t = 1,2,3, \ldots 8$ months) to test the hypothesis that the intercept is zero and the slope coefficient is equal to one. The regression results indicated little difference between the forecasting performance of the corn and cattle futures contracts.

In addition, Leuthold compared the performance of the current *futures* price with that of the current *spot* price as a predictor of the future spot price. This was accomplished by computing mean square errors for weekly cash and futures prices of corn and cattle. The results indicated that for corn the mean square errors for cash and futures prices are similar for all 36 weeks prior to delivery. This held for cattle only during the first 15 weeks prior to delivery. During the 15th to the 36th week prior to delivery, the mean square error for the futures price on cattle got progressively larger than the cash price. The author concluded that for cattle the deferred futures contracts (i.e., contracts that are 15 to 36 weeks away from delivery) were poor predictors of the future spot price relative to the current spot price.

It is, however, not clear whether the poor forecasting ability of deferred

[18] Raymond M. Leuthold, "The Price Performance on the Futures Market of a Nonstorable Commodity: Live Beef Cattle," in *Selected Writings on Futures Markets,* ibid., 375–386.

contracts is the result of nonstorability of the underlying commodity or is due to the limited open interest and volume of trading in distant delivery contracts. In sum, we may conclude that the futures price of a near-delivery (i.e., up to three months from delivery) contract on both storable and nonstorable commodities generates a market consensus forecast with negligible bias of the delivery-time spot price. Notably, its forecasting performance is comparable to that of the current spot price. The amount of bias and the forecast error tend to increase with the distance to delivery of futures contracts (i.e., as the length of the forecast horizon increases). One apparent reason for this tendency is the thinness of the market for distant delivery contracts. This suggests that the current spot price is a more reliable predictor of the future spot price of nonstorable commodities over longer horizons than a distant delivery futures contract with a thin market.

Peck[19] examined the forecasting performance of the shell egg futures (traded on the Chicago Mercantile Exchange) during June 1971 and December 1973. She reports that forecast errors (root mean squared errors) increase as the forecast horizon lengthens from one to five months prior to delivery. She concluded that the performance measured by the root mean squared error of the futures forecast is comparable to that of subjective point forecast. It is far more reliable over the five-month horizon than a simple regression forecast of the future spot price.

The foregoing discussion raises an important question. If the current spot price is as good as the current futures price in predicting the expected future spot price, does this mean the value added (to economic activity) by futures trading is virtually negligible? To answer this question, recall that active futures trading provides professional traders with a low cost mechanism to formulate their (future spot price) forecasts. It increases market information and thereby enables producers, processors, and distributors in the spot market to respond faster to expected supply and demand conditions. This helps integrate the spot and futures markets. As a result, the current spot price reflects the information contained in the current futures price. Clearly, the operations of an active futures market tend to increase the efficiency of the underlying spot market.

Hedging and Speculative Transactions

As discussed earlier, individuals and institutions involved in commodities trading can be categorized into one of two groups: hedgers or speculators. Hedgers enter into a futures contract to offset another risk. This will be dealt with more fully below. In contrast, a speculator attempts to derive a rate of return on the purchase and sale of the asset in line with the risk he accepts in the transaction. In this regard, the speculator is like the typical common stock investor who buys stock when he expects a price increase and sells stock short if he expects a price decline. Let us first discuss a few broad examples of hedging and speculation and then examine the theory of hedging and speculation.

A hedger enters into a futures transaction to reduce the risk of loss from price fluctuations of the cash asset. A *naive* hedge is a futures position that is *equal* in size but *opposite* to the one you have in the spot market; i.e., if you have a long

---

[19] Anne E. Peck, "Hedging and Income Stability: Concepts, Implications, and an Example," in *Selected Writings on Futures Markets,* 237–250.

position in the spot market, you go short on the futures contract. In the futures market, to *go long* means to buy a contract and to *go short* means to sell a contract. Because of deferred delivery and payment, you are not acquiring (relinquishing) title to the underlying asset when you buy (sell) a futures contract. In contrast, in the spot market to *go long* means to buy the *underlying asset,* i.e., a long position means you already own the asset. Further, to *go short* on spot means that you sell an asset you do not own. Two examples of the naive hedging strategy in the commodities futures are: the farmer hedging his crop (a short hedge) and a processor of commodities who wants to hedge an order for future delivery (a long hedge). To simplify the discussion, we will not consider the details of margin maintenance costs that arise from marking-to-market of the futures contract and other transactions costs and taxes.

Examples of Hedging Transactions in Commodities.   Consider the example of a farmer who grows corn. As of June he expects to harvest about 10,000 bushels in August. In June, the September futures for corn are selling for 294 ($2.94 a bushel). If the farmer thinks that $2.94 is a reasonable price and does not want to gamble on possibly higher *or* lower prices at harvest time, he can *sell* futures contracts to hedge his current long position; i.e., the farmer is basically long in the crop that he owns and is going to harvest. Therefore, by selling a futures contract in that commodity he has offset his own long position. For our example, assume that he sells two September corn contracts for 10,000 bushels. Let us now consider what happens if the price of corn goes up or down between June and August when he harvests the 10,000 bushels of corn.

If the price of corn decreases to $2.80 a bushel between June and August, the farmer will *lose* on his harvested crop relative to what he expected to receive (which is what he was concerned about), but he will *gain* a comparable amount on the contract he sold short, as shown.

```
Revenue from cash crop:   10,000 × $2.80 = $28,000
Sale of 2 contracts at $2.94 =        $29,400
Purchase of 2 contracts at $2.80 = $28,000
    Gain on short sale                     $ 1,400
Total revenue (before transactions
and margin costs)                          $29,400
```

By entering into the hedge the farmer has assured himself of the $2.94 a bushel because what he loses on the cash market he gains in the futures market.

If the price of corn *increases* to $3.05 a bushel between June and August, the opposite occurs. In this instance, the farmer will *gain* on his cash crop relative to what he expected to receive but will *lose* on his futures contract, as shown.

```
Revenue from cash crop:   10,000 × $3.05 = $30,500
Sale of 2 contracts at $2.94 =        $29,400
Purchase of 2 contracts at $3.05 = $30,500
    Loss on short sale                     $ (1,100)
Total revenue (before transaction
costs)                                     $29,400
```

In this instance the farmer has likewise assured himself of $2.94 a bushel and thereby *forgone the added gain* due to the price rise. It is just this sort of possibility that causes some farmers to avoid using the futures market as a means to hedge some or all of their crop. When they do not hedge, they are basically speculators in the commodity because by definition they are long in the commodity that they are growing.

It is seldom possible to hedge a position completely because of uncertainty about the size of the harvest transactions, margin costs, and differential price movements. Specifically, it would be a *partial* hedge if the harvest turns out to be a different quantity than anticipated. In addition, there are going to be commissions and margin costs on the futures transaction that will add to the loss or detract from the gain. Still, these costs will be small compared to the gain or loss on a large crop. Finally, futures prices may not move completely with the cash price, which could mean it will not be a complete offset. As an example, consider the first case in which the cash price declined to $2.80 a bushel. If we assume that the September futures contract only declined to $2.82 a bushel, the gain on the short sale would have been only $1,200 so there would not be a complete offset.

A second group that consistently enters into hedging positions is commodity processors who are basically forced to be short some required commodity due to the nature of their business. Consider the example of a flour producer who signs a contract in April with a food processing firm to deliver a certain amount of flour the following July. Because the contract is for July delivery, the price quoted will be based upon the July wheat price. Assume that the flour is going to require the type of wheat sold on the Kansas City Board of Trade. (The type of wheat traded on each of the exchanges differs — hard red winter wheat, soft red winter wheat, etc. Each of these wheats is used to produce a flour that has different uses.) At the time the contract is signed, the price for a July Kansas City wheat contract is 440 ($4.40 a bushel). Therefore, the commodity processor will quote a price for the flour that assumes he will buy the wheat required at $4.40 a bushel. If the contract requires 20,000 bushels of wheat, once the contract is signed the processor is basically short 20,000 bushels of Kansas City wheat at $4.40 a bushel; i.e., he has agreed to deliver flour that will require 20,000 bushels of wheat and he does not own the wheat. To hedge his position he would immediately *buy* four July wheat contracts on the Kansas City Exchange. Assume that between April and June (when the processor must buy the wheat in the cash market to fulfill his flour contract) the price of wheat has increased to $4.75 a bushel. The processor's cash flows will be as shown.

Cost of 20,000 bushels at $4.75	= $95,000
Cost of 4 contracts at $4.40 = $88,000	
Sale of 4 contracts at $4.75 = $95,000	
Gain on futures contracts	$ 7,000
Total cost of wheat for flour contract (before transaction and margin costs)	$88,000

As shown, although the processor had to pay more for his cash wheat than the contract price, he made a gross profit on his futures contract. As a result, his total cost before transactions and margin costs was $88,000 or $4.40 a bushel, which is consistent with his contract.

In contrast, assume that the price of wheat declined from $4.40 to $4.20. The processor's costs will be as shown.

Cost of 20,000 bushels at $4.20	= $84,000	
Cost of 4 contracts at $4.40 = $88,000		
Sale of 4 contracts at $4.20 = $84,000		
Loss on futures transaction	$(4,000)	
Total cost of wheat for flour contract (before transactions and margin costs)	$88,000	

In this instance, the processor did not have to pay as much for the wheat in the spot market, but lost on his futures transaction so that the total cost was $88,000 or $4.40 a bushel. Obviously he would have been better off if he had not entered into the futures contract because he would have made more on the flour contract. The fact is this would have required the processor to *speculate* on the future price of wheat. The whole point of a naive hedge is to *avoid* speculation. The processor wants to make his income from processing the wheat and does *not* want to be required to accept the possible *price* risk related to his basic commodity. With the hedge he has avoided this price risk.

Again, the hedge may not work perfectly due to transaction and margin costs involved in the futures investment. Also, prices in the cash market and futures market may not move perfectly together.

Why Speculate in Commodities?

As mentioned, besides using the futures market to hedge a position, an investor can speculate in commodities futures. The reasons for entering into speculative commodity transactions are similar to the reasons for investing in other investment instruments. Specifically, you want to either reduce the risk involved in your overall portfolio while holding expected return constant, or you attempt to increase your return for a given level of risk. There is potential for risk reduction in commodities trading because the prices and returns on commodities are not very highly correlated with those in other securities markets (i.e., stocks and bonds). Chapter 2 showed that the correlation between *commodity* prices and *stock* prices was about 0.29. Therefore, although the *total* variability of commodity returns is rather high, the movements are not related to other potential investments so the variance of your *total* portfolio could be reduced.

As the examples will show, there is the potential for large rates of return on your investment in a short period of time with commodities because of the substantial leverage involved. Therefore, for the investor with the time, temperment, and discipline required for commodities investing, the rewards can be substantial. After we have considered several examples of potential commodity trades, we will discuss some common rules that a speculator in commodities should keep in mind.

Speculative Transactions

In the case of speculation, it is necessary to consider what commodities to deal in and what approach to use in analysis. Regarding commodities to consider, a quick analysis of the *Wall Street Journal* indicates there are about 30 different commodities that can be traded in a wide range of categories (e.g., grains, foods, metals). Few traders ever attempt to trade more than 5 or 6 at a time because of the diverse nature of the markets and the difference in supply and demand analysis factors. Trying to analyze and trade wheat, orange juice, and pork bellies would be like trying to analyze industrials, railroads, and banks at the same time. Therefore, you would normally concentrate on commodities within a given group (e.g., corn and soybeans) or between groups that might be related (e.g., corn and livestock).

After you have selected a limited number of commodities that you want to trade, you must decide how you are going to make your trading decisions. Similar to stock investors, commodity investors are basically divided between fundamentalists and technicians. *Fundamentalists* attempt to analyze changes in the supply and demand for the commodity. Factors influencing supply would include the amount of acreage planted, the weather during the growing season in the major areas for the crop in question, and the carryover of the crop from the previous season. Regarding demand, the analyst would consider the domestic demand for the product based upon secular population growth and also demand for animal feed. In addition, an important aspect of demand is that from foreign countries. Hence, it is necessary to consider foreign supply and demand for the commodity and its residual impact on our market.

Some investors adhere to *technical analysis;* i.e., future price movements can be predicted on the basis of past price changes and volume changes. Some investors consider a combination of fundamental and technical analysis most useful. There is a stronger preference for the technical approach in commodity analysis than there is in stock analysis, although there is a fair amount of empirical support for random changes in commodity prices.[20]

Examples of Speculative Transactions in Commodities.   At this point, let us consider some examples, assuming you have decided what commodity you are going to trade and your method of analysis. *Long on Soybeans:* Assume you have become interested in soybeans and, based upon your analysis, you expect soybean prices to increase over the next six months (from January to July). Therefore, you want to be long in July soybeans and decide to buy two contracts (10,000 bushels). After making your decision, you call your commodities broker and place a market order for two July soybean contracts. Like a common stock transaction, your order is transmitted to the firm's representative on the floor of the Chicago Board of Trade (CBT). This floor broker proceeds to the soybean pit and calls out that he wants to buy two July contracts. After bargaining with several other brokers or traders, he completes the transaction at 660 ($6.60 a bushel). If

[20] Holbrook Working, "Prices of Cash Wheat and Futures at Chicago since 1883," *Wheat Studies,* 2 (1934): 75–134.

we assume that the current margin on soybeans at the CBT is 15 percent, it would be necessary to send the broker $9,900 (.15 × $66,000). Because each contract is for 5,000 bushels, each one-cent change in the price of soybeans is worth $50 per contract or $100 to you because you control two contracts. Subsequently, if the futures price rises (falls), the speculator with a long futures position stands to gain (lose). The customer's account would be adjusted on a *daily* basis for futures price changes, and the brokerage house would ask the customer to deposit more margin (margin calls) if the account balance falls below the maintenance margin level. This shows the speculator is exposed to an added cost, namely, the interest on variable margins.

After the purchase, the investor can enter a stop-loss order, as is done with stocks, or simply watch the market closely. One difference between trading stocks and commodities is that limits are placed on the daily price changes of each commodity. These limits ensure that no major price change occurs due to an unexpected catastrophe. The idea is that this daily price limit allows time for new investors or speculators to enter the market to help stabilize the price following the major event that caused the abrupt price change.

Assume that in March, the price of July soybeans has gone to $6.85 a bushel, which is your target price, so you decide to take your profit. You call your broker and tell him to close out your long July soybean position by *selling* two July soybean contracts on the market. Again, the broker contacts his representative on the floor of the CBT who sells two contracts at $6.85 a bushel. Your position is cleared and your return is as shown.

Bought 2 July contracts at $6.60 a bushel = $66,000 (you deposited 15 percent: $9,900)	
Sold 2 July contracts at $6.85 a bushel	= $68,500
Gross profit	$ 2,500
Less estimated round trip commission ($30/contract)	$ 60
Profit before margin costs	$ 2,440
Rate of return on the initial amount committed (before interest on variable margins): 2,440/$9,900 = 24.6%	

This 24.6 percent return was generated during a two-month period, which means the annual return would be approximately six times as large. Also, consider the impact of leverage: you received a 24.6 percent return on your investment when the price of soybeans only increased by 3.8 percent ($6.85 versus $6.60).

Now consider the same investment but assume the price of soybeans does not rise but begins to decline during February. As do most commodity traders, assume that after the purchase you automatically put in a stop-loss order at $6.45 a bushel; this means if soybeans ever hit this price the broker is instructed to put in a market sell order for you. The purpose is to ensure that you cut any losses short; i.e., the maximum loss should be approximately 15 cents a bushel. If the price declines to this level, the broker puts in a market sell, and let us assume that he sells the two contracts for $6.44 a bushel. (He is not able to get the $6.45 at that point.) Under these assumptions your results would be as follows:

Bought 2 July contracts at $6.60 a bushel = $66,000
(you deposited 15 percent: $9,900)
Sold 2 July contracts at $6.44 a bushel = $64,400

Gross loss $(1,600)
Less estimated round trip commission
($30/contract) $ 60

Loss before interest on variable margins $(1,660)
Rate of return on initial margin (subject
to interest on variable margins):
($1,660)/$9,900 = (16.8%)

In this example you have a return of minus 16.8 percent in approximately one month, which would convert to an annual loss of about 12 times this number. Again, it is possible to see the impact of leverage. You experienced a negative return of 16.8 percent on your investment when soybean prices only declined 2.5 percent ($6.44 versus $6.60). *Short Pork Bellies:* In contrast to being optimistic about soybeans, assume that, based upon your fundamental and/or technical analysis, you are pessimistic about the future price of pork bellies (uncured bacon). According to the quotation section, pork bellies are traded on the Chicago Mercantile Exchange (CME), and the standard contract is 38,000 pounds. In November you decide to *sell* three May pork-belly contracts that are selling for 44.00 (44 cents a pound). This means each contract is worth $16,720 ($.44 × 38,000). In this instance, a one-cent change in the price of pork bellies changes the value of the contract by $380. To protect yourself if you are wrong, assume you put in a stop-gain order at 48 cents. Such an order means you want to *buy* three contracts to offset your prior sale if pork belly futures reach this price. It is not certain that you will receive 48 cents, but it should be fairly close.

Assume that prices increase, your stop-gain order is enacted, and you sell at 48.5 cents a pound in February. Your return would be as follows:

Sale of 3 May pork-belly contracts at 44¢/lb. = $50,160
(you deposited 15 percent: $7,524)
Purchase of 3 May pork-belly contracts   = $55,290
at 48.5¢/lb.

Gross loss $(5,130)
Less estimated round trip commission
($30/contract) $ 90

Total loss before interest on variable margins $(5,220)
Rate of return on initial deposits (Subject to
interest on variable margins)
(5,220)/7,524 = (69.4%)

In this instance, pork bellies increased in price by 10.2 percent, and you experienced a negative rate of return of over 69 percent on your investment in three months.

These examples are meant to indicate the opportunities and risks involved in commodities trading as a speculator.

Basic Rules for Commodity Trading

A large brokerage firm devoted to commodities trading has run a series of ads containing rules for commodities trading.[21] The following is a composite list of suggestions derived from them.

1. Have a basic money management plan that takes into account your financial needs and risk preferences.
2. Establish your trading plans *before* engaging in any trading, and stick to your plan regardless of short-run market changes. If you want to change your plan, do so only after reconsideration of all aspects and not when under pressure.
3. Your trading plan should be detailed in terms of specifying such factors as entry point, objective of the trade, and exit price. This includes extensive use of stop-loss or stop-gain orders that ensure discipline and will not allow you to get caught up in the emotion of the market.
4. In general, your trading plan should be an attempt to cut your losses short and let profits run. Most commodities traders lose on most trades but hope to make the losses up on a few big winners. Therefore, the key is to have a number of *small losses* but a few *big gains*.
5. Select a broker whose psychology of trading is consistent with yours. In many instances, the best recommendation for a broker is another satisfied customer. In most cases, the broker's main task is to protect you from yourself and your impulse not to stick to your plan.
6. Keep in constant contact with your broker so that when action is required you will not hesitate.
7. Be sure you begin with enough money to accomplish your plan. If not, you may not be able to stay through temporary setbacks; i.e., a string of small losses may wipe you out before you make a big gain.

GENERAL THEORY OF HEDGING AND SPECULATION

Now that you have an elementary understanding of the operational aspects of hedging and speculation, we can consider some basic issues. Two of the important issues are: (1) could hedging stabilize income; i.e., could it reduce the variability of expected returns from a spot futures portfolio? (2) what are the risk-return characteristics of futures contracts?

In our earlier discussion, we described a hedger as one who assumes a futures position that is equal in quantity but opposite to his spot market position. A speculator, in contrast, is one who trades a futures contract without a corresponding position in the underlying spot asset in hopes of earning a profit for bearing the risk of futures price fluctuations. However, in trying to reduce spot price variability the hedger is indeed *speculating* on movements in the *basis*— the difference between the current spot and futures prices. If the basis does not change over the hedging period (i.e., the price changes are perfectly correlated), the spot and futures price changes cancel out and the hedger's net cash

---

[21] Conti Commodity Services, Inc., 1800 Board of Trade Building, Chicago, Illinois, 60604.

flow is equal to the transaction costs and the margin maintenance costs. But, if the basis at the time of lifting the hedge is larger (smaller) than the initial basis, the short hedger experiences a price gain (price loss). In effect, the short hedger is exchanging *basis risk,* which is the variability in the spot price relative to the futures price, for *price risk,* which is the variability of spot price.

The Portfolio Approach

The portfolio approach to futures trading does not distinguish between hedging and speculation. It assumes that the basic motivation for trading futures contracts is the same as that for trading stocks and bonds. The objective of a futures contract holder is to maximize expected return at a given level of risk or to minimize risk given the expected return. Under this approach, both the hedger and the speculator are concerned with expected return as well as risk in trading futures contracts. The holding period dollar return, *DR*, on a portfolio consisting of χ units of the spot asset and y units of a futures contract is:

(24.12) $\qquad E[DR] = \chi E(S_{t+1} - S_t) + yE(F_{t+1} - F_t).$

The variance of this spot futures portfolio is:

(24.13) $\qquad \sigma^2(DR) = \chi^2\sigma_i^2 + y^2\sigma_j^2 + 2\chi y\sigma_{ij},$

where: σ_i^2 = the variance of expected spot price changes.

$\qquad \sigma_j^2$ = the variance of expected futures price changes.

$\qquad \sigma_{ij}$ = the covariance of spot and futures price changes.

In the Markowitz mean-variance portfolio analysis, the holder of the spot futures portfolio seeks to maximize Q:[22]

$$Q = E(DR) + \lambda\sigma^2(DR),$$

where: λ = the risk parameter representing the investor's subjective weighting of expected return relative to the risk involved. Since the investor is assumed to be risk averse, λ assumes negative values.

If the basic motivation for trading futures contracts is to *minimize* portfolio variance, we can derive the optimal number of contracts to trade given the spot position. To do so, differentiate $\sigma^2(DR)$ with respect to y, set it equal to zero, and solve. The optimal number of futures contracts is y^*:

(24.14) $\qquad\qquad y^* = \chi\sigma_{ij}/\sigma_j^2.$

This means that the variance minimizing hedge ratio, H^*, is[23]

---

[22] Peck, "Hedging and Income Stability: Concepts, Implications, and an Example," in *Selected Writings on Futures Markets,* 237–250.

[23] See Leland L. Johnson, "The Theory of Hedging and Speculation in Commodity Futures," *Review of Economic Studies,* 27 (1959–1960): 139–160; Jerome L. Stein, "The Simultaneous Determination of Spot and Futures Prices," *American Economic Review,* 51 no. 5 (December 1961): 1012–1025.

(24.15)
$$H^* = (y^*/\chi) = -(\sigma_{ij}/\sigma_j^2)$$
$$= \rho_{ij}\sigma_i/\sigma_j,$$

where: ρ_{ij} = the correlation coefficient of spot and futures price changes.

Given that the spot and futures price changes are positively correlated ($\rho_{ij} > 0$), H^* is negative. The negative sign indicates that for the hedger to minimize variance he must hold a futures position which is opposite to that held in the cash market. In a variance-minimizing hedge the futures position need not necessarily be equal in size to the spot position; i.e., the absolute value of H^* need not necessarily be equal to one. Specifically, the value of H^* depends on the correlation and the relative variability of spot and futures price changes. If the standard deviations of spot and futures price changes are comparable, the absolute value of the hedge ratio is less than one.

The variance of the minimum-variance hedge portfolio, $\sigma^2(DR)^*$, can be obtained by substituting the value of y^* for y in Equation 24.13:

(24.16)
$$\sigma^2(DR)^* = \chi^2\sigma_i^2[1 - \rho_{ij}^2],$$

where: ρ_{ij}^2 = the coefficient of determination of spot and futures price changes.

This means $\sigma^2(DR)^*$ is only a fraction of the variance of the unhedged spot position, $\chi^2\sigma_i^2$. The percentage risk reduction obtained from the minimum-variance hedge is a measure of the effectiveness of the hedge:

(24.17)
$$e = [(\chi^2\sigma_i^2 - \sigma^2(DR)^*)/\chi^2\sigma_i^2] = \rho_{ij}^2.$$

Thus the coefficient of determination of spot and futures price changes provides a measure of the effectiveness of the minimum-variance hedge. It is often used as one measure of the hedging performance of a futures contract. The portfolio approach can be extended to cover several cash assets and futures contracts.

A major limitation of the Markowitz mean-variance portfolio model of hedging is the assumption that the spot position to be hedged is *known*. While this assumption is realistic for a processor with a known future delivery commitment, it does not hold for a producer since the size of the harvest is unknown at planting time. Further, the model abstracts from the marking-to-market of futures positions and ignores the covariance of daily futures price changes and interest rates. It does not account for transaction costs and taxes. Nevertheless, it provides a useful guide in determining the number of futures contracts to trade and in evaluating the hedging performance of futures contracts.

An Application of the Portfolio Approach

Peck[24] employed the Markowitz mean-variance portfolio model to examine if a routine system of optimal hedging of expected egg productions in the shell egg futures market (CME) on a monthly basis succeeded in stabilizing producer

[24] Peck, "Hedging and Income Stability: Concepts, Implications, and an Example," ibid.

income during the 1971–1973 period. Her major findings were:

1. The average optimal hedge ratios of hedges lasting one to five months ranged from 55 to 90 percent of production; the longer the hedge horizon, the higher the optimal hedge ratio.
2. The relevant measure of risk is the root mean squared error—the root of the squared deviations of actual returns from their expected values. It is not the standard deviation of returns. Based on the root mean squared error, optimal hedging substantially reduced the risk confronting a producer.
3. The results obtained from a scheme of *total* routine hedging (i.e., a hedge ratio equal to one) compared favorably with the optimal hedging strategy.

In summary, the hedger is concerned with both expected return and risk. Based on his subjective risk aversion and expectations about spot and futures price movements, he decides how much of his spot position to hedge in the futures market in order to attain a mean-variance efficient spot futures hedge portfolio.

An optimal hedging routine substantially reduces the variability of actual portfolio returns from their expected values. Even a naive strategy of hedging total spot positions is quite successful in reducing unpredictable variability of portfolio returns. Futures trading facilitates the production and marketing of commodities by providing a form of insurance against unpredictable price fluctuations. It reduces the probability of bankruptcy[25] and enables the hedger to obtain credit at more favorable terms, thereby reducing costs of capital. While the hedger is exposed to additional costs in trading futures, such as commissions, bid-ask spreads in futures prices, and lost interest on margins, futures trading provides the *lowest cost* means of insuring against unexpected price movements.

Risk and Return on Futures Contracts

Our earlier discussion indicated that under the Keynesian hypothesis of normal backwardation, the variability of futures prices is used as measure of risk associated with futures trading. Under this theory, speculators expect to earn a positive return on their long futures positions. In contrast, the CAPM holds that only the *systematic risk* and not the *total price risk* is relevant. The systematic risk (the futures beta) of a futures contract is measured by the covariance of the futures price change with the return on the market portfolio divided by the variance of the market return. Because the futures contract requires no initial investment of funds but only good faith margin deposits, the futures contract is not a part of the market portfolio of all assets. If the futures beta is close to zero, then the expected return from trading the futures contract must be close to zero. Expected returns to hedgers, speculators and spreaders in futures contracts are also close to zero. To make consistent profits on the futures positions, these traders must be able to forecast prices better than other market participants.

In a study of corn, wheat, and soybean futures during the 1952–1967 period,

[25] Scholes, "The Economics of Hedging and Spreading," *The Journal of Futures Market,* 1 (1981): 265–286.

Dusak found the futures betas and semimonthly returns close to zero.[26] Recently, Bodie and Rosansky examined quarterly returns on 23 commodity futures contracts over the period 1950 to 1976.[27] The futures returns are computed assuming that the investor used treasury bills to post 100 percent margin. The annual rates of return are presented in Table 24.1. The table shows that the mean and standard deviation of returns on an equally weighted commodity futures portfolio is comparable to those on common stocks. The futures returns have low to negative correlations with returns on T-bills, long-term government bonds, and common stocks, indicating the diversification potential of commodity futures contracts. The study revealed that a portfolio with 60 percent in common stocks and 40 percent in commodity futures has about the same mean rate of return, but the standard deviation of such a portfolio is only two thirds that of a pure common stock portfolio. Further, the positive correlation of commodity futures returns with inflation rates means they are a better hedge against inflation than common stocks.

Table 24.2 indicates the mean annual returns on most commodity futures are positive but the returns are relatively volatile. Many of the futures betas are negative and close to zero indicating that the systematic risk of commodity futures is relatively small. The authors concluded that these results favor the Keynesian normal backwardation hypothesis rather than the CAPM.

Effects of Futures Trading on Underlying Spot Asset Prices

The history of futures trading reveals that regulatory authorities (and others) have been concerned that futures markets encourage excessive speculation and thereby destabilize the underlying spot asset price. In contrast, economic theory argues that futures trading creates a centralized minimum cost mechanism that enables traders with special forecasting skills to determine the future price of the underlying asset. As futures price information is widely disseminated, the market participants are better informed. Consequently, they can react more judiciously to changes in supply and demand factors, which, in turn, reduces the random element in price movements. The futures price provides guidance in production decisions for farmers, processors, mortgage bankers, and others. It facilitates temporal allocation of inventories of seasonally produced, storable commodities by providing a forecast of the storage cost. Carrying inventories over time makes it possible to absorb the difference between production and consumption. With adequate controls to prevent corners and squeezes, futures trading should *reduce* interseasonal as well as short-run price fluctuations.

Empirical testing of these effects is difficult because the behavior of spot prices subsequent to the institution of futures trading is influenced by many other factors. In a study of the effects of futures trading on spot onion prices

---

[26] Dusak, "Futures Trading and Investor Returns: An Investigation of Commodity Marketing Premiums," *Journal of Political Economy*, 81 no. 4 (December 1973): 1387–1406.

[27] Zvi Bodie and Victor Rosansky, "Risk and Return in Commodity Futures," *Financial Analysts Journal*, 36 no. 3 (May–June 1980): 27–39.

TABLE 24.1
Distributions of Annual Rates of Return on Alternative Investments, 1950–1976

Series	Mean[a]	Standard Deviation
A. Nominal Returns (percent per year)		
Common Stocks	13.05	18.95
Commodity Futures	13.83	22.43
Commodity Futures with Treasury Bills		
Long-Term Government Bonds	2.84	6.53
U.S. Treasury Bills	3.63	1.95
Rate of Inflation	3.43	2.90
B. Real Returns[b] (percent per year)		
Common Stocks	9.58	19.65
Commodity Futures with Treasury Bills	9.81	19.44
Long-Term Government Bonds	-.51	6.81
U.S. Treasury Bills	.22	1.80
C. Excess Returns[c] (percent per year)		
Common Stocks	9.42	20.12
Commodity Futures	9.77	21.39
Long-Term Government Bonds	-.79	6.43

Correlation Matrix

Series	Commodity Futures	Long-Term Government Bonds	Treasury Bills	Inflation
A. Nominal Returns				
Common Stocks	-.24	-.10	-.57	-.43
Commodity Futures		-.16	.34	.58
Long-Term Government Bonds			.20	.03
Treasury Bills				.76
B. Real Returns				
Common Stocks	-.25	.14	.18	-.54
Commodity Futures		-.36	-.48	.48
Long-Term Government Bonds			.46	-.38
Treasury Bills				-.75
C. Excess Returns				
Common Stocks	-.20	.08	—	-.48
Commodity Futures		-.26	—	.52
Long-Term Government Bonds			—	-.20

[a] The mean annual loss is defined as the sum of the annual losses (negative rates of return) divided by the number of years in which losses occurred.
[b] The real rate of return. R_r is defined by:

$$1 + R_r = \frac{1 + R_n}{1 + i},$$

where R_n = the nominal rate of return i = the rate of inflation as measured by the proportional change in the Consumer Price Index.
[c] The excess return is the difference between the nominal rate of return and the treasury bill rate.

SOURCE: Zvi Bodie and Victor I. Rosansky, "Risk and Return in Commodity Futures," Financial Analysts Journal, 36 no. 3 (May–June 1980): 27–39.

TABLE 24.2
Distributions of Annual Rates of Return on 23 Commodity Futures Contracts
(percent per year), 1950–1976

Commodity	Arithmetic Mean	Standard Deviation	Standard Error	Beta (Standard Error of beta)
Wheat	3.181	30.745	5.917	−.370 (.296)
Corn	2.130	26.310	5.063	−.429 (.247)
Oats	1.681	19.492	3.751	.000 (.194)
Soybeans	13.576	32.318	6.220	−.266 (.317)
Soybean Oil	25.839	57.672	11.099	−.650 (.558)
Soybean Meal	11.870	35.599	6.851	.239 (.351)
Broilers	13.065	39.202	13.860	−1.692 (.395)
Plywood	17.968	39.962	16.314	.660 (.937)
Potatoes	6.905	42.111	8.104	−.610 (.400)
Platinum	.641	25.185	7.594	.221 (.411)
Wool	7.436	36.955	7.12	.307 (.362)
Cotton	8.937	36.236	6.974	−.015 (.360)
Orange Juice	2.515	31.771	10.047	.117 (.557)
Propane	68.260	202.088	71.449	−3.851 (3.788)
Cocoa	15.713	54.630	11.391	−.291 (.589)
Silver	3.587	25.622	7.106	−.272 (.375)
Copper	19.785	47.205	9.843	.005 (.492)
Cattle	7.362	21.609	6.238	.365 (.319)
Hogs	13.280	36.617	11.579	−.148 (.641)
Pork Bellies	16.098	39.324	11.352	−.062 (.618)
Egg	−4.741	27.898	5.369	−.293 (.271)
Lumber	13.070	34.667	13.101	−.131 (.768)
Sugar	25.404	116.215	24.232	−2.403 (1.146)

SOURCE: Zvi Bodie and Victor I. Rosansky, "Risk and Return in Commodity Futures," *Financial Analysts Journal*, 36 no. 3 (May–June 1980): 27–39.

during 1930–1968, Johnson[28] found that the pattern of within-season, seasonal, year-to-year, and within-month price changes has remained essentially *unchanged.* In another study, Taylor and Leuthold[29] divided their sample period into two equal parts: 1957 through 1964 with no futures trading and 1965 through 1972 with futures trading. They compared the variability of cash prices for live beef cattle during the two periods and reported a significant *reduction* in monthly and weekly price fluctuations.

Recently, Froewiss[30] examined the effects of futures trading on GNMA spot prices. The study covered two time periods: May 1973 through October 1975 without futures trading and October 1975 through December 1977 with futures trading. He regressed weekly percentage changes in spot GNMA prices on that of ten year U.S government bonds. There was an insignificant difference between the regression slope coefficients for the two periods, which indicated futures trading has *not increased* the variability of cash GNMA prices relative to the bond market. There was also a significant decrease in the standard error of regression in the latter subperiod, which implied the GNMA market has become more integrated with the rest of the bond market. Finally, a regression of the current week's percentage spot price change over that of the previous week showed the slope coefficient was significant in the first subperiod but not in the second. This suggests new information is rapidly incorporated into spot prices, and futures trading has made the GNMA cash market *more* efficient.

SUMMARY

In this chapter you were introduced to commodities futures specifically, but also the overall terminology and theory of futures markets that will carry over to the next chapter concerned with financial futures. The initial discussion involved the definition of spot, forward, and future contracts and the difference among them. Subsequently, given your background in stocks and bonds, we provided general background on the futures market by discussing the similarities and differences between trading in stocks versus trading in futures. This was followed by a brief discussion of the futures markets and market quotations.

Following this general background, there was an extended section on what determines forward and future prices and also the theoretical and empirical relationship among spot, forward, and futures prices. The discussion of the economic consequences of futures markets indicated several important functions of these markets. Because of the importance of understanding hedging and speculating as related to futures markets, the notion of why and how one hedges or speculates with commodities was discussed and demonstrated with several examples. The final section presented the general theory of hedging and specu-

[28] Aaron C. Johnson, "Effects of Futures Trading on Price Performance in the Cash Onion Market, 1930–1968," in *Selected Writings on Futures Markets:* 329–336.

[29] Gregory S. Taylor and Raymond M. Leuthold, "The Influence of Futures Trading on Cash Cattle Price Variations," in *Selected Studies on Futures Markets:* 367–373.

[30] Kenneth C. Froewiss, "GMMA Futures: Stabilizing or Destabilizing?" San Francisco Federal Reserve Bank *Economic Review* (Spring 1978): 20–29.

lating including the portfolio approach and its application. The chapter concluded with a discussion of some empirical studies of the returns and risk experienced in commodities trading alone or as part of a total investment portfolio. In general, the results were encouraging in a portfolio context as suggested in Chapter 2. Also, several empirical studies have concluded that generally the existence of these futures markets are beneficial to spot market participants.

QUESTIONS

1. Discuss two areas in which trading commodities and trading common stocks are similar.
2. Discuss two differences in trading commodities and trading common stocks.
3. Discuss one advantage that commodities have over stocks; an advantage that stocks have over commodities.
4. Based upon prices listed in *The Wall Street Journal,* compute the value of a soybeans contract for delivery in about six months (or a length of time close to this). Assuming a 15 percent margin, compute what you must deposit with your broker.
5. Given the conditions in Question 4, compute your rate of return if you buy the contract and prices *increase* by 10 percent. What is your rate of return if prices *decline* by 10 percent?
6. Assume a margin of 10 percent and that you sell the soybean contract. What is your rate of return if prices decline by 15 percent? What is your return if they rise by 8 percent?
7. What is the purpose of a stop-gain order? Give an example for a current three-month soybean meal contract.
8. You are a Kansas wheat farmer. In June you decide to hedge 15,000 bushels of your August harvest. Using the September Kansas City contract shown in Figure 24.1, show what would happen if you did it and prices increased by 15 cents a bushel.
9. In January, July wheat on the Kansas City Board of Trade (KC) is selling for 484 ($4.84 a bushel). You are bullish on wheat and buy three contracts (15,000 bushels).
   a. Assuming a 15 percent margin, how much must you deposit with your broker?
   b. In April, the price of wheat is 496. Assuming the commission is $30 per contract, compute your annualized rate of return if you close out this contract. Discuss the impact of leverage on this trade.
   c. Assume that in March the price of wheat is 475 and you think you should close out your trade. Assuming a commission of $30 per contract, compute the annualized rate of return on your investment. Discuss the impact of leverage.
10. In February you read reports about the number of cattle that will come to market over the next nine months. You believe that cattle prices will probably decline from current levels. Therefore, you decide to sell two August live cattle contracts (40,000 lbs. per contract) on the Chicago Mercantile Exchange (CME). Currently, the price of August live cattle is 71.00 (71 cents a pound). Given a margin

of 15 percent on live cattle and a commission of $30 a contract:

    a.   Assume you put in a stop-gain order at 76 cents a pound and you get closed out at that price in June. Compute the rate of return on your investment for this trade. What is your annualized rate of return?

    b.   Assume cattle prices decline to 65 cents a pound in July and you decide to close out your position. Compute the annualized rate of return on your investment.

    c.   Compute your annualized rate of return for the conditions in Part b if the margin were 10 percent rather than 15 percent. Discuss the difference in leverage effect between Parts b and c.

11. Discuss the results of at least one empirical study on the forecasting performance of commodity futures contracts.

12. Discuss the effects of futures trading on the spot market.

13. What is the difference between the value of a futures contract and its price?

14. Is the forward price equal to the futures price? Assume that both contracts are written on the same underlying asset and have identical delivery months.

REFERENCES

Black, Fischer. "The Pricing of Commodity Contracts." *Journal of Financial Economics.* 3 nos. 1, 2 (January–March 1976).

Bodie, Zvi, and Victor Rosansky. "Risk and Return in Commodity Futures." *Financial Analysts Journal.* 36 no. 3 (May–June 1980).

Brennan, M. T. "The Supply of Storage." *American Economic Review.* 48 no. 1 (March 1958).

Cootner, Paul H. "Speculation and Hedging." Stanford University Ford Research Institute Studies. Supplement (1967).

Cox, John C., Jonathan E. Ingersoll, Jr., and Stephen A. Ross. "The Relation between Forward Prices and Futures Prices." *Journal of Financial Economics.* 9 no. 4 (December 1981).

Dusak, Katherine. "Futures Trading and Investor Returns: An Investigation of Commodity Market Risk Premiums." *Journal of Political Economy.* 81 no. 4 (December 1973).

Froewiss, Kenneth C. "GNMA Futures: Stabilizing or Destabilizing?" *San Francisco Federal Reserve Bank Economic Review.* (Spring 1978).

Gold, G. *Modern Commodities Futures Trading* (New York: Commodity Research Bureau, 1968).

Hicks, J. R. *Value and Capital* 2nd ed. Oxford: Oxford University Press, 1953.

Jarrow, Robert A., and George S. Oldfield. "Forward Contracts and Futures Contracts." *Journal of Financial Economics.* 9 no. 4 (December 1981).

Johnson, Aaron C. "Effects of Futures Trading on Price Performance in the Cash Onion Market, 1930–1968." in *Selected Writings on Futures Markets.* A. E. Peck (ed.) Chicago: Chicago Board of Trade, 1977.

PART 6 ALTERNATIVE INVESTMENTS

796

Johnson, Leland L. "The Theory of Hedging and Speculation in Commodity Futures." *Review of Economic Studies.* 27 (1959–1960).

Keynes, T. M. *Treatise on Money.* 2. London: Macmillan, 1930.

Khoury, Sarkis J. *Speculative Markets.* New York: Macmillan Publishing Co., 1984.

Labys, Walter C., and C. W. T. Granger. *Speculation, Hedging, and Commodity Price Forecasts.* Lexington, Mass.: D.C. Heath and Company, 1970.

Larson, Arnold B. "Measurement of a Random Process in Futures Prices." in *Selected Writings on Futures Markets.* A. E. Peck (ed.) Chicago: Chicago Board of Trade, 1977.

Leuthold, Raymond M. "The Price Performance on the Futures Market of a Nonstorable Commodity: Live Beef Cattle." in *Selected Writings on Futures Markets.* A. E. Peck (ed.) Chicago: Chicago Board of Trade, 1977.

Peck, Anne E. "Hedging and Income Stability: Concepts, Implications, and an Example." in *Selected Writings on Futures Markets.* A. E. Peck (ed.) Chicago: Chicago Board of Trade, 1977.

Richard, Scott F., and M. Sundaresan. "A Continuous Time Equilibrium Model of Forward Prices and Futures Prices in a Multigood Economy." *Journal of Financial Economics.* 9 no. 4 (December 1981).

Rockwell, Charles S. "Normal Backwardation Forecasting and the Returns to Commodity Futures Traders." in *Selected Writings on Futures Markets.* A. E. Peck (ed.) Chicago: Chicago Board of Trade, 1977.

Scholes, Myron S. "The Economics of Hedging and Spreading in Futures Markets." *The Journal of Futures Markets.* 1 no. 2 (Summer 1981).

Smidt, Seymour. "A Test of the Serial Independence of Price Changes in Soybean Futures." in *Selected Writings on Futures Markets.* A. E. Peck (ed.) Chicago: Chicago Board of Trade, 1977.

Stein, Jerome L. "The Simultaneous Determination of Spot and Futures Prices." *American Economic Review.* 51 no. 6 (December 1961).

Stevenson, Richard A., and Robert M. Bear. "Commodity Futures: Trends or Random Walk?" *Journal of Finance.* 25 no. 1 (March 1970).

Taylor, Gregory S., and Raymond M. Leuthold. "The Influence of Futures Trading on Cash Cattle Price Variations." in *Selected Writings on Futures Markets.* A. E. Peck (ed.) Chicago: Chicago Board of Trade, 1977.

Teweles, R., C. Harlow, and H. Stone. *The Commodity Futures Game.* New York: McGraw-Hill, 1977.

Working, Holbrook. "Prices of Cash Wheat and Futures at Chicago since 1883." *Wheat Studies.* 2 (1934).

Working, Holbrook. "The Theory of Price of Storage," *American Economics Review.* 39 no. 5 (December, 1949).

Appendix 24.1

Commodity and Financial Futures Glossary

Arbitrage The simultaneous purchase and sale of similar financial instruments or commodity futures in order to benefit from an anticipated change in their price relationship.

Basis The spread or difference between the spot or cash price and the price of the future.

Buy In To cover or liquidate a sale.

Carrying Charges Those charges incurred in carrying the actual commodity generally including interest, insurance, and storage.

CFTC The Commodity Futures Trading Commission is the independent federal agency created by Congress to regulate futures trading. The CFTC Act of 1974 became effective April 21, 1975. Previously, futures trading had been regulated by the Commodity Exchange Authority of the USDA.

Clearinghouse An adjunct to a futures exchange through which transactions executed on the floor of the exchange are settled using a process of matching purchases and sales. A clearing organization is also charged with the proper conduct of delivery procedures and the adequate financing of the entire operation.

Clearing Member A member of the clearinghouse or organization. Each clearing member must also be a member of the exchange. Not all members of the exchange, however, are members of the clearing organization. All trades of a non-clearing member must be registered with, and eventually settled through, a clearing member.

Close The period at the end of the trading session during which all trades are officially declared as having been executed *at or on the close.* The closing range is the range of actual sales during this period.

Contract A term of reference describing a unit of trading for a financial commodity future. Also, actual bilateral agreement between the buyer and seller of a futures transaction as defined by an exchange.

Cover The buying of a commodity or a financial instrument to offset sales previously made.

Current Delivery Delivery during the current month.

Day Orders Those limited orders that are to be executed on a specific day and are automatically canceled at the close of that day.

Delivery The tender and receipt of an actual commodity or financial instrument or cash in settlement of a futures contract.

Delivery Month The calendar month during which a futures contract matures.

Delivery Points Those locations designated by futures exchanges at which the commodity covered by a futures contract may be delivered in fulfillment of the contract.

Discount Commodity or bond prices that are below the future, deliveries at a lesser price than others (e.g., May price is below the July price), or a lesser price owing to quality differences.

Evening Up Buying or selling to offset an existing market position.

Floor Trader A member who generally trades only for his own account, for an account controlled by him or who has such a trade made for him. Also referred to as a "local."

Hedging The sale of a futures contract against the physical commodity, an existing bond position, or its equivalent as protection against a price decline. Alternatively, it is the purchase of a futures contract against anticipated prices of the physical commodity or bond as protection against a price advance.

Inverted Market A futures market in which the nearer months are selling at premiums to the more distant months.

Last Trading Day The final day under an exchange's rules during which trading may take place in a particular delivery futures month. Futures contracts outstanding at the end of the last trading day must be settled by delivery of underlying physical commodities or financial instruments, or by agreement for monetary settlement if the former is impossible.

Life of Delivery (or Contract) The period between the beginning of trading in a particular futures contract and the expiration of that contract.

Liquidation Sale of a previously bought contract, otherwise known as *long liquidation.* It may also be the repurchase of a previously sold contract, generally referred to as *short covering.*

Long Hedge The purchase of a futures contract(s) in anticipation of actual purchases in the cash market. Used by processors or exporters as protection against an advance in the cash price.

Maintenance Margin A sum, usually smaller than — but part of — the original margin. At all times if a customer's equity in any futures position drops to, or under, the maintenance margin level, the broker must issue a "margin call" for the amount of money required to restore the customer's equity in the account to the original margin level.

Margin The amount deposited by a client with his broker to protect the broker against losses on contracts being carried or to be carried by the broker. A *margin call* is a request to deposit either the original margin at the time of the transaction or to restore the margin to the maintenance levels required for the duration of the time the contract is held.

Opening Range/Closing Range In open auction with many buyers and sellers, commodities are often traded at several prices at the opening or close of the market. Buying or selling orders might be filled at any point within such a price range.

Open Interest The total of unfilled or unsatisfied contracts on either side of the market. In any delivery month, the short interest equals the long interest; in other words, the total number of contracts sold equals the total number bought.

Pit The designated location on the trading floor where futures trading in a specific commodity takes place.

Round-turn Procedure by which the long or short position of an individual is offset by an opposite transaction or by accepting or making delivery of the actual financial instrument or physical commodity.

Scalper A speculator operating on the trading floor who provides market liquidity by buying and selling rapidly with small profits or losses and who holds his position for a short time.

Settlement Price The daily price at which the clearinghouse clears all the day's trades in a given commodity; also the price established by the exchange to settle contracts unliquidated because of acts of God, such as floods or other causes.

Short Hedge The sale of a futures contract(s) to eliminate or lessen the possible decline in value of ownership of an approximately equal amount of the actual financial instrument or physical commodity.

Speculator One who attempts to anticipate price changes and, through market activities, to profit from these changes.

Spot Commodity Goods available for immediate delivery.

Trading Limit The maximum price change permitted for a single session. These limits vary in the different markets. After prices have advanced or have declined to the permissible daily limits, trading automatically ceases unless offers appear at the permissible upper trading limit or bids appear at the permissible lower limit.

Volume of Trading The purchases or sales of a commodity future during a specified period.

Chapter 25   *Financial Futures*

B ased on the material in Chapter 24, you should have a good background in the basic makeup of the futures markets as well as an understanding of the theoretical relationship among spot, forward, and futures prices. This chapter applies and extends these concepts to some new financial instruments that have enjoyed enormous growth. Specifically, since their introduction in 1975, we have witnessed phenomenal growth in the number of financial futures instruments and the trading in these new instruments. Because of the many uses available for these instruments, most observers expect this growth to continue and even accelerate in the years ahead.

The same is true for stock index futures and foreign currency futures. In all cases these are relatively new instruments that promise to change the way that investors, money managers, and financial managers function. Needless to say, it is very important that you understand how to use these financial futures.

INTEREST RATE FUTURES

Futures contracts on various commodities have existed for many decades as a means of hedging against price changes in these commodities. Another set of futures contracts is relatively new: futures contracts on financial instruments such as government bonds and commercial paper. The basic idea and purpose of these contracts is the same as those for commodity contracts. Specifically, an interest rate futures contract promises delivery of a specified amount of a particular financial instrument at some future time. As an example, if you buy a September treasury bond contract on the Chicago Board of Trade, this contract specifies that, if you hold it to maturity, you will receive $100,000 face value of 8 percent, 20-year U.S. treasury bonds. (The specific characteristics of the bonds are set forth for all contracts.)

The reason for creating such futures contracts is the same as for commodities: the futures contract allows market participants to hedge against price risk in the underlying instrument. Since the mid–1970s, the volatility of interest rates had increased markedly. This was further accentuated in October 1979 when the Federal Reserve Board changed the basic premise of monetary policy from controlling interest rates to attempting to control the growth rate of alternative monetary aggregates (e.g., money supply, monetary base). This has caused a sharp increase in the price volatility of short- and long-term debt instruments. The mortgage banking industry was the first and by far the worst victim of a higher level of interest rates and greater volatility. Accordingly, an interest rate futures contract based on the GNMA pass-through certificates was first introduced by the Chicago Board of Trade (CBT) in October 1975 to provide mortgage bankers with a mechanism to hedge against unexpected interest rate fluctuations. In January 1976, the International Monetary Market (IMM), a subsidiary of the Chicago Mercantile Exchange, initiated the 90-day T-bill futures contract. This was followed by the introduction of the T-bond futures contract in August 1977 by the CBT.

Because of the exceptional growth in trading experienced by these two exchanges, other exchanges have initiated contracts, but the volume on those exchanges has been relatively light. Specifically, the New York Commodity Exchange (COMEX) began trading financial futures in 1979, but the volume is relatively small. In addition, the New York Futures Exchange (NYFE, pronounced "knife"), which is part of the New York Stock Exchange, was started in 1980 but apparently is not enjoying very large volume.[1]

Characteristics of Interest Rate Contracts

Currently, there are numerous interest rate futures contracts being traded on several exchanges. Of these, the ones with a relatively larger trading volume and open interest are: T-bill futures (IMM), T-bond futures (CBT), and GNMA futures (CBT). All three contracts have quarterly delivery cycles and the delivery months are March, June, September, and December. There are eight T-bill futures, eleven T-bond futures, and nine GNMA futures contracts trading at any given time. The T-bill futures contract calls for delivery of T-bills having $1 million face value with 90–92 days to maturity. During the delivery month the T-bill futures contract matures on the Wednesday following the third Monday of the month. The IMM T-bill futures index value is derived as follows (see the *Wall Street Journal* quotations in Chapter 24, Figure 24.1):

$$\text{IMM T-Bill Futures Index value} = 100 - \text{T-Bill Futures Discount Yield}$$
$$\text{(in percent)}.$$

That is, if the T-bill futures discount yield is 10.00 percent, the corresponding IMM index value is 90.00 (= 100 − 10.00). The price of a T-bill futures contract

[1] Roger Lowenstein, "Commodities Trader Pushes a New Market for Financial Futures," *Wall Street Journal*, December 29, 1980, p. 1; "NYSE Seat Prices Hit Low Amid Uncertainty," *Wall Street Journal*, March 30, 1981, p. 28.

with the IMM index value of 90.00 is:

$$= \$1,000,000 - \left(1,000,000 \times \text{T-bill futures yield} \times \frac{90}{360}\right)$$

$$= 1,000,000 - \left(1,000,000 \times .10 \times \frac{90}{360}\right)$$

$$= \$975,000.$$

The T-bond futures contract (CBT) requires delivery of $100,000 face value T-bonds with at least 15 years to call or maturity. The published quotes assume that the underlying spot bond has 20 years to maturity and bears an 8 percent coupon. A T-bond futures quote of 70–16 means 70 16/32 percent of par value. The corresponding market price of the contract is: $100,000 × 70 16/32 percent = $70,500. Currently, the prescribed minimum price movement on a contract is 1/32 of one percent of $100,000, which is equal to $31.25. The CBT limits the maximum daily price change to ±2.00 points from the previous day's settle price, which is worth $2,000 per contract. The exchange has stipulated a 3-day delivery process, which allows the contract seller to deliver on any business day during the delivery month. The specifications of the contract permit delivery of bonds bearing coupons other than 8 percent with proper price adjustment. Further, in computing the final settlement price, interest accrued since the last interest payment date is added to the published settlement price.

The financial instrument underlying the GNMA futures contract (CBT) is the GNMA pass-through certificate with a face value of $100,000. The futures quotes are based on 8 percent GNMA pass-throughs with an assumed maturity of 12 years. These certificates represent shares in a pool of single family, FHA-insured or VA-guaranteed mortgages that are collected by a mortgage banker and deposited with a custodial agent. The mortgage institution originating the GNMAs collects monthly payments from homeowners and passes them through to the certificate holders. The term to maturity of these certificates is uncertain because of mortgage prepayments by homeowners. The limits on daily price moves, interpretation of quotations, and delivery procedures (to a large extent) pertaining to the GNMA futures are similar to those of the T-bond futures contract.

Given this background, we are in a position to discuss various futures trades: (1) short hedges, (2) long hedges, and (3) speculation.

Short Hedges

A short hedge involves the sale of an interest rate futures contract to hedge a current position in the underlying financial instrument. The following examples of how various participants can use a short hedge will help you understand the procedure.

a. A bond dealer with an inventory of bonds can use a short hedge to reduce price risk in a volatile interest rate market by selling interest rate futures contracts against the inventory.

b. An investment banker can sell interest rate futures contracts against a recent bond issue that is not completely sold out. A prime example of this was an IBM bond issued in October 1979 that suffered a major price decline shortly after the offering because of a Federal Reserve policy change. Fortunately, investment bankers had sold futures contracts against part of the unsold offering, so the loss on the unsold issue was partially offset by a gain on the futures contracts.

c. A bond portfolio manager can sell futures contracts against a unique holding in the portfolio that is expected to decline. In this case, rather than sell the issue and then have to buy it back later, the portfolio manager would sell futures contracts against the issue and would offset the expected loss by a gain on the futures sale.

d. A bond portfolio manager can enter into a short hedge as protection against a price decline when attempting to liquidate an illiquid issue. Assume that he decides to sell a large position but knows that, because the market for this bond issue is thin, it will take two weeks to complete the sale. To protect against a price decline during this period, he could sell futures contracts against the position.

e. A corporate financial manager who anticipates a bond financing could use financial futures to hedge against higher rates before the actual financing. By selling a futures position you will gain on the futures transaction (if interest rates increase) and this will help offset the higher interest rate on the corporate bond issue.

The following is an example of a short-hedge transaction:

Intent: Sell futures contracts short against a cash position to hedge an unexpected increase in interest rates.

Cash	Futures	Basis
		(cash-future)
Nov. 1: You own $1 million of 15-yr., 8 3/8% U.S. bonds at 82–17 (Yield: 10.45%) (Value: $825,312.50)	Sell 10 March bond futures contracts at 80–09	+2–8
Mar. 3: You sell the 8 3/8% bonds at 70–26 (Yield: 12.31%) (Value: $708,125) Loss: 11–23 per bond $117,187.50	Buy 10 March bond futures contracts at 66–29 Gain: 13–12 per contract $133,750	+3–29

Conclusion: Overall gain before margins and transaction costs on the hedge is $16,562.50 because the basis moved in your direction.

Long Hedges

A long hedge involves the purchase of interest rate futures contracts to offset adverse price movements related to the future purchase of bonds (i.e., a future cash position). Long hedges are not as widespread as short hedges. The most obvious instance in which a long hedge is useful would involve a portfolio manager who expects a future cash flow will be available to buy bonds. Given this expectation, if the portfolio manager thinks yields might decline between now and the time when the cash flows are available, it is possible to "lock in" the higher yield through a long hedge, i.e., buy futures contracts on the bonds.

The following example of a Long Hedge shows how this would work:

Intent: Buy futures contracts against a future cash position.

Cash	Futures	Basis
June 1: A 20-year treasury bond currently yields 12.45%. Price for 20-yr., 8 1/4% bond is 67–28 (current cost is $678,750)	Buy 10 Dec. bond futures contracts at 66–13 Cost: $66,406.25	(cash-future) +1–15
Dec. 3: Buy $1 million of 20-yr., 8 1/4% U.S. bonds at 83–23 (Yield: 10.03%) (Cost of $837,187.50) Loss: $837,187.50 — 678,750.00 — $158,437.50	Sell 10 Dec. bond futures contracts at 81–22 Revenue: $81,687.50 Gain: $81,687.50 — 66,406.25 — $15,281.25/contract $152,812.50 Total	+2–1

Conclusion: Overall loss before margin and transaction costs on the hedge is $5,625 because the basis moved against you — i.e., the basis increased which means that the price of futures did not increase as much as the prices in the cash market.

Speculative Transactions

Investors can engage in speculative interest rate futures transactions when they anticipate a rise or decline in interest rates and want to buy or sell bonds to profit from this change. The use of futures contracts allows you to speculate on this expectation with a small capital outlay and derive all the benefits and/or risks of substantial leverage.

The following examples will demonstrate the large profit potential available because of the leverage; i.e., you control a large amount of bonds with a relatively small margin. As a result, a small change in price results in a large percentage gain or loss on your capital investment. Never forget — when there is a potential for a large gain, there is *also* the potential for a large loss.

Example of a Speculative Trade

Outlook: You expect a decline in interest rates over the next three months.

April 1: You buy a 90-day T-bill futures contract at 87 (13 percent discount). Your initial margin on this contract is $1,500. The contract unit is $1,000,000; a one-basis-point change on this contract is worth $25.

July 10: You were correct and rates declined from 13 percent to 11 percent. You can sell your contract at 89 (11 percent discount). The 200-basis-point change is worth $5,000 (200 × $25). You made $5,000 on the initial deposit of $1,500 (ignoring maintenance margin and transaction costs).
Note: If you were wrong and the rates increased to 15 percent, you would sell the contract for 85 and lose $5,000 on a $1,500 deposit.

The final example is for a speculator who expects an increase in interest rates. This situation is somewhat unique because typically, if you are in such a position, you have no way to make money on the expectation of a price decline: about all you can do is either avoid buying bonds or sell those you currently own. As shown, with futures contracts you can make money on the price decline. In addition, you may also use intramarket (between delivery months) and inter-market spreads.

Example of a Speculative Trade

Outlook: You expect an increase in interest rates over the next three months.

Sept. 1: You sell a long-term treasury bond future at 89–00. Your initial margin on this contract is $2,000. The contract unit is $100,000; a change of 1/32nd in this contract is worth $31.25.

Oct. 15: You were correct and rates increase. As a result, the futures price declines to 86–00. You buy back the contract at 86–00. This offsets the original sale. The three-point change is equal to 96 32nds (3×32). The total gain is: $96 \times 31.25 = \$3,000$. This $3,000 gain is on a deposit of $2,000 (ignoring maintenance margin and transaction costs). Again if interest rates had declined, prices would have increased, you would have to buy the contract at a higher price, and you would have lost on the trade.

ALTERNATIVE FORWARD LOANS

As we observed in Chapter 24, if we could assume that financial markets are *perfect* and carrying costs are *constant* (i.e., deterministic) over the life of a futures contract, then the current futures price would be equal to the current forward price. Since the carrying costs of T-bills in perfect markets consist of only interest rates, the above assumption implies that interest rates are constant over the life of the contract. If these assumptions hold, then we can show that there are three ways of creating forward loans that are *perfect substitutes* for one another:[2]

1. Buy and hold a T-bill futures contract that would deliver a 13-week T-bill in 13 weeks (at $t + 13$).
2. Enter into a repurchase agreement; i.e., buy a 26-week bill, sell it, and simultaneously agree to buy it back 13 weeks later at the current market price on a 13-week T-bill. The document specifying this arrangement is referred to as a *Repo*.
3. Buy a 26-week T-bill and sell short an appropriate number of 13-week T-bills.

The cash flows (per $100 par value) involved in these transactions are:

1. Futures market

$$\begin{array}{ccc} & F(t,\, t+13) & \$100 \\ \vdash & \dashv & \dashv \\ t & t+13 & t+26 \text{ weeks} \end{array}$$

2. Repo (forward) market

$$\begin{array}{ccc} & FO(t,\, t+13) & \$100 \\ \vdash & \dashv & \dashv \\ t & t+13 & t+26 \text{ weeks} \end{array}$$

[2] Edward J. Kane, "Market Incompleteness and Divergences between Forward and Futures Interest Rates," *Journal of Finance*, 35 no. 2 (May 1980): 221–234.

That is, the current forward price on a 13-week T-bill to be delivered 13 weeks later is $FO(t, t+13)$.

3. Spot market

$$\left[\frac{S(t,t+26)}{S(t,t+13)}\right] \times 100 \qquad \$100$$

$$\vdash\!\!\!\!-\!\!\!\!-\!\!\!\!-\!\!\!\!-\!\!\!\!-\!\!\!\!\!+\!\!\!\!-\!\!\!\!-\!\!\!\!-\!\!\!\!-\!\!\!\!-\!\!\!\dashv$$
$$t \qquad\qquad t+13 \qquad\qquad\qquad t+26$$

At t, short $[s(t, t+26)/s(t, t+13)]$ number of 13-week bills. This transaction will generate cash flows worth $[S(t, t+26)/S(t, t+13) \times S(t, t+13)$, which is equal to $\$S(t, t+26)$. Using the proceeds from this short sale, you could buy a 26-week T-bill and hold it to maturity. At $t+13$, settle the short sale by paying $\$100 \times [S(t, t+26)/S(t, t+13)]$.

Observe that the three transactions have an identical cash flow of $100 at $t+26$. According to the law of one price discussed in Chapter 24, these three transactions must have the same price at time t. That is:

(25.1) $F(t, t+13) = FO(t, t+13) = 100[S(t, t+26)/S(t, t+13)]$.

The last term in the above equation $[S(t, t+26)/S(t, t+13)]$ is the implied forward price; i.e., the forward price implied in the current yield curve. Since the repo market is very illiquid relative to the spot and futures markets, we will limit our analysis to the relationship between the current futures price and the current implied forward price.

If the current futures price is not equal to the current implied forward price, we can show that arbitrage opportunities exist. For instance, if the current futures price is less than the current implied forward price, one could set up the following arbitrage:

A basic rule of arbitrage is to buy the underpriced and sell the overpriced instruments as shown in Equation 25.1. That is:

At t:

a. Sell short the 26-week T-bill. $\$S(t, t+26)$
b. Buy $[S(t, t+26)/S(t, t+13)]$ number of 13-week T-bills.
                                                            $-\$S(t, t+26)$
c. Buy a futures contract.   0
d. Net cash flow: 0

At t + 13:

e. The maturing T-bills produce: $\$[S(t, t+26)/S(t, t+13)]$.
f. Take delivery (of a 13-week T-bill) on the futures contract.

$$-\$F(t, t+13)$$

g. Net cash flow:

$$\${[S(t, t+26)/S(t, t+13)] - F(t, t+13)} > 0$$

The net cash flow is positive because the current futures price is less than the current implied forward price. When interest rates are deterministic, as assumed earlier, interest on variable margins could be ignored. An easy way to demonstrate this is to assume that the term structure of interest rates is flat over the life of the contract. In this idealized case, the futures price remains fixed until delivery.

At t + *26:*

h.   The maturing 13-week T-bill produces: $100
i.   Settle the original short sale of a 26-week T-bill.   − 100
j.   Net cash flow: 0

In this example the arbitrageur does not invest any capital at time *t*, and yet he is *assured* of a positive cash flow at *t* + 13. *This means that this arbitrage transaction produces a riskless return without requiring any capital investment.* Such profit opportunities rarely exist in efficient markets. The increased demand for the futures contract and for the 13-week bills along with the excess supply of the 26-week bill would exert pressure on market prices such that the equilibrium condition is reestablished quickly.

Now that we have seen the fundamental and somewhat unrealistic relationship between the current futures price and the current forward price implied by the corresponding spot bills, we can relax the simplifying assumptions. With stochastic interest rates, we would have to account for interest on margins arising from the daily marking-to-market of the futures contract. Further, we have to consider taxes and transaction costs, such as commissions, short selling costs, and bid-ask spreads, in the spot and futures markets. Although these transaction costs are relatively fixed over the life of the contract, the interest margin on daily margin flows are not. Therefore, the transactions discussed above are *not* perfect substitutes. They are indeed *speculative* in nature and thus, they are *not arbitrage* transactions.

In general, it is difficult to profit from minor deviations of the current futures price from the implied forward price because of market imperfections and margin maintenance costs. There could be profits *only* if the difference between the current futures and forward prices exceeds the costs due to market frictions and the interest paid on variable margins. If one can obtain a reasonable estimate of the total of such costs, say K, then it is possible to compute an upper and a lower boundary for the futures price. That is:

$$(25.2) \quad 100 \times [S(t,\, t+26)/S(t,\, t+13)] - K < F(t,\, t+13) < \\ 100 \times [S(t,\, t+26)/S(t,\, t+13)] + K.$$

The lower and upper boundaries for the futures price are expressed in terms of the implied forward price adjusted for K. Within these bounds, it is not possible to profit from the futures-forward price deviations. Alternatively, if the futures price falls below the lower boundary or lies above the upper boundary, it would be profitable to set up strategies similar to the arbitrage transactions illustrated earlier.

Empirical Evidence

Using daily data from January 1976 to March 1978, Rendleman and Carabini[3] compared the T-bill futures price of the first three contracts (maturing in the following nine months at quarterly intervals) with the corresponding implied forward price. Their findings are summarized in Table 25.1. Panel A indicates that the annualized mean basis point differential between the futures and the implied forward price (not adjusted for transaction costs) is 5.775 basis points, worth about $578 on a $1 million contract. This implies that on average the futures contract is overpriced relative to the implied forward price. Notice, however, that the third contract is generally underpriced. The average absolute differentials are 15.868 basis points. That is, if one held the futures long when they are underpriced and replaced them with the implied forward instrument when the former are overpriced, an average annual return of $1,587 per contract would be produced.

Panel B shows the basis point differentials adjusted for transaction costs (exclusive of short selling costs in the cash T-bill market). These results indicate that 66 percent of the differences for all contracts are within the upper and lower boundaries. This implies that, in the remaining 34 percent of the cases, an investor with the required T-bills in his portfolio could have profited by arbitraging between the futures and the spot T-bill markets. These arbitrage possibilities are called *quasi-arbitrage* opportunities, because it is assumed that the arbitrageur already has the required spot T-bills in his portfolio and thus is not obliged to incur the short selling costs. In contrast, a pure arbitrage opportunity exists only when the difference between the futures and forward prices exceeds *all* transaction costs, including short selling costs in the spot market. Typically, it costs about 50 basis points per annum to sell T-bills short. After adjusting for short selling costs, Rendleman and Carabini found that all of the futures-forward price differences lie within the no-arbitrage (lower-upper) boundaries. They concluded that while there are some quasi-arbitrage opportunities, pure arbitrage opportunities seldom exist in the T-bill futures market for the first three contracts. The absence of pure arbitrage opportunities supports the hypothesis that the T-bill futures market is efficient in pricing the first three contracts relative to the corresponding implied forward prices.

Evidence on Hedging with Interest Rate Futures

Another topic of empirical research is the hedging performance of interest rate futures contracts. We discussed in Chapter 24 that the mean-variance portfolio approach can be used to measure the variance-minimizing hedge ratio, H^*, and the hedging effectiveness of futures contracts, e. Using weekly data over the period from January 1976 to December 1977, Ederington[4] examined the hedging

---

[3] Richard Rendleman and Christopher Carabini, "The Efficiency of the Treasury Bill Futures Market," *Journal of Finance,* 34 no. 4 (September 1979): 895–914.

[4] Louis H. Ederington, "The Hedging Performance of the New Futures Market," *Journal of Finance,* 34 no. 1 (March 1979): 157–170.

TABLE 25.1

Summary Statistics for Basis Points Differential Between T-Bill Futures and Implied Forward Prices, 1976–1978

		1st Contract Month	2nd Contract Month	3rd Contract Month	All Contracts
		Contract			
A. Annual basis point differentials *unadjusted* for transaction costs.	μ	21.244	3.426	−9.192	5.775
	$|\mu|$	24.902	10.867	11.277	15.868
	σ	26.952	13.308	10.114	22.319
	σ_ϵ	23.460	5.498	3.516	N/A
	ϕ_1, ϕ_2	.308,.280	.755,.167	.863,.074	N/A
	N	558	559	489	1606
	t	8.813	1.149	−3.642[a]	N/A
	$Q(21,N)$	25.031	24.072	35.341[b]	N/A

Legend:

μ = sample mean

$|\mu|$ = sample mean of absolute value

σ = sample standard deviation

σ_ϵ = standard error of estimate of second order autoregressive process

ϕ_1, ϕ_2 = first and second order autocorrelation coefficients

N = sample size

$t = \mu(1 - \phi_1 - \phi_2)/(\sigma_\epsilon/\sqrt{N})$

$Q(21,N)$ = Box-Pierce Q statistic using 21 residual autocorrelations with sample size N.

[a] Significantly different from zero at 5 percent level.

[b] Null hypothesis that residuals follow a white noise process is rejected at the 5 percent level.

	Contract		N	Percent	μ	μ_a
B. Basis point differentials adjusted for transaction costs.	1st Contract Month	B	1	0	−.574	−.582
		W	391	70	4.108	14.590
		A	166	30	8.204	13.425
			558	100		
	2nd Contract Month	B	51	9	−8.404	−4.879
		W	396	71	.626	.878
		A	112	22	11.822	9.830
			559	100		
	3rd Contract Month	B	212	43	−19.350	−7.539
		W	266	54	−7.441	3.257
		A	11	3	10.031	3.724
			489	100		
	All Contracts	B	264	16	−17.164	−6.999
		W	1053	66	−.119	4.925
		A	289	18	9.676	11.662
			1606	100		

Legend:

N = number of observations

Percent = percent of total observations within cell

μ = sample mean, not annualized

μ_a = sample mean, annualized

B = below lower index boundary (Means are differences between actual IMM index values.)

W = within index boundaries (Means are differences between actual and no-transaction cost.)

A = above upper index boundary. (Means are differences between actual IMM index values.)

SOURCE: Richard Rendleman and Christopher Carabini, "The Efficiency of the Treasury Bill Futures Market," *Journal of Finance*, 34 no. 4 (September 1979): 895–914.

TABLE 25.2
Hedging Performance Results (two-week hedges)

The Futures Contract	Estimated e	Estimated H*
8% GNMA's (46 observations)		
The Nearby Contract	.664	.801*
3- to 6-Month Contract	.675	.832
6- to 9-Month Contract	.677	.854
9- to 12-Month Contract	.661	.852
90-Day Treasury Bills (41 observations)		
The Nearby Contract	.272	.307*
3- to 6-Month Contract	.256	.237*
6- to 9-Month Contract	.178	.143*
9- to 12-Month Contract	.140	.116
Wheat (45 observations)		
The Nearby Contract	.898	.864*
3- to 6-Month Contract	.889	.815*
4- to 8-Month Contract	.868	.784
6- to 10-Month Contract	.841	.778*
Corn (45 observations)		
The Nearby Contract	.649	.915
2- to 6-Month Contract	.605	.905
4- to 8-Month Contract	.541	.868
6- to 10-Month Contract	.450	.764

* Significantly different from 1 at .05 level.
SOURCE: Louis H. Ederington, "The Hedging Performance of the New Futures Market." *Journal of Finance*, 24 no. 1 (March 1979): 157–170.

performance of futures contracts on GNMAs, T-bills, wheat, and corn. His results are reported in Table 25.2.

The results for the GNMA futures indicate that the variance-minimizing hedge ratio of a two-week hedge involving the nearby futures contract is about 80 percent of the spot position. That is, the hedger has to trade futures with a face value equal to 80 percent of the par value of the cash GNMAs. For example, a savings and loan association with $1 million par value GNMA in its portfolio needs to sell 8 futures contracts with a total face value of $800,000. Such a hedge reduces the price variability of the unhedged spot GNMA portfolio by 66 percent, as revealed by the measure of hedging effectiveness, e. From the evidence reported in Table 25.2, it appears that the hedging performance of the GNMA futures is quite comparable to those of wheat and corn futures. Franckle[5] has shown that the low performance of T-bill futures shown in Table 25.2 is due to some errors in data and methodology. He contends that when the results are corrected, the T-bill futures are as effective in hedging as other contracts.

[5] Charles T. Franckle, "The Hedging Performance of the New Futures Market: Comment," *Journal of Finance*, 35 no. 5 (December 1980): 1273–1279.

812 Price Sensitivity Approach to Hedging Interest Rates

Under the mean-variance portfolio approach to hedging, one must estimate the expected correlation between the spot and future price changes in order to establish the optimal hedge ratio (See Equation 24.15). In certain situations, such as the flotation of a new debt with term to maturity and coupon quite different from the existing debt instruments, the correlation coefficient may be difficult to estimate. This problem arises frequently in cross-hedging, i.e., hedging financial instruments that have terms to maturity, coupons, default-risk ratings, and tax features that are different from those of the spot asset underlying the futures contract. It can be overcome by using the *price sensitivity* approach to hedging. With this approach, *the hedge ratio is computed as a ratio of the expected price volatility of the spot asset being hedged to the expected volatility of the futures contract.* That is, the hedge ratio, h, is determined such that the expected change in the spot price, ΔS, is *offset completely* by the expected price change in the futures contract, ΔF.[6]

$$(25.3) \qquad \Delta S + h\Delta F = 0$$

$$h = -[\Delta S/\Delta F] = -[dS/dF].$$

We know from the discussion on bond durations that bond price volatility is related to its duration. For the sake of simplicity, assume that the term structure of interest rates is *flat* over the hedging horizon and undergoes only *a small parallel* change. This enables us to express the relationship between price volatility and yield volatility of a bond using Macaulay's duration.[7] For a small change in the bond's yield:

$$(25.4) \qquad dS = -D(S)\ S\ dR(S)/R(S)$$

$$dF = -D(F)\ F\ dR(F)/R(F),$$

where:

> $D(S)$ = the duration of the spot asset being hedged
>
> $D(F)$ = the duration of the asset underlying the futures contract
>
> $R(S)$ = 1 + (spot bond yield to maturity)
>
> $R(F)$ = 1 + (futures rate).

The sensitivity of the spot and futures prices to a small change in the *risk-free rate of interest* is given by:

$$(25.5) \qquad dS/dR = -D(S)\ S\ dR(S)/(R(S)\ dR)$$

$$dF/dR = -D(F)\ F\ dR(F)/(R(F)\ dR),$$

---

[6] Robert Kolb and Raymond Chiang, "Improving Hedging Performance Using Interest Rate Futures," *Financial Management* (Autumn 1981): 72–79; Robert Kolb and Raymond Chiang, "Duration, Immunization, and Hedging with Interest Rate Futures," *Journal of Financial Research*, 5 no. 2 (Summer 1982): 161–170.

[7] Michael H. Hopewell and George G. Kaufman, "Bond Price Volatility and Term to Maturity: A Generalized Respecification," *American Economic Review*, 64 no. 4 (September 1973): 749–753.

where:

$$R = 1 + \text{(risk-free rate of interest)}.$$

Substituting these values into Equation 25.3 we obtain:

$$b = \frac{(-)D(S)\ S\ R(F)\ [dR(S)/dR]}{D(F)\ F\ R(S)\ [dR(F)/dR]}$$

When $[dR(S)/dR] = [dR(F)/dR]$, i.e., when the spot yield to maturity and the futures rate are equally sensitive to a change in the risk-free rate, the hedge ratio simplifies to:

(25.6)
$$b = \frac{(-)D(S)\ S\ R(F)}{D(F)\ F\ R(S)}$$

A major shortcoming of the price sensitivity approach is its underlying assumption that the term structure of interest rates is flat over the hedge horizon and that it undergoes only one parallel shift. The margin of error in estimating the hedge ratio can be large when the term structure is markedly nonlinear and volatile over time. Yet, the price sensitivity hedge ratio has convenient practical applications relative to the historical hedge ratio based on the portfolio approach and the naive hedge ratio.

Empirical Evidence on Price Sensitive Hedge. Gay, Kolb and Chiang[8] hedged a random sample of New York Exchange bonds with the nearby T-bond futures contract during the period 1979–1980. They compared the performance of the following alternative strategies of hedging a planned investment of $1 million in a bond at the end of the hedge horizon:
1. Do not hedge the planned investment.
2. Buy ten T-bond futures contracts with a total face value of $1,000,000 (Naive Strategy 1).
3. Buy ($1,000,000/F) T-bond futures contracts, where F is the current futures price (Naive Strategy 2).
4. Buy T-bond futures contracts as per the price sensitive hedge ratio (Price Sensitive Strategy).

The dollar performance of these alternative strategies is reported in Table 25.3. The results indicate that the price sensitive strategy produces the minimum absolute wealth change (i.e., the minimum absolute difference between the actual and the expected bond prices). By employing the price sensitive strategy, the investor can reduce the variability of the unhedged position by 73 percent, which is greater than the risk reduction produced by the naive strategies.

Using Futures to Adjust Portfolio Duration

The hedging examples above assume that the investor intends to *minimize* price risk. This is not an optimal or desirable investment objective under all market

---

[8] Gerald Gay, Robert Kolb, and Raymond Chiang, "Interest Rate Hedging: An Empirical Test of Alternative Strategies," *Journal of Financial Research*, 6 no. 3 (Fall 1983): 187–197.

TABLE 25.3
Hedging Performance of the Price-Sensitive Strategy (absolute wealth change)

	Unhedged	Naive 1	Naive 2	Price Sensitive
Mean	$ 80,781.09	$ 32,637.10	$ 34,538.05	$25,292.15
Standard Deviation	73,398.15	26,075.53	31,321.98	19,477.25
Minimum	57.89	59.62	453.94	123.30
Maximum	294,102.69	150,838.50	178,059.00	79,558.44
Range	294,044.80	150,777.88	177,605.06	79,435.14
Mean Percentage of Wealth Hedged	—	$ 59.60	$ 57.24	$ 68.69
Percentage Reduction Standard Deviation of Wealth Change	—	$ 64.47	$ 57.33	$ 73.46

SOURCE: Gerald Gay, Robert Kolb, and Raymond Chiang, "Interest Rate Hedging: An Empirical Test of Alternative Strategies," *Journal of Financial Research*, 6 no. 3 (Fall 1983): 187–197.

situations. As discussed in Chapter 19 an active bond portfolio manager would like to change the duration of the bond portfolio in line with his interest rate forecasts. If he expects a decline in interest rates, he would attempt to maximize the expected price gain by increasing the duration of the bond portfolio. On the other hand, when he expects an increase in market rates, he would try to reduce the portfolio duration to minimize the expected price loss. If the credit market conditions are such that he is uncertain which way interest rates will go, he would seek to immunize the bond portfolio by equating the portfolio duration with the length of the holding period (i.e., the investment horizon). In contrast, a passive portfolio manager would construct a portfolio with a duration that is consistent with his client's risk-return preferences and hold it over time.

In the absence of futures trading, altering a portfolio's duration by shifting funds from low to high duration securities and vice versa is expensive in terms of transaction costs, including short selling, liquidity costs, and taxes. Interest rate futures provide a convenient and inexpensive mechanism for adjusting the portfolio duration because of their low transaction costs and high liquidity. To demonstrate this, consider the following example. We know that the duration of a bond portfolio is a weighted average of the durations of individual bonds included in the portfolio. In the case of a portfolio consisting of X units of a given T-bond and h' units of the T-bond futures contract, the price change of this bond-futures portfolio for an instantaneous change in the level of market rates of interest is given by these alternative strategies:

(25.7) $$dP = X \, dS + h' \, dF,$$

where:

$dP =$ the change in price of the bond–futures portfolio

$dS =$ the change in the spot T-bond price

$dF =$ the change in the T-bond futures price.

Assuming a flat term structure of interest rates that experiences a parallel shift and also perfect markets, we can represent the above price changes as:

(25.8) $- DP\, dR/R = - X\, D(S)\, S\, dR/R - h'D(F)\, F\, dR/R$

$$DP = XD(S)S + h'\, D(F)F$$

where:

D = the portfolio duration

P = the price of the bond-futures portfolio

$D(S)$ = the duration of the spot T-bond

$D(F)$ = the duration of the bond underlying the T-bond futures contract.

We know the duration of the spot T-bond and the T-bond futures contract. Also, we know X, S, F, and P. Given our interest rate forecast, we want to alter the portfolio duration to a target level. Therefore, we also know the target duration of this bond-futures portfolio, D. (Assume that it is 5 years.) What we must determine is the number of T-bond futures contracts required to obtain the desired portfolio duration:

(25.9) $h' = [DP - X\, D(S)\, S]/D(F)F.$

While the change in the portfolio price over a *small interval* of time is the sum of price changes in the spot and futures positions, the price of the bond-futures portfolio *at any given moment in time* is exactly equal to the price of the spot position. This is because the margins on the futures contracts are treated as good faith deposits and the holder of a futures contract does *not* own the underlying asset until he takes delivery. Therefore:

(25.10) $P \equiv X \cdot S.$

When we recognize this identity, we can infer the following from Equation 25.8, assuming that one holds a long spot position (i.e., $X > 0$):
— If $D > D(S)$, $h' > 0$, buy futures.
— If $D < D(S)$, $h' < 0$, sell futures.
— If $D = D(S)$, $h' = 0$, no futures trading.
For example, if the target portfolio duration exceeds the duration of the spot T-bond, then one has to buy h' futures contracts to obtain the desired change in the portfolio price. Although we have made several restrictive assumptions in the above example, the insights gained are quite helpful in using interest rate futures in the portfolio management of fixed-income securities.[9]

[9] For a further use of futures to immunize bond portfolios, see Robert W. Kolb and Gerald D. Gay, "Immunizing Bond Portfolios with Interest Rate Futures," *Financial Management,* 11 no. 3 (Summer 1982): 81–89; and Gerald D. Gay and Robert W. Kolb, "Interest Rate Futures as a Tool for Immunizing," *Journal of Portfolio Management,* 10 no. 1 (Fall 1983): 65–70.

STOCK INDEX FUTURES

It is well known that the variability of stock prices, although less than that of many commodities, is much higher than the variability of bond prices. An investor owning a well-diversified portfolio of stocks bears little unsystematic (i.e., firm specific) risk but is fully exposed to systematic risk (i.e., sensitivity of the expected portfolio return to fluctuations in the rate of return on the market portfolio). This market sensitivity is measured by the beta of the portfolio. It is possible for the holder of a diversified portfolio to protect against his subjective forecast of a market decline by *selling short* shares in a diversified stock mutual fund. Since the returns on the investor's portfolio would be highly correlated with the returns on the mutual fund, the loss (gain) on the long stock position would be reduced by the gain (loss) on the short mutual fund position. The investor who employs this strategy is subjected to *costs and restrictions on short sales* in the stock market, particularly the requirement that a stock can be shorted only on an uptick.

Alternatively, the investor with a bearish outlook for the market could sell part of his stock portfolio and could invest the proceeds in liquid assets. The costs of this strategy would involve commissions, bid-ask spreads, taxes, and potential liquidity costs in thin markets. Another alternative is that the investor could buy put options on individual stocks in his portfolio or options on a stock market index.

Two major problems with the above strategies are high transaction costs and taxes and the difficulties involved in executing these strategies. A solution is to *trade futures contracts on a stock market index.* The liquidity and leverage of a stock index futures market provide a *convenient low cost mechanism* for hedging *market risk.* For index futures contracts, going short is as easy as going long.

The Kansas City Board of Trade introduced the first stock index futures contract on the Value Line Composite Average (VLA) in February 1982. Currently, there are three popular index futures contracts: (1) The Standard and Poor's 500 (S&P 500) index futures traded on the Chicago Mercantile Exchange, (2) the New York Stock Exchange (NYSE) Composite Index futures traded on the New York Futures Exchange, and (3) the VLA index futures. Table 25.4 highlights the specifications of these contracts.

As indicated in Table 25.4 the market price of the three futures contracts is 500 times the value of the underlying stock index. The instrument underlying index futures contracts is *not* an asset, such as a commodity or a bond that is traded in the spot market, but a stock market index. Accordingly, index futures *do not require delivery of the underlying instrument;* instead, they call for a *cash settlement* at contract expiration. At the end of the last day of trading, the quote on the index futures contract is *set equal to the value of the underlying stock index,* and gains/losses on futures positions are settled in cash.

Use of Stock Index Futures

In terms of the CAPM, the *ex post* return on a stock or a portfolio of stocks has two components: a market component and a firm-specific component.

TABLE 25.4
A Comparison of Stock Index Futures Contracts Currently Traded

Feature	Kansas City Board of Trade (KCBT)	Chicago Mercantile Exchange (CME)	New York Futures Exchange (NYFE)
1. Location	Kansas City	Chicago	New York
2. Underlying Market Index	Value Line Composite Average (VLA). This is an equally weighted index of approximately 1700 stocks. Geometric average is used.	Standard and Poor's 500 index (S&P 500). This is a value-weighted index of 500 stocks. Arithmetic average is used.	NYSE Composite Index. It is a value-weighted average of *all* common stocks listed on the NYSE. Arithmetic average is used.
3. Contract Size (value of contract)	Five hundred times the Value Line average (about $88,500).	Five hundred times the S&P index (about $75,000).	Five hundred times the NYSE composite index (about $45,000).
4. Minimum Price Change	Tick size is 0.01 points. The minimum change would cause the value of the contract to change by $5.	Tick size is 0.05 points. This represents a change of $25 per tick.	Tick size is 0.05 points. This represents a change of $25 per tick.
5. Daily Price Change Limits	Five points daily price limit is in effect. Each point represents $500.	Five points daily price limit[a] is in effect. Each point represents $500.	No limits currently in effect.
6. Margins (minimum customer margin set by the exchange)	Initial Margin $6500 2500 400 / Maintenance Margin $2000 1500 200 / Trader Speculator Hedger Spreaders	Initial Margin $6000 2500 400 / Maintenance Margin $2500 1500 200 / Trader Speculator Hedger Spreaders	Initial Margin $3500 1500 200 / Maintenance Margin $1500 750 100 / Trader Speculator Hedger Spreaders
7. Delivery Concept	Cash settlement. Actual value of VLA determines the payment. Final settlement is the last trading day of the expiring month. Delivery months are March, June, September, and December.	Cash settlement. Actual value of S&P 500 index determines the payment. Final settlement of open contracts occurs on the third Thursday of the delivery month. Delivery months are March, June, September, and December.	Cash settlement. Actual value of NYSE composite determines the payment. Settlement is based on the difference between the settlement price on the next to the last day of trading in the month and the value of NYSE composite index at the close of trading. Delivery months are March, June, September, and December.
8. Volume of Trading and Approximate Dollar Value February 22, 1984	4031 $365 million	46,737 $3.5 billion	15,902 $715 million

[a] If the limit is reached on two consecutive days, the limit on the third day is 7.5 points; if reached for three consecutive days, the limit on the fourth day is 10 points if reached on four consecutive days, there is no limit on the fifth day.

SOURCE: Modest Sundaresan, Journal of Futures Market, copyright 1983. Reprinted by permission of John Wiley & Sons, Inc.

(25.11) $$R(p) = R_f + \beta(p)[R(M) - R] + \epsilon,$$

where:

$R(p)$ = the return on the portfolio

R_f = the return on a risk-free asset

$\beta(P)$ = the beta of the portfolio

$R(M)$ = the return on the market portfolio

ϵ = the return due to firm-specific factors; it has a zero mean and a constant variance.

The market component of the portfolio return is $R + \beta(P)[R(M) - R]$. The components of the portfolio return are related to two sources of risk: market risk and unsystematic risk.

(25.12) $$\sigma^2(P) = \beta^2(P)\sigma^2(M) + \sigma^2(\epsilon)$$

The first term on the right side of Equation 25.12 is a measure of the portfolio's market risk, and the second term denotes nonmarket (unsystematic) risk which is eliminated in a diversified portfolio.

Active portfolio management involves stock analysis and market timing. An active portfolio manager analyzes stocks in order to discover underpriced and overpriced securities. Market timing calls for predicting the overall movement of the stock market and altering the stock position to take advantage of the market forecast. An active portfolio manager with a bullish market outlook would *increase* the beta of his portfolio in order to maximize his gain from the expected market rally. When he is bearish on the market, he would *reduce* the portfolio beta to minimize the price loss. If he is uncertain which way the market will go, he would prefer a *zero-beta* portfolio where the return is *immunized* against uncertain market fluctuations. Through these strategies, an active portfolio manager with superior skills in forecasting firm-specific factors and/or market turns would experience above average risk-adjusted returns. In contrast, a passive portfolio manager would construct a portfolio with a beta that is consistent with his client's risk-return preferences and would hold that portfolio over time.[10]

Using Futures to Alter the Portfolio Beta.   In the absence of futures trading, altering the portfolio beta by shifting funds from low- to high-beta stocks and vice versa necessitates a large turnover of the portfolio. The accompanying transaction costs (including short selling costs and liquidity costs and taxes) are very high. As noted previously, stock index futures provide an inexpensive yet effective way of altering the portfolio beta without affecting its essential composition.

[10] Stephen Figlewski and Stanley Kon, "Portfolio Management with Stock Index Futures," *Financial Analysts Journal,* 38 no. 1 (January–February 1982): 52–60. For an overview of these, see Victor Niederhoff and Richard Zeckhauser, "Market Index Futures Contracts," *Financial Analysts Journal,* 36 no. 1 (January–February 1980): 49–55. An excellent set of readings on this topic is contained in, Frank J. Fabozzi and Gregory M. Kipnis, (eds) *Stock Index Futures* (Homewood, Ill.: Dow Jones-Irwin, 1984).

To see this, assume that the S&P 500 portfolio is a *perfect* proxy for the market portfolio and that you hold shares in an index fund portfolio that is identical to the S&P 500 index. The expected dollar return on a portfolio of the index fund and index futures is:

(25.13) $$E(DR) = XE(\Delta S) + yE(\Delta F),$$

where:

$E(DR)$ = the expected price change in the portfolio of index fund and index futures over a short interval of time

X,y = number of units of the index fund and the index futures contract, respectively (assume that each unit of trading on both the spot and the futures market has the same dollar value)

$E(\Delta S)$ = the expected price change in the index fund shares

$E(\Delta F)$ = the expected price change in the index futures contract based on the S&P 500.

As shown earlier, the variance minimizing hedge ratio is given by:

(25.14) $$H^* = (y^*/X) = \rho_{ij}\sigma_i/\sigma_j,$$

where:

ρ_{ij} = the correlation coefficient of spot and futures price changes

σ_i,σ_j = the standard deviations of spot and futures price changes, respectively.

Further, under the CAPM:

(25.15) $$E(\Delta S) = R \times S + \beta(S)[E(R(M)) - R]$$

(25.16) $$E(\Delta F) = \beta F[ER(M) - R],$$

where:

$$R = \text{the risk-free rate of interest}$$

$$\beta(S) = Cov[\Delta S, R(M)]/\sigma^2[R(M)]$$

$$\beta(F) = Cov(\Delta F, R(M)/\sigma^2(R(M)).$$

The spot and futures betas are represented in terms of the covariance of *dollar* price changes with the market return and, therefore, are different from the betas based on *percentage* price changes. Also, $B(S) = B(F) = 1$, because the index fund is assumed to be identical to the S&P 500 index on which the futures contract is based. Then, H^* would be equal to one and the spot-futures hedge would be *perfect*. Substituting Equations 25.14, 25.15, and 25.16 in Equation 25.13 we obtain

(25.17) $$E(DR) = R_f \cdot S.$$

That is, the expected dollar return on the *perfect* spot-futures hedge portfolio is equal to the dollar risk-free interest income on the spot investment. In this ideal case, the index fund has no unsystematic risk because it is a *fully diversified* portfolio. Its systematic risk is equal to that of the market portfolio. The perfect hedge in the index futures contract has enabled us to *eliminate completely* its market risk.

Obviously, it is seldom possible to construct the perfect hedge in the real world, because the assumptions of the CAPM are rarely satisfied and the index fund and the index futures contract are not identical to the true market portfolio (which is a value-weighted portfolio of *all* forms of wealth). Besides, the perfect hedge is mostly irrelevant, because an *active* portfolio manager rarely wants to hold the zero-beta portfolio of spot and futures instruments. Instead, he seeks to hold a portfolio with desired levels of systematic and unsystematic risk and return. Through *security analysis,* he selects stocks with desirable *firm-specific characteristics* and by employing *market-timing* strategies he tries to control the exposure of the portfolio to general market movements. Until the advent of index futures trading, it was not feasible to *separate systematic risk from unsystematic risk.* For example, consider an active portfolio manager who has selected a portfolio of stocks with desirable firm-specific factors but with high betas. If the manager is bearish on the market, he would not want to hold this portfolio because of its high systematic risk. By trading index futures, he could alter the systematic risk of the portfolio to obtain a desired beta.

Determining the Hedge Ratio.   One important decision in using stock index futures to manage a portfolio's systematic risk is the number of futures contracts to trade. For a two-asset portfolio it can be derived as:

(25.18) $\beta(P) = Cov(DR, R(M))/\sigma^2(R(M)),$

where:

$\beta(P) =$ the dollar beta of the spot-futures portfolio

$DR =$ the dollar price change in the spot futures portfolio.
$= X[(1 - \beta(S)R \times S + \beta(S)R(M) + \epsilon(S)] +$
$y\{[R(M) - R]\beta(F) + \epsilon(F)\}.$

Substituting for *DR* in Equation 25.18:

(25.19) $\beta(P) = X\beta(S) + y\beta(F).$

That is, the dollar beta of the two-asset portfolio is the sum of the product of the spot dollar beta and the number of units of the spot asset and of the futures dollar beta and the number of units of the futures contract. For purposes of this example, $X = 1$ in Equation 25.19. The active portfolio manager knows the values of $\beta(S)$, and $\beta(F)$ and determines the desired value $\beta(p)$ consistent with his *market outlook.* So he could solve the equation to determine the number of index futures contracts required to obtain the desired portfolio dollar beta:

(25.20) $y = [\beta(P) - X\beta(S)]/\beta(F).$

The hedge ratio, H, is given by:

(25.21) $H = (y/X) = [\beta(P) - X\beta(S)]/X \cdot \beta(F).$

In Equation 25.21, $\beta(S)$ and $\beta(F)$ are positive because they relate to portfolios of stocks. Further, X is positive when the manager holds a long position in the spot portfolio. This means that:
1. If $\beta(P) > \beta(S)$, buy index futures.
2. If $\beta(P) < \beta(S)$, sell index futures.
3. If $\beta(P) = \beta(S)$, do not trade futures.

Therefore, the decision whether to buy or sell index futures contracts depends on the relationship between the target spot-futures portfolio dollar beta and the spot portfolio dollar beta.

To see the impact of such an eclectic hedging strategy on the risk and return on the spot futures portfolio, we need to substitute for y in Equation 25.13:

(25.22) $E(DR) = XE(\Delta S) + HX\,E(\Delta F).$

(25.23) $\sigma^2(DR) = X^2\sigma^2(\Delta S) + H^2 X^2\sigma^2(\Delta F) + 2HX^2 Cov(\Delta S, \Delta F).$

The ratio of the variance of the spot futures portfolio to that of the unhedged spot portfolio is:

(25.24) $\dfrac{\sigma^2(DR)}{X^2\sigma^2(\Delta S)} = 1 + \dfrac{H[H\sigma^2(\Delta F) + 2Cov(\Delta S,\Delta F)}{\sigma^2(\Delta S)}.$

If the hedge ratio, H, is equal to the variance-minimizing hedge ratio, H^*, given in Equation 25.14, then:

(25.25) $\dfrac{\sigma^2(DR)}{X^2\sigma^2(\Delta S)} = 1 - \rho_{ij}^2,$

where:

$\rho_{ij}^2 =$ the coefficient of determination of the spot and futures price changes.

This indicates that the higher the correlation between the spot portfolio and the index futures price changes, the more effective the hedge in minimizing the dollar return variability on the spot-futures portfolio. Although the hedging model discussed above has ignored transaction costs, margins, taxes, and dividends, it is quite helpful in understanding the role of stock index futures in the management of systematic risk.

Example of a Stock Index Futures Hedge.   Let us now illustrate the defensive use of stock index futures with a simple example. Assume that the price behavior of the stock index futures contract is identical to the underlying stock index, there is 100 percent margin on futures, and percentage price changes are used instead of *dollar* price changes. In this case, the variance-minimizing hedge ratio in Equation 25.14 is equal to the beta of the spot portfolio. That is:

(25.26) $H^{*\prime} = Cov(R(S),R(M))/\sigma^2(R(M))$
$= \beta'(S).$

TABLE 25.5
An Illustration of a Stock Index Futures Hedge

Spot Market		Futures Market	
January 16, value of the spot portfolio:	$1,500,000	Sell 26 nearby S&P 500 futures contracts with market price of 26 × 75,000: Initial margins 26 × 2500 = $65,000	$1,950,000
March 10, sale of spot portfolio:	1,480,000	S&P 500 Index futures is at 148. Buy back 26 nearby futures contracts at 26 × 148 × 500:	1,924,000
Gross loss on spot portfolio:	($20,000)	Gross gain on futures:	$ 26,000

Total gain subject to margin and transaction costs = $6,000.

It follows that:

(25.27)
$$y^* = (-)\frac{X \times S}{F}\beta'(S)$$
$$= (-)\frac{V(S)}{F}\beta'(S),$$

where:

$V(S)$ = the value of the (spot) stock portfolio

F = the price of a stock index futures contract

$B'(S)$ = the beta of the spot portfolio (based on percentage price changes).

In Equation 25.27, the first term, $V(S)/F$, expresses the value of the spot portfolio in terms of the number of index futures contracts. The second term, $B'(S)$, adjusts the number of index futures contracts for the market sensitivity of the spot portfolio.

Now, consider a market-maker in stocks who holds a diversified portfolio of stocks with a beta of 1.3. The current value of this portfolio is $1.5 million, and the dealer expects a decline in the market in the near future. Currently, the S&P 500 stock index futures contract has a value of 150, which means the contract price is $75,000 (150 × 500). To minimize the variance of his spot-futures portfolio, the dealer needs to sell 26 futures contracts as shown below:

$$y^* = (-)\frac{V(S)}{F}B'(S) = \frac{1,500,000}{75,000} \times 1.3$$
$$= 26.$$

The hedging transactions are illustrated in Table 25.5.

OPTIONS ON FUTURES

A recent development in the innovation of financial contracts is the advent of put and call options based on futures instruments. The owner of a put (call) option has the *right* (but not the obligation) to sell (buy) a futures contract at a predetermined striking price during a specified time period. These options expire at the same time as their underlying futures contracts. They are American options so they can be exercised prior to their expiration. On exercising the option, a call owner assumes a long position in the futures contract, and a put owner takes a short futures position. Market quotes on some of the more popular futures options are contained in Figure 25.1.

The first set of quotes in Figure 25.1 pertains to puts and calls on the CBOT T-bond futures contract. The strike prices range from 64 to 80 per 100 par value of the futures contract. The June 66 call is quoted at 4 – 04; this means the premium on the call that expires in June is $4062.50 (= $100,000 × 4 4/64 × 1/100) per contract. The call owner has the right to buy a June T-bond futures contract at $66,000. Suppose that the call owner exercises the option in early June when the futures contract is trading at 72. On exercise, he assumes a long futures position at the strike price of 66. He can take profit by selling a futures contract at the current price of 72. His price gain is $6000 − 4062.50 = $1,937.50, unadjusted for transaction costs and taxes.

The June 66 put is quoted at 0 – 05, which is equal to a premium of $78.125 per futures contract. The put owner has the right to sell a futures contract at 66, and on exercise, he assumes a short futures position. He can close out his short futures position by executing a reverse trade or he can elect to give delivery at the time of final settlement.

As another example, consider the options on S&P 500 stock index futures. The June 155 call and put are quoted at 6.00 and 2.20, which amount to $3,000 and $1100 per futures contract, respectively. If at expiration in June, the S&P 500 index is at 155, both options will remain unexercised. If the index is at 150, the call is worthless, but the put is worth $2500 per contract. In contrast, if the index is at 160, the put is worthless, and the call is worth $2500 per contract.

A Comparison of Options and Futures

At this juncture, it is important to note some of the essential similarities and differences between options and futures.

1. Both are *deferred delivery* instruments. Positions in both options and futures can be terminated prior to expiration by executing a reverse trade. Delivery on a futures contract takes place *only* during the delivery period prescribed by the futures exchange. In contrast, options are American and may be exercised at *any* time prior to expiration.

2. Ignoring transaction costs and taxes, the maximum possible loss at expiration to an option buyer (put or call) is the amount of the option premium. The call buyer (put buyer) has insured himself against the downside (upside) variability of the futures price. The downside (upside) risk is the variability of the futures price below (above) the level of the call's exercise price.

FIGURE 25.1

Quotes for Options on Futures Contracts

Futures Options

Wednesday, February 8, 1984

Chicago Board of Trade

TREASURY BONDS—$100,000; points and 64ths of 100%

Strike	Calls—Last			Puts—Last		
Price	Mar	Jun	Sep	Mar	Jun	Sep
64	....	....	....	....	0-01	0-12
66	4-44	4-04	3-54	0-01	0-05	0-28
68	2-44	2-22	2-24	0-01	0-23	0-58
70	0-53	1-07	1-23	0-07	1-02	1-57
72	0-03	0-26	0-45	1-21	2-16	3-10
74	0-01	0-07	0-22	3-20	3-59	4-46
76	0-01	0-02	0-08	5-20	....	....
78	0-01	....	0-05	7-20	....	....
80	0-01	....	0-02	....	....	....

Est. total vol. 17,500
Calls: Tues. vol. 11,029; open int. 78,565
Puts: Tues. vol. 6,585; open int. 47,623

Comex, New York

GOLD—100 troy ounces; dollars per troy ounce.

Strike	Calls—Last			Puts—Last		
Price	Apr	Jun	Aug	Apr	Jun	Aug
340	47.50	54.00	....	.20	1.10	1.80
360	28.00	35.00	42.00	1.10	2.60	3.80
380	12.00	20.70	27.00	4.70	6.50	7.80
400	3.00	10.30	17.00	15.50	15.50	16.00
420	1.10	4.50	9.00	34.00	30.00	27.50
440	.40	2.20	5.00	53.50	47.00	43.00
460	.20	....	3.00	....	....	60.00
480	.10	....	1.60	....	....	80.00
500	.10	....	1.00	....	....	100.00
530	.10	....	.80	....	....	....

Est. total vol. 4,000
Calls: Tues. vol. 1,767; open int. 27,435
Puts: Tues. vol. 932; open int. 14,121

Chicago Mercantile Exchange

S&P 500 STOCK INDEX—Price = $500 times premium.

Strike	Calls—Settle			Puts—Settle		
Price	Mar	Jun	Sep	Mar	Jun	Sep
135	....	....	....	....	....	....
140	....	....	....	....	....	....
145	....	....	....	....	....	....
150	....	....	....	.35	....	....
155	3.00	6.00	....	1.55	2.20	....
160	1.10	3.20	....	4.55	5.00	3.90
165	.25	1.40	....	8.65	7.70	....
170	.05	.50	3.00	13.50	11.70	....
175	.05	.30	1.50	18.45	16.40	....
180	.05	.10	.95	....	....	....
185	.002	.10	....	....	....	....

Estimated total vol. 4,174
Calls: Tues. vol. 1,300; open int. 12,357
Puts: Tues. vol. 1,866; open int. 19,703

W. GERMAN MARK—125,000 marks, cents per mark

Strike	Calls—Settle		Puts—Settle	
Price	Mar	Jun	Mar	Jun
34	2.55	....	0.01	0.04
35	1.55	2.05	0.02	0.15
36	0.72	1.29	0.17	0.36
37	0.19	0.74	0.61	0.76
38	0.04	0.35	1.46	1.36
39	0.01	0.17	....	....
Futures	.3656	.3692		

Estimated total vol. 1,996.
Calls: Tues. vol. 1,921; open int. 4,905.
Puts: Tues. vol. 581; open int. 2,613.

SOURCE: *The Wall Street Journal*, February 9, 1984. Reprinted by permission of *The Wall Street Journal*, © Dow Jones & Company, Inc., 1984. All rights reserved.

The maximum possible gain at expiration on a purchased put is limited to the option exercise price, while the potential gain on a purchased call is equal to the excess of the futures price over the option strike price. The option seller's position at expiration is opposite to that of the option buyer. For instance, the option seller's maximum possible gain at expiration is limited to the premium received. In contrast, the buyer (seller) of a futures contract gains (loses) dollar for dollar with an increase in futures price. Therefore, the distribution of returns on options is different from the distribution of futures returns.

3. In general, a purchased option is less risky than a written option, because the maximum possible loss on a purchased option is limited to the premium paid. Except for some delivery privileges enjoyed by the futures contract seller, the riskiness of a long futures position is comparable to that of a short futures position.

4. The option premium is paid up-front, but the payment on a futures contract is postponed until final settlement. Purchased options do not require any margins and are not marked-to-market on a daily basis. Margins on written options are generally higher than those on futures and are marked-to-market daily.

5. Writing an option generates premium income, but selling a futures contract does not.

6. Options provide a flexible hedging mechanism. The holder of a long spot position can insure against a price decline by buying a put option with a desired strike price. In doing so, the investor continues to enjoy the benefit of capital appreciation on the spot position. Alternatively, he can obtain limited protection against price declines by writing calls. Any subsequent price decline will be reduced by the amount of premium received. He can also vary the number of calls written per unit of spot position. It is possible to transform his spot position into a relatively riskless position by buying a put and writing a call, both with identical exercise price and expiration date.

When one sells an appropriate number of futures contracts against a long spot position, one accomplishes something similar to buying a put and selling a call. That is, a *single* futures trade is sufficient to minimize variability of returns on the hedge portfolio.[11] However, the hedger in the futures market is obliged to give up the benefits of capital appreciation on the spot position. Unlike options, a futures contract does not provide the trader with an opportunity to separate downside risk from upside potential.

Pricing of Options on Futures

Black[12] has extended the Black-Scholes stock option pricing model to valuation of options on futures. To understand this relationship, it is convenient to assume

[11] Eugene Moriarty, Susan Philips, and Paula Tosini, "A Comparison of Options and Futures in the Management of Portfolio Risk," *Financial Analysts Journal,* 37 no. 1 (January–February 1981): 61–67.

[12] Fischer Black, "The Pricing of Commodity Contracts," *Journal of Financial Economics,* 3 no. 1,2 (January-March 1976): 167–179.

that capital markets are perfect, there are no transaction costs, margin costs, and taxes, the riskless rate is constant over the life of the option, and the returns on the futures contract is lognormally distributed with a constant variance. Under these assumptions, one can construct a portfolio combining a long position in the futures contract and a short position in options with the same expiration date as the futures. When continuously rebalanced, this becomes a *riskless* hedge. In efficient markets, options will be priced in such a way that the hedge portfolio earns a riskless rate of return.

According to this model, the value of a European call is given by:

(25.28) $$C[F,\tau,K] = e^{-\gamma\tau} FF(t,T)N(d_1) - KN(d_2),$$

where:

$C[F,\tau,K]$ = the call price

e = the base of the natural log

γ = the riskless rate

$\tau = T - t$, the term to expiration of the option

$F(t,T)$ = the futures price

$d_1 = \{ln[F(t,T)/K] + (\sigma^2/2)\tau\}/\sigma\sqrt{\tau}$

$N(.)$ = the cumulative standard normal probability

K = the exercise price on the call

$d_2 = d_1 - \sigma\sqrt{\tau}$

σ = the standard deviation of percentage changes in the futures price.

The value of a European put is equal to:

(25.29) $$P[F,\tau,K] = e^{-\gamma\tau} KN(-d_2) - F(t,T)N(-d_1).$$

The value of a European call in Equation 25.28 is comparable to the value of a call option on a stock that pays a continuous dividend over the life of the option at a rate equal to the risk-free rate times the stock price. This model does not give an exact value of options on futures because they are American options, which can be exercised early. Still, it is a useful model since it provides a lower boundary on the value of American options.

CURRENCY FUTURES

The rapid growth of international trade and travel has led to development of an active market for foreign currencies centered primarily in New York. In the foreign exchange market, international currencies are traded for spot as well as deferred delivery by exporters, importers, banks, and travelers. The spot and forward foreign exchange quotes reported in *The Wall Street Journal* are presented in Figure 25.2. These rates pertain to transactions among a few large

FIGURE 25.2
Spot and Forward Foreign Exchange Rates

Foreign Exchange

Wednesday, February 22, 1984

The New York foreign exchange selling rates below apply to trading among banks in amounts of $1 million and more, as quoted at 3 p.m. Eastern time by Bankers Trust Co. Retail transactions provide fewer units of foreign currency per dollar.

Country	U.S. $ equiv. Wed	Tues	Currency per U.S. $ Wed	Tues
Argentina (Peso)	.03636	.03636	27.506	27.506
Australia (Dollar)	.9430	.9510	1.0604	1.0515
Austria (Schilling)	.05330	.05241	18.76	19.08
Belgium (Franc)				
Commercial rate	.01838	.01815	54.420	55.110
Financial rate	.01768	.01757	56.55	56.900
Brazil (Cruzeiro)	.0008985	.0008985	1113.00	1113.00
Britain (Pound)	1.4545	1.4473	.6875	.6909
30-Day Forward	1.4554	1.4483	.6871	.6905
90-Day Forward	1.4578	1.4505	.6860	.6894
180-Day Forward	1.4615	1.4542	.6842	.6877
Canada (Dollar)	.8017	.8004	1.2474	1.2494
30-Day Forward	.8018	.8005	1.2472	1.2492
90-Day Forward	.8021	.8008	1.2468	1.2488
180-Day Forward	.8025	.8012	1.2461	1.2481
Chile (Official rate)	.01135	.01135	88.10	88.10
China (Yuan)	.4898	.4898	2.0417	2.0417
Colombia (Peso)	.01087	.01087	92.00	92.00
Denmark (Krone)	.1028	.1012	9.7250	9.8800
Ecuador (Sucre)				
Official rate	.01801	.01801	55.52	55.52
Floating rate	.01126	.01126	88.80	88.80
Finland (Markka)	.1746	.1731	5.7275	5.7770
France (Franc)	.1221	.1199	8.1875	8.3400
30-Day Forward	.1216	.1195	8.2255	8.3660
90-Day Forward	.1204	.1184	8.3050	8.4490
180-Day Forward	.1187	.1168	8.4225	8.5600
Greece (Drachma)	.009926	.009814	100.75	101.90
Hong Kong (Dollar)	.1283	.1283	7.7930	7.7960
India (Rupee)	.0929	.0931	10.7643	10.7411
Indonesia (Rupiah)	.001006	.001006	994.00	994.00
Ireland (Punt)	1.1355	1.1430	.8807	.8749
Israel (Shekel)	.007547	.007686	132.50	130.10
Italy (Lira)	.0006086	.0005986	1643.00	1670.50
Japan (Yen)	.004290	.004274	233.08	234.00
30-Day Forward	.004303	.004286	232.40	233.33
90-Day Forward	.004329	.004312	231.01	231.90
180-Day Forward	.004370	.004354	228.81	229.68
Lebanon (Pound)	.1645	.1645	6.08	6.08
Malaysia (Ringgit)	.4284	.4278	2.3345	2.3375
Mexico (Peso)				
Floating rate	.005961	.005961	167.75	167.75
Netherlands (Guilder)	.3337	.3280	2.9965	3.0485
New Zealand (Dollar)	.6614	.6600	1.5119	1.5152
Norway (Krone)	.1312	.1301	7.6240	7.6875
Pakistan (Rupee)	.07463	.07463	13.40	13.40
Peru (Sol)	.0004130	.0004130	2421.19	2421.19
Philippines (Peso)	.07133	.07133	14.02	14.02
Portugal (Escudo)	.007533	.007440	132.75	134.40
Saudi Arabia (Riyal)	.2850	.2849	3.5090	3.5100
Singapore (Dollar)	.4705	.4697	2.1255	2.1290
South Africa (Rand)	.8290	.8170	1.2063	1.2240
South Korea (Won)	.001255	.001255	796.90	796.90
Spain (Peseta)	.006557	.006477	152.50	154.40
Sweden (Krona)	.1259	.1252	7.9450	7.9890
Switzerland (Franc)	.4570	.4510	2.1880	2.2175
30-Day Forward	.4596	.4534	2.1758	2.2058
90-Day Forward	.4645	.4583	2.1528	2.1820
180-Day Forward	.4719	.4655	2.1191	2.1482
Taiwan (Dollar)	.02489	.02489	40.18	40.18
Thailand (Baht)	.04353	.04353	22.975	22.975
Uruguay (New Peso)				
Financial	.02139	.02139	46.75	46.75
Venezuela (Bolivar)				
Official rate	.1942	.1942	5.15	5.15
Floating rate	.07758	.07758	12.89	12.89
W. Germany (Mark)	.3765	.3698	2.6558	2.7045
30-Day Forward	.3779	.3710	2.6462	2.6954
90-Day Forward	.3805	.3736	2.6278	2.6764
180-Day Forward	.3847	.3776	2.5996	2.6486
SDR	1.05083	1.04638	.951631	.955672

Special Drawing Rights are based on exchange rates for the U.S., West German, British, French and Japanese currencies. Source: International Monetary Fund.

z-Not quoted.

SOURCE: *The Wall Street Journal*, February 23, 1984. Reprinted by permission of *The Wall Street Journal*, © Dow Jones & Company, Inc., 1984. All rights reserved.

FIGURE 25.3
Prices on Foreign Currency Futures

Futures

Prices

Thursday, June 21, 1984

Open Interest Reflects Previous Trading Day.

– FINANCIAL –

BRITISH POUND (IMM) – 25,000 pounds; $ per pound

Sept	1.3680	1.3790	1.3675	1.3730	+ .0005	1.5240	1.3675	11,229
Dec	1.3760	1.3880	1.3760	1.3830	+ .0005	1.5100	1.3760	381
Mar85	1.3900	1.3990	1.3840	1.3935	+ .0005	1.5170	1.3840	205

Est vol 3,734; vol Wed 5,086; open int 11,815, –4,773.

CANADIAN DOLLAR (IMM) – 100,000 dlrs.; $ per Can $

Sept	.7678	.7680	.7669	.7671	–.0015	.8147	.7669	5,470
Dec	.7680	.7680	.7671	.7672	–.0014	.8048	.7671	1,735
Mar85	.7676	.7676	.7671	.7672	–.0014	.8050	.7671	1,508
June				.7672	–.0014	.7835	.7683	20

Est vol 983; vol Wed 573; open int 8,773, –2,023.

JAPANESE YEN (IMM) 12.5 million yen; $ per yen (.00)

Sept	.4314	.4325	.4312	.4318	–.0007	.4615	.4312	16,238
Dec	.4377	.4389	.4377	.4383	–.0006	.4663	.4377	1,405
Mar85	.4343	.4349	.4343	.4345	–.0013	.4695	.4343	76
June				.4545		.4570	.4570	1

Est vol 5,590; vol Wed 6,703; open int 17,720, –4,974.

SWISS FRANC (IMM) – 125,000 francs-$ per franc

Sept	.4394	.4413	.4388	.4403	–.0011	.5020	.4388	16,327
Dec	.4485	.4507	.4481	.4493	–.0011	.5000	.4481	1,019
Mar85	.4580	.4590	.4580	.4588	–.0010	.5035	.4580	45
June	.4691	.4691	.4683	.4683	–.0009	.4900	.4683	22
Sept	.4800	.4800	.4800	.4793	–.0008	.4830	.4800	0

Est vol 16,041; vol Wed 12,791; open int 17,413, –4,406.

W. GERMAN MARK (IMM) – 125,000 marks; $ per mark

Sept	.3639	.3659	.3636	.3648	–.0001	.4037	.3602	22,240
Dec	.3694	.3717	.3693	.3706	+.0001	.4080	.3640	1,393
Mar85				.3767	+.0002	.4110	.3699	230

Est vol 17,778; vol Wed 22,500; open int 23,863, –6,469.

EURODOLLAR (IMM) – $1 million; pts of 100%

	Open	High	Low	Settle	Chg	Yield Settle	Chg	Open Interest
Sept	86.86	86.93	86.76	86.77	– .11	13.23	+ .11	42,871
Dec	86.26	86.31	86.08	86.10	– .17	13.90	+ .17	23,413
Mar85	85.87	85.92	85.69	85.70	– .17	14.30	+ .17	9,588
June	85.62	85.62	85.41	85.41	– .18	14.59	+ .18	3,922
Sept	85.36	85.37	85.18	85.18	– .16	14.82	+ .16	1,769
Dec	85.19	85.19	85.02	85.00	– .16	15.00	+ .16	15

Est vol 20,823; vol Wed 35,197; open int 81,578, +3,933.

EURODOLLAR (LIFFE) – $1 million; pts of 100%

Sept	87.10	87.24	87.10	87.20	...	89.63	86.70	8,020
Dec	86.55	86.64	86.54	86.62	– .02	89.36	85.92	3,580
Mar85	86.16	86.25	86.16	86.22	– .02	88.85	85.49	1,365
June	85.91	85.93	85.91	85.93	– .02	88.13	85.66	265
Sept				85.69	– .02	86.20	85.52	2

Est vol 5,058; vol Wed 9,343; open int 13,232, +217.

STERLING DEPOSIT (LIFFE) – £250,000; pts of 100%

Sept	89.85	89.90	89.78	89.89	– .03	91.06	89.10	5,021
Dec	89.32	89.32	89.28	89.31	– .09	90.91	88.60	2,939
Mar85	88.90	88.90	88.88	88.87	– .08	90.86	88.25	865
June				88.69	– .08	90.60	88.10	25

Est vol 593; vol Wed 1,513; open int 8,850, +35.

LONG GILT (LIFFE) – £50,000; pts of 100%

June	103-09	103-23	103-09	103-23	+ 0-05	110-10	101-04	3,697
Sept	102-06	102-17	101-29	102-09	....	109-12	100-10	4,847
Dec				101-24	....	108-31	99-30	125
Mar85				101-14	....	108-19	100-00	6
June				101-06	....	105-26	99-27	147

Est vol 3,027; vol Wed 3,889; open int 8,822, +314.

SOURCE: *The Wall Street Journal*, June 22, 1984. Reprinted by permission of *The Wall Street Journal*, © Dow Jones & Company, Inc., 1984. All rights reserved.

banks who make up the forward market. As an example, the figure shows that the spot exchange rate per British pound is $1.4545, while the 180-day forward rate is $1.4615.

The holder of foreign currencies is exposed to a new type of business risk, namely, uncertain fluctuations in exchange rates. One way to minimize exposure to exchange rate risk is to try to balance foreign currency denominated assets and liabilities. Any net exposure, i.e., the excess of foreign assets over foreign liabilities, or vice versa, can be covered by a hedge — short or long — in the forward currency market. While the *forward* market can provide a hedging tool that is tailored to the trader's needs, it suffers from low liquidity relative to the currency *futures* market.

The primary currency futures market is the International Monetary Market (IMM), a subsidiary of the Chicago Mercantile Exchange. Sample currency futures quotations reported in *The Wall Street Journal* are shown in Figure 25.3. It shows that the futures contract on British pounds is for £25,000 with four delivery months a year: March, June, September, and December. The settle quote on the March contract is $1.3935, amounting to $34,837.50 per contract.

Like other futures instruments, the major economic functions of currency forward and futures markets are price discovery and hedging. The general conclusion of empirical studies is the current forward rate provides an unbiased forecast of the future spot rate, but its forecasting performance is no better than the current spot rate.[13] The hedging performance of currency futures compared quite favorably with that of commodity futures and interest rate futures.[14]

SUMMARY

Following the background material regarding futures markets and alternative prices provided in Chapter 24, this chapter was concerned with financial futures, one of the newest and fastest growing instruments in our financial markets. Following a brief description of interest rate contracts, we considered instances where one might consider using them as hedges, and provided examples of short and long hedges as well as speculative transactions. Because it is important to understand price relationships, we considered alternative instruments. The empirical evidence supported the theoretical models and subsequent evidence supported the ability to hedge with interest rate futures.

In Chapter 24 we discussed the portfolio approach to determining hedge ratios. In this chapter we considered an alternative price sensitive approach. The empirical evidence indicates that this technique works very well compared to several naive strategies. As a follow-up to Chapter 19, we also saw that financial futures can be used to adjust bond portfolio duration and thereby assist in immunizing portfolios.

---

[13] Tamir Agmon and Yakov Amihud, "The Forward Exchange Rate and the Prediction of the Future Spot Rate," *Journal of Banking and Finance,* 5 no. 3 (September 1981): 425–437.

[14] Charles Dale, "The Hedging Effectiveness of Currency Futures Markets," *The Journal of Futures Markets,* 1 no. 1 (Spring 1981): 77–88.

In addition to interest rate futures, another major development has been the creation of stock index futures, serving a multitude of purposes for individuals and institutional money managers. We described these index futures and discussed several important uses including information about their implementation.

The enormous innovation possible in the financial markets is exemplified by the creation of options on futures. As discussed, these provide all the advantages and opportunities of these two instruments. We considered the method by which these options are priced and examined the differences and similarities of options and futures.

The concluding section deals with currency futures, another area of growing importance and activity. As the world becomes more a united business community, it is essential that financial managers and money managers understand how to use these currency futures to hedge against the volatility of foreign exchange rates.

QUESTIONS

1. You have been reading about the diversification benefits of gold as well as the returns enjoyed by some "gold bugs." In June, you decide to take the plunge and buy a March contract in gold (100 troy ounces) on the International Monetary Market (IMM) at the Chicago Mercantile Exchange (CME). March gold on the IMM is 465 ($465 an ounce), the margin on gold is 10 percent, and the commission is $30 a contract:
   a. In September there is an outbreak in the Middle East and the price of March gold goes to 525. Compute the rate of return on your investment.
   b. When you bought the gold contract in June you put in a stop-loss order at 455. In November, over the weekend, there are several very optimistic announcements by the government regarding the inflationary outlook, interest rates, and peace in the Middle East. Gold closes down the limit for five days and the price goes right through your limit order to 440 before your broker can sell your contract. Compute the rate of return on your investment. Discuss the leverage involved.
2. Discuss the portfolio approach and the price-sensitivity approach to hedging.
3. How could one use interest rate futures and stock index futures in active portfolio management? What are the advantages of futures over other methods of altering a portfolio beta?
4. Differentiate between stock options on futures contracts. Discuss Black's model of pricing options on futures.
5. What are the two important economic functions of currency futures? Give an example of each.
6. CFA Examination III — (June 1982) In each of the following cases, **discuss** how you as a portfolio manager would use financial futures to protect the portfolio.
   a. You own a large postition in a relatively illiquid bond that you want to sell.
   b. You have a large gain on one of your long Treasuries and want to sell it, but would like to defer the gain until the next accounting period which begins in four weeks.

    c.   You will receive a large contribution next month that you hope to invest in long-term corporate bonds on a yield basis as favorable as is now available.

(15 minutes)

7.   CFA Examination III — (June 1983) In February 1983, the United American Co. is considering the sale of $100 million in 10-year debentures that will probably be rated AAA like the firm's other bond issues. The firm is anxious to proceed at today's rate of 10.5%.

    As Treasurer, you know that it will take about 12 weeks (May 1983) to get the issue registered and sold. Therefore, you suggest that the firm hedge the pending bond issue using Treasury bond futures contracts. (Each Treasury bond contract is for $100,000.)

    Explain how you would go about hedging the bond issue, and **describe** the results assuming that the following two sets of future conditions actually occur. (Ignore commissions and margin costs, and assume a 1-to-1 hedge ratio.) **Show** all calculations.

	Case 1	Case 2
Current Values — February 1983		
Bond rate	10.5%	10.5%
June '83 Treasury Bond Futures	78.875	78.875
Estimated Values — May 1983		
Bond rate	11.0%	10.0%
June '83 Treasury Bond Futures	75.93	81.84
Present Value of a $1 Annuity		
10 years at 10.5%	6.021	6.021

(15 minutes)

REFERENCES

Agmon, Tamir, and Yakov Amihud. "The Forward Exchange Rate and the Prediction of the Future Spot Rate." *Journal of Banking and Finance.* 5 no. 3 (September 1981).

Bacon, Peter W., and R. E. Williams. "Interest Rate Futures: New Tool for the Financial Manager." *Financial Management.* 5 no. 1 (Spring 1976).

Black, Fischer. "The Pricing of Commodity Contracts." *Journal of Financial Economics.* 3 no. 1, 2 (January-March 1976).

Dale, Charles. "The Hedging Effectiveness of Currency Futures Markets." *The Journal of Futures Markets.* 1 no. 1 (Spring 1981).

Ederington, Louis H. "The Hedging Performance of the New Futures Market." *Journal of Finance.* 34 no. 1 (March 1979).

Fabozzi, Frank J., and Gregory M. Kipnis (eds.) *Stock Index Futures.* Homewood, Ill.: Dow Jones-Irwin, 1984.

Figlewski, Stephen, and Stanley Kon. "Portfolio Management with Stock Index Futures." *Financial Analysts Journal.* 38 no. 1 (January–February 1982).

Franckle, Charles T. "The Hedging Performance of the New Futures Market: Comment." *Journal of Finance.* 35 no. 5 (December 1980).

Gay, Gerald D., and Robert W. Kolb. "Interest Rate Futures as a Tool for Immunization." *Journal of Portfolio Management.* 10 no. 1 (Fall 1983).

Gay, Gerald D., and Robert W. Kolb (eds.). *Interest Rate Futures: Concepts and Issues.* Richmond, Va.: Robert F. Dame, Inc. 1982.

Gay, Gerald, Robert Kolb, and Raymond Chiang. "Interest Rate Hedging: An Empirical Test of Alternative Strategies." *Journal of Financial Research.* 6 no. 3 (Fall 1983).

Hopewell, Michael H., and George G. Kaufman. "Bond Price Volatility and Term to Maturity: A Generalized Respecification." *American Economic Review.* 64 no. 4 (September 1973).

Kane, Edward J. "Market Incompleteness and Divergencies Between Forward and Futures Interest Rates," *Journal of Finance.* 35 no. 2 (May 1980).

Kolb, Robert W. *Interest Rate Futures.* Richmond, Va.: Robert F. Dame, Inc. 1982.

Kolb, Robert W., and Gerald D. Gay. "Immunizing Bond Portfolios with Interest Rate Futures," *Financial Management.* 11 no. 3 (Summer 1982).

Kolb, Robert, and Raymond Chiang. "Improving Hedging Performance Using Interest Rate Futures." *Financial Management.* 10 no. 4 (Autumn 1981).

Kolb, Robert, and Raymond Chiang. "Duration, Immunization and Hedging with Interest Rate Futures." *Journal of Financial Research.* 5 no. 2 (Summer 1982).

McEnally, Richard W., and Michael L. Rice, "Hedging Possibilities in the Flotation of Debt Securities." *Financial Management.* 8 no. 4 (Winter 1979).

Moriarity, Eugene, Susan Phillips, and Paula Tosini, "A Comparison of Options and Futures in the Management of Portfolio Risk." *Financial Analysts Journal.* 37 no. 1 (January–February 1981).

Niederhoffer, Victor, and Richard Zeckhauser, "Market Index Futures Contracts." *Financial Analysts Journal.* 36 no. 1 (January–February 1980).

Rendleman, Richard, and Christopher Carabini. "The Efficiency of the Treasury Bill Futures Market." *Journal of Finance.* 34 no. 4 (September 1979).

Schwarz, Edward W. *How to Use Interest Rate Futures Contracts.* Homewood, Ill.: Dow Jones-Irwin, 1979.

Chapter 26   *Investment Companies*

U p until fairly recently, most investment texts were limited in their discussion of investment companies. This was due to the assumption that most readers would prefer to make their own investment decisions. However, recent studies of efficient capital markets have indicated that it is difficult for an individual investor to outperform the aggregate market averages, making professionally managed investment companies an appealing alternative. In addition, there are a number of different types of investment companies which offer a wide variety of options to the investor in terms of risk and return. Therefore, the reader should be aware of what investment companies are, how they operate, what types of companies there are, and how they have performed in the past. These are the topics of our concluding chapter.

We will begin by defining investment companies, discussing their basic management organization, and describing the major types of companies. These different types, ranging from very conservative to common stock funds, are the subject of the second section. In the third section, some studies that have examined the historical performance of mutual funds, using the composite performance measures will be discussed. The final section considers sources of information on investment companies.

INVESTMENT COMPANY DEFINED

An investment company is a pool of funds belonging to many individuals that is used to acquire a collection of individual investments such as stocks, bonds, and other publicly traded securities. As an example, 10 million shares of an investment company might be sold to the public at $10 a share for a total of $100 million. Assuming that this is a common stock fund, the managers of the company might then invest the funds in the stock of companies like American Telephone and Telegraph, General Motors, IBM, Xerox, and General Electric. As a result, each of the individuals that bought shares of the investment company would own a percentage of the total portfolio of the investment company. In other words, they would have acquired shares of a diversified portfolio of securities. The value of the investor's shares depends upon what happens to the portfolio of assets acquired by the managers of the fund. If we assume no transactions are made, and the total market value of all the stocks in the portfolio increased to $105 million, then the per share value of each of the original shares would be $10.50 ($105 million ÷ 10 million shares).This figure is referred to as the *net asset value (NAV)* and is equal to the total market value of all the assets of the fund divided by the number of shares of the fund outstanding.

Management of Investment Companies

The investment company is typically a corporation whose major assets are the portfolio of marketable securities. The *management* of the portfolio, and most of the other administrative duties related to the company and its portfolio of securities, are handled by a *separate* management company hired by the board of directors of the investment company. While this is the legal description, the actual management usually begins with a group of managers or an investment advisor who start an investment company and select a board of directors for the fund that will then hire the investment advisory firm as the fund manager. The contract between the investment company (fund) and the management company indicates the duties of the management company and the fee it will receive for these services. Major responsibilities include *research, portfolio management,* and *administrative duties* such as issuing securities and handling redemptions and dividends. The fee is generally stated in terms of a percentage of the value of the fund. Fees typically range from one quarter of one percent to one half of one percent of the total value, with a sliding scale as funds get larger. As an example, assuming that a fund had a total market value of $200 million and a one half of one percent fee, the management company would receive $100,000 to perform all the duties mentioned. If the management company has to pay out less than $100,000 in salaries and other costs, it will make money. Because there are substantial economies of scale involved in money management, it is in the interest of the management company to have the fund get larger. If the fund grew to $500 million, and the fee scale did not change, the management company would receive $250,000, and it is likely that management expenses would not increase very much because it does not cost much more to manage a $500 million fund than it does a $200 million fund.

The concept of economies of scale is the reason that many management companies start *several* funds with different characteristics.[1] This allows the management group to appeal to many different types of investors, provides the investors with the flexibility to switch between funds, and increases the total capital managed.

[1] For an interesting discussion of cases in which insurance companies acquired management companies, see David Armstrong, "Were Mutual Funds Worth the Candle?" *Journal of Portfolio Management,* 2 no. 4 (Summer 1976): 46–51.

Open-End vs. Closed-End Funds

Investment companies are begun like any other company—by selling an issue of common stock to a group of investors. In the case of an investment company, the proceeds are used to purchase the securities of other publicly held companies rather than buildings and equipment. The difference between an open-end investment company (often referred to as a *mutual fund*) and a closed-end investment company is how they operate *after* the initial public offering is sold.

A closed-end investment company operates like any other public firm, since its stock is bought and sold on the regular secondary market and the market price of the investment company shares is determined by supply and demand. There are typically no further shares offered by the investment company, and it does *not* repurchase the shares on demand. There are *no* subsequent additions to the investment company unless it makes another public sale of securities. Also, there is *no withdrawal* of funds unless the investment company decides to repurchase its stock, which is quite unusual.

There are two prices of importance for shares of a closed-end investment company. The first is the *net asset value (NAV)* for the shares which is computed as discussed earlier. The investment company's net asset value is computed twice a day based upon prevailing market prices for the securities in the portfolio. The second price is the *market price* of shares in the fund, which is determined by the relative supply and demand for investment company stock in the market. When buying or selling shares of a closed-end investment company, the investor pays this *market* price plus or minus a regular trading commission. It is very important to recognize that *the two prices (NAV and market price) are almost never the same!* The long-run historical relationship has been that the market price for closed-end investment companies is from 5 to 20 percent *below* the net asset value. Figure 26.1 contains a list of closed-end funds from *Barron's*. (They are currently referred to as *publicly traded funds.*) As shown, at the time of this figure, the division between premium and discount funds was evenly split. Based upon the historical relationship, this is unusual. A lingering question has been why these funds sell at a discount and why the discounts differ between funds. Of even more importance are the returns available to investors from funds that sell at large discounts since, given the fact that an investor is acquiring a portfolio at a price below market value, the returns from such an investment would be expected to exceed average returns.[2] In addition to closed-end stock

[2] Eugene J. Pratt, "Myths Associated with Closed-End Investment Company Discounts," *Financial Analysts Journal,* 22 no. 3 (July–August 1966): 79–82; Julian L. Simon, "Does 'Good Portfolio Management' Exist?" *Management Science,* 15 no. 6 (February 1969): B308–B319; Morris Mendelson, "Closed-End Fund Discounts Revisited," *The Financial Review* (Spring 1978): 48–72; Burton Malkiel, "The Valuation of Closed-End Investment Company Shares," *Journal of Finance,* 32 no. 3 (June 1977): 847–859; Malcolm Richards, Donald Fraser, and John Groth, "Winning Strategies for Closed-End Funds," *Journal of Portfolio Management,* 7 no.1 (Fall 1980): 50–55; Malcolm Richards, Donald Fraser, and John Groth, "Premiums, Discounts, and the Volatility of Closed-End Mutual Funds," *The Financial Review,* 14 no. 3 (Fall 1979): 26–33; Rodney Roenfeldt and Donald Tuttle, "An Examination of the Discounts and Premium of Closed-End Investment Companies," *Journal of Business Research,* 5 no. 1 (Fall 1973): 129–140; Rex Thompson, "The Information Content of Discounts and Premiums on Closed-End Fund Shares," *Journal of Financial Economics,* 6 no. 2/3 (June–September 1978): 151–186.

FIGURE 26.1
Sample Quotations on Publicly Traded Funds

PUBLICLY TRADED FUNDS

Friday, February 17, 1984
Following is a weekly listing of unaudited net asset values of publicly traded investment fund shares, reported by the companies as of Friday's close. Also shown is the closing listed market price or a dealer-to-dealer asked price of each fund's shares, with the percentage of difference.

	N.A. Value	Stk Price	% Diff.
Diversified Common Stock Funds			
Adams Express	16.65	15⅞	- 4.7
Baker Fentress	38.17	32	- 16.2
Equity Strat.	bz	z	z
CenAInv	15.92	16¼	+ 2.1
Lehman	.14.10	15⅛	+ 7.3
Niagara Share	16.95	17⅛	+ 1.0
Overseas Sec	6.30	7¼	+ 15.1
Source	a31.20	30⅛	- 3.4
Tri-Continental	23.39	23½	+ 0.5
US & Foreign	22.53	21¼	- 5.7
Specialized Equity and Convertible Funds			
Amer Cap Cv	29.93	30¾	+ 2.7
ASA	b62.78	60⅝	-- 3.4
Bancroft Conv	24.54	22⅞	- 6.8
Castle Conv	30	31½	+ .5
Central Sec	13.45	12	- 10.8
Claremont	34.46	28⅞	- 16.2
CLAS	.01	1⅛	z
CLAS PFD	39.19	z	z
Cyprus	.53	3½	+ 560.4
Engex	22.36	17	- 23.9
Japan Fund	12.52	12⅝	+ 0.8
Mexico	b3.31	3¼	-- 1.8
Nautilus	31.24	33½	+ 7.2
New American Fd	36.66	32¼	- 12.0
Pete & Res	28.25	28⅝	+ 1.3

a-Ex-Dividend. b-As of Thursday's close. z-Not available.

CLOSED-END BOND FUNDS

Unaudited net asset values of closed-end bond fund shares, reported by the companies as of Friday, February 10, 1984. Also shown is the closing listed market price or a dealer-to-dealer asked price of each fund's shares, with percentage of difference.

	N.A. Value	Stk Price	% Diff.
AmCapBd	19.36	18⅞	- 2.5
BunkerHill	17.43	17½	+ 0.4
CircleInc	12.33	13¾	+ 11.5
CNAInc	10.84	10⅛	- 6.6
CurrentI	b10.10	9⅜	- 7.2
DrexelBd	17.26	17¾	+ 2.8
Excelsior	16.47	15⅝	- 5.1
FtDearInc	12.30	11½	- 6.5
Hatteras	a15.37	15¾	+ 2.5
INAInvS	16.60	16½	- 0.6
IndSqls	15.81	16¾	+ 6.0
Intercap	18.00	18¼	+ 1.4
JHanInv	18.88	18⅛	- 4.0
JHanSec	14.10	12⅞	- 8.7
LincInNatl	22.68	20½	- 9.6
MMIncInv	11.05	11½	+ 4.1
MntgSt	17.14	17	- 0.8
MuOmahI	12.90	12⅞	- 0.2
PacAmInc	14.03	12⅜	- 11.8
StPaulS	10.14	10⅛	- 0.2
StateMSec	10.74	10	- 6.9
Transaml	19.15	18⅝	- 2.7
USLIFE	a9.52	8⅞	- 6.8

a-Ex-dividend. b-Thursday's close.

SOURCE: *Barron's Weekly,* February 20, 1984, p. 132. Reprinted by permission.

funds, a number of closed-end bond funds were initiated, and a listing of them also appears in Figure 26.1.[3]

Open-end investment companies are funds for which shares continue to be bought and sold *after* the initial public offering is made. They stand ready to *sell* additional shares at the *net asset value* of the fund with or without a sales charge. In addition, open-end investment companies stand ready to buy back shares of the fund (redeem shares) at the *net asset value* at any time with or without a redemption fee.

Open-end mutual funds have enjoyed substantial growth during the post-war period, as shown by the figures in Table 26.1. As can be seen, there was a steady increase in the number of funds until 1973 followed by a decline in 1974 and 1975 due to mergers. The growth in the number of funds resumed in 1976 and continued through 1983. Clearly, open-end funds account for a substantial portion of investment assets and provide a very important service for almost 10 million accounts.

[3] Malcolm Richards, Donald Fraser, and John Groth, "The Attractions of Closed-End Bond Funds," *Journal of Portfolio Management,* 8 no. 2 (Winter 1982): 56–61.

TABLE 26.1
Open-End Investment Company Assets 1945–1983

Year End	Number of Reporting Funds[a]	Assets (billions)	Year End	Number of Reporting Funds[a]	Assets (billions)
1945	72	$ 1.3	1965	170	$ 35.2
1946	74	1.3	1966	182	34.8
1947	80	1.4	1967	204	44.7
1948	87	1.5	1968	240	52.7
1949	91	2.0	1969	269	48.3
1950	98	2.5	1970	361	47.6
1951	103	3.1	1971	392	55.0
1952	110	3.9	1972	410	59.8
1953	110	4.1	1973	421	46.5
1954	115	6.1	1974	416	34.1
1955	125	7.8	1975	390	42.2
1956	135	9.0	1976	404	47.6
1957	143	8.7	1977	427	45.0
1958	151	13.2	1978	444	45.0
1959	155	15.8	1979	446	49.0
1960	161	17.0	1980	458	58.4
1961	170	22.8	1981	486	55.2
1962	169	21.3	1982	539	76.8
1963	165	25.2	1983	653	113.4
1964	160	29.1			

[a] The figures are for conventional funds; money market funds are *not* included.
SOURCE: *Mutual Fund Fact Book* (Washington, D.C.: Investment Company Institute, 1984). Reprinted by permission.

Load vs. No-Load Open-End Funds. One distinction between open-end funds is whether they charge a sales fee when the fund is initially offered. In the case of a *load fund,* the offering price for a share is equal to the net asset value of the share *plus* a sales charge, typically 7.5–8.0 percent of the NAV. Therefore, assuming an 8 percent sales charge *(load),* an individual investing $1,000 in such a fund would only receive $920 worth of stock. In such cases, the funds generally do *not* charge a redemption fee, which means the shares can be redeemed at their net asset value. Therefore, the funds are typically quoted in the paper with a bid and ask price. The bid price is the redemption price and is equal to the net asset value of the shares. The ask price is the offering price and is equal to the net asset value divided by 0.92. The percent of the load typically declines with the size of the order.

There is no initial sales charge on *a no-load fund,* so the shares are sold at their net asset value. In some instances, there is a small redemption charge on these funds (one half of one percent). When examining the prices of mutual funds listed in *The Wall Street Journal,* the reader will see the bid price is listed as *NAV* and, in the case of a no-load fund, in the offering price column, there is the designation *NL* (no-load). A number of no-load funds have been established in recent years. The mutual fund listing in *The Wall Street Journal* indicated more than 220 no-load funds quoted. A directory of such funds is available.[4]

TYPES OF INVESTMENT COMPANIES BASED ON PORTFOLIO MAKEUP

Common Stock Funds

Some funds invest almost solely in common stocks, as contrasted to those that invest in preferred stocks, bonds, etc. Within this category of common stock funds there are wide differences in terms of whether their emphasis is on the common stock of growth companies, or on the stock of companies in specific industries (e.g., Chemical Fund, Oceanography Fund), or certain areas (e.g., Technology Fund). In some instances, funds will even concentrate their investments in given geographic areas (e.g., Northeast Fund). Within the general category of common stock funds *there is a very wide variety of types of funds to suit almost any taste or investment desire.* Therefore, the first decision an investor must make is whether he wants a fund that only invests in common stock; then he must consider the type of common stock desired.

Balanced Funds

Balanced funds contain a combination of common stock *and* fixed-income securities which could include government bonds, corporate bonds, convertible bonds, or preferred stock. The idea is to balance the commitment of the fund and not restrict the portfolio to only one kind of security. Therefore, managers diversify outside of the stock market. The ratio of stocks to fixed-income securities will vary by fund as stated in the prospectus for the fund. Given the balanced nature of these funds, one would expect them to have a beta factor less than one, which means they would not rise as much as the aggregate stock market will rise during bull markets, but they also should not decline as much during bear markets.[5]

Bond Funds

As indicated by the title, bond funds are concentrated in various types of bonds in order to generate high current income with a minimum of risk. As is true of common stock funds, there is a difference in the bond investment policy of different funds. Some concentrate in only high-grade corporate bonds, while others hold a mixture of investment grades. Some portfolio managers may engage in more trading of the bonds in the portfolio. In addition to corporate bond funds, a change in the tax law in 1976 made it possible to establish *municipal*

---

[4] No-Load Mutual Fund Association, Inc., Valley Forge, Pa., 19481.

[5] An article on these funds is Jill Bettner, "Stodgy Image of Old 'Balanced' Mutual Funds Could Change with Rally in Both Stocks, Bonds," *Wall Street Journal,* June 29, 1981, p. 42.

bond funds. A number of these funds have been established and provide investors with monthly interest checks that are exempt from federal income taxes (although some of the interest may be subject to state and local taxes).

Money Market Funds

Another relatively recent addition to the universe of investment companies is money market funds. These funds were initiated during 1973 when interest rates on short-term money market securities were at record levels. Managers of these funds attempt to provide current income and safety of principal by investing in short-term securities such as treasury bills, bank certificates of deposit, bank acceptances, and commercial paper. The intent is to provide a diversified portfolio of such investments to investors who are concerned with liquidity and safety. Many conservative investors, who normally invest in savings accounts or savings and loan shares, switched into money market securities because the yields had risen substantially above the ceiling allowed banks and savings and loan associations. During 1980 and early 1981 the annual return ranged between 14 percent and 17 percent for the typical money market fund. In addition, all of these are no-load funds and there is no penalty for withdrawal at any time. Finally, as an option, most of them allow the holder to write checks against the account; typically a $500 minimum investment is required.[6]

The significant growth of these funds is documented in Table 26.2. Because of the interest in money market funds, *The Wall Street Journal* on Mondays carries a special section within the mutual fund section titled "Money Market Funds." This section indicates the average maturity of the portfolio for the various funds and the average current yield for these funds.

TABLE 26.2
Statistics on Money Market Funds (millions of dollars)

Year End	Total Number of Funds	Total Accounts Outstanding	Average Maturity (days)	Total Net Assets
1974	15	n.a.	n.a.	$ 1,715.1
1975	36	208,777	93	3,695.7
1976	48	180,676	110	3,685.8
1977	50	177,522	76	3,887.7
1978	61	467,803	42	10,858.0
1979	76	2,307,852	34	45,214.2
1980	96	4,745,572	24	74,447.7
1981	159	10,282,095	34	181,910.4
1982	281	13,101,347	37	206,607.5
1983	307	12,276,639	37	162,552.1

SOURCE: *Mutual Fund Fact Book* (Washington, D.C.: Investment Company Institute, 1984).

[6] For a list of names and addresses of money market funds, write to Investment Company Institute, 1775 K Street N.W., Washington, D.C. 20006. A service that concentrates on money market funds is *Donoghue's Money Letter,* 770 Washington Street, Holliston, MA 01746. An analysis of performance is contained in Michael G. Ferri and H. Dennis Oberhelman, "How Well Do Money Market Funds Perform?" *Journal of Portfolio Management,* 7 no. 3 (Spring 1981): 18–26.

Breakdown by Fund Characteristics

The figures in Table 26.3 break down the funds in terms of how they market their funds and by investment objectives. *Broker-dealer* means that these funds are sold through brokers, while *direct selling* means that the fund has its own sales force. The figures on methods of distribution attest to *the growth of no-load funds* in absolute terms (they almost doubled during the period) and in relative terms: over 30 percent of the total. These figures reflect the creation of new no-load funds and the conversion of some load funds to no-load funds.

The breakdown by investment objective indicates a shift in investor emphasis and a response to this shift by the investment company industry. The aggressive growth funds have experienced significant growth in absolute dollar value and as a percentage of the total. In contrast there has been a notable movement away from growth and income and balanced funds into the income and bond funds. The data also reveal investor interest in the new municipal bond funds. Finally, almost 2 percent of the total is in option income funds that specialize in writing covered call options.

Dual Funds.   Dual funds are special purpose closed-end funds that issue two classes of stock, income shares and capital shares. An investor in a dual fund indicates whether he wants the income shares or the capital shares. Holders of the income shares receive a stated dividend income from *all* investments, but they give up potential capital gain. Investors in the capital shares do not receive any income during the life of the fund, but they receive the capital value of all the shares at the end of the life of the fund.

Problems can arise for these funds if they are not balanced in terms of the proportion of income to capital appreciation stocks. Additional problems can arise if stock prices decline, in which case the income required on the remaining capital is above normal expectations.[7] Like the closed-end fund, these funds typically sell at deep discounts from their NAV.[8]

PERFORMANCE OF INVESTMENT COMPANIES

A number of studies have examined the historical performance of mutual funds for a variety of reasons. One is that the funds are a prime example of what can be accomplished by professional money managers. Another very important reason is that data on the funds are available for a long period. Consequently, two of the three major portfolio evaluation techniques were derived in connection with a study of mutual fund performance.

[7] See John P. Shelton, Eugene F. Brigham, and Alfred E. Hofflander, Jr., "An Evaluation and Appraisal of Dual Funds," *Financial Analysts Journal,* 23 no. 3 (May–June 1967): 131–139; and James A. Gentry and John R. Pike, "Dual Funds Revisited," *Financial Analysts Journal,* 24 no. 2 (March–April 1968): 149–157.

[8] For an analysis and evaluation of dual funds, see Robert Litzenberger and Howard B. Sosin, "The Structure and Management of Dual Purpose Funds." *Journal of Financial Economics,* 4 no. 1 (May 1977): 203–230; "The Performance and Potential of Dual Purpose Funds," *Journal of Portfolio Management,* 4 no. 3 (Spring 1978): 56–68; "The Theory of Recapitalizations and the Evidence of Dual Purpose Funds," *Journal of Finance,* 32 no. 5 (December 1977); 1433–1456.

TABLE 26.3
Total Net Assets by Fund Characteristics (millions of dollars)

	1980		1981		1982		1983	
	Dollars	Percent	Dollars	Percent	Dollars	Percent	Dollars	Percent
Total Net Assets	$58,399.6	100.0	$55,207.3	100.0	$76,840.6	100.0	$113,403.9	100.0
Method of Distribution								
Broker-Dealer	32,032.4	54.9	30,636.6	55.5	42,337.4	55.1	62,651.5	55.2
Direct Selling	9,176.7	15.7	8,600.4	15.5	11,556.1	14.6	14,444.9	12.7
No-Load	15,647.5	26.8	14,548.4	26.4	21,883.6	28.5	34,459.6	30.4
Other	1,543.0	2.6	1,421.9	2.6	1,363.5	1.8	1,847.9	1.6
Investment Objective								
Aggressive Growth	4,681.3	8.0	4,966.5	9.0	9,562.0	12.5	18,801.6	16.6
Growth	16,823.4	28.8	15,221.3	27.6	18,971.8	24.7	25,614.3	22.6
Growth and Income	19,522.6	33.4	18,226.8	33.0	22,029.8	28.7	29,256.1	25.8
Balanced	3,389.2	5.8	2,778.3	5.0	3,065.1	4.0	3,102.1	2.7
Income	4,801.8	8.2	4,487.3	8.1	5,865.7	7.6	8,906.1	7.1
Bond	5,712.6	9.8	5,913.3	10.7	9,094.7	11.8	12,014.7	10.6
Municipal Bond	2,908.3	5.0	3,062.5	5.6	7,455.6	9.7	14,607.0	12.9
Option Income	$ 560.4	1.0	$ 551.6	1.0	$ 795.9	1.0	$ 1,911.9	1.7

SOURCES: *Mutual Fund Fact Book* (Washington, D.C.: Investment Company Institute, 1984). Reprinted by permission.

842   Sharpe Study

A study of mutual funds done by Sharpe includes a discussion of the CAPM and a derivation of performance measure based upon the fact that all efficient portfolios will be on the CML.[9] Therefore, the best portfolios are those with the highest value of the ratio:

$$S_i = \frac{R_i - RFR}{V_i},$$

where:

R_i = average rate of return on fund i

RFR = risk-free rate

V_i = standard deviation of rates of return for fund i.

This is also referred to as the *reward-to-variability ratio* (R/V), because the numerator is the risk premium $(R_i - RFR)$ and the denominator is the total variability of returns. Sharpe used the measure to evaluate the performance of 34 open-end mutual funds during the period 1944–1963. The rate of return included price change, dividend, and capital distribution, which is considered a *net* return because it is calculated after the costs of administration and management have been subtracted. It does *not* include the load fee. The reward-to-variability ratio (R/V) for the sample of funds varied from 0.43 to 0.78 compared to the DJIA's performance of 0.667. For the total period, only 11 of the 34 funds had superior performance compared to the DJIA. Sharpe compared the ranks of the various funds during the first part of the sample period (1944–1953) to the rank during the second half (1954–1963) to determine the ability to predict performance. The results indicated some relationship (rank correlation of 0.36), but the predictions were imperfect. He concluded that past performance in terms of the R/V ratio was not the best predictor of future performance. Sharpe also predicted rank using the Treynor measure, and showed that the Treynor measure, which only considers systematic risk, is a better predictor. (The rank correlation between the two periods using the Treynor measure was 0.454.)

The consistency in ranking could be attributable to the consistent performance of the managers (good or bad) *or* consistent differences in expense ratio (e.g., certain funds could always be low because they spend too much on research and administration). Therefore, Sharpe examined the relationship between performance and the expense ratio. The results indicated that *good performance was associated with low expense ratios;* the rank correlation coefficient was 0.505. There was only a slight relationship between size and performance.

Because it is important for an investor to know his risk class, Sharpe analyzed the consistency of the variability of returns over time. There was reasonable consistency with the rank correlation between periods being 0.528.

---

[9] William F. Sharpe, "Mutual Fund Performance," *Journal of Business,* 39 no. 1, Part 2 (January 1966): 119–138.

Finally, Sharpe analyzed *gross* performance with expenses added back to the returns. This comparison indicated that 19 of the 34 funds did better than the DJIA. He concluded:

> it appears that the average mutual fund manager selects a portfolio at least as good as the Dow-Jones Industrials, but that the results actually obtained by the holder of mutual fund shares (after the costs associated with the operations of the fund have been deducted) fall somewhat short of those from the Dow-Jones Industrials.[10]

Jensen Study

A study by Jensen developed a portfolio evaluation technique from the CAPM as shown in Chapter 22 and then used this performance measure to evaluate 115 open-end mutual funds during the period 1945–1964.[11] The basic performance model is:

$$R_{it} - RFR_t = \alpha_i + \beta_i(R_{mt} - RFR_t),$$

where:

R_{it} = rate of return for fund i during the time period t

RFR_t = risk-free rate during the time period t

α_i = the abnormal return for fund i allowing for the systematic risk of the portfolio

β_i = the systematic risk for fund $i (Cov_{im}/\sigma_m^2)$

R_{mt} = rate of return for the market portfolio during time period t.

If the α_i for a fund is a statistically significant positive value, it indicates that the fund has experienced abnormally good returns during the period involved, allowing for the systematic risk of the portfolio. This superior performance can be due to the manager's ability to consistently select undervalued stocks or due to a superior job of predicting market turns.

The summary results for the 115 mutual funds, using all the data available for the period 1945–1964, indicated that the mean alpha value (α_i) was -0.011, with a minimum of -0.078, and a maximum of 0.058. This indicated that, on average, the funds earned 1.1 percent less per year than they should have earned for their level of systematic risk. The frequency distribution of the alphas is contained in Figure 26.2. Note that these returns are *net* of expenses (i.e., after deducting expenses). There was also an analysis of *gross* returns with expenses added back each year. In this instance, the average alpha (α) was -0.004. Therefore, on the basis of *net* returns, 39 funds (34 percent) had a positive alpha and 76 had a negative alpha. Using *gross* returns, 48 funds (42 percent) had positive alphas, and 67 had negative alphas. The results with gross returns indicate the forecasting ability of all the funds, because this analysis does not penalize the funds for operating expenses. All the funds have to do is cover the brokerage

[10] Ibid., p. 137.

[11] Michael C. Jensen, "The Performance of Mutual Funds in the Period 1945–1964," *Journal of Finance*, 23 no. 2 (May 1968): 389–416.

FIGURE 26.2

Frequency Distribution of Estimated Intercepts (α) for 115 Mutual Funds for All Years Available for Each Fund. Fund Returns Calculated *Net* of All Expenses.

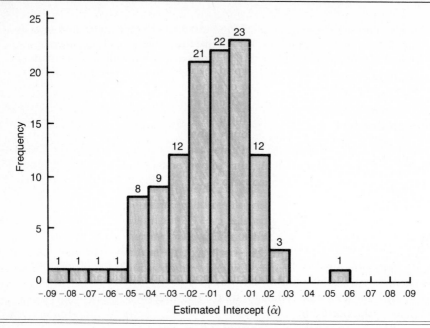

SOURCE: Michael C. Jensen, "The Performance of Mutual Funds in the Period 1945–1964," *Journal of Finance*, 23 no. 2 (May 1968), p. 404. Reprinted by permission.

commissions. The preponderance of negative alphas indicates the inability of the funds to forecast well enough to cover commissions.

Because data were not available for all the funds for the full 20 years, he examined the total sample for the ten years 1955–1964. The analysis of *gross* returns indicated an average alpha of −0.001 and an almost even split for funds. Given the various alpha values, how many are statistically significant? An analysis of the 115 funds indicated 14 funds had *significant negative* alphas and only three had significant positive alphas. An analysis of 56 funds for which data was available for the full 20 years indicated that none of them had substantial forecasting ability. Jensen concluded:

> The evidence on mutual fund performance discussed above indicates not only that these 115 mutual funds were *on average* not able to predict security prices well enough to outperform a buy-the-market-and-hold policy, but also that there is very little evidence that any *individual* fund was able to do significantly better than that which we expected from mere random chance.[12]

Mains Comment.   A comment by Mains on the Jensen study questioned several of the estimates made by Jensen that apparently biased the results against

---

[12] Ibid., p. 415.

mutual funds.[13] The specific objections were:

1. Jensen assumed that all dividend payments and capital distributions were made at the end of the year for the funds and for the market. Mains believed that the returns for the funds were underestimated as a result.

2. When Jensen computed the gross returns by adding back expenses, he likewise assumed all of this was done at the year end rather than throughout the year. Again this results in an understatement of gross returns for the funds.

3. Jensen computed the systematic risk for the funds for a 20-year period and, when he subsequently examined the performance over the last ten years, he assumed that the systematic risk for the funds during the ten-year period was the same as it was for the 20-year span. Although Jensen's test for stability showed significant correlation, it was shown that risk was generally lower during the later period, and this could definitely influence the results given the importance of the systematic risk in the performance measure. An overstatement of systematic risk would cause an understatement of fund performance.

To test the effect of these objections, Mains examined the performance of 70 funds (all in the Jensen sample) using monthly rates of return for the ten-year period 1955–1964 and adjusted for the biases. Comparing the basic returns, the Mains subsample had a slightly higher return and lower risk. Because of these differences, the Mains monthly data produced an annual performance measure, using net returns, of 0.09 (not significantly different from zero) compared to an average performance measure of −0.62 for Jensen's data. In addition, 40 of the funds had positive alphas and 30 were negative. One would probably interpret this as an even split using net returns.

To derive gross returns, Mains added back expenses and an estimate of brokerage commissions on a monthly basis. It was noted that expenses and commissions averaged about one percent a year for all the funds, but the effect varied widely. Using gross returns, the annual average alpha for the Mains sample was 1.07, which indicates abnormal returns of 10.7 percent above expectations. Fifty-five of the funds posted positive alphas and 15 had negative values. This compared to an average alpha of 0.009 for the full Jensen sample with 60 of the 115 having positive results.

The author contended that, after the Jensen results are corrected for several biases, the performance of the funds on a net return basis is neutral. Further, on the basis of gross returns, the results indicate that the majority of fund managers demonstrated above average performance owing either to stock selection or timing ability. It is contended that these results do not support the strong efficient market hypothesis.

Carlson Study

Carlson examined the overall performance of mutual funds during the period 1948–1967 with an emphasis on analyzing the effect of the market series used

---

[13] Norman E. Mains, "Risk, the Pricing of Capital Assets, and the Evaluation of Investment Portfolios: Comment," *Journal of Business,* 50 no. 3 (July 1977): 371–384.

TABLE 26.4
Index Comparisons — Mutual Funds vs. the Market, 1948–1967[a]

Index	No. of Funds 1948	No. of Funds 1967	Riskless Return R^*	Mean Return $\bar{R}$	Variability Standard Deviation V	Performance θ
Balanced Fund–Gross	23	25	2.92	9.92	9.22	0.7595
Balanced Fund–Net	23	25	2.92	9.15	9.22	0.6762
Common Stock Fund–Gross	33	136	2.92	13.66	14.61	0.7352
Common Stock Fund–Net	33	136	2.92	12.89	14.63	0.6811
S&P Stock Price Index			2.92	13.34	14.71	0.7086
NYSE Composite Index			2.92	13.02	14.49	0.6971
Dow-Jones Industrial Average			2.92	12.39	14.51	0.6526
Income Fund–Gross	6	17	2.92	11.01	12.79	0.6328
Income Fund–Net	6	17	2.92	10.24	12.79	0.5725

[a] Returns for each market index include estimated dividends. The riskless rate, R^*, is the average annual rate of return for United States Government 9- to 12-month certificates.
SOURCE: Robert S. Carlson, "Aggregate Performance of Mutual Funds, 1948–1967," *Journal of Financial and Quantitative Analysis,* 5 no. 1 (March 1970): 8. © March 1970. Reprinted by permission.

and the difference in results depending on the time period.[14] After providing evidence of a linear risk-return relationship, the author categorized the funds as one of three types: (1) diversified common stock, (2) balanced funds, and (3) income funds. When each of the fund groups are compared to the market using a return to total variability measure, it is shown, in Table 26.4 that the results are heavily dependent upon which market series is used: the S&P 500, the NYSE composite, or the DJIA. For the total period, almost all the fund groups outperformed the DJIA, but only a few had *gross* returns that were better than those for the S&P 500 or the NYSE composite. Using net returns, *none* of the groups did better than the S&P 500 or the NYSE composite. Also, the balanced and income funds were consistently inferior to the full common stock funds, which indicates that the fund's objective did make a difference. An analysis of various ten-year subperiods showed that the relative results were clearly dependent on the time interval examined.

Carlson examined the computation of systematic risk for the funds and contended that investigators should consider using an index of common stock funds, because the correlation with such an index is superior to that with the S&P 500. Such a practice would also eliminate some adjustments that have to be made relative to the S&P 500. Finally, he showed that, during this 20-year period, the computed alpha relative to the S&P 500 was positive and about 59 percent of the funds had a positive alpha (the author did not indicate how many were "significant").

The author's final analysis considered the factors related to performance during this period. Although there was consistency over time for return or risk taken alone, there was *no* consistency in the risk-adjusted performance measure. Less than one third of the funds that experienced above average performance

[14] Robert S. Carlson, "Aggregate Performance of Mutual Funds, 1948–1967," *Journal of Financial and Quantitative Analysis,* 5 no. 1 (March 1970): 1–32.

during the first half did so in the second half. An analysis of five-year periods indicated there was *more* consistency for the shorter intervals than there was for ten-year intervals. Notably, consistency *declined* over time. An analysis of performance relative to size, expense ratios, and a new funds factor indicated *no* relationship with size or the expense ratio. On the other hand, there was a relationship between performance and a measure of new cash into the fund. This relationship with new cash inflows was not related to age. There was no difference in performance of new versus old funds. Finally, he examined the performance of eight no-load funds compared to that of the other 74 funds. The results indicated that the no-loads experienced a significantly *higher* performance measure, but the conclusion must be tentative because the sample was limited.

Impact of Fund Objectives

McDonald examined the performance of 123 mutual funds using monthly returns for the period 1960–1969.[15] In addition to an analysis of the performance of the total group, the author examined performance relative to the stated objective of the fund. Each fund was categorized according to objective: (1) maximum capital gain, (2) growth, (3) income growth, (4) balanced, and (5) income. The results indicated a positive relationship between stated objectives and measures of beta and total variability. The risk measures increased as objectives became more aggressive. The second question concerned the relationship between objectives and the average monthly excess return without considering risk. Again, the results were generally as one would expect since the returns increased with the aggressiveness of the objective, except at the lower end where the income fund return was slightly higher than the balanced fund return. Given the earlier results with risk and return taken alone, it should be no surprise that there was a positive relationship between return and either systematic risk or total variability. The relationship was especially strong when the author combined several funds in a risk class.

The third consideration was the relationship between fund objective and overall risk-adjusted performance as indicated by the Sharpe, Treynor, and Jensen measures. The results in Table 26.5 indicate that, for all the composite performance measures, *the portfolios with the more aggressive objectives appeared to outperform the more conservative funds during this period.* Regarding overall fund performance relative to the aggregate market, four measures were considered: excess return alone plus the three composite performance measures. One third of the funds had an excess return above the market's, and the mean excess return for all the funds was below the market's. This was not too surprising because the average beta was only 0.92. The analysis using the Treynor measure indicated an average value for all the funds of 0.518 versus 0.510 for the market, and approximately half the funds had a value above the market's. The results with the Jensen measure indicated that 67 of 123 (54 percent) had positive alphas during this period, and the average alpha was 0.052

[15] John G. McDonald, ''Objectives and Performance of Mutual Funds, 1960–1969,'' *Journal of Financial and Quantitative Analysis*, 9 no. 3 (June 1974): 311–333.

TABLE 26.5
Objectives and Performance

	Risk			Performance Measures		
Objective of Fund	Systematic Risk (beta)	Total Variability (std. dev.)	Mean Monthly Excess Return (%)	Sharpe[a] Measure	Treynor[b] Measure	Jensen[c] Measure
Maximum Capital Gain	1.22	5.90	.693	.117	.568	.122
Growth	1.01	4.57	.565	.124	.560	.099
Growth-Income	.90	3.93	.476	.121	.529	.058
Income-Growth	.86	3.80	.398	.105	.463	.004
Balanced	.68	3.05	.214	.070	.314	−.099
Income	.55	2.67	.252	.094	.458	−.002
Sample Means	.92	4.17	.477	.112	.518	.051
Market-Based Portfolios	—	—	—	.133	.510	0
Stock Market Index	1.00	3.83	.510	.133	.510	0
Bond Market Index[d]	.18	1.42	.093	.065	.516	Not Available

[a] Reward-to-variability ratio: mean excess return divided by the standard deviation of fund return.
[b] Reward-to-volatility ratio: mean excess return divided by beta.
[c] Alpha: estimated constant from least-squares regression of fund excess returns on market excess returns (Jensen's delta).
[d] Proxy measure based on arithmetic means of results for Keystone B-1 and B-4 funds, with returns adjusted for 0.042 percent per month average management fee.
SOURCE: John G. McDonald, "Objectives and Performance of Mutual Funds, 1960–1969," *Journal of Financial and Quantitative Analysis,* 9 no. 3 (June 1974): 319. © June 1974. Reprinted by permission.

percent per month, which is about one half of one percent a year above expectations. Only six of the funds had a statistically significant alpha, which is what one would expect on the basis of chance. Finally, the results with Sharpe's measure indicated that two thirds of the funds had a performance measure below the market value (0.133), and the mean value for all the funds was below the market (0.112 vs. 0.133). The poorer performance with the Sharpe measure was because the funds did not diversify completely.

The final question was the relationship between the market line that prevailed during the period (based upon the risk-free return and the market return) and the fund line during the period, as indicated by the relationship between risk and return for the sample of funds. If the market was in equilibrium, the two lines should coincide. The results showed that the fund line was *steeper* than the market line. This means that the low risk portfolios did *not* do as well as expected relative to the market line, and the high risk funds did *better* than expected on a risk-adjusted basis. It was noted that the difference in the slope is not significant. However, the difference in slope is contrary to that found by Friend and Blume[16] and consistent with the difference indicated in the Klemkosky study.[17] These

[16] Irwin Friend and Marshall Blume, "Measurement of Portfolio Performance under Uncertainty," *American Economic Review,* 60 no. 4 (September 1970): 561–575.

[17] Robert C. Klemkosky, "The Bias in Composite Performance Measures," *Journal of Financial and Quantitative Analysis,* 8 no. 3 (June 1973): 505–514.

results support the notion that, although there may be a bias in the composite performance measures, *the direction of the bias is unknown.*

Ang and Chua examined the consistency of performance for mutual funds with different objectives.[18] Through the use of stochastic dominance they determined that there could be alternative groups of investors with different objectives and different funds at one time or another provided an investment medium that was as good as or better than the market portfolio. Given this result, they questioned whether these funds were *consistent* in their performance. In this test, the results indicated that *less than half* the funds in their sample could meet the consistency condition. Therefore, they concluded that funds do fulfill the function of serving alternative objectives, but they don't do it well based on consistency.

Martin, Keown, and Farrell examined the impact of alternative fund objectives on the diversification policies of mutual funds—i.e., is there more extra-market covariation for specialized funds?[19] They examined 72 mutual funds representing five investment objective classifications (aggressive growth, growth, growth and income, income, and other). The results indicated that there was a definite difference in the extra-market variation for the funds in alternative classifications. Still, while the authors found a large amount of extra-market variation for some funds, the fund objective only explained a small proportion of this variation (15 percent), which implied there were other important factors contributing to this phenomenon.

Market-Timing Ability

In addition to an analysis of overall performance and risk analysis, several studies have examined the ability of mutual funds to *time market cycles and react accordingly.* Specifically, an ideal fund portfolio manager would increase the beta of the portfolio in anticipation of a bull market and reduce the beta prior to a bear market. An early study by Treynor and Mazuy did not derive any evidence that the funds were able to time market changes and change their risk levels accordingly.[20] Fabozzi and Francis likewise could not find evidence that there was a shift in the beta for funds in line with expectations as noted above.[21]

A more recent study by Veit and Cheney also considered the ability of mutual funds to time market changes by examining portfolio betas during bull and bear markets and also by examining the alpha for these funds assuming that the alpha will be lower during rising markets and *vice versa.*[22] They computed the alphas

---

[18] James S. Ang and Jess H. Chua, "Mutual Funds: Different Strokes for Different Folks?" *Journal of Portfolio Management,* 8 no. 2 (Winter 1982): 43–47.

[19] John D. Martin, Arthur J. Keown, Jr. and James L. Farrell, "Do Fund Objectives Affect Diversification Policies?" *Journal of Portfolio Management,* 8 no. 2 (Winter 1982): 19–28.

[20] Jack L. Treynor and Kay K. Mazuy, "Can Mutual Funds Outguess the Market?" *Harvard Business Review,* 44 no. 4 (July–August 1966): 131–136.

[21] Frank J. Fabozzi and Jack C. Francis, "Mutual Fund Systematic Risk for Bull and Bear Markets," *Journal of Finance,* 34 no. 5 (December 1979): 1243–1250.

[22] E. Theodore Veit and John M. Cheney, "Are Mutual Funds Market Timers?" *Journal of Portfolio Management,* 8 no. 2 (Winter 1982): 35–42.

and betas during bull markets, bear markets, and the total period and determined if the differences were as hypothesized for good market timers. The sample was 74 mutual funds using annual data for the period 1944–1978. They used four different schemes to define bull and bear markets. After an extended discussion of different results depending on the definition of bull and bear markets, it is concluded that mutual funds do *not* successfully alter their characteristic lines (i.e., their alphas and betas) in an attempt to employ timing strategies. Clearly, the strongest evidence was for no change in the characteristic lines which would support the efficient market hypothesis.

A study by Kon and Jen considered not only timing but also the idea of selectivity by mutual fund managers.[23] They examined the performance of 49 mutual funds during the period 1960–1971 using both the Sharpe–Lintner–Mossin CAPM and the Black equilibrium model as benchmarks. They specifically examined the ability to change portfolio composition to take advantage of market cycles and the ability to select undervalued securities. The results indicated that many sample funds experienced a significant change in their risk levels during the test period. This evidence that a number of funds (eleven) exhibited superior timing ability was in sharp contrast to Jensen's earlier results. While this evidence of several superior funds and the average results would be evidence against the EMH, it is noteworthy that no individual fund was able to *consistently* generate superior results. The results regarding selectivity also indicated that many *individual* funds were able to generate superior performance, but in this case, the *average* performance was negative relative to a naive policy. Finally, there was evidence that mutual fund portfolio managers did attempt to time the market based upon risk changes and diversification changes. Overall, the results were mixed regarding the EMH. While *on average* the funds appeared to select superior portfolios, this can be partially explained by the bias in the model toward low-risk securities. Further, there is a question whether this superior selection is enough to cover research expenses, management fees, and commission expenses.

A study by Shawky likewise provided some encouraging evidence for mutual funds.[24] He examined the performance of 255 funds using monthly data during the period 1973–1977. Similar to earlier studies, the author found that the risk is consistent with fund objectives. Regarding overall performance, the results are similar to Jensen's in that only about 10 percent of the alphas are significant (25 out of 255), and 16 of these are negative and 9 are positive. The author contended (without much justification) that this is an improvement from earlier periods. He also found strong correlation between alternative performance measures (Jensen, Sharpe, Treynor). Finally, the results indicated that the funds have been able to reduce the unsystematic risk in their portfolios based upon an increase in the average R^2 with the market from about 0.59 in the 1960s to about 0.75 in the 1970s.

[23] Stanley J. Kon and Frank C. Jen, "The Investment Performance of Mutual Funds: An Empirical Investigation of Timing, Selectivity, and Market Efficiency," *Journal of Business,* 52 no. 2 (April 1979): 263–289.

[24] Hany A. Shawky, "An Update on Mutual Funds: Better Grades," *Journal of Portfolio Management,* 8 no. 2 (Winter 1982): 29–34.

Two recent studies examined the macro market forecasting and the micro stock selection ability of fund managers using a technique suggested by Henriksson and Merton.[25] In turn, this technique was based on some earlier work by Merton.[26] They basically specified two tests. The first was a nonparametric test that did not require any assumption about the distribution of security prices or the way in which individual security prices are formed. This test can be used if the market timer's forecasts are observable. Alternatively, if the analyst only has access to the time series of realized returns and not the forecasts themselves, they derived a parametric test of market timing that requires the assumption of a specific generating process for returns on securities.

A study by Chang and Lewellen used the following parametric model from Henriksson and Merton to examine the performance of mutual funds during the period 1971–1979:[27]

$$Z_p(t) - R(t) = \alpha_{pt} + \beta_1 X_1(t) + \beta_2 X_2(t) + \epsilon_p(t),$$

where:

$Z_p(t)$ = the observed rate of return on the portfolio during the period

$R(t)$ = the contemporaneous return on a riskless asset

α_p = the average residual or abnormal component on that portfolio's return due to the manager's security selection ability

β_1 = the average down market beta for the portfolios

X_1 = the excess market return (Z_m) during down markets $[Z_m(t) < R(t)]$

β_2 = the average up market beta for the portfolios

X_2 = the excess market return (Z_m) during up markets $[Z_m(t) > R(t)]$

$\epsilon_p(t)$ = a random error term.

The test for market timing analyzes the difference between β_1 and β_2 (i.e., it tests whether there is an attempt to change the portfolio beta over time) and whether the changes are in the rational direction (i.e., whether $\beta_1 < \beta_2$). The test for micro forecasting (stock selection) is whether the α_p is positive and statistically significant after taking account of the timing decisions.

The results provided little evidence of any market timing ability by fund managers. In fact, the average estimated down market beta (0.993) was slightly *higher* than the up market beta (0.955). There were only four instances where there was a statistically significant difference in the down market, up market betas, and in three of these cases the down market beta was higher. Based on this

[25] Roy D. Henriksson and Robert C. Merton, "On Market Timing and Investment Performance, II. Statistical Procedures for Evaluating Forecasting Skills," *Journal of Business,* 54 no. 4 (October 1981): 513–533.

[26] Robert C. Merton, "On Market Timing and Investment Performance, I. An Equilibrium Theory of Value for Market Forecasts," *Journal of Business,* 54 no. 3 (July 1981): 313–406.

[27] Eric C. Chang and Wilbur G. Lewellen, "Market Timing and Mutual Fund Investment Performance," *Journal of Business,* 57 no. 1, part 1 (January 1984): 57–72.

the authors concluded:

> Apparently, then, there was really not much macro-price forecasting going on within the sample or, if there was, it was either not being acted on or was overwhelmed by other portfolio design factors.[28]

The results related to security selection were similar. While 41 of the 67 funds had positive alphas, only five of the 67 were statistically significant, and three of these were negative. The overall results using quarterly data rather than monthly were very similar. Their overall conclusion is:

> Nonetheless, those same results suggest that neither skillful market timing nor clever security selection abilities are evident in abundance in observed mutual fund return data, and the general conclusion of the prior literature that mutual funds have been unable collectively to outperform a passive investment strategy still seems valid.[29]

A study by Henriksson employed a parametric model similar to that suggested by Henriksson and Martin and used by Chang and Lewellen, except that he adjusted the model for potential heteroscedasticity.[30] Besides this parametric model, he also considered a nonparametric model to examine the performance of 116 open-end mutual funds using monthly data during the period February 1968–June 1980. In addition to the entire period, he also considered two subperiods: February 1968–April 1974 and May 1974–June 1980. These subperiods were analyzed to determine the ability of any funds to enjoy consistent success.

The initial results for the parametric tests showed little evidence of market-timing ability (i.e., 62 percent of the funds had negative results for β_2, and there were only three significant positive values). The results for the α value for the overall period was similar. The results for the subperiod analysis were similarly discouraging—it was not possible to reject the hypothesis that the α's and the β_2's for each fund were independent for the two periods. When market timing was ignored, only one of the 116 funds had a significant α for both subperiods. Further, the results without adjustment for heteroscedasticity were similar, and a test to determine if managers could forecast large changes likewise did not provide a positive result. Equally discouraging, there was a negative correlation between estimates of α and β_2 which implied that funds that earn superior returns from stock selection have negative market-timing ability.

The author used an equally weighted market index and an expanded model to isolate a mutual fund factor that helped explain returns for many funds, but it did not explain the negative correlation between α and β_2. Because of potential problems with the specified model of returns required by the parametric test, the author employed a nonparametric test that required knowledge of forecasts. He proxied these forecasts by using actual returns as a measure of total performance

[28] Ibid., p. 64.

[29] Ibid., p. 67.

[30] Roy D. Henriksson, "Market Timing and Mutual Fund Performance: An Empirical Investigation," *Journal of Business*, 57 no. 1, part 1 (January 1984): 73–96.

(not only market timing) compared with performance of a feasible passive strategy. Again, on average, the funds did slightly worse than the passive strategy which implies no forecasting ability. As before, there was little relationship between performance during the first and second subperiods for individual funds. Also, there was no evidence that the fund managers were able to forecast large changes better than small changes. The author concluded:

> The empirical results . . . do not support the hypothesis that mutual fund managers are able to follow an investment strategy that successfully times the return on the market portfolio. . . . Strong evidence of nonstationarity in the performance parameters was found in both the parametric and nonparametric tests. In addition, no evidence was found that forecasters are more successful in their market-timing activity with respect to predicting large changes . . . relative to small changes.[31]

Klemkosky on Consistency

A study by Klemkosky specifically examined the question of the performance consistency by mutual fund managers.[32] The author analyzed the risk-adjusted performance for a sample of 158 mutual funds using monthly data for the eight-year period 1968–1975. To test consistency, Klemkosky compared the ranking using the Sharpe and Treynor measures for adjacent two-year periods and the two four-year periods. The results indicated some consistency in the four-year periods, but relatively low consistency between the adjacent two-year periods (only one of the three correlations was significant). As a test of consistency with the Jensen measure, Klemkosky analyzed the proportion of funds that had positive or negative alphas in adjacent periods. Again, there was no significant association in the proportion of positive and negative alphas between successive two-year periods. In contrast, there was consistency for the two four-year periods, mainly due to the great consistency in the negative results.

The author concluded that the investor should exercise caution in using past performance (either relative to other funds or to the market) to predict future performance. This is especially true for short periods of time.

Implications of Performance Studies

Assume that you had your own personal portfolio manager and consider the functions you would want him to perform for you. Some of these we talked about in the portfolio performance chapter. The list would probably include:

1. Determine your risk-return preferences and develop a portfolio that will be consistent with your desires.
2. Diversify the securities in your portfolio in order to eliminate unsystematic risk.

---

[31] Ibid., pp. 92–93.

[32] Robert C. Klemkosky, "How Consistently Do Managers Manage?" *Journal of Portfolio Management,* 3 no. 2 (Winter 1977): 11–15.

3. Control your portfolio in order to maintain diversification and ensure that you remain in your desired risk class. At the same time, allow flexibility so you can shift between investment instruments, if you desire.

4. Attempt to derive a risk-adjusted performance record that is superior to aggregate market performance. As noted, this can be done by either consistently selecting undervalued stocks or by proper timing of market swings. For some investors, assuming that they have other diversified investments, they may be willing to sacrifice diversification for this superiority.

5. Administer the account, keep records of costs, provide timely information for tax purposes, and reinvest dividends, if desired.

The reader will recognize that most of the performance studies were concerned with Number 4 — risk-adjusted performance. Still, it seems appropriate to consider all of the functions in order to put performance into perspective.

The first function of *determining* your risk preference is *not* performed by mutual funds. However, once you have determined what you want, it is clear that the industry *does* provide a large variety of funds that can meet almost any goal in the area of marketable securities. The empirical studies indicated that *the funds were generally consistent in meeting their stated goals;* i.e., the risk and returns *were* consistent with the stated objectives.

The second function is to diversify your portfolio in order to eliminate unsystematic risk. One of the major benefits of mutual funds is *instant diversification.* This is especially beneficial to the new, small investor who does not have the resources to acquire 100 shares of 10 or 12 different issues and thereby reduce unsystematic risk. With most mutual funds, it is possible to start with about $1,000 and acquire a portfolio of securities that is correlated about 0.90 with the market portfolio (about 90 percent diversified). As noted in the studies, there is a range of diversification, but typically some three quarters of the funds in any sample have a correlation about 0.90, so *most funds provide excellent diversification,* especially if they state this as an objective.

The third function is to maintain diversification and keep you in your desired risk class. Mutual funds have been quite good in terms of the stability of their correlation with the market. This is not too surprising since, once you have a reasonably well-diversified portfolio, it is difficult to change its makeup substantially. Further, the evidence is quite strong regarding the consistency of the risk class. Recall that even the studies that indicated there was not much consistency in risk-adjusted performance did indicate *consistency in risk alone.* Finally, on the flexibility to change investment instruments, the initiation of a number of funds by a given management company helps accomplish this goal. Typically, these investment groups will allow an investor to shift between their funds without a charge simply by calling the fund. Therefore, it is possible to shift from an aggressive stock fund to a money market fund and back again for much less than it would cost you if you did it yourself.

The fourth function is to derive a record of risk-adjusted performance that is superior to the aggregate market (i.e., naive buy and hold). The reader will probably not be surprised when I conclude that the news on this function is not very good. A reasonable summary of the evidence is that, on average, the results achieved by portfolio managers through their ability to select securities or time the market are *about as good as* or only *slightly better* than would be achieved with a naive buy-and-hold policy. This conclusion is based upon evidence using *gross* returns. Unfortunately, the evidence regarding *net* returns, which is what the investor receives, indicates that the majority of funds do *not* do as well as a naive buy-and-hold policy. The shortfall in performance is about one percent a year, which is roughly the average cost of expenses and commissions. For the investor who would like to find one of the superior funds, the news is likewise not very encouraging. Most studies show a lack of consistency in performance over time except among inferior funds. Apparently if the poor performance is due to excessive expenses, this state of affairs will continue, so such funds should be avoided. In general, an investor should *not* expect to consistently enjoy superior risk-adjusted performance from investment in a mutual fund.

The final objective is administration of the account. This is a major benefit of most mutual funds, since they allow automatic reinvestment of dividends with no charge and consistently provide a record of total cost. Further, each year they supply a statement which indicates the dividend income and capital gain distribution for tax purposes.

Most investors have a set of functions they want their portfolio manager to perform. *Typically, mutual funds can help the investor accomplish four of the five at a cost lower in terms of time and money than it would be if they did it on their own.* Unfortunately the price of this is about one percent a year in loss of performance. The studies we discussed did not take into account the sales load of many funds, which also detracts from performance. An obvious way to avoid this loss is to acquire a no-load fund, since most evidence indicates that their performance on average is about equal to that of load funds.

SOURCES OF INFORMATION

Given the wide variety of types and number of funds available, it is important to be able to determine the performance of various funds over time and derive some understanding of their goals and management philosophy.

Daily quotations on a large number of open-end funds are contained in *The Wall Street Journal*. A more comprehensive weekly list of quotations and the dividend income and capital gain for the past 12 months are carried in *Barron's,* which also includes a quarterly update on performance over the past ten years for a number of funds. *Barron's* contains a list of closed-end funds with current net asset values, current market quotes on the funds, and indicated percentage of difference between the two figures. As mentioned, the market price is typically about 5–10 percent below the net asset value. Finally, for those interested in dual funds, *Barron's* contains a brief list of these, giving their current net asset value, market quotation, and the percentage of difference between the two. The discounts on these funds are generally close to 10 percent.

The major source of comprehensive historical information is an annual publication issued by Arthur Wiesenberger Services entitled *Investment Companies.* This book is published each year and currently contains vital statistics for over 600 mutual funds arranged alphabetically. The description of each fund includes: a brief history, investment objectives and portfolio analysis, statistical

FIGURE 26.3
Sample Page from *Investment Companies*

TECHNOLOGY FUND, INC.

Organized in 1948 as Television Fund, Technology Fund became Television-Electronics Fund in 1951 and adopted its present name in January 1968. On December 10, 1976, the name of the fund's adviser (then Supervised Investors Services, Inc.) was changed to Kemper Financial Services, Inc., a wholly owned subsidiary of Kemper Corp., an insurance and financial services holding company.

Under the policy revised in early 1968, the fund invests primarily in securities of companies expected to benefit from technological advances and improvements in such fields as aerospace, astrophysics, chemistry, electricity, electronics, geology, mechanical engineering, metallurgy, nuclear physics and oceanography. Management may, however, seek investment opportunities in virtually any industry in which they may be found. An advisory board provides information of a technical nature relating to new inventions and developments.

At the end of 1981, the fund had 85% of its assets in common stocks, of which the major proportion was concentrated in five industry groups: petroleum services (13.9% of assets), communications & entertainment (11%), electronic data processing & instruments (10.7%), transportation (9%), and insurance & finance

(6.6%). The five largest individual common stock holdings were American International Group (7.1% of assets), Schlumberger (6.1%), Burlington Northern (4.5%), Teledyne (4.3%), and Warner Communications (2.8%). The rate of portfolio turnover during the latest fiscal year was 20.7% of average assets. Unrealized appreciation was 37% of calendar year-end assets.

Special Services: An open account system serves for accumulation and automatic dividend reinvestment. Minimum initial investment is $1,000; subsequent investments must be at least $100. Income dividends are invested at net asset value. Plan payments may be made by way of pre-authorized checks against the investor's checking account. Arrangements may be made for payroll deduction. A monthly or quarterly withdrawal plan is available without charge to accounts worth $5,000 at the offering price; payments may be of any designated amount. Shares may be exchanged for those of other funds in the Kemper Financial group without service fee. Tax-deferred retirement plans are available for corporations and the self-employed, as well as Individual Retirement Account plans. A one-time account reinstatement privilege is available to redeeming shareholders within a specified time.

Statistical History

Year	Total Net Assets ($)	Number of Share-holders	Net Asset Value Per Share ($)	Offer-ing Price ($)	Yield (%)	Cash & Equiv-alent	Bonds & Pre-ferreds	Com-mon Stocks	Income Div-idends ($)	Capital Gains Distribu-tion ($)	Expense Ratio (%)	Offering Price ($) High	Low
1981	478,771,015	52,758	11.11	12.14	2.6	12	3	85	0.33	0.76	0.52	15.53	11.64
1980	588,946,604	54,967	14.18	15.50	1.9	5	1	94	0.31	0.62	0.57	16.07	10.38
1979	427,059,368	58,190	10.17	11.11	2.3	4	1	95	0.26	0.43	0.60	11.45	8.86
1978	375,341,502	63,590	8.26	9.03	2.7	14	2	84	0.25	0.20†	0.62	9.67	6.56
1977	358,694,594	70,491	7.14	7.80	2.5	8	2*	90	0.20	0.10	0.60	8.31	7.17
1976	432,029,805	77,716	7.58	8.28	2.3	3	6*	91	0.19	—	0.59	8.42	5.12
1975	416,490,321	86,336	6.20	6.78	2.8	6	3*	91	0.19	—	0.64	7.42	5.12
1974	338,514,102	91,141	4.67	5.12	3.5	12	3*	85	0.18	—	0.67	7.01	4.66
1973	489,644,043	96,032	6.21	6.81	2.2	8	2*	90	0.15	—	0.59	8.47	6.30
1972	665,113,022	100,312	7.66	8.39	1.6	6	4*	90	0.14	0.36	0.56	9.24	8.02
1971	667,760,452	106,008	7.47	8.14	2.1	5	6*	89	0.18	0.30	0.54	9.02	7.06

* Includes a substantial proportion in convertible issues.   † Includes $0.01 short-term capital gains.

Directors: John Hawkinson, Pres.; Thomas R. Anderson, Vice President; David W. Belin; Lewis A. Burnham; Harry C. De Muth; Donald L. Dunaway; James W. Harding; Robert B. Hoffman; Thomas L. Martin, Jr.; Christian G. Schmidt; William P. Sommers. Advisory Board: Dr. William L. Everitt; Dr. Jerome B. Wiesner.

Investment Adviser: Kemper Financial Services, Inc. Compensation to the Adviser is ½ of 1% annually of average daily net assets on first $215 million; 0.375% on the next $335 million; 0.30% on the next $250 million; and 0.25% on all assets over $800 million.

Custodian and Transfer Agent: United Missouri Bank of Kansas City N.A., Kansas City, MO 64141.

Shareholder Service Agent: DST, Inc., Kansas City, MO 64141.

Distributor: Kemper Financial Services, Inc., 120 South La Salle Street, Chicago, IL 60603.

Sales Charge: Maximum is 8½% of offering price; minimum is 1% at $1 million. Reduced charges begin at $10,000 and are applicable to combined purchases of the fund and other of the Kemper Mutual Funds.

Dividends: Income dividends are paid in cash or shares quarterly in the months of February, May, August and November. Capital gains, if any, are paid optionally in shares or cash in November.

Shareholder Reports: Issued quarterly. Fiscal year ends October 31. The 1982 prospectus was effective in February.

Qualified for Sale: In all states and DC.

Address: 120 South LaSalle St., Chicago, IL 60603.

Telephone: (312) 781-1121.

An assumed investment of $10,000 in this fund, with capital gains accepted in shares and income dividends reinvested, is illustrated below. The explanation on Page 155 must be read in conjunction with this illustration.

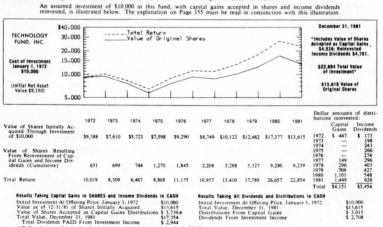

	1972	1973	1974	1975	1976	1977	1978	1979	1980	1981
Value of Shares Initially Acquired Through Investment of $10,000	$9,388	$7,610	$5,723	$7,598	$9,290	$8,749	$10,122	$12,462	$17,377	$13,615
Value of Shares Resulting From Reinvestment of Capital Gains and Income Dividends (Cumulative)	631	699	744	1,270	1,845	2,208	3,288	5,327	9,280	9,239
Total Return	10,019	8,309	6,467	8,868	11,135	10,957	13,410	17,789	26,657	22,854

Dollar amounts of distributions reinvested:

	Capital Gains	Income Dividends
1972	$ 447	$ 173
1973		198
1974	—	243
1975	—	266
1976	—	274
1977	149	296
1978	296	403
1979	709	427
1980	1,101	548
1981	1,449	626
Total	$4,151	$3,454

Results Taking Capital Gains in SHARES and Income Dividends in CASH
Initial Investment At Offering Price, January 1, 1972 ... $10,000
Value as of 12/31/81 of Shares Initially Acquired ... $13,615
Value of Shares Accepted as Capital Gains Distributions $ 3,739#
Total Value, December 31, 1981 ... $17,354
Total Dividends PAID From Investment Income ... $ 2,944
\# Dollar Amount of these distributions at the time shares were acquired: $3,373

Results Taking All Dividends and Distributions in CASH
Initial Investment At Offering Price, January 1, 1972 ... $10,000
Total Value, December 31, 1981 ... $13,615
Distributions From Capital Gains ... $ 3,015
Dividends From Investment Income ... $ 2,708

SOURCE: *Investment Companies* (Boston, Mass.: Arthur Wiesenberger Companies Services, 1982), p. 414. Reprinted with permission from Wiesenberger Investment Companies Service, 42nd ed. copyright 1982. Warren, Gorham & Lamont, 210 South Street, Boston, Mass. All rights reserved.

FIGURE 26.4
Sample Fund Page from *Forbes*

1983 Fund Ratings

Performance			Investment results			Total assets		Maximum	Annual
			Average annual total return 1973-83	Latest 12 months		6/30/83 (millions)	% change '83 vs '82	sales charge	expenses per $100
in UP markets	in DOWN markets			return from capital growth	return from income dividends				
		Standard & Poor's 500 stock average	8.3%	53.4%	4.1%				
		FORBES stock fund composite	10.8%	63.3%	2.9%				
		FORBES balanced fund composite	8.8%	36.4%	7.3%				
		FORBES bond and preferred stock fund composite	7.6%	19.8%	11.4%				
		Stock funds (load)	Group averages						
			10.6%	64.0%	2.9%				
C	C	Affiliated Fund (212-425-8720)	11.8%	44.2%	5.5%	$2,023.8	41.5%	7.25%	$0.36
C	D	Alpha Fund (800-241-1662)	8.6	92.7	1.9	23.4	90.2	5.00	1.50
B	B	AMCAP Fund (213-486-9200)	14.9	53.9	2.4	907.3	130.3	8.50	0.76
C	C	American Birthright Trust (800-327-4508)	11.6	63.6	none	177.1	54.9	8.50	1.09
B	A	American General Comstock Fund (713-522-1111)	20.4	58.3	3.8	393.1	156.3	8.50	0.72
A	F	American General Enterprise Fund (713-522-1111)	12.2	64.7	2.0	748.7	67.9	8.50	0.69
B	B	American General Pace Fund (713-522-1111)	17.6	60.6	3.2	1,072.0	726.5	8.50	0.71
B	B	American General Venture Fund (713-522-1111)	17.5	65.2	3.5	359.1	336.3	8.50	0.78
D	A	American Growth Fund (800-525-2406)	13.7	44.7	5.1	52.8	75.4	8.50	1.50
D	C	American Leaders Fund (800-245-5051)	8.0	44.6	5.2	47.3	22.2	6.50	1.45
D	B	American Mutual Fund (213-486-9200)	14.1	47.5	5.0	797.5	66.7	8.50	0.51
B	B	American National Growth Fund (409-766-6577)	14.7	87.8	1.7	103.3	97.5	8.50	0.76
•D	•C	American National Income Fund (409-766-6577)	—*	46.2	5.2	37.2	91.8	8.50	0.80
B	D	Axe-Houghton Stock Fund (800-431-1030)	11.7	118.2	0.1	203.3	93.8	8.50	0.88
B	F	BLC Growth Fund (515-247-5711)	8.7	64.1	2.5	19.0	62.4	8.50	1.01
D	B	BLC Income Fund (515-247-5711)	12.1	54.3	5.0	21.7	58.4	8.50	1.00
C	C	Bullock Fund (800-221-5757)	9.4	47.6	3.7	160.5	43.2	8.50	0.82
C	D	The Cardinal Fund (614-464-6811)	9.9	62.3	3.3	17.7	53.9	8.50	1.06
A	F	Centennial Growth Fund (303-770-2345)	9.1	108.9	1.0	30.0	75.4	8.50	1.33
C	F	Chemical Fund (800-221-5233)	6.5	57.2	2.4	1,273.8	43.0	8.50	0.59
B	F	CIGNA Growth Fund[1] (800-225-5151)	8.1	60.5	2.6	199.3	65.5	7.50	0.69
B	F	Colonial Growth Shares (800-225-2365)	6.6	60.5	2.0	72.7	42.6	8.50	1.17
D	C	Commonwlth Fund Indent Plans A&B (617-482-6500)	6.8	31.5	6.9	10.4	20.9	7.50	0.32
D	C	Commonwlth Fund Indent Plan C (617-482-6500)	8.0	32.2	6.1	38.2	24.4	7.50	0.75
D	D	Corp Leaders Tr Fund Certificates Ser B (800-526-4791)	8.3	41.3	5.6	53.5	28.9	†	0.08
C	D	Country Capital Growth Fund (309-557-2444)	6.8	58.6	2.6	61.2	54.2	7.50	0.93
D	B	Decatur Income Fund (800-523-1918)	12.6	36.7	7.3	487.2	39.4	8.50	0.68
D	C	Delaware Fund (800-523-1918)	12.7	63.1	5.8	354.1	61.3	8.50	0.76
B	C	Delta Trend Fund (800-523-1918)	12.7	114.1	0.5	49.0	257.7	8.50	1.40
D	D	Dividend Shares (800-221-5757)	7.6	47.5	4.6	291.5	33.8	8.50	0.82
C	C	The Dreyfus Fund (800-645-6561)	10.3	35.9	4.9	1,880.9	24.1	8.50	0.77
C	C	The Dreyfus Leverage Fund (800-645-6561)	10.2	32.3	6.5	389.3	35.7	8.50	1.00
C	•B	Eagle Growth Shares (212-668-8107)	—*	45.8	4.0	6.3	40.0	8.50	1.33
D	F	Eaton & Howard Stock Fund (617-482-8260)	3.3	40.1	4.5	72.4	25.9	7.25	0.85
C	C	Eaton Vance Growth Fund (617-482-8260)	10.2	58.6	2.5	83.3	72.1	8.50	0.85
B	D	Eaton Vance Special Equities[2] (617-482-8260)	6.7	58.8	1.5	54.4	63.9	7.25	0.99
A+	F	Fairfield Fund (800-223-7757)	12.0	106.2	0.5	67.7	158.4	8.50	1.07
A	B	Fidelity Destiny Fund (800-225-6190)	18.8	86.5	2.3	520.6	111.8	‡	0.70
A+	B	Fidelity Magellan Fund (800-225-6190)	22.2	112.4	0.7	1,365.2	830.0	3.00	0.85
B	D	First Investors Discovery Fund (212-825-7900)	10.9	149.0	0.9	27.5	461.2	8.50	1.50
A	F	First Investors Fund for Growth (212-825-7900)	8.9	98.5	1.7	108.5	113.2	8.50	0.98
D	F	First Investors Natural Resources Fund (212-825-7900)	3.4	62.6	2.2	14.1	74.1	8.50	1.29
D	A	First Investors Option Fund (212-825-7900)	6.5	18.4	3.5	119.1	2.1	†	0.97
D	D	Founders Mutual Fund (800-525-2440)	7.0	56.9	3.8	144.9	42.6	4.00	0.47
A	F	Franklin Custodian-Dynatech Ser (800-227-6350)	10.2	98.2	1.2	40.6	290.4	7.25	1.06

•Fund rated for two periods only; maximum allowable rating A. *Fund not in operation for full period. †Fund not currently selling new shares. ‡Available only through contractual plans. [1]Formerly CG Fund. [2]Formerly Eaton & Howard Growth Fund.

SOURCE: *Forbes*, August 29, 1983. Reprinted by permission.

858

FIGURE 26.5

Sample Page from *United Mutual Fund Selector*

UNITED Mutual Fund Selector   May 15, 1984

INVESTMENT COMPANY PERFORMANCE COMPARISONS

(This supplement appears in the first issue of every month)

NO LOAD FUNDS

% Change in Net Asset Value ■

	4 Mos. 1984	1 Mo. Jan. 84	1 Mo. Feb. 84	1 Mo. Mar. 84	1 Mo. Apr. 84	% Yield°
Acorn Fund	− 5.7	− 2.8	− 3.9	+ 0.9	− 0.1	2.6
ADV Fund	− 9.9	− 4.7	− 5.3	+ 0.9	− 1.1	1.6
Afuture Fund	−14.4	− 3.4	− 8.6	− 0.9	− 4.3	0.8
American Express Growth	− 8.3	− 3.2	− 4.8	− 0.2	− 0.3	0.5
American Investors Gr.	−11.5	− 5.5	− 4.3	− 0.1	− 2.0	0.0
American Investors Inc.	− 7.2	+ 1.9	− 3.1	+ 4.6	−10.3	13.0
Armstrong Associates	−11.3	− 3.1	− 7.8	− 0.4	− 0.4	4.0
Babson Funds:						
Growth	− 4.9	− 3.7	− 4.7	+ 3.5	+ 0.1	2.9
Income Trust	+ 0.7	+ 2.0	0.0	− 1.4	0.0	11.9
Beacon Hill Mutual	− 6.7	− 4.4	− 3.6	− 0.7	+ 1.9	0.2
Boston Co. Cap. Appr.	− 5.0	− 2.7	− 3.4	+ 1.7	− 0.9	2.1
Bull & Bear Group:						
Capital Growth	− 8.3	− 4.3	− 5.9	+ 1.7	+ 0.3	0.8
Equity Income	− 2.9	0.0	− 3.7	+ 0.3	+ 0.6	8.7
Golconda Investors	+ 3.1	− 3.4	+11.8	− 1.5	− 3.1	1.5
Calvert Social Investments	− 5.3	− 0.7	+ 0.1	− 1.8	− 3.0	0.0
Century Shares Trust	+ 0.7	− 0.7	− 0.7	+ 5.3	− 2.9	5.0
Charter Fund	− 9.9	− 5.5	− 5.0	+ 2.5	− 2.0	2.9
★Columbia Growth Fund	−10.3	− 5.6	− 7.2	+ 2.1	− 0.4	0.9
Composite Bond & Stock	− 4.2	+ 0.5	− 4.7	+ 0.9	− 0.9	5.9
Composite Fund	− 5.9	− 1.5	− 5.2	+ 2.9	− 2.1	3.5
Constellation Growth	−17.5	− 8.8	− 9.0	− 0.1	− 0.6	0.0
Dodge & Cox Bal. Fd.	− 1.7	− 0.3	− 1.5	+ 0.5	− 0.4	6.8
Dodge & Cox Stock Fund	− 0.1	+ 0.8	− 3.3	+ 3.6	+ 0.9	4.2
Drexel Burnham Fund	− 3.1	− 0.6	− 2.8	+ 0.2	+ 0.1	3.9
Dreyfus Funds:						
Growth Opportunity	− 3.3	+ 0.9	− 5.2	+ 3.3	− 2.4	1.7
Special Income	+ 2.4	+ 2.1	− 0.6	+ 0.7	+ 0.2	8.2
Third Century	− 3.2	− 0.7	− 3.4	+ 3.2	− 2.3	3.7
Energy & Utility Shares	− 5.3	0.0	− 1.6	− 0.6	− 3.3	10.5
★Evergreen Fund	− 6.1	− 2.5	− 5.4	+ 0.8	+ 0.4	1.9
Evergreen Total Return	− 2.9	+ 0.7	− 4.1	+ 0.1	+ 0.3	4.2
Fidelity Group Funds:						
Contrafund	−15.8	− 7.6	− 8.6	− 0.3	− 1.0	6.1
Corporate Bond	− 0.8	+ 2.5	− 1.0	− 1.8	− 0.5	11.9
Discoverer	−13.1	− 3.0	− 9.5	+ 1.0	− 1.9	1.5
Freedom	− 5.2	− 1.6	− 5.6	+ 1.6	+ 0.4	0.4
Fidelity Fund	− 5.7	− 3.2	− 4.9	+ 4.3	− 2.5	5.7
Government Securities	− 1.8	+ 0.8	− 1.3	− 0.8	− 0.4	8.8
High Income	+ 0.6	+ 3.4	− 1.4	− 0.9	− 0.6	13.0
Puritan	− 2.1	+ 0.7	− 3.6	+ 1.0	− 0.3	8.6
Thrift Trust	+ 0.1	+ 1.6	− 0.4	− 0.7	− 0.4	11.1
Trend	− 8.4	− 4.2	− 6.9	+ 2.8	− 0.1	2.2
Financial Programs:						
Dynamics	−11.8	− 4.6	− 7.4	+ 1.3	− 1.4	2.2
Industrial	− 8.7	− 2.9	− 5.2	+ 0.3	− 1.0	4.0
Industrial Income	− 2.6	0.0	− 3.2	+ 0.5	+ 0.2	5.6
44 Wall Street	−26.4	−14.1	−16.3	+ 5.5	− 2.9	0.0
Founders Group Funds:						
Growth	−13.3	− 6.7	− 6.2	+ 0.9	− 1.8	2.4
Income	− 1.5	+ 1.2	− 1.5	+ 0.4	− 1.6	6.0
Mutual	− 5.2	− 3.5	− 4.4	+ 2.4	+ 0.2	4.2
Special	−14.4	− 5.5	− 7.4	− 0.2	− 2.0	8.1
G.T. Pacific Fund	+ 6.3	+ 3.9	+ 0.7	+ 4.7	− 3.0	2.3
Gateway Option Income	− 1.1	− 0.4	− 2.9	+ 1.9	+ 0.4	15.3

% Change in Net Asset Value ■

	4 Mos. 1984	1 Mo. Jan. 84	1 Mo. Feb. 84	1 Mo. Mar. 84	1 Mo. Apr. 84	% Yield°
General Electric S&S	− 3.9	− 1.5	− 4.1	+ 1.0	+ 0.5	5.0
General Securities	− 2.3	− 3.6	+ 1.2	+ 0.3	− 0.1	5.0
★Gintel ERISA	+ 0.9	+ 0.4	− 4.0	+ 4.9	+ 0.4	2.2
Gintel Fund	− 1.2	+ 0.8	− 6.2	+ 5.9	− 1.4	3.2
Growth Industry Shares	− 7.4	− 6.6	− 4.7	+ 3.1	+ 0.8	2.0
Hartwell Growth Fund	−12.4	−10.5	− 0.7	− 0.4	− 1.3	0.0
Hartwell Leverage Fund	−22.4	− 6.6	−10.1	− 5.7	− 2.0	0.0
Horace Mann Growth	− 2.6	− 2.2	− 4.2	+ 1.8	+ 2.0	1.3
Istel Fund	+ 0.6	− 2.2	− 1.5	+ 3.4	+ 1.3	4.4
Ivy Growth	− 1.5	+ 1.0	− 3.6	+ 1.5	0.0	6.1
Janus Fund	− 6.0	− 2.9	− 4.2	+ 1.2	− 0.3	8.6
Keystone Mass Group:						
Investment Bond B-1	− 3.1	+ 2.1	− 2.5	− 1.6	− 1.2	11.4
Medium Grade Bd. B-2	− 5.9	− 0.6	− 2.1	+ 1.6	− 4.8	12.6
Discount Bond B-4	− 4.4	+ 2.2	− 1.6	− 3.6	− 1.4	9.2
Income K-1	− 0.1	+ 3.4	− 4.4	+ 2.0	− 0.9	8.5
Growth K-2	−14.7	− 2.3	− 4.6	+ 2.6	−10.8	2.2
High Gr. Com. Stk. S-1	− 6.9	− 3.5	− 5.6	+ 3.3	− 1.1	2.5
Growth Com. Stock S-3	− 8.5	− 3.8	− 5.6	+ 2.2	− 1.4	2.3
Low Pr. Com. Stk. S-4	−17.7	− 7.9	− 8.4	− 0.2	− 2.3	0.3
International	− 2.1	+ 1.7	− 2.4	+ 1.2	− 2.5	1.0
Legg Mason Value Trust	− 2.0	− 0.7	− 5.2	+ 2.6	+ 1.4	1.4
Lehman Capital	− 5.2	− 0.5	− 5.6	+ 1.6	− 0.7	12.5
Lehman Investors	− 4.3	− 2.0	− 4.8	+ 0.8	+ 1.3	3.6
Leverage Fund of Boston	−16.3	− 5.6	− 6.1	− 0.4	− 5.2	0.0
Lexington Group:						
GNMA	− 0.3	+ 2.1	− 0.1	− 2.0	− 0.3	8.0
Growth	−16.9	− 2.7	− 9.4	− 4.0	− 2.5	4.0
Research	−10.3	− 3.6	− 6.1	− 0.5	− 0.7	5.5
Lindner Fund	+ 4.4	+ 2.4	− 0.5	+ 0.6	+ 1.9	4.6
Loomis-Sayles Funds:						
Capital Development	− 9.6	− 4.8	− 6.9	+ 3.6	− 3.3	0.7
Mutual	− 6.0	− 0.1	− 4.2	+ 0.5	− 3.1	5.0
Mathers Fund	− 6.4	− 2.2	− 5.8	+ 1.3	− 0.6	5.7
Mutual Qualified Income	+ 6.7	+ 3.6	+ 1.2	+ 1.0	+ 0.8	1.7
★Mutual Shares	+ 6.4	+ 3.8	+ 0.3	+ 1.7	+ 0.5	5.6
National Aviation & Tech.	−11.0	− 3.5	− 8.0	− 0.2	+ 0.1	2.9
National Industries	− 5.7	− 3.3	− 5.2	+ 0.8	+ 1.6	3.4
Neuberger & Berman:						
★Energy	+ 3.3	+ 1.6	− 2.1	+ 2.6	+ 1.2	5.5
★Guardian Mutual	− 3.9	− 1.7	− 4.9	+ 2.1	+ 0.7	4.3
Liberty	− 0.3	+ 0.7	0.0	− 1.0	0.0	7.6
Manhattan	− 4.0	− 2.1	− 5.0	+ 3.5	− 0.2	3.1
Partners	− 2.9	− 0.3	− 3.6	+ 1.7	− 0.6	5.9
Newton Growth	− 9.3	− 6.9	− 5.9	+ 3.9	− 0.4	0.8
Newton Income	+ 1.2	+ 1.5	+ 0.4	− 0.3	− 0.4	11.1
Nicholas Fund	− 4.6	− 2.5	− 4.5	+ 1.7	+ 0.8	3.7
Nicholas Income Fund	− 0.6	+ 1.9	− 0.8	0.0	− 1.7	12.9
Northeast Investors:						
Growth	− 7.3	− 4.1	− 6.0	+ 3.5	− 0.8	1.6
★Trust	+ 0.5	+ 3.5	− 0.3	− 1.4	− 1.3	13.0
★Nova Fund	− 9.4	+14.8	−24.9	+ 1.0	− 2.0	1.6
Omega Fund	− 8.9	− 3.6	− 6.2	+ 1.5	− 0.7	1.0
One Hundred Fund	−15.3	− 8.6	− 8.0	+ 1.4	− 0.6	0.8
Pax World Fund	− 1.5	− 0.3	− 3.2	+ 2.3	− 0.3	4.6
Penn Square Mutual	− 1.4	− 1.4	− 3.6	+ 3.3	+ 0.4	4.9

SOURCE: *United Mutual Fund Selector* (Boston, Mass.: United Business Service Co., May 15, 1984), p. 84. Reprinted by permission.

history, special services available, personnel, advisors and distributors, sales charges, and a hypothetical $10,000 investment charted over 10 years for major funds. A sample page for the Technology Fund is contained in Figure 26.3 on page 856. In addition, the Wiesenberger book contains a summary table that lists the annual rates of return and price volatility for a number of funds. Recently, Wiesenberger has added two additional services. Every three months the firm publishes *Management Results,* which is an update of the long-term perform- ance of more than 400 mutual funds, arranged alphabetically according to the investment objective of the fund. Every month the firm also publishes *Current Performance and Dividend Record,* which contains the dividend and short-run performance of more than 400 funds. The funds are listed alphabetically with the objective indicated.[33]

Another source of analytical historical information on funds is *Forbes,* a biweekly financial publication that usually contains information about individ- ual companies and their investment philosophy. In addition, the magazine con- ducts an annual survey of mutual funds in August. A sample page is contained in Figure 26.4 on page 857. As shown, the survey not only considers recent and 10-year returns, but it also indicates sales charge and the annual expense ratio for each fund.

Because of the interest in mutual funds, United Business Service Company publishes a semimonthly service called *United Mutual Fund Selector.* Each issue contains several articles on specific mutual funds or classes of mutual funds (e.g., municipal bond funds). The first issue of each month contains a four-page supplement entitled, ''Investment Company Performance Comparisons,'' that gives recent and historical changes in NAV for load and no-load funds. A sample page is contained in Figure 26.5.[34]

SUMMARY

This chapter described the general characteristics of investment companies and discussed the historical performance of mutual funds. The first section defined investment companies and discussed typical management arrangements. A breakdown of types of investment companies, including closed-end, open-end, load, no-load, and dual funds, was then considered. This was followed by a discussion of the wide variety of funds available. Almost any investment objec- tive or combination of objectives can currently be matched by some investment companies.

The major portion of the chapter was a discussion of the results of a number of studies examining the historical performance of mutual funds. Most of the studies indicated that less than half the funds did as well as the aggregate market did on a risk-adjusted basis using net returns, while the results with gross returns generally indicated an average risk-adjusted return about equal to the market's, and about half the funds did better than the market did. There were also some

---

[33] These services are currently published by Wiesenberger Investment Companies Services, 210 South St., Boston, Mass., 02111.

[34] This service is available from United Business Service Company, 210 Newbury St., Boston, Mass., 02116.

studies that indicated performance was superior when gross returns were considered. Following a discussion of the implications of the results for an individual investor, the chapter concluded with a discussion of sources of information on mutual funds.

QUESTIONS

1. How do you compute the net asset value of an investment company?
2. Discuss the difference between an open-end investment company and a closed-end investment company.
3. What are the two prices of importance to a closed-end investment company? How do these prices typically differ?
4. What is the difference between a load and no-load fund?
5. What are the differences between a common stock fund and a balanced fund? How would you expect their risk and return characteristics to compare?
6. Why would anyone buy a money market fund?
7. What is the purpose of dual funds? What are some potential problems for these funds? What has been the typical relationship between NAV and market price?
8. Do you care about how well a mutual fund is diversified? Why or why not? How could you quickly measure the extent of diversification?
9. Why is the stability of risk for a mutual fund important to an investor? Discuss. What is the empirical evidence in this regard—i.e., is the risk measure for mutual funds generally stable?
10. Do you think the performance of mutual funds should be judged on the basis of return alone or on a risk-adjusted basis? Why? Discuss using examples.
11. Define the net return and gross return for a mutual fund. Discuss how you would compute each of these.
12. a. As an investor in a mutual fund, is net return or gross return relevant to you?
    b. As an investigator attempting to determine the ability of mutual fund managers to select undervalued stocks or project market returns, which return is relevant: net or gross?
13. You are told that, on the basis of the Treynor composite measure of performance, about half the mutual funds did better than the market and, on the basis of the Sharpe measure, only 35 percent did better than the market. Explain in detail *why* this happened.
14. Based upon the numerous tests of mutual fund performance, you are convinced that only about half of them do better than a naive buy-and-hold policy. Does this mean you would forget about investing in them? Why or why not?
15. a. You are told that Fund X experienced above average performance over the past two years. Do you think it will continue over the next two years? Why or why not?
    b. You are told that Fund Y experienced consistently poor performance over the past two years. Would you expect this to continue over the next two years? Why or why not?
16. Assume that you see advertisements for two mutual funds which indicate that the investment objectives of the funds are consistent with yours.

a. Indicate where you would go to get a quick view of how these two funds have performed over the past two or three years.

b. Where would you go to get more in-depth information on the funds, including an address so you can write for a prospectus?

REFERENCES

Ang, James S. and Jess H. Chua. "Mutual Funds: Different Strokes for Different Folks?" *Journal of Portfolio Management.* 8 no. 2 (Winter 1982).

Bogle, John C. "Mutual Fund Performance Evaluation." *Financial Analysts Journal.* 26 no. 6 (November–December 1970).

Carlson, Robert S. "Aggregate Performance of Mutual Funds 1948–1967." *Journal of Financial and Quantitative Analysis.* 5 no. 1 (March 1970).

Chang, Eric C. and Wilbur G. Lewellen. "Market Timing and Mutual Fund Investment Performance." *Journal of Business.* 57 no. 1, part 1 (January 1984).

Fabozzi, Frank J. and Jack C. Francis. "Mutual Fund Systematic Risk for Bull and Bear Markets." *Journal of Finance.* 34 no. 5 (December 1979).

Friend, Irwin, Marshall Blume, and Jean Crockett. *Mutual Funds and Other Institutional Investors.* New York: McGraw-Hill, 1970.

Gaumnitz, Jack E. "Appraising Performance of Investment Portfolios." *Journal of Finance.* 25 no. 3 (June 1970).

Gentry, James A. and John R. Pike. "Dual Funds Revisited." *Financial Analysts Journal.* 24 no. 2 (March–April 1968).

Greeley, Robert E. "Mutual Fund Management Companies." *Financial Analysts Journal.* 23 no. 5 (September–October 1967).

Henriksson, Roy D. "Mutual Timing and Mutual Fund Performance: An Empirical Investigation." *Journal of Business.* 57 no. 1, part 1 (January 1984).

Henriksson, Roy D. and Robert C. Merton. "On Market Timing and Investment Performance, II. Statistical Procedures for Evaluating Forecasting Skills," *Journal of Business.* 54 no. 4 (October 1981).

Horowitz, Ira. "A Model for Mutual Fund Evaluation." *Industrial Management Review.* 6 no. 3 (Spring 1965).

Horowitz, Ira. "The Reward-to-Variability Ratio and Mutual Fund Performance." *Journal of Business.* 39 no. 4 (October 1966).

Horowitz, Ira and Harold B. Higgins. "Some Factors Affecting Investment Fund Performance." *Quarterly Review of Economics and Business.* 3 no. 1 (Spring 1963).

Jensen, Michael C. "The Performance of Mutual Funds in the Period 1945–1964." *Journal of Finance.* 23 no. 2 (May 1968).

Kon, Stanley J. and Frank C. Jen. "The Investment Performance of Mutual Funds: An Empirical Investigation of Timing, Selectivity and Market Efficiency." *Journal of Business.* 52 no. 2 (April 1979).

Litzenberger, Robert H. and Howard B. Sosin. "The Performance and Potential of Dual Purpose Funds." *Journal of Portfolio Management.* 4 no. 3 (Spring 1978).

Litzenberger, Robert H. and Howard B. Sosin. "The Structure and Management of Dual Purpose Funds." *Journal of Financial Economics.* 4 no. 1 (May 1977).

Litzenberger, Robert H. and Howard B. Sosin. "The Theory of Recapitalizations and the Evidence of Dual Purpose Funds." *Journal of Finance.* 32 no. 5 (December 1977).

Malkiel, Burton. "The Valuation of Closed-End Investment Company Shares." *Journal of Finance.* 32 no. 3 (June 1977).

Martin, John D., Arthur J. Keown, Jr., and James L. Farrell. "Do Fund Objectives Affect Diversification Policies?" *Journal of Portfolio Management.* 8 no. 2 (Winter 1982).

McDonald, John G. "Objectives and Performance of Mutual Funds, 1960–1969." *Journal of Financial and Quantitative Analysis.* 9 no. 3 (June 1974).

Merton, Robert C. "On Market Timing and Investment Performance, I. An Equilibrium Theory of Value for Market Forecasts." *Journal of Business.* 54 no. 3 (July 1981).

Mills, Harlan D. "On the Measurement of Fund Performance." *Journal of Finance.* 25 no. 5 (December 1970).

Netter, Joseph, II. "Dual-Purpose Funds." *Financial Analysts Journal.* 23 no. 4 (July–August 1967).

Pratt, Eugene J. "Myths Associated with Closed-End Investment Company Discounts." *Financial Analysts Journal.* 22 no. 4 (July–August 1966).

Richards, Malcolm, Donald Fraser, and John Groth. "Winning Strategies for Closed-End Funds." *Journal of Portfolio Management.* 7 no. 1 (Fall 1980).

Richards, Malcolm, Donald Fraser, and John Groth. "Premiums, Discounts, and the Volatility of Closed-End Mutual Funds." *The Financial Review.* 14 no. 3 (Fall 1979).

Richards, Malcolm, Donald Fraser, and John Groth. "The Attractions of Closed-End Bond Funds." *Journal of Portfolio Management.* 8 no. 2 (Winter 1982).

Roenfeldt, Rodney and Donald Tuttle. "An Examination of the Discounts and Premiums of Closed-End Investment Companies." *Journal of Business Research.* 5 no. 1 (Fall 1973).

Sharpe, William F. "Mutual Fund Performance." *Journal of Business, Supplement on Security Prices.* 39 no. 1 (January 1966).

Shawky, Hany A. "An Update on Mutual Funds: Better Grades." *Journal of Portfolio Management.* 8 no. 2 (Winter 1982).

Shelton, John P., Eugene F. Brigham, and Alfred E. Hofflander. "An Evaluation and Appraisal of Dual Funds." *Financial Analysts Journal.* 23 no. 3 (May–June 1967).

Simonson, Donald G. "The Speculative Behavior of Mutual Funds" *Journal of Finance.* 27 no. 2 (May 1972).

Thompson, Rex. "The Information Content of Discounts and Premiums on Closed-End Fund Shares." *Journal of Financial Economics.* 6 no. 2/3 (June–September 1978).

Treynor, Jack L. "How to Rate Management of Investment Funds." *Harvard Business Review.* 43 no. 1 (January–February 1965).

Treynor, Jack L. and Kay K. Mazuy. "Can Mutual Funds Outguess the Market?" *Harvard Business Review.* 24 no. 4 (July–August 1966).

Veit, E. Theodore and John M. Cheney. "Are Mutual Funds Market Timers?" *Journal of Portfolio Management.* 8 no. 2 (Winter 1982).

Williamson, Peter J. "Measuring Mutual Fund Performance." *Financial Analysts Journal.* 28 no. 6 (November–December 1972).

Appendix 26.1

Glossary of Mutual Funds

Accumulation Plan (Periodic Payment Plan)   Enables an investor to purchase mutual fund shares periodically in large or small amounts, usually with provisions for the reinvestment of income dividends and capital gains distributions in additional shares.

Adviser   The organization employed by a mutual fund to give professional advice on its investments and management of its assets.

Asked or Offering Price   The price at which a mutual fund's shares can be purchased. The asked or offering price means the net asset value per share plus, at times, a sales charge.

Automatic Reinvestment   The option available to mutual fund shareholders whereby fund income dividends and capital gains distributions are automatically put back into the fund to buy new shares and thereby build up holdings.

Balanced Fund   A mutual fund which has an investment policy of balancing its portfolio, generally by including bonds, preferred stocks, and common stocks.

Bid or Redemption Price   The price at which a mutual fund's shares are redeemed (bought back) by the fund. The bid or redemption price usually means the net asset value per share.

Bond Fund   A mutual fund with a portfolio consisting primarily of bonds. The emphasis of such funds is normally on income rather than growth.

Bookshares   A modern share recording system that eliminates the need for mutual fund share certificates but gives the fund shareowner a record of his holdings.

Broker-Dealer (or Dealer)   A firm that retails mutual fund shares and other securities to the public.

Capital Gains Distributions   Payments to mutual fund shareholders of gains realized on the sale of the fund's portfolio securities. These amounts usually are paid once a year.

Capital Growth   An increase in the market value of a mutual fund's securities which is reflected in the net asset value of fund shares. This is a specific long-term objective of many mutual funds.

Closed-End Investment Company   Unlike mutual funds (known as *open-end*), closed-end companies issue only a limited number of shares and do not redeem them (buy them back). Instead, closed-end shares are traded in the securities markets with supply and demand determining the price.

Common Stock Fund   A mutual fund with a portfolio consisting primarily of common stocks. The emphasis of such funds is usually on growth.

Contractual Plan   A program for the accumulation of mutual fund shares in which the investor agrees to invest a fixed amount on a regular basis for a specified number of years. A substantial portion of the sales charge applicable to the total investment is usually deducted from early payments.

Conversion Privilege (Exchange Privilege)   Enables a mutual fund shareholder to transfer his investment from one fund to another within the same fund group if his needs or objectives change, sometimes with a small transaction charge.

Custodian   The organization (usually a bank) that holds in custody and safekeeping the securities and other assets of a mutual fund.

Diversification   The mutual fund policy of spreading investments among a number of different securities to reduce the risks inherent in investing.

Dollar-Cost Averaging   Investing equal amounts of money at regular intervals regardless of whether the stock market is moving upward or downward. This reduces average share costs in periods of lower securities prices and number of shares in periods of higher prices.

Exchange Privilege   *See* Conversion Privilege.

Growth Fund   A mutual fund with the primary investment objective of growth of capital. Invests principally in common stocks with growth potential.

Growth-Income Fund   A mutual fund with the aim of providing for a degree of both income and long-term growth.

Income Dividends   Payments to mutual fund shareholders of dividends, interest, and short-term capital gains earned on the fund's portfolio securities after deduction of operating expenses.

Income Fund   A mutual fund with the primary investment objective of current income rather than growth of capital. It invests in stocks and bonds that normally pay higher dividends and interest.

Individual Retirement Account   A retirement program for individuals who are not covered under employer or government retirement plans. An individual may contribute and deduct from his or her income tax an amount up to $2,000. An individual retirement account may be funded with mutual fund shares.

Investment Adviser   *See* Adviser.

Investment Company   A corporation, trust, or partnership in which investors may pool their money to obtain professional management and diversification of their investments. Mutual funds are the most popular type of investment company.

Investment Objective   The goal (e.g., long-term capital growth, current income, etc.) that an investor or a mutual fund pursues.

Keogh Plan   A retirement program for self-employed individuals and their employees based on tax-saving provisions. An individual can contribute 15 percent of income to a maximum of $15,000. A Keogh plan may be funded with mutual fund shares.

Liquid Asset Fund   *See* Money Market Fund.

Management Fee   The amount paid by a mutual fund to the investment adviser for its services. The average cost to the shareholder industry-wide is about one half of one percent of his investment a year.

Money Market (Cash Management) Fund   A mutual fund that invests primarily in short-term instruments, such as instruments issued or guaranteed by the U.S. government or its agencies and instrumentalities, bank certificates of deposit, banker's acceptances, and commercial paper. The fund's primary objective is current income.

Municipal Bond Fund   A mutual fund that invests in a broad range of tax-exempt bonds issued by states, cities, and other local governments. The interest obtained from these bonds is passed through to shareowners free of federal tax. The fund's primary objective is current income.

Mutual Fund   An investment company that ordinarily stands ready to buy back (redeem) its shares at their current net asset value; the value of the shares depends on the market value of the fund's portfolio securities at the time. Also, mutual funds generally continuously offer new shares to investors.

Net Asset Value Per Share   The market worth of a mutual fund's total resources (securities, cash, and any accrued earnings) after deduction of liabilities and divided by the number of shares outstanding.

No-Load Fund   A mutual fund selling its shares at net asset value without the addition of sales charges.

Open-End Investment Company   The more formal name for a mutual fund, indicating that it continuously offers new shares to investors and redeems them (buys them back) on demand.

Payroll Deduction Plan   An arrangement whereby an employee may accumulate shares in a mutual fund by authorizing his employer to deduct and transfer to a fund a specified amount from his salary at stated times.

Periodic Payment Plan   *See* Accumulation Plan.

Prospectus   A booklet describing the mutual fund and offering its shares for sale. It contains information required by the Securities and Exchange Commission on such subjects as the fund's investment objective and policies, services, investment restrictions, officers and directors, how shares can be bought and redeemed, its charges, and its financial statements.

Qualified Retirement Plan   A private retirement plan that meets the rules and regulations of the Internal Revenue Service. Contributions to a qualified retirement plan are in almost all cases tax deductible, and earnings on such contributions are always tax sheltered until the investor retires.

Redemption Price   The amount per share the mutual fund shareholder receives when he cashes in his shares (also known as *bid price*). The value of the shares depends on the market value of the fund's portfolio securities at the time.

Reinvestment Privilege   A service provided by most mutual funds for the automatic reinvestment of a shareholder's income dividends and capital gains distributions in additional shares.

Sales Charge   An amount charged to purchase shares in most mutual funds. Typically the charge is 8.5 percent of the initial investment. The charge is added to the net asset value per share in determining the offering price. (Some funds, which do not have sales representatives, have no sales charge and are called *no-load funds.*)

Specialty Fund   A mutual fund specializing in the securities of certain industries, special types of securities, or in regional investments.

Split Funding   A program that combines the purchase of mutual fund shares with the purchase of life insurance contracts or other investment instruments.

Transfer Agent   The organization employed by a mutual fund to prepare and maintain records relating to the accounts of fund shareholders.

Underwriter (Principal Underwriter)   The organization that acts as the distributor of a mutual fund's shares to broker-dealers and the public.

Variable Annuity   A contract under which an annuity is purchased with a fixed number of dollars that are converted into a varying number of accumulation units. At retirement, the annuitant is paid a fixed number of monthly units which are converted into a varying number of dollars. The value of both accumulation and annuity units varies in accordance with the performance of a portfolio invested in equity securities.

Variable Life Insurance   An equity-based life insurance policy in which the reserves may be invested in common stocks. The death benefit is guaranteed never to fall below the face value, but it could increase if the value of the securities increased. There may be no guaranteed cash surrender value under this kind of policy.

Voluntary Plan   A flexible accumulation plan in which there is no definite time period or total amount to be invested.

Withdrawal Plans   Many mutual funds offer withdrawal programs whereby shareholders receive payments from their investments at regular intervals. These payments typically are drawn from the fund's dividends and capital gains distributions, if any, and from principal, to the extent necessary.

Appendix A

Interest Tables

TABLE A.1
Present Value of $1: $PVIF = 1/(1 + k)^t$

Period	1%	2%	3%	4%	5%	6%	7%	8%	9%	10%	12%	14%	15%	16%	18%	20%	24%	28%	32%	36%
1	.9901	.9804	.9709	.9615	.9524	.9434	.9346	.9259	.9174	.9091	.8929	.8772	.8696	.8621	.8475	.8333	.8065	.7813	.7576	.7353
2	.9803	.9612	.9426	.9246	.9070	.8900	.8734	.8573	.8417	.8264	.7972	.7695	.7561	.7432	.7182	.6944	.6504	.6104	.5739	.5407
3	.9706	.9423	.9151	.8890	.8638	.8396	.8163	.7938	.7722	.7513	.7118	.6750	.6575	.6407	.6086	.5787	.5245	.4768	.4348	.3975
4	.9610	.9238	.8885	.8548	.8227	.7921	.7629	.7350	.7084	.6830	.6355	.5921	.5718	.5523	.5158	.4823	.4230	.3725	.3294	.2923
5	.9515	.9057	.8626	.8219	.7835	.7473	.7130	.6806	.6499	.6209	.5674	.5194	.4972	.4761	.4371	.4019	.3411	.2910	.2495	.2149
6	.9420	.8880	.8375	.7903	.7462	.7050	.6663	.6302	.5963	.5645	.5066	.4556	.4323	.4104	.3704	.3349	.2751	.2274	.1890	.1580
7	.9327	.8706	.8131	.7599	.7107	.6651	.6227	.5835	.5470	.5132	.4523	.3996	.3759	.3538	.3139	.2791	.2218	.1776	.1432	.1162
8	.9235	.8535	.7894	.7307	.6768	.6274	.5820	.5403	.5019	.4665	.4039	.3506	.3269	.3050	.2660	.2326	.1789	.1388	.1085	.0854
9	.9143	.8368	.7664	.7026	.6446	.5919	.5439	.5002	.4604	.4241	.3606	.3075	.2843	.2630	.2255	.1938	.1443	.1084	.0822	.0628
10	.9053	.8203	.7441	.6756	.6139	.5584	.5083	.4632	.4224	.3855	.3220	.2697	.2472	.2267	.1911	.1615	.1164	.0847	.0623	.0462
11	.8963	.8043	.7224	.6496	.5847	.5268	.4751	.4289	.3875	.3505	.2875	.2366	.2149	.1954	.1619	.1346	.0938	.0662	.0472	.0340
12	.8874	.7885	.7014	.6246	.5568	.4970	.4440	.3971	.3555	.3186	.2567	.2076	.1869	.1685	.1372	.1122	.0757	.0517	.0357	.0250
13	.8787	.7730	.6810	.6006	.5303	.4688	.4150	.3677	.3262	.2897	.2292	.1821	.1625	.1452	.1163	.0935	.0610	.0404	.0271	.0184
14	.8700	.7579	.6611	.5775	.5051	.4423	.3878	.3405	.2992	.2633	.2046	.1597	.1413	.1252	.0985	.0779	.0492	.0316	.0205	.0135
15	.8613	.7430	.6419	.5553	.4810	.4173	.3624	.3152	.2745	.2394	.1827	.1401	.1229	.1079	.0835	.0649	.0397	.0247	.0155	.0099
16	.8528	.7284	.6232	.5339	.4581	.3936	.3387	.2919	.2519	.2176	.1631	.1229	.1069	.0930	.0708	.0541	.0320	.0193	.0118	.0073
17	.8444	.7142	.6050	.5134	.4363	.3714	.3166	.2703	.2311	.1978	.1456	.1078	.0929	.0802	.0600	.0451	.0258	.0150	.0089	.0054
18	.8360	.7002	.5874	.4936	.4155	.3503	.2959	.2502	.2120	.1799	.1300	.0946	.0808	.0691	.0508	.0376	.0208	.0118	.0068	.0039
19	.8277	.6864	.5703	.4746	.3957	.3305	.2765	.2317	.1945	.1635	.1161	.0829	.0703	.0596	.0431	.0313	.0168	.0092	.0051	.0029
20	.8195	.6730	.5537	.4564	.3769	.3118	.2584	.2145	.1784	.1486	.1037	.0728	.0611	.0514	.0365	.0261	.0135	.0072	.0039	.0021
25	.7798	.6095	.4776	.3751	.2953	.2330	.1842	.1460	.1160	.0923	.0588	.0378	.0304	.0245	.0160	.0105	.0046	.0021	.0010	.0005
30	.7419	.5521	.4120	.3083	.2314	.1741	.1314	.0994	.0754	.0573	.0334	.0196	.0151	.0116	.0070	.0042	.0016	.0006	.0002	.0001
40	.6717	.4529	.3066	.2083	.1420	.0972	.0668	.0460	.0318	.0221	.0107	.0053	.0037	.0026	.0013	.0007	.0002	.0001	*	*
50	.6080	.3715	.2281	.1407	.0872	.0543	.0339	.0213	.0134	.0085	.0035	.0014	.0009	.0006	.0003	.0001	*	*	*	*
60	.5504	.3048	.1697	.0951	.0535	.0303	.0173	.0099	.0057	.0033	.0011	.0004	.0002	.0001	*	*	*	*	*	*

* The factor is zero to four decimal places.

Copyright © 1985 The Dryden Press
A division of CBS College Publishing

TABLE A.2

Present Value of an Annuity of $1 Per Period for n Periods: $PVIFA = \sum_{t=1}^{n} \dfrac{1}{(1+k)^t} = \dfrac{1 - \dfrac{1}{(1+k)^n}}{k}$

Number of Payments	1%	2%	3%	4%	5%	6%	7%	8%	9%	10%	12%	14%	15%	16%	18%	20%	24%	28%	32%
1	0.9901	0.9804	0.9709	0.9615	0.9524	0.9434	0.9346	0.9259	0.9174	0.9091	0.8929	0.8772	0.8696	0.8621	0.8475	0.8333	0.8065	0.7813	0.7576
2	1.9704	1.9416	1.9135	1.8861	1.8594	1.8334	1.8080	1.7833	1.7591	1.7355	1.6901	1.6467	1.6257	1.6052	1.5656	1.5278	1.4568	1.3916	1.3315
3	2.9410	2.8839	2.8286	2.7751	2.7232	2.6730	2.6243	2.5771	2.5313	2.4869	2.4018	2.3216	2.2832	2.2459	2.1743	2.1065	1.9813	1.8684	1.7663
4	3.9020	3.8077	3.7171	3.6299	3.5460	3.4651	3.3872	3.3121	3.2397	3.1699	3.0373	2.9137	2.8550	2.7982	2.6901	2.5887	2.4043	2.2410	2.0957
5	4.8534	4.7135	4.5797	4.4518	4.3295	4.2124	4.1002	3.9927	3.8897	3.7908	3.6048	3.4331	3.3522	3.2743	3.1272	2.9906	2.7454	2.5320	2.3452
6	5.7955	5.6014	5.4172	5.2421	5.0757	4.9173	4.7665	4.6229	4.4859	4.3553	4.1114	3.8887	3.7845	3.6847	3.4976	3.3255	3.0205	2.7594	2.5342
7	6.7282	6.4720	6.2303	6.0021	5.7864	5.5824	5.3893	5.2064	5.0330	4.8684	4.5638	4.2883	4.1604	4.0386	3.8115	3.6046	3.2423	2.9370	2.6775
8	7.6517	7.3255	7.0197	6.7327	6.4632	6.2098	5.9713	5.7466	5.5348	5.3349	4.9676	4.6389	4.4873	4.3436	4.0776	3.8372	3.4212	3.0758	2.7860
9	8.5660	8.1622	7.7861	7.4353	7.1078	6.8017	6.5152	6.2469	5.9952	5.7590	5.3282	4.9464	4.7716	4.6065	4.3030	4.0310	3.5655	3.1842	2.8681
10	9.4713	8.9826	8.5302	8.1109	7.7217	7.3601	7.0236	6.7101	6.4177	6.1446	5.6502	5.2161	5.0188	4.8332	4.4941	4.1925	3.6819	3.2689	2.9304
11	10.3676	9.7868	9.2526	8.7605	8.3064	7.8869	7.4987	7.1390	6.8052	6.4951	5.9377	5.4527	5.2337	5.0286	4.6560	4.3271	3.7757	3.3351	2.9776
12	11.2551	10.5753	9.9540	9.3851	8.8633	8.3838	7.9427	7.5361	7.1607	6.8137	6.1944	5.6603	5.4206	5.1971	4.7932	4.4392	3.8514	3.3868	3.0133
13	12.1337	11.3484	10.6350	9.9856	9.3936	8.8527	8.3577	7.9038	7.4869	7.1034	6.4235	5.8424	5.5831	5.3423	4.9095	4.5327	3.9124	3.4272	3.0404
14	13.0037	12.1062	11.2961	10.5631	9.8986	9.2950	8.7455	8.2442	7.7862	7.3667	6.6282	6.0021	5.7245	5.4675	5.0081	4.6106	3.9616	3.4587	3.0609
15	13.8651	12.8493	11.9379	11.1184	10.3797	9.7122	9.1079	8.5595	8.0607	7.6061	6.8109	6.1422	5.8474	5.5755	5.0916	4.6755	4.0013	3.4834	3.0764
16	14.7179	13.5777	12.5611	11.6523	10.8378	10.1059	9.4466	8.8514	8.3126	7.8237	6.9740	6.2651	5.9542	5.6685	5.1624	4.7296	4.0333	3.5026	3.0882
17	15.5623	14.2919	13.1661	12.1657	11.2741	10.4773	9.7632	9.1216	8.5436	8.0216	7.1196	6.3729	6.0472	5.7487	5.2223	4.7746	4.0591	3.5177	3.0971
18	16.3983	14.9920	13.7535	12.6593	11.6896	10.8276	10.0591	9.3719	8.7556	8.2014	7.2497	6.4674	6.1280	5.8178	5.2732	4.8122	4.0799	3.5294	3.1039
19	17.2260	15.6785	14.3238	13.1339	12.0853	11.1581	10.3356	9.6036	8.9501	8.3649	7.3658	6.5504	6.1982	5.8775	5.3162	4.8435	4.0967	3.5386	3.1090
20	18.0456	16.3514	14.8775	13.5903	12.4622	11.4699	10.5940	9.8181	9.1285	8.5136	7.4694	6.6231	6.2593	5.9288	5.3527	4.8696	4.1103	3.5458	3.1129
25	22.0232	19.5235	17.4131	15.6221	14.0939	12.7834	11.6536	10.6748	9.8226	9.0770	7.8431	6.8729	6.4641	6.0971	5.4669	4.9476	4.1474	3.5640	3.1220
30	25.8077	22.3965	19.6004	17.2920	15.3725	13.7648	12.4090	11.2578	10.2737	9.4269	8.0552	7.0027	6.5660	6.1772	5.5168	4.9789	4.1601	3.5693	3.1242
40	32.8347	27.3555	23.1148	19.7928	17.1591	15.0463	13.3317	11.9246	10.7574	9.7791	8.2438	7.1050	6.6418	6.2335	5.5482	4.9966	4.1659	3.5712	3.1250
50	39.1961	31.4236	25.7298	21.4822	18.2559	15.7619	13.8007	12.2335	10.9617	9.9148	8.3045	7.1327	6.6605	6.2463	5.5541	4.9995	4.1666	3.5714	3.1250
60	44.9550	34.7609	27.6756	22.6235	18.9293	16.1614	14.0392	12.3766	11.0480	9.9672	8.3240	7.1401	6.6651	6.2402	5.5553	4.9999	4.1667	3.5714	3.1250

Copyright © 1985 The Dryden Press
A division of CBS College Publishing

TABLE A.3
Future Value of $1 at the End of *n* Periods: $FVIF_{k,n} = (1 + k)^n$

Period	1%	2%	3%	4%	5%	6%	7%	8%	9%	10%	12%	14%	15%	16%	18%	20%	24%	28%	32%	36%
1	1.0100	1.0200	1.0300	1.0400	1.0500	1.0600	1.0700	1.0800	1.0900	1.1000	1.1200	1.1400	1.1500	1.1600	1.1800	1.2000	1.2400	1.2800	1.3200	1.3600
2	1.0201	1.0404	1.0609	1.0816	1.1025	1.1236	1.1449	1.1664	1.1881	1.2100	1.2544	1.2996	1.3225	1.3456	1.3924	1.4400	1.5376	1.6384	1.7424	1.8496
3	1.0303	1.0612	1.0927	1.1249	1.1576	1.1910	1.2250	1.2597	1.2950	1.3310	1.4049	1.4815	1.5209	1.5609	1.6430	1.7280	1.9066	2.0972	2.3000	2.5155
4	1.0406	1.0824	1.1255	1.1699	1.2155	1.2625	1.3108	1.3605	1.4116	1.4641	1.5735	1.6890	1.7490	1.8106	1.9388	2.0736	2.3642	2.6844	3.0360	3.4210
5	1.0510	1.1041	1.1593	1.2167	1.2763	1.3382	1.4026	1.4693	1.5386	1.6105	1.7623	1.9254	2.0114	2.1003	2.2878	2.4883	2.9316	3.4360	4.0075	4.6526
6	1.0615	1.1262	1.1941	1.2653	1.3401	1.4185	1.5007	1.5869	1.6771	1.7716	1.9738	2.1950	2.3131	2.4364	2.6996	2.9860	3.6352	4.3980	5.2899	6.3275
7	1.0721	1.1487	1.2299	1.3159	1.4071	1.5036	1.6058	1.7138	1.8280	1.9487	2.2107	2.5023	2.6600	2.8262	3.1855	3.5832	4.5077	5.6295	6.9826	8.6054
8	1.0829	1.1717	1.2668	1.3686	1.4775	1.5938	1.7182	1.8509	1.9926	2.1436	2.4760	2.8526	3.0590	3.2784	3.7589	4.2998	5.5895	7.2058	9.2170	11.703
9	1.0937	1.1951	1.3048	1.4233	1.5513	1.6895	1.8385	1.9990	2.1719	2.3579	2.7731	3.2519	3.5179	3.8030	4.4355	5.1598	6.9310	9.2234	12.166	15.916
10	1.1046	1.2190	1.3439	1.4802	1.6289	1.7908	1.9672	2.1589	2.3674	2.5937	3.1058	3.7072	4.0456	4.4114	5.2338	6.1917	8.5944	11.805	16.059	21.646
11	1.1157	1.2434	1.3842	1.5395	1.7103	1.8983	2.1049	2.3316	2.5804	2.8531	3.4785	4.2262	4.6524	5.1173	6.1759	7.4301	10.657	15.111	21.198	29.439
12	1.1268	1.2682	1.4258	1.6010	1.7959	2.0122	2.2522	2.5182	2.8127	3.1384	3.8960	4.8179	5.3502	5.9360	7.2876	8.9161	13.214	19.342	27.982	40.037
13	1.1381	1.2936	1.4685	1.6651	1.8856	2.1329	2.4098	2.7196	3.0658	3.4523	4.3635	5.4924	6.1528	6.8858	8.5994	10.699	16.386	24.758	36.937	54.451
14	1.1495	1.3195	1.5126	1.7317	1.9799	2.2609	2.5785	2.9372	3.3417	3.7975	4.8871	6.2613	7.0757	7.9875	10.147	12.839	20.319	31.691	48.756	74.053
15	1.1610	1.3459	1.5580	1.8009	2.0789	2.3966	2.7590	3.1722	3.6425	4.1772	5.4736	7.1379	8.1371	9.2655	11.973	15.407	25.195	40.564	64.358	100.71
16	1.1726	1.3728	1.6047	1.8730	2.1829	2.5404	2.9522	3.4259	3.9703	4.5950	6.1304	8.1372	9.3576	10.748	14.129	18.488	31.242	51.923	84.953	136.96
17	1.1843	1.4002	1.6528	1.9479	2.2920	2.6928	3.1588	3.7000	4.3276	5.0545	6.8660	9.2765	10.761	12.467	16.672	22.186	38.740	66.461	112.13	186.27
18	1.1961	1.4282	1.7024	2.0258	2.4066	2.8543	3.3799	3.9960	4.7171	5.5599	7.6900	10.575	12.375	14.462	19.673	26.623	48.038	85.070	148.02	253.33
19	1.2081	1.4568	1.7535	2.1068	2.5270	3.0256	3.6165	4.3157	5.1417	6.1159	8.6128	12.055	14.231	16.776	23.214	31.948	59.567	108.89	195.39	344.53
20	1.2202	1.4859	1.8061	2.1911	2.6533	3.2071	3.8697	4.6610	5.6044	6.7275	9.6463	13.743	16.366	19.460	27.393	38.337	73.864	139.37	257.91	468.57
21	1.2324	1.5157	1.8603	2.2788	2.7860	3.3996	4.1406	5.0338	6.1088	7.4002	10.803	15.667	18.821	22.574	32.323	46.005	91.591	178.40	340.44	637.26
22	1.2447	1.5460	1.9161	2.3699	2.9253	3.6035	4.4304	5.4365	6.6586	8.1403	12.100	17.861	21.644	26.186	38.142	55.206	113.57	228.35	449.39	866.67
23	1.2572	1.5769	1.9736	2.4647	3.0715	3.8197	4.7405	5.8715	7.2579	8.9543	13.552	20.361	24.891	30.376	45.007	66.247	140.83	292.30	593.19	1178.6
24	1.2697	1.6084	2.0328	2.5633	3.2251	4.0489	5.0724	6.3412	7.9111	9.8497	15.178	23.212	28.625	35.236	53.108	79.496	174.63	374.14	783.02	1602.9
25	1.2824	1.6406	2.0938	2.6658	3.3864	4.2919	5.4274	6.8485	8.6231	10.834	17.000	26.461	32.918	40.874	62.668	95.396	216.54	478.90	1033.5	2180.0
26	1.2953	1.6734	2.1566	2.7725	3.5557	4.5494	5.8074	7.3964	9.3992	11.918	19.040	30.166	37.856	47.414	73.948	114.47	268.51	612.99	1364.3	2964.9
27	1.3082	1.7069	2.2213	2.8834	3.7335	4.8223	6.2139	7.9881	10.245	13.110	21.324	34.389	43.535	55.000	87.259	137.37	332.95	784.63	1800.9	4032.2
28	1.3213	1.7410	2.2879	2.9987	3.9201	5.1117	6.6488	8.6271	11.167	14.421	23.883	39.204	50.065	63.800	102.96	164.84	412.86	1004.3	2377.2	5483.8
29	1.3345	1.7758	2.3566	3.1187	4.1161	5.4184	7.1143	9.3173	12.172	15.863	26.749	44.693	57.575	74.008	121.50	197.81	511.95	1285.5	3137.9	7458.0
30	1.3478	1.8114	2.4273	3.2434	4.3219	5.7435	7.6123	10.062	13.267	17.449	29.959	50.950	66.211	85.849	143.37	237.37	634.81	1645.5	4142.0	10143.
40	1.4889	2.2080	3.2620	4.8010	7.0400	10.285	14.974	21.724	31.409	45.259	93.050	188.88	267.86	378.72	750.37	1469.7	5455.9	19426.	66520.	*
50	1.6446	2.6916	4.3839	7.1067	11.467	18.420	29.457	46.901	74.357	117.39	289.00	700.23	1083.6	1670.7	3927.3	9100.4	46890.	*	*	*
60	1.8167	3.2810	5.8916	10.519	18.679	32.987	57.946	101.25	176.03	304.48	897.59	2595.9	4383.9	7370.1	20555.	56347.	*	*	*	*

* $FVIF > 99.999$

Copyright © 1985 The Dryden Press
A division of CBS College Publishing

TABLE A.4

Sum of an Annuity of $1 Per Period for *n* Periods: $FVIFA_{k,n} = \sum_{t=1}^{n}(1+k)^{t-1} = \dfrac{(1+k)^{n}-1}{k}$

Number of Periods	1%	2%	3%	4%	5%	6%	7%	8%	9%	10%	12%	14%	15%	16%	18%	20%	24%	28%	32%	36%
1	1.0000	1.0000	1.0000	1.0000	1.0000	1.0000	1.0000	1.0000	1.0000	1.0000	1.0000	1.0000	1.0000	1.0000	1.0000	1.0000	1.0000	1.0000	1.0000	1.0000
2	2.0100	2.0200	2.0300	2.0400	2.0500	2.0600	2.0700	2.0800	2.0900	2.1000	2.1200	2.1400	2.1500	2.1600	2.1800	2.2000	2.2400	2.2800	2.3200	2.3600
3	3.0301	3.0604	3.0909	3.1216	3.1525	3.1836	3.2149	3.2464	3.2781	3.3100	3.3744	3.4396	3.4725	3.5056	3.5724	3.6400	3.7776	3.9184	4.0624	4.2096
4	4.0604	4.1216	4.1836	4.2465	4.3101	4.3746	4.4399	4.5061	4.5731	4.6410	4.7793	4.9211	4.9934	5.0665	5.2154	5.3680	5.6842	6.0156	6.3624	6.7251
5	5.1010	5.2040	5.3091	5.4163	5.5256	5.6371	5.7507	5.8666	5.9847	6.1051	6.3528	6.6101	6.7424	6.8771	7.1542	7.4416	8.0484	8.6999	9.3983	10.146
6	6.1520	6.3081	6.4684	6.6330	6.8019	6.9753	7.1533	7.3359	7.5233	7.7156	8.1152	8.5355	8.7537	8.9775	9.4420	9.9299	10.980	12.135	13.405	14.798
7	7.2135	7.4343	7.6625	7.8983	8.1420	8.3938	8.6540	8.9228	9.2004	9.4872	10.089	10.730	11.066	11.413	12.141	12.915	14.615	16.533	18.695	21.126
8	8.2857	8.5830	8.8923	9.2142	9.5491	9.8975	10.259	10.636	11.028	11.435	12.299	13.232	13.726	14.240	15.327	16.499	19.122	22.163	25.678	29.731
9	9.3685	9.7546	10.159	10.582	11.026	11.491	11.978	12.487	13.021	13.579	14.775	16.085	16.785	17.518	19.085	20.798	24.712	29.369	34.895	41.435
10	10.462	10.949	11.463	12.006	12.577	13.180	13.816	14.486	15.192	15.937	17.548	19.337	20.303	21.321	23.521	25.958	31.643	38.592	47.061	57.351
11	11.566	12.168	12.807	13.486	14.206	14.971	15.783	16.645	17.560	18.531	20.654	23.044	24.349	25.732	28.755	32.150	40.237	50.398	63.121	78.998
12	12.682	13.412	14.192	15.025	15.917	16.869	17.888	18.977	20.140	21.384	24.133	27.270	29.001	30.850	34.931	39.580	50.894	65.510	84.320	108.43
13	13.809	14.680	15.617	16.626	17.713	18.882	20.140	21.495	22.953	24.522	28.029	32.088	34.351	36.786	42.218	48.496	64.109	84.852	112.30	148.47
14	14.947	15.973	17.086	18.291	19.598	21.015	22.550	24.214	26.019	27.975	32.392	37.581	40.504	43.672	50.818	59.195	80.496	109.61	149.23	202.92
15	16.096	17.293	18.598	20.023	21.578	23.276	25.129	27.152	29.360	31.772	37.279	43.842	47.580	51.659	60.965	72.035	100.81	141.30	197.99	276.97
16	17.257	18.639	20.156	21.824	23.657	25.672	27.888	30.324	33.003	35.949	42.753	50.980	55.717	60.925	72.939	87.442	126.01	181.86	262.35	377.69
17	18.430	20.012	21.761	23.697	25.840	28.212	30.840	33.750	36.973	40.544	48.883	59.117	65.075	71.673	87.068	105.93	157.25	233.79	347.30	514.66
18	19.614	21.412	23.414	25.645	28.132	30.905	33.999	37.450	41.301	45.599	55.749	68.394	75.836	84.140	103.74	128.11	195.99	300.25	459.44	700.93
19	20.810	22.840	25.116	27.671	30.539	33.760	37.379	41.446	46.018	51.159	63.439	78.969	88.211	98.603	123.41	154.74	244.03	385.32	607.47	954.27
20	22.019	24.297	26.870	29.778	33.066	36.785	40.995	45.762	51.160	57.275	72.052	91.024	102.44	115.37	146.62	186.68	303.60	494.21	802.86	1298.8
21	23.239	25.783	28.676	31.969	35.719	39.992	44.865	50.422	56.764	64.002	81.698	104.76	118.81	134.84	174.02	225.02	377.46	633.59	1060.7	1767.3
22	24.471	27.299	30.536	34.248	38.505	43.392	49.005	55.456	62.873	71.402	92.502	120.43	137.63	157.41	206.34	271.03	469.05	811.99	1401.2	2404.6
23	25.716	28.845	32.452	36.617	41.430	46.995	53.436	60.893	69.531	79.543	104.60	138.29	159.27	183.60	244.48	326.23	582.62	1040.3	1850.6	3271.3
24	26.973	30.421	34.426	39.082	44.502	50.815	58.176	66.764	76.789	88.497	118.15	158.65	184.16	213.97	289.49	392.48	723.46	1332.6	2443.8	4449.9
25	28.243	32.030	36.459	41.645	47.727	54.864	63.249	73.105	84.700	98.347	133.33	181.87	212.79	249.21	342.60	471.98	898.09	1706.8	3226.8	6052.9
26	29.525	33.670	38.553	44.311	51.113	59.156	68.676	79.954	93.323	109.18	150.33	208.33	245.71	290.08	405.27	567.37	1114.6	2185.7	4260.4	8233.0
27	30.820	35.344	40.709	47.084	54.669	63.705	74.483	87.350	102.72	121.09	169.37	238.49	283.56	337.50	479.22	681.85	1383.1	2798.7	5624.7	11197.9
28	32.129	37.051	42.930	49.967	58.402	68.528	80.697	95.338	112.96	134.20	190.69	272.88	327.10	392.50	566.48	819.22	1716.0	3583.3	7425.6	15230.2
29	33.450	38.792	45.218	52.966	62.322	73.639	87.346	103.96	124.13	148.63	214.58	312.09	377.16	456.30	669.44	984.06	2128.9	4587.6	9802.9	20714.1
30	34.784	40.568	47.575	56.084	66.438	79.058	94.460	113.28	136.30	164.49	241.33	356.78	434.74	530.31	790.94	1181.8	2640.9	5873.2	12940.	28172.2
40	48.886	60.402	75.401	95.025	120.79	154.76	199.63	259.05	337.88	442.59	767.09	1342.0	1779.0	2360.7	4163.2	7343.8	22728.	69377.	*	*
50	64.463	84.579	112.79	152.66	209.34	290.33	406.52	573.76	815.08	1163.9	2400.0	4994.5	7217.7	10435.	21813.	45497.	*	*	*	*
60	81.669	114.05	163.05	237.99	353.58	533.12	813.52	1253.2	1944.7	3034.8	7471.6	18535.	29219.	46057.	*	*	*	*	*	*

* $FVIFA > 99{,}999$

Copyright © 1985 The Dryden Press
A division of CBS College Publishing

Appendix B

Cumulative Probability Distributions

Values of $N(x)$ for Given Values of x for a Cumulative Normal Probability Distribution with Zero Mean and Unit Variance

x	$N(x)$	x	$N(x)$	x	$N(x)$	x	$N(x)$	x	$N(x)$	x	$N(x)$
		-1.00	.1587	1.00	.8413	-2.00	.0228	.00	.5000	2.00	.9773
-2.95	.0016	$-.95$	.1711	1.05	.8531	-1.95	.0256	.05	.5199	2.05	.9798
-2.90	.0019	$-.90$	.1841	1.10	.8643	-1.90	.0287	.10	.5398	2.10	.9821
-2.85	.0022	$-.85$	.1977	1.15	.8749	-1.85	.0322	.15	.5596	2.15	.9842
-2.80	.0026	$-.80$	.2119	1.20	.8849	-1.80	.0359	.20	.5793	2.20	.9861
-2.75	.0030	$-.75$	.2266	1.25	.8944	-1.75	.0401	.25	.5987	2.25	.9878
-2.70	.0035	$-.70$	.2420	1.30	.9032	-1.70	.0446	.30	.6179	2.30	.9893
-2.65	.0040	$-.65$	.2578	1.35	.9115	-1.65	.0495	.35	.6368	2.35	.9906
-2.60	.0047	$-.60$	.2743	1.40	.9192	-1.60	.0548	.40	.6554	2.40	.9918
-2.55	.0054	$-.55$	.2912	1.45	.9265	-1.55	.0606	.45	.6736	2.45	.9929
-2.50	.0062	$-.50$	.3085	1.50	.9332	-1.50	.0668	.50	.6915	2.50	.9938
-2.45	.0071	$-.45$	.3264	1.55	.9394	-1.45	.0735	.55	.7088	2.55	.9946
-2.40	.0082	$-.40$	.3446	1.60	.9452	-1.40	.0808	.60	.7257	2.60	.9953
-2.35	.0094	$-.35$	.3632	1.65	.9505	-1.35	.0885	.65	.7422	2.65	.9960
-2.30	.0107	$-.30$	.3821	1.70	.9554	-1.30	.0968	.70	.7580	2.70	.9965
-2.25	.0122	$-.25$	.4013	1.75	.9599	-1.25	.1057	.75	.7734	2.75	.9970
-2.20	.0139	$-.20$	.4207	1.80	.9641	-1.20	.1151	.80	.7881	2.80	.9974
-2.15	.0158	$-.15$	.4404	1.85	.9678	-1.15	.1251	.85	.8023	2.85	.9978
-2.10	.0179	$-.10$	.4602	1.90	.9713	-1.10	.1357	.90	.8159	2.90	.9981
-2.05	.0202	$-.05$	.4801	1.95	.9744	-1.05	.1469	.95	.8289	2.95	.9984

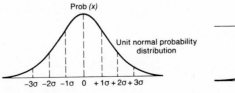

Prob (x)

Unit normal probability distribution

-3σ -2σ -1σ 0 $+1\sigma$ $+2\sigma$ $+3\sigma$

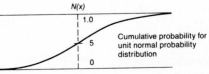

N(x)

1.0

5

0

Cumulative probability for unit normal probability distribution

Name Index

Friend, Irwin, 64n, 87, 449, 616, 638n, 643n, 650, 678n, 685n, 707, 848n, 861
Froewiss, Kenneth C., 793n, 795
Fruhan, William E., Jr., 419
Fuller Russel, Jr., 259
Fuller, Russell J., 384n, 468n, 470
Furst, Richard W., 176n, 208

Galai, Dan, 730n, 740n, 753, 754, 756
Garbisch, Michael W., 490
Garrone, Francois, 675
Gastineau, Gary, 754
Gaumnitz, Jack E., 101n, 117, 235, 246n, 259, 396n, 419, 861
Gay, Gerald, 813n, 815n, 832
Gentry, James A., 333, 840n, 861
Geske, Robert, 754
Gibson, William E., 378, 579
Gipson, James H., 266n
Gladstein, Mathew L., 733n, 735n, 754
Glauber, Robert, 449
Glickstein, David A., 483n, 491
Goff, William, 483
Gold, G., 793
Gombola, M. J., 724n, 754
Gonedes, Nicholas J., 22, 331
Goodman, David A., 188n, 209
Gordon, C. E., II, 128n
Gordon, Myron J., 278n, 449
Gould, Alex, 491
Gould, J. P., 754
Goulet, Waldemar M., 177n, 208
Graham, Benjamin, 449
Granger, C. W. T., 777n, 796
Granito, Michael, 616
Grant, Dwight, 491
Grant, J. A., 564n
Gray, H. Peter, 357n, 358n, 377
Gray, Jean M., 565n
Gray, William S., III, 378
Greeley, Robert E., 861
Green, David, 758
Greenbaum, Mary, 37n, 535
Griepentrog, Gary L., 630n, 651
Grier, Paul, 208
Griggs, Frank T., 368n, 379
Gross, LeRoy, 756
Groth, John, 835n, 836n, 862
Grove, Myron A., 579
Grube, R., 754
Grubel, Herbert G., 52, 657n, 658n, 675
Gruber, Martin J., 234, 642n, 646n, 650
Gultekin, N. Bulent, 391n, 643n, 650
Gupta, Manak, 378
Guy, James, 295

Hafer, R. W., 557n, 655n
Hagerman, Robert L., 77n, 87, 108n, 168n, 186n, 208
Hagin, Robert, 235, 259
Hakansson, Nils H., 235
Hamada, Robert, 22, 294, 331

Hamburger, Michael J., 343n, 378
Hamilton, James L., 77n, 87, 88, 109n, 117
Hamilton, Kevin J., 717n
Hamilton, Mary T., 134, 199n
Hammond, Carl T., 175n, 209
Hangen, Robert A., 426n
Hardy, C. Colburn, 491
Hardy, J. Donald, 699n
Harlow, Charles V., 36n, 52, 53, 796
Harris, Maury, 378
Harris, R. S., 547n
Hass, Jerome, 535
Hastie, Larry K., 559n, 579
Hatfield, Kenneth, 53, 175n, 210
Haugen, Robert A., 22, 579
Hausman, W. H., 175n, 208
Hawawini, Gabriel A., 616
Hawkins, C. A., 758
Hayes, Samuel L., III, 64n
Hays, Patrick A., 66n
Heathcotte, Bryan, 341n, 378
Heins, John, 38n
Helfert, Erich, 302n, 330
Hendershott, Patric H., 567n
Henriksson, Roy D., 851n, 852n, 853n, 861
Hershkoff, R. A., 178n
Hertzberg, Daniel, 36n, 113n, 513n, 670n
Hess, A. P., Jr., 64n, 87
Hettenhouse, George W., 611n, 754
Hickman W. Braddock, 331, 500n, 509n, 536, 608n, 616
Hicks, J. R., 770n, 795
Higgins, Harold B., 861
Hilliard, Jimmy E., 756
Hirsch, Michael D., 16n, 22, 378
Hirshleifer, J., 3n
Hodes, D. A., 399n, 419
Hodges, Stewart D., 235
Hofflander, Alfred E., Jr., 840n, 862
Holt, Charles C., 427n, 659n, 470
Homa, Kenneth E., 343n, 378
Homer, Sidney, 507n, 536, 542n, 543n, 546n, 570n, 579, 586n, 588n, 593n, 616
Hopewell, Michael H., 84n, 88, 572n, 579, 812n, 832
Horowitz, Ira, 707, 861
Horrigan, James O., 303n, 330, 332, 509n, 536
Horton, Joseph J., Jr., 559n
Hover, Roger D., 757
Hsia, Chi-Chang, 754
Huberman, 650
Hudson, Richard, 110n, 113n
Hurt, Ron, 181n, 210

Ibbotson, Roger G., 44n, 45, 52, 53, 175n, 208, 362n, 388n, 607n, 608, 616
Ingersoll, Jonathon E., 616, 617, 758
Ingersoll, Jonathon E., Jr., 768n, 771n, 774n, 795

Jacquillat, Bertrand, 629n, 649, 668n
Jaedicke, Robert K., 330
Jaffee, Dwight A., 343n, 378, 567n
Jaffe, Jeffrey F., 175n, 191n, 208, 390n
Jahnke, William W., 383n
James, Christopher, 188n, 208
James, F. E., Jr., 485n, 491
Jamroz, Deborah, 378
Jarrow, Robert A., 65n, 756, 771n, 795
Jen, Frank C., 560n, 579, 850n, 861
Jennings, Edward H., 758
Jensen, M., 172n, 173n, 207
Jensen, Michael C., 193n, 208, 259, 632n, 633, 649, 650, 682n, 707, 843n, 844n, 861
Jessup, Paul F., 134, 135
Jiler, William L., 491
Jobson, J. D., 647n, 650
Joehnk, Michael D., 65n, 66n, 105n, 117, 512n, 514n, 536, 541n, 560n, 567n, 570n, 579, 609n, 610, 617
Johannesen, Richard I., Jr., 580
Johnson, Aaron C., 793n, 795
Johnson, Craig G., 333
Johnson, Glenn L., 389n
Johnson, Keith B., 65n
Johnson, Leland L., 787n, 796
Johnson, Ramon E., 580
Jones, Charles P., 134, 181n, 182n, 208, 209
Jordan, Jerry L., 342n, 377
Jordan, Ronald J., 208
Joy, O. Maurice, 15n, 181n, 182n, 208, 209, 315n, 663n, 664, 666, 675

Kaish, Stanley, 478n, 491
Kalay, Avner, 754
Kalotay, A. J., 547n, 560n, 580
Kane, Edward J., 566n, 580, 806n, 832
Kaplan, Mortimer, 536
Kaplan, Robert S., 180n, 208, 332, 511n
Karna, Adi S., 66n
Karnosky, Denis S., 14n, 23, 380, 581
Katz, Steven, 209, 535, 611n
Kaufman, George G., 572n, 574n, 578, 579, 580, 595n, 596n, 615, 616, 812n, 832
Kavesh, Robert A., 377
Keller, Myron, 39n
Keller, Werner E., 485, 490
Kendall, Maurice G., 167n, 209
Kennedy, William, 755
Keown, Arthur J., Jr., 847n, 860
Keran, Michael W., 343n, 378
Keresztes, Peter, 39n
Kerr, H. S., 491
Kerrigan, Thomas J., 482n, 491
Kessel, Reuben, 65n, 386n, 565n, 580

Subject Index